Contents

II European driving: cut through the confusion
IV Driving regulations
VIII Ski resorts
X Sights of Europe
XXIV European politics and economics

1 Route planning maps

1 Key to route planning map pages

24 Road maps

24 Key to road map pages · Distance table

201 City plans and approach maps

Alicante C	201	Luxembourg C	215
Amsterdam C U	202	Lyon C U	215
Antwerpen C	201	Madrid U C	215
Athina U C	202	Málaga C	216
Barcelona C U	203	Marseille C	216
Basel C	203	Milano C U	217
Beograd C	205	Moskva C U	218
Berlin C U	204	München C U	218
Bordeaux C U	205	Nápoli C U	219
Bruxelles U C	205	Oslo U C	219
Budapest C U	206	Paris C U	220
Dublin C U	207	Praha C U	222
Düsseldorf C U	207	Roma C U	223
Edinburgh C	207	Rotterdam C	222
Firenze Florence C	209	Sankt Peterburg U	222
Frankfurt C	209	Sevilla C	224
Genève Geneva C	209	Stockholm C U	225
Génova Genoa C	209	Strasbourg C U	224
Göteborg C	210	Stuttgart C	224
Granada C	210	Torino U C	226
Hamburg C U	210	Venézia C	226
Helsinki C U	211	Warszawa C U	227
İstanbul U	211	Wien U C	227
København C U	212	Zagreb C	228
Köln Cologne C	212	Zürich C	228
Lisboa C U	213	C City street plan	
London C U	213	U Urban area map	

229 Index to road maps

www.philips-maps.co.uk

First published in 2007 as **Philip's EasyRead Europe** by Philip's, a division of Octopus Publishing Group Ltd
www.octopusbooks.co.uk
Endeavour House, 189 Shaftesbury Avenue, London WC2H 8JY
An Hachette UK Company · www.hachette.co.uk

Fifth edition 2014, first impression 2014

*Independent research survey, from research carried out by Outlook Research Limited, 2005/06.
**Nielsen BookScan Travel Publishing Year Book 2013 data.

Photographic acknowledgements: *Page II, top left* Raimund Kutter / imageBROKER / Alamy · *centre* Lipowski Milan / Shutterstock · *bottom right* mladn61 / iStockphoto · *Page III, top centre* Baiaz / iStockphoto · *centre* zstock / Shutterstock; *left* Lya_Cattel / iStockphoto · *bottom* Hugo Maes / iStockphoto.

Printed in China

Legend to route planning maps pages 2–23

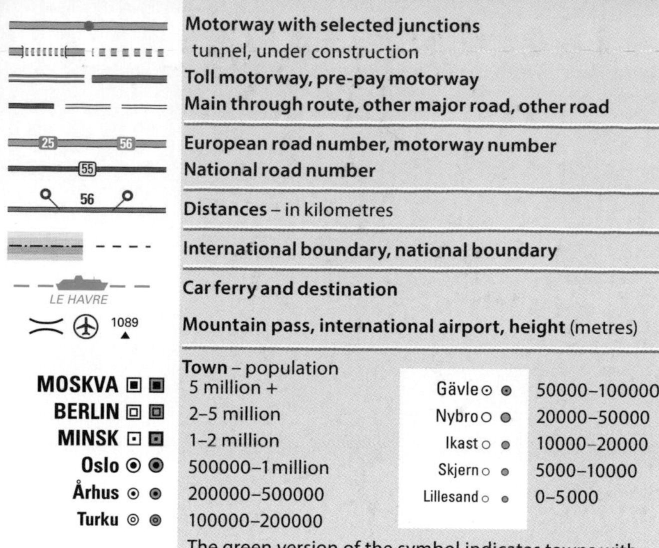

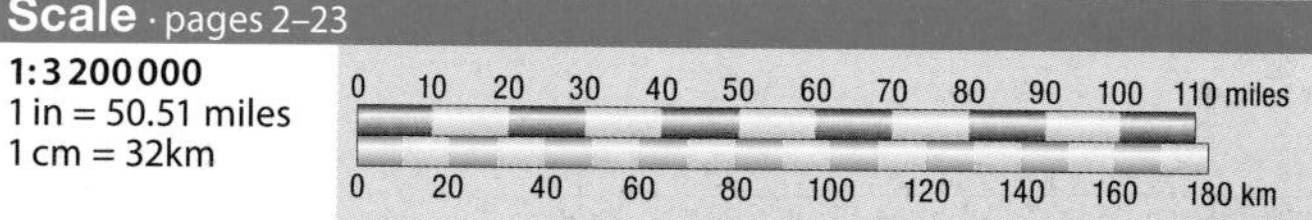

Legend to road maps pages 26–200

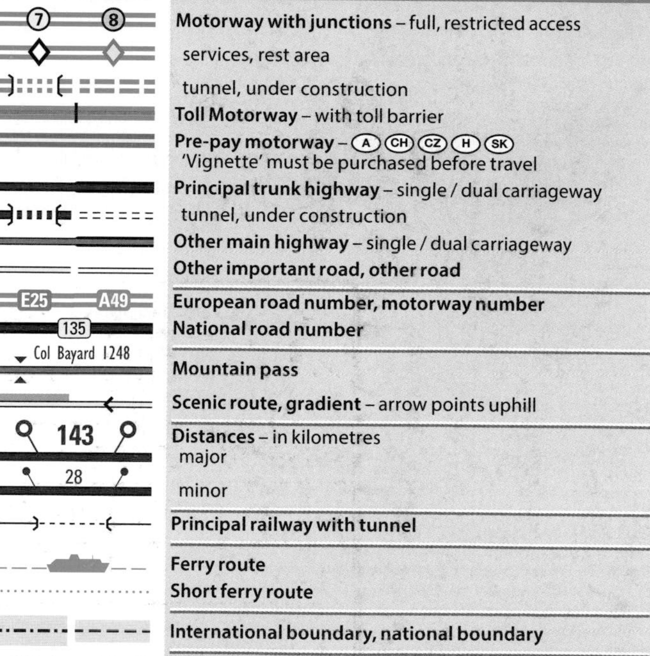

Airport
Ancient monument
Beach
Castle or house
Cave
Other place of interest
Park or garden
Religious building
Ski resort
Theme park
World Heritage site
1754 Spot height
Sevilla World Heritage town
Verona Town of tourist interest
City or town with Low Emission Zone

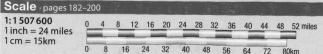

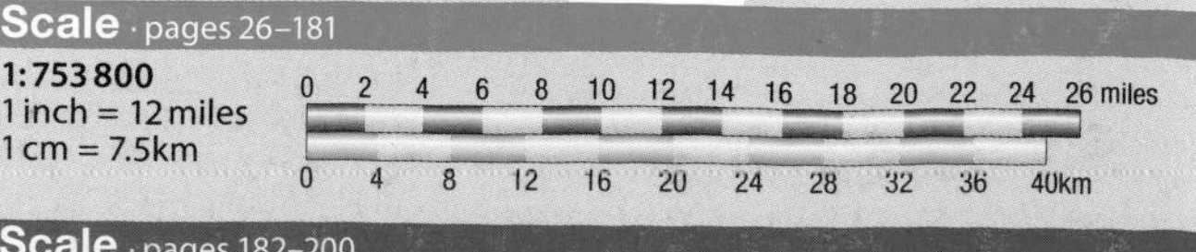

Scale · pages 182–200
1:1 507 600
1 inch = 24 miles
1 cm = 15km
0 4 8 12 16 20 24 28 32 36 40 44 48 52 miles
0 8 16 24 32 40 48 56 64 72 80km

European driving: cut through the confusion

Stay safe with GEM Motoring Assist

- Are you confused about European driving laws?
- How will you know what speed limits apply?
- Are you new to driving on the right hand side?
- Do you need advice about equipment requirements and which documents to take?
- Who do you call if you have an accident or break down?

Since its foundation in 1932, GEM Motoring Assist has been at the forefront of road safety in the UK. Now one of the largest member-led road safety organisations, GEM provides a wide range of discounts and benefits for its 75,000+ members, including the UK's best-value range of breakdown recovery insurance products for motorists, motorcyclists and caravanners. GEM members also benefit from discounts on European breakdown cover and travel insurance, as well as enjoying free access to GEM's Accident Management Service, which provides free-of-charge legal help following any road traffic collision. Members receive Good Motoring, a free quarterly magazine and access to an excellent line-up of road safety leaflets and web-based advice.

Why not make GEM Motoring Assist your one-stop shop for trouble-free motoring! Visit www.motoringassist.com/philipsmaps today.

Millions of us drive abroad on holiday each year. Perhaps it's a long motorway trip to the Mediterranean, a selection of historic cities and sites or a gentle tour along quiet country lanes. Whatever the purpose, it makes sense to ensure that both we and our vehicles are properly prepared for the journey.

It's not easy getting to grips with the finer points of driving in other countries, however experienced you may be as a motorist. Whether you have notched up thousands of miles of European driving or are preparing to make your first journey, the chances are you will always manage to find some road sign or legal requirement that will cause confusion.

What's more, 'driving in Europe' covers such a huge area. There are 28 countries in the European Union alone, each with its own set of road traffic laws and motoring customs. Driving in Europe can mean a spectacular and sunny coastal road that's within sight of Africa, or a snowy track amid the biting cold of the Arctic Circle, where the only others on the road are reindeer. Add to this some of the world's most congested cities, dense clusters of motorways (many with confusing numbers) and a big variation in safety standards and attitudes to risk. No wonder we often risk getting lost, taking wrong turnings or perhaps stopping where we shouldn't.

Depending on the country we're in, our errors at the wheel or our lack of familiarity with the rules of the road can sometimes bring unwelcome consequences. In any country, foreign drivers are subject to the same traffic rules as residents, enforceable in many situations by hefty on-the-spot fines and other sanctions. The situation across Europe is complex, simply because of the number of different sets of rules. For example, failure to carry a specific piece of breakdown equipment may be an offence in one country, but not in another. It's easy to see why the fun and excitement of a road trip in Europe could be spoilt by a minefield of regulations.

But we want to ensure that doesn't happen. Preparation and planning are key to a great holiday. It certainly pays to do a bit of research before you go, just to ensure you and your vehicle are up to the journey, your documents are in order and you're carrying the correct levels of equipment to keep the law enforcers happy.

Before you go

Some sensible planning will help make sure your European journey is enjoyable and – we hope – stress-free. So take some time before departure to ensure everything is in good shape: and that includes you, your travelling companions and your vehicle.

For you:

Try to become familiar with the driving laws of your holiday destination, including the local speed limits and which side of the road to drive on. You will be subject to these laws when driving abroad and if you are stopped by the police, it is not an excuse to say that you were unaware of them. Police officers in many countries have the power to impose (and collect) substantial on-the-spot fines for motoring offences, whether you are a resident or a visitor.

GEM Motoring Assist can link you direct with up-to-date information on driving in 27 different European countries (including Norway and Switzerland, who are not members of the European Union). For each country, you will find an attractive, downloadable three-page PDF document containing detailed information on driving facts, traffic laws, document and equipment requirements – and even a few simple, emergency phrases to help you if you're in difficulty. Go to www.motoringassist.com/europe

The Foreign and Commonwealth Office also gives country-specific travel advice (www.gov.uk/driving-abroad) with information on driving.

Passports

Check everyone's passport to make sure they are all valid.

Don't wait for your passport to expire. Unused time, rounded up to whole months (minimum one month, maximum nine months), will usually be added to your new passport.

New passports usually take two weeks to arrive. The Passport Office (0300 222 0000, www.gov.uk/renew-adult-passport) offers a faster service if you need a replacement passport urgently, but you'll have to pay a lot more.

Driving Licence

The new style photocard driving licence is valid in all European Union countries. However, you must ensure you carry both parts: the credit card-size photocard and the paper licence. The previously used pink EU format UK licence is also valid, though it may not be recognized in some areas. So if you haven't already done so, now is the time to update your old licence. For more information, contact the DVLA (0300 790 6801, www.dft.gov.uk/dvla)

Travel Insurance

Travel insurance is vital as it covers you against medical emergencies, accidents, thefts and cancellations, and repatriation. Ask for details before buying any travel insurance policy. Find out what it covers you for, and to what value. More important, check what's not covered. One of the key benefits of GEM membership is the excellent discount you can get on travel insurance. For more details, please visit: www.motoringassist.com/philipsmaps

European Breakdown Cover

Don't risk letting a breakdown ruin your European trip. Ensure you purchase a policy that will cover you for roadside assistance, emergency repair and recovery of your vehicle to the UK, wherever in Europe you may be heading. Once again, GEM members enjoy a specially discounted rate. You'll find the details at www.motoringassist.com/philipsmaps

EHIC

The E111 medical treatment form is no longer valid. Instead, you need an EHIC card for everyone travelling. These are free and cover you for any medical treatment you may need during a trip to another EU country or Switzerland. However, do check at the time of requiring assistance that your EHIC will be accepted. Apply online (www.ehic.org.uk), by telephone (0845 606 2030) or complete an application form, available from a Post office. Allow up to 14 days for the cards to arrive.

For your vehicle:

Service

It makes sense to get your car serviced before you travel. As a minimum, ensure the tyres have plenty of tread left and that water and oil levels are checked and topped up if required. Check them regularly during your time away.

Vehicle Registration Document

Police in many countries can demand that you prove you have the right to be driving your car. That means you need to show the registration document, or a suitable letter of authorization if the registration document is not in your name. Remember you should never leave the registration document in the car.

Nationality plate

Your vehicle must display a nationality plate of an approved pattern, design and size.

MOT

If your car is more than three years old, make sure you take its current MOT test certificate with you.

Insurance

If you are planning a trip to Europe, you should find that your car insurance policy provides you with the minimum amount of cover you need. But it's important to contact your insurer before you go, to confirm exactly what level of cover you have and for how many days it will be valid.

Mechanical adjustments

Check the adjustments required for your headlights before you go. Beam deflectors are a legal requirement if you drive in Europe. They are generally sold at the ports, on ferries and in the Folkestone Eurotunnel terminal, but be warned – the instructions can be a little confusing! The alternative is to ask a local garage to do the job for you before you go. If you choose this, then make sure you shop around as prices for undertaking this very simple task vary enormously.

Equipment check-list

This checklist represents GEM's suggestions for what you should take with you in the car. Different countries have different rules about what's compulsory and these rules change from time to time. So it's important to check carefully before you set out. For country-by-country guidance, visit www.motoringassist.com/europe or see page IV of this atlas.

- Fire extinguisher
- First aid kit
- High-visibility jacket – one for each occupant
- Two warning triangles
- Replacement bulbs and fuses
- Spare spectacles (if worn) for each driver
- Snow chains for winter journeys into the mountains
- Disposable camera and notebook. Keep in your glove compartment and record any collisions or damage for insurance purposes (if it is safe).

Contact details

Make sure you have all relevant emergency helpline numbers with you, including emergency services, breakdown assistance, the local British consulate and your insurance company. There are links to embassies and consulates around the world from the Foreign Office website. (www.fco.gov.uk) For information, the European emergency telephone number (our equivalent of 999) is 112.

HELP ME, PLEASE!

If you're in a difficult situation and need local help, then the following words and phrases might prove useful if language is a problem:

Do you speak English?	Parlez-vous anglais?	¿Habla usted inglés?	Parla inglese?	Sprechen Sie Englisch?
Thank you (very much)	Merci (beaucoup)	(Muchas) Gracias	Grazie (mille)	Danke (sehr)
Is there a police station near here?	Est-ce qu'il y a un commissariat de police près d'ici?	¿Hay una comisaría cerca?	C'e' un commissariato qui vicino?	Gibt es ein Polizeirevier hier in der Nähe?
I have lost my passport.	J'ai perdu mon passeport.	He perdido mi pasaporte	Ho perso il mio passaporto.	Ich have meinen Reisepass verloren.
I have broken down.	Je suis tombé en panne	Mi coche se ha averiado.	Ho un guasto.	Ich habe eine Panne.
I have run out of fuel.	Je suis tombé en panne d'essence.	Me he quedado sin gasolina.	Ho terminato la benzina.	Ich habe kein Benzin mehr.
I feel ill.	Je me sens malade.	Me siento mal.	Mi sento male.	Mir ist schlecht.

WORTH KNOWING

You will need a separate GB sticker in EU countries if your car doesn't have a registration plate containing the GB euro-symbol.

Fuel is generally most expensive at motorway service areas and cheapest at supermarkets. However, these are usually shut on Sundays and Bank Holidays. So-called '24 hour' regional fuel stations in France seldom accept payment by UK credit card, so don't rely on them if your tank is running low during a night-time journey.

If you see several fuel stations in short succession before a national border, it's likely that fuel on the other side will be more expensive, so take the opportunity to fill up.

Radar speed camera detectors are illegal in most European countries.

The insurance 'green card' is no longer required for journeys in Europe, but it is important to make sure you have contact details for your insurer in case of an accident or claim.

Speed limits in France are enforced vigorously. Radar controls are frequent, and any driver (including non-residents) detected at more than 25km/h above the speed limit can have their licence confiscated on the spot. Furthermore, if you are caught exceeding the speed limit by 50km/h, even on a first offence, you will face a term of imprisonment. • New legislation introduced in France in 2012 required every driver to carry a self-breathalyser test kit. However, the imposition of a €11 fine for failing to produce a breathalyser when required has been postponed indefinitely. So, in theory, you are required to carry a breathalyser kit, but no fine can be imposed if you don't.

In Spain you must carry two warning triangles, plus a spare pair of glasses for every driver who needs to use them.

In Luxembourg, there are specific rules relating to how you fix a satnav device to your windscreen. Get it wrong and you could be fined on the spot.

In Germany it is against the law to run out of fuel on the motorway. If you do run out, then you face an on-the-spot fine.

Norway and Sweden have particularly low limits for drink-driving: just 20mg per 100ml of blood (compared to 80 in the UK). In Slovakia, the limit is zero.

In Hungary, the limit is also zero. If you are found to be drink-driving, your driving licence will be withdrawn by police officers on the spot.

In most countries, maps and signs will have the European road number (shown in white on a green background) alongside the appropriate national road number. However, in Sweden and Belgium only the E-road number will be shown.

Denmark Cars towing caravans and trailers are prohibited from overtaking on motorways at certain times of day.

Finland Speeding fines are worked out according to your income. Access to a national database allows police at the roadside to establish a Finnish resident's income and number of dependants. Officers then impose a fine based on a specific number of days' income. • If you hit an elk or deer, you must report the collision to the police.

TOP TIPS FOR STAYING SAFE

Collisions abroad occur not just because of poor driving conditions locally, but also because we do not always take the same safety precautions as we might expect to take at home, for example by not wearing a seatbelt or by drinking and driving.

1. Plan your route before you go. That includes the journey you make to reach your destination (with sufficient breaks built in) and any excursions or local journeys you make while you're there.

2. Remember that, wherever you drive, you will be subject to the same laws as local drivers. Claiming ignorance of these laws will not be accepted as an excuse.

3. Take extra care at junctions when you're driving on the 'right side' of the road. If driving in a family group, involve every member in a quick 'junction safety check' to help reduce the risk of a collision. Having everybody in the car call out a catchphrase such as "DriLL DriLL DriLL" (Driver Look Left) on the approach to junctions and roundabouts is a small but potentially life-saving habit.

4. Take fatigue seriously. The excellent European motorway network means you can cover big distances with ease. But you must also make time for proper breaks (experts recommend a break of at least 15 minutes after every two hours of driving). If possible, share the driving and set strict daily limits to the number of driving hours. Watch a short video that explains the risks of driver fatigue: **www.motoringassist.com/fatigue**

5. Drink-driving limits across Europe are lower than those in the UK. The only exception is Malta, where the limit is the same (0.8mg per ml). Bear this in mind if you're flying to a holiday or business destination and plan to have a drink on the plane, as the combination of unfamiliar roads and alcohol in your bloodstream is not a safe one. It's also worth remembering that drivers who cause collisions because they were drinking are likely to find their insurance policy will not cover them.

6. Expect the unexpected. Styles of driving in your destination country are likely to be very different from those you know in the UK. Drive defensively and certainly don't get involved in any altercations on the road.

7. Don't overload your car while away, however tempting the local bargains may appear. Also, make sure you have good all-round visibility by ensuring you don't pile up items on the parcel shelf or boot, and keep your windscreen clear of dirt and dust.

8. Always wear a seatbelt and ensure everyone else on board wears one. Check specific regulations regarding the carriage of children: in some countries children under the age of 12 are not permitted to travel in the front of the car.

9. Don't use your mobile phone while driving. Even though laws on phone use while driving differ from country to country, the practice is just as dangerous wherever you are.

10. When you're exploring on foot, be wise to road safety as a pedestrian. You may get into trouble for 'jay-walking', so don't just wander across a road. Use a proper crossing, but remember that drivers may not stop for you! And don't forget that traffic closest to you approaches from the LEFT.

STOP AND GIVE WAY

Who has priority?
Make sure you keep a watchful eye on signs telling you who has priority on the road. Look for a yellow diamond sign, which tells you that traffic already on the road has priority. If you see the yellow diamond sign crossed out, then you must give way to traffic joining the road.

Priorité a droite
Despite the use of the yellow diamond signs, be aware that on some French roads (especially roundabouts in Paris), the traditional 'priorité a droite' practice is followed, even though it may no longer be legal. In theory these days, the rule no longer applies unless it is clearly signed. In practice, though, it makes sense to anticipate a driver pulling out in front of you, even though the priority may be yours.

Stop means stop!
If you come to a solid white line with an octagonal 'STOP' sign, then you must come to a complete stop. In other words your wheels must stop turning. Adherence to the 'STOP' sign is generally much more rigorously enforced in European countries than you may be used to here.

Headlight flash
Bear in mind that the practice of flashing headlights at a junction in France does not mean the same thing as it might in the UK. If another motorists flashes his headlights at you, he's telling you that he has priority and will be coming through in front of you.

Other laws and motoring advice to be aware of across Europe:

Austria Recent rules require the mandatory use of winter tyres between 1 November and 15 April.

Belgium You will have to pay to use most public toilets – including those at motorway service stations • You are not permitted to use cruise control on motorways when traffic is heavy • There are also specific penalties for close-following on motorways • Roadside drug-testing of drivers (using oral fluid testing devices) forms a regular part of any police controls.

Cyprus There have been important changes in how speeding and drink-driving are sanctioned. Cyprus now has a graduated system of speeding fines, ranging from one euro per km/h over the limit in marginal cases through to fines of up to €5,000 and a term of imprisonment for the most severe infringements. There are also graduated fines for drink-driving, ranging from fixed penalties for being slightly over the limit to terms of imprisonment and fines of up to €5,000 for the most severe.

France Any driver must be in possession of a valid breathalyser (displaying an 'BF' number), either electronic or chemical, to be shown to a police officer in case of control • All motorcycle riders and passengers must wear reflective clothing, measuring a minimum 150 square centimetres and worn on the upper part of the body. This must also be worn if they have had to stop at the side of the road • Jail terms for drivers caught at more than 50km/h above the speed limit – even first time offenders • The banning of radar detectors, with fines of €1500 for anyone using them • Increased penalties for driving while using a mobile phone.

Germany Check your fuel contents regularly as it's an offence to run out of fuel on a German motorway • It's also an offence to make rude signs to other road users.

Greece has Europe's highest accident rate in terms of the number of crashes per vehicle. Pay particular attention at traffic light junctions, as red lights are frequently ignored • All drivers detected with more than 1.10 g/l of alcohol in blood, or more than 0.60mg/l in breath will be prosecuted for the offence • Carrying a petrol can in a vehicle is forbidden.

Ireland The drink-drive limit was reduced in 2011 from 0.8 mg per ml to 0.5. • Beware of rural three-lane roads, where the middle overtaking lane is used by traffic travelling in both directions. On wider rural roads it's the accepted practice for slower vehicles to pull over to let faster traffic through.

Italy Police can impound your vehicle if you cannot present the relevant ownership documents when requested • You will need a red and white warning sign if you plan to use any rear-mounted luggage rack such as a bike rack • Zero alcohol tolerance is now applied for drivers who have held a driving licence for less than three years, as well as to drivers aged 18 to 21, professional drivers, taxi drivers and truckers.

Norway Under new legislation, police officers can perform roadside drug impairment saliva tests. There are specific limits set for the presence of 20 common non-alcohol drugs. • You'll find what amounts to a zero tolerance where drinking and driving is concerned. Only 0.1mg of alcohol per millilitre of blood is permitted (compared to 0.8 in the UK) • Speeding fines are high. For example, a driver caught at 25 km/h over the 80 km/h speed limit on a national road could expect a fine of around £600.

Portugal If you are towing a caravan, you must have a current inventory of the caravan's contents to show a police officer if requested.

Slovakia It is now mandatory to use dipped headlights on every road journey, regardless of the time of day, season or weather conditions.

Spain Motorway speed limits in Spain are 120km/h • If you need glasses for driving, then the law requires you to carry a spare pair with you in the car • It's compulsory to carry two spare warning triangles, spare bulbs for your car and reflective jackets.

Turkey Take great caution if you're driving at dusk. Many local drivers put off using their lights until it's properly dark, so you may find oncoming traffic very hard to spot • During the time of Ramadan, many people will do without food and water between the hours of sunrise and sunset. This can seriously reduce levels of alertness, especially among people driving buses, trucks and taxis.

Driving regulations

A national vehicle identification plate is always required when taking a vehicle abroad. It is important for your own safety and that of other drivers to fit headlamp converters or beam deflectors when taking a right-hand drive car to a country where driving is on the right (every country in Europe except the UK and Ireland). When the headlamps are dipped on a right-hand drive car, the lenses of the headlamps cause the beam to shine upwards to the left – and so, when driving on the right, into the eyes of oncoming motorists.

Where compulsory visibility vests should be kept in the passenger compartment and put on before exiting the vehicle in breakdowns or emergencies. All countries require that you carry a driving licence, green card/insurance documentation, registration document or hire certificate, and passport. Minimum driving ages are often higher for people holding foreign licences.

The penalties for infringements of regulations vary considerably from one country to another. In many countries the police have the right to impose on-the-spot fines (you should always request a receipt for any fine paid). Penalties can be severe for serious infringements, particularly for drinking when driving which in some countries can lead to immediate imprisonment. Insurance is important, and you may be forced to take out cover at the frontier if you cannot produce acceptable proof that you are insured. Please note that driving regulations often change.

Symbols

- [Motorway] Motorway
- [Dual carriageway] Dual carriageway
- [Single carriageway] Single carriageway
- [Surfaced road] Surfaced road
- [Unsurfaced road] Unsurfaced / gravel road
- [Urban area] Urban area
- [Speed] Speed limit in kilometres per hour (kph)
- [Seat belts] Seat belts
- [Children] Children
- [Blood alcohol] Blood alcohol level
- △ Warning triangle
- [First aid] First aid kit
- [Spare bulb] Spare bulb kit
- [Fire extinguisher] Fire extinguisher
- ⊖ Minimum driving age
- [Documents] Additional documents required
- [Mobile phones] Mobile phones
- LEZ Low Emission Zone
- ★ Other information

The publishers have made every effort to ensure that the information given here was correct at the time of going to press. No responsibility can be accepted for any errors or their consequences.

Andorra (AND)

	Motorway	Dual carriageway	Single carriageway	Urban area
Speed	n/a	90	60/90	50

- [Seat belts] Compulsory
- [Children] Under 10 and below 150 cm must travel in an EU-approved restraint system adapted to their size in the rear
- [Blood alcohol] 0.05% △ Compulsory
- [First aid] Recommended [Spare bulb] Compulsory
- [Fire extinguisher] Recommended ⊖ 18
- [Mobile phones] Not permitted whilst driving
- ★ Dipped headlights compulsory for motorcycles during day and for other vehicles during poor daytime visibility.
- ★ On-the-spot fines imposed
- ★ Visibility vests compulsory
- ★ Winter tyres or snow chains compulsory in poor conditions or when indicated by signs

Austria (A)

	Motorway	Dual carriageway	Single carriageway	Urban area
Speed	130	100	100	50
If towing trailer under 750kg / over 750 kg				
Speed	100	100	100/80	50

- [Seat belts] Compulsory
- [Children] Under 14 and under 150cm cannot travel as a front or rear passenger unless they use a suitable child restraint; under 14 over 150cm must wear adult seat belt
- [Blood alcohol] 0.049%; 0.01% if licence held less than 2 years
- △ Compulsory
- [First aid] Compulsory [Spare bulb] Recommended
- [Fire extinguisher] Recommended ⊖ 18 (16 for mopeds)
- [Mobile phones] Only allowed with hands-free kit
- LEZ On A12 motorway non-compliant vehicles banned and certain substances banned, night-time speed restrictions; Steermark province has LEZs affecting lorries
- ★ Dipped headlights must be used during the day by all road users. Headlamp converters compulsory
- ★ On-the-spot fines imposed
- ★ Radar detectors prohibited
- ★ Snow chains recommended in winter. Winter tyres compulsory 1 Nov–15 Apr in poor driving conditions
- ★ To drive on motorways or expressways, a motorway sticker must be purchased at the border or main petrol station. These are available for 10 days, 2 months or 1 year. Vehicles 3.5 tonnes or over must display an electronic tag.
- ★ Visibility vests compulsory

Belarus (BY)

	Motorway	Dual carriageway	Single carriageway	Urban area
Speed	110	90	90	60*
If towing trailer under 750kg				
Speed	90	70	70	

*In residential areas limit is 20 km/h • Vehicle towing another vehicle 50 kph limit • If full driving licence held for less than two years, must not exceed 70 kph

- [Seat belts] Compulsory in front seats, and rear seats if fitted
- [Children] Under 12 not allowed in front seat and must use appropriate child restraint
- [Blood alcohol] 0.00% △ Compulsory
- [First aid] Compulsory [Spare bulb] Recommended
- [Fire extinguisher] Compulsory ⊖ 18
- [Documents] Visa, vehicle technical check stamp, international driving permit, green card, health insurance. Even with a green card, local third-party insurance may be imposed at the border
- [Mobile phones] Use prohibited
- ★ A temporary vehicle import certificate must be purchased on entry and driver must be registered
- ★ Dipped headlights are compulsory during the day Nov–Mar and at all other times in conditions of poor visibility or when towing or being towed.
- ★ Fees payable for driving on highways
- ★ It is illegal for vehicles to be dirty
- ★ On-the-spot fines imposed
- ★ Radar-detectors prohibited
- ★ Winter tyres compulsory; snow chains recommended

Belgium (B)

	Motorway	Dual carriageway	Single carriageway	Urban area
Speed	120*	120*	90	50**
If towing trailer				
Speed	90	90	60	50
Over 3.5 tonnes				
Speed	90	90	60	50

*Minimum speed of 70kph may be applied in certain conditions on motorways and some dual carriageways

**Near schools, hospitals and churches the limit may be 30kph

- [Seat belts] Compulsory
- [Children] All under 19s under 135 cm must wear an appropriate child restraint. Airbags must be deactivated if a rear-facing child seat is used in the front
- [Blood alcohol] 0.05% △ Compulsory
- [First aid] Recommended [Spare bulb] Recommended
- [Fire extinguisher] Compulsory ⊖ 18
- [Mobile phones] Only allowed with a hands-free kit
- ★ Cruise control is not permitted on motorways
- ★ Dipped headlights mandatory at all times for motorcycles and advised during the day in poor conditions for other vehicles
- ★ On-the-spot fines imposed
- ★ Radar detectors prohibited
- ★ Sticker indicating recommended maximum speed for winter tyres must be displayed on dashboard if using them
- ★ Visibility vest compulsory

Bosnia and Herzegovina (BIH)

	Motorway	Dual carriageway	Single carriageway	Urban area
Speed	120	90	90	60

- [Seat belts] Compulsory if fitted
- [Children] Under 12 not allowed in front seat; under 5 must use appropriate child restraint
- [Blood alcohol] 0.03% △ Compulsory
- [First aid] Compulsory [Spare bulb] Compulsory
- ⊖ 18
- [Documents] Visa, International Driving Permit; if driver's insurance not valid for the country, cover may be obtained at most border crossings
- [Mobile phones] Prohibited
- ★ Dipped headlights compulsory for all vehicles at all times
- ★ GPS must have fixed speed camera function deactivated; radar detectors prohibited.
- ★ On-the-spot fines imposed
- ★ Visibility vest compulsory
- ★ Winter tyres compulsory 15 Nov–15 Apr, snow chains recommended

Bulgaria (BG)

	Motorway	Dual carriageway	Single carriageway	Urban area
Speed	130	90	90	50
If towing trailer				
Speed	100	70	70	50

- [Seat belts] Compulsory in front and rear seats
- [Children] Under 3 not permitted in vehicles without child restraints; age 3–10 must sit in rear
- [Blood alcohol] 0.05% △ Compulsory
- [First aid] Compulsory [Spare bulb] Recommended
- [Fire extinguisher] Compulsory ⊖ 18
- [Documents] Photo driving licence with translation and International Driving Permit; vehicle insurance specific to Bulgaria
- [Mobile phones] Only allowed with a hands-free kit
- ★ Dipped headlights compulsory
- ★ Fee at border
- ★ GPS must have fixed speed camera function deactivated; radar detectors prohibited
- ★ On-the-spot fines imposed
- ★ Road tax stickers (annual, monthly or weekly) must be purchased at the border and displayed prominently with the vehicle registration number written on them.
- ★ Visibility vest compulsory

Croatia (HR)

	Motorway	Dual carriageway	Single carriageway	Urban area
Speed	130	110	90	50
Under 24				
Speed	120	100	80	50
If towing				
Speed	110	80	80	50

- [Seat belts] Compulsory if fitted
- [Children] Children under 12 not permitted in front seat and must use appropriate child seat or restraint in rear.
- [Blood alcohol] 0.00% △ Compulsory [First aid] Compulsory
- [Spare bulb] Compulsory [Fire extinguisher] Recommended ⊖ 18
- [Mobile phones] Only allowed with hands-free kit
- ★ Dipped headlights compulsory
- ★ In winter, snow chains compulsory in the mountains; snow tyres compulsory everywhere else Nov–Apr
- ★ On-the-spot fines imposed
- ★ Radar detectors prohibited
- ★ Tow bar and rope compulsory
- ★ Visibility vest compulsory

Czech Republic (CZ)

	Motorway	Dual carriageway	Single carriageway	Urban area
Speed	130	130	90	50
If towing				
Speed	80	80	80	50

- [Seat belts] Compulsory in front and, if fitted, in rear
- [Children] Children: Children under 36 kg and 150 cm must use appropriate child restraint. Only front-facing child retraints are permitted in the front in vehicles with airbags fitted. Airbags must be deactivated if a rear-facing child seat is used in the front.
- [Blood alcohol] 0.00% △ Compulsory [First aid] Compulsory
- [Spare bulb] Compulsory [Fire extinguisher] Compulsory
- ⊖ 18 (17 for motorcycles under 125 cc)
- [Mobile phones] Only allowed with a hands-free kit
- LEZ Two-stage LEZ in Prague for vehicles over 3.5 and 6 tonnes. Permit system.
- ★ Dipped headlights compulsory at all times
- ★ GPS must have fixed speed camera function deactivated; radar detectors prohibited
- ★ On-the-spot fines imposed
- ★ Vignette needed for motorway driving, available for 1 year, 60 days, 15 days. Toll specific to lorries introduced 2006, those over 12 tonnes must buy an electronic tag
- ★ Visibility vest compulsory
- ★ Spectacles or contact lens wearers must always carry a spare pair in their vehicle
- ★ Winter tyres or snow chains compulsory between Nov and Apr

Denmark (DK)

	110-130	80	80	50
If towing				
	80	70	70	50

- Compulsory front and rear
- Under 135cm must use appropriate child restraint; in front permitted only in an appropriate rear-facing seat with any airbags disabled.
- 0.05%
- Compulsory
- Recommended Recommended
- Recommended 18
- Only allowed with a hands-free kit
- LEZ Aalborg, Arhus, Copenhagen, Frederiksberg and Odense. Proofs of emissions compliance/compliant filter needed to obtain sticker. Non-compliant vehicles banned.
- ★ Dipped headlights must be used at all times
- ★ On-the-spot fines imposed
- ★ Radar detectors prohibited
- ★ Tolls apply on the Storebaeltsbroen and Oresundsbron bridges.
- ★ Visibility vest recommended

Estonia (EST)

	n/a	90*	90	50
If full driving licence held for less than two years				
	90	90	90	50

*In summer, the speed limit on some dual carriageways may be raised to 100/110 kph

- Compulsory if fitted
- Children too small for adult seatbelts must wear a seat restraint appropriate to their size. Rear-facing safety seats must not be used in the front if an air bag is fitted, unless this has been deactivated.
- 0.00%
- 2 compulsory
- Compulsory
- Recommended
- Compulsory 18
- Only allowed with a hands-free kit
- ★ A toll system is in operation in Tallinn
- ★ Dipped headlights compulsory at all times
- ★ On-the-spot fines imposed
- ★ Winter tyres are compulsory from Dec–Mar. Studded winter tyres are allowed from 15 Oct–31 Mar, but this can be extended to start 1 October and/or end 30 April

Finland (FIN)

	120	100	80*	30/60
If towing				
	80	80	80	30/60

*100 in summer • If towing a vehicle by rope, cable or rod, max speed limit 60 kph. •Maximum of 80 kph for vans and lorries •Speed limits are often lowered in winter

- Compulsory in front and rear
- Below 135 cm must use a child restraint or seat
- 0.05%
- Compulsory
- Recommended
- Recommended
- Recommended
- 18 (motorbikes below 125cc 16)
- Only allowed with hands-free kit
- ★ Dipped headlights must be used at all times
- ★ On-the-spot fines imposed
- ★ Radar-detectors are prohibited
- ★ Visibility vest compulsory
- ★ Winter tyres compulsory Dec–Feb

France (F)

	130	110	90	50
On wet roads or if full driving licence held for less than 2 years				
	110	100	80	50
If towing below / above 3.5 tonnes gross				
	110/90	100/90	90/80	50

50kph on all roads if fog reduces visibility to less than 50m • Licence will be lost and driver fined for exceeding speed limit by over 40kph

- Compulsory in front and, if fitted, in rear
- In rear, 4 or under must have a child safety seat (rear facing if up to 9 months); if 5–10 must use an appropriate restraint system. Under 10 permitted in the front only if rear seats are fully occupied by other under 10s or there are no rear safety belts. In front, if child is in rear-facing child seat, any airbag must be deactivated.
- 0.05%. If towing or with less than 2 years with full driving licence, 0.00% • All drivers/motorcyclists must carry 2 unused breathalysers to French certification standards, showing an NF number.
- Compulsory Recommended
- Recommended 18
- Use not permitted whilst driving
- LEZ An LEZ operates in the Mont Blanc tunnel
- ★ Dipped headlights compulsory in poor daytime visibility and at all times for motorcycles
- ★ GPS must have fixed speed camera function deactivated; radar-detection equipment is prohibited
- ★ It is compulsory to carry a French-authority-recognised (NF) breathalyser.
- ★ On-the-spot fines imposed
- ★ Tolls on motorways. Electronic tag needed if using automatic tolls.
- ★ Visibility vests must be carried in the passenger compartment; legislation making visibility vests compulsory for motorcyclists and passengers may be reintroduced.
- ★ Winter tyres recommended. Carrying snow chains recommended in winter as these may have to be fitted if driving on snow covered roads, in accordance with signage.

Germany (D)

	*	*	100	50
If towing				
	80	80	80	50

*no limit, 130 kph recommended

- Compulsory
- Under 150 cm and 12 or under must use an appropriate child seat or restraint. In front if child is in rear facing child seat, airbags must be deactivated.
- 0.05%, 0.0% for drivers 21 or under or with less than two years full licence
- Compulsory Compulsory
- Recommended Recommended
- 18 (motorbikes: 16 if under 50cc)
- Use permitted only with hands-free kit – also applies to motorcyclists and cyclists
- LEZ More than 60 cities have or are planning LEZs. Proof of compliance needed to acquire sticker. Non-compliant vehicles banned.
- ★ Dipped headlights compulsory in poor weather conditions and tunnels; recommended at other times
- ★ GPS must have fixed speed camera function deactivated; radar detectors prohibited
- ★ Motorcyclists must use dipped headlights at all times; other vehicles must use dipped headlights during poor daytime visibility.
- ★ On-the-spot fines imposed
- ★ Tolls on autobahns for lorries
- ★ Winter tyres compulsory in all winter weather conditions; snow chains recommended

Greece (GR)

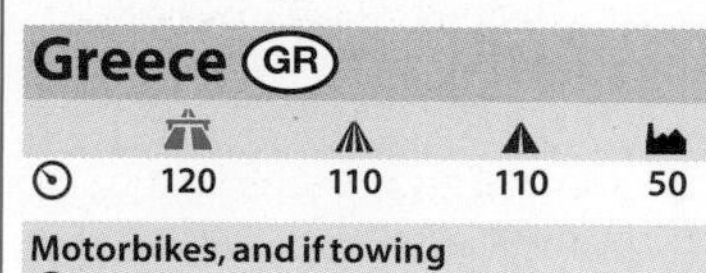

	120	110	110	50
Motorbikes, and if towing				
	90	70	70	40

- Compulsory in front seats and, if fitted, in rear
- Under 12 or below 135cm must use appropriate child restraint. In front if child is in rear-facing child seat, any airbags must be deactivated.
- 0.05%, 0.00% for drivers with less than 2 years' full licence and motorcyclists
- Compulsory Compulsory
- Recommended
- Compulsory
- 18
- Not permitted.
- ★ Dipped headlights compulsory during poor daytime visibility and at all times for motorcycles
- ★ On-the-spot fines imposed
- ★ Radar-detection equipment is prohibited
- ★ Tolls on several newer motorways.

Hungary (H)

	130	110	90	50
If towing				
	80	70	70	50

- Compulsory in front seats and if fitted in rear seats
- Under 150cm and over 3 must be seated in rear and use appropriate child restraint. Under 3 allowed in front only in rear-facing child seat with any airbags deactivated.
- 0.00%
- Compulsory
- Compulsory
- Compulsory
- Recommended 17
- Only allowed with a hands-free kit
- LEZ Budapest has vehicle restrictions on days with heavy dust and is planning an LEZ.
- ★ All motorways are toll and operate electronic vignette system with automatic number plate recognition, tickets are available for 4 days, 7 days, 1 month, 1 year
- ★ During the day dipped headlights compulsory outside built-up areas; compulsory at all times for motorcycles
- ★ Electronic vignette system in use for tolls on several motorways
- ★ On-the-spot fines issued
- ★ Snow chains compulsory where conditions dictate
- ★ Visibility vest compulsory

Iceland (IS)

	n/a	90	80	50

- Compulsory in front and rear seats
- Under 12 or below 150cm not allowed in front seat and must use appropriate child restraint.
- 0.05% Compulsory
- Compulsory Compulsory
- Compulsory
- 18; 21 to drive a hire car; 25 to hire a jeep
- Only allowed with a hands-free kit
- ★ Dipped headlights compulsory at all times
- ★ Driving off marked roads is forbidden
- ★ Highland roads are not suitable for ordinary cars
- ★ On-the-spot fines imposed
- ★ Winter tyres compulsory c.1 Nov–14 Apr (variable)

Ireland (IRL)

	120	100	80	50
If towing				
	80	80	80	50

- Compulsory where fitted. Driver responsible for ensuring passengers under 17 comply
- Children 3 and under must be in a suitable child restraint system. Airbags must be deactivated if a rear-facing child seat is used in the front. Those under 150 cm and 36 kg must use appropriate child restraint in cars with seatbelts.
- 0.05%, 0.02% for novice and professional drivers
- Compulsory
- Recommended
- Recommended
- Recommended
- 17 (16 for motorbikes up to 125cc; 18 for over 125cc; 18 for lorries; 21 bus/minibus)
- Only allowed with a hands-free kit
- ★ Dipped headlights are compulsory during daylight hours
- ★ Dipped headlights compulsory for motorbikes at all times and in poor visibility for other vehicles
- ★ Driving is on the left
- ★ GPS must have fixed speed camera function deactivated; radar detectors prohibited
- ★ On-the-spot fines imposed
- ★ Tolls are being introduced on some motorways; the M50 Dublin has barrier-free tolling with number-plate recognition.

Italy (I)

	130	110	90	50
If towing				
	80	70	70	50
Less than three years with full licence				
	100	90	90	50
When wet				
	100	90	80	50

Some motorways with emergency lanes have speed limit of 150 kph

- Compulsory in front seats and, if fitted, in rear
- Under 12 not allowed in front seats except in child safety seat; children under 3 must have special seat in the back
- 0.05%, but 0.00% for professional drivers or with less than 3 years full licence
- Compulsory
- Recommended
- Compulsory
- Recommended
- 18 (14 for mopeds, 16 up to 125cc, 20 up to 350cc)
- Only allowed with hands-free kit
- LEZ Most northern and several southern regions operate seasonal LEZs and many towns and cities have various schemes that restrict access. There is an LEZ in the Mont Blanc tunnel
- ★ Dipped headlights compulsory outside built-up areas, in tunnels, on motorways and dual carriageways and in poor visibility; compulsory at all times for motorcycles
- ★ On-the-spot fines imposed
- ★ Radar-detection equipment is prohibited
- ★ Snow chains compulsory where signs indicate Nov–April
- ★ Tolls on motorways. Blue lanes accept credit cards; yellow lanes restricted to holders of Telepass pay-toll device.
- ★ Visibility vest compulsory

Kosovo (RKS)

	120	100	100	60

- Compulsory
- Under 12 must sit in rear seats
- 0.03%, 0.00% for professional, business and commercial drivers
- Compulsory
- Compulsory Compulsory
- Compulsory
- 18 (16 for motorbikes less than 125 cc, 14 for mopeds)
- International driving permit, locally purchased third-party insurance (green card is not recognised), documents with proof of ability to cover costs and valid reason for visiting. Visitors from many non-EU countries require a visa.
- Only allowed with a hands-free kit
- ★ Dipped headlights compulsory at all times
- ★ Winter tyres or snow chains compulsory in poor winter weather conditions

Latvia (LV)

	90/100	90	90	50
If towing				
	90/100	90	90	50

In residential areas limit is 20kph • If full driving licence held for less than two years, must not exceed 80 kph

- Compulsory in front seats and if fitted in rear
- If under 12 years and 150cm must use child restraint in front and rear seats
- 0.05%, 0.02% with less than 2 years experience
- Compulsory
- Compulsory Recommended
- Compulsory 18
- Only allowed with hands-free kit
- ★ Dipped headlights must be used at all times all year round
- ★ On-the-spot fines imposed
- ★ Pedestrians have priority
- ★ Visibility vests compulsory
- ★ Winter tyres compulsory for vehicles up to 3.5 tonnes Dec–Feb, but illegal May–Sept

Lithuania (LT)

	130	110	90	50
If towing				
	n/a	70	70	50

In winter speed limits are reduced by 10–20 km/h

- Compulsory in front seats and if fitted in rear seats
- Under 12 not allowed in front seats unless in a child safety seat; under 3 must use appropriate child seat and sit in rear
- 0.04%, 0.02% for those with less than 2 years' full licence
- Compulsory
- Compulsory Recommended
- Compulsory 18
- Only allowed with a hands-free kit
- ★ Dipped headlights must be used at all times
- ★ On-the-spot fines imposed
- ★ Visibility vest compulsory
- ★ Winter tyres compulsory 10 Nov–1 Apr

Luxembourg (L)

	130/110	90	90	50
If towing				
	90	75	75	50

If full driving licence held for less than two years, must not exceed 75 kph • In 20 km/h zones, pedestrians have right of way.

- Compulsory
- Children under 3 must use an appropriate restraint system. Airbags must be disabled if a rear-facing child seat is used in the front. Children 3 to 18 and / or under 150 cm must use a restraint system appropriate to their size. If over 36kg a seatbelt may be used in the back only
- 0.05%, 0.02 for young drivers, drivers with less than 2 years experience and drivers of taxis and commercial vehicles
- Compulsory
- Compulsory (buses) Compulsory
- Compulsory (buses, transport of dangerous goods) 18
- Use permitted only with hands-free kit
- ★ Dipped headlights compulsory for motorcyclists and in poor visibility for other vehicles
- ★ On-the-spot fines imposed
- ★ Visibility vest compulsory
- ★ Winter tyres compulsory in winter weather

Macedonia (MK)

	120	100	60	60
Newly qualified drivers				
	100	80	60	60
If towing				
	80	70	50	50

- Compulsory in front seats; compulsory if fitted in rear seats
- Under 12 not allowed in front seats
- 0.05%, 0.00% for business, commercial and professional drivers and with less than 2 years experience
- Compulsory
- Compulsory Compulsory
- Recommended; compulsory for LPG vehicles
- 18 (mopeds 16)
- International driving permit; visa
- Use not permitted whilst driving
- ★ Dipped headlights compulsory at all times
- ★ GPS must have fixed speed camera function deactivated; radar detectors prohibited
- ★ Novice drivers may only drive between 11pm and 5am if there is someone over 25 with a valid licence in the vehicle.
- ★ On-the-spot fines imposed
- ★ Tolls apply on many roads
- ★ Visibility vest must be kept in the passenger compartment and worn to leave the vehicle in the dark outside built-up areas
- ★ Winter tyres or snow chains compulsory 15 Nov–15 Mar

Moldova (MD)

	90	90	90	60
If towing or if licence held under 1 year				
	70	70	70	60

- Compulsory in front seats and, if fitted, in rear seats
- Under 12 not allowed in front seats
- 0.00% Compulsory
- Compulsory Recommended
- Compulsory
- 18 (mopeds and motorbikes, 16; vehicles with more than eight passenger places, taxis or towing heavy vehicles, 21)
- International Driving Permit (preferred), visa
- Only allowed with hands-free kit
- ★ Motorcyclists must use dipped headlights at all times
- ★ Winter tyres recommended Nov–Feb

Montenegro (MNE)

	n/a	100	80	60

80kph speed limit if towing a caravan

- Compulsory in front and rear seats
- Under 12 not allowed in front seats
- 0.05% Compulsory
- Compulsory Compulsory
- Compulsory
- 18 (16 for motorbikes less than 125cc; 14 for mopeds)
- Prohibited
- ★ An 'eco' tax vignette must be obtained when crossing the border and displayed in the upper right-hand corner of the windscreen
- ★ Dipped headlights must be used at all times
- ★ From mid-Nov to March, driving wheels must be fitted with winter tyres
- ★ On-the-spot fines imposed
- ★ Tolls on some primary roads and in the Sozina tunnel between Lake Skadar and the sea
- ★ Visibility vest compulsory

Netherlands (NL)

	120/100	80/100	80/100	50

- Compulsory
- Under 3 must travel in the back, using an appropriate child restraint; 3-12 or under 135cm must use an appropriate child restraint
- 0.05%, 0.02% with less than 5 years experience or moped riders under 24
- Compulsory
- Recommended Recommended
- Recommended 18
- Only allowed with a hands-free kit
- LEZ About 20 cities operate or are planning LEZs. A national scheme is planned.
- ★ Dipped headlights compulsory for motorcycles and recommended in poor visibility and on open roads for other vehicles.
- ★ On-the-spot fines imposed
- ★ Radar-detection equipment is prohibited

Norway (N)

	90/100	80	80	30/50
If towing trailer with brakes				
	80	80	80	50
If towing trailer without brakes				
	60	60	60	50

- Compulsory in front seats and, if fitted, in rear
- Children less than 150cm tall must use appropriate child restraint. Children under 4 must use child safety seat or safety restraint (cot)
- 0.01% Compulsory
- Recommended Recommended
- Recommended
- 18 (heavy vehicles 18/21)
- Only allowed with a hands-free kit
- LEZ Planned for Bergen, Oslo and Trondheim
- ★ Dipped headlights must be used at all times
- ★ On-the-spot fines imposed
- ★ Radar-detectors are prohibited
- ★ Tolls apply on some bridges, tunnels and access roads into Bergen, Oslo, Trondheim and Stavangar. Several use electronic fee collection only.
- ★ Visibility vest compulsory
- ★ Winter tyres or summer tyres with snow chains compulsory for snow- or ice-covered roads

Poland (PL)

Motor-vehicle only roads[1], under/over 3.5 tonnes				
	130[2]/80[2]	110/80	100/80	n/a
Motor-vehicle only roads[1] if towing				
	n/a	80	80	n/a
Other roads, under 3.5 tonnes				
	n/a	100	90	50/60[3]
Other roads, 3.5 tonnes or over				
	n/a	80	70	50/60[3]
Other roads, if towing				
	n/a	60	60	30

[1]Indicated by signs with white car on blue background. [2]Minimum speed 40 kph. [3]50 kph 05.00–23.00; 60 kph 23.00–05.00; 20 kph in marked residential areas

- Compulsory in front seats and, if fitted, in rear
- Under 12 not allowed in front seats unless in a child safety seat; in rear seats children under 12 and less than 150 cm must use child safety seat. Rear-facing child seats not permitted in vehicles with airbags.
- 0.02% Compulsory
- Recommended Recommended
- Compulsory
- 18 (mopeds and motorbikes – 16)
- Only allowed with a hands-free kit
- ★ Dipped headlights compulsory for all vehicles
- ★ On-the-spot fines imposed
- ★ Radar-detection equipment is prohibited
- ★ Visibility vests compulsory for drivers of Polish-registered vehicles

Portugal (P)

	120*	90	90	50
If towing				
	100*	90	80	50

*40kph minimum; 90kph maximum if licence held under 1 year

- Compulsory in front seats; compulsory if fitted in rear seats
- Under 12 and below 150cm must travel in the rear in an appropriate child restraint; rear-facing child seats permitted in front only if airbags deactivated
- 0.05% Compulsory
- Recommended Recommended
- Recommended
- 18 (motorcycles under 50cc 17)
- MOT certificate for vehicles over 3 years old, photographic proof of identity (e.g. driving licence or passport) must be carried at all times.
- Only allowed with hands-free kit
- LEZ An LEZ prohibits vehicles without catalytic converters from certain parts of Lisbon. There are plans to extend the scheme to the whole of the city
- ★ Dipped headlights compulsory for motorcycles, compulsory for other vehicles in poor visibility and tunnels
- ★ On-the-spot fines imposed
- ★ Radar-detectors prohibited
- ★ Tolls on motorways; do not use green lanes, these are reserved for auto-payment users. Some motorways require an automatic toll device.
- ★ Visibility vest compulsory
- ★ Wearers of spectacles or contact lenses should carry a spare pair

Romania (RO)

Cars and motorcycles				
	120/130	100	90	50
Vans				
	110	90	80	50
Motorcycles				
	100	80	80	50

For motor vehicles with trailers or if full driving licence has been held for less than one year, speed limits are 20kph lower than those listed above •Jeep-like vehicles: 70kph outside built-up areas but 60kph in all areas if diesel

- Compulsory
- Under 12 not allowed in front seats
- 0.00% Compulsory Compulsory
- Compulsory Compulsory 18
- Only allowed with hands-free kit
- ★ Dipped headlights compulsory outside built-up areas, compulsory everywhere for motorcycles
- ★ Electronic road tax system; price depends on emissions category and length of stay
- ★ It is illegal for vehicles to be dirty
- ★ On-the-spot fines imposed
- ★ Tolls on motorways
- ★ Visibility vest compulsory
- ★ Winter tyres compulsory Nov–Mar if roads are snow- or ice-covered, especially in mountainous areas

Russia (RUS)

	110	90	90	60
If licence held for under 2 years				
	70	70	70	60

- Compulsory if fitted
- Under 12 permitted in front seat only in an appropriate child restraint
- 0.00% Compulsory Compulsory
- Compulsory Compulsory 18
- International Driving Permit with Russian translation, visa, green card endorsed for Russia, International Certificate for Motor Vehicles
- Only allowed with a hands-free kit
- ★ Dipped headlights compulsory during the day
- ★ On-the-spot fines imposed
- ★ Picking up hitchhikers is prohibited
- ★ Radar detectors/blockers prohibited
- ★ Road tax payable at the border

Serbia (SRB)

	120	100	80	60

- Compulsory in front and rear seats
- Age 3–12 must be in rear seats and wear seat belt or appropriate child restraint; under 3 in rear-facing child seat permitted in front only if airbag deactivated
- 0.03% Compulsory Compulsory
- Compulsory Compulsory
- 18 (16 for motorbikes less than 125cc; 14 for mopeds)
- International Driving Permit, green card or locally bought third-party insurance
- No legislation
- ★ 3-metre tow bar or rope
- ★ 80km/h speed limit if towing a caravan
- ★ Dipped headlights compulsory
- ★ On-the-spot fines imposed
- ★ Radar detectors prohibited
- ★ Tolls on motorways and some primary roads
- ★ Visibility vest compulsory
- ★ Winter tyres compulsory Nov–Apr for vehicles up to 3.5 tonnes. Carrying snow chains recommended in winter as these may have to be fitted if driving on snow-covered roads, in accordance with signage.

Slovak Republic (SK)

	130	90	90	60

- Compulsory
- Under 12 or below 150cm must be in rear in appropriate child restraint
- 0.0 Compulsory
- Compulsory Compulsory
- Recommended 18 (15 for mopeds)
- International driving permit, proof of health insurance
- Only allowed with a hands-free kit
- ★ Dipped headlights compulsory at all times
- ★ On-the-spot fines imposed
- ★ Radar-detection equipment is prohibited
- ★ Tow rope recommended
- ★ Vignette required for motorways, car valid for 1 year, 30 days, 7 days; lorry vignettes carry a higher charge.
- ★ Visibility vests compulsory
- ★ Winter tyres compulsory

Slovenia (SLO)

	130	90*	90*	50
If towing				
	80	80*	80*	50

*70kph in urban areas

- Compulsory in front and, if fitted, in rear
- Under 12 and below 150cm must use appropriate child restraint; babies must use child safety seat
- 0.05% Compulsory Compulsory
- Compulsory Recommended
- 18 (motorbikes up to 125cc – 16, up to 350cc – 18)
- Only allowed with hands-free kit
- ★ Dipped headlights must be used at all times
- ★ On-the-spot fines imposed
- ★ Snow chains or winter tyres compulsory mid-Nov to mid-March, and in wintery conditions at other times
- ★ Vignettes valid for variety of periods compulsory for vehicles below 3.5 tonnes for toll roads. Write your vehicle registration number on the vignette before displaying it. For heavier vehicles electronic tolling system applies; several routes are cargo-traffic free during high tourist season.
- ★ Visibility vest compulsory

Spain (E)

	110	100	90	50
If towing				
	80	80	70	50

- Compulsory in front seats and if fitted in rear seats
- Under 135cm and below 12 must use appropriate child restraint
- 0.05%, 0.03% if less than 2 years full licence or if vehicle is over 3.5 tonnes or carries more than 9 passengers
- Two compulsory (one for in front, one for behind)
- Recommended Compulsory
- Recommended
- 18 (18/21 heavy vehicles; 18 for motorbikes over 125cc; 16 for motorbikes up to 125cc; 14 for mopeds up to 75cc)
- Only allowed with hands-free kit
- ★ Dipped headlights compulsory for motorcycles and in poor daytime visibility for other vehicles.
- ★ It is recommended that spectacles or contact lens wearers carry a spare pair.
- ★ Radar-detection equipment is prohibited
- ★ Snow chains recommended for mountainous areas in winter
- ★ Spare tyre compulsory
- ★ Tolls on motorways
- ★ Visibility vest compulsory

Sweden (S)

	110–120	80	70–100	30–60
If towing trailer with brakes				
	80	80	70	50

- Compulsory in front and rear seats
- Under 16 or below 135cm must use appropriate child restraint; below 140cm may travel in front only if airbag deactivated; rear-facing child seat permitted only if airbag deactivated.
- 0.02%
- Compulsory
- Recommended
- Recommended
- Recommended
- 18
- No legislation
- LEZ Gothenberg, Helsingborg, Lund, Malmo, Mölndal and Stockholm have LEZs, progressively prohibiting vehicles 6 or more years old.
- ★ 1 Dec–31 Mar winter tyres, anti-freeze and shovel compulsory
- ★ Dipped headlights must be used at all times
- ★ On-the-spot fines imposed
- ★ Radar-detection equipment is prohibited

Switzerland (CH)

	120	80	80	50/30
If towing up to 1 tonne / over 1 tonne				
	80	80	60/80	30/50

- Compulsory in front and, if fitted, in rear
- Up to 12 years and below 150 cm must use an appropriate child restraint. Children 6 and under must sit in the rear.
- 0.05%
- Compulsory
- Recommended
- Recommended
- Recommended
- 18 (mopeds up to 50cc – 16)
- Only allowed with a hands-free kit
- ★ Dipped headlights compulsory
- ★ GPS must have fixed speed camera function deactivated; radar detectors prohibited
- ★ Motorways are all toll and for vehicles below 3.5 tonnes a vignette must be purchased at the border. The vignette is valid for one calendar year. Vehicles over 3.5 tonnes must have an electronic tag for travel on any road.
- ★ On-the-spot fines imposed
- ★ Pedestrians have right of way
- ★ Picking up hitchhikers is prohibited on motorways and main roads
- ★ Spectacles or contact lens wearers must carry a spare pair in their vehicle at all times
- ★ Winter tyres recommended Nov–Mar; snow chains compulsory in designated areas in poor winter weather

Turkey (TR)

	120	90	90	50
If towing				
	70	70	70	40

- Compulsory in front seats
- Under 150 cm and below 36kg must use suitable child restraint. If above 136 cm may sit in the back without child restraint. Under 3s can only travel in the front in a rear facing seat if the airbag is deactivated. Children 3–12 may not travel in the front seat.
- 0.00%
- Two compulsory (one in front, one behind)
- Compulsory
- Compulsory
- Compulsory
- 18
- International driving permit advised; note that Turkey is in both Europe and Asia, green card/UK insurance that covers whole of Turkey or locally bought insurance, e-visa obtained in advance.
- Prohibited
- ★ Dipped headlights compulsory in daylight hours
- ★ On-the-spot fines imposed
- ★ Several motorways, and the Bosphorus bridges are toll roads
- ★ Tow rope and tool kit must be carried

Ukraine (UA)

	130	90	90	60
If towing				
	80	80	80	60

Speed limit in pedestrian zone 20 kph

- Compulsory in front and rear seats
- Under 12 and below 145cm must use an appropriate child restraint and sit in rear
- 0.02% – if use of medication can be proved. Otherwise 0.00%
- Compulsory
- Compulsory
- Optional
- Compulsory
- 18 cars; 16 motorbikes
- International Driving Permit, visa, International Certificate for Motor Vehicles, green card
- No legislation
- ★ A road tax is payable on entry to the country.
- ★ Dipped headlights compulsory in poor daytime visibility
- ★ On-the-spot fines imposed
- ★ Tow rope and tool kit recommended
- ★ Winter tyres compulsory Nov–Apr in snowy conditions

United Kingdom (GB)

	112	112	96	48
If towing				
	96	96	80	48

- Compulsory in front seats and if fitted in rear seats
- Under 3 not allowed in front seats except with appropriate restraint, and in rear must use child restraint if available; in front 3–12 or under 135cm must use appropriate child restraint, in rear must use appropriate child restraint (or seat belt if no child restraint is available, e.g. because two occupied restraints prevent fitting of a third).
- 0.08% (may change to 0.05% in Scotland)
- Recommended
- Recommended
- Recommended
- Recommended
- 17 (16 for mopeds)
- Only allowed with hands-free kit
- LEZ London's LEZ operates by number-plate recognition; non-compliant vehicles face hefty daily charges. Foreign-registered vehicles must register.
- ★ Driving is on the left
- ★ On-the-spot fines imposed
- ★ Smoking is banned in all commercial vehicles
- ★ Some toll motorways and bridges

Ski resorts

The resorts listed are popular ski centres, therefore road access to most is normally good and supported by road clearing during snow falls. However, mountain driving is never predictable and drivers should make sure they take suitable snow chains as well as emergency provisions and clothing. Listed for each resort are: the atlas page and grid square; the resort/minimum piste altitude (where only one figure is shown, they are at the same height) and maximum altitude of its own lifts; the number of lifts and gondolas (the total for lift-linked resorts); the season start and end dates (snow cover allowing); whether snow is augmented by cannon; the nearest town (with its distance in km) and, where available, the website and/or telephone number of the local tourist information centre or ski centre ('00' prefix required for calls from the UK).

The ❄ symbol indicates resorts with snow cannon

Andorra

Pyrenees

Pas de la Casa / Grau Roig 146 B2 ❄ 2050–2640m • 65 lifts • Dec–Apr • Andorra La Vella (30km) www.pasdelacasa-andorra.com • *Access via Envalira Pass (2407m), highest in Pyrenees, snow chains essential.*

Austria

Alps

Bad Gastein 109 B4 ❄ 1050/1100–2700m • 50 lifts • Dec–Mar • St Johann im Pongau (45km) i +43 6432 3393 0 www.gastein.com

Bad Hofgastein 109 B4 ❄ 860–2295m • 50 lifts • Dec–Mar • St Johann im Pongau (40km) i +43 6432 3393 0 www.gastein.com/en/region-orte/bad-hofgastein

Bad Kleinkirchheim 109 C4 ❄ 1070–2310m • 25 lifts • Dec–Mar • Villach (35km) i +43 4240 8212 www.badkleinkirchheim.at

Ehrwald 108 B1 ❄ 1000–2965m • 24 lifts • Dec–Apr • Imst (30km) i +43 5673 2395 www.wetterstein-bahnen.at/en

Innsbruck 108 B2 ❄ 574/850–3200m • 79 lifts • Dec–Apr • Innsbruck i + 43 512 56 2000 www.innsbruck-pauschalen.com • *Motorway normally clear. The motorway through to Italy and through the Arlberg Tunnel are both toll roads.*

Ischgl 107 B5 ❄ 1340/1380–2900m • 42 lifts • Dec–May • Landeck (25km) i +43 50990 100 www.ischgl.com • *Car entry to resort prohibited between 2200hrs and 0600hrs.*

Kaprun 109 B3 ❄ 885/770–3030m, • 53 lifts • Nov–Apr • Zell am See (10km) i +43 6542 770 www.zellamsee-kaprun.com

Kirchberg in Tirol 109 B3 860–2000m • 60 lifts • Nov–Apr • Kitzbühel (6km) i +43 57507 2100 www.kitzbueheler-alpen.com/en • *Easily reached from Munich International Airport (120 km)*

Kitzbühel (Brixen im Thale) 109 B3 ❄ 800/1210–2000m • 60 lifts • Dec–Apr • Wörgl (40km) i +43 57057 2200 www.kitzbueheler-alpen.com/en

Lech/Oberlech 107 B5 ❄ 1450–2810m • 62 lifts • Dec–Apr • Bludenz (50km) i +43 5583 2161 0 www.lechzuers.com • *Roads normally cleared but keep chains accessible because of altitude.*

Mayrhofen 108 B2 ❄ 630–2500m • 75 lifts • Dec–Apr • Jenbach (35km) i +43 5285 6760 www.mayrhofen.at • *Chains rarely required.*

Obertauern 109 B4 ❄ 1740/1640–2350m • 26 lifts • Dec–Apr • Radstadt (20km) i +43 6456 7252 www.obertauern.com • *Roads normally cleared but chain accessibility recommended. Camper vans and caravans not allowed; park these in Radstadt*

Saalbach Hinterglemm 109 B3 ❄ 1030/1100–2100m • 52 lifts • Nov–Apr • Zell am See (19km) i +43 6852 70660 www.saalbach.com • *Both village centres are pedestrianised and there is a good ski bus service during the daytime*

St Anton am Arlberg 107 B5 ❄ 1300–2810m • 84 lifts • Dec–Apr • Innsbruck (104km) i +43 5446 22690 www.stantonamarlberg.com

Schladming 109 B4 ❄ 745–1900m • 88 lifts • Dec–Mar • Schladming i + 43 36 87 233 10 www.schladming-dachstein.at

Serfaus 108 B1 ❄ 1427/1200–2820m • 70 lifts • Dec–Apr • Landeck (30km) i +43 5476 6239 www.serfaus-fiss-ladis.at • *Private vehicles banned from village. Use Dorfbahn Serfaus, an underground funicular which runs on an air cushion.*

Sölden 108 C2 ❄ 1380–3250m, • 33 lifts • Sep–Apr (glacier); Nov–Apr (main area) • Imst (50km) i +43 572 000 200 www.soelden.com • *Roads normally cleared but snow chains recommended because of altitude. The route from Italy and the south over the Timmelsjoch via Obergurgl is closed Oct–May and anyone arriving from the south should use the Brenner Pass motorway.*

Zell am See 109 B3 ❄ 750–1950m • 53 lifts • Dec–Mar • Zell am See i +43 6542 770 www.zellamsee-kaprun.com • *Low altitude, so good access and no mountain passes to cross.*

Zell im Zillertal (Zell am Ziller) 109 B3 ❄ 580/930–2410m • 22 lifts • Dec–Apr • Jenbach (25km) i +43 5282 7165–226 www.zillertalarena.com

Zürs 107 B5 ❄ 1720/1700–2450m • 62 lifts • Dec–Apr • Bludenz (30km) i +43 5583 2245 www.lech-zuers.at • *Roads normally cleared but keep chains accessible because of altitude. Village has garage with 24-hour self-service gas/petrol, breakdown service and wheel chains supply.*

France

Alps

Alpe d'Huez 118 B3 ❄ 1860–3330m • 85 lifts • Dec–Apr • Grenoble (63km) i +33 4 76 11 44 44 www.alpedhuez.com • *Snow chains may be required on access road to resort.*

Avoriaz 118 A3 ❄ 1800/1100–2280m • 35 lifts • Dec–May • Morzine (14km) i +33 4 50 74 02 11 www.morzine-avoriaz.com • *Chains may be required for access road from Morzine. Car-free resort, park on edge of village. Horse-drawn sleigh service available.*

Chamonix-Mont-Blanc 119 B3 ❄ 1035–3840m • 49 lifts • Dec–Apr • Martigny (38km) i +33 4 50 53 00 24 www.chamonix.com

Chamrousse 118 B2 ❄ 1700–2250m • 26 lifts • Dec–Apr • Grenoble (30km) i +33 4 76 89 92 65 www.chamrousse.com • *Roads normally cleared, keep chains accessible because of altitude.*

Châtel 119 A3 ❄ 1200/1110–2200m • 41 lifts • Dec–Apr • Thonon-Les-Bains (35km) i +33 4 50 73 22 44 http://info.chatel.com/english-version.html

Courchevel 118 B3 ❄ 1750/1300–2470m • 67 lifts • Dec–Apr • Moûtiers (23km) www.courchevel.com • *Roads normally cleared but keep chains accessible. Traffic 'discouraged' within the four resort bases.*

Flaine 118 A3 ❄ 1600–2500m • 26 lifts • Dec–Apr • Cluses (25km) i +33 4 50 90 80 01 www.flaine.com • *Keep chains accessible for D6 from Cluses to Flaine. Car access for depositing luggage and passengers only. 1500-space car park outside resort. Near Sixt-Fer-á-Cheval.*

La Clusaz 118 B3 ❄ 1100–2600m • 55 lifts • Dec–Apr • Annecy (32km) i +33 4 50 32 65 00 www.laclusaz.com • *Roads normally clear but keep chains accessible for final road from Annecy.*

La Plagne 118 B3 ❄ 2500/1250–3250m • 109 lifts • Dec–Apr Moûtiers (32km) i +33 4 79 09 79 79 www.la-plagne.com • *Ten different centres up to 2100m altitude. Road access via Bozel, Landry or Aime normally cleared. Linked to Les Arcs by cablecar*

Les Arcs 119 B3 ❄ 1600/1200–3230m • 77 lifts • Dec–May • Bourg-St-Maurice (15km) i +33 4 79 07 12 57 www.lesarcs.com • *Four base areas up to 2000 metres; keep chains accessible. Pay parking at edge of each base resort. Linked to La Plagne by cablecar*

Les Carroz d'Araches 118 A3 ❄ 1140–2500m • 80 lifts • Dec–Apr • Cluses (13km) i + 33 4 50 90 00 04 www.lescarroz.com

Les Deux-Alpes 118 C3 ❄ 55 lifts • Dec–Apr • 1650/1300–3600m • Grenoble (75km) i +33 4 76 79 22 00 www.les2alpes.com • *Roads normally cleared, however snow chains recommended for D213 up from valley road (D1091).*

Les Gets 118 A3 ❄ 1170/1000–2000m • 52 lifts • Dec–Apr • Cluses (18km) i +33 4 50 75 80 80 www.lesgets.com

Les Ménuires 118 B3 ❄ 1815/1850–3200m • 40 lifts • Dec–Apr • Moûtiers (27km) i +33 4 00 63 77 www.lesmenuires.com • *Keep chains accessible for D117 from Moûtiers.*

Les Sept Laux Prapoutel 118 B3 ❄ 1350–2400m, • 24 lifts • Dec–Apr • Grenoble (38km) i +33 4 76 08 17 86 www.les7laux.com • *Roads normally cleared, however keep chains accessible for mountain road up from the A41 motorway. Near St Sorlin d'Arves.*

Megève 118 B3 ❄ 1100/1050–2350m • 79 lifts • Dec–Apr • Sallanches (12km) i +33 4 50 21 27 28 www.megeve.com • *Horse-drawn sleigh rides available.*

Méribel 118 B3 ❄ 1400/1100–2950m • 61 lifts • Dec–May • Moûtiers (18km) i +33 4 79 08 60 01 www.meribel.net • *Keep chains accessible for 18km to resort on D90 from Moûtiers.*

Morzine 118 A3 ❄ 1000–2460m • 67 lifts • Dec–Apr • Thonon-Les-Bains (30km) i +33 4 50 74 72 72 www.morzine-avoriaz.com

Pra Loup 132 A2 ❄ 1600/1500–2500m • 53 lifts • Dec–Apr • Barcelonnette (10km) i +33 4 92 84 10 04 www.praloup.com • *Roads normally cleared but chains accessibility recommended.*

Risoul 118 C3 ❄ 1850/1650–2750m • 51 lifts • Dec–Apr • Briançon (40km) i +33 4 92 46 02 60 www.risoul.com • *Keep chains accessible. Near Guillestre. Linked with Vars Les Claux*

St-Gervais Mont-Blanc 118 B3 ❄ 850/1150–2350m • 27 lifts • Dec–Apr • Sallanches (10km) www.st-gervais.com

Serre Chevalier 118 C3 ❄ 1350/1200–2800m • 77 lifts • Dec–Apr • Briançon (10km) i + 33 4 92 24 98 98 www.serre-chevalier.com • *Made up of 13 small villages along the valley road, which is normally cleared.*

Tignes 119 B3 ❄ 2100/1550–3450m • 97 lifts • Jan–Dec • Bourg St Maurice (26km) i +33 4 79 40 04 40 www.tignes.net • *Keep chains accessible because of altitude.*

Val d'Isère 119 B3 ❄ 1850/1550–3450m • 97 lifts • Dec–Apr • Bourg-St-Maurice (30km) i +33 4 79 06 06 60 www.valdisere.com • *Roads normally cleared but keep chains accessible.*

Schladming ski resort, Austria nikolpetr / Shutterstock

Val Thorens 118 B3 2300/1850–3200m • 29 lifts • Dec–Apr • Moûtiers (37km) www.valthorens.com • *Chains essential – highest ski resort in Europe. Obligatory paid parking on edge of resort.*

Valloire 118 B3 1430–2600m • 34 lifts • Dec–Apr • Modane (20km) +33 4 79 59 03 96 www.valloire.net • *Road normally clear up to the Col du Galbier, to the south of the resort, which is closed from 1st November to 1st June. Linked to Valmeinier.*

Valmeinier 118 B3 1500–2600m • 34 lifts • Dec–Apr • St Michel de Maurienne (47km) +33 4 79 59 53 69 www.valmeinier.com • *Access from north on D1006 / D902. Col du Galbier, to the south of the resort closed from 1st November to 1st June. Linked to Valloire.*

Valmorel 118 B3 1400–2550m • 90 lifts • Dec–Apr • Moûtiers (15km) +33 4 79 09 85 55 www.valmorel.com • *Near St Jean-de-Belleville. Linked with ski areas of Doucy-Combelouvière and St François-Longchamp.*

Vars Les Claux 118 C3 1850/1650–2750m • 51 lifts • Dec–Apr • Briançon (40km) +33 4 92 46 51 31 www.vars-ski.com • *Four base resorts up to 1850 metres. Keep chains accessible. Linked with Risoul.*

Villard de Lans 118 B2 1050/1160–2170m • 28 lifts • Dec–Apr • Grenoble (32km) +33 4 76 95 10 38 www.villarddelans.com

Pyrenees

Font-Romeu 146 B3 1800/1600–2200m • 25 lifts • Nov–Apr • Perpignan (87km) +33 4 68 30 68 30 www.font-romeu.fr • *Roads normally clear but keep chains accessible.*

Saint-Lary Soulan 145 B4 Dec–Mar • 31 lifts • 830/1650/1700–2515m • Tarbes (75km) +33 5 62 39 50 81 www.saintlary.com • *Access roads constantly cleared of snow.*

Vosges

La Bresse-Hohneck 106 A1 Dec–Mar • 500/900–1350m • 33 lifts • Cornimont (6km) +33 3 29 25 41 29 www.labresse.net

Germany

Alps

Garmisch-Partenkirchen 108 B2 700–2830m • 38 lifts • Dec–Apr • Munich (95km) +49 8821 180 700 www.gapa.de • *Roads usually clear, chains rarely needed.*

Oberaudorf 108 B3 480–1850m • 30 lifts • Dec–Apr • Kufstein (15km) +49 8033 301 20 www.oberaudorf.de • *Motorway normally kept clear. Near Bayrischzell.*

Oberstdorf 107 B5 815m • 26 lifts • Dec–Apr • Sonthofen (15km) +49 8322 7000 http://oberstdorf.de

Rothaargebirge

Winterberg 81 A4 700/620–830m • 19 lifts • Dec–Mar • Brilon (30km) +49 2981 925 00 www.winterberg.de • *Roads usually cleared, chains rarely required.*

Greece

Central Greece

Mount Parnassos: Kelaria-Fterolakka 182 E4 1640–2260m • 14 lifts • Dec–Apr • Amfiklia +30 22340 22694-5 www.parnassos-ski.gr (Greek only)

Mount Parnassos: Gerondovrahos 182 E4 1800–1900m • 14 lifts • Dec–Apr • Amfiklia +30 29444 70371

Peloponnisos

Mount Helmos: Kalavrita Ski Centre 184 A3 1650–2100m • 7 lifts • Dec–Mar • Kalavrita +30 26920 2261 www.kalavrita-ski.gr (Greek only)

Mount Menalo: Ostrakina 184 B3 1500–1600m • 5 lifts • Dec–Mar • Tripoli +30 27960 22227

Macedonia

Mount Falakro: Agio Pneuma 183 B6 1720/1620–2230m • 7 lifts • Dec–Apr • Drama +30 25210 23691 www.falakro.gr (Greek only)

Mount Vasilitsa: Vasilitsa 182 C3 1750/1800–2113m • 3 lifts • Dec–Mar • Konitsa +30 24620 26100 www.vasilitsa.com (Greek only)

Mount Vermio: Seli 182 C4 1500–1900m • 8 lifts • Dec–Mar • Kozani +30 23320 71234 www.seli-ski.gr (in Greek)

Mount Vermio: Tria-Pente Pigadia 182 C3 1420–2005m • 7 lifts • Dec–Mar • Ptolemaida +30 23320 44464 www.3-5pigadia.gr

Mount Verno: Vigla 182 C3 1650–1900m • 5 lifts • Dec–Mar • Florina +30 23850 22354 www.vigla-ski.gr (in Greek)

Mount Vrondous: Lailias 183 B5 4 lifts • 1600–1850m • Dec–Mar • Serres +30 23210 53790

Thessalia

Mount Pilio: Agriolefkes 183 D5 4 lifts • 1300–1500m • Dec–Mar • Volos +30 24280 73719

Italy

Alps

Bardonecchia 118 B3 1312–2750m • 21 lifts • Dec–Apr • Bardonecchia www.bardonecchiaski.com + 39 0122 99137 • *Resort reached through the 11km Frejus tunnel from France, roads normally cleared.*

Bórmio 107 C5 1200/1230–3020m • 24 lifts • Dec–Apr • Tirano (40km) +39 342 902424 www.bormio.com • *Tolls payable in Ponte del Gallo Tunnel, open 0800hrs–2000hrs.*

Breuil-Cervinia 119 B4 2050–3500m • 21 lifts • Jan–Dec • Aosta (54km) +39 166 944311 www.cervinia.it • *Snow chains strongly recommended. Bus from Milan airport.*

Courmayeur 119 B3 1200–2760m • 21 lifts • Dec–Apr • Aosta (40km) +39 165 846658 www.courmayeur-montblanc.com • *Access through the Mont Blanc tunnel from France. Roads constantly cleared.*

Limone Piemonte 133 A3 1000/1050–2050m • 29 lifts • Dec–Apr • Cuneo (27km) + 39 171 925281 www.limonepiemonte.it • *Roads normally cleared, chains rarely required.*

Livigno 107 C5 1800–3000m • 31 lifts • Nov–May • Zernez (CH) (27km) +39 342 052200 www.livigno.com • *Keep chains accessible. The direction of traffic through Munt la Schera Tunnel to/from Zernez is regulated on Saturdays. Check in advance.*

Sestrière 119 C3 2035/1840–2840m • 92 lifts • Dec–Apr • Oulx (22km) +39 122 755444 www.visitsestriere.com • *One of Europe's highest resorts; although roads are normally cleared keep chains accessible.*

Appennines

Roccaraso – Aremogna 169 B4 1285/1240–2140m • 39 lifts • Dec–Apr • Castel di Sangro (7km) +39 864 62210 www.roccaraso.net (in Italian)

Dolomites

Andalo – Fai della Paganella 121 A3 1042/1050/2125m • 19 lifts • Dec–Apr • Trento (40km) www.visitdolomitipaganella.it +39 461 585836

Arabba 108 C2 1600/1450–2950m • 29 lifts • Dec–Mar • Brunico (45km) +39 436 780019 www.arabba.it • *Roads normally cleared but keep chains accessible.*

Cortina d'Ampezzo 108 C3 1224/1050–2930m • 37 lifts • Dec–Apr • Belluno (72km) +39 436 869086 www.cortina.dolomiti.org • *Access from north on route 51 over the Cimabanche Pass may require chains.*

Corvara (Alta Badia) 108 C2 1568–2500m • 52 lifts • Dec–Apr • Brunico (38km) +39 471 836176 www.altabadia.it • *Roads normally clear but keep chains accessible.*

Madonna di Campiglio 121 A3 1550/1500–2600m • 72 lifts • Dec–Apr • Trento (60km) +39 465 447501 www.campigliodolomiti.it/homepage • *Roads normally cleared but keep chains accessible. Linked to Folgarida and Marilleva.*

Moena di Fassa (Sorte/Ronchi) 108 C2 1184/1450–2520m • 8 lifts • Dec–Apr • Bolzano (40km) +39 462 609770 www.fassa.com

Selva di Val Gardena/Wolkenstein Groden 108 C2 1563/1570–2450m • 84 lifts • Dec–Apr • Bolzano (40km) +39 471 777777 www.valgardena.it • *Roads normally cleared but keep chains accessible.*

Norway

Hemsedal 47 B5 700/640–1450m • 24 lifts • Nov–May • Honefoss (150km) +47 32 055030 www.hemsedal.com • *Be prepared for extreme weather conditions.*

Slovak Republic

Chopok (Jasna-Chopok) 99 C3 900/950–1840m • 17 lifts • Dec–Apr • Jasna +421 907 886644 www.jasna.sk

Donovaly 99 C3 913–1360m • 17 lifts • Nov–Apr • Ruzomberok +421 48 4199900 www.parksnow.sk/zima

Martinské Hole 98 B2 1250/1150–1456m • 8 lifts • Nov–May • Zilina +421 43 430 6000 www.martinky.com (in Slovak only)

Plejsy 99 C4 470–912m • 9 lifts • Dec–Mar • Krompachy +421 53 429 8015 www.plejsy.sk

Strbske Pleso 99 B4 1380–1825m • 7 lifts • Dec–Mar • Poprad +421 917 682 260 www.vt.sk

Slovenia

Julijske Alpe

Kanin (Bovec) 122 A2 460/1600–2389m • 12 lifts • Dec–Apr • Bovec +386 5 384 1919 www.boveckanin.si

Kobla (Bohinj) 122 A2 512/530–1495m • 6 lifts • Dec–Mar • Bohinjska Bistrica +386 4 5747 100 www.bohinj.si/kobla/en/naprave.html

Kranjska Gora 122 A2 800–1210m • 19 lifts • Dec–Mar • Kranjska Gora +386 4 5809 440 www.kranjska-gora.si

Vogel 122 A2 570–1800m • 8 lifts • Dec–Apr • Bohinjska Bistrica +386 4 5729 712 www.vogel.si

Kawiniške Savinjske Alpe

Krvavec 122 A3 1450–1970m • 10 lifts • Dec–Apr • Kranj 386 4 25 25 911 www.rtc-krvavec.si

Pohorje

Rogla 123 A4 1517/1050–1500m • 13 lifts • Dec–Apr • Slovenska Bistrica +386 3 75 77 100 www.rogla.eu

Spain

Pyrenees

Baqueira-Beret/Bonaigua 145 B4 1500–2500m • 33 lifts • Dec–Apr • Vielha (15km) +34 902 415 415 www.baqueira.es • *Roads normally clear but keep chains accessible. Near Salardú.*

Sistema Penibetico

Sierra Nevada 163 A4 2100–3300m • 24 lifts • Dec–May • Granada (32km) +34 902 70 80 90 http://sierranevada.es • *Access road designed to be avalanche safe and is snow cleared.*

Sweden

Idre Fjäll 199 D9 590–890m • 33 lifts • Nov–Apr • Mora (140km) +46 253 41000 www.idrefjall.se • *Be prepared for extreme weather conditions.*

Sälen 49 A5 360m • 100 lifts • Nov–Apr • Malung (70km) +46 771 84 00 00 www.skistar.com/salen • *Be prepared for extreme weather conditions.*

Switzerland

Alps

Adelboden 106 C2 1353m • 55 lifts • Dec–Apr • Frutigen (15km) +41 33 673 80 80 www.adelboden.ch • *Linked with Lenk.*

Arosa 107 C4 1800m • 16 lifts • Dec–Apr • Chur (30km) +41 81 378 70 20 www.arosa.ch (German only) • *Roads cleared but keep chains accessible due to high altitude.*

Crans Montana 119 A4 1500–3000m • 34 lifts • Dec–Apr, Jul–Oct • Sierre (15km) www.crans-montana.ch +41 848 22 12 12 • *Roads normally cleared but keep chains accessible for ascent from Sierre.*

Davos 107 C4 1560/1100–2840m • 38 lifts • Nov–Apr • Davos +41 81 415 21 21 www.davos.ch

Engelberg 106 C3 1000/1050–3020m • 26 lifts • Nov–May • Luzern (39km) +41 41 639 77 77 www.engelberg.ch • *Straight access road normally cleared.*

Flums (Flumserberg) 107 B4 17 lifts • 1400/1000–2220m • Dec–Apr • Buchs (25km) +41 81 720 18 18 www.flumserberg.ch • *Roads normally cleared, but 1000-metre vertical ascent; keep chains accessible.*

Grindelwald 106 C3 1050–2950m • 39 lifts • Dec–Apr • Interlaken (20km) +41 33 854 12 12 www.jungfrauregion.ch

Gstaad – Saanenland 106 C2 1050/950–3000m • 74 lifts • Dec–Apr • Gstaad +41 33 748 81 81 www.gstaad.ch • *Linked to Anzère.*

Klosters 107 C4 1191/1110–2840m • 52 lifts • Dec–Apr • Davos (10km) +41 81 410 20 20 www.klosters.ch • *Roads normally clear but keep chains accessible.*

Leysin 119 A4 2263/1260–2330m • 16 lifts • Dec–Apr • Aigle (6km) +41 24 493 33 00 www.leysin.ch

Mürren 106 C2 1650–2970m • 12 lifts • Dec–Apr • Interlaken (18km) +41 33 856 86 86 www.mymuerren.ch • *No road access. Park in Strechelberg (1500 free places) and take the two-stage cable car.*

Nendaz 119 A4 1365/1400–3300m • 20 lifts • Nov–Apr • Sion (16km) +41 27 289 55 89 www.nendaz.ch • *Roads normally cleared, however keep chains accessible for ascent from Sion. Near Vex.*

Saas-Fee 119 A4 1800–3500m • 23 lifts • Jan–Dec • Brig (35km) +41 27 958 18 58 www.saas-fee.ch • *Roads normally cleared but keep chains accessible because of altitude.*

St Moritz 107 C4 1856/1730–3300m • 24 lifts • Nov–May • Chur (89km) +41 81 837 33 33 www.stmoritz.ch • *Roads normally cleared, keep chains accessible.*

Samnaun 107 C5 1846/1400–2900m • 40 lifts • Dec–May • Scuol (30km) +41 81 861 88 30 www.engadin.com • *Roads normally cleared, keep chains accessible.*

Verbier 119 A4 1500–3330m • 17 lifts • Nov–Apr • Martigny (27km) +41 27 775 38 70 www.verbier.ch • *Roads normally cleared.*

Villars-Gryon 119 A4 1253/1200–2100m • 16 lifts • Dec–Apr, Jun–Jul • Montreux (35km) +41 24 495 32 32 www.villars.ch • *Roads normally cleared but keep chains accessible for ascent from N9. Near Bex.*

Wengen 106 C2 1270–2320m • 39 lifts • Dec–Apr • Interlaken (12km) +41 33 856 85 85 http://wengen.ch • *No road access. Park at Lauterbrunnen and take mountain railway.*

Zermatt 119 A4 1620–3900m • 40 lifts, • all year • Brig (42km) +41 27 966 81 00 www.zermatt.ch • *Cars not permitted in resort, park in Täsch (3km) and take shuttle train.*

Turkey

North Anatolian Mountains

Uludag 186 B4 1770–2320m • 13 lifts • Dec–Mar • Bursa (36km) +90 224 285 21 11 http://skiingturkey.com/resorts/uludag.html

300 greatest sights of Europe

For entries with no website listed, use that given for the national tourist board.

Albania Shqipëria

www.albaniantourism.com

Berat

Fascinating old town with picturesque Ottoman Empire buildings and traditional Balkan domestic architecture. **www.albaniantourism.com/berat 182 C1**

Tirana Tiranë

Capital of Albania. Skanderbeg Square has main historic buildings. Also: 18c Haxhi Ethem Bey Mosque; Art Gallery (Albanian); National Museum of History. Nearby: medieval Krujë; Roman monuments. **www.albaniantourism.com/tirane 182 B1**

Austria Österreich

www.austria.info

Bregenz

Lakeside town bordering Germany, Liechtenstein, Switzerland. Locals, known as Vorarlbergers, have their own dialect. The Martinsturm Roman to 17c tower, 17c town hall and Seekapelle, Kunsthaus modern art museum, Vorarlberger Landesmuseum, Festspielhaus. **www.bregenz.travel 107 B4**

Graz

University town, seat of imperial court to 1619. Historic centre around Hauptplatz. Imperial monuments: Burg; mausoleum of Ferdinand II; towers of 16c schloss; 17c Schloss Eggengerg (with Old Gallery). Also: 16c Town Hall; Zeughaus; 15c cathedral; New Gallery (good 19–20c); Kunsthaus (modern art). **www.graztourismus.at 110 B2**

Innsbruck

Old town is reached by Maria-Theresien-Strasse with famous views. Buildings: Goldenes Dachl (1490s); 18c cathedral; remains of Hofburg imperial residence; 16c Hofkirche (tomb of Maximilian I). **www.innsbruckaustria.co.uk 108 B2**

Krems

On a hill above the Danube, medieval quarter has Renaissance mansions. Also: Gothic Piaristenkirche; Museumkrems; Kunsthalle (modern art). **www.krems.gv.at 97 C3**

Linz

Port on the Danube. Historic buildings are concentrated on Hauptplatz below the imperial 15c schloss. Notable: Baroque Old Cathedral; 16c Town Hall; Old Castle Museum; Lentos Art Museum. **www.linz.at 96 C2**

▲ **Maholicahaus, Vienna, Austria**

Melk

Set on a rocky hill above the Danube, the fortified abbey is the greatest Baroque achievement in Austria – particularly the Grand Library and abbey church. **www.stiftmelk.at 110 A2**

Salzburg

Set in subalpine scenery, the town was associated with powerful 16–17c prince-archbishops. The 17c cathedral has a complex of archiepiscopal buildings: the Residence and its gallery (19c); the 13c Franciscan Church (notable altar). Also: Mozart's birthplace; Schloss Mirabell; Salzburg Museum; the Hohensalzburg fortress; the Collegiate Church of St Peter (cemetery, catacombs); Museum of Modern Art at the Mönschberg and Rupertinum. **www.salzburg.info/en 109 B4**

Salzkammergut

Natural beauty with 76 lakes (Wolfgangersee, Altersee, Traunsee, Grundlsee) in mountain scenery. Attractive villages (St Wolfgang) and towns (Bad Ischl, Gmunden) include Hallstatt, famous for Celtic remains. **www.salzkammergut.at 109 B4**

Vienna Wien

Capital of Austria, the historic centre lies within the Ring. Churches: Gothic St Stephen's Cathedral; 17c Imperial Vault; 14c Augustine Church; 14c Church of the Teutonic Order (treasure); 18c Baroque churches (Jesuit Church, Franciscan Church, St Peter, St Charles). Imperial residences: Hofburg; Schönbrunn. Architecture of Historicism on Ringstrasse (from 1857). Art Nouveau: station pavilions, Secession Building, Postsparkasse, Looshaus, Majolicahaus. Museums: Art History Museum (antiquities, old masters), Cathedral and Diocesan Museum (15c), Albertina (graphic arts), Liechtenstein Museum (old masters), Museum of Applied Arts, Museum of Modern Art (MUMOK), Leopold Museum, Belvedere (Gothic, Baroque, 19–20c); AzW (architecture); Vienna Museum. **www.wien.info 111 A3**

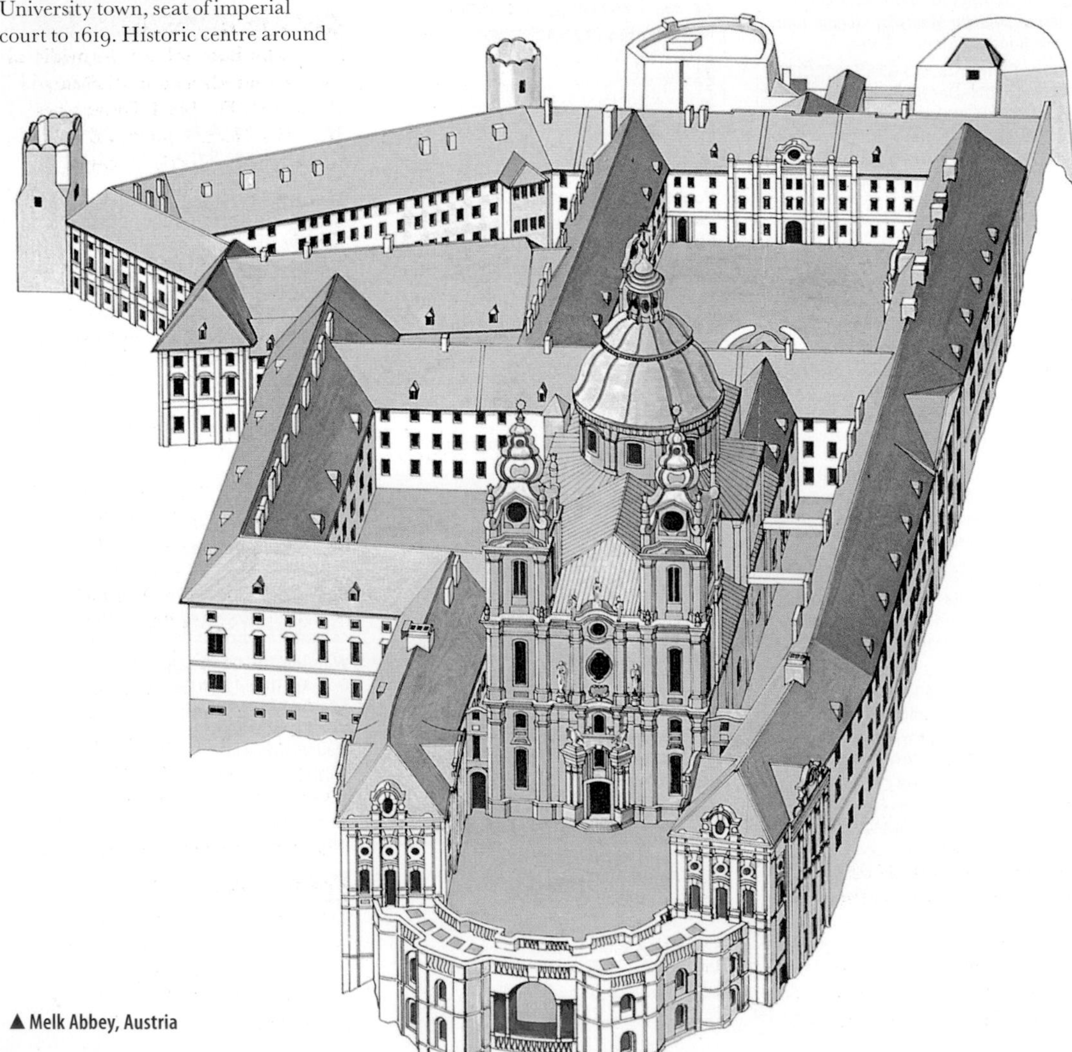

▲ **Melk Abbey, Austria**

Belgium Belgique

www.visitbelgium.com

Antwerp Antwerpen

City with many tall gabled Flemish houses on the river. Heart of the city is Great Market with 16–17c guildhouses and Town Hall. Charles Borromeus Church (Baroque). 14–16c Gothic cathedral has Rubens

▼ Town Hall, Antwerp, Belgium

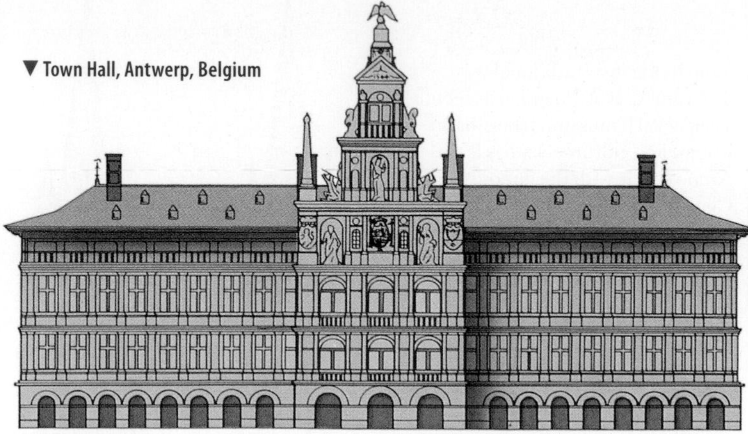

paintings. Rubens also at the Rubens House and his burial place in St Jacob's Church. Excellent museums: Mayer van den Bergh Museum (applied arts); Koninklijk Museum of Fine Arts (Flemish, Belgian); MAS (ethnography, folklore, shipping); Muhka (modern art). www.visitantwerpen.be 79 A4

Bruges Brugge

Well-preserved medieval town with narrow streets and canals. Main squares: the Market with 13c Belfort and covered market; the Burg with Basilica of the Holy Blood and Town Hall. The collections of Groeninge Museum and Memling museum in St Jans Hospital include 15c Flemish masters. The Onze Lieve Vrouwekerk has a famous *Madonna and Child* by Michelangelo http://visitbruges.be 78 A3

Brussels Bruxelles

Capital of Belgium. The Lower Town is centred on the enormous Grand Place with Hôtel de Ville and rebuilt guildhouses. Symbols of the city include the 'Manneken Pis' and Atomium (giant model of a molecule). The 13c Notre Dame de la Chapelle is the oldest church. The Upper Town contains: Gothic cathedral; Neoclassical Place Royale; 18c King's Palace; Royal Museums of Fine Arts (old and modern masters) Magritte Museum; MRAH (art and historical artefacts); BELvue museum (in the Bellevue Residence). Also: much Art Nouveau (Horta Museum, Hôtel Tassel, Hôtel Solvay); Place du Petit Sablon and Place du Grand Sablon; 19c Palais de Justice. http://visitbrussels.be 79 B4

Ghent Gent

Medieval town built on islands surrounded by canals and rivers. Views from Pont St-Michel. The Graslei and Koornlei quays have Flemish guild houses. The Gothic cathedral has famous Van Eyck altarpiece. Also: Belfort; Cloth Market; Gothic Town Hall; Gravensteen. Museums: STAM Museum in Bijloke Abbey (provincial and applied art); Museum of Fine Arts (old masters). www.visitgent.be 79 A3

Namur

Reconstructed medieval citadel is the major sight of Namur, which also has a cathedral and provincial museums. www.namurtourisme.be/index.php 79 B4

Tournai

The Romanesque-Gothic cathedral is Belgium's finest (much excellent art). Fine Arts Museum has a good collection (15–20c). www.tournai.be/en/officiel 78 B3

Bulgaria Bulgariya

www.bulgariatravel.org

Black Sea Coast

Beautiful unspoiled beaches (Zlatni Pyasŭtsi). The delightful resort Varna is popular. Nesebŭr is famous for Byzantine churches. Also: Danube Delta in Hungary. 17 D7

Koprivshtitsa

Beautiful village known both for its half-timbered houses and links with the April Rising of 1876. Six house museums amongst which the Lyutov House and the Oslekov House, plus the birthplaces of Georgi Benkovski, Dimcho Debelyanov, Todor Kableshkov, and Lyuben Karavelov. www.eng.koprivshtitza.com

Plovdiv

City set spectacularly on three hills. The old town has buildings from many periods: 2c Roman stadium and amphitheatre; 14c Dzumaiya Mosque; Archaeological Museum; 19c Ethnographic Museum. Nearby: Bačkovo Monastery (frescoes). www.bulgariatravel.org/en/object/306/plovdiv_grad 183 A6

Rila

Bulgaria's finest monastery, set in the most beautiful scenery of the Rila mountains. The church is richly decorated with frescoes. www.rilamonastery.pmg-blg.com 183 A5

Sofia Sofiya

Capital of Bulgaria. Sights: exceptional neo-Byzantine cathedral; Church of St Sofia; St Alexander Nevsky Cathedral; Boyana church; 4c rotunda of St George (frescoes); Byzantine Boyana Church (frescoes) on panoramic Mount Vitoša. Museums: National Historical Museum (particularly for Thracian artefacts); National Art Gallery (icons, Bulgarian art). 17 D5 www.bulgariatravel.org/en/object/234/sofia

Veliko Tŭrnovo

Medieval capital with narrow streets. Notable buildings: House of the Little Monkey; Hadji Nicoli Inn; ruins of medieval citadel; Baudouin Tower; churches of the Forty Martyrs and of SS Peter and Paul (frescoes); 14c Monastery of the Transfiguration. www.bulgariatravel.org/en/object/15/veliko_tyrnovo_grad 17 D6

Croatia Hrvatska

http://croatia.hr

Dalmatia Dalmacija

Exceptionally beautiful coast along the Adriatic. Among its 1185 islands, those of the Kornati Archipelago and Brijuni Islands are perhaps the most spectacular. Along the coast are several attractive medieval and Renaissance towns, most notably Dubrovnik, Split, Šibenik, Trogir, Zadar. www.dalmacija.net 138 B2

Dubrovnik

Surrounded by medieval and Renaissance walls, the city's architecture dates principally from 15–16c. Sights: many churches and monasteries including Church of St Blaise and Dominican monastery (art collection); promenade street of Stradun, Dubrovnik Museums; Renaissance Rector's Palace; Onofrio's fountain; Sponza Palace. The surrounding area has some eighty 16c noblemen's summer villas. http://experience.dubrovnik.hr/eng 139 C4

Islands of Croatia

There are over 1,000 islands off the coast of Croatia among which there is Brač, known for its white marble and the beautiful beaches of Bol (www.bol.hr); Hvar (www.tzhvar.hr/en/) is beautifully green with fields of lavender, marjoram, rosemary, sage and thyme; Vis (www.tz-vis.hr) has the beautiful towns of Komiža and Vis Town, with the Blue Cave on nearby Biševo. 123 & 137–138

Istria Istra

Peninsula with a number of ancient coastal towns (Rovinj, Poreč, Pula, Piran in Slovene Istria) and medieval hill-top towns (Motovun). Pula has Roman monuments (exceptional 1c amphitheatre). Poreč has narrow old streets; the mosaics in 6c Byzantine basilica of St Euphrasius are exceptional. See also Slovenia. www.istra.hr 122 B2

Plitvička Jezera

Outstandingly beautiful world of water and woodlands with 16 lakes and 92 waterfalls interwoven by canyons. Archaeological museums; art gallery; Gallery of Ivan Meštrović. www.tzplitvice.hr 123 C4

Split

Most notable for the exceptional 4c palace of Roman Emperor Diocletian, elements of which are incorporated into the streets and buildings of the town itself. The town also has a cathedral (11c baptistry) and a Franciscan monastery. www.split.info 138 B2

Trogir

The 13–15c town centre is surrounded by medieval city walls. Romanesque-Gothic cathedral includes the chapel of Ivan the Blessed. Dominican and Benedictine monasteries house art collections; Ćipiko palace; Lučić palace. http://tztrogir.hr 138 B2

Zagreb

Capital city of Croatia with cathedral and Archbishop's Palace in Kaptol and to the west Gradec with Baroque palaces. Donji Grad – The Lower Town – is home to the Archaological Museum, Art Pavilion, Museum of Arts and Crafts, Ethnographic Museum, Mimara Museum and National Theatre; Modern Gallery; Museum of Contemporary Art. www.zagreb-touristinfo.hr 124 B1

Czech Republic Česka Republica

www.czechtourism.com

Brno

Capital of Moravia. Sights: Vegetable Market and Old Town Hall; Capuchin crypt decorated with bones of dead monks; hill of St Peter with Gothic cathedral; Church of St James; Mies van der Rohe's buildings (Bata, Avion Hotel, Togendhat House). Museums: Moravian Museum; Moravian Gallery; City Art Gallery; Brno City Museum in Spilberk Castle. www.brno.cz 97 B4

České Budějovice

Famous for Budvar beer, the medieval town is centred on náměsti Přemysla Otokara II. The Black Tower gives fine views. Nearby: medieval Český Krumlov. www.c-budejovice.cz/en 96 C2

Kutná Hora

A town with strong silver mining heritage shown in the magnificent Cathedral of sv Barbara which was built by the miners. See also the ossuary with 40,000 complete sets of bones moulded into sculptures and decorations. www.czechtourism.com/t/kutna-hora 97 B3

Olomouc

Well-preserved medieval university town of squares and fountains. The Upper Square has the Town Hall. Also: 18c Holy Trinity; Baroque Church of St Michael. http://tourism.olomouc.eu 98 B1

Pilsen Plzeň

Best known for Plzeňský Prazdroj (Pilsener Urquell), beer has been brewed here since 1295. An industrial town with eclectic architecture shown in the railway stations and the namesti Republiky (main square). www.czechtourism.com/a/pilsen-area 96 B1

Prague Praha

Capital of Czech Republic and Bohemia. The Castle Quarter has a complex of buildings behind the walls (Royal Castle; Royal Palace; cathedral). The Basilica of St George has a fine Romanesque interior. The Belvedere is the best example of Renaissance architecture. Hradčani Square has aristocratic palaces and the National Gallery. The Little Quarter has many Renaissance (Wallenstein Palace) and Baroque mansions and the Baroque Church of St Nicholas. The Old Town has its centre at the Old Town Square with the Old Town Hall (astronomical clock), Art Nouveau Jan Hus monument and Gothic Týn church. The Jewish quarter has 14c Staranova Synagogue and Old Jewish Cemetery. The Charles Bridge is famous. The medieval New Town has many Art Nouveau buildings and is centred on Wenceslas Square. www.prague.cz **84 B2**

Spas of Bohemia
Spa towns of Karlovy Vary (Carlsbad: www.karlovyvary.cz), Márianske Lázně (Marienbad: www.marianskelazne.cz) and Frantiskovy Lázně **83 B4**

Denmark Danmark
www.visitdenmark.com

Århus
Second largest city in Denmark with a mixture of old and new architecture that blends well, Århus has been dubbed the culture capital of Denmark with the Gothic Domkirke; Latin Quarter; 13th Century Vor Frue Kirke; Den Gamle By, open air museum of traditional Danish life; ARoS (art museum). www.visitaarhus.com **59 B3**

Copenhagen København
Capital of Denmark. Old centre has fine early 20c Town Hall. Latin Quarter has 19c cathedral. 18c Kastellet has statue of the Little Mermaid nearby. The 17c Rosenborg Castle was a royal residence, as was the Christianborg (now government offices). Other popular sights: Nyhavn canal; Tivoli Gardens. Excellent art collections: Ny Carlsberg Glypotek; National Gallery; National Museum. www.visitcopenhagen.dk **61 D2**

Hillerød
Frederiskborg (home of the national history museum) is a fine red-brick Renaissance castle set among three lakes. www.visitnorthsealand.com/ln-int/north-sealand/hilleroed **61 D2**

Roskilde
Ancient capital of Denmark. The marvellous cathedral is a burial place of the Danish monarchy. The Viking Ship Museum houses the remains of five 11c Viking ships excavated in the 1960s. www.visitroskilde.com **61 D2**

Estonia Eesti
www.visitestonia.com

Kuressaare
Main town on the island of Saaremaa with the 14c Kuressaare Kindlus. www.visitestonia.com/en/kuressaare-tourist-information-centre **8 C3**

Pärnu
Sea resort with an old town centre. Sights: 15c Red Tower; neoclassical Town Hall; St Catherine's Church. www.visitparnu.com **8 C4**

Tallinn
Capital of Estonia. The old town is centred on the Town Hall Square. Sights: 15c Town Hall; Toompea Castle; Three Sisters houses. Churches: Gothic St Nicholas; 14c Church of the Holy Spirit; St Olaf's Church; Kumu Art Museum; Maritime Museum. www.tourism.tallinn.ee **8 C4**

Tartu
Historic town with 19c university. The Town Hall Square is surrounded by neoclassical buildings. Also: remains of 13c cathedral; Estonian National Museum. www.visittartu.com **8 C5**

Finland Suomi
www.visitfinland.com

Finnish Lakes
Area of outstanding natural beauty covering about one third of the country with thousands of lakes, of which Päijänne and Saimaa are the most important. Tampere, industrial centre of the region, has numerous museums, including the Tampere Art Museum (modern). Savonlinna has the medieval Olavinlinna Castle. Kuopio has the Orthodox and Regional Museums. **8 A5**

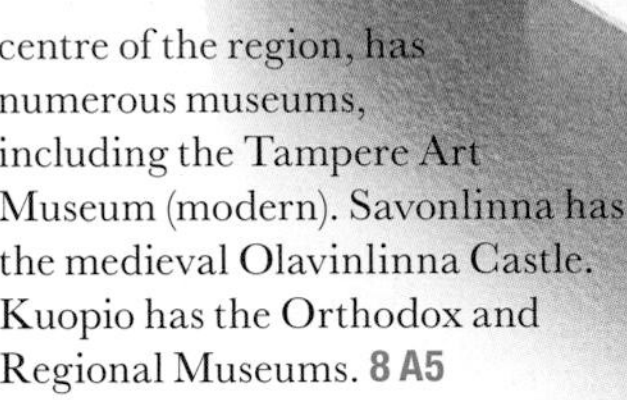

Helsinki
Capital of Finland. The 19c neoclassical town planning between the Esplanade and Senate Square includes the Lutheran cathedral. There is also a Russian Orthodox cathedral. The Constructivist Stockmann Department Store is the largest in Europe. The main railway station is Art Nouveau. Gracious 20c buildings in Mannerheimintie avenue include Finlandiatalo by Alvar Aalto. Many good museums: Art Museum of the Ateneum (19–20c); National Museum; Design Museum; Helsinki City Art Museum (modern Finnish); Open Air Museum (vernacular architecture); 18c fortress of Suomenlinna has several museums. www.visithelsinki.fi **8 B4**

Lappland (Finnish)
Vast unspoiled rural area. Lappland is home to thousands of nomadic Sámi living in a traditional way. The capital, Rovaniemi, was rebuilt after WWII; museums show Sámi history and culture. Nearby is the Arctic Circle with the famous Santa Claus Village. Inari is a centre of Sámi culture. See also Norway and Sweden. www.lapland.fi/en/travel **192–193**

France
http://us.rendezvousenfrance.com/

Albi
Old town with rosy brick architecture. The vast Cathédrale Ste-Cécile (begun 13c) holds some good art. The Berbie Palace houses the Toulouse-Lautrec museum. www.albi-tourisme.fr **130 B1**

Alps
Grenoble, capital of the French Alps, has a good 20c collection in the Museum of Grenoble. The Vanoise Massif has the greatest number of resorts (Val d'Isère, Courchevel). Chamonix has spectacular views on Mont Blanc, France's and Europe's highest peak. www.thealps.com **118 B2**

▲ Abbaye aux Hommes, Caen, France

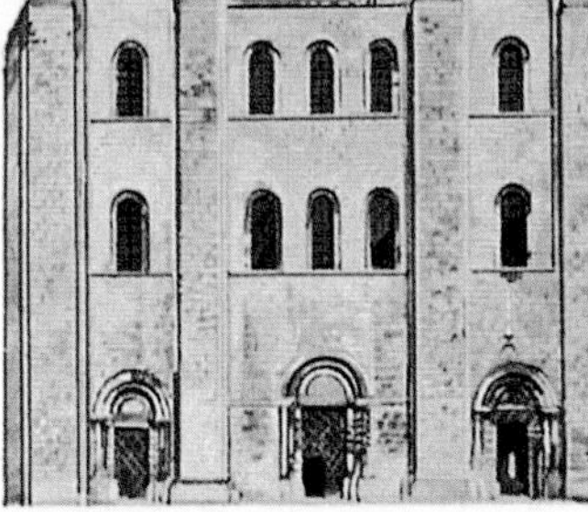

◄ Château de Chenonceaux, Châteaux of the Loire, France

Amiens
France's largest Gothic cathedral has beautiful decoration. The Museum of Picardy has unique 16c panel paintings. www.visit-amiens.com **90 B2**

Arles
Ancient, picturesque town with Roman relics (1c amphitheatre), 11c cathedral, Archaeological Museum (Roman art); Van Gogh centre. www.arlestourisme.com **131 B3**

Avignon
Medieval papal capital (1309–77) with 14c walls and many ecclesiastical buildings. Vast Palace of the Popes has stunning frescoes. The Little Palace has fine Italian Renaissance painting. The 12–13c Bridge of St Bénézet is famous. www.ot-avignon.fr **131 B3**

Bourges
The Gothic Cathedral of St Etienne, one of the finest in France, has a superb sculptured choir. Also notable is the House of Jacques Coeur. www.bourgestourisme.com **103 B4**

Burgundy Bourgogne
Rural wine region with a rich Romanesque, Gothic and Renaissance heritage. The 12c cathedral in Autun and 12c basilica in Vézelay

have fine Romanesque sculpture. Monasteries include 11c L'Abbaye de Cluny (ruins) and L'Abbaye de Fontenay. Beaune has beautiful Gothic Hôtel-Dieu and 15c Nicolas Rolin hospices.
www.burgundy-tourism.com **104 B3**

Brittany Bretagne

Brittany is famous for cliffs, sandy beaches and wild landscape. It is also renowned for megalithic monuments (Carnac) and Celtic culture. Its capital, Rennes, has the Palais de Justice and good collections in the Museum of Brittany (history) and Museum of Fine Arts. Also: Nantes; St-Malo. www.bretagne.com **100–101**

Caen

City with two beautiful Romanesque buildings: Abbaye aux Hommes; Abbaye aux Dames. The château has two museums (15–20c painting; history). The *Bayeux Tapestry* is displayed in nearby Bayeux.
www.tourisme.caen.fr **89 A3**

Carcassonne

Unusual double-walled fortified town of narrow streets with an inner fortress. The fine Romanesque Church of St Nazaire has superb stained glass.
www.tourism-carcassonne.co.uk **130 B1**

Chartres

The 12–13c cathedral is an exceptionally fine example of Gothic architecture (Royal Doorway, stained glass, choir screen). The Fine Arts Museum has a good collection.
www.chartres.com **90 C1**

Clermont-Ferrand

The old centre contains the cathedral built out of lava and Romanesque basilica. The Puy de Dôme and Puy de Sancy give spectacular views over some 60 extinct volcanic peaks (*puys*).
www.clermontferrandtourism.com **116 B3**

Colmar

Town characterised by Alsatian half-timbered houses. The Unterlinden Museum has excellent German religious art including the famous Isenheim altarpiece. The Dominican church also has a fine altarpiece. Espace André Malraux (contemporary arts). www.ot-colmar.fr **106 A2**

Corsica Corse

Corsica has a beautiful rocky coast and mountainous interior. Napoleon's birthplace of Ajaccio has: Fesch Museum with Imperial Chapel and a large collection of Italian art; Maison Bonaparte; cathedral. Bonifacio, a medieval town, is spectacularly set on a rock over the sea.
www.visit-corsica.com **180**

Côte d'Azur

The French Riviera is best known for its coastline and glamorous resorts. There are many relics of artists who worked here: St-Tropez has Musée de l'Annonciade; Antibes has 12c Château Grimaldi with the Picasso Museum; Cagnes has the Renoir House and Mediterranean Museum of Modern Art; St-Paul-de-Vence has the excellent Maeght Foundation and Matisse's Chapelle du Rosaire. Cannes is famous for its film festival. Also: Marseille, Monaco, Nice.
www.frenchriviera-tourism.com **133 B3**

Dijon

Great 15c cultural centre. The Palais des Ducs et des Etats is the most notable monument and contains the Museum of Fine Arts. Also: the Charterhouse of Champmol.
www.visitdijon.com **105 B4**

Disneyland Paris

Europe's largest theme park follows in the footsteps of its famous predecessors in the United States.
www.disneylandparis.com **90 C2**

Le Puy-en-Velay

Medieval town bizarrely set on the peaks of dead volcanoes. It is dominated by the Romanesque cathedral (cloisters). The Romanesque chapel of St-Michel is dramatically situated on the highest rock. www.ot-lepuyenvelay.fr **117 B3**

Loire Valley

The Loire Valley has many 15–16c châteaux built amid beautiful scenery by French monarchs and members of their courts. Among the most splendid are Azay-le-Rideau, Chenonceaux and Loches. Also: Abbaye de Fontévraud. www.lvo.com **102 B2**

Lyon

France's third largest city has an old centre and many museums including the Museum of the History of Textiles and the Museum of Fine Arts (old masters). www.lyon-france.com **117 B4**

Marseilles Marseille

Second lagest city in France. Spectacular views from the 19c Notre-Dame-de-la-Garde. The Old Port has 11-12c Basilique St Victor (crypt, catacombs). Cantini Museum has major collection of 20c French art. Château d'If was the setting of Dumas' *The Count of Monte Cristo.*
www.marseille-tourisme.com **131 B4**

Mont-St-Michel

Gothic pilgrim abbey (11–12c) set dramatically on a steep rock island rising from mud flats and connected to the land by a road covered by the tide. The abbey is made up of a complex of buildings.
www.ot-montsaintmichel.com **101 A4**

Nancy

A centre of Art Nouveau. The 18c Place Stanislas was constructed by dethroned Polish king Stanislas. Museums: School of Nancy Museum (Art Nouveau furniture); Fine Arts Museum. www.ot-nancy.fr **92 C2**

Nantes

Former capital of Brittany, with the 15c Château des ducs de Bretagne. The cathedral has a striking interior.
www.nantes-tourisme.com **101 B4**

Nice

Capital of the Côte d'Azur, the old town is centred on the old castle on the hill. The seafront includes the famous 19c Promenade des Anglais. The aristocratic quarter of the Cimiez Hill has the Marc Chagall Museum and the Matisse Museum. Also: Museum of Modern and Contemporary Art (especially neo-Realism and Pop Art).
www.nicetourism.com **133 B3**

Paris

Capital of France, one of Europe's most interesting cities. The Île de la Cité area, an island in the River Seine has the 12–13c Gothic Notre Dame (wonderful stained glass) and La Sainte-Chapelle (1240–48), one of the jewels of Gothic art. The Left Bank area: Latin Quarter with the famous Sorbonne university; Museum of Cluny housing medieval art; the Panthéon; Luxembourg Palace and Gardens; Montparnasse, interwar artistic and literary centre; Eiffel Tower; Hôtel des Invalides with Napoleon's tomb. Right Bank: the great boulevards (Avenue des Champs-Élysées joining the Arc de Triomphe and Place de la Concorde); 19c Opéra Quarter; Marais, former aristocratic quarter of elegant mansions (Place des Vosges); Bois de Boulogne, the largest park in Paris; Montmartre, centre of 19c bohemianism, with the Basilique Sacré-Coeur. The Church of St Denis is the first gothic church and the mausoleum of the French monarchy. Paris has three of the world's greatest art collections: The Louvre (to 19c, *Mona Lisa*), Musée d'Orsay (19–20c) and National Modern Art Museum in the Pompidou Centre. Other museums include: Orangery Museum; Paris Museum of Modern Art; Rodin Museum; Picasso Museum. Notable cemeteries with graves of the famous: Père-Lachaise, Montmartre, Montparnasse. Near Paris are the royal residences of Fontainebleau and Versailles. www.parisinfo.com **90 C2**

Pyrenees

Beautiful unspoiled mountain range. Towns include: delightful sea resorts of St-Jean-de-Luz and Biarritz; Pau, with access to the Pyrenees National Park; pilgrimage centre Lourdes.
144–145

Reims

Together with nearby Epernay, the centre of champagne production. The 13c Gothic cathedral is one of the greatest architectural achievements in France (stained glass by Chagall). Other sights: Palais du Tau with cathedral sculpture, 11c Basilica of St Rémi; cellars on Place St-Niçaise and Place des Droits-des-Hommes.
www.reims-tourisme.com **91 B4**

Rouen

Old centre with many half-timbered houses and 12–13c Gothic cathedral and the Gothic Church of St Maclou with its fascinating remains of a dance macabre on the former cemetery of Aître St-Maclou. The Fine Arts Museum has a good collection.
www.rouentourisme.com **89 A5**

St-Malo

Fortified town (much rebuilt) in a fine coastal setting. There is a magnificent boat trip along the river Rance to Dinan, a splendid well-preserved medieval town.
www.saint-malo-tourisme.com **101 A3**

Strasbourg

Town whose historic centre includes a well-preserved quarter of medieval half-timbered Alsatian houses, many of them set on the canal. The cathedral is one of the best in France. The Palais Rohan contains several museums. www.otstrasbourg.fr **93 C3**

Toulouse

Medieval university town characterised by flat pink brick (Hôtel Assézat). The Basilique St Sernin, the largest Romanesque church in France, has many art treasures. Church of the Jacobins holds the body of St Thomas Aquinas. www.toulouse-tourisme.com **129 C4**

Tours

Historic town centred on Place Plumereau. Good collections in the Guilds Museum and Fine Arts Museum. www.tours-tourisme.fr **102 B2**

Versailles

Vast royal palace built for Louis XIV, primarily by Mansart, set in large formal gardens with magnificent fountains. The extensive and much-imitated state apartments include the famous Hall of Mirrors and the exceptional Baroque chapel.
www.chateauversailles.fr **90 C2**

Vézère Valley Caves

A number of prehistoric sites, most notably the cave paintings of Lascaux (some 17,000 years old), now only seen in a duplicate cave, and the cave of Font de Gaume. The National Museum of Prehistory is in Les Eyzies. www.lascaux-dordogne.com/en **129 B4**

Germany Deutschland

www.germany.travel

Northern Germany

Aachen

Once capital of the Holy Roman Empire. Old town around the Münsterplatz with magnificent cathedral. An exceptionally rich treasure is in the Schatzkammer. The Town Hall is on the medieval Market. www.aachen.de **80 B2**

Berlin

Capital of Germany. Sights include: the Kurfürstendamm avenue; Brandenburg Gate, former symbol of the division between East and West Germany; Tiergarten; Unter den

Linden; 19c Reichstag. Berlin has many excellent art and history collections. Museum Island: Pergamon Musem (classical antiquity, Near and Far East, Islam; Bode Museum (sculpture, Byzantine art); Altes Museum (Greek and Roman); New National Gallery (20th-c European); Old National Gallery (19th-c German); New Museum (Egyptian, prehistoric). Dahlem: Museum of Asian Art; Museum of European Cultures; Museum of Ethnology; Die Brücke Museum (German Expressionism). Tiergarten: Picture Gallery (old masters); Decorative Arts Museum (13–19c); New National Gallery (19–20c); Bauhaus Archive. Kreuzberg: Gropius Building with Jewish Museum and Berlin Gallery; remains of Berlin Wall and Checkpoint Charlie House. Unter den Linden: German Guggenheim (commissioned contemporary works). http://visitberlin.de **74 B2**

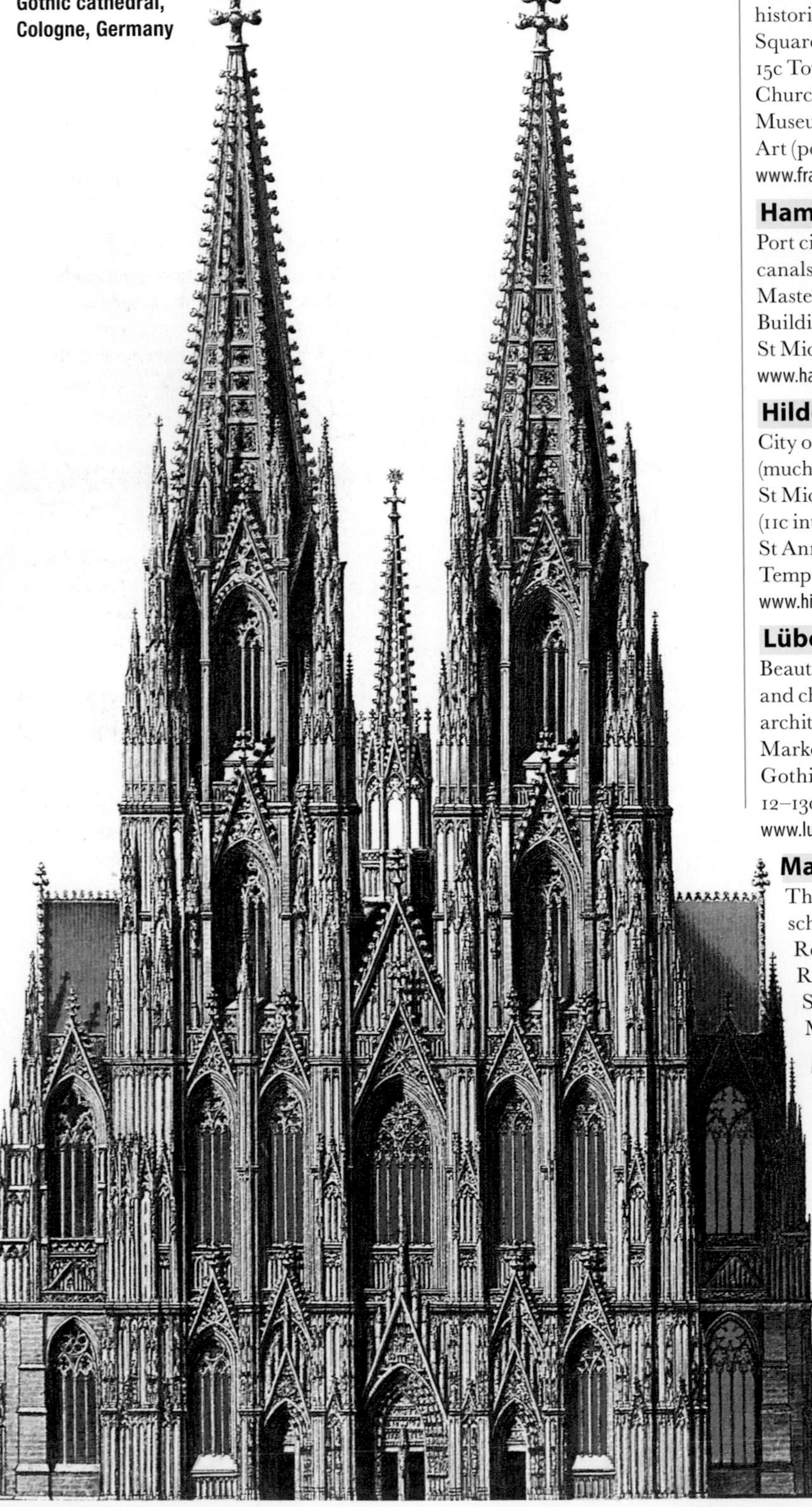

Gothic cathedral, Cologne, Germany

Cologne Köln

Ancient city with 13–19c cathedral (rich display of art). In the old town are the Town Hall and many Romanesque churches (Gross St Martin, St Maria im Kapitol, St Maria im Lyskirchen, St Ursula, St Georg, St Severin, St Pantaleon, St Apostolen). Museums: Diocesan Museum (religious art); Roman-German Museum (ancient history); Wallraf-Richartz and Ludwig Museum (14–20c art). www.cologne-tourism.com **80 B2**

Dresden

Historic centre with a rich display of Baroque architecture. Major buildings: Castle of the Electors of Saxony; 18c Hofkirche; Zwinger Palace with fountains and pavilions (excellent old masters); Albertinum with excellent Gallery of New Masters; treasury of Grünes Gewölbe. The Baroque-planned New Town contains the Japanese Palace and Schloss Pillnitz. www.dresden.de **84 A1**

Frankfurt

Financial capital of Germany. The historic centre around the Römerberg Square has 13–15c cathedral, 15c Town Hall, Gothic St Nicholas Church, Saalhof (12c chapel). Museums: Museum of Modern Art (post-war); State Art Institute. www.frankfurt-tourismus.de **81 B4**

Hamburg

Port city with many parks, lakes and canals. The Kunsthalle has Old Masters and 19-20c German art. Buildings: 19c Town Hall; Baroque St Michael's Church. www.hamburg-tourism.de **72 A3**

Hildesheim

City of Romanesque architecture (much destroyed). Principal sights: St Michael's Church; cathedral (11c interior, sculptured doors, St Anne's Chapel); superb 15c Tempelhaus on the Market Place. www.hildesheim.de **72 B2**

Lübeck

Beautiful old town built on an island and characterised by Gothic brick architecture. Sights: 15c Holsten Gate; Market with the Town Hall and Gothic brick St Mary's Church; 12–13c cathedral; St Ann Museum. www.luebeck-tourism.de **65 C3**

Mainz

The Electoral Palatinate schloss and Market fountain are Renaissance. Churches: 12c Romanesque cathedral; Gothic St Steven's (with stained glass by Marc Chagall). www.mainz.de **93 A4**

Marburg

Medieval university town with the Market Place and Town Hall, St Elizabeth's Church (frescoes, statues, 13c shrine), 15–16c schloss. www.marburg.de **81 B4**

Münster

Historic city with well-preserved Gothic and Renaissance buildings: 14c Town Hall; Romanesque-Gothic cathedral. The Westphalian Museum holds regional art. **71 C4** www.muenster.de/stadt/tourismus/en

Potsdam

Beautiful Sanssouci Park contains several 18–19c buildings including: Schloss Sanssouci; Gallery (European masters); Orangery; New Palace; Chinese Teahouse. http://www.potsdam-tourism.com **74 B2**

Rhein Valley Rheintal

Beautiful 80km gorge of the Rhein Valley between Mainz and Koblenz with rocks (Loreley), vineyards (Bacharach, Rüdesheim), white medieval towns (Rhens, Oberwesel) and castles. Some castles are medieval (Marksburg, Rheinfles, island fortress Pfalzgrafenstein) others were built or rebuilt in the 19c (Stolzenfles, Rheinstein). **80 B3**

Weimar

The Neoclassical schloss, once an important seat of government, now houses a good art collection. Church of SS Peter and Paul has a Cranach masterpiece. Houses of famous people: Goethe, Schiller, Liszt. The famous Bauhaus was founded at the School of Architecture and Engineering. www.weimar.de **82 B3**

Southern Germany

Alpine Road Deutsche Alpenstrasse

German Alpine Road in the Bavarian Alps, from Lindau on Bodensee to Berchtesgaden. The setting for 19c fairy-tale follies of Ludwig II of Bavaria (Linderhof, Hohenschwangau, Neuschwanstein), charming old villages (Oberammergau) and Baroque churches (Weiss, Ottobeuren). Garmisch-Partenkirchen has views on Germany's highest peak, the Zugspitze. **108 B2**

Augsburg

Attractive old city. The Town Hall is one of Germany's finest Renaissance buildings. Maximilianstrasse has several Renaissance houses and Rococo Schaezler Palace (good art collection). Churches: Romanesque-Gothic cathedral; Renaissance St Anne's Church. The Fuggerei, founded 1519 as an estate for the poor, is still in use. www.augsburg-tourismus.de **94 C2**

Bamberg

Well-preserved medieval town. The island, connected by two bridges, has the Town Hall and views of Klein Venedig. Romanesque-Gothic cathedral (good art) is on an exceptional square of Gothic, Renaissance and Baroque buildings – Alte Hofhalttung; Neue Residenz with State Gallery (German masters); Ratstube. http://en.bamberg.info **94 B2**

Black Forest Schwarzwald

Hilly region between Basel and Karlsruhe, the largest and most picturesque woodland in Germany, with the highest summit, Feldberg, lake resorts (Titisee), health resorts (Baden-Baden) and clock craft (Triberg). Freiburg is the regional capital. www.schwarzwald.de **93 C4**

Freiburg
Old university town with system of streams running through the streets. The Gothic Minster is surrounded by the town's finest buildings. Two towers remain of the medieval walls. The Augustine Museum has a good collection. **106 B2**
www.freiburg.de/pb/,Len/225797.html

Heidelberg
Germany's oldest university town, majestically set on the banks of the river and romantically dominated by the ruined schloss. The Gothic Church of the Holy Spirit is on the Market Place with the Baroque Town Hall. Other sights include the 16c Knight's House and the Baroque Morass Palace with the Museum of the Palatinate.
www.tourism-heidelberg.com **93 B4**

Lake Constance Bodensee
Lake Constance, with many pleasant lake resorts. Lindau, on an island, has numerous gabled houses. Birnau has an 18c Rococo church. Konstanz (Swiss side) has the Minster set above the Old Town. www.bodensee.eu **107 B4**

Munich München
Old town centred on the Marienplatz with 15c Old Town Hall and 19c New Town Hall. Many richly decorated churches: St Peter's (14c tower); Gothic red-brick cathedral; Renaissance St Michael's (royal portraits on the façade); Rococo St Asam's. The Residenz palace consists of seven splendid buildings holding many art objects. Schloss Nymphenburg has a palace, park, botanical gardens and four beautiful pavilions. Superb museums: Old Gallery (old masters), New Gallery (18–19c), Lenbachhaus (modern German). Many famous beer gardens.
www.munich-touristinfo.de **108 A2**

Nuremberg Nürnberg
Beautiful medieval walled city dominated by the 12c Kaiserburg. Romanesque-Gothic St Sebaldus Church and Gothic St Laurence Church are rich in art.
On Hauptmarkt is the famous 14c Schöner Brunnen. Also notable is 15c Dürer House. The German National Museum has excellent German medieval and Renaissance art.
www.nuernberg.de/internet/portal_e **94 B3**

Regensburg
Medieval city set majestically on the Danube. Views from 12c Steinerne Brücke. Churches: Gothic cathedral; Romanesque St Jacob's; Gothic St Blaisius; Baroque St Emmeram. Other sights: Old Town Hall (museum); Haidplatz; Schloss Thurn und Taxis; State Museum.
www.regensburg.de **95 B4**

Romantic Road
Romantische Strasse

Romantic route between Aschaffenburg and Füssen, leading through picturesque towns and villages of medieval Germany. The most popular section is the section between Würzburg and Augsburg, centred on Rothenburg ob der Tauber. Also notable are Nördlingen, Harburg Castle, Dinkelsbühl, Creglingen.
www.romantischestrasse.de **94 B2**

Rothenburg ob der Tauber
Attractive medieval walled town with tall gabled and half-timbered houses on narrow cobbled streets. The Market Place has Gothic-Renaissance Town Hall, Rattrinke-stubbe and Gothic St Jacob's Church (altarpiece).
www.tourismus.rothenburg.de **94 B2**

Speyer
The 11c cathedral is one of the largest and best Romanesque buildings in Germany. 12c Jewish Baths are well-preserved.
www.speyer.de/sv_speyer/en/Tourism **93 B4**

Stuttgart
Largely modern city with old centre around the Old Schloss, Renaissance Alte Kanzlei, 15c Collegiate Church and Baroque New Schloss.
Museums: Regional Museum; Old and New State Galleries.
The 1930s Weissenhofsiedlung is by several famous architects.
www.stuttgart-tourist.de/en **94 C1**

Trier
Superb Roman monuments: Porta Nigra; Aula Palatina (now a church); Imperial Baths; amphitheatre. The Regional Museum has Roman artefacts. Also, Gothic Church of Our Lady; Romanesque cathedral.
www.trier-info.de **92 B2**

Ulm
Old town with half-timbered gabled houses set on a canal. Gothic 14–19c minster has tallest spire in the world (161m). www.tourismus.ulm.de **94 C1**

Würzburg
Set among vineyard hills, the medieval town is centred on the Market Place with the Rococo House of the Falcon. The 18c episcopal princes' residence (frescoes) is magnificent. The cathedral is rich in art. Work of the great local Gothic sculptor, Riemenschneider, is in Gothic St Mary's Chapel, Baroque New Minster, and the Mainfränkisches Museum.
www.wuerzburg.de/en/index.html **94 B1**

Greece Ellas

www.visitgreece.gr

Athens Athina
Capital of Greece. The Acropolis, with 5c BC sanctuary complex (Parthenon, Propylaia, Erechtheion, Temple of Athena Nike), is the greatest architectural achievement of antiquity in Europe. The Agora was a public meeting place in ancient Athens. Plaka has narrow streets and small Byzantine churches (Kapnikarea). The Olympeum was the largest temple in Greece. Also: Olympic Stadium; excellent collections of ancient artefacts (Museum of Cycladic and Ancient Greek Art; New Acropolis Museum; National Archeological Museum; Benaki Museum). www.visitgreece.gr **185 B4**

Corinth Korinthos
Ancient Corinth (ruins), with 5c BC Temple of Apollo, was in 44 BC made capital of Roman Greece by Julius Caesar. Set above the city, the Greek-built acropolis hill of Acrocorinth became the Roman and Byzantine citadel (ruins). **184 B3**

Crete Kriti
Largest Greek island, Crete was home to the great Minoan civilization (2800–1100 BC). The main relics are the ruined Palace of Knossos and Malia. Gortys was capital of the Roman province. Picturesque Rethimno has narrow medieval streets, a Venetian fortress and a former Turkish mosque. Matala has beautiful beaches and famous caves cut into cliffs. Iraklio (Heraklion), the capital, has a good Archeological Museum. **185 D6**

Delphi
At the foot of the Mount Parnassos, Delphi was the seat of the Delphic Oracle of Apollo, the most important oracle in Ancient Greece. Delphi was also a political meeting place and the site of the Pythian Games. The Sanctuary of Apollo consists of: Temple of Apollo, led to by the Sacred Way; Theatre; Stadium. The museum has a display of objects from the site (5c BC Charioteer). **182 E4**

Epidavros
Formerly a spa and religious centre focused on the Sanctuary of Asclepius (ruins). The enormous 4c BC theatre is probably the finest of all ancient theatres. **184 B4**

Greek Islands
Popular islands with some of the most beautiful and spectacular beaches in Europe. The many islands are divided into various groups and individual islands: The major groups are the Kiklades and Dodekanisa in the Aegean Sea, the largest islands are Kerkyra (Corfu) in the Ionian Sea and Kriti. **182–185 & 188**

Meteora
The tops of bizarre vertical cylinders of rock and towering cliffs are the setting for 14c Cenobitic monasteries, until recently only accessible by baskets or removable ladders. Mega Meteoro is the grandest and set on the highest point. Roussánou has the most extraordinary site. Varlaám is one of the oldest and most beautiful, with the Ascent Tower and 16c church with frescoes. Aghiou Nikolaou also has good frescoes.
www.meteora-greece.com **182 D3**

Mistras
Set in a beautiful landscape, Mistras is the site of a Byzantine city, now in ruins, with palaces, frescoed churches, monasteries and houses.
184 B3

Mount Olympus
Oros Olymbos

Mount Olympus, mythical seat of the Greek gods, is the highest, most dramatic peak in Greece. **182 C4**

Mycenae Mikines
The citadel of Mycenae prospered between 1950 BC and 1100 BC and consists of the royal complex of Agamemnon: Lion Gate, royal burial site, Royal Palace, South House, Great Court. **184 B3**

Olympia
In a stunning setting, the Panhellenic Games were held here for a millennium. Ruins of the sanctuary of Olympia consist of the Doric temples of Zeus and Hera and the vast Stadium. There is also a museum (4c BC figure of Hermes). **184 B2**

Rhodes
One of the most attractive islands with wonderful sandy beaches.
The city of Rhodes has a well-preserved medieval centre with the Palace of the Grand Masters and the Turkish Süleymaniye Mosque
www.rhodestravels.com **188 C2**

Salonica Thessaloniki
Largely modern city with Byzantine walls and many fine churches: 8c Aghia Sofia; 11c Panaghia Halkeo; 14c Dodeka Apostoli; 14c Aghios Nikolaos Orfanos; 5c Aghios Dimitrios (largest in Greece, 7c Mosaics). **183 C5**

Hungary Magyarország
http://gotohungary.com

Balaton
The 'Hungarian sea', famous for its holiday resorts: Balatonfüred, Tihany, Badasconytomaj, Keszthely.
http://gotohungary.com **111 C4**

Budapest
Capital of Hungary on River Danube, with historic area centring on the Castle Hill of Buda district. Sights include: Matthias church; Pest district with late 19c architecture, centred on Ferenciek tere; neo-Gothic Parliament Building on river; Millennium Monument. The Royal Castle houses a number of museums: Hungarian National Gallery, Budapest History Museum; Ludwig Collection. Other museums: National Museum of Fine Arts (excellent Old and Modern masters); Hungarian National Museum (Hungarian history). Famous for public thermal baths: Király and Rudas baths, both made under Turkish rule; Gellért baths, the most visited. http://budapest.gotohungary.com/budapest-and-surroundings **112 B3**

Esztergom
Medieval capital of Hungary set in scenic landscape. Sights: Hungary's largest basilica (completed 1856); royal palace ruins. **112 B2**

Pécs
Attractive old town with Europe's fifth oldest university (founded 1367). Famous for Turkish architecture (Mosque of Gazi Kasim Pasha, Jakovali Hassan Mosque).
http://en.pecs.hu/idegenforgalom/ **125 A4**

Sopron
Beautiful walled town with many Gothic and Renaissance houses. Nearby: Fertöd with the marvellous Eszergázy Palace.
http://portal.sopron.hu **111 B3**

Ireland
www.discoverireland.com

Aran Islands
Islands with spectacular cliffs and notable pre-Christian and Christian sights, especially on Inishmore.
www.aranislands.ie **26 B2**

Cashel
Town dominated by the Rock of Cashel (61m) topped by ecclesiastical ruins including 13c cathedral; 15c Halls of the Vicars; beautiful Romanesque 12c Cormac's Chapel (fine carvings). www.cashel.ie **29 B4**

Connemara
Beautiful wild landscape of mountains, lakes, peninsulas and beaches. Clifden is the capital.
www.connemara.ie/en **28 A1**

Cork
Pleasant city with its centre along St Patrick's Street and Grand Parade lined with fine 18c buildings. Churches: Georgian St Anne's Shandon (bell tower); 19c cathedral.
www.corkcity.ie/traveltourism **29 C3**

County Donegal
Rich scenic landscape of mystical lakes and glens and seascape of cliffs (Slieve League cliffs are the highest in Europe). The town of Donegal has a finely preserved Jacobean castle.
www.govisitdonegal.com **26 B2**

Dublin
Capital of Ireland. City of elegant 18c neoclassical and Georgian architecture with gardens and parks (St Stephen's Green, Merrion Square with Leinster House – now seat of Irish parliament). City's main landmark, Trinity College (founded 1591), houses in its Old Library fine Irish manuscripts (7c Book of Durrow, 8c Book of Kells). Two Norman cathedrals: Christ Church; St Patrick's. Other buildings: originally medieval Dublin Castle with State Apartments; James Gandon's masterpieces: Custom House; Four Courts. Museums: National Museum (archaeology, decorative arts, natural history); National Gallery (old masters, Impressionists); Museum of Modern Art; Dublin Writers' Museum. www.visitdublin.com **30 A2**

Glendalough
Impressive ruins of an important early Celtic (6c) monastery with 9c cathedral, 12c St Kevin's Cross, oratory of St Kevin's Church.
www.glendalough.ie **30 A2**

Kilkenny
Charming medieval town, with narrow streets dominated by 12c castle (restored 19c). The 13c Gothic cathedral has notable tomb monuments. www.kilkennytourism.ie **30 B1**

Newgrange
Part of a complex that also includes the sites of Knowth, Dowth, Fourknocks, Loughcrew and Tara, Newgrange is one of the best passage graves in Europe, the massive 4500-year-old tomb has stones richly decorated with patterns. **30 A2**
www.knowth.com/newgrange.htm

Ring of Kerry
Route around the Iveragh peninsula with beautiful lakes (Lough Leane), peaks overlooking the coastline and islands (Valencia Island, Skelling). Also: Killarney; ruins of 15c Muckross Abbey. **29 B2**
www.ringofkerrytourism.com

Italy Italia

www.italia.it

Northern Italy

Alps
Wonderful stretch of the Alps running from the Swiss and French borders to Austria. The region of Valle d'Aosta is one of the most popular ski regions, bordered by the highest peaks of the Alps. www.thealps.com
108–109 & 119–120

Arezzo
Beautiful old town set on a hill dominated by 13c cathedral. Piazza Grande is surrounded by medieval and Renaissance palaces. Main sight: Piero della Francesca's frescoes in the choir of San Francesco.
www.arezzocitta.com **135 B4**

Assisi
Hill-top town that attracts pilgrims to the shrine of St Francis of Assisi at the Basilica di San Francesco, consisting of two churches, Lower and Upper, with superb frescoes.
www.assisionline.com **136 B1**

Bologna
Elegant city with oldest university in Italy. Historical centre around Piazza Maggiore and Piazza del Nettuno with the Town Hall, Palazzo del Podestà, Basilica di San Petronio. Other churches: San Domenico; San Giacomo Maggiore. The two towers (one incomplete) are symbols of the city. Good collection in the National Gallery (Bolognese). **135 A4**
www.bolognawelcome.com

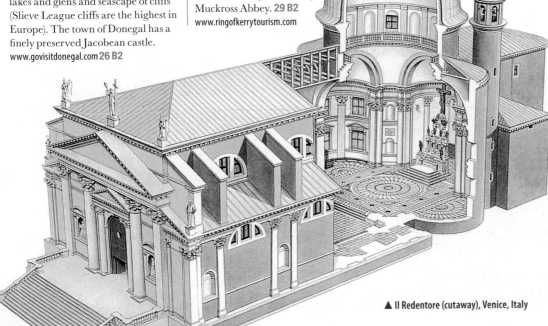

Dolomites Dolomiti
Part of the Alps, this mountain range spreads over the region of Trentino-Alto Adige, with the most picturesque scenery between Bolzano and Cortina d'Ampezzo. www.dolomiti.it **121 A4**

Ferrara
Old town centre around Romanesque-Gothic cathedral and Palazzo Communale. Also: Castello Estenese; Palazzo Schifanoia (frescoes); Palazzo dei Diamanti housing Pinacoteca Nazionale.
www.ferrarataterraeacqua.it **121 C4**

Florence Firenze
City with exceptionally rich medieval and Renaissance heritage. Piazza del Duomo has:13–15c cathedral (first dome since antiquity); 14c campanile; 11c baptistry (bronze doors). Piazza della Signoria has: 14c Palazzo Vecchio (frescoes); Loggia della Signoria (sculpture); 16c Uffizi Gallery with one of the world's greatest collections (13–18c). Other great paintings: Museo di San Marco; Palatine Gallery in 15–16c Pitti Palace surrounded by Boboli Gardens. Sculpture: Cathedral Works Museum; Bargello Museum; Academy Gallery (Michelangelo's *David*). Among many other Renaissance palaces: Medici-Riccardi; Rucellai; Strozzi. The 15c church of San Lorenzo has Michelangelo's tombs of the Medici. Many churches have richly frescoed chapels: Santa Maria Novella, Santa Croce, Santa Maria del Carmine. The 13c Ponte Vecchio is one of the most famous sights. www.firenzeturismo.it **135 B4**

Italian Lakes
Beautiful district at the foot of the Alps, most of the lakes with holiday resorts. Many lakes are surrounded by aristocratic villas (Maggiore, Como, Garda). **120–121**

Mantua Mántova
Attractive city surrounded by three lakes. Two exceptional palaces: Palazzo Ducale (Sala del Pisanello; Camera degli Sposi, Castello San Giorgio); luxurious Palazzo Tè (brilliant frescoes). Also: 15c Church of Sant'Andrea; 13c law courts.
www.turismo.mantova.it **121 B3**

Milan Milano
Modern city, Italy's fashion and design capital (Corso and Galleria Vittoro Emmanuelle II). Churches include: Gothic cathedral (1386–1813), the world's largest (4c baptistry); Romanesque St Ambrose; 15c San Satiro; Santa Maria delle Grazie with Leonardo da Vinci's *Last Supper* in the convent refectory. Great art collections, Brera Gallery, Ambrosian Library, Museum of Modern Art. Castello Sforzesco (15c, 19c) also has a gallery. The famous La Scala opera house opened in 1778.
Nearby: monastery at Pavia.
www.visitamilano.it/turismo **120 B2**

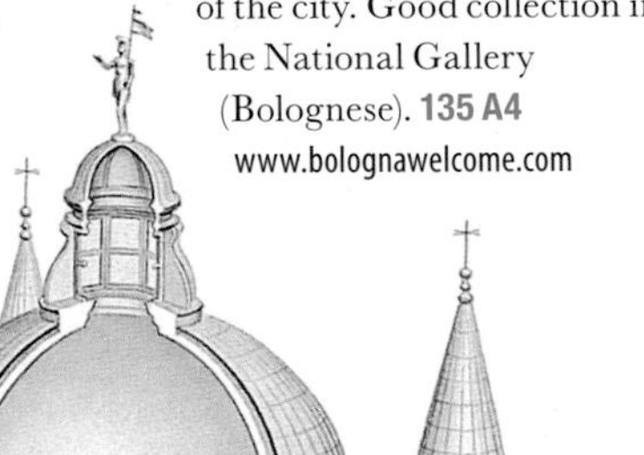

▲ Il Redentore (cutaway), Venice, Italy

Padua Pádova
Pleasant old town with arcaded streets. Basilica del Santo is a place of pilgrimage to the tomb of St Anthony. Giotto's frescoes in the Scrovegni chapel are exceptional. Also: Piazza dei Signori with Palazzo del Capitano; vast Palazzo della Ragione; church of the Eremitani (frescoes).
www.turismopadova.it **121 B4**

Parma
Attractive city centre, famous for Corregio's frescoes in the Romanesque cathedral and church of St John the Evangelist, and Parmigianino's frescoes in the church of Madonna della Steccata. Their works are also in the National Gallery.
www.turismo.comune.parma.it **120 C3**

Perúgia
Hill-top town centred around Piazza Quattro Novembre with the cathedral, Fontana Maggiore and Palazzo dei Priori. Also: Collegio di Cambio (frescoes); National Gallery of Umbria; many churches.
www.perugiaonline.com **136 B1**

Pisa
Medieval town centred on the Piazza dei Miracoli. Sights: famous Romanesque Leaning Tower, Romanesque cathedral (excellent façade, Gothic pulpit); 12–13c Baptistry; 13c Camposanto cloistered cemetery (fascinating 14c frescoes).
www.turismo.pisa.it **134 B3**

Ravenna
Ancient town with exceptionally well-preserved Byzantine mosaics. The finest are in 5c Mausoleo di Galla Placidia and 6c Basilica di San Vitale. Good mosaics also in the basilicas of Sant'Apollinare in Classe and Sant'Apollinare Nuovo.
www.turismo.ra.it/eng **135 A5**

▼ Romanesque cathedral, Pisa, Italy

Siena
Outstanding 13–14c medieval town centred on beautiful Piazza del Campo with Gothic Palazzo Publico (frescoes of secular life). Delightful Romanesque-Gothic Duomo (Libreria Piccolomini, baptistry, art works). Many other richly decorated churches. Fine Sienese painting in Pinacoteca Nazionale and Museo dell'Opera del Duomo.
www.sienaonline.com **135 B4**

Turin Torino
City centre has 17-18c Baroque layout dominated by twin Baroque churches. Also: 15c cathedral (holds Turin Shroud); Palazzo Reale; 18c Superga Basilica; Academy of Science with rich Egyptian Museum.
www.turismotorino.org **119 B4**

Urbino
Set in beautiful hilly landscape, Urbino's heritage is mainly due to the 15c court of Federico da Montefeltro at the magnificent Ducal Palace (notable Studiolo), now also a gallery. www.turismo.pesarourbino.it **136 B1**

Venice Venezia
Stunning old city built on islands in a lagoon, with some 150 canals. The Grand Canal is crossed by the famous 16c Rialto Bridge and is lined with elegant palaces (Gothic Ca'd'Oro and Ca'Foscari, Renaissance Palazzo Grimani, Baroque Rezzonico). The district of San Marco has the core of the best known sights and is centred on Piazza San Marco with 11c Basilica di San Marco (bronze horses, 13c mosaics); Campanile (exceptional views) and Ducal Palace (connected with the prison by the famous Bridge of Sighs). Many churches (Santa Maria Gloriosa dei Frari, Santa Maria della Salute, Redentore, San Giorgio Maggiore, San Giovanni e Paolo) and scuole (Scuola di San Rocco, Scuola di San Giorgio degli Schiavoni) have excellent works of art. The Gallery of the Academy houses superb 14–18c Venetian art. The Guggenheim Museum holds 20c art.
http://en.turismovenezia.it **122 B1**

Verona
Old town with remains of 1c Roman Arena and medieval sights including the Palazzo degli Scaligeri; Arche Scaligere; Romanesque Santa Maria Antica; Castelvecchio; Ponte Scaliger. The famous 14c House of Juliet has associations with *Romeo and Juliet.* Many churches with fine art works (cathedral; Sant'Anastasia; basilica di San Zeno Maggiore).
www.tourism.verona.it **121 B4**

Vicenza
Beautiful town, famous for the architecture of Palladio, including the Olympic Theatre (extraordinary stage), Corso Palladio with many of his palaces, and Palazzo Chiericati. Nearby: Villa Rotonda, the most influential of all Palladian buildings. www.vicenzae.org **121 B4**

Southern Italy

Naples Napoli
Historical centre around Gothic cathedral (crypt). Spaccanapoli area has numerous churches (bizarre Cappella Sansevero, Gesù Nuovo, Gothic Santa Chiara with fabulous tombs). Buildings: 13c Castello Nuovo; 13c Castel dell'Ovo; 15c Palazzo Cuomo. Museums: National Archeological Museum (artefacts from Pompeii and Herculaneum); National Museum of Capodimonte (Renaissance painting). Nearby: spectacular coast around Amalfi; Pompeii; Herculaneum.
www.inaples.it **170 C2**

Orvieto
Medieval hill-top town with a number of monuments including the Romanesque-Gothic cathedral (façade, frescoes).
www.inorvieto.it/en **168 A2**

▼ Palazzo Publico, Siena, Italy

Rome Roma
Capital of Italy, exceptionally rich in sights from many eras. Ancient sights: Colosseum; Arch of Constantine; Trajan's Column; Roman and Imperial fora; hills of Palatino and Campidoglio (Capitoline Museum shows antiquities); Pantheon; Castel Sant' Angelo; Baths of Caracalla). Early Christian sights: catacombs (San Calisto, San Sebastiano, Domitilla); basilicas (San Giovanni in Laterano, Santa Maria Maggiore, San Paolo Fuori le Mura). Rome is known for richly decorated Baroque churches: il Gesù, Sant'Ignazio, Santa Maria della Vittoria, Chiesa Nuova. Other churches, often with art treasures: Romanesque Santa Maria in Cosmedin, Gothic Santa Maria Sopra Minerva, Renaissance Santa Maria del Popolo, San Pietro in Vincoli. Several Renaissance and Baroque palaces and villas house superb art collections (Palazzo Barberini, Palazzo Doria Pamphilj, Palazzo Spada, Palazzo Corsini, Villa Giulia, Galleria Borghese) and are beautifully frescoed (Villa Farnesina). Fine Baroque public spaces with fountains: Piazza Navona; Piazza di Spagna with the Spanish Steps; also Trevi Fountain. Nearby: Tivoli; Villa Adriana. Rome also contains the Vatican City (Città del Vaticano). www.turismoroma.it **168 B2**

Volcanic Region

Region from Naples to Sicily. Mount Etna is one of the most famous European volcanoes. Vesuvius dominates the Bay of Naples and has at its foot two of Italy's finest Roman sites, Pompeii and Herculaneum, both destroyed by its eruption in 79 AD. Stromboli is one of the beautiful Aeolian Islands.

Sardinia Sardegna

Sardinia has some of the most beautiful beaches in Italy (Alghero). Unique are the nuraghi, some 7000 stone constructions (Su Nuraxi, Serra Orios), the remains of an old civilization (1500–400 BC). Old towns include Cagliari and Sássari.
www.sardi.it **178–179**

Sicily Sicilia

Surrounded by beautiful beaches and full of monuments of many periods, Sicily is the largest island in the Mediterranean. Taormina with its Greek theatre has one of the most spectacular beaches, lying under the mildly active volcano Mount Etna. Also: Agrigento; Palermo, Siracusa.
www.sicilytourism.com **176–177**

Agrigento

Set on a hill above the sea and famed for the Valley of the Temples. The nine originally 5c BC Doric temples are Sicily's best-preserved Greek remains. www.agrigento-sicilia.it **176 B2**

Palermo

City with Moorish, Norman and Baroque architecture, especially around the main squares (Quattro Canti, Piazza Pretoria, Piazza Bellini). Sights: remains of Norman palace (12c Palatine Chapel); Norman cathedral; Regional Gallery (medieval); some 8000 preserved bodies in the catacombs of the Cappuchin Convent. Nearby: 12c Norman Duomo di Monreale.
www.palermotourism.com **176 A2**

Syracuse Siracusa

Built on an island connected to the mainland by a bridge, the old town has a 7c cathedral, ruins of the Temple of Apollo; Fountain of Arethusa; archaeological museum. On the mainland: 5c BC Greek theatre with seats cut out of rock; Greek fortress of Euralus; 2c Roman amphitheatre; 5–6c Catacombs of St John. **177 B4**

Latvia Latvija

www.latvia.travel/en

Riga

Well-preserved medieval town centre around the cathedral. Sights: Riga Castle; medieval Hanseatic houses; Great Guild Hall; Gothic Church of St Peter; Art Nouveau buildings in the New Town. Nearby: Baroque Rundale Castle.
www.latvia.travel/en/riga **8 D4**

Lithuania Lietuva

http://lietuva.lt/en/tourism

Vilnius

Baroque old town with fine architecture including: cathedral; Gediminas Tower; university complex; Archbishop's Palace; Church of St Anne. Also: remains of Jewish life; Vilnius Picture Gallery (16–19c regional); Lithuanian National Museum. www.vilnius.com **13 A6**

Luxembourg

www.visitluxembourg.com

Luxembourg

Capital of Luxembourg, built on a rock with fine views. Old town is around the Place d'Armes. Buildings: Grand Ducal Palace; fortifications of Rocher du Bock; cathedral. Museum of History and Art holds an excellent regional collection.
www.visitluxembourg.com **92 B2**

Macedonia Makedonija

www.exploringmacedonia.com

Ohrid

Old town, beautifully set by a lake, with houses of wood and brick, remains of a Turkish citadel, many churches (two cathedrals; St Naum south of the lake).
www.ohridinfo.com/?osnovni=2&lg=en **182 B2**

Skopje

Historic town with Turkish citadel, fine 15c mosques, oriental bazaar, ancient bridge. Superb Byzantine churches nearby. **182 A3**

Malta

www.visitmalta.com

Valletta

Capital of Malta. Historic walled city, founded in 16c by the Maltese Knights, with 16c Grand Master's Palace and a richly decorated cathedral. **175 C3**

Monaco

www.visitmonaco.com

Monaco

Major resort area in a beautiful location. Sights include: Monte Carlo casino, Prince's Palace at Monaco-Ville; 19c cathedral; oceanographic museum. **133 B3**

Netherlands Nederland

http://holland.com

Amsterdam

Capital of the Netherlands. Old centre has picturesque canals lined with distinctive elegant 17–18c merchants' houses. Dam Square has 15c New Church and Royal Palace. Other churches include Westerkerk. The Museumplein has three world-famous museums: the newly restored Rijksmuseum (several art collections including 15–17c painting); Van Gogh Museum; Municipal Museum (art from 1850 on). Other museums: Anne Frank House; Jewish Historical Museum; Rembrandt House; Hermitage Museum (exhibitions). http://holland.com **70 B1**

Delft

Well-preserved old Dutch town with gabled red-roofed houses along canals. Gothic churches: New Church; Old Church. Famous for Delftware (two museums).
www.delft.nl **70 B1**

Haarlem

Many medieval gabled houses centred on the Great Market with 14c Town Hall and 15c Church of St Bavon. Museums: Frans Hals Museum; Teylers Museum.
www.haarlemmarketing.co.uk **70 B1**

The Hague Den Haag

Seat of Government and of the royal house of the Netherlands. The 17c Mauritshuis houses the Royal Picture Gallery (excellent 15–18c Flemish and Dutch). Other museums: Escher Museum; Meermanno Museum (books); Municipal Museum. www.denhaag.nl **70 B1**

Het Loo

Former royal palace and gardens set in a vast landscape (commissioned by future the future King and Queen of England, William and Mary).
www.paleishetloo.nl **70 B2**

Keukenhof

In spring, landscaped gardens, planted with bulbs of many varieties, are the largest flower gardens in the world. www.keukenhof.nl **70 B1**

Leiden

University town of beautiful gabled houses set along canals. The Rijksmuseum Van Oudheden is Holland's most important home to archaeological artefacts from the Antiquity. The 16c Hortus Botanicus is one of the oldest botanical gardens in Europe. The Cloth Hall with van Leyden's *Last Judgement*.
http://leidenholland.com **70 B1**

Rotterdam

The largest port in the world. The Boymans-van Beuningen Museum has a huge and excellent decorative and fine art collection (old and modern). Nearby: 18c Kinderdijk with 19 windmills. www.rotterdam.info **79 A4**

Utrecht

Delightful old town centre along canals with the Netherlands' oldest university and Gothic cathedral. Good art collections: Central Museum; National Museum.
www.utrecht.nl **70 B2**

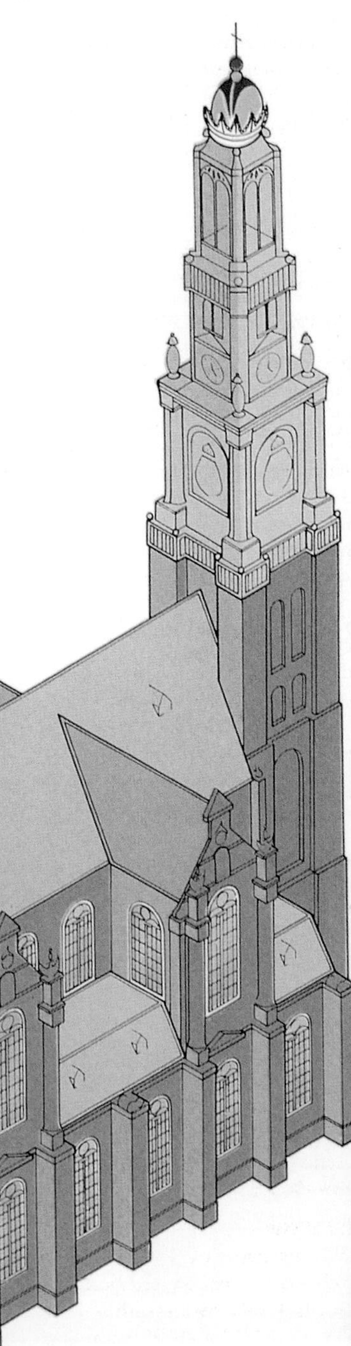

▼ **Westerkerk, Amsterdam, Netherlands**

Norway Norge

www.visitnorway.com

Bergen

Norway's second city in a scenic setting. The Quay has many painted wooden medieval buildings. Sights: 12c Romanesque St Mary's Church; Bergenhus fortress with 13c Haakon's Hall; Rosenkrantz Tower; Grieghallen; Bergen Art Museum (Norwegian art); Bryggens Museum. www.visitbergen.com **46 B2**

Lappland (Norwegian)

Vast land of Finnmark is home to the Sámi. Nordkapp is the northern point of Europe. Also Finland, Sweden. **192–193**

Norwegian Fjords

Beautiful and majestic landscape of deep glacial valleys filled by the sea. The most thrilling fjords are between Bergen and Ålesund. www.fjords.com **46 & 198**

Oslo

Capital of Norway with a modern centre. Buildings: 17c cathedral; 19c city hall, 19c royal palace; 19c Stortinget (housing parliament); 19c University; 13c Akershus (castle); 12c Akerskirke (church). Museums: National Gallery; Munch Museum; Viking Ship Museum; Folk Museum (reconstructed buildings). www.visitoslo.com **48 C2**

Stavkirker

Wooden medieval stave churches of bizarre pyramidal structure, carved with images from Nordic mythology. Best preserved in southern Norway.

Tromsø

Main arctic city of Norway with a university and two cathedrals. www.visittromso.no **192 C3**

Trondheim

Set on the edge of a fjord, a modern city with the superb Nidaros cathedral (rebuilt 19c). Also: Stiftsgaard (royal residence); Applied Arts Museum. www.trondheim.com **199 B7**

Poland Polska

www.poland.travel/en-gb

Częstochowa

Centre of Polish Catholicism, with the 14c monastery of Jasna Góra a pilgrimage site to the icon of the Black Madonna for six centuries. www.jasnagora.pl **86 B3**

Gdańsk

Medieval centre with: 14c Town Hall (state rooms); Gothic brick St Mary's Church, Poland's largest; Long Market has fine buildings (Artus Court); National Museum. www.gdansk.pl/en **69 A3**

Kraków

Old university city, rich in architecture, centred on superb 16c Marketplace with Gothic-Renaissance Cloth Hall containing the Art Gallery (19c Polish), Clock Tower, Gothic red-brick St Mary's Church (altarpiece). Czartoryski Palace has city's finest art collection. Wawel Hill has the Gothic cathedral and splendid Renaissance Royal Palace. The former Jewish ghetto in Kazimierz district has 16c Old Synagogue, now a museum. www.krakow.pl/english **99 A3**

Poznań

Town centred on the Old Square with Renaissance Town Hall and Baroque mansions. Also: medieval castle; Gothic cathedral; National Museum (European masters). www.poznan.pl/mim/public/turystyka/index.html?lang=en **76 B1**

Tatry

One of Europe's most delightful mountain ranges with many beautiful ski resorts (Zakopane). Also in Slovakia. **99 B3**

Warsaw Warszawa

Capital of Poland, with many historic monuments in the Old Town with the Royal Castle (museum) and Old Town Square surrounded by reconstructed 17–18c merchants' houses. Several churches including: Gothic cathedral; Baroque Church of the Nuns of Visitation. Richly decorated royal palaces and gardens: Neoclassical Łazienki Palace; Baroque palace in Wilanów. The National Museum has Polish and European art. www.warsawtour.pl/en **77 C6**

Wrocław

Historic town centred on the Market Square with 15c Town Hall and mansions. Churches: Baroque cathedral; St Elizabeth; St Adalbert. National Museum displays fine art. Vast painting of Battle of Racławice is specially housed. www.wroclaw.pl **85 A5**

Portugal

www.visitportugal.com

Alcobaça

Monastery of Santa Maria, one of the best examples of a Cistercian abbey, founded in 1147 (exterior 17–18c). The church is Portugal's largest (14c tombs). http://whc.unesco.org/en/list/505 **154 A1**

Algarve

Modern seaside resorts among picturesque sandy beaches and rocky coves (Praia da Rocha). Old towns: Lagos; Faro. www.visitalgarve.pt/visitalgarve/vEN **160 B1**

Batalha

Abbey is one of the masterpieces of French Gothic and Manueline architecture (tombs, English Perpendicular chapel, unfinished pantheon). http://whc.unesco.org/en/list/264 **154 A2**

Braga

Historic town with cathedral and large Archbishop's Palace. **148 A1**

Coimbra

Old town with narrow streets set on a hill. The Romanesque cathedral is particularly fine (portal). The university (founded 1290) has a fascinating Baroque library. Also: Museum of Machado de Castro; many monasteries and convents. **148 B1**

Évora

Centre of the town, surrounded by walls, has narrow streets of Moorish character and medieval and Renaissance architecture. Churches: 12–13c Gothic cathedral; São Francisco with a chapel decorated with bones of some 5000 monks; 15c Convent of Dos Lóis. The Jesuit university was founded in 1559. Museum of Évora holds fine art (particularly Flemish and Portugese). http://whc.unesco.org/en/list/361 **154 B3**

Guimarães

Old town with a castle with seven towers on a vast keep. Churches: Romanesque chapel of São Miguel; São Francisco. Alberto Sampaio Museum and Martins Sarmento Museum are excellent. http://whc.unesco.org/en/list/1031 **148 A1**

Lisbon Lisboa

Capital of Portugal. Baixa is the Neoclassical heart of Lisbon with the Praça do Comércio and Rossio squares. São Jorge castle (Visigothic, Moorish, Romanesque) is surrounded by the medieval quarters. Bairro Alto is famous for *fado* (songs). Monastery of Jerónimos is exceptional. Churches: 12c cathedral; São Vicente de Fora; São Roque (tiled chapels); Torre de Belém; Convento da Madre de Deus. Museums: Gulbenkian Museum (ancient, oriental, European), National Museum of Ancient Art; Design Museum; Modern Art Centre; Azulego Museum (decorative tiles). Nearby: palatial monastic complex Mafra; royal resort Sintra. www.visitlisboa.com **154 B1**

Porto

Historic centre with narrow streets. Churches: São Francisco; cathedral. Soares dos Reis Museum holds fine and decorative arts (18–19c). The suburb of Vila Nova de Gaia is the centre for port wine. Views from Clérigos Tower. www.portoturismo.pt **148 A1**

Tomar

Attractive town with the Convento de Cristo, founded in 1162 as the headquarters of the Knights Templar (Charola temple, chapter house, Renaissance cloisters). **154 A2**

Romania

www.romaniatourism.com

Bucovina

Beautiful region in northern Romanian Moldova renowned for a number of 15–16c monasteries and their fresco cycles. Of particular note are Moldovita, Voroneţ and Suceviţa. **17 B6**

Bucharest Bucureşti

Capital of Romania with the majority of sites along the Calea Victoriei and centring on Piaţa Revoluţei with 19c Romanian Athenaeum and 1930s Royal Palace housing the National Art Gallery. The infamous 1980s Civic Centre with People's Palace is a symbol of dictatorial aggrandisement. www.romaniatourism.com/bucharest.html **17 C7**

Carpathian Mountains Carpaţii

The beautiful Carpathian Mountains have several ski resorts (Sinaia) and peaks noted for first-rate mountaineering (Făgă raşuiui, Rodnei). Danube Delta Europe's largest marshland, a spectacular nature reserve. Travel in the area is by boat, with Tulcea the starting point for visitors. The Romanian Black Sea Coast has a stretch of resorts (Mamaia, Eforie) between Constantaţ and the border, and well-preserved Roman remains in Histria. **17 B6**

Transylvania Transilvania

Beautiful and fascinating scenic region of medieval citadels (Timişoara, Sibiu) provides a setting for the haunting image of the legendary Dracula (Sighişoara, Braşov, Bran Castle). Cluj-Napoca is the main town. **17 B5**

Russia Rossiya

www.russia-travel.com

Moscow Moskva

Capital of Russia, with many monuments. Within the Kremlin's red walls are: 15c Cathedral of the Dormition; 16c Cathedral of the Archangel; Cathedral of the Annunciation (icons), Armour Palace. Outside the walls, Red Square has the Lenin Mausoleum and 16c St Basil's Cathedral. There are a number of monasteries (16c Novodevichi). Two superb museums: Tretiakov Art Gallery (Russian); Pushkin Museum of Fine Art (European); also State Historical Museum. Kolomenskoe, once a royal summer retreat, has the Church of the Ascension. www.russia-travel.com **9 E10**

Novgorod

One of Russia's oldest towns, centred on 15c Kremlin with St Sophia Cathedral (iconostasis, west door). Two other cathedrals: St Nicholas; St George. Museum of History, Architecture and Art has notable icons and other artefacts. http://visitnovgorod.com **9 C7**

Peterhof

Peterhof, also known as Petrodvorets, is a grand palace with numerous pavilions (Monplaisir) set in beautiful parkland interwoven by a system of fountains, cascades and waterways connected to the sea. www.peterhofmuseum.ru/ **9 C6**

▼ El Escorial (cutaway), Spain

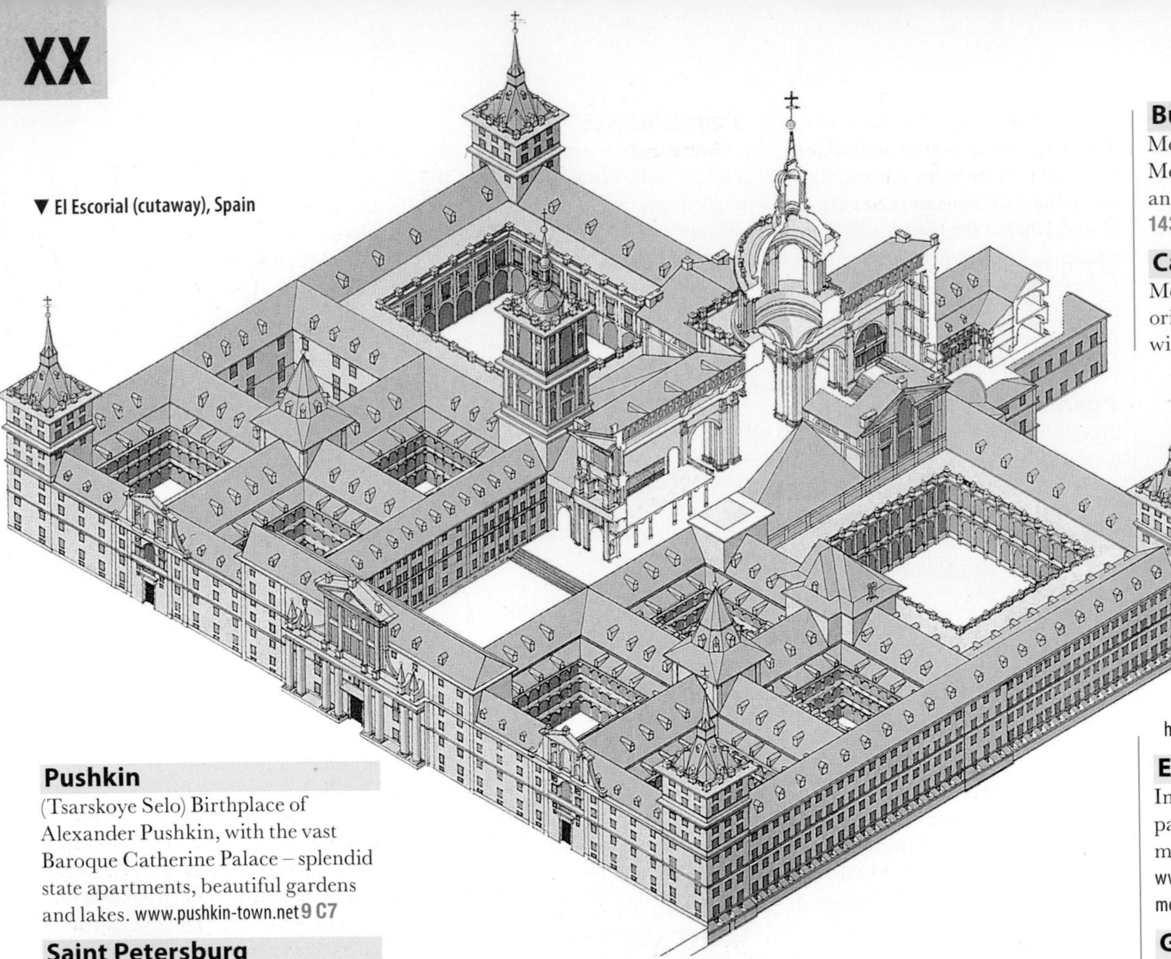

Pushkin

(Tsarskoye Selo) Birthplace of Alexander Pushkin, with the vast Baroque Catherine Palace – splendid state apartments, beautiful gardens and lakes. www.pushkin-town.net 9 C7

Saint Petersburg
Sankt Peterburg

Founded in 1703 with the SS Peter and Paul Fortress and its cathedral by Peter the Great, and functioning as seat of court and government until 1918. Many of the most famous sights are around elegant Nevski Prospekt. The Hermitage, one of the world's largest and finest art collections is housed in several buildings including the Baroque Winter and Summer palaces. The Mikhailovsky Palace houses the Russian Museum (Russian art). Other sights: neoclassical Admiralty; 19c St Isaac's Cathedral and St Kazan Cathedral; Vasilievsky Island with 18c Menshikov Palace; Alexander Nevsky Monastery; 18c Smolny Convent. www.saint-petersburg.com 9 C7

Sergiev Posad

(Zagorsk) Trinity St Sergius monastery with 15c cathedral. 9 D11

Serbia Srbija

www.serbia.travel

Belgrade Beograd

Capital of Serbia. The largely modern city is set between the Danube and Sava rivers. The National Museum holds European art. To the south there are numerous fascinating medieval monasteries, richly embellished with frescoes. www.tob.co.rs/en/index.php 127 C2

Slovak Republic
Slovenska Republika

www.slovakia.travel

Bratislava

Capital of Slovakia, dominated by the castle (Slovak National Museum, good views). Old Town centred on the Main Square with Old Town Hall and Jesuit Church. Many 18–19c palaces (Mirbach Palace, Pálffy Palace, Primate's Palace), churches (Gothic cathedral, Corpus Christi Chapel) and museums (Slovak National Gallery). http://visit.bratislava.sk/en 111 A4

Košice

Charming old town with many Baroque and neoclassical buildings and Gothic cathedral. www.kosice.info 12 D4

Spišské Podhradie

Region, east of the Tatry, full of picturesque medieval towns (Levoča, Kežmarok, Prešov) and architectural monuments (Spišský Castle). 99 B4

Tatry

Beautiful mountain region. Poprad is an old town with 19c villas. Starý Smokovec is a popular ski resort. See also Poland. 99 B3

Slovenia Slovenija

www.slovenia.info

Istria Istra

Two town centres, Koper and Piran, with medieval and Renaissance squares and Baroque palaces. See also Croatia. www.slovenia.info 122 B2

Julian Alps Julijske Alpe

Wonderfully scenic section of the Alps with lakes (Bled, Bohinj), deep valleys (Planica, Vrata) and ski resorts (Kranjska Gora, Bohinjska Bistrica). 122 A2

Karst Caves

Numerous caves with huge galleries, extraordinary stalactites and stalagmites, and underground rivers. The most spectacular are Postojna (the most famous, with Predjamski Castle nearby) and Škocjan. http://www.postojnska-jama.eu/en 123 B3

Ljubljana

Capital of Slovenia. The old town, dominated by the castle (good views), is principally between Prešeren Square and Town Hall (15c, 18c), with the Three Bridges and colonnaded market. Many Baroque churches (cathedral, St Jacob, St Francis, Ursuline) and palaces (Bishop's Palace, Seminary, Gruber Palace). Also: 17c Križanke church and monastery complex; National Gallery and Modern Gallery show Slovene art. www.visitljubljana.si 123 A3

Spain España

www.spain.info

Ávila

Medieval town with 2km-long 11c walls. Pilgrimage site to shrines to St Teresa of Ávila (Convent of Santa Teresa, Convent of the Incarnation). www.avila.com/avila_tourism 150 B3

Barcelona

Showcase of Gothic ('Barri Gòtic': cathedral; Santa María del Mar; mansions on Carrer de Montcada) and *modernista* architecture ('Eixample' area with Manzana de la Discòrdia; Sagrada Familia, Güell Park, La Pedrera). Many elegant boulevards. Museums: Modern Catalan Art, Catalan Archaeology, Picasso Museum, Miró Museum, Tàpies Museum. Nearby: monastery of Montserrat (Madonna); Figueres (Dali Museum). www.barcelonaturisme.com 147 C3

Burgos

Medieval town with Gothic cathedral, Moorish-Gothic Royal Monastery and Charterhouse of Miraflores. 143 B3

Cáceres

Medieval town surrounded by originally Moorish walls and with several aristocratic palaces with solars. 155 A4

Córdoba

Capital of Moorish Spain with a labyrinth of streets and houses with tile-decorated patios. The 8–10c Mezquita is the finest mosque in Spain. A 16c cathedral was added at the centre of the building and a 17c tower replaced the minaret. The old Jewish quarter has 14c synagogue http://english.turismodecordoba.org 156 C3

El Escorial

Immense Renaissance complex of palatial and monastic buildings and mausoleum of the Spanish monarchs. www.turismomadrid.es/en/component/guides/monumento/55 151 B3

Granada

The Alhambra was hill-top palace-fortress of the rulers of the last Moorish kingdom and is the most splendid example of Moorish art and architecture in Spain. The complex has three principal parts: Alcazaba fortress (11c); Casa Real palace (14c, with later Palace of Carlos V); Generalife gardens. Also: Moorish quarter; gypsy quarter; Royal Chapel with good art in the sacristy. www.turgranada.es 163 A4

León

Gothic cathedral has notable stained glass. Royal Pantheon commemorates early kings of Castile and León. 142 B1

Madrid

Capital of Spain, a mainly modern city with 17–19c architecture at its centre around Plaza Mayor. Sights: Royal Palace with lavish apartments; Descalzas Reales Convent (tapestries and other works); Royal Armoury museum. Spain's three leading galleries: Prado (15–18c); Queen Sofia Centre (20c Spanish, Picasso's *Guernica*); Thyssen-Bornemisza Museum (medieval to modern). www.turismomadrid.es/en 151 B4

Oviedo

Gothic cathedral with 12c sanctuary. Three Visigoth (9c) churches: Santullano, Santa María del Naranco, San Miguel de Lillo. 141 A5

Palma

Situated on Mallorca, the largest and most beautiful of the Balearic islands, with an impressive Gothic cathedral. www.palmademallorca.es 166 B2

Picos de Europa
Mountain range with river gorges and peaks topped by Visigothic and Romanesque churches. 142 A2

Pyrenees
Unspoiled mountain range with beautiful landscape and villages full of Romanesque architecture (cathedral of Jaca). The Ordesa National Park has many waterfalls and canyons. 144–145

Salamanca
Delightful old city with some uniquely Spanish architecture: Renaissance Plateresque is famously seen on 16c portal of the university (founded 1215); Baroque Churrigueresque on 18c Plaza Mayor; both styles at the Convent of San Esteban. Also: Romanesque Old Cathedral; Gothic-Plateresque New Cathedral; House of Shells. www.salamanca.es 150 B2

Santiago di Compostela
Medieval city with many churches and religious institutions. The famous pilgrimage to the shrine of St James the Apostle ends here in the magnificent cathedral, originally Romanesque with many later elements (18c Baroque façade). www.santiagodecompostela.org 140 B2

Segovia
Old town set on a rock with a 1c Roman aqueduct. Also: 16c Gothic cathedral; Alcázar (14–15c, rebuilt 19c); 12-sided 13c Templar church of Vera Cruz. 151 B3

Seville Sevilla
City noted for festivals and flamenco. The world's largest Gothic cathedral (15c) retains the Orange Court and minaret of a mosque. The Alcazar is a fine example of Moorish architecture. The massive 18c tobacco factory, now part of the university, was the setting for Bizet's *Carmen*. Barrio de Santa Cruz is the old Jewish quarter with narrow streets and white houses. Casa de Pilatos (15–16c) has a fine domestic patio. The Museum of Fine Arts is in a former convent. Nearby: Roman Italica with amphitheatre. 162 A2

Tarragona
The city and its surroundings have some of the best-preserved Roman heritage in Spain. Also: Gothic cathedral (cloister); Archaeological Museum. www.tarragonaturisme.cat 147 C2

Toledo
Historic city with Moorish, Jewish and Christian sights. The small 11c mosque of El Cristo de la Luz is one of the earliest in Spain. Two synagogues have been preserved: Santa María la Blanca; El Tránsito. Churches: San Juan de los Reyes; Gothic cathedral (good artworks). El Greco's *Burial of the Count of Orgaz* is in the Church of Santo Tomé. More of his works are in the El Greco house and, with other art, in Hospital de Santa Cruz. 151 C3

Valencia
The old town has houses and palaces with elaborate façades. Also: Gothic cathedral and Lonja de la Seda church. www.turisvalencia.es 159 B3

Zaragoza
Town notable for Moorish architecture (11c Aljafería Palace). The Basilica de Nuestra Señora del Pilar, one of two cathedrals, is highly venerated. www.zaragoza.es/turismo 153 A3

Sweden Sverige
www.visitsweden.com/sweden

Abisko
Popular resort in the Swedish part of Lapland set in an inspiring landscape of lakes and mountains. www.visitabisko.com 194 B9

Gothenburg Göteborg
Largest port in Sweden, the historic centre has 17–18c Dutch architectural character (Kronhuset). The Art Museum has interesting Swedish works. www.goteborg.com 60 B1

Gotland
Island with Sweden's most popular beach resorts (Ljugarn) and unspoiled countryside with churches in Baltic Gothic style (Dahlem, Bunge). Visby is a pleasant walled medieval town. www.gotland.info/language/eng 57 C4

Lappland (Swedish)
Swedish part of Lappland with 18c Arvidsjaur the oldest preserved Sámi village. Jokkmokk is a Sámi cultural centre, Abisko a popular resort in fine scenery. Also Finland, Norway. www.kirunalapland.se 192–193

Lund
Charming university city with medieval centre and a fine 12c Romanesque cathedral (14c astronomical clock, carved tombs). www.visitlund.se/en 61 D3

Malmö
Old town centre set among canals and parks dominated by a red-brick castle (museums) and a vast market square with Town Hall and Gothic Church of St Peter. www.malmotown.com/en 61 D3

Mora
Delightful village on the shores of Siljan Lake in the heart of the Dalarna region, home to folklore and traditional crafts. 50 A1

Stockholm
Capital of Sweden built on a number of islands. The Old Town is largely on three islands with 17–18c houses, Baroque Royal Castle (apartments and museums), Gothic cathedral, parliament. Riddarholms church has tombs of the monarchy. Museums include: National Museum; Modern Museum (one of world's best modern collections); Nordiska Museet (cultural history); open-air Skansen (Swedish houses). Baroque Drottningholm Castle is the residence of the monarchy. www.visitstockholm.com 57 A4

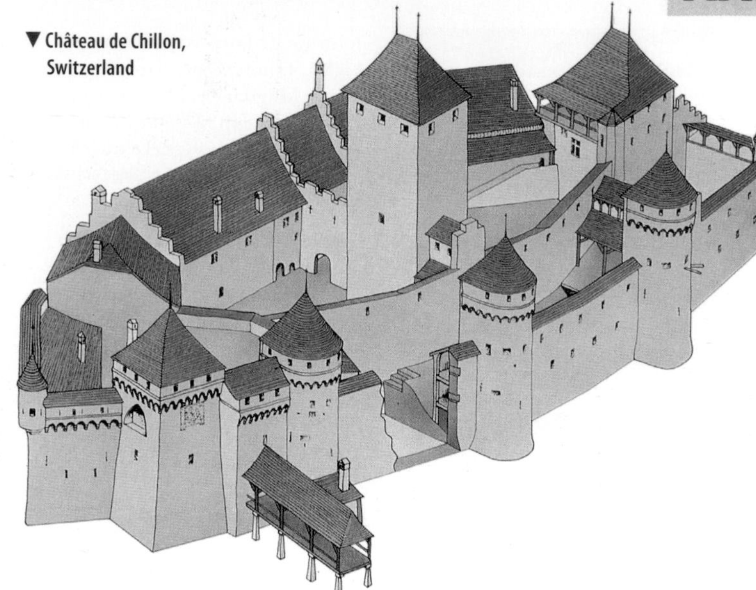
▼ Château de Chillon, Switzerland

Swedish Lakes
Beautiful region around the Vättern and Vänern Lakes. Siljan Lake is in the Dalarna region where folklore and crafts are preserved (Leksand, Mora, Rättvik). 55 B4

Uppsala
Appealing university town with a medieval centre around the massive Gothic cathedral. www.destinationuppsala.se/en 51 C4

Switzerland Schweiz
www.myswitzerland.com

Alps
The most popular Alpine region is the Berner Oberland with the town of Interlaken a starting point for exploring the large number of picturesque peaks (Jungfrau). The valleys of the Graubünden have famous ski resorts (Davos, St Moritz). Zermatt lies below the most recognizable Swiss peak, the Matterhorn. www.thealps.com 119 A4

Basle Basel
Medieval university town with Romanesque-Gothic cathedral (tomb of Erasmus). Superb collections: Art Museum; Museum of Contemporary Art. www.basel.com/en 106 B2

Bern
Capital of Switzerland. Medieval centre has fountains, characteristic streets (Spitalgasse) and tower-gates. The Bärengraben is famed for its bears. Also: Gothic cathedral; Fine Arts Museum. www.bern.com/en 106 C2

Geneva Genève
The historic area is centred on the Romanesque cathedral and Place du Bourg du Four. Excellent collections: Art and History Museum; new Museum of Modern and Contemporary Art. On the lake shore: splendid medieval Château de Chillon. www.geneve-tourisme.ch 118 A3

Interlaken
Starting point for excursions to the most delightful part of the Swiss Alps, the Bernese Oberland, with Grindelwald and Lauterbrunnen – one of the most thrilling valleys leading up to the ski resort of Wengen with views on the Jungfrau. www.interlaken.ch 106 C2

Lucerne Luzern
On the beautiful shores of Vierwaldstättersee, a charming medieval town of white houses on narrow streets and of wooden bridges (Kapellbrücke, Spreuerbrücke). It is centred on the Kornmarkt with the Renaissance Old Town Hall and Am Rhyn-Haus (Picasso collection). www.luzern.com 106 C1

Zürich
Set on Zürichsee, the old quarter is around Niederdorf with 15c cathedral. Gothic Fraumünster has stained glass by Chagall. Museums: Swiss National Museum (history); Art Museum (old and modern masters); Rietberg Museum (non-European cultures). www.zuerich.com 107 B3

Turkey Türkiye
www.gototurkey.co.uk

Istanbul
Divided by the spectcular Bosphorus, the stretch of water that separates Europe from Asia, the historic district is surrounded by the Golden Horn, Sea of Marmara and the 5c wall of Theodosius. Major sights: 6c Byzantine church of St Sophia (converted first to a mosque in 1453 and then a museum in 1934); 15c Topkapi Palace; treasury and Archaeological Museum; 17c Blue Mosque; 19c Bazaar; 16c Süleymaniye Mosque; 12c Kariye Camii; European district with Galata Tower and 19c Dolmabahçe Palace. http://english.istanbul.com 186 A3

Ukraine Ukraina

www.ukraine.com

Kiev Kyïv

Capital of Ukraine, known for its cathedral (11c, 17c) with Byzantine frescoes and mosaics. The Monastery of the Caves has churches, monastic buildings and catacombs. www.kiev.info **13 C9**

United Kingdom

www.visitbritain.com

England

www.visitengland.com

Bath

Elegant spa town with notable 18c architecture: Circus, Royal Crescent, Pulteney Bridge, Assembly Rooms; Pump Room. Also: well-preserved Roman baths; superb Perpendicular Gothic Bath Abbey. Nearby: Elizabethan Longleat House; exceptional 18c landscaped gardens at Stourhead. http://visitbath.co.uk **43 A4**

Brighton

Resort with a sea-front of Georgian, Regency and Victorian buildings, Palace Pier and old town of narrow lanes. The main sight is the Oriental-style Royal Pavilion. Nearby: South Downs National Park. www.visitbrighton.com **44 C3**

Bristol

Old port city with the fascinating Floating Harbour. Major sights include Gothic 13–14c Church of St Mary Redcliffe and 19c Clifton Suspension Bridge. http://visitbristol.co.uk **43 A4**

Cambridge

City with university founded in the early 13c. Peterhouse (1284) is the oldest college. Most famous colleges were founded in 14–16c: Queen's, King's (with the superb Perpendicular Gothic 15–16c King's College Chapel), St John's (with famous 19c Bridge of Sighs), Trinity, Clare, Gonville and Caius, Magdalene. Museums: excellent Fitzwilliam Museum (classical, medieval, old masters). Kettle's Yard (20c British). www.visitcambridge.org **45 A4**

Canterbury

Medieval city and old centre of Christianity. The Norman-Gothic cathedral has many sights and was a major medieval pilgrimage site (as related in Chaucer's *Canterbury Tales*). St Augustine, sent to convert the English in 597, founded St Augustine's Abbey, now in ruins. www.canterbury.co.uk **45 B5**

Chatsworth

One of the richest aristocratic country houses in England (largely 17c) set in a large landscaped park. The palatial interior has some 175 richly furnished rooms and a major art collection. www.chatsworth.org **40 B2**

Chester

Charming medieval city with complete walls. The Norman-Gothic cathedral has several abbey buildings. www.visitchester.com **38 A4**

Cornish Coast

Scenic landscape of cliffs and sandy beaches with picturesque villages (Fowey, Mevagissey). St Ives has the Tate Gallery with work of the St Ives Group. St Michael's Mount is reached by causeway at low tide. www.visitcornwall.com **42 B1**

Dartmoor

Beautiful wilderness area in Devon with tors and its own breed of wild pony as well as free-ranging cattle and sheep. www.dartmoor-npa.gov.uk **42 B3**

Durham

Historic city with England's finest Norman cathedral and a castle, both placed majestically on a rock above the river. www.thisisdurham.com **37 B5**

Eden Project

Centre showing the diversity of plant life on the planet, built in a disused clay pit. Two biomes, one with Mediterranean and Southern African focus and the larger featuring a waterfall, river and tropical trees plants and flowers. Outdoors also features plantations including bamboo and tea. www.edenproject.com **42 B2**

Hadrian's Wall

Built to protect the northernmost border of the Roman Empire in the 2c AD, the walls originally extended some 120km with castles every mile and 16 forts. Best-preserved walls around Hexam; forts at Housesteads and Chesters. www.visithadrianswall.co.uk **37 A4**

Lake District

Beautiful landscape of lakes (Windermere, Coniston) and England's high peaks (Scafell Pike, Skiddaw, Old Man), famous for its poets, particularly Wordsworth. www.lakedistrict.gov.uk **36 B3**

Leeds Castle

One of the oldest and most romantic English castles, standing in the middle of a lake. Most of the present appearance dates from 19c. www.leeds-castle.com **45 B4**

Lincoln

Old city perched on a hill with narrow streets, majestically dominated by the Norman-Gothic cathedral and castle. www.visitlincolnshire.com **40 B3**

Liverpool

City on site of port founded in 1207 and focused around 1846 Albert Dock, now a heritage attraction. Croxteth Hall and Country Park; Speke Hall; Sudley House; Royal Liver Building; Liverpool Cathedral; Walker Art Gallery; Tate Liverpool; University of Liverpool Art Gallery. www.visitliverpool.com **38 A4**

London

Capital of UK and Europe's largest city. To the east of the medieval heart of the city – now the largely modern financial district and known as the City of London – is the Tower of London (11c White Tower, Crown Jewels) and 1880s Tower Bridge. The popular heart of the city and its entertainment is the West End, around Piccadilly Circus, Leicester Square and Trafalgar Square (Nelson's Column). Many sights of political and royal power: Whitehall (Banqueting House, 10 Downing Street, Horse Guards); Neo-Gothic Palace of Westminster (Houses of Parliament) with Big Ben; The Mall leading to Buckingham Palace (royal residence, famous ceremony of the Changing of the Guard). Numerous churches include: 13–16c Gothic Westminster Abbey (many tombs, Henry VII's Chapel); Wren's Baroque St Paul's Cathedral, St Mary-le-Bow, spire of St Bride's, St Stephen Walbrook. Museums of world fame: British Museum (prehistory, oriental and classical antiquity, medieval); Victoria and Albert Museum (decorative arts); National Gallery (old masters to 19c); National Portrait Gallery (historic and current British portraiture); Tate – Britain and Modern; Science Museum; Natural History Museum. Madame Tussaud's waxworks museum is hugely popular. Other sights include: London Eye, Kensington Palace; Greenwich with Old Royal Observatory (Greenwich meridian), Baroque Royal Naval College, Palladian Queen's House; Tudor Hampton Court Palace; Syon House. Nearby: Windsor Castle (art collection, St George's Chapel). www.visitlondon.com **44 B3**

◀ Salisbury Cathedral, England

Longleat
One of the earliest and finest Elizabethan palaces in England. The palace is richly decorated. Some of the grounds have been turned into a pleasure park, with the Safari Park, the first of its kind outside Africa. www.longleat.co.uk **43 A4**

Manchester
Founded on a Roman settlement of 79AD and a main player in the Industrial Revolution. Victorian Gothic Town Hall; Royal Exchange; Cathedral. Many museums including Imperial War Museum North, Lowry Centre and Manchester Art Gallery. www.visitmanchester.com **40 B1**

Newcastle upon Tyne
A key player in the Industrial Revolution with 12th century cathedral and many museums as well as strong railway heritage. www.newcastlegateshead.com **37 B5**

Norwich
Medieval quarter has half-timbered houses. 15c castle keep houses a museum and gallery. Many medieval churches include the Norman-Gothic cathedral. www.visitnorwich.co.uk **41 C5**

Oxford
Old university city. Earliest colleges date from 13c: University College; Balliol; Merton. 14–16c colleges include: New College; Magdalen; Christ Church (perhaps the finest). Other buildings: Bodleian Library; Radcliffe Camera; Sheldonian Theatre; cathedral. Good museums: Ashmolean Museum (antiquity to 20c); Museum of the History of Science; Museum of Modern Art; Christ Church Picture Gallery (14–17c). Nearby: outstanding 18c Blenheim Palace. www.visitoxfordandoxfordshire.com **44 B2**

Petworth
House (17c) with one of the finest country-house art collections (old masters), set in a huge landscaped park. www.nationaltrust.org.uk **44 C3**

Salisbury
Pleasant old city with a magnificent 13c cathedral built in an unusually unified Gothic style. Nearby: Wilton House. www.visitwiltshire.co.uk **44 B2**

Stonehenge
Some 4000 years old, one of the most famous and haunting Neolithic monuments in Europe. Many other Neolithic sites are nearby. www.english-heritage.org.uk **44 B2**

Stourhead
Early 18c palace famous for its grounds, one of the finest examples of neoclassical landscaped gardening, consisting of a lake surrounded by numerous temples. www.nationaltrust.org.uk **43 A4**

Stratford-upon-Avon
Old town of Tudor and Jacobean half-timbered houses, famed as the birth and burial place of William Shakespeare and home of the Royal Shakespeare Company. www.shakespeare-country.co.uk **44 A2**

Wells
Charming city with beautiful 12–16c cathedral (west facade, scissor arches, chapter house, medieval clock). Also Bishop's Palace; Vicar's Close. www.wellssomerset.com **43 A4**

Winchester
Historic city with 11–16c cathedral. Also: 13c Great Hall, Winchester College, St Cross almshouses. Western gateway to the South Downs National Park. www.visitwinchester.co.uk **44 B2**

York
Attractive medieval city surrounded by well-preserved walls with magnificent Gothic 13–15c Minster. Museums: York City Art Gallery (14–19c); Jorvik Viking Centre. Nearby: Castle Howard. www.visityork.org **40 B2**

Northern Ireland
www.discovernorthernireland.com

Antrim Coast
Spectacular coast with diverse scenery of glens (Glenarm, Glenariff), cliffs (Murlough Bay) and the famous Giant's Causeway, consisting of some 40,000 basalt columns. Carrickefergus Castle is the largest and best-preserved Norman castle in Ireland. www.causewaycoastandglens.com **27 A4**

Belfast
Capital of Northern Ireland. Sights: Donegall Square with 18c Town Hall; neo-Romanesque Protestant cathedral; University Square; Ulster Museum (European painting). http://visit-belfast.com **27 B5**

Giant's Causeway
Spectacular and unique rock formations in the North Antrim coast, formed by volcanic activity 50–60 million years ago. World Heritage Site. www.nationaltrust.org.uk **27 A4**

Scotland
www.visitscotland.com

Edinburgh
Capital of Scotland, built on volcanic hills. The medieval Old Town is dominated by the castle set high on a volcanic rock (Norman St Margaret's Chapel, state apartments, Crown Room). Holyrood House (15c and 17c) has lavishly decorated state apartments and the ruins of Holyrood Abbey (remains of Scottish monarchs). The 15c cathedral has the Crown Spire and Thistle Chapel. The New Town has good Georgian architecture (Charlotte Square, Georgian House). Excellent museums: Scottish National Portrait Gallery, National Gallery of Scotland; Scottish National Gallery of Modern Art. **35 C4**

Glamis Castle
In beautiful, almost flat landscaped grounds, 14c fortress, rebuilt 17c, gives a fairy-tale impression. www.strathmore-estates.co.uk **35 B5**

Glasgow
Scotland's largest city, with centre around George Square and 13–15c Gothic cathedral. The Glasgow School of Art (currently closed for repair after a fire) is the masterpiece of Charles Rennie Mackintosh. Fine art collections: Glasgow Museum and Art Gallery; Hunterian Gallery; Burrell Collection; Kelvingrove Art Gallery and Museum. **35 C3**

Loch Ness
In the heart of the Highlands, the lake forms part of the scenic Great Glen running from Inverness to Fort William. Famous as home of the fabled Loch Ness Monster (exhibition at Drumnadrochit). Nearby: ruins of 14–16c Urquhart Castle. www.lochness.com **32 D2**

Wales
www.visitwales.com

Caernarfon
Dominated by magnificent 13c castle, one of a series built by Edward I in Wales. www.visitcaernarfon.com **38 A2**

Cardiff
Capital of Wales, most famous for its medieval castle, restored 19c in Greek, Gothic and Oriental styles. Also: National Museum and Gallery. www.visitcardiff.com **39 C3**

Vatican City
Città del Vaticano
www.vatican.va

Independent state within Rome. On Piazza San Pietro is the 15–16c Renaissance-Baroque Basilica San Pietro (Michelangelo's dome and *Pietà*), the world's most important Roman Catholic church. The Vatican Palace contains the Vatican Museums with many fine art treasures including Michelangelo's frescoes in the Sistine Chapel. **168 B2**

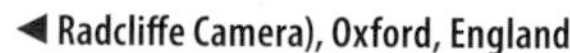
◀ Radcliffe Camera), Oxford, England

▼ The facade of Basilica San Pietro, Vatican City

European politics and economics

The figures given for capitals' populations are for the whole metropolitan area.

Albania Shqipëria

Area 28,748 km² (11,100 mi²)
Population 3,011,000
Capital Tirana / Tiranë (764,000)
Languages Albanian (official), Greek, Vlach, Romani and Slavic
GDP $4,000
Currency Lek = 100 Quindars
Government multiparty republic
Head of state Bujar Nishani, 2012
Head of government Prime Minister Edi Rama, Socialist Party, 2013
Website www.km.gov.al/?gj=gj2

Events In the 2005 general elections, the Democratic Party and its allies won a decisive victory on pledges of reducing crime and corruption, promoting economic growth and decreasing the size of government. The party retained power by a narrow margin in 2009, amid disputes over electoral procedure. After three years of talks, a Stabilisation and Association Agreement was signed with the EU in June 2006, and the country formally applied for membership in April 2009, the same month as it became a member of NATO. Protests at alleged official corruption and vote-rigging led to violent clashes in 2011. The Socialist Party won 53% of the vote in 2013 elections. Albania was formally recommended as an EU candidate in June 2014

Economy Although economic growth has begun, Albania is still one of the poorest countries in Europe. 56% of the workforce are engaged in agriculture. Private ownership of land has been encouraged since 1991 and foreign investment is encouraged.

Andorra Principat d'Andorra

Area 468 km² (181 mi²)
Population 85,000
Capital Andorra la Vella (44,000)
Languages Catalan (official), French, Castilian and Portuguese
GDP $46,418 (2012)
Currency Euro = 100 cents
Government independent state and co-principality
Head of state co-princes: Joan Enric Vives i Sicilia, Bishop of Urgell, 2003 and François Hollande (see France), 2012
Head of government Chief Executive Antoni Martí Petit, Democrats for Andorra, 2011
Website http://visitandorra.com

Events In 1993 a new democratic constitution was adopted that reduced the roles of the President of France and the Bishop of Urgell to constitutional figureheads. In 2010, the OECD removed Andorra from its list of uncooperative tax havens. Personal income tax was introduced in 2013.

Economy About 80% of the work force are employed in the services sector, but tourism accounts for about 80% of GDP with an estimated 9 million visiting annually, attracted by its duty-free status and its summer and winter resorts. Agricultural production is limited (2% of the land is arable) and most food has to be imported. The principal livestock activity is sheep rearing. Manufacturing output consists mainly of cigarettes, cigars and furniture.

Austria Österreich

Area 83,859 km² (32,377 mi²)
Population 8,505,000
Capital Vienna / Wien (2,419,000)
Languages German (official)
GDP $48,956 (2013)
Currency Euro = 100 cents
Government federal republic
Head of state President Heinz Fischer, 2004
Head of government Federal Chancellor Werner Faymann, Social Democratic Party, 2008
Website www.austria.gv.at

Events Since general elections in 1999, the extreme right Freedom Party has made gains at the expense of the Social Democrats and their successive coalition partners. In 2013 parliamentary elections, the coalition received just over 50% of the vote and the Freedom Party 21%.

Economy Has a well-developed market economy and high standard of living. The economy grew in 2013. The leading economic activities are the manufacture of metals and tourism. Dairy and livestock farming are the principal agricultural activities.

Belarus

Area 207,600 km² (80,154 mi²)
Population 9,609,000
Capital Minsk (2,002,000)
Languages Belarusian, Russian (both official)
GDP $7,577 (2013)
Currency Belarussian ruble = 100 kopek
Government Republic
Head of state President Alexander Lukashenko, 1994
Head of government Prime Minister Mikhail Myasnikovich, independent, 2010
Website www.belarus.by/en/government

Events Belarus attained its independence in 1991. As a result of a referendum in 1996 the president increased his power at the expense of parliament. In 1997, Belarus signed a Union Treaty committing it to political and economic integration with Russia. Since his election in July 1994 as the country's first president, Alexander Lukashenko, has steadily consolidated his power through authoritarian means. Government restrictions on freedom of speech, the press and religion continue and in early 2005, the US listed Belarus as an outpost of tyranny. Belarus joined the EU's Eastern Partnership in 2009. In 2010, it signed a customs union with Russia and Kazakhstan. Alexander Lukashenko was declared to have won a fourth term as president in December 2010 in elections, described internationally as flawed, which provoked protests. The arrests and beatings of opposition candidates and protesters led to EU sanctions, but clamp-downs on personal and political freedoms have continued.

Economy Belarus has faced problems in the transition to a free-market economy. After relaxation of currency rules in early 2011, the value of the ruble dropped sharply and the country's large foreign debts and lack of hard currency led to negotiations with Russia over substantial loans. Agriculture, especially meat and dairy farming, is important. In 2011, the country was forced to apply to the IMF for funds and for a Russian-led bailout.

Belgium Belgique

Area 30,528 km² (11,786 mi²)
Population 12,000,000
Capital Brussels/Bruxelles (1,830,000)
Languages Dutch, French, German (all official)
GDP $45,383 (2013)
Currency Euro = 100 cents
Government federal constitutional monarchy
Head of state Philippe I, 2013
Head of government Prime Minister (caretaker) Elio Di Rupo, Socialist Party, 2011
Website www.belgium.be/en

Events In 1993 Belgium adopted a federal system of government. Elections in June 2007 led to the Christian Democrats gaining almost 30% of the vote in Flanders. An uneasy coalition was eventually formed in March 2008, but negotiations for constitutional reform stalled. Former PM Leterme replaced Herman van Rompuy when the latter became President of the European Council. The coalition collapsed in April 2010. Elections in June resulted in gains for the pro-separatist New Flemish Alliance and the Socialist Party in Wallonia. Negotiations to form a coalition lasted until December 2011. After parliamentary elections in May 2014 and PM Elio di Rupo resigned, but was asked to stay on as caretaker until a new government could be negotiated.

Economy Belgium is a major trading nation with a modern, private-enterprise economy, which grew slightly in 2013. The leading activity is manufacturing i.e. steel and chemicals. With few natural resources, it imports substantial quantities of raw materials and export a large volume of manufactures.

Bosnia-Herzegovina Bosna i Hercegovina

Area 51,197 km² (19,767 mi²)
Population 3,872,000
Capital Sarajevo (608,000)
Languages Bosnian/Croatian/Serbian
GDP $4,597 (2013)
Currency Convertible Marka = 100 convertible pfenniga
Government federal republic
Head of state Chairman of the Presidency - rotates between Presidency members Bakir Izetbegović (Party of Democratic Action), Željko Komšić (Social Democratic Party) and Nebojša Radmanović (Political party Alliance of Independent Social Democrats)
Head of government Prime Minister Vjekoslav Bevanda, Croatian Democratic Union of Bosnia and Herzegovina, 2012
Website www.fbihvlada.gov.ba/english/index.php

Events In 1992 a referendum approved independence from the Yugoslav federation. The Bosnian Serb population was against independence and in the resulting war occupied over two-thirds of the land. Croat forces seized other parts of the area. The 1995 Dayton Peace Accord ended the war and set up the Bosnian Muslim/Croat Federation and the Bosnian Serb Republic, each with their own president, government, parliament, military and police. There is also a central Bosnian government and rotating presidency. The office of High Representative has the power to impose decisions where the authorities are unable to agree or where political or economic interests are affected; the current incumbent, Valentin Inzko took charge in 2009. EUFOR troops took over from the NATO-led force in 2004. In late 2005, agreement was reached to set up state-wide police defence and security forces, a state court and state taxation system, and the EU initiated its Stabilisation and Association Agreement with Bosnia in 2007. Application for full EU membership has been delayed. In December 2006 Bosnia joined NATO's Partnership for Peace programme and in April 2010 received its Membership Action Plan. Elections in 2010 resulted in a 14-month stalemate before a new government could be agreed. High unemployment and perceptions of official corruption led to riots in early 2014.

Economy Excluding Macedonia, Bosnia was the least developed of the former republics of Yugoslavia. Currently receiving substantial aid, though this will be reduced. The country attracts considerable foreign direct investment and the Convertible Marka is Euro-pegged. The economy remained stagnant in 2013.

Bulgaria Bulgariya

Area 110,912 km² (42,822 mi²)
Population 6,925,000
Capital Sofia (1,454,000)
Languages Bulgarian (official), Turkish
GDP $7,328 (2013)
Currency Lev = 100 stotinki
Government multiparty republic
Head of state President Rosen Asenov Plevneliev, Citizens for European Development of Bulgaria GERB, 2012
Head of government Prime Minister Plamen Oresharski, independent, 2013
Website www.government.bg

Events In 1990 the first non-communist president for 40 years, Zhelyu Zhelev, was elected. A new constitution in 1991 saw the adoption of free-market reforms. Bulgaria joined NATO in 2004. The president was re-elected in 2006. Bulgaria joined the EU in January 2007, but lack of progress in tackling corruption has led to the delay, then scrapping of a large proportion of EU funding. The GERB-led coalition fell in early 2012 after street protests and was replaced in May 2013 by a technocratic government. Protests over official corruption sprang up in the summer of 2013.

Economy The Lev has been pegged to the Euro since 2002. The economy has begun to attract significant amounts of foreign direct investment. Bulgaria experienced macroeconomic stability and strong growth from 1996 to early 2008, and after a sharp decline in GDP in 2009, the economy returned to slight growth from 2010. Manufacturing is the leading economic activity but has outdated technology. The main products are chemicals, metals, machinery and textiles. The valleys of the Maritsa are ideal for winemaking, plums and tobacco. Tourism is increasing rapidly.

Croatia Hrvatska

Area 56,538 km² (21,829 mi²)
Population 4,471,000
Capital Zagreb (1,111,000)
Languages Croatian
GDP $13,561 (2013)
Currency Kuna = 100 lipa
Government multiparty republic
Head of state President Ivo Josipović, SDP, 2010
Head of government Prime Minister Zoran Milanović, Social Democratic Party of Croatia (SDP), 2011.
Website http://croatia.hr

Events A 1991 referendum voted overwhelmingly in favour of independence from Yugoslavia. Serb-dominated areas took up arms to remain in the federation. Serbia armed Croatian Serbs, war broke out between Serbia and Croatia, and Croatia lost much territory. In 1992 United Nations peacekeeping troops were deployed. Following the Dayton Peace Accord of 1995, Croatia and Yugoslavia established diplomatic relations. An agreement between the Croatian government and Croatian Serbs provided for the eventual reintegration of Krajina into Croatia in 1998. PM Kosor leads a minority government with the support of many smaller parties, promising to continue the policies of her predecessor. Croatia joined NATO in 2009 and, after a referendum in 2012, joined the EU in 2013.

Economy The wars badly disrupted Croatia's economy but it emerged from a mild recession in 2000, with tourism, banking and public investment leading the way. The economy continues to struggle and unemployment is high.

Czech Republic Česka Republica

Area 78,864 km² (30,449 mi²)
Population 10,627,000
Capital Prague/Praha (2,300,000)
Languages Czech (official), Moravian
GDP $18,857 (2013)
Currency Czech Koruna = 100 haler
Government multiparty republic
Head of state President Milos Zeman, 2013
Head of government Prime Minister Bohuslav Sobotka, SDP, 2014
Website www.vlada.cz/en/

Events In 1992 the government agreed to the secession of the Slovak Republic, and on 1 January 1993 the Czech Republic was created. The Czech Republic was granted full membership of NATO in 1999 and joined the EU in May 2004. Governments have been characterized by short-lived coalitions. PM Petr Nečas was forced to resign in June 2013 over allegations of corruption. After early parliamentary elections in October, Bohuslav Sobotka of the Social Democrats was appointed head of a coalition government in January 2014.

Economy The country has deposits of coal, uranium, iron ore, tin and zinc. Industries include chemicals, beer, iron and steel. Private ownership of land is gradually being restored. Agriculture employs 12% of the workforce. Inflation is under control. Intensified restructuring among large enterprises, improvements in the financial sector and effective use of available EU funds served to strengthen output growth until the onset of the worldwide economic downturn, because of reduced exports. Prague is now a major tourist destination.

Denmark Danmark

Area 43,094 km² (16,638 mi²)
Population 5,627,000
Capital Copenhagen / København (1,997,000)
Languages Danish (official)
GDP $59,190 (2013)
Currency Krone = 100 øre
Government parliamentary monarchy
Head of state Queen Margrethe II, 1972
Head of government Prime Minister Helle Thorning-Schmidt, Social Democrats, 2011.
Website www.denmark.dk/en

Events In 1992 Denmark rejected the Maastricht Treaty, but reversed the decision in a 1993 referendum. In 1998 the Amsterdam Treaty was ratified by a further referendum. In 2009 Greenland assumed responsibility for many domestic competencies. The government is a coalition formed by the Social Democrats, Danish Social Liberal Party and the Socialist People's Party, which narrowly beat the rightwing coalition led by Lars Lokke Rasmussen in 2011.

Economy Danes enjoy a high standard of living with a thoroughly modern market economy

featuring high-tech agriculture, up-to-date small-scale and corporate industry, comfortable living standards and a stable currency, which is pegged to the Euro, but still independent. Economic growth gained momentum in 2004, but slowed in 2007. GDP has continued to grow slightly since 2012. Denmark is self-sufficient in oil and natural gas. Services, including tourism, form the largest sector (63% of GDP). Farming employs only 4% of the workforce but is highly productive. Fishing is also important.

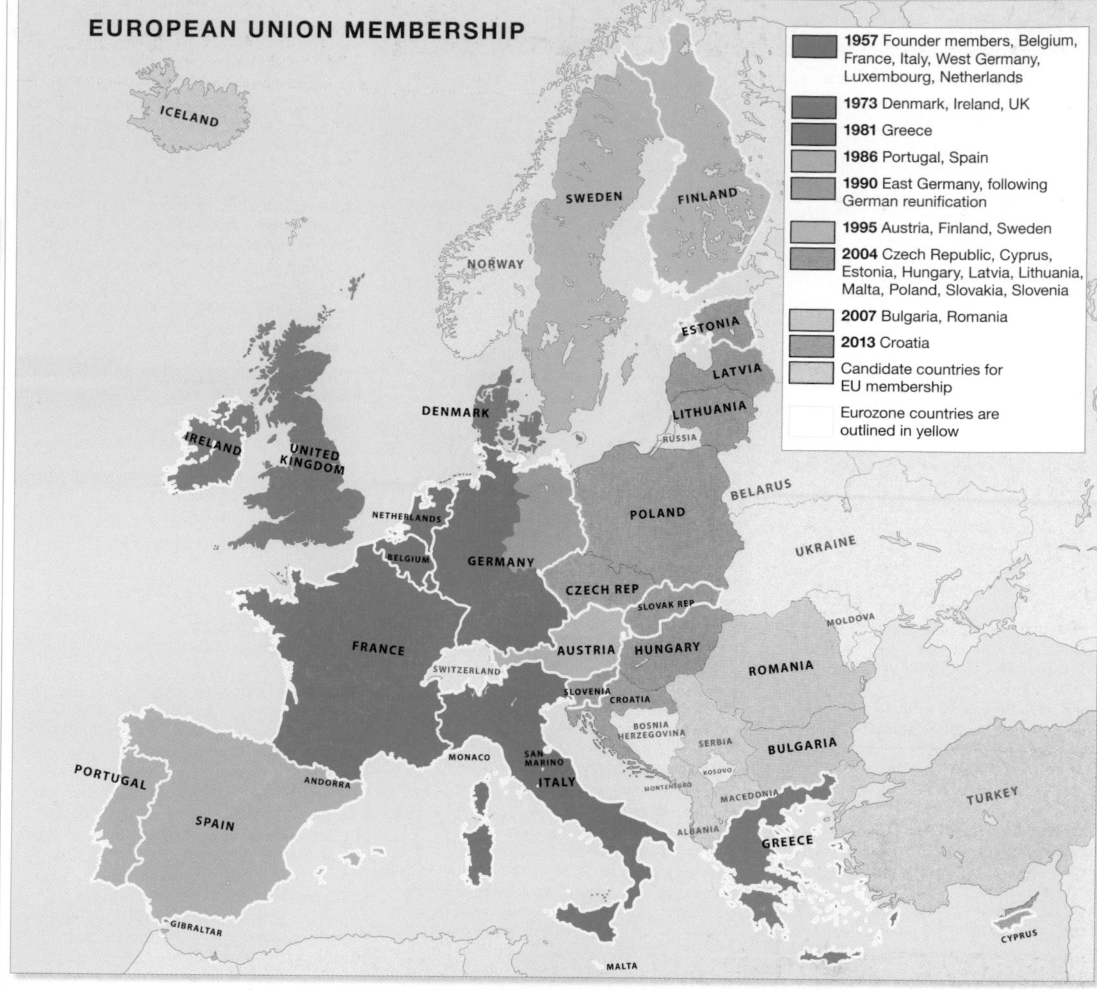

Estonia Eesti

Area 45,100 km² (17,413 mi²)
Population 1,314,000
Capital Tallinn (543,000)
Languages Estonian (official), Russian
GDP $19,031 (2013)
Currency Euro = 100 cents
Government multiparty republic
Head of state President Toomas Hendrik Ilves, 2006
Head of government Prime Minister Taavi Roivas, Reform Party, 2014
Website http://valitsus.ee/en

Events In 1992 Estonia adopted a new constitution and multiparty elections were held. Estonia joined NATO in March 2004 and the EU in May 2004. In 2005 a treaty defining the border with Russia was signed, but Russia refused to ratify it after Estonia introduced a reference to the Russian occupation of Estonia. Long-standing coalition PM Andrus Ansip resigned as leader in early 2014 and was replaced by 34-year-old Taavi Roivas. Estonia joined the OECD in 2010 and adopted the Euro in January 2011. Strict language laws are regarded by Russian-speakers as discriminatory.
Economy Privatisation and free-trade reforms after independence increased foreign investment and trade. Chief natural resources are oil shale and forests. Manufactures include petrochemicals, fertilisers and textiles. Estonia has led the way among new EU states with a strong electronics and communications sector. Since the country emerged from the global financial crisis in 2010, the economy has grown strongly.

Finland Suomi

Area 338,145 km² (130,557 mi²)
Population 5,457,000
Capital Helsinki (1,403,000)
Languages Finnish, Swedish (both official)
GDP $47, 129 (2013) **Currency** Euro = 100 cents
Government multiparty republic
Head of state President Sauli Niinistö, National Coalition Party, 2012
Head of government Prime Minister Alexander Stubb, National Coalition Party, 2014
Website http://government.fi/etusivu/en.jsp

Events In 1986 Finland became a member of EFTA and in 1995 joined the EU. A new constitution was established in March 2000. The Finnish Parliament voted for the EU constitution in 2006. Successive governments have been in the form of multi-party coalitions. In the presidential election of 2012, Sauli Niinistö defeated Pekka-Haavisto of the Green Party.
Economy Forests are Finland's most valuable resource, with wood and paper products accounting for 35% of exports. Engineering, shipbuilding and textile industries have grown. Finland excels in high-tech exports and is a leading light in the telecoms industry. Farming employs 9% of the workforce. Unemployment remains high, although the economy returned to growth in 2011.

France

Area 551,500 km² (212,934 mi²)
Population 66,616,000
Capital Paris (12,162,000)
Languages French (official), Breton, Occitan
GDP $42,999 (2013)
Currency Euro = 100 cents
Government multiparty republic
Head of state President François Hollande, Socialist Party, 2012
Head of government Prime Minister Manuel Valls, Socialist Party, 2014
Website www.diplomatie.gouv.fr/en/

Events France was a founder member of both the EU and NATO. Its post-war governments have swung between socialist and centrist/right. Widespread dissatisfaction with François Sarkozy's austerity measures led to a return to power for the Socialist Party in 2012.
Economy France is a leading industrial nation. Industries include chemicals and steel. It is the leading producer of farm products in western Europe. Livestock and dairy farming are vital sectors. The French economy was badly affected by the global financial downturn. In May 2013 it entered its second recession in four years. It is the world's second largest producer of cheese and wine. Tourism is a major industry.

Germany Deutschland

Area 357,022 km² (137,846 mi²)
Population 80,716,000
Capital Berlin (6,000,000)
Languages German (official)
GDP $44,999 (2013) **Currency** Euro = 100 cents
Government federal multiparty republic
Head of state President Joachim Gauck, independent, 2012
Head of government Chancellor Angela Merkel, Christian Democratic Union, 2005
Website www.bundesregierung.de

Events Germany is a major supporter of the European Union, and former chancellor Helmut Köhl was the driving force behind the creation of the Euro. The grand coalition government formed in 2005 between the CDU, CSU and Social Democrats was replaced by one of the CDU, CSU and FDP after elections in 2009. Repeated calls upon German funds in support of weaker Eurozone economies have caused widespread anger. In 2012, after Christian Wulff was forced to resign because of corruption charges the consensus candidate former Lutheran pastor and civil rights activist Joacham Glauk was elected president. Angela Merkel's CDU only narrowly missed winning an outright majority in 2013 elections.
Economy Germany has long been one of the world's greatest economic powers. In 2013, the economy shrank slightly because of a reduction in industrial output. Services form the largest economic sector. Machinery and transport equipment account for 50% of exports. It is the world's third-largest car producer. Other major products include ships, iron, steel, petroleum and tyres. It has the world's second-largest lignite mining industry. Other minerals are copper, potash, lead, salt, zinc and aluminium. Germany is the world's second-largest producer of hops and beer, and fifth-largest of wine. Other products are cheese and milk, barley, rye and pork.

Greece Ellas

Area 131,957 km² (50,948 mi²)
Population 10,816,000
Capital Athens / Athina (3,758,000)
Languages Greek (official)
GDP $21,857 (2013)
Currency Euro = 100 cents
Government multiparty republic
Head of state President Karolos Papoulias, Panhellenic Socialist Movement (PASOK), 2005
Head of government Prime Minister Antonis Samaris, New Democracy
Website www.primeminister.gr/english

Events In 1981 Greece joined the EU and Andreas Papandreous became Greece's first Socialist prime minister. His son was re-elected in 2009, but lost power in 2012 as a result of his handling of the economic crisis and the deep unpopularity of the austerity measures imposed by the Eurozone and IMF as a condition of bailout funds. After inconclusive election results, the president asked Antonis Samaris to form a government, resulting in continued uncertainty about Greece's remaining within the Eurozone. Strikes and protests continued through 2012 and 2013.
Economy Greece is one of the poorest members of the European Union. Manufacturing is important. Products: textiles, cement, chemicals, metallurgy. Minerals: lignite, bauxite, chromite. Farmland covers 33% of Greece, grazing land 40%. Major crops: tobacco, olives, grapes, cotton, wheat. Livestock are raised. Tourism provides 15% of GDP. Severely hit by the global downturn, from 2010 it was repeatedly in danger of defaulting on debt repayments, forcing multiple bailouts by other Eurozone countries and the IMF and putting extreme pressure on the Euro. The economy continued to contract through 2013, but a return to growth was projected by the government for 2014.

Hungary Magyarország

Area 93,032 km² (35,919 mi²)
Population 9,879,000
Capital Budapest (3,284,000)
Languages Hungarian (official)
GDP $13,404 (2013)
Currency Forint = 100 filler
Government multiparty republic
Head of state President János Áder, Fidesz, 2012.
Head of government Prime Minister Viktor Orban, Fidesz, 2010
Website www.kormany.hu/en

Events In 1990 multiparty elections were held for the first time. In 1999 Hungary joined NATO and in 2004 it acceded to the EU.
In 2012 attempts to change the electoral system led to widespread protests, as have austerity measures imposed by successive governments. Relations with the EU bodies and IMF remain fractious because of the effect of terms imposed for Euro accession and financial bailouts.
Economy Since the early 1990s, Hungary has adopted market reforms and partial privatisation programmes. High levels of public debt meant that Hungary had to appeal for repeated loans from the IMF and EU to prevent economic collapse when the world economic crisis struck. The manufacture of machinery and transport is the most valuable sector. Hungary's resources include bauxite, coal and natural gas.
Major crops include grapes for wine-making, maize, potatoes, sugar beet and wheat. Tourism is a growing sector.

Iceland Ísland

Area 103,000 km² (39,768 mi²)
Population 326,000
Capital Reykjavik (209,000)
Languages Icelandic
GDP $45,535 (2013)
Currency Krona = 100 aurar
Government multiparty republic
Head of state President Olafur Ragnar Grimmson, 1996
Head of government Prime Minister Sigmundur Gunnlaugsson, Progresssive Party, 2013
Website www.government.is/

Events In 1944, a referendum decisively voted to sever links with Denmark, and Iceland became a fully independent republic. In 1946 it joined NATO. In 1970 Iceland joined the European Free Trade Association. The last post-war US military personnel left in September 2006, the same year that the government voted to resume commercial whaling. There are concerns among environmentalists about

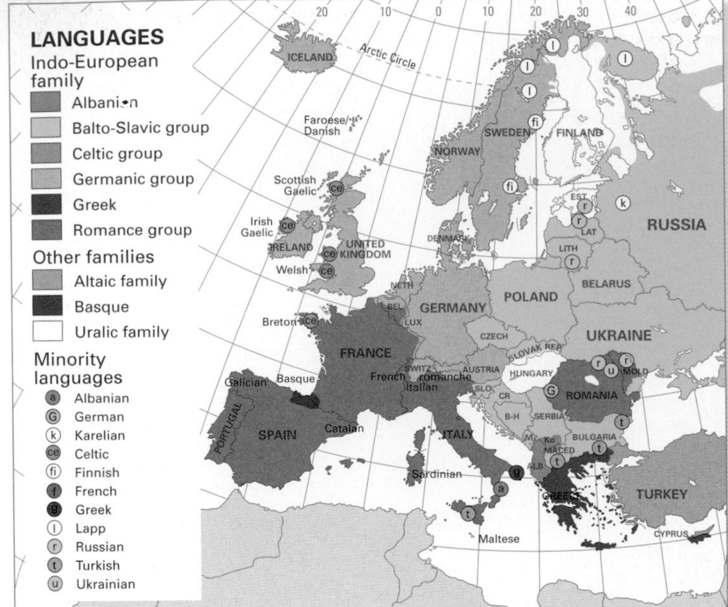

the impact of major new industrial complexes powered by Iceland's abundant thermal energy. Even though Sigurdardottir's Social Democratic Alliance had returned some stability to the economy,the Social Democrats were defeated in 2013 parliamentary elections.
Economy The economy has long been sensitive to declining fish stocks as well as to fluctuations in world prices for its main exports: fish and fish products, aluminum and ferrosilicon. There has traditionally been low unemployment, and remarkably even distribution of income. Risky levels of investment in overseas companies left Iceland's banks with high debts when the global credit crunch hit, and the government had to apply for IMF funding.

Ireland Eire

Area 70,273 km^2 (27,132 mi^2)
Population 4,593,000
Capital Dublin (1,804,000)
Languages Irish, English (both official)
GDP $45,620 (2013)
Currency Euro = 100 cents
Government multiparty republic
Head of state
President Michael Higgins, Independent (formerly Labour Party), 2011
Head of government
Taoiseach Enda Kenny, Fine Gael, 2011
Website www.gov.ie/en/
Events In 1948 Ireland withdrew from the British Commonwealth and joined the European Community in 1973. The Anglo-Irish Agreement (1985) gave Ireland a consultative role in the affairs of Northern Ireland. Following a 1995 referendum, divorce was legalised. Abortion remains a contentious political issue. In the Good Friday Agreement of 1998 the Irish Republic gave up its constitutional claim to Northern Ireland and a North-South Ministerial Council was established. Sinn Fein got its first seats in the European elections of June 2004. In 2008, long-standing PM Bertie Ahern stood down and Brian Cowen of Fianna Fáil formed a coalition. This fell in early 2011 because of public anger at the bailout from the EU and IMF.
Economy Ireland benefited greatly from its membership of the European Union. It joined in circulating the Euro in 2002. Grants have enabled the modernisation of farming, which employs 14% of the workforce. Major products include cereals, cattle and dairy products, sheep, sugar beet and potatoes. Fishing is important. Traditional sectors, such as brewing, distilling and textiles, have been supplemented by high-tech industries, such as electronics. Tourism is the most important component of the service industry. The economy also benefited from a rise in consumer spending, construction and business investment, but growth slowed in 2007 and the country went into recession in 2008, and the joint banking and debt crisis eventually led to the government of Brian Cowen requesting a bailout from the EU and IMF. The economy returned to recession in 2013, but at the end of the year Ireland became the first country to exit from its EU bailout programme.

Italy Italia

Area 301,318 km^2 (116,338 mi^2)
Population 60,783,000
Capital Rome / Roma (4,194,000)
Languages Italian (official)
GDP $34,714 (2013)
Currency Euro = 100 cents
Government social democracy
Head of state Giorgio Napolitano, 2006
Head of government Matteo Renzi, Democratic Party, 2014
Website www.italia.it
Events Since World War II Italy has had a succession of unstable, short-lived governments. Silvio Berlusconi regained control in 2008, but was forced to resign in late 2011 because of the ongoing economic crisis and alleged personal scandals. His successor, Mario Monti, was defeated in 2013 elections that resulted in a coalition between the Democrats and Berlusconi's Freedom Party. In October, Berlusconi's attempt to topple the coalition backfired when several colleagues refused to resign in relation to his expulsion from the Senate. In December, mayor of Florence Matteo Renzi was elected Secretary of the Democrat Party in December 2013 and appointed PM two months later at the head of a broad coalition.
Economy Italy's main industrial region is the north-western triangle of Milan, Turin and Genoa. It is the world's eighth-largest car and steel producer. Machinery and transport equipment account for 37% of exports. Agricultural production is important. Italy is the world's largest producer of wine. Tourism is a vital economic sector. Italy emerged from a two-year recession at the end of 2013, but unemployment remains high.

Kosovo (Republika e Kosoves/Republika Kosovo)

Area 10,887 km^2 (4203 mi^2)
Population 1,859,000
Capital Pristina (465,000)
Languages Albanian, Serbian (both official), Bosnian, Turkish, Roma
GDP $3,454 (2013)
Currency Euro (Serbian dinar in Serb enclaves)
Government Multiparty republic
Head of state President Atifete Jahjaga (2011)
Head of government
Prime Minister Hashim Thaci (2008)
Website www.kryeministri-ks.net/?page=2,1
Events An autonomous province with a mainly ethnic Albanian Muslim population, Kosovo first declared independence from Serbia in 1990, leading to years of increased ethnic tension and violence. In 1998 conflict between Serb police and the Kosovo Liberation Army led to a violent crackdown by Serbia, which ceased only after more than two months' aerial bombardment by Nato in 1999, during which hundreds of thousands of Kosovo Albanians were massacred or expelled before Serbia agreed to withdraw and a UN peacekeeping force and administration were sent in, which remained in place until 2008. Talks on the status of the province took place in 2003 and 2006. In 2008, independence was declared again and a new constitution was adopted that transferred power from the UN to the ethnic Albanian government, a move that was rejected by Serbia and Russia but recognised by the US and major European countries. The UN referred Kosovo's declaration of independence to the International Court of Justice, which declared in 2010 that it was not illegal. In March 2011, direct talks between Serbia and Kosovo began. In 2013, the EU brokered an agreement on policing for the Serb minority. PM Thaci claimed victory after early results of parliamentary elections in June 2014.
Economy Kosovo is one of the poorest areas of Europe, with a high proportion of the population classed as living in poverty. It possesses some mineral resources but the chief economic activity is agriculture.

Latvia Latvija

Area 64,589 km^2 (24,942 mi^2)
Population 1,998,000
Capital Riga (1,018,000)
Languages Latvian (official), Russian
GDP $15,205 (2013)
Currency Euro = 100 cents
Government multiparty republic
Head of state
President Andris Bērziņš, Independent, 2011, Independent, 2011
Head of government
Prime Minister Laimdota Straujuma, People's Party 2014
Website www.mk.gov.lv/en
Events Latvia became a member of NATO and the EU in spring 2004. People applying for citizenship are now required to pass a Latvian language test, which has caused much upset amongst the one third of the population who are Russian speakers. After Ivars Godmanis resigned in February 2009 over his handling of the economic crisis, including having to apply for aid from the IMF, a 6-party coalition was approved by parliament. After the previous coalition government fell in May 2011, elections resulted in the formation of a new coalition, again led by Valdis. Latvia adopted the Euro on 1 January 2014.
Economy Latvia has to import many of the materials needed for manufacturing. It produces only 10% of the electricity it needs, and the rest has to be imported from Belarus, Russia and Ukraine. Manufactures include electronic goods, farm machinery and fertiliser. Farm exports include beef, dairy products and pork. The majority of companies, banks, and real estate have been privatised. Unemployment remains very high.

Liechtenstein

Area 157 km^2 (61 mi^2)
Population 36,000
Capital Vaduz (5,300)
Languages German (official)
GDP $134,617 (2012)
Currency Swiss franc = 100 centimes
Government independent principality
Head of state Prince Hans Adam II (1989)
Head of government
Prime Minister Adrian Hasler, Progressive Citizens Party, 2013
Website www.liechtenstein.li
Events Women finally got the vote in 1984. The principality joined the UN in 1990. In 2003 the people voted in a referendum to give Prince Hans Adam II new political powers, rendering the country Europe's only absolute monarchy with the prince having power of veto over the government. Its status as a tax haven has been criticised as it has been alleged that many billions are laundered there each year. The law has been reformed to ensure that anonymity is no longer permitted when opening a bank account. In August 2004 Prince Hans Adam II transferred the day-to-day running of the country to his son Prince Alois, though he did not abdicate and remains titular head of state. The OECD removed Liechtenstein from its list of uncooperative tax havens in 2010. In 2013, the Progressive Citizens Party came first in parliamentary elections.
Economy Liechtenstein is the fourth-smallest country in the world and one of the richest per capita. Since 1945 it has rapidly developed a specialised manufacturing base. It imports more than 90% of its energy requirements. The economy is widely diversified with a large number of small businesses. Tourism is increasingly important.

Lithuania Lietuva

Area 65,200 km^2 (25,173 mi^2)
Population 2,944,000
Capital Vilnius (806,000)
Languages Lithuanian (official), Russian, Polish
GDP $16,003 (2013)
Currency Litas = 100 centai
Government multiparty republic
Head of state
President Dalia Grybauskaite, 2009
Head of government Algirdas Butkevicius, Social Democratic Party, 2012
Website www.lrvk.lt/en
Events The Soviet Union recognised Lithuania's independence in September 1991. Lithuania joined NATO in March 2004 and the EU that May. Elections in autumn 2012 led to a change in the make-up of the ruling coalition. Adoption of the Euro is likely to take place in 2015.
Economy Lithuania is dependent on Russian raw materials. Manufacturing is the most valuable export sector and major products include chemicals, electronic goods and machine tools. Dairy and meat farming and fishing are also important activities. More than 80% of enterprises have been privatised. The economy was badly hit by the 2008 global economic crisis.

Luxembourg

Area 2,586 km^2 (998 mi^2)
Population 550,000
Capital Luxembourg (165,000)
Languages Luxembourgian / Letzeburgish (official), French, German
GDP $110,423 (2013) **Currency** Euro = 100 cents
Government constitutional monarchy (or grand duchy)
Head of state Grand Duke Henri, 2000
Head of government Prime Minister Xavier Bettel, Democratic Party, 2013
Website www.visitluxembourg.com
Events Governments have mostly been coalitions led by the Christian Social People's Party under Jean-Claude Juncker. In July 2013, the Social Workers Party withdrew from the latest coalition, provoking early elections. These resulted in a coalition between the Social Democrats, Socialists and Greens.
Economy It has a stable, high-income economy, benefiting from its proximity to France, Germany and Belgium. The city of Luxembourg is a major centre of European administration and finance. In 2009, it implemented stricter laws on transparency in the banking sector. There are rich deposits of iron ore, and is a major producer of iron and steel. Other industries include chemicals, textiles, tourism, banking and electronics.

Macedonia Makedonija

Area 25,713 km^2 (9,927 mi^2)
Population 2,100,000
Capital Skopje (669,000)
Languages Macedonian (official), Albanian
GDP $4,943 (2013) **Currency** Denar = 100 deni
Government multiparty republic
Head of state President Gjorge Ivanov, VMRO-DPMNE, 2009
Head of government Nikola Gruevski, VMRO-DPMNE, 2006
Website www.vlada.mk/?language=en-gb
Events In 1993 the UN accepted the new republic as a member. It formally retains the FYR prefix because of Greek fears that the name implies territorial ambitions towards the Greek region named Macedonia. In August 2004, proposed expansion of rights and local autonomy for Albanians provoked riots by Macedonian nationalists, but the measures went through. In December 2005, EU leaders agreed that Macedonia should become a candidate for membership, if corruption was stamped out, but in February 2007 expressed alarm at political developments during 2006 and continuing problems about rights for ethnic Albanians. In 2008 Greece vetoed NATO's invitation of membership to Macedonia, in a move ruled illegal by the International Court of Justice in 2011. After snap elections in 2014, Gruevski's VMRO-DPMNE won a fourth successive term in government.
Economy Macedonia is a developing country. The poorest of the six former republics of Yugoslavia, its economy was devastated by UN trade sanctions against Yugoslavia and by the Greek embargo. The economy returned to growth in 2013. Manufactures, especially metals, dominate exports. Agriculture employs 17% of the workforce. Major crops include cotton, fruits, maize, tobacco and wheat.

Malta

Area 316 km² (122 mi²)
Population 453,000
Capital Valetta (6,700)
Languages Maltese, English (both official)
GDP $22,872 (2013)
Currency Euro = 100 cents
Government multiparty republic
Head of state President Marie Louise Coleiro Preca, Labour Party, 2014
Head of government Prime Minister Joseph Muscat, Labour Party, 2013
Website www.gov.mt
Events In 1990 Malta applied to join the EU. In 1997 the newly elected Malta Labour Party pledged to rescind the application. The Christian Democratic Nationalist Party, led by the pro-European Edward Fenech Adami, regained power in 1998 elections and won again by a narrow margin in March 2008. Malta joined the EU in May 2004 and adopted the Euro on 1 January 2008. In 2013, the Labour Party defeated Lawrence Gonzi's Nationalists to return to power for the first time in 15 years.
Economy Malta produces only about 20% of its food needs, has limited fresh water supplies and has few domestic energy sources. Machinery and transport equipment account for more than 50% of exports. Malta's historic naval dockyards are now used for commercial shipbuilding and repair. Manufactures include chemicals, electronic equipment and textiles. The largest sector is services, especially tourism. The economy remains at risk from the Eurozone crisis.

Moldova

Area 33,851 km² (13,069 mi²)
Population 3,600,000
Capital Chisinau (801,000)
Languages Moldovan / Romanian (official)
GDP 2,229 (2013)
Currency Leu = 100 bani
Government multiparty republic
Head of state President Nicolae Timofti, independent, 2012.
Head of government Prime Minister Iurie Leancă, Liberal Democratic Party, 2013
Website www.moldova.md
Events In 1994 a referendum rejected reunification with Romania and Parliament voted to join the CIS. A new constitution established a presidential parliamentary republic. The Transnistria region mainly inhabited by Russian and Ukrainian speakers declared independence in 1990. This independence has never been recognised and a regional referendum in Transnistria in 2006 that supported eventual union of the region with Russia is similarly being ignored. Relations between Chisinau and Moscow remain strained. Moldova joined the EU's Eastern Partnership in 2009 and aims to sign its Association Agreement in late 2014. In September 2010, a referendum on the appointment of a president failed because of a low turnout. It took nearly 18 months to appoint a new president before Parliament elected Nicolae Timofti in March 2012. Iurie Leancă was confirmed as PM some two months after Vlad Filat was dismissed by a vote of no confidence in April 2013.
Economy There is a favourable climate and good farmland but no major mineral deposits. Agriculture is important and major products include fruits and grapes for wine-making. Farmers also raise livestock, including dairy cattle and pigs. Moldova has to import materials and fuels for its industries. Exports include food, wine, tobacco and textiles. The economy remains vulnerable to high fuel prices and poor agricultural weather. The economy grew strongly in 2013.

Monaco

Area 1.5 km² (0.6 mi²)
Population 36,000
Capital Monaco-Ville (1150)
Languages French (official), Italian, Monegasque
GDP 163,026 (2012)
Currency Euro = 100 cents
Government principality
Head of state Prince Albert II, 2005
Head of government Minister of State Michel Roger, independent, 2010
Website www.gouv.mc
Events Monaco has been ruled by the Grimaldi family since the end of the 13th century and been under the protection of France since 1860.
Economy The chief source of income is tourism. The state retains monopolies in tobacco, the telephone network and the postal service. There is some light industry, including printing, textiles and postage stamps. Also a major banking centre, residents live tax free. Prince Albert wishes to attract high-tech industries and to prove that Monaco is not a haven for money-launderers, and in 2010 the OECD removed Monaco from its list of uncooperative tax havens.

Montenegro Crna Gora

Area 13,812 km² (5,333 mi²)
Population 625,000
Capital Podgorica (186,000)
Languages Serbian (of the Ijekavian dialect)
GDP $7,026 (2013)
Currency Euro = 100 cents
Government federal republic
Head of state President Filip Vujanovic, 2003
Head of government Prime Minister Milo Djukanovich, Democratic Party of Socialists, 2012
Website www.gov.me/en/homepage
Events In 1992 Montenegro went into federation with Serbia, first as Federal Republic of Yugoslavia, then as a looser State Union of Serbia and Montenegro. Montenegro formed its own economic policy and adopted the Deutschmark as its currency in 1999. It currently uses the Euro, though it is not formally part of the Eurozone. In 2002, Serbia and Montenegro came to a new agreement regarding continued cooperation. On 21 May 2006, the status of the union was decided as 55.54% of voters voted for independence of Montenegro, narrowly passing the 55% threshold needed to validate the referendum under rules set by the EU. On 3 June 2006 the Parliament of Montenegro declared independence. Montenegro was rapidly admitted to the UN, the World Bank and the IMF, joined NATO's Partnership for Peace and applied for EU membership. It was formally named as an EU candidate country in 2010 and accession negotiations started in 2012, just after it joined the WTO.
Economy A rapid period of urbanisation and industrialisation was created within the communism era of Montenegro. During 1993, two thirds of the Montenegrin population lived below the poverty line. Financial losses under the effects of the UN sanctions on the economy of Montenegro are estimated to be $6.39 billion. Today there is faster and more efficient privatisation, introduction of VAT and usage of the Euro.

The Netherlands Nederland

Area 41,526 km² (16,033 mi²)
Population 16,820,000
Capital Amsterdam (2,400,000); administrative capital 's-Gravenhage (The Hague) (1,051,000)
Languages Dutch (official), Frisian
GDP $47,633 (2013)
Currency Euro = 100 cents
Government constitutional monarchy
Head of state King Willem-Alexander, 2013
Head of government Prime Minister Mark Rutte, People's Party for Freedom and Democracy, 2010
Website www.government.nl
Events A founding member of NATO and the EU. Jan Peter Balkenende's coalition cabinet with the Labour Party and the Christian Union collapsed in early 2010 after Labour refused to sanction continued military deployment in Afghanistan. In 2010 the former junior coalition partner, the Party for Freedom and Democracy, took power, winning again in 2012. In 2013, Queen Beatrix abdicated.
Economy The Netherlands has prospered through its close European ties. Private enterprise has successfully combined with progressive social policies. It is highly industrialised. Products include aircraft, chemicals, electronics and machinery. Agriculture is intensive and mechanised, employing only 5% of the workforce. Dairy farming is the leading agricultural activity. It continues to be one of the leading European nations for attracting foreign direct investment.

Norway Norge

Area 323,877 km² (125,049 mi²)
Population 5,138,000
Capital Oslo (1,503,000)
Languages Norwegian (official), Lappish, Finnish
GDP $100,318 (2013)
Currency Krone = 100 øre
Government constitutional monarchy
Head of state King Harald V, 1991
Head of government Prime Minister Erna Solberg, Conservative Party, 2013
Website www.norway.org.uk
Events In referenda in 1972 and 1994 Norway rejected joining the EU. A centre-left coalition, the Labour-led 'Red-Green Alliance' won closely contested elections in September 2005, and retained power in 2009. It was ousted by a Conservative-led minority government in 2013.
Economy Norway has one of the world's highest standards of living. Discovery of oil and gas in adjacent waters in the late 1960s boosted its economic fortunes, with its chief exports now oil and natural gas. Per capita, it is the world's largest producer of hydroelectricity. It is possible oil and gas will begin to run out in Norway in the next two decades but it has been saving its oil budget surpluses and is invested abroad in a fund, valued at more than $250 billion at its height, although this fell rapidly as a result of the global financial crisis. Major manufactures include petroleum products, chemicals, aluminium, wood pulp and paper.

Poland Polska

Area 323,250 km² (124,807 mi²)
Population 38,545,000
Capital Warsaw / Warszawa (2,666,000)
Languages Polish (official)
GDP $13,393 (2013)
Currency Zloty = 100 groszy
Government multiparty republic
Head of state President Bronislaw Komorowski, Civic Platform, 2010
Head of government Prime Minister Donald Tusk, Civic Platform, 2007
Website http://en.polska.pl
Events Poland joined the OECD in 1996, NATO in 1999 and the EU in 2004. The death of President Lech Kaczynski and large numbers of the country's military and civilian leadership in a plane crash in April 2010 brought forward presidential elections to June. The first round was inconclusive, with Mr Komorowski gaining more votes than the ex-president's brother, Jaroslaw, but in the second round, he gained 53% of the vote to secure a mandate.
Economy Of the workforce, 27% is employed in agriculture and 37% in industry. Poland is the world's fifth-largest producer of lignite and ships. Copper ore is also a vital resource. Manufacturing accounts for 24% of exports. Agriculture remains important. Economic growth began to speed up in 2013 in response to record low interest rates.

Portugal

Area 88,797 km² (34,284 mi²)
Population 10,427,000
Capital Lisbon / Lisboa (3,035,000)
Languages Portuguese (official)
GDP $20,727 (2013)
Currency Euro = 100 cents
Government multiparty republic
Head of state President Anibal Cavaco Silva, Social Democratic Party, 2006
Head of government Pedro Passos Coelho, Social Democratic Party, 2011
Website www.portugal.gov.pt/en.aspx
Events In 1986 Portugal joined the EU. In 2002 the Social Democrat Party won the election and formed a coalition government with the Popular Party. The opposition Socialist Party were clear victors in European elections of June 2004, a result attributed in part to the ruling party's support for the war in Iraq. The Socialist Party's minority government collapsed in 2011 when Parliament rejected further austerity measures. Since their return to power they have instigated several further tranches, leading to instability in both the coalition and the country.
Economy Portugal was hit by the economic downturn and in April 2011 it became the third Eurozone country to ask for a financial bailout. Public debt rose above the 3% threshold allowed by Eurozone regulations and in March 2010 the government introduced further budget cuts. Manufacturing accounts for 33% of exports. Textiles, footwear and clothing are major exports. Portugal is the world's fifth-largest producer of tungsten and eighth-largest producer of wine. Olives, potatoes and wheat are also grown. Tourism is very important.

Romania

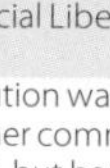

Area 238,391 km² (92,042 mi²)
Population 20,122,000
Capital Bucharest / Bucuresti (2,272,000)
Languages Romanian (official), Hungarian
GDP $8,910 (2013)
Currency Romanian leu = 100 bani
Government multiparty republic
Head of state President Traian Basescu, 2004
Head of government Prime Minister Victor-Viorel Ponta, Social Liberal Union, 2012
Website www.gov.ro
Events A new constitution was introduced in 1991. Ion Iliescu, a former communist official, was re-elected in 2000, but barred from standing again in 2004, when he was replaced by Traian Basescu. After losing a vote of no confidence after just 10 months as PM, Boc was reappointed in December 2009. Romania joined NATO in 2004 and joined the EU in January 2007 after making progress towards tackling corruption, although because of this issue France and Germany blocked its Schengen area accession in December 2010. Protests in 2012 led to PM Emil Boc's resignation. Interim PM Ungureanu was toppled in weeks and elections in September were won by Victor Ponta. Euro adoption is set for 2015 at the earliest. The Romany minority still suffers from discrimination.
Economy The currency was re-valued in 2005. Despite a period of strong economic growth, Romania's large public debt led to the need for substantial IMF loans in 2009, necessitating severe cuts in public services.

Russia Rossiya

Area 17,075,000 km² (6,592,800 mi²)
Population 143,700,000
Capital Moscow / Moskva (11,511,000)
Languages Russian (official), and many others
GDP $14,818 (2013)
Currency Russian ruble = 100 kopeks
Government federal multiparty republic
Head of state President Vladimir Putin 2012
Head of government Prime Minister Dimitry Medvedev, 2012
Website http://government.ru/en/
Events In 1992 the Russian Federation became a co-founder of the CIS (Commonwealth of Independent States). A new Federal Treaty was signed between the central government and the autonomous republics within the Russian Federation, Chechnya refused to sign and declared independence. In December 1993 a new democratic constitution was adopted. From 1994 to 1996, Russia fought a civil war in Chechnya which flared up again in 1999. Putin's chosen successor, Medvedev, was elected by a landslide in elections that were criticised by outside observers for biased media coverage. In 2011 Putin was re-elected as President, after the law that prevented serving a third term was revoked. He appointed former president Medvedev as PM. Critics allege that freedom of speech and dissent are being repressed amid crackdowns on NGOs and opponents of the ruling party. Russia joined the WTO in 2012. In February 2014, in response to events in Ukraine, Russian forces took over the Crimean Peninsula and Sevastopol, leading to accusations of illegal annexation from the West (see Ukraine)
Economy In 1993 mass privatisation began. By 1996, 80% of the Russian economy was in private hands. A major problem remains the size of Russia's foreign debt. It is reliant on world oil prices to keep its economy from crashing and the sudden fall in oil prices in the second half of 2008 forced it to devalue the ruble several times. Industry employs 46% of the workforce and contributes 48% of GDP. Mining is the most valuable activity. Russia is the world's leading producer of natural gas and nickel, the second largest producer of aluminium and phosphates, and the third-largest of crude oil, lignite and brown coal. Most farmland is still government-owned or run as collectives, with important products barley, oats, rye, potatoes, beef and veal. In 2006, the ruble became a convertable currency.

San Marino

Area 61 km² (24 mi²)
Population 33,000 **Capital** San Marino (4,100)
Languages Italian (official)
GDP $62,188 (2012)
Currency Euro = 100 cents
Government multiparty republic
Head of state co-Chiefs of State: Luca Beccari and Valeria Ciavatta

…d of government Secretary of State for …eign and Political Affairs and Economic Planning Pasquale Valentini, 2012
Website www.visitsanmarino.com
Events World's smallest republic and perhaps Europe's oldest state, San Marino's links with Italy led to the adoption of the Euro. Its 60-member Great and General Council is elected every five years and headed by two captains regent, who are elected by the council every six months. In 2013 a narrow majority of recorded votes were in favour of joining the EU, but the low turnout invalidated the result.
Economy The economy is largely agricultural. Tourism is vital to the state's income, contributing over 50% of GDP. The economy is generally stable.

Serbia Srbija

Area 77,474 km² (29,913 mi²)
Population 7,187,000
Capital Belgrade / Beograd (1,659,000)
Languages Serbian
GDP $5,906 (2013)
Currency Dinar = 100 paras
Government federal republic
Head of state President Tomislav Nikolić, Serbian Progresssive Party,
Head of government Prime Minister Aleksandar Vucic, Progressive Party, 2014
Website www.srbija.gov.rs
Events Serbian attempts to control the Yugoslav federation led to the secession of Slovenia and Croatia in 1991 and to Bosnia-Herzegovina's declaration of independence in 1992 and the three-year war that ended only with the signing of the Dayton Peace Accord. Slobodan Milosovic became president of Yugoslavia in 1997. Kostunica won the elections of September 2000: Milosevic refused to hand over power, but was ousted after a week. From 2003 to 2006, Serbia was part of the State Union of Serbia and Montenegro, After a referendum in May 2006, the Parliament of Montenegro declared Montenegro independent. Serbia assumed the State Union's UN membership. In 2006 Serbia joined the NATO Partnership for Peace programme and in 2008 signed a Stability and Association Agreement with the EU, to which it applied formally for membership in December 2009. Serbia became a candidate member of the EU in 2012 and accession talks began in early 2014. In May of the latter year, the pro-EU Progressive Party scored a landslide victory in parliamentary elections.
Economy The lower-middle income economy was devastated by war and economic sanctions. Industrial production collapsed. Natural resources include bauxite, coal and copper. There is some oil and natural gas. Manufacturing includes aluminium, cars, machinery, plastics, steel and textiles. Agriculture is important. In 2008 Serbia and Russia signed an energy deal, and in October 2009 the latter granted the former a 1 billion Euro loan to ease its budgetary problems.

Slovak Republic Slovenska

Area 49,012 km² (18,923 mi²)
Population 5,416,000
Capital Bratislava (660,000)
Languages Slovak (official), Hungarian
GDP $17,706 (2013)
Currency Euro = 100 cents
Government multiparty republic
Head of state President Andrej Kiska, independent, 2014
Head of government Prime Minister Robert Fico, Direction - Social Democracy (Smer), 2012.
Website www.government.gov.sk
Events In 1993 the Slovak Republic became a sovereign state, breaking peaceably from the Czech Republic, with whom it maintains close relations. In 1996 the Slovak Republic and Hungary ratified a treaty confirming their borders and stipulating basic rights for the 560,000 Hungarians in the country. The Slovak Republic joined NATO in March 2004 and the EU two months later. There is still a problem with the Romany population. The country adopted the Euro in January 2009. In elections in April 2012 Smer returned to power with a parliamentary majority. Former businessman and philanthropist Andrej Kiska won the presidential election against PM Fico in 2014.
Economy The transition from communism to private ownership was initially painful with industrial output falling, unemployment and inflation rising, but the economy has become more stable. Manufacturing employs 33% of the workforce. Bratislava and Košice are the chief industrial cities. Major products include ceramics, machinery and steel. Farming employs 12% of the workforce. Crops include barley and grapes. Tourism is growing.

Slovenia Slovenija

Area 20,256 km² (7,820 mi²)
Population 2,062,000
Capital Ljubljana (275,000)
Languages Slovene
GDP $22,756 (2013)
Currency Euro = 100 cents
Government multiparty republic
Head of state President Borut Pahor, Social Democratic Party, 2012
Head of government Prime Minister (outgoing) Alenka Bratusek, Positive Slovenia, 2013
Website www.gov.si
Events In 1990 Slovenia declared itself independent, which led to brief fighting between Slovenes and the federal army. In 1992 the EU recognised Slovenia's independence. Janez Drnovsek was elected president in December 2002. Slovenia joined NATO in March 2004 and the EU two months later. In June 2004 the value of the Tolar was fixed against the Euro, which it joined in 2007. The 2008 general election resulted in a coalition government led by the Social Democratic Party. A referendum in June 2010 narrowly approved the settlement of the border dispute with Croatia. After two years of political instability, Ivan Janša was appointed PM in February 2012, leading a centre-right coalition, but his government fell the following year. The succeeding administration fell in May 2014 leading to early elections.
Economy The transformation of a centrally planned economy and the fighting in other parts of former Yugoslavia caused problems for Slovenia but the economy eventually experienced strong growth in per capita GDP until this was badly hit by the gobal financial crisis. Manufacturing is the leading activity. Major manufactures include chemicals, machinery, transport equipment, metal goods and textiles. Major crops include maize, fruit, potatoes and wheat.

Spain España

Area 497,548 km² (192,103 mi²)
Population 46,704,000
Capital Madrid (6,369,000)
Languages Castilian Spanish (official), Catalan, Galician, Basque
GDP 29,150 (2013)
Currency Euro = 100 cents
Government constitutional monarchy
Head of state King Felipe VI, 2014
Head of government Prime Minister Mariano Rajoy, Spanish People's Party, 2011
Website www.lamoncloa.gob.es/home.htm
Events From 1959-98 the militant Basque organisation ETA waged a campaign of terror. Its first ceasefire was broken in 2000 and a second - declared in 2006 - with a bomb attack on Madrid airport at the end of the year. A third ceasefire was declared in September 2010. In March 2004 Al qaeda-related bombers killed 191 people in Madrid, resulting in an election win for the opposition Socialist Party. In the 2008 elections, the socialists increased their numbers in Parliament, but did not gain a majority. Austerity measures brought in to tackle public debt, and as condition of the country's financial bailout, changes to pensions and benefits and rising unemployment led to widespread protests in 2010 and 2011. Local and regional elections in May 2011 resulted in heavy losses for the socialists and the Popular Party won a sweeping majority in general elections in November. King Juan Carlos abdicated in favour of Prince Felipe in 2014.
Economy Spain's transformation from a largely poor, agrarian society to a prosperous nation came to an end with the economic downturn of 2008. The country's debt burden became untenable and financial bailouts from the international community in 2010 and the Eurozone in 2012 were necessary. Unemployment is more than double the European average. Agriculture now employs only 10% of the workforce and the sector is shrinking further because of recurrent droughts. Spain is the world's third-largest wine producer. Other crops include citrus fruits, tomatoes and olives. Industries: cars, ships, chemicals, electronics, metal goods, steel, and textiles.

Sweden Sverige

Area 449,964 km² (173,731 mi²)
Population 9,658,000 **Capital** Stockholm (2,127,000) **GDP** $57,909 (2013)
Languages Swedish (official), Finnish
Currency Swedish krona = 100 ore
Government constitutional monarchy
Head of state King Carl Gustaf XVI, 1973
Head of government Prime Minister Fredrik Reinfeldt, Moderate Party, 2006
Website www.sweden.gov.se
Events In 1995 Sweden joined the European Union. The cost of maintaining Sweden's extensive welfare services has become a major political issue. In 2003 Sweden rejected adoption of the Euro. The elections of 2010 saw a rise in votes for the far right.
Economy Sweden is a highly developed industrial country. It has rich iron ore deposits. Privately owned firms account for about 90% of industrial output. Steel is a major product, used to manufacture aircraft, cars, machinery and ships. Forestry and fishing are important. Agriculture accounts for 2% of GDP and jobs. The Swedish central bank focuses on price stability with its inflation target of 2%.

Switzerland Schweiz

Area 41,284 km² (15,939 mi²)
Population 8,014,000 **Capital** Bern (356,000)
Languages French, German, Italian, Romansch (all official) **GDP** $81,323 (2013)
Currency Swiss Franc = 100 centimes / rappen
Government federal republic
Head of state Federal President Didier Burkhalter, 2014 **Website** www.admin.ch
Events Priding themselves on their neutrality, Swiss voters rejected membership of the UN in 1986 and the EU in 1992 and 2001. However, Switzerland finally became a partner country of NATO in 1997 and joined the organisation in 2002, when it also joined the UN. The federal council is made up of seven federal ministers from whom the president is chosen on an annual basis. A 2005 referendum backed membership of EU Schengen and Dublin agreements, bringing Switzerland into the European passport-free zone and increasing co-operation on crime and asylum seekers. Immigration is becoming an increasingly divisive issue.
Economy Switzerland is a wealthy and stable modern market economy with low unemployment, and per capita GDP grew slightly in 2013. Manufactures include chemicals, electrical equipment, machinery, precision instruments, watches and textiles. Livestock, notably dairy farming, is the chief agricultural activity. Tourism is important, and Swiss banks remain a safe haven for investors. In November 2011, the government announced that the Swiss franc would be pegged to the Euro.

Turkey Türkiye

Area 774,815 km² (299,156 mi²)
Population 76,668,000
Capital Ankara (5,045,000)
Languages Turkish (official), Kurdish
GDP $10,815 (2013)
Currency New Turkish lira = 100 kurus
Government multiparty republic
Head of state President Abdullah Gül, Justice and Development Party (AK), 2007
Head of government Prime Minister Recep Tayyip Erdogan, Justice and Development Party (AK), 2003
Website www.mfa.gov.tr/default.en.mfa
Events The Kurdistan Workers Party (PKK) carried out terrorist activities throughout the 1980s and 1990s, but declared a ceasefire in 1999, changed their name to Congress for Freedom and Democracy in Kurdistan (KADEK) and said they wanted to campaign peacefully for Kurdish rights. In September 2003 they ended a 4-year ceasefire, but declared another in 2006, although this did not hold. In October 2005, the EU opened accession negotiations with Ankara. Membership of the EU is an aim but human rights, the Cyprus issue and the hostility of successive French and Austrian governments are barriers, but it was announced in October that talks would recommence the following month.. The PM and President are both former Islamists, although they say they are committed to secularism. The escalating civil war in Syria has caused a refugee crisis on the border. In 2013, the proposed introduction of laws seen as being anti-secular and the proposed development of one of Istanbul's few green spaces led to widespread protests and calls for the resignation of the government.
Economy Turkey is an upper-middle-income country. Agriculture employs 47% of the workforce, but is becoming less important to the economy. Turkey is a leading producer of citrus fruits, barley, cotton, wheat, tobacco and tea. It is a major producer of chromium and phosphate fertilisers. Tourism is a vital source of foreign exchange. In January 2005, the New Turkish lira was introduced at a rate of 1 to 1,000,000 old Turkish lira. The economy grew strongly in 2013.

Ukraine Ukraina

Area 603,700 km² (233,088 mi²)
Population 44,573,000 **Capital** Kiev / Kyviv (3,275,000) **Languages** Ukrainian (official), Russian **GDP** $3,919 (2013)
Currency Hryvnia = 100 kopiykas
Government multiparty republic
Head of state Petro Poroshenko, independent, 2014
Head of government Prime Minister (acting) Mykola Azarov, Party of the Regions, 2010
Website www.kmu.gov.ua/control/en
Events The Chernobyl disaster of 1986 contaminated large areas of Ukraine. Independence was achieved in 1991 with the dissolution of the USSR. Leonid Kuchma was elected president in 1994. He continued the policy of establishing closer ties with the West and sped up the pace of privatisation. In 2010, the coalition governent of Yulia Tymoshenko fell, and the Party of the Regions formed a coalition with the Communists and the centrist Lytvyn Bloc. Former PM Victor Yanukovic beat Tymoshenko in the presidential elections. Ukraine joined the EU's Eastern Partnership in 2009, but has abandoned plans to join NATO. President Yanukovich's decision to abandon plans for closer ties with the EU led to riots from late 2013, followed by his escape to Russia in February 2014. The following month, Russia sent forces into the Crimean Peninsula to assist separatists. A few days later, after a partially boycotted referendum, the administrations of Crimea and Sevastopol asked Russia for the right to accede, which Russia granted and annexed the region and city. The West has refused to recognise the annexation as legal. Pro-Russian elements, which Russia is accused of supporting, promoted separatism in the east and south-west in the lead-up to presidential election, which was won by chocolate magnate Petro Poroshenko.
Economy Ukraine is a lower-middle-income economy. Agriculture is important. It is the world's leading producer of sugar beet, the second-largest producer of barley, and a major producer of wheat. Ukraine has extensive raw materials, including coal (though many mines are exhausted), iron ore and manganese ore. Ukraine is reliant on oil and natural gas imports. The economy's dependence on steel exports made it vulnerable to the 2008 global economic downturn and it was offered a massive loan by the IMF.

United Kingdom

Area 241,857 km² (93,381 mi²)
Population 63,705,000
Capital London (15,011,000)
Languages English (official), Welsh (also official in Wales), Gaelic **GDP** $39,567 (2013)
Currency Sterling (pound) = 100 pence
Government constitutional monarchy
Head of state Queen Elizabeth II, 1952
Head of government Prime Minister David Cameron, Conservative Party, 2010
Website www.gov.uk
Events The United Kingdom of Great Britain and Northern Ireland is a union of four countries – England, Northern Ireland, Scotland and Wales. Since 1997, Scotland and Wales have had their own legislative assemblies. The Good Friday Agreement of 1998 offered the best chance of peace in Northern Ireland for a generation. In 2005 the IRA anounced a permanent cessation of hostilities and the Northern Ireland Assembly was finally reinstated in early 2007. Right-wing political parties have gained some ground, fuelled by worries of rising levels of immigration and anti-EU rhetoric.
Economy The UK is a major industrial and trading nation. A producer of oil, petroleum products, natural gas, potash and salt. Financial services and tourism are the leading service industries. The economic downturn of 2008 led to the government effectively nationalising several banks and bailing out others with massive loans. Although the economy emerged from recession in late 2009, economic recovery remains weak.

Key to route planning map pages

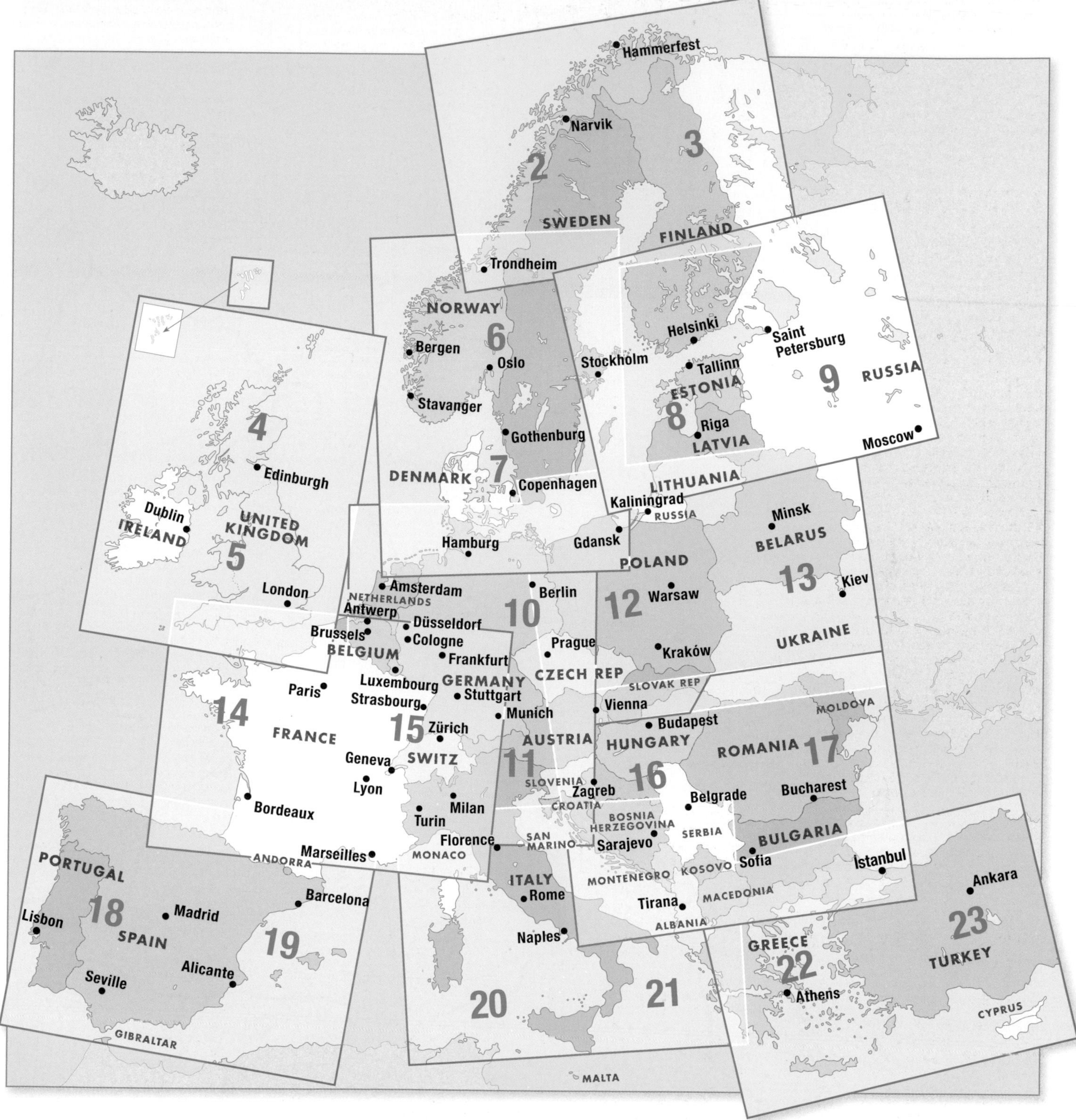

Motorway vignettes

Some countries require you to purchase (and in some cases display) a vignette before using motorways.

In Austria you will need to purchase and display a vignette on the inside of your windscreen. Vignettes are available for purchase at border crossings and petrol stations.
More details from **www.austria.info/uk/how-to-get-there/** and **www.asfinag.at/en/maut/vignette**.

In the Czech Republic, you can buy a vignette at the border and also at petrol stations. Make sure you write your vehicle registration number on the vignette before displaying it. The roads without toll are indicated by a traffic sign saying "Bez poplatku". More details from **www.motorway.cz**.

In Hungary a new e-vignette system was introduced in 2008. It is therefore no longer necessary to display the vignette, though you should make doubly sure the information you give on your vehicle is accurate. Vignettes are sold at petrol stations throughout the country.
Buy online at **www.motorway.hu**.

In Slovakia, a vignette is also required to be purchased before using the motorways. This is sold in two kinds at the Slovak border and petrol stations. You will need to write your vehicle registration plate on the vignette before displaying it. More details from **www.slovensko.com**.

In Switzerland, you will need to purchase and display a vignette before you drive on the motorway. Bear in mind you will need a separate vignette if you are towing a caravan. Purchase the Swiss vignette in advance from **www.autobahnen.ch**.

0 40 80 120 160 km
ARCTIC CIRCLE
NORWAY
SWEDEN
FINLAND
Lofoten
Vesterålen
Helgeland
Trøndelag
Jämtland
Lappland
Norrbotten
Västerbotten
Lopphavet
Moskenstraumen
Vestfjorden
Saltfjorden
Trondheimsfjorden
Tromsø
Narvik
Bodø
Kiruna
Gällivare
Mo i Rana
Mosjøen
Fauske
Harstad
Andenes
Svolvær
Trondheim
Steinkjer
Grong
Namsos
Östersund
Umeå
Skellefteå
Luleå
Piteå
Boden
Lycksele
Vilhelmina
Storuman
Arvidsjaur
Arjeplog
Jokkmokk
Örnsköldsvik
Sollefteå
Åre
Storlien
Vaasa
Senja
Hinnøya
Andøya
Langøya
Austvågøy
Vestvågøy
Moskenesøya
Værøy
Røst
Kvaløy
Ringvassøy
Vanna
Arnøy
Kebnekaise
Svartisen
Halti
Torneträsk
Abisko
Sulitjelma
Raippaluoto

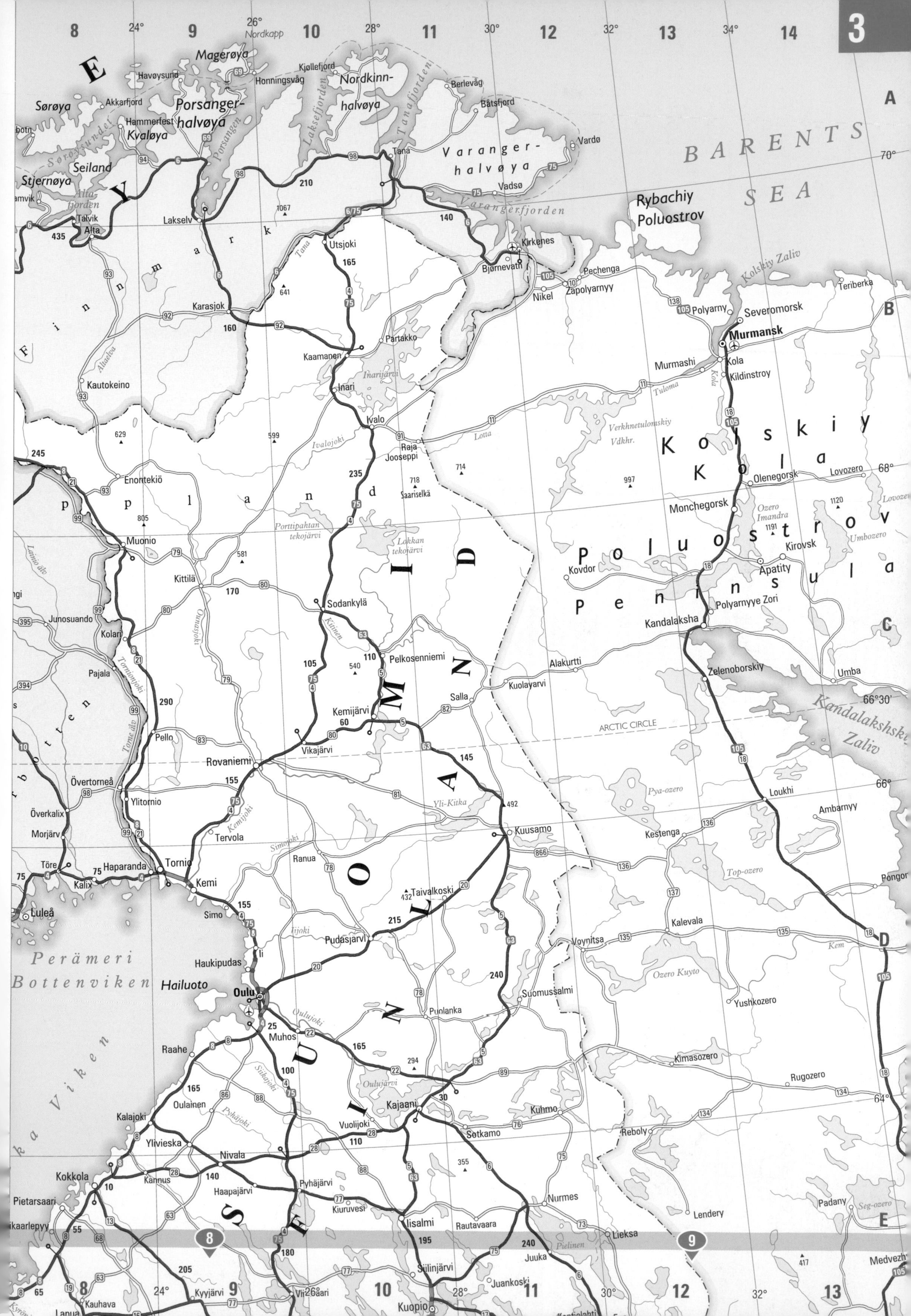
8
9
10
11
12
13
14
24°
26°
28°
30°
32°
34°
Nordkapp
A
B
C
D
E
70°
68°
66°30'
66°
64°
ARCTIC CIRCLE
BARENTS SEA
Magerøya
Havøysund
Honningsvåg
Kjøllefjord
Nordkinn-halvøya
Berlevåg
Båtsfjord
Sørøya
Akkarfjord
Porsanger-halvøya
Hammerfest
Kvaløya
Sørøysundet
Porsangen
Laksefjorden
Tanafjorden
Vardø
Varanger-halvøya
Tana
Vadsø
Varangerfjorden
Seiland
Stjernøya
Altafjorden
Talvik
Alta
Lakselv
Finnmark
Rybachiy Poluostrov
Utsjoki
Kirkenes
Bjørnevatn
Pechenga
Nikel
Zapolyarnyy
Kolskiy Zaliv
Teriberka
Karasjok
Polyarny
Severomorsk
Murmansk
Partakko
Kaamanen
Inarijärvi
Murmashi
Kola
Kildinstroy
Kautokeino
Tuloma
Inari
Ivalo
Raja Jooseppi
Lotta
Verkhnetulomskiy Vdkhr.
Kolskiy Kola Poluostrov Peninsula
Ivalojoki
Saariselkä
Olenegorsk
Lovozero
Enontekiö
Lappland
Monchegorsk
Ozero Imandra
Umbozero
Porttipahtan tekojärvi
Lokkan tekojärvi
Kirovsk
Apatity
Muonio
Kovdor
Kittilä
Sodankylä
Polyarnyye Zori
Junosuando
Kolari
Kandalaksha
Ounasjoki
Kitinen
Pelkosenniemi
Pajala
Alakurtti
Zelenoborskiy
Umba
Torniojoki
Kuolayarvi
Salla
Kemijärvi
Kandalakshskiy Zaliv
Norrbotten
Pello
Vikajärvi
Torne älv
Rovaniemi
Övertorneå
Ylitornio
Yli-Kitka
Loukhi
Pya-ozero
Överkalix
Morjärv
Kemijoki
Tervola
Kuusamo
Kestenga
Ambarnyy
Simojoki
Ranua
Töre
Haparanda
Tornio
Kalix
Kemi
Top-ozero
Pongoma
Taivalkoski
Luleå
Simo
Kalevala
Iijoki
Pudasjärvi
Voynitsa
Perämeri
Bottenviken
Ii
Haukipudas
Kem
Ozero Kuyto
Hailuoto
Oulu
Suomussalmi
Yushkozero
Oulujoki
Puolanka
Muhos
Raahe
Kimasozero
Siikajoki
Oulujärvi
Rugozero
Oulainen
Pyhäjoki
Kajaani
Kuhmo
Kalajoki
Vuolijoki
Sotkamo
Reboly
Ylivieska
Nivala
Kokkola
Kannus
Pyhäjärvi
Haapajärvi
Kiuruvesi
Nurmes
Padany
Seg-ozero
Pietarsaari
Iisalmi
Rautavaara
Lendery
Uusikaarlepyy
Lieksa
Pielinen
Juuka
Siilinjärvi
Juankoski
Medvezh
Kyyjärvi
Viitasaari
Kauhava
Lapua
Kuopio
SUOMI FINLAND
Pohjanlahti Botniska Viken
8
9

4
Føroyar (Danmark)
Færoe Islands (Denmark)
Norðoyar
Slættaratindur
882
Klaksvík
Streymoy
Mykines
Eysturoy
Vágar
Tórshavn
Sandoy
Suðuroy
SEYÐISFJÖRÐUR
Shetland Is. (U.K.)
Unst
Yell
Fetlar
Mainland
Lerwick
Foula
Sumburgh Hd.
Fair Isle
Orkney Is.
Westray
Sanday
Stronsay
Mainland
Kirkwall
Stromness
Hoy
South Ronaldsay
Pentland Firth
Thurso
John o' Groats
Wick
C. Wrath
Tongue
Helmsdale
Lochinver
Lairg
Loch Shin
Ullapool
Golspie
Tain
Invergordon
Dingwall
Moray Firth
Buckie
Banff
Fraserburgh
Rattray Hd.
Peterhead
Elgin
Nairn
Huntly
Inverness
Inverurie
Aberdeen
Stonehaven
North West Highlands
North Minch
SCOTLAND
Grampian Mts.
L. Ness
Spey
Don
Dee
Fort Augustus
Aviemore
Ben Macdhui
Braemar
Ballater
Newtonmore
Fort William
Ben Nevis
Ballachulish
Pitlochry
Aberfeldy
Forfar
Brechin
Montrose
Arbroath
Blairgowrie
Dundee
Perth
L. Tay
St. Andrews
Glenrothes
Firth of Forth
Dunfermline
Kirkcaldy
Stirling
L. Lomond
Dumbarton
Greenock
Glasgow
Edinburgh
North Berwick
Dunbar
Paisley
East Kilbride
Hamilton
Dunoon
Rothesay
Ardrossan
Irvine
Kilmarnock
Ayr
Cumnock
Peebles
Galashiels
Coldstream
Berwick-upon-Tweed
Southern Uplands
Hawick
Jedburgh
Moffat
Alnwick
Ashington
Rubha Robhanais
Stornoway
Eilean Leodais
789
Tairbeart
Na Hearadh
St. Kilda
Outer Hebrides
Uibhist a Tuath
Loch nam Madadh
Beinn na Faoghla
Uibhist a Deas
Loch Baghasdail
Bagh a Chaisteil
Eilean Bharraigh
Inner Hebrides
Uig
Portree
Kyle of Lochalsh
Skye
Armadale
Mallaig
Rum
Eigg
Coll
Tobermory
Tiree
Mull
Oban
F. of Lorn
Colonsay
Lochgilphead
Jura
Port Askaig
Islay
Port Ellen
Tarbert
Arran
Brodick
Campbeltown
Firth of Clyde
Mull of
Malin Hd.
North Channel
North Sea
0 20 40 60 80 100 miles
0 40 80 120 160 km

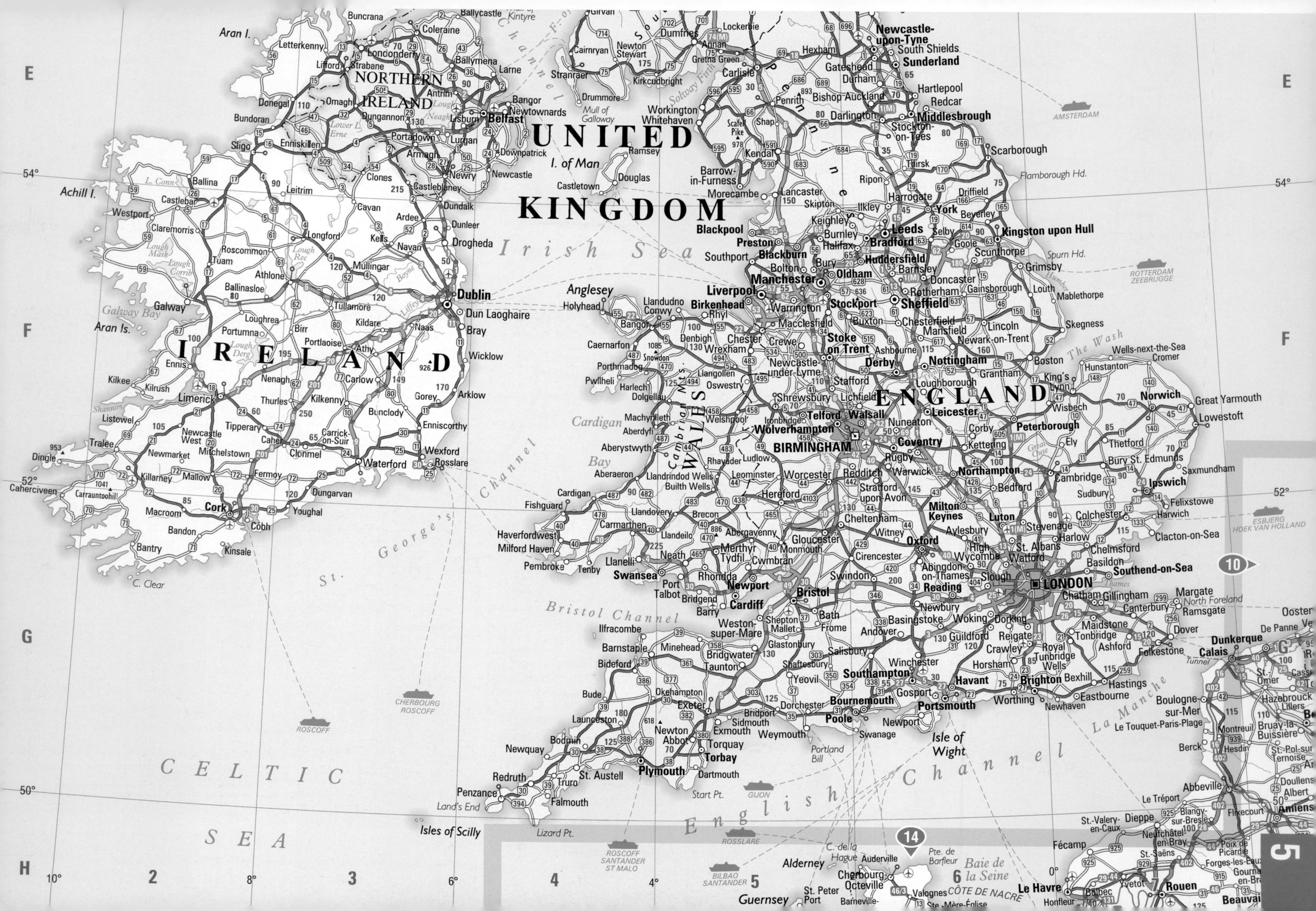
5
UNITED KINGDOM
IRELAND
NORTHERN IRELAND
ENGLAND
WALES
Irish Sea
CELTIC SEA
St. George's Channel
Bristol Channel
English Channel
La Manche
North Channel
Cardigan Bay
Galway Bay
The Wash
I. of Man
Anglesey
Isle of Wight
Isles of Scilly
Alderney
Guernsey
Aran I.
Aran Is.
Achill I.
Flamborough Hd.
Spurn Hd.
Land's End
Lizard Pt.
Start Pt.
Portland Bill
C. Clear
C. de la Hague
Baie de la Seine
CÔTE DE NACRE
LONDON
Birmingham
Manchester
Liverpool
Leeds
Sheffield
Bradford
Newcastle-upon-Tyne
Sunderland
Middlesbrough
Kingston upon Hull
York
Nottingham
Leicester
Coventry
Derby
Stoke on Trent
Wolverhampton
Northampton
Peterborough
Norwich
Ipswich
Cambridge
Oxford
Reading
Southampton
Portsmouth
Bournemouth
Brighton
Plymouth
Bristol
Cardiff
Swansea
Newport
Belfast
Dublin
Cork
Limerick
Galway
Waterford
Dun Laoghaire
Rosslare
Dunkerque
Calais
Boulogne-sur-Mer
Le Havre
Rouen
Amiens
Dieppe
Cherbourg-Octeville
AMSTERDAM
ROTTERDAM ZEEBRUGGE
ESBJERG HOEK VAN HOLLAND
CHERBOURG ROSCOFF
ROSCOFF
ROSCOFF SANTANDER ST MALO
BILBAO SANTANDER
ROSSLARE
GIJON
54°
52°
50°
10°
8°
6°
4°
0°
E
F
G
H
2
3
4
5
6

NORWAY
SWEDEN
Trøndelag
Jämtland
Norrland
Svealand
Telemark
Fosna
Frohavet
Hustadvika
Gulf of Bothnia
Pohjanlahti
Selkämeri
Bottenhavet
Ålands hav
Åland
Frøya
Hitra
Smøla
Stord
Bømlo
0
40
80
120
160 km
Trondheim
Oslo
Bergen
STOCKHOLM
Uppsala
Västerås
Örebro
Karlstad
Östersund
Sundsvall
Umeå
Ålesund
Molde
Kristiansund
Stavanger
Sandnes
Haugesund
Drammen
Lillehammer
Hamar
Gjøvik
Elverum
Kongsvinger
Fredrikstad
Sarpsborg
Halden
Moss
Tønsberg
Sandefjord
Larvik
Skien
Porsgrunn
Kongsberg
Hønefoss
Lillestrøm
Røros
Oppdal
Dombås
Steinkjer
Namsos
Levanger
Stjørdalshalsen
Gävle
Falun
Borlänge
Mora
Hudiksvall
Söderhamn
Härnösand
Örnsköldsvik
Sollefteå
Ljusdal
Sveg
Bollnäs
Sala
Avesta
Ludvika
Köping
Eskilstuna
Södertälje
Nyköping
Norrtälje
Sigtuna
Märsta
Enköping
Karlskoga
Kristinehamn
Arvika
Säffle
Åmål
Torsby
Hagfors
Filipstad
Strömsund
Åre
Storlien
Funäsdalen
Idre
Särna
Sälen
Malung
Trysil
Engerdal
Tynset
Koppang
Fagernes
Gol
Geilo
Voss
Odda
Rjukan
Lom
Stryn
Florø
Måløy
Førde
Sogndalsfjorda
Gudvangen
Flåm
Lærdalsøyri
Åndalsnes
Sunndalsøra
Snøhetta 2286
Galdhøpiggen 2469
Skagastølstindane 2403
Gausta 1883
Sylarna 1766
Mjøsa
Femunden
Siljan
Storsjön
Vänern
Hjälmaren
Mälaren
Oslofjorden
Sognefjorden
Hardangerfjorden
Boknafjorden
Trondheimsfjorden
Glåma
Klarälven
Österdalälven
Västerdalälven
Dalälven
Indalsälven
Ljusnan
Ljungan
HIRTSHALS
RIGA

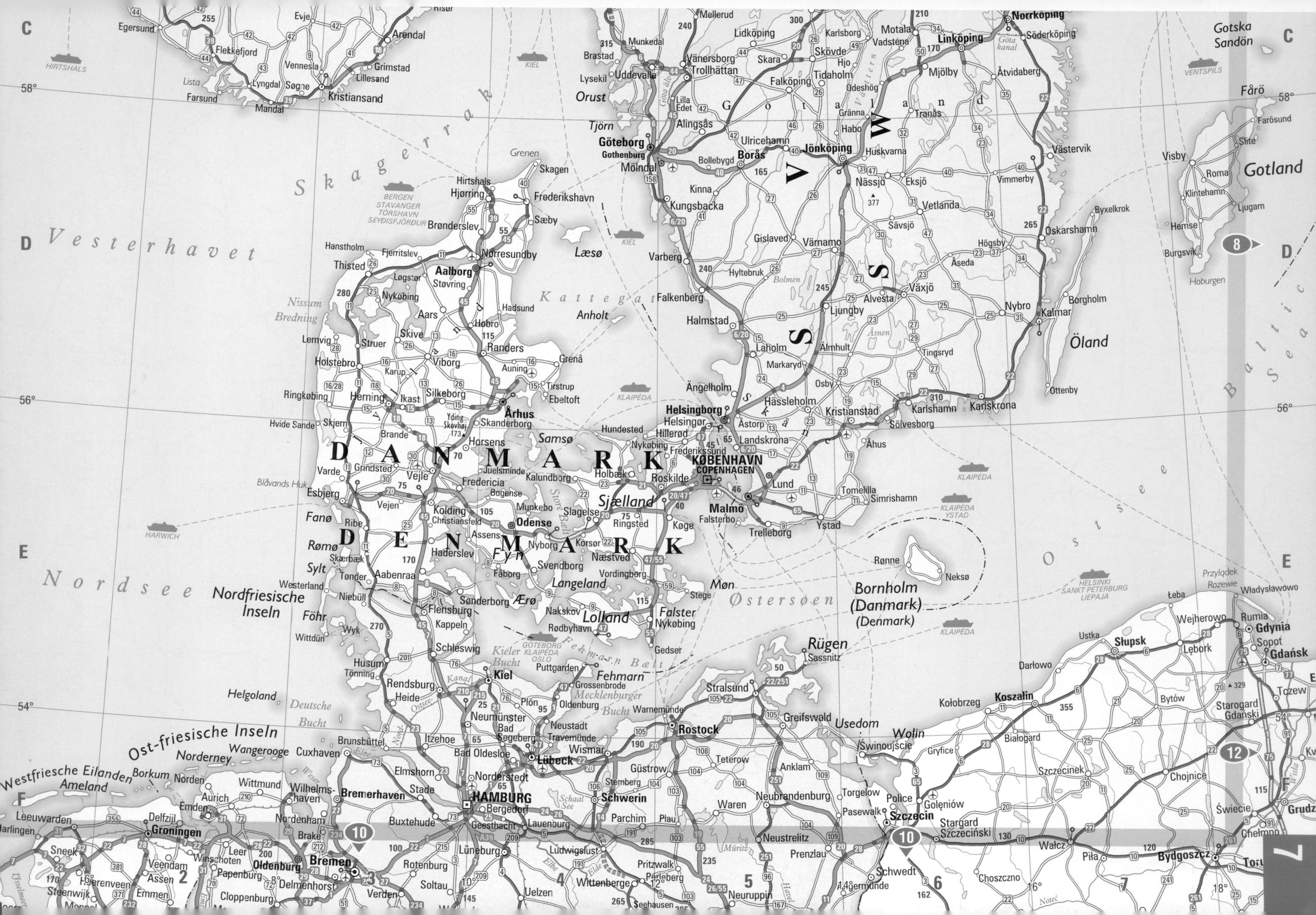
Skagerrak
Vesterhavet
Kattegat
Nordsee
Østersøen
Ostsee
Baltic Sea
Fehmarn Bælt
DANMARK
DENMARK
KØBENHAVN
COPENHAGEN
Sjælland
Fyn
Odense
Lolland
Falster
Møn
Langeland
Ærø
Samsø
Anholt
Læsø
Aalborg
Århus
Randers
Viborg
Silkeborg
Herning
Esbjerg
Vejle
Kolding
Fredericia
Skagen
Frederikshavn
Hirtshals
Hjørring
Fanø
Rømø
Sylt
Föhr
Nordfriesische Inseln
Ost-friesische Inseln
Westfriesche Eilanden
Helgoland
Deutsche Bucht
Kiel
Lübeck
HAMBURG
Bremen
Bremerhaven
Oldenburg
Groningen
Leeuwarden
Rostock
Schwerin
Stralsund
Rügen
Usedom
Wolin
Szczecin
Koszalin
Słupsk
Gdynia
Gdańsk
Bydgoszcz
Bornholm (Danmark) (Denmark)
Rønne
Neksø
Göteborg
Gothenburg
Borås
Jönköping
Linköping
Norrköping
Halmstad
Helsingborg
Malmö
Lund
Ystad
Kristianstad
Karlskrona
Kalmar
Växjö
Öland
Gotland
Visby
Fårö
Gotska Sandön
Orust
Tjörn
Kristiansand
Arendal
Mandal
Egersund
Flekkefjord
58°
56°
54°
C
D
E
F
7

8
Örnsköldsvik
Kramfors
Härnösand
Sundsvall
Hudiksvall
Iggesund
Söderhamn
Ljusne
Gävle
Älvkarleby
Uppsala
Norrtälje
Sigtuna
Märsta
Kappelskär
STOCKHOLM
Södertälje
Tumba
Vendelso
Nynäshamn
Grisslehamn
Eckerö
Geta
Mariehamn
Åland
Ålands hav
Selkämeri
Bottenhavet
Pohjanlahti
Gulf of Bothnia
Raippaluoto
Vaasa
Lapua
Kauhava
Ilmajoki
Seinäjoki
Kurikka
Kauhajoki
Alavus
Jalasjärvi
Kaskinen
Kristiinankaupunki
Kyyjärvi
Viitasaari
Saarijärvi
Äänekoski
Laukaa
Keuruu
Jyväskylä
Pieksämäki
Iisalmi
Siilinjärvi
Kuopio
Kallavesi
Leppävirta
Varkaus
Rautavaara
Parkano
Mänttä
Jämsä
Kankaanpää
Pori
Nokia
Tampere
Kangasala
Kuhmoinen
Päijänne
Mikkeli
Rauma
Vammala
Kokemäenjoki
Valkeakoski
Huittinen
Hämeenlinna
Heinola
Tuohikotti
Joutseno
Lappeenranta
Uusikaupunki
Loimaa
Forssa
Janakkala
Lahti
Kuusankoski
Kouvola
Anjalankoski
Riihimäki
Hyvinkää
Naantali
Raisio
Turku
Somero
Järvenpää
Hamina
Kotka
Loviisa
Porvoo
Kerava
Vantaa
Karkkila
Salo
Parainen
Lohja
Espoo
Helsinki
Kirkkonummi
Tammisaari
Hanko
Primorsk
ROSTOCK
Suomenlahti
Gulf of Finland
Finskaviken
LÜBECK TRAVEMÜNDE
RIGA
Naissaar
Tallinn
Paldiski
Keila
Kunda
Rakvere
Tapa
Kohtla-Järve
Jõhvi
Sillamäe
Narva
Ust Luga
Sosnovyy Bor
Slantsy
Gdov
Vormsi
Kärdla
Hiiumaa
Haapsalu
Rapla
EESTI
ESTONIA
Paide
Jõgeva
Muhu
Virtsu
Orissaare
Kuivastu
Saaremaa
Põltsamaa
Kuressaare
Parnu
Viljandi
Tartu
Ozero Chudskoye
Võrts Järv
Kihnu
Moisaküla
Ozero Pskovskoye
Polna
Pečory
Võru
Munamägi
Ruhnu saar
Ainaži
Kolkasrags
Valka
Valga
VENTSPILS
Gotska Sandön
Fårö
Farösund
Visby
Slite
Roma
Gotland
Klintehamn
Ljugarn
Hemse
Burgsvik
Hoburgen
Östersjön
Baltic Sea
NYNÄSHAMN
Ovišrags
Rizhskiy Zaliv
Valmiera
Limbaži
Ventspils
Roja
Talsi
LATVIJA
Cēsis
Alūksne
Gulbene
Ostrov
STOCKHOLM
Pāvilosta
Kuldīga
Tukums
Jūrmala
Rīga
Sigulda
Ērgli
Balvi
Pytalovo
Aizpute
Saldus
LATVIA
Ogre
Madona
Lubānas Ezers
Liepāja
Jelgava
Dobele
Plavinas
Aizkraukle
Bauska
Jēkabpils
Rēzekne
Ludza
Priekule
Skuodas
Mažeikiai
Preiļi
Daugava
Joniškis
Biržai
Palanga
Kretinga
Plungė
Telšiai
Šiauliai
Radviliškis
Rokiškis
Krāslava
Klaipėda
Daugavpils
LIETUVA
LITHUANIA
Panevėžys
Zarasai
Verkhnyadzvinsk
Druya
Braslaw
Dzisna
Navapolatsk
Neringa
Šilute
Raseiniai
Utena
Vidzy
Kurshskiy Zaliv
Tauragė
Kėdainiai
Ukmergė
Sovetsk
Jurbarkas
Neman
Šakiai
Jonava
Pastavy
Hlybokaye
Lyntupy
Mys Taran
Zelenogradsk
Polessk
Władysławowo
SASSNITZ KIEL KØBENHAVN FREDERICIA
LÜBECK

9
ROSSIYA
RUSSIA
Lendery
Lieksa
Pielinen
Juuka
Juankoski
Kontiolahti
Outokumpu
Eno
Joensuu
Ilomantsi
Liperi
Vyartsilya
Kitee
Savonlinna
Puruvesi
Pihlajavesi
Sortavala
Parikkala
Ruokolahti
Imatra
Valaam
Pitkyaranta
Suoyarvi
Padany
Seg-ozero
Medvezhyegorsk
Povenets
Petrovskiy Yam
Belomorsko-Baltiyskiy Kanal
Chelmuzhi
Kondopaga
Petrozavodsk
Onezhskoye Ozero
Shalskiy
Pudozh
Savinskiy
Oksovskiy
Konevo
Nyandoma
Kargopol
Vytegra
Voznesenye
Svir
Podporozhy
Olonets
Lodeinoye Pole
Annenskiy Most
Volgo-Baltiyskiy Kanal
Ozero Vozhe
Priozersk
Ladozhskoye Ozero
Lake Ladoga
Svirtsa
Vyborg
Zelenogorsk
Sestroretsk
Kronshtadt
SANKT-PETERBURG
ST. PETERSBURG
Novaya Ladoga
Syasstroy
Volkhov
Sosnovyy Bor
Petrodvorets
Neva
Pushkin
Kolpino
Gatchina
Volosovo
Tosno
Lyuban
Kirishi
Kingisepp
Shugozero
Pasha
Tikhvin
Pikalevo
Boksitogorsk
Nebolchy
Megra
Ozero Beloye
Belozersk
Kirillov
Ozero Kubenskoye
Suda
Babayevo
Chebsara
Kaduy
Cherepovets
Seksna
Chagoda
Khvoynaya
Ustyuzhna
Chudovo
Luga
Malaya Vishera
Lyubytino
Torkovichi
Tolmachevo
Vesyegonsk
Rybinskoye Vdkhr.
Pestovo
Msta
Volkhov
Novgorod
Parakhino Paddubye
Okulovka
Borovichi
Plyusa
Strugi Krasnyye
Ozero Ilmen
Shimsk
Soltsy
Krettsy
Lesnoye
Krasnyy Kholm
Rybinsk
Volga
Shelon
Staraya Russa
Parfino
Lychkova
Pola
Valday
Bologoye
Sonkovo
Bezhetsk
Pskov
Porkhov
Dno
Demyansk
Vyshniy Volochek
Uglich
Dedovichi
Lovat
Ozero Seliger
Valdayskaya Vozvyshennost
Medveditsa
Kashin
Kalyazin
Likhoslavl
Goritsy
Kholm
Ostashkov
Torzhok
Kimry
Velikaya
Novorzhev
Kuvshinovo
Tver
Ivankovskoye Vdkhr.
Dubna
Peno
Selizharovo
Redkino
Konakovo
Opochka
Loknya
Andreapol
Staritsa
Krasnozavodsk
Dmitrov
Sergiyev Posad
Toropets
Vysokovsk
Klin
Solnechnogorsk
Velikiye Luki
Pustoshka
Idritsa
Rzhev
Zubtsov
Pushkino
Zapadnaya Dvina
Nelidovo
Olenino
Volokolamsk
Zelenograd
Khimki
Mytishchi
Noginsk
Sebezh
Novosokolniki
Nevel
Sychevka
MOSKVA
Moscow
Elektrostal
Odintsovo
Lyubertsy
Ramenskoye
Yezerishche
Belyy
Zharkovskiy
Tupik
Mezha
Gagarin
Borodino
Moskva
Mozhaysk
Naro Fominsk
Podolsk
Borovsk
Klimovsk
Velizh
Polatsk
Haradok
Surazh
Demidov
Dukhovshchina
Obninsk
Mikhnevo
Stupino
Vitsyebsk
Vitebsk
Vyazma
Yartsevo
Safonovo
Maloyaroslavets
Serpukhov
Kashira
0 40 80 120 160 km

DANMARK
DEUTSCHLAND
GERMANY
NEDERLAND
NETHERLANDS
BELGIQUE
BELGIUM
ČESKÁ
CZECH
LUX.
Nordsee
Noordzee
Østersøen
Nordfriesische Inseln
Ost-friesische Inseln
Westfriesische Eilanden
Bornholm (Danmark)
(Denmark)
Rügen
Usedom
Wolin
Fehmarn
Lolland
Falster
Langeland
Fyn
Ærø
Møn
Helgoland
Sylt
Föhr
Texel
Terschelling
Ameland
Borkum
Norderney
Wangerooge
Deutsche Bucht
Mecklenburger Bucht
Kieler Bucht
BERLIN
HAMBURG
PRAHA
PRAGUE
AMSTERDAM
ROTTERDAM
BRUXELLES
BRUSSELS
's-Gravenhage
The Hague
Bremen
Hannover
Kiel
Lübeck
Rostock
Schwerin
Szczecin
Magdeburg
Leipzig
Dresden
Erfurt
Kassel
Frankfurt
Köln
Cologne
Düsseldorf
Dortmund
Essen
Bremerhaven
Braunschweig
Wolfsburg
Potsdam
Chemnitz
Halle
Jena
Gera
Würzburg
Utrecht
Antwerpen
Liège
Aachen
Bonn
Koblenz
Mainz
Wiesbaden
Darmstadt
Odense
Koszalin
Zielona Góra
Gorzów Wielkopolski
Liberec
Ústí nad Labem
Hradec Králové
Plzeň
0 40 80 120 160 km

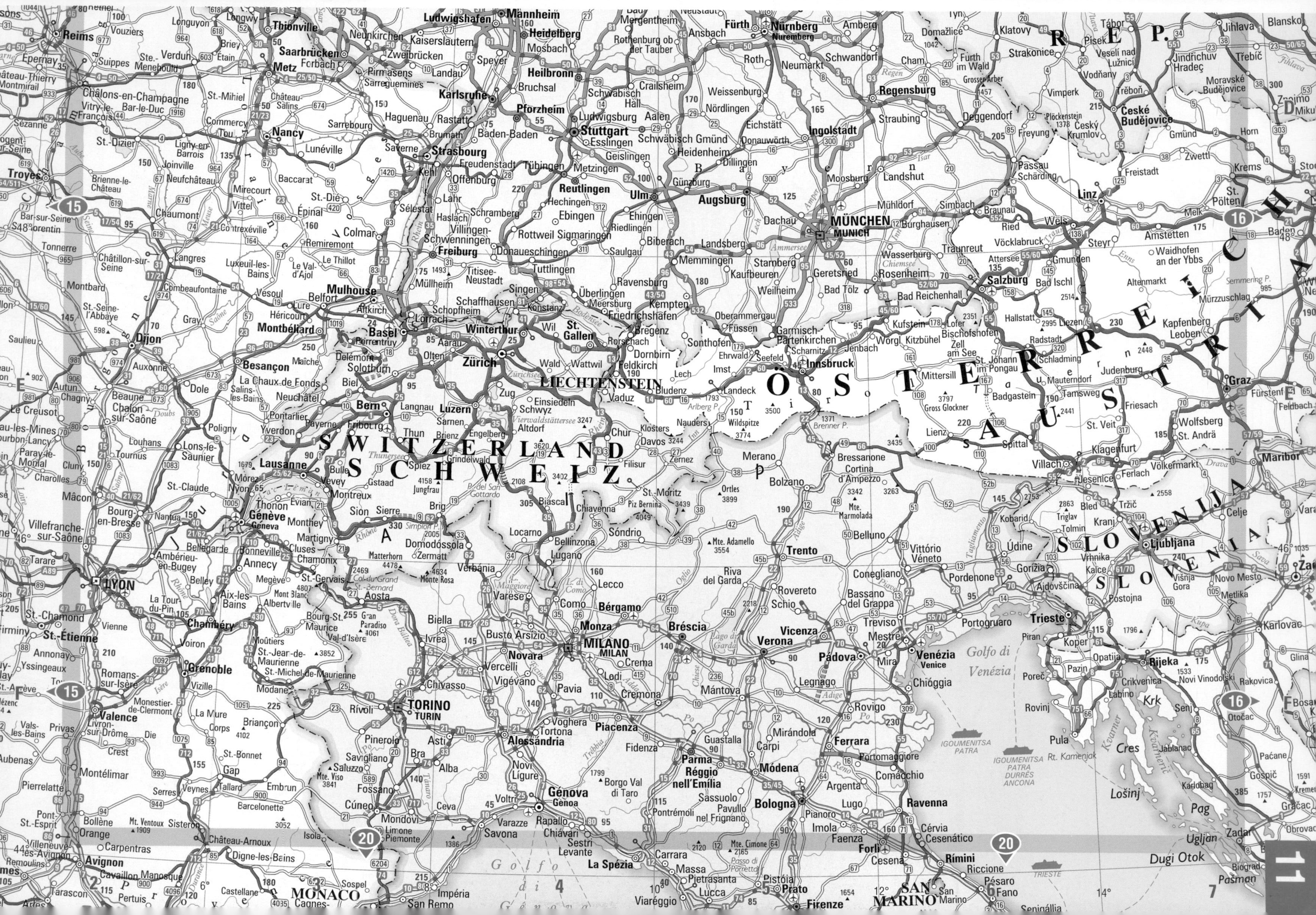

11
ÖSTERREICH
AUSTRIA
SWITZERLAND
SCHWEIZ
SLOVENIJA
SLOVENIA
LIECHTENSTEIN
SAN MARINO
MONACO
Tirol
Bayern
Golfo di Venézia
Reims
Metz
Nancy
Strasbourg
Karlsruhe
Mannheim
Heidelberg
Ludwigshafen
Saarbrücken
Heilbronn
Stuttgart
Pforzheim
Reutlingen
Ulm
Augsburg
Ingolstadt
Nürnberg
Fürth
Regensburg
MÜNCHEN
MUNICH
Salzburg
Linz
Graz
Innsbruck
Klagenfurt
Villach
Ljubljana
Rijeka
Trieste
Zürich
Basel
Bern
Luzern
St. Gallen
Winterthur
Lausanne
Genève
Geneva
Mulhouse
Freiburg
Besançon
Dijon
Montbéliard
LYON
Grenoble
Chambéry
St.-Étienne
Valence
Avignon
Troyes
TORINO
TURIN
MILANO
MILAN
Génova
Genoa
Bréscia
Bérgamo
Monza
Verona
Vicenza
Pádova
Venézia
Venice
Trento
Bolzano
Parma
Réggio nell'Emília
Módena
Bologna
Ferrara
Ravenna
Rímini
Prato
Firenze
La Spézia
Alessándria
Novara
Maribor
Karlovac
České Budějovice
Jihlava
Plzeň
Dugi Otok
Krk
Cres
Pag

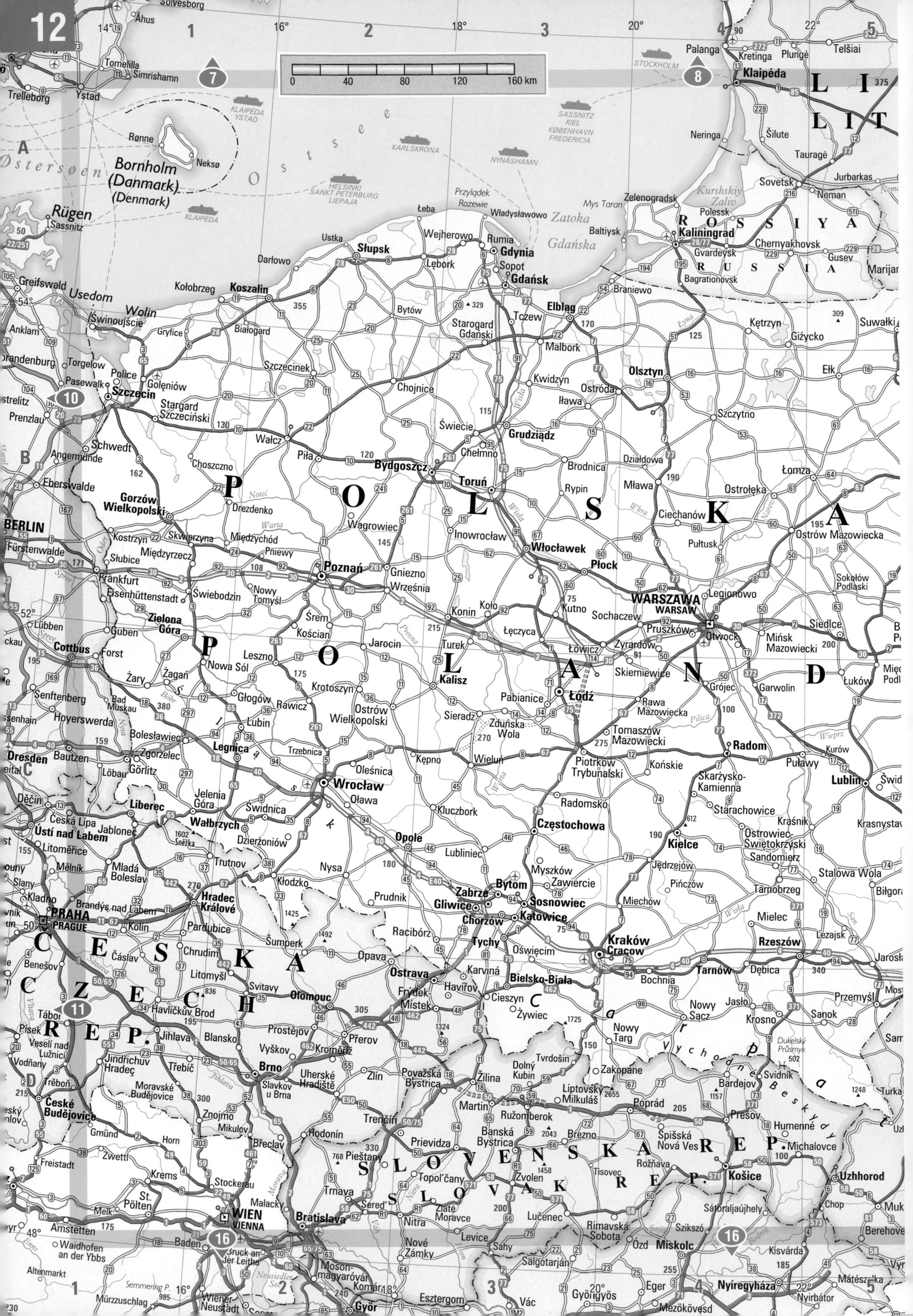

12
Sölvesborg
Åhus
Tomelilla
Simrishamn
Trelleborg
Ystad
0
40
80
120
160 km
STOCKHOLM
Palanga
Kretinga
Plungė
Telšiai
Klaipėda
L I
L I T
KLAIPĖDA YSTAD
SASSNITZ KIEL KØBENHAVN FREDERICIA
Neringa
Šilutė
Tauragė
Rønne
Nexø
KARLSKRONA
NYNÄSHAMN
A
Østersøen
Bornholm (Danmark) (Denmark)
Ostsee
HELSINKI SANKT PETERBURG LIEPAJA
Przylądek Rozewie
Mys Taran
Zelenogradsk
Kurshskiy Zaliv
Sovetsk
Jurbarkas
Neman
KLAIPĖDA
Rügen
Sassnitz
Łeba
Władysławowo
Zatoka Gdańska
Polessk
ROSSIYA
RUSSIA
Kaliningrad
Baltiysk
Gvardeysk
Chernyakhovsk
Gusev
Ustka
Słupsk
Wejherowo
Rumia
Gdynia
Sopot
Gdańsk
Darłowo
Lębork
Bagrationovsk
Braniewo
Greifswald
Usedom
Kołobrzeg
Koszalin
Wolin
Świnoujście
Bytów
Starogard Gdański
Tczew
Elbląg
Malbork
Kętrzyn
Giżycko
Suwałki
Anklam
Gryfice
Białogard
Szczecinek
Brandenburg
Torgelow
Pasewalk
Police
Goleniów
Szczecin
Chojnice
Kwidzyn
Ostróda
Olsztyn
Ełk
Iława
Szczytno
Prenzlau
Stargard Szczeciński
Wałcz
Świecie
Grudziądz
Chełmno
Schwedt
Angermünde
Choszczno
Piła
Bydgoszcz
Toruń
Brodnica
Działdowo
Łomża
Eberswalde
Gorzów Wielkopolski
Drezdenko
Noteć
Rypin
Mława
Ostrołęka
POLSKA
POLAND
Warta
Wągrowiec
Ciechanów
Pułtusk
Ostrów Mazowiecka
BERLIN
Fürstenwalde
Kostrzyn
Skwierzyna
Międzychód
Inowrocław
Włocławek
Płock
Słubice
Międzyrzecz
Pniewy
Poznań
Gniezno
Września
Frankfurt
Eisenhüttenstadt
Świebodzin
Nowy Tomyśl
Konin
Koło
Kutno
Sochaczew
WARSZAWA WARSAW
Legionowo
Sokołów Podlaski
Lübben
Zielona Góra
Guben
Śrem
Kościan
Jarocin
Turek
Łęczyca
Pruszków
Otwock
Mińsk Mazowiecki
Siedlce
Cottbus
Forst
Leszno
Nowa Sól
Kalisz
Łowicz
Żyrardów
Skierniewice
Garwolin
Łuków
Żary
Żagań
Krotoszyn
Ostrów Wielkopolski
Pabianice
Łódź
Rawa Mazowiecka
Grójec
Senftenberg
Hoyerswerda
Bad Muskau
Głogów
Rawicz
Sieradz
Zduńska Wola
Tomaszów Mazowiecki
Radom
Kurów
Bolesławiec
Lubin
Legnica
Trzebnica
Kępno
Wieluń
Piotrków Trybunalski
Końskie
Puławy
Lublin
Dresden
Bautzen
Zgorzelec
Görlitz
Löbau
Oleśnica
Wrocław
Oława
Skarżysko-Kamienna
Jelenia Góra
Liberec
Wałbrzych
Świdnica
Kluczbork
Radomsko
Starachowice
Kraśnik
Krasnystaw
Děčín
Česká Lípa
Jablonec
Ústí nad Labem
Litoměřice
Sněžka
Dzierżoniów
Opole
Częstochowa
Kielce
Ostrowiec-Świętokrzyski
Mělník
Mladá Boleslav
Trutnov
Kłodzko
Nysa
Lubliniec
Myszków
Zawiercie
Jędrzejów
Sandomierz
Stalowa Wola
Hradec Králové
Prudnik
Bytom
Zabrze
Gliwice
Sosnowiec
Chorzów
Katowice
Pińczów
Miechów
Tarnobrzeg
Biłgoraj
PRAHA PRAGUE
Kladno
Brandýs nad Labem
Kolín
Pardubice
Šumperk
Racibórz
Tychy
Mielec
Leżajsk
ČESKÁ
CZECH REP.
Čáslav
Chrudim
Opava
Oświęcim
Kraków Cracow
Rzeszów
Jarosław
Benešov
Litomyšl
Ostrava
Karviná
Havířov
Bielsko-Biała
Tarnów
Dębica
Svitavy
Olomouc
Frýdek-Místek
Cieszyn
Żywiec
Bochnia
Nowy Sącz
Jasło
Krosno
Przemyśl
Sanok
Tábor
Havlíčkův Brod
Písek
Jihlava
Blansko
Prostějov
Přerov
Nowy Targ
Veselí nad Lužnicí
Vodňany
Jindřichův Hradec
Třebíč
Vyškov
Kroměříž
Brno
Tvrdošín
Zakopane
Dukelský Průsmyk
Vychodné Beskydy
Třeboň
Moravské Budějovice
Slavkov u Brna
Uherské Hradiště
Zlín
Považská Bystrica
Žilina
Dolný Kubín
Liptovský Mikuláš
Svidník
Bardejov
České Budějovice
Znojmo
Mikulov
Martin
Ružomberok
Poprad
Prešov
Humenné
Gmünd
Horn
Břeclav
Hodonín
Trenčín
Prievidza
Banská Bystrica
Brezno
Spišská Nová Ves
Michalovce
Zwettl
Freistadt
Piešťany
SLOVENSKÁ REP.
SLOVAK REP.
Rožňava
Košice
Uzhhorod
Krems
Stockerau
Topoľčany
Zvolen
Tisovec
Chop
St. Pölten
Malacky
Trnava
Sereď
Zlaté Moravce
Lučenec
Sátoraljaújhely
Melk
WIEN VIENNA
Bratislava
Nitra
Levice
Rimavská Sobota
Szikszó
Amstetten
Baden
Waidhofen an der Ybbs
Bruck an der Leitha
Nové Zámky
Šahy
Ózd
Miskolc
Kisvárda
Berehove
Mosonmagyaróvár
Salgótarján
Altenmarkt
Semmering P.
Neusiedler See
Komárno
Esztergom
Gyöngyös
Eger
Nyíregyháza
Mátészalka
Nyírbátor
Mürzzuschlag
Wiener Neustadt
Győr
Vác
Mezőkövesd

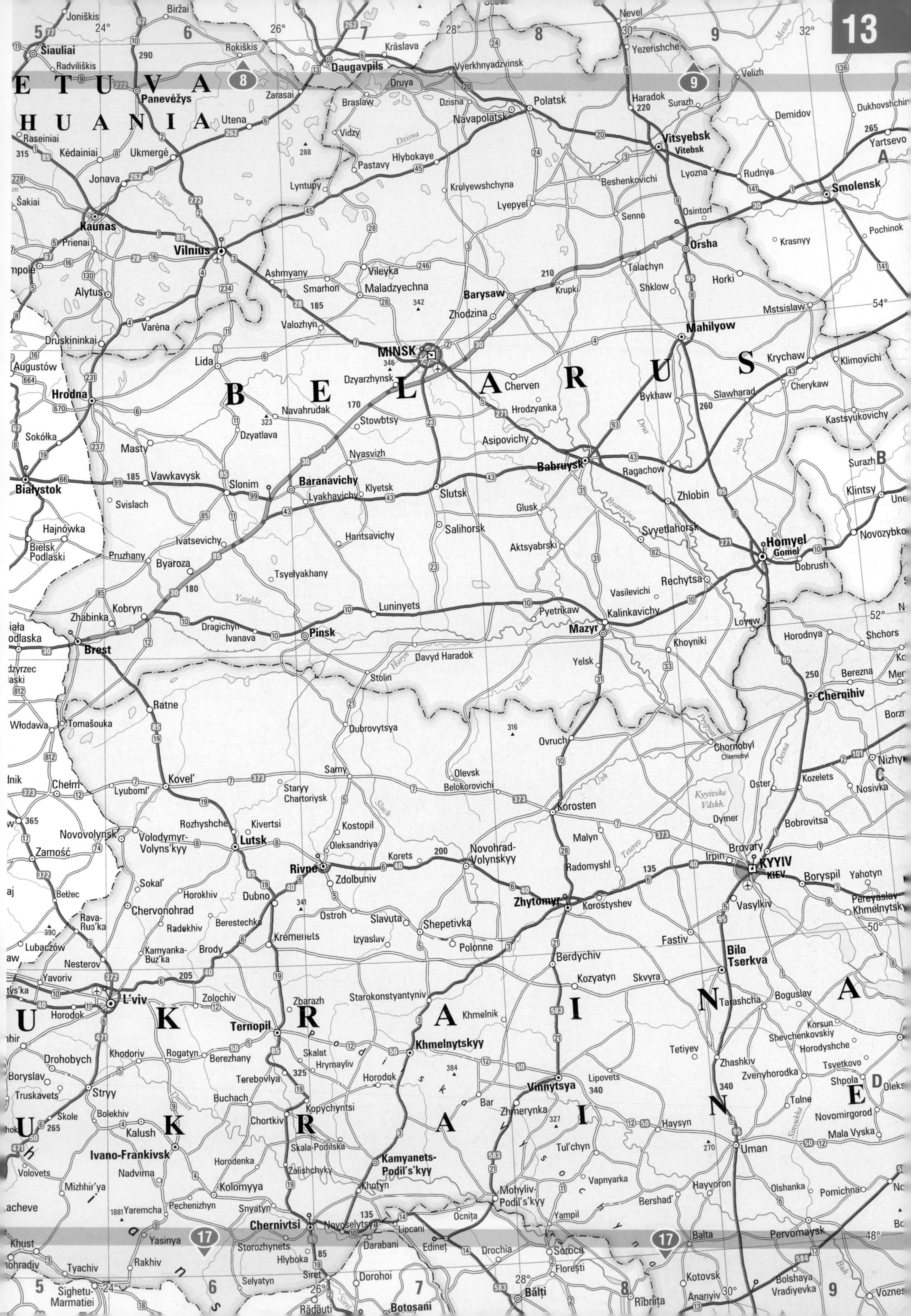
LITHUANIA
BELARUS
UKRAINE
Podil's'ka Vysochyna
Šiauliai
Joniškis
Biržai
Radviliškis
Rokiškis
Panevėžys
Zarasai
Utena
Raseiniai
Kėdainiai
Ukmergė
Jonava
Šakiai
Kaunas
Prienai
Vilnius
Alytus
Varėna
Druskininkai
Augustów
Hrodna
Sokółka
Białystok
Hajnówka
Bielsk Podlaski
Daugavpils
Krāslava
Vyerkhnyadzvinsk
Druya
Braslaw
Dzisna
Navapolatsk
Polatsk
Vidzy
Pastavy
Hlybokaye
Lyntupy
Krulyewshchyna
Lyepyel
Ashmyany
Smarhon
Vileyka
Maladzyechna
Valozhyn
Barysaw
Zhodzina
Krupki
MINSK
Dzyarzhynsk
Lida
Navahrudak
Dzyatlava
Stowbtsy
Nyasvizh
Masty
Vawkavysk
Slonim
Baranavichy
Lyakhavichy
Klyetsk
Slutsk
Salihorsk
Hantsavichy
Svislach
Ivatsevichy
Pruzhany
Byaroza
Tsyelyakhany
Kobryn
Zhabinka
Brest
Biała Podlaska
Dragichyn
Ivanava
Pinsk
Luninyets
Davyd Haradok
Stolin
Cherven
Hrodzyanka
Asipovichy
Babruysk
Glusk
Aktsyabrski
Pyetrikaw
Mazyr
Kalinkavichy
Yelsk
Khoyniki
Vasilevichi
Rechytsa
Svyetlahorsk
Zhlobin
Ragachow
Bykhaw
Homyel
Gomel
Dobrush
Loyew
Nevel
Yezerishche
Velizh
Haradok
Surazh
Vitsyebsk
Vitebsk
Beshenkovichi
Senno
Lyozna
Rudnya
Demidov
Dukhovshchina
Yartsevo
Smolensk
Osintorf
Orsha
Talachyn
Shklow
Horki
Krasnyy
Pochinok
Mstsislaw
Mahilyow
Krychaw
Klimovichi
Cherykaw
Slawharad
Kastsyukovichy
Surazh
Klintsy
Novozybkov
Horodnya
Shchors
Berezna
Chernihiv
Nizhyn
Kozelets
Nosivka
Oster
Bobrovitsa
Chornobyl
Chernobyl
Kyyivske Vdskh.
Dymer
Brovary
KYYIV
KIEV
Irpin
Boryspil
Yahotyn
Pereyaslav-Khmelnytskyy
Vasylkiv
Fastiv
Bila Tserkva
Skvyra
Boguslav
Tarashcha
Korsun Shevchenkovskiy
Horodyshche
Tetiyev
Zhashkiv
Zvenyhorodka
Shpola
Tsvetkovo
Talne
Novomirgorod
Mala Vyska
Uman
Haysyn
Olshanka
Pomichna
Hayvoron
Bershad
Balta
Pervomaysk
Kotovsk
Bolshaya Vradiyevka
Voznesensk
Ananyiv
Ratne
Włodawa
Tomašouka
Dubrovytsya
Ovruch
Olevsk
Belokorovichi
Sarny
Staryy Chartoriysk
Korosten
Malyn
Radomyshl
Kovel'
Lyuboml'
Chełm
Zamość
Bełżec
Novovolynsk
Volodymyr-Volyns'kyy
Rozhyshche
Kivertsi
Lutsk
Kostopil
Oleksandriya
Rivne
Zdolbuniv
Korets
Novohrad-Volynskyy
Zhytomyr
Korostyshev
Berdychiv
Kozyatyn
Sokal'
Horokhiv
Dubno
Chervonohrad
Rava-Rus'ka
Radekhiv
Berestechko
Kremenets
Ostroh
Slavuta
Shepetivka
Izyaslav
Polonne
Lubaczów
Kamyanka-Buz'ka
Brody
Nesterov
Yavoriv
L'viv
Horodok
Zolochiv
Zbarazh
Starokonstyantyniv
Khmelnik
Ternopil
Khmelnytskyy
Skalat
Hrymayliv
Drohobych
Khodoriv
Rogatyn
Berezhany
Boryslav
Truskavets'
Stryy
Terebovlya
Horodok
Bar
Vinnytsya
Lipovets
Zhmerynka
Skole
Bolekhiv
Kalush
Buchach
Chortkiv
Kopychyntsi
Ivano-Frankivsk
Horodenka
Skala-Podilska
Kamyanets-Podil's'kyy
Zalishchyky
Tul'chyn
Vapnyarka
Volovets
Nadvirna
Mizhhir'ya
Kolomyya
Khotyn
Mohyliv-Podil's'kyy
Yampil
Svalyava
Yaremcha
Pechenizhyn
Snyatyn
Chernivtsi
Novoselytsya
Lipcani
Ocnița
Khust
Yasinya
Storozhynets
Hlyboka
Darabani
Edineț
Drochia
Soroca
Vynohradiv
Rakhiv
Tyachiv
Siret
Dorohoi
Florești
Sighetu-Marmatiei
Selyatyn
Rădăuti
Botoșani
Bălți
Ribnița
Dzisna
Viliya
Ptsich
Byarezina
Drut
Sozh
Yaselda
Haryn
Ubort
Prypyat
Uzh
Sluch
Teterev
Desna
Dnister
Siret
Sinyukha
Buh
Mezha
24°
26°
28°
30°
32°
54°
52°
50°
48°
5
6
7
8
9
A
B
C
D
E

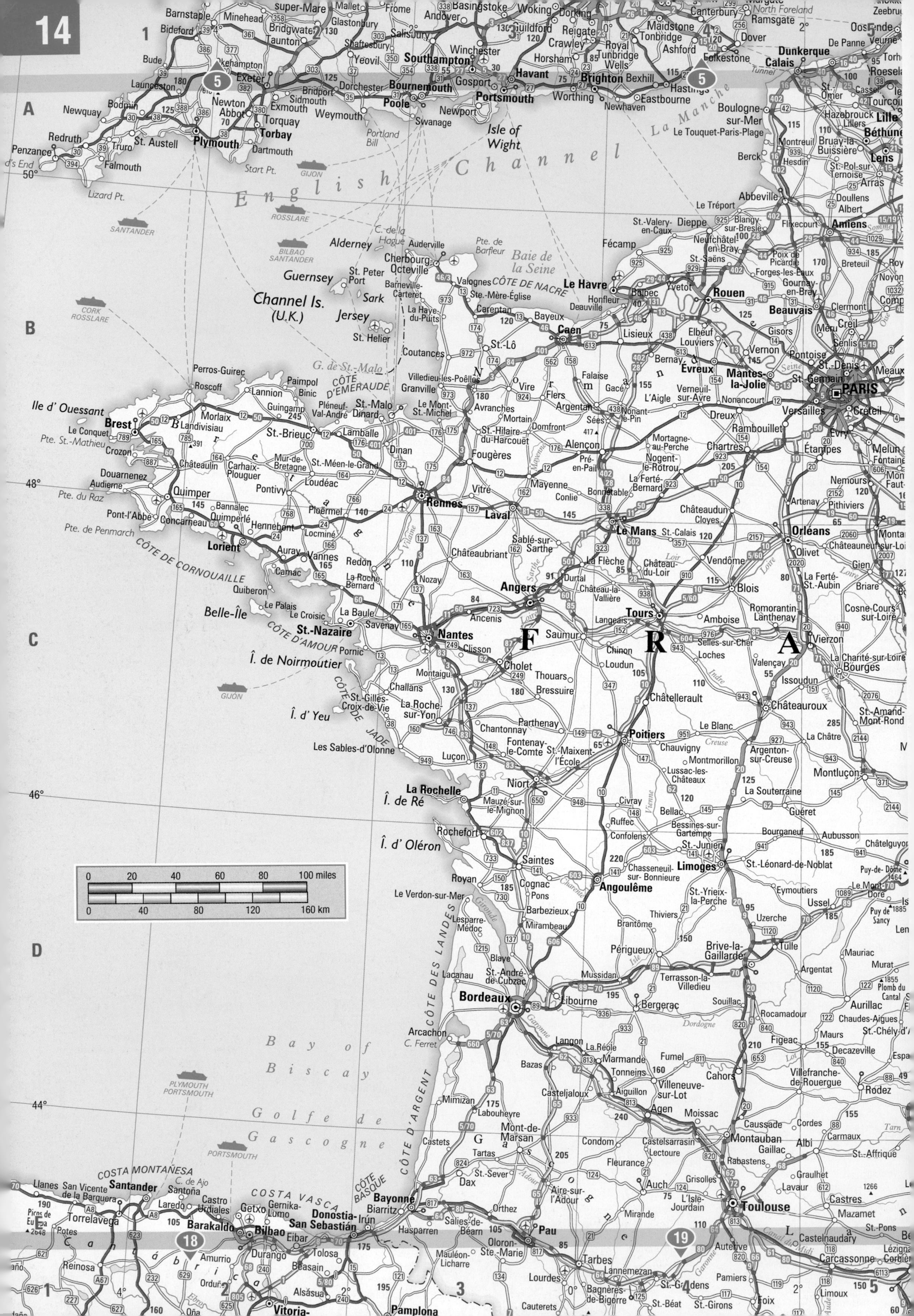
Barnstaple
Minehead
Bideford
Bridgwater
Taunton
Glastonbury
Frome
Mallet
Basingstoke
Woking
Dorking
Andover
Guildford
Reigate
Canterbury
Margate
North Foreland
Zeebrugge
Ramsgate
Maidstone
Tonbridge
Royal Tunbridge Wells
Ashford
Dover
Folkestone
Crawley
Horsham
Salisbury
Shaftesbury
Winchester
Southampton
Yeovil
Bude
Okehampton
Exeter
Launceston
Newquay
Bodmin
Newton Abbot
Exmouth
Sidmouth
Bridport
Dorchester
Bournemouth
Poole
Weymouth
Swanage
Gosport
Portsmouth
Havant
Brighton
Bexhill
Hastings
Worthing
Newhaven
Eastbourne
Newport
Isle of Wight
Torquay
Torbay
Dartmouth
Plymouth
St. Austell
Truro
Redruth
Penzance
Falmouth
Lizard Pt.
Start Pt.
Portland Bill
50°
English Channel
La Manche
Tunnel
Dunkerque
Calais
De Panne
Oostende
Veurne
Roeselare
St.-Omer
Cassel
Tourcoing
Hazebrouck
Lillers
Lille
Béthune
Boulogne-sur-Mer
Le Touquet-Paris-Plage
Montreuil
Bruay-la-Buissière
Lens
Hesdin
St.-Pol-sur-Ternoise
Arras
Berck
Doullens
Albert
Abbeville
Le Tréport
Amiens
Somme
St.-Valery-en-Caux
Dieppe
Blangy-sur-Bresle
Flixecourt
Neufchâtel-en-Bray
Poix-de-Picardie
Forges-les-Eaux
St.-Saëns
Breteuil
Roye
Noyon
Gournay-en-Bray
Fécamp
Yvetot
Bolbec
Rouen
Beauvais
Clermont
Compiègne
Creil
Senlis
Méru
Gisors
Le Havre
Honfleur
Deauville
Pont-l'Évêque
Lisieux
Elbeuf
Louviers
Vernon
Pontoise
St.-Denis
Meaux
St.-Germain
PARIS
Créteil
Versailles
Évry
Melun
Fontainebleau
Étampes
Rambouillet
Dreux
Nonancourt
Évreux
Mantes-la-Jolie
Bernay
L'Aigle
Verneuil-sur-Avre
Gacé
Nonant-le-Pin
Sées
Alderney
C. de la Hague
Auderville
Pte. de Barfleur
Baie de la Seine
Cherbourg-Octeville
Valognes
Côte de Nacre
Ste.-Mère-Église
Guernsey
St. Peter Port
Sark
Barneville-Carteret
Jersey
St. Helier
Channel Is. (U.K.)
La Haye-du-Puits
Carentan
Bayeux
Caen
Coutances
St.-Lô
G. de St.-Malo
Côte d'Émeraude
Perros-Guirec
Roscoff
Lannion
Paimpol
Binic
Guingamp
Morlaix
Landivisiau
Ile d'Ouessant
Brest
Le Conquet
Pte. St.-Mathieu
Crozon
Châteaulin
Carhaix-Plouguer
Douarnenez
Audierne
Pte. du Raz
Quimper
Pont-l'Abbé
Pte. de Penmarch
Concarneau
Quimperlé
Bannalec
Lorient
Hennebont
Pontivy
Mur-de-Bretagne
St.-Brieuc
Lamballe
Pléneuf-Val-André
St.-Malo
Dinard
Dinan
Granville
Villedieu-les-Poêles
Le Mont-St.-Michel
Avranches
Vire
Flers
Falaise
Argentan
Domfront
St.-Hilaire-du-Harcouët
Mortain
Fougères
Alençon
Mortagne-au-Perche
Pré-en-Pail
Nogent-le-Rotrou
Chartres
La Ferté-Bernard
Mayenne
Vitré
Rennes
Laval
Loudéac
St.-Méen-le-Grand
Ploërmel
Locminé
Vannes
Auray
Carnac
Quiberon
Belle-Île
Le Palais
Le Croisic
La Baule
St.-Nazaire
Savenay
Redon
La Roche-Bernard
Nozay
Châteaubriant
Ancenis
Nantes
Clisson
Pornic
Côte d'Amour
Côte de Cornouaille
Î. de Noirmoutier
Challans
Montaigu
Cholet
St.-Gilles-Croix-de-Vie
La Roche-sur-Yon
Î. d'Yeu
Côte de Jade
Les Sables-d'Olonne
Luçon
Chantonnay
Fontenay-le-Comte
Angers
Saumur
Sablé-sur-Sarthe
La Flèche
Le Mans
Bonnétable
Conlie
Château-du-Loir
Durtal
Château-la-Vallière
Tours
Langeais
Chinon
Loudun
Thouars
Bressuire
Parthenay
St.-Maixent-l'École
Niort
La Rochelle
Î. de Ré
Mauzé-sur-le-Mignon
Rochefort
Î. d'Oléron
Royan
Saintes
Cognac
Pons
Le Verdon-sur-Mer
Barbezieux
Mirambeau
Lesparre-Médoc
Blaye
St.-André-de-Cubzac
Lacanau
Bordeaux
Libourne
Arcachon
C. Ferret
Châteaudun
Cloyes
St.-Calais
Vendôme
Blois
Amboise
Loches
Orléans
Olivet
Pithiviers
Artenay
Nemours
Montargis
Châteauneuf-sur-Loire
Gien
La Ferté-St.-Aubin
Briare
Cosne-Cours-sur-Loire
Romorantin-Lanthenay
Vierzon
Selles-sur-Cher
Valençay
Issoudun
Bourges
La Charité-sur-Loire
Châtellerault
Poitiers
Chauvigny
Montmorillon
Lussac-les-Châteaux
Le Blanc
Châteauroux
Argenton-sur-Creuse
La Châtre
St.-Amand-Mont-Rond
Montluçon
La Souterraine
Guéret
Civray
Ruffec
Confolens
Bellac
Bessines-sur-Gartempe
St.-Junien
Limoges
St.-Léonard-de-Noblat
Bourganeuf
Aubusson
Châtelguyon
Chasseneuil-sur-Bonnieure
Angoulême
St.-Yrieix-la-Perche
Eymoutiers
Ussel
Thiviers
Uzerche
Brantôme
Périgueux
Brive-la-Gaillarde
Tulle
Mussidan
Terrasson-la-Villedieu
Bergerac
Souillac
Rocamadour
Figeac
Aurillac
Mauriac
Argentat
Maurs
Decazeville
Villefranche-de-Rouergue
Rodez
Cahors
Fumel
Villeneuve-sur-Lot
Marmande
Tonneins
La Réole
Langon
Bazas
Aiguillon
Agen
Moissac
Casteljaloux
Caussade
Montauban
Gaillac
Albi
Cordes
Carmaux
Castelsarrasin
Lectoure
Condom
Fleurance
Auch
Grisolles
L'Isle-Jourdain
Toulouse
Rabastens
Graulhet
Lavaur
Castres
Mazamet
St.-Pons
Castelnaudary
Carcassonne
Limoux
Pamiers
Foix
Mimizan
Labouheyre
Mont-de-Marsan
Castets
Tartas
Dax
St.-Sever
Aire-sur-l'Adour
Orthez
Pau
Tarbes
Lannemezan
Mirande
Salies-de-Béarn
Bayonne
Biarritz
Hasparren
Oloron-Ste.-Marie
Mauléon-Licharre
Lourdes
Bagnères-de-Bigorre
Cauterets
St.-Gaudens
St.-Girons
St.-Béat
Autevive
Côte d'Argent
Côte des Landes
Côte Basque
Bay of Biscay
Golfe de Gascogne
Costa Montañesa
Costa Vasca
Llanes
San Vicente de la Barquera
Santander
C. de Ajo
Santoña
Castro Urdiales
Laredo
Torrelavega
Barakaldo
Getxo
Bilbao
Gernika-Lumo
Eibar
Durango
Donostia-San Sebastián
Irún
Tolosa
Beasain
Amurrio
Reinosa
Potes
Orduña
Alsásua
Vitoria-Gasteiz
Pamplona
Cantabria
Ebro
Canal du Midi
FRANCE
Normandie
Bretagne
Gascogne
SANTANDER
ROSSLARE
BILBAO SANTANDER
CORK ROSSLARE
GIJON
PLYMOUTH PORTSMOUTH
PORTSMOUTH
48°
46°
44°
0 20 40 60 80 100 miles
0 40 80 120 160 km
Loire
Seine
Garonne
Dordogne
Charente
Vienne
Sarthe
Mayenne
Vilaine
Indre
Cher
Creuse
Lot
Tarn
Adour
Gironde
Isle

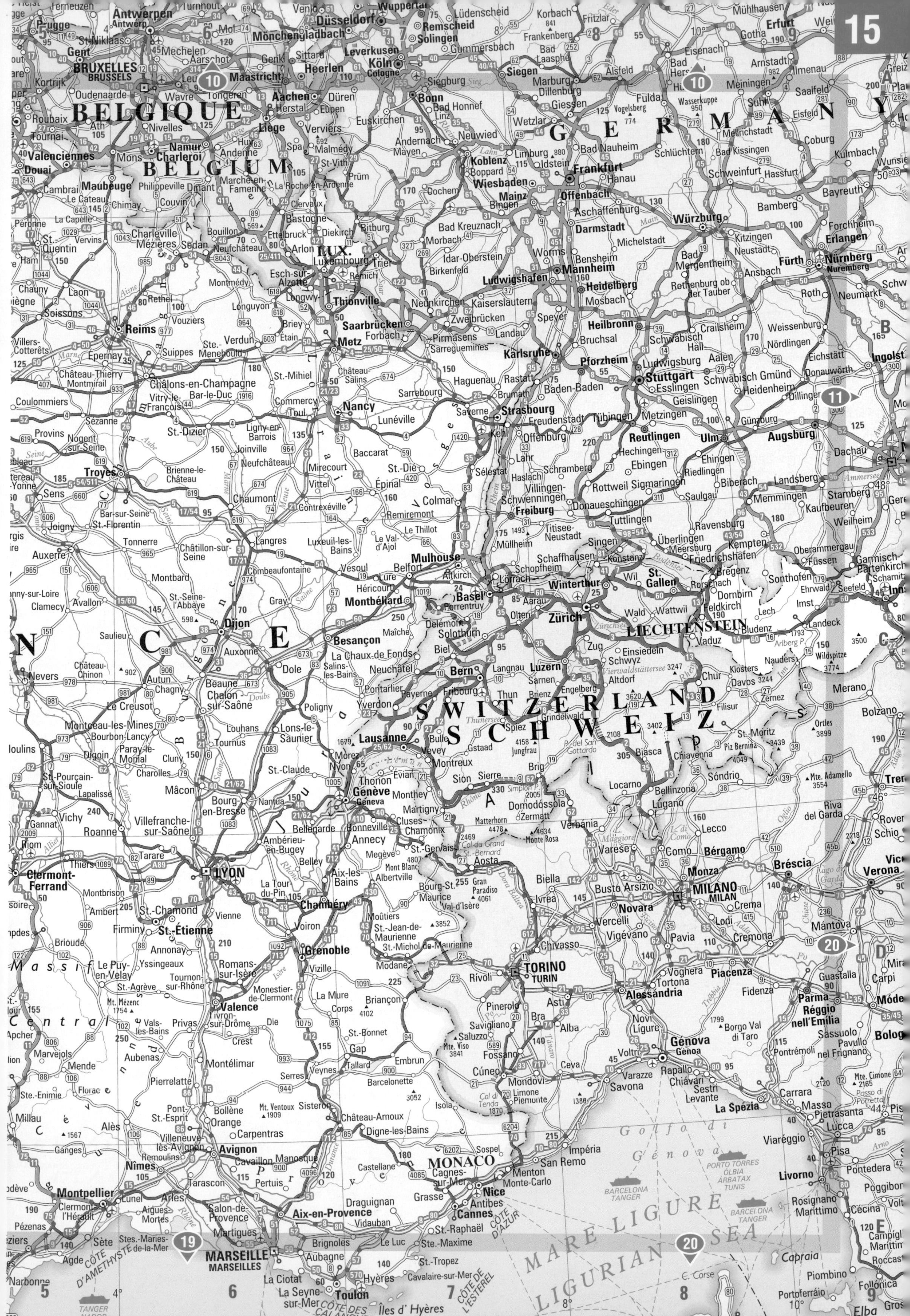
BELGIQUE
BELGIUM
GERMANY
SWITZERLAND
SCHWEIZ
LIECHTENSTEIN
LUX.
MONACO
Massif Central
MARE LIGURE
LIGURIAN SEA
Golfo di Génova
CÔTE D'AZUR
CÔTE D'AMETHYSTE
CÔTE DE L'ESTEREL
CÔTE DES CALANQUES
Îles d'Hyères
Capraia
Elba
Antwerpen
Antwerp
Brugge
Gent
BRUXELLES
BRUSSELS
Mechelen
Aarschot
Kortrijk
Oudenaarde
Leuven
Maastricht
Tongeren
Wavre
Roubaix
Tournai
Ath
Nivelles
Namur
Charleroi
Mons
Valenciennes
Douai
Cambrai
Maubeuge
Liège
Herstal
Aachen
Düren
Eupen
Verviers
Spa
Malmedy
St-Vith
Huy
Andenne
Dinant
Philippeville
Marche-en-Famenne
La Roche-en-Ardenne
Chimay
Couvin
Bastogne
Clervaux
Diekirch
Ettelbruck
Bitburg
Arlon
Luxembourg
Esch-sur-Alzette
Remich
Trier
Düsseldorf
Mönchengladbach
Leverkusen
Köln
Cologne
Heerlen
Sittard
Genk
Venlo
Wuppertal
Remscheid
Solingen
Lüdenscheid
Gummersbach
Siegburg
Bonn
Bad Honnef
Euskirchen
Andernach
Mayen
Neuwied
Koblenz
Boppard
Limburg
Idstein
Wiesbaden
Mainz
Bingen
Frankfurt
Hanau
Offenbach
Aschaffenburg
Darmstadt
Michelstadt
Bad Kreuznach
Morbach
Idar-Oberstein
Birkenfeld
Cochem
Prüm
Siegen
Marburg
Dillenburg
Giessen
Wetzlar
Bad Nauheim
Korbach
Fritzlar
Frankenberg
Bad Laasphe
Alsfeld
Fulda
Vogelsberg
Wasserkuppe
Eisenach
Bad Hersfeld
Gotha
Erfurt
Mühlhausen
Arnstadt
Ilmenau
Meiningen
Suhl
Eisfeld
Saalfeld
Mellrichstadt
Coburg
Kulmbach
Bad Kissingen
Schlüchtern
Schweinfurt
Hassfurt
Bayreuth
Bamberg
Würzburg
Forchheim
Erlangen
Kitzingen
Neustadt
Fürth
Nürnberg
Nuremberg
Bad Mergentheim
Ansbach
Rothenburg ob der Tauber
Roth
Neumarkt
Worms
Bensheim
Mannheim
Ludwigshafen
Heidelberg
Mosbach
Kaiserslautern
Neunkirchen
Zweibrücken
Pirmasens
Saarbrücken
Forbach
Sarreguemines
Landau
Speyer
Heilbronn
Crailsheim
Bruchsal
Karlsruhe
Pforzheim
Schwäbisch Hall
Ludwigsburg
Stuttgart
Esslingen
Aalen
Schwäbisch Gmünd
Heidenheim
Nördlingen
Weissenburg
Eichstätt
Ingolstadt
Donauwörth
Dillingen
Geislingen
Günzburg
Augsburg
Ulm
Dachau
Rastatt
Baden-Baden
Brumath
Haguenau
Saverne
Strasbourg
Kehl
Offenburg
Freudenstadt
Tübingen
Metzingen
Reutlingen
Hechingen
Ebingen
Lahr
Haslach
Schramberg
Rottweil
Sigmaringen
Ehingen
Riedlingen
Biberach
Saulgau
Landsberg
Memmingen
Kaufbeuren
Starnberg
Weilheim
Villingen-Schwenningen
Donaueschingen
Tuttlingen
Sélestat
Colmar
Freiburg
Titisee-Neustadt
Müllheim
Singen
Konstanz
Überlingen
Meersburg
Friedrichshafen
Ravensburg
Kempten
Oberammergau
Füssen
Garmisch-Partenkirchen
Bodensee
Schaffhausen
Schopfheim
Lörrach
Basel
Altkirch
Mulhouse
Belfort
Montbéliard
Héricourt
Lure
Vesoul
Porrentruy
Delémont
Solothurn
Olten
Aarau
Zürich
Winterthur
Wil
St. Gallen
Rorschach
Bregenz
Dornbirn
Feldkirch
Vaduz
Bludenz
Landeck
Imst
Ehrwald
Seefeld
Sonthofen
Lech
Arlberg P.
Wildspitze
Wald
Wattwil
Zug
Zürichsee
Einsiedeln
Schwyz
Vierwaldstättersee
Altdorf
Luzern
Langnau
Sarnen
Engelberg
Chur
Klosters
Davos
Zernez
Filisur
Biel
Bern
Neuchâtel
Thun
Spiez
Grindelwald
Thunersee
Jungfrau
La Chaux-de-Fonds
Maîche
Pontarlier
Payerne
Fribourg
Yverdon
Bulle
Gstaad
Lausanne
Vevey
Montreux
Morez
Nyon
Thonon
Evian
Genève
Geneva
Monthey
Martigny
Sion
Sierre
Brig
Simplon P.
Domodossola
Zermatt
Matterhorn
Monte Rosa
P. del San Gottardo
Biasca
Locarno
Bellinzona
Lugano
Chiavenna
St. Moritz
Piz Bernina
Sóndrio
Merano
Bolzano
Ortles
Mte. Adamello
Trento
Riva del Garda
Rovereto
Schio
Lago di Garda
Verona
Vicenza
Brescia
Bérgamo
Lecco
Como
Varese
Verbania
L. Maggiore
Monza
MILANO
MILAN
Busto Arsizio
Biella
Ivrea
Novara
Vercelli
Vigévano
Pavia
Lodi
Crema
Cremona
Mántova
Guastalla
Carpi
Parma
Réggio nell'Emilia
Módena
Bologna
Sassuolo
Pavullo nel Frignano
Fidenza
Piacenza
Voghera
Tortona
Alessándria
Asti
Alba
Bra
Chivasso
TORINO
TURIN
Rívoli
Pinerolo
Savigliano
Saluzzo
Mte. Viso
Fossano
Cúneo
Mondovì
Limone Piemonte
Col di Tenda
Ceva
Savona
Varazze
Voltri
Génova
Genoa
Novi Lígure
Rapallo
Chiávari
Sestri Levante
La Spézia
Borgo Val di Taro
Pontrémoli
Carrara
Massa
Pietrasanta
Viaréggio
Lucca
Pisa
Pontedera
Livorno
Poggibonsi
Rosignano Marittimo
Cécina
Campiglia Marittima
Roccastrada
Piombino
Follonica
Portoferráio
Imperia
San Remo
Menton
Monte-Carlo
Nice
Antibes
Cannes
Cagnes-sur-Mer
Grasse
Sospel
St.-Raphaël
Ste.-Maxime
St.-Tropez
Cavalaire-sur-Mer
Hyères
Toulon
La Seyne-sur-Mer
La Ciotat
Le Luc
Draguignan
Vidauban
Brignoles
Aubagne
MARSEILLE
MARSEILLES
Martigues
Aix-en-Provence
Salon-de-Provence
Pertuis
Manosque
Cavaillon
Avignon
Villeneuve-lès-Avignon
Remoulins
Nîmes
Tarascon
Arles
Aigues-Mortes
Stes.-Maries-de-la-Mer
Sète
Agde
Pézenas
Montpellier
Lunel
Clermont-l'Hérault
Narbonne
Ganges
Alès
Millau
Ste.-Enimie
Florac
Mende
Marvejols
Castellane
Digne-les-Bains
Château-Arnoux
Sisteron
Mt. Ventoux
Carpentras
Orange
Bollène
Pont-St.-Esprit
Pierrelatte
Montélimar
Crest
Die
Valence
Livron-sur-Drôme
Privas
Vals-les-Bains
Aubenas
Mt. Mézenc
St.-Agrève
Tournon-sur-Rhône
Romans-sur-Isère
Le Puy-en-Velay
Yssingeaux
Annonay
St.-Étienne
Firminy
St.-Chamond
Vienne
Brioude
Ambert
Montbrison
Clermont-Ferrand
Thiers
Riom
Gannat
Vichy
Roanne
Lapalisse
St.-Pourçain-sur-Sioule
Moulins
Digoin
Paray-le-Monial
Charolles
Cluny
Mâcon
Tournus
Louhans
Bourg-en-Bresse
Villefranche-sur-Saône
Tarare
LYON
Nantua
Oyonnax
St.-Claude
Lons-le-Saunier
Poligny
Salins-les-Bains
Dole
Bellegarde
Ambérieu-en-Bugey
Belley
La Tour-du-Pin
Chambéry
Aix-les-Bains
Annecy
Cluses
Chamonix
St.-Gervais
Megève
Mont Blanc
Albertville
Bourg-St.-Maurice
Val-d'Isère
Gran Paradiso
Aosta
Col du Grand St.-Bernard
Moûtiers
St.-Jean-de-Maurienne
St.-Michel-de-Maurienne
Modane
Voiron
Grenoble
Vizille
La Mure
Corps
Monestier-de-Clermont
Briançon
St.-Bonnet
Gap
Embrun
Barcelonette
Tallard
Serres
Veynes
Isola
Besançon
Auxonne
Dijon
Beaune
Chagny
Chalon-sur-Saône
Autun
Le Creusot
Montceau-les-Mines
Bourbon-Lancy
Nevers
Château-Chinon
Saulieu
Avallon
Clamecy
Auxerre
Joigny
Sens
St.-Florentin
Tonnerre
Châtillon-sur-Seine
Montbard
St.-Seine-l'Abbaye
Bar-sur-Seine
Troyes
Langres
Chaumont
Joinville
Neufchâteau
Brienne-le-Château
St.-Dizier
Vitry-le-François
Bar-le-Duc
Châlons-en-Champagne
St.-Mihiel
Commercy
Toul
Nancy
Lunéville
Baccarat
St.-Dié
Mirecourt
Épinal
Vittel
Contrexéville
Remiremont
Le Thillot
Luxeuil-les-Bains
Le Val-d'Ajol
Combeaufontaine
Gray
Sarrebourg
Château-Salins
Metz
Thionville
Longwy
Longuyon
Briey
Étain
Verdun
Ste.-Menehould
Suippes
Vouziers
Rethel
Reims
Épernay
Château-Thierry
Montmirail
Sézanne
Provins
Nogent-sur-Seine
Coulommiers
Villers-Cotterêts
Soissons
Laon
Chauny
Ham
St.-Quentin
Péronne
Vervins
La Capelle
Le Cateau
Charleville-Mézières
Sedan
Bouillon
Neufchâteau
Montmédy

SLOVENSKÁ REP.
SLOVAK REP.
MAGYARORSZÁG
HUNGARY
HRVATSKA
CROATIA
BOSNA I HERCEGOVINA
BOSNIA HERZEGOVINA
SRBIJA
SERBIA
CRNA GORA
MONTENEGRO
KOSOVO
SHQIPERIA
ALBANIA
MAKEDONIJA
MACEDONIA
MARE ADRIATICO
ADRIATIC SEA
WIEN
VIENNA
BUDAPEST
BEOGRAD
BELGRADE
Bratislava
Ljubljana
Zagreb
Sarajevo
Podgorica
Tiranë
Tirana
Skopje
Priština
Košice
Miskolc
Debrecen
Oradea
Arad
Timișoara
Győr
Székesfehérvár
Kecskemét
Szeged
Pécs
Graz
Maribor
Osijek
Novi Sad
Subotica
Niš
Split
Dubrovnik
Bari
Fóggia
Táranto
Bríndisi
Banja Luka
Mostar
Zadar
Rijeka
Durrës
Shkodër
Bitola
Ohrid
Kragujevac
Nyíregyháza
Sopron
Szombathely
ANCONA
TRIESTE

Ivano-Frankivsk
Kamyanets-Podil's'kyy
Uman
Mukacheve
Chernivtsi
Mohyliv-Podil's'kyy
MOLDOVA
Satu Mare
Baia Mare
Suceava
Botoşani
Bălţi
Bistriţa
Iaşi
Chişinău
Khisinev
Tiraspol
Tighina
Cluj-Napoca
Piatra Neamţ
Târgu Mureş
Bacău
ODESA
ODESSA
Sighişoara
Alba-Iulia
ROMÂNIA
Sibiu
Braşov
Focşani
Galaţi
Brăila
Tulcea
Râmnicu Vâlcea
Piteşti
Ploieşti
Buzău
Craiova
BUCUREŞTI
BUCHAREST
Constanţa
Ruse
Pleven
Dobrich
Varna
Shumen
BULGARIYA
BULGARIA
SOFIYA
SOFIA
Plovdiv
Stara Zagora
Sliven
Burgas
Edirne
Kırklareli
ISTANBUL
İstanbul Boğazı
Marmara Denizi
Kocaeli
Sakarya
Thessaloniki
Kavala
Alexandroupoli
Thasos
Tekirdağ
0
40
80
120
160 km

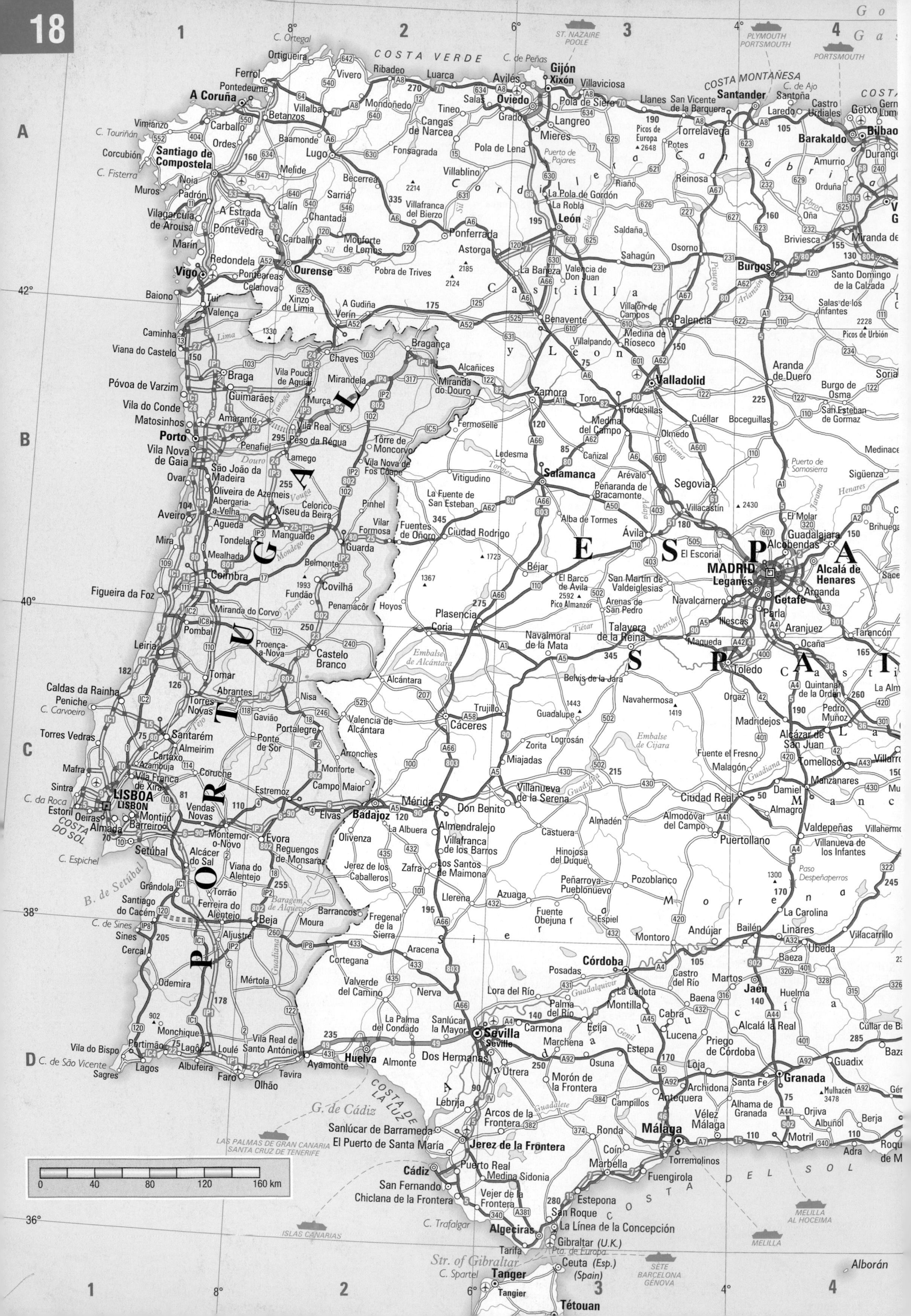

COSTA VERDE
C. Ortegal
C. de Peñas
ST. NAZAIRE POOLE
PLYMOUTH PORTSMOUTH
PORTSMOUTH
COSTA MONTAÑESA
Ortigueira
Ferrol
Vivero
Ribadeo
Luarca
Avilés
Gijón
Xixón
Villaviciosa
Pontedeume
A Coruña
Betanzos
Villalba
Mondoñedo
Tineo
Salas
Oviedo
Grado
Pola de Siero
Llanes
San Vicente de la Barquera
Santander
Laredo
Santoña
C. de Ajo
Castro Urdiales
Getxo
Bilbao
Barakaldo
Durango
Vimianzo
C. Touriñán
Carballo
Ordes
Baamonde
Cangas de Narcea
Langreo
Mieres
Picos de Europa
2648
Torrelavega
Potes
Corcubión
Santiago de Compostela
Lugo
Fonsagrada
Pola de Lena
Puerto de Pajares
Cordillera Cantábrica
Amurrio
Orduña
C. Fisterra
Melide
Villablino
Riaño
Reinosa
Muros
Noia
Padrón
Becerrea
Sarriá
Lalín
Villafranca del Bierzo
La Pola de Gordón
La Robla
Vilagarcía de Arousa
A Estrada
Chantada
León
Oña
Ebro
Pontevedra
O Carballino
Monforte de Lemos
Ponferrada
Saldaña
Briviesca
Miranda de Ebro
Marín
Astorga
Sahagún
Osorno
Redondela
Ourense
Sil
Pobra de Trives
La Bañeza
Valencia de Don Juan
Burgos
Vigo
Ponteareas
Celanova
Santo Domingo de la Calzada
Baiona
Tui
Xinzo de Limia
Castilla y León
Arlanzón
Pisuerga
Salas de los Infantes
Valença
A Gudiña
Verín
Benavente
Villalón de Campos
Palencia
Picos de Urbión
Caminha
Lima
Medina de Rioseco
Viana do Castelo
Bragança
Villalpando
Chaves
Alcañices
Aranda de Duero
Soria
Braga
Vila Pouca de Aguiar
Mirandela
Miranda do Douro
Valladolid
Póvoa de Varzim
Guimarães
Zamora
Toro
Burgo de Osma
Vila do Conde
Murça
Tordesillas
San Esteban de Gormaz
Matosinhos
Amarante
Vila Real
Medina del Campo
Cuéllar
Boceguillas
Porto
Peso da Régua
Torre de Moncorvo
Fermoselle
Olmedo
Vila Nova de Gaia
Penafiel
Douro
Lamego
Ledesma
Cañizal
Medinaceli
Ovar
São João da Madeira
Vila Nova de Foz Côa
Vitigudino
Salamanca
Arévalo
Puerto de Somosierra
Sigüenza
Oliveira de Azeméis
Peñaranda de Bracamonte
Segovia
Henares
Aveiro
Abergaria-a-Velha
Vouga
Celorico da Beira
Pinhel
La Fuente de San Esteban
Alba de Tormes
Villacastín
Águeda
Viseu
Vilar Formosa
El Molar
Brihuega
Mira
Tondela
Mangualde
Fuentes de Oñoro
Ciudad Rodrigo
Ávila
Guadalajara
Alcobendas
Mealhada
Mondego
Guarda
El Escorial
MADRID
Alcalá de Henares
Coimbra
Belmonte
1723
Béjar
Leganés
Getafe
Arganda
PORTUGAL
ESPAÑA
SPAIN
Figueira da Foz
Fundão
Covilhã
1367
El Barco de Ávila
San Martín de Valdeiglesias
Pico Almanzor
2592
Arenas de San Pedro
Navalcarnero
Miranda do Corvo
Zêzere
Penamacor
Hoyos
Plasencia
Illescas
Parla
Aranjuez
Pombal
Coria
Navalmoral de la Mata
Talavera de la Reina
Tiétar
Alberche
Maqueda
Ocaña
Tarancón
Leiria
Proença-a-Nova
Castelo Branco
Embalse de Alcántara
Toledo
Castilla-La Mancha
Tomar
Alcántara
Belvis de la Jara
Quintanar de la Orden
Caldas da Rainha
Peniche
C. Carvoeiro
Abrantes
Nisa
Trujillo
Navahermosa
Orgaz
Pedro Muñoz
Torres Novas
Tejo
Gavião
Valencia de Alcántara
Guadalupe
1443
1419
Madridejos
Torres Vedras
Santarém
Portalegre
Cáceres
Alcázar de San Juan
Almeirim
Ponte de Sor
Zorita
Logrosán
Embalse de Cijara
Fuente el Fresno
Mafra
Cartaxo
Azambuja
Arronches
Miajadas
Malagón
Tomelloso
Villarrobledo
Vila Franca de Xira
Coruche
Monforte
Guadiana
Sintra
LISBOA
LISBON
Estremoz
Campo Maior
Villanueva de la Serena
Ciudad Real
Manzanares
Daimiel
C. da Roca
Estoril
Oeiras
Montijo
Vendas Novas
Mérida
Don Benito
Almagro
Almada
Barreiro
COSTA DO SOL
Elvas
Badajoz
Almendralejo
Almadén
Almodóvar del Campo
Valdepeñas
Setúbal
Montemor-o-Novo
Évora
La Albuera
Olivenza
Villafranca de los Barros
Castuera
Puertollano
Villanueva de los Infantes
C. Espichel
Alcácer do Sal
Reguengos de Monsaraz
Jerez de los Caballeros
Zafra
Los Santos de Maimona
Hinojosa del Duque
Paso Despeñaperros
B. de Setúbal
Viana do Alentejo
Peñarroya-Pueblonuevo
Pozoblanco
Grândola
Torrão
Llerena
Azuaga
Sierra Morena
Santiago do Cacém
Ferreira do Alentejo
Barragem de Alqueva
Barrancos
Fregenal de la Sierra
Fuente Obejuna
Espiel
La Carolina
C. de Sines
Sines
Beja
Moura
Montoro
Andújar
Bailén
Linares
Villacarrillo
Cercal
Aljustrel
Aracena
Córdoba
Úbeda
Cortegana
Baeza
Odemira
Mértola
Valverde del Camino
Nerva
Posadas
Castro del Río
Martos
Jaén
Lora del Río
Guadalquivir
La Carlota
Palma del Río
Montilla
Baena
Huelma
Monchique
La Palma del Condado
Sanlúcar la Mayor
Sevilla
Seville
Carmona
Écija
Cabra
Lucena
Alcalá la Real
Cúllar de Baza
Vila do Bispo
Portimão
Lagoa
Loulé
Vila Real de Santo António
Marchena
Genil
Priego de Córdoba
Baza
C. de São Vicente
Sagres
Lagos
Albufeira
Faro
Olhão
Tavira
Ayamonte
Huelva
Almonte
Dos Hermanas
Utrera
Osuna
Estepa
Loja
Guadix
COSTA DE LA LUZ
Morón de la Frontera
Archidona
Santa Fe
Granada
Mulhacén
3478
Lebrija
Antequera
Alhama de Granada
G. de Cádiz
Arcos de la Frontera
Guadalete
Campillos
Vélez Málaga
Orjiva
Albuñol
Berja
Sanlúcar de Barrameda
Ronda
Málaga
Motril
Adra
LAS PALMAS DE GRAN CANARIA
SANTA CRUZ DE TENERIFE
El Puerto de Santa María
Jerez de la Frontera
Coín
Torremolinos
COSTA DEL SOL
Cádiz
Puerto Real
Marbella
San Fernando
Medina Sidonia
Fuengirola
Chiclana de la Frontera
Vejer de la Frontera
Estepona
San Roque
C. Trafalgar
ISLAS CANARIAS
Algeciras
La Línea de la Concepción
MELILLA AL HOCEIMA
MELILLA
Tarifa
Gibraltar (U.K.)
Pta. de Europa
Str. of Gibraltar
C. Spartel
Tanger
Tangier
Ceuta (Esp.)
(Spain)
SÈTE BARCELONA GÉNOVA
Alborán
Tétouan
0
40
80
120
160 km
42°
40°
38°
36°
8°
6°
4°
A
B
C
D
1
2
3
4

Golfe de Gascogne
Mont-de-Marsan
Montauban
Albi
Nîmes
Castets
Condom
Castelsarrasin
Lectoure
Gaillac
St.-Affrique
Remoulins
Tartas
Fleurance
Rabastens
Graulhet
Lodève
Montpellier
Lunel
Arles
Dax
St.-Sever
Grisolles
Lavaur
Salon-de-Provence
Aigues-Mortes
Martigues
CÔTE BASQUE
Aire-sur-l'Adour
Auch
L'Isle-Jourdain
Toulouse
Castres
Mazamet
Pézenas
Clermont-l'Hérault
Bayonne
Biarritz
Orthez
Pau
Mirande
St.-Pons
Béziers
Sète
Stes.-Maries-de-la-Mer
MARSEILLE
MARSEILLES
Donostia-San Sebastián
Irún
Salies-de-Béarn
Castelnaudary
Agde
CÔTE D'AMETHYSTE
Hasparren
Oloron-Ste.-Marie
Tarbes
Autérive
Lézignan-Corbières
Carcassonne
Narbonne
Golfe du Lion
Eibar
Tolosa
Mauléon-Licharre
Lannemezan
St.-Gaudens
Pamiers
Limoux
Beasain
Lourdes
Bagnères-de-Bigorre
St.-Girons
Foix
Alsasua
Cauterets
St.-Béat
Quillan
TANGER NADOR
Vitoria-Gasteiz
Pamplona
Lavelanet
Perpignan
Pyrénées
Bagnères-de-Luchon
Pico de Aneto
Ax-les-Thermes
Argelès-sur-Mer
Port-Vendres
Cerbère
Portbou
CÔTE VERMEILLE
PORTO-VECCHIO TUNIS
Ebro
Jaca
Mte. Perdido
ANDORRA
Andorra La Vella
Le Perthus
Mt. Canigou
ORAN
Logroño
Tafalla
Puigcerdà
Ribes de Freser
Figueras
C. de Creus
La Seu d'Urgell
Banyoles
G. de Roses
Calahorra
Ayerbe
Ripoll
Olot
Alfaro
Torrecilla en Cameros
Huesca
Tremp
Berga
Girona
42°
ALGER BEJAIA SKIKDA ANNABA
Tudela
Barbastro
Solsona
Gironella
Palafrugell
Tarazona
Palamós
Monzón
Sallent
Vic
San Felíu de Guíxols
Balaguer
Manresa
Granollers
Tossa
Lloret de Mar
Zaragoza
Cervera
Terrassa
Blanes
COSTA BRAVA
Fraga
Lleida
Tàrrega
Sabadell
Mataró
CALELLA
Igualada
Badalona
Almazán
La Almunia de Doña Godina
Vilafranca del Penedès
Cariñena
Montblanc
BARCELONA
Calatayud
Valls
Sitges
El Prat de Llobregat
Alhama de Aragón
Belchite
Reus
Arcos de Jalón
Hijar
Caspe
Falset
Vilanova i la Geltrú
B
Daroca
Alcañiz
Tarragona
GÉNOVA CIVITAVÉCCHIA TANGER LIVORNA
Alcolea del Pinar
Gandesa
Calamocha
G. de Sant Jordi
COSTA DORADA
Montalbán
Tortosa
C. Tortosa
Monreal del Campo
Morella
Sant Mateu
Vinarós
Benicarló
Teruel
Albocàcer
Alcalá de Xivert
Islas Baleares
Menorca
Minorca
Fornells
40°
Cuenca
Cañete
COSTA DEL AZAHAR
C. de Formentor
Ciudadela de Menorca
Maó
Onda
Castelló de la Plana
Is. Columbretes
Sóller
Alcúdia
Vila-real de los Infantes
Chelva
La Vall de Uxió
Palma de Mallorca
Inca
Manacor
Olivares
Liria
Sagunt
Golfo de Valencia
Calviá
Llucmajor
Mallorca
Majorca
Utiel
Chiva
San Clemente
Motilla del Palancar
Minglanilla
Requena
Valencia
Torrent
B. de Palma
Casas Ibáñez
L'Albufera
Sueca
Cabrera
C
Algemesí
Cullera
Eivissa
La Roda
Xúquer
Alberic
Alcira
Sant Antoni de Portmany
Ibiza
Albacete
Gandía
Chinchilla de Monte Aragón
Xátiva
Denia
Almansa
Alcoy
Formentera
Robledo
Villena
C. de la Nao
Tobarra
Yecla
Altea
Alcaraz
Hellín
Elda
Benidorm
Balearic Islands
Jumilla
Villajoyosa
Yeste
Elche de la Sierra
Novelda
COSTA BLANCA
Caravaca de la Cruz
Cieza
Alicante
Elche
38°
Mula
Orihuela
ALGER
Alcantarilla
Murcia
Torrevieja
Totana
San Pedro del Pinatar
San Javier
MARSEILLE ALICANTE
Huéscar
Vélez Rubio
Cartagena
Mar Menor
Lorca
La Unión
C. de Palos
Huércal Overa
Aguilas
MAR MEDITERRANEO
Cuevas del Almanzora
Vera
D
Sorbas
Dellys
Azeffoun
Níjar
Bordj el Kiffan
C. Matifou
Bordj Menaiel
Azazga
Almería
Aïn Benian
ALGER
ALGIERS
Thenia
Tizi-Ouzou
Koléa
Bou Ismael
El Arba
Cherchell
Blida
Boufarik
C. de Gata
C. Ténès
Ténès
Damous
Gouraya
MARSEILLE
C. Kramis
Beni-Haoua
Bouïra
Miliana
Médéa
Sour el Ghozlane
Djendel
Ech Cheliff
Khemis Miliana
Berrouaghia
MELILLA
36°
Mansourah
Aïn Tédelès
O. Chéliff
Mostaganem
Oued Rhiou
Theniet el Had
Ksar el Boukhari
Sidi-Aïssa
Arzew
4
5
6
7
Oran
Relizane
Tissemsilt
Aïn el Hadjel
Chabounia
Mohammadia

A
B
C
D
E
1
2
3
4
5
42°
40°
38°
8°
10°
12°
14°
Pinerolo
Savigliano
Saluzzo
Viso
3841
Embrun
Cúneo
Mondovì
Fossano
Bra
Asti
Alba
Alessándria
Tortona
Voghera
Piacenza
Fidenza
Novi Lígure
Ceva
Voltri
Génova
Genoa
Varazze
Savona
Rapallo
Chiavari
Sestri Levante
Borgo Val di Taro
Pontrémoli
La Spézia
Carrara
Massa
Pietrasanta
Viaréggio
Lucca
Pisa
Livorno
Parma
Réggio nell'Emília
Módena
Guastalla
Carpi
Mirándola
Ferrara
Portomaggiore
Comacchio
Argenta
Bologna
Sassuolo
Pavullo nel Frignano
Mte. Cimone
2165
Pianoro
Imola
Faenza
Lugo
Ravenna
Forlì
Cesena
Cérvia
Cesenático
Rímini
Riccione
Pésaro
Fano
San Marino
SAN MARINO
Urbino
Sansepolcro
Città di Castello
Senigállia
Falconara Maríttima
Ancona
Fossombrone
Cagli
Jesi
Loreto
Macerata
Civitanova Marche
Fermo
Sarnano
Áscoli Piceno
San Benedetto del
Giulianova
Téramo
Mte. Vettore
2476
Acquasanta Terme
Montesilvano
Pescara
Gran Sasso d'Italia
2912
L'Áquila
Chieti
Pópoli
Mte. Amaro
2793
Sulmona
Avezzano
Agnone
Sora
Isérnia
Venafro
Cassino
Pistóia
Prato
Firenze
Florence
Scandicci
Pontedera
Montevarchi
Poggibonsi
Volterra
Siena
Arezzo
Cortona
Gúbbio
Fabriano
Gualdo Tadino
Perúgia
Assisi
Foligno
Spoleto
Magione
Chiusi
L. Trasimeno
Terni
Narni
Rieti
Orvieto
L. di Bolsena
Montefiascone
Viterbo
Vetralla
Acquapendente
Mte. Amiata
1738
Rosignano Maríttimo
Cécina
Campíglia Maríttima
Roccastrada
Piombino
Follónica
Grosseto
Orbetello
Porto Santo Stéfano
Mte. Argentário
Tarquínia
Civitavécchia
Santa Marinella
L. di Bracciano
CITTÀ DEL VATICANO
VATICAN CITY
ROMA
ROME
Tívoli
Guidónia-Montecélio
Lido di Óstia
Pomézia
Aprília
Velletri
Frosinone
Alatri
Latina
Ánzio
Terracina
Fondi
Gaeta
Fórmia
Mondragone
Cápua
Caserta
Marcianise
Aversa
Pozzuoli
NÁPOLI
NAPLES
Castellammare di Stábia
Sorrento
Capri
Íschia
Ventotene
Ísole Ponziane
G. di Gaeta
Capraia
Portoferráio
Elba
Pianosa
Giglio
Montecristo
Rovinj
Pula
Rt. Kamenjak
Cres
Lošinj
Kvarner
Monaco
MONACO
Cagnes-sur-Mer
Grasse
Nice
Antibes
Cannes
St.-Raphaël
Ste.-Maxime
St.-Tropez
Cavalaire-sur-Mer
CÔTE D'AZUR
CÔTE DE L'ESTEREL
Menton
Monte-Carlo
San Remo
Impéria
Sospel
Isola
Limone Piemonte
Col di Tenda
1870
Golfo di Génova
MARE LIGURE
LIGURIAN SEA
MARE ADRIATICO
C. Corse
Bastia
Calvi
L'Ile-Rousse
Mte. Cinto
2710
Corte
Corse
Corsica
Ajaccio
Aléria
Propriano
Porto-Vecchio
Bonifacio
Maddalena
Asinara
Golfo dell' Asinara
C. Falcone
Porto Tórres
Sássari
Alghero
Témpio Pausánia
Palau
Golfo Aranci
Ólbia
Ozieri
Budoni
Siniscóla
C. Comino
Orosei
Bosa
Macomer
Núoro
Dorgali
Sardegna
Sardinia
Sorgono
Mti. del Gennargentu
1834
C. di Monte Santu
Oristano
G. di Oristano
Terralba
Gúspini
Nurallao
Árbatax
Lanusei
Sanluri
Senorbì
Villaputzu
Iglésias
Sestu
Quartu Sant'Élena
Cágliari
San Pietro
Portoscuso
Carbónia
Sant'Antíoco
Giba
Teulada
Pula
G. di Cágliari
C. Carbonara
G. di Pálmas
C. Spartivento
MARE TIRRENO
TYRRHENIAN SEA
MEDITERRANEAN SEA
Ústica
Ísole Égadi
Favignana
C. San Vito
Érice
Trápani
Paceco
Castellammare del Golfo
Palermo
Bagheria
Términi Imerese
Cefalù
Partinico
Alcamo
Calatafimi
Corleone
Castelbuono
Marsala
Castelvetrano
Mazara del Vallo
Menfi
Lercara Friddi
Mussomeli
Sciacca
Caltanissetta
Enna
Raffadali
Porto Empédocle
Agrigento
Canicattì
Favara
Piazza Armerina
Licata
Gela
Vittória
Caltagirone
Sicilia
Pantelleria
Is. de la Galite
C. Blanc
C. Serrat
Bizerte
Menzel-Bourguiba
Mateur
Golfe de Tunis
Ra's at Tib
C. Rosa
Annaba
El Kala
Tabarka
Manouba
Ariana
La Marsa
Tébourba
Tunis
Béja
Bou Salem
Bardo
Ben Arous
Kelibia
Ra's Muṣṭafá
Menzel-Temime
Korba
Ghardimaou
BARCELONA TANGER
PORTO TORRES ÓLBIA ÁRBATAX TUNIS
BARCELONA TANGER
BARCELONA TRAPANI TUNIS
MARSEILLE
PALERMO
GÉNOVA
GÉNOVA
CATÁNIA
GÉNOVA SALERNO CIVITAVÉCCHIA TUNIS
CIVITAVÉCCHIA
GÉNOVA PALERMO SALERNO
MARSEILLE
MARSEILLE
LINOSA LAMPEDUSA
TRIESTE

BOSNA I
BOSNIA
HERCEGOVINA
HERZEGOVINA
SRBIJA
SERBIA
CRNA GORA
MONTENEGRO
KOSOVO
SHQIPËRIA
ALBANIA
MAKEDONIJA
MACEDONIA
ADRIATICO
ADRIATIC SEA
Jadransko more
MARE IONIO
IONIO PELAGOS
IONIAN SEA
Ionioi Nisoi
Ionian Islands
Golfo di Táranto
G. di Sant' Eufémia
G. di Squillace
Str. di Messina
Kiparissiakos Kolpos
Isole Eólie
Senj
Otočac
Jablanac
Karlobag
Pag
Gospić
Pаćane
Gračac
Zadar
Ugljan
Dugi Otok
Obrovac
Benkovac
Biograd
Pašman
Knin
Drniš
Šibenik
Troglav
Sinj
Split
Trogir
Omiš
Šolta
Brač
Makarska
Hvar
Vrgorac
Pelješac
Vis
Korčula
Lastovo
Mljet
Palagruža
Bosanski Novi
Bosanska Krupa
Bihać
Prijedor
Sanski Most
Drvar
Bosanska Gradiška
Banja Luka
Derventa
Brod
Doboj
Tuzla
Žepče
Jajce
Travnik
Donji Vakuf
Bugojno
Zenica
Prozor
Sarajevo
Sokolac
Jablanica
Konjic
Mostar
Čapljina
Stolac
Metković
Bileća
Slano
Trebinje
Dubrovnik
Herceg-Novi
Zvornik
Vlasenica
Srebrenica
Han Pijesak
Rogatica
Goražde
Foča
Višegrad
Brčko
Bijeljina
Sremska Mitrovica
Šabac
Loznica
Valjevo
Zemun
Pančevo
Crkva
BEOGRAD
BELGRADE
Smederevo
Požarevac
Berzasca
Negotin
Bor
Zaječar
Kragujevac
Jagodina
Užice
Čačak
Kraljevo
Kruševac
Priboj
Prijepolje
Sjenica
Novi Pazar
Prokuplje
Niš
Leskovac
Kosovska Mitrovica
Priština
Vranje
Peć
Đakovica
Uroševac
Prizren
Pljevlja
Žabljak
Durmitor
Nikšić
Kolašin
Andrijevica
Danilovgrad
Podgorica
Cetinje
Risan
Kotor
Budva
Bar
Ulcinj
Skadarsko Jezero
Shkodër
Kukës
Pukë
Lezhë
Peshkopi
Durrës
Tiranë
Tirana
Kavajë
Elbasan
Lushnjë
Fier
Berat
Patos
Tomorit
Vlorë
Sazanit
Korçë
Gjirokastër
Himarë
Delvinë
Sarandë
Mathraki
Kumanovo
Skopje
Tetovo
Kočani
Štip
Veles
Solunska Glava
Debar
Prilep
Bitola
Ohrid
Ohridsko Jezero
Prespansko Jezero
Kyustendil
Edessa
Florina
Ptolemaida
Kastoria
Kozani
Grevena
Smolikas
Ioannina
Kalambaka
Trikala
Kerkyra
Corfu
Igoumenitsa
Parga
Paxi
Preveza
Vonitsa
Arta
Amfilochia
Agrinio
Lefkada
Ithaki
Kefalonia
Cephalonia
Sami
Argostoli
Mesologi
Nafpaktos
Patra
Patras
Erimanthos
Amaliada
Pirgos
Zakynthos
Zante
Kiparissia
Filiatra
Gargaliani
Pilos
Vasto
Térmoli
San Severo
Sannicandro Gargánico
Vieste
Apricena
Monte Sant' Ángelo
Gargano
Manfredónia
Campobasso
Lucera
Fóggia
Cerignola
Barletta
Trani
Bisceglie
Molfetta
Andria
Corato
Bitonto
Bari
Mola di Bari
Monópoli
Putignano
Fasano
Ostuni
Martina Franca
Gravina in Púglia
Altamura
Benevento
Ariano Irpino
Lavello
Rionero in Vúlture
Avellino
Pompei
Potenza
Salerno
Eboli
Battipaglia
G. di Salerno
Agrópoli
Castellabate
Vallo della Lucánia
Pisciotta
Polla
Sala Consilina
Matera
Ginosa
Montescaglioso
Pisticci
Táranto
Bríndisi
Francavilla Fontana
Mesagne
Squinzano
Lecce
Mandúria
Galatina
Otranto
Nardò
Gallípoli
Máglie
C. d' Otranto
Casarano
Gagliano del Capo
C. Santa Maria di Leuca
Policoro
Sapri
Lauria
Maratea
Práia a Mare
Castrovillari
Trebisacce
Rossano
Corigliano Cálabro
Cariati
Cirò Marina
Cetraro
Páola
Cosenza
Rende
San Giovanni in Fiore
Crotone
Amantea
Nicastro
Cutro
C. Rizzuto
Tiriolo
Sambiase
Catanzaro
Máida
Vibo Valéntia
Tropea
Soverato
Rosarno
Palmi
Caulónia
Taurianova
Siderno
Locri
Scilla
Réggio di Calábria
Mélito di Porto Salvo
C. Spartivento
Strómboli
Salina
Lípari
Vulcano
Milazzo
Barcellona Pozzo di Gotto
Messina
Tortorici
Patti
Taormina
Etna
Giarre
Acireale
Adrano
Paternò
Catánia
Scordia
Lentini
Augusta
Sortino
Siracusa
Ragusa
Módica
Ávola
Ispica
Pachino
C. Passero
KERKYRA IGOUMENITSA PATRA
TRIESTE
ANCONA VENEZIA TRIESTE DUBROVNIK
PATRA
PALERMO TUNIS MESSINA
SALERNO
NAPOLI
16°
18°
20°
0 40 80 120 160 km

16
22
34

MAKEDONIJA
MACEDONIA
GREECE
ELLAS
Skopje
Kumanovo
Kyustendil
Tetovo
Kočani
Veles
Štip
Strumica
Prilep
Bitola
Ohrid
Prespansko Jezero
Valandovo
Gevgelija
Dupnitsa
Samokov
Blagoevgrad
Sandanski
Gotse Delchev
Petrich
Pazardzhik
Plovdiv
Asenovgrad
Stara Zagora
Dimitrovgrad
Khaskovo
Kharmanli
Kŭrdzhali
Smolyan
Rudozem
Zlatograd
Momchilgrad
Svilengrad
Yambol
Burgas
Sozopol
Pomorie
Sredets
Malko Tŭrnovo
Bŭlgari
Rezovo
Rhodopi Planina
Maritsa
Tundzha
Arda
Edirne
Kırklareli
Pınarhisar
Vize
Demirköy
İğneada
Babaeski
Lüleburgaz
Saray
Çerkezköy
Çorlu
Silivri
Büyükçekmece
Hayrabolu
Muratlı
Uzunköprü
Tekirdağ
Malkara
Keşan
İpsala
Enez
Şarköy
Marmara
Marmara Denizi
Saros Körfezi
Gelibolu
Eceabat
Lapseki
Çanakkale
Biga
Karabiga
Erdek
Bandırma
Gönen
Çan
Yenice
Bayramiç
Ezine
Ayvacık
Edremit
Edremit Körfezi
Burhaniye
Ayvalık
Balya
Susurluk
Balıkesir
Bergama
Soma
Kınık
Akhisar
Bigadiç
Aliağa
Foça
Menemen
Manisa
Turgutlu
Salihli
İZMIR
Karaburun
Çeşme
Urla
Seferihisar
Torbalı
Bayındır
Ödemiş
Tire
Selçuk
Kuşadası
Aydın
Nazilli
Söke
Çine
Milas
Yatağan
Muğla
Bodrum
Güllük
Ören
Kerme Körfezi
Datça
Yenihisar
Orestiada
Didimoticho
Soufli
Alexandroupoli
Komotini
Sapes
Xanthi
Drama
Kavala
Serres
Sidirokastro
Nigrita
Kilkis
Amfipoli
Edessa
Florina
Giannitsa
Ptolemaida
Veria
Kastoria
Kozani
Grevena
Smolikas
Thessaloniki
Salonica
Katerini
Litochoro
Olymbos
Poligiros
Nea Moudania
Ierissos
Athos
Akra Pines
Akra Paliouri
Thessaloniki Kolpos
Orfanos Kolpos
Kasandra Kolpos
Aghiou Orous Kolpos
Tirnavos
Larisa
Ossa
Aghia
Kalambaka
Trikala
Karditsa
Velestino
Volos
Farsala
Pagastikos Kolpos
Domokos
Lamia
Arta
Amfilochia
Agrinio
Mesologi
Nafpaktos
Patra
Egio
Korinthiakos Kolpos
Oros Giona
Parnassos
Livadia
Thiva
Halkida
Istiea
Mandoudi
Kimi
Dirfis
Evia
Karistos
Kavo Doro
Aharnes
ATHINA
ATHENS
Pireas
Megara
Salamina
Saronikos
Lavrio
Kiato
Korinthos
Killini
Erimanthos
Amaliada
Pirgos
Peloponnisos
Tripoli
Argos
Nafplio
Nea Epidavros
Galatas
Kranidi
Argolikos Kolpos
Kiparissia
Filiatra
Gargaliani
Pilos
Methoni
Messini
Kalamata
Sparti
Githio
Monemvasia
Messiniakos Kolpos
Lakonikos Kolpos
Akra Tenaro
Akra Maleas
Kythira
Cerigo
Antikythira
Thasos
Samothraki
Gökçeada
Limnos
Moudros
Bozcaada
Baba Burnu
Aghios Efstratios
Vories Sporades
North Sporades
Skiathos
Skopelos
Skiros
Skyros
Lesbos
Mitilini
Psara
Hios
Chios
Andros
Tinos
Mykonos
Ikaria
Samos
Fourni
Patmos
Kea
Kithnos
Syros
Serifos
Sifnos
Paros
Naxos
Milos
Sikinos
Ios
Thira
Santorini
Amorgos
Astipalea
Kalimnos
Kos
Timos
Simi
Rhodes
Lindos
Karpathos
Kasos
Hydra
EGEO PELAGOS
AEGEAN SEA
Kiklades
Cyclades
Dodekanisa
Dodecanese
VENEZIA
BRINDISI TRIESTE
Akra Spatha
Kolpos Chanion
Ormos Almyrou
Kastelli
Platanos
Chania
Lekva Ori
Paleochora
Chora Sfakion
Rethimno
Idi Oros
Timbaki
Akra Lithino
Iraklio
Dikti Oros
Kolpos Merabello
Akra Sideros
Sitia
Ierapetra
Gavdos
Kriti

5
6
7
8
30°
32°
34°
36°
38°
40°
A
B
C
D
TURKEY
CYPRUS
ISTANBUL
ANKARA
İstanbul Boğazı
SINOP
ISTANBUL
HAIFA
Sinop
İnce Burun
Kerempe Burnu
Bafra Burnu
Çatalzeytin
Abana
İnebolu
Cide
Kurucaşile
Ayancık
Gerze
Bafra
Alaçam
Küre
Küre Dağları
Devrekâni
Taşköprü
Gökırmak
Boyabat
Durağan
Samsun
Amasra
Bartin
Kilimli
Zonguldak
Kozlu
Çaycuma
Daday
Kastamonu
Ereğli
Devrek
Safranbolu
Karabük
Araç
Kargı
Kızıl Irmak
Vezirköprü
Kavak
Havza
Ladik
Suluova
Merzifon
Gümüşhaciköy
Osmancık
Tosya
Ilgaz
Çerkeş
Kurşunlu
Devrez
Çankırı
İskilip
Amasya
Yeşilırmak
Turhal
Mecitözü
Çorum
Zile
Sarıyer
Beykoz
Şile
Çatalca
Kandıra
Karasu
Akçakoca
Düzce
Kocaeli
İzmit
Sakarya
Hendek
Kartal
Gebze
Yalova
Gölcük
Sapanca
Akyazı
Bolu
Gerede
Orhangazi
Gemlik
Mudanya
Bursa
İznik
İznik Gölü
Geyve
Göynük
Mudurnu
Seben
Köroğlu Dağları
Kızılcahamam
Çubuk
Kızılırmak
Sungurlu
Alaca
Boğazkale
Yozgat
Sorgun
Akdağmadeni
Ulubat Gölü
Uludağ
İnegöl
Yenişehir
Gölpazarı
Nallıhan
Beypazarı
Ayaş
Sincan
Bilecik
Söğüt
Kemalpaşa
Orhaneli
Domaniç
Bozüyük
Eskişehir
Sarıyar Barajı
Mihalıççık
Gölbaşı
Elmadağ
Kırıkkale
Kalecik
Delice
Keskin
Alpu
Polatlı
Sivrihisar
Bâlâ
Yerköy
Sarıkaya
Çayıralan
Tavşanlı
Dursunbey
Kütahya
Emet
Seyitgazi
Çifteler
Haymana
Kaman
Kırşehir
Boğazlıyan
Kırka
Sakarya
Yenice
Hirfanlı Barajı
Mucur
Kayseri
Talas
Hacılar
Simav
Demirci
Gediz
Altıntaş
Emirdağ
Sülüklü
Kulu
Şereflikoçhisar
Hacıbektaş
Gülşehir
Ortaköy
Nevşehir
Tomarza
Afyonkarahisar
Bolvadin
Yunak
Eber Gölü
Tuz Gölü
Cihanbeyli
Derinkuyu
Develi
Kula
Uşak
Banaz
Şuhut
Çay
Akşehir Gölü
Aksaray
Yeşilhisar
Bakırdağı
Alaşehir
Ulubey
Sandıklı
Akşehir
Ilgın
Sarayönü
Kadınhanı
Gölcük
Yahyalı
Eşme
Sarıgöl
Çivril
Yalvaç
Obruk
Buldan
Çal
Senirkent
Gelendost
Eğridir Gölü
Dinar
Uluborlu
Eğridir
Bor
Niğde
Menderes
Sarayköy
Karacasu
Denizli
Çardak
Acıgöl
Burdur Gölü
Burdur
Isparta
Ağlasun
Konya
Çumra
Karapınar
Ulukışla
Kozan
Beyşehir Gölü
Beyşehir
Ereğli
Pozanti
Karaisali
İmamoğlu
Tavas
Kızılhisar
Yeşilova
Bucak
Akören
Kale
Boz Dağ
Tefenni
Sütçüler
Seydişehir
Suğla Gölü
Ayrancı
Karaman
Seyhan Barajı
Ceyhan
Bozkır
Aksu
Dalaman
Köyceğiz
Çameli
Korkuteli
Hadım
Göksu
Toros Dağları
Tarsus
Adana
Yumurtalık
Seyhan
Serik
İçel
Ortaca
Dalaman
Elmalı
Ak Dağ
Antalya
Manavgat
Ermenak
Mut
Tuzla
Karataş
Karataş Burnu
Erdemli
Fethiye
Kemer
Alanya
Silifke
Antalya Körfezi
Kumluca
Gülnar
Taşucu
İncekum Burnu
Kalkan
Kaş
Finike
Gazipaşa
Anamur
Gelidonya Burnu
Megiste
Anamur Burnu
C. Apostolos Andreas
Yialousa
Kyrenia
Nicosia
Morphou
Famagusta
Polis
Olympus
Larnaca
Paphos
Limassol
0
40
80
120
160 km

Key to road map pages

● **Florence** *Firenze*	City plan	97	**Map pages** at 1:750000
□ **İstanbul**	City approach map	182	**Map pages** at 1:1 500000
■ **Milan** *Milano*	City plan and approach map See pages 201–228 for city plans and approach maps		

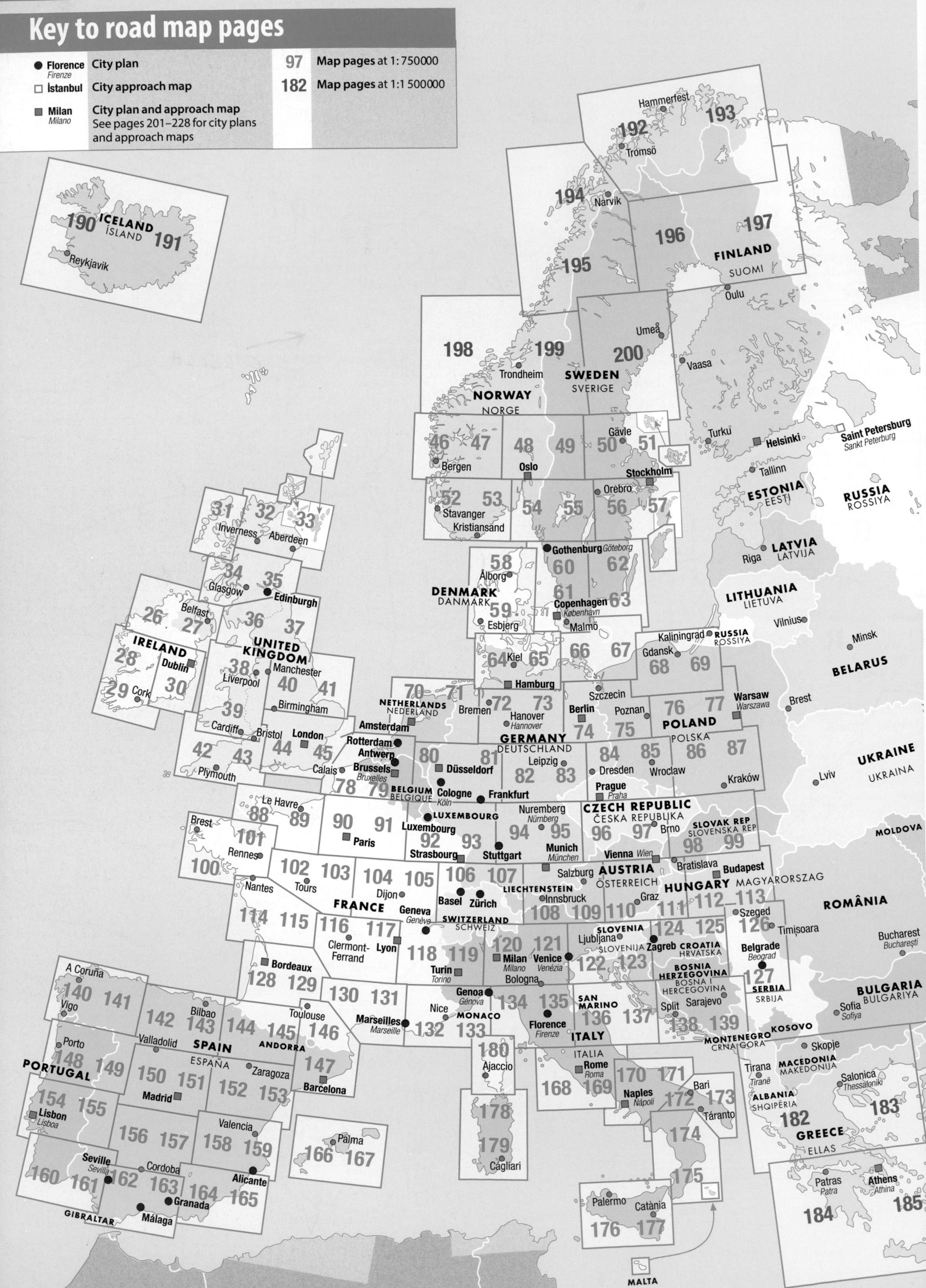

Distance table

Dublin ▶ Göteborg = 477 km

	Dublin	Edinburgh	Frankfurt	Göteborg	Hamburg
Dublin					
Edinburgh	548				
Frankfurt	726	346			
Göteborg	575	1123	1301		
Hamburg	1342	477	176	1067	
	760	477	1486	485	582

Distances shown in blue involve at least one ferry journey

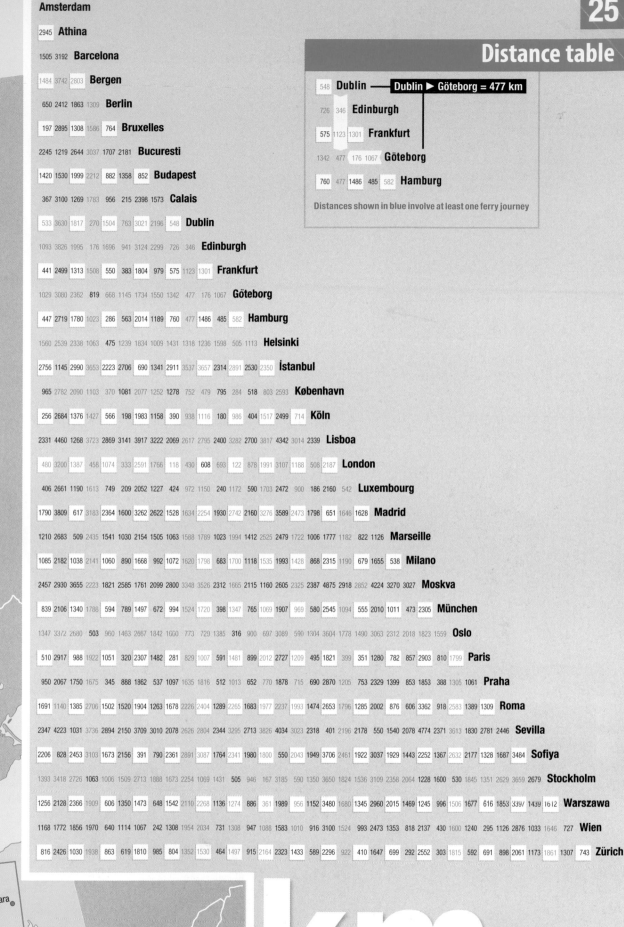

City	Amsterdam	Athina	Barcelona	Bergen	Berlin	Bruxelles	Bucuresti	Budapest	Calais	Dublin	Edinburgh	Frankfurt	Göteborg	Hamburg	Helsinki	İstanbul	København	Köln	Lisboa	London	Luxembourg	Madrid	Marseille	Milano	Moskva	München	Oslo	Paris	Praha	Roma	Sevilla	Sofiya	Stockholm	Warszawa	Wien
Amsterdam																																			
Athina	2945																																		
Barcelona	1505	3192																																	
Bergen	1484	3742	2803																																
Berlin	650	2412	1863	1309																															
Bruxelles	197	2895	1308	1586	764																														
Bucuresti	2245	1219	2644	3037	1707	2181																													
Budapest	1420	1530	1999	2212	882	1358	852																												
Calais	367	3100	1269	1783	956	215	2398	1573																											
Dublin	533	3630	1817	270	1504	763	3021	2196	548																										
Edinburgh	1093	3826	1995	176	1696	941	3124	2299	726	346																									
Frankfurt	441	2499	1313	1508	550	383	1804	979	575	1123	1301																								
Göteborg	1029	3080	2362	819	668	1145	1734	1550	1342	477	176	1067																							
Hamburg	447	2719	1780	1023	286	563	2014	1189	760	477	1486	485	582																						
Helsinki	1560	2539	2338	1063	475	1239	1834	1009	1431	1318	1236	1598	505	1113																					
İstanbul	2756	1145	2990	3653	2223	2706	690	1341	2911	3537	3657	2314	2891	2530	2350																				
København	965	2782	2090	1103	370	1081	2077	1252	1278	752	479	795	284	518	803	2593																			
Köln	256	2684	1376	1427	566	198	1983	1158	390	938	1116	180	986	404	1517	2499	714																		
Lisboa	2331	4460	1268	3723	2869	3141	3917	3222	2069	2617	2795	2400	3282	2700	3817	4342	3014	2339																	
London	480	3200	1387	458	1074	333	2591	1766	118	430	608	693	122	878	1991	3107	1188	508	2187																
Luxembourg	406	2661	1190	1613	749	209	2052	1227	424	972	1150	240	1172	590	1703	2472	900	186	2160	542															
Madrid	1790	3809	617	3183	2364	1600	3262	2622	1528	1634	2254	1930	2742	2160	3276	3589	2473	1798	651	1646	1628														
Marseille	1210	2683	509	2435	1541	1030	2154	1505	1063	1588	1789	1023	1994	1412	2525	2479	1722	1006	1777	1182	822	1126													
Milano	1085	2182	1038	2141	1060	890	1668	992	1072	1620	1798	683	1700	1118	1535	1993	1428	868	2315	1190	679	1655	538												
Moskva	2457	2930	3655	2223	1821	2585	1761	2099	2800	3348	3526	2312	1665	2115	1160	2605	2325	2387	4875	2918	2852	4224	3270	3027											
München	839	2106	1340	1788	594	789	1497	672	994	1524	1720	398	1347	765	1069	1907	969	580	2545	1094	555	2010	1011	473	2305										
Oslo	1347	3372	2680	503	960	1463	2667	1842	1660	773	729	1385	316	900	697	3089	590	1304	3604	1778	1490	3063	2312	2018	1823	1559									
Paris	510	2917	988	1922	1051	320	2307	1482	281	829	1007	591	1481	899	2012	2727	1209	495	1821	399	351	1280	782	857	2903	810	1799								
Praha	950	2067	1750	1675	345	888	1362	537	1097	1635	1816	512	1013	652	770	1878	715	690	2870	1205	753	2329	1399	853	1853	388	1305	1061							
Roma	1691	1140	1385	2706	1502	1520	1904	1263	1678	2226	2404	1289	2265	1683	1977	2237	1993	1474	2653	1796	1285	2002	876	606	3362	918	2583	1389	1309						
Sevilla	2347	4223	1031	3736	2894	2150	3709	3010	2078	2626	2804	2344	3295	2713	3826	4034	3023	2318	401	2196	2178	550	1540	2078	4774	2371	3613	1830	2781	2446					
Sofiya	2206	828	2453	3103	1673	2156	391	790	2361	2891	3087	1764	2341	1980	1800	550	2043	1949	3706	2461	1922	3037	1929	1443	2252	1367	2632	2177	1328	1687	3484				
Stockholm	1393	3418	2726	1063	1006	1509	2713	1888	1673	2254	1069	1431	505	946	167	3185	590	1350	3650	1824	1536	3109	2358	2064	1228	1600	530	1845	1351	2629	3659	2679			
Warszawa	1256	2128	2366	1909	606	1350	1473	648	1542	2110	2268	1136	1274	886	361	1989	956	1152	3480	1680	1345	2960	2015	1469	1245	996	1506	1677	616	1853	3397	1439	1612		
Wien	1168	1772	1856	1970	640	1114	1067	242	1308	1954	2034	731	1308	947	1088	1583	1010	916	3100	1524	993	2473	1353	818	2137	430	1600	1240	295	1126	2876	1033	1646	727	
Zürich	816	2426	1030	1938	863	619	1810	985	804	1352	1530	464	1497	915	2164	2323	1433	589	2296	922	410	1647	699	292	2552	303	1815	592	691	898	2061	1173	1861	1307	743

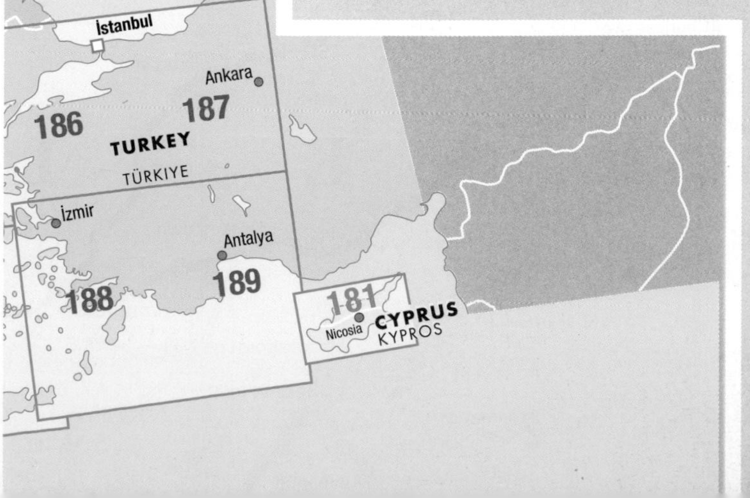

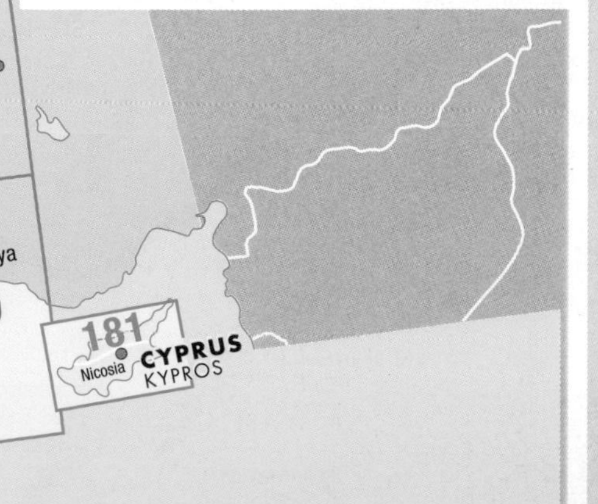

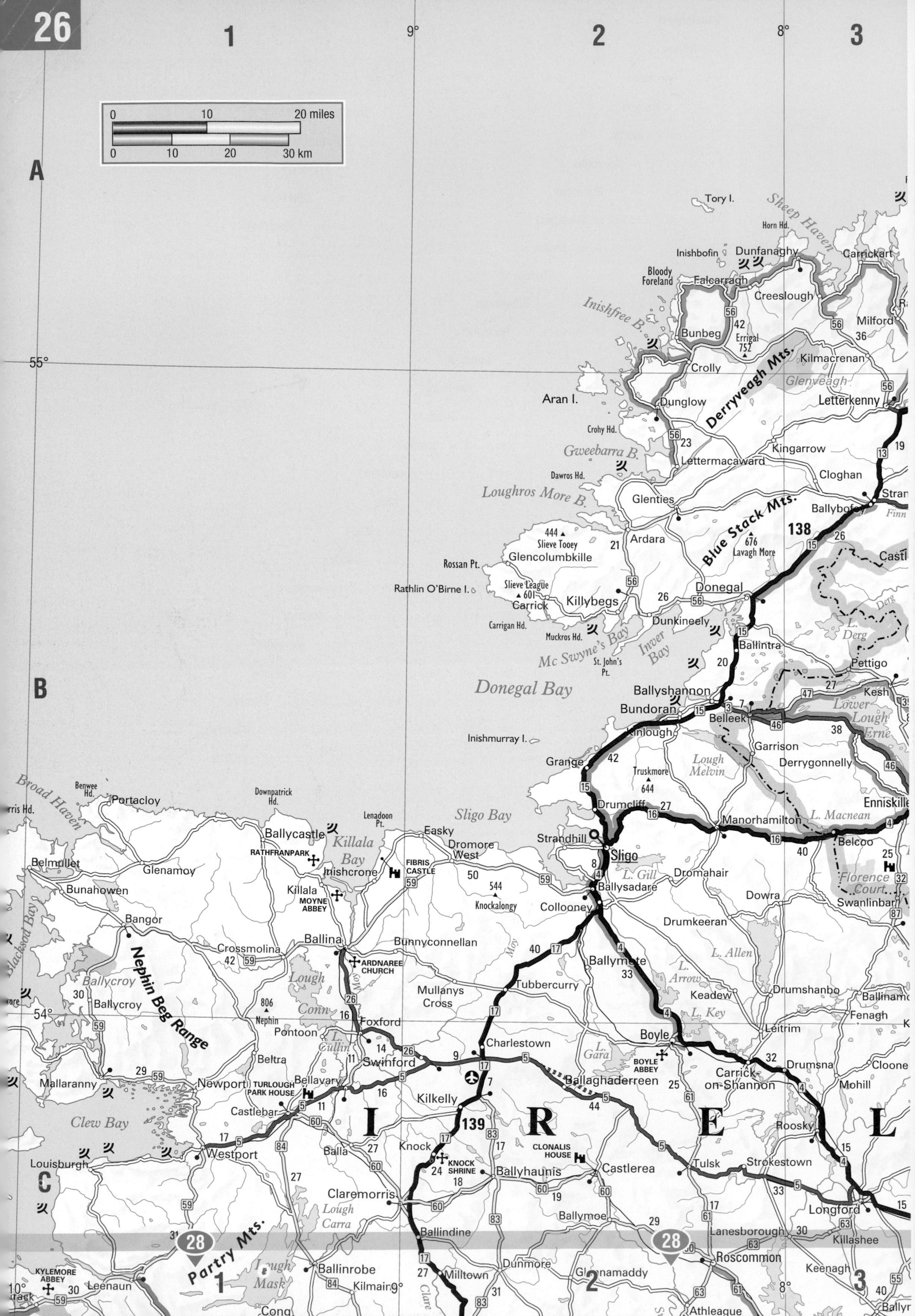

1
2
3
A
B
C
9°
8°
55°
54°
10°
0 10 20 miles
0 10 20 30 km
Tory I.
Sheep Haven
Horn Hd.
Inishbofin
Dunfanaghy
Carrickart
Bloody Foreland
Falcarragh
Creeslough
Inishfree B.
Bunbeg
Errigal 752
Milford
Derryveagh Mts.
Kilmacrenan
Crolly
Glenveagh
Aran I.
Dunglow
Letterkenny
Crohy Hd.
Gweebarra B.
Lettermacaward
Kingarrow
Dawros Hd.
Cloghan
Loughros More B.
Glenties
Blue Stack Mts.
Ballybofey
Finn
Slieve Tooey
Ardara
Lavagh More
Rossan Pt.
Glencolumbkille
Slieve League
Rathlin O'Birne I.
Carrick
Killybegs
Donegal
Carrigan Hd.
Muckros Hd.
Dunkineely
Mc Swyne's Bay
Inver Bay
St. John's Pt.
Ballintra
L. Derg
Pettigo
Donegal Bay
Ballyshannon
Kesh
Bundoran
Belleek
Lower Lough Erne
Inishmurray I.
Kinlough
Garrison
Grange
Truskmore
Lough Melvin
Derrygonnelly
Broad Haven
Benwee Hd.
Portacloy
Downpatrick Hd.
Lenadoon Pt.
Sligo Bay
Drumcliff
Enniskillen
Manorhamilton
L. Macnean
Ballycastle
Killala Bay
Easky
Strandhill
Dromore West
Belcoo
Belmullet
Glenamoy
Rathfranpark
Inishcrone
Fibris Castle
Sligo
L. Gill
Dromahair
Florence Court
Bunahowen
Killala
Moyne Abbey
Knockalongy
Ballysadare
Collooney
Dowra
Swanlinbar
Blacksod Bay
Bangor
Drumkeeran
Nephin Beg Range
Crossmolina
Ballina
Bunnyconnellan
Ardnaree Church
L. Allen
Ballycroy
Lough Conn
Moy
Ballymote
Tubbercurry
L. Arrow
Mullanys Cross
Keadew
Drumshanbo
Ballycroy
Nephin
Foxford
L. Key
Fenagh
Pontoon
L. Cullin
Boyle
Leitrim
Beltra
Charlestown
Swinford
L. Gara
Boyle Abbey
Carrick-on-Shannon
Drumsna
Cloone
Mallaranny
Newport
Turlough Park House
Bellavary
Ballaghaderreen
Mohill
Castlebar
Kilkelly
Clew Bay
I R E L
Rooskey
Westport
Knock
Clonalis House
Louisburgh
Knock Shrine
Ballyhaunis
Castlerea
Tulsk
Strokestown
Balla
Claremorris
Lough Carra
Ballymoe
Longford
Ballindine
Lanesborough
Killashee
Partry Mts.
Roscommon
Kylemore Abbey
Lough Mask
Ballinrobe
Dunmore
Glennamaddy
Keenagh
Leenaun
Kilmaine
Milltown
Clare
Cong
Athleague
28
28

3
4
5
7°
6°
A
B
C
34
30
55°
54°
Saddell
Campbeltown
Machrihanish
Southend
Mull of Kintyre
Sanda I.
Torrylin Cairn
Malin Hd.
Glengad Hd.
Trawbreaga B.
Dunaff Hd.
Fanad Hd.
Malin
Clonmany
Carndonagh
Inishowen
Slieve Snaght 615
Peninsula
Greencastle
Moville
Magilligan
Inishowen Hd.
Lough Swilly
Buncrana
Rathmullan
Lough Foyle
Muff
Rathmelton
Eglinton
Derry/Londonderry
Newtown Cunningham
St. Johnstown
Lifford
Strabane
Sion Mills
Rathlin Island
Causeway Coast
Benbane Hd.
Giants Causeway
Dunluce Castle
Portstewart
Portrush
Bushmills
Downhill
Hezlett House
Coleraine
Binevenagh
Limavady
Ballymoney
Dervock
Armoy
Fair Hd.
Ballycastle
Bonamargy Friary
Knocklayd 517
Mountains of Antrim
Antrim Coast
Cushendall
Red B. & Garron Pt.
Glens
Trostan 554
Carnlough
Glenarm
North Channel
Troon
Cairnryan
Liverpool
Douglas
Dunloy
Garvagh
Kilrea
Dungiven
Claudy
Feeny
Sperrin Mts.
Sawel 683
Swatragh
Portglenone
Bann
Ballymena
Broughshane
Agnews Hill 476
Larne
Larne Lough
Maghera
Tobermore
Ahoghill
L. Beg
Draperstown
Plumbridge
Sperrin
Gortin
Newtownstewart
Magherafelt
Randalstown
Ballyclare
Ballycarry
Ballynure
I. Magee
Whitehead
Carrickfergus
Greenisland
Belfast Lough
Bangor
Copeland I.
Donaghadee
NORTHERN IRELAND
Moneymore
Springhill House
Creeve
Cookstown
Coagh
Lough Neagh
Antrim
Belfast International
Newtownabbey
Crumlin
Glenavy
Holywood
George Best Belfast City
Belfast
Newtownards
Mount Stewart House
Dunmurry
Comber
Ballywalter
Strangford Lough
Ards Peninsula
Kircubbin
Portavogie
Drumquin
Mountfield
Omagh
Pomeroy
Castle Caulfield
Coalisland
Dromore
Seskinore
Beragh
Fintona
Aghalee
Lisburn
Lagan
Carryduff
Ballygowan
Saintfield
Rowallane
Killyleagh
Dungannon
Ballygawley
Chambered Cairn
Augher
Clogher
Aughnacloy
Moy
Portadown
Lurgan
Dromore
Hillsborough
Irvinestown
Enniskillen Castle
Castle Coole
Lisbellaw
Fivemiletown
Navan Fort
Caledon
Armagh
Gilford
Banbridge
Ballynahinch
Inch Abbey
Portaferry
Strangford
Strangford Lough
Ballyquintin Pt.
Audley's Castle
Leganany Dolmen
Downpatrick
Loughbrickland
Gosford
Emyvale
Cooneen
Maguiresbridge
Upper Lough Erne
Lisnaskea
Rosslea
Monaghan
Middletown
Markethill
Keady
Poyntz Pass
Clough
Castlewellan
Dundrum
Ardglass
Jordan's Castle
Lecale Coast
St. John's Pt.
Rathfriland
Drumena Cashel
Dundrum Bay
Newcastle
Newtownhamilton
Derrylin
Newtownbutler
Clones
Newbliss
Ballybay
Castleblaney
Ring of Gullion
Newry
Mourne Mts.
Slieve Donard 852
Mourne
Annalong
Warrenpoint
Kilkeel
Belturbet
Cootehill
Butler's Bridge
Culloville
Fane
Kilcurry
Carlingford
Carlingford Lough
Dundalk
King John's Castle
Cavan
Killashandra
Shercock
Carrigallen
Carrickmacross
Dundalk Bay
Bellananagh
Bailieborough
Bracklin
Kingscourt
Castlebellingham
Ballyjamesduff
Ardee
Dunany Pt.
Kilnaleck
Lough Gowna
Virginia
Dunleer
IRELAND
L. Sheelin
L. Ramor
Granard
Finnea
Oldcastle
Collon
Clogher Hd.
Termonfeckin
Kells
Crossakiel
Slane
Drogheda
Edgeworthstown
Newgrange
Julianstown
Castlepollard
Clonmellon
Navan
Duleek
L. Derravaragh
Ballinalack
Delvin
Athboy
Boyne
Balbriggan
Ardgillan Castle
Naul
Skerries
L. Owel
Tayto Park
112
197
162
204

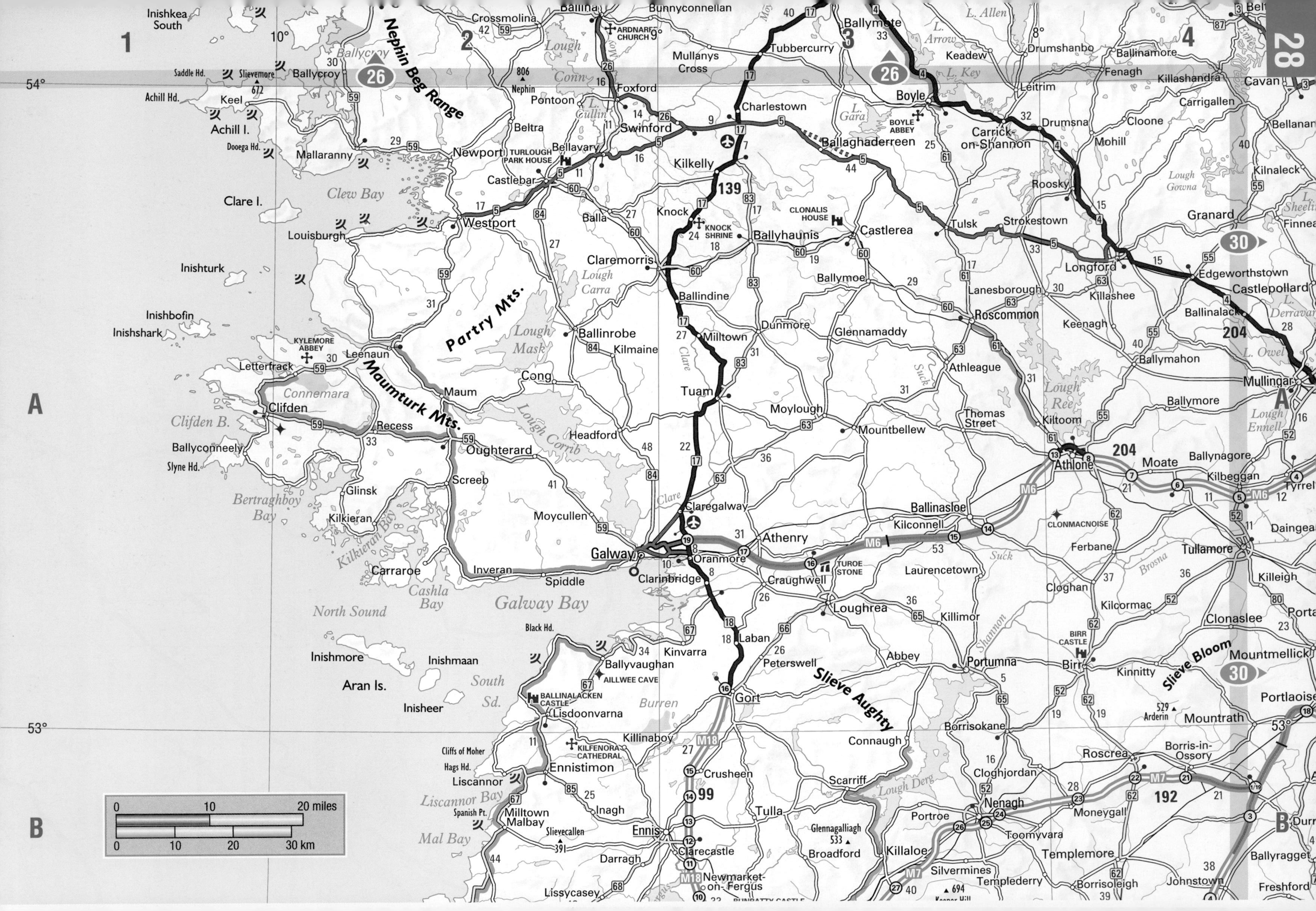
Nephin Beg Range
Partry Mts.
Maumturk Mts.
Slieve Aughty
Slieve Bloom
Inishkea South
Achill I.
Clare I.
Inishturk
Inishbofin
Inishshark
Clew Bay
Galway Bay
North Sound
Aran Is.
Inishmore
Inishmaan
Inisheer
Lough Mask
Lough Corrib
Lough Ree
Lough Derg
Connemara
Burren
Ballina
Crossmolina
Foxford
Swinford
Castlebar
Westport
Newport
Louisburgh
Clifden
Oughterard
Galway
Tuam
Claremorris
Ballinrobe
Knock
Ballyhaunis
Castlerea
Charlestown
Tubbercurry
Ballymote
Boyle
Carrick-on-Shannon
Longford
Roscommon
Athlone
Ballinasloe
Athenry
Loughrea
Portumna
Gort
Ennis
Lisdoonvarna
Ennistimon
Birr
Tullamore
Nenagh
Roscrea
Mullingar
Portlaoise
Cavan
0 10 20 miles
0 10 20 30 km

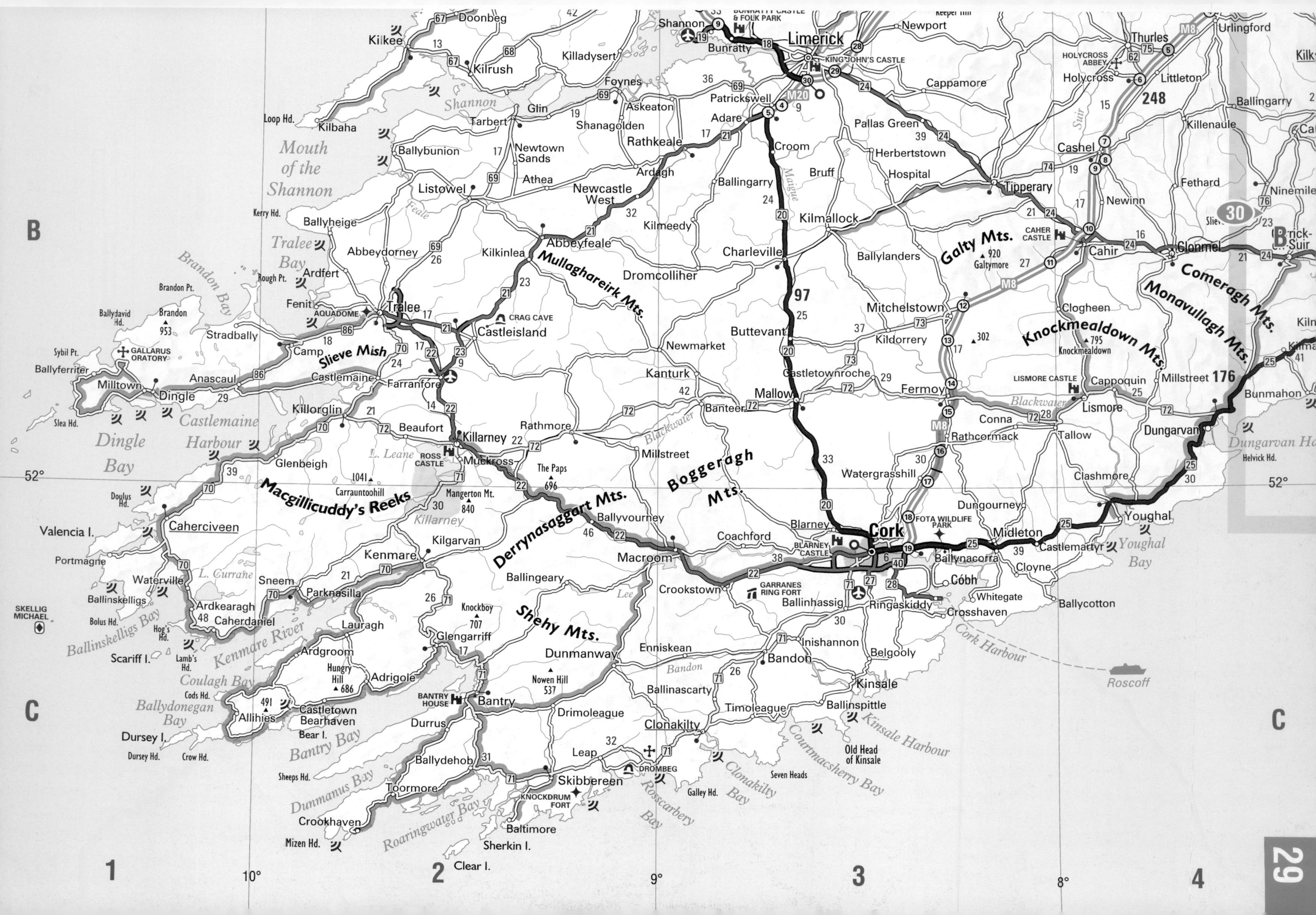

29
Limerick
Shannon
Bunratty
BUNRATTY CASTLE & FOLK PARK
KING JOHN'S CASTLE
Newport
Patrickswell
Adare
Croom
Bruff
Kilmallock
Charleville
Buttevant
Mallow
Blarney
BLARNEY CASTLE
Cork
Cóbh
Midleton
Youghal
Dungarvan
Clonmel
Cahir
CAHER CASTLE
Cashel
Tipperary
Thurles
Holycross
HOLYCROSS ABBEY
Littleton
Urlingford
Fethard
Killenaule
Ninemile
Newinn
Cappamore
Pallas Green
Herbertstown
Hospital
Ballylanders
Mitchelstown
Kildorrery
Fermoy
Lismore
LISMORE CASTLE
Cappoquin
Millstreet
Bunmahon
Helvick Hd.
Tallow
Conna
Rathcormack
Watergrasshill
Dungourney
FOTA WILDLIFE PARK
Clashmore
Castlemartyr
Ballynacorra
Cloyne
Ballycotton
Whitegate
Crosshaven
Ringaskiddy
Ballinhassig
GARRANES RING FORT
Inishannon
Belgooly
Kinsale
Ballinspittle
Old Head of Kinsale
Bandon
Timoleague
Ballinascarty
Enniskean
Clonakilty
DROMBEG
Leap
Skibbereen
KNOCKDRUM FORT
Baltimore
Sherkin I.
Clear I.
Ballydehob
Toormore
Crookhaven
Mizen Hd.
Durrus
Bantry
BANTRY HOUSE
Drimoleague
Dunmanway
Nowen Hill 537
Glengarriff
Knockboy 707
Adrigole
Hungry Hill 686
Ardgroom
Lauragh
Castletown Bearhaven
Bear I.
Allihies
Dursey I.
Dursey Hd.
Crow Hd.
Cods Hd.
Sheeps Hd.
Kenmare
Kilgarvan
Sneem
Parknasilla
Ardkearagh
Caherdaniel
Waterville
Ballinskelligs
Bolus Hd.
Hog's Hd.
Lamb's Hd.
Scariff I.
SKELLIG MICHAEL
Portmagne
Valencia I.
Caherciveen
Doulus Hd.
Glenbeigh
Killorglin
Beaufort
Killarney
Muckross
ROSS CASTLE
Carrauntoohill 1041
Mangerton Mt. 840
The Paps 696
Rathmore
Millstreet
Ballyvourney
Macroom
Ballingeary
Coachford
Crookstown
Banteer
Kanturk
Newmarket
Castletownroche
Castleisland
CRAG CAVE
Farranfore
Castlemaine
Tralee
AQUADOME
Fenit
Ardfert
Abbeydorney
Ballyheige
Kerry Hd.
Rough Pt.
Brandon Pt.
Brandon 953
Ballydavid Hd.
GALLARUS ORATORY
Stradbally
Camp
Anascaul
Dingle
Milltown
Ballyferriter
Sybil Pt.
Slea Hd.
Kilkinlea
Abbeyfeale
Newcastle West
Ardagh
Rathkeale
Kilmeedy
Dromcolliher
Ballingarry
Listowel
Ballybunion
Athea
Newtown Sands
Tarbert
Glin
Shanagolden
Askeaton
Foynes
Killadysert
Kilrush
Kilkee
Doonbeg
Kilbaha
Loop Hd.
Galtymore 920
Knockmealdown 795
Galty Mts.
Knockmealdown Mts.
Comeragh Mts.
Monavullagh Mts.
Boggeragh Mts.
Mullaghareirk Mts.
Derrynasaggart Mts.
Shehy Mts.
Macgillicuddy's Reeks
Slieve Mish
Mouth of the Shannon
Shannon
Tralee Bay
Brandon Bay
Dingle Bay
Castlemaine Harbour
L. Leane
Killarney
L. Currane
Kenmare River
Ballinskelligs Bay
Coulagh Bay
Ballydonegan Bay
Bantry Bay
Dunmanus Bay
Roaringwater Bay
Rosscarbery Bay
Clonakilty Bay
Courtmacsherry Bay
Seven Heads
Galley Hd.
Kinsale Harbour
Cork Harbour
Roscoff
Youghal Bay
Dungarvan Harbour
Blackwater
Lee
Bandon
Feale
Maigue
Suir
B
C
1
2
3
4
52°
8°
9°
10°

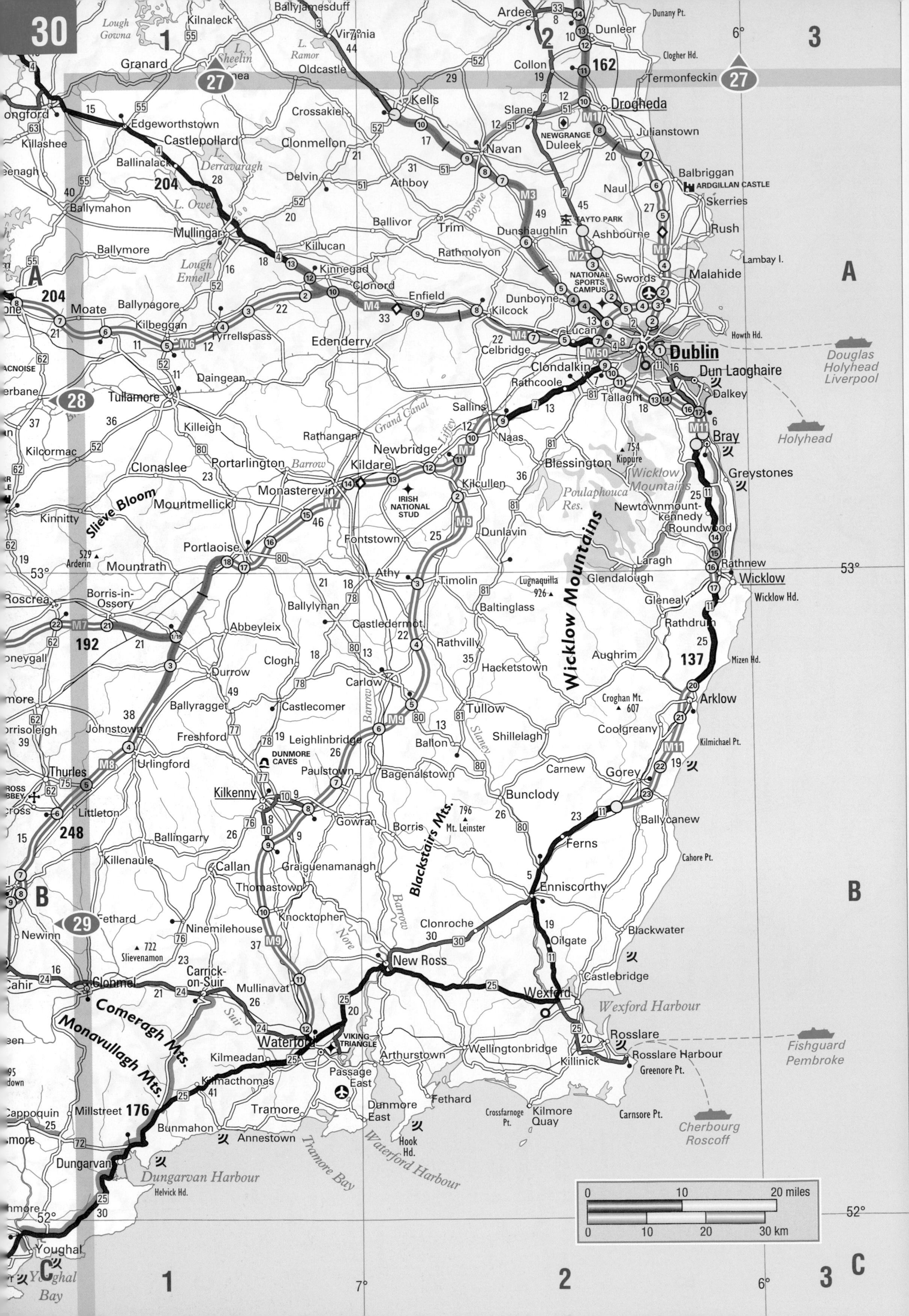

1
2
3
A
B
C
Lough Gowna
Kilnaleck
Ballyjamesduff
Virginia
L. Ramor
Oldcastle
Ardee
Dunleer
Dunany Pt.
Clogher Hd.
Termonfeckin
Collon
L. Sheelin
Granard
27
Kells
Drogheda
Slane
Newgrange
Duleek
Julianstown
Crossakiel
Edgeworthstown
Longford
Killashee
Castlepollard
Clonmellon
Navan
L. Derravaragh
Ballinalack
Delvin
Athboy
Balbriggan
Ardgillan Castle
Skerries
Naul
Ballymahon
L. Owel
Mullingar
Ballivor
Trim
Boyne
Fayto Park
Dunshaughlin
Ashbourne
Rush
Killucan
Rathmolyon
Ballymore
Lough Ennell
Kinnegad
Clonord
Lambay I.
Malahide
National Sports Campus
Swords
Moate
Ballynagore
Enfield
Dunboyne
Kilcock
Kilbeggan
Tyrrellspass
Edenderry
Celbridge
Lucan
Howth Hd.
Dublin
Clondalkin
Dun Laoghaire
Dalkey
Douglas
Holyhead
Liverpool
Daingean
Rathcoole
Tallaght
Tullamore
28
Sallins
Grand Canal
Liffey
Naas
Bray
Holyhead
Killeigh
Rathangan
Newbridge
Kilcormac
Portarlington
Barrow
Kildare
Blessington
Kippure
Greystones
Clonaslee
Wicklow Mountains
Irish National Stud
Kilcullen
Poulaphouca Res.
Monasterevin
Newtownmountkennedy
Roundwood
Slieve Bloom
Mountmellick
Kinnitty
Fontstown
Dunlavin
Wicklow Mountains
Portlaoise
Laragh
Arderin
Mountrath
Athy
Timolin
Lugnaquilla
Glendalough
Rathnew
Wicklow
Wicklow Hd.
Roscrea
Borris-in-Ossory
Ballylynan
Baltinglass
Glenealy
Castledermot
Rathdrum
Abbeyleix
Rathvilly
Aughrim
Mizen Hd.
Clogh
Hacketstown
Durrow
Carlow
Arklow
Croghan Mt.
Ballyragget
Castlecomer
Tullow
Johnstown
Freshford
Leighlinbridge
Ballon
Shillelagh
Coolgreany
Slaney
Kilmichael Pt.
Urlingford
Dunmore Caves
Paulstown
Bagenalstown
Carnew
Gorey
Thurles
Holycross
Kilkenny
Bunclody
Littleton
Gowran
Borris
Blackstairs Mts.
Mt. Leinster
Ballycanew
Ballingarry
Ferns
Killenaule
Callan
Graiguenamanagh
Cahore Pt.
Thomastown
Enniscorthy
Fethard
Knocktopher
Nore
Clonroche
Newinn
29
Ninemilehouse
Slievenamon
Oilgate
Blackwater
New Ross
Castlebridge
Cahir
Clonmel
Carrick-on-Suir
Mullinavat
Wexford
Wexford Harbour
Comeragh Mts.
Suir
Monavullagh Mts.
Waterford
Viking Triangle
Rosslare
Rosslare Harbour
Greenore Pt.
Fishguard
Pembroke
Kilmeadan
Arthurstown
Wellingtonbridge
Killinick
Passage East
Kilmacthomas
Fethard
Cappoquin
Millstreet
Tramore
Dunmore East
Crossfarnoge Pt.
Kilmore Quay
Carnsore Pt.
Cherbourg
Roscoff
Bunmahon
Annestown
Tramore Bay
Waterford Harbour
Hook Hd.
Dungarvan
Dungarvan Harbour
Helvick Hd.
Youghal
Youghal Bay
0 10 20 miles
0 10 20 30 km
53°
52°
6°
7°

1
2
3
7°
6°
0 10 20 miles
0 10 20 30 km
A
B
C
Butt of Lewis
Port Nis
Dail bho Dheas
Barabhas
Tolastadh bho Thuath
Tolsta Hd.
Siabost
Carlabhagh
Broad Bay
Bac
Tiumpan Hd.
Port Nan Giuran
Gallan Hd.
Great Bernera
292
Ben Mholach
Newmarket
Timsgearraidh
Calanais
Stornoway
Mealabost
Chicken Hd.
Lewis
574
Mealisval
Giosla
Crosbost
Kintarvie
Scarp
Grabhair
Leumrabhagh
Kebock Hd.
Ullapool
58°
Husinish
799
Clisham
572
Beinn Mhor
West L. Tarbert
Ardhasig
Taransay
Aird Asaig
Tairbeart
Harris
Shiant Is.
Scalpay
East L. Tarbert
Toe Hd.
Sgarasta Mhor
Pabbay
Sd. of Pabbay
Sound of Harris
An t-Ob
Roghadal
Renish Pt.
Berneray
South Lewis, Harris & North Uist
Outer Hebrides
North Minch
Little Minch
Rubha Hunish
DUNTULM CASTLE
Solas
North Uist
Loch nam Madadh
Staffin
Vaternish Pt.
Trotternish
Sound of Monach
Geary
L. Snizort
Uig
Clachan na Luib
Monach Is.
Dunvegan Hd.
Stein
The Storr
719
Baleshare
Ronay
DUNVEGAN CASTLE
Dunvegan
Carbost
Sound of Raasay
Lephin
Benbecula
Roskhill
Portree
Wiay
Creag Ghoraidh
Bracadale
Skye
Raasay
Clachan
Tobha Mor
L. Bracadale
Scalpay
Sconser
Drynoch
Carbost
South Uist
Cuillin Hills
South Uist Machair
Broadford
Glenbrittle
The Cuillin Hills
Dalabrog
Loch Baghasdail
L. Eishort
Soay
Elgol
Pol a Charra
Sound of Barra
Eriskay
Canna
Sanday
Rùm
Kinloch
Inner Hebrides
57°
Barra
Bagh a Chaisteil
Vatersay
Sandray
Mingulay
The Small Isles
Sound of Rùm
Eigg
Galmisdale
Muck
Coll
Sorisdale
Ballyhaugh
Arinagour
Arileod
Tiree
Calgary
Tobermory
Dervaig
Loch na Keal
Inner Sound
Pt. of Stoer
Stoer
Enard B.
Rubha Coigeach
Achiltibuie
HYDROPONICUM GARDENS
32
Gruinard B.
Greenstone Pt.
L. Ewe
Cove
Aultbea
Melvaig
INVEREWE GARDEN
Poolewe
Fionn Loch
Longa I.
Gairloch
L. Gairloch
L. Maree
Wester Ross
Port Henderson
Kerrysdale
Red Point
Talladale
L. Torridon
Kinlochewe
Rona
Torridon
Shieldaig
Achnashellach
Applecross
Coulags
Ardarroch
Lochcarron
L. Carron
Stromeferry
WOODLAND GARDEN
Kyle of Lochalsh
Auchtertyre
Dornie
CASTLE MOIL
Kyleakin
L. Alsh
EILEAN CASTLE
Glenelg
Shiel B
Kylerhea
KNOCK CASTLE
Sd. of Sleat
L. Hourn
Teangue
Armadale
ARMADALE GARDENS
Knoydart
L. Nevis
Pt. of Sleat
Mallaig
57°
Arisaig
L. Morar
Lochailort
Glenfinn
LOCH NAN UAMH CAIRN
Rhois-Bheinn
Morar, Moidart & Ardnamurchan
Shona I.
Kinlochmoidart
Loch Shiel
Achosnich
Acharacle
Kilchoan
MINGARY CASTLE
Salen
L. Sunart
Strontian
34
Claggan
Lochaline
Loch Linnhe
857
858
859
866
865
867
855
850
863
87
851
888
832
896
890
830
882
861
884
848
24
16
51
48
38
23
32
34
15
53
18
28
12
8
21
26
46
30
62
29
20
27

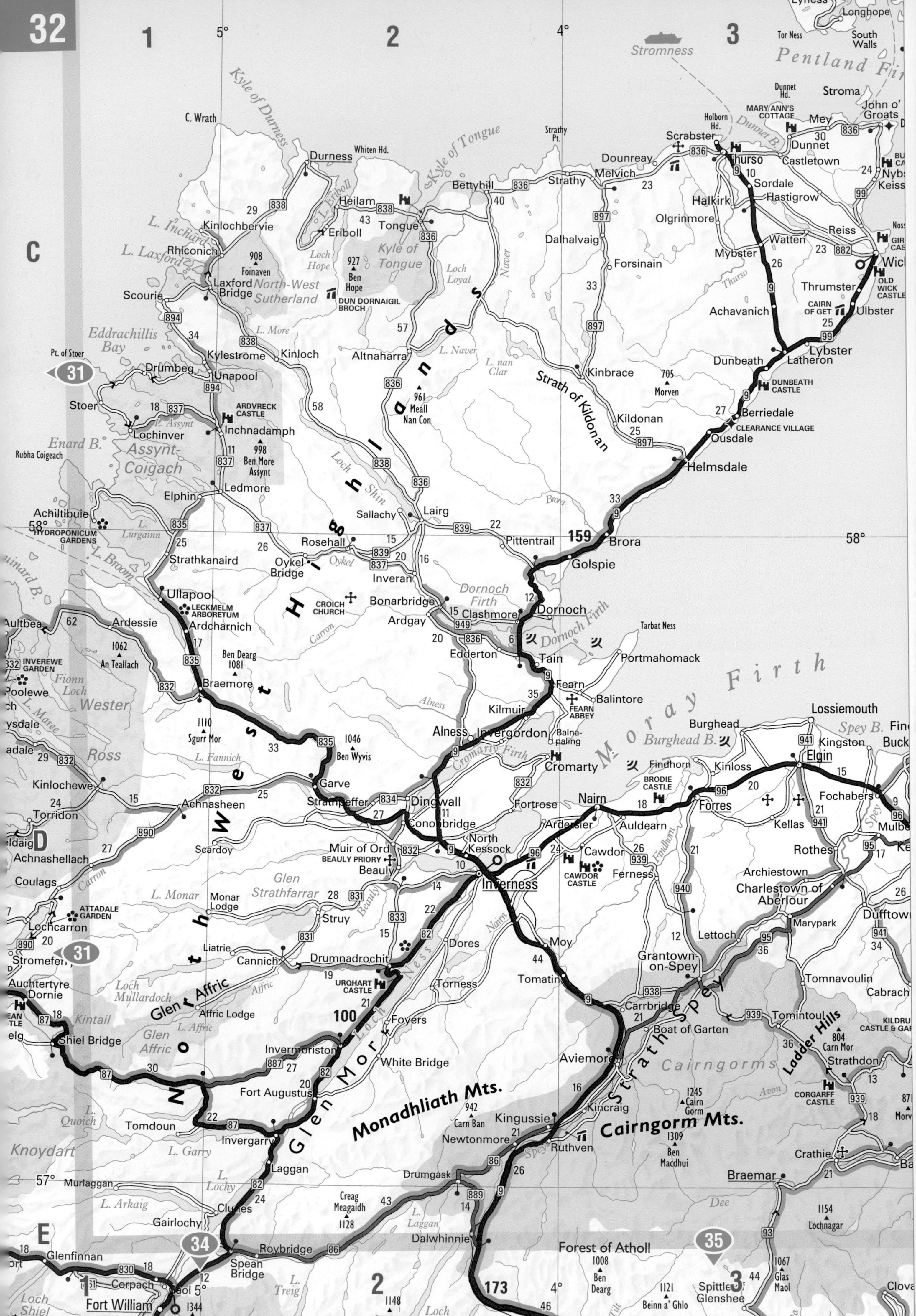

32
1
2
3
C
D
E
5°
4°
58°
57°
Lyness
Longhope
Tor Ness
South Walls
Stromness
Pentland Fir
Dunnet Hd.
Stroma
John o' Groats
MARY ANN'S COTTAGE
Mey
Dunnet
Holborn Hd.
Scrabster
Dunnet B.
Thurso
Castletown
Dounreay
Melvich
Strathy
Strathy Pt.
Bettyhill
Sordale
Hastigrow
Halkirk
Olgrinmore
Reiss
Watten
Mybster
Wick
OLD WICK CASTLE
Thrumster
CAIRN OF GET
Ulbster
Achavanich
Lybster
Latheron
Dunbeath
DUNBEATH CASTLE
Berriedale
CLEARANCE VILLAGE
Ousdale
Helmsdale
Kildonan
Strath of Kildonan
Kinbrace
705 Morven
Forsinain
Dalhalvaig
Naver
Loch Loyal
L. Naver
L. nan Clar
C. Wrath
Kyle of Durness
Durness
Whiten Hd.
Kyle of Tongue
L. Eriboll
Heilam
Eriboll
Tongue
DUN DORNAIGIL BROCH
927 Ben Hope
Loch Hope
Kinlochbervie
L. Inchard
L. Laxford
Rhiconich
908 Foinaven
Laxford Bridge
North-West Sutherland
Scourie
Eddrachillis Bay
L. More
Kylestrome
Kinloch
Altnaharra
Pt. of Stoer
31
Drumbeg
Unapool
Stoer
ARDVRECK CASTLE
Inchnadamph
L. Assynt
Lochinver
Enard B.
Rubha Coigeach
Assynt-Coigach
998 Ben More Assynt
961 Meall Nan Con
Loch Shin
Ledmore
Elphin
Achiltibuie
HYDROPONICUM GARDENS
L. Lurgainn
Lairg
Sallachy
Rosehall
Pittentrail
Brora
Golspie
159
Strathkanaird
L. Broom
Oykel Bridge
Inveran
Ullapool
LECKMELM ARBORETUM
CROICH CHURCH
Bonarbridge
Dornoch Firth
Dornoch
Clashmore
Ardgay
Edderton
Tain
Tarbat Ness
Portmahomack
Moray Firth
Aultbea
Ardessie
Ardcharnich
1062 An Teallach
Ben Dearg 1081
INVEREWE GARDEN
Fionn Loch
Poolewe
Braemore
Wester Ross
L. Maree
1110 Sgurr Mor
1046 Ben Wyvis
Fearn
Balintore
FEARN ABBEY
Kilmuir
Alness
Invergordon
Balnapaling
Cromarty Firth
Cromarty
Lossiemouth
Burghead
Burghead B.
Spey B.
Kingston
Elgin
Findhorn
Kinloss
BRODIE CASTLE
Nairn
Forres
Fochabers
Kellas
Rothes
L. Fannich
Kinlochewe
Garve
Torridon
Achnasheen
Strathpeffer
Dingwall
Fortrose
Ardersier
Auldearn
Conon Bridge
North Kessock
Achnashellach
Scardoy
Muir of Ord
BEAULY PRIORY
Beauly
Inverness
Cawdor
CAWDOR CASTLE
Ferness
Coulags
L. Monar
Monar Lodge
Glen Strathfarrar
Archiestown
Charlestown of Aberlour
ATTADALE GARDEN
Lochcarron
Stromeferry
Struy
Liatrie
Cannich
Dores
Moy
Lettoch
Marypark
Dufftown
Drumnadrochit
URQUHART CASTLE
Grantown-on-Spey
Tomatin
Tomnavoulin
Cabrach
Auchtertyre
Dornie
Loch Mullardoch
Glen Affric
Affric Lodge
L. Affric
Torness
Loch Ness
Carrbridge
Strathspey
Tomintoul
Ladder Hills
Kintail
Shiel Bridge
Foyers
Boat of Garten
804 Carn Mor
Invermoriston
White Bridge
Aviemore
Cairngorms
Strathdon
Glen Mor
North West Highlands
Monadhliath Mts.
Fort Augustus
942 Carn Ban
Kingussie
Kincraig
1245 Cairn Gorm
Cairngorm Mts.
CORGARFF CASTLE
L. Quoich
Tomdoun
Invergarry
Newtonmore
Ruthven
1309 Ben Macdhui
Knoydart
L. Garry
Laggan
Drumgask
Crathie
Braemar
Murlaggan
L. Lochy
L. Arkaig
Clunes
Creag Meagaidh 1128
L. Laggan
Dee
1154 Lochnagar
Gairlochy
Dalwhinnie
Forest of Atholl
35
34
Glenfinnan
Roybridge
Spean Bridge
1008 Ben Dearg
Corpach
Caol
Loch Shiel
Fort William
1344
L. Treig
1148
173
Loch
1121 Beinn a' Ghlo
Spittle of Glenshee
1067 Glas Maol
Clova

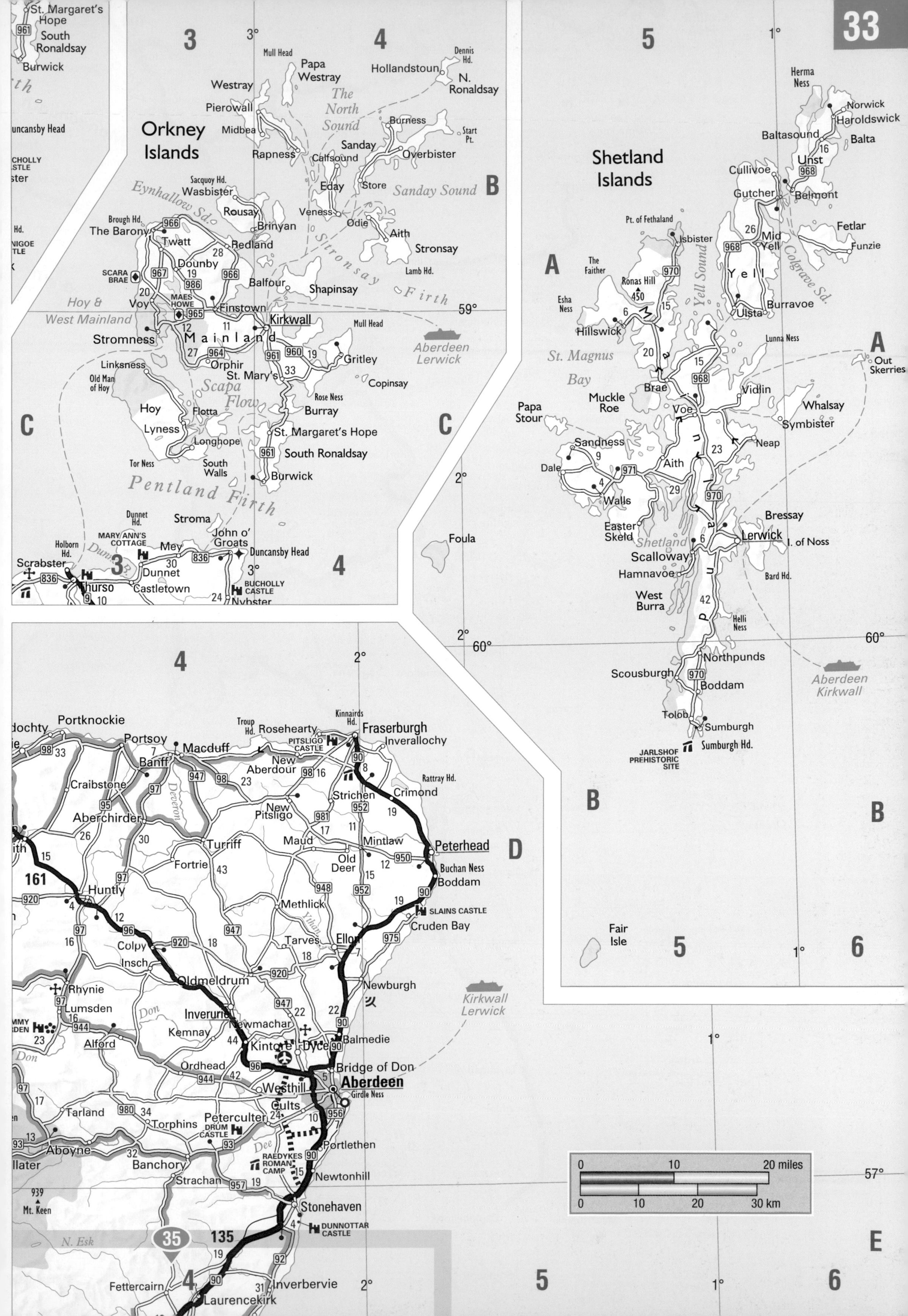

Orkney Islands
Shetland Islands
St. Margaret's Hope
South Ronaldsay
Burwick
Duncansby Head
Mull Head
Papa Westray
Hollandstoun
Dennis Hd.
N. Ronaldsay
Westray
Pierowall
Midbea
The North Sound
Burness
Start Pt.
Sanday
Rapness
Calfsound
Overbister
Sacquoy Hd.
Wasbister
Eynhallow Sd.
Eday
Store
Sanday Sound
Rousay
Veness
Brough Hd.
The Barony
Twatt
Brinyan
Odie
Aith
Redland
Stronsay
Dounby
SCARA BRAE
MAES HOWE
Balfour
Shapinsay
Lamb Hd.
Stronsay Firth
Hoy & West Mainland
Voy
Finstown
Kirkwall
59°
Stromness
Mainland
Mull Head
Aberdeen Lerwick
Linksness
Orphir
St. Mary's
Gritley
Old Man of Hoy
Scapa Flow
Copinsay
Rose Ness
Hoy
Flotta
Burray
Lyness
Longhope
Tor Ness
South Walls
Pentland Firth
Dunnet Hd.
Stroma
MARY ANN'S COTTAGE
Holborn Hd.
Mey
John o' Groats
Duncansby Head
Scrabster
Dunnet
Thurso
Castletown
BUCHOLLY CASTLE
Nybster
Herma Ness
Norwick
Haroldswick
Baltasound
Balta
Unst
Cullivoe
Gutcher
Belmont
Pt. of Fethaland
Isbister
Mid Yell
Fetlar
Funzie
Yell Sound
Yell
Colgrave Sd.
The Faither
Ronas Hill
Esha Ness
Burravoe
Ulsta
Hillswick
Lunna Ness
Out Skerries
St. Magnus Bay
Mainland
Brae
Vidlin
Muckle Roe
Papa Stour
Voe
Whalsay
Symbister
Sandness
Neap
Dale
Aith
Walls
Easter Skeld
Bressay
Shetland
Lerwick
I. of Noss
Foula
Scalloway
Hamnavoe
Bard Hd.
West Burra
Helli Ness
Northpunds
Scousburgh
Boddam
Aberdeen Kirkwall
Tolob
Sumburgh
JARLSHOF PREHISTORIC SITE
Sumburgh Hd.
Fair Isle
60°
1°
2°
Portknockie
Cullen
Portsoy
Troup Hd.
Rosehearty
Kinnairds Hd.
Fraserburgh
Inverallochy
PITSLIGO CASTLE
Macduff
Banff
New Aberdour
Craibstone
Rattray Hd.
Crimond
Strichen
Aberchirder
Deveron
New Pitsligo
Turriff
Maud
Mintlaw
Peterhead
Old Deer
Fortrie
Buchan Ness
Boddam
Huntly
Methlick
SLAINS CASTLE
Cruden Bay
Ythan
Tarves
Ellon
Colpy
Insch
Oldmeldrum
Newburgh
Rhynie
Kirkwall Lerwick
Lumsden
Inverurie
Newmachar
Don
Kemnay
Balmedie
Alford
Kintore
Dyce
Ordhead
Bridge of Don
Aberdeen
Westhill
Girdle Ness
Cults
Tarland
Torphins
Peterculter
DRUM CASTLE
Aboyne
Dee
Portlethen
Ballater
Banchory
RAEDYKES ROMAN CAMP
Newtonhill
Strachan
Mt. Keen
Stonehaven
DUNNOTTAR CASTLE
N. Esk
Fettercairn
Inverbervie
Laurencekirk
57°
0 10 20 miles
0 10 20 30 km

Cuillin Hills
Glenbrittle
The Cuillin Hills
Broadford
Kyleakin
Kylerhea
EILEAN CASTLE
Glenelg
Kintail
Shiel Bridge
Glen Affric
Affric Lodge
Invermoriston
Foyers
White Bridge
Fort Augustus
Glen Mor
Monadhliath
Soay
Elgol
L. Eishort
KNOCK CASTLE
L. Hourn
Teangue
Sd. of Sleat
Canna
Armadale
ARMADALE GARDENS
Knoydart
L. Quoich
Tomdoun
Invergarry
Sanday
Rùm
Kinloch
57°
Pt. of Sleat
Mallaig
L. Nevis
L. Garry
Laggan
Drumgask
Murlaggan
L. Lochy
The Small Isles
Sound of Rùm
L. Arkaig
Clunes
Creag Meagaidh
1128
L. Laggan
Dalwhinnie
Eigg
Arisaig
L. Morar
Gairlochy
Roybridge
Galmisdale
LOCH NAN UAMH CAIRN
Lochailort
Glenfinnan
Spean Bridge
Muck
Morar, Moidart & Ardnamurchan
882
Rhois-Bheinn
Corpach
Caol
Shona I.
Kinlochmoidart
Loch Shiel
Fort William
1344
Ben Nevis
L. Treig
Grampian
1148
Ben Alder
Loch Ericht
Bagh a Chaisteil
Loch Baghasdail
Achosnich
Acharacle
Corran
Kinlochleven
Blackwater Res.
Sorisdale
Kilchoan
MINGARY CASTLE
Salen
Strontian
Onich
Glencoe
Rannoch Station
Ballyhaugh
Arinagour
L. Sunart
Ballachulish
L. Rannoch
Loch Rannoch & Glen Lyon
Arileod
Coll
Tobermory
Calgary
Drimnin
Loch Linnhe
1150
Bidean Nam Bian
Ben Nevis & Glen Coe
Dervaig
Sound of Mull
Portnacroish
Glen Lyon
Loch na Keal, Isle of Mull
Claggan
Lochaline
Lynn of Lorn
Loch Etive
Bridge of Orchy
Gometra
Ulva
Oskamull
Salen
Lismore I.
Craignure
ARDCHATTAN PRIORY
Bonawe
Connel
Ben Cruachan
1126
KILCHURN CASTLE
SCOT
MULL
966
Ben More
Staffa
Oban
Taynuilt
Tyndrum
Ardchyle
Kerrera
Dalmally
1130
Ben Lui
Crianlarich
Lochearnhead
Iona
Fionnphort
Pennyghael
Bunessan
ST COLUMBA EXHIBITION
GLENFEOCHAN GARDENS
Cladich
INISHAIL CHAPEL
1174
Ben More
Firth of Lorn
Kilninver
Seil
Balvicar
Loch Awe
Ardlui
Loch Lomond
Strathyre
Luing
Kilmelford
ARDCHONNELL CASTLE
Cairndow
Stronachlachar
L. Katrine
1011
Ben Ime
Scarba
Toberonochy
Inveraray
Arrochar
Tarbet
974
Ben Lomond
Aberfoyle
FINCHAIRN CASTLE
Ford
Strachur
Lochgoilhead
Aird
GLEBE CAIRN
Kilmartin
The Trossachs
Loch Lomond
Luss
Garbhallt
CARRICK CASTLE
Colonsay
Scalasaig
ROCK MARKINGS
Garelochhead
Drymen
Jura
Ardlussa
Lochgilphead
Coulport
Killearn
56°
Oronsay
Ardrishaig
Otter Ferry
Helensburgh
Alexandria
Knapdale
Kilcreggan
Sandbank
Gourock
Lennox
Sd. of Jura
Keillmore
Dunoon
Dumbarton
Lagg
785
Paps of Jura
Tighnabruaich
Greenock
Port Glasgow
Clydebank
Ardnave Pt.
Loch Fyne
Rhubodach
Innellan
Renfrew
Sanaigmore
Port Askaig
Feolin Ferry
Craighouse
Portavadie
Port Bannatyne
Skelmorlie
Paisley
Islay
Kilberry
Tarbert
Rothesay
Clyde-Muirsheil
Johnstone
Bridgend
Bowmore
Kennacraig
Bute
Largs
Barrhead
Port Charlotte
491
Ben Bheigeir
SKIPNESS CASTLE
Skipness
Claonaig
Millport
Kilbirnie
Beith
Kilchattan
Fairlie
Portnahaven
Gigha
Lochranza
ST. BLANE'S CHAPEL
West Kilbride
Dalry
Dunlop
Stewarton
Ardbeg
Port Ellen
DISTILLERIES
The Oa
Mull of Oa
Tayinloan
Pirnmill
North Arran
874
Goat Fell
Kilbrannan Sound
Ardrossan
Saltcoats
Kilwinning
Kilmaurs
Fenwick
Kilmarnock
Arran
Brodick
Irvine
Galston
Glenbarr
Saddell
Holy I.
Troon
Hurlford
Mauchline
0
10
20 miles
0
10
20
30 km
Blackwaterfoot
CARN BAN
Firth of Clyde
Monkton
Prestwick
Tarbolton
Ochiltree
Ayr
Larne
Drongan
Dippen
TORRYLINN CAIRN
Machrihanish
Campbeltown
Dalrymple
Patna
CULZEAN CASTLE
Maybole
Kirkoswald
Crosshill
Dalmellington
Causeway Coast
Benbane Hd.
GIANTS CAUSEWAY
Rathlin Island
6°
Southend
Mull of Kintyre
Sanda I.
5°
Turnberry
Bellsbank
31
32
27
36

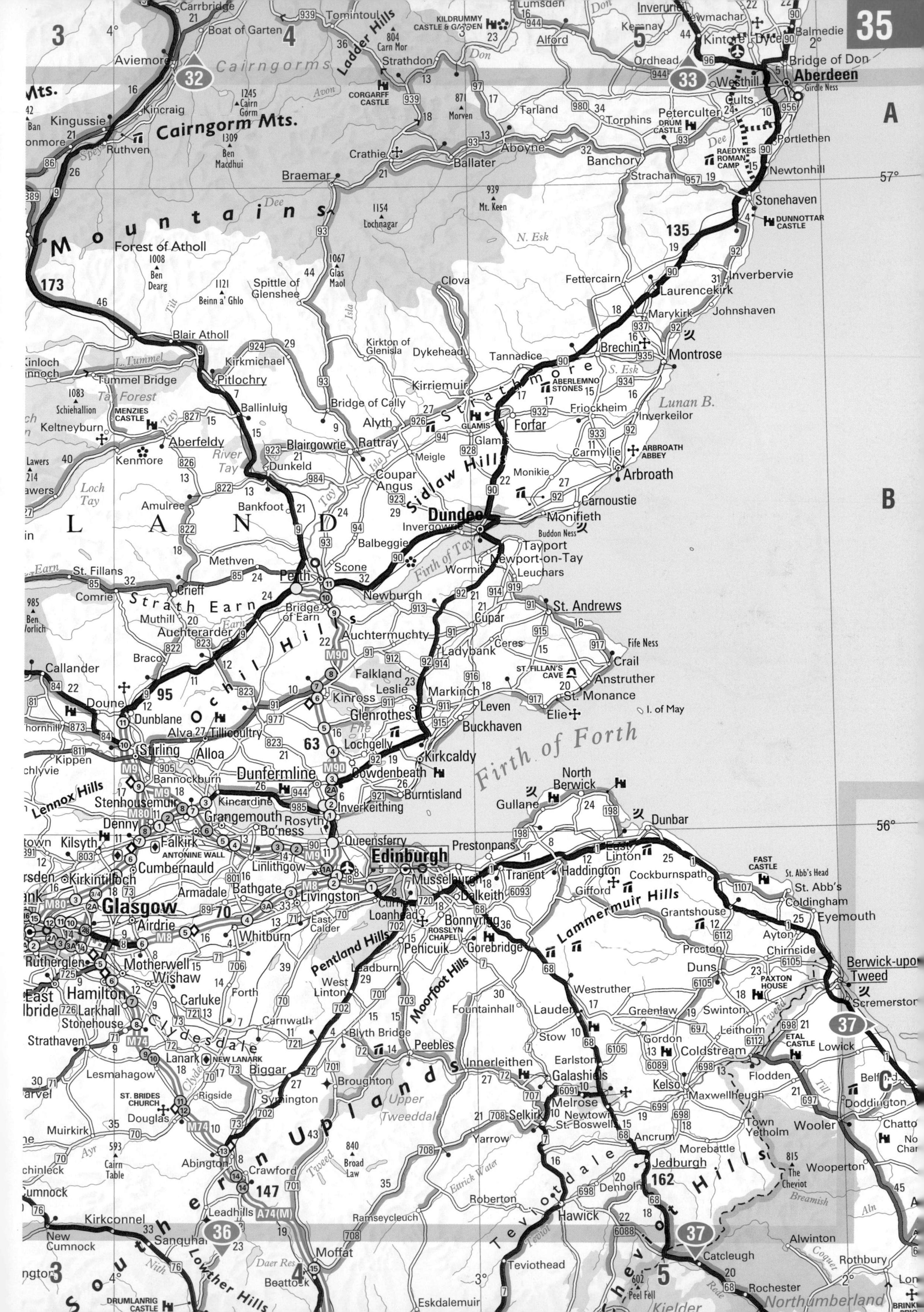

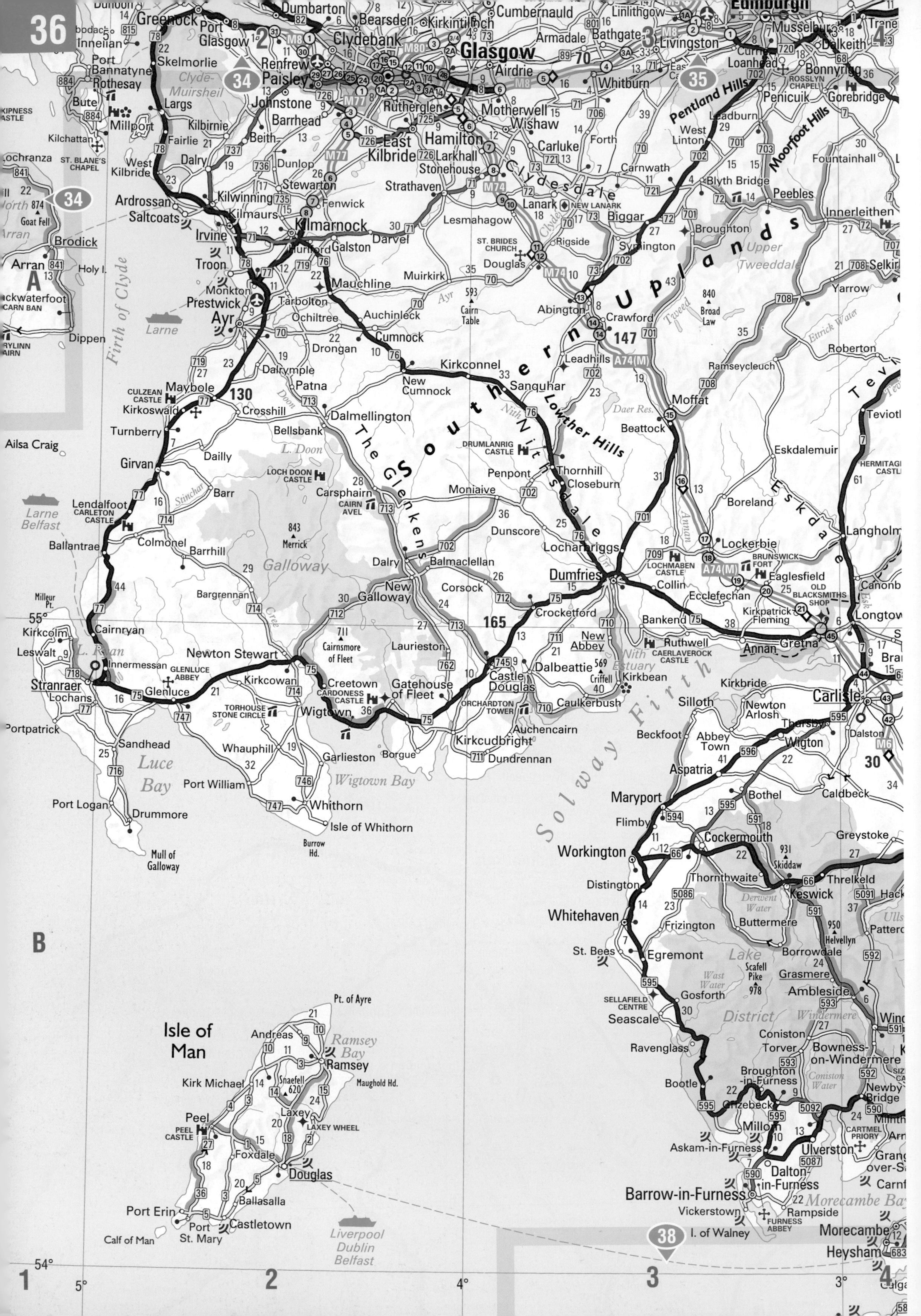

Greenock
Port Glasgow
Dumbarton
Bearsden
Kirkintilloch
Cumbernauld
Linlithgow
Edinburgh
Musselburgh
Tranent
Inverkip
Innellan
Clydebank
Glasgow
Armadale
Bathgate
Livingston
Dalkeith
Port Bannatyne
Skelmorlie
Renfrew
Paisley
Airdrie
Whitburn
Loanhead
Bonnyrigg
Rothesay
Clyde-Muirsheil
Johnstone
Rutherglen
Motherwell
Pentland Hills
Penicuik
ROSSLYN CHAPEL
Gorebridge
Bute
Largs
Millport
Barrhead
Wishaw
Leadburn
Kilbirnie
East Kilbride
Hamilton
Carluke
Forth
West Linton
Moorfoot Hills
Kilchattan
Fairlie
Beith
Larkhall
Stonehouse
Fountainhall
Lochranza
ST. BLANE'S CHAPEL
West Kilbride
Dalry
Dunlop
Clydesdale
Carnwath
Stewarton
Strathaven
Blyth Bridge
Peebles
Goat Fell
Ardrossan
Saltcoats
Kilwinning
Kilmaurs
Fenwick
Lanark
NEW LANARK
Innerleithen
Arran
Irvine
Kilmarnock
Darvel
Lesmahagow
Biggar
Broughton
Brodick
Troon
Hurlford
Galston
ST. BRIDES CHURCH
Rigside
Symington
Southern Uplands
Upper Tweeddale
Selkirk
Holy I.
Firth of Clyde
Monkton
Prestwick
Tarbolton
Mauchline
Muirkirk
Douglas
Yarrow
Blackwaterfoot
CARN BAN
Ayr
Larne
Ochiltree
Auchinleck
Cairn Table
Abington
Crawford
Broad Law
Ettrick Water
Dippen
Drongan
Cumnock
Leadhills
Roberton
Dalrymple
Patna
Kirkconnel
New Cumnock
Sanquhar
Ramseycleuch
CULZEAN CASTLE
Maybole
Kirkoswald
Crosshill
Dalmellington
Lowther Hills
Moffat
Teviot
Turnberry
Bellsbank
The Glenkens
Daer Res.
Beattock
Ailsa Craig
L. Doon
DRUMLANRIG CASTLE
Nithsdale
Eskdalemuir
HERMITAGE CASTLE
Girvan
Dailly
LOCH DOON CASTLE
Penpont
Thornhill
Closeburn
Stinchar
Barr
Carsphairn
CAIRN AVEL
Moniaive
Boreland
Eskdale
Lendalfoot
CARLETON CASTLE
Larne
Belfast
Merrick
Dunscore
Annan
Langholm
Ballantrae
Colmonel
Barrhill
Galloway
Dalry
Balmaclellan
Lochanbriggs
Lockerbie
BRUNSWICK FORT
LOCHMABEN CASTLE
Eaglesfield
Dumfries
Collin
Canonbie
Millfeur Pt.
Bargrennan
New Galloway
Corsock
Ecclefechan
OLD BLACKSMITHS SHOP
Kirkpatrick-Fleming
Cairnryan
Crocketford
Bankend
Longtown
Kirkcolm
Cree
Cairnsmore of Fleet
Laurieston
New Abbey
Ruthwell
Annan
Gretna
Leswalt
L. Ryan
Newton Stewart
CAERLAVEROCK CASTLE
Innermessan
GLENLUCE ABBEY
Dalbeattie
Nith Estuary
Criffell
Kirkbean
Solway Firth
Kirkbride
Stranraer
Lochans
Kirkcowan
Creetown
Gatehouse of Fleet
Castle Douglas
Glenluce
CARDONESS CASTLE
Carlisle
Silloth
Newton Arlosh
TORHOUSE STONE CIRCLE
Wigtown
ORCHARDTON TOWER
Caulkerbush
Thursby
Dalston
Portpatrick
Auchencairn
Beckfoot
Abbey Town
Sandhead
Whauphill
Kirkcudbright
Wigton
Garlieston
Borgue
Dundrennan
Luce Bay
Aspatria
Port William
Wigtown Bay
Caldbeck
Port Logan
Maryport
Bothel
Drummore
Whithorn
Isle of Whithorn
Flimby
Greystoke
Mull of Galloway
Burrow Hd.
Workington
Cockermouth
Skiddaw
Threlkeld
Distington
Thornthwaite
Keswick
Derwent Water
Whitehaven
Frizington
Buttermere
Ullswater
Patterdale
Helvellyn
St. Bees
Egremont
Lake District
Borrowdale
Scafell Pike
West Water
Grasmere
Ambleside
SELLAFIELD CENTRE
Gosforth
Seascale
Windermere
Pt. of Ayre
Isle of Man
Andreas
Ramsey Bay
Ramsey
Coniston
Torver
Bowness-on-Windermere
Ravenglass
Maughold Hd.
Kirk Michael
Snaefell
Broughton-in-Furness
Coniston Water
Bootle
Newby Bridge
Laxey
LAXEY WHEEL
Grizebeck
Peel
PEEL CASTLE
Millom
CARTMEL PRIORY
Foxdale
Askam-in-Furness
Ulverston
Grange-over-Sands
Douglas
Dalton-in-Furness
Ballasalla
Barrow-in-Furness
Morecambe Bay
Port Erin
Castletown
Vickerstown
Rampside
FURNESS ABBEY
Calf of Man
Port St. Mary
Liverpool
Dublin
Belfast
I. of Walney
Morecambe
Heysham

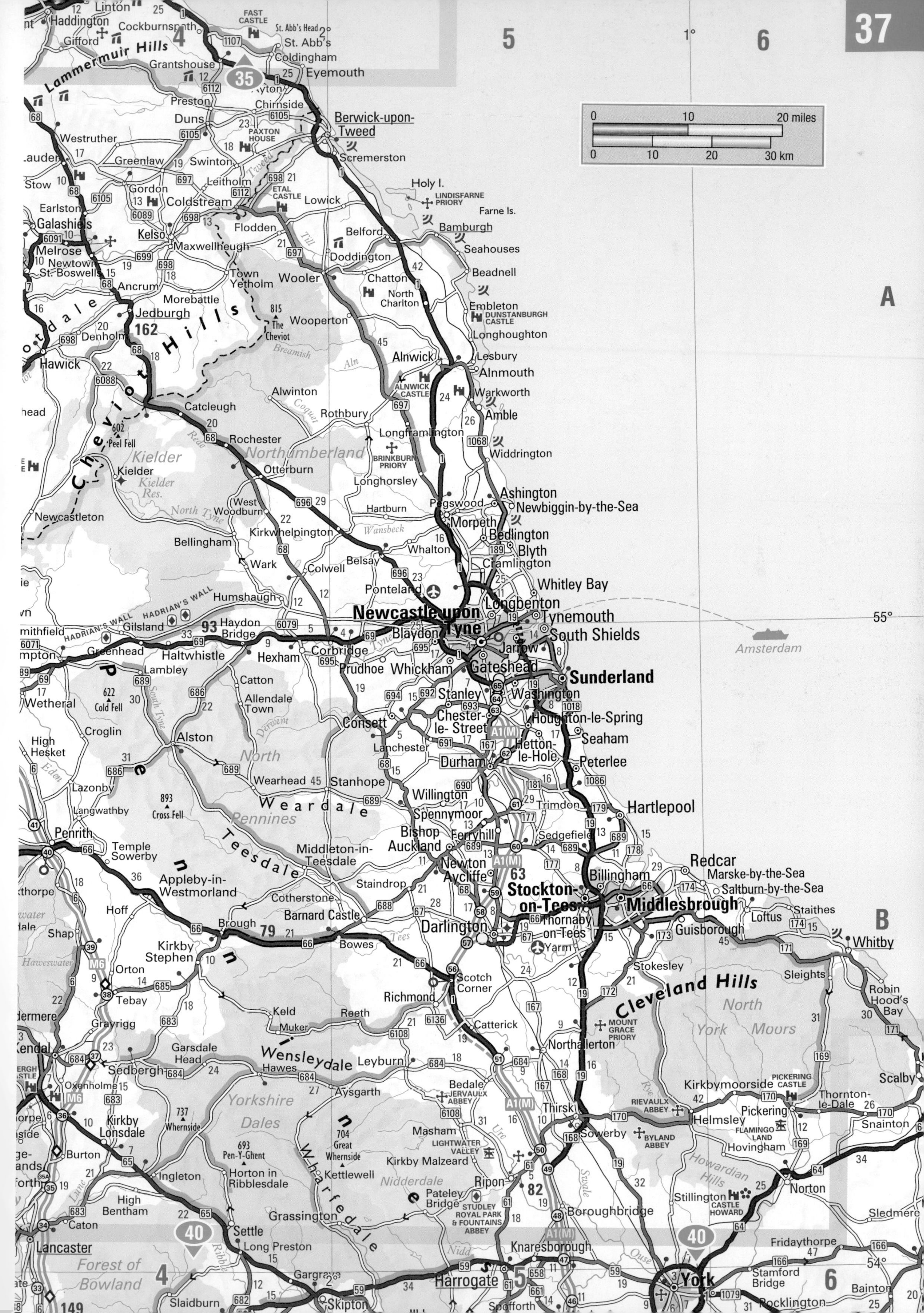

5
6
1°
A
B
55°
54°
4
0 10 20 miles
0 10 20 30 km
Linton
Haddington
Cockburnspath
Gifford
Lammermuir Hills
Fast Castle
St. Abb's Head
St. Abb's
Coldingham
Grantshouse
Eyemouth
Ayton
Preston
Chirnside
Duns
Paxton House
Berwick-upon-Tweed
Westruther
Scremerston
Lauder
Greenlaw
Swinton
Tweed
Stow
Leitholm
Gordon
Coldstream
Etal Castle
Lowick
Holy I.
Lindisfarne Priory
Farne Is.
Earlston
Galashiels
Kelso
Flodden
Belford
Bamburgh
Melrose
Maxwellheugh
Till
Seahouses
Newtown St. Boswells
Doddington
Beadnell
Ancrum
Town Yetholm
Wooler
Chatton
North Charlton
Morebattle
Embleton
Dunstanburgh Castle
Jedburgh
The Cheviot
Wooperton
Longhoughton
Denholm
Cheviot Hills
Breamish
Aln
Alnwick
Lesbury
Hawick
Alnmouth
Alnwick Castle
Warkworth
Alwinton
Coquet
Rothbury
Amble
Catcleugh
Peel Fell
Rede
Rochester
Longframlington
Kielder
Northumberland
Brinkburn Priory
Widdrington
Kielder Res.
Otterburn
Longhorsley
Ashington
Newcastleton
North Tyne
West Woodburn
Hartburn
Pegswood
Newbiggin-by-the-Sea
Morpeth
Wansbeck
Bedlington
Bellingham
Kirkwhelpington
Whalton
Blyth
Wark
Colwell
Belsay
Cramlington
Ponteland
Whitley Bay
Humshaugh
Hadrian's Wall
Longbenton
Newcastle upon Tyne
Tynemouth
Gilsland
Haydon Bridge
South Shields
Blaydon
Amsterdam
Greenhead
Haltwhistle
Hexham
Corbridge
Jarrow
Prudhoe
Whickham
Gateshead
Sunderland
Lambley
Catton
Washington
Stanley
Wetheral
Cold Fell
Allendale Town
Chester-le-Street
Houghton-le-Spring
Croglin
Consett
Seaham
High Hesket
Alston
Derwent
South Tyne
Lanchester
Hetton-le-Hole
North
Durham
Peterlee
Eden
Wearhead
Stanhope
Lazonby
Cross Fell
Willington
Hartlepool
Langwathby
Weardale
Spennymoor
Trimdon
Pennines
Bishop Auckland
Ferryhill
Sedgefield
Penrith
Temple Sowerby
Middleton-in-Teesdale
Teesdale
Newton Aycliffe
Redcar
Marske-by-the-Sea
Appleby-in-Westmorland
Staindrop
Billingham
Saltburn-by-the-Sea
Cotherstone
Stockton-on-Tees
Middlesbrough
Staithes
Hoff
Barnard Castle
Loftus
Brough
Darlington
Thornaby-on-Tees
Guisborough
Whitby
Shap
Kirkby Stephen
Bowes
Tees
Yarm
Orton
Stokesley
Sleights
Haweswater
Scotch Corner
Cleveland Hills
Robin Hood's Bay
Tebay
Richmond
North York Moors
Keld
Reeth
Grayrigg
Muker
Catterick
Mount Grace Priory
Northallerton
Kendal
Garsdale Head
Wensleydale
Leyburn
Sedbergh
Hawes
Scalby
Oxenholme
Aysgarth
Bedale
Jervaulx Abbey
Kirkbymoorside
Pickering Castle
Thornton-le-Dale
Yorkshire Dales
Thirsk
Rievaulx Abbey
Pickering
Helmsley
Kirkby Lonsdale
Whernside
Masham
Sowerby
Byland Abbey
Flamingo Land
Snainton
Great Whernside
Lightwater Valley
Hovingham
Pen-Y-Ghent
Ure
Burton
Kirkby Malzeard
Howardian Hills
Horton in Ribblesdale
Kettlewell
Nidderdale
Ripon
Ingleton
Lune
Norton
High Bentham
Pateley Bridge
Studley Royal Park & Fountains Abbey
Swale
Stillington
Castle Howard
Grassington
Wharfedale
Boroughbridge
Sledmere
Caton
Settle
Lancaster
Long Preston
Ribble
Knaresborough
Nidd
Ouse
Fridaythorpe
Forest of Bowland
Gargrave
Harrogate
York
Stamford Bridge
Bainton
Slaidburn
Skipton
Spofforth
Pocklington

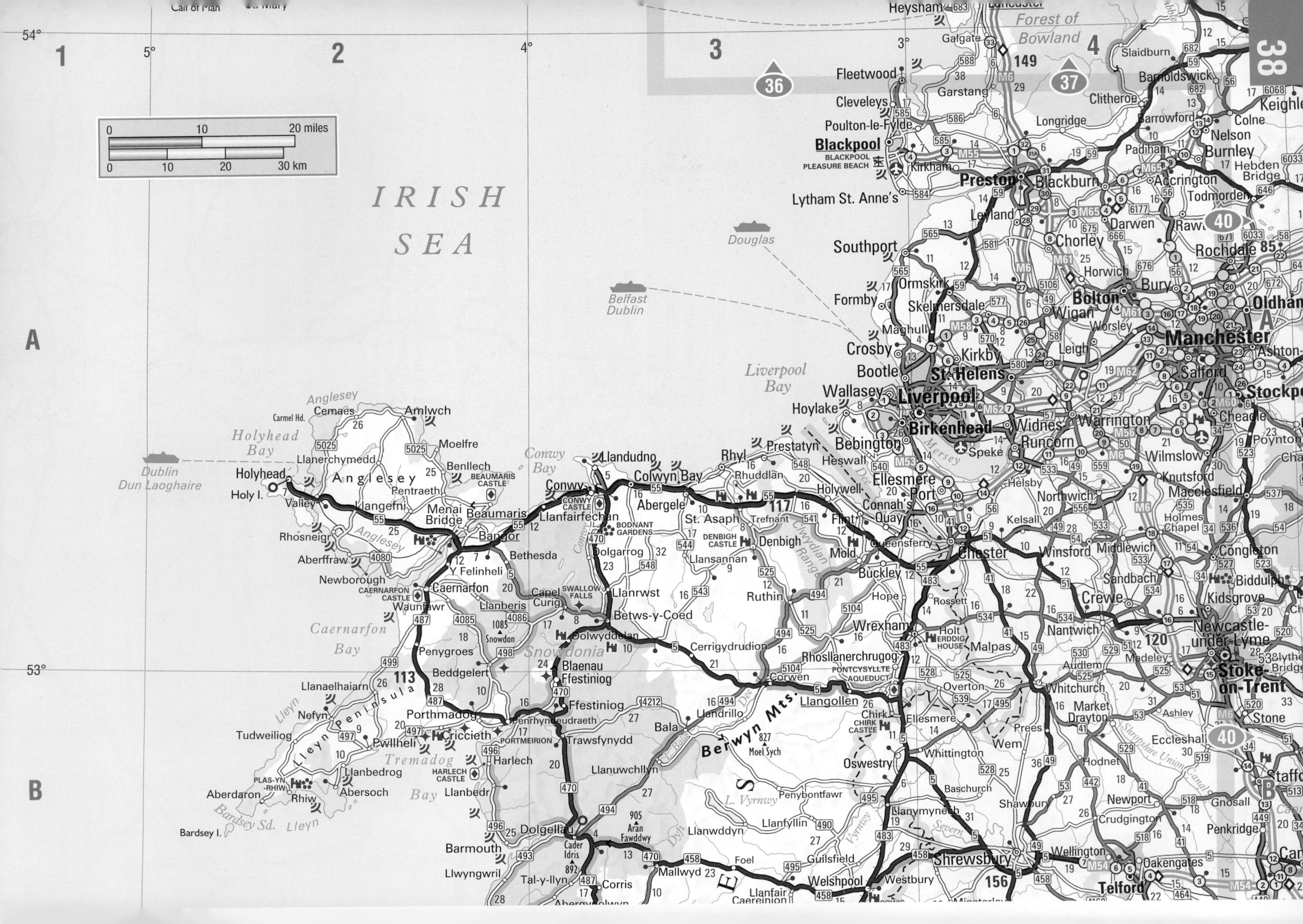
38
IRISH SEA
Liverpool Bay
Caernarfon Bay
Tremadog Bay
Conwy Bay
Holyhead Bay
Anglesey
Snowdonia
Berwyn Mts.
Forest of Bowland
Clwydian Range
Lleyn Peninsula
Bardsey Sd.
Blackpool
Preston
Southport
Liverpool
Birkenhead
St. Helens
Wigan
Bolton
Manchester
Stockport
Warrington
Chester
Wrexham
Crewe
Stoke-on-Trent
Shrewsbury
Telford
Bangor
Caernarfon
Holyhead
Conwy
Llandudno
Rhyl
Colwyn Bay
Dolgellau
Barmouth
Pwllheli
Porthmadog
Bala
Llangollen
Welshpool
Oswestry
Dublin
Dun Laoghaire
Belfast
Dublin
Douglas
20 miles
30 km
54°
53°
5°
4°
3°

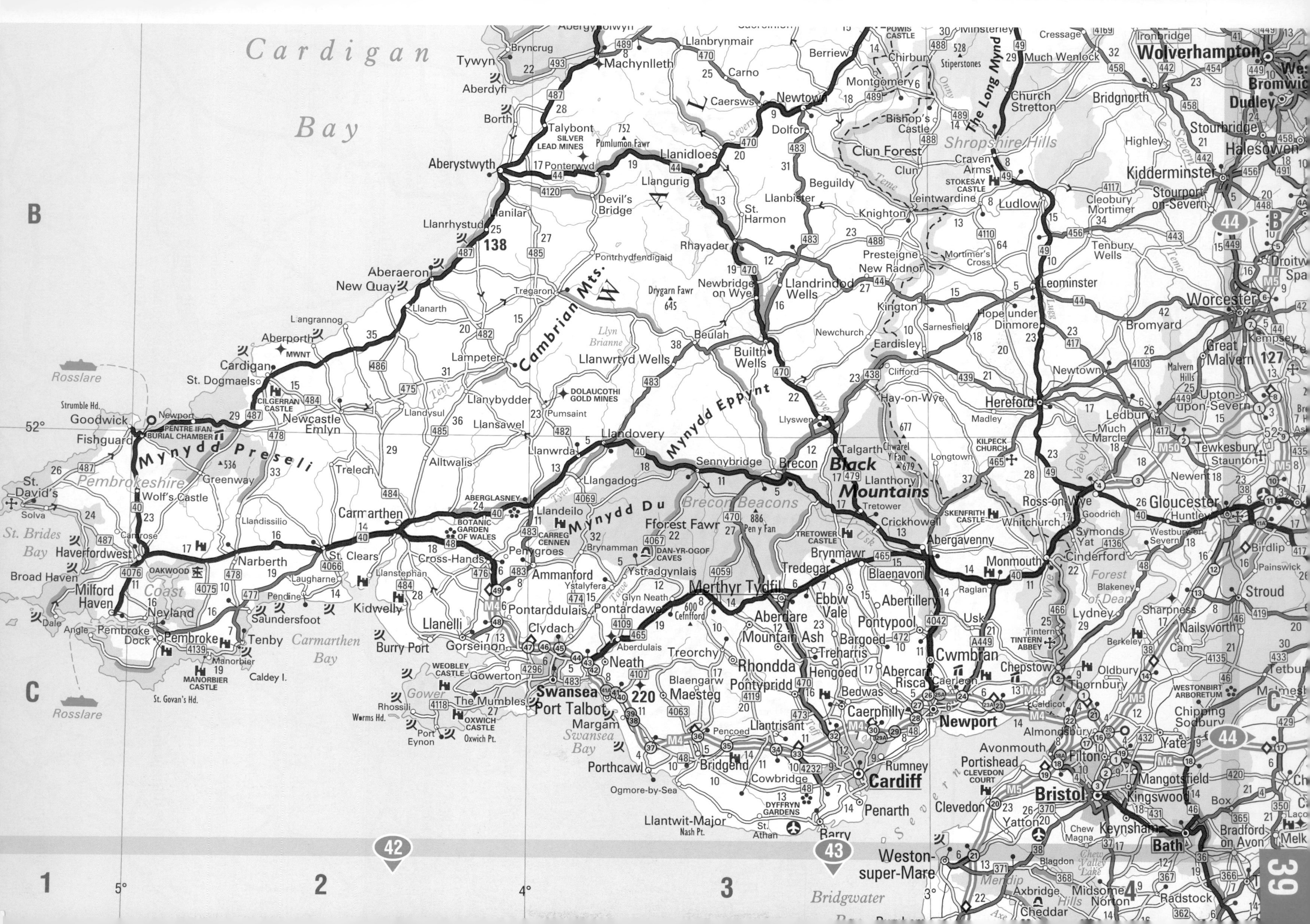
Cardigan Bay
Aberystwyth
Machynlleth
Tywyn
Aberdyfi
Borth
Talybont
Llanidloes
Newtown
Llangurig
Devil's Bridge
Rhayader
Llandrindod Wells
Builth Wells
Cambrian Mts.
Mynydd Eppynt
Llandovery
Lampeter
Tregaron
Aberaeron
New Quay
Cardigan
Fishguard
Goodwick
St. David's
Haverfordwest
Milford Haven
Pembroke
Tenby
Narberth
St. Clears
Carmarthen
Llandeilo
Ammanford
Llanelli
Swansea
Port Talbot
Neath
Bridgend
Cardiff
Newport
Merthyr Tydfil
Brecon
Black Mountains
Brecon Beacons
Abergavenny
Monmouth
Hereford
Leominster
Ludlow
Kidderminster
Worcester
Gloucester
Stroud
Chepstow
Bristol
Bath
Weston-super-Mare
Wolverhampton
Dudley
Mynydd Preseli
Mynydd Du
Pembrokeshire Coast
Carmarthen Bay
Swansea Bay
Bridgwater
Rosslare
Shropshire Hills
The Long Mynd
Clun Forest
Forest of Dean
B
C
1
2
3
4
42
43
44
52°
5°
4°
3°

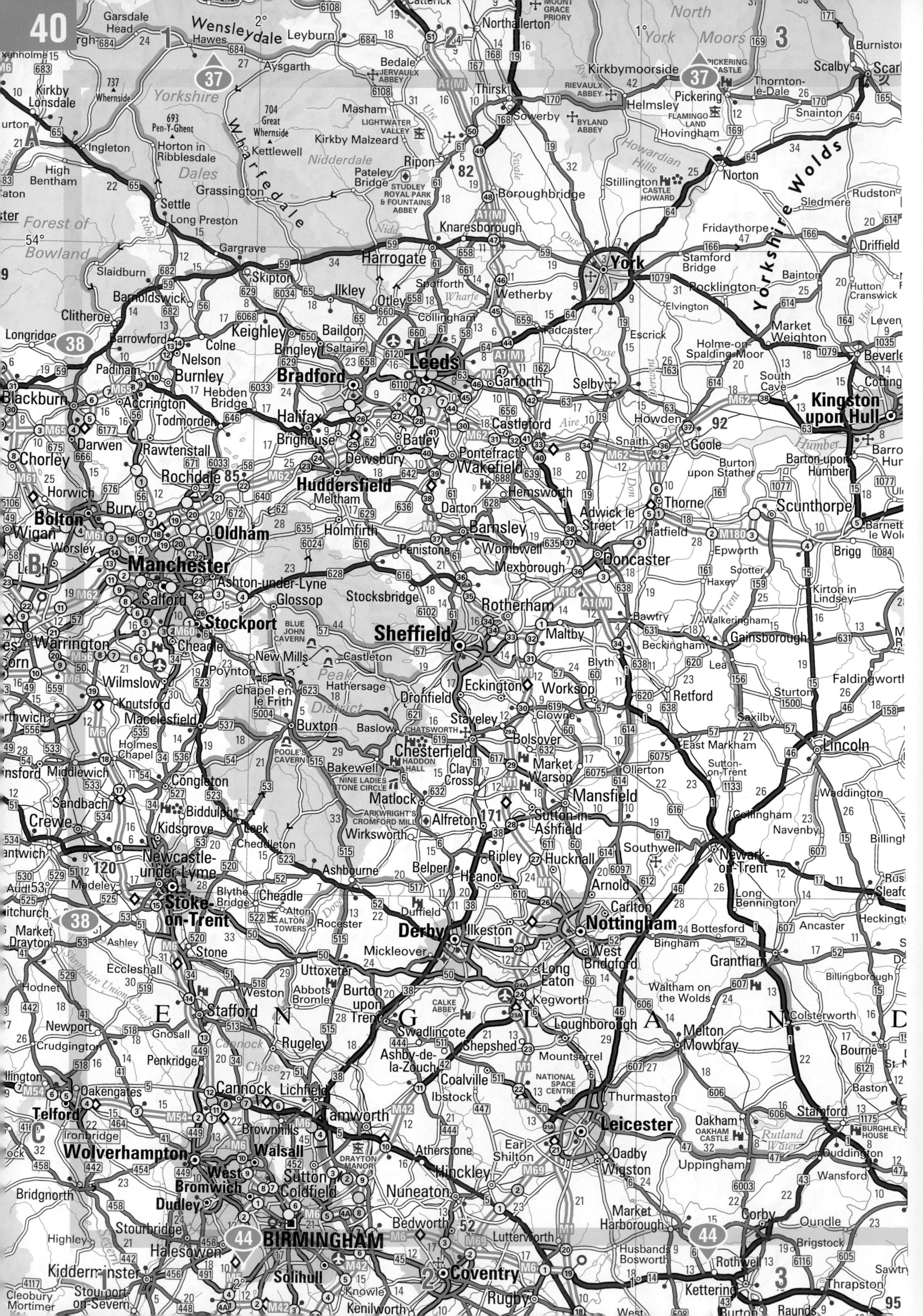

NORTH SEA
The Wash
Norfolk Coast
Bridlington Bay
Lincolnshire Wolds
The Fens
Breckland
The Broads
Rotterdam
Zeebrugge
Spurn Hd.
0 10 20 miles
0 10 20 30 km
Filey
Flamborough
Bridlington
Burton Agnes
Skipsea
North Frodingham
Hornsea
Aldbrough
Sproatley
Hedon
Withernsea
Keyingham
Patrington
Easington
Immingham
Grimsby
Cleethorpes
Humberston
Laceby
Caistor
North Thoresby
North Somercotes
Saltfleet
Binbrook
ST. JAMES CHURCH
Louth
Mablethorpe
Withern
Sutton-on-Sea
Wragby
Scamblesby
Huttoft
Alford
Bardney
Horncastle
Partney
Woodhall Spa
Burgh le Marsh
Skegness
Mareham le Fen
Spilsby
Coningsby
Wainfleet All Saints
Sibsey
Wrangle
Benington
Boston
Kirton
Gosberton
Pinchbeck
Spalding
Holbeach
Long Sutton
Deeping St Nicholas
Crowland
Market Deeping
Wisbech
Eye
Peterborough
Whittlesey
Yaxley
March
Chatteris
Ramsey
Somersham
Ely
Littleport
Outwell
Downham Market
Hilgay
Methwold
Lakenheath
Brandon
GRIMES GRAVES
Thetford
Hunstanton
Heacham
Brancaster
Docking
Dersingham
SANDRINGHAM
Burnham Market
HOLKHAM HALL
Wells-next-the-Sea
Little Walsingham
Cley
Sheringham
Cromer
Holt
King's Lynn
Gayton
CASTLE ACRE PRIORY
Fakenham
Litcham
Swaffham
Fincham
OXBURGH HALL
Stoke Ferry
Dereham
Watton
Attleborough
BICKLING HALL
Saxthorpe
Reepham
Aylsham
DINOSAUR ADVENTURE PARK
Drayton
New Costessey
Norwich
Wymondham
Mundesley
North Walsham
Stalham
Coltishall
Wroxham
Acle
Martham
Caister-on-Sea
Great Yarmouth
BURGH CASTLE
Gorleston-on-sea
Oulton
Corton
Oulton Broad
Lowestoft
Beccles
Harleston
Diss
Scole
Wrentham
Ouse
Nene
Welland
Witham
Wensum
Bure
Yare
A1(M)
0°
1°
53°
54°
A
B
C
3
4
5
45
69

St. David's Hd.
St. David's
Ramsey I.
Solva
Pembrokeshire
Greenway
Wolf's Castle
St. Brides Bay
Haverfordwest
Camrose
Broad Haven
Skomer I.
Skokholm I.
Milford Haven
Dale
Angle
Pembroke Dock
Neyland
Pembroke
OAKWOOD
Coast
Narberth
Llandissilio
Carmarthen
St. Clears
Laugharne
Pendine
Saundersfoot
Tenby
Manorbier
MANORBIER CASTLE
St. Govan's Hd.
Caldey I.
Carmarthen Bay
Rosslare
Llanstephan
Kidwelly
Burry Port
Llanelli
Gorseinon
Cross-Hands
ABERGLASNEY
BOTANIC GARDEN OF WALES
Llandeilo
CARREG CENNEN
Penygroes
Ammanford
Ystalyfera
Pontarddulais
Clydach
WEOBLEY CASTLE
Gowerton
Gower
Swansea
The Mumbles
Port Talbot
Rhossili
Worms Hd.
Port Eynon
OXWICH CASTLE
Oxwich Pt.
Swansea Bay

A

Bristol Channel

Lundy
North Devon
Lynmouth
Lynton
Ilfracombe
Morte Pt.
Morte Bay
Woolacombe
Croyde
Barnstaple or Bideford Bay
Barnstaple
Instow
Appledore
Westward Ho!
Hartland Pt.
Hartland
Clovelly
Bideford
South Molton
Great Torrington
Stibb Cross
Chulmleigh
Morwenstow
Venn Green
Winkleigh
Bude Bay
Bude
Stratton
Hatherleigh
North Tawton
Widemouth
Holsworthy
Okehampton
South Tawton
Poundstock
Roadford Res.
High Willhays
Chagford
Boscastle
Tintagel Hd.
Tintagel
TINTAGEL CASTLE
Hallworthy
Launceston
LAUNCESTON CASTLE
Lydford
Moretonhampstead
Dartmoor
Delabole
Port Isaac
Port Isaac Bay
Pentire Pt.
Camelford
Marytavy
Brown Willy
Padstow
St. Teath
Bodmin Moor
Tavistock
Princetown
Trevose Hd.
Wadebridge
SLATE CAVERNS
Gunnislake
BUCKFAST ABBEY
Buckfastleigh
Ashburton
St. Issey
Bodmin
Callington
Tamar
Yelverton
Dobwalls
Bere Alston
Valley
BUCKLAND ABBEY
Newquay
St. Columb Major
Liskeard
Saltash
South Brent
RESTORMEL CASTLE
Lostwithiel
Torpoint
Plymouth
Ivybridge
St. Enoder
St. Blazey
EDEN PROJECT
Devonport
Plymstock
Perranporth
St. Austell
Bodinnick
Looe
ROYAL CITADEL
Yealmpton
St. Agnes
Fowey
Polruan
Polperro
Whitesand Bay
Wembury
Newton Ferrers
Charlestown
Perranzabuloe
Mevagissey Bay
Bigbury
Portreath
HELIGAN GDNS.
Probus
Mevagissey
Bigbury Bay
Redruth
GWENNAP PIT
Truro
Tregony
Gorran Haven
Marlborough
St. Ives
Carbis Bay
Gwennap
Veryan
Hayle
Camborne
Zennor
Penryn
Pendeen
POLDARK MINE
St. Mawes
St. Just
Marazion
Falmouth
Helston
Falmouth Bay
Newlyn
Penzance
Sennen
Mousehole
HALLIGGYE FOGOU
Land's End
Porthleven
St. Keverne
TREGIFFIAN BURIAL CHAMBER
Mount's Bay
The Manacles
Mullion
GOONHILLY
Coverack
Lizard
Lizard Pt.
Wolf Rock
Roscoff
Santander
St Malo
Cornwall

B

Isles of Scilly
Tresco
St. Martin's
Hugh Town
Crow Sound
St. Mary's

51°
50°
5°
4°
6°
1
2
3

Brecon Beacons
Fforest Fawr
Pen y Fan
Llanthony
Tretower
Crickhowell
Tretower Castle
Skenfrith Castle
Whitchurch
Ross-on-Wye
Goodrich
Symonds Yat
Gloucester
Huntley
Westbury-on-Severn
Cheltenham
Cleeve Cloud
Cotswold
Charlton Kings
Northleach
Burford
Birdlip
Painswick
Stroud
Cirencester
Fairford
Bibury
Lechlade-on-Thames
Dan-yr-Ogof Caves
Ystradgynlais
Glyn Neath
Merthyr Tydfil
Brynmawr
Tredegar
Blaenavon
Abergavenny
Monmouth
Cinderford
Forest of Dean
Blakeney
Lydney
Raglan
Abertillery
Ebbw Vale
Aberdare
Mountain Ash
Pontypool
Usk
Tintern Abbey
Sharpness
Nailsworth
Berkeley
Cam
Neath
Aberdulais
Treorchy
Rhondda
Treharris
Bargoed
Cwmbran
Chepstow
Oldbury
Tetbury
Cricklade
Faringdon
Blaengarw
Maesteg
Pontypridd
Hengoed
Abercarn
Risca
Caerleon
Bedwas
Caerphilly
Newport
Caldicot
Thornbury
Westonbirt Arboretum
Malmesbury
Chipping Sodbury
Swindon
Llantrisant
Pencoed
Bridgend
Cowbridge
Porthcawl
Almondsbury
Avonmouth
Portishead
Clevedon Court
Filton
Yate
Lyneham
Chippenham
Marlborough Downs
Ogmore-by-Sea
Cardiff
Rumney
Dyffryn Gardens
Penarth
Clevedon
Bristol
Kingswood
Mangotsfield
Box
Calne
Avebury
Silbury Hill
Tan Hill
Marlborough
Llantwit-Major
Nash Pt.
St. Athan
Barry
Severn
Yatton
Chew Magna
Keynsham
Bath
Bradford on Avon
Lacock
Melksham
Vale of Pewsey
Weston-super-Mare
Blagdon
Chew Valley Lake
Devizes
Pewsey
Mendip Hills
Axbridge
Midsomer Norton
Radstock
Trowbridge
Upavon
Bridgwater Bay
Cheddar
Wookey Hole
Salisbury Plain
Westbury
Warminster
Burnham-on-Sea
Hinkley Pt.
Minehead
Porlock
Exmoor
Dunster
Watchet
Wells
Shepton Mallet
Frome
Longleat
Woodhenge
Stonehenge
Heytesbury
Amesbury
Dunkery Beacon
Dunster Castle
Brendon Hills
Nether Stowey
Glastonbury
Polden Hills
Evercreech
Maiden Bradley
Porton
Old Sarum
Bridgwater
Quantock Hills
North Petherton
Street
Stourhead
Wylye
Wilton
Salisbury
Middlezoy
Castle Cary
Bruton
Mere
Cranborne
Bishops Lydeard
Somerton
Wincanton
Gillingham
Wilton House
Chase & West
Wiveliscombe
Dulverton
North Molton
Milverton
Taunton
Sparkford
Shaftesbury
Wiltshire Downs
Fordingbridge
Wellington
Knightshayes Court
Staple Hill
Blackdown Hills
South Petherton
Ilchester
Yeovil
Sherborne
Sturminster Newton
Blackmoor Vale
New Forest
Tiverton
Halberton
Uffculme
Ilminster
Chard
Crewkerne
Blandford Forum
Verwood
Ringwood
Lapford
Cullompton
Yarcombe
Pilsdon Pen
North Dorset Downs
Cerne Abbas Giant
Cerne Abbas
Wimborne Minster
Brockenhurst
Ferndown
Crediton
Silverton
Honiton
Beaminster
Maiden Newton
Dorset
Broadclyst
Ottery St. Mary
Axminster
East Devon
Charminster
Tolpuddle
Bere Regis
Broadstone
Christchurch
Priory Church
Exeter
Pinhoe
Colyford
Bridport
Maiden Castle
Dorchester
Wareham
Poole
Bournemouth
Sandbanks
Dunsford
Topsham
Exminster
Beer
Seaton
Lyme Regis
Burton Bradstock
Abbotsbury
Poor Lot Barrows
South Dorset Downs
Wool
Poole Harbour
Studland
I. of Purbeck
Corfe Castle
Swanage
Durlston Hd.
Sidmouth
Lyme Bay
Chesil Beach
West Lulworth
Weymouth
Fortuneswell
Portland Castle
Easton
Portland Bill
I. of Portland
St. Alban's Head
Budleigh Salterton
Bovey Tracey
Exmouth
Dawlish
Teignmouth
Shaldon
Kingsteignton
Newton Abbot
Dartington
Torquay
Paignton
Tor Bay
Totnes
Galmpton
Brixham
Kingswear
Dartmouth
Stoke Fleming
Kingsbridge
Start Bay
Torcross
Salcombe
Start Pt.
Guernsey
Jersey
St. Malo
Cherbourg
Gijon
0 10 20 miles
0 10 20 30 km
50°
3°
2°
3
4
5
A
B
39
44

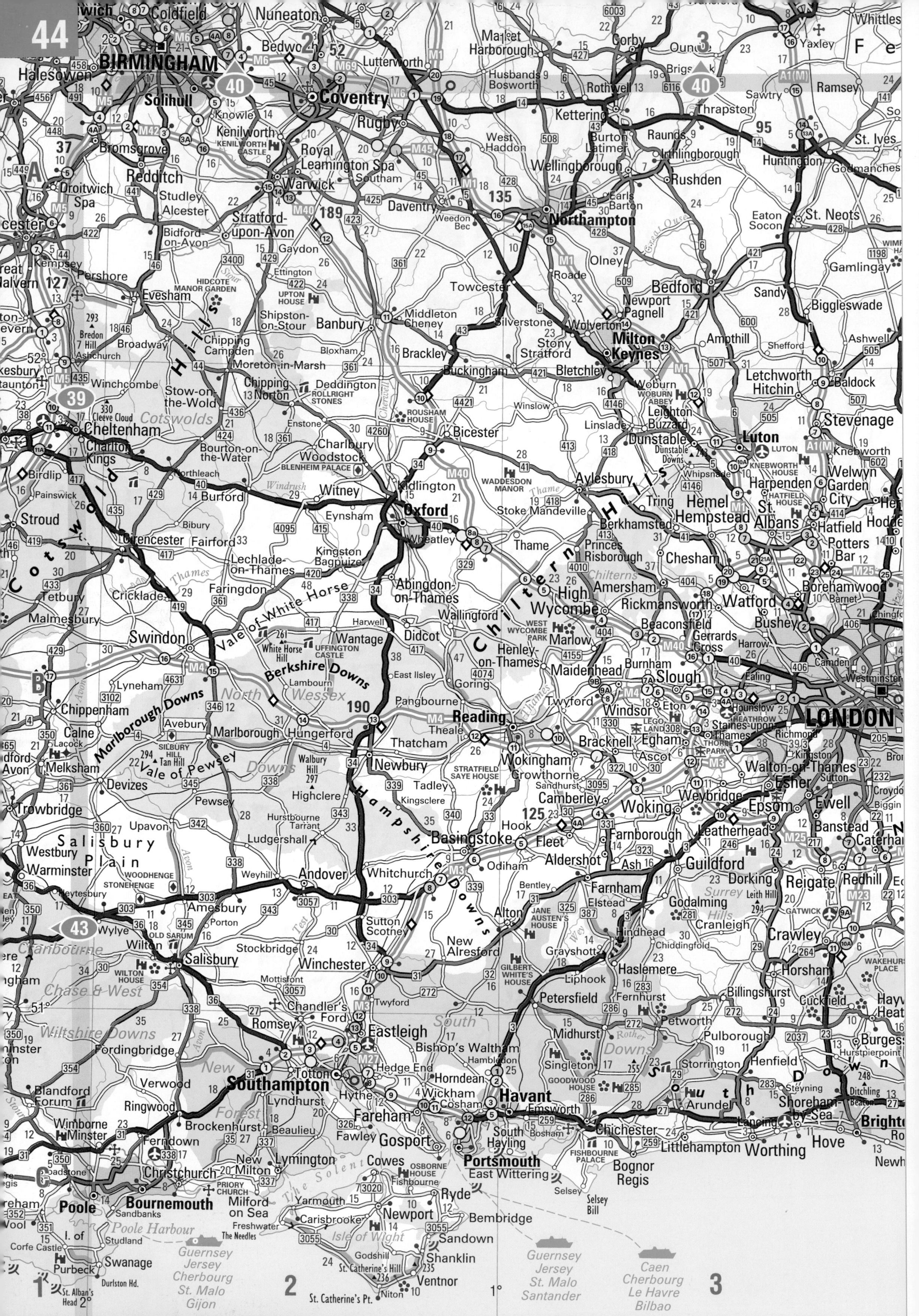

March
Hilgay
Methwold
Attleborough
Wymondham
Corton
Oulton
Oulton Broad
Lowestoft
2°
Chatteris
Littleport
Breckland
GRIMES GRAVES
Brandon
Thetford
Bungay
Beccles
Wrentham
Ely
Lakenheath
Diss
Scole
Harleston
Mildenhall
Halesworth
Southwold
Needingworth
Soham
Isleham
Eye
Blythburgh
Cottenham
Burwell
Fordham
Ixworth
A
Newmarket
NATIONAL STUD
Bury St. Edmunds
Framlingham
Saxmundham
Cambridge
ICKWORTH HOUSE
Stowmarket
LEISTON ABBEY
Leiston
Aldeburgh
Hartest
Needham Market
Wickham Market
Suffolk Coast And Heaths
Tunstall
ORFORD CASTLE
Lavenham
Ipswich
Woodbridge
SUTTON HOO
Orford Ness
DUXFORD
Haverhill
Long Melford
Kesgrave
Royston
Saffron Walden
Sudbury
Hadleigh
Dedham Vale
Bawdsey
52°
AUDLEY END HOUSE
Finchingfield
HEADINGHAM CASTLE
Felixstowe
Thaxted
Halstead
Shotley Gate
Harwich
Stansted Mountfitchet
Manningtree
Esbjerg
Hoek van Holland
STANSTED
ST. JAMES THE LESS
Colchester
Bishop's Stortford
Braintree
Coggeshall
The Naze
Great Dunmow
Wivenhoe
Walton-on-the-Naze
Frinton-on-Sea
Ware
Sawbridgeworth
Tiptree
Great Waltham
Witham
Brightlingsea
Clacton-on-Sea
Harlow
West Mersea
Cheshunt
Chelmsford
Waltham Abbey
Epping
Chipping Ongar
Danbury
Maldon
ST. PETERS ON THE WALL
South Woodham Ferrers
Shenfield
Billericay
Burnham-on-Crouch
0
10
20 miles
30 km
Chigwell
Wickford
Rayleigh
Foulness Island
Romford
Brentwood
Havering
Basildon
B
Newham
South Ockendon
Stanford le Hope
Hadleigh
Southend-on-Sea
Shoeburyness
Woolwich
Canvey
Thames
Greenwich
Purfleet
Grays
Grain
Sheerness
Northfleet
Dartford
Gravesend
Swanley
Leysdown-on-Sea
Rochester
Gillingham
Herne Bay
Margate
EYNSFORD CASTLE
Whitstable
North Foreland
Orpington
Chatham
Rainham
Sittingbourne
Broadstairs
Faversham
Ramsgate
Oostende
Canterbury
Ash
RICHBOROUGH CASTLE
Sevenoaks
Sandwich
Oxted
Hadlow
Maidstone
Wingham
LEEDS CASTLE
Deal
Sutton Valence
Walmer
Barham
HEVER CASTLE
Tonbridge
Headcorn
Wye
Southborough
Staplehurst
SISSINGHURST CASTLE
Ashford
St. Margaret's at Cliffe
South Foreland
Royal Tunbridge Wells
EUROTUNNEL TERMINAL
Hawkinge
East Grinstead
Goudhurst
Newington
Dover
Dunkerque
Lamberhurst
Tenterden
Folkestone
Weald
Lympne
Hamstreet
Hythe
Crowborough
Hawkhurst
Romney Marsh
Dymchurch
Gravelines
High Weald
Bodiam
Calais
Marck
Uckfield
Heathfield
Peasmarsh
Lydd
New Romney
Sangatte
Rye
Halland
Battle
Winchelsea
Wissant
EUROTUNNEL TERMINAL
Dungeness
Lewes
Herstmonceux
Rye Bay
Cap Gris-Nez
Ardres
MICHELHAM PRIORY
Hailsham
St. Leonards
Guînes
Polegate
Bexhill
Hastings
Ambleteuse
Marquise
Licques
Wimereux
Seaford
Pevensey Bay
NAUSICAA
Caps et Marais d'Opale
Eastbourne
Boulogne-sur-Mer
Le Portel
Escoeuilles
Lumbres
Beachy Hd.
Outreau
Desvres
Hardelot Plage
Samer
Fauquembergues
Dieppe
Hucqueliers
4
1°
5
Étaples
6
Strait of Dover
Downs
Kent
North Downs

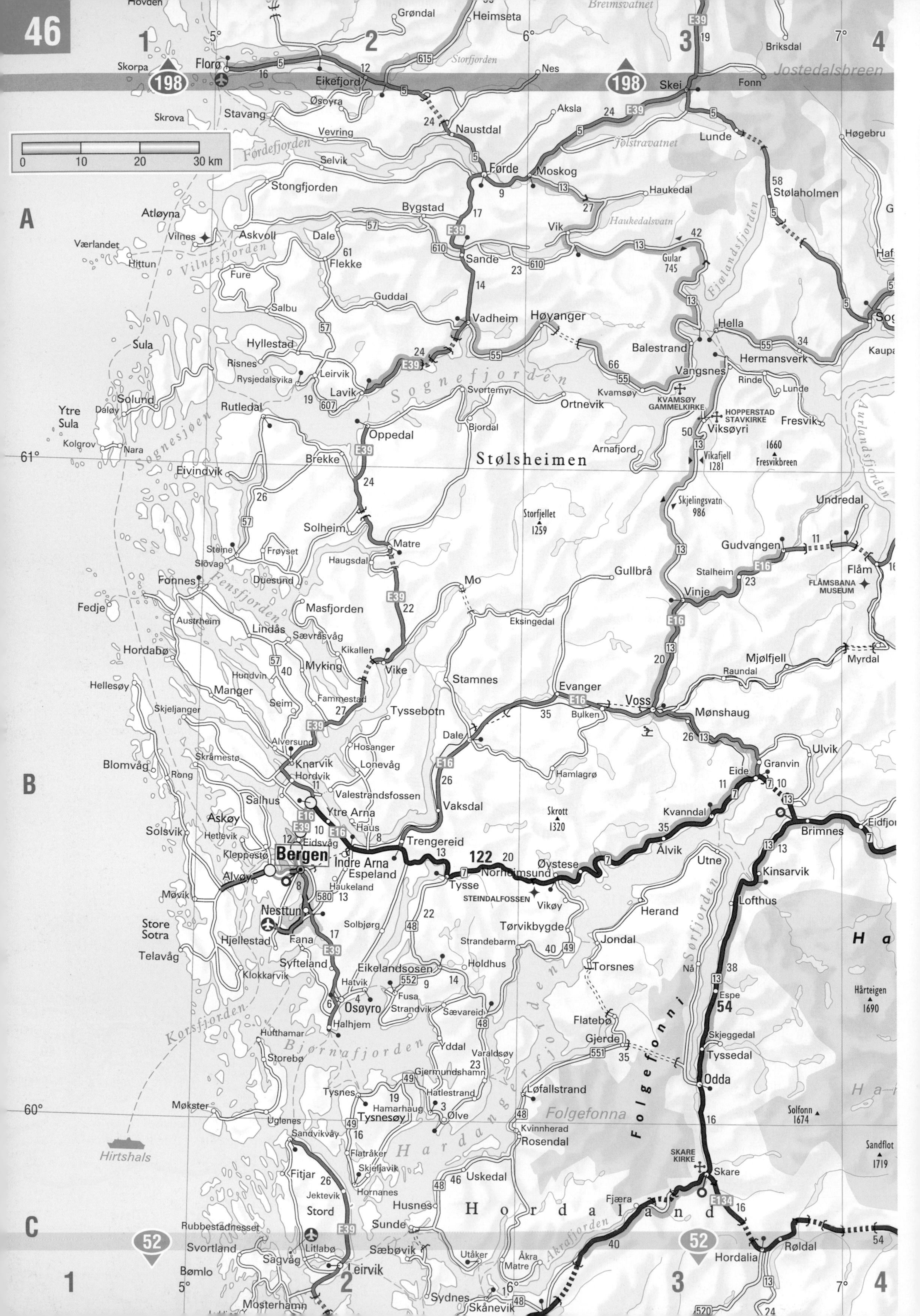
46
1
2
3
4
5°
6°
7°
Hovden
Grøndal
Heimseta
Breimsvatnet
Briksdal
Jostedalsbreen
Skorpa
Florø
198
Eikefjord
Storfjorden
Nes
Skei
Fonn
Øsoyra
Stavang
Skrova
Vevring
Naustdal
Aksla
Førdefjorden
Jølstravatnet
Lunde
Høgebru
0
10
20
30 km
Selvik
Førde
Moskog
Stongfjorden
Haukedal
58
Stølaholmen
A
Atløyna
Bygstad
Haukedalsvatn
Vik
Værlandet
Vilnes
Askvoll
Dale
Vilnesfjorden
Hittun
Flekke
Sande
Gular
745
Fjærlandsfjorden
Fure
Salbu
Guddal
Vadheim
Høyanger
Sula
Hyllestad
Hella
Balestrand
Hermansverk
Risnes
Rysjedalsvika
Leirvik
Lavik
Sognefjorden
Vangsnes
Rinde
Kvamsøy
KVAMSØY GAMMELKIRKE
Solund
Ytre Sula
Daløy
Rutledal
Svortemyr
Ortnevik
HOPPERSTAD STAVKIRKE
Viksøyri
Fresvik
Aurlandsfjorden
Kolgrov
Nara
Sognesjøen
Bjordal
Oppedal
Arnafjord
1660
Fresvikbreen
61°
Brekke
Stølsheimen
Vikafjell
1281
Eivindvik
Skjelingsvatn
986
Undredal
Storfjellet
1259
Solheim
Matre
Gudvangen
Steine
Frøyset
Haugsdal
Stalheim
Flåm
Sløvag
Fensfjorden
Gullbrå
FLÅMSBANA MUSEUM
Fonnes
Duesund
Mo
Vinje
Fedje
Austrheim
Masfjorden
Eksingedal
Lindås
Sævråsvåg
Hordabø
Kikallen
Mjølfjell
Raundal
Myrdal
Hundvin
Myking
Vike
Hellesøy
Manger
Stamnes
Evanger
Voss
Seim
Fammestad
Bulken
Mønshaug
Skjeljanger
Tyssebotn
Dale
Alversund
Skråmestø
Hosanger
Ulvik
Blomvåg
Knarvik
Lonevåg
Granvin
Rong
Hordvik
Eide
Hamlagrø
B
Salhus
Valestrandsfossen
Askøy
Vaksdal
Skrott
1320
Kvanndal
Ytre Arna
Eidfjord
Solsvik
Hetlevik
Haus
Brimnes
Eidsvåg
Trengereid
Ålvik
Kleppestø
Bergen
Indre Arna
122
Øystese
Utne
Alvøy
Espeland
Norheimsund
Kinsarvik
Haukeland
Tysse
Møvik
STEINDALFOSSEN
Vikøy
Lofthus
Nesttun
Herand
Store Sotra
Solbjørg
Tørvikbygde
Hjellestad
Fana
Strandebarm
Jondal
Telavåg
Syfteland
Holdhus
Torsnes
Sørfjorden
Klokkarvik
Eikelandsosen
Nå
Hatvik
Fusa
Espe
Hårteigen
1690
Osøyro
Strandvik
Sævareid
Flatebø
Korsfjorden
Halhjem
Hufthamar
Bjørnafjorden
Skjeggedal
Gjerde
Folgefonni
Yddal
Varaldsøy
Tyssedal
Storebø
Gjermundshamn
Odda
Hatlestrand
Løfallstrand
Tysnes
Hamarhaug
Møkster
Ølve
60°
Tysnesøy
Folgefonna
Solfonn
1674
Uglenes
Sandvikvåg
Kvinnherad
Rosendal
Hardangerfjorden
Sandflot
1719
Hirtshals
Flatråker
Skjeljavik
SKARE KIRKE
Skare
Fitjar
Uskedal
Jektevik
Hornanes
Husnes
Fjæra
Stord
Hordaland
C
Rubbestadnesset
Sunde
Akrafjorden
52
Svortland
Litlabø
Sæbøvik
Utåker
Røldal
Sagvåg
Åkra
Hordalia
Bømlo
Matre
Leirvik
Sydnes
Mosterhamn
Skånevik

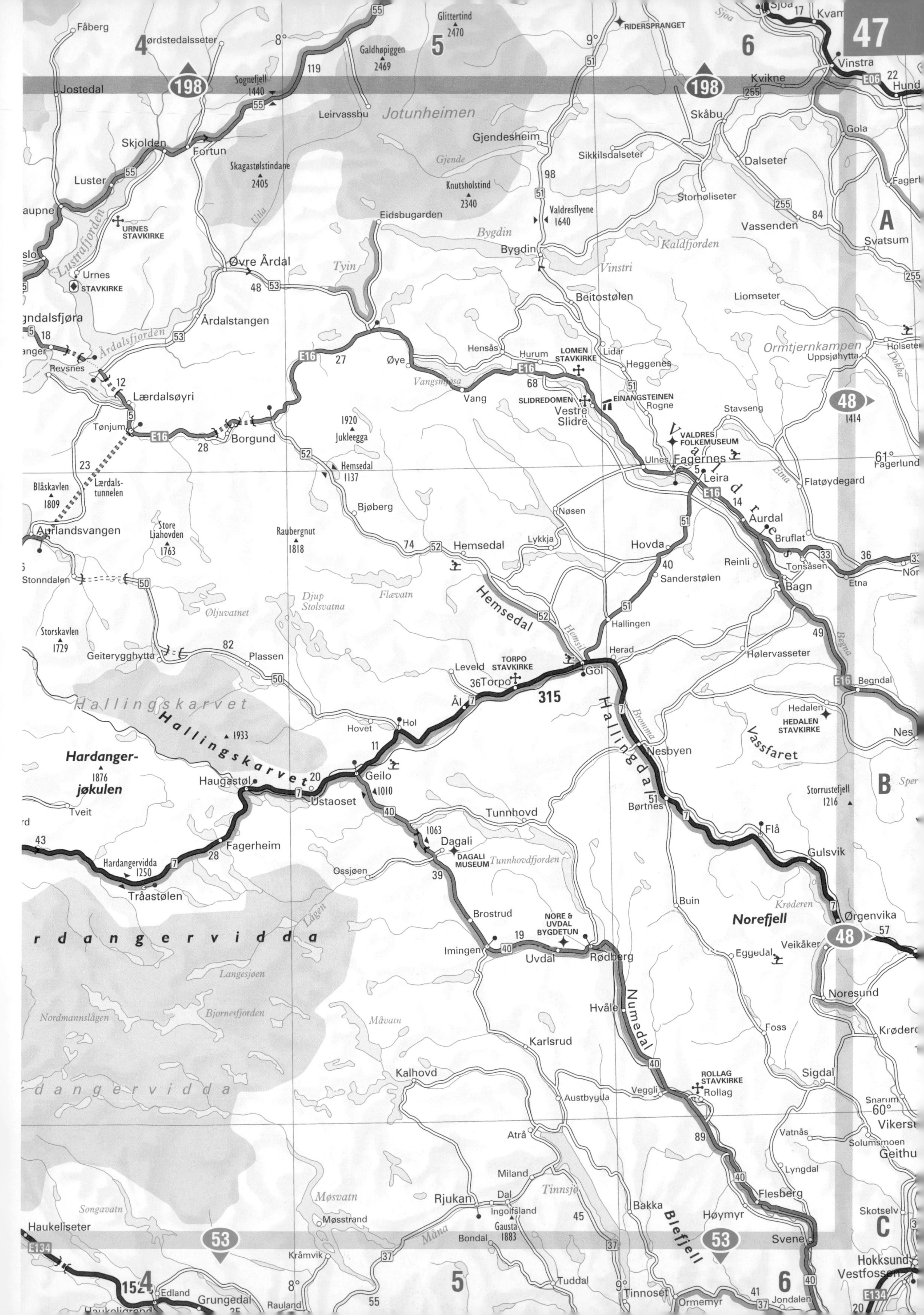
Jotunheimen
Glittertind 2470
Galdhøpiggen 2469
Sognefjell 1440
Jostedal
Fåberg
Skjolden
Fortun
Luster
Skagastølstindane 2405
Leirvassbu
Gjendesheim
Gjende
Knutsholstind 2340
Eidsbugarden
Bygdin
Tyin
Urnes Stavkirke
Øvre Årdal
Årdalstangen
Årdalsfjorden
Revsnes
Lærdalsøyri
Tønjum
Borgund
Lærdalstunnelen
Blåskavlen 1809
Aurlandsvangen
Stonndalen
Store Liahovden 1763
Raubergnut 1818
1920 Jukleegga
Hemsedal 1137
Bjøberg
Hemsedal
Vang
Øye
Vangsmjøsa
Hensås
Hurum
Lomen Stavkirke
Slidredomen
Vestre Slidre
Einangsteinen
Rogne
Lidar
Heggenes
Beitostølen
Valdresflyene 1640
Vinstri
Kaldfjorden
Ridersspranget
Sjoa
Kvam
Vinstra
Kvikne
Skåbu
Sikkilsdalseter
Dalseter
Gola
Storhøliseter
Vassenden
Svatsum
Liomseter
Ormtjernkampen
Holsetet
Uppsjøhytta
Stavseng
Valdres Folkemuseum
Fagernes
Ulnes
Leira
Aurdal
Bruflat
Tonsåsen
Reinli
Bagn
Etna
Flatøydegard
Fagerlund
Valdres
Nøsen
Lykkja
Hovda
Sanderstølen
Hallingen
Herad
Hølervasseter
Begndal
Begna
Gol
Torpo Stavkirke
Torpo
Leveld
Ål
Hol
Hovet
Geilo
Ustaoset
Haugastøl
Hallingskarvet
1933
Hardangerjøkulen 1876
Tveit
Fagerheim
Hardangervidda 1250
Tråastølen
Hardangervidda
Storskavlen 1729
Geiterygghytta
Plassen
Oljuvatnet
Djup Stolsvatna
Flævatn
Hemsedal
Hallingdal
Nesbyen
Bromma
Vassfaret
Hedalen
Hedalen Stavkirke
Nes
Storrustefjell 1216
Børtnes
Flå
Gulsvik
Krøderen
Ørgenvika
Norefjell
Eggedal
Veikåker
Noresund
Buin
Tunnhovd
Dagali
Dagali Museum
Tunnhovdfjorden
1063
1010
Ossjøen
Brostrud
Nore & Uvdal Bygdetun
Imingen
Uvdal
Rødberg
Numedal
Hvåle
Lågen
Langesjøen
Bjornesfjorden
Nordmannslågen
Måvatn
Karlsrud
Kalhovd
Austbygda
Veggli
Rollag Stavkirke
Rollag
Foss
Sigdal
Krøderen
Snarum
Vikersund
Vatnås
Solumsmoen
Geithus
Lyngdal
Atrå
Miland
Tinnsjø
Møsvatn
Møsstrand
Rjukan
Dal
Ingolfsland
Gausta 1883
Bondal
Måna
Songavatn
Haukeliseter
Kråmvik
Bakka
Blefjell
Flesberg
Høymyr
Svene
Skotselv
Hokksund
Vestfossen
Tuddal
Tinnoset
Ormemyr
Jondalen
Edland
Grungedal
Rauland
Haukeligrend
61°
60°
8°
9°
A
B
C
4
5
6
198
53
48
1414

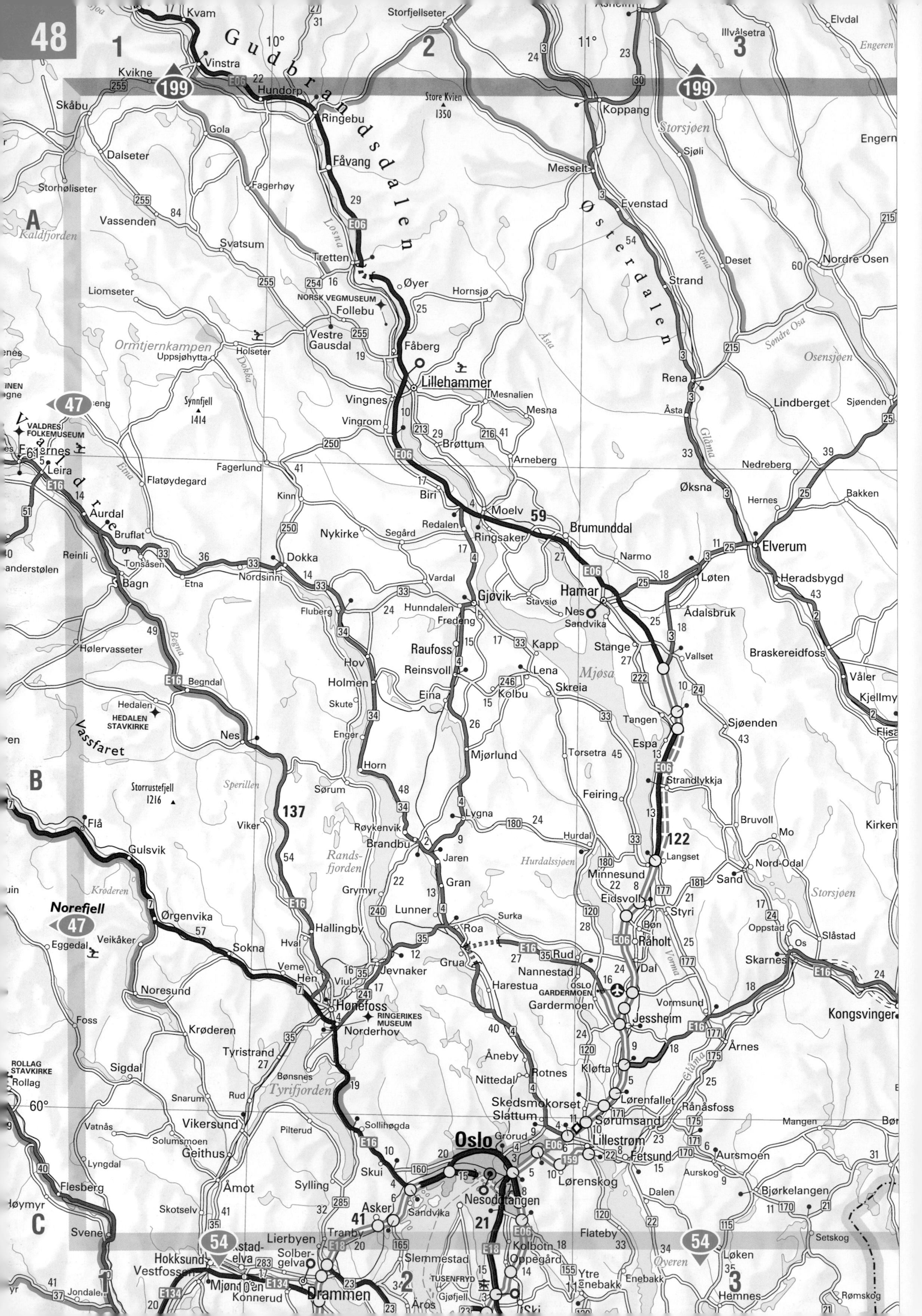
48
1
2
3
Gudbrandsdalen
Østerdalen
Valdres
10°
11°
60°
Kvam
Vinstra
Kvikne
Hundorp
Storfjellseter
Store Kvien
1350
Ringebu
Koppang
Illvålsetra
Elvdal
Engeren
Skåbu
Gola
Storsjøen
Sjøli
Engern
Dalseter
Fåvang
Messelt
Storhøliseter
Fagerhøy
Evenstad
A
Kaldfjorden
Vassenden
Losna
Svatsum
Tretten
Rena
Deset
Nordre Osen
Strand
Liomseter
Øyer
Hornsjø
NORSK VEGMUSEUM
Follebu
Vestre
Gausdal
Fåberg
Åsta
Søndre Osa
Osensjøen
Ormtjernkampen
Holseter
Uppsjøhytta
Dokka
Lillehammer
Synnfjell
1414
Vingnes
Mesnalien
Mesna
Lindberget
Sjøenden
Åsta
VALDRES FOLKEMUSEUM
Vingrom
Brøttum
Glåma
Fagernes
Leira
Eina
Flatøydegard
Fagerlund
Arneberg
Nedreberg
Kinn
Biri
Øksna
Hernes
Bakken
Aurdal
Bruflat
Nykirke
Segård
Redalen
Moelv
Ringsaker
Brumunddal
Elverum
Reinli
Tonsåsen
Dokka
Narmo
Heradsbygd
Bagn
Etna
Nordsinni
Vardal
Løten
Hamar
Fluberg
Hunndalen
Gjøvik
Fredeng
Stavsiø
Nes
Sandvika
Ådalsbruk
Begna
Hølervasseter
Raufoss
Kapp
Stange
Vallset
Braskereidfoss
Hov
Reinsvoll
Lena
Mjøsa
Våler
Holmen
Begndal
Eina
Kolbu
Skreia
Kjellmy
Hedalen
HEDALEN STAVKIRKE
Skute
Tangen
Sjøenden
Vassfaret
Nes
Enger
Espa
Mjørlund
Torsetra
Strandlykkja
B
Horn
Storrustefjell
1216
Sperillen
Sørum
Feiring
Flå
Viker
Lygna
Bruvoll
Mo
Kirken
Røykenvik
Hurdal
Brandbu
Jaren
Randsfjorden
Hurdalssjøen
Langset
Gulsvik
Nord-Odal
Gran
Minnesund
Sand
Krøderen
Grymyr
Eidsvoll
Storsjøen
Norefjell
Lunner
Styri
Ørgenvika
Surka
Bøn
Oppstad
Slåstad
Eggedal
Veikåker
Hallingby
Roa
Råholt
Os
Hval
Rud
Skarnes
Sokna
Veme
Jevnaker
Grua
Dal
Hen
Viul
Nannestad
Vorma
Noresund
Harestua
OSLO GARDERMOEN
Hønefoss
Gardermoen
Vormsund
RINGERIKES MUSEUM
Foss
Norderhov
Jessheim
Kongsvinger
Krøderen
Åneby
Årnes
Tyristrand
ROLLAG STAVKIRKE
Sigdal
Rollag
Bønsnes
Kløfta
Nittedal
Rotnes
Tyrifjorden
Snarum
Rud
Skedsmokorset
Lørenfallet
Rånåsfoss
Slattum
Sørumsand
Vatnås
Vikersund
Pilterud
Sollihøgda
Grorud
Mangen
Solumsmoen
Geithus
Oslo
Lillestrøm
Fetsund
Aursmoen
Lyngdal
Skui
Aurskog
Flesberg
Sylling
Åmot
Nesoddtangen
Lørenskog
Dalen
Bjørkelangen
Høymyr
C
Skotselv
Asker
Sandvika
Flateby
Sveine
Lierbyen
Tranby
Kolbotn
Setskog
Hokksund
Solbergelva
Slemmestad
Oppegård
Øyeren
Løken
Vestfossen
Mjøndalen
TUSENFRYD
Ytre Enebakk
Enebakk
Jondalen
Konnerud
Drammen
Gjøfjell
Åros
Ski
Hemnes
Rømskog
199
47
54
E06
E16
E18
E134
122
137
59
41
21

Särna
Fulufjällets
Trysil
Grundforsen
Sälen
Älvdalen
Orsa
Mora
Transtrand
Stavåsnäs
Limedsforsen
Dalarna
Malung
Sysslebäck
Höljes
Vansbro
Tiomilaskogen
Östmark
Torsby
Hagfors
Ekshärad
VÄRMLAND
Sunne
Rottneros
Munkfors
Filipstad
Hällefors
Eda glasbruk
Charlottenberg
Östbyrsåsen
Östersdalälven
STORSLAGEN KRAFTVERKSDAM
SANTAWORLD
SELMA LAGERLÖFSEM
0 10 20 30 km

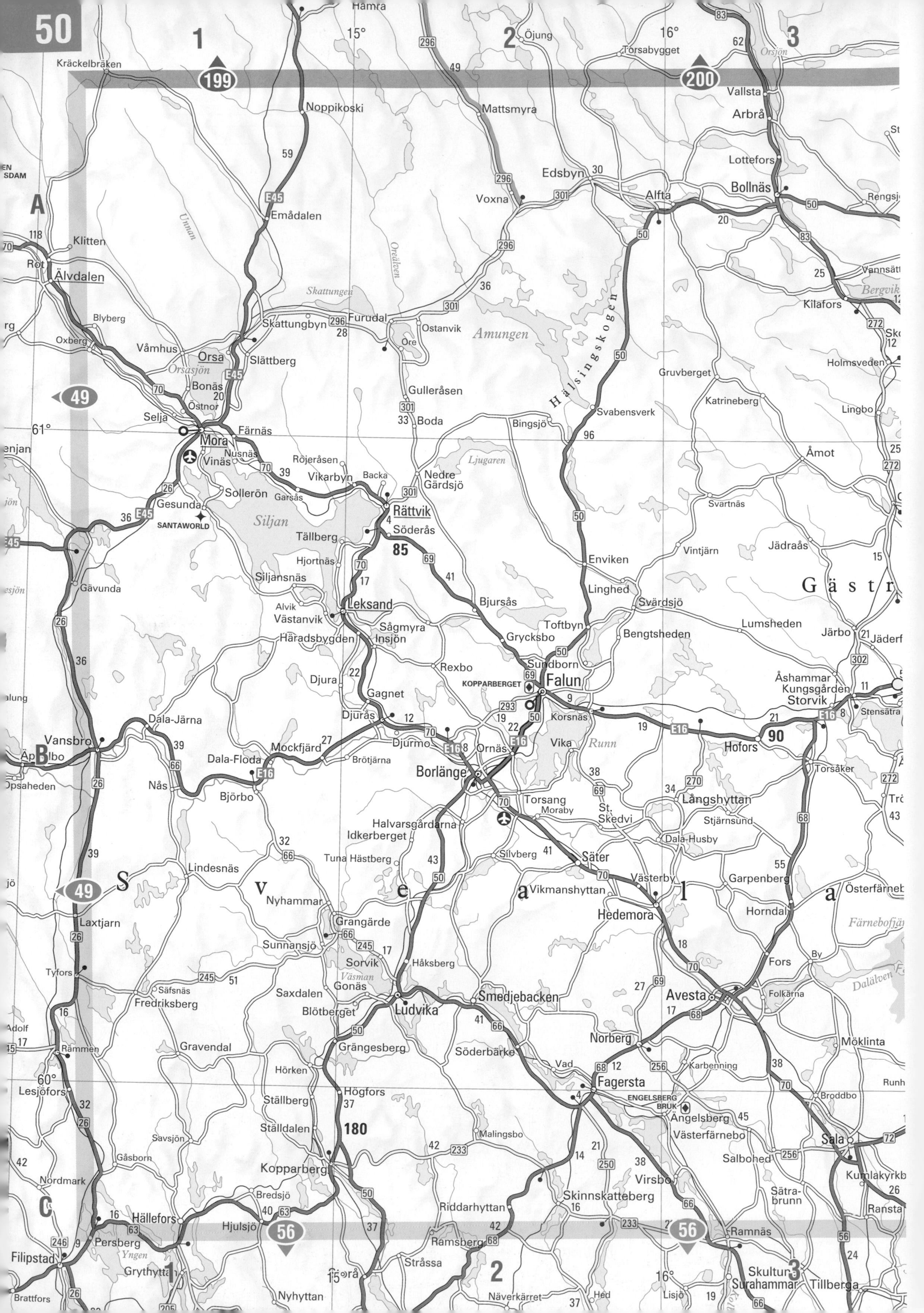

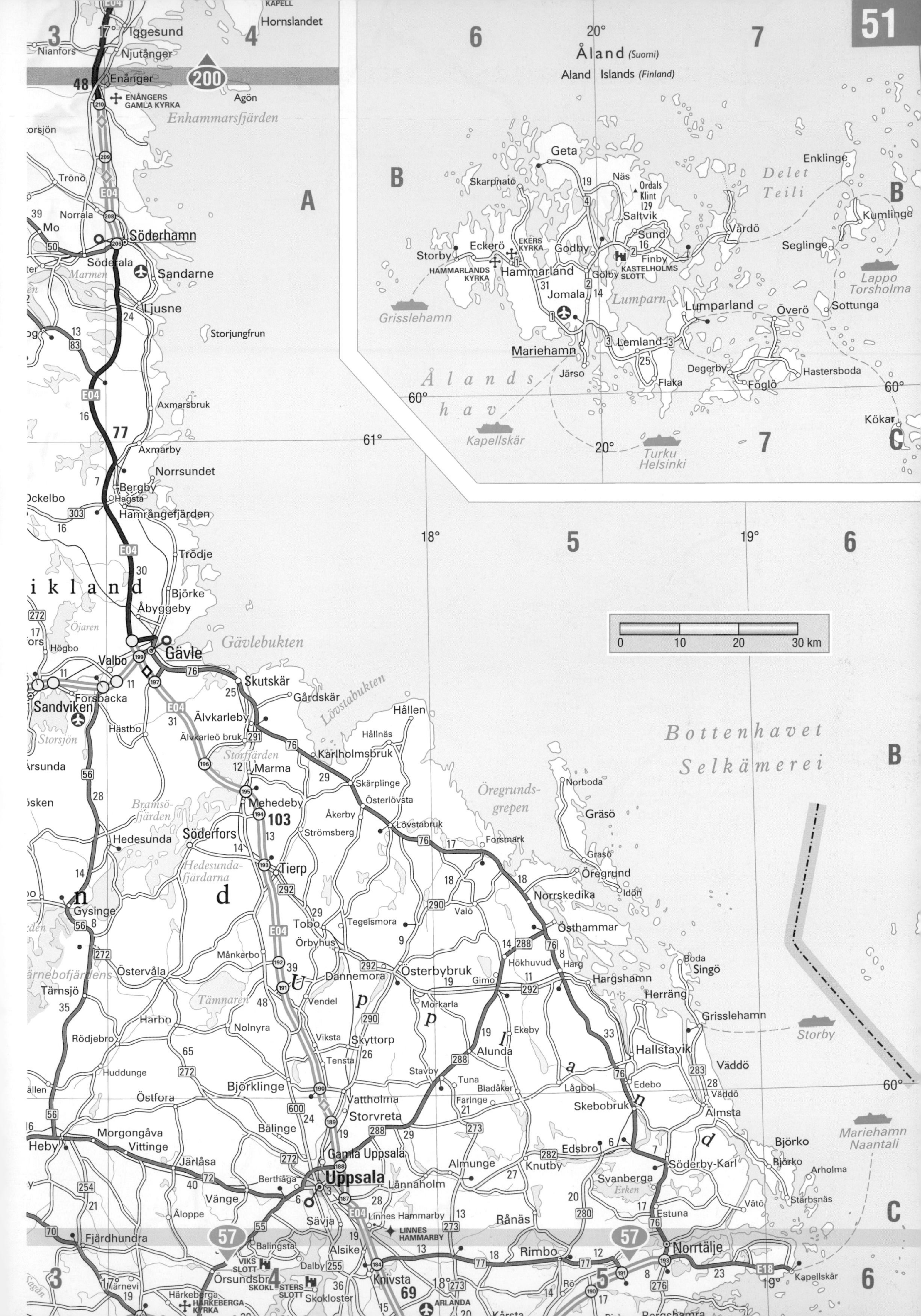

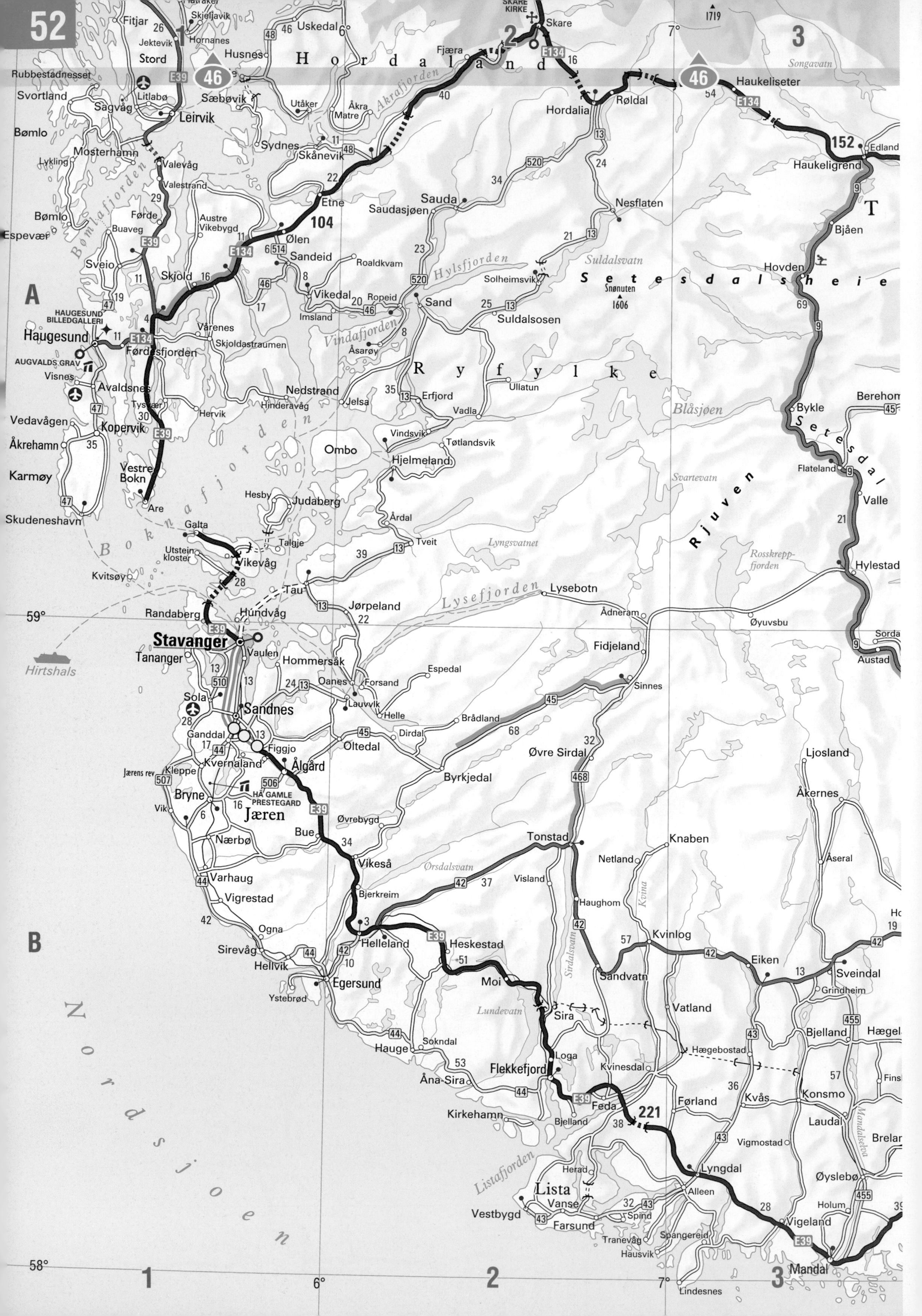

Fitjar
Skjeljavik
Jektevik
Hornanes
Stord
Husnes
Uskedal
Hordaland
Skare
Fjæra
Rubbestadnesset
Svortland
Litlabø
Sagvåg
Sæbøvik
Leirvik
Utåker
Åkra
Matre
Akrafjorden
Hordalia
Røldal
Haukeliseter
Songavatn
Bømlo
Mosterhamn
Lykling
Sydnes
Skånevik
Valevåg
Valestrand
Edland
Haukeligrend
Etne
Sauda
Saudasjøen
Nesflaten
Bømlo
Førde
Austre Vikebygd
Espevær
Buaveg
Bømlafjorden
Ølen
Sandeid
Roaldkvam
Hylsfjorden
Suldalsvatn
Bjåen
Hovden
Sveio
Skjold
Vikedal
Ropeid
Imsland
Sand
Solheimsvik
Setesdalsheie
Snønuten
1606
Suldalsosen
HAUGESUND BILLEDGALLERI
Haugesund
Vårenes
Skjoldastraumen
Førdesfjorden
Vindafjorden
Åsarøy
AUGVALDS GRAV
Visnes
Avaldsnes
Ryfylke
Ullatun
Nedstrand
Hinderavåg
Jelsa
Erfjord
Vadla
Tysvær
Hervik
Blåsjøen
Berehom
Bykle
Vedavågen
Kopervik
Åkrehamn
Karmøy
Vindsvik
Tøtlandsvik
Ombo
Hjelmeland
Setesdal
Flateland
Vestre Bokn
Hesby
Judaberg
Svartevatn
Rjuven
Valle
Skudeneshavn
Are
Årdal
Boknafjorden
Galta
Tveit
Lyngsvatnet
Talgje
Utstein kloster
Vikevåg
Kvitsøy
Tau
Rosskrepp-fjorden
Hylestad
Lysefjorden
Lysebotn
Jørpeland
Ådneram
Øyuvsbu
59°
Randaberg
Hundvåg
Stavanger
Tananger
Vaulen
Fidjeland
Sorda
Austad
Hirtshals
Hommersåk
Oanes
Forsand
Espedal
Lauvvik
Sinnes
Sola
Sandnes
Helle
Brådland
Ganddal
Dirdal
Oltedal
Figgjo
Kvernaland
Ålgård
Øvre Sirdal
Ljosland
Jærens rev
Kleppe
Byrkjedal
Bryne
HÅ GAMLE PRESTEGARD
Åkernes
Vik
Jæren
Øvrebygd
Bue
Tonstad
Knaben
Nærbø
Vikeså
Ørsdalsvatn
Netland
Åseral
Varhaug
Visland
Kvina
Vigrestad
Bjerkreim
Haughom
Sirdalsvatn
Ogna
Helleland
Heskestad
Kvinlog
Sirevåg
Hellvik
Sandvatn
Eiken
Sveindal
Egersund
Moi
Grindheim
Ystebrød
Lundevatn
Vatland
Sira
Nordsjøen
Hauge
Sokndal
Hægebostad
Bjelland
Hægeland
Loga
Flekkefjord
Kvinesdal
Åna-Sira
Konsmo
Finsland
Kvås
Kirkehamn
Feda
Førland
Bjelland
Laudal
Mandalselva
Brelan
Vigmostad
Listafjorden
Herad
Lyngdal
Øyslebø
Lista
Vanse
Alleen
Holum
Vestbygd
Farsund
Spind
Vigeland
Spangereid
Tranevåg
Hausvik
Mandal
Lindesnes
58°
6°
7°

Telemark
Rjukan
Møsvatn
Tinnsjø
Gausta 1883
Blefjell
Kongsberg
Drammen
Notodden
Skrimfjella 871
Lifjell
Seljord
Kviteseid
Bø
Lunde
Skien
Porsgrunn
Brevik
Larvik
Sandefjord
Stavern
Nisser
Fyresdal
Nissedal
Drangedal
Kragerø
Risør
Tvedestrand
Arendal
Grimstad
Lillesand
Kristiansand
Vennesla
Birkeland
Åmli
Evje
Bygland
Byglandsfjord
Sandes
Hirtshals
0 10 20 30 km

Oslo
Skui
Asker
Sand
Nesoddtangen
Lillestrøm
Fetsund
Aursmoen
Aurskog
Dalen
Bjørkelangen
Magnor
Vestmarka
Eda glasbruk
Charlottenberg
Eda
Gunnars
Köla
Åmotfors
Koppom
Sulvik
Arvika
Jössefors
Glafsfjorden
Glava
Lierbyen
Tranby
Solbergelva
Slemmestad
Kolbotn
Oppegård
Flateby
Øyeren
Løken
Setskog
Ytre Enebakk
Enebakk
Hemnes
Rømskog
Drammen
Konnerud
TUSENFRYD
Gjøfjell
Åros
Ski
Sætre
Tomter
Drøbak
Ås
Svelvik
Eidsfoss
Sande
Selvik
Holmsbu
Filtvet
Knapstad
Trøgstad
Spydeberg
Askim
Skjønhaug
Kroksund
Östervallskog
Vännacka
Hof
Hillestad
Tofte
Hølen
Son
Slitu
Mysen
Töcksfors
Lenungshammar
Holmestrand
Gullhaug
Våler
Eidsberg
Skiptvet
Glomma
Ørje
Holmedal
Stora Gla
Horten
Moss
Skoppum
Fuglevik
RYGGE
Svindal
Rakkestad
Øymark
Fölsbyn
Årjäng
Finntorp
Høyjord
Ramnes
Borre
Åsgårdstrand
Rygge
Karlshus
Degernes
Foxen
Larkollen
Lennartsfors
Sillerud
Långserud
Andebu
Sem
Bårkåker
Spetalen
Lervik
Greåker
Sarpsborg
Ise
Blomskog
V. Silen
Tønsberg
Stokke
Kodal
Gressvik
Aremark
Ö. Silen
Skjeberg
Gustavsfors
Skogen
Kjopmannskjaer
Oterbekk
Vikane
Fredrikstad
Vårvik
TORP
Årøysund
Øyenkilen
Ingedal
FREDRIKSTEN FESTNING
Halden
Torrskog
Svanskog
Sandefjord
Tjøme
Framnes
Ormelet
Sponvika
Tistedal
Holmegil
Sund
Nössemark
Letäng
Idd
Korshavn
Lund
Larvik
Sandøysund
Spjærøy
Stora Le
Verdens Ende
Hvaler
Edsleskog
Åmål
Østre Halsen
Skjærhalden
Hogdal
Trestickland
Bengtsfors
Skåpafors
59°
Stavern
Bjørnerod
Enningdal
Fengersfors
Prestebakke
Billingsfors
Strömstad
Skee
Kornsjø
Håbol
Dals Långed
Tisselskog
Søndre Enningdal
Kappel
Ed
Ånimskog
Hirtshals
Töftedal
Dalsland
Håverud
Frederikshavn
København
Kiel
Tanum
Naverstad
Bäckefors
Åsensbruk
Havstenssund
Lerdal
Dalskog
Tanumshede
Kynnefjäll
Kroppefjäll
Dals Rostock
HÄLLRISTNINGAR TANUM
Mo
Grebbestad
Mellerud
Hedekas
Högsäter
Fjällbacka
Kville
Hällevadsholm
Brålanda
Hambergsund
Färgelanda
Stigen
Bolstad
Dingle
Ödeborg
Bovallstrand
Frändefors
Vänersnäs
Hunnebostrand
Munkedal
Brodalen
Bohuslän
Väjern
Brastad
Smögen
Kungshamn
Rixo
Malmon
Uddevalla
Vänersborg
Vargön
Herrestad
Hunneberg
Trollhättan
Lysekil
Fiskebäckskil
Väne-Åsaka
Henån
Grundsund
Ljungskile
Orust
Ellös
Sjuntorp
Nossebro
Upphärad
Hälleviksstrand
Svanesund
Lilla Edet
Sollebrunn
Göta
Mollösund
Stenungsund
Ucklum
Gräfsnäs
Tjörn
Långared
Kyrkesund
Hakefjord
Skärhamn
Jörlanda
Skepplanda
Klädesholmen
BOHUS
58°
11°
12°
0
10
20
30 km

Värmland
Närke
Västergötland
Vänern
Vättern
Dalbosjön
Uddheden
Sunne
Sunnemo
Munkfors
Bosjön
Nordmark
Gåsborn
Savsjön
Ställdalen
Kopparberg
Bredsjö
Hjulsjö
Hällefors
Persberg
Yngen
Grythyttan
Filipstad
Rottneros
Manskog
Rottneros Park
Mårbacka
Selma Lagerlöfsem
Östra Ämtervik
Västra Ämtervik
Ransäter
Alvsbacka
Svartå
Övre Ullerud
Brattfors
Nykroppa
Mellan Fryken
Edane
Deje
Molkom
Blombacka
Värmeln
Boda
Forshaga
Laggartorp
Storfors
Lundsberg
Fagerås
Kil
Stavnäs
Värmskog
Edsvalla
Skåre
Kappstad
Hulteby
Bjurtjärn
Norsbron
Vålberg
Segerstad
Karlstad
Skattkärr
Väse
Ölme
Borgvik
Grums
Aspberg
Hammarö
Slottsbron
Skoghall
Kristinehamn
Karlskoga
Kilsbergen
Nysäter
Segmon
Takene
Värmlands Bro
Säffle
Värmlandsnäs
Södra Ny
Botilsäter
Olserud
Eskilsäter
Ekenäs
Djurö
Degerfors
Björneborg
Bäckhammar
Visnums-Kil
Medhamn
Nybble
Åtorp
Svartå
Mullhyttan
Hasselfors
Rudskoga
Gullspång
Södra Råda
Skagern
Skagersvik
Otterbäcken
Finnerödja
Laxå
Röfors
Vretstorp
Åsbro
Kårberg
Skyllberg
Rönneshytta
Askersund
Åmmeberg
Zinkgruvan
Gårdsjö
Hova
Sjötorp
Älgarås
Lyrestad
Tived
Unden
Tivedens
Hammar
Sänna
Olshammar
Laxhall
Torsö
Göta kanal
Töreboda
Mariestad
Ullervad
Moholm
Undenäs
Medevi
Nykyrke
Godegård
Ljusfalls
Läckö
Kållandsö
Årnäs
Hällekis
Lugnås
Gössäter
Kinneviken
Sunnersberg
Stenhammar
Kinne-Kleva
Tofta
Lidköping
Götene
Timmersdala
Tidan
Väring
Forsvik
Hanken
Karlsborgs fästning
Karlsborg
Mölltorp
Motala
Boren
Fornås
Örslösa
Råda
Källby
Vinninga
Eggby
Fagersanna
Tibro
Brevik
Vadstena
Fågelsta
Tun
Järpås
Saleby
Ardala
Skara
Axvall
Skövde
Varnhem
Hörnebo
Borghamn
Skänninge
Tåkern
Hogstad
Väderstad
Mjölby
Grästorp
Jung
St. Levene
Kvänum
Skultorp
Stenstorp
Blikstorp
Korsberga
Hjo
Hästholmen
Hellas
Vara
Tråvad
Arentorp
Gudhem
Ödeshög
Strålsnäs
Vedum
Torbjörntorp
Boxholm
Tidaholm
Falköping
Madängsholm
Ålleberg 335
Hålaveden
Sommen
Björke
Floby
Fåglavik
Vartofta
Visingsö
Herrljunga
Härja
Hökensås
Duvebo
Kinnarp
Tunnerstad
Tranås
Kattilstorp
Gränna
Vårgårda
Annelund
Åsarp
Orserum
Gripenberg
Ljung
Trädet
Sandhem
Frinnaryd
Lindesberg
Stråssa
Storå
Nyhyttan
Gusselby
Striberg
Nora
Gyttorp
Vedevåg
Ramsberg
Riddarhyttan
Ölmbro
Hovsta
Glanshammar
Garphyttan
Vintrosa
Örebro
Lanna
Marieberg
Ekeby
Fjugesta
Åbytorp
Kumla
Hällabrottet
Hallsberg
E45
E18
E20
E04
49
56
60
62
A
B
3
4
5
6
13°
14°
15°
58°

Malingsbo
Västerfärnebo
Sala
Heby
Vittinge
Salbohed
Virsbo
Kumlakyrkby
Skinnskatteberg
Sätra-brunn
Ransta
Vänge
Åloppe
Fjärdhundra
Ramnäs
Ramsberg
Stråssa
Storå
Bredsjö
Nyhyttan
Skultuna
Surahammar
Tillberga
Härnevi
Örsundsbro
Härkeberga
HARKEBERGA KYRKA
VIKS SLOTT
Balingsta
Näverkärret
Hed
Lisjö
Kolbäcksån
Sagån
Gusselby
Lindesberg
Kåfalla
Kolsva
Hallstahammar
VÄSTERÅS
Västerås
Irsta
Hummelsta
Enköping
Grillby
Bålsta
Striberg
Vedevåg
Nora
Gyttorp
Rockhammar
Munktorp
Kolbäck
Dingtuna
Kärrbo
Angsö
Lillkyrka
Kungs-Husby
Frövi
Köping
Kvicksund
VÄSTMANLAND
Mälaren
Fellingsbro
Kungsör
Torshälla
Fogdö
Norra Björkfjärden
Ölmbrotorp
Kilsbergen
Kil
Hovsta
ÖREBRO SLOTT
Glanshammar
Arboga
Hällbybrunn
Eskilstuna
Strängnäs
Stallarholmen
HOVGÅRDEN
Adelsö
Sjölunda
Skogstorp
Hällberga
Ärla
Malmby
GRIPSHOLMS SLOTT
Mariefred
Övergran
Vintrosa
Örebro
Ålberga
Hällsta
Merlånna
Lanna
Ekeby-Almby
Marieberg
Hjälmaren
Åkers Styckebruk
Gripsholm
Södertälje
Kvismarkanal
Närke
Fjugesta
Åbytorp
Odensbacken
Dunker
Hälleforsnäs
Nykvarn
Kumla
Sköllersta
Läppe
Äsköping
Malmköping
Hällabrottet
Pålsboda
Kilsmo
Bie
Mellösa
Sparreholm
Stjärnhov
Björnlunda
Mölnbo
Hallsberg
Flen
Skebokvarn
Gnesta
Hölö
Åsbro
Svennevad
Bevensbruk
Högsjö
Vingåker
Valla
Sköldinge
Båven
Kårberg
Baggetorp
Katrineholm
Forssjöbruk
Ripsa
Skyllberg
Rönneshytta
Tisnaren
Skedevi
Hjortkvarn
Bettna
Ludgo
Lästringe
Åmmeberg
Regna
Strångsjö
Yngaren
Runtuna
Igelfors
Zinkgruvan
Rejmyre
Björkvik
Tystberga
Grytgöl
Stigtomta
SKAVSTA
Svärta
Oppeby
Hammar
Sänna
Ljusfallshammar
Simonstorp
Hällestad
Borggård
Sonstorp
Lotorp
Jönåker
Enstaberga
Nyköping
Godegård
Tjällmo
Ålberga
Medevi
Falla
Finspång
Strömsfors
Krokek
Arno
Åby
Jursla
Buskhyttan
Oxelösund
Svärtinge
Glan
Bråviken
Nävekvarn
Nykyrke
Östergötland
Lindö
Norrköping
Ljunga
Östra Husby
Borensberg
Boren
Skärblacka
Kimstad
Motala
Ljungsbro
Roxen
Norsholm
Göta kanal
Vester Husby
Kuddby
Jonsberg
Norrköpingsdjupet
Fågelsta
Fornåsa
Bergs slussar
Gistad
Söderköping
Mogata
Arkösund
Linghem
Rönö
Slätbaken
Skänninge
Malmslätt
Linköping
Östra Ryd
Bankekind
Vikingstad
DOM
Hogstad
Mantorp
Björsäter
Ringarum
St. Anna
N. Finnö
Tyrislöt
Mjölby
Sya
Yxnerum
Häljelöt
S. Finnö
Nykil
Gusum
Strålsnäs
Bestorp
Yxningen
Valdemarsvik
Boxholm
Berg
Brokind
Åtvidaberg
Gryt
Björke
Järnlunden
Rumma
Tryserum
Rimforsa
Falerum
Sommen
Ulrika
Söderö
Ekevik
Ukna
Långrådna
Tranås
Malexander
Oppeby
Risebo
Edsbruk
Marek
Kisa
Åsunden
Överum
Hulta
Flatvarp
St. Askö
Gripenberg
Sundhultsbrunn
Tidersrum
Hycklinge
16°
17°
15°
58°

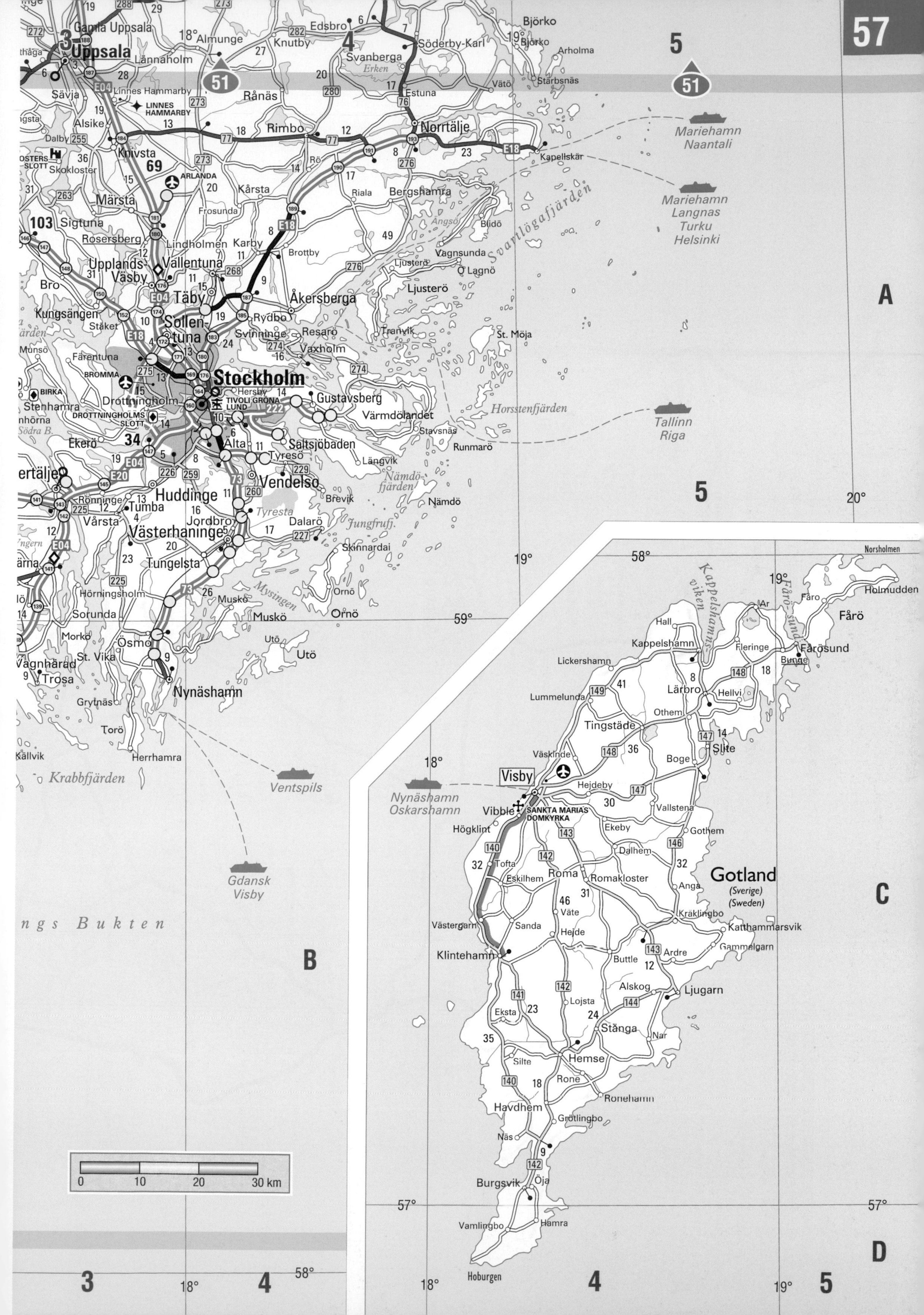
Gamla Uppsala
Uppsala
Almunge
Knutby
Edsbro
Söderby-Karl
Björko
Arholma
Svanberga
Erken
Lännaholm
Linnes Hammarby
LINNES HAMMARBY
Sävja
Rånäs
Estuna
Vätö
Starbsnäs
Alsike
Rimbo
Norrtälje
Mariehamn
Naantali
Dalby
Knivsta
Kapellskär
SKOKLOSTERS SLOTT
Skokloster
ARLANDA
Kårsta
Riala
Bergshamra
Märsta
Frösunda
Mariehamn
Langnas
Turku
Helsinki
Sigtuna
Rosersberg
Lindholmen
Karby
Brottby
Angsö
Blidö
Svartlögafjärden
Upplands-Väsby
Vallentuna
Vagnsunda
Ljusterö
Lagnö
Bro
Täby
Åkersberga
Kungsängen
Stäket
Sollentuna
Rydbo
Svinninge
Resarö
Tranvik
St. Möja
Munsö
Färentuna
Vaxholm
BROMMA
Stockholm
Hersby
Gustavsberg
BIRKA
Stenhamra
Drottningholm
DROTTNINGHOLMS SLOTT
TIVOLI GRÖNA LUND
Värmdölandet
Horsstenfjärden
Södra B.
Stavsnäs
Tallinn
Riga
Ekerö
Älta
Saltsjöbaden
Runmarö
Tyresö
Längvik
Nämdöfjärden
Huddinge
Vendelso
Brevik
Nämdö
Rönninge
Tumba
Tyresta
Vårsta
Jordbro
Dalarö
Jungfrufj.
Västerhaninge
Skinnardai
Tungelsta
Hörningsholm
Mysingen
Muskö
Sorunda
Ornö
Morkö
Utö
St. Vika
Ösmo
Vagnhärad
Trosa
Nynäshamn
Grytnäs
Torö
Källvik
Herrhamra
Krabbfjärden
Ventspils
Gdansk
Visby
ngs Bukten
0
10
20
30 km
Norsholmen
Kappelshamnsviken
Fårösund
Holmudden
Fårö
Ar
Hall
Kappelshamn
Fleringe
Fårösund
Bunge
Lickershamn
Lärbro
Lummelunda
Hellvi
Othem
Tingstäde
Slite
Väskinde
Boge
Visby
Hejdeby
Nynäshamn
Oskarshamn
Vibble
SANKTA MARIAS DOMKYRKA
Vallstena
Högklint
Ekeby
Gothem
Dalhem
Tofta
Eskilhem
Roma
Romakloster
Anga
Gotland
(Sverige)
(Sweden)
Väte
Kräklingbo
Västergarn
Sanda
Hejde
Katthammarsvik
Gammelgarn
Klintehamn
Ardre
Buttle
Alskog
Ljugarn
Lojsta
Eksta
Stånga
Nar
Silte
Hemse
Rone
Ronehamn
Havdhem
Grötlingbo
Näs
Burgsvik
Öja
Vamlingbo
Hamra
Hoburgen

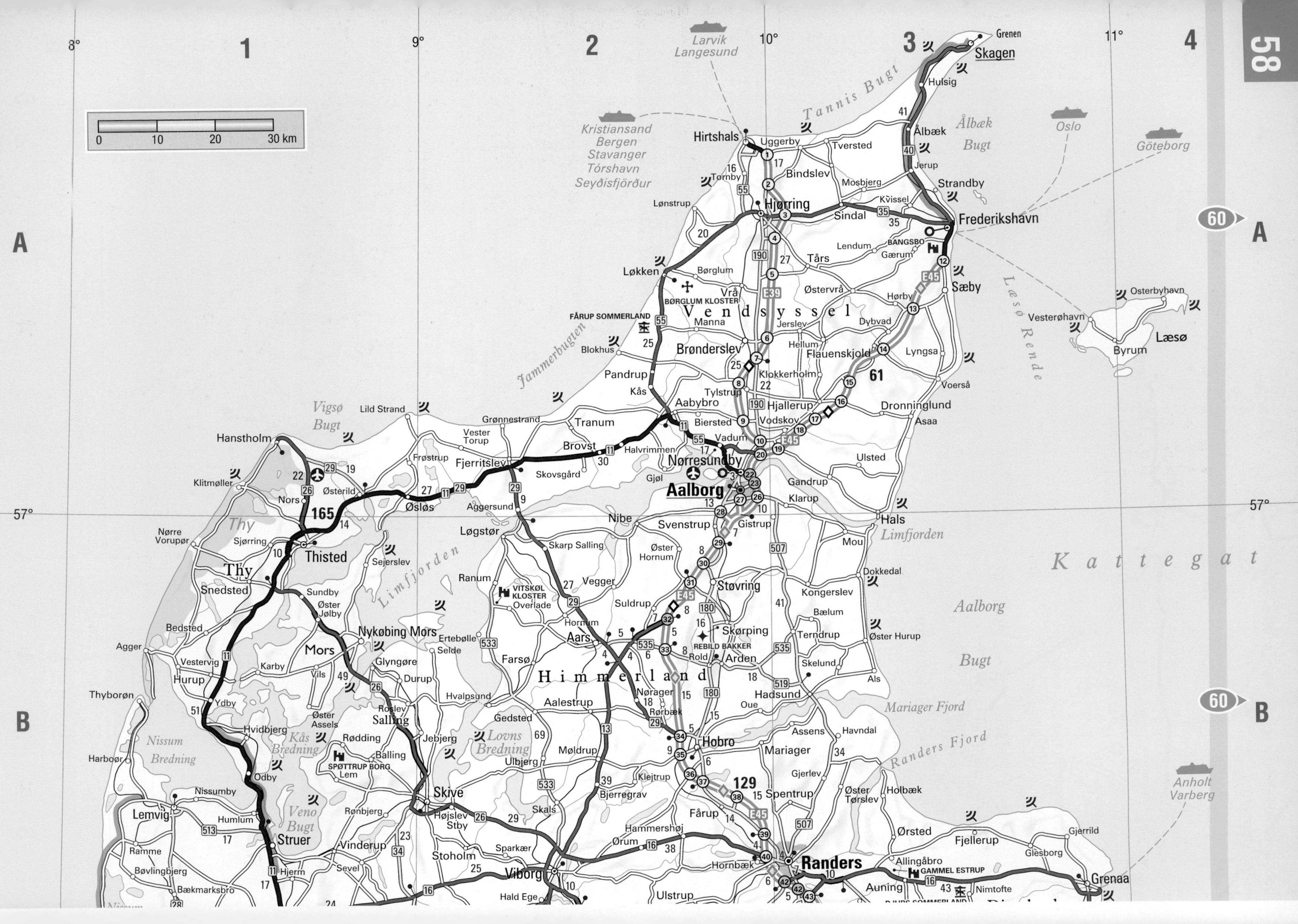

Skagen
Grenen
Hulsig
Ålbæk
Ålbæk Bugt
Strandby
Frederikshavn
Sæby
Jerup
Tannis Bugt
Tversted
Bindslev
Uggerby
Hirtshals
Tornby
Hjørring
Sindal
Mosbjerg
Kvissel
Bangsbo
Gærum
Lendum
Tårs
Østervrå
Hørby
Dybvad
Lyngsa
Voerså
Dronninglund
Asaa
Flauenskjold
Hellum
Jerslev
Klokkerholm
Hjallerup
Vodskov
Vendsyssel
Vrå
Børglum
Børglum Kloster
Manna
Brønderslev
Lønstrup
Løkken
Fårup Sommerland
Blokhus
Pandrup
Kås
Aabybro
Tylstrup
Biersted
Vadum
Nørresundby
Aalborg
Gistrup
Gandrup
Ulsted
Klarup
Hals
Limfjorden
Jammerbugten
Tranum
Brovst
Halvrimmen
Skovsgård
Gjøl
Svenstrup
Øster Hornum
Nibe
Støvring
Skørping
Rebild Bakker
Rold
Arden
Suldrup
Vegger
Skarp Salling
Aars
Hornum
Himmerland
Aalestrup
Møldrup
Nørager
Rørbæk
Hobro
Oue
Hadsund
Skelund
Terndrup
Bælum
Kongerslev
Dokkedal
Øster Hurup
Als
Mariager Fjord
Mariager
Havndal
Assens
Gjerlev
Spentrup
Randers
Randers Fjord
Øster Tørslev
Holbæk
Ørsted
Allingåbro
Gammel Estrup
Auning
Fjellerup
Nimtofte
Glesborg
Gjerrild
Grenaa
Fårup
Hammershøj
Ørum
Ulstrup
Hornbæk
Klejtrup
Bjerregrav
Viborg
Hald Ege
Skals
Sparkær
Ulbjerg
Gedsted
Lovns Bredning
Farsø
Vitskøl Kloster
Overlade
Ranum
Løgstør
Aggersund
Ertebølle
Selde
Hvalpsund
Fjerritslev
Vester Torup
Grønnestrand
Frøstrup
Lild Strand
Østerild
Vigsø Bugt
Øsløs
Sejerslev
Nykøbing Mors
Glyngøre
Durup
Roslev
Salling
Jebjerg
Skive
Højslev Stby
Stoholm
Balling
Rødding
Spøttrup Borg
Lem
Øster Assels
Rønbjerg
Vinderup
Sevel
Thisted
Sundby
Øster Jølby
Mors
Vils
Karby
Kås Bredning
Hvidbjerg
Venø Bugt
Struer
Hjerm
Odby
Ydby
Hurup
Vestervig
Bedsted
Snedsted
Thy
Sjørring
Hanstholm
Nors
Klitmøller
Nørre Vorupør
Agger
Thyborøn
Harboør
Nissum Bredning
Nissumby
Humlum
Lemvig
Bøvlingbjerg
Bækmarksbro
Ramme
Læsø
Østerbyhavn
Vesterøhavn
Byrum
Læsø Rende
Kattegat
Aalborg Bugt
Oslo
Göteborg
Larvik Langesund
Kristiansand Bergen Stavanger Tórshavn Seyðisfjörður
Anholt Varberg
8°
9°
10°
11°
57°
1
2
3
4
A
B
60
0
10
20
30 km
E45
E39

Jylland
Djursland
Holstebro
Herning
Ikast
Silkeborg
Århus
Skanderborg
Horsens
Odder
Vejle
Fredericia
Kolding
Middelfart
Esbjerg
Varde
Ribe
Skjern
Ringkøbing
Grindsted
Billund
Brande
Haderslev
Aabenraa
Vojens
Odense
Nyborg
Svendborg
Fåborg
Assens
Bogense
Kerteminde
Fyn
Kalundborg
Slagelse
Korsør
Skælskør
Samsø
Tunø
Endelave
Sejerø
Fanø
Rømø
Mandø
Langeland
Ebeltoft
Randers
Grenaa
Århus Bugt
Ebeltoft Vig
Horsens Fjord
Vejle Fjord
Ringkøbing Fjord
Fanø Bugt
Vadehavet
Knudedyb
Lille Bælt
Store Bælt
Samsø Bælt
Sejerø Bugt
Aabenraa Fjord
LEGOLAND
KONGERNES JELLING
FREDERICIA MUSEUM
HIMMELBJERGET
EGESKOV SLOT
GRAM SLOT
HADERSLEV DOMKIRKE
KOLDINGHUS
HARRIDSLEVGAARD SLOT
MANNEKIN PIS
LADBYSKIBET
FREGATTEN JYLLAND
ROSENHOLM
KALØ SLOT
VOR FRUE KIRKE
København Klaipeda
Harwich
56°
55°
8°
9°
10°
11°
B
C
1
2
3
4
61
64
65
E20
E45

Västergötland
Halland
Kattegat
Göteborg
Gothenburg
Borås
Jönköping
Huskvarna
Kungsbacka
Mölndal
Varberg
Falkenberg
Alingsås
Kungälv
Ulricehamn
Värnamo
Gislaved
Ljungby
Kinna
Svenljunga
Tranemo
Vaggeryd
Skillingaryd
Anderstorp
Hyltebruk
Lerum
Mölnlycke
Kållered
Lindome
Anneberg
Torslanda
Öckerö
Hönö
Styrsö
Vrångö
Särö
Billdal
Vickan
Onsala
Åsa
Frillesås
Veddige
Bua
Tvååker
Träslövsläge
Glommen
Skogstorp
Skrea
Heberg
Sloinge
Getinge
Kvibille
Harplinge
Sennan
Åled
Oskarström
Torup
Rydöbruk
Kinnared
Landeryd
Fegen
Ätran
Ullared
Kungsäter
Överlida
Mjöbäck
Oxaback
Björketorp
Horred
Berghem
Fritsla
Rydal
Sätila
Skene
Rävlanda
Bollebygd
Hindås
Härryda
Sandared
Sjömarken
Dalsjöfors
Viskafors
Rydboholm
Gånghester
Fristad
Rångedala
Hedared
Tollered
Floda
Gråbo
Jonsered
Surte
Nödinge
Nol
Älvängen
Skepplanda
Lödöse
Jörlanda
Kode
Stenungsund
Tjörn
Kyrkesund
Skärhamn
Klädesholmen
Rönnäng
Marstrand
Kärna
Säve
Röro
Björkö
Mollösund
Vårgårda
Långared
Tarabo
Ljung
Annelund
Borgstena
Dalum
Hökerum
Timmele
Kinnarp
Åsarp
Trädet
Sandhem
Kattilstorp
Blidsberg
Mullsjö
Furusjö
Habo
Bankeryd
Gränna
Tunnerstad
Vireda
Skärstad
Kaxholmen
Lekeryd
Forserum
Tenhult
Barnarp
Odensjö
Norrahammar
Taberg
Bottnaryd
Månsarp
Mulseryd
Marbäck
Vegby
Rånnaväg
Gällstad
Dalstorp
Hillared
Länghem
Sexdrega
Limmared
Uddebo
Ambjörnarp
Grimsås
Hestra
Nissafors
Gnosjö
Hillerstorp
Sjötofta
Karshult
Kalv
Burseryd
Smålandsstenar
Skeppshult
Broaryd
Reftele
Forsheda
Bredaryd
Lanna
Åminne
Hånger
Bor
Hörle
Store Mosse
Klevshult
Vrigstad
Osbruk
Rusken
Malmbäck
Hok
Tranhult
Bondstorp
N Unnaryd
Ljungsarp
Kållerstad
Dannäs
Vidöstern
Långaryd
Sunnaryd
Unnaryd
Tannåker
Vittaryd
Bolmen
Odensjö
Flåren
Lagan
Ryssby
Hjortsberga
Rydaholm
Moheda
Torpsbruk
Horda
Agunnaryd
Vislanda
Annerstad
Hamneda
Enneryda
Torpa
Vrå
Lidhult
Femsjö
Gräsås
Vessigebro
Vinberg
Långås
Köinge
Trönningeby
Skällinge
Åsby
Älvsered
Holsljunga
Ästad
Värö
Lygnern
Viskan
Nissan
Ätran
Göta älv
Mjörn
Kungsbackafjord
Hökensås
BOHUS FÄSTNING
CARLSTENS FÄSTNING
LISEBERG
HABO KYRKA
VARBERG RADIOSTATION
Frederikshavn
Kiel
Læsø
Osterbyhavn
Byrum
Anholt
Västra-Bodarne
11°
12°
14°
57°
54
55
58
62
142
210
230
A
B
C
1
2
3
4

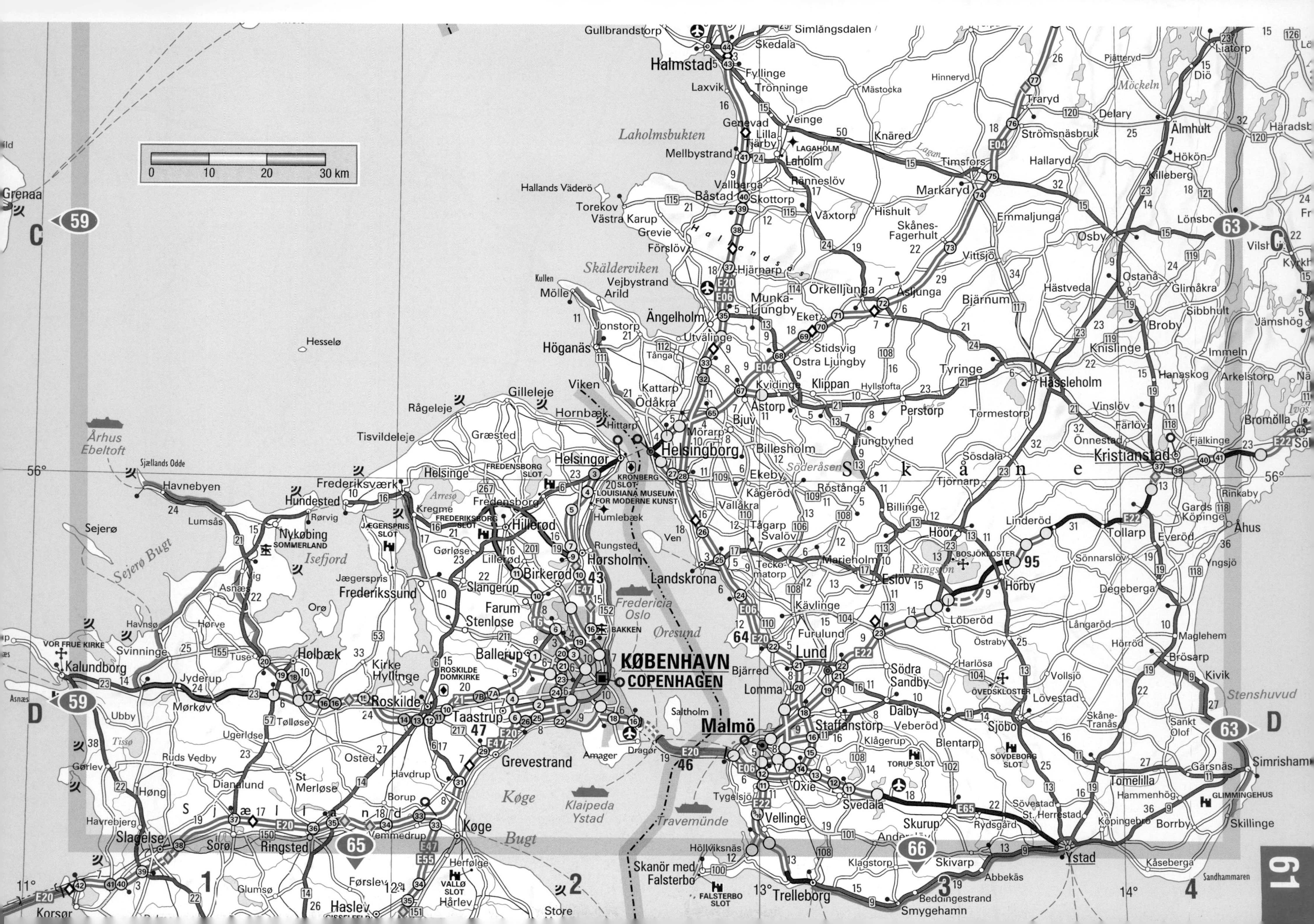
61
KØBENHAVN
COPENHAGEN
Malmö
Helsingborg
Helsingør
Lund
Landskrona
Trelleborg
Ystad
Kristianstad
Hässleholm
Ängelholm
Halmstad
Roskilde
Hillerød
Køge
Kalundborg
Slagelse
Holbæk
Laholmsbukten
Skälderviken
Øresund
Køge Bugt
Sejerø Bugt
Isefjord
Skåne
Sjælland
0 10 20 30 km

1
2
3
4
5
A
B
Visby
Ölands norra udde
Nabbelund
Byxelkrok
Böda
Löttorp
Köpingsvik
Borgholm
Västervik
Gamleby
Almvik
Loftahammar
Blankaholm
Figeholm
Oskarshamn
Påskallavik
Emsfors
Mönsterås
Timmernabben
Ålem
Rockneby
Överum
Risebo
Ekevik
Södra Vi
Vimmerby
Frödinge
Totebo
Tuna
Hultsfred
Vena
Kristdala
Målilla
Rosenfors
Mörlunda
Virserum
Högsby
Berga
Bockara
Döderhult
Kisa
Horn
Oppeby
Söderö
Tranås
Gripenberg
Aneby
Eksjö
Vetlanda
Nässjö
Huskvarna
Jönköping
Gränna
Habo
Bankeryd
Taberg
Vaggeryd
Skillingaryd
Värnamo
Sävsjö
Vrigstad
Lammhult
Alvesta
Växjö
Rottne
Braås
Åseda
Lenhovda
Kosta
Lessebo
Nybro
Orrefors
Ljungby
Lagan
Vislanda
Moheda
Rydaholm
Hjortsberga
Ingelstad
Hovmantorp
Småland
Hökensås
Norra Kvill
Blå Jungfrun
Store Mosse
Emån
Helgasjön
Åsnen
Sommen
57°
58°
14°
15°
16°
17°
E04
E22
56
60
63
134
204
230
HABO KYRKA
DOMKYRKAN I VÄXJÖ

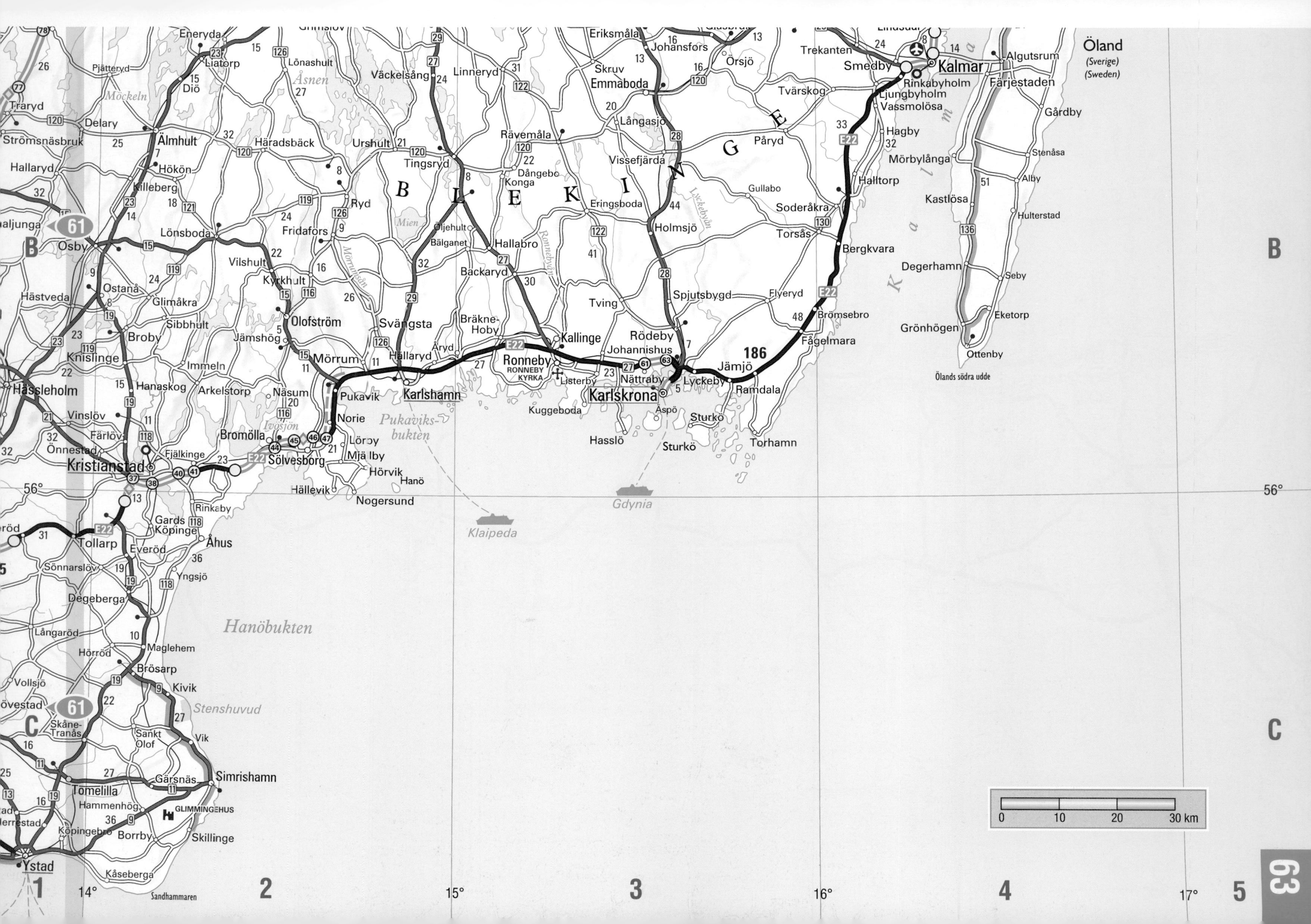

Öland
(Sverige)
(Sweden)
Kalmar
Färjestaden
Algutsrum
Gårdby
Stenåsa
Alby
Hulterstad
Seby
Eketorp
Ottenby
Ölands södra udde
Grönhögen
Degerhamn
Kastlösa
Mörbylånga
Rinkabyholm
Ljungbyholm
Vassmolösa
Smedby
Trekanten
Hagby
Halltorp
Bergkvara
Brömsebro
Fågelmara
Söderåkra
Torsås
Tvärskog
Påryd
Gullabo
Flyeryd
Jämjö
Ramdala
Torhamn
Sturkö
Lyckeby
Karlskrona
Nättraby
Hasslö
Aspö
Gdynia
Klaipeda
Rödeby
Johannishus
Spjutsbygd
Holmsjö
Lyckebyån
Vissefjärda
Emmaboda
Johansfors
Örsjö
Eriksmåla
Skruv
Långasjö
Eringsboda
Tving
Kallinge
Ronneby
RONNEBY KYRKA
Listerby
Kuggeboda
Ronnebyån
Hallabro
Backaryd
Bräkne-Hoby
Dångebo
Konga
Rävemåla
Linneryd
Tingsryd
Väckelsång
Urshult
Bälganet
Öljehult
Mien
B L E K I N G E
Karlshamn
Pukaviksbukten
Hällaryd
Åryd
Svängsta
Mörrumsån
Ryd
Mörrum
Pukavik
Norie
Hörvik
Hanö
Nogersund
Mjällby
Sölvesborg
Hällevik
Ivösjön
Bromölla
Näsum
Olofström
Jämshög
Kyrkhult
Fridafors
Lönashult
Åsnen
Häradsbäck
Vilshult
Älmhult
Liatorp
Diö
Eneryda
Möckeln
Pjätteryd
Delary
Hökön
Killeberg
Lönsboda
Glimåkra
Sibbhult
Broby
Östanå
Hanaskog
Immeln
Arkelstorp
Hanöbukten
Åhus
Rinkaby
Gärds Köpinge
Yngsjö
Fjälkinge
Kristianstad
Färlöv
Vinslöv
Önnestad
Knislinge
Hästveda
Hässleholm
Osby
Strömsnäsbruk
Traryd
Hallaryd
Tollarp
Everöd
Degeberga
Sönnarslöv
Maglehem
Brösarp
Kivik
Stenshuvud
Vik
Simrishamn
Gärsnäs
GLIMMINGEHUS
Skillinge
Sankt Olof
Tomelilla
Hammenhög
Borrby
Köpingebro
Kåseberga
Sandhammaren
Ystad
Hörröd
Långaröd
Vollsjö
Skåne-Tranås
186
56°
14°
15°
16°
17°
0
10
20
30 km
B
C
1
2
3
4
5
63

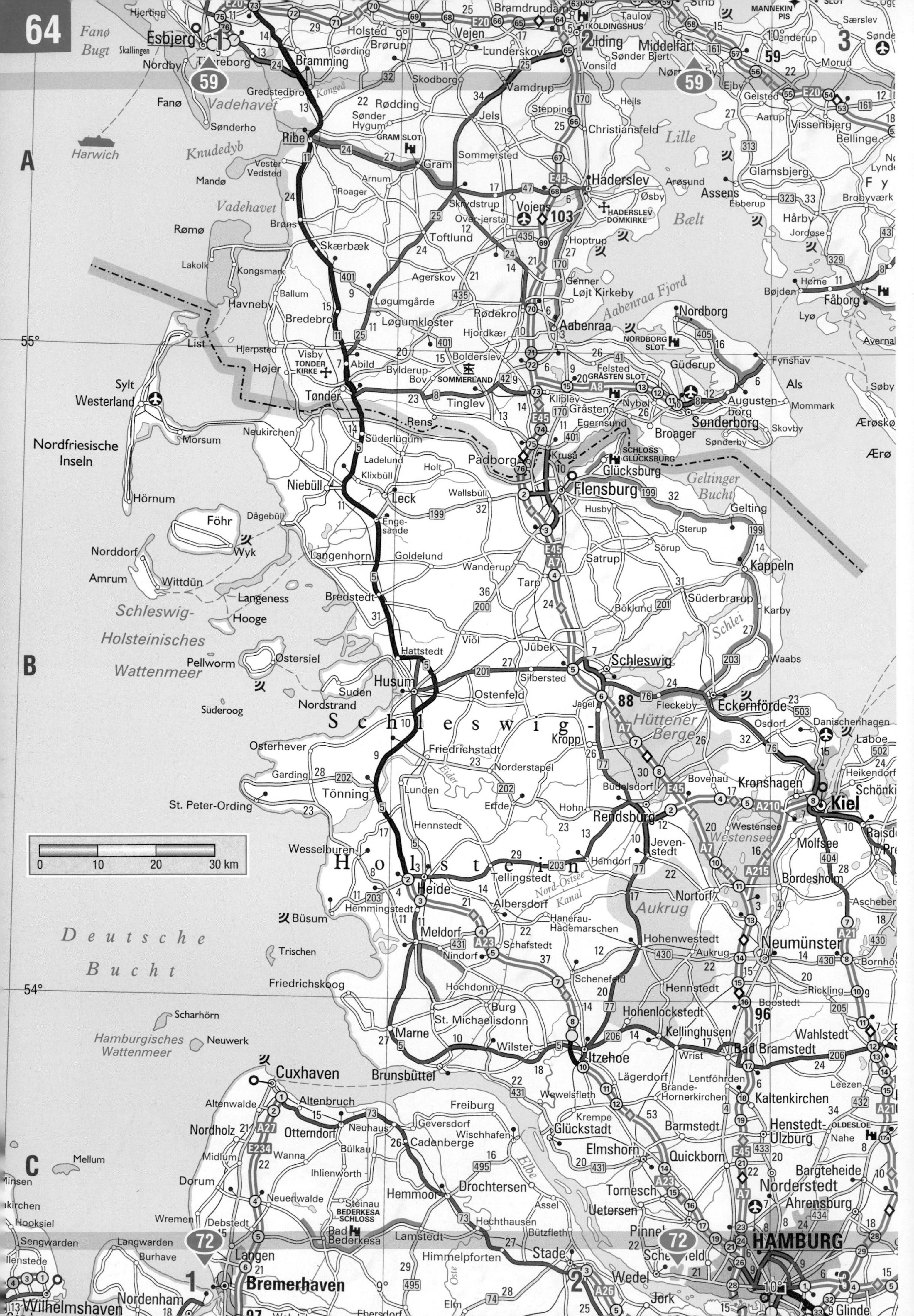

Fanø Bugt
Esbjerg
Skallingen
Nordby
Tjæreborg
Bramming
Gørding
Holsted
Brørup
Vejen
Bramdrupdam
Taulov
KOLDINGSHUS
Kolding
Middelfart
Sønder Bjert
Vonsild
Lunderskov
Skodborg
Vamdrup
Fanø
Vadehavet
Sønderho
Gredstedbro
Kongeå
Rødding
Sønder Hygum
GRAM SLOT
Jels
Stepping
Christiansfeld
Lille
Harwich
Knudedyb
Ribe
Gram
Sommersted
Haderslev
Vester Vedsted
Mandø
Arnum
Roager
Skrydstrup
Vojens
Øsby
HADERSLEV DOMKIRKE
Bælt
Assens
Ebberup
Glamsbjerg
Vissenbjerg
Bellinge
Aarup
Gelsted
Ejby
Særslev
Morud
Brobyværk
Hårby
Jordløse
Vadehavet
Brøns
Over-jerstal
Toftlund
Hoptrup
Rømø
Skærbæk
Lakolk
Kongsmark
Agerskov
Genner
Løjt Kirkeby
Aabenraa Fjord
Ballum
Havneby
Bredebro
Løgumgårde
Løgumkloster
Rødekro
Hjordkær
Aabenraa
Nordborg
NORDBORG SLOT
Horne
Bøjden
Fåborg
Lyø
55°
List
Hjerpsted
Visby
TONDER KIRKE
Højer
Abild
Bylderup-Bov
SOMMERLAND
Bolderslev
Felsted
GRÅSTEN SLOT
Guderup
Fynshav
Als
Avernak
Sylt
Westerland
Tønder
Tinglev
Kliplev
Gråsten
Nybøl
Augustenborg
Mommark
Søby
Ærøskø
Sønderborg
Skovby
Rens
Egernsund
Broager
Sønderby
Ærø
Neukirchen
Morsum
Nordfriesische Inseln
Süderlügum
Ladelund
Holt
Padborg
Kruså
SCHLOSS GLÜCKSBURG
Glücksburg
Geltinger Bucht
Niebüll
Klixbüll
Wallsbüll
Flensburg
Leck
Hörnum
Husby
Gelting
Föhr
Dägebüll
Enge-sande
Sterup
Norddorf
Wyk
Langenhorn
Goldelund
Sörup
Satrup
Kappeln
Amrum
Wittdün
Wanderup
Tarp
Langeness
Bredstedt
Süderbrarup
Böklund
Karby
Schleswig-Holsteinisches Wattenmeer
Hooge
Schlei
Viöl
Jübek
Pellworm
Ostersiel
Hattstedt
Schleswig
Waabs
Silberstedt
Suden
Husum
Nordstrand
Ostenfeld
Süderoog
Jagel
Fleckeby
Eckernförde
Osdorf
Danischenhagen
Laboe
Schleswig-Holstein
Hüttener Berge
Kropp
Osterhever
Friedrichstadt
Heikendorf
Schönkirchen
Garding
Norderstapel
Eider
Büdelsdorf
Bovenau
Kronshagen
Kiel
Tönning
Lunden
Erfde
Hohn
Rendsburg
St. Peter-Ording
Hennstedt
Westensee
Raisdorf
Wesselburen
Jeven-stedt
Hamdorf
Molfsee
Tellingstedt
Nord-Ostsee Kanal
Bordesholm
0
10
20
30 km
Heide
Hemmingstedt
Albersdorf
Nortorf
Aukrug
Büsum
Hanerau-Hademarschen
Meldorf
Schafstedt
Hohenwestedt
Neumünster
Deutsche Bucht
Trischen
Nindorf
Bornhöved
Friedrichskoog
Schenefeld
Hennstedt
Rickling
54°
Hochdonn
Burg
Hohenlockstedt
Boostedt
Scharhörn
St. Michaelisdonn
Kellinghusen
Wahlstedt
Hamburgisches Wattenmeer
Neuwerk
Marne
Wilster
Wrist
Bad Bramstedt
Itzehoe
Cuxhaven
Brunsbüttel
Lägerdorf
Lentföhrden
Brande-Hörnerkirchen
Leezen
Kaltenkirchen
Altenwalde
Altenbruch
Freiburg
Wewelsfleth
Krempe
Barmstedt
Henstedt-Ulzburg
OLDESLOE
Nahe
Nordholz
Otterndorf
Neuhaus
Geversdorf
Wischhafen
Cadenberge
Glückstadt
Elmshorn
Quickborn
Bargteheide
Mellum
Midlum
Wanna
Bülkau
Ihlienworth
Elbe
Norderstedt
Ahrensburg
Dorum
Hemmoor
Drochtersen
Tornesch
Uetersen
Neuenwalde
Steinau
BEDERKESA SCHLOSS
Assel
Hooksiel
Wremen
Debstedt
Hechthausen
Sengwarden
Langwarden
Bad Bederkesa
Lamstedt
Bützfleth
Pinneberg
Schenefeld
HAMBURG
Burhave
Langen
Himmelpforten
Stade
Bremerhaven
Oste
Wedel
Nordenham
Wilhelmshaven
Elm
Jork
Glinde

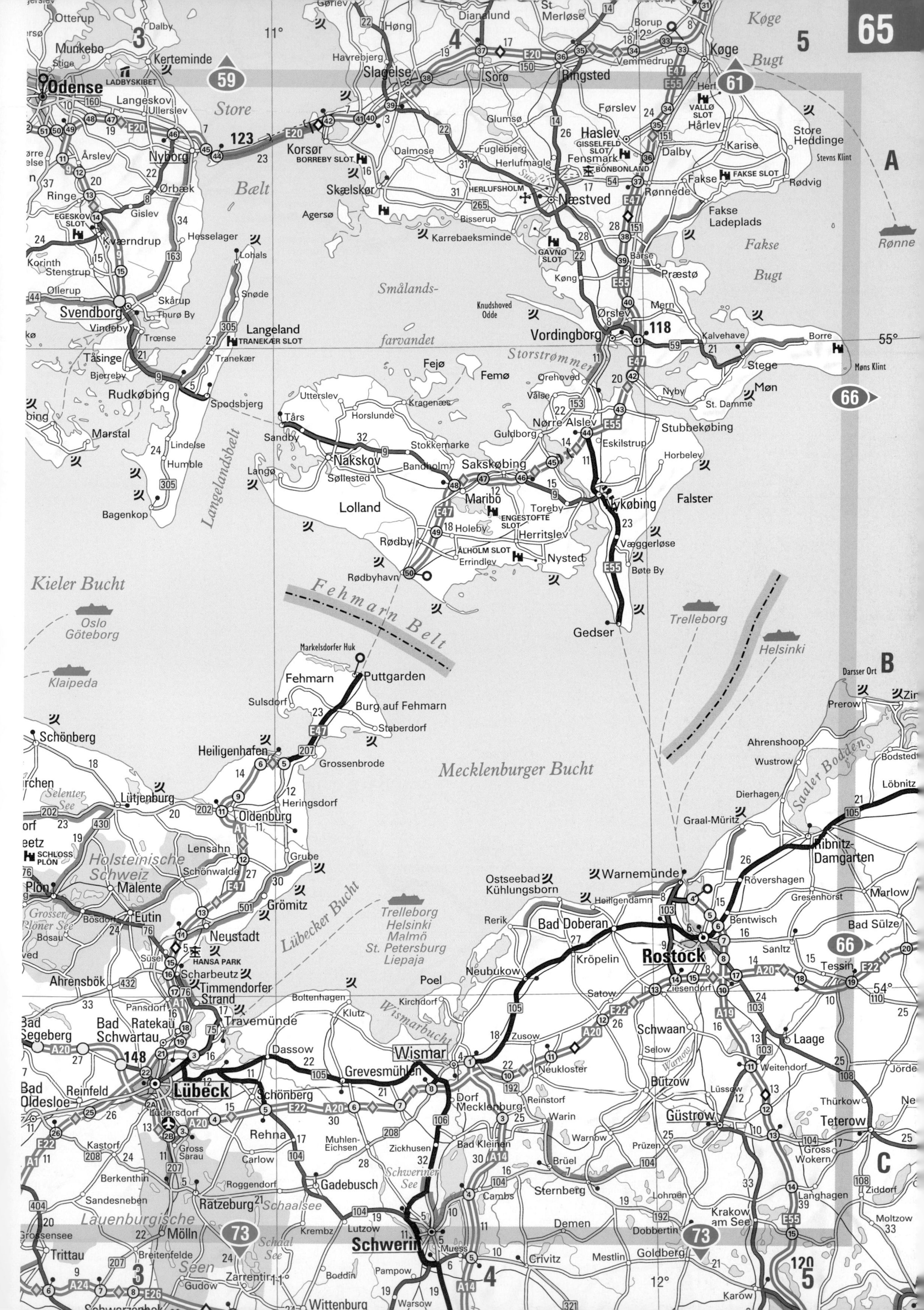
Odense
Kerteminde
Nyborg
Svendborg
Rudkøbing
Marstal
Langeland
Store Bælt
Korsør
Slagelse
Sorø
Ringsted
Køge
Køge Bugt
Haslev
Næstved
Skælskør
Vordingborg
Præstø
Fakse
Fakse Bugt
Stege
Møn
Smålands-farvandet
Storstrømmen
Nakskov
Lolland
Maribo
Sakskøbing
Nykøbing
Falster
Rødby
Rødbyhavn
Gedser
Kieler Bucht
Fehmarn Belt
Fehmarn
Puttgarden
Burg auf Fehmarn
Heiligenhafen
Oldenburg
Lütjenburg
Mecklenburger Bucht
Lübecker Bucht
Neustadt
Eutin
Plön
Bad Segeberg
Bad Schwartau
Travemünde
Lübeck
Ratzeburg
Mölln
Wismar
Grevesmühlen
Schwerin
Bad Doberan
Warnemünde
Rostock
Ribnitz-Damgarten
Güstrow
Teterow
Trelleborg
Helsinki
Rønne
Oslo Göteborg
Klaipeda
Trelleborg Helsinki Malmö St. Petersburg Liepaja
55°
54°
11°
12°
A
B
C
59
61
66
73

KØBENHAVN
COPENHAGEN
Malmö
Taastrup
Grevestrand
Køge
Køge Bugt
Roskilde Domkirke
Osted
Havdrup
Borup
Vemmedrup
Herfølge
Vallø Slot
Hårlev
Store Heddinge
Stevns Klint
Karise
Dalby
Fakse
Fakse Slot
Rødvig
Rønnede
Fakse Ladeplads
Fakse Bugt
Præstø
Mern
Ørslev
Kalvehave
Borre
Stege
Møns Klint
Møn
Nyby
St. Damme
Stubbekøbing
Eskilstrup
Horbelev
Falster
Væggerløse
Bøte By
Gedser
Amager
Dragør
Saltholm
Bjärred
Lomma
Södra Sandby
Dalby
Staffanstorp
Veberöd
Klågerup
Torup Slot
Blentarp
Sjöbo
Lövestad
Vollsjö
Övedskloster
Harlösa
Skåne-Tranås
Sankt Olof
Tomelilla
Hammenhög
Gärsnäs
Sövdeborg Slot
Sövestad
St. Herrestad
Köpingebro
Borrby
Ystad
Kåseberga
Sandhammaren
Rydsgård
Skurup
Anderslöv
Svedala
Oxie
Tygelsjö
Vellinge
Höllviksnäs
Skanör med Falsterbo
Falsterbo Slot
Trelleborg
Klagstorp
Skivarp
Abbekås
Beddingestrand
Smygehamn
Klaipeda Ystad
Travemünde
Rønne
Rostock Travemünde
København
Swinoujście
Bornholm
Trelleborg
Helsinki
Klaipeda
Wittow
Kap Arkona
Dranske
Altenkirchen
Wiek
Kloster
Hiddensee
Neuendorf
Jasmund
Trent
Sagard
Sassnitz
Rügen
Gingst
Bergen
Binz
Sellin
Göhren
Putbus
Samtens
Garz
Thiessow
Zudar
Brandshagen
Greifswalder Bodden
Darsser Ort
Vorpommersche Boddenlandschaft
Prerow
Zingst
Ahrenshoop
Wustrow
Saaler Bodden
Barth
Bodstedt
Hohendorf
Stralsund
Löbnitz
Dierhagen
Graal-Müritz
Veglast
Ribnitz-Damgarten
Richtenberg
Franzburg
Miltzow
Reinberg
Warnemünde
Rövershagen
Gresenhorst
Marlow
Bentwisch
Grimmen
Greifswald
Lubmin
Peenemünde
Kröslin
Rostock
Sanitz
Tessin
Bad Sülze
Tribsees
Rakow
Poggendorf
Kemnitz
Zinnowitz
Koserow
Wolgast
Ziesendorf
Glewitz
Görmin
Loitz
Gnoien
Trebel
Züssow
Zemitz
Usedom
Bansin
Ahlbeck
Lassan
Schwaan
Selow
Laage
Warnow
Demmin
Dargun
Tutow
Jarmen
Gützkow
Murchin
Swinoujście
Bützow
Weitendorf
Jördenstorf
Verchen
Tollense
Peene
Anklam
Lüssow
Neukalen
Thürkow
Güstrow
Teterow
Kummerower See
Albinshof
Leopoldshagen
Mönkebude
Stettiner Haff
Prüzen
Gross Wokern
Malchin
Abbaue
Burow
Spantekow
Ducherow
Sarnow
Rathebur
Ueckermünde
Lohmen
Gielow
Eggesin
Mecklenburg

3
4
5
15°
16°
A
B
C
55°
54°
0 10 20 30 km
Stenshuvud
Vik
Simrishamn
Skillinge
holmsgattet
Hammeren
HAMMARSHUS
Sandvig-Allinge
Tejn
Ertholmene
Bornholm
(Danmark)
(Denmark)
Hasle
Rø
Gudhjem
Klemensker
Nyker
Svaneke
Øster-marie
Køge
Rønne
Nylars
Åkirkeby
Neksø
Pedersker
Snogebaek
Ystad
Jaroslawiec
J. Kopań
Wieprza
Darłowo
Stary Jaroslaw
Dąbki
MUZEUM DARŁOWO
Sławno
68
J. Bukowo
Łazy
Ostrowiec
Mielno
J. Jamno
Jamno
Sarbinowo
Lejkowo
Sianów
Ustronie Morskie
Koszalin
Kołobrzeg
Bonin
Nacław
Dobrzyca
ZAMEK W. KOSZALINIE
Manowo
Mrzezyno
Dygowo
Wrzosowo
Biesiekierz
Niechorze
Rewal
Trzebiatów
Gościno
Karlino
Niedalino
Rosnowo
Mostowo
Pobierowo
Dziwnów
Międzywodzie
Cerkwica
Białogard
Dargiń
Kamień Pomorski
Gorawino
Wolinski
Kolczewo
Swierzno
Rega
Rymań
Bobolice
Międzyzdroje
Rzesznikowo
Sławoborze
Tychowo
Mechowo
Gryfice
Tychówka
Parsęta
Lubin
Rabino
Ząbrowo
Grzmiąca
Wolin
Gołczewo
Połczyn-Zdrój
Białowąs
Haff
Płoty
75
Resko
Rusinowo
Sława
Zalew Szczeciński
Świdwin
ZAMEK W. POŁCZYNIE
Barwice
Przybiernów
Żabowo
Starogard
Bierzwnica
Nowe Warpno
Brzeżno
Radowo
Drawsko
Ostropole
E28
E65
219

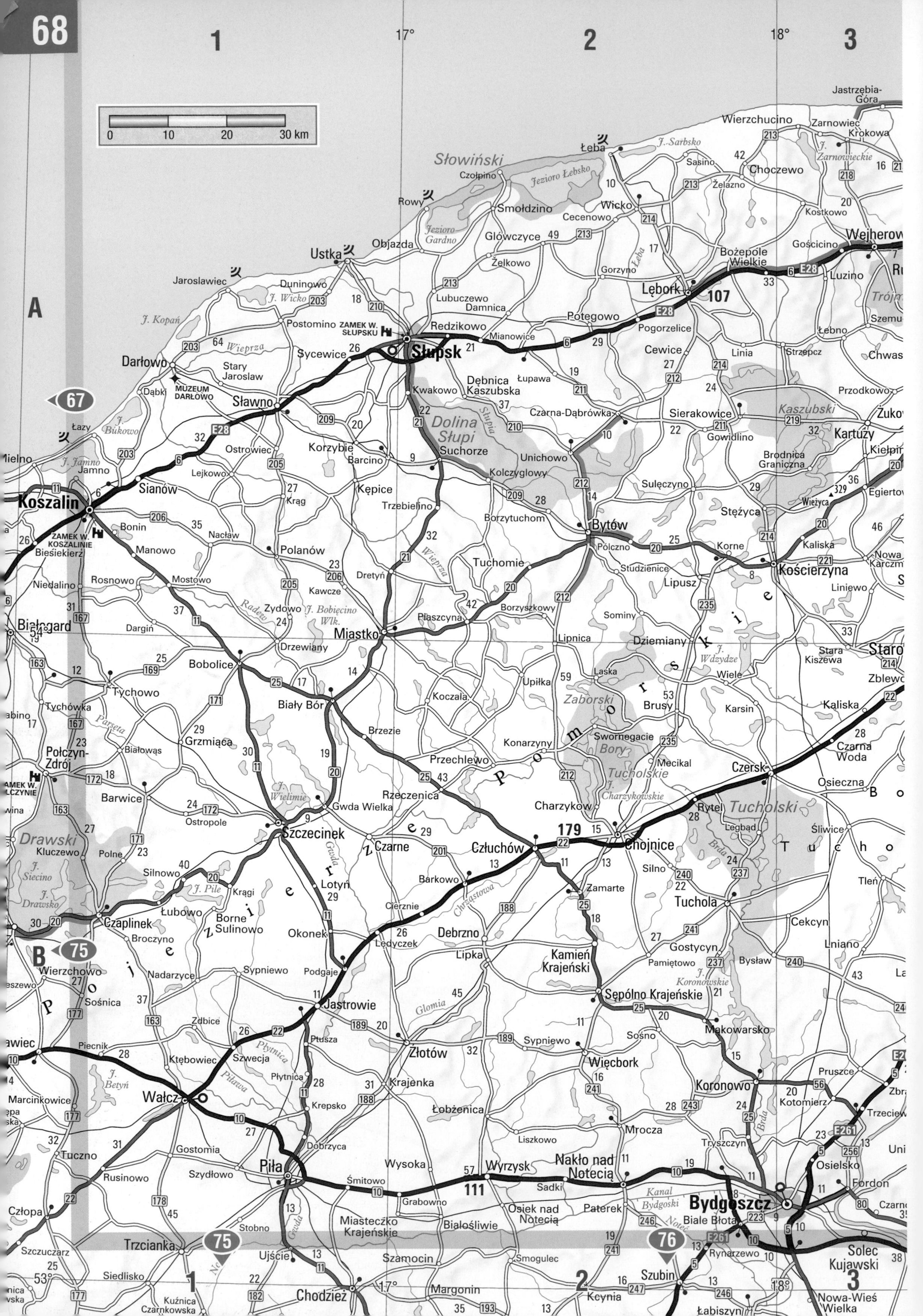
1
2
3
17°
18°
A
B
0 10 20 30 km
Jastrzębia-Góra
Wierzchucino
Żarnowiec
Krokowa
J. Żarnowieckie
Łeba
J. Sarbsko
Sasino
Choczewo
Słowiński
Czołpino
Jezioro Łebsko
Żelazno
Rowy
Smołdzino
Wicko
Cecenowo
Kostkowo
Jezioro Gardno
Główczyce
Wejherowo
Gościcino
Ustka
Objazda
Bożepole Wielkie
Żelkowo
Gorzyno
Łeba
Jarosławiec
Duninowo
J. Wicko
Lębork
107
Luzino
Lubuczewo
Damnica
Trójmiasto
J. Kopań
Postomino
ZAMEK W. SŁUPSKU
Redzikowo
Potęgowo
Pogorzelice
Łebno
Szemud
Mianowice
Wieprza
Słupsk
Cewice
Sycewice
Linia
Strzepcz
Chwaszczyno
Darłowo
Stary Jarosław
Dębnica Kaszubska
Łupawa
MUZEUM DARŁOWO
Dąbki
Kwakowo
Sławno
Przodkowo
Kaszubski
Czarna-Dąbrówka
Sierakowice
Żukowo
J. Bukowo
Dolina Słupi
Słupia
E28
Łazy
Gowidlino
Kartuzy
Korzybie
Kiełpino
Ostrowiec
Suchorze
Unichowo
Brodnica Graniczna
Mielno
J. Jamno
Jamno
Barcino
Kolczygłowy
Sulęczyno
Lejkowo
Sianów
Kępice
Egiertowo
Wieżyca
Koszalin
Krąg
Trzebielino
Stężyca
Bonin
Nacław
Borzytuchom
Bytów
ZAMEK W. KOSZALINIE
Biesiekierz
Manowo
Polanów
Pólczno
Korne
Kaliska
Nowa Karczma
Tuchomie
Studzienice
Kościerzyna
Rosnowo
Wieprza
Niedalino
Mostowo
Kawcze
Dretyń
Lipusz
Liniewo
Radew
Zydowo
J. Bobięcino Wlk.
Borzyszkowy
Sominy
Płaszczyna
Białogard
Dargiń
Miastko
Lipnica
Dziemiany
Stara Kiszewa
Starogard
Drzewiany
J. Wdzydze
Wiele
Bobolice
Laska
Zblewo
Upiłka
Tychowo
Koczała
Brusy
Kaliska
Tychówka
Biały Bór
Zaborski
Karsin
Parsęta
Grzmiąca
Brzezie
Swornegacie
Bory
Czarna Woda
Białowąs
Konarzyny
Połczyn-Zdrój
Tucholskie
Mecikal
Czersk
ZAMEK W. POŁCZYNIE
Przechlewo
J. Wielimie
Rzeczenica
J. Charzykowskie
Osieczna
Barwice
Charzykowy
Rytel
Tucholski
Gwda Wielka
Legbąd
Śliwice
Ostropole
Szczecinek
Czarne
Człuchów
Chojnice
Tuchola
Drawski
Kluczewo
Polne
Gwda
Silno
Tleń
Silnowo
J. Siecino
J. Pile
Kręgi
Lotyń
Barkowo
Zamarte
J. Drawsko
Łubowo
Cierznie
Chrząstowa
Tuchola
Czaplinek
Borne Sulinowo
Okonek
Debrzno
Cekcyn
Broczyno
Lędyczek
Gostycyn
Lniano
Kamień Krajeński
Lipka
Pamiętowo
Bysław
Wierzchowo
Nadarzyce
Sypniewo
Podgaje
J. Koronowskie
Sępólno Krajeńskie
Sośnica
Jastrowie
Glomia
Makowarsko
Zdbice
Ptusza
Sypniewo
Sosno
Wałcz
Piecnik
Szwecja
Płytnica
Złotów
Więcbork
Pruszcz
Kłębowiec
Piława
Koronowo
J. Betyń
Krajenka
Kotomierz
Marcinkowice
Krepsko
Łobżenica
Trzeciewnica
Mrocza
Tuczno
Gostomia
Dobrzyca
Liszkowo
Tryszczyn
Osielsko
Piła
Wysoka
Wyrzysk
Nakło nad Notecią
Fordon
Rusinowo
Szydłowo
Śmiłowo
Sadki
Kanał Bydgoski
Bydgoszcz
Człopa
Grabowno
111
Osiek nad Notecią
Paterek
Białe Błota
Miasteczko Krajeńskie
Białośliwie
Noteć
Stobno
Trzcianka
Ujście
Rynarzewo
Solec Kujawski
Szczuczarz
Szamocin
Smogulec
Siedlisko
Szubin
Chodzież
Margonin
Kcynia
Kuźnica Czarnkowska
Łabiszyn
Nowa-Wieś Wielka
53°
54°
Pomorskie
Pojezierze
Tucholskie
B o

67
75
75
76

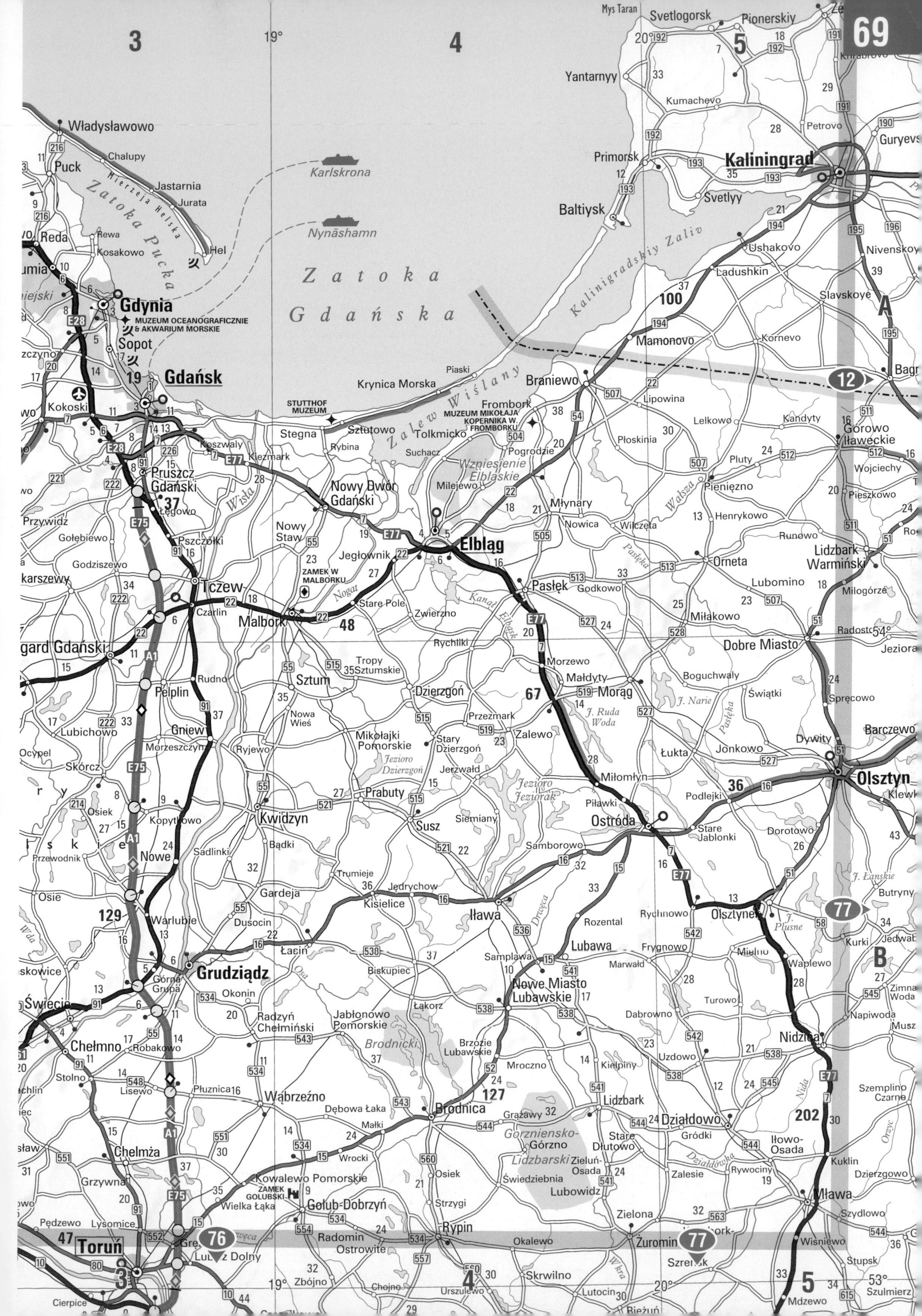
69
3
4
5
19°
20°
Mys Taran
Svetlogorsk
Pionerskiy
Yantarnyy
Kumachevo
Petrovo
Guryevsk
Primorsk
Kaliningrad
Svetlyy
Baltiysk
Kaliningradskiy Zaliv
Ushakovo
Nivenskoye
Ladushkin
Slavskoye
Mamonovo
Kornevo
Władysławowo
Chalupy
Puck
Mierzeja Helska
Jastarnia
Jurata
Zatoka Pucka
Rewa
Reda
Kosakowo
Hel
Karlskrona
Nynäshamn
Zatoka Gdańska
Gdynia
MUZEUM OCEANOGRAFICZNE & AKWARIUM MORSKIE
Sopot
Gdańsk
Kokoski
Piaski
Krynica Morska
Braniewo
Lipowina
STUTTHOF MUZEUM
Stegna
Sztutowo
Zalew Wiślany
Frombork
MUZEUM MIKOŁAJA KOPERNIKA W. FROMBORKU
Tolkmicko
Suchacz
Rybina
Kiezmark
Koszwały
Pogrodzie
Płoskinia
Lelkowo
Kandyty
Górowo Iławeckie
Wzniesienie Elbląskie
Milejewo
Pruszcz Gdański
Łęgowo
Nowy Dwór Gdański
Pieniężno
Pluty
Wojciechy
Pieszkowo
Przywidz
Gołębiewo
Pszczółki
Nowy Staw
Jegłownik
Elbląg
Młynary
Nowica
Wilczęta
Henrykowo
Runowo
Lidzbark Warmiński
Godziszewo
Tczew
ZAMEK W MALBORKU
Nogat
Pasłęk
Godkowo
Orneta
Lubomino
Miłogórze
Czarlin
Malbork
Stare Pole
Zwierzno
Kanał Elbląski
Miłakowo
Radostowo
Dobre Miasto
Jeziorany
Starogard Gdański
Rychliki
Tropy Sztumskie
Sztum
Dzierzgoń
Morzewo
Małdyty
Morąg
Boguchwały
Świątki
Sręcowo
Pelplin
Rudno
Nowa Wieś
J. Ruda Woda
J. Narie
Lubichowo
Gniew
Przezmark
Zalewo
Barczewo
Ocypel
Morzeszczyn
Ryjewo
Mikołajki Pomorskie
Stary Dzierzgoń
Łukta
Jonkowo
Dywity
Skórcz
Jezioro Dzierzgoń
Jerzwałd
Jezioro Jeziorak
Miłomłyn
Olsztyn
Prabuty
Osiek
Kopytkowo
Kwidzyn
Susz
Siemiany
Piławki
Ostróda
Podlejki
Stare Jabłonki
Dorotowo
Klewki
Przewodnik
Nowe
Sadlinki
Bądki
Samborowo
Trumieje
J. Łańskie
Osie
Gardeja
Jędrychowo
Kisielice
Iława
Rozental
Rychnowo
Olsztynek
J. Plusne
Butryny
Warlubie
Dusocin
Drwęca
Kurki
Jedwabno
Łasin
Lubawa
Frygnowo
Mielno
Grudziądz
Górna Grupa
Biskupiec
Samplawa
Marwałd
Waplewo
Okonin
Nowe Miasto Lubawskie
Turowo
Zimna Woda
Świecie
Radzyń Chełmiński
Jabłonowo Pomorskie
Łąkorz
Dąbrowno
Napiwoda
Chełmno
Robakowo
Brodnicki
Brzozie Lubawskie
Uzdowo
Nidzica
Stolno
Mroczno
Kiełpiny
Lisewo
Płużnica
Wąbrzeźno
Lidzbark
Szemplino Czarne
Dębowa Łąka
Małki
Brodnica
Grążawy
Działdowo
Chełmża
Wrocki
Górzno
Gorznieńsko-Lidzbarski
Stare Dłutowo
Gródki
Iłowo-Osada
Kuklin
Grzywna
Kowalewo Pomorskie
Osiek
Świedziebnia
Zieluń-Osada
Zalesie
Rywociny
Dzierzgowo
ZAMEK GOLUBSKI
Wielka Łąka
Golub-Dobrzyń
Strzygi
Lubowidz
Mława
Pędzewo
Lysomice
Zielona
Szydłowo
Toruń
Radomin
Ostrowite
Rypin
Okalewo
Żuromin
Wiśniewo
Lubicz Dolny
Stupsk
Zbójno
Skrwilno
Wkra
Chojno
Urszulewo
Lutocin
Mdzewo
Szulmierz
Cierpice
Bieżuń
Szreńsk
53°
54°
E28
E75
E77
A1
12
76
77

1
2
3
5°
6°
A
B
C
0
10
20
30 km
Waddeneilanden
Schiermonnikoog
Ameland
Nes
Hollum
Terschelling
Oosterend
West-Terschelling
Vlieland
Oost-Vlieland
De Cocksdorp
Texel
De Koog
Den Burg
Duinen van Texel
Waddenzee
53°
Den Helder
Julianadorp
Den Oever
Hippolytushoef
Slootdorp
Schagen
Nieuwe Niedorp
Medemblik
Andijk
Langedijk
Opmeer
Hoogkarspel
Enkhuizen
Stede Broek
Bergen
Heerhugowaard
Alkmaar
Egmond aan Zee
Stompetoren
Hoorn
Newcastle (Amsterdam)
Heiloo
Castricum
Uitgeest
Oosthuizen
Purmerend
Krommenie
Wormer
Edam
Volendam
Monnickendam
Beverwijk
IJmuiden
Zaanstad
Zuid-Kennemerland
Haarlem
Zandvoort
Amsterdam
Heemstede
Amstelveen
Hoofddorp
Schiphol
Hillegom
Keukenhof
Noordwijkerhout
Lisse
Aalsmeer
Weesp
Bussum
Almere
Noordwijk
Katwijk
Uithoorn
Hilversum
Oegstgeest
Leiden
Kasteel Sypesteyn
Wassenaar
Leidschendam
Voorschoten
Alphen a.d. Rijn
Breukelen
Rietveld Schröderhuis
Scheveningen
's-Gravenhage
The Hague
Boskoop
Woerden
Utrecht
Zoetermeer
Monster
Gouda
's-Gravenzande
Hoek van Holland
Delft
Pijnacker
Naaldwijk
Oudewater
Nieuwegein
Europoort
Krimpen a.d. IJssel
Schoonhoven
Schiedam
Rotterdam
Ridderkerk
Spijkenisse
Oud-Beijerland
Lek
Leerdam
Geldermalsen
Tiel
Culemborg
Wijk bij Duurstede
Amerongen
Rhenen
Doorn
Zeist
Bilthoven
Soest
Baarn
Amersfoort
Leusden
Scherpenzeel
Veenendaal
Wageningen
Ede
Rijn
Lunteren
Barneveld
Nijkerk
Huizen
Blaricum
Spakenburg
Putten
Ermelo
Harderwijk
Dolfinarium
Nunspeet
Elspeet
Het Loo
Apeldoorn
Vaassen
Epe
Heerde
Twello
Deventer
Beekbergen
Hoenderlo
De Hoge Veluwe
Veluwezoom
Dieren
Velp
Arnhem
Elst
Huissen
Zevenaar
Bemmel
Doetinchem
Nijmegen
Zutphen
Eerbeek
Lelystad
Flevoland
Dronten
Biddinghuizen
Walibi World
Swifterbant
Elburg
Kampen
IJsselmuiden
Zwolle
Hattem
Wijhe
Raalte
IJsselmeer
D.F. Woudagemaal
Urk
Emmeloord
Noord-oost-Polder
Nagele
Ens
Museum Schokland
Vollenhove
Genemuiden
Zwartsluis
Hasselt
Kuinre
Steenwijk
Weerribben-Wieden
Blokzijl
Marknesse
Giethoorn
Meppel
Lemmer
Oudemirdum
Balk
St. Nicolaasga
Tjeukemeer
Wolvega
Stavoren
Koudum
Woudsend
Workum
Makkum
Bolsward
Sneek
Akkrum
Joure
Heerenveen
Oldeboorn
Tijnje
Gorredijk
Beetsterzwaag
Drachten
Grouw
Opeinde
De Alde Feanen
Witmarsum
Harlingen
Franeker
Winsum
Dronrijp
Warga
Leeuwarden
Hardegarijp
Bergum
Berlikum
Tzummarum
St. Annaparochie
Stiens
Damwoude
Dokkum
Kollum
Marrum
Ferwerd
Holwerd
Metslawier
Buitenpost
Grootegast
Surhuisterveen
Oldeberkoop
Noordwolde
Drents-Friese
Kuinder of Tjonger
Tjongerkanaal
173
39
54
65
79
80
72
E22
A7
A31
A32
A6
A9
A5
A10
A1
A2
A4
A12
A13
A15
A20
A27
A28
A30
A44
A50
A325
A348
E19
E25
E30
E31
E35
E231
E232

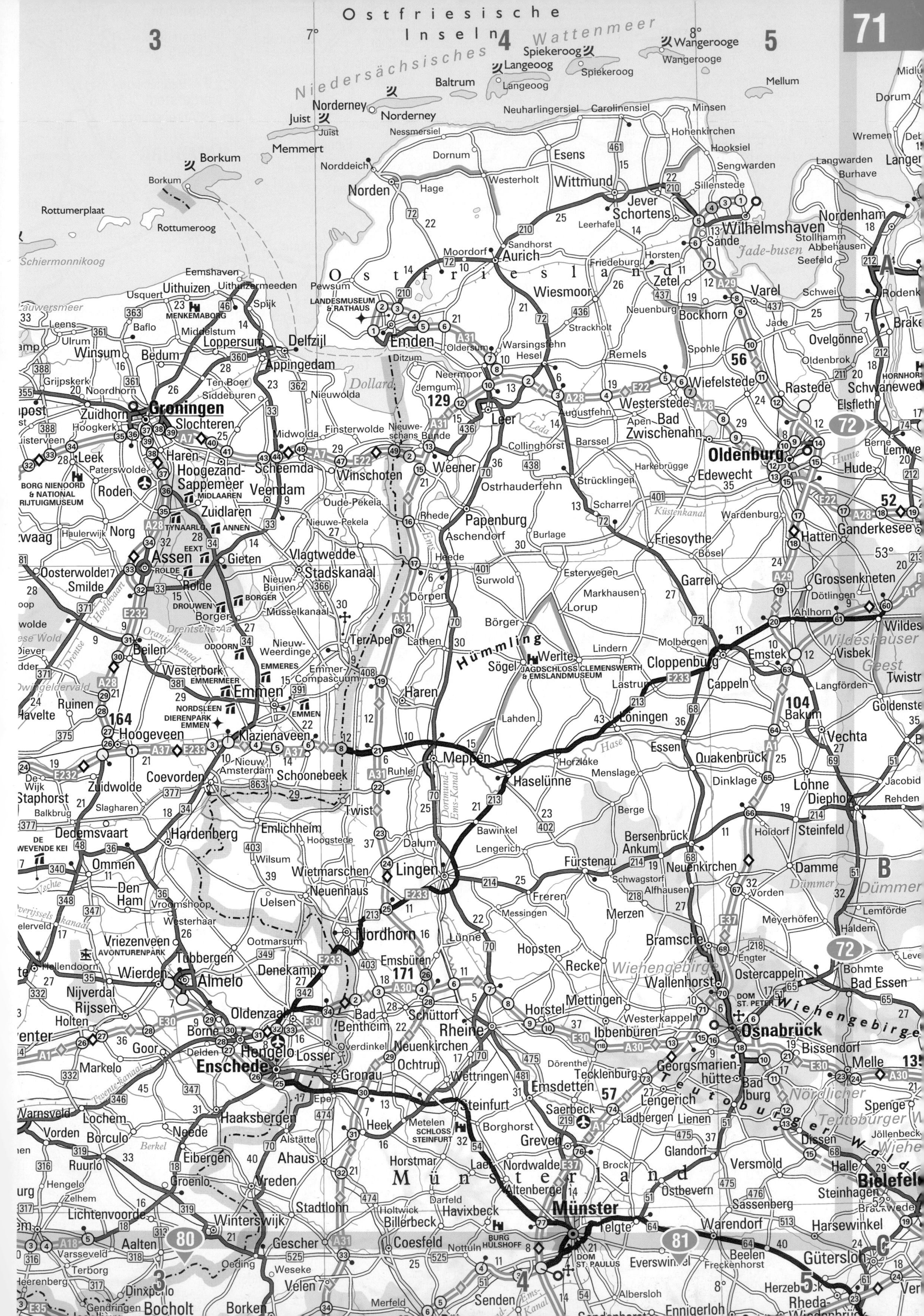
Ostfriesische
Inseln
Niedersächsisches Wattenmeer
Wangerooge
Spiekeroog
Langeoog
Baltrum
Norderney
Juist
Memmert
Borkum
Rottumerplaat
Rottumeroog
Schiermonnikoog
Mellum
Minsen
Carolinensiel
Neuharlingersiel
Nessmersiel
Hohenkirchen
Hooksiel
Sengwarden
Dornum
Esens
Norddeich
Norden
Hage
Westerholt
Wittmund
Jever
Schortens
Leerhafe
Wilhelmshaven
Sande
Jade-busen
Nordenham
Stollhamm
Abbehausen
Seefeld
Langwarden
Burhave
Wremen
Dorum
Midlum
Aurich
Moordorf
Sandhorst
Ostfriesland
Friedeburg
Horsten
Zetel
Varel
Schweiburg
Rodenkirchen
Brake
Ovelgönne
Jade
Wiesmoor
Neuenburg
Bockhorn
Strackholt
Remels
Spohle
Oldenbrok
Rastede
Schwanewede
Elsfleth
Pewsum
LANDESMUSEUM & RATHAUS
Emden
Oldersum
Warsingsfehn
Hesel
Ditzum
Dollard
Neermoor
Jemgum
Leer
Leda
Augustfehn
Apen
Westerstede
Wiefelstede
Bad Zwischenahn
Oldenburg
Hunte
Hude
Berne
Lemwerder
Barssel
Harkebrügge
Edewecht
Collinghorst
Weener
Bunde
Nieuweschans
Ostrhauderfehn
Strücklingen
Scharrel
Küstenkanaal
Wardenburg
Ganderkesee
Hatten
Papenburg
Aschendorf
Rhede
Burlage
Friesoythe
Bösel
Heede
Surwold
Esterwegen
Garrel
Grossenkneten
Dötlingen
Ahlhorn
Wildeshausen
Wildeshauser Geest
Dörpen
Markhausen
Lorup
Börger
Hümmling
Werlte
JAGDSCHLOSS CLEMENSWERTH & EMSLANDMUSEUM
Sögel
Lindern
Molbergen
Cloppenburg
Emstek
Visbek
Cappeln
Lastrup
Lathen
Haren
Meppen
Löningen
Lahden
Essen
Quakenbrück
Bakum
Vechta
Goldenstedt
Langförden
Lohne
Dinklage
Diepholz
Rehden
Haselünne
Herzlake
Menslage
Hase
Twist
Berge
Bersenbrück
Ankum
Holdorf
Steinfeld
Damme
Dümmer
Lemförde
Bawinkel
Lengerich
Dalum
Lingen
Fürstenau
Schwagstorf
Neuenkirchen
Alfhausen
Vorden
Freren
Messingen
Merzen
Bramsche
Hopsten
Recke
Wiehengebirge
Wallenhorst
Ostercappeln
Bohmte
Bad Essen
Mettingen
Westerkappeln
Osnabrück
DOM ST. PETER
Ibbenbüren
Hörstel
Rheine
Tecklenburg
Georgsmarienhütte
Bissendorf
Melle
Bad Iburg
Nördlicher Teutoburger Wald
Teutoburger Wald
Lengerich
Lienen
Ladbergen
Saerbeck
Emsdetten
Dissen
Spenge
Halle
Bielefeld
Steinhagen
Versmold
Glandorf
Greven
Nordwalde
Altenberge
Brock
Ostbevern
Münsterland
Münster
Telgte
Warendorf
Sassenberg
Harsewinkel
Gütersloh
Beelen
Everswinkel
Freckenhorst
DOM ST. PAULUS
Steinfurt
Borghorst
Metelen
SCHLOSS STEINFURT
Horstmar
Laer
Darfeld
Holtwick
Billerbeck
Havixbeck
BURG HÜLSHOFF
Coesfeld
Nottuln
Senden
Albersloh
Enniger
Rheda-Wiedenbrück
Herzebrock
Schüttorf
Emsbüren
Bad Bentheim
Ochtrup
Wettringen
Neuenkirchen
Gronau
Heek
Epe
Ahaus
Alstätte
Vreden
Stadtlohn
Gescher
Velen
Borken
Weseke
Oeding
Merfeld
Nordhorn
Lünne
Neuenhaus
Uelsen
Wietmarschen
Emlichheim
Hoogstede
Wilsum
Schoonebeek
Ter Apel
Emmer-Compascuum
Nieuw-Weerdinge
Stadskanaal
Vlagtwedde
Musselkanaal
Nieuw-Buinen
Oude-Pekela
Nieuwe-Pekela
Winschoten
Finsterwolde
Midwolda
Nieuwolda
Scheemda
Veendam
Hoogezand-Sappemeer
MIDLAAREN
Zuidlaren
TYNAARLO
ANNEN
Gieten
Assen
ROLDE
Rolde
EEXT
DROUWEN
BORGER
Borger
Drentsche Aa
Oranjekanaal
ODOORN
EMMERES
EMMERMEER
Westerbork
Emmen
NORDSLEEN
DIERENPARK EMMEN
Klazienaveen
Nieuw Amsterdam
Coevorden
Slagharen
Hardenberg
Dedemsvaart
DE WEVENDE KEI
Ommen
Vechte
Den Ham
Vroomshoop
Westerhaar
Vriezenveen
AVONTURENPARK
Tubbergen
Ootmarsum
Denekamp
Hellendoorn
Wierden
Almelo
Nijverdal
Rijssen
Holten
Oldenzaal
Borne
Hengelo
Losser
Overdinkel
Enschede
Delden
Goor
Markelo
Twentekanaal
Haaksbergen
Neede
Eibergen
Berkel
Groenlo
Lochem
Borculo
Vorden
Ruurlo
Hengelo
Zelhem
Lichtenvoorde
Winterswijk
Aalten
Varsseveld
Terborg
Dinxperlo
Bocholt
Gendringen
Doetinchem
Hoogeveen
Zuidwolde
Staphorst
Balkbrug
De Wijk
Havelte
Ruinen
Dwingelderveld
Diever
Beilen
Smilde
Oosterwolde
Hoofdvaart
Drentse Wold
Norg
Haulerwijk
Roden
Leek
Paterswolde
BORG NIENOORD & NATIONAL RIJTUIGMUSEUM
Groningen
Zuidhorn
Hoogkerk
Slochteren
Haren
Siddeburen
Ten Boer
Appingedam
Delfzijl
Loppersum
Middelstum
Bedum
Winsum
Baflo
Ulrum
Leens
Usquert
Uithuizen
Uithuizermeeden
Spijk
MENKEMABORG
Eemshaven
Lauwersmeer
Grijpskerk
Noordhorn
Niedersachsen
Ems
Dortmund-Ems-Kanal
Emmerikanal

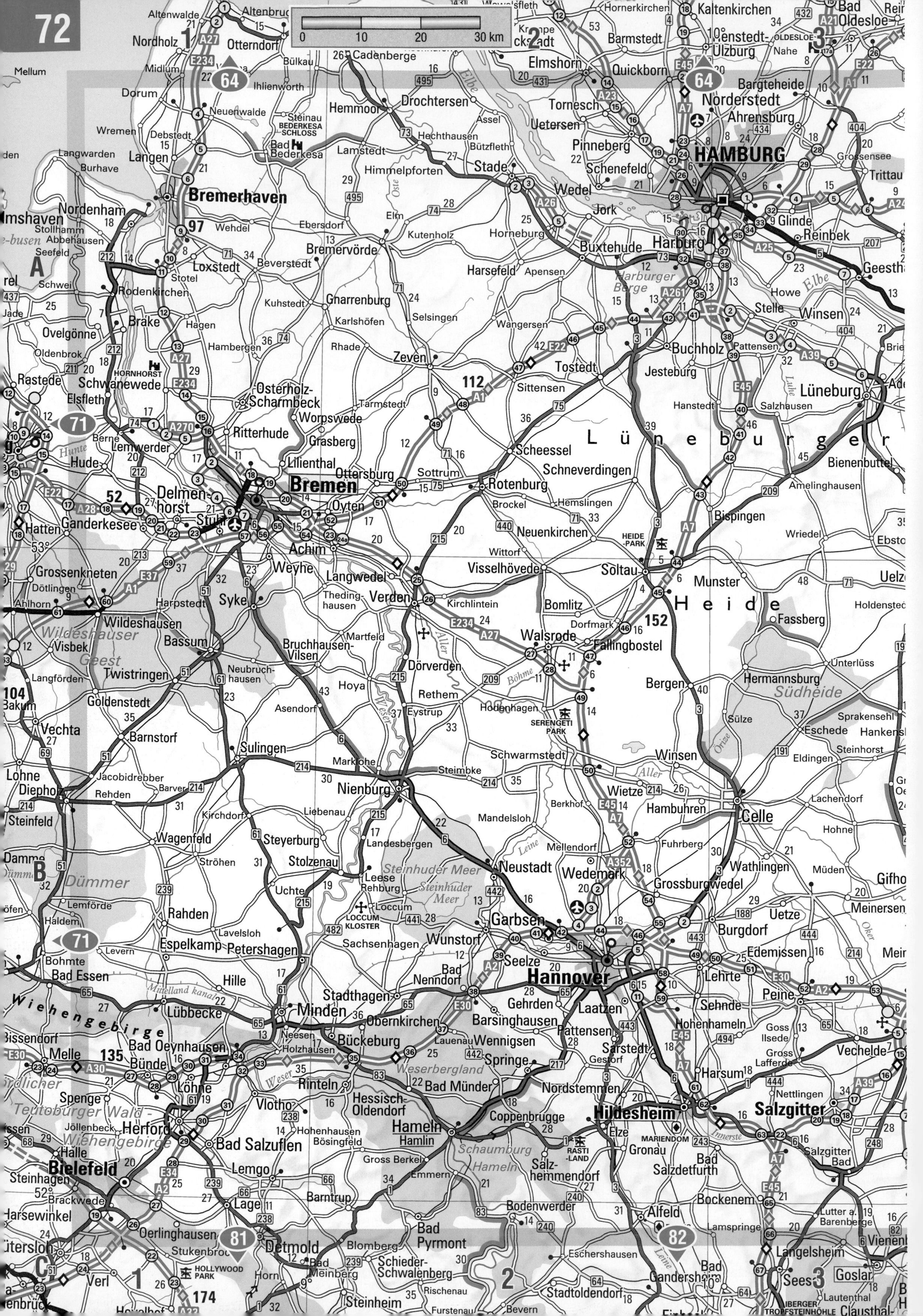
0 10 20 30 km
Altenwalde
Altenbruch
Nordholz
Otterndorf
Cadenberge
Mellum
Midlum
Bülkau
Ihlienworth
Dorum
Neuenwalde
Steinau
BEDERKESA SCHLOSS
Wremen
Debstedt
Bad Bederkesa
Langen
Langwarden
Burhave
Bremerhaven
Nordenham
Stollhamm
Abbehausen
Seefeld
Wehdel
Ebersdorf
Bremervörde
Loxstedt
Stotel
Beverstedt
Rodenkirchen
Schwei
Jade
Ovelgönne
Oldenbrok
Brake
Hagen
Hamberger
Kuhstedt
Gnarrenburg
Karlshöfen
Rhade
Selsingen
Zeven
Rastede
Schwanewede
HORNHORST
Elsfleth
Osterholz-Scharmbeck
Worpswede
Tarmstedt
Ritterhude
Berne
Lemwerder
Hude
Grasberg
Lilienthal
Ottersburg
Bremen
Delmenhorst
Ganderkesee
Hatten
Stuhr
Oyten
Achim
Sottrum
Rotenburg
Brockel
Hemslingen
Neuenkirchen
Grossenkneten
Dötlingen
Ahlhorn
Wildeshausen
Harpstedt
Syke
Weyhe
Langwedel
Theding-hausen
Verden
Kirchlintein
Wittorf
Visselhövede
Bomlitz
Dorfmark
Walsrode
Fallingbostel
Wildeshauser Geest
Visbek
Bassum
Bruchhausen-Vilsen
Martfeld
Dörverden
Neubruchhausen
Twistringen
Langförden
Bakum
Goldenstedt
Hoya
Asendorf
Rethem
Eystrup
Hodenhagen
SERENGETI PARK
Vechta
Barnstorf
Sulingen
Lohne
Jacobidrebber
Diepholz
Rehden
Barver
Markloh
Nienburg
Steimbke
Schwarmstedt
Steinfeld
Kirchdorf
Liebenau
Mandelsloh
Wagenfeld
Steyerburg
Landesbergen
Damme
Dümmer
Ströhen
Stolzenau
Steinhuder Meer
Neustadt
Uchte
Leese
Rehburg
Loccum
LOCCUM KLOSTER
Lemförde
Haldem
Rahden
Lavelsloh
Espelkamp
Petershagen
Sachsenhagen
Wunstorf
Garbsen
Levern
Bohmte
Bad Essen
Hille
Bad Nenndorf
Seelze
Hannover
Mittelland kanal
Stadthagen
Minden
Gehrden
Laatzen
Lübbecke
Obernkirchen
Barsinghausen
Pattensen
Wiehengebirge
Bad Oeynhausen
Bückeburg
Lauenau
Wennigsen
Sarstedt
Melle
Bünde
Neesen
Holzhausen
Springe
Gestorf
Löhne
Rinteln
Weserbergland
Bad Münder
Nordstemmen
Spenge
Teutoburger Wald
Vlotho
Hessisch-Oldendorf
Coppenbrügge
Hildesheim
Jöllenbeck
Herford
Hohenhausen
Hameln
Hamlin
Elze
MARIENDOM
Halle
Bad Salzuflen
Bösingfeld
Schaumburg
RASTI-LAND
Gronau
Bielefeld
Lemgo
Gross Berkel
Salzhemmendorf
Bad Salzdetfurth
Steinhagen
Brackwede
Lage
Barntrup
Emmern
Bodenwerder
Harsewinkel
Oerlinghausen
Alfeld
Bad Pyrmont
Lamspringe
Gütersloh
Stukenbrock
Detmold
Blomberg
Eschershausen
HOLLYWOOD PARK
Bad Meinberg
Horn
Schieder-Schwalenberg
Bad Gandersheim
Verl
Steinheim
Rischenau
Stadtoldendorf
Furstenau
Bevern
Wewelsfleth
Krempe
Glückstadt
Hornerkirchen
Kaltenkirchen
Barmstedt
Henstedt-Ulzburg
Bad Oldesloe
Elmshorn
Quickborn
Bargteheide
Drochtersen
Hemmoor
Tornesch
Norderstedt
Uetersen
Ahrensburg
Assel
Hechthausen
Pinneberg
HAMBURG
Bützfleth
Lamstedt
Stade
Schenefeld
Grossensee
Himmelpforten
Trittau
Wedel
Oste
Jork
Glinde
Elm
Kutenholz
Horneburg
Harburg
Reinbek
Buxtehude
Harsefeld
Apensen
Harburger Berge
Geesthacht
Elbe
Howe
Stelle
Winsen
Wangersen
Buchholz
Pattensen
Tostedt
Jesteburg
Sittensen
Lüneburg
Hanstedt
Salzhausen
Scheessel
Lüneburger Heide
Bienenbüttel
Schneverdingen
Amelinghausen
Bispingen
Wriedel
Ebstorf
HEIDE-PARK
Soltau
Munster
Uelzen
Holdenstedt
Fassberg
Unterlüss
Hermannsburg
Südheide
Bergen
Sülze
Sprakensehl
Eschede
Hankensbüttel
Steinhorst
Eldingen
Winsen
Aller
Wietze
Berkhof
Hambühren
Celle
Lachendorf
Hohne
Mellendorf
Fuhrberg
Wathlingen
Wedemark
Grossburgwedel
Müden
Gifhorn
Uetze
Meinersen
Burgdorf
Edemissen
Lehrte
Peine
Sehnde
Hohenhameln
Gross Ilsede
Gross Lafferde
Vechelde
Harsum
Nettlingen
Salzgitter
Innerste
Salzgitter-Bad
Bockenem
Lutter a. Barenberge
Langelsheim
Vienenburg
Goslar
Seesen
Lautenthal
Clausthal
Sarstedt

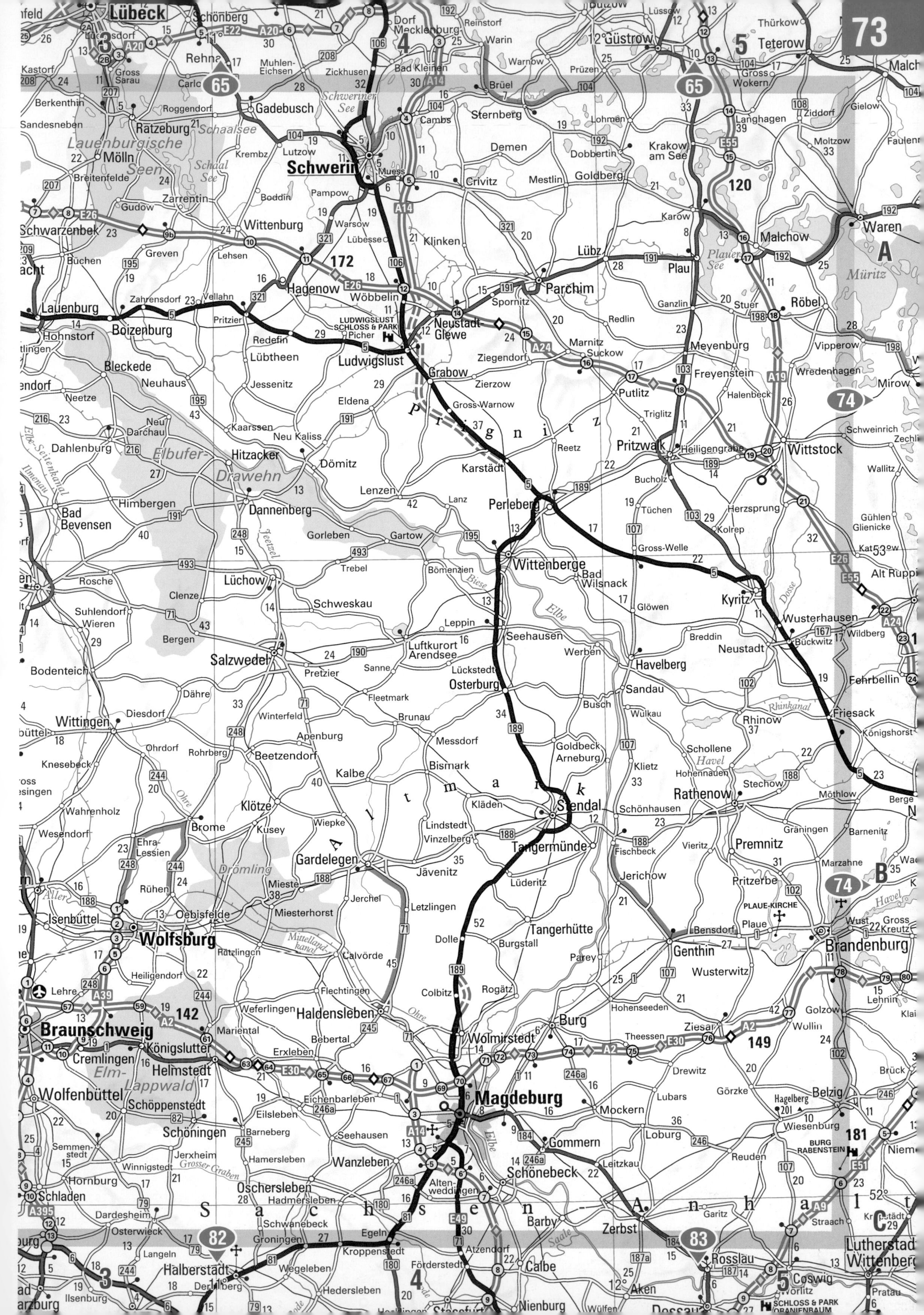
Lübeck
Schwerin
Wittenberge
Salzwedel
Stendal
Wolfsburg
Braunschweig
Magdeburg
Brandenburg
Prignitz
Altmark
Sachsen Anhalt
Ludwigslust
Parchim
Perleberg
Gardelegen
Haldensleben
Helmstedt
Wolfenbüttel
Halberstadt
Schönebeck
Burg
Genthin
Rathenow
Havelberg
Kyritz
Wittstock
Pritzwalk
Güstrow
Teterow
Waren
Müritz
Ratzeburg
Mölln
Gadebusch
Hagenow
Boizenburg
Lauenburg
Lüchow
Dannenberg
Hitzacker
Uelzen
Oschersleben
Wanzleben
Tangermünde
Osterburg
Klötze
Belzig
Zerbst
Rosslau
Dessau
Lutherstadt Wittenberg

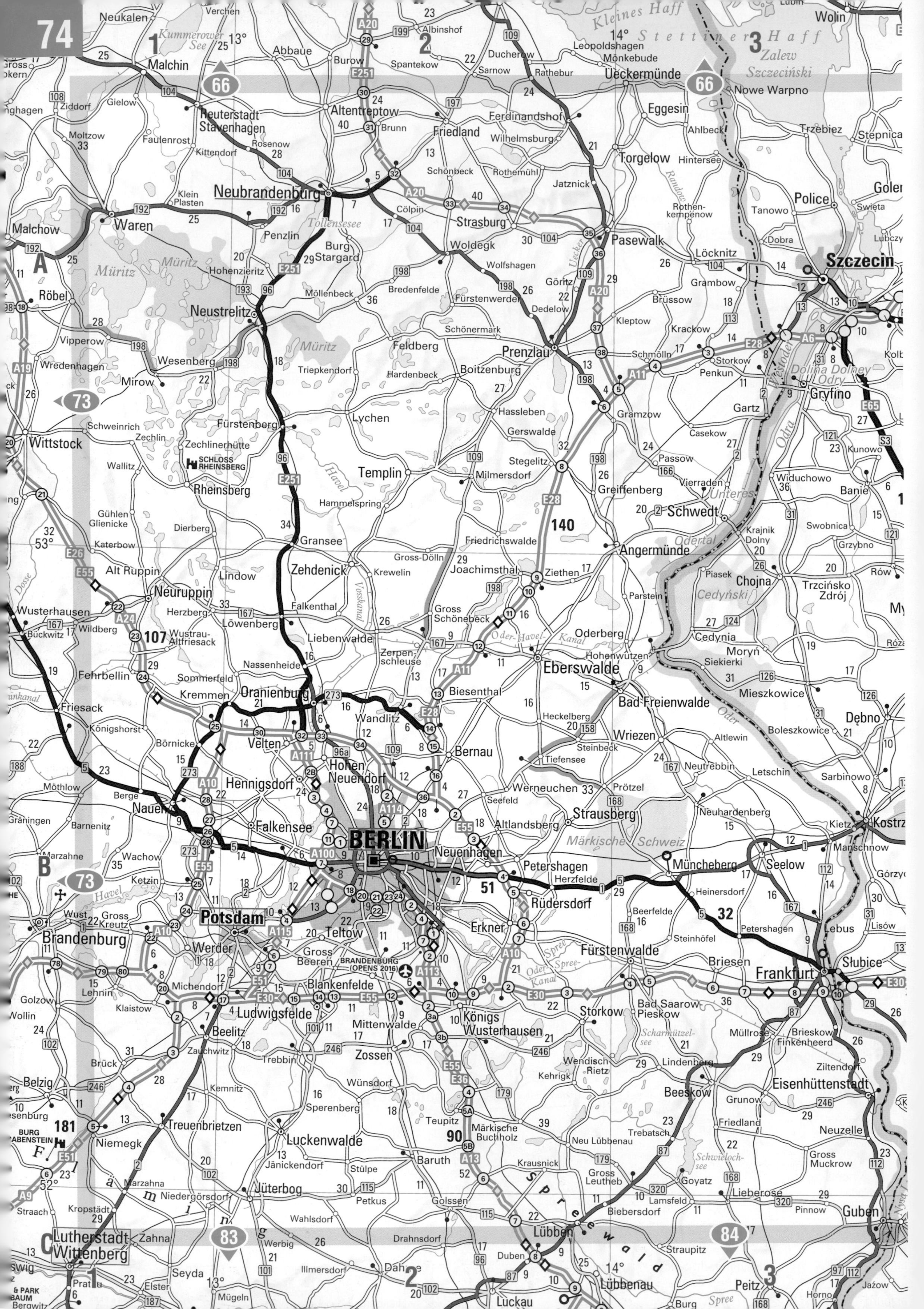

Neukalen
Verchen
Kummerower See
Malchin
Abbaue
Burow
Albinshof
Spantekow
Ducherow
Sarnow
Kleines Haff
Leopoldshagen
Mönkebude
Stettiner Haff
Zalew Szczeciński
Wolin
Rathebur
Ueckermünde
Nowe Warpno
Reuterstadt Stavenhagen
Altentreptow
Friedland
Ferdinandshof
Eggesin
Ahlbeck
Trzebież
Stepnica
Gielow
Ziddorf
Moltzow
Faulenrost
Rosenow
Kittendorf
Brunn
Wilhelmsburg
Torgelow
Hintersee
Schönbeck
Rothemühl
Jatznick
Neubrandenburg
Klein Plasten
Cölpin
Strasburg
Rothenkempenow
Tanowo
Police
Święta
Goleniów
Malchow
Waren
Penzlin
Tollensesee
Burg Stargard
Woldegk
Pasewalk
Löcknitz
Dobra
Lubczyna
Szczecin
Müritz
Hohenzieritz
Wolfshagen
Grambow
Röbel
Möllenbeck
Bredenfelde
Fürstenwerder
Görlitz
Dedelow
Brüssow
Neustrelitz
Kleptow
Krackow
Schönermark
Vipperow
Feldberg
Prenzlau
Schmölln
Storkow
Penkun
Wesenberg
Wredenhagen
Mirow
Triepkendorf
Hardenbeck
Boitzenburg
Dolina Dolnej Odry
Westoder
Gryfino
Gartz
Hassleben
Gramzow
Schweinrich
Wittstock
Zechlin
Fürstenberg
Zechlinerhütte
Lychen
Gerswalde
Casekow
Kunowo
Schloss Rheinsberg
Wallitz
Rheinsberg
Templin
Milmersdorf
Stegelitz
Passow
Widuchowo
Banie
Greiffenberg
Vierraden
Unteres Odertal
Hammelspring
Gühlen Glienicke
Dierberg
Katerbow
Gransee
Friedrichswalde
Schwedt
Krajnik Dolny
Swobnica
Grzybno
Angermünde
Odertal
Gross-Dölln
Joachimsthal
Ziethen
Alt Ruppin
Zehdenick
Krewelin
Lindow
Neuruppin
Piasek
Chojna
Trzcińsko Zdrój
Parstein
Cedyński
Wusterhausen
Herzberg
Falkenthal
Gross Schönebeck
Löwenberg
Bückwitz
Wildberg
Wustrau-Altfriesack
Liebenwalde
Oderberg
Cedynia
Moryń
Siekierki
Zerpenschleuse
Oder-Havel-Kanal
Hohenwutzen
Eberswalde
Fehrbellin
Nassenheide
Sommerfeld
Kremmen
Oranienburg
Biesenthal
Bad Freienwalde
Mieszkowice
Friesack
Wandlitz
Heckelberg
Dębno
Königshorst
Börnicke
Velten
Bernau
Wriezen
Altlewin
Boleszkowice
Steinbeck
Tiefensee
Hohen Neuendorf
Neutrebbin
Letschin
Sarbinowo
Möthlow
Hennigsdorf
Werneuchen
Prötzel
Berge
Nauen
Seefeld
Strausberg
Neuhardenberg
Kietz
Kostrzyn
Gräningen
Barnenitz
Falkensee
Altlandsberg
Märkische Schweiz
BERLIN
Neuenhagen
Müncheberg
Seelow
Manschnow
Marzahne
Wachow
Ketzin
Petershagen
Herzfelde
Heinersdorf
Görzyca
Havel
Rüdersdorf
Wust
Gross Kreutz
Potsdam
Teltow
Erkner
Beerfelde
Lebus
Lisów
Brandenburg
Werder
Steinhöfel
Fürstenwalde
Briesen
Frankfurt
Słubice
Gross Beeren
Brandenburg (Opens 2016)
Blankenfelde
Lehnin
Michendorf
Oder-Spree-Kanal
Golzow
Klaistow
Ludwigsfelde
Königs Wusterhausen
Storkow
Bad Saarow-Pieskow
Wollin
Mittenwalde
Beelitz
Scharmützelsee
Müllrose
Brieskow Finkenheerd
Zossen
Trebbin
Zauchwitz
Wendisch Rietz
Lindenberg
Brück
Ziltendorf
Belzig
Kemnitz
Wünsdorf
Kehrigk
Beeskow
Eisenhüttenstadt
Sperenberg
Grunow
Teupitz
Märkische Buchholz
Trebatsch
Friedland
Neuzelle
Treuenbrietzen
Burg Rabenstein
Niemegk
Luckenwalde
Neu Lübbenau
Jänickendorf
Baruth
Stülpe
Krausnick
Schwielochsee
Gross Leuthen
Gross Muckrow
Goyatz
Marzahna
Niedergörsdorf
Jüterbog
Petkus
Golssen
Spreewald
Biebersdorf
Lamsfeld
Lieberose
Pinnow
Guben
Straach
Kropstädt
Wahlsdorf
Lübben
Lutherstadt Wittenberg
Zahna
Werbig
Drahnsdorf
Straupitz
Duben
Seyda
Illmersdorf
Dahme
Lübbenau
Peitz
Jaźow
Elster
Mügeln
Luckau
Burg
Spree
Horno
Neisse
Fläming

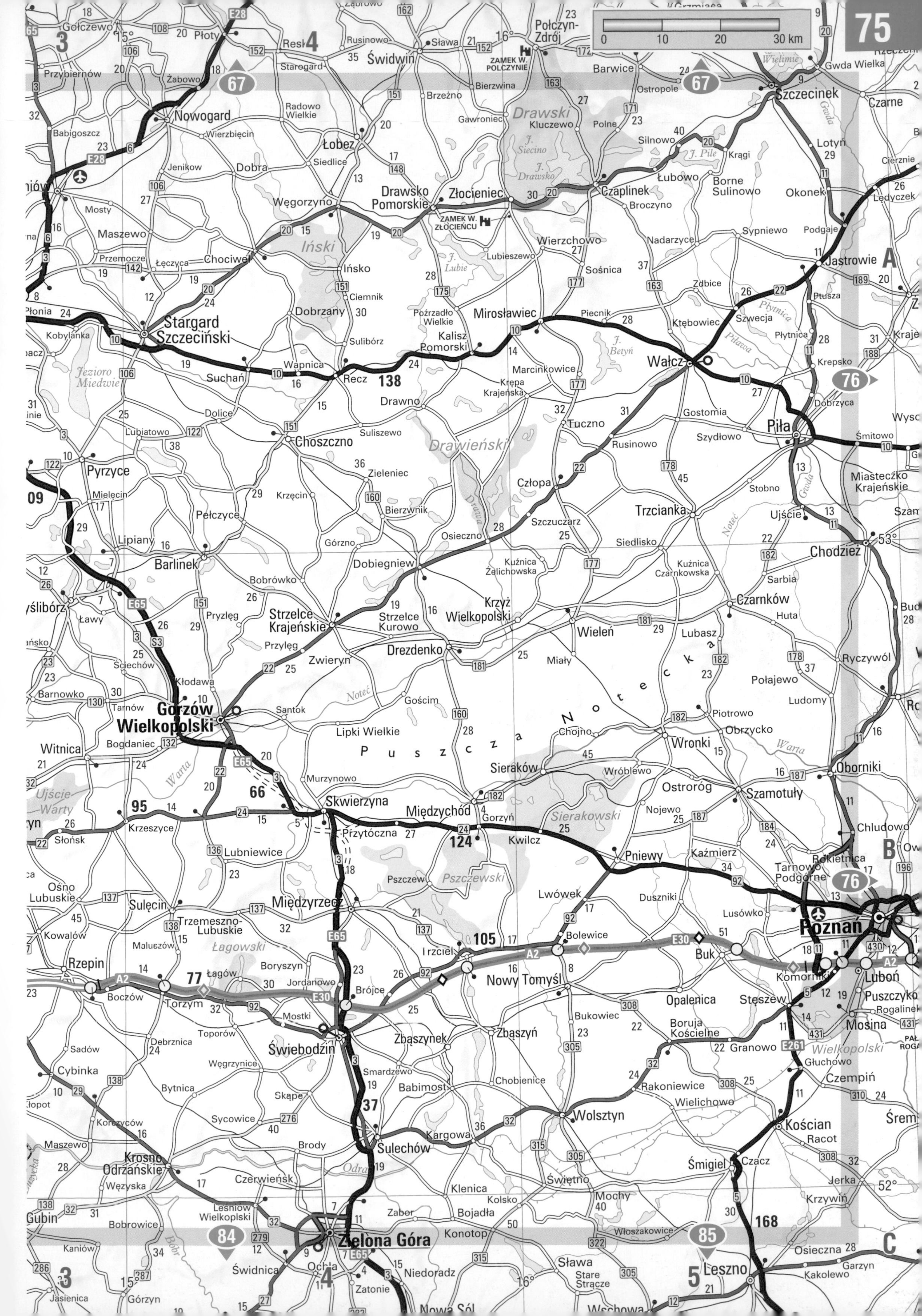

75
0 10 20 30 km
Gołczewo
Płoty
Resko
Rusinowo
Sława
Świdwin
Połczyn-Zdrój
ZAMEK W. POŁCZYNIE
Barwice
Szczecinek
Gwda Wielka
Przybiernów
Żabowo
Starogard
Bierzwina
Ostropole
Nowogard
Radowo Wielkie
Brzeżno
Gawroniec
Drawski
Kluczewo
Polne
Silnowo
Czarne
Babigoszcz
Wierzbięcin
Łobez
J. Siecino
J. Pile
Krągi
Lotyń
Siedlice
Jenikowo
Dobra
J. Drawsko
Łubowo
Borne Sulinowo
Okonek
Mosty
Węgorzyno
Drawsko Pomorskie
Złocieniec
Czaplinek
Broczyno
Lędyczek
ZAMEK W. ZŁOCIEŃCU
Maszewo
Iński
Nadarzyce
Sypniewo
Podgaje
Wierzchowo
Przemocze
Łęczyca
Chociwel
J. Lubie
Lubieszewo
Sośnica
Jastrowie
Ińsko
Zdbice
Ciemnik
Płusza
Płonia
Stargard Szczeciński
Dobrzany
Poźrzadło Wielkie
Mirosławiec
Piecnik
Kłębowiec
Szwecja
Płytnica
Kobylanka
Kalisz Pomorski
Sulibórz
J. Betyń
Wałcz
Krepsko
Jezioro Miedwie
Wapnica
Suchań
Recz
Marcinkowice
Krępa Krajeńska
Drawno
Tuczno
Gostomia
Dobrzyca
Piła
Dolice
Lubiatowo
Suliszewo
Choszczno
Drawieński
Rusinowo
Szydłowo
Śmitowo
Pyrzyce
Zieleniec
Człopa
Stobno
Miasteczko Krajeńskie
Mielęcin
Krzęcin
Bierzwnik
Pełczyce
Trzcianka
Ujście
Szczuczarz
Lipiany
Górzno
Osieczno
Siedlisko
Chodzież
Barlinek
Dobiegniew
Kuźnica Żelichowska
Kuźnica Czarnkowska
Bobrówko
Sarbia
Myślibórz
Czarnków
Ławy
Przyzęg
Strzelce Krajeńskie
Strzelce Kurowo
Krzyż Wielkopolski
Huta
Wieleń
Lubasz
Przyłęg
Zwierzyn
Drezdenko
Miały
Ryczywół
Ściechów
Połajewo
Kłodawa
Barnówko
Tarnów
Noteć
Gościm
Ludomy
Gorzów Wielkopolski
Santok
Piotrowo
Lipki Wielkie
Puszcza Notecka
Chojno
Obrzycko
Witnica
Bogdaniec
Wronki
Warta
Sieraków
Oborniki
Wróblewo
Murzynowo
Ostroróg
Szamotuły
Ujście Warty
Skwierzyna
Międzychód
Gorzyń
Sierakowski
Nojewo
Krzeszyce
Przytóczna
Kwilcz
Chludowo
Słońsk
Lubniewice
Pniewy
Kaźmierz
Rokietnica
Pszczew
Pszczewski
Tarnowo Podgórne
Ośno Lubuskie
Sulęcin
Międzyrzecz
Lwówek
Duszniki
Trzemeszno Lubuskie
Lusówko
Poznań
Kowalów
Maluszów
Łagowski
Trzciel
Bolewice
Buk
Rzepin
Boryszyn
Jordanowo
Nowy Tomyśl
Komorniki
Luboń
Łagów
Boczów
Torzym
Brójce
Opalenica
Stęszew
Puszczykowo
Rogalinek
Mostki
Bukowiec
Boruja Kościelne
Mosina
Toporów
Świebodzin
Zbąszynek
Zbąszyń
Sadów
Debrznica
Granowo
Wielkopolski
Cybinka
Węgrzynice
Smardzewo
Głuchowo
Bytnica
Babimost
Chobienice
Rakoniewice
Czempiń
Skąpe
Wielichowo
Korczyców
Sycowice
Wolsztyn
Śrem
Kościan
Maszewo
Kargowa
Racot
Brody
Sulechów
Krosno Odrzańskie
Odra
Śmigiel
Czacz
Węzyska
Czerwieńsk
Świętno
Jerka
Klenica
Mochy
Gubin
Lesniów Wielkopolski
Bojadła
Kolsko
Krzywiń
Bobrowice
Zabór
Zielona Góra
Konotop
Włoszakowice
Kaniów
Bóbr
Osieczna
Ochla
Niedoradz
Sława
Garzyn
Świdnica
Leszno
Kakolewo
Stare Strącze
Jasienica
Górzyn
Zatonie
Nowa Sól
Wschowa

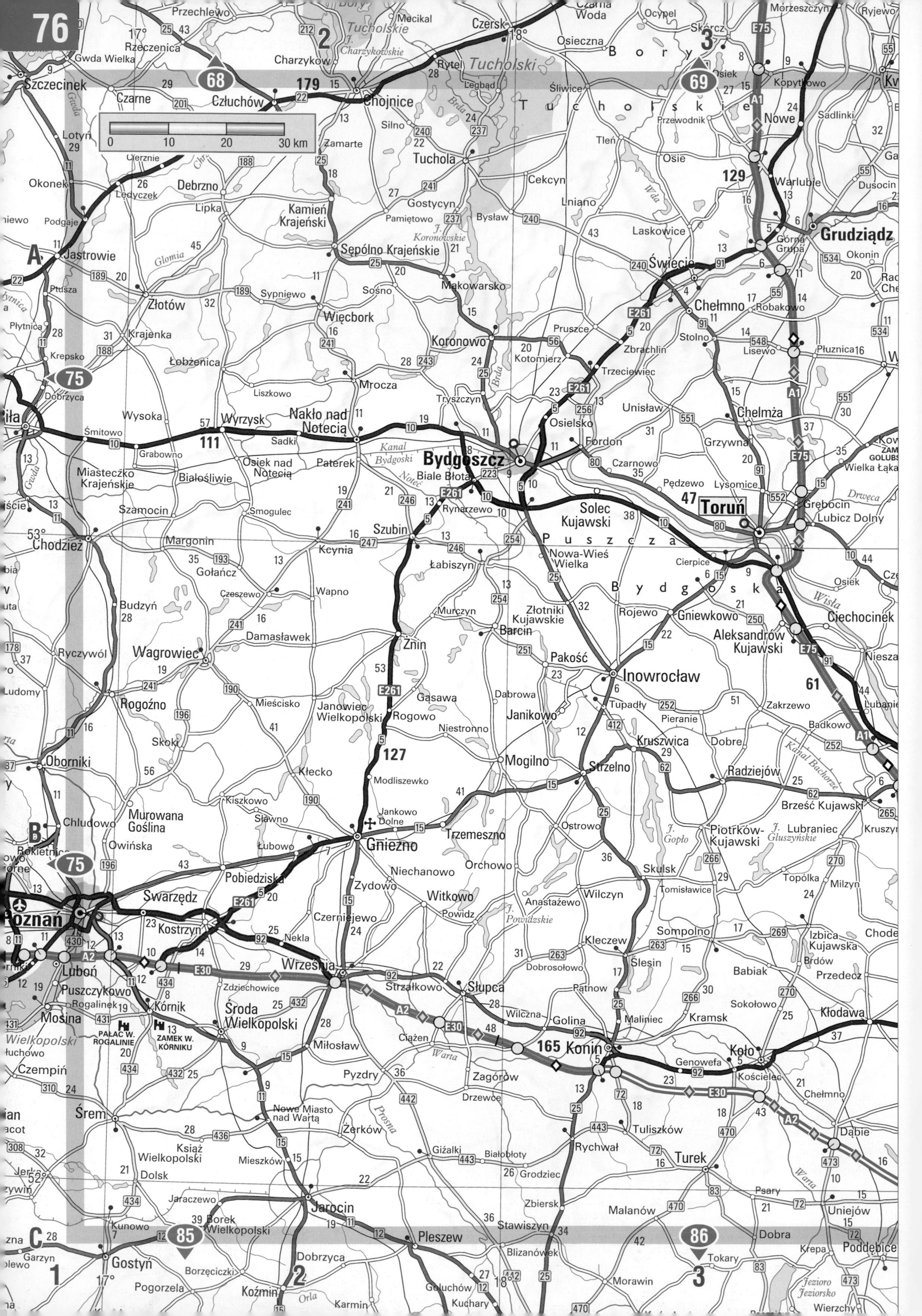

Przechlewo
Rzeczenica
Gwda Wielka
Szczecinek
Czarne
Człuchów
Chojnice
Charzykowy
Czersk
Rytel
Tucholskie
Bory Tucholskie
Osieczna
Śliwice
Skórcz
Nowe
Grudziądz
0 10 20 30 km
Lotyń
Okonek
Debrzno
Lipka
Kamień Krajeński
Tuchola
Cekcyn
Gostycyn
Lniano
Laskowice
Jastrowie
Sępólno Krajeńskie
Świecie
Chełmno
Złotów
Sypniewo
Więcbork
Sośno
Mąkowarsko
Koronowo
Krajenka
Łobżenica
Mrocza
Pruszce
Zbrachlin
Płużnica
Wysoka
Wyrzysk
Nakło nad Notecią
Osielsko
Fordon
Unisław
Chełmża
Piła
Bydgoszcz
Biale Błota
Czarnowo
Toruń
Solec Kujawski
Miasteczko Krajeńskie
Białośliwie
Szamocin
Smogulec
Szubin
Rynarzewo
Lubicz Dolny
Chodzież
Margonin
Kcynia
Łabiszyn
Puszcza Bydgoska
Nowa-Wieś Wielka
Gołańcz
Wapno
Budzyń
Damasławek
Żnin
Barcin
Złotniki Kujawskie
Rojewo
Gniewkowo
Aleksandrów Kujawski
Ciechocinek
Wągrowiec
Ryczywół
Pakość
Inowrocław
Rogoźno
Mieścisko
Janowiec Wielkopolski
Gąsawa
Rogowo
Janikowo
Kruszwica
Skoki
Oborniki
Kłecko
Mogilno
Strzelno
Radziejów
Brześć Kujawski
Murowana Goślina
Kiszkowo
Trzemeszno
Gniezno
Piotrków-Kujawski
Lubraniec
Swarzędz
Pobiedziska
Niechanowo
Witkowo
Orchowo
Skulsk
Poznań
Kostrzyn
Nekla
Września
Czerniejewo
Kleczew
Sompolno
Izbica Kujawska
Luboń
Kórnik
Środa Wielkopolska
Strzałkowo
Słupca
Golina
Ślesin
Kłodawa
Mosina
Czempiń
Miłosław
Konin
Koło
Pyzdry
Zagórów
Śrem
Nowe Miasto nad Wartą
Żerków
Tuliszków
Książ Wielkopolski
Dolsk
Turek
Rychwał
Jaraczewo
Jarocin
Borek Wielkopolski
Pleszew
Stawiszyn
Malanów
Uniejów
Dobra
Poddębice
Gostyń
Dobrzyca
Koźmin
Gołuchów
Pogorzela

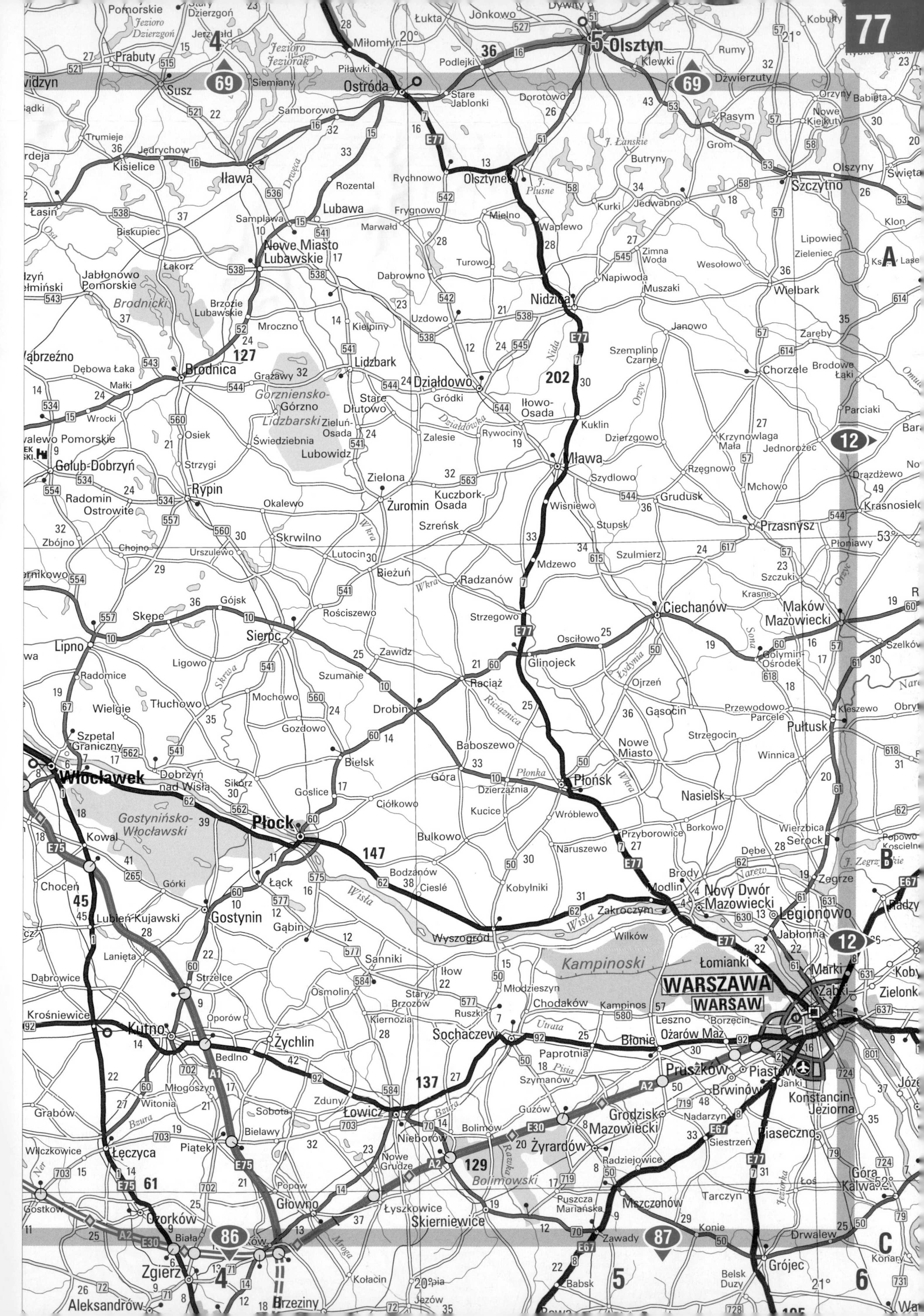
Olsztyn
Ostróda
Iława
Lubawa
Nowe Miasto Lubawskie
Olsztynek
Nidzica
Działdowo
Lidzbark
Brodnica
Golub-Dobrzyń
Rypin
Żuromin
Mława
Szczytno
Wielbark
Chorzele
Przasnysz
Ciechanów
Maków Mazowiecki
Pułtusk
Płońsk
Sierpc
Lipno
Włocławek
Płock
Gostynin
Kutno
Żychlin
Łowicz
Sochaczew
Łęczyca
Ozorków
Zgierz
Głowno
Skierniewice
Żyrardów
Grodzisk Mazowiecki
Pruszków
Piaseczno
Grójec
Nowy Dwór Mazowiecki
Legionowo
Marki
Ząbki
Łomianki
Błonie
Ożarów Maz.
Konstancin-Jeziorna
Zakroczym
Wyszogród
Raciąż
Drobin
Bielsk
Kowal
Lubień Kujawski
Nasielsk
Serock
Prabuty
Susz
Kisielice
Rychnowo
Lubowidz
Bieżuń
Radzanów
Glinojeck
Mszczonów
Brzeziny
Aleksandrów
WARSZAWA
WARSAW
Kampinoski
Gostynińsko-Włocławski
Brodnicki
Gorznieńsko-Lidzbarski
Bolimowski
Wisła
Narew
Wkra
Bzura
Skrwa
Drwęca
E77
E75
E67
E30
A1
A2
69
86
87
12
A
B
C
4
5
6
20°
21°
53°
52°

Woodbridge
Sutton Hoo
Orford Ness
Deben
Bawdsey
Felixstowe
Shotley Gate
Harwich
Esbjerg
Hoek van Holland
The Naze
Walton-on-the-Naze
Frinton-on-Sea
Clacton-on-Sea
0 10 20 miles
0 10 20 30 km
45
A
Westkapelle
Hull
Margate
North Foreland
Broadstairs
Ramsgate
Stour
Richborough Castle
Ash
Oostende
Wingham
Sandwich
Deal
Walmer
St. Margaret's at Cliffe
South Foreland
Hawkinge
Dover
Folkestone
Strait of Dover
Ramsgate
Knokke-Heist
Zeebrugge
Blankenberge
De Haan
Oostende
Brugge
Middelkerke
Oudenburg
Oostkamp
Gistel
Beernem
Nieuwpoort
Koksijde
Ichtegem
De Panne
Plopsaland
Bray-Dunes
Veurne
Koekelare
Torhout
Ruddervoorde
Wingene
Diksmuide
Adinkerke
Lichtervelde
Dunkerque
Dunkirk
Gravelines
Loone-Plage
Woumen
Zarren
Tielt
Calais
Marck
Sangatte
Bergues
Hondschoote
Staden
Roeselare
Ardooie
Izegem
Ingelmunster
Bourbourg
Vleteren
Eurotunnel Terminal
Wissant
Cap Gris-Nez
Audruicq
Langemark-Poelkapelle
Roesbrugge
Wormhout
Poperinge
Moorslede
Kortrijk
Ardres
Guînes
Watten
Steenvoorde
Ieper
Ypres
Cathédrale St. Martin
Bellewaerde
Ambleteuse
Marquise
Licques
Nordausques
Wimereux
Nausicaa
Caps et Marais d'Opale
Cassel
Menen
Comines
Avelgem
Boulogne-sur-Mer
Le Portel
Outreau
St. Omer
Arques
Bailleul
Halluin
Mouscron
Escoeuilles
Hazebrouck
Armentières
Tourcoing
Dottignies
Lumbres
La Coupole
Desvres
Hardelot Plage
Merville
Roubaix
Villeneuve-d'Ascq
Aire-sur-la-Lys
Samer
Thérouanne
St. Venant
Estaires
Fauquembergues
Norrent-Fontes
Lille
Estrée-Blanche
Lillers
Béthune
Tournai
Antoing
Hucqueliers
Étaples
Le Touquet-Paris-Plage
Auchy-au-Bois
Seclin
La Bassée
Carvin
Fruges
Bruay-la-Buissière
Pont-à-Marcq
Orchies
St. Amand-les-Eaux
Merlimont Plage
Bagatelle
Montreuil
Heuchin
Divion
Noeux-les-Mines
Houdain
Anvin
Berck
Maresquel
Canche
Liévin
Lens
Flines-lez-Raches
Scarpe
St. Pol-sur-Ternoise
Hesdin
Vimy
Hénin-Beaumont
Le Parcq
Cambligeu
Fort-Mahon-Plage
Wallers
Somain
Denain
Tincques
Aubigny-en-Artois
Douai
Vron
Authie
Vitry-en-Artois
Aniche
Avesnes-le-Comte
Rue
Arras
Bouchain
Baie de la Somme
Crécy-en-Ponthieu
Auxi-le-Château
Frévent
Beaumetz-lès-Loges
Citadelle d'Arras
Aubigny-au-Bac
Le Crotoy
Noyelles-sur-Mer
Nouvion
Bouquemaison
La Herlière
Marquion
St. Valéry-sur-Somme
Iwuy
Cayeux-sur-Mer
Ayette
Cambrai
St. Riquier
Bernaville
Doullens
Vaulx Vraucourt
Ault
Abbeville
Puisieux
Caudry
Marieux
Bapaume
Beauval
Acheux-en-Amiénois
Bertincourt
Fressenville
Walincourt
B
1
2
3
51°
52°
2°
3°
90

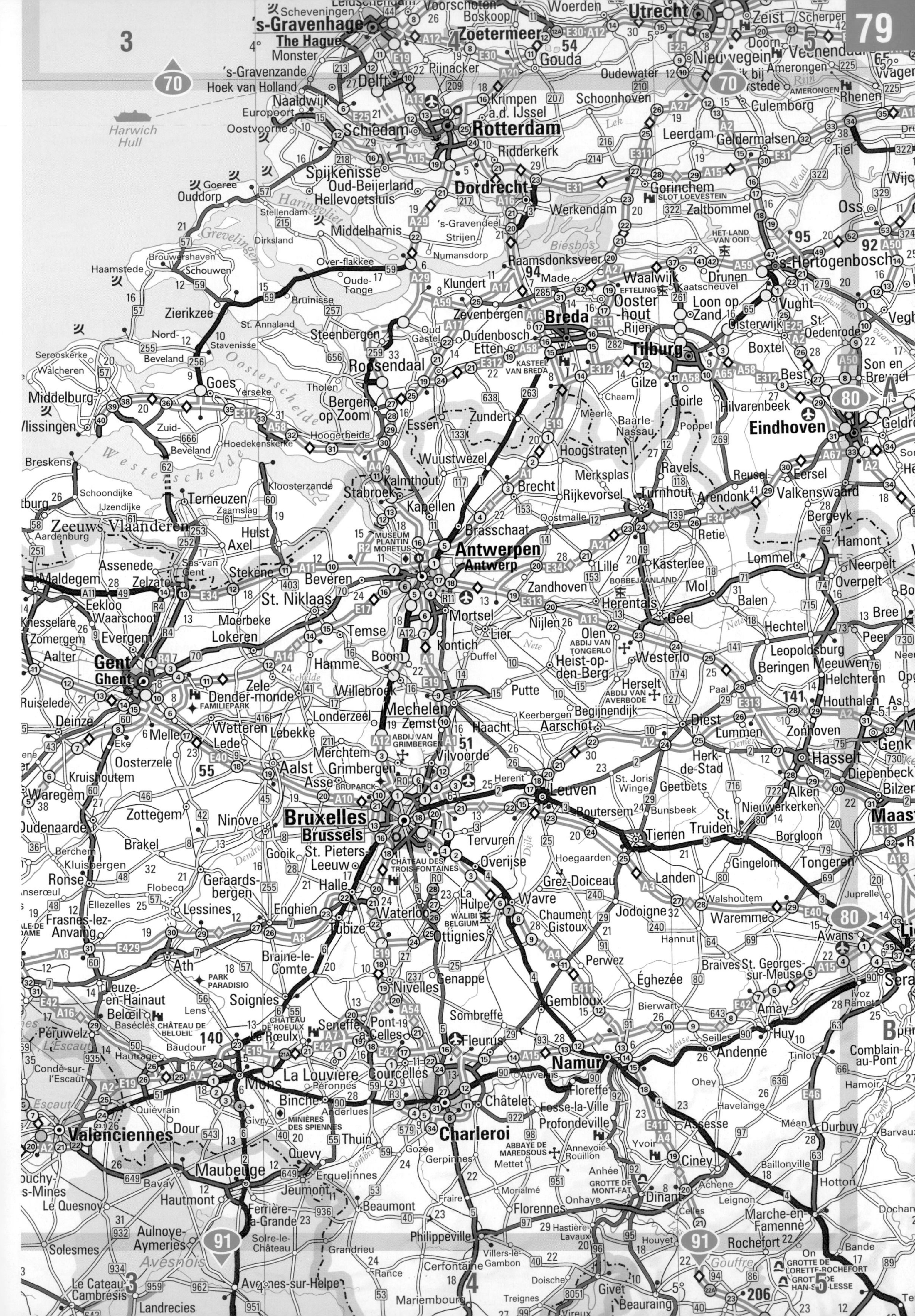

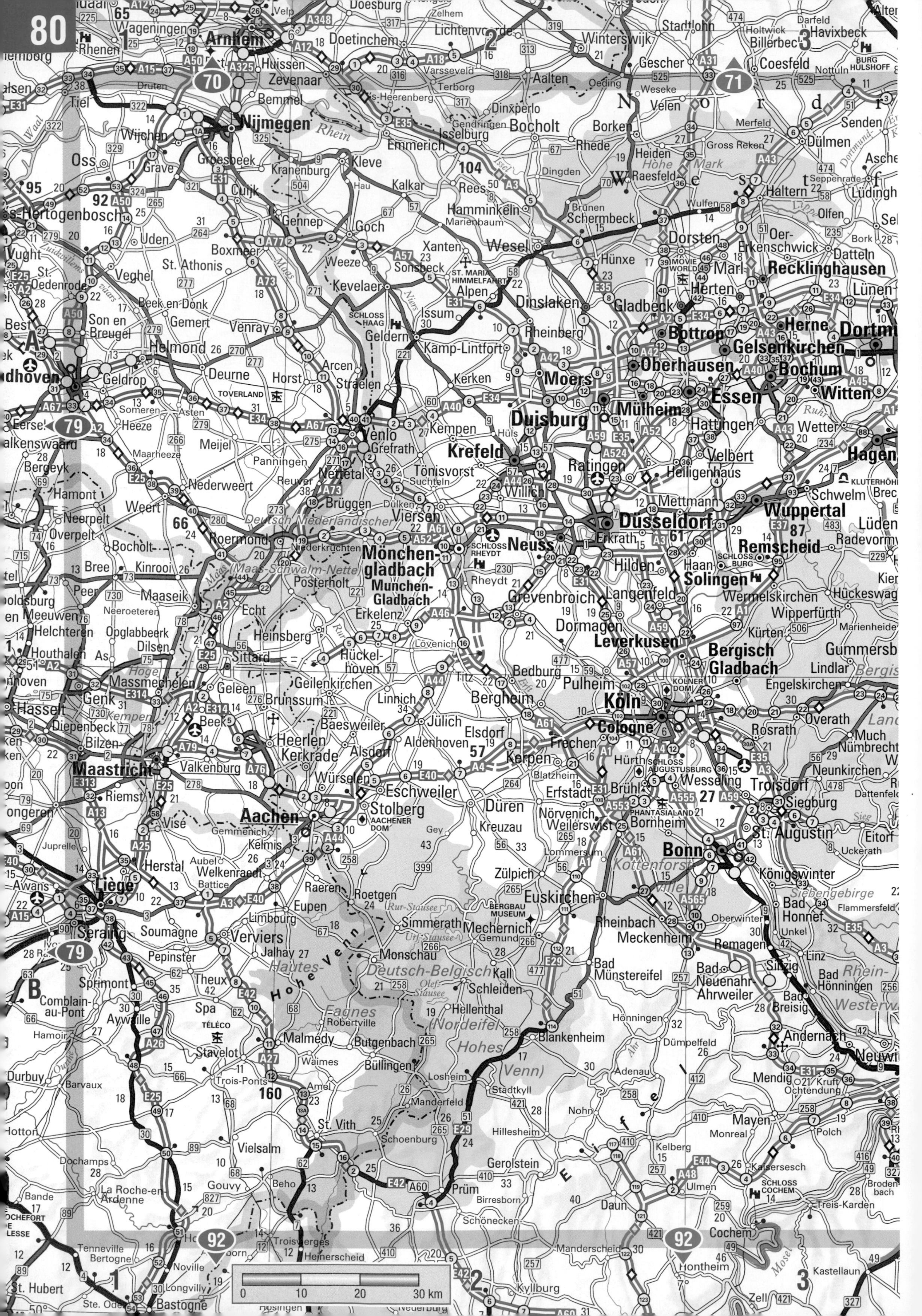

Arnhem
Wageningen
Rhenen
Doetinchem
Doesburg
Lichtenvoorde
Winterswijk
Stadtlohn
Billerbeck
Havixbeck
Coesfeld
Nottuln
Tiel
Zevenaar
Aalten
Gescher
Nijmegen
Bocholt
Borken
Velen
Dülmen
Senden
Nordrhein-Westfalen
Oss
Grave
Kleve
Emmerich
Isselburg
Rhede
Heiden
Haltern
Lüdinghausen
's-Hertogenbosch
Uden
Gennep
Goch
Kalkar
Rees
Hamminkeln
Schermbeck
Dorsten
Marl
Recklinghausen
Datteln
Lünen
Vught
Veghel
Boxmeer
Weeze
Kevelaer
Xanten
Sonsbeck
Wesel
Hünxe
Herten
Gladbeck
Bottrop
Herne
Dortmund
Eindhoven
Helmond
Geldrop
Venray
Geldern
Kamp-Lintfort
Rheinberg
Dinslaken
Moers
Oberhausen
Gelsenkirchen
Bochum
Witten
Deurne
Horst
Straelen
Kerken
Duisburg
Mülheim
Essen
Hattingen
Wetter
Hagen
Venlo
Kempen
Krefeld
Ratingen
Velbert
Heiligenhaus
Weert
Nederweert
Nettetal
Tönisvorst
Willich
Mettmann
Wuppertal
Schwelm
Roermond
Brüggen
Viersen
Düsseldorf
Erkrath
Remscheid
Mönchengladbach
München-Gladbach
Neuss
Hilden
Solingen
Haan
Maaseik
Heinsberg
Erkelenz
Grevenbroich
Langenfeld
Wermelskirchen
Wipperfürth
Hückeswagen
Dormagen
Leverkusen
Bergisch Gladbach
Gummersbach
Sittard
Hückelhoven
Bedburg
Pulheim
Genk
Geleen
Brunssum
Geilenkirchen
Bergheim
Köln
Cologne
Engelskirchen
Hasselt
Heerlen
Kerkrade
Jülich
Elsdorf
Frechen
Overath
Maastricht
Valkenburg
Alsdorf
Aldenhoven
Kerpen
Hürth
Troisdorf
Würselen
Eschweiler
Brühl
Wesseling
Siegburg
Aachen
Stolberg
Düren
Erftstadt
Bornheim
St. Augustin
Tongeren
Visé
Kelmis
Kreuzau
Bonn
Eitorf
Herstal
Zülpich
Königswinter
Liège
Eupen
Roetgen
Euskirchen
Bad Honnef
Seraing
Verviers
Simmerath
Mechernich
Rheinbach
Meckenheim
Remagen
Spa
Monschau
Schleiden
Bad Münstereifel
Bad Neuenahr-Ahrweiler
Sinzig
Hohe Venn
Hautes-Fagnes
Malmedy
Stavelot
Bütgenbach
Blankenheim
Andernach
Neuwied
Eifel
Mayen
Mendig
St. Vith
Hillesheim
Gerolstein
Daun
Vielsalm
Prüm
Cochem
La Roche-en-Ardenne
Bastogne
St. Hubert
Kyllburg
Zell
0 10 20 30 km

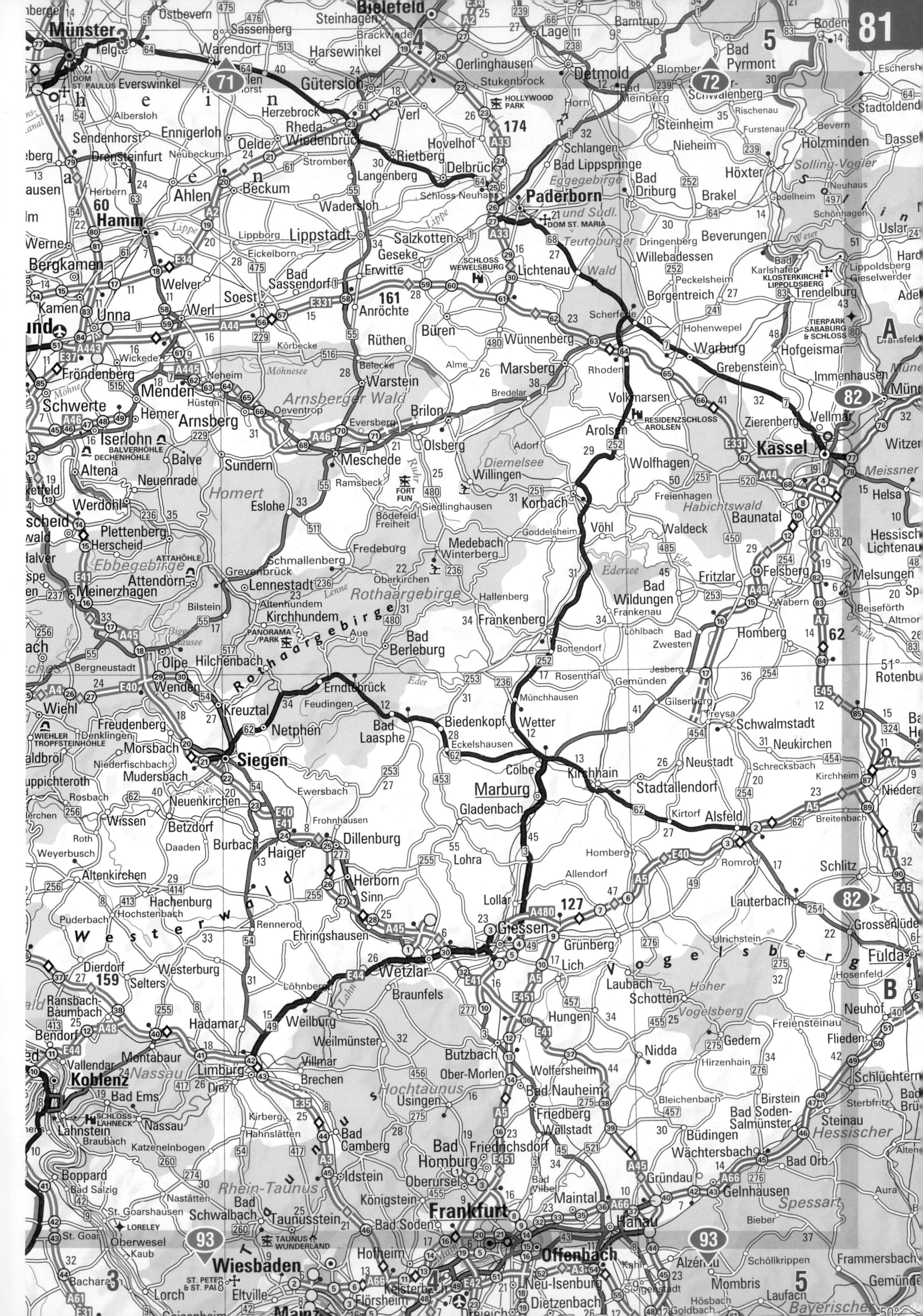
Münster
Bielefeld
Gütersloh
Detmold
Paderborn
Hamm
Lippstadt
Soest
Unna
Arnsberg
Brilon
Meschede
Marsberg
Warburg
Kassel
Korbach
Bad Wildungen
Frankenberg
Siegen
Marburg
Gießen
Wetzlar
Limburg
Koblenz
Wiesbaden
Frankfurt
Offenbach
Hanau
Fulda
Alsfeld
Höxter
Holzminden
Bad Pyrmont
Rothaargebirge
Westerwald
Vogelsberg
Taunus
Sauerland

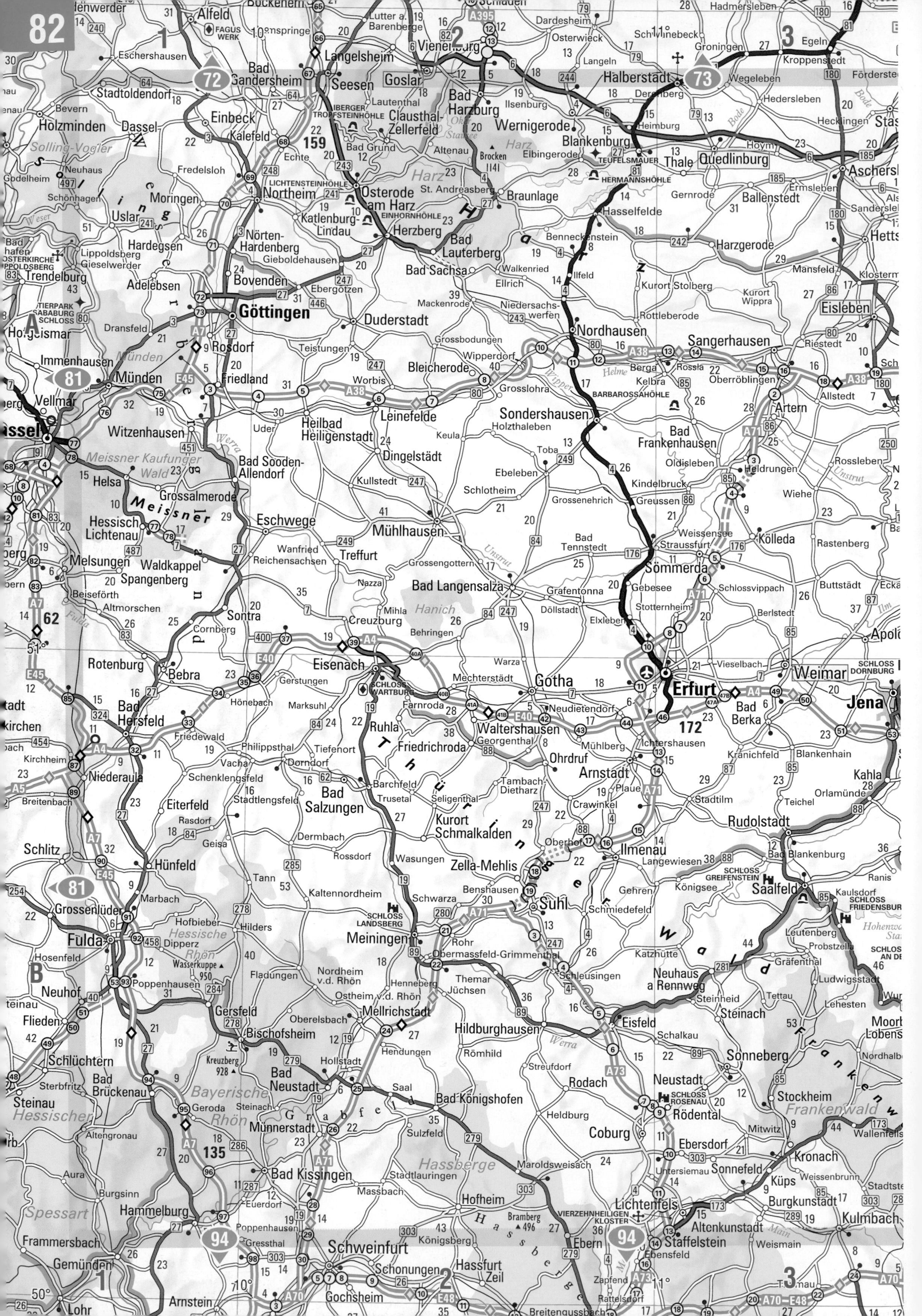

Alfeld
Eschershausen
Bad Gandersheim
Stadtoldendorf
Holzminden
Dassel
Einbeck
Kalefeld
Langelsheim
Seesen
Goslar
Vienenburg
Bad Harzburg
Clausthal-Zellerfeld
Wernigerode
Osterwieck
Halberstadt
Blankenburg
Thale
Quedlinburg
Aschersleben
Egeln
Kroppenstedt
Wegeleben
Hedersleben
Ballenstedt
Harzgerode
Northeim
Osterode am Harz
Katlenburg-Lindau
Herzberg
Bad Lauterberg
Braunlage
St. Andreasberg
Moringen
Uslar
Hardegsen
Nörten-Hardenberg
Gieboldehausen
Bad Sachsa
Trendelburg
Bovenden
Adelebsen
Göttingen
Duderstadt
Hasselfelde
Benneckenstein
Ilfeld
Ellrich
Walkenried
Nordhausen
Kurort Stolberg
Mansfeld
Eisleben
Sangerhausen
Rosdorf
Friedland
Hann. Münden
Immenhausen
Vellmar
Kassel
Witzenhausen
Bleicherode
Worbis
Leinefelde
Heilbad Heiligenstadt
Dingelstädt
Bad Sooden-Allendorf
Sondershausen
Bad Frankenhausen
Artern
Allstedt
Helsa
Grossalmerode
Hessisch Lichtenau
Eschwege
Mühlhausen
Schlotheim
Ebeleben
Greussen
Kindelbruck
Heldrungen
Kölleda
Melsungen
Waldkappel
Spangenberg
Treffurt
Bad Tennstedt
Sömmerda
Bad Langensalza
Sontra
Creuzburg
Rotenburg
Bebra
Eisenach
Gotha
Erfurt
Weimar
Jena
Apolda
Bad Hersfeld
Ruhla
Friedrichroda
Waltershausen
Ohrdruf
Arnstadt
Bad Berka
Kranichfeld
Blankenhain
Kahla
Niederaula
Vacha
Bad Salzungen
Eiterfeld
Schmalkalden
Zella-Mehlis
Ilmenau
Rudolstadt
Bad Blankenburg
Saalfeld
Schlitz
Hünfeld
Suhl
Meiningen
Grossenlüder
Fulda
Neuhof
Schleusingen
Neuhaus a Rennweg
Flieden
Gersfeld
Mellrichstadt
Hildburghausen
Eisfeld
Sonneberg
Schlüchtern
Bischofsheim
Bad Neustadt
Bad Königshofen
Rodach
Neustadt
Bad Brückenau
Steinau
Münnerstadt
Coburg
Rödental
Stockheim
Kronach
Bad Kissingen
Hammelburg
Lichtenfels
Burgkunstadt
Kulmbach
Schweinfurt
Hassfurt
Zeil
Staffelstein
Gemünden
Arnstein
Lohr
Gochsheim
Harz
Thüringer Wald
Frankenwald
Rhön
Spessart
Hassberge

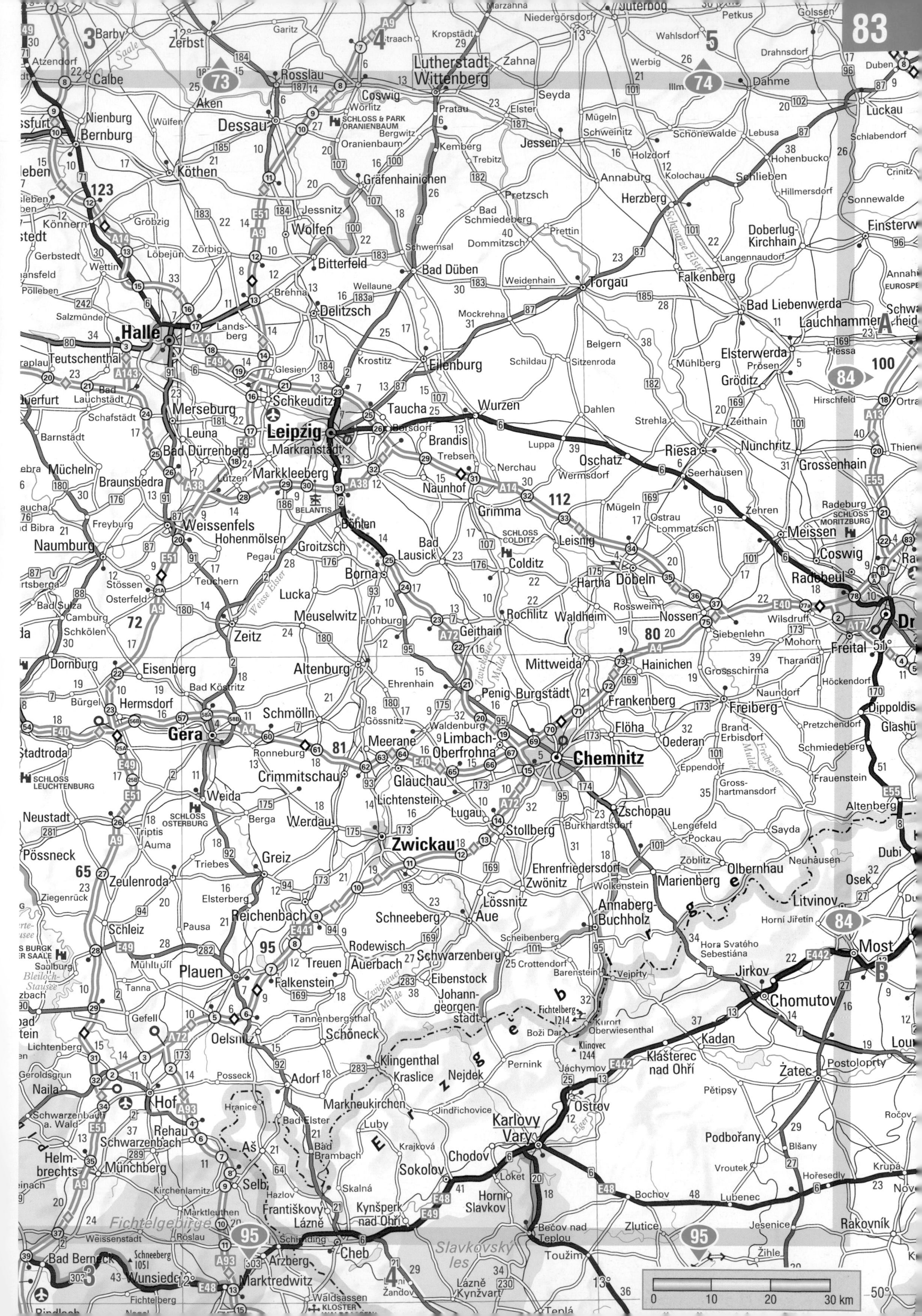

83
Barby
Zerbst
Calbe
Rosslau
Lutherstadt Wittenberg
Zahna
Coswig
Wörlitz
Schloss & Park Oranienbaum
Oranienbaum
Aken
Dessau
Nienburg
Bernburg
Köthen
Gräfenhainichen
Kemberg
Jessen
Seyda
Elster
Mügeln
Schweinitz
Schönewalde
Lebusa
Holzdorf
Kolochau
Schlieben
Hohenbucko
Herzberg
Annaburg
Pretzsch
Bad Schmiedeberg
Prettin
Dommitzsch
Doberlug-Kirchhain
Falkenberg
Torgau
Bad Liebenwerda
Lauchhammer
Elsterwerda
Prösen
Gröditz
Mühlberg
Belgern
Schildau
Sitzenroda
Jüterbog
Niedergörsdorf
Petkus
Golssen
Wahlsdorf
Drahnsdorf
Dahme
Luckau
Schlabendorf
Crinitz
Sonnewalde
Hillmersdorf
Finsterwalde
Langennaudorf
Plessa
Hirschfeld
Ortrand
Könnern
Gröbzig
Löbejün
Zörbig
Wettin
Gerbstedt
Salzmünde
Halle
Teutschenthal
Landsberg
Brehna
Bitterfeld
Wolfen
Jessnitz
Schwemsal
Bad Düben
Wellaune
Delitzsch
Mockrehna
Eilenburg
Krostitz
Glesien
Schkeuditz
Taucha
Wurzen
Leipzig
Markranstädt
Borsdorf
Brandis
Trebsen
Naunhof
Merseburg
Leuna
Bad Lauchstädt
Schafstädt
Querfurt
Barnstädt
Mücheln
Braunsbedra
Bad Dürrenberg
Lützen
Markkleeberg
Belantis
Böhlen
Grimma
Nerchau
Dahlen
Luppa
Oschatz
Wermsdorf
Strehla
Riesa
Zeithain
Nünchritz
Seerhausen
Grossenhain
Mügeln
Ostrau
Lommatzsch
Zehren
Meissen
Radeburg
Schloss Moritzburg
Coswig
Radebeul
Dresden
Weissenfels
Hohenmölsen
Freyburg
Naumburg
Bad Bibra
Groitzsch
Pegau
Bad Lausick
Schloss Colditz
Colditz
Leisnig
Döbeln
Hartha
Waldheim
Rochlitz
Geithain
Borna
Lucka
Meuselwitz
Frohburg
Zeitz
Teuchern
Stössen
Osterfeld
Bad Sulza
Camburg
Schkölen
Dornburg
Eisenberg
Bad Köstritz
Hermsdorf
Bürgel
Stadtroda
Schloss Leuchtenburg
Gera
Ronneburg
Schmölln
Gössnitz
Altenburg
Ehrenhain
Meerane
Crimmitschau
Glauchau
Waldenburg
Limbach-Oberfrohna
Penig
Burgstädt
Mittweida
Hainichen
Frankenberg
Flöha
Chemnitz
Oederan
Freiberg
Brand-Erbisdorf
Rosswein
Nossen
Siebenlehn
Wilsdruff
Mohorn
Tharandt
Freital
Grossschirma
Höckendorf
Naundorf
Dippoldiswalde
Pretzschendorf
Glashütte
Schmiedeberg
Frauenstein
Weida
Schloss Osterburg
Triptis
Auma
Berga
Werdau
Zwickau
Lichtenstein
Lugau
Stollberg
Burkhardtsdorf
Zschopau
Eppendorf
Grosshartmannsdorf
Lengefeld
Pockau
Sayda
Zöblitz
Olbernhau
Neuhausen
Marienberg
Wolkenstein
Ehrenfriedersdorf
Zwönitz
Annaberg-Buchholz
Neustadt
Pössneck
Zeulenroda
Triebes
Greiz
Ziegenrück
Schleiz
Elsterberg
Reichenbach
Pausa
Plauen
Treuen
Rodewisch
Auerbach
Falkenstein
Schneeberg
Lössnitz
Aue
Schwarzenberg
Scheibenberg
Crottendorf
Bärenstein
Vejprty
Eibenstock
Johanngeorgenstadt
Fichtelberg 1214
Kurort Oberwiesenthal
Boži Dar
Klínovec 1244
Jáchymov
Tannenbergsthal
Schöneck
Oelsnitz
Mühltroff
Tanna
Gefell
Saalburg
Bleiloch-Stausee
Lichtenberg
Geroldsgrün
Naila
Hof
Schwarzenbach a. Wald
Rehau
Schwarzenbach
Helmbrechts
Münchberg
Kirchenlamitz
Marktleuthen
Selb
Asch
Hranice
Adorf
Posseck
Markneukirchen
Klingenthal
Kraslice
Nejdek
Pernink
Jindřichovice
Luby
Bad Elster
Bad Brambach
Krajková
Skalná
Hazlov
Františkovy Lázně
Kynšperk nad Ohří
Sokolov
Chodov
Loket
Karlovy Vary
Ostrov
Horní Slavkov
Bečov nad Teplou
Toužim
Slavkovský les
Lázně Kynžvart
Cheb
Schirnding
Arzberg
Marktredwitz
Waldsassen
Kloster Waldsassen
Wunsiedel
Bad Berneck
Schneeberg 1051
Weissenstadt
Röslau
Fichtelgebirge
Fichtelberg
Bindlach
Zlutice
Jesenice
Rakovník
Žihle
Krupá
Lubenec
Bochov
Hořesedly
Blšany
Vroutek
Podbořany
Žatec
Postoloprty
Louny
Pětipsy
Kadaň
Klášterec nad Ohří
Chomutov
Jirkov
Most
Litvínov
Horní Jiřetín
Hora Svatého Šebestiána
Osek
Dubí
Altenberg
Erzgebirge
Saale
Weisse Elster
Zwickauer Mulde
Freiberger Mulde
Schwarze Elster
Eger
0 10 20 30 km

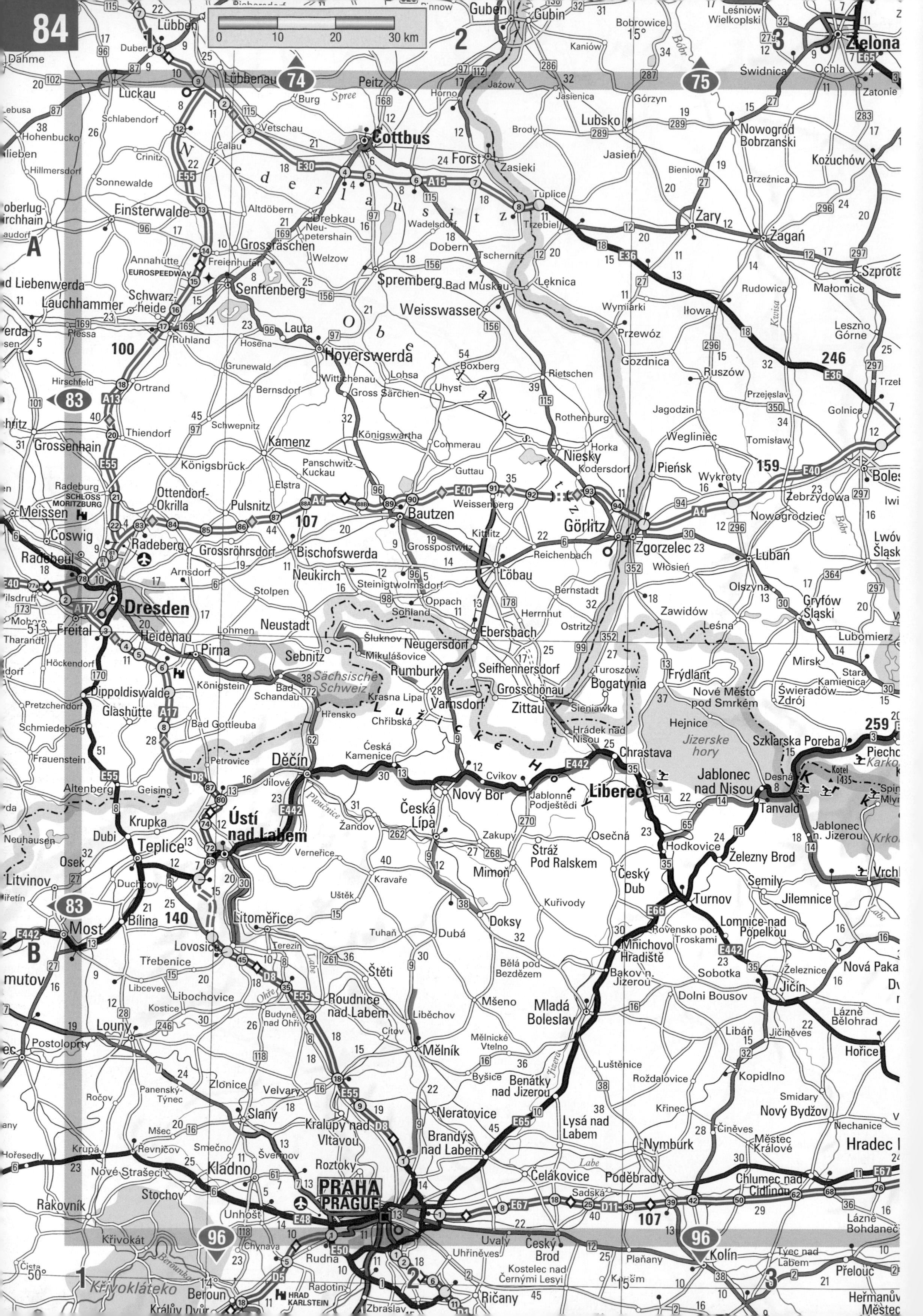
0 10 20 30 km
74
75
83
96
Lübben
Lübbenau
Luckau
Dahme
Guben
Gubin
Bobrowice
Leśniów Wielkopolski
Zielona
Świdnica
Ochla
Zatonie
Peitz
Burg
Spree
Cottbus
Forst
Zasieki
Brody
Lubsko
Jasień
Gorzyn
Nowogród Bobrzański
Kożuchów
Schlabendorf
Vetschau
Calau
Hohenbucko
Crinitz
Hillmersdorf
Sonnewalde
Niederlausitz
Finsterwalde
Altdöbern
Drebkau
Neupetershain
Grossräschen
Welzow
Dobern
Tschernitz
Tuplice
Trzebiel
Żary
Żagań
Bieniow
Brzeźnica
Szprotawa
Małomice
Annahütte
EUROSPEEDWAY
Freienhufen
Senftenberg
Spremberg
Bad Muskau
Łęknica
Wymiarki
Iłowa
Rudowica
Leszno Górne
Bad Liebenwerda
Lauchhammer
Schwarzheide
Plessa
Ruhland
Hosena
Lauta
Hoyerswerda
Weisswasser
Oberlausitz
Przewóz
Gozdnica
Ruszów
Boxberg
Rietschen
Wittichenau
Lohsa
Gross Särchen
Uhyst
Grunewald
Bernsdorf
Ortrand
Hirschfeld
Thiendorf
Schwepnitz
Königswartha
Commerau
Rothenburg
Jagodzin
Przejęslav
Golnice
Tomisław
Węgliniec
Horka
Niesky
Kodersdorf
Pieńsk
Wykroty
Grossenhain
Kamenz
Königsbrück
Panschwitz-Kuckau
Guttau
Elstra
Radeburg
SCHLOSS MORITZBURG
Ottendorf-Okrilla
Pulsnitz
Bautzen
Weissenberg
Görlitz
Zgorzelec
Żebrzydowa
Nowogrodziec
Meissen
Coswig
Radebeul
Radeberg
Grossröhrsdorf
Bischofswerda
Grosspostwitz
Kittlitz
Reichenbach
Lubań
Lwówek Śląski
Arnsdorf
Neukirch
Steinigtwolmsdorf
Löbau
Włosień
Olszyna
Gryfów Śląski
Dresden
Stolpen
Oppach
Sohland
Bernstadt
Herrnhut
Zawidów
Leśna
Wilsdruff
Mohorn
Freital
Tharandt
Heidenau
Lohmen
Neustadt
Ostritz
Lubomierz
Pirna
Sebnitz
Šluknov
Neugersdorf
Mikulášovice
Ebersbach
Rumburk
Seifhennersdorf
Turoszów
Bogatynia
Frýdlant
Nové Město pod Smrkem
Świeradów-Zdrój
Mirsk
Stara Kamienica
Höckendorf
Königstein
Bad Schandau
Sächsische Schweiz
Dippoldiswalde
Krasna Lipa
Varnsdorf
Grossschönau
Zittau
Sieniawka
Pretzschendorf
Glashütte
Hřensko
Chřibská
Hrádek nad Nisou
Hejnice
Jizerske hory
Szklarska Poreba
Piechowice
Schmiedeberg
Bad Gottleuba
Lužické Hory
Chrastava
Frauenstein
Petrovice
Děčín
Česká Kamenice
Cvikov
Liberec
Jablonec nad Nisou
Desná
Kotel 1435
Tanvald
Altenberg
Geising
Jílové
Nový Bor
Jablonné Podještědí
Ploučnice
Krupka
Ústí nad Labem
Česká Lípa
Žandov
Osečná
Hodkovice
Jablonec n. Jizerou
Neuhausen
Dubí
Teplice
Zakupy
Stráž Pod Ralskem
Železný Brod
Osek
Verneřice
Mimoň
Český Dub
Semily
Litvínov
Duchcov
Kravaře
Turnov
Jilemnice
Úštěk
Kuřivody
Bílina
Litoměřice
Doksy
Lomnice nad Popelkou
Most
Lovosice
Terezín
Tuhaň
Dubá
Rovensko pod Troskami
Mnichovo Hradiště
Třebenice
Štětí
Bělá pod Bezdězem
Sobotka
Železnice
Nová Paka
Chomutov
Libceves
Libochovice
Ohře
Roudnice nad Labem
Bakov n. Jizerou
Jičín
Kostice
Budyně nad Ohří
Mšeno
Mladá Boleslav
Dolni Bousov
Lázně Bělohrad
Louny
Postoloprty
Cítov
Liběchov
Mělník
Mělnické Vtelno
Libáň
Jičíněves
Hořice
Zlonice
Panenský-Týnec
Velvary
Byšice
Benátky nad Jizerou
Luštěnice
Kopidlno
Rožďalovice
Ročov
Slaný
Kralupy nad Vltavou
Neratovice
Lysá nad Labem
Křinec
Smidary
Nový Bydžov
Nechanice
Mšec
Hořesedly
Krupá
Řevničov
Smečno
Švermov
Brandýs nad Labem
Nymburk
Čiňeves
Městec Králové
Hradec Králové
Nové Strašecí
Kladno
Roztoky
Čelákovice
Poděbrady
Chlumec nad Cidlinou
Rakovník
Stochov
PRAHA PRAGUE
Sadská
Unhošť
Křivoklát
Chýnava
Rudna
Uhříněves
Uvaly
Český Brod
Plaňany
Kolín
Týec nad Labem
Přelouč
Lázně Bohdaneč
Čista
Křivoklátsko
Beroun
Radotín
HRAD KARLSTEIN
Zbraslav
Kostelec nad Černými Lesy
Kouřim
Říčany
Heřmanův Městec
Králův Dvůr
Berounka
100
107
140
159
246
259

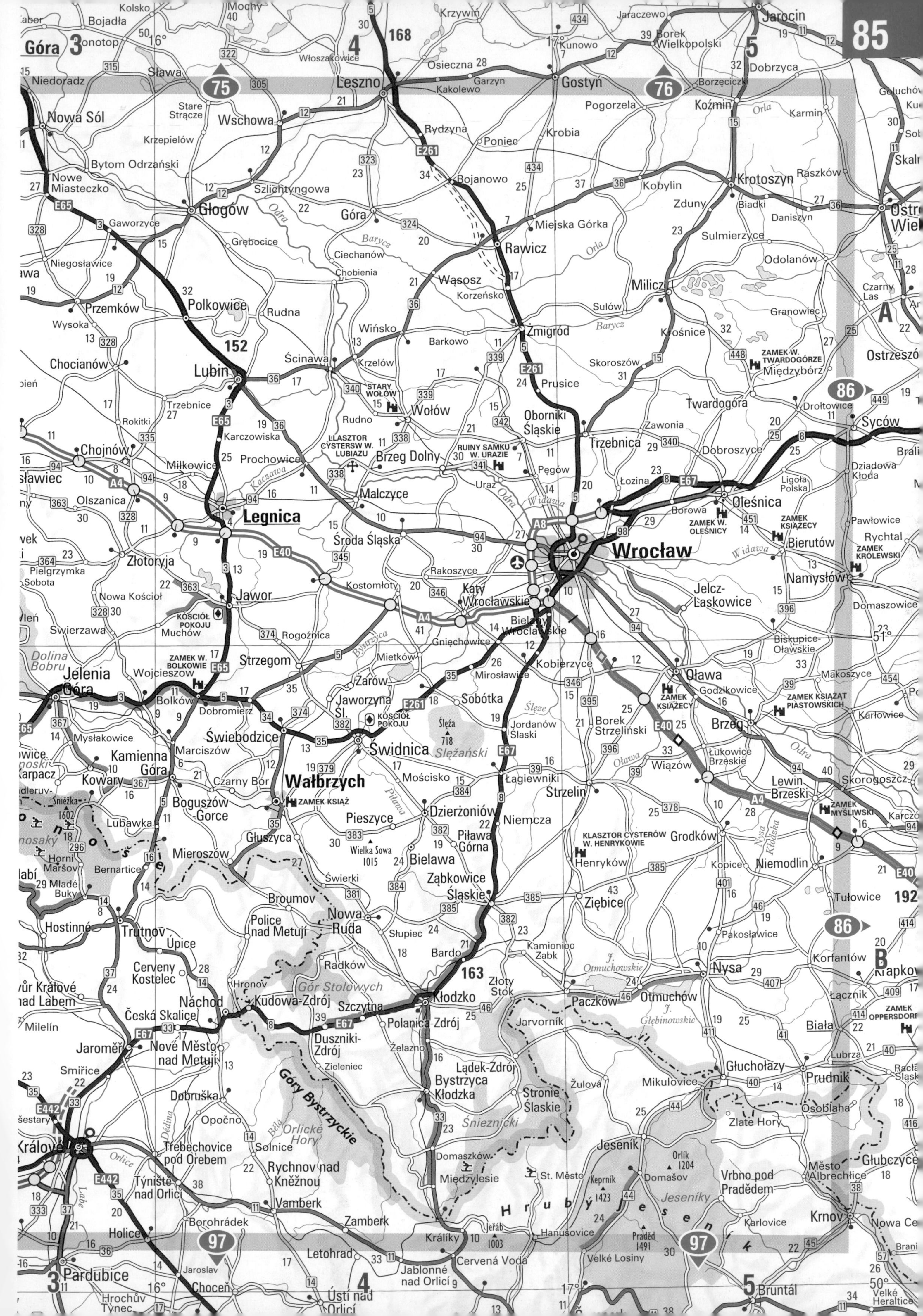
Góra
Bojadła
Kolsko
Mochy
Sława
Niedoradz
Nowa Sól
Stare Strącze
Wschowa
Krzepielów
Bytom Odrzański
Nowe Miasteczko
Szlichtyngowa
Głogów
Gaworzyce
Grębocice
Niegosławice
Przemków
Wysoka
Polkowice
Rudna
Chocianów
Lubin
Trzebnice
Rokitki
Chojnów
Karczowiska
Prochowice
Miłkowice
Olszanica
Legnica
Złotoryja
Pielgrzymka
Sobota
Nowa Kościół
Jawor
Kościół Pokoju
Muchów
Swierzawa
Rogoźnica
Strzegom
Zamek w. Bolkowie
Wojcieszów
Bolków
Dobromierz
Jelenia Góra
Dolina Bobru
Mysłakowice
Kamienna Góra
Marciszów
Świebodzice
Karpacz
Kowary
Czarny Bór
Wałbrzych
Zamek Książ
Boguszów-Gorce
Lubawka
Sněžka 1602
Mieroszów
Bernartice
Horní Maršov
Mladé Buky
Głuszyca
Hostinné
Trutnov
Úpice
Broumov
Police nad Metují
Nowa Ruda
Červený Kostelec
Hronov
Náchod
Kudowa-Zdrój
Česká Skalice
Jaroměř
Nové Město nad Metují
Smiřice
Dobruška
Opočno
Hradec Králové
Třebechovice pod Orebem
Týniště nad Orlicí
Rychnov nad Kněžnou
Solnice
Vamberk
Borohrádek
Holice
Žamberk
Pardubice
Letohrad
Choceň
Ústí nad Orlicí
Králíky
Jablonné nad Orlicí
Červená Voda
Góry Bystrzyckie
Orlické Hory
Zieleniec
Duszniki-Zdrój
Szczytna
Polanica Zdrój
Kłodzko
Radków
Gór Stołowych
Słupiec
Bardo
Złoty Stok
Żelazno
Lądek-Zdrój
Bystrzyca Kłodzka
Stronie Śląskie
Śnieżnicki
Domaszków
Międzylesie
Jeřáb 1003
St. Město
Hanušovice
Králíky
Leszno
Włoszakowice
Krzywiń
Osieczna
Kąkolewo
Garzyn
Rydzyna
Poniec
Krobia
Gostyń
Kunowo
Jaraczewo
Borek Wielkopolski
Jarocin
Dobrzyca
Borzęciczki
Pogorzela
Koźmin
Karmin
Bojanowo
Kobylin
Krotoszyn
Raszków
Zduny
Biadki
Daniszyn
Miejska Górka
Rawicz
Sulmierzyce
Odolanów
Milicz
Wąsosz
Korzeńsko
Sułów
Granowiec
Ciechanów
Chobienia
Góra
Wińsko
Barkowo
Żmigród
Krośnice
Zamek w. Twardogórze
Międzybórz
Ścinawa
Krzelów
Stary Wołów
Wołów
Rudno
Prusice
Skoroszów
Twardogóra
Oborniki Śląskie
Zawonia
Klasztor Cystersów w. Lubiążu
Brzeg Dolny
Ruiny Samku w. Urazie
Uraz
Pęgów
Trzebnica
Dobroszyce
Łozina
Oleśnica
Borowa
Zamek w. Oleśnicy
Zamek Książęcy
Bierutów
Malczyce
Środa Śląska
Wrocław
Rakoszyce
Kostomłoty
Kąty Wrocławskie
Bielany Wrocławskie
Jelcz-Laskowice
Gniechowice
Mietków
Żarów
Mirosławice
Kobierzyce
Oława
Zamek Książęcy
Jaworzyna Śl.
Kościół Pokoju
Sobótka
Ślęża 718
Ślężański
Jordanów Śląski
Borek Strzeliński
Świdnica
Mościsko
Łagiewniki
Strzelin
Wiązów
Dzierżoniów
Pieszyce
Niemcza
Pilawa Górna
Wielka Sowa 1015
Bielawa
Ząbkowice Śląskie
Świerki
Klasztor Cysterów w. Henrykowie
Henryków
Ziębice
Kamieniec Ząbk.
J. Otmuchowskie
Paczków
Otmuchów
J. Głębinowskie
Javorník
Žulová
Mikulovice
Głuchołazy
Zlaté Hory
Jeseník
Orlík 1204
Keprník 1423
Domašov
Hrubý Jeseník
Jeseníky
Praděd 1491
Velké Losiny
Vrbno pod Pradědem
Karlovice
Krnov
Město Albrechtice
Bruntál
Grodków
Kopice
Niemodlin
Nysa
Pakosławice
Korfantów
Łącznik
Biała
Prudnik
Osobłaha
Głubczyce
Zamek Oppersdorf
Brzeg
Łukowice Brzeskie
Lewin Brzeski
Zamek Myśliwski
Skorogoszcz
Godzikowice
Zamek Książąt Piastowskich
Karłowice
Makoszyce
Biskupice Oławskie
Namysłów
Zamek Królewski
Rychtal
Pawłowice
Domaszowice
Ligota Polska
Dziadowa Kłoda
Syców
Drołtowice
Ostrzeszów
Czarny Las
Ostrów Wielkopolski
Gołuchów
Tułowice
Krapkowice
Nowa Cerekwia
Velké Heraltice
Wrocław
Odra
Barycz
Orla
Widawa
Kaczawa
Bystrzyca
Ślęza
Oława
Piława
Nysa Kłodzka
Orlice
Labe
Dědina
Bělá
75
76
86
97
A4
A8
E40
E65
E67
E261
E442
3
4
5
A
B
16°
17°
51°
50°

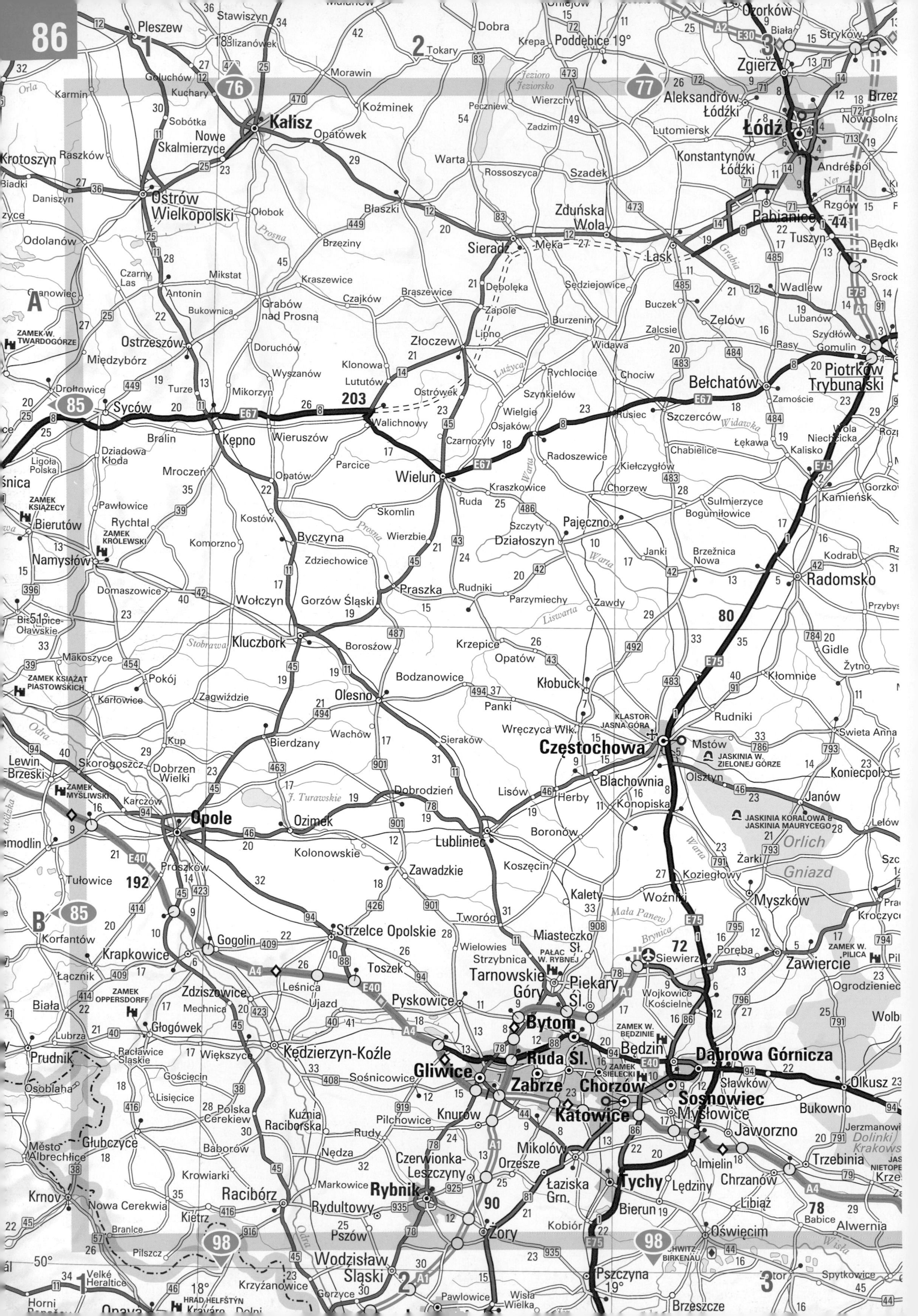

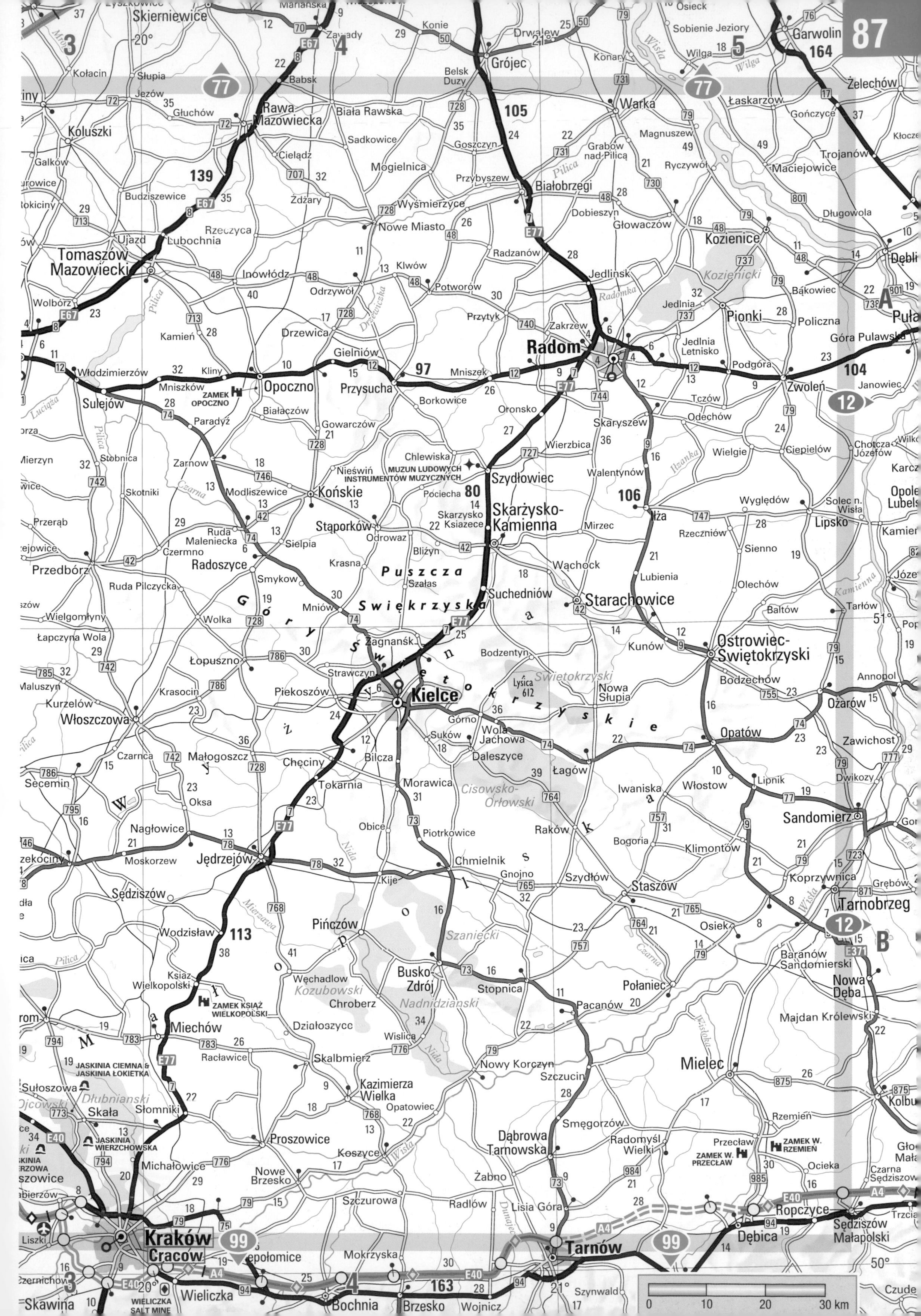
Skierniewice
Grójec
Warka
Garwolin
Tomaszów Mazowiecki
Rawa Mazowiecka
Koluszki
Białobrzegi
Kozienice
Radom
Opoczno
Przysucha
Zwoleń
Końskie
Szydłowiec
Skarżysko-Kamienna
Starachowice
Ostrowiec-Świętokrzyski
Kielce
Włoszczowa
Jędrzejów
Sandomierz
Tarnobrzeg
Pińczów
Busko-Zdrój
Miechów
Mielec
Dąbrowa Tarnowska
Tarnów
Kraków
Cracow
Bochnia
Brzesko
Wieliczka
Dębica
Puszcza Świękrzyska
Góry Świętokrzyskie
Małopolska
ZAMEK OPOCZNO
MUZUN LUDOWYCH INSTRUMENTÓW MUZYCZNYCH
ZAMEK KSIĄŻ WIELKOPOLSKI
JASKINIA CIEMNA & JASKINIA ŁOKIETKA
JASKINIA WIERZCHOWSKA
ZAMEK W. PRZECŁAW
ZAMEK W. RZEMIEŃ
WIELICZKA SALT MINE
0 10 20 30 km

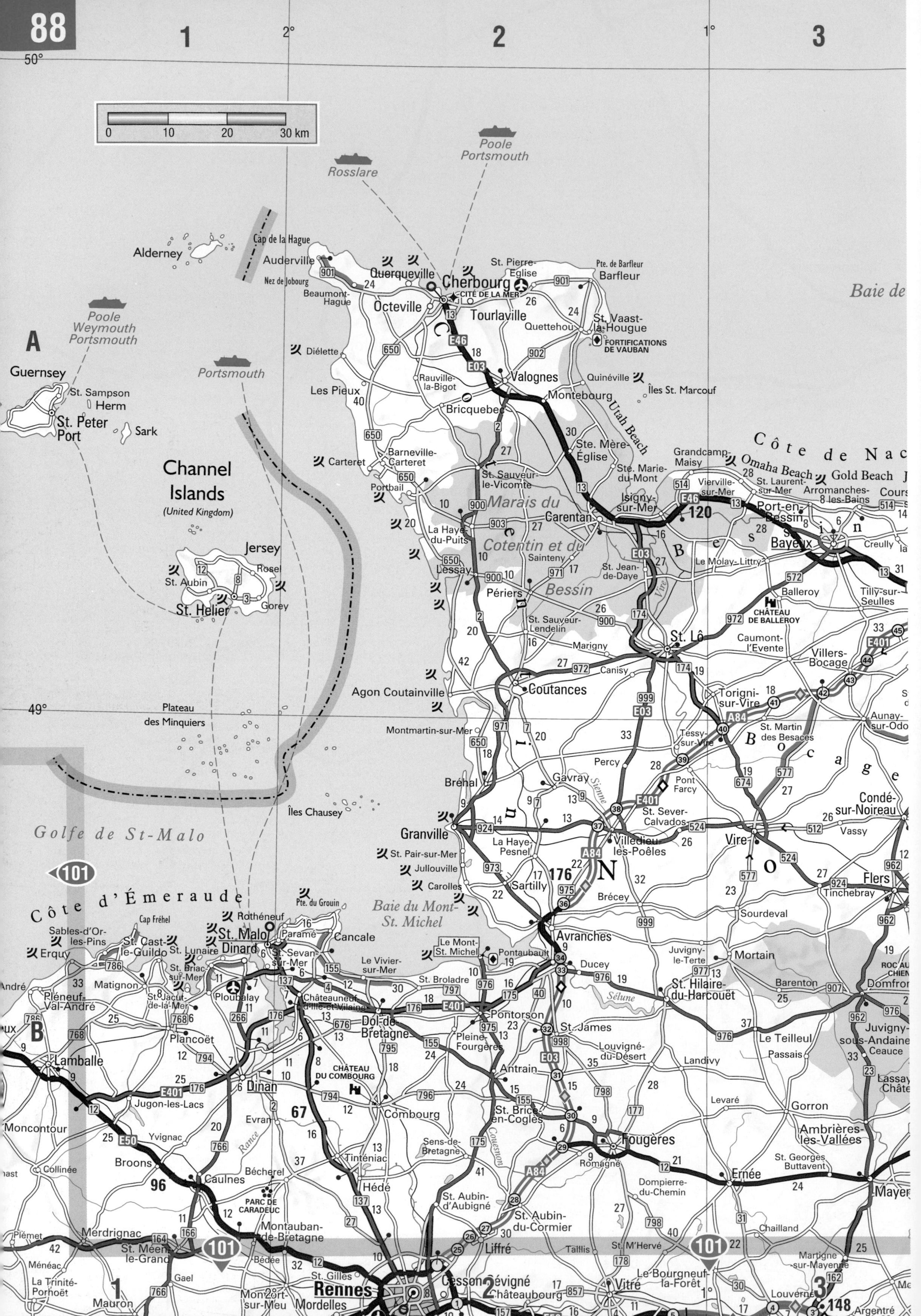

Channel Islands
(United Kingdom)
Guernsey
St. Peter Port
St. Sampson
Herm
Sark
Alderney
Jersey
St. Helier
St. Aubin
Rosel
Gorey
Cherbourg
Octeville
Querqueville
Tourlaville
Valognes
Barfleur
St. Vaast-la-Hougue
Bricquebec
Les Pieux
Barneville-Carteret
Carentan
Isigny-sur-Mer
Bayeux
Port-en-Bessin
Omaha Beach
Gold Beach
Utah Beach
Marais du Cotentin et du Bessin
Lessay
Périers
St. Lô
Coutances
Agon Coutainville
Gavray
Villedieu-les-Poêles
Granville
Vire
Flers
Avranches
Mortain
Pontorson
St. Malo
Dinard
Cancale
Dinan
Dol-de-Bretagne
Combourg
Fougères
Lamballe
Rennes
Vitré
Ernée
Golfe de St-Malo
Côte d'Émeraude
Baie du Mont-St. Michel
Plateau des Minquiers
Îles Chausey
Poole
Portsmouth
Weymouth
Rosslare

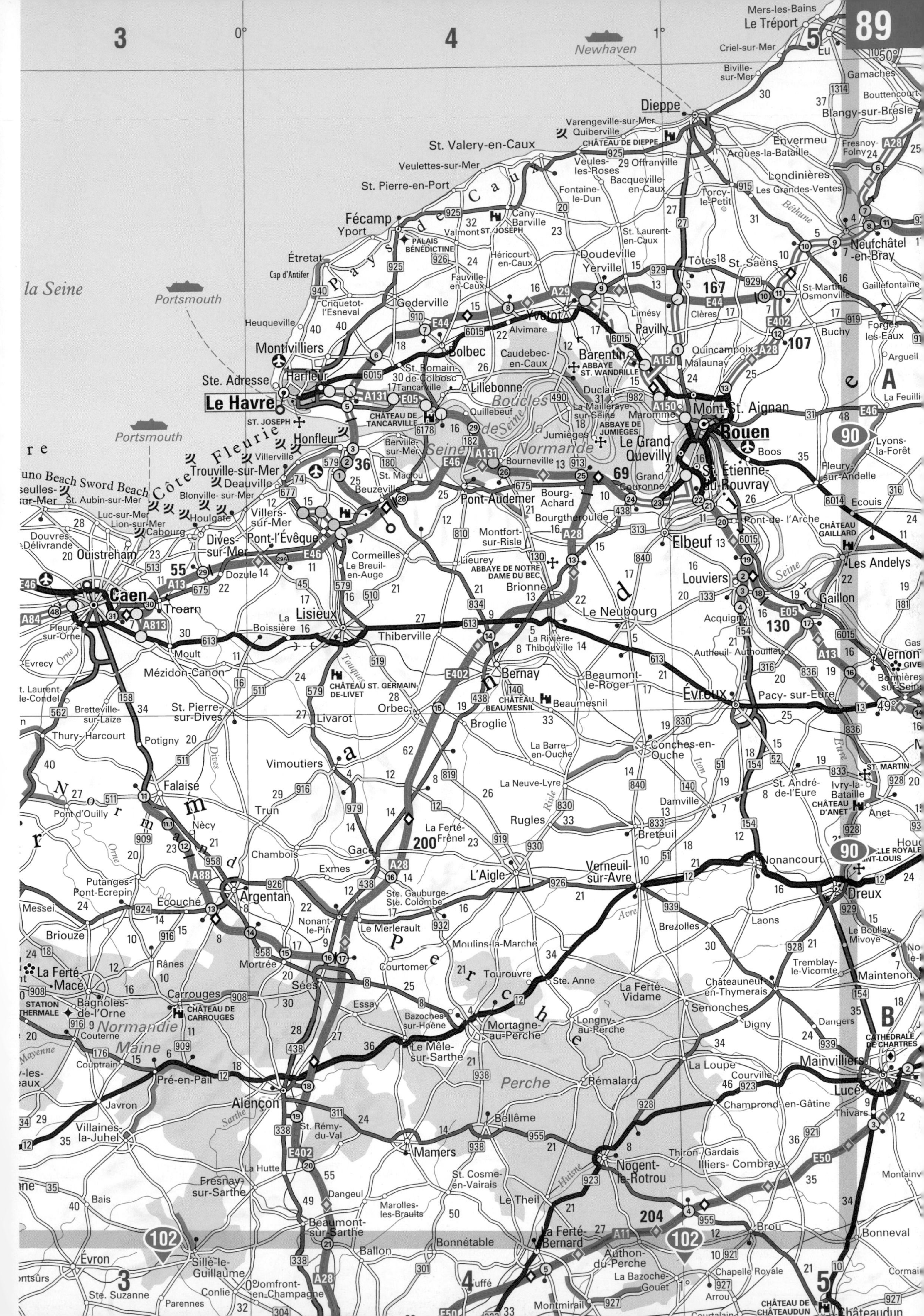

Abbeville
Le Tréport
Eu
Doullens
Bapaume
Albert
Amiens
Péronne
Ham
Neufchâtel-en-Bray
Aumale
Poix-de-Picardie
Montdidier
Roye
Noyon
Chauny
Tergnier
Beauvais
Gournay-en-Bray
Clermont
Compiègne
Soissons
Gisors
Les Andelys
Creil
Senlis
Chantilly
Crépy-en-Valois
Villers-Cotterêts
Vernon
Mantes-la-Jolie
Pontoise
Cergy
St. Denis
Meaux
PARIS
Versailles
Créteil
Dreux
Rambouillet
Évry
Melun
Chartres
Étampes
Fontainebleau
Provins
Nemours
Montereau-Faut-Yonne
Coulommiers
Picardie
Pays de Bray
Vexin Français
Forêt de Fontainebleau
0 10 20 30 km

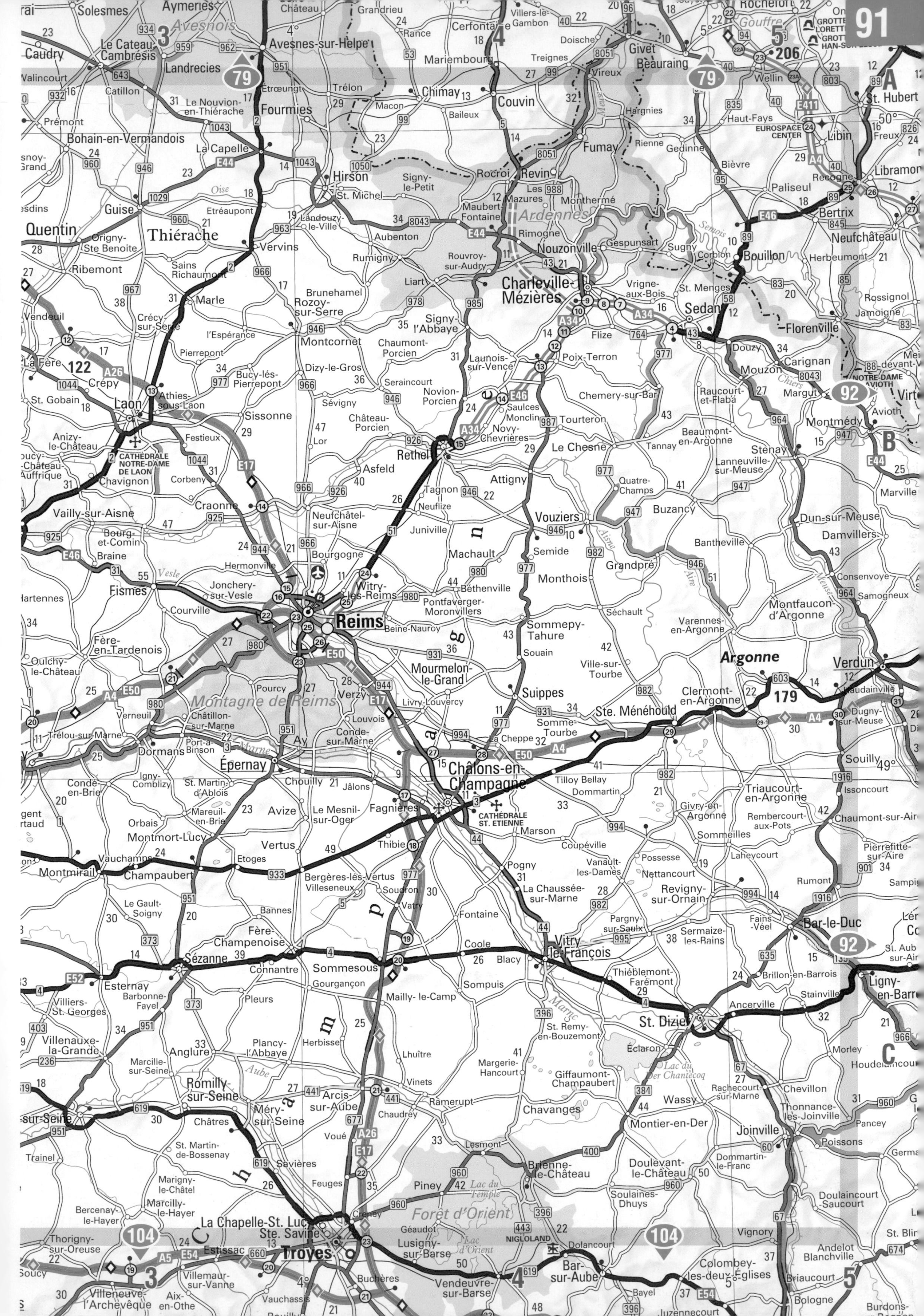
Solesmes
Aymeries
Avesnois
Château
Grandrieu
Rance
Cerfontaine
Villers-le-Gambon
Doische
Givet
Beauraing
Rochefort
Gouffre
GROTTE LORETTE
GROTTE HAN-SUR-LESSE
Le Cateau-Cambrésis
Caudry
Avesnes-sur-Helpe
Mariembourg
Treignes
Vireux
Landrecies
Walincourt
Catillon
Etrœungt
Trélon
Chimay
Couvin
Wellin
St. Hubert
Le Nouvion-en-Thiérache
Fourmies
Macon
Baileux
Hargnies
Haut-Fays
EUROSPACE CENTER
Libin
Prémont
Bohain-en-Vermandois
La Capelle
Fumay
Rienne
Gedinne
Freux
Hirson
Signy-le-Petit
Rocroi
Revin
Bièvre
Libramont
Recogne
St. Michel
Guise
Oise
Etréaupont
Les Mazures
Monthermé
Paliseul
Maubert-Fontaine
Ardennes
Bertrix
Quentin
Origny-Ste Benoite
Thiérache
Landouzy-le-Ville
Aubenton
Rimogne
Neufchâteau
Vervins
Rumigny
Nouzonville
Gespunsart
Semois
Sugny
Corbion
Bouillon
Herbeumont
Ribemont
Sains Richaumont
Rouvroy-sur-Audry
Liart
Charleville-Mézières
Vrigne-aux-Bois
St. Menges
Sedan
Rossignol
Jamoigne
Florenville
Marle
Brunehamel
Rozoy-sur-Serre
Signy-l'Abbaye
Vendeuil
Crécy-sur-Serre
l'Espérance
Montcornet
Chaumont-Porcien
Flize
Douzy
Mouzon
Carignan
Pierrepont
Launois-sur-Vence
Poix-Terron
La Fère
Crépy
Bucy-lès-Pierrepont
Dizy-le-Gros
Seraincourt
Novion-Porcien
Chemery-sur-Bar
Raucourt-et-Flaba
Chiers
Margut
NOTRE-DAME AVIOTH
Virton
St. Gobain
Laon
Athies-sous-Laon
Sévigny
Saulces Monclin
Tourteron
Avioth
Montmédy
Sissonne
Château-Porcien
Novy-Chevrières
Beaumont-en-Argonne
Anizy-le-Château
Festieux
Lor
Rethel
Le Chesne
Tannay
Stenay
Coucy-le-Château-Auffrique
CATHÉDRALE NOTRE-DAME DE LAON
Asfeld
Attigny
Lanneuville-sur-Meuse
Chavignon
Corbeny
Quatre-Champs
Marville
Tagnon
Neuflize
Craonne
Buzancy
Vailly-sur-Aisne
Neufchâtel-sur-Aisne
Juniville
Vouziers
Dun-sur-Meuse
Bourg-et-Comin
Damvillers
Braine
Bourgogne
Machault
Semide
Aisne
Grandpré
Bantheville
Hermonville
Witry-lès-Reims
Béthenville
Monthois
Aire
Consenvoye
Fismes
Vesle
Jonchery-sur-Vesle
Pontfaverger-Moronvilliers
Meuse
Samogneux
Hartennes
Courville
Reims
Beine-Nauroy
Sommepy-Tahure
Séchault
Montfaucon-d'Argonne
Varennes-en-Argonne
Fère-en-Tardenois
Souain
Argonne
Verdun
Oulchy-le-Château
Mourmelon-le-Grand
Ville-sur-Tourbe
Haudainville
Clermont-en-Argonne
Pourcy
Montagne de Reims
Verzy
Livry-Louvercy
Suippes
Ste. Ménéhould
Dugny-sur-Meuse
Verneuil
Châtillon-sur-Marne
Louvois
Somme-Tourbe
Trélou-sur-Marne
Port-à-Binson
Marne
Ay
Conde-sur-Marne
La Cheppe
Dormans
Épernay
Châlons-en-Champagne
Souilly
Condé-en-Brie
Igny-Comblizy
St. Martin-d'Ablois
Chouilly
Jâlons
Tilloy Bellay
Dommartin
Triaucourt-en-Argonne
Isoncourt
Orbais
Mareuil-en-Brie
Avize
Le Mesnil-sur-Oger
Fagnières
CATHÉDRALE ST. ETIENNE
Marson
Givry-en-Argonne
Rembercourt-aux-Pots
Chaumont-sur-Aire
Montmort-Lucy
Vertus
Thibie
Coupéville
Sommeilles
Pierrefitte-sur-Aire
Vauchamps
Montmirail
Champaubert
Etoges
Bergères-lès-Vertus
Villeseneux
Pogny
Vanault-les-Dames
Possesse
Nettancourt
Laheycourt
Rumont
Le Gault-Soigny
Soudron
Vatry
La Chaussée-sur-Marne
Revigny-sur-Ornain
Bannes
Fontaine
Pargny-sur-Saulx
Fains-Véel
Bar-le-Duc
Fère-Champenoise
Coole
Sermaize-les-Bains
Sézanne
Connantre
Sommesous
Blacy
Vitry-le-François
St. Aubin-sur-Aire
Esternay
Gourgançon
Sompuis
Thiéblemont-Farémont
Brillon-en-Barrois
Ligny-en-Barrois
Villiers-St. Georges
Barbonne-Fayel
Pleurs
Mailly-le-Camp
Stainville
Ancerville
St. Dizier
Marne
St. Remy-en-Bouzemont
Villenauxe-la-Grande
Herbisse
Anglure
Plancy-l'Abbaye
Lhuître
Eclaron
Lac du Der Chantecoq
Morley
Houdelaincourt
Marcilly-sur-Seine
Aube
Margerie-Hancourt
Giffaumont-Champaubert
Romilly-sur-Seine
Arcis-sur-Aube
Vinets
Ramerupt
Chavanges
Wassy
Rachecourt-sur-Marne
Chevillon
Thonnance-les-Joinville
Pancey
Méry-sur-Seine
Châtres
Chaudrey
Montier-en-Der
Joinville
Poissons
Voué
St. Martin-de-Bossenay
Lesmont
Dommartin-le-Franc
Trainel
Savières
Brienne-le-Château
Doulevant-le-Château
Marigny-le-Châtel
Feuges
Piney
Lac du Temple
Soulaines-Dhuys
Doulaincourt-Saucourt
Marcilly-le-Hayer
Bercenay-le-Hayer
Creney
Forêt d'Orient
La Chapelle-St. Luc
Ste. Savine
Géraudot
Lac d'Orient
NIGLOLAND
Vignory
St. Blin
Thorigny-sur-Oreuse
Estissac
Troyes
Lusigny-sur-Barse
Dolancourt
Andelot Blanchville
Soucy
Villemaur-sur-Vanne
Bar-sur-Aube
Colombey-les-deux-Eglises
Briaucourt
Bréviandes
Buchères
Vendeuvre-sur-Barse
Bayel
Villeneuve-l'Archevêque
Aix-en-Othe
Vauchassis
Bologne
Juzennecourt
Burdons

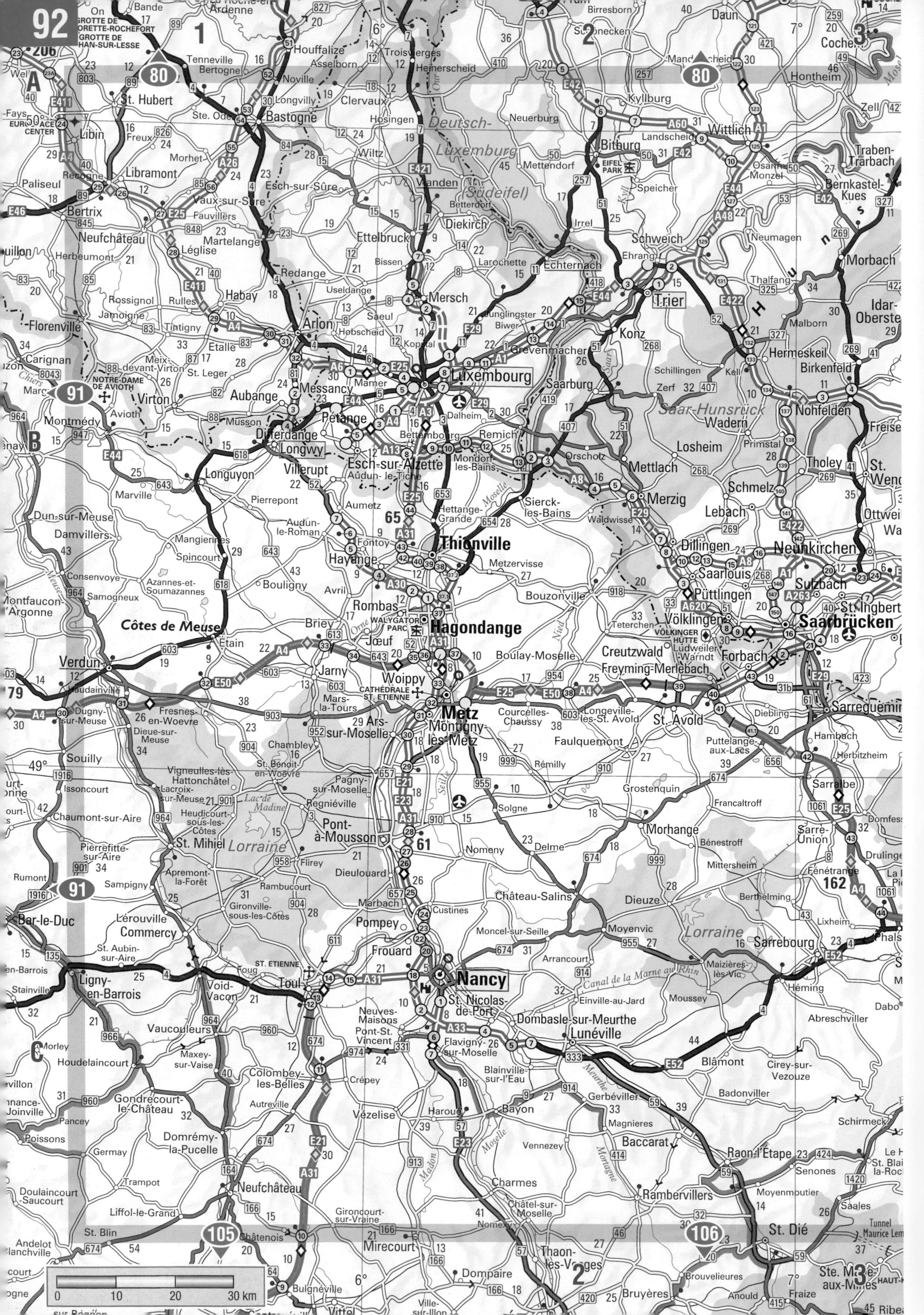
Luxembourg
Metz
Nancy
Thionville
Saarbrücken
Trier
Verdun
Hagondange
Arlon
Bastogne
Longwy
Esch-sur-Alzette
Pont-à-Mousson
Toul
Lunéville
Bar-le-Duc
Commercy
St. Mihiel
Sarrebourg
Sarreguemines
Forbach
St. Avold
Neufchâteau
Mirecourt
St. Dié
Côtes de Meuse
Lorraine
Saar-Hunsrück
Deutsch-Luxemburg (Südeifel)
Hunsrück
0 10 20 30 km

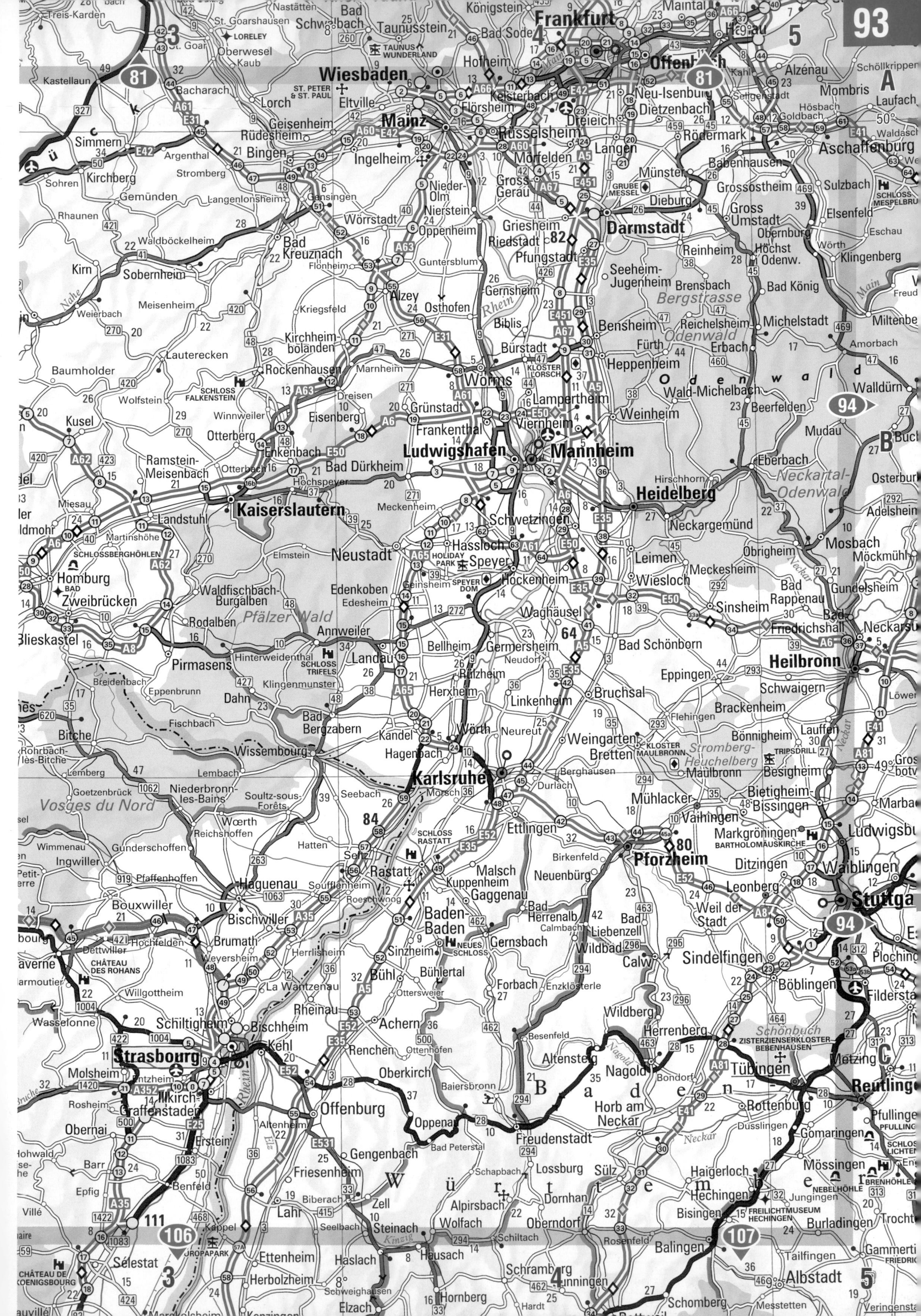
Frankfurt
Wiesbaden
Mainz
Offenbach
Darmstadt
Rüsselsheim
Bingen
Ingelheim
Bad Kreuznach
Alzey
Worms
Ludwigshafen
Mannheim
Heidelberg
Kaiserslautern
Neustadt
Speyer
Landau
Karlsruhe
Pforzheim
Stuttgart
Heilbronn
Baden-Baden
Rastatt
Offenburg
Strasbourg
Tübingen
Reutlingen
Freudenstadt
Aschaffenburg
Homburg
Zweibrücken
Pirmasens
Haguenau
Sélestat
Kehl
Bruchsal
Sinsheim
Mosbach
Eberbach
Weinheim
Bensheim
Worms
Frankenthal
Schwetzingen
Hockenheim
Wiesloch
Bretten
Ettlingen
Gaggenau
Calw
Sindelfingen
Böblingen
Herrenberg
Nagold
Rottenburg
Hechingen
Balingen
Albstadt
Simmern
Kirn
Kusel
Bad Dürkheim
Grünstadt
Eisenberg
Wissembourg
Bad Bergzabern
Germersheim
Pfälzer Wald
Vosges du Nord
Odenwald
Bergstrasse
Neckartal-Odenwald
Stromberg-Heuchelberg
Schönbuch
Baden-Württemberg
Rhein
Main
Neckar
Nahe
81
94
106
107
A
B
C
3
4
5

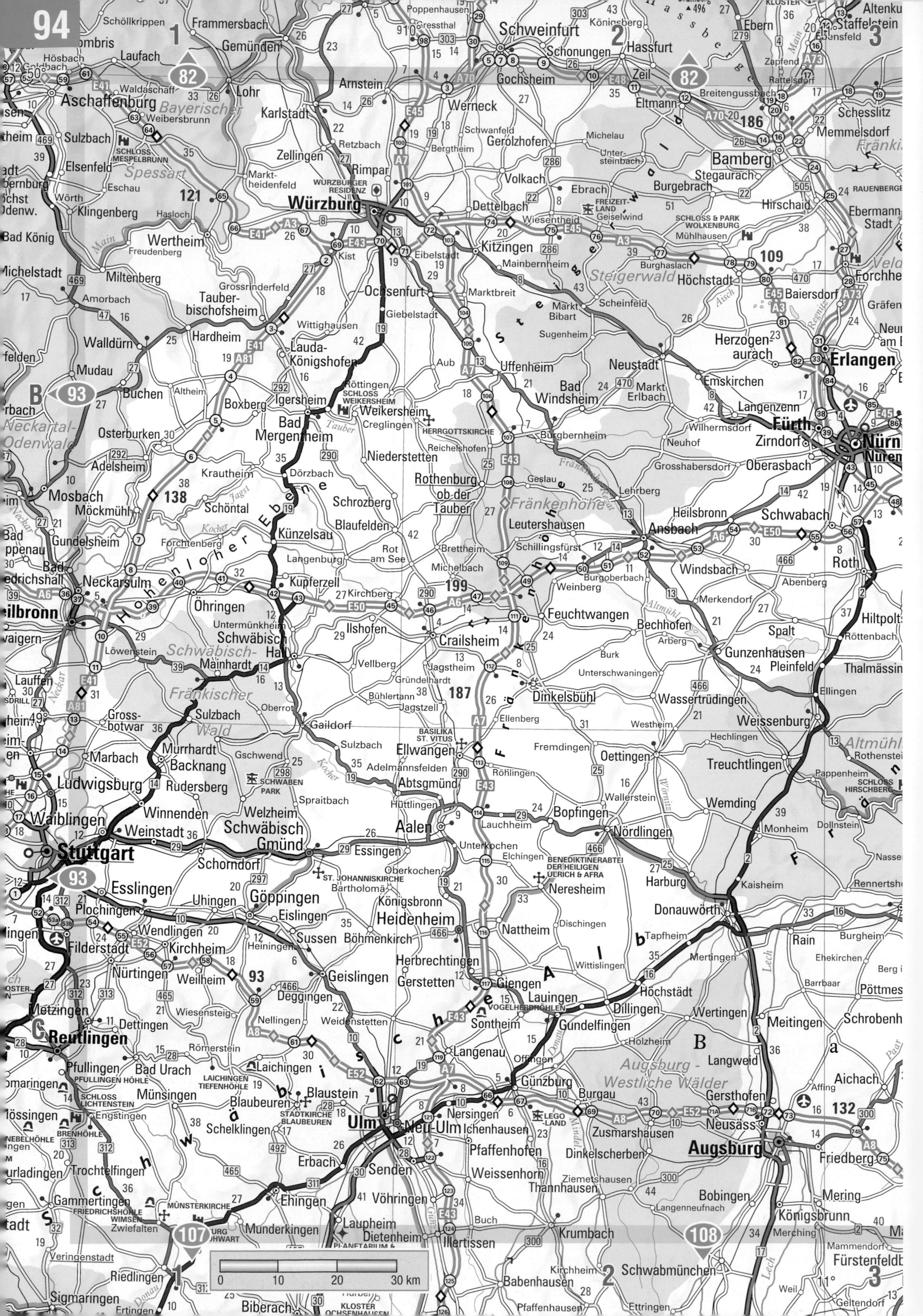

Schöllkrippen
Frammersbach
Gemünden
Poppenhausen
Gressthal
Schweinfurt
Königsberg
Schonungen
Hassfurt
Ebern
Staffelstein
Altenkunstadt
Hösbach
Laufach
Lohr
Arnstein
Gochsheim
Zeil
Rattelsdorf
Breitengussbach
Aschaffenburg
Bayerischer
Weibersbrunn
Karlstadt
Werneck
Eltmann
Schesslitz
Memmelsdorf
Sulzbach
Schloss Mespelbrunn
Zellingen
Retzbach
Schwanfeld
Gerolzhofen
Michelau
Bergtheim
Untersteinbach
Bamberg
Elsenfeld
Spessart
Markt-heidenfeld
Rimpar
Volkach
Stegaurach
Eschau
Würzburger Residenz
Ebrach
Burgebrach
Wörth
Klingenberg
Hasloch
Würzburg
Dettelbach
Freizeit-Land Geiselwind
Hirschaid
Ebermannstadt
Bad König
Wertheim
Freudenberg
Wiesentheid
Schloss & Park Wolkenburg
Mühlhausen
Kist
Eibelstadt
Kitzingen
Michelstadt
Miltenberg
Mainbernheim
Burghaslach
Steigerwald
Höchstadt
Forchheim
Amorbach
Grossrinderfeld
Tauber-bischofsheim
Ochsenfurt
Marktbreit
Baiersdorf
Gräfenberg
Giebelstadt
Markt Bibart
Scheinfeld
Walldürn
Hardheim
Wittighausen
Sugenheim
Herzogen-aurach
Lauda-Königshofen
Aub
Uffenheim
Neustadt
Erlangen
Mudau
Röttingen
Emskirchen
Buchen
Altheim
Boxberg
Igersheim
Schloss Weikersheim
Weikersheim
Bad Windsheim
Markt Erlbach
Langenzenn
Fürth
Bad Mergentheim
Creglingen
Herrgottskirche
Wilhermsdorf
Neckartal-Odenwald
Osterburken
Reichelshofen
Burgbernheim
Neuhof
Zirndorf
Nürnberg
Adelsheim
Niederstetten
Grosshabersdorf
Oberasbach
Krautheim
Dörzbach
Rothenburg ob der Tauber
Geslau
Mosbach
Lehrberg
Möckmühl
Schöntal
Schrozberg
Frankenhöhe
Heilsbronn
Schwabach
Jagst
Leutershausen
Ansbach
Gundelsheim
Forchtenberg
Künzelsau
Blaufelden
Rot am See
Schillingsfürst
Brettheim
Windsbach
Roth
Bad Friedrichshall
Langenburg
Michelbach
Neckarsulm
Kupferzell
Kirchberg
Burgoberbach
Abenberg
Heilbronn
Öhringen
Weinberg
Merkendorf
Hiltpoltstein
Untermünkheim
Feuchtwangen
Bechhofen
Schwäbisch Hall
Ilshofen
Crailsheim
Altmühl
Spalt
Röttenbach
Löwenstein
Schwäbisch-Fränkischer Wald
Arberg
Burk
Gunzenhausen
Mainhardt
Vellberg
Jagstheim
Unterschwaningen
Pleinfeld
Thalmässing
Lauffen
Gründelhardt
Dinkelsbühl
Bühlertann
Jagstzell
Wassertrüdingen
Ellingen
Oberrot
Gross-bottwar
Sulzbach
Gaildorf
Ellenberg
Westheim
Weissenburg
Basilika St. Vitus
Hechlingen
Ellwangen
Fremdingen
Oettingen
Marbach
Murrhardt
Gschwend
Adelmannsfelden
Treuchtlingen
Backnang
Röhlingen
Rothenstein
Pappenheim
Schloss Hirschberg
Ludwigsburg
Rudersberg
Schwaben Park
Abtsgmünd
Spraitbach
Wallerstein
Hüttlingen
Wemding
Winnenden
Welzheim
Bopfingen
Waiblingen
Aalen
Monheim
Dollnstein
Weinstadt
Schwäbisch Gmünd
Lauchheim
Nördlingen
Stuttgart
Essingen
Unterkochen
Elchingen
Schorndorf
Oberkochen
Benediktinerabtei der Heiligen Ulrich & Afra
St. Johanniskirche
Bartholomä
Neresheim
Harburg
Esslingen
Uhingen
Göppingen
Königsbronn
Kaisheim
Plochingen
Eislingen
Heidenheim
Donauwörth
Wendlingen
Dischingen
Nattheim
Rain
Burgheim
Filderstadt
Kirchheim
Heiningen
Sussen
Böhmenkirch
Tapfheim
Ehekirchen
Herbrechtingen
Mertingen
Nürtingen
Weilheim
Geislingen
Gerstetten
Giengen
Wittislingen
Höchstädt
Pöttmes
Metzingen
Deggingen
Lauingen
Vogelherdhöhlen
Dillingen
Wertingen
Wiesensteig
Nellingen
Weidenstetten
Sontheim
Gundelfingen
Meitingen
Schrobenhausen
Dettingen
Reutlingen
Römerstein
Langenau
Holzheim
Offingen
Donau
Pfullingen
Bad Urach
Laichingen
Augsburg - Westliche Wälder
Langweid
Aichach
Pfullingen Höhle
Laichingen Tiefenhöhle
Blaustein
Günzburg
Burgau
Gersthofen
Affing
Münsingen
Schloss Lichtenstein
Blaubeuren
Stadtkirche Blaubeuren
Nersingen
Lego-Land
Zusmarshausen
Neusäss
Engstingen
Ulm
Neu-Ulm
Ichenhausen
Bärenhöhle
Nebelhöhle
Schelklingen
Pfaffenhofen
Dinkelscherben
Augsburg
Friedberg
Trochtelfingen
Erbach
Senden
Weissenhorn
Ziemetshausen
Thannhausen
Mering
Gammertingen
Münsterkirche
Ehingen
Vöhringen
Bobingen
Langenneufnach
Königsbrunn
Friedrichshöhle Wimsen
Zwiefalten
Munderkingen
Laupheim
Dietenheim
Buch
Krumbach
Merching
Veringenstadt
Illertissen
Mammendorf
Riedlingen
Kirchheim
Schwabmünchen
Fürstenfeldbruck
Sigmaringen
Babenhausen
Biberach
Kloster Ochsenhausen
Pfaffenhausen
Ettringen
Weil
Geltendorf
Neckar
Main
Tauber
Kocher
Wörnitz
Lech
Günz
Mindel
Frankenhöhe
Hassberge
Steigerwald
Hohenloher Ebene
Schwäbische Alb
Fränkische Alb
0 10 20 30 km

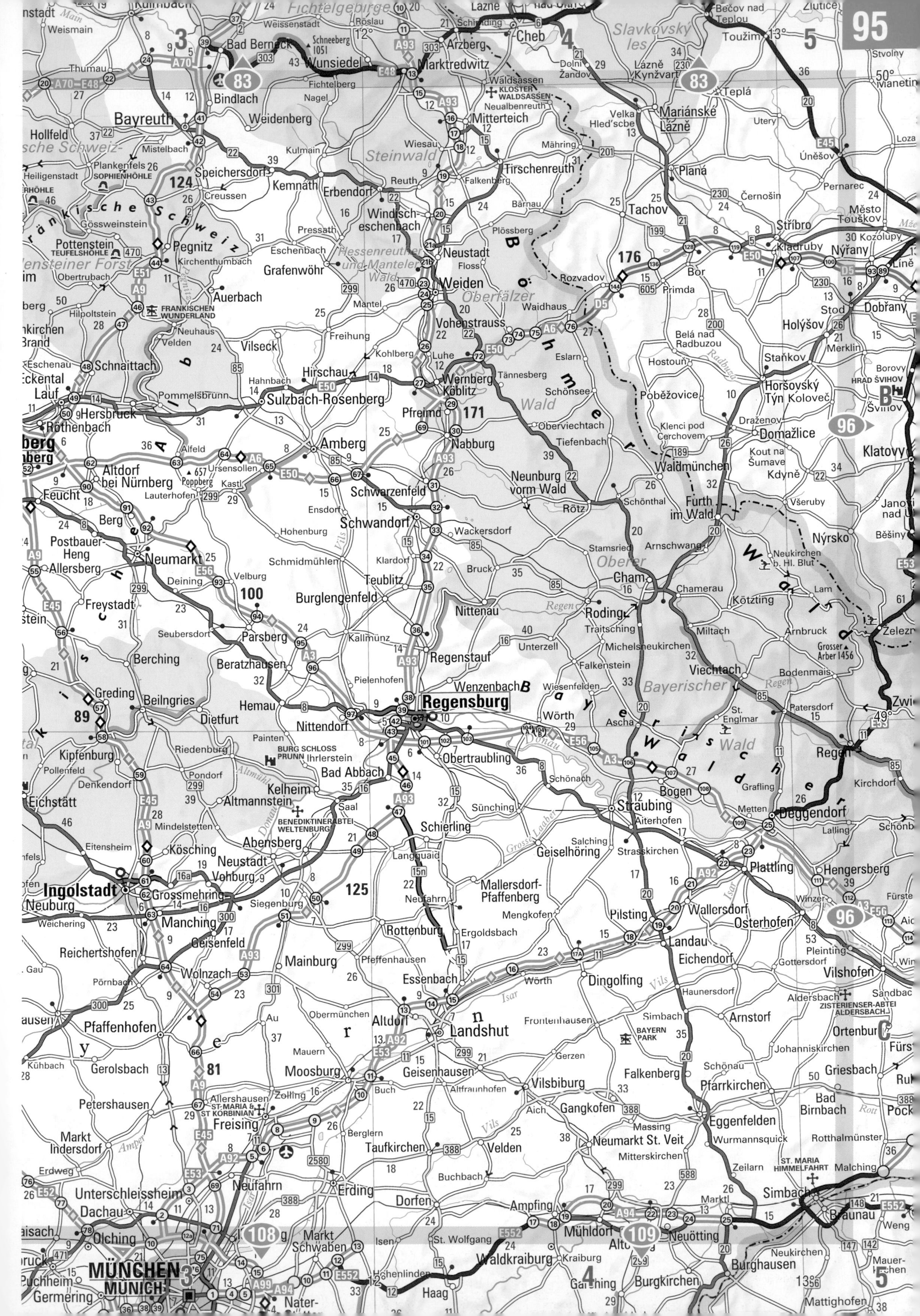
Fichtelgebirge
Bad Berneck
Wunsiedel
Marktredwitz
Arzberg
Cheb
Slavkovský les
Bečov nad Teplou
Toužim
Mariánské Lázně
Bindlach
Bayreuth
Hollfeld
Weidenberg
Mitterteich
Waldsassen
KLOSTER WALDSASSEN
Steinwald
Tirschenreuth
Planá
Tachov
Speichersdorf
Kemnath
Erbendorf
Windischeschenbach
Neustadt
Weiden
Oberpfälzer Wald
Pegnitz
Grafenwöhr
Auerbach
FRÄNKISCHEN WUNDERLAND
Pottenstein
TEUFELSHÖHLE
Fränkische Schweiz
Stříbro
Nýřany
Kladruby
Bor
Rozvadov
Primda
Holýšov
Dobřany
Stod
Vohenstrauss
Vilseck
Schnaittach
Lauf
Hersbruck
Sulzbach-Rosenberg
Hirschau
Wernberg Köblitz
Pfreimd
Böhmer Wald
Horšovský Týn
Poběžovice
Domažlice
Klatovy
Amberg
Nabburg
Oberviechtach
Altdorf bei Nürnberg
Feucht
Neumarkt
Schwarzenfeld
Schwandorf
Neunburg vorm Wald
Rötz
Waldmünchen
Furth im Wald
Kdyně
Nýrsko
Burglengenfeld
Teublitz
Nittenau
Cham
Roding
Chamerau
Kötzting
Bayerischer Wald
Grosser Arber 1456
Parsberg
Berching
Beratzhausen
Regenstauf
Viechtach
Bodenmais
Hemau
Regensburg
Wenzenbach
Wörth
Greding
Beilngries
Dietfurt
Nittendorf
Kipfenburg
Eichstätt
Kelheim
Bad Abbach
Obertraubling
BURG SCHLOSS PRUNN
Altmannstein
BENEDIKTINERABTEI WELTENBURG
Straubing
Bogen
Deggendorf
Regen
Abensberg
Schierling
Geiselhöring
Plattling
Hengersberg
Ingolstadt
Neuburg
Grossmehring
Vohburg
Neustadt
Manching
Siegenburg
Mallersdorf-Pfaffenberg
Wallersdorf
Osterhofen
Rottenburg
Geisenfeld
Reichertshofen
Mainburg
Landau
Eichendorf
Vilshofen
Wolnzach
Essenbach
Dingolfing
Pfaffenhofen
Landshut
Altdorf
Frontenhausen
Arnstorf
ZISTERIENSER-ABTEI ALDERSBACH
Ortenburg
Moosburg
Geisenhausen
Vilsbiburg
Falkenberg
Pfarrkirchen
Griesbach
Gerolsbach
Freising
ST.-MARIA & ST KORBINIAN
Gangkofen
Eggenfelden
Bad Birnbach
Taufkirchen
Velden
Neumarkt St. Veit
Erding
Dorfen
Ampfing
Simbach
Braunau
Unterschleissheim
Dachau
Olching
Mühldorf
Altötting
Neuötting
MÜNCHEN MUNICH
Waldkraiburg
Burghausen
Haag
Burgkirchen
Garching

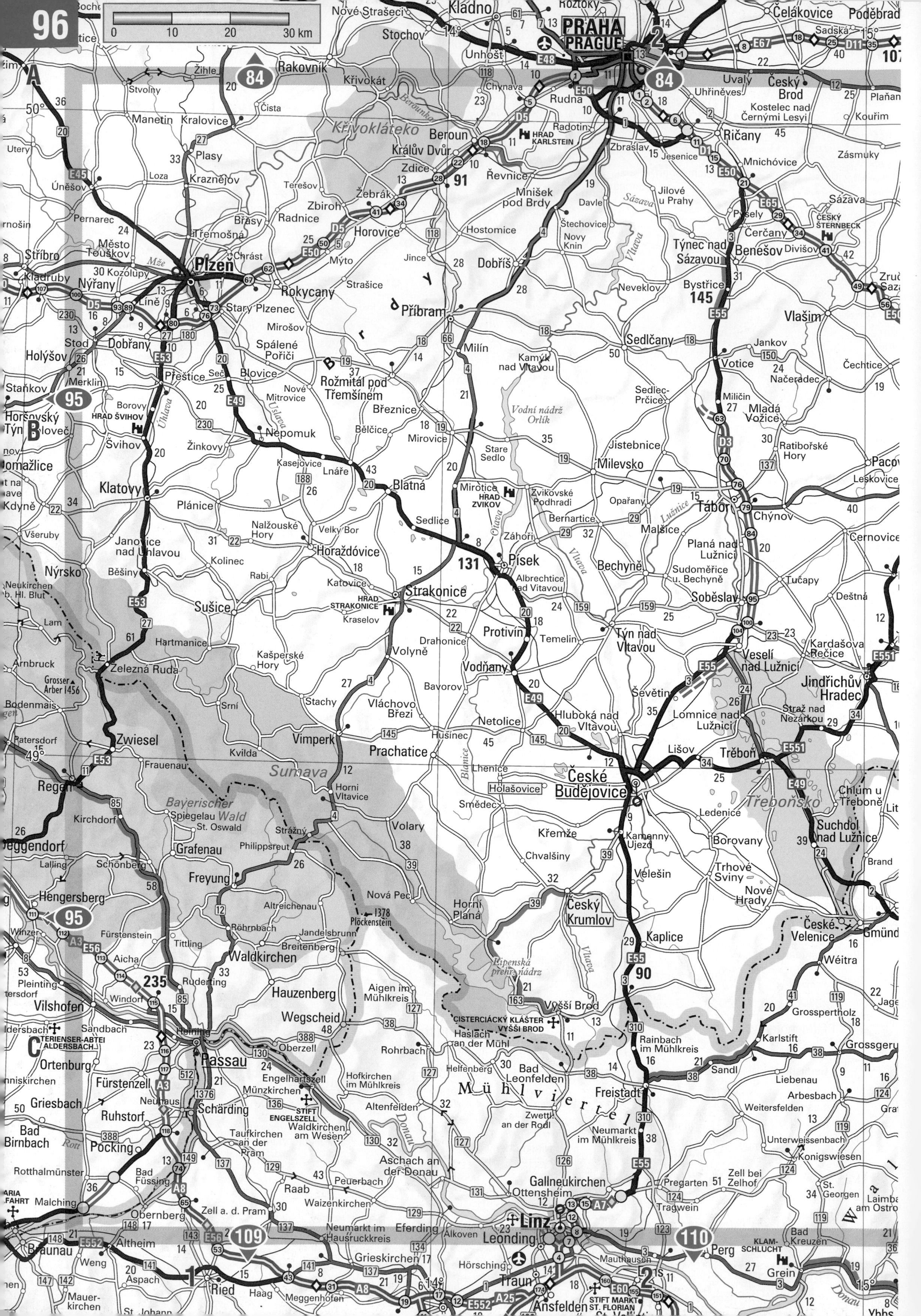
0 10 20 30 km
Kladno
Nové Strašecí
Stochov
Roztoky
PRAHA
PRAGUE
Čelákovice
Poděbrady
Sadská
Unhošť
Rakovník
Křivoklát
Žihle
Stvolny
Čista
Manetin
Kralovice
Křivoklátsko
Beroun
Králův Dvůr
Zdice
Řevnice
HRAD KARLŠTEJN
Radotín
Rudná
Chýnava
Zbraslav
Jesenice
Uhříněves
Uvaly
Český Brod
Kostelec nad Černými Lesy
Kouřim
Plaňany
Říčany
Mnichóvice
Zásmuky
Plasy
Kraznějov
Loza
Úněšov
Utery
Tēresov
Žebrák
Zbiroh
Radnice
Břasy
Třemošná
Pernarec
Město Touškov
Chrást
Plzeň
Stříbro
Kladruby
Nýřany
Kozolupy
Líně
Rokycany
Mýto
Hořovice
Jince
Hostomice
Mníšek pod Brdy
Davle
Štěchovice
Nový Knín
Jílové u Prahy
Sázava
Týnec nad Sázavou
Benešov
Pyšely
Čerčany
Divišov
ČESKÝ ŠTERNBECK
Dobříš
Strašice
Příbram
Neveklov
Bystřice
Vlašim
Stary Plzenec
Mirošov
Spálené Poříčí
Holýšov
Stod
Dobřany
Přeštice
Seč
Blovice
Merklin
Staňkov
Horšovský Týn
Bělověc
Domažlice
Borovy
HRAD ŠVIHOV
Švihov
Nové Mitrovice
Rožmitál pod Třemšínem
Milín
Kamýk nad Vltavou
Sedlčany
Jankov
Votice
Načeradec
Čechtice
Sedlec-Prčice
Miličín
Mladá Vožice
Březnice
Bělčice
Mirovice
Nepomuk
Žinkovy
Kasejovice
Lnáře
Blatná
Vodní nádrž Orlík
Stare Sedlo
Jistebnice
Milevsko
Ratibořské Hory
Pacov
Leskovice
Klatovy
Kdyně
Plánice
Všeruby
Nalžouské Hory
Velký Bor
Sedlice
Mirotice
HRAD ZVIKOV
Zvíkovské Podhradí
Opařany
Tábor
Chýnov
Bernartice
Záhoří
Malšice
Planá nad Lužnicí
Janovice nad Úhlavou
Horaždovice
Kolinec
Rabí
Písek
Albrechtice nad Vltavou
Bechyně
Sudoměřice u. Bechyně
Černovice
Tučapy
Nýrsko
Běšiny
Katovice
Strakonice
HRAD STRAKONICE
Kraselov
Sušice
Soběslav
Deštná
Neukirchen b. Hl. Blut
Lam
Hartmanice
Drahonice
Protivín
Temelín
Týn nad Vltavou
Veselí nad Lužnicí
Kardašova Řečice
Arnbruck
Grosser Arber 1456
Železná Ruda
Kašperské Hory
Volyně
Vodňany
Bavorov
Ševětín
Jindřichův Hradec
Bodenmais
Srní
Stachy
Vláchovo Březí
Netolice
Hluboká nad Vltavou
Lomnice nad Lužnicí
Stráž nad Nežárkou
Ratersdorf
Zwiesel
Kvilda
Vimperk
Prachatice
Husinec
Lišov
Třeboň
Frauenau
Šumava
Lhenice
České Budějovice
Holašovice
Regen
Bayerischer Wald
Spiegelau
St. Oswald
Horní Vltavice
Smědec
Třeboňsko
Chlum u Třeboně
Kirchdorf
Strážný
Volary
Křemže
Kamenny Ujezd
Ledenice
Borovany
Suchdol nad Lužnicí
Deggendorf
Grafenau
Philippsreut
Chvalšiny
Velešin
Trhové Sviny
Brand
Lalling
Schönberg
Freyung
Nová Pec
Horní Planá
Nové Hrady
Hengersberg
Altreichenau
1378 Plöckenstein
Český Krumlov
České Velenice
Gmünd
Winzer
Fürstenstein
Röhrnbach
Jandelsbrunn
Kaplice
Tittling
Breitenberg
Weitra
Aicha
Waldkirchen
Lipenská přehr. nádrž
Plenting
Ruderting
Hauzenberg
Aigen im Mühlkreis
Vyšší Brod
Grosspertholz
Vilshofen
Windorf
Wegscheid
CISTERCIÁCKÝ KLÁŠTER VYŠŠÍ BROD
Rainbach im Mühlkreis
Karlstift
Sandbach
Passau
Oberzell
Rohrbach
Haslach an der Mühl
Grossgerungs
Ortenburg
Engelhartszell
Helfenberg
Bad Leonfelden
Sandl
Liebenau
Fürstenzell
Hofkirchen im Mühlkreis
Mühlviertel
Freistadt
Arbesbach
Griesbach
Neuhaus
Münzkirchen
Schärding
STIFT ENGELSZELL
Altenfelden
Weitersfelden
Ruhstorf
Waldkirchen am Wesen
Zwettl an der Rodl
Neumarkt im Mühlkreis
Bad Birnbach
Pocking
Taufkirchen an der Pram
Donau
Unterweissenbach
Königswiesen
Rotthalmünster
Bad Füssing
Aschach an der Donau
Gallneukirchen
Zell bei Zelhof
Malching
Raab
Peuerbach
Pregarten
St. Georgen
Ottensheim
Tragwein
Obernberg
Zell a. d. Pram
Waizenkirchen
Linz
Laimbach am Ostrong
Braunau
Altheim
Neumarkt im Hausruckkreis
Eferding
Alkoven
Leonding
Perg
KLAM-SCHLUCHT
Bad Kreuzen
Weng
Ried
Grieskirchen
Hörsching
Mauthausen
Aspach
Haag
Traun
Grein
Mauerkirchen
Meggenhofen
Ansfelden
STIFT MARKT ST. FLORIAN
Ybbs

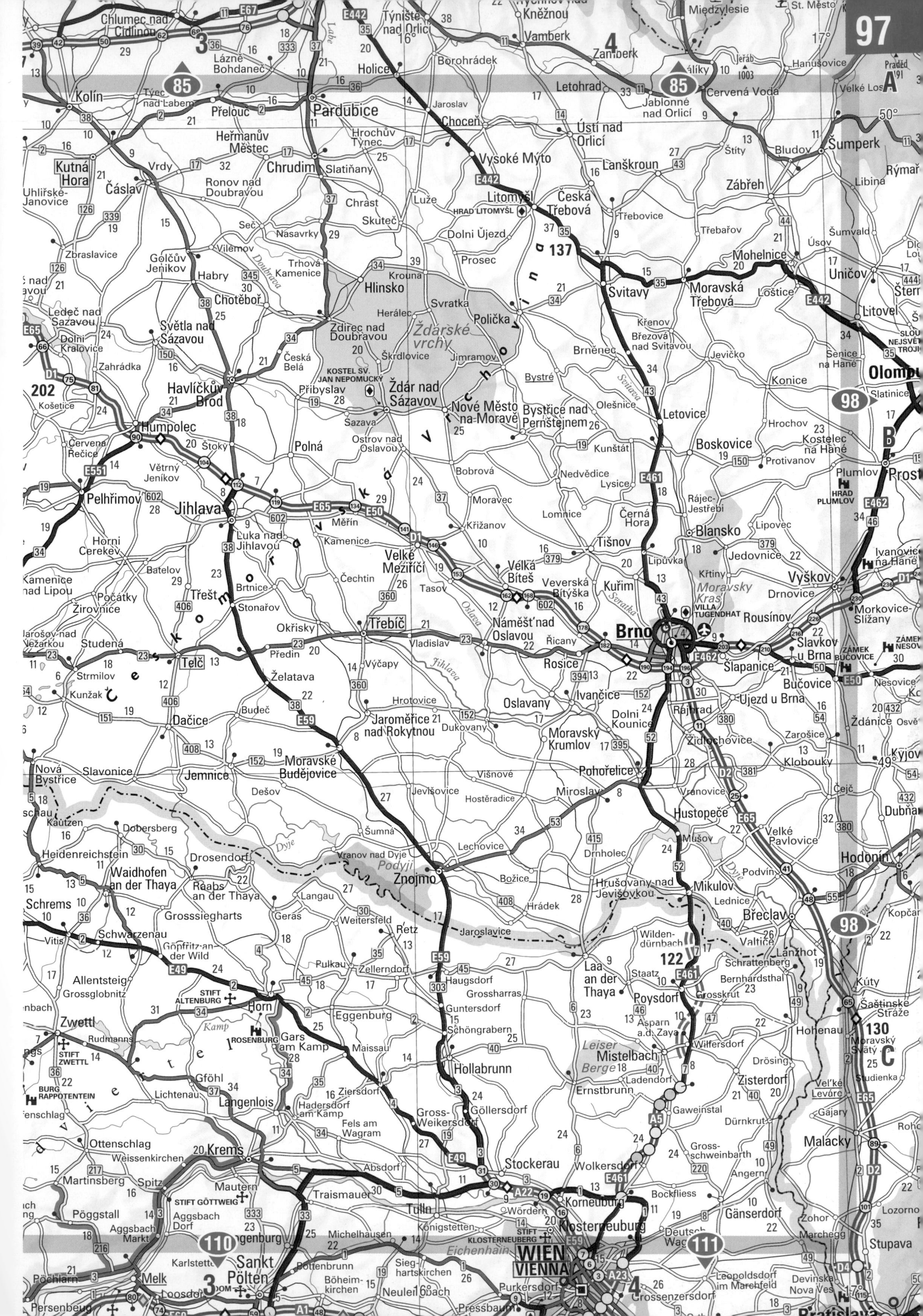

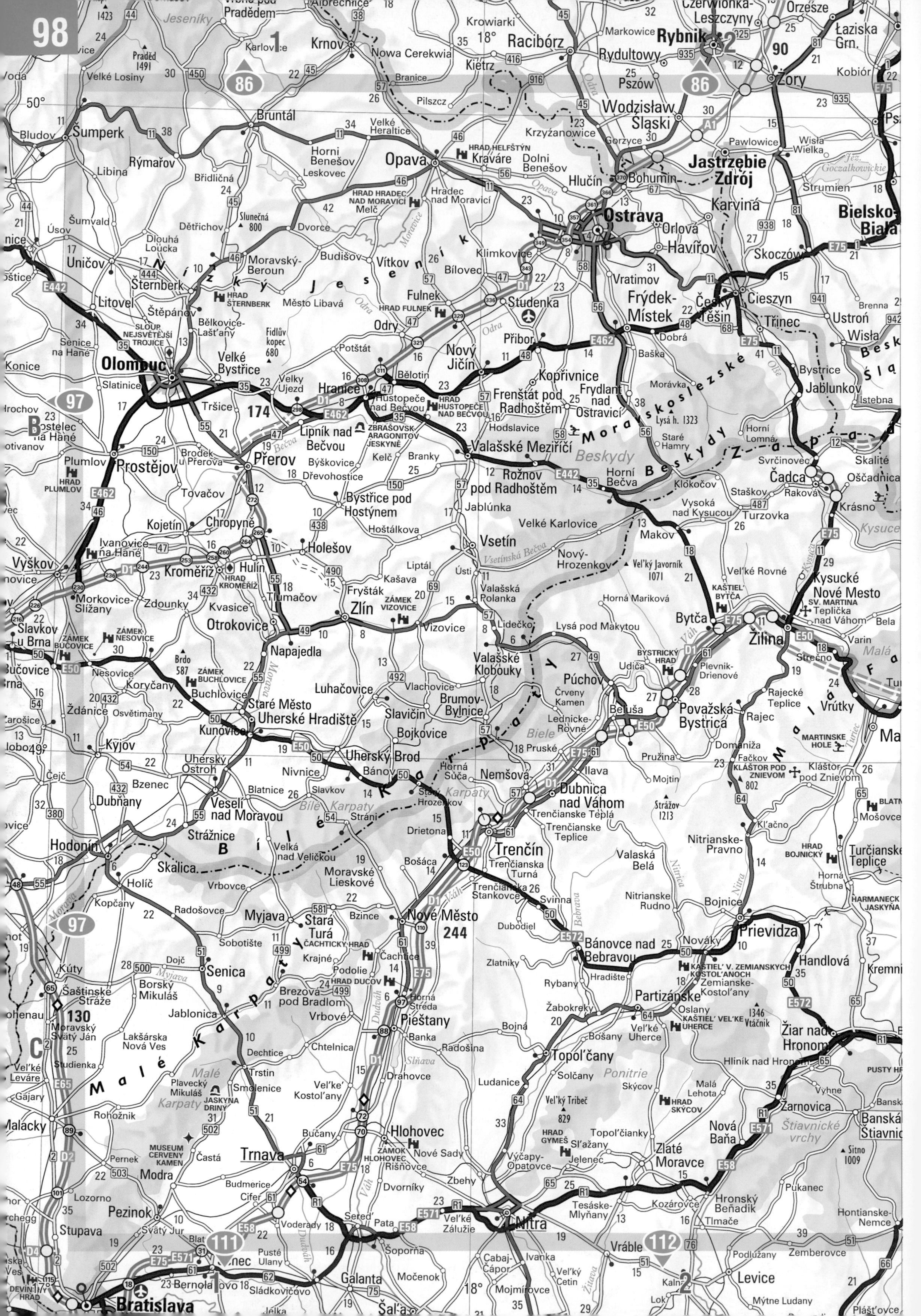

86
97
111
112
130
174
244
Jeseníky
Praděd 1491
Krnov
Racibórz
Rybnik
Žory
Łaziska Grn.
Wodzisław Śląski
Jastrzębie Zdrój
Bielsko-Biała
Šumperk
Bruntál
Opava
Hlučín
Bohumín
Ostrava
Orlová
Havířov
Karviná
Cieszyn
Český Těšín
Třinec
Skoczów
Ustroń
Wisła
Uničov
Šternberk
Litovel
Olomouc
Nízký Jeseník
Studénka
Frýdek-Místek
Příbor
Nový Jičín
Odry
Hranice
Kopřivnice
Frenštát pod Radhoštěm
Moravskoslezské Beskydy
Lysá h. 1323
Jablunkov
Prostějov
Přerov
Valašské Meziříčí
Rožnov pod Radhoštěm
Čadca
Vsetín
Kroměříž
Holešov
Zlín
Otrokovice
Vyškov
Slavkov u Brna
Bučovice
Kysucké Nové Mesto
Bytča
Žilina
Púchov
Považská Bystrica
Uherské Hradiště
Uherský Brod
Kyjov
Veselí nad Moravou
Hodonín
Bílé Karpaty
Trenčín
Dubnica nad Váhom
Skalica
Senica
Myjava
Nové Mesto
Prievidza
Bánovce nad Bebravou
Partizánske
Piešťany
Handlová
Žiar nad Hronom
Topoľčany
Malé Karpaty
Malacky
Trnava
Hlohovec
Žarnovica
Banská Štiavnica
Nová Baňa
Zlaté Moravce
Pezinok
Modra
Nitra
Vráble
Galanta
Levice
Bratislava

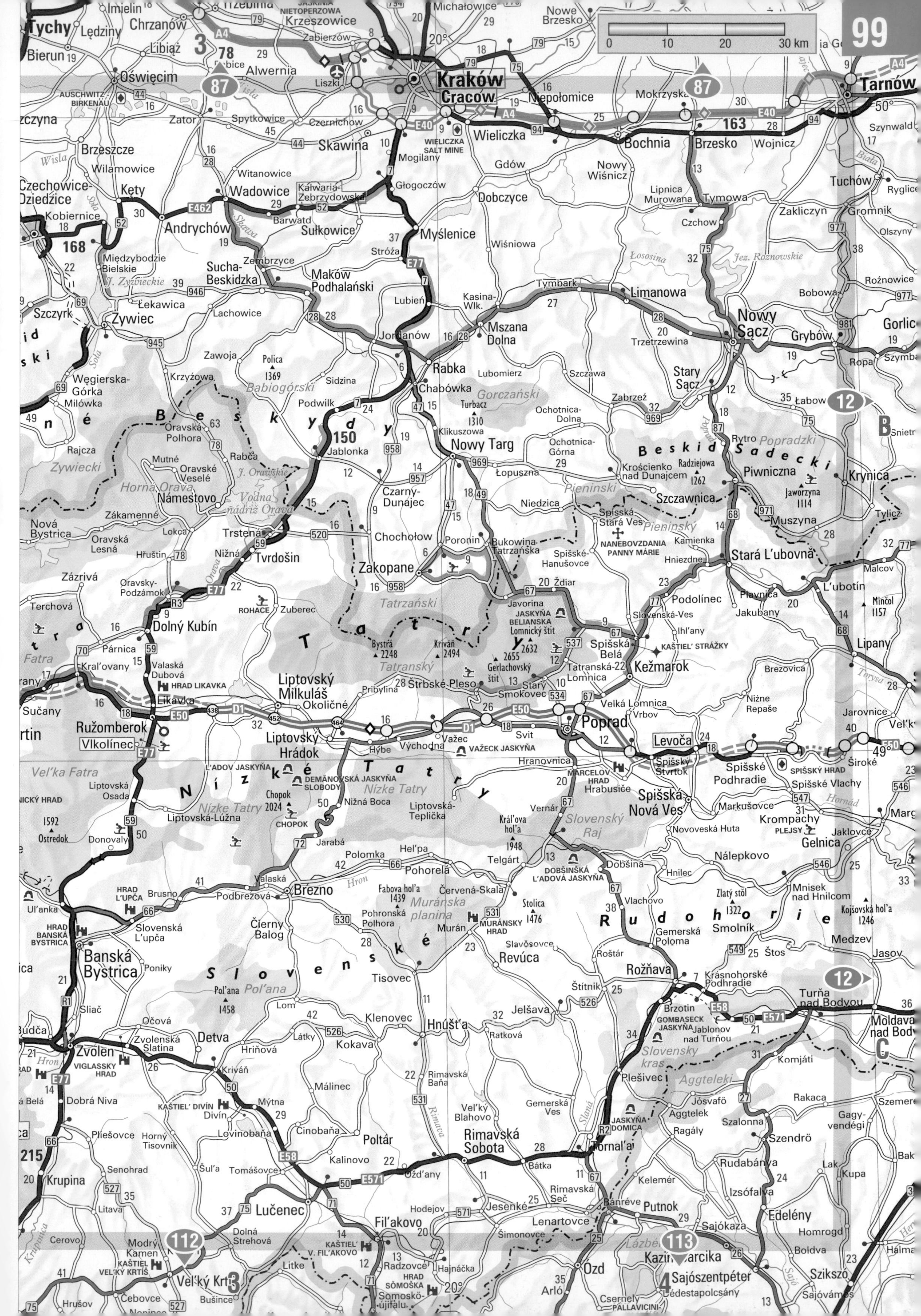
0
10
20
30 km
Tychy
Lędziny
Chrzanów
Krzeszowice
Michałowice
Nowe Brzesko
Bierun
Libiąż
Oświęcim
Alwernia
Liszki
Kraków
Cracow
Niepołomice
Mokrzyska
Tarnów
AUSCHWITZ-BIRKENAU
Zator
Spytkowice
Czernichów
Skawina
WIELICZKA SALT MINE
Wieliczka
Bochnia
Brzesko
Wojnicz
Szynwałd
Brzeszcze
Wilamowice
Mogilany
Gdów
Nowy Wiśnicz
Czechowice-Dziedzice
Kęty
Witanowice
Wadowice
Kalwaria-Zebrzydowska
Głogoczów
Dobczyce
Lipnica Murowana
Tymowa
Tuchów
Ryglice
Kobiernice
Andrychów
Barwałd
Sułkowice
Myślenice
Zakliczyn
Gromnik
Czchów
Olszyny
Międzybrodzie Bielskie
Stróża
Wiśniowa
Łososina
Jez. Rożnowskie
Sucha-Beskidzka
Zembrzyce
Maków Podhalański
Tymbark
Limanowa
Rożnowice
Bobowa
Łękawica
Lubień
Kasina-Wlk.
Szczyrk
Żywiec
Lachowice
Jordanów
Mszana Dolna
Nowy Sącz
Grybów
Gorlice
Trzetrzewina
Zawoja
Polica 1369
Rabka
Stary Sącz
Ropa
Szymbark
Krzyżowa
Sidzina
Chabówka
Lubomierz
Szczawa
Węgierska-Górka
Milówka
Babiogórski
Gorczański
Turbacz 1310
Ochotnica-Dolna
Zabrzeż
Łabów
Podwilk
Klikuszowa
Beskydy
Oravská Polhora
Rajcza
Żywiecki
Mutné
Oravské Veselé
Rabča
Jablonka
Nowy Targ
Ochotnica-Górna
Beskid Sądecki
Popradzki
Rytro
Krościenko nad Dunajcem
Radziejowa 1262
Piwniczna
Krynica
Łopuszna
Horná Orava
Námestovo
J. Oravské
Vodná nádriž Orava
Czarny-Dunajec
Pieninski
Szczawnica
Jaworzyna 1114
Niedzica
Zákamenné
Spišská Stará Ves
Pieninský
Muszyna
Tylicz
Nová Bystrica
Oravská Lesná
Lokca
Trstená
Chochołów
Poronin
Bukowina Tatrzańska
NANEBOVZDANIA PANNY MÁRIE
Kamienka
Hniezdne
Stará Ľubovňa
Malcov
Hruštín
Nižná
Tvrdošín
Zakopane
Spišské-Hanušovce
Zázrivá
Oravsky-Podzámok
Ždiar
Ľubotín
Terchová
ROHÁČE
Zuberec
Tatrzański
Javorina
JASKYŇA BELIANSKA
Lomnický štít 2632
Podolínec
Plavnica
Mincol 1157
Dolný Kubín
Tatry
Jakubany
Slovenská-Ves
Ihľany
KAŠTIEĽ STRÁŽKY
Lipany
Fatra
Párnica
Bystrá 2248
Kriváň 2494
Gerlachovský štít 2655
Spišská Belá
Kraľovany
Valaská Dubová
Tatranský
Tatranská-Lomnica
Kežmarok
Brezovica
Torysa
HRAD LIKAVKA
Liptovský Mikuláš
Pribylina
Štrbské Pleso
Starý Smokovec
Likavka
Okoličné
Veľká Lomnica
Nižné Repaše
Sučany
Vrbov
Jarovnice
Ružomberok
Liptovský Hrádok
Važec
Svit
Poprad
Levoča
Vlkolínec
Hýbe
Východná
VAŽECKÁ JASKYŇA
Veľ'ka Fatra
Hranovnica
Spišský Štvrtok
Spišské Podhradie
SPIŠSKÝ HRAD
Široké
ĽADOVÁ JASKYŇA
Nízke Tatry
DEMÄNOVSKÁ JASKYŇA SLOBODY
Liptovská Osada
MARCELOV HRAD
Hrabušice
Spišské Vlachy
Nižná Boca
Chopok 2024
Liptovská-Teplička
Spišská Nová Ves
Markušovce
Krompachy
Liptovská-Lúžna
Vernár
Slovenský Raj
Novoveská Huta
PLEJSY
Jaklovce
Gelnica
Ostredok 1592
Donovaly
CHOPOK
Kráľova hoľa 1948
Jarabá
Heľpa
Polomka
Pohorelá
Telgárt
Dobšiná
Nálepkovo
DOBŠINSKÁ ĽADOVÁ JASKYŇA
Hnilec
Valaská
Hron
Brezno
Podbrezová
Brusno
HRAD ĽUPČA
Ul'anka
Fabova hoľa 1439
Červená-Skala
Vlachovo
Zlatý stôl 1322
Mnisek nad Hnilcom
Kojšovská hoľa 1246
Stolica 1476
Slovenská Ľupča
HRAD BANSKÁ BYSTRICA
Pohronská Polhora
Muránska planina
MURÁNSKY HRAD
Murán
Rudohorie
Smolník
Čierny Balog
Gemerská Poloma
Medzev
Banská Bystrica
Poniky
Slovenské
Slavošovce
Roštár
Štos
Jasov
Tisovec
Revúca
Rožňava
Krásnohorské Podhradie
Poľana 1458
Štítnik
Turňa nad Bodvou
Sliač
Lom
Jelšava
Brzotín
Moldava nad Bodvou
Očová
Klenovec
Hnúšťa
Ratková
GOMBASECK JASKYŇA
Jablonov nad Turňou
Zvolenská Slatina
Detva
Látky
Kokava
Zvolen
Hriňová
Slovenský kras
Komjáti
VIGLASSKÝ HRAD
Kriváň
Rimavská Baňa
Plešivec
Aggteleki
Dobrá Niva
KAŠTIEĽ DIVÍN
Divín
Málinec
Mýtna
Veľký Blahovo
Gemerská Ves
Jósvafő
Aggtelek
Rakaca
Szalonna
Gagyvendégi
Lovinobaňa
Cinobaňa
JASKYŇA DOMICA
Ragály
Szendrő
Pliešovce
Horný Tisovník
Poltár
Rimavská Sobota
Tornaľa
Senohrad
Šuľa
Tomášovce
Kalinovo
Ožďany
Bátka
Rudabánya
Lak
Kupa
Krupina
Kelemér
Izsófalva
Litava
Lučenec
Hodejov
Jesenké
Rimavská Seč
Bánréve
Putnok
Edelény
Cerovo
Dolná Strehová
Fiľakovo
Lenartovce
Šimonovce
Sajókaza
Homrogd
Modrý Kameň
KAŠTIEĽ VEĽKÝ KRTÍŠ
KAŠTIEĽ V. FIĽAKOVO
Radzovce
Hajnáčka
Ózd
Kazincbarcika
Boldva
Halmaj
Litke
Veľký Krtíš
HRAD SÖMÖSKA
Somoskőújfalu
Arló
Sajószentpéter
Szikszó
Hrušov
Čebovce
Bušince
Csernely
Ládbesenyő
Sajóvámos
Lénárddaróc
Edestapolcsány
PALLAVICINI

1
2
3
A
B
4°
3°
48°
47°
Cork
Rosslare
Plymouth
Côte de Granit Rose
Sillon de Talbert
Île de Bréhat
Plougrescant
Ploumanach
Perros-Guirec
Trégastel- Plage
Pleubian
Pte. de l'Arcouest
Ploubazlanec
Tréguier
Lézardrieux
Paimpol
Trébeurden
Pleumeur-Bodou
Lannion
La Roche Derrien
LA ROCHE JAGU
Ploučzec
Île de Batz
Roscoff
St. Pol-de-Léon
Primel-Trégastel
Plougasnou
Locquirec
St. Efflam
St. Michel-en-Grève
Plestin-les-Grèves
Pontrieux
Plouha
Brignogan-Plage
Kerlouan
Cléder
Plouescat
Carantec
Lanmeur
Bégard
Lanvollon
Plouguerneau
NOTRE DAME
Lesneven
Lannilis
Portsall
Plouzévédé
CHÂTEAU DE KERJEAN
Taulé
Plouaret
Binic
Porspoder
Le Folgoet
Ploudalmézeau
St. Thégonnec
Morlaix
Plouigneau
Louargat
Guingamp
Châtelaudren
Plougonven
Belle-Isle-en-Terre
Plabennec
Landivisiau
Pleyber-Christ
Lannéanou
Plougonver
Mousteru
Plouagat
St. Brieuc
Lanildut
Plouarzel
St. Renan
Ploudiry
Landerneau
Guipavas
Brest
Sizun
St. Sauveur
Mts. d'Arrée
Callac
Bourbriac
Quintin
Le Conquet
Plougastel-Daoulas
Daoulas
Kérien
Pte. de St. Mathieu
Camaret-sur-Mer
TOUR VAUBAN
Landévennec
Le Faou
Huelgoat
Poullaouen
B
Armorique
Brasparts
St. Nicolas-du-Pélem
Corlay
Uzel
Pte. de Penhir
Crozon
Morgat
Pont-de-Buis-lès-Quimerch
Carhaix-Plouguer
Maël-Carhaix
Plounévez-Quintin
Rostrenen
Mer d'Iroise
Châteaulin
Playben
Glomel
Gouarec
Baie de Douarnenez
Châteauneuf-du-Faou
Spézet
Mur-de-Bretagne
Aulne
Mts. Noires
ST. RONAN
Locronan
Gourin
Roudouallec
Plouray
Cléguérec
Douarnenez
Briec
Noyal-Pontivy
Plogoff
Pte. du Raz
Pont-Croix
Coray
Guiscriff
Odet
Le Faouët
Guémené-sur-Scorff
Pontivy
Audierne
Plouhinec
Quimper
Llandudec
Scaër
Kernascléden
Plozévet
Plogastel-St. Germain
Rosporden
Bannalec
Scorff
Bubry
Pluméliau
Blavet
Ploinéour-Lanvern
Fouesnant
CHÂTEAU DE KRIOLET
Concarneau
Arzano
Plouay
Pont-l'Abbé
Bénodet
Quimperlé
Baud
Locminé
St. Guénolé
Penmarch
Loctudy
Trégunc
Névez
Pont-Aven
Riec-sur-Belon
Moëlan-sur-Mer
Pont Scorff
Languidic
Camors
Pte. de Penmarch
Lesconil
Guilvinec
Port Manech
Clohars-Carnoët
Hennebont
Lanester
Landévant
Pluvigner
Le Pouldu
Lorient
Ploemeur
Îles de Glénan
Larmor-Plage
Port Louis
Ste. Anne-d'Auray
Auray
Vannes
Belz
Groix
Île de Groix
Carnac
La Trinité
Locmariaquer
Port-Navalo
Côte Sauvage
Presqu'île de Quiberon
Baie de Quiberon
St. Pierre-Quiberon
St. Gildas-de-Rhuys
Quiberon
Île de Houat
Sauzon
Le Palais
Bangor
Locmaria
Belle-Île
E50
E60
138
129
0
10
20
30 km

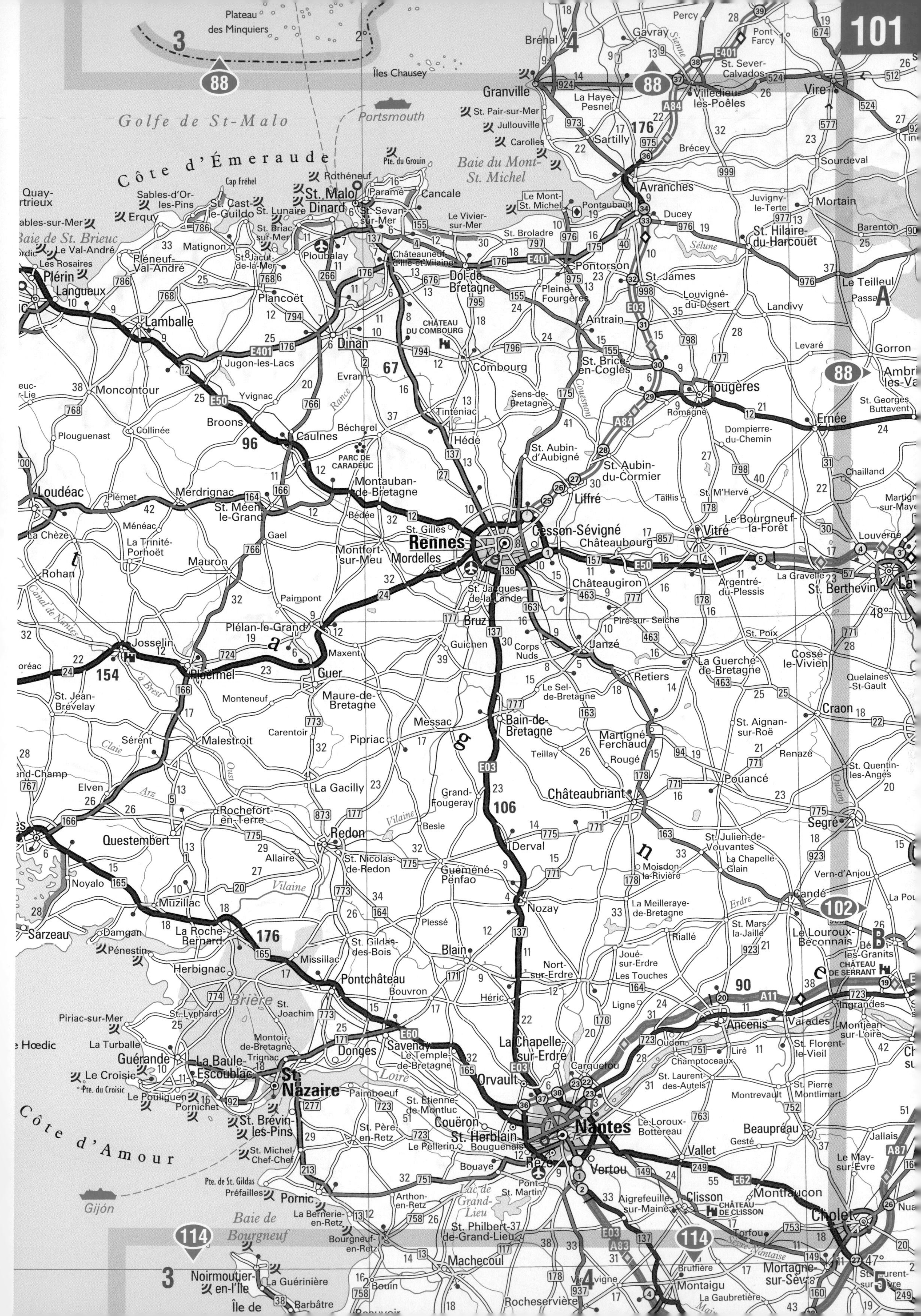

Plateau des Minquiers
Îles Chausey
Golfe de St-Malo
Portsmouth
Côte d'Émeraude
Cap Fréhel
Baie du Mont-St. Michel
Pte. du Grouin
Granville
St. Pair-sur-Mer
Jullouville
Carolles
Bréhal
Gavray
Percy
Pont Farcy
Villedieu-les-Poêles
St. Sever-Calvados
Vire
La Haye-Pesnel
Sartilly
Brécey
Sourdeval
Avranches
Juvigny-le-Terte
Mortain
Ducey
St. Hilaire-du-Harcouët
Barenton
Le Mont-St. Michel
Pontaubault
Le Vivier-sur-Mer
St. Broladre
Pontorson
St. James
Le Teilleul
Cancale
Rothéneuf
St. Malo
Paramé
Dinard
St. Sevan-sur-Mer
St. Lunaire
St. Briac-sur-Mer
Sables-d'Or-les-Pins
St. Cast-le-Guildo
Erquy
Baie de St. Brieuc
Le Val-André
Les Rosaires
Pléneuf-Val-André
Matignon
St. Jacut-de-la-Mer
Ploubalay
Châteauneuf-d'Ille-et-Vilaine
Dol-de-Bretagne
Pleine-Fougères
Louvigné-du-Désert
Landivy
Plérin
Langueux
Lamballe
Plancoët
Dinan
Château du Combourg
Combourg
Antrain
St. Brice-en-Coglès
Fougères
Levaré
Gorron
Jugon-les-Lacs
Moncontour
Yvignac
Evran
Tinténiac
Sens-de-Bretagne
Romagné
Ernée
St. Georges-Buttavent
Plouguenast
Collinée
Broons
Caulnes
Bécherel
Parc de Caradeuc
Hédé
St. Aubin-d'Aubigné
St. Aubin-du-Cormier
Dompierre-du-Chemin
Chailland
Loudéac
Plémet
Merdrignac
St. Méen-le-Grand
Montauban-de-Bretagne
Liffré
Taillis
St. M'Hervé
Ménéac
La Trinité-Porhoët
Gael
Bédée
St. Gilles
Rennes
Cesson-Sévigné
Châteaubourg
Vitré
Le Bourgneuf-la-Forêt
Louverné
La Chèze
Rohan
Mauron
Montfort-sur-Meu
Mordelles
Châteaugiron
Argentré-du-Plessis
La Gravelle
St. Berthevin
Canal de Nantes à Brest
Paimpont
St. Jacques-de-la-Lande
Piré-sur-Seiche
Plélan-le-Grand
Bruz
St. Poix
Josselin
Maxent
Guichen
Corps Nuds
Janzé
Cossé-le-Vivien
Ploërmel
Guer
La Guerche-de-Bretagne
Retiers
Quelaines-St-Gault
St. Jean-Brévelay
Monteneuf
Maure-de-Bretagne
Le Sel-de-Bretagne
Craon
Messac
Bain-de-Bretagne
St. Aignan-sur-Roë
Sérent
Malestroit
Carentoir
Pipriac
Martigné-Ferchaud
Claie
Oust
Teillay
Rougé
Renazé
Elven
La Gacilly
Grand-Fougeray
St. Quentin-les-Anges
Pouancé
Arz
Châteaubriant
Rochefort-en-Terre
Redon
Vilaine
Besle
Segré
Questembert
Allaire
Derval
St. Julien-de-Vouvantes
La Chapelle-Glain
St. Nicolas-de-Redon
Guémené-Penfao
Moisdon-la-Rivière
Vern-d'Anjou
Noyalo
Muzillac
Nozay
La Meilleraye-de-Bretagne
Candé
Erdre
Sarzeau
Damgan
La Roche-Bernard
Plessé
St. Mars-la-Jaille
Le Louroux-Béconnais
Pénestin
St. Gildas-des-Bois
Blain
Rialle
Joué-sur-Erdre
Les Touches
Château de Serrant
Herbignac
Missillac
Pontchâteau
Nort-sur-Erdre
Bouvron
Héric
Ligné
Ancenis
Varades
Ingrandes
Montjean-sur-Loire
Brière
St. Joachim
St-Lyphard
Piriac-sur-Mer
La Turballe
Hoedic
Montoir-de-Bretagne
Trignac
Donges
Savenay
Le Temple-de-Bretagne
La Chapelle-sur-Erdre
Oudon
Liré
St. Florent-le-Vieil
Guérande
La Baule-Escoublac
Le Croisic
Pte. du Croisic
Le Pouliguen
Pornichet
St. Nazaire
Paimboeuf
Orvault
Carquefou
Champtoceaux
St. Laurent-des-Autels
St. Pierre Montlimart
Montrevault
St. Étienne-de-Montluc
Loire
Côte d'Amour
St. Brévin-les-Pins
St. Père-en-Retz
Couëron
St. Herblain
Nantes
Le Loroux-Bottereau
Beaupréau
Jallais
St. Michel-Chef-Chef
Le Pellerin
Bouguenais
Vallet
Gesté
Le May-sur-Evre
Bouaye
Rezé
Vertou
Pte. de St. Gildas
Préfailles
Pornic
Gijón
Baie de Bourgneuf
La Bernerie-en-Retz
Arthon-en-Retz
Lac de Grand-Lieu
Pont-St. Martin
Aigrefeuille-sur-Maine
Clisson
Château de Clisson
Montfaucon
Cholet
Bourgneuf-en-Retz
St. Philbert-de-Grand-Lieu
Torfou
Sèvre-Nantaise
Machecoul
Noirmoutier-en-l'Île
La Guérinière
Barbâtre
Île de
Bouin
Rocheservière
Vieillevigne
Montaigu
Brufière
La Gaubretière
Mortagne-sur-Sèvre
St. Laurent-sur-Sèvre
48°
47°
2°
88
114
102
A
B

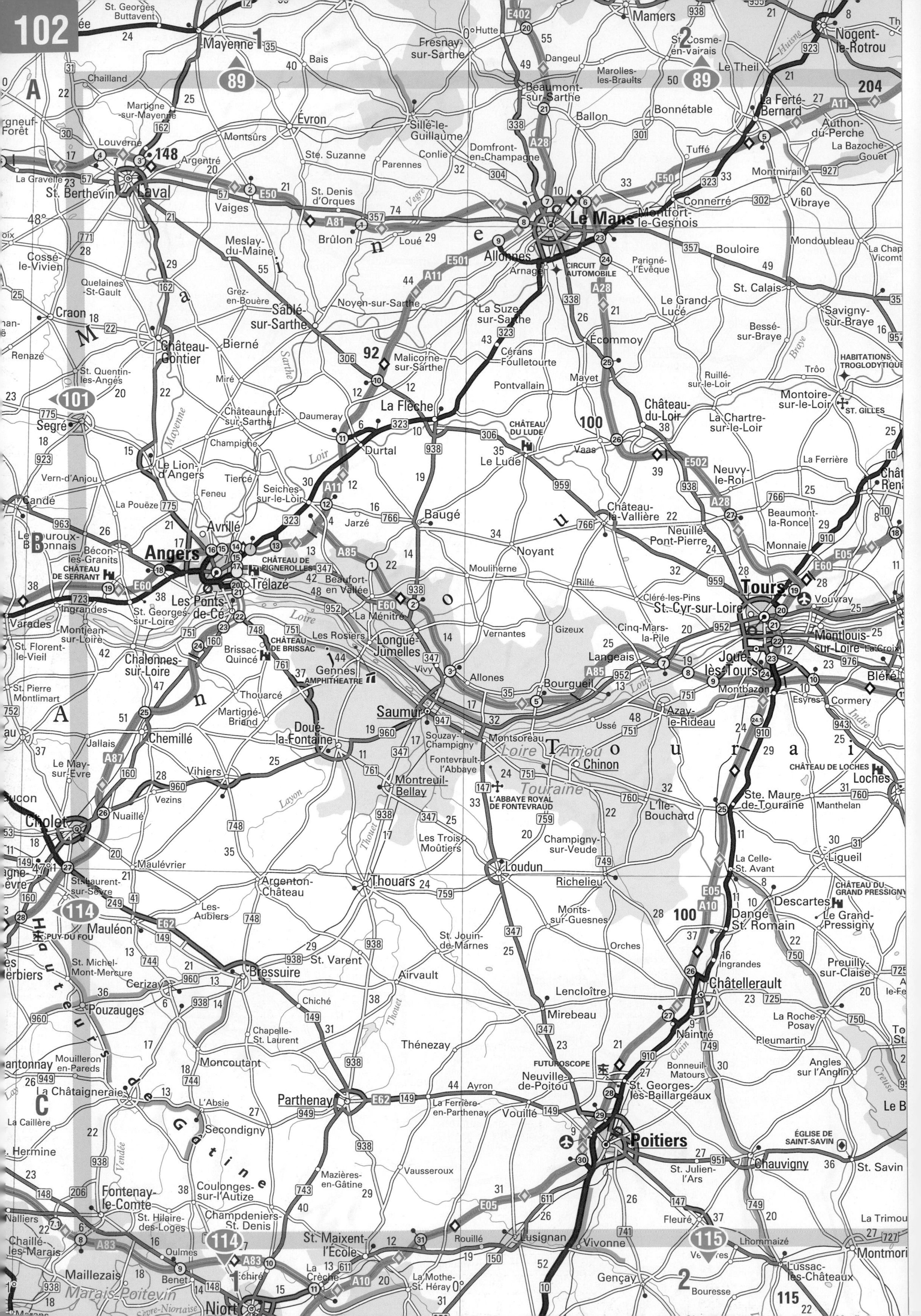
St. Georges-Buttavent
Mayenne
Hutte
Fresnay-sur-Sarthe
Mamers
St. Cosme-en-Vairais
Nogent-le-Rotrou
Bais
Chailland
Dangeul
Marolles-les-Braults
Le Theil
Beaumont-sur-Sarthe
Martigné-sur-Mayenne
Évron
Sillé-le-Guillaume
Ballon
Bonnétable
La Ferté-Bernard
Authon-du-Perche
Louverné
Montsûrs
Domfront-en-Champagne
Tuffé
La Bazoche-Gouet
Argentré
Ste. Suzanne
Conlie
Parennes
Montmirail
La Gravelle
St. Berthevin
Laval
Vaiges
St. Denis d'Orques
Connerré
Vibraye
Le Mans
Montfort-le-Gesnois
Brûlon
Loué
Meslay-du-Maine
Cossé-le-Vivien
Allonnes
Arnage
Circuit Automobile
Parigné-l'Évêque
Bouloire
Mondoubleau
Quelaines-St-Gault
Grez-en-Bouère
Sablé-sur-Sarthe
Noyen-sur-Sarthe
La Suze-sur-Sarthe
Le Grand-Lucé
St. Calais
Savigny-sur-Braye
Bessé-sur-Braye
Craon
Renazé
Château-Gontier
Bierné
Malicorne-sur-Sarthe
Cérans-Foulletourte
Écommoy
St. Quentin-les-Anges
Miré
Pontvallain
Mayet
Ruillé-sur-le-Loir
Trôo
Habitations Troglodytiques
Segré
Châteauneuf-sur-Sarthe
Daumeray
La Flèche
Château-du-Loir
La Chartre-sur-le-Loir
Montoire-sur-le-Loir
St. Gilles
Champigné
Château du Lude
Le Lude
Vaas
Durtal
Le Lion-d'Angers
Vern-d'Anjou
Tiercé
Seiches-sur-le-Loir
Neuvy-le-Roi
La Ferrière
Candé
La Pouëze
Feneu
Baugé
Jarzé
Château-la-Vallière
Neuillé-Pont-Pierre
Beaumont-la-Ronce
Monnaie
Le Louroux-Béconnais
Avrillé
Angers
Bécon-les-Granits
Château de Serrant
Château de Pignerolles
Noyant
Mouliherne
Trélazé
Beaufort-en-Vallée
Rillé
Cléré-les-Pins
St. Cyr-sur-Loire
Tours
Vouvray
Varades
Ingrandes
St. Georges-sur-Loire
Les Ponts-de-Cé
La Ménitré
Montjean-sur-Loire
Les Rosiers
Longué-Jumelles
Vernantes
Gizeux
Cinq-Mars-la-Pile
Montlouis-sur-Loire
St. Florent-le-Vieil
Chalonnes-sur-Loire
Brissac-Quincé
Château de Brissac
Gennes
Amphithéâtre
Vivy
Allonnes
Langeais
Joué-lès-Tours
Bléré
St. Pierre-Montlimart
Thouarcé
Bourgueil
Montbazon
Esvres
Cormery
Martigné-Briand
Saumur
Azay-le-Rideau
Ussé
Chemillé
Jallais
Doué-la-Fontaine
Souzay-Champigny
Montsoreau
Chinon
Fontevrault-l'Abbaye
Le May-sur-Èvre
Vihiers
Montreuil-Bellay
L'Abbaye Royal de Fontevraud
L'Île-Bouchard
Ste. Maure-de-Touraine
Château de Loches
Loches
Manthelan
Cholet
Nuaillé
Vezins
Les Trois Moûtiers
Champigny-sur-Veude
Maulévrier
Loudun
Richelieu
La Celle-St. Avant
Ligueil
St. Laurent-sur-Sèvre
Argenton-Château
Thouars
Château du Grand Pressigny
Descartes
Le Grand-Pressigny
Mauléon
Puy-du-Fou
Les Aubiers
Monts-sur-Guesnes
Dangé-St. Romain
St. Jouin-de-Marnes
Orches
St. Michel-Mont-Mercure
St. Varent
Bressuire
Airvault
Ingrandes
Preuilly-sur-Claise
Cerizay
Pouzauges
Chiché
Lencloître
Châtellerault
Mirebeau
La Roche-Posay
Chapelle-St. Laurent
Thénezay
Naintré
Pleumartin
Mouilleron-en-Pareds
Moncoutant
Futuroscope
Bonneuil-Matours
Angles sur l'Anglin
La Châtaigneraie
Neuville-de-Poitou
Parthenay
Ayron
La Ferrière-en-Parthenay
St. Georges-lès-Baillargeaux
L'Absie
Vouillé
La Caillère
Secondigny
Poitiers
Église de Saint-Savin
Chauvigny
St. Savin
St. Julien-l'Ars
Vausseroux
Mazières-en-Gâtine
Fontenay-le-Comte
Coulonges-sur-l'Autize
St. Hilaire-des-Loges
Champdeniers-St. Denis
Fleuré
La Trimouille
Chaillé-les-Marais
St. Maixent-l'École
Rouillé
Lusignan
Vivonne
Lhommaizé
Montmorillon
Oulmes
Maillezais
Benet
La Crèche
La Mothe-St. Héray
Gençay
Lussac-les-Châteaux
Marais Poitevin
Niort
Bouresse
Maine
Anjou
Touraine
Haute Gâtine

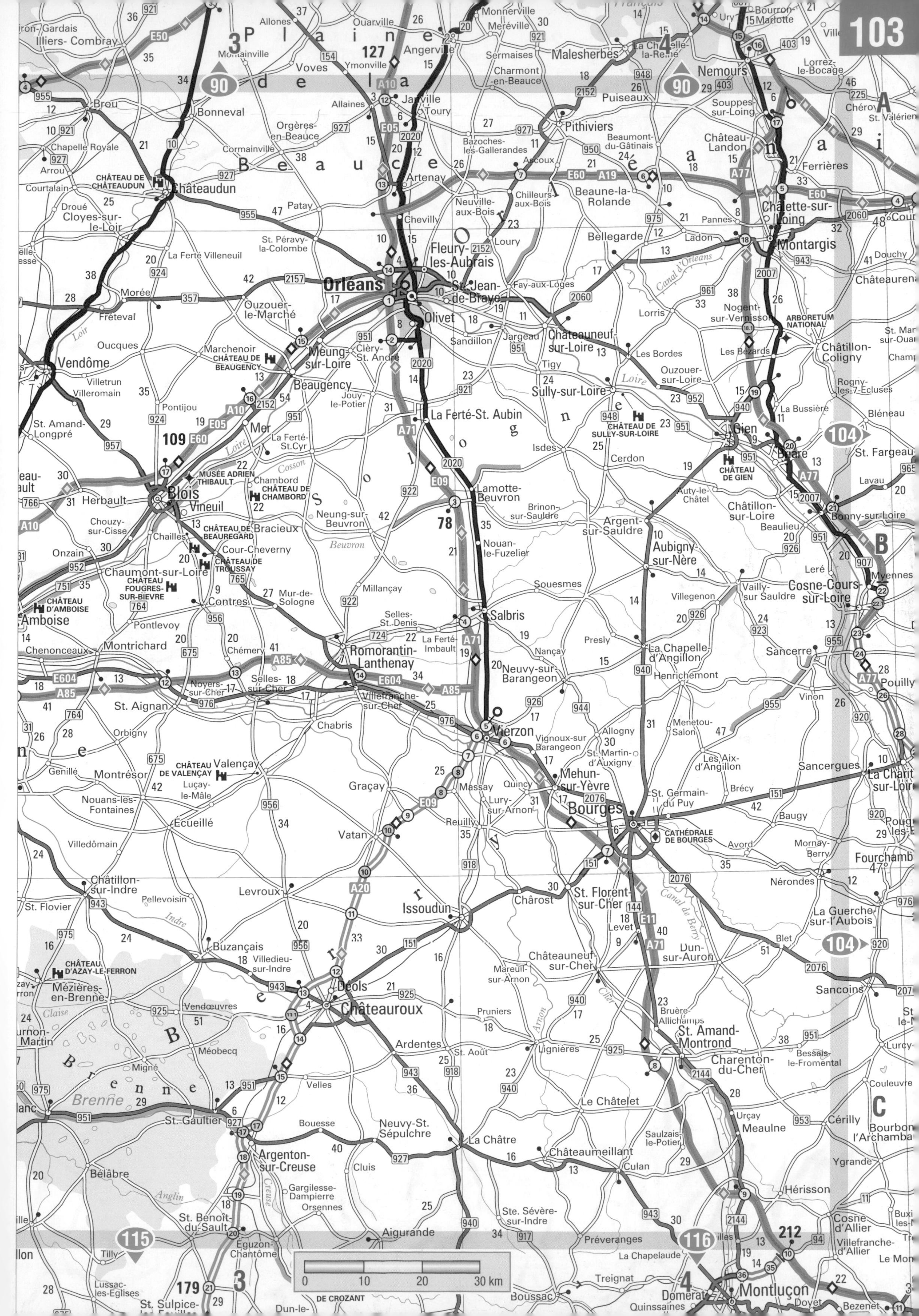

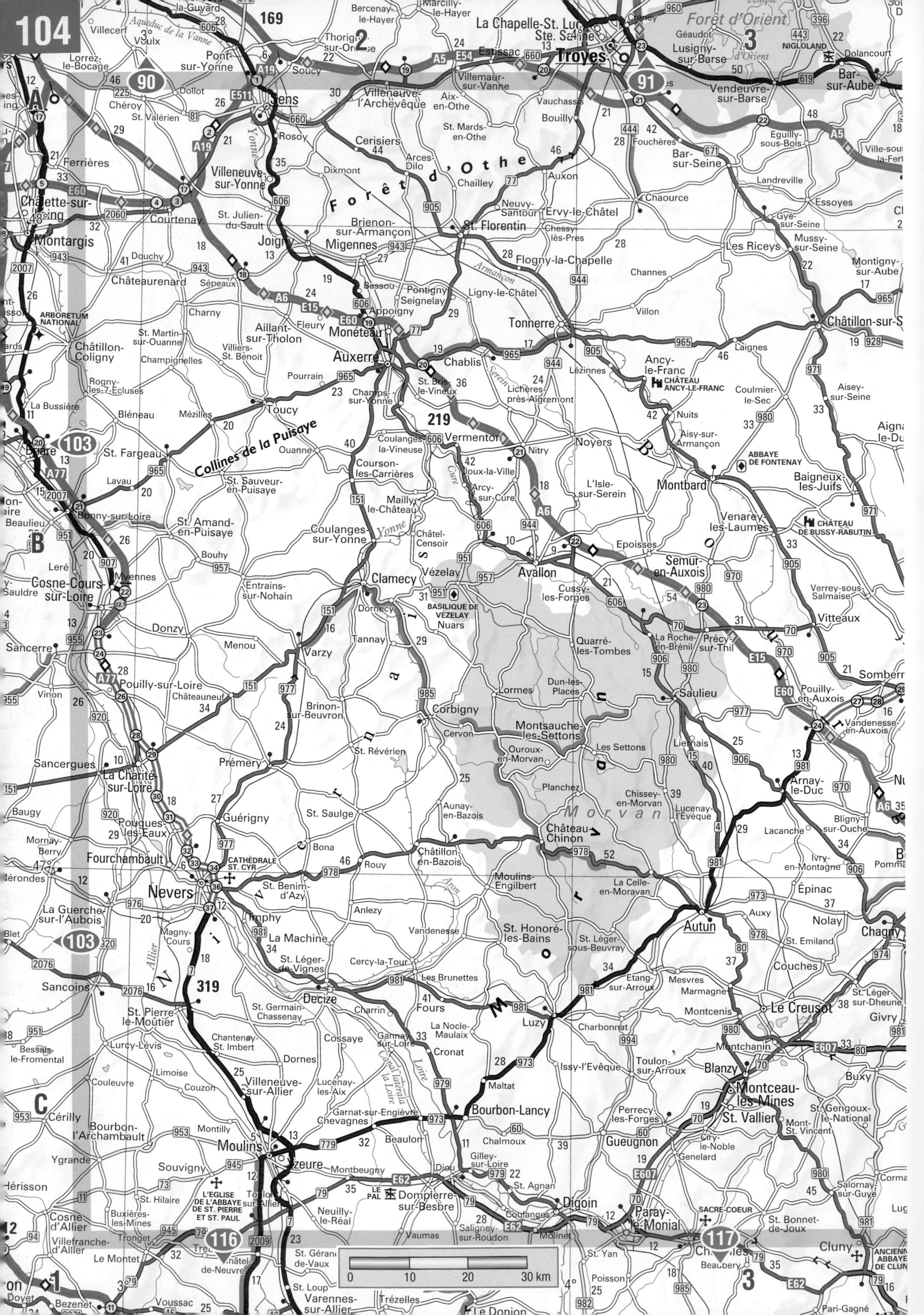
Villecerf
Voulx
Lorrez-le-Bocage
Pont-sur-Yonne
Aqueduc de la Vanne
Bercenay-le-Hayer
Marcilly-le-Hayer
Thorigny-sur-Oreuse
La Chapelle-St. Luc
Ste. Savine
Troyes
Forêt d'Orient
Géraudot
Lusigny-sur-Barse
NIGLOLAND
Dolancourt
Bar-sur-Aube
Estissac
Soucy
Sens
Dollot
Chéroy
St. Valérien
Villeneuve-l'Archevêque
Villemaur-sur-Vanne
Aix-en-Othe
Vauchassis
Bouilly
Vendeuvre-sur-Barse
Eguilly-sous-Bois
Ville-sous-la-Ferté
Rosoy
Cerisiers
St. Mards-en-Othe
Fouchères
Bar-sur-Seine
Ferrières
Villeneuve-sur-Yonne
Dixmont
Arces-Dilo
Forêt d'Othe
Chailley
Auxon
Landreville
Châlette-sur-Loing
Montargis
Courtenay
St. Julien-du-Sault
Joigny
Brienon-sur-Armançon
Migennes
Neuvy-Sautour
St. Florentin
Ervy-le-Châtel
Chessy-lès-Prés
Chaource
Gyé-sur-Seine
Essoyes
Les Riceys
Mussy-sur-Seine
Montigny-sur-Aube
Douchy
Châteaurenard
Sépeaux
Bassou
Pontigny
Seignelay
Appoigny
Flogny-la-Chapelle
Armançon
Channes
Ligny-le-Châtel
Villon
ARBORETUM NATIONAL
Charny
St. Martin-sur-Ouanne
Aillant-sur-Tholon
Fleury
Monéteau
Tonnerre
Châtillon-sur-Seine
Laignes
Châtillon-Coligny
Champignelles
Villiers-St. Benoit
Auxerre
Chablis
Lézinnes
Ancy-le-Franc
CHÂTEAU ANCY-LE-FRANC
Coulmier-le-Sec
Aisey-sur-Seine
Rogny-les-7-Ecluses
Pourrain
Champs-sur-Yonne
St. Bris-le-Vineux
Lichères-près-Aigremont
Serein
La Bussière
Bléneau
Mézilles
Toucy
Nuits
Collines de la Puisaye
Coulanges-la-Vineuse
Vermenton
Nitry
Noyers
Aisy-sur-Armançon
ABBAYE DE FONTENAY
Briare
St. Fargeau
Ouanne
Courson-les-Carrières
Joux-la-Ville
Arcy-sur-Cure
Cure
L'Isle-sur-Serein
Montbard
Baigneux-les-Juifs
Lavau
St. Sauveur-en-Puisaye
Mailly-le-Château
Venarey-les-Laumes
CHÂTEAU DE BUSSY-RABUTIN
Bonny-sur-Loire
Beaulieu
St. Amand-en-Puisaye
Coulanges-sur-Yonne
Yonne
Châtel-Censoir
Epoisses
Semur-en-Auxois
Bouhy
Avallon
Léré
Cosne-Cours-sur-Loire
Myennes
Entrains-sur-Nohain
Clamecy
Vézelay
BASILIQUE DE VÉZELAY
Cussy-les-Forges
Verrey-sous-Salmaise
Dornecy
Nuars
Donzy
Sancerre
Menou
Varzy
Tannay
Quarré-les-Tombes
La Roche-en-Brénil
Précy-sous-Thil
Vitteaux
Pouilly-sur-Loire
Vinon
Châteauneuf
Brinon-sur-Beuvron
Corbigny
Lormes
Dun-les-Places
Saulieu
Pouilly-en-Auxois
Sombernon
Vandenesse-en-Auxois
Cervon
Montsauche-les-Settons
Ouroux-en-Morvan
Les Settons
Liernais
Sancergues
La Charité-sur-Loire
Prémery
St. Révérien
Planchez
Arnay-le-Duc
Chissey-en-Morvan
Morvan
Lucenay-l'Evêque
Baugy
Pougues-les-Eaux
Guérigny
St. Saulge
Aunay-en-Bazois
Château-Chinon
Bligny-sur-Ouche
Lacanche
Mornay-Berry
Fourchambault
Bona
Rouy
Châtillon-en-Bazois
CATHÉDRALE ST. CYR
Ivry-en-Montagne
Nevers
St. Benim-d'Azy
Moulins-Engilbert
La Celle-en-Moravan
Epinac
La Guerche-sur-l'Aubois
Imphy
Anlezy
Aron
Auxy
Nolay
Autun
Magny-Cours
Allier
La Machine
Vandenesse
St. Honoré-les-Bains
St. Léger-sous-Beuvray
St. Emiland
Chagny
St. Léger-de-Vignes
Cercy-la-Tour
Couches
Sancoins
Decize
Les Brunettes
Etang-sur-Arroux
Mesvres
Marmagne
St. Léger-sur-Dheune
St. Pierre-le-Moûtier
St. Germain-Chassenay
Charrin
Fours
Luzy
Montcenis
Le Creusot
Givry
Nivernais
La Nocle-Maulaix
Charbonnat
Bessais-le-Fromental
Lurcy-Lévis
Chantenay-St. Imbert
Cossaye
Garnay-sur-Loire
Cronat
Montchanin
Limoise
Dornes
Issy-l'Evêque
Toulon-sur-Arroux
Blanzy
Couleuvre
Couzon
Villeneuve-sur-Allier
Lucenay-les-Aix
Canal latéral à la Loire
Loire
Maltat
Montceau-les-Mines
Buxy
Cérilly
Bourbon-l'Archambault
Montilly
Garnat-sur-Engièvre
Chevagnes
Bourbon-Lancy
Perrecy-les-Forges
St. Vallier
St. Gengoux-le-National
Mont-St. Vincent
Moulins
Beaulon
Chalmoux
Gueugnon
Ciry-le-Noble
Genelard
Ygrande
Souvigny
Yzeure
Montbeugny
Dio
Gilley-sur-Loire
St. Agnan
Hérisson
L'EGLISE DE L'ABBAYE DE ST. PIERRE ET ST. PAUL
Toulon-sur-Allier
LE PAL
Dompierre-sur-Besbre
Digoin
Salornay-sur-Guye
St. Hilaire
Buxières-les-Mines
Cosne-d'Allier
Villefranche-d'Allier
Neuilly-le-Réal
Coulanges
SACRE-COEUR
Paray-le-Monial
St. Bonnet-de-Joux
Tronget
Vaumas
Saligney-sur-Roudon
Molinet
Cluny
ANCIENNE ABBAYE DE CLUNY
Le Montet
St. Gérand-de-Vaux
St. Yan
Charolles
Beaubery
Châtel-de-Neuvre
Poisson
Doyet
Bezenet
Voussac
St. Loup
Varennes-sur-Allier
Trézelles
Le Donjon
Pari-Gagné
0
10
20
30 km

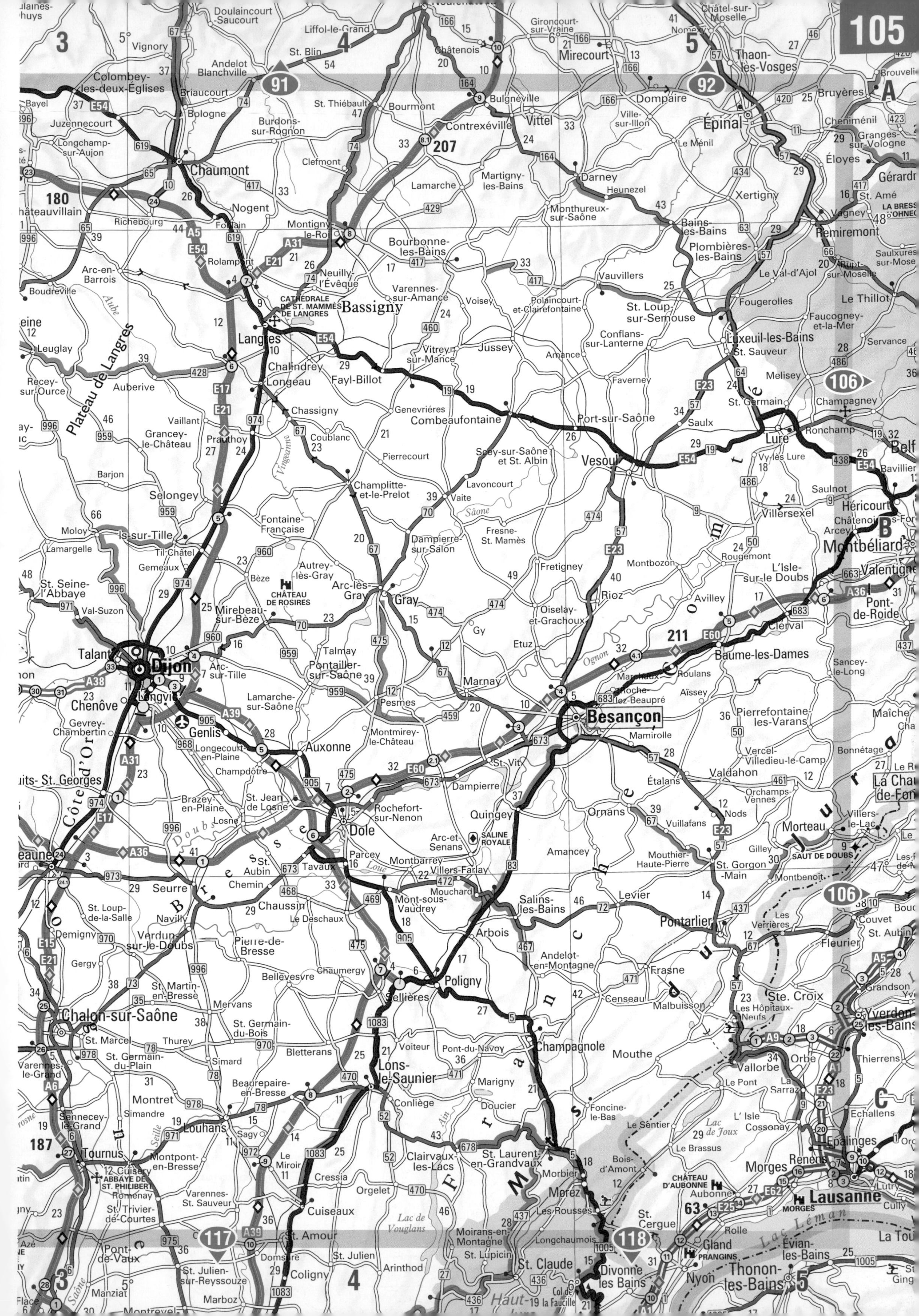

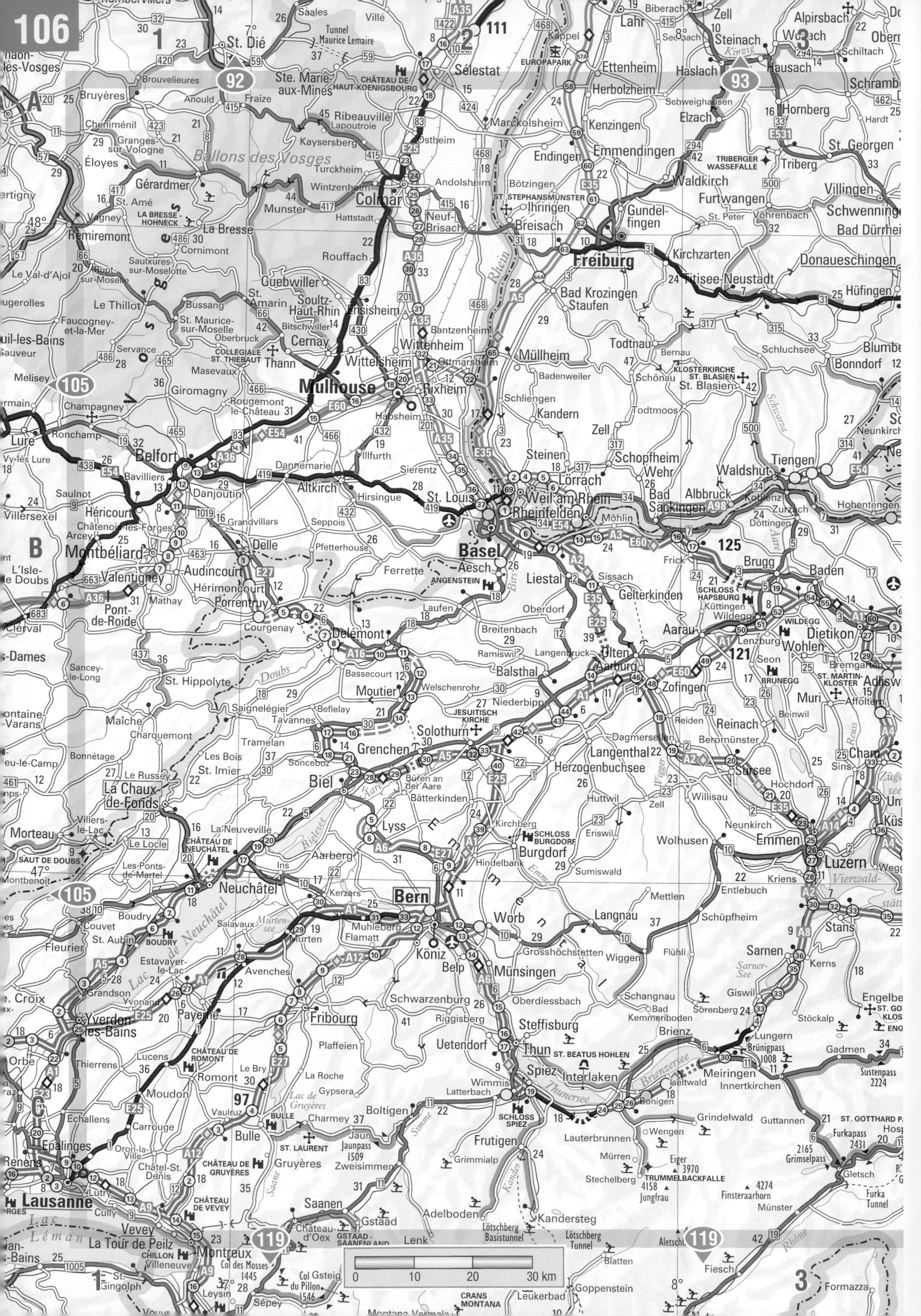
St. Dié
Saales
Villé
Tunnel Maurice Lemaire
Sélestat
Ste. Marie-aux-Mines
Château de Haut-Koenigsbourg
Brouvelieures
Bruyères
Anould
Fraize
Ribeauvillé
Lapoutroie
Kaysersberg
Cheniménil
Granges-sur-Vologne
Ballons des Vosges
Éloyes
Gérardmer
St. Amé
Vagney
La Bresse-Hohneck
La Bresse
Remiremont
Cornimont
Le Val-d'Ajol
Rupt-sur-Moselle
Saulxures-sur-Moselotte
Le Thillot
Bussang
St. Maurice-sur-Moselle
Oberbruck
Faucogney-et-la-Mer
Servance
Collegiale St. Thiebaut
Thann
Masevaux
Melisey
Giromagny
Rougemont-le-Château
Champagney
Lure
Ronchamp
Belfort
Bavilliers
Danjoutin
Héricourt
Villersexel
Saulnot
Châtenois-les-Forges
Arcey
Montbéliard
Valentigney
Audincourt
Hérimoncourt
L'Isle-le-Doubs
Pont-de-Roide
Mathay
Clerval
Sancey-le-Long
St. Hippolyte
Doubs
Maîche
Charquemont
Bonnétage
Le Russey
La Chaux-de-Fonds
Le Locle
Morteau
Villers-le-Lac
Saut de Doubs
Les-Ponts-de-Martel
Montbenoît
Neuchâtel
Château de Neuchâtel
Boudry
Couvet
St. Aubin
Fleurier
Lac de Neuchâtel
Estavayer-le-Lac
Grandson
Yvonand
Yverdon-les-Bains
Orbe
Thierrens
Moudon
Echallens
Epalinges
Renens
Lausanne
Lutry
Cully
Vevey
La Tour de Peilz
Montreux
Chillon
Villeneuve
Lac Léman
St. Gingolph
Leysin
Col des Mosses
Sépey
Col Gstaig du Pillon
Château-d'Oex
Gstaad-Saanenland
Gstaad
Saanen
Lenk
Zweisimmen
Jaunpass
Charmey
Bulle
Château de Gruyères
Gruyères
St. Laurent
Oron-la-Ville
Châtel-St.-Denis
Château de Vevey
Romont
Château de Romont
Lucens
Le Bry
La Roche
Gypsera
Lac de Gruyères
Vaulruz
Payerne
Avenches
Murten
Murtensee
Salavaux
Fribourg
Schwarzenburg
Riggisberg
Plaffeien
Boltigen
Latterbach
Wimmis
Spiez
Schloss Spiez
Thun
St. Beatus Hohlen
Interlaken
Thunersee
Brienzersee
Iseltwald
Bönigen
Brienz
Meiringen
Innertkirchen
Grindelwald
Wengen
Lauterbrunnen
Mürren
Stechelberg
Eiger 3970
Trummelbackfalle
Jungfrau 4158
Finsteraarhorn 4274
Grimselpass 2165
Furkapass 2431
Gletsch
Furka Tunnel
Münster
Guttannen
Sustenpass 2224
Gadmen
St. Gotthard Pass
Frutigen
Grimmialp
Kandersteg
Adelboden
Lötschberg Basistunnel
Lötschberg Tunnel
Goppenstein
Leukerbad
Crans Montana
Blatten
Aletsch
Fiesch
Formazza
Rhône
Uetendorf
Steffisbury
Oberdiessbach
Münsingen
Belp
Köniz
Bern
Muhleberg
Flamatt
Worb
Grosshöchstetten
Langnau
Schangnau
Bad Kemmeriboden
Sörenberg
Flühli
Schüpfheim
Wiggen
Emmental
Trubschachen
Burgdorf
Schloss Burgdorf
Kirchberg
Hindelbank
Sumiswald
Eriswil
Huttwil
Lyss
Aarberg
Ins
Kerzers
Biel
Bielersee
La Neuveville
Büren an der Aare
Bätterkinden
Grenchen
Solothurn
Jesuitisch Kirche
Niederbipp
Welschenrohr
Moutier
Tavannes
Bassecourt
Saignelégier
Beflelay
Tramelan
Les Bois
St. Imier
Sonceboz
Delémont
Courgenay
Porrentruy
Delle
Grandvillars
Laufen
Breitenbach
Balsthal
Oberdorf
Langenbruck
Olten
Aarburg
Zofingen
Langenthal
Herzogenbuchsee
Dagmersellen
Reiden
Willisau
Zell
Wolhusen
Neunkirch
Emmen
Luzern
Kriens
Entlebuch
Mettlen
Sursee
Beromünster
Reinach
Hochdorf
Sins
Cham
Zugersee
Küssnacht
Vierwaldstättersee
Stans
Sarnen
Kerns
Sarnersee
Giswil
Lungern
Brünigpass 1008
Engelberg
St. Goth. Kloster
Stöckalp
Muri
Beinwil
Affoltern
Adliswil
Bremgarten
Wohlen
St. Martin-Kloster
Seon
Brunegg
Lenzburg
Wildegg
Dietikon
Aarau
Küttingen
Schloss Habsburg
Brugg
Baden
Frick
Zurzach
Döttingen
Koblenz
Hohentengen
Gelterkinden
Sissach
Liestal
Aesch
Angenstein
Basel
Ferrette
Pfetterhouse
Seppois
Hirsingue
Altkirch
Dannemarie
Illfurth
Sierentz
St. Louis
Weil am Rhein
Lörrach
Rheinfelden
Möhlin
Bad Säckingen
Wehr
Schopfheim
Steinen
Kandern
Zell
Todtmoos
Waldshut
Albbruck
Tiengen
Bonndorf
Schluchsee
St. Blasien
Klosterkirche St. Blasien
Schönau
Todtnau
Bernau
Blumberg
Neunkirch
Hüfingen
Donaueschingen
Titisee-Neustadt
Kirchzarten
Freiburg
Gundelfingen
St. Peter
Vöhrenbach
Furtwangen
Villingen-Schwenningen
Bad Dürrheim
Waldkirch
Triberg
Triberger Wassefalle
St. Georgen
Hornberg
Elzach
Schramberg
Hardt
Hausach
Haslach
Schiltach
Steinach
Kinzig
Alpirsbach
Wolfach
Oberndorf
Zell
Biberach
Lahr
Seelbach
Kappel
Europapark
Ettenheim
Herbolzheim
Kenzingen
Emmendingen
Endingen
Schweighausen
Marckolsheim
Bötzingen
St. Stephansmünster
Ihringen
Breisach
Neuf-Brisach
Bad Krozingen
Staufen
Müllheim
Badenweiler
Schliengen
Ottmarsheim
Bantzenheim
Rhein
Mulhouse
Rixheim
Habsheim
Wittenheim
Wittelsheim
Ensisheim
Cernay
Bitschwiller
Soultz-Haut-Rhin
St. Amarin
Guebwiller
Rouffach
Hattstadt
Colmar
Andolsheim
Wintzenheim
Turckheim
Munster
Ostheim
Vosges
Sausheim
Leukerbad
Jaun
Sepey
0
10
20
30 km

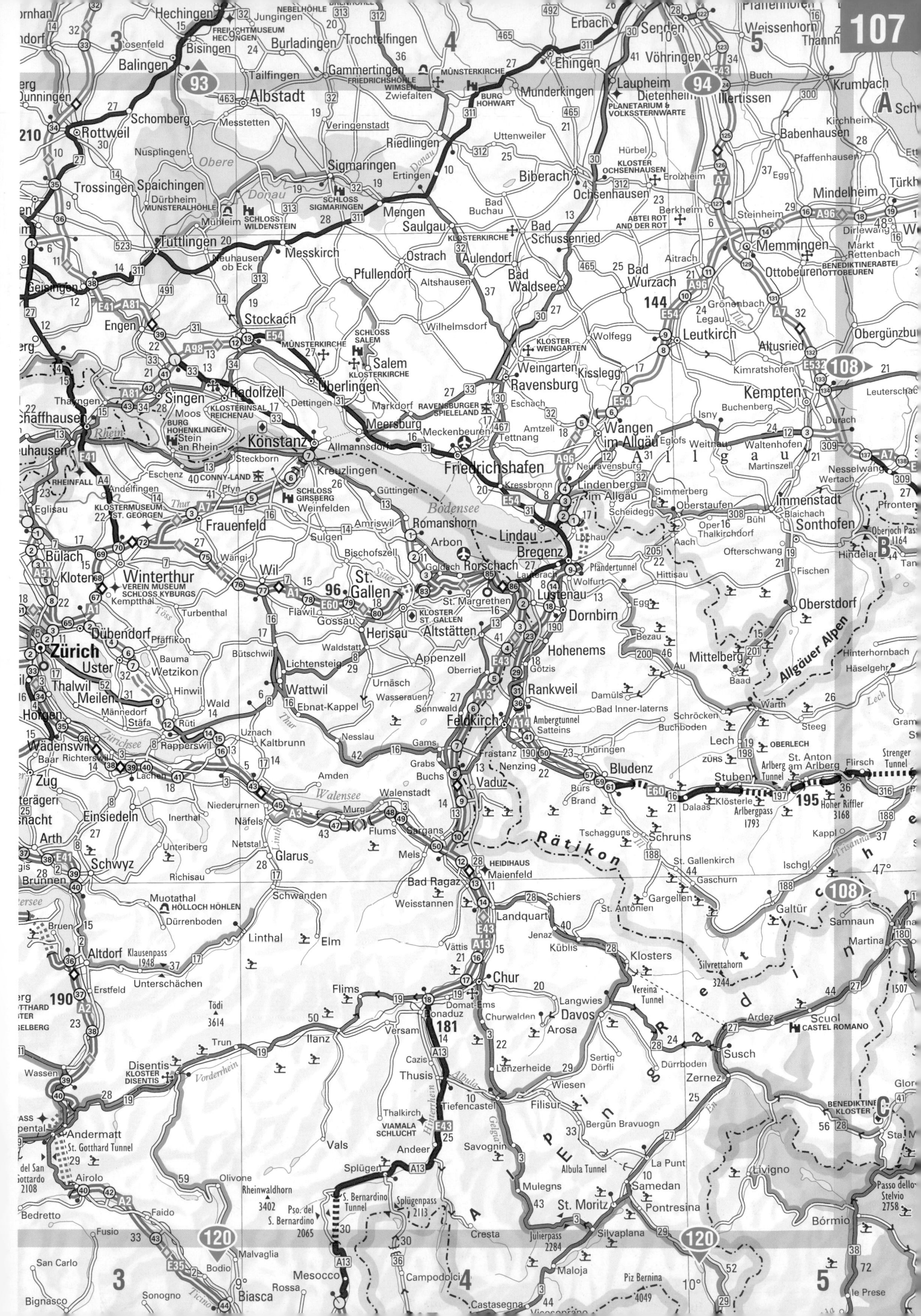

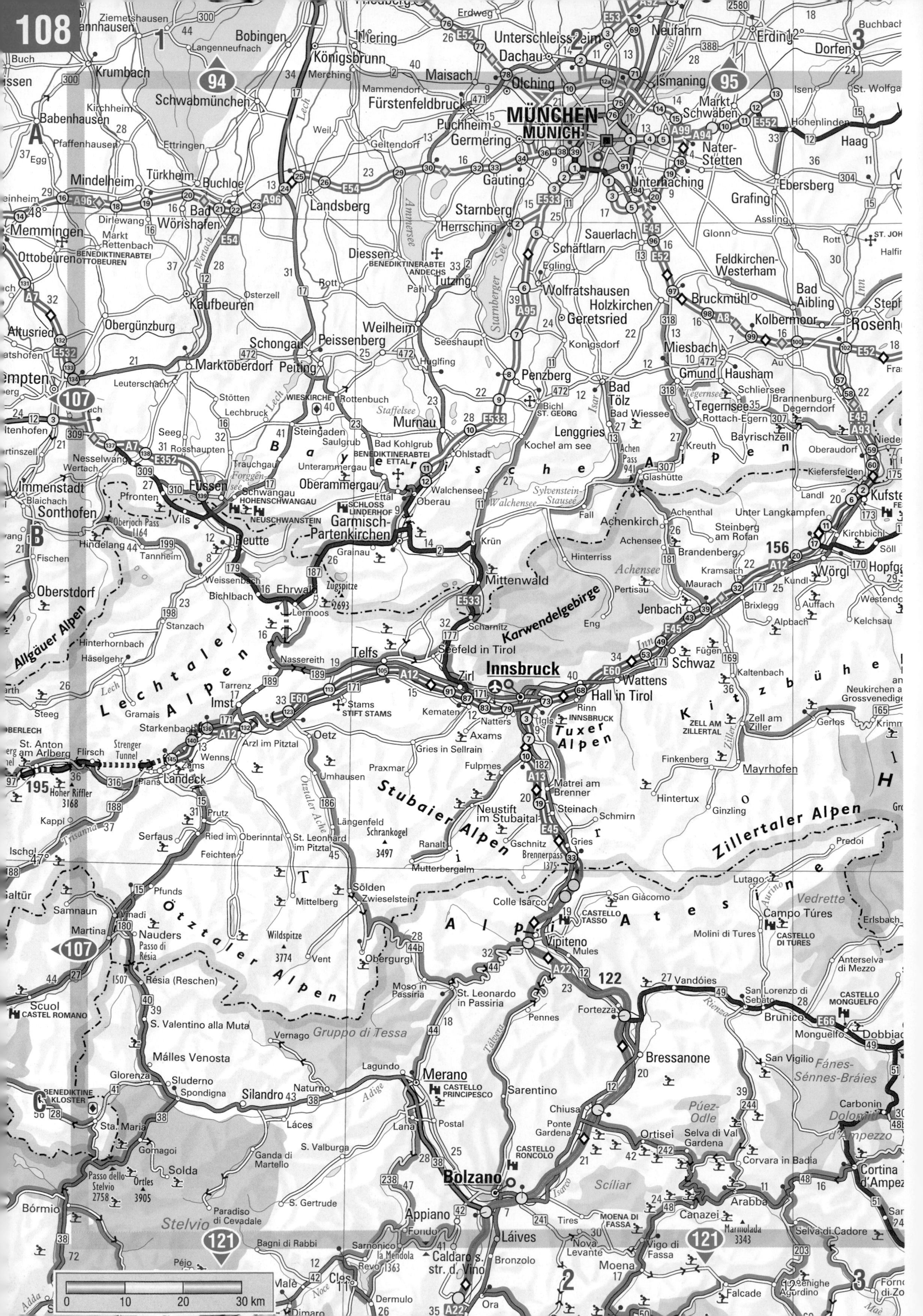
Ziemetshausen
Bobingen
Langenneufnach
Krumbach
Königsbrunn
Merching
Maisach
Olching
Dachau
Unterschleissheim
Neufahrn
Erding
Dorfen
Ismaning
Erdweg
Buchbach
Schwabmünchen
Mammendorf
Fürstenfeldbruck
MÜNCHEN
MUNICH
Markt Schwaben
Isen
St. Wolfgang
Kirchheim
Babenhausen
Pfaffenhausen
Ettringen
Weil
Geltendorf
Puchheim
Germering
Nater-Stetten
Hohenlinden
Haag
Mindelheim
Türkheim
Buchloe
Landsberg
Gauting
Unterhaching
Ebersberg
Grafing
Bad Wörishofen
Dirlewang
Memmingen
Markt Rettenbach
Ottobeuren
BENEDIKTINERABTEI OTTOBEUREN
Ammersee
Starnberg
Herrsching
Diessen
BENEDIKTINERABTEI ANDECHS
Sauerlach
Schäftlarn
Glonn
Assling
Rott
Feldkirchen-Westerham
Egling
Tutzing
Wolfratshausen
Holzkirchen
Geretsried
Bruckmühl
Bad Aibling
Kolbermoor
Rosenheim
Starnberger See
Kaufbeuren
Osterzell
Rott
Pähl
Obergünzburg
Altusried
Weilheim
Schongau
Peissenberg
Seeshaupt
Königsdorf
Miesbach
Marktoberdorf
Peiting
Hugfing
Penzberg
Gmund
Hausham
Kempten
Leuterschach
Stötten
WIESKIRCHE
Rottenbuch
Staffelsee
Bichl
ST. GEORG
Bad Tölz
Bad Wiessee
Tegernsee
Schliersee
Brannenburg-Degerndorf
Lechbruck
Murnau
Seeg
Steingaden
Saulgrub
Bad Kohlgrub
Lenggries
Rottach-Egern
Bayrischzell
Kreuth
Oberaudorf
Rosshaupten
Nesselwang
Wertach
Trauchgau
Forggensee
Unterammergau
BENEDIKTINERABTEI ETTAL
Ohlstadt
Kochel am see
Achen Pass
Glashütte
Kiefersfelden
Immenstadt
Blaichach
Pfronten
Füssen
Schwangau
HOHENSCHWANGAU
Oberammergau
Ettal
Walchensee
Sylvenstein-Stausee
Landl
Kufstein
Sonthofen
Oberjoch Pass
Vils
NEUSCHWANSTEIN
SCHLOSS LINDERHOF
Oberau
Garmisch-Partenkirchen
Fall
Achenthal
Unter Langkampfen
Achenkirch
Steinberg am Rofan
Kirchbichl
Hindelang
Tannheim
Reutte
Grainau
Krün
Hinterriss
Achensee
Brandenberg
Söll
Fischen
Weissenbach
Mittenwald
Kramsach
Wörgl
Hopfgarten
Oberstdorf
Ehrwald
Zugspitze
Pertisau
Maurach
Kundl
Bichlbach
Lermoos
Karwendelgebirge
Brixlegg
Auffach
Westendorf
Stanzach
Scharnitz
Eng
Jenbach
Alpbach
Kelchsau
Allgäuer Alpen
Hinterhornbach
Seefeld in Tirol
Fügen
Häselgehr
Nassereith
Telfs
Zirl
Innsbruck
Schwaz
Kaltenbach
Wattens
Hall in Tirol
Neukirchen am Grossvenediger
Tarrenz
Imst
Stams
STIFT STAMS
Kematen
Natters
Rinn
Igls
INNSBRUCK
Steeg
Gramais
Lechtaler Alpen
Tuxer Alpen
ZELL AM ZILLERTAL
Zell am Ziller
Gerlos
Krimml
Starkenbach
Oetz
Axams
Gries in Sellrain
Flirsch
St. Anton am Arlberg
Strenger Tunnel
Arzl im Pitztal
Wenns
Zams
Pians
Landeck
Praxmar
Fulpmes
Matrei am Brenner
Finkenberg
Mayrhofen
Hoher Riffler
Umhausen
Stubaier Alpen
Neustift im Stubaital
Steinach
Schmirn
Hintertux
Ginzling
Zillertaler Alpen
Kappl
Prutz
Längenfeld
Schrankogel
Serfaus
Ried im Oberinntal
St. Leonhard im Pitztal
Ranalt
Gschnitz
Gries
Brennerpass
Predoi
Ischgl
Feichten
Mutterbergalm
Ötztaler Ache
Trisanna
Galtür
Pfunds
Sölden
Zwieselstein
Mittelberg
Lutago
San Giacomo
Colle Isarco
CASTELLO TASSO
Vedrette
Campo Túres
Erlsbach
Samnaun
Vinadi
Ötztaler Alpen
Martina
Nauders
Passo di Résia
Wildspitze
Vipiteno
Mules
Molini di Tures
CASTELLO DI TURES
Vent
Obergurgl
Anterselva di Mezzo
Résia (Reschen)
Moso in Passíria
St. Leonardo in Passiria
Vandóies
San Lorenzo di Sebato
CASTELLO MONGUELFO
Scuol
CASTEL ROMANO
Fortezza
Brunico
Monguelfo
Dobbiaco
S. Valentino alla Muta
Vernago
Gruppo di Tessa
Pennes
Rienza
Bressanone
Málles Venosta
Lagundo
Merano
CASTELLO PRINCIPESCO
San Vigilio
Fánes-Sénnes-Bráies
Glorenza
Sluderno
Spondigna
Silandro
Naturno
Sarentino
Carbonin
BENEDIKTINE KLOSTER
Sta. Maria
Láces
Lana
Postal
Chiusa
Ponte Gardena
Púez-Odle
Ortisei
Selva di Val Gardena
Dolomiti d'Ampezzo
Gomagoi
Solda
Ganda di Martello
S. Valburga
CASTELLO RONCOLO
Corvara in Badia
Passo dello Stelvio
Ortles
Bolzano
Sciliar
Cortina d'Ampezzo
S. Gertrude
Arabba
Bórmio
Paradiso di Cevadale
Appiano
Tires
MOENA DI FASSA
Canazei
Marmolada
Selva di Cadore
Stelvio
Fondo
Láives
Nova Levante
Bagni di Rabbi
Sarnonico
la Mendola
Caldaro s. str. d. Vino
Vigo di Fassa
Moena
Péio
Revò
Bronzolo
Malè
Cles
Dermulo
Ora
Falcade
Agordino
Forno di Zoldo
Adige
Isarco
Noce
Adda
Inn
Isar
Lech
Wertach
Ziller
Mae
Bayerische Alpen
Alpi Atesine
Kitzbüheler
0
10
20
30 km

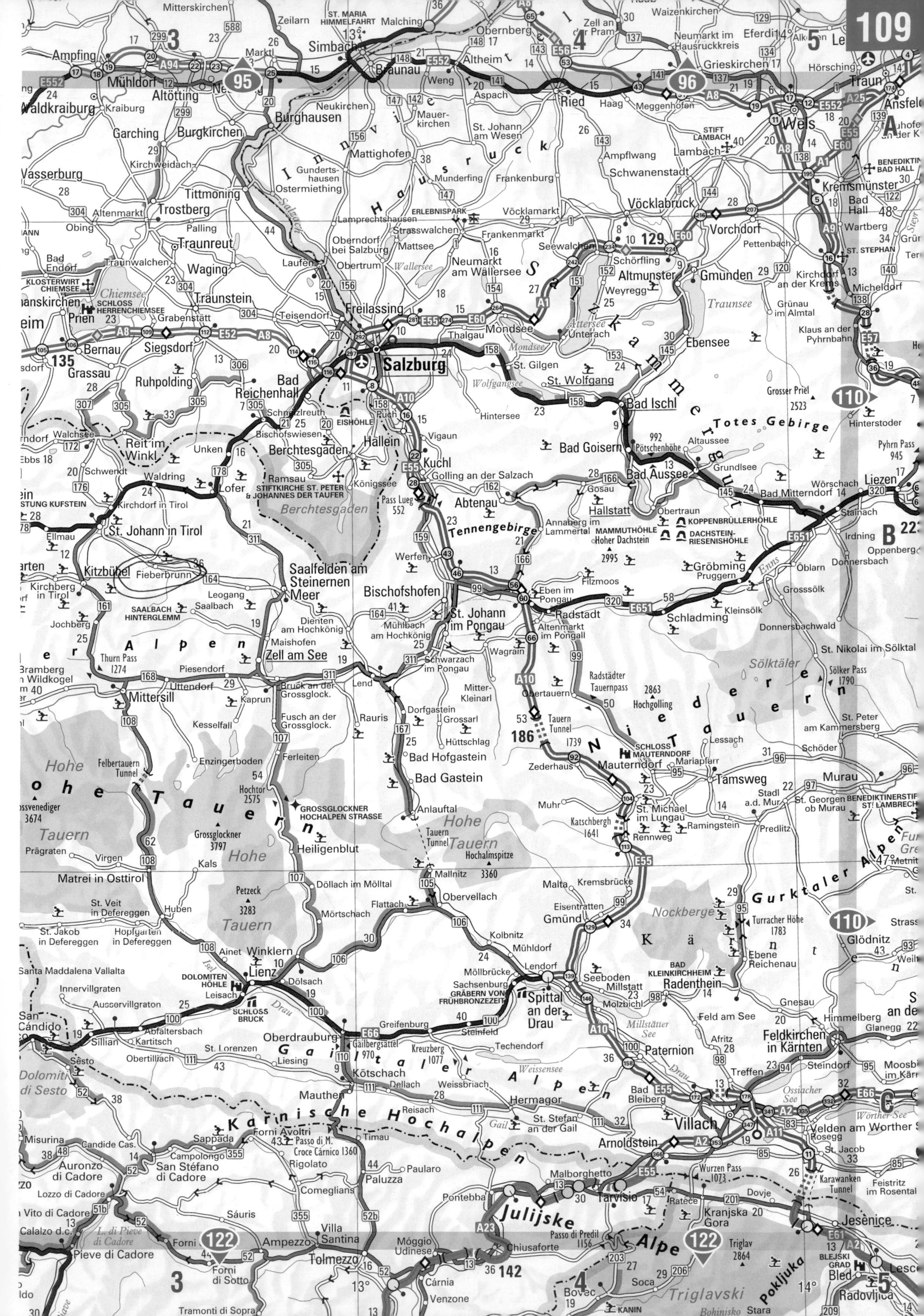
Mitterskirchen
Zeilarn
ST. MARIA HIMMELFAHRT
Malching
Obernberg
Zell an der Pram
Waizenkirchen
Neumarkt im Hausruckkreis
Eferding
Ampfing
Simbach
Braunau
Altheim
Grieskirchen
Mühldorf
Altötting
Neuötting
Weng
Aspach
Ried
Haag
Meggenhofen
Traun
Hörsching
Waldkraiburg
Kraiburg
Neukirchen
Burghausen
Mauerkirchen
Wels
Ansfelden
Garching
Burgkirchen
St. Johann am Wesen
Mattighofen
STIFT LAMBACH
Lambach
Kirchweidach
Ampflwang
Schwanenstadt
BENEDIKTINERSTIFT BAD HALL
Wasserburg
Gundertshausen
Ostermiething
Munderfing
Frankenburg
Kremsmünster
Tittmoning
Bad Hall
Trostberg
Altenmarkt
Lamprechtshausen
ERLEBNISPARK
Vöcklamarkt
Vöcklabruck
Obing
Palling
Strasswalchen
Frankenmarkt
Vorchdorf
Wartberg
Oberndorf bei Salzburg
Mattsee
Seewalchen
ST. STEPHAN
Traunreut
Neumarkt am Wallersee
Schörfling
Pettenbach
Bad Endorf
Traunwalchen
Waging
Laufen
Obertrum
Wallersee
Altmunster
Gmunden
Kirchdorf an der Krems
KLOSTERWIRT CHIEMSEE
Weyregg
Chiemsee
SCHLOSS HERRENCHIEMSEE
Traunstein
Micheldorf
Prien
Grabenstätt
Freilassing
Traunsee
Grünau im Almtal
Teisendorf
Mondsee
Attersee
Unterach
Bernau
Siegsdorf
Thalgau
Klaus an der Pyhrnbahn
Ebensee
Grassau
Salzburg
St. Gilgen
St. Wolfgang
Ruhpolding
Bad Reichenhall
Wolfgangsee
Grosser Priel 2523
Hintersee
Bad Ischl
Schneizlreuth
EISHÖHLE
Puch
Hinterstoder
Walchsee
Bischofswiesen
Totes Gebirge
Reit im Winkl
Unken
Hallein
Vigaun
Bad Goisern
Pötschenhöhe
Altaussee
Pyhrn Pass 945
Ebbs
Berchtesgaden
Kuchl
Bad Aussee
Grundlsee
Schwendt
Waldring
Lofer
Ramsau
STIFTKIRCHE ST. PETER & JOHANNES DER TAUFER
Königssee
Golling an der Salzach
Wörschach
Liezen
Gosau
Bad Mitterndorf
FESTUNG KUFSTEIN
Kirchdorf in Tirol
Berchtesgaden
Pass Lueg 552
Abtenau
Hallstatt
Obertraun
KOPPENBRÜLLERHÖHLE
Stainach
St. Johann in Tirol
Tennengebirge
Annaberg im Lammertal
MAMMUTHÖHLE Hoher Dachstein
DACHSTEIN-RIESENEISHÖHLE
Ellmau
Irdning
Oppenberg
Werfen
2995
Gröbming
Pruggern
Donnersbach
Kitzbühel
Fieberbrunn
Saalfelden am Steinernen Meer
Enns
Öblarn
Kirchberg in Tirol
Leogang
Bischofshofen
Filzmoos
Eben im Pongau
Grosssölk
SAALBACH HINTERGLEMM
Saalbach
St. Johann im Pongau
Radstadt
Kleinsölk
Jochberg
Dienten am Hochkönig
Mühlbach am Hochkönig
Altenmarkt im Pongau
Schladming
Donnersbachwald
Maishofen
Alpen
Zell am See
Wagrain
St. Nikolai im Sölktal
Thurn Pass 1274
Schwarzach im Pongau
Sölktäler
Sölker Pass 1790
Bramberg am Wildkogel
Piesendorf
Lend
Mitter-Kleinarl
Radstädter Tauernpass
Mittersill
Uttendorf
Bruck an der Grossglock.
Kaprun
Obertauern
2863 Hochgolling
Niedere Tauern
Dorfgastein
Grossarl
Tauern Tunnel
Kesselfall
Fusch an der Grossglock.
Rauris
Hüttschlag
1739
SCHLOSS MAUTERNDORF
Lessach
St. Peter am Kammersberg
Schöder
Enzingerboden
Ferleiten
Bad Hofgastein
Zederhaus
Mauterndorf
Mariapfarr
Hohe
Felbertauern Tunnel
Bad Gastein
Tamsweg
Murau
Hohe Tauern
Hochtor 2575
Stadl a.d. Mur
St. Georgen ob Murau
BENEDIKTINERSTIFT ST. LAMBRECHT
Grossvenediger 3674
GROSSGLOCKNER HOCHALPEN STRASSE
Anlauftal
Muhr
St. Michael im Lungau
Katschbergh 1641
Ramingstein
Predlitz
Tauern
Grossglockner 3797
Heiligenblut
Tauern Tunnel
Hohe Tauern
Rennweg
Prägraten
Virgen
Hochalmspitze 3360
Kals
Hohe
Mallnitz
Matrei in Osttirol
Döllach im Mölltal
Malta
Kremsbrücke
Gurktaler Alpen
St. Veit in Defereggen
Petzeck 3283
Obervellach
Huben
Mörtschach
Flattach
Eisentratten
Gmünd
Nockberge
Turracher Höhe 1783
Tauern
St. Jakob in Defereggen
Hopfgarten in Defereggen
Kolbnitz
Mühldorf
Glödnitz
Ainet
Winklern
Ebene Reichenau
Kärnten
Santa Maddalena Vallalta
Lienz
Lendorf
Seeboden
BAD KLEINKIRCHHEIM
Radenthein
DOLOMITEN HÖHLE
Dölsach
Möllbrücke
Sachsenburg
Millstatt
Innervillgraten
Leisach
GRÄBERN VON FRÜHBRONZEZEIT
Spittal an der Drau
Molzbichl
Gnesau
Ausservillgraton
SCHLOSS BRUCK
Drau
Himmelberg
San Cándido
Sillian
Abfaltersbach
Kartitsch
Greifenburg
Steinfeld
Millstätter See
Feld am See
Glanegg
Oberdrauburg
Gailbergsattel 970
Kreuzberg 1077
Techendorf
Afritz
Feldkirchen in Kärnten
Sesto
Obertilliach
St. Lorenzen
Liesing
Gailtaler Alpen
Weissensee
Paternion
Dolomiti di Sesto
Kötschach
Treffen
Steindorf
Moosburg
Mauthen
Dellach
Weissbriach
Bad Bleiberg
Ossiacher See
Hermagor
Reisach
Karnische Hochalpen
St. Stefan an der Gail
Villach
Velden am Worther See
Wörther-See
Misurina
Candide Cas.
Sappada
Forni Avoltri
Passo di M. Croce Cárnico 1360
Timau
Arnoldstein
Rosegg
St. Jacob
Auronzo di Cadore
Campolongo
San Stéfano di Cadore
Rigolato
Paularo
Malborghetto
Wurzen Pass 1073
Karawanken Tunnel
Feistritz im Rosental
Paluzza
Comeglians
Pontebba
Tarvisio
Ratece
Dovje
Lozzo di Cadore
Kranjska Gora
Jesenice
Vito di Cadore
Sáuris
Julijske Alpe
Calalzo d.C.
L. di Pieve di Cadore
Villa Santina
Passo di Predil 1156
Triglav 2864
Pieve di Cadore
Forni
Ampezzo
Móggio Udinese
Chiusaforte
BLEJSKI GRAD
Forni di Sotto
Tolmezzo
Cárnia
Soca
Pokljuka
Bled
Lesce
Venzone
Bovec
Triglavski
KANIN
Bohinjsko
Stara
Radovljica
Tramonti di Sopra
13°
14°
47°
48°

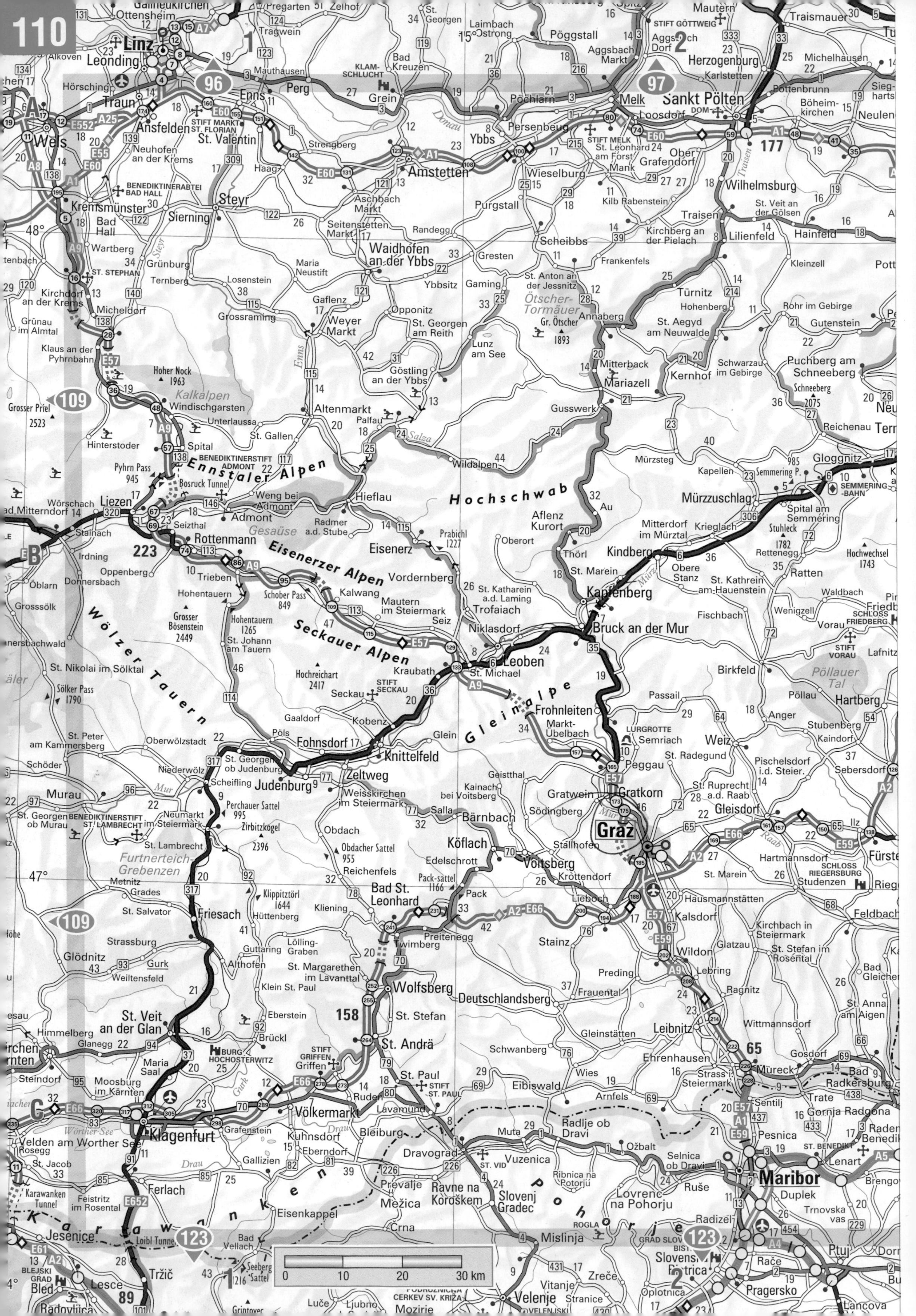

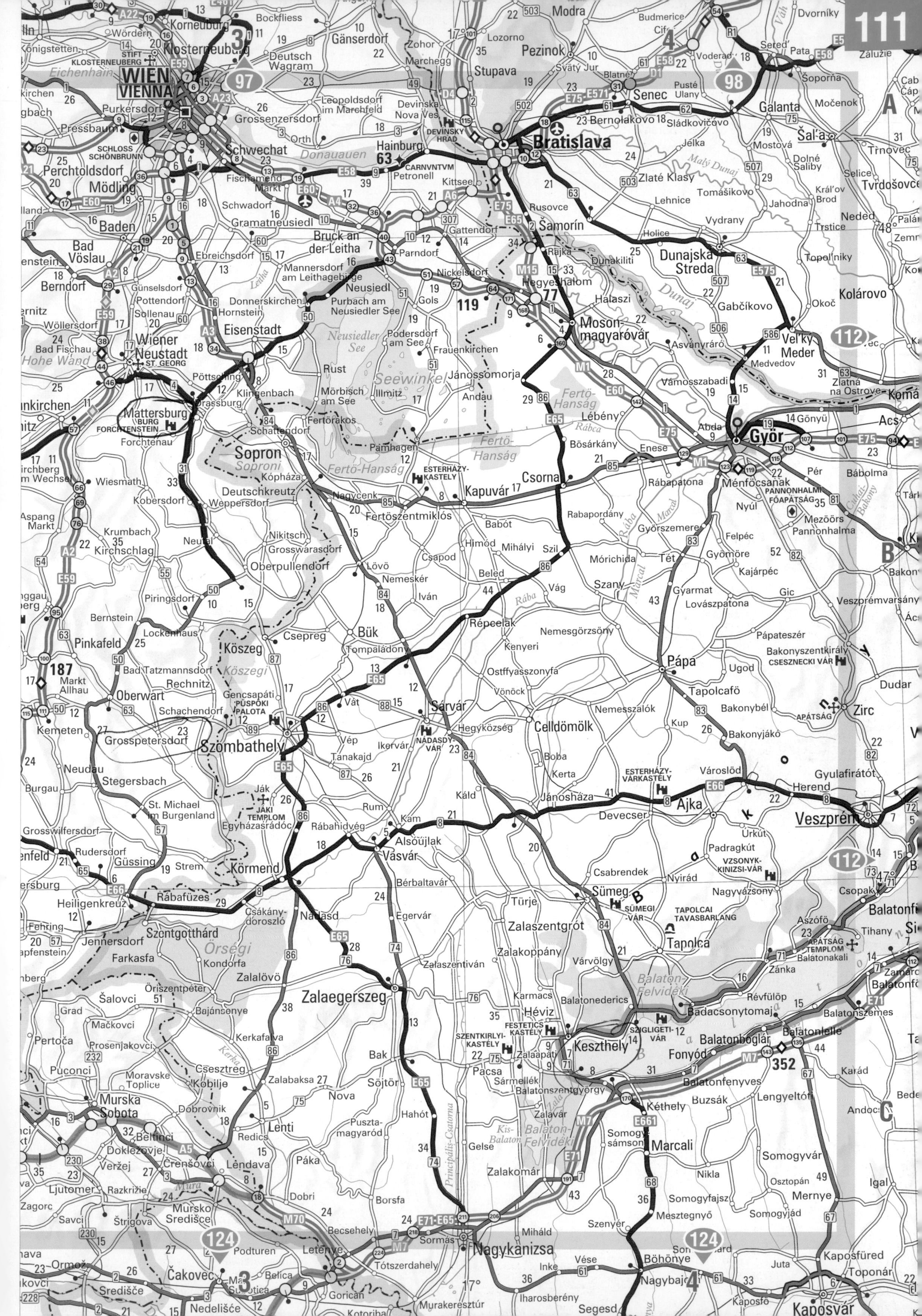
Korneuburg
Bockfliess
Gänserdorf
Zohor
Lozorno
Modra
Budmerice
Cifer
Dvorníky
Wördern
Königstetten
Klosterneuburg
STIFT KLOSTERNEUBERG
Deutsch Wagram
Marchegg
Stupava
Pezinok
Svätý Jur
Blatné
Voderady
Sered'
Pata
Záluzie
Eichenhain
WIEN
VIENNA
97
98
Senec
Pusté Úľany
Šoporňa
Purkersdorf
Leopoldsdorf im Marchfeld
Devínska Nová Ves
Galanta
Močenok
Grossenzersdorf
DEVÍNSKY HRAD
Bratislava
Bernolákovo
Sládkovičovo
Pressbaum
Orth
Jelka
Mostová
Šaľa
Trnovec
SCHLOSS SCHÖNBRUNN
Schwechat
Donauauen
Hainburg
Maly Dunaj
Dolné Saliby
Perchtoldsdorf
Fischamend Markt
CARNVNTVM
Petronell
Kittsee
Zlaté Klasy
Tomášikovo
Selice
Tvrdošovce
Mödling
Schwadorf
Rusovce
Lehnice
Jahodná
Kráľov Brod
Gramatneusiedl
Šamorín
Vydrany
Neded
Trstice
Baden
Bruck an der Leitha
Parndorf
Gattendorf
Rajka
Holice
Bad Vöslau
Ebreichsdorf
Mannersdorf am Leithagebirge
Nickelsdorf
Dunakiliti
Dunajská Streda
Topoľníky
Berndorf
Günselsdorf
Pottendorf
Neusiedl
Hegyeshalom
Dunaj
Gabčíkovo
Kolárovo
Sollenau
Donnerskirchen
Purbach am Neusiedler See
Gols
119
77
Halaszi
Okoč
Wöllersdorf
Hornstein
Eisenstadt
Podersdorf am See
Moson-magyaróvár
Vel'ky Meder
112
Bad Fischau
Wiener Neustadt
ST. GEORG
Hohe Wand
Neusiedler See
Frauenkirchen
Ásványráró
Medvedov
Rust
Seewinkel
Jánossomorja
Vámosszabadi
Zlatná na Ostrove
Komárno
Pöttsching
Mörbisch am See
Illmitz
Andau
Fertő-Hanság
Mattersburg
Klingenbach
Drassburg
BURG FORCHTENSTEIN
Forchtenau
Fertőrákos
Schattendorf
Lébény
Abda
Győr
Gönyű
Ács
Pamhagen
Rábca
Bősárkány
Enese
Sopron
Fertő-Hanság
Kópháza
ESTERHÁZY-KASTÉLY
Csorna
Wiesmath
Deutschkreutz
Nagycenk
Kapuvár
Rábapatona
Ménfőcsanak
Pér
Bábolma
Kobersdorf
Weppersdorf
PANNONHALMI FŐAPÁTSÁG
Aspang Markt
Fertőszentmiklós
Rabapordány
Nyúl
Mezőörs
Krumbach
Kirchschlag
Babót
Győrszemere
Pannonhalma
Neutal
Nikitsch
Grosswarasdorf
Himód
Mihályi
Szil
Felpéc
Csapod
Mórichida
Tét
Gyömöre
Kajárpéc
Oberpullendorf
Lövő
Beled
Nemeskér
Vág
Szany
Gyarmat
Lovászpatona
Gic
Iván
Veszprémvarsány
Piringsdorf
Bernstein
Lockenhaus
Répcelak
Nemesgörzsöny
Pápateszér
Pinkafeld
Kőszeg
Csepreg
Bük
Tompaládony
Kenyeri
Bakonyszentkirály
CSESZNECKI VÁR
Bad Tatzmannsdorf
Pápa
Ugod
Markt Allhau
Rechnitz
Ostffyasszonyfa
Dudar
Oberwart
Gencsapáti
PÜSPÖKI PALOTA
Vönöck
Tapolcafő
Vát
Sárvár
Nemesszalók
Bakonybél
Zirc
Kemeten
Schachendorf
APÁTSÁG
Grosspetersdorf
Szombathely
Vép
Hegyközség
Celldömölk
Kup
Bakonyjákó
Neudau
Tanakajd
Ikervár
NÁDASDY-VÁR
Boba
Stegersbach
Városlőd
Gyulafirátót
Kerta
ESTERHÁZY-VÁRKASTÉLY
Herend
Burgau
Ják
St. Michael im Burgenland
JÁKI TEMPLOM
Rum
Káld
Jánosháza
Ajka
Veszprém
Grosswilfersdorf
Egyházasrádóc
Rábahidvég
Kam
Devecser
Úrkút
Rudersdorf
Alsóújlak
Padragkút
Güssing
Strem
Körmend
Vasvár
Csabrendek
Nyirád
VZSONYK-KINIZSI-VÁR
Heiligenkreuz
Rábafüzes
Bérbaltavár
Sümeg
SÜMEGI VÁR
Nagyvázsony
Csopak
Balatonfüred
Fehring
Jennersdorf
Szentgotthárd
Csákánydoroszló
Nádasd
Egervár
Türje
TAPOLCAI TAVASBARLANG
Aszófő
Tihany
Őrségi
Farkasfa
Zalaszentgrót
Tapolca
APÁTSÁG TEMPLOM
Kondorfa
Zalakoppány
Várvölgy
Balatonakali
Zalalövő
Zalaszentiván
Zánka
Balaton-Felvidéki
Őriszentpéter
Šalovci
Grad
Bajánsenye
Zalaegerszeg
Karmacs
Balatonederics
Révfülöp
Balatonszemes
Mačkovci
Hévíz
Badacsonytomaj
Pertoča
Prosenjakovci
FESTETICS-KASTÉLY
SZENTKIRLYI-KASTÉLY
Kerkafalva
SZIGLIGETI-VÁR
Keszthely
Balatonboglár
Balatonlelle
Bak
Zalaapáti
Fonyód
352
Puconci
Moravske Toplice
Csesztreg
Pacsa
Sármellék
Balatonfenyves
Karád
Kobilje
Zalabaksa
Söjtör
Balatonszentgyörgy
Buzsák
Lengyeltóti
Murska Sobota
Dobrovnik
Nova
Zalavár
Kéthely
Andocs
Beltinci
Redics
Hahót
Kis-Balaton
Balaton-Felvidéki
Somogysámson
Marcali
Lenti
Pusztamagyaród
Principális-Csatorna
Gelse
Somogyvár
Dokležovje
Veržej
Črenšovci
Lendava
Páka
Zalakomár
Nikla
Ljutomer
Razkrižje
Mura
Osztopán
Igal
Mernye
Murska Sredisce
Dobri
Borsfa
Somogyfajsz
Zagorc
Savci
Štrigova
Mesztegnyő
Somogyjád
Becsehely
Szenyér
Miháld
124
Sormás
Nagykanizsa
Podturen
Letenye
Tótszerdahely
Böhönye
Kaposfüred
Ormož
Čakovec
Belica
Inke
Vése
Juta
Toponár
Sredisce
Mala Subotica
Goričan
Iharosberény
Nagybajom
Kaposfő
Kaposvár
Nedelišće
Kotoriba
Murakeresztúr
Segesd

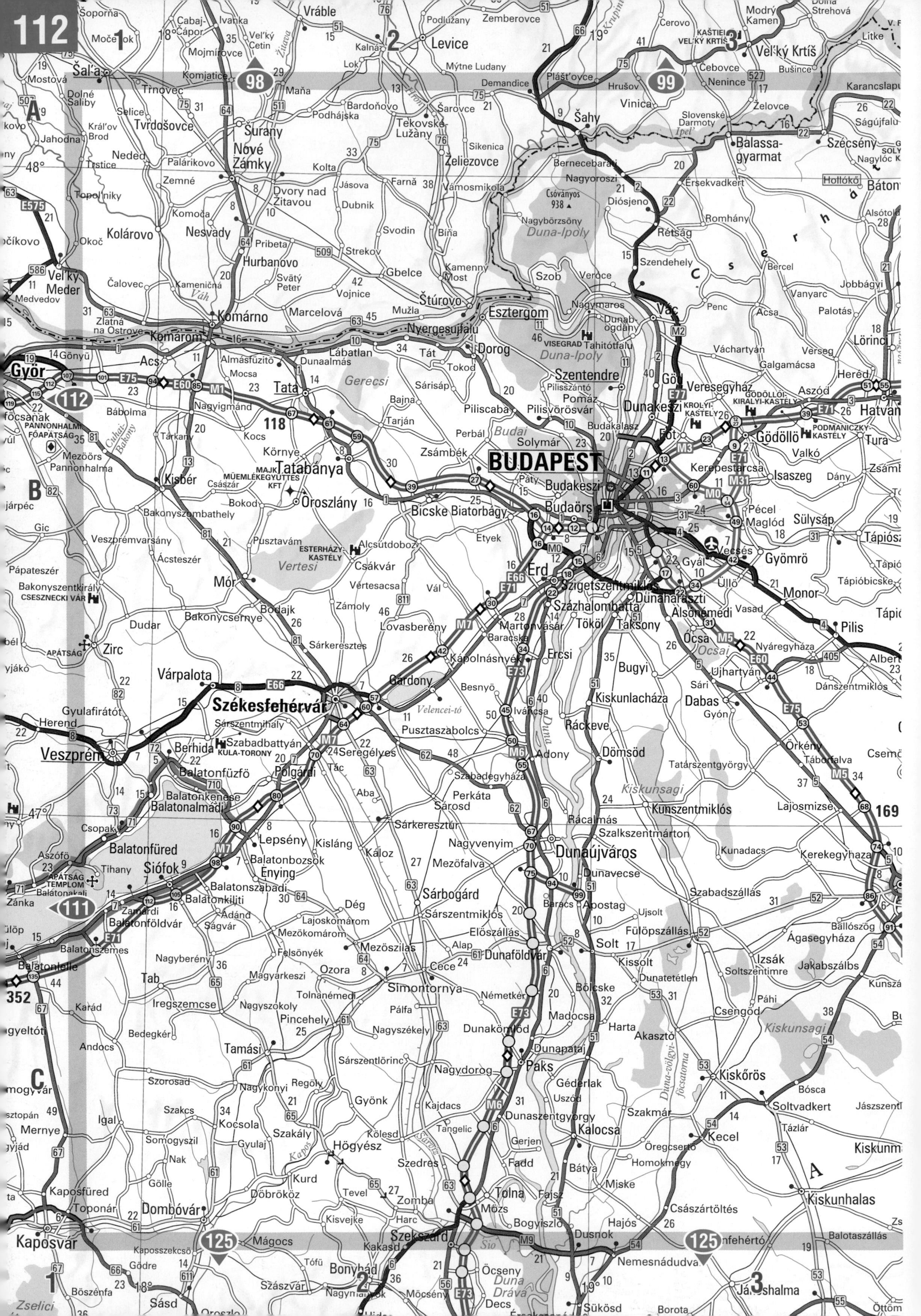
Šoporňa
Cabaj-Čápor
Ivanka
Vráble
Podlužany
Zemberovce
Modrý Kameň
Dolná Strehová
Močenok
Veľký Cetin
Mojmírovce
Kalná
Levice
Cerovo
KAŠTIEĽ VEĽKÝ KRTÍŠ
Veľký Krtíš
Litke
Šaľa
Komjatice
98
Lok
Mýtne Ludany
Demandice
Plášťovce
Hrušov
99
Cebovce
Nenince
Bušince
Karancslapu
Mostová
Trnovec
Maňa
Dolné Saliby
Selice
Bardoňovo
Podhájska
Šarovce
Vinica
Želovce
Slovenské Darmoty
Ipeľ
Ságújfalu
Kráľov Brod
Tvrdošovce
Šurany
Tekovské Lužany
Šahy
Balassagyarmat
Szécsény
Nagylóc
Jahodná
Neded
Nové Zámky
Sikenica
Želiezovce
48°
Trstice
Palárikovo
Kolta
Bernecebaráti
Ersekvadkert
Hollókő
Bátonyterenye
Zemné
Dvory nad Žitavou
Jásova
Farná
Vámosmikola
Nagyoroszi
Diósjeno
Csóványos 938
Topoľníky
Dubník
Komoča
Nagybörzsöny
Duna-Ipoly
Romhány
Alsótold
Kolárovo
Nesvady
Svodin
Bíňa
Rétság
Okoč
Pribeta
Strekov
Hurbanovo
Szendehely
Cserhát
Bercel
Kamenný Most
Gbelce
Szob
Verőce
Jobbágyi
Veľký Meder
Čalovec
Kameničná
Svätý Peter
Vojnice
Štúrovo
Vanyarc
Medvedov
Váh
Komárno
Marcelová
Mužla
Esztergom
Nagymaros
Dunabogdány
Vác
Penc
Acsa
Palotás
Zlatná na Ostrove
Komárom
Nyergesújfalu
VISEGRAD
Tahitótfalu
Lőrinci
Gönyű
Lábatlan
Tát
Dorog
Váchartyán
Verseg
Győr
Ács
Almásfüzitő
Dunaalmás
Tokod
Szentendre
Göd
Veresegyház
Galgamácsa
Heréd
Mocsa
Tata
Gerecsi
Sárisáp
Pilisszántó
Pomáz
GÖDÖLLŐI KIRÁLYI-KASTÉLY
Aszód
Hatvan
112
Bábolma
Nagyigmánd
Bajna
Piliscaba
Pilisvörösvár
Dunakeszi
KROLYI-KASTÉLY
Fót
Gödöllő
PODMANICZKY-KASTÉLY
Tura
PANNONHALMI FŐAPÁTSÁG
Tárkány
Kocs
Tarján
Perbál
Budai
Solymár
Budakalász
Valkó
Mezőörs
Pannonhalma
Környe
Zsámbék
BUDAPEST
Kerepestarcsa
Isaszeg
Dány
MAJK MŰEMLÉKEGYÜTTES KFT
Tatabánya
Kisbér
Császár
Páty
Budakeszi
Oroszlány
Bokod
Bicske
Biatorbágy
Budaörs
Pécel
Maglód
Sülysáp
Bakonyszombathely
Tápió
Gic
Veszprémvarsány
Pusztavám
Alcsútdoboz
Etyek
Vecsés
Gyömrő
ESTERHÁZY-KASTÉLY
Ácsteszér
Vertesi
Csákvár
Erd
Gyál
Pápateszér
Üllő
Bakonyszentkirály
CSESZNECKI VÁR
Mór
Vértesacsa
Vál
Szigetszentmiklós
Dunaharaszti
Tápióbicske
Monor
Zámoly
Százhalombatta
Alsónémedi
Vasad
Dudar
Bakonycsernye
Bodajk
Lovasberény
Martonvásár
Tököl
Taksony
Pilis
Zirc
APÁTSÁG
Sárkeresztes
Baracska
Ócsa
Nyáregyháza
Albertirsa
Kápolnásnyék
Ercsi
Ocsai
Bugyi
Újhartyán
Dánszentmiklós
Várpalota
Gárdony
Besnyő
Kiskunlacháza
Sári
Dabas
Gyón
Székesfehérvár
Velencei-tó
Iváncsa
Gyulafirátót
Herend
Sárszentmihály
Pusztaszabolcs
Ráckeve
Veszprém
Berhida
Szabadbattyán
KULA-TORONY
Seregélyes
Adony
Dömsöd
Örkény
Táborfalva
Csemő
Balatonfűzfő
Polgárdi
Tác
Szabadegyháza
Tatárszentgyörgy
Aba
Perkáta
Kiskunsagi
Balatonkenese
Balatonalmádi
Sárosd
Kunszentmiklós
Lajosmizse
169
47°
Csopak
Sárkeresztúr
Rácalmás
Szalkszentmárton
Lepsény
Kisláng
Nagyvenyim
Balatonfüred
Káloz
Dunaújváros
Kunadacs
Kerekegyháza
Aszófő
Tihany
Siófok
Balatonbozsok
Enying
Mezőfalva
Dunavecse
APÁTSÁG TEMPLOM
Balatonakali
Balatonszabadi
Sárbogárd
Zánka
111
Zamárdi
Balatonkiliti
Adánd
Dég
Baracs
Apostag
Szabadszállás
Ujsolt
Balatonföldvár
Ságvár
Lajoskomárom
Sárszentmiklós
Fülöpszállás
Ballószög
Mezőkomárom
Előszállás
Solt
Ágasegyháza
Balatonszemes
Mezőszilas
Alap
Dunaföldvár
Kissolt
Izsák
Nagyberény
Felsőnyék
Balatonlelle
Cece
Soltszentimre
Jakabszállás
Tab
Ozora
Dunatetétlen
352
Magyarkeszi
Simontornya
Németkér
Bölcske
Kunszállás
Karád
Tolnanémedi
Iregszemcse
Nagyszokoly
Pálfa
Harta
Páhi
Csengőd
Pincehely
Madocsa
Kiskunsági
Bedegkér
Nagyszékely
Dunakömlőd
Akasztó
Andocs
Tamási
Dunapataj
Sárszentlőrinc
Paks
Nagydorog
Duna-völgyi-főcsatorna
Kiskőrös
Szorosad
Nagykónyi
Regöly
Gédelak
Bócsa
Uszód
Gyönk
Kajdacs
Soltvadkert
Jászszentlászló
Szakcs
Igal
Kocsola
Dunaszentgyörgy
Szakmár
Tázlár
Mernye
Somogyszil
Szakály
Tangelic
Kalocsa
Kecel
Gyulaj
Kölesd
Gerjen
Öregcsertő
Kiskunmajsa
Nak
Högyész
Kapos
Sárvíz
Fadd
Homokmégy
Szedres
Bátya
Kaposfüred
Gölle
Kurd
Tevel
Miske
Toponár
Dombóvár
Döbrököz
Zomba
Tolna
Fajsz
Kiskunhalas
Kaposvár
Kisvejke
Harc
Mözs
Bogyiszló
Hajós
Császártöltés
Mágocs
Szekszárd
Dusnok
Kaposszekcső
125
Kakasd
Sió
Balotaszállás
Gödre
Tófű
Bonyhád
Őcsény
Nemesnádudvar
Kisszállás
Szászvár
Duna-Dráva
Böszénfa
Zselici
Sásd
Nagymányok
Mőcsény
Decs
Sükösd
Jánoshalma
Borota
Öttömös

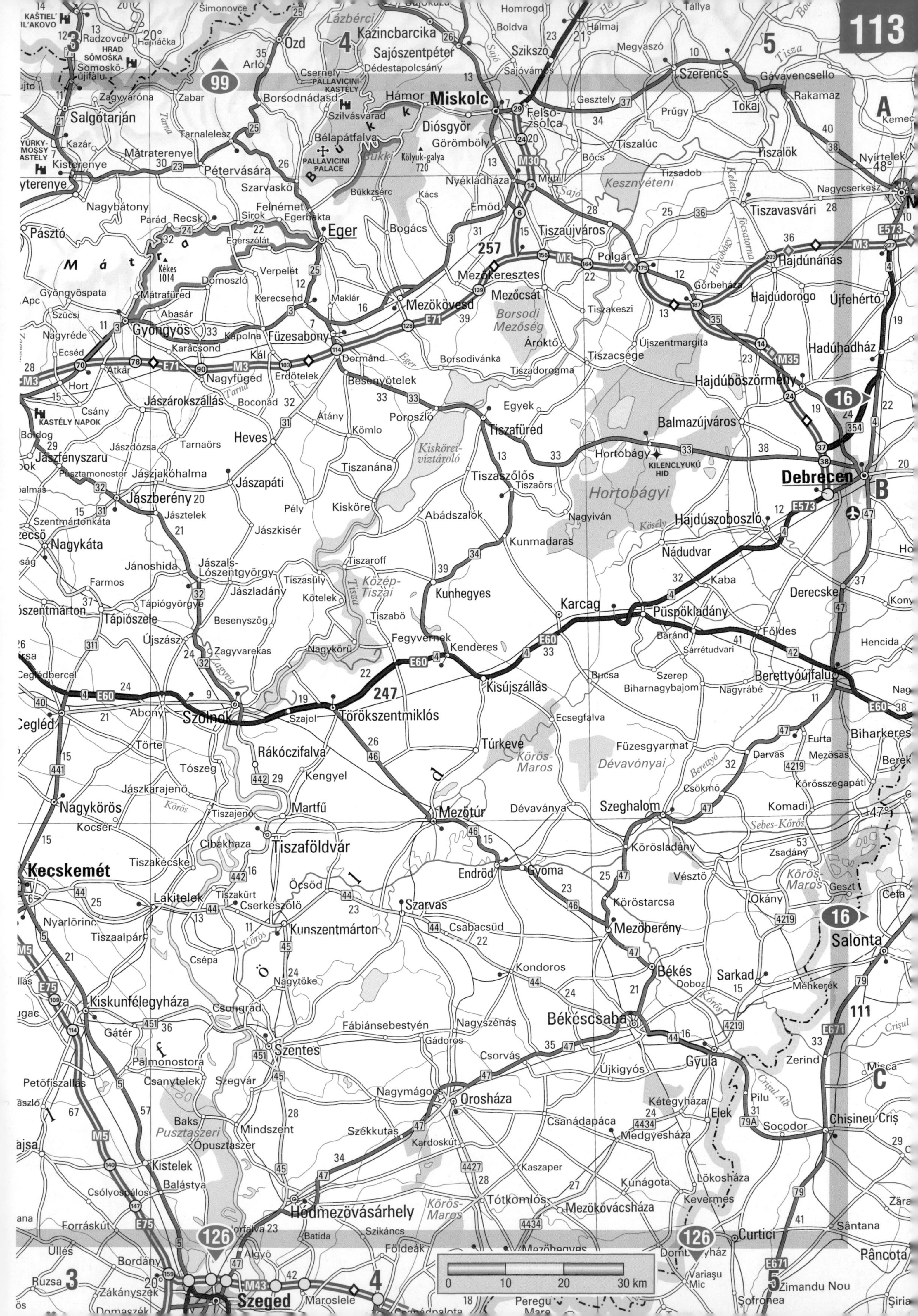
Miskolc
Eger
Debrecen
Kecskemét
Szeged
Békéscsaba
Szolnok
Ózd
Kazincbarcika
Sajószentpéter
Salgótarján
Szerencs
Tokaj
Rakamaz
Gávavencsello
Tiszalök
Nyírtelek
Tiszavasvári
Hajdúnánás
Hajdúdorogo
Újfehértó
Hadúhadház
Hajdúböszörmény
Balmazújváros
Hortobágy
KILENCLYUKÚ HID
Hortobágyi
Hajdúszoboszló
Nádudvar
Kaba
Derecske
Püspökladány
Karcag
Kunhegyes
Kunmadaras
Tiszafüred
Tiszaújváros
Polgár
Mezőkeresztes
Mezőcsát
Mezőkövesd
Borsodi Mezőség
Füzesabony
Gyöngyös
Heves
Jászberény
Jászapáti
Nagykáta
Tápiószele
Cegléd
Abony
Törökszentmiklós
Kisújszállás
Berettyóújfalu
Mezőtúr
Tiszaföldvár
Martfű
Nagykörös
Kiskunfélegyháza
Csongrád
Szentes
Szarvas
Kunszentmárton
Gyoma
Endrőd
Szeghalom
Körösladány
Mezőberény
Békés
Gyula
Sarkad
Salonta
Orosháza
Hódmezővásárhely
Mezőkovácsháza
Tótkomlós
Kistelek
Curtici
Chişineu Criş
Pâncota
Kiskörei-víztároló
Közép-Tiszai
Körös-Maros
Dévaványai
Pusztaszeri
Kesznyéteni
Mátra
Kékes 1014
Bükk
PALLAVICINI PALACE
KASTÉLY NAPOK
Szerencs
0 10 20 30 km
A
B
C
3
4
5
99
126
16
111
257
247

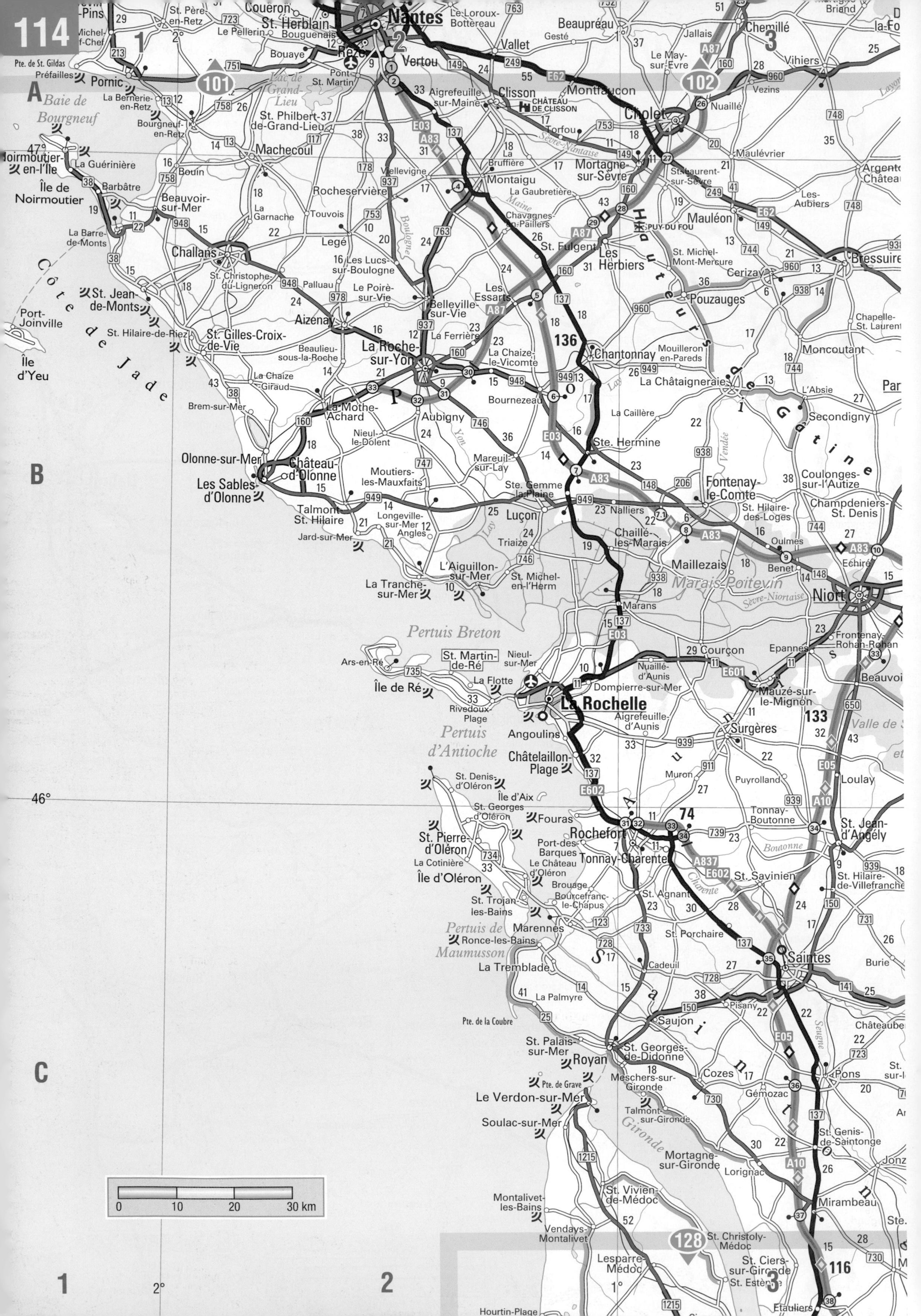
Nantes
St. Herblain
Rezé
Vertou
Pornic
Pte. de St. Gildas
Préfailles
Baie de Bourgneuf
La Bernerie-en-Retz
Bourgneuf-en-Retz
St. Philbert-de-Grand-Lieu
Lac de Grand-Lieu
Machecoul
Noirmoutier-en-l'Île
La Guérinière
Île de Noirmoutier
Barbâtre
Beauvoir-sur-Mer
La Barre-de-Monts
Challans
St. Jean-de-Monts
Port-Joinville
Île d'Yeu
Côte de Jade
St. Hilaire-de-Riez
St. Gilles-Croix-de-Vie
Aizenay
La Roche-sur-Yon
Brem-sur-Mer
La Mothe-Achard
Olonne-sur-Mer
Château-d'Olonne
Les Sables-d'Olonne
Talmont-St. Hilaire
Jard-sur-Mer
Longeville-sur-Mer
Angles
La Tranche-sur-Mer
L'Aiguillon-sur-Mer
St. Michel-en-l'Herm
Luçon
Triaize
Clisson
CHÂTEAU DE CLISSON
Aigrefeuille-sur-Maine
Montaigu
Vallet
Beaupréau
Montfaucon
Cholet
Chemillé
Vihiers
Maulévrier
Mortagne-sur-Sèvre
St. Laurent-sur-Sèvre
Les Herbiers
St. Fulgent
PUY-DU FOU
Mauléon
Bressuire
Pouzauges
Cerizay
Chantonnay
Les Essarts
La Châtaigneraie
Moncoutant
Secondigny
Hauteurs de la Gâtine
Coulonges-sur-l'Autize
Fontenay-le-Comte
Ste. Hermine
Mareuil-sur-Lay
Bournezeau
Maillezais
Marais Poitevin
Niort
Marans
Pertuis Breton
St. Martin-de-Ré
Ars-en-Ré
Île de Ré
La Flotte
Rivedoux-Plage
La Rochelle
Dompierre-sur-Mer
Aigrefeuille-d'Aunis
Angoulins
Châtelaillon-Plage
Pertuis d'Antioche
Surgères
Mauzé-sur-le-Mignon
St. Denis-d'Oléron
Île d'Aix
St. Georges-d'Oléron
Fouras
St. Pierre-d'Oléron
La Cotinière
Île d'Oléron
Rochefort
Tonnay-Charente
St. Trojan-les-Bains
Marennes
Bourcefranc-le-Chapus
Ronce-les-Bains
Pertuis de Maumusson
La Tremblade
La Palmyre
Pte. de la Coubre
Saujon
St. Palais-sur-Mer
Royan
St. Georges-de-Didonne
Meschers-sur-Gironde
Talmont-sur-Gironde
Pte. de Grave
Le Verdon-sur-Mer
Soulac-sur-Mer
Gironde
Mortagne-sur-Gironde
Cozes
Saintes
St. Jean-d'Angély
Tonnay-Boutonne
St. Savinien
Pons
Gémozac
St. Genis-de-Saintonge
Mirambeau
St. Vivien-de-Médoc
Montalivet-les-Bains
Vendays-Montalivet
Lesparre-Médoc
St. Christoly-Médoc
St. Ciers-sur-Gironde
Hourtin-Plage
Etauliers
46°
47°
0 10 20 30 km
A
B
C
1
2
3

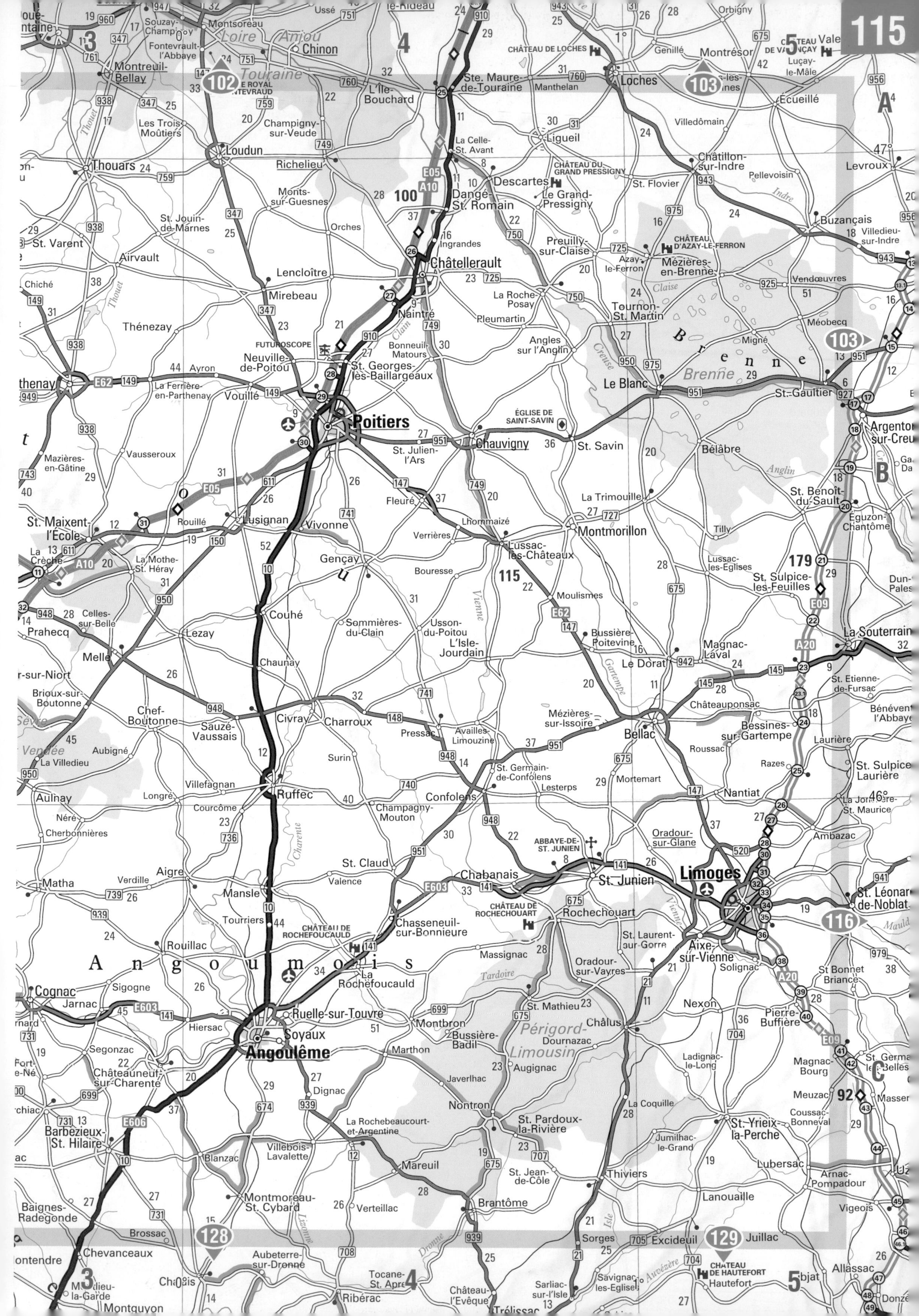
Ussé
le-Rideau
Orbigny
Souzay-Champigny
Montsoreau
Loire
Anjou
Chinon
Fontevrault-l'Abbaye
Montreuil-Bellay
Château de Loches
Genillé
Montrésor
Château de Valençay
Luçay-le-Mâle
102
Touraine
Abbaye Royale de Fontevraud
L'Ile-Bouchard
Ste. Maure-de-Touraine
Manthelan
Loches
103
Écueillé
Les Trois-Moûtiers
Champigny-sur-Veude
Villedômain
Thouet
Loudun
Richelieu
La Celle-St. Avant
Ligueil
Thouars
Châtillon-sur-Indre
Château du Grand Pressigny
Levroux
Monts-sur-Guesnes
Descartes
Le Grand-Pressigny
St. Flovier
Pellevoisin
Dangé-St. Romain
Indre
St. Jouin-de-Marnes
Orches
Ingrandes
Preuilly-sur-Claise
Buzançais
Villedieu-sur-Indre
St. Varent
Airvault
Châtellerault
Château d'Azay-le-Ferron
Azay-le-Ferron
Mézières-en-Brenne
Lencloître
Chiché
Mirebeau
La Roche-Posay
Claise
Vendœuvres
Naintré
Tournon-St. Martin
Thénezay
Pleumartin
Méobecq
Futuroscope
Clain
Angles sur l'Anglin
Migné
Brenne
Bonneuil-Matours
Neuville-de-Poitou
St. Georges-lès-Baillargeaux
Creuse
Ayron
Parthenay
La Ferrière-en-Parthenay
Vouillé
Le Blanc
St. Gaultier
Poitiers
Église de Saint-Savin
Argenton-sur-Creuse
Chauvigny
St. Savin
St. Julien-l'Ars
Bélâbre
Vausseroux
Mazières-en-Gâtine
Anglin
Fleuré
La Trimouille
St. Benoît-du-Sault
St. Maixent-l'École
Rouillé
Lusignan
Vivonne
Lhommaizé
Montmorillon
Éguzon-Chantôme
Verrières
Tilly
La Crèche
Gençay
Lussac-les-Châteaux
La Mothe-St. Héray
Bouresse
Lussac-les-Eglises
St. Sulpice-les-Feuilles
Vienne
Moulismes
Celles-sur-Belle
Couhé
Prahecq
Lezay
Sommières-du-Clain
Usson-du-Poitou
L'Isle-Jourdain
Bussière-Poitevine
Magnac-Laval
La Souterraine
Melle
Chaunay
Le Dorat
St. Etienne-de-Fursac
Gartempe
Brioux-sur-Boutonne
Châteauponsac
Bénévent-l'Abbaye
Chef-Boutonne
Sauzé-Vaussais
Civray
Charroux
Pressac
Availles-Limouzine
Mézières-sur-Issoire
Bellac
Bessines-sur-Gartempe
Sèvre
Vendée
Aubigné
La Villedieu
Surin
St. Germain-de-Confolens
Roussac
Laurière
Razes
St. Sulpice-Laurière
Villefagnan
Ruffec
Mortemart
Longré
Aulnay
Courcôme
Champagny-Mouton
Confolens
Lesterps
Nantiat
La Jonchère-St. Maurice
Néré
Cherbonnières
Charente
Abbaye-de-St. Junien
Oradour-sur-Glane
Ambazac
Matha
Verdille
Aigre
St. Claud
Valence
Chabanais
St. Junien
Limoges
St. Léonard-de-Noblat
Mansle
Château de Rochechouart
Rochechouart
Tourriers
Château de Rochefoucauld
Chasseneuil-sur-Bonnieure
St. Laurent-sur-Gorre
Aixe-sur-Vienne
Rouillac
Angoumois
Massignac
Oradour-sur-Vayres
Solignac
St Bonnet Briance
La Rochefoucauld
Tardoire
Cognac
Sigogne
Jarnac
St. Mathieu
Nexon
Ruelle-sur-Touvre
Hiersac
Montbron
Châlus
Périgord-Limousin
Pierre-Buffière
Soyaux
Angoulême
Bussière-Badil
Dournazac
Segonzac
Marthon
Augignac
Ladignac-le-Long
Magnac-Bourg
Châteauneuf-sur-Charente
Javerlhac
Dignac
Meuzac
Nontron
La Coquille
Coussac-Bonneval
La Rochebeaucourt-et-Argentine
St. Pardoux-la-Rivière
St. Yrieix-la-Perche
Barbezieux-St. Hilaire
Jumilhac-le-Grand
Villebois-Lavalette
Blanzac
Mareuil
St. Jean-de-Côle
Thiviers
Lubersac
Arnac-Pompadour
Montmoreau-St. Cybard
Baignes-Ste. Radegonde
Verteillac
Brantôme
Lanouaille
Vigeois
Brossac
128
Isle
129
Juillac
Chevanceaux
Montendre
Aubeterre-sur-Dronne
Lizonne
Dronne
Sorges
Excideuil
Château de Hautefort
Auvézère
Allassac
Montlieu-la-Garde
Chalais
Tocane-St. Apre
Ribérac
Château-l'Evêque
Sarliac-sur-l'Isle
Savignac-les-Eglises
Hautefort
Montguyon
Trélissac
Donzenac

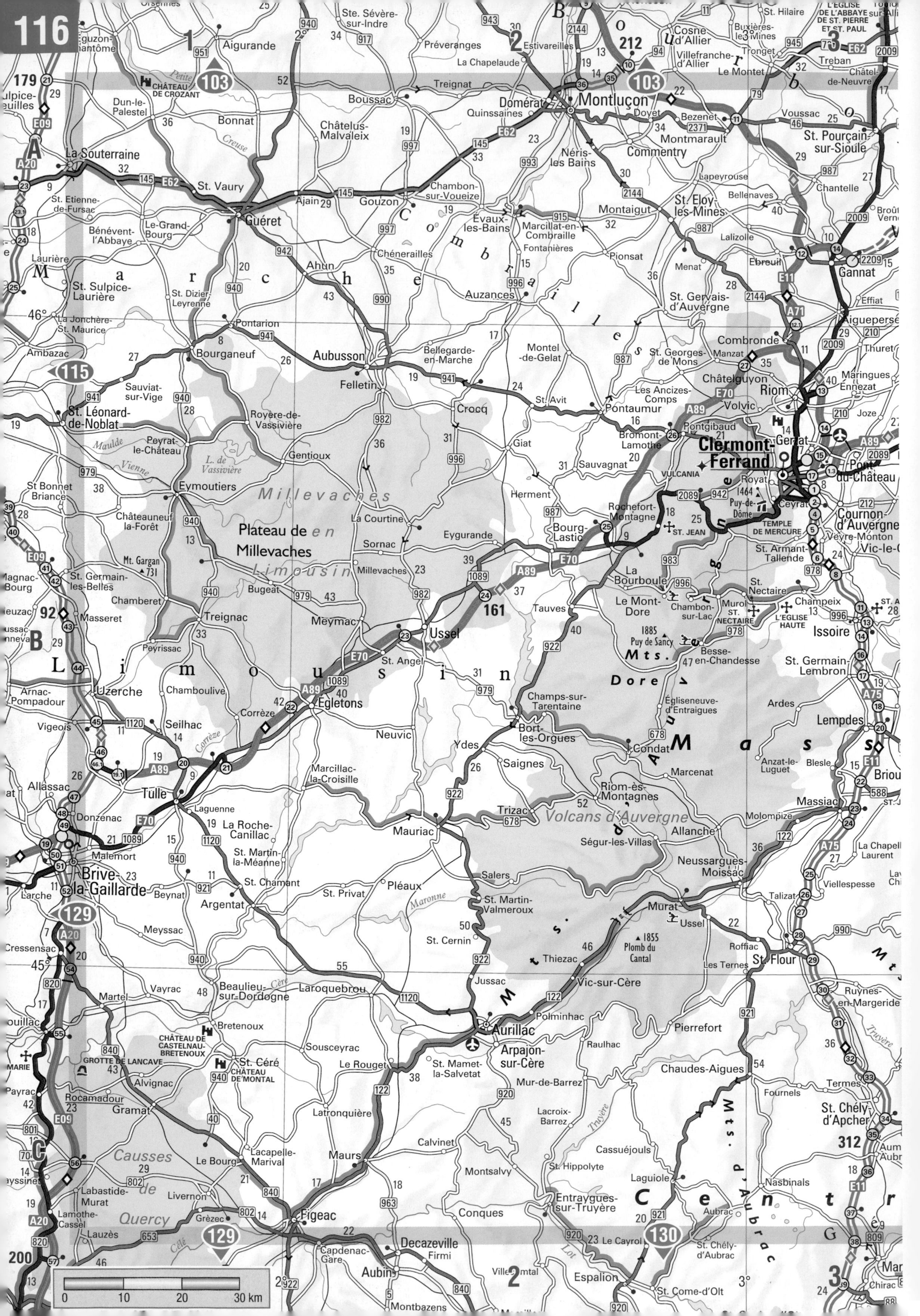
Aigurande
Préveranges
Estivareilles
Cosne d'Allier
Villefranche-d'Allier
Buxières-les-Mines
Montluçon
Domérat
Quinssaines
Boussac
Treignat
Château de Crozant
Dun-le-Palestel
Bonnat
Châtelus-Malvaleix
La Souterraine
St. Vaury
Guéret
Ajain
Gouzon
Chambon-sur-Voueize
Évaux-les-Bains
Néris-les-Bains
Commentry
Montmarault
Montaigut
St. Eloy-les-Mines
St. Pourçain-sur-Sioule
Chantelle
Gannat
Ebreuil
Menat
Pionsat
St. Gervais-d'Auvergne
Aigueperse
Combronde
Châtelguyon
Riom
Volvic
Pontgibaud
Clermont-Ferrand
Royat
Puy-de-Dôme
Cournon-d'Auvergne
Bourganeuf
Aubusson
Felletin
Bellegarde-en-Marche
Auzances
Crocq
Pontaumur
St. Léonard-de-Noblat
Eymoutiers
Plateau de Millevaches
Millevaches
Limousin
Meymac
Ussel
Bort-les-Orgues
La Bourboule
Le Mont-Dore
Puy de Sancy
Mts. Dore
Besse-en-Chandesse
Issoire
Treignac
Uzerche
Égletons
Tulle
Brive-la-Gaillarde
Argentat
Mauriac
Salers
Murat
Plomb du Cantal
St. Flour
Aurillac
Arpajon-sur-Cère
Beaulieu-sur-Dordogne
St. Céré
Rocamadour
Gramat
Figeac
Decazeville
Conques
Entraygues-sur-Truyère
Laguiole
Chaudes-Aigues
St. Chély-d'Apcher
Espalion
Massif Central
Volcans d'Auvergne
Monts d'Aubrac
Causses de Quercy
0 10 20 30 km

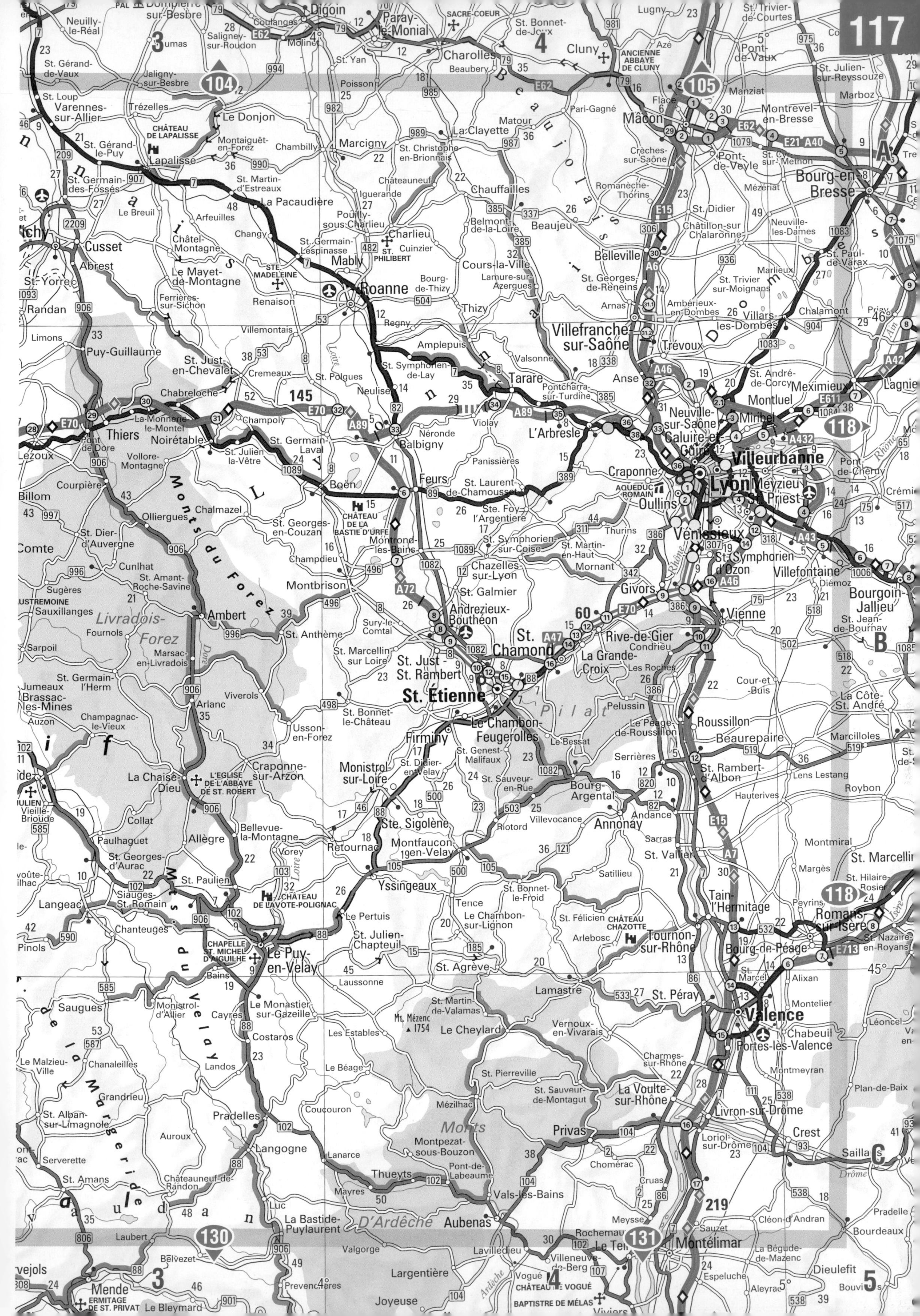
Digoin
Paray-le-Monial
Sacré-Coeur
Charolles
Cluny
Ancienne Abbaye de Cluny
Mâcon
Pont-de-Vaux
Manziat
Montrevel-en-Bresse
Bourg-en-Bresse
La Clayette
Chauffailles
Beaujeu
Beaujolais
Belleville
Villefranche-sur-Saône
Trévoux
Villars-les-Dombes
Dombes
Meximieux
Montluel
Miribel
Neuville-sur-Saône
Caluire-et-Cuire
Villeurbanne
Lyon
Oullins
Vénissieux
St. Priest
Meyzieu
Aqueduc Romain
Givors
Vienne
Bourgoin-Jallieu
Villefontaine
St. Symphorien-d'Ozon
Varennes-sur-Allier
Le Donjon
Château de Lapalisse
Lapalisse
Vichy
Cusset
La Pacaudière
Roanne
Charlieu
St. Philibert
Ste. Madeleine
Mably
Tarare
L'Arbresle
Thiers
Noirétable
Boën
Feurs
Château de la Bastie d'Urfé
Montbrison
Monts du Forez
Livradois-Forez
Ambert
Montrond-les-Bains
Andrezieux-Bouthéon
St. Chamond
Rive-de-Gier
St. Étienne
Firminy
Le Chambon-Feugerolles
Pilat
Annonay
Roussillon
Beaurepaire
Monistrol-sur-Loire
Yssingeaux
Château de Lavoûte-Polignac
La Chaise-Dieu
L'Eglise de l'Abbaye de St. Robert
Le Puy-en-Velay
Chapelle St. Michel d'Aiguilhe
Monts du Velay
Langeac
Tain-l'Hermitage
Tournon-sur-Rhône
Château Chazotte
Romans-sur-Isère
Bourg-de-Péage
Valence
Portes-lès-Valence
Mt. Mézenc 1754
Le Cheylard
Lamastre
St. Péray
La Voulte-sur-Rhône
Privas
Livron-sur-Drôme
Crest
Monts du Margeride
Langogne
Pradelles
Thueyts
Aubenas
Vals-les-Bains
D'Ardèche
Montélimar
Mende
Ermitage de St. Privat
Château de Vogüé
Baptistre de Mélas
Viviers
104
105
118
130
131
145
219

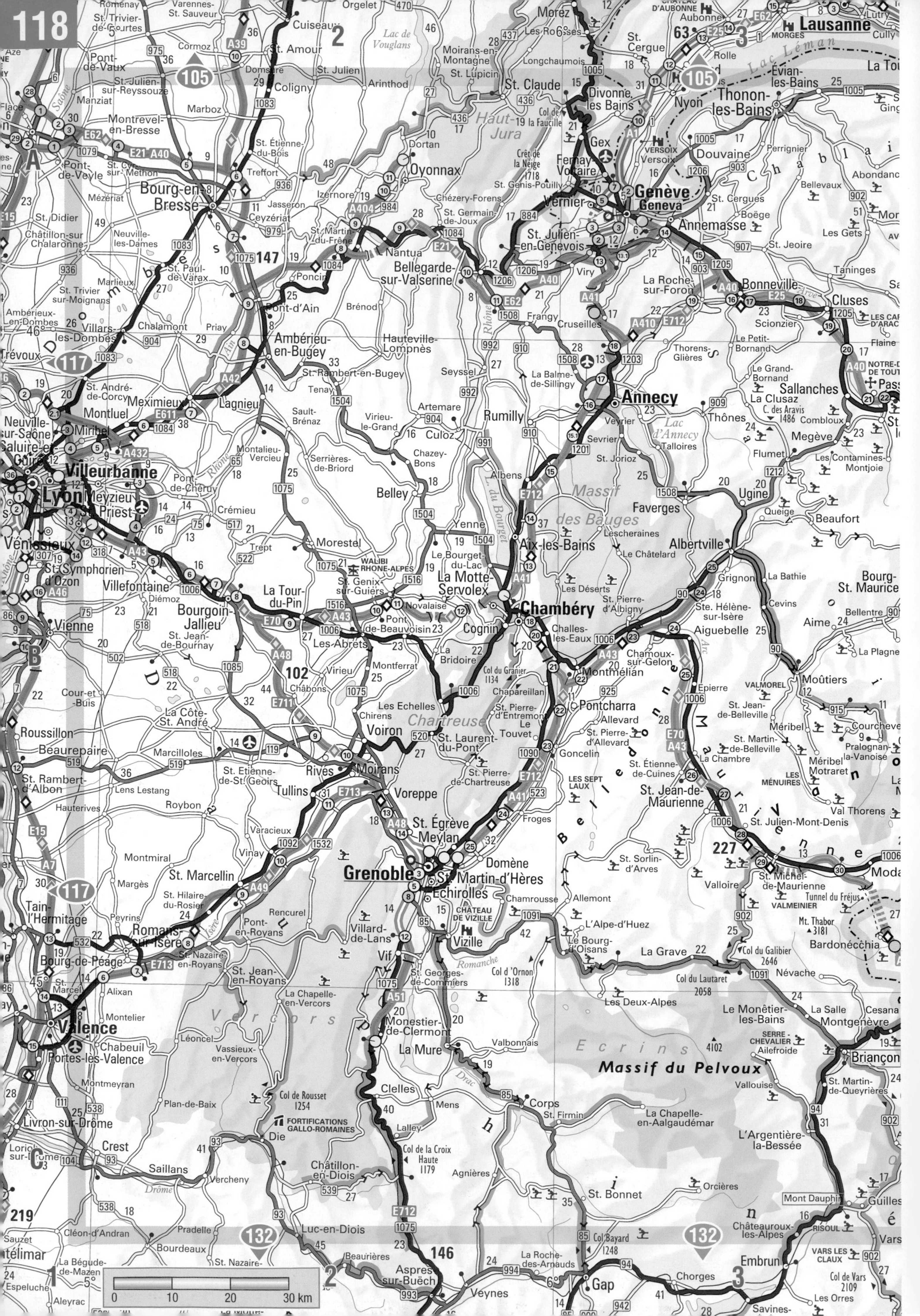
Lausanne
Lac Léman
Genève
Geneva
Annemasse
Thonon-les-Bains
Évian-les-Bains
Nyon
Divonne-les Bains
Gex
Ferney-Voltaire
Vernier
St. Julien-en-Genevois
Bonneville
Cluses
Sallanches
La Roche-sur-Foron
Cruseilles
Annecy
Lac d'Annecy
Thônes
Megève
Ugine
Faverges
Albertville
Massif des Bauges
Aix-les-Bains
Chambéry
Montmélian
Pontcharra
Grenoble
St. Martin-d'Hères
Échirolles
Meylan
St. Égrève
Voiron
Moirans
Voreppe
Chartreuse
Bourgoin-Jallieu
La Tour-du-Pin
Lyon
Villeurbanne
Vénissieux
Vienne
Valence
Romans-sur-Isère
Bourg-de-Péage
Tain-l'Hermitage
Crest
Die
Vercors
Bourg-en-Bresse
Oyonnax
Nantua
Bellegarde-sur-Valserine
St. Claude
Haut-Jura
Ambérieu-en-Bugey
Belley
Rumilly
Seyssel
Culoz
Moûtiers
Bourg-St. Maurice
Aiguebelle
St. Jean-de-Maurienne
St. Michel-de-Maurienne
Modane
Maurienne
Belledonne
Bardonécchia
Briançon
Massif du Pelvoux
Écrins
L'Argentière-la-Bessée
Embrun
Gap
Veynes
Aspres-sur-Buëch
Corps
La Mure
Vizille
Le Bourg-d'Oisans
L'Alpe-d'Huez
Les Deux-Alpes
La Grave
Col du Lautaret 2058
Col du Galibier 2646
Montélimar
0 10 20 30 km

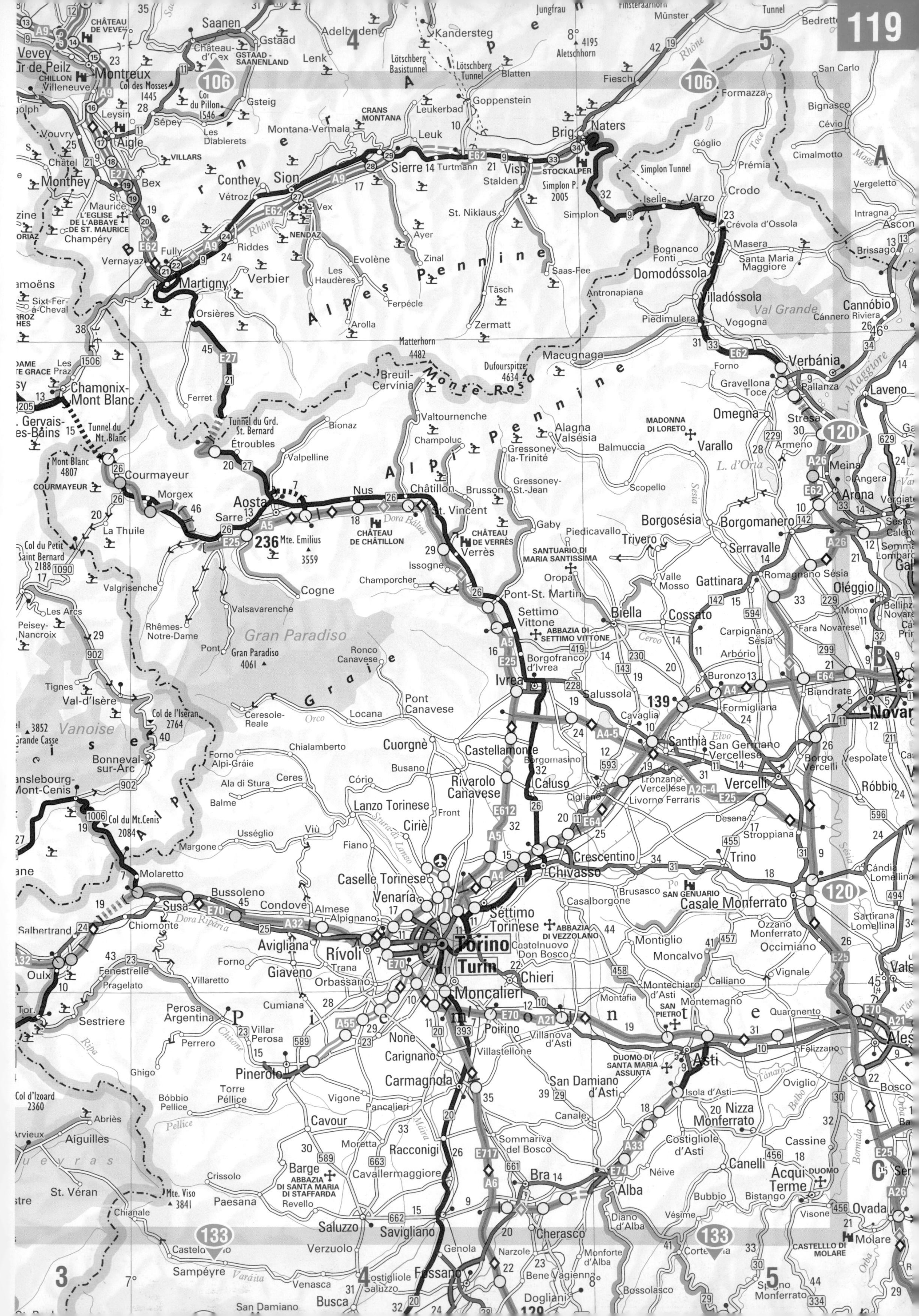
Vevey
Montreux
Chillon
Villeneuve
Saanen
Gstaad
Château-d'Œx
Adelboden
Kandersteg
Lötschberg Basistunnel
Lötschberg Tunnel
Blatten
Jungfrau
Aletschhorn
4195
Münster
Tunnel
Bedretto
Fiesch
Formazza
San Carlo
Bignasco
Cévio
Col des Mosses
1445
Col du Pillon
1546
Gsteig
Leysin
Sépey
Aigle
Les Diablerets
Vouvry
Châtel
Monthey
Bex
Villars
Crans Montana
Montana-Vermala
Leukerbad
Goppenstein
Leuk
Brig
Naters
Sierre
Turtmann
Visp
Stockalper
Góglio
Cimalmotto
Simplon Tunnel
Prémia
Vergeletto
Sion
Conthey
Vétroz
St. Maurice
Champéry
Stalden
Simplon P.
2005
Simplon
Iselle
Varzo
Crodo
Crévola d'Ossola
Intragna
Ascona
Brissago
Vex
Nendaz
Riddes
Fully
Vernayaz
Martigny
Verbier
Orsières
St. Niklaus
Ayer
Zinal
Evolène
Les Haudères
Ferpècle
Arolla
Täsch
Zermatt
Saas-Fee
Bognanco Fonti
Masera
Santa Maria Maggiore
Domodóssola
Villadóssola
Antronapiana
Piedimulera
Vogogna
Val Grande
Cannóbio
Cánnero Riviera
Alpes Pennine
Matterhorn
4482
Dufourspitze
4634
Monte Rosa
Macugnaga
Sixt-Fer-à-Cheval
Les Praz
Chamonix-Mont Blanc
St. Gervais-les-Bains
Tunnel du Mt. Blanc
Mont Blanc
4807
Courmayeur
Ferret
Tunnel du Grd. St. Bernard
Étroubles
Bionaz
Breuil-Cervínia
Valtournenche
Champoluc
Alagna Valsésia
Gressoney-la-Trinité
Gressoney-St.-Jean
Balmuccia
Madonna di Loreto
Varallo
Omegna
Stresa
Armeno
Meina
Angera
Arona
Verbánia
Pallanza
Gravellona Toce
Forno
Laveno
L. Maggiore
L. d'Orta
Valpelline
Morgex
Aosta
Sarre
Nus
Châtillon
St. Vincent
Brusson
Scopello
La Thuile
Col du Petit Saint Bernard
2188
Mte. Emilius
3559
Château de Châtillon
Château de Verrès
Verrès
Issogne
Champorcher
Cogne
Valgrisenche
Les Arcs
Peisey-Nancroix
Rhêmes-Notre-Dame
Valsavarenche
Gran Paradiso
4061
Pont
Gaby
Piedicavallo
Trivero
Santuario di Maria Santissima
Oropa
Borgosésia
Borgomanero
Serravalle
Gattinara
Romagnano Sésia
Oléggio
Valle Mosso
Pont-St. Martin
Settimo Vittone
Abbazia di Settimo Vittone
Biella
Cossato
Carpignano Sésia
Fara Novarese
Arbório
Borgofranco d'Ivrea
Ivrea
Salussola
Buronzo
Biandrate
Novara
Formigliana
Cavaglia
Santhià
San Germano Vercellese
Vercelli
Borgo Vercelli
Vespolate
Róbbio
Ronco Canavese
Alpi Graie
Tignes
Val-d'Isère
Col de l'Iseran
2764
Vanoise
3852
Grande Casse
Bonneval-sur-Arc
Lanslebourg-Mont-Cenis
Col du Mt.Cenis
2084
Ceresole-Reale
Locana
Pont Canavese
Orco
Forno Alpi-Gráie
Chialamberto
Cuorgnè
Castellamonte
Borgomasino
Caluso
Tronzano-Vercellese
Livorno Ferraris
Cigliano
Desana
Stroppiana
Trino
Ala di Stura
Ceres
Cório
Busano
Rivarolo Canavese
Balme
Lanzo Torinese
Front
Ciriè
Usséglio
Viù
Fiano
Margone
Molaretto
Caselle Torinese
Venaría
Crescentino
Chivasso
Brusasco
San Genuario
Casalborgone
Casale Monferrato
Cándia Lomellina
Sartirana Lomellina
Bussoleno
Susa
Condove
Almese
Alpignano
Settimo Torinese
Abbazia di Vezzolano
Castelnuovo Don Bosco
Montiglio
Ozzano Monferrato
Occimiano
Moncalvo
Salbertrand
Chiomonte
Dora Ripária
Avigliana
Rívoli
Torino
Turin
Chieri
Oulx
Fenestrelle
Pragelato
Forno
Villaretto
Giaveno
Trana
Orbassano
Moncalieri
Montechiaro d'Asti
Calliano
Vignale
Valenza
Sestriere
Perosa Argentina
Villar Perosa
Cumiana
None
Poirino
Villanova d'Asti
Montafia
San Pietro
Montemagno
Quargnento
Alessandria
Perrero
Pinerolo
Carignano
Villastellone
Duomo di Santa Maria Assunta
Asti
Felizzano
Col d'Izoard
2360
Ghigo
Torre Péllice
Bóbbio Pellice
Carmagnola
San Damiano d'Asti
Isola d'Asti
Nizza Monferrato
Oviglio
Bosco
Abriès
Aiguilles
Vigone
Pancalieri
Cavour
Canale
Costigliole d'Asti
Cassine
Moretta
Racconigi
Sommariva del Bosco
Barge
Abbazia di Santa Maria di Staffarda
Cavallermaggiore
Crissolo
Bra
Alba
Néive
Canelli
Acqui Terme
Duomo
St. Véran
Mte. Viso
3841
Paesana
Revello
Chianale
Diano d'Alba
Bubbio
Bistango
Vésime
Visone
Ovada
Saluzzo
Savigliano
Cherasco
Verzuolo
Genola
Narzole
Monforte d'Alba
Castello di Molare
Molare
Casteldelfino
Sampéyre
Varáita
Venasca
Costigliole Saluzzo
Fossano
Bene Vagienna
Busca
San Damiano
Dogliani
Bossolasco
Spigno Monferrato

Faido
Fusio
Pso. del S. Bernardino 2065
Tunnel
Splügenpass 2113
St. Moritz
Pontresina
Cresta
Bórmio
San Carlo
Bodio
Malvaglia
Mesocco
Julierpass 2284
Silvaplana
Maloja
Piz Bernina 4049
Bignasco
Cévio
Sonogno
Biasca
Rossa
Campodolcino
Castasegna
Vicosoprano
Chiaréggio
Poschiavo
Grósio
Sóndalo
Chiavenna
Villa di Chiavenna
Maggia
Vergeletto
Grono
Castione
Bellinzona
Novate Mezzola
Bagni del Másino
Chiesa in Valmalenco
Brusio
Mazzo di Valtellina
Górdola
Cataéggio
Tirano
Intragna
Ascona
Locarno
Cadenazzo
L. di Mezzola
Valtellina
Sóndrio
Tresenda
Edolo
Ossola
Brissago
Vira
Gravedona
Dongo
Berbenno di Valtellina
Aprica
Pso. dell'Aprica 1176
Bogno
Cólico
Morbegno
Alpi Orobie
Cannóbio
Cánnero Riviera
Maccagno-Agra
Agno
Lugano
Taverne
Porlezza
Menággio
Tremezzo
Bellano
Varenna
Gerola Alta
Mezzoldo
Fóppolo
Carona
Órobie Valtellinesi
Valbondione
Schilpário
Luino
Castagnola
L. di Lugano
Bellágio
Branzi
Bergamasche
Verbánia
Pallanza
Melide
Argegno
L. di Lecco
Introbio
Valtorta
Bárzio
Gromo
Dezzo
Breno
L. Maggiore
Laveno
Nesso
Mandello d. Lário
Piazza Brembana
Stresa
Porto Cerésio
Mendrisio
Láglio
Asso
Vedeseta
San Giovanni Bianco
Clusone
Boario Terme
Gavirate
Chiasso
Cernóbbio
Lecco
Serina
Darfo
Varese
L. di Varese
Erba
Brumano
San Pellegrino Terme
Gandino
Lóvere
Meina
Angera
Malnate
Olgiate Comasco
Como
Olginate
Oggiono
Calolziocorte
Zogno
Selvino
Pisogne
Bóvegno
Arona
Vergiate
Tradate
Cantù
Lurago d'Erba
Almenno S. Bart
Albino
Casazza
L. d'Iseo
Marone
Sesto Calende
Somma Lombardo
Cassano Magnago
Brianza Carate
Calco
Merate
Bérgamo
Seriate
Trescore Balneário
Tavernola Bergamasca
Gardone Val Trómpia
Gallarate
Malpensa
Séveso
Meda
Seregno
Trezzo sull'Adda
Ponte S. Pietro
Sárnico
Iseo
Oléggio
Saronno
Désio
Monza
Vimercate
Lombardia
Stezzano
Cologne al Serio
Rovato
Sarezzo
Busto Arsízio
Legnano
Crespi d'Adda
Vaprio d'Adda
Martinengo
Palazzolo sull'Oglio
Bréscia
Bellinzago Novarese
Castano Primo
Inveruno
Rho
Duomo di San Giovanni Battista
Gorgonzola
Treviglio
Romano di Lombardia
Chiari
Ospitaletto
Rezzato
Galliate
Sesto San Giovanni
Cassano d'Adda
Caravággio
Oglio Nord
Novara
Trecate
Magenta
Milano
Milan
Linate
Córsico
Rivolta d'Adda
Santuario della Madonna di Caravaggio
Mozzanica
Antegnate
Lograto
Bagnolo Mella
Castenédolo
Ghedi
Cerano
Abbiategrasso
Paullo
Pandino
Orzinuovi
Orzivécchi
Rozzano
Melegnano
Crema
Offanengo
Soncino
Manérbio
Leno
Carpenédolo
Borgo Vercelli
Vespolate
Cassolnovo
Vigévano
Siziano
Duomo di Lodi
Lodi
Quinzano d'Oglio
Róbbio
Binasco
Landriano
Castelleone
Verolanuova
Motta Visconti
Sant'Angelo Lodigiano
Soresina
Pontevico
Pralboino
Gambolò
Mortara
Bereguardo
Castiglione d'Adda
Casalbuttano ed Uniti
Gámbara
Tromello
Garlasco
Villantério
Ostiano
Cándia Lomellina
San Giorgio di Lomellina
Pavia
San Colombano al Lambro
Casalpusterlengo
Pizzighettone
Levata
Oglio Sud
Canneto sull'Oglio
Gropello Cairoli
Belgioioso
Santa Cristina
Codogno
Cremona
Cicognolo
Lomello
Zinasco
Monticelli d'Ongina
Piádena
Sartirana Lomellina
Mede
Sannazzaro de'Burgondi
Bressana
Cingia de'Botti
Pieve del Cáiro
Broni
Stradella
Castel San Giovanni
Rottofreno
Piacenza
Caorso
San Giovanni in Croce
Scandolara Ravara
Valenza
Castelnuovo Scrivia
Casteggio
Santa Maria della Versa
Borgonovo Val Tidone
Cortemaggiore
Roccabianca
Casalmaggiore
Sale
Voghera
Montalto Pavese
Busseto
Alessándria
Rivanazzano
Agazzano
Pianello Val Tidone
Podenzano
Grazzano Visconti
Pontenure
Carpaneto Piacentino
Fiorenzuola d'Arda
Soragna
San Secondo Parmense
Tortona
Godiasco
Nibbiano
Rivergaro
Fidenza
Bosco
Zavattarello
Travo
Ponte dell'Olio
Castell'Arquato
Salsomaggiore Terme
Noceto
Parma
Villaggio Medievale di Novi Ligure
Cassano Spinola
Varzi
Perino
Lugagnano Val d'Arda
Basaluzzo
San Sebastiano Curone
Vernasca
Tabiano Bagni
Novi Ligure
Bóbbio
Béttola
Medesano
Serravalle Scrívia
Brallo di Pregola
Pellegrino Parmense
Collécchio
Sala Baganza
Caldirola
Farini
Cabella Ligure
Marságlia
Bore
Varano de'Melegari
Gavi
Fornovo di Taro
Ovada
Ronco Scrivia
Montaldo di Cósola
Varsi
Molare
Voltággio
Ottone
Ferriere
Bardi
Langhirano
Traversétolo
Busalla
Calestano
Rossiglione
Campo Ligure
Casella
Passo dei Giovi
Masone
Pontedécimo
Torriglia
Bedónia
Berceto
0 10 20 30 km

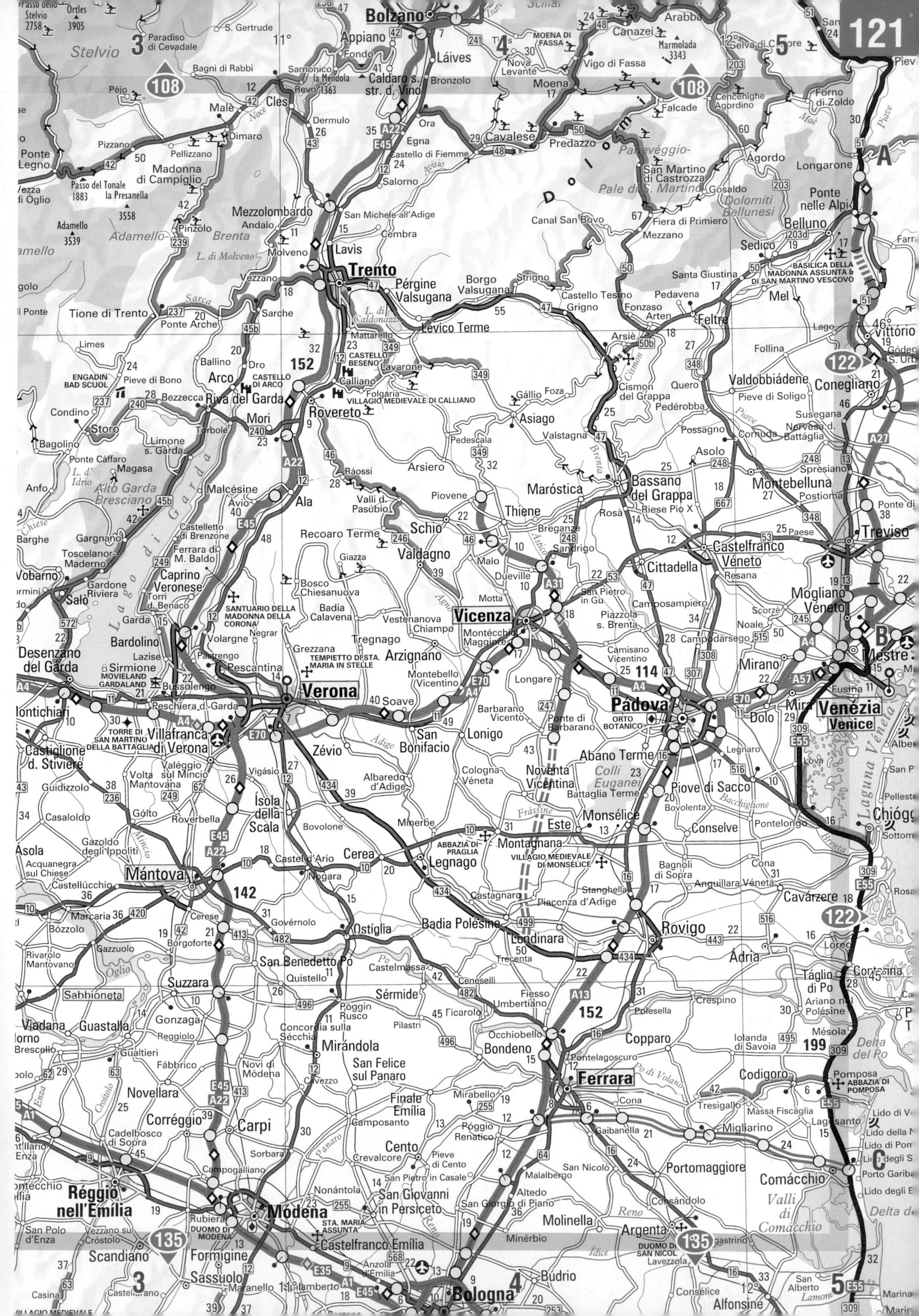

Bolzano
Ortles 3905
Stelvio
Paradiso di Cevadale
S. Gertrude
Appiano
Fondo
Láives
Moena di Fassa
Nova Levante
Canazei
Arabba
Marmolada 3343
Selva di Cadore
Vigo di Fassa
Bagni di Rabbi
Sarnonico
la Mendola
Revò 1363
Caldaro s. str. d. Vino
Bronzolo
Moena
Péjo
Malè
Cles
Noce
Dermulo
Ora
Egna
Cavalese
Predazzo
Falcade
Cencenighe Agordino
Forno di Zoldo
Piave
Pizzano
Pellizzano
Dimaro
Ponte di Legno
Castello di Fiemme
Avisio
Paneveggio-
Ágordo
Longarone
Madonna di Campiglio
Passo del Tonale 1883
la Presanella 3558
Salorno
San Martino di Castrozza
Pale di S. Martino
Gosaldo
Dolomiti Bellunesi
Ponte nelle Alpi
Dolomiti
Vezza d'Oglio
Adamello 3539
Adamello-Brenta
Pinzolo
Mezzolombardo
Andalo
San Michele all'Adige
Cembra
Canal San Bovo
Fiera di Primiero
Mezzano
Belluno
Sedico
Basilica della Madonna Assunta & di San Martino Vescovo
L. di Molveno
Molveno
Lavis
Trento
Pérgine Valsugana
Borgo Valsugana
Strigno
Castello Tesino
Grigno
Santa Giustina
Pedavena
Mel
Vezzano
Sarca
Tione di Trento
Ponte Arche
Sarche
L. di Caldonazzo
Levico Terme
Fonzaso
Arten
Feltre
Lago
Vittório
Limes
Mattarello
Castello Beseno
Arsiè
Cismon
Follina
Engadin Bad Scuol
Pieve di Bono
Ballino
Dro
Arco
Castello di Arco
Lavarone
Calliano
Folgaria
Villaggio Medievale di Calliano
Cismon del Grappa
Quero
Valdobbiádene
Conegliano
Pieve di Soligo
Condino
Bezzecca
Riva del Garda
Rovereto
Gállio
Foza
Asiago
Pederobba
Susegana
Storo
Torbole
Mori
Limone s. Garda
Nervesa d. Battáglia
Cornuda
Possagno
Bagolino
Pedescala
Valstagna
Brenta
Asolo
Ponte Cáffaro
L. d'Idrio
Magasa
Ráossi
Arsiero
Bassano del Grappa
Montebelluna
Spresiano
Anfo
Alto Garda Bresciano
Malcésine
Avio
Ala
Valli d. Pasúbio
Piovene
Maróstica
Postioma
Riese Pio X
Chiese
Castelletto di Brenzone
Thiene
Rosà
Ponte di Piave
Barghe
Gargnano
Lago di Garda
Recoaro Terme
Schio
Breganze
Treviso
Paese
Toscolano-Maderno
Ferrara di M. Baldo
Giazza
Valdagno
Malo
Sandrigo
Castelfranco Véneto
Cittadella
Resana
Vobarno
Caprino Veronese
Gardone Riviera
Salò
Torri d. Benaco
Bosco Chiesanuova
Badia Calavena
Dueville
San Pietro in Gu
Camposampiero
Mogliano Véneto
Scorzè
Santuario della Madonna della Corona
Garda
Motta
Vicenza
Vestenanova
Chiampo
Agno
Piazzola s. Brenta
Noale
Bardolino
Volargne
Negrar
Montécchio Maggiore
Camposampiero
Campodársego
Mestre
Desenzano del Garda
Lazise
Pastrengo
Grezzana
Tempietto di Sta. Maria in Stelle
Tregnago
Arzignano
Camisano Vicentino
Mirano
Sirmione
Movieland Gardaland
Bussolengo
Pescantina
Verona
Montebello Vicentino
Longare
Pádova
Fusina
Venézia Venice
Montichiari
Peschiera d. Garda
Soave
Barbarano Vicentino
Ponte di Barbarano
Orto Botanico
Dolo
Mira
Torre di San Martino della Battaglia
Villafranca di Verona
San Bonifacio
Lonigo
Castiglione d. Stiviere
Zévio
Adige
Abano Terme
Legnaro
Laguna Véneta
Guidizzolo
Volta Mantovana
Valéggio sul Mincio
Vigásio
Albaredo d'Adige
Cologna Véneta
Noventa Vicentina
Colli Euganei
Piove di Sacco
Battaglia Terme
Bovolenta
Bacchiglione
Chiógg
Casaloldo
Góito
Roverbella
Ísola della Scala
Bovolone
Minerbe
Frássine
Monsélice
Este
Conselve
Pontelongo
Sottom
Ásola
Gazoldo degli Ippoliti
Mincio
Abbazia di Praglia
Montagnana
Villaggio Medievale di Monsélice
Acquanegra sul Chiese
Cerea
Castel d'Ario
Legnago
Bagnoli di Sopra
Cona
Mántova
Castellúcchio
Nogara
Anguillara Véneta
Cavárzere
Marcaria
Cerese
Castagnaro
Stanghella
Piacenza d'Adige
Bózzolo
Borgoforte
Gazzuolo
Govérnolo
Ostíglia
Badia Polésine
Lendinara
Rovigo
Rivarolo Mantovano
Oglio
San Benedetto Po
Quistello
Po
Castelmassa
Trecenta
Ádria
Loreo
Sabbioneta
Suzzara
Sérmide
Ceneselli
Fiesso Umbertiano
Crespino
Táglio di Po
Contarina
Poggio Rusco
Ficarolo
Polesella
Ariano nel Polésine
Viadana
Guastalla
Gonzaga
Concordia sulla Sécchia
Pilastri
Occhiobello
Mésola
Delta del Po
Reggiolo
Mirándola
Bondeno
Copparo
Iolanda di Savoia
Brescello
Gualtieri
Fábbrico
Novi di Módena
San Felice sul Panaro
Pontelagoscuro
Po di Volano
Ferrara
Codigoro
Pompósa
Abbazia di Pompósa
Cavezzo
Novellara
Enza
Crostolo
Finale Emília
Mirabello
Cona
Tresigallo
Massa Fiscáglia
Lido di Volano
Corréggio
Carpi
Camposanto
Póggio Renatico
Gaibanella
Migliarino
Lagosanto
Lido delle Nazioni
Lido di Pomposa
Lido degli Scacchi
Cadelbosco di Sopra
Sorbara
Cento
Pieve di Cento
Crevalcore
Panaro
Portomaggiore
Comácchio
Porto Garibaldi
Campogalliano
San Pietro in Casale
Malalbergo
San Nicolò
Lido degli Estensi
Réggio nell'Emília
Montécchio Emília
Nonántola
San Giovanni in Persiceto
Altedo
San Giorgio di Piano
Consándolo
Valli di Comácchio
Delta del Po
Rubiera
Duomo di Módena
Módena
Sta. Maria Assunta
Castelfranco Emília
Reno
Molinella
Argenta
Duomo di San Nicolò
Minérbio
Ídice
San Polo d'Enza
Vezzano sul Crostolo
Scandiano
Formígine
Sassuolo
Maranello
Spilamberto
Anzola d'Emília
Búdrio
Lavezzola
Conselice
Alfonsine
San Alberto
Lamone
Casina
Castellarano
Bologna

San Vito di Cadore
Calalzo d.c.
L. di Pieve di Cadore
Pieve di Cadore
Sáuris
Forni di Sopra
Ampezzo
Villa Santina
Forni di Sotto
Tolmezzo
Pontebba
Tarvisio
Rateče
Kranjska Gora
Dovje
Julijske
Alpe
Passo di Predil
Chiusaforte
Móggio Udinese
Cárnia
Venzone
Triglav 2864
Bovec
Soca
Triglavski
Pokljuka
Bohinjsko jezero
Stara Fužina
Ukanc
KANIN
Žaga
Kobarid
VOGEL
KOBLA
Podbrdo
Tolmin
Forno di Zoldo
Tramonti di Sopra
Cimoláis
Cláut
Gemona del Friuli
Lusévera
Artegna
Tarcento
Nimis
Tricésimo
Faédis
Pulfero
Volče
Grahovo
Most na Soči
Longarone
Ponte nelle Alpi
Belluno
Sedico
Dolomiti Bellunesi
Farra d'Alpago
Bárcis
Maniago
Meduno
Sequals
Pinzano al Tagliamento
Buia
Montereale Valcellina
San Daniele del Friuli
Fagagna
DUOMO DI CIVIDALE DEL FRIULI
STA MARIA MAGGIORE
BASILICA DELLA MADONNA ASSUNTA & DI SAN MARTINO VESCOVO
Mel
Aviano
Spilimbergo
Dignano
Údine
Cividale del Friuli
Kanal
Slap
San Martino di Campagna
San Giorgio d. Richinvelda
Campofórmido
Deskle
Cepovan
Lago
Vittório Véneto
Follina
Gódega di S. Urbano
Sacile
Pordenone
Cordenons
San Vito al Tagliamento
Mortegliano
Codróipo
Cormòns
CASTELLO DI GORIZIA
Gorizia
Nova Gorica
Grgar
Solkan
Predmeja
Črni
Valdobbiádene
Pieve di Soligo
Conegliano
Susegana
Nervesa d. Battáglia
Cornuda
Prata di Pordenone
Castions di Strada
Palmanova
Gradisca d'Isonzo
Ajdovščina
Azzano Décimo
Rivignano
Cervignano del Friuli
Ronchi dei Legionari
Monfalcone
Branik
Spresiano
Montebelluna
Postioma
Oderzo
Cordovado
Portogruaro
Muzzano del Turgnano
San Giorgio di Nogaro
Aquiléia
AQUILEIA
Komen
Dutovlje
Motta di Livenza
Concordia Sagittária
Latisana
Marano Lagunare
Duino
Sistiana
Ponte di Piave
Treviso
Paese
Castelfranco
San Stino di Livenza
Céggia
L. di Marano
Grignano
Sežana
Divača
Opicina
Bašovizza
BASILICA DI SANT'EUFEMIA
Lignano Sabbiadoro
Grado
Trieste
Noventa di Piave
La Salute di Livenza
Bibione
San Donà di Piave
Múggia
Mogliano Véneto
Scorzè
Caposile
Eraclea
Cáorle
G. di Trieste
Ankaran
Koper
Izola
Piran
Eraclea Mare
Portegrandi
Jésolo
Burano
Mestre
Murano
Lido di Jésolo
Savudrija
Lucija
Igoumenitsa
Patra
Durrës
Ancona
Mira
Fusina
Cavallino
Punta Sabbioni
Oragonja
Dolo
Venézia
Venice
Lido
Umag
Buje
Oprtalj
Buzet
Alberoni
Golfo di Venézia
Brtonigla
Lova
Laguna Véneta
San Pietro in Volta
Novigrad
Motovun
Vižinada
Karojba
Cerovlje
Pellestrina
Istra
Višnjan
Pontelongo
Chióggia
Sottomarina
Pazin
Poreč
Baderna
Cavárzere
Rosalina Mare
Kanfanar
Žminj
Vrsar
Loreo
Rovinj
Svetvinčenat
Bale
Contarina
Ariano nel Polésine
Ca'Pisani
Porto Tolle
Barbariga
Vodnjan
Mésola
Delta del Po
Scardovari
Foci del Po
Brijuni
Brionski
Pula
Pomposa
ABBAZIA DI POMPOSA
PULA ANTIČKI NALAZIŠTE
Lido di Volano
Lagosanto
Lido della Nazioni
Lido di Pomposa
Lido degli Scacchi
Porto Garibaldi
Lido degli Estensi
Comácchio
Valli di Comácchio
Premantura
Rt. Kamenjak
0 10 20 30 km
San Alberto
Marina Romea
Marina di Ravenna
13°
46°
45°

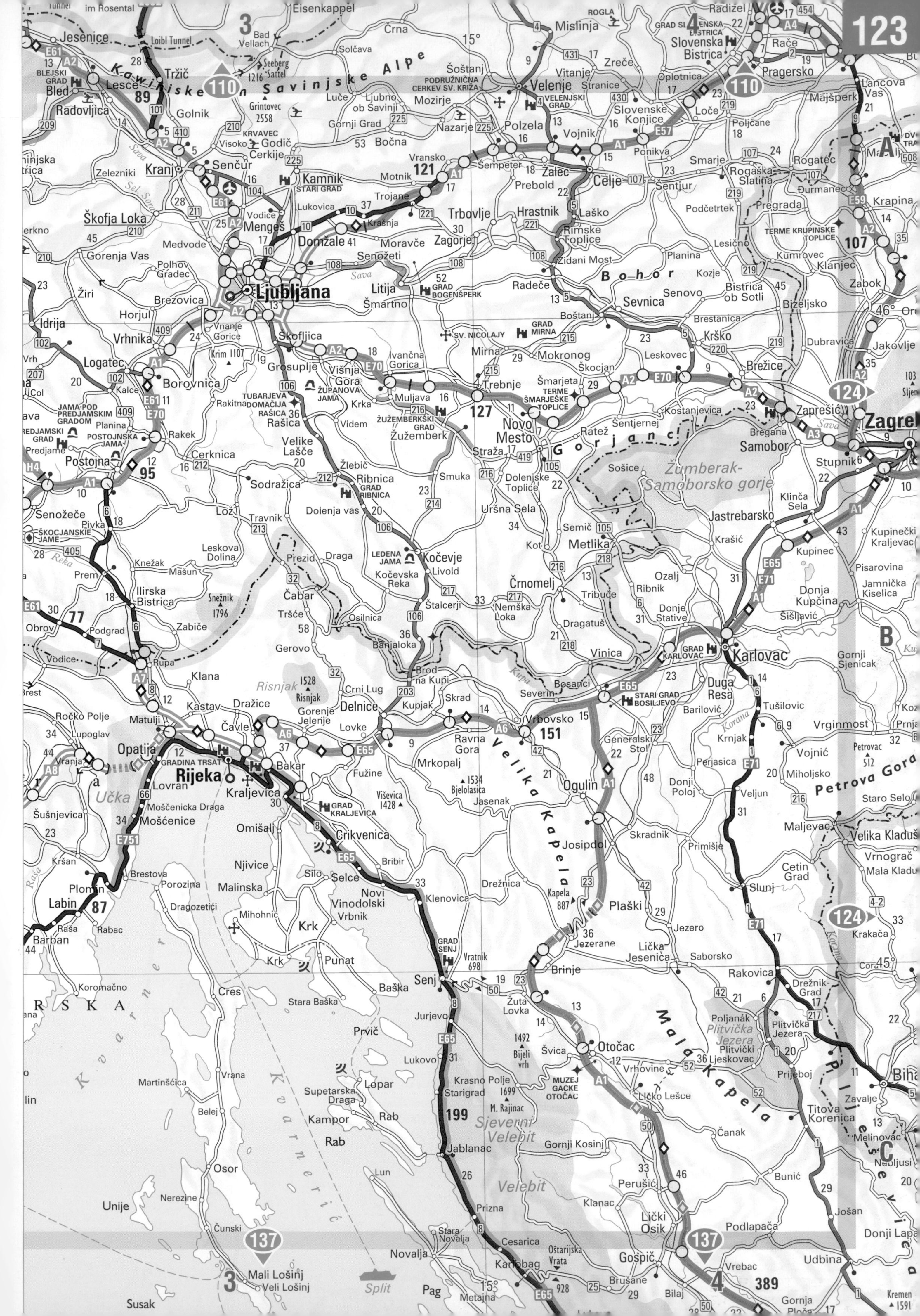

Nagykanizsa
Ptuj
Čakovec
Varaždin
Zagreb
Koprivnica
Bjelovar
Đurđevac
Virovitica
Barcs
Nagyatád
Csurgo
Križevci
Sesvete
Velika Gorica
Dugo Selo
Ivanić Grad
Čazma
Daruvar
Sisak
Petrinja
Kutina
Novska
Pakrac
Lipik
Okučani
Nova Gradiška
Glina
Velika Kladuša
Bosanski Novi
Prijedor
Bosanska Dubica
Bosanska Gradiška
Bosanska Krupa
Bihać
Cazin
Sanski Most
Banja Luka
Bosanski Petrovac
Ključ
Kotor Varoš
Ivanščica
Kalnik
Medvednica
Moslavačka Gora
Bilo Gora
Papuk
Zrinska Gora
Petrova Gora
Kozara
Krajina
Grmeč Planina
Plješevica
Lonjsko Polje
0
10
20
30 km

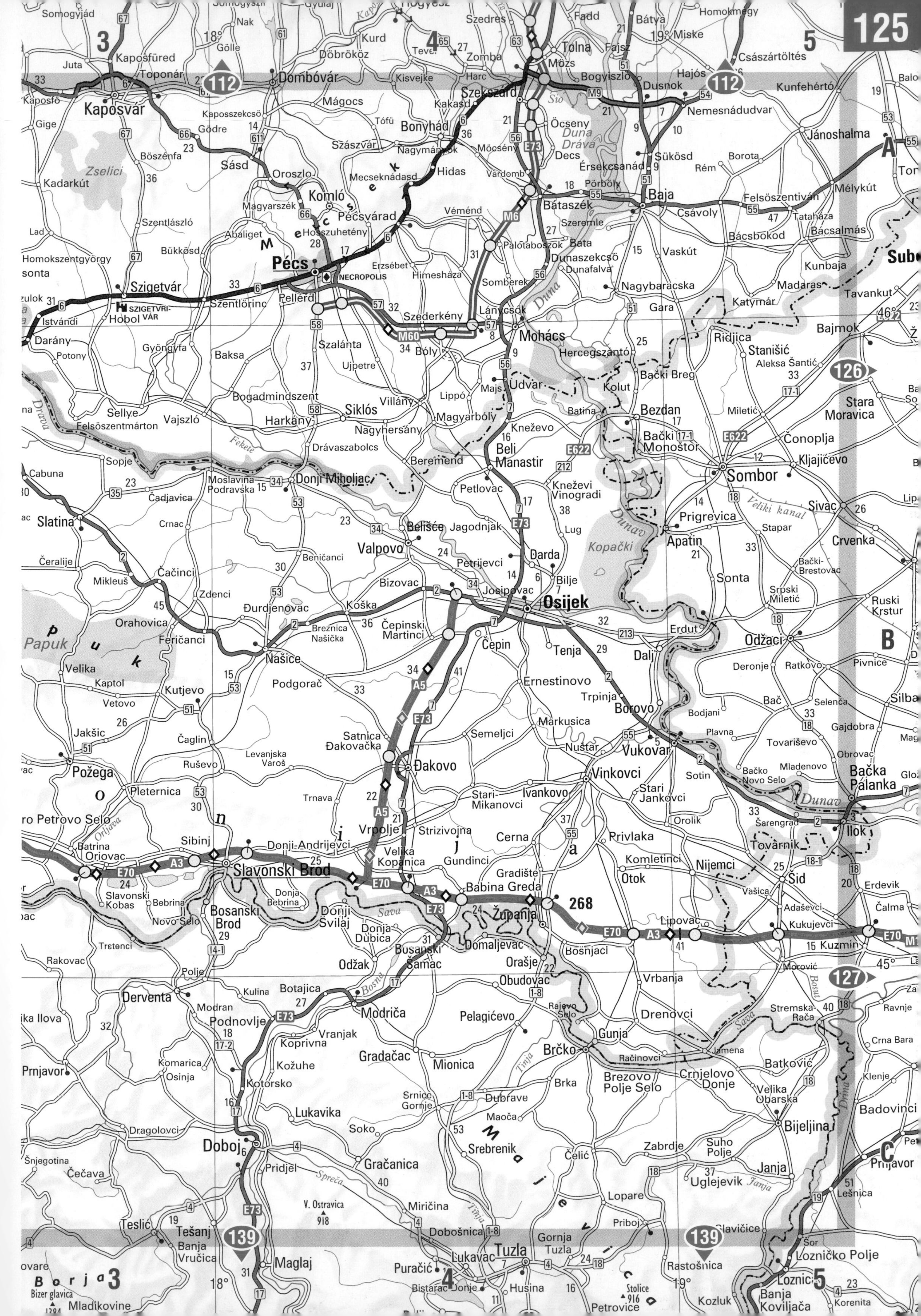

Kaposvár
Dombóvár
Szekszárd
Tolna
Bonyhád
Komló
Pécs
Pécsvárad
Szigetvár
Mohács
Baja
Bátaszék
Sombor
Siklós
Harkány
Beli Manastir
Osijek
Valpovo
Našice
Đakovo
Vinkovci
Vukovar
Slavonski Brod
Bosanski Brod
Županja
Požega
Slatina
Bačka Palanka
Ilok
Šid
Odžaci
Apatin
Brčko
Bijeljina
Doboj
Gradačac
Modriča
Tuzla
Lukavac
Gračanica
Srebrenik
Derventa
Teslić
Maglaj
Orašje
Kopački rit
Dunav
Drava
Sava
Papuk
Mecsek
Majevica
E70
E73
A3
A5
M6
M60
268
NECROPOLIS
SZIGETVÁRI VÁR
112
126
127
139

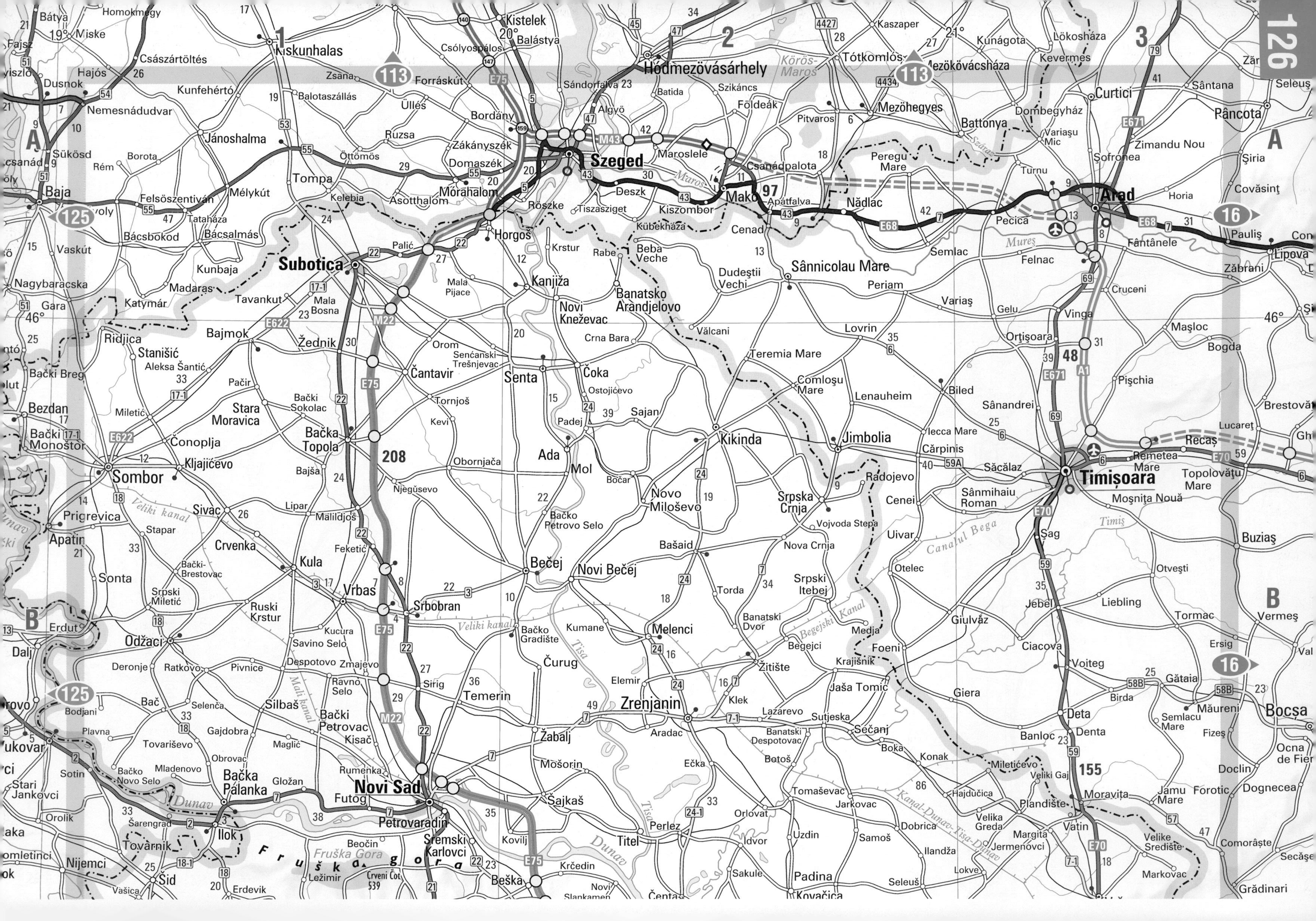
A
B
1
2
3
Arad
Timişoara
Szeged
Subotica
Novi Sad
Zrenjanin
Kikinda
Sombor
Hódmezővásárhely
Kiskunhalas
Baja
Makó
Curtici
Pâncota
Lipova
Pauliş
Zăbrani
Recaş
Buziaş
Bocşa
Vermeş
Deta
Jimbolia
Sânnicolau Mare
Nădlac
Pecica
Battonya
Mezőkovácsháza
Mezőhegyes
Tótkomlós
Kunágota
Dombegyház
Lőkösháza
Kevermes
Sofronea
Zimandu Nou
Sântana
Şiria
Covăsânţ
Fântânele
Vinga
Felnac
Orţişoara
Sânandrei
Săcălaz
Şag
Biled
Periam
Lovrin
Lenauheim
Comloşu Mare
Teremia Mare
Dudeştii Vechi
Cenad
Kiszombor
Maroslele
Deszk
Kübekháza
Beba Veche
Banatsko Arandjelovo
Novi Kneževac
Čoka
Senta
Ada
Mol
Bečej
Novi Bečej
Novo Miloševo
Srpska Crnja
Nova Crnja
Srpski Itebej
Žitište
Melenci
Bašaid
Čurug
Žabalj
Titel
Perlez
Aradac
Sečanj
Jaša Tomić
Sutjeska
Lazarevo
Kanjiža
Horgoš
Röszke
Mórahalom
Ásotthalom
Palić
Bačka Topola
Čantavir
Srbobran
Vrbas
Kula
Crvenka
Temerin
Ruski Krstur
Bački Petrovac
Bačka Palanka
Ilok
Šid
Futog
Petrovaradin
Sremski Karlovci
Beočin
Fruška Gora
Odžaci
Bač
Apatin
Sonta
Bezdan
Bački Monoštor
Kljajićevo
Čonoplja
Stanišić
Ridjica
Bajmok
Tavankut
Mala Bosna
Žednik
Kelebia
Tompa
Jánoshalma
Mélykút
Bácsalmás
Kunbaja
Madaras
Katymár
Kistelek
Balástya
Forráskút
Üllés
Ruzsa
Öttömös
Zákányszék
Domaszék
Bordány
Algyő
Sándorfalva
Csanádpalota
Földeák
Pitvaros
Zsana
Balotaszállás
Kunfehértó
Császártöltés
Hajós
Nemesnádudvar
Borota
Rém
Felsőszentiván
Bácsbokod
Vaskút
Nagybaracska
Gara
Dusnok
Sükösd
Erdut
Dalj
Sivac
Srpski Miletić
Deronje
Ratkovo
Selenča
Gajdobra
Obrovac
Tovariševo
Mladenovo
Despotovo
Pivnice
Silbaš
Kisač
Rumenka
Šajkaš
Mošorin
Kovilj
Beška
Banatski Dvor
Torda
Elemir
Ečka
Orlovat
Tomaševac
Padina
Vatin
Banloc
Denta
Voiteg
Giera
Foeni
Otelec
Uivar
Giulvăz
Jebel
Ciacova
Liebling
Cărpiniş
Cenei
Moşniţa Nouă
Topolovăţu Mare
Remetea Mare
Maşloc
Bogda
Mureş
Maros
Tisa
Dunav
Timiş
Canalul Bega
Veliki kanal
Mali kanal
Kanal-Dunav-Tisa-Dunav
E68
E70
E75
E671
E622
M43
M22
A1
16
113
125
155
208
48
97
46°
20°
21°

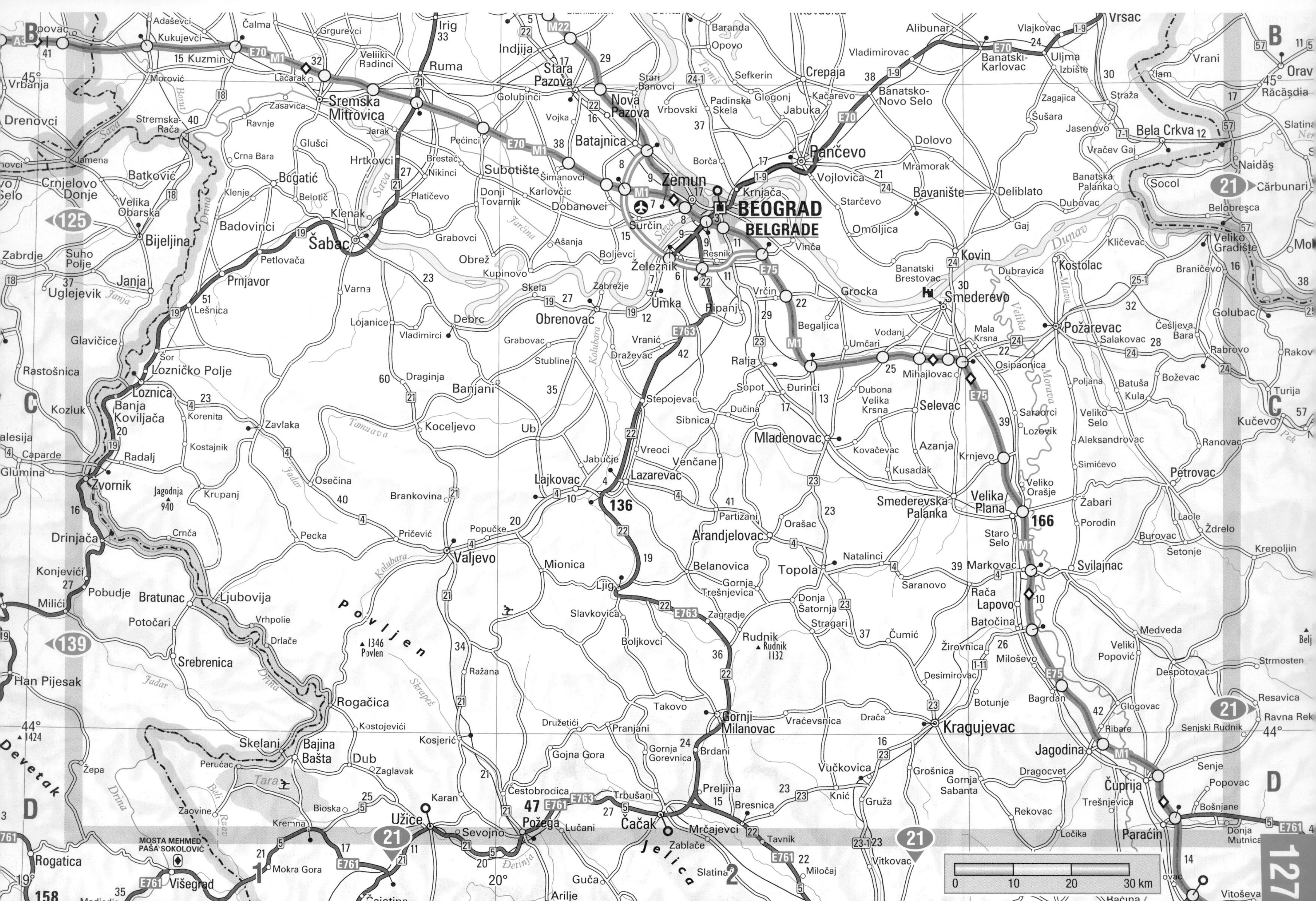
BEOGRAD
BELGRADE
Zemun
Pančevo
Novi Sad
Vršac
Bela Crkva
Smederevo
Požarevac
Kostolac
Kovin
Veliko Gradište
Golubac
Kučevo
Petrovac
Svilajnac
Velika Plana
Smederevska Palanka
Mladenovac
Arandjelovac
Topola
Kragujevac
Jagodina
Ćuprija
Paraćin
Lapovo
Batočina
Markovac
Gornji Milanovac
Čačak
Požega
Užice
Valjevo
Lajkovac
Lazarevac
Obrenovac
Šabac
Sremska Mitrovica
Ruma
Indjija
Stara Pazova
Nova Pazova
Batajnica
Subotište
Bijeljina
Zvornik
Loznica
Banja Koviljača
Ljubovija
Bratunac
Srebrenica
Bajina Bašta
Rogačica
Višegrad
Rogatica
Han Pijesak
Mionica
Ljig
Rudnik
Koceljevo
Ub
Banjani
Prnjavor
Bogatić
Crepaja
Banatski Karlovac
Alibunar
Deliblato
Bavanište
Jelica
Povljen
Devetak
Drina
Sava
Dunav
Morava
Mlava
Kolubara
Jadar
MOSTA MEHMED PAŠA SOKOLOVIĆ
0
10
20
30 km
21
125
139
158
166
136
47
44°
45°
20°
19°
B
C
D

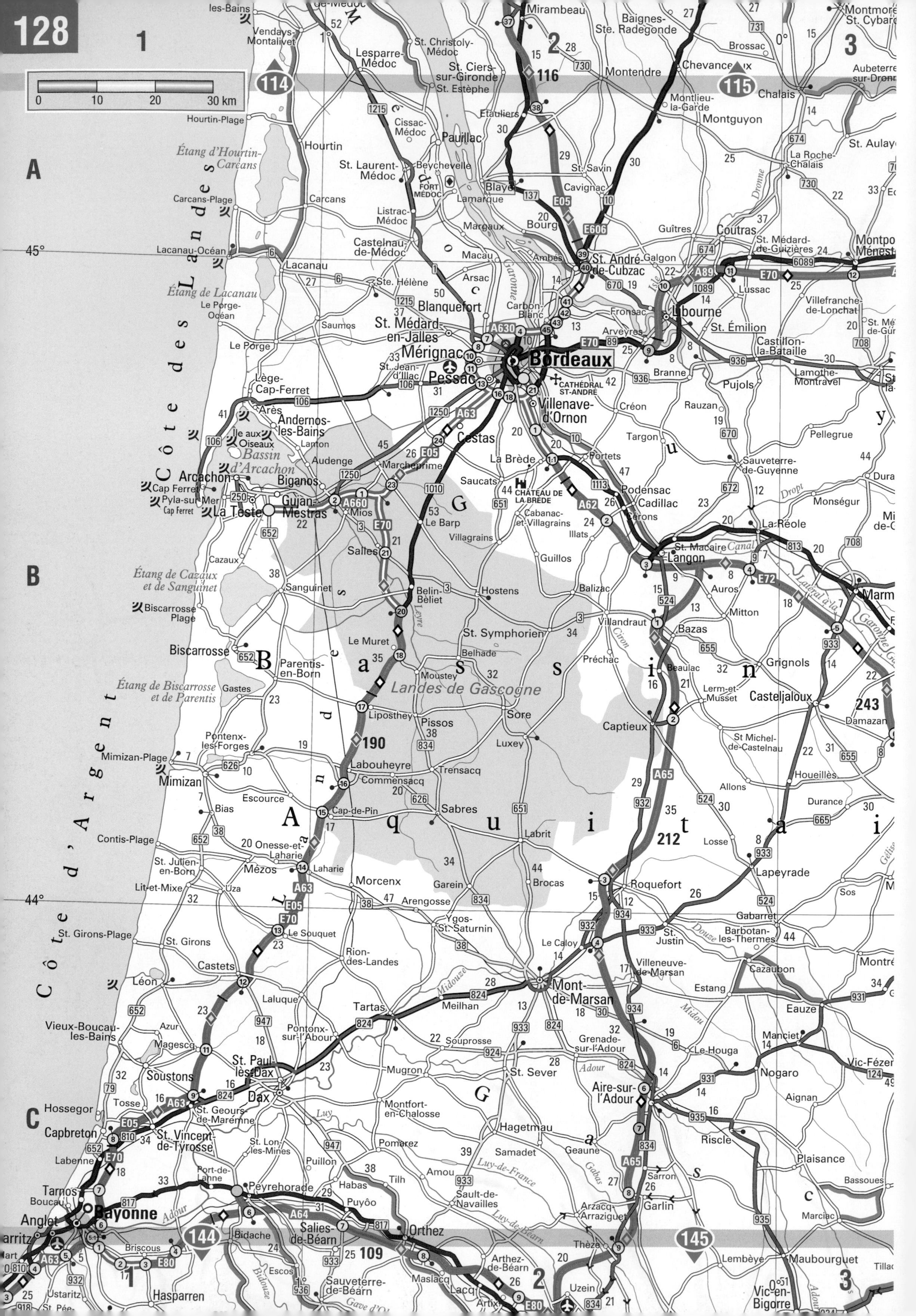
0 10 20 30 km
Côte des Landes
Côte d'Argent
Landes de Gascogne
Aquitaine
Gascogne
Landes
Médoc
Bassin d'Arcachon
Étang d'Hourtin-Carcans
Étang de Lacanau
Étang de Cazaux et de Sanguinet
Étang de Biscarrosse et de Parentis
Vendays-Montalivet
Lesparre-Médoc
St. Christoly-Médoc
St. Ciers-sur-Gironde
St. Estèphe
Mirambeau
Baignes-Ste. Radegonde
Montendre
Brossac
Chevanceaux
Chalais
Montlieu-la-Garde
Montguyon
Aubeterre-sur-Dronne
St. Aulaye
La Roche-Chalais
Hourtin-Plage
Hourtin
Cissac-Médoc
Pauillac
Etauliers
St. Laurent-Médoc
Beychevelle
FORT MÉDOC
Blaye
Lamarque
St. Savin
Cavignac
Carcans-Plage
Carcans
Listrac-Médoc
Margaux
Bourg
Guîtres
Coutras
St. Médard-de-Guizières
Lacanau-Océan
Castelnau-de-Médoc
Macau
Ambès
St. André-de-Cubzac
Galgon
Lacanau
Ste. Hélène
Arsac
Lussac
Villefranche-de-Lonchat
Le Porge-Océan
Blanquefort
Carbon-Blanc
Fronsac
Libourne
St. Émilion
Saumos
St. Médard-en-Jalles
Arveyres
Castillon-la-Bataille
Le Porge
Mérignac
Bordeaux
St. Jean-d'Illac
Pessac
CATHÉDRAL ST-ANDRÉ
Branne
Pujols
Lamothe-Montravel
Lège-Cap-Ferret
Arès
Andernos-les-Bains
Villenave-d'Ornon
Créon
Rauzan
Île aux Oiseaux
Lanton
Cestas
Targon
Pellegrue
Audenge
Marcheprime
La Brède
Portets
Sauveterre-de-Guyenne
Arcachon
Cap Ferret
Pyla-sur-Mer
Biganos
Saucats
CHÂTEAU DE LA BRÈDE
Podensac
Cadillac
Monségur
La Teste
Gujan-Mestras
Mios
Le Barp
Cabanac-et-Villagrains
Cérons
La Réole
Villagrains
Illats
Salles
St. Macaire
Langon
Cazaux
Guillos
Auros
Sanguinet
Belin-Bèliet
Hostens
Balizac
Mitton
Biscarrosse Plage
Villandraut
Bazas
Le Muret
St. Symphorien
Belhade
Préchac
Grignols
Biscarrosse
Parentis-en-Born
Moustey
Beaulac
Gastes
Lerm-et-Musset
Casteljaloux
Liposthey
Pissos
Sore
Captieux
Damazan
Pontenx-les-Forges
Luxey
St Michel-de-Castelnau
Mimizan-Plage
Labouheyre
Trensacq
Mimizan
Commensacq
Houeillès
Escource
Allons
Cap-de-Pin
Sabres
Durance
Bias
Contis-Plage
Onesse-et-Laharie
Labrit
Losse
St. Julien-en-Born
Laharie
Mézos
Lapeyrade
Lit-et-Mixe
Uza
Morcenx
Garein
Brocas
Roquefort
Arengosse
Sos
Ygos-St. Saturnin
Gabarret
St. Girons-Plage
St. Girons
Le Souquet
Le Caloy
St. Justin
Barbotan-les-Thermes
Rion-des-Landes
Castets
Villeneuve-de-Marsan
Cazaubon
Léon
Mont-de-Marsan
Estang
Laluque
Midouze
Tartas
Meilhan
Eauze
Vieux-Boucau-les-Bains
Azur
Pontonx-sur-l'Adour
Grenade-sur-l'Adour
Manciet
Magescq
Souprosse
Le Houga
Soustons
St. Paul-lès-Dax
Mugron
St. Sever
Nogaro
Vic-Fézensac
Dax
Aire-sur-l'Adour
Hossegor
Tosse
Montfort-en-Chalosse
Aignan
St. Geours-de-Maremne
Capbreton
St. Vincent-de-Tyrosse
Hagetmau
Riscle
St. Lon-les-Mines
Labenne
Pomarez
Samadet
Geaune
Plaisance
Puillon
Port-de-Lanne
Amou
Tarnos
Habas
Tilh
Sarron
Boucau
Peyrehorade
Sault-de-Navailles
Garlin
Bassoues
Puyôo
Arzacq-Arraziguet
Marciac
Anglet
Bayonne
Salies-de-Béarn
Orthez
Bidache
Thèze
Biarritz
Briscous
Lembeye
Maubourguet
Escos
Arthez-de-Béarn
Sauveterre-de-Béarn
Maslacq
Lacq
Artix
Hasparren
Ustaritz
Uzein
Vic-en-Bigorre
Garonne
Dordogne
Dronne
Isle
Dropt
Leyre
Ciron
Adour
Luy
Midou
Douze
Gabas
Luy-de-France
Luy-de-Béarn
Canal Latéral à la Garonne
114
115
116
144
145
190
212
243
109
45°
44°
A
B
C
1
2
3

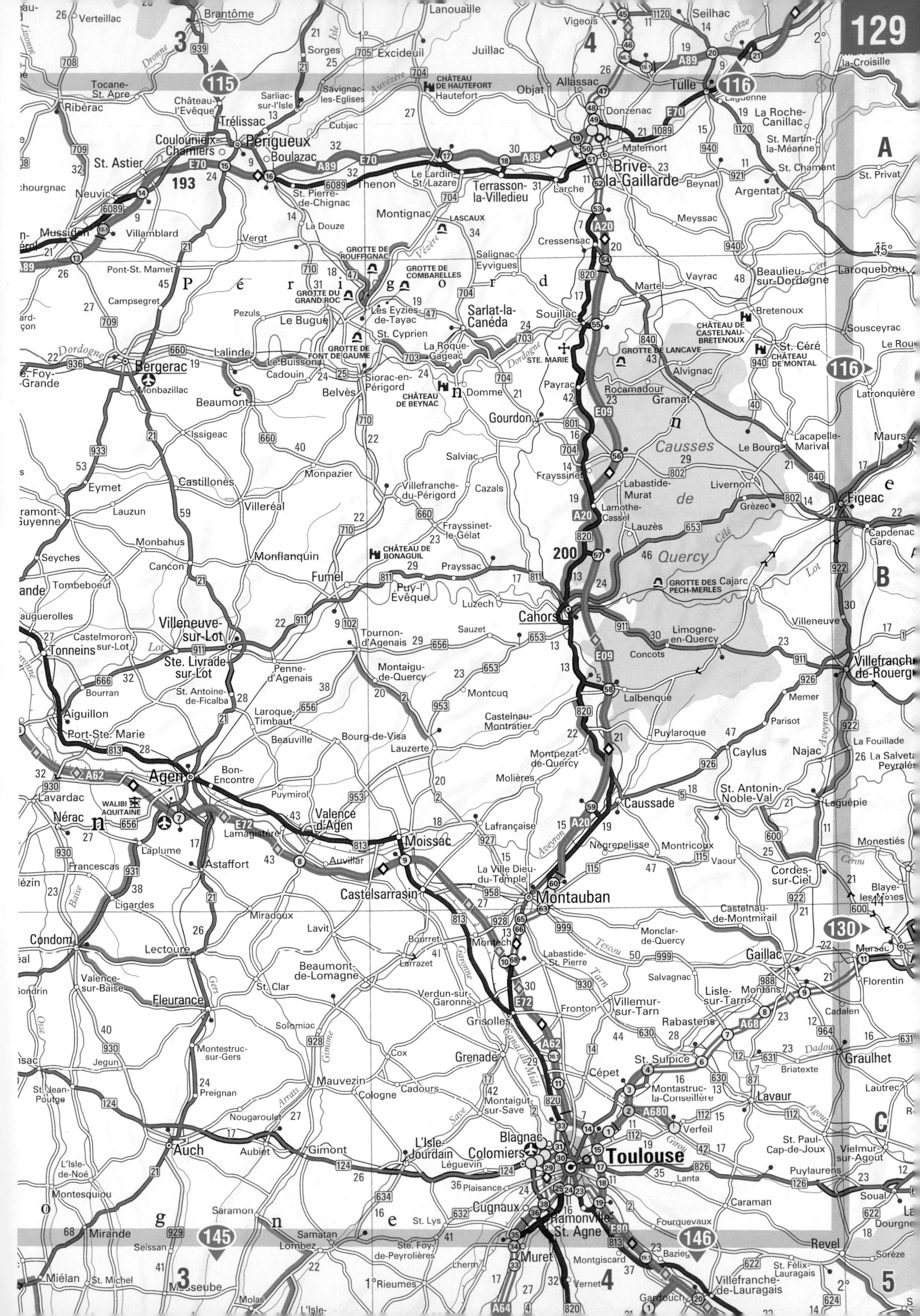
Brantôme
Verteillac
Lanouaille
Vigeois
Seilhac
Sorges
Excideuil
Juillac
Tocane-St. Apre
115
Château-l'Evêque
Sarliac-sur-l'Isle
Savignac-les-Eglises
CHÂTEAU DE HAUTEFORT
Hautefort
Objat
Allassac
Tulle
116
Laguenne
Ribérac
Trélissac
Cubjac
Donzenac
La Roche-Canillac
Coulounieix-Chamiers
Périgueux
Boulazac
Malemort
St. Martin-la-Méanne
St. Astier
Brive-la-Gaillarde
St. Chamant
St. Privat
Neuvic
193
Thenon
Le Lardin-St. Lazare
Terrasson-la-Villedieu
Larche
Beynat
Argentat
St. Pierre-de-Chignac
Mussidan
Villamblard
La Douze
Montignac
LASCAUX
Meyssac
Vergt
GROTTE DE ROUFFIGNAC
Salignac-Eyvigues
Cressensac
Pont-St. Mamet
GROTTE DE COMBARELLES
Vayrac
Beaulieu-sur-Dordogne
Laroquebrou
Périgord
Martel
GROTTE DU GRAND ROC
Campsegret
Les Eyzies-de-Tayac
Sarlat-la-Canéda
Souillac
Bretenoux
Pezuls
Le Bugue
St. Cyprien
CHÂTEAU DE CASTELNAU-BRETENOUX
Sousceyrac
GROTTE DE FONT DE GAUME
La Roque-Gageac
GROTTE DE LANCAVE
St. Céré
CHÂTEAU DE MONTAL
Le Rouget
Lalinde
Bergerac
Le Buisson
Cadouin
Siorac-en-Périgord
STE. MARIE
Ste.-Foy-la-Grande
Monbazillac
Beaumont
Belvès
CHÂTEAU DE BEYNAC
Domme
Payrac
Rocamadour
Gramat
Alvignac
Latronquière
Gourdon
Issigeac
Salviac
Causses
Le Bourg
Lacapelle-Marival
Maurs
Eymet
Monpazier
Castillonès
Villefranche-du-Périgord
Cazals
Frayssinet
Labastide-Murat
Livernon
Figeac
Lauzun
Villeréal
Lamothe-Cassel
Grèzec
de
Lauzès
Capdenac Gare
Miramont-de-Guyenne
Monbahus
Frayssinet-le-Gélat
Seyches
Cancon
Monflanquin
CHÂTEAU DE BONAGUIL
Quercy
Célé
Fumel
Prayssac
Tombeboeuf
Puy-l'Évêque
Luzech
GROTTE DES PECH-MERLES
Cajarc
Lot
Villeneuve-sur-Lot
Cahors
Limogne-en-Quercy
Villeneuve
Marmande
Castelmoron-sur-Lot
Tonneins
Sauzet
Tournon-d'Agenais
Concots
Villefranche-de-Rouergue
Ste. Livrade-sur-Lot
Penne-d'Agenais
Montaigu-de-Quercy
Bourran
St. Antoine-de-Ficalba
Montcuq
Lalbenque
Memer
Aiguillon
Laroque-Timbaut
Castelnau-Montratier
Parisot
Port-Ste. Marie
Beauville
Bourg-de-Visa
Lauzerte
Puylaroque
Caylus
Najac
La Fouillade
La Salvetat-Peyralès
Agen
Bon-Encontre
Montpezat-de-Quercy
Molières
St. Antonin-Noble-Val
Laguépie
Lavardac
WALIBI AQUITAINE
Puymirol
Caussade
Nérac
Valence-d'Agen
Lamagistère
Lafrançaise
Monestiés
Moissac
Nègrepelisse
Montricoux
Vaour
Laplume
Astaffort
Auvillar
La Ville Dieu-du-Temple
Cordes-sur-Ciel
Francescas
Montauban
Castelsarrasin
Blaye-les-Mines
Mézin
Ligardes
Castelnau-de-Montmirail
Miradoux
Lavit
Montech
Monclar-de-Quercy
130
Condom
Lectoure
Bourret
Labastide-St. Pierre
Gaillac
Mursac
Larrazet
Valence-sur-Baïse
Beaumont-de-Lomagne
Salvagnac
Florentin
Gondrin
St. Clar
Lisle-sur-Tarn
Montans
Fleurance
Verdun-sur-Garonne
Fronton
Villemur-sur-Tarn
Cadalen
Grisolles
Rabastens
Solomiac
Montestruc-sur-Gers
Grenade
St. Sulpice
Briatexte
Graulhet
Jegun
Cox
Cépet
St. Jean-Poutge
Mauvezin
Cadours
Montastruc-la-Conseillère
Lautrec
Cologne
Lavaur
Preignan
Montaigut-sur-Save
Nougaroulet
Blagnac
Verfeil
Auch
Aubiet
Gimont
L'Isle-Jourdain
Colomiers
Toulouse
St. Paul-Cap-de-Joux
Vielmur-sur-Agout
L'Isle-de-Noé
Léguevin
Lanta
Puylaurens
Plaisance
Montesquiou
Caraman
Soual
Saramon
Cugnaux
Ramonville-St. Agne
Fourquevaux
Dourgne
Mirande
145
Samatan
St. Lys
146
Seissan
Lombez
Ste. Foy-de-Peyrolières
Revel
Lherm
Muret
Bazieg
Sorèze
Montgiscard
St. Félix-Lauragais
Miélan
St. Michel
Masseube
Rieumes
Vernet
Villefranche-de-Lauragais
Molas
Gardouch
L'Isle-
A
B
C
3
4
5

Conques
Entraygues-sur-Truyère
Aubrac
Decazeville
Firmi
Capdenac-Gare
Aubin
Villecomtal
Espalion
Le Cayrol
St. Chély-d'Aubrac
Marvejols
Mende
Laubert
Bleymard
Chirac
ERMITAGE DE ST. PRIVAT
Le Bleymard
St. Come-d'Olt
Montbazens
Roussennac
Marcillac-Vallon
Bozouls
Gabriac
St. Geniez-d'Olt
Chanac
La Canourgue
Col de Montmirat 1046
Villeneuve
Rignac
Sebazac-Concourès
St.-Saturnin-de-Lenne
Ste. Enimie
Ispagnac
Le Pont-de-Montvert
Villefranche-de-Rouergue
Rodez
Laissac
Recoules-Prévinquières
Sévérac-le-Château
Le Massegros
Florac
Cévennes
La Primaube
Lac de Pont-de-Salars
La Malène
Rieupeyroux
Baraqueville
Pont-de-Salars
Vézins-de-Lévézou
Les Vignes
Causse-Méjean
Cassagnas
La Fouillade
La Salvetat-Peyralès
Lac de Pareloup
Mostuéjouls
Barre-des-Cevennes
Najac
Naucelle
Salmiech
Salles-Curan
Le Rozier
Rousses
Laguépie
Cassagnes-Bégonhès
Meyrueis
St. André-de-Valborgne
Mt. Aigoual 1567
St Beauzély
Aguessac
La Roque-Ste. Marguerite
Viaur
Tanus
Montjaux
Millau
Monestiés
Villefranche-de-Panat
St. Georges-de-Luzençon
Creissels
l'Esperou
Valleraugue
Causse du Larzac
Carmaux
Réquista
St. Rome-de-Tarn
Nant
St. Jean-du-Bruel
Lasalle
Blaye-les-Mines
Valence-d'Albigeois
Broquies
Grands
St. Rome-de-Cernon
La Cavalerie
St. Hippolyte-du-Fort
Le Vigan
St. Juéry
St. Izaire
Marsac
Albi
Tarn
L'Hospitalet-du-Larzac
St. Affrique
Montdardier
Ganges
St. Bauzille-de-Putois
Plaisance
St. Sernin-sur-Rance
St. Felix-de-Sorgues
Cornus
Florentin
Villefranche-d'Albigeois
Alban
Causses
St. Pierre
Le Caylar
St. Maurice-Navacelles
Cadalen
Teillet
Col Notre-Dame 667
Camarès
Belmont-sur-Rance
Fayet
Ceilhes-et-Rocozels
Causse-de-la-Selle
Graulhet
Réalmont
Brusque
St. Pierre-de-la-Fage
St. Martin-de-Londres
Montredon-Labessonnié
Lodève
Lautrec
Lacaune
Col de la Bassine 885
Vabre
Murat-sur-Vèbre
Le Bousquet-d'Orb
Lunas
Aniane
Roquecourbe
Mts. de Lacaune
Lac de Laouzas
Lac du Salagou
Gignac
Montpell
Vielmur-sur-Agout
Brassac
St. Gervais-sur-Mare
Clermont-l'Hérault
St. André-de-Sangonis
Castres
Hérépian
Bédarieux
Pignan
Canet
Anglès
La Salvetat-sur-Agout
Olargues
Poujol-sur-Orb
Fabrègues
Cournonterral
Soual
Haut-Languedoc
Paulhan
Labruguière
Dourgne
Thoré
Labastide-Rouairoux
St. Pons-de-Thomières
Roquebrun
Villeveyrac
Montagnac
Mazamet
Montagne Noire
Roujan
Lezignan-la-Cèbe
St. Amans-Soult
Courniou
Col des Usclats 575
Murviel-lès-Béziers
Pézenas
Frontignan
Sorèze
Col de Serieres 681
St. Chinian
Cessenon
Cazouls-lès-Béziers
Servian
Mèze
Saissac
Mas-Cabardès
Puisserguier
Florensac
Sète
Castelnaudary
Caunes-Minervois
Béziers
Bessan
Marseillan
Bassin de Thau
Montolieu
Aigues-Vives
Maureilhan
Capestang
Agde
Peyriac-Minervois
Nissan-lez-Enserune
Alzonne
Bram
Conques-sur-Orbiel
Olonzac
Canal du Midi
Coursan
Sérignan
Le Cap d'Agde
C. d'Agde
Carcassonne
Aude
Valras-Plage
Fleury
Côte d'A
Montréal
Lézignan-Corbières
Capendu
Narbonne
Narbonne-Plage
Ferrals-les-Corbières
Thézar-les-Corbières
Narbonnaise
Gruissan
St. Hilaire
Lagrasse
Limoux
St. Laurent-de-la-Cabrerisse
ABBAYE DE FONTFROIDE
Ajac
Sigean
Port-la-Nouvelle
Tanger
Nador
Chalabre
Vignevieille
Méditerranée
Alet-les-Bains
Durban-Corbières
Mouthoumet
Espéraza
Villeneuve-les-Corbières
La Palme
Puivert
Couiza
Rennes-les-Bains
Leucate
Tuchan
Corbières
Soulatgé
Quillan
Paziols
Étang de Leucate
St. Paul-de-Fenouillet
FORTERESS DE SALSES
Salses-le-Château
Axat
Vingrau
Maury
Caudiès-de-Fenouillèdes
Rivesaltes
Port-Barcarès
Usson-les-Bains
Agly
St. Laurent-de-la-Salanque
Estagel
Sournia
Millas
Perpignan
Ille-sur-Têt
Têt
Canet-Plage
Quérigut
Madrès

Vals-les-Bains
Aubenas
Luc
La Bastide-Puylaurent
Valgorge
Largentière
Prevenchères
Joyeuse
Lablachère
Ruoms
Villefort
Les Vans
Vallon-Pont-d'Arc
St. Paul-le-Jeune
Barjac
Orgnac-l'Aven
AVEN MARZAL-GROTTE, MUSÉE ET ZOO PRÉHISTORIQUE
Bessèges
Le Collet-de-Deze
St. Ambroix
Les Mages
St. Germain-de-Calberte
La Grand-Combe
Salindres
Alès
Lussan
St. André-de-Roquepertuis
St. Christol-lès-Alès
Vézenobres
Anduze
Seynes
Connaux
St. Quentin-la-Poterie
Serviers
Uzès
Lédignan
Moussac
Sauve
Quissac
La Calmette
PONT DU GARD
Remoulins
Montmirat
Sauteyrargues
Valflaunes
Sommières
Calvisson
St. Mathieu-de-Tréviers
Boisseron
Nîmes
Marguerittes
Beaucaire
Bouillargues
Uchaud
Vauvert
St. Gilles
Castries
Lunel
Aimargues
L'EGLISE DE L'ABBAYE DE ST. GILLES
St. Laurent-d'Aigouze
MURS DU MOYEN-AGE
Mauguio
Pérols
Carnon-Plage
La Grande-Motte
Aigues-Mortes
Le Grau-du-Roi
Palavas-les-Flots
Port-Camargue
Golfe d'Aigues-Mortes
Étang de Vic
Mayres
D'Ardèche
Lavilledieu
Villeneuve-de-Berg
Vogüé
CHÂTEAU DE VOGÜÉ
BAPTISTRE DE MÉLAS
Viviers
Rochemaure
Le Teil
Meysse
Montélimar
Sauzet
Donzère
St.-Montant
Pierrelatte
Bourg-St. Andéol
Pont-St. Esprit
St. Just
Bagnols-sur-Cèze
Orange
Roquemaure
Villeneuve-lès-Avignon
Sorgues
Avignon
Aramon
Barbentane
CHÂTEAU DE TARASCON
Tarascon
Graveson
Noves
Châteaurenard
Bellegarde
Les Baux-de-Provence
RUINES ROMAINES DE GLANUM
St. Rémy-de-Provence
Alpilles
Maussane-les-Alpilles
Arles
Mouriès
St. Martin-de-Crau
Camargue
Étang de Vaccarès
Rhône
La Crau
Stes. Maries-de-la-Mer
STES. MARIES DE LA MER
Port-St.-Louis-du-Rhône
Fos-sur-Mer
Port-de-Bouc
Istres
Miramas
St. Chamas
Salon-de-Provence
Eyguières
Sénas
Orgon
Plan-d'Orgon
Cavaillon
Lançon-Provence
Étang de Berre
Berre-l'Etang
Marignane
Martigues
Carro
C. Couronne
Sausset-les-Pins
Carry-le-Rouet
CHÂTEAU D'IF
Marseille
Marseilles
Cap Croisette
Cassis
Calanques
La Ciotat
Aubagne
Allauch
Roquevaire
Auriol
Gémenos
Gardanne
Aix-en-Provence
Trets
Vauvenargues
Venelles
Éguilles
Pélissanne
Lambesc
Rognes
St. Cannat
Le Puy-Ste. Réparade
Meyrargues
Peyrolles-en-Provence
Pertuis
Mallemort
Cadenet
Lourmarin
Cucuron
La Tour d'Aigues
Bonnieux
Luberon
Apt
Cereste
Reillanne
La Bastide-des-Jourdans
Manosque
Ste. Tulle
Rustrel
St. Saturnin-lès-Apt
Fontaine de Vaucluse
L'Isle-sur-la-Sorgue
Pernes-les-Fontaines
Carpentras
Mazan
Bédarrides
Châteauneuf-du-Pape
Vacqueyras
Camaret-sur-Aigues
Mondragon
Bollène
Suze-la-Rousse
Tulette
Vaison-la-Romaine
VILLE ROMAINE RUIN
Malaucène
Bédoin
Mt. Ventoux
Sault
St. Christol
ST. CHRISTOL
Banon
Revest-du-Bion
Montbrun-les-Bains
Séderon
Les Omergues
Buis-les-Baronnies
Mirabel-aux-Baronnies
Nyons
Valréas
St. Paul-Trois-Châteaux
Grignan
CHÂTEAU DE GRIGNAN
Taulignan
Aleyrac
Espeluche
La Bégude-de-Mazenc
Cléon-d'Andran
Dieulefit
Bouvières
Pradelle
Bourdeaux
St. Nazaire-le-Désert
Luc-en-Diois
Bellegarde-en-Diois
La Motte-Chalançon
La Charce
Rémuzat
Ste. Jalle
Rosans
Verclause
L'Epine
Serres
Aspres-sur-Buëch
Laragne-Monte
La Rochette
Barret-le-Bas
St. Etienne-les-Orgues
Golfe du Lion
Améthyste
Oran
Alger
Annaba
Bejaia
Skikda
Tunis
Porto Tórres
Ajaccio
Bastia
l'Ile Rousse
Porto-Vecchio
Propriano
0
10
20
30 km
43°
44°
4°
5°
A
B
C
2
3
4
118
132

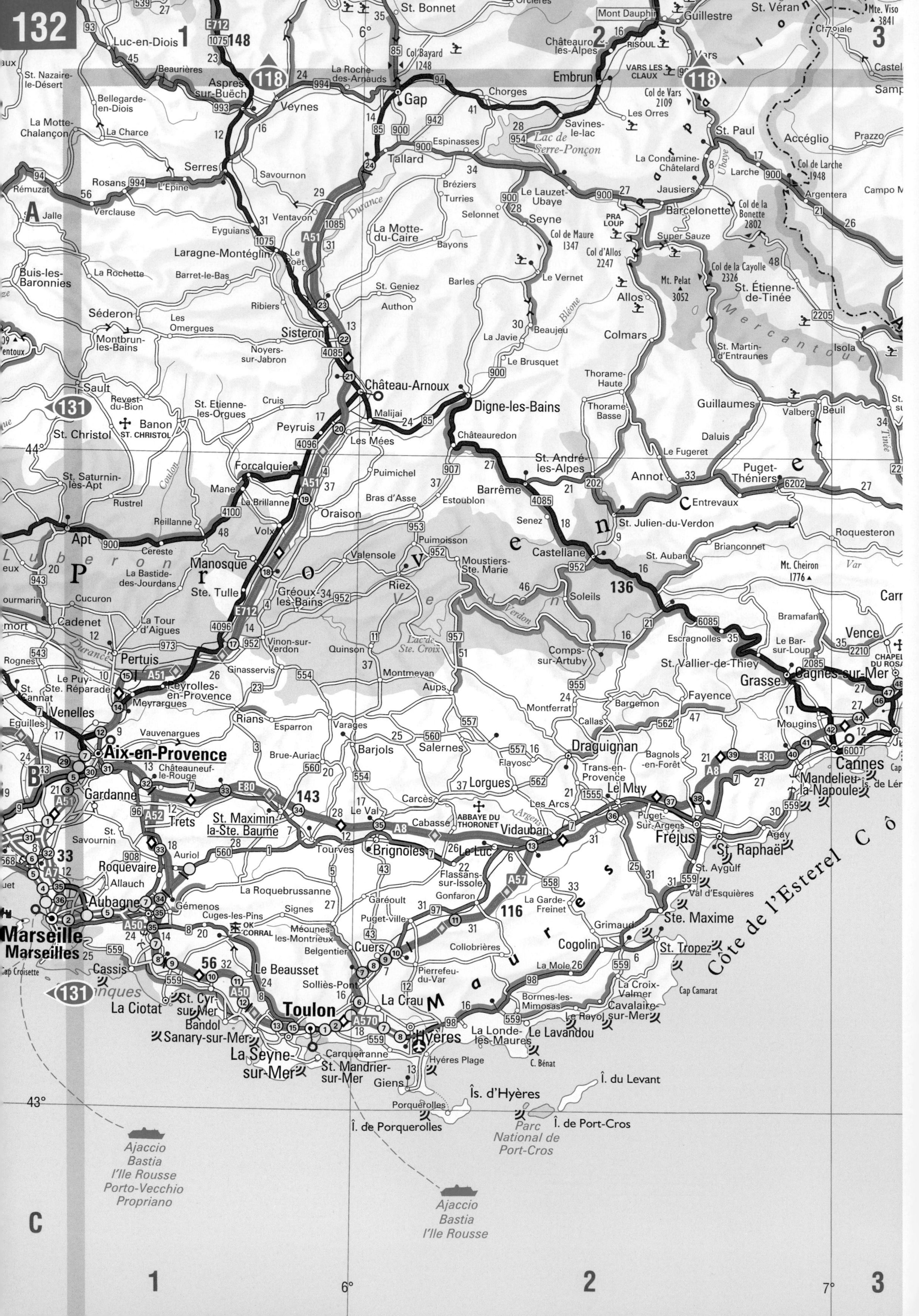

Alba
Saluzzo
Savigliano
Fossano
Cherasco
Bra
Dogliani
Carrù
Mondovì
Cúneo
Borgo San Dalmazzo
Dronero
Caráglio
Busca
Centallo
Ceva
Millesimo
Cairo Montenotte
Ovada
Molare
Gavi
Busalla
Génova
Genoa
Nervi
Voltri
Pegli
Arenzano
Varazze
Celle Ligure
Albisola Marina
Savona
Vado Lígure
Spotorno
Noli
Finale Lígure
Pietra Ligure
Loano
Borghetto Santo Spirito
Albenga
Alássio
Laiguéglia
Diano Marina
Impéria
San Lorenzo al Mare
Riva Lígure
Tággia
San Remo
Ospedaletti
Bordighera
Ventimiglia
Menton
Monte-Carlo
MONACO
Beaulieu-sur-Mer
Villefranche-sur-Mer
Cap Ferrat
Nice
MARINELAND
Antibes
Sospel
Breil-sur-Roya
Saorge
Tende
Limone Piemonte
Colle di Tenda 1279
Tunnel de Tende
Alpes Maritimes
Mercantour
St. Martin-Vésubie
Roquebilière
Triora
Pieve di Teco
Ormea
Garéssio
Bagnasco
Calizzano
Golfo di Génova
Bastia
Calvi
Árbatax
Barcelona
Olbia
Palermo
Porto Tórres
Tanger
Tunis
l'Ile Rousse
Ajaccio
Riviera di Ponente
Côte d'Azur
MARE LIGURE
LIGURIAN SEA
134
44°
43°
8°
9°
A
B
C
3
4
0
10
20
30 km

Ligure
Montaldo di Cósola
Ottone
Aveto
Ferriere
Geno
Varsi
Bardi
Fornovo di Taro
Langhirano
Traversetolo
Montecchio Emília
Réggio nell'Emília
San Polo d'Enza
Vezzano sul Cróstolo
Ciano d'Enza
Calestano
Scandiano
Busalla
Mte. Maggiorasca 1799
Casella
Torriglia
Rezzoáglio
Montebruno
Santo Stefano d'Aveto
Bedónia
Taro
Berceto
Corníglio
Pso. della Cisa 1039
Borgo Val di Taro
Palanzano
Castelnovo ne' Monti
Vetto
Casina
VILLAGIO MEDIEVALE DI CASTELNOVO NE' MONTI
Carpineti
Masone
Passo dei Giovi
Pontedécimo
Bolzaneto
Molassano
Gattorna
Cicagna
Santa Maria del Taro
Borzonasca
Varese Ligure
Voltri
Pegli
Génova
Genoa
Nervi
Recco
Camogli
Rapallo
Carasco
Santa Margherita Ligure
Portofino
Chiávari
Lavagna
Sestri Levante
San Pietro Vara
Castiglione Chiavarese
Monte Góttero 1640
Sesta Godano
Pontrémoli
Mónchio della Corti
Collagna
Busana
Villa Minozzo
Toano
Montefiorino
Lama Mocogno
Alto Appennino Reggiano
Villafranca in Lunigiana
Licciana Nardi
Mte. Cusna 2120
Golfo di Génova
Riviera di Levante
Monéglia
Déiva Marina
Bonassola
Lévanto
Borghetta di Vara
Ricco Del Golfo
Aulla
Fivizzano
Orecchiella
Piazza al Sérchio
Piandelagotti
Pievepélago
Alto Appennino Modenese
Monterosso al Mare
Vernazza
Riomaggiore
Cinque Terre
Santo Stefano di Magra
Fosdinovo
Sarzana
Castelnuovo di Garfagnana
M. Giovo 1991
Árbatax
Barcelona
Bastia
Olbia
Palermo
Porto Tórres
Tanger
Tunis
La Spézia
Portovénere
Lérici
Carrara
Alpi Apuane
Barga
Gallicano
Sérchio
Marinella di Sarzana
Marina di Carrara
Marina di Massa
Massa
Seravezza
Bagni di Lucca
Borgo a Mozzano
44°
Pietrasanta
Camaiore
Forte dei Marmi
Ponte a Moriano
Lido di Camaiore
Massarosa
Lucca
Capánnori
Viaréggio
Torre del Lago Puccini
Migliarino S. Rossore Massaciúccoli
San Giuliano Terme
MUSEO NAZ. CERTOSA DI
Pisa
Vicopisano
Cascina
Arno
Marina di Pisa
Tirrénia
Vicarello
Collesalvetti
Livorno
Lari
Ardenza
Casciana Terme
MARE LIGURE
LIGURIAN SEA
Barcelona
Tanger
Gorgona
Quercianella
Rosignano Maríttimo
Castiglioncello
Rosignano Solvay
Castellina Maríttima
Bastia
Vada
San Pietro in Palazzi
Cécina
Marina di Cécina
M. di Castagneto-Donorático
Donorático
0 10 20 30 km
Golfo Aranci
Ólbia
San Vincenzo
Capraia
C. Corse
43°
Ersa
Macinaggio
Rogliano
Marseille
Toulon
Nice
Génova
Savona
Livorno
Populónia
Canale di Piombino
Piombino
G. di Follónica
Pino
Luri
Santa Severa
COUVENT ANCIEN DE SANTA CATALINA
Marine de Sisco
Cavo
Rio Marina
Marciana Marina
Portoferráio
Nonza
Brando
Erbalunga
Prócchio
Pomonte
Porto Azzurro
San-Martino-di-Lota
Ville-di-Pietrabugno
Patrimonio
St. Florent
Bastia
Marina di Campo
Elba
9°
10°

Modena
Nonántola
San Giovanni in Persiceto
San Giorgio di Piano
Altedo
Molinella
Consándolo
Argenta
Valli di Comácchio
Lido degli Estensi
Castelfranco Emília
Formígine
Sassuolo
Maranello
Spilamberto
Anzola d'Emilia
Bologna
Búdrio
Minérbio
Longastrino
Lavezzola
Conselice
Alfonsine
San Alberto
Marina Romea
Marina di Ravenna
Punta Marina
Vignola
Bazzano
Monteveglio
Casalécchio di Reno
San Lazzaro di Sávena
Medicina
Massa Lombarda
Mezzano
Bagnacavallo
Ravenna
Delta del Po
Serramazzoni
Guiglia
Pavullo nel Frignano
Sasso Marconi
Castel San Pietro Terme
Ímola
Lugo
Russi
Mirabilandia
Lido di Classe
Lido di Savio
Milano Marittima
Cérvia
Zocca
Marzabotto
Pianoro
Monterénzio
Castel Bolognese
Faenza
Vergato
Vado
Loiano
Castel d'Aiano
Riola
Sassoleone
Fontanélice
Forlì
Forlimpopoli
Cesenático
Pinerella
Gatteo a Mare
Bellária
Igea Marina
Sestola
Fanano
Mte. Cimone 2165
Alto Appennino Modenese
Lagaro
Monghidoro
Castel di Rio
Cásola Valsénio
Brisighella
Castrocaro Terme
Modigliana
Bertinoro
Méldola
Cesena
Savignano sul Rubicone
Santarcángelo di Romagna
Abetone
Lizzano in Belvedere
Porretta Terme
Castiglione dei Pépoli
Corno alle Scale
Pso. d. Raticosa 968
Covigliáio
Firenzuola
Palazzuolo sul Senio
Predáppio
Montepiano
Pso. d. Futa 903
Marradi
Tredózio
Rocca San Casciano
Borello
San Marcello Pistoiese
Vérnio
Barberino di Mugello
Abbazia di Sta. Reparata
Portico di Romagna
Civitella di Romagna
Prunetta
Passo di Collina 932
Scarperia
Galeata
Mercato Saraceno
Soglianello al Rubicone
Duomo di San Zeno
Pistóia
Vaiano
San Piero a Sieve
Borgo San Lorenzo
Vicchio
San Benedetto in Alpe
Ránchio
San-Marino
Montecatini Terme
Prato
Vaglia
Pieve di Sta. Maria Felicita
San Godenzo
Corniolo
Santa Sofia
Sársina
Talamello
Novaféltria
Monsummano Terme
Campi Bisénzio
Sesto Fiorentino
Dicomano
Foreste Casentinesi-Monte Falterona-Campigna
San Piero in Bagno
Sant'Agata Feltria
Pennabilli
Altopáscio
Póggio a Caiano
Rufina
Bagno di Romagna
Galleno
Vinci
Firenze
Florence
Pontassieve
Stia
Consuma
Badia Pratáglia
Borgo alla Collina
Carpegna
Signa
Scandicci
Émpoli
Montelupo Fiorentino
Vallombrosa
Poppi
Abbazia di San Fedele
Bibbiena
Sestino
Badia Tedalda
Fucécchio
San Miniato
Cerbaia
Reggello
Croce di Pratomagno 1592
Pieve S. Stefano
Borgo Pace
Sant'Angelo in Vado
San Casciano in V. di Pesa
Castelfiorentino
Montespértoli
Figline Valdarno
Loro Ciuffenna
Rássina
Paláia
Tavarnelle val di Pesa
Greve in Chianti
San Giovanni Valdarno
Talla
Subbiano
Sansepolcro
Péccioli
Gambassi Terme
Certaldo
Castiglion Fibocchi
Anghiari
Villagio Medievale di Subbiano
San Giustino
Poggibonsi
Radda in Chianti
Montevarchi
Arezzo
le Ville
Città di Castello
San Gimignano
Castellina in Chianti
Ponticino
Palazzo del Pero
Pietralunga
Volterra
Città Estrusca
Colle di Val d'Elsa
Castelnuovo Berardenga
Monte San Savino
Rigutino
Trestina
Saline di Volterra
Cásole d'Elsa
Pianella
Siena
Castiglion Fiorentino
Niccone
Colline Metallifere
Pomarance
Sovicille
Rapolano Terme
Lucignano
Foiano della Chiana
Cortona
Umbértide
Radicóndoli
Rosia
Monteroni d'Arbia
Asciano
Sinalunga
Mercatale
Tuoro sul Trasimeno
Passignano sul Trasimeno
Castelnuovo di Val di Cécina
Torrita di Siena
Villagio Medievale di Buonconvento
L. Trasimeno
Magione
Sant' Agostino di Monticiano
San Lorenzo a Merse
Monticiano
Buonconvento
Acquaviva
Castiglione del Lago
Ponte Felcino
Monterotondo Maríttimo
Montieri
Montepulciano
Pozzuolo
Perúgia
Suvereto
Torniella
Montalcino
San Quírico d'Órcia
Pienza
Chianciano Terme
Chiusi
Mugnano
Tavernelle
Deruta
Massa Maríttima
Duomo San Cerbone
Roccatederighi
Roccastrada
Villagio Medievale di Montalcino
Castiglione d'Órcia
Sarteano
Città della Pieve
Piegaro
Casalina
Valpiana
Ribolla
Sticciano Scalo
Pagánico
Sasso d'Ombrone
Castel d. Piano
Abbadia San Salvatore
Radicófani
Monteleone d'Orvieto
Cerqueto
Marsciano
Follónica
Gavorrano
Cinigiano
Campagnático
Montepescali
Mte. Amiata 1738
Piazze
San Casciano d. Bagni
San Venanzo
Fratta Todina
Città Etrusca di Vetulonia
Batignano
Arcidosso
Piancastagnáio
Ficulle
Castello di Castiglione della Pescáia
Arcille
Cana
Sant' Caterina
Santa Fiora
Castell'Azzara
M. Rufino
Tévere
Grosseto
Castiglione della Pescáia
Istia d'Ombrone
Roccalbegna
Acquapendente
Orvieto
Prodo
Capretta
Todi
Marina di Grosseto
Sorano
Onano
Acquasparta
Maremma
Chianti
Casentino
Val di Chiana
Romagna
Appennino Tosco-Emiliano

1
13°
2
14°
122
122
MARE
ADRIATICO
Marina Romea
Marina di Ravenna
Punta Marina
Ravenna
Delta del Po
MIRABILANDIA
Lido di Classe
Lido di Savio
Savio
Milano Marittima
Cérvia
Casemurate
Pinerella
Cesenático
Gatteo a Mare
Bellária
Igea Marina
ITALIA IN MINIATURA
Viserba
Cesena
Savignano sul Rubicone
Santarcángelo di Romagna
Borello
Rímini
FIABILANDIA
Miramare
Riccione
135
Sogliano al Rubicone
Cattólica
SAN MARINO
San Marino
Talamello
San Leo
Novaféltria
Morciano di Romagna
Saludécio
Mercatino Conca
Pésaro
Fano
Montécchio
105
Mombaróccio
Pennabilli
Macerata Féltria
Carpegna
Sassocorvaro
Foglia
Marotta
Saltara
Calcinelli
Metauro
San Costanzo
Mondolfo
Senigállia
Urbino
Fossombrone
Sestino
Badia Tedalda
Lunano
Borgo Pace
Urbánia
Sant'Angelo in Vado
Monte Porzio
Cesano
Marzocca
Rocca Priora
Falconara Maríttima
Ancona
Mondavio
Corinaldo
Chiaravalle
Ostra
Piobbico
Pérgola
San Lorenzo in Campo
San Marcello
Cónero
SAN PIETRO
Camerano
VILLAGGIO MEDIEVALE DI SIROLO
Sirolo
Numana
Igoumenitsa Patra
Apecchio
Cagli
Montecarotto
Jesi
Móie
Agugliano
Ósimo
Castelfidardo
Loreto
Porto Recanati
Sansepolcro
San Giustino
Appennino Umbro-Marchigiano
Città di Castello
Arcévia
Cantiano
SAN GIOVANNI BATTISTA
Mte. Cátria 1701
Serra S. Quírico
SAN FRANCESCO DI SASSOFERRATO
GROTTA DI FRASSASSI
Sassoferrato
Cupramontana
Filottrano
Montefano
Recanati
Pietralunga
Scheggia
Apiro
Cíngoli
Monte Cucco
Montecassiano
Potenza Picena
Porto Potenza Picena
Gúbbio
Camporeggiano
Sigillo
Fabriano
Cerreto d'Esi
Civitanova Alta
Macerata
Tréia
Passo di Tréia
SAN CLAUDIO AL CHIENTI
Civitanova Marche
Niccone
Umbértide
Fossato di Vico
Branca
Matélica
San Severino Marche
Sforzacosta
Chienti
Porto Sant'Elpídio
Scritto
Trasimeno
Castiglione del Lago
Gualdo Tadino
Tolentino
Corridónia
Sant'Elpídio a Mare
Lido di Fermo
Casa Castalda
Castelraimondo
Serrapetrona
Abbadia di Fiastra
Montegranaro
Mogliano
ABBAZIA DI CHIARAVALLE DI FIASTRA
Porto San Giórgio
Piccione
Valfabbrica
Pióraco
Camerino
Caldarola
Ponte Felcino
Nocera Umbra
Montegiórgio
Fermo
Perúgia
Ponte San Giovanni
Monte Subásio
Mte. Pennino 1571
Serravalle di Chienti
Múccia
San Ginésio
Tenna
Bastia
Assisi
Servigliano
Monterubbiano
Pedaso
Valtopina
Pieve Torina
Sarnano
Bettona
Spello
Colfiorito
Santa Vittória in Matenano
152
Cupra Maríttima
Deruta
Cannara
Montalto d. Marche
Ripatransone
Grottammare
Casalina
Casenove
Appennino
Bolognola
Amándola
MADONNA DEL PIANO
Bevagna
Foligno
Monti Sibillini
Montefortino
Comunanza
Rotella
San Benedetto del Tronto
Marsciano
Collepepe
Visso
Offida
Acquaviva Picena
Porto d'Ascoli
San Venanzo
Bastardo
Montefalco
Trevi
Sellano
Castelsantángelo
Montemónaco
Áscoli Piceno
Martinsicuro
Fratta Todina
Mte. Vettore 2476
Balzo
Tronto
Nereto
Alba Adriática
Triponzo
Nórcia
Arquata del Tronto
Sant'Egídio alla Vibrata
Tortoreto Lido
Massa Martana
San Giácomo
Piedipaterno
Prodo
Todi
Serravalle
Civitella di Tronto
Spoleto
168
169
Acquasanta Terme
Giulianova
Mosciano Sant'Angelo
Acquasparta
Cáscia
Accúmoli
Gran Sasso e Monti della Laga
Valle Castellana
CATTEDRALE DI SAN BERNARDO
Campli
Baschi
Montecastrilli
Monteleone di Spoleto
Cívita
Téramo
Roseto
A
B
C
E55
E45
E78
A14

Unije
Nerezine
Čunski
Pula
Mali Lošinj
Veli Lošinj
Susak
Novalja
Stara Novalja
Prizna
Cesarica
Karlobag
Oštarijska Vrata
Klanac
Lički Osik
Gospić
Podlapača
Udbina
Jošan
Vrebac
Brušane
Bilaj
Pag
Metajna
AENONA
Lukovo Šugorje
Medak
Vaganski vrh
1757
Gornja Ploča
Kremen
1591
Mazin
Bruvno
Raduc
Sveti Rok
Silba
Olib
Gorica
Barič Draga
Tribanj Kruščica
Paklenica
Starigrad-Paklenica
Premuda
Vir
Povljana
Virsko more
Ist
Molat
Ražanac
Velebit
Gračac
Privlaka
Vrsi
Nin
Jasenice
Posedarje
Obrovac
Zrmanja
Kaštel Zegarski
Sestrunj
Petrčane
Poličnik
Novigrad
Ancona
Božava
Zadar
Murvica
Zemunik Donji
Medvide
Ervenik
Ugljan
Preko
TVRĐAVA SV. MIHOVILA
Kali
Bibinje
Sukošan
Benkovac
ASSERIA
BURNUM
Brbinj
Kukljica
Dugi Otok
Miranje
Turanj
Pašman
Đevrske
Krka
Kistanje
Biograd na Moru
Pakoštane
Stankovci
Zaglav
Sali
Tkon
MANASTIR KRKA
Telašćica
Vransko Jezero
Žut
Pirovac
Skradin
Murter
Prokljansko Jezero
Kornati
Kornat
Tisno
Vodice
Šibenik
KATEDRALA SV JAKOVA
Zablaće
Krapanj
Žirje
Primošten
Rogoznica
Rijeka
Ancona
Split
Starigrad
Durrës
Trieste
ADRIATICO
MARE ADRIATICO
Jabucka
Svetac
el Tronto
degli Abruzzi
E65
A1
8
25
27
50
502
56
54
33
1
123
138
149
389
928
15°
43°
44°
0
10
20
30 km
3
4
A
B
C

Donji Lapac
Kulen Vakuf
Bosanski Petrovac
Kapljuh
Ključ
Čadavica
Mrkonjić Grad
Krupa na Vrbasu
Vrbanjci
Orahova
Skender Vakuf
Vlatkovići
Barevo
Jajce
Jezero
Kremen 1591
Osječenica 1795
124
Kolunić
Drinić
1961 Klekovača
Mazin
Doljani
Bruvno
Sveti Rok
Donji Srb
Kupirovo
Drvar
Potoci
Protić
Šipovo
Pliva
Gračac
Velebit
Prekaja
Vijenac 1650
Poljice
Barači
Mliništa
Krezluk
Zrmanja
1443 Kučina kosa
Otrić
Bosansko Grahovo
Preodac
Rore
Kaštel Žegarski
Plavno
Strmica
Korita
Šator 1872
Medena Selista
Todorici
Novi
Donji Vakuf
Medvide
Ervenik
Padene
Crni Lug
Vitorog 1907
Mokro Polje
Glamoč
Bugojno
BURNUM
Krka
Vrbnik
Knin
Kijevo
Donji Kazanci
Čelebič
1509
Skucani
Kupres
Kistanje
Oklaj
Golija 1891
1913 Troglav
Vrlika
Donji-Rujani
Lusnić
Priluka
Rilić
Gornji Vakuf
Idovac 1956
Vrbas
Đevrske
Stankovci
Siverić
Koljane
Cincar
Donji Malovan
Gornji Ravno
MANASTIR KRKA
Skradin
Drniš
Peručko Jezero
Šuica
Rumboci
Prokljansko Jezero
Ružic
Svilaja 1508
Livno
Trolog
Vodice
Konjevrate
Umljanovic
Hrvace
Zagoričani
Ramsko Jezero
KATEDRALA SV JAKOVA
Šibenik
Zablaće
ROGOZNICA
Unešić
Obrovac Sinjski
Sinj
Prisoje
Tomislavgrad
Ljubuša
149
Krapanj
Perković
Kladnice
Muć
Otok
Brnaze
Buško Jezero
Mandino Selo
Donje Brišnik
V. Vran 2074
Primošten
Lećevica
Trilj
Kamensko
Blidinje jezero
Čvrsnica
Prapatnica
Dugopolje
Kaštel-Stari
SALONA
Solin
Klis
Aržano
Rogoznica
Ugljane
Vir
Marina
Trogir
Split
Žrnovica
Blato na Cetini
Studenci
Rijeka
Čiovo
Stobreč
Lovreć
Posušje
Splitski Kan.
Gata
Šestanovac
Imotski
Bročanac
Dugi Rat
Grabovac
Sovići
Omiš
Cetina
Zagvozd
Zmijavci
Kočerin
Maslinica
Rogač
Sutivan
Supetar
Mimice
Donja Brela
Grude
Ancona
Šolta
Grohote
Brački Kanal
Sveti Jure 1762
Drinovci
Postira
Pučišća
Baška Voda
Biokovo
Milna
Nerežišća
Povlja
Selca
113
Makarska
Kozica
DOMINIKANSKI SAMOSTAN
Gornji Humac
Sumartin
Tučepi
Hvarski Kanal
Bol
Brač
Podgora
Vitina
Trebižat
Ravča
Radiš
SV. STJPAN
Starigrad
Vrgorac
Vrboska
Hvar
Jelsa
SV. IVAN
TOR
Drvenik
Gdinj
Gradac
Viški Kanal
Šćedro
Sućuraj
Vis
Komiža
Korčulanski Kanal
Neretvanski Kanal
Ploče
Svetac
Loviste
Biševo
GALERIJA CENTRA ZA KULTURU
Vela Luka
Prigradica
Kuciste
Sv. Ilija 962
Trpanj
Orebić
Korčula
Pelješac
Janjina
Blato
SV. ANTUN
Lumbarda
Žuljana
Lastovski Kanal
Mljetski
SV. KUZMA & DAMJAN
Lastovo
Govedari
Mljet
Sušac
Kopište
Ubli
0
10
20
30 km
A
B
C
1
2
3
16°
17°
44°
43°
137

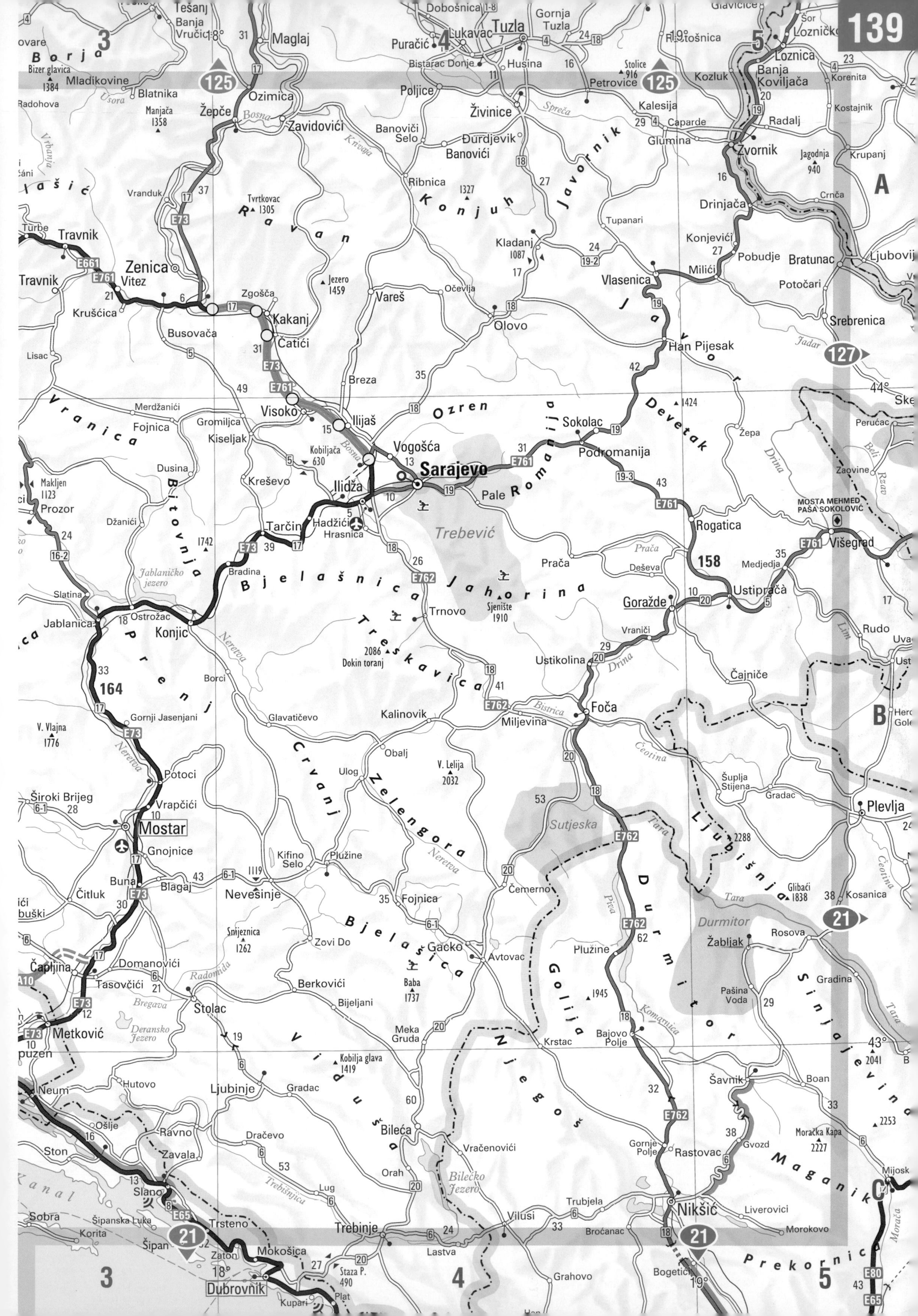

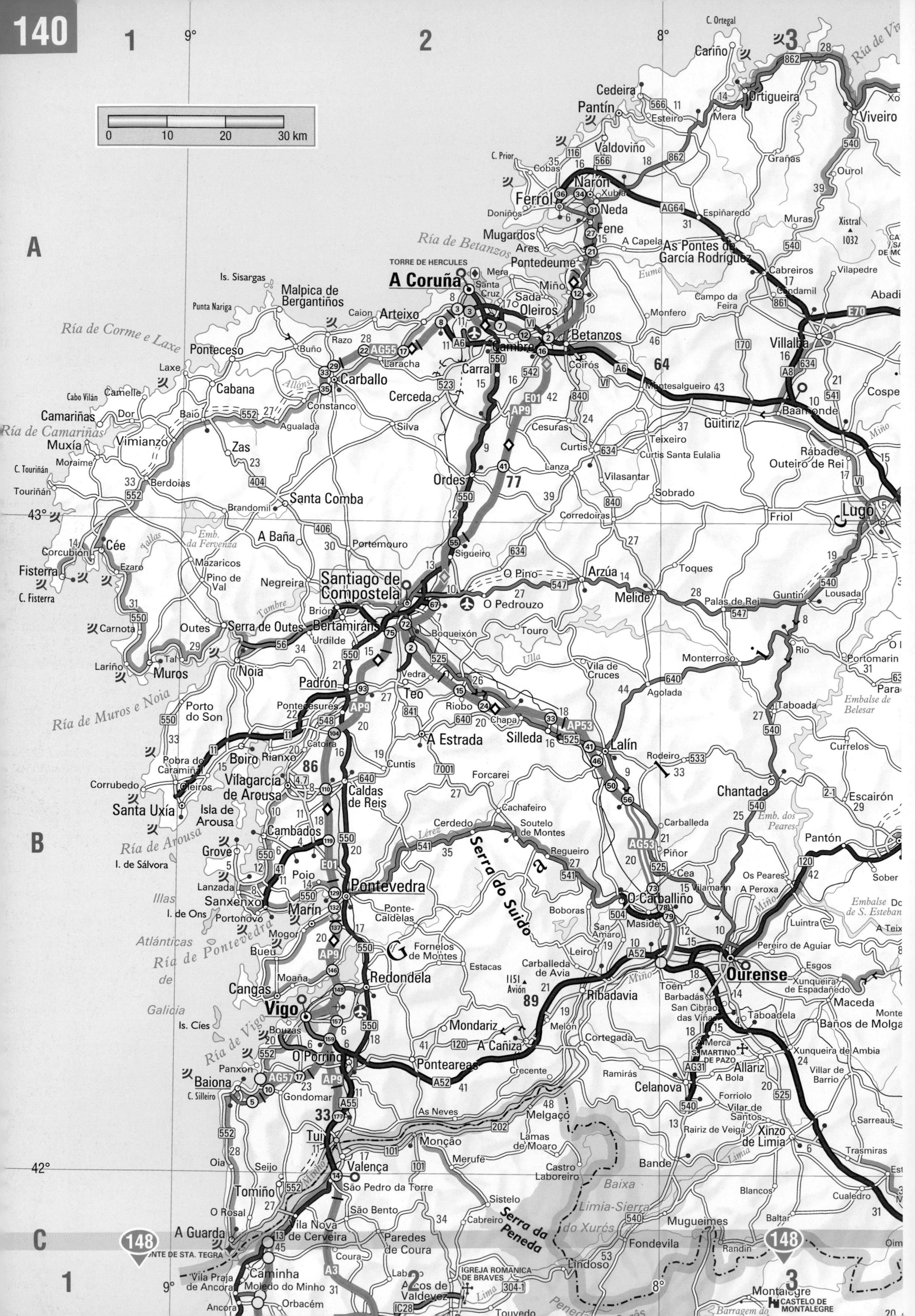

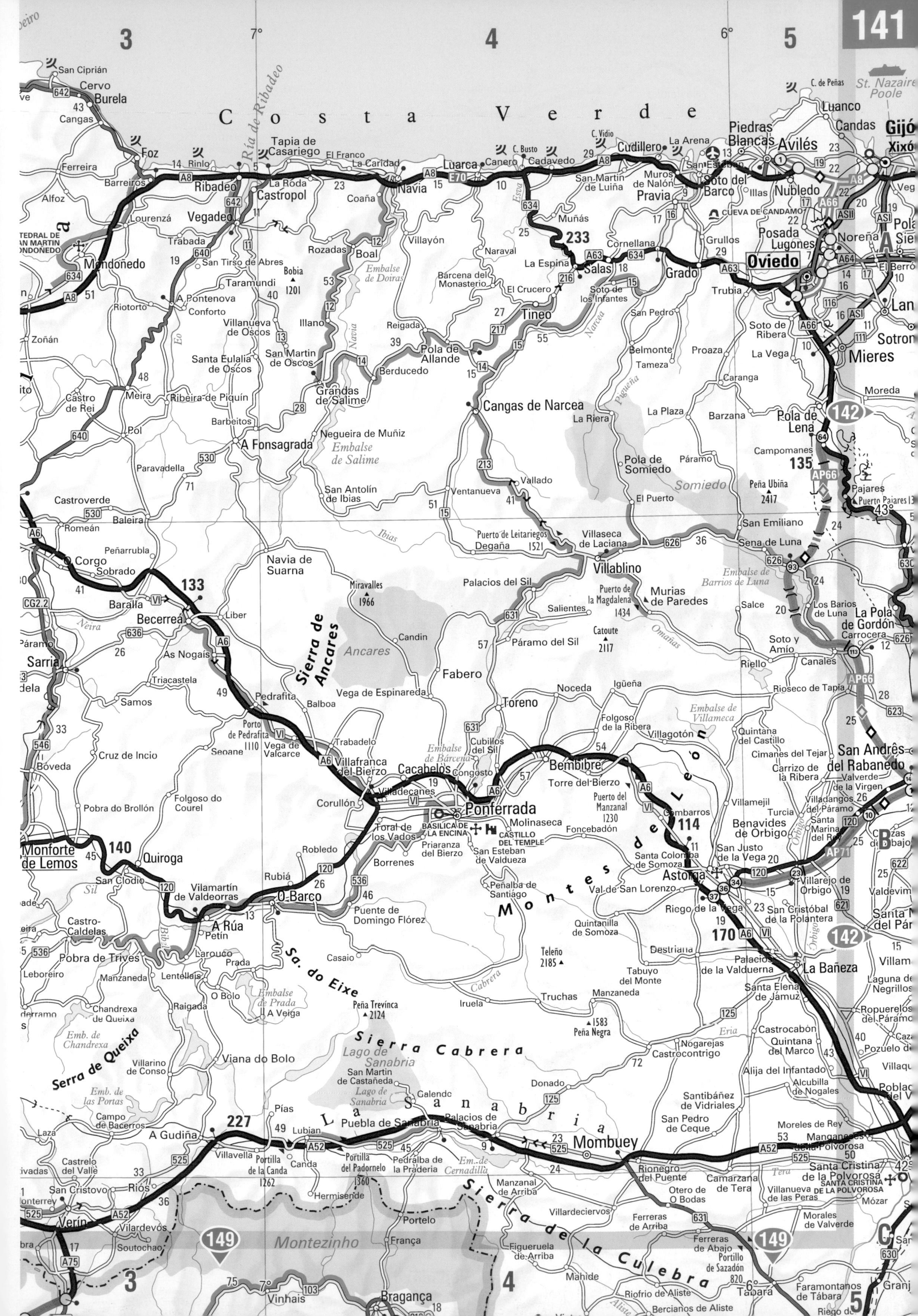
3
4
5
7°
6°
Costa Verde
Ría de Ribadeo
San Ciprián
Cervo
Burela
Cangas
Foz
Rinlo
Tapia de Casariego
El Franco
La Caridad
Ferreira
Barreiros
Ribadeo
La Roda
Castropol
Coaña
Navia
Luarca
Canero
C. Busto
Cadavedo
C. Vidio
Cudillero
La Arena
San Esteban
San Martín de Luiña
Muros de Nalón
Pravia
Soto del Barco
Piedras Blancas
Avilés
Illas
Nubledo
C. de Peñas
Luanco
Candas
Gijón
Xixón
St. Nazaire
Poole
Alfoz
Lourenzá
Vegadeo
Mondoñedo
Trabada
San Tirso de Abres
Bobia
1201
Taramundi
A Pontenova
Conforto
Riotorto
Villanueva de Oscos
Illano
Rozadas
Boal
Embalse de Doiras
Villayón
Naraval
Bárcena del Monasterio
La Espina
Salas
El Crucero
Soto de los Infantes
Muñás
Cornellana
Grado
Grullos
Posada
Lugones
Noreña
Oviedo
Trubia
CUEVA DE CANDAMO
El Berrón
Zoñán
Santa Eulalia de Oscos
San Martín de Oscos
Reigada
Pola de Allande
Berducedo
Tineo
San Pedro
Belmonte
Tameza
Proaza
Soto de Ribera
La Vega
Mieres
Sotrondio
Castro de Rei
Meira
Ribeira de Piquín
Grandas de Salime
Cangas de Narcea
La Riera
La Plaza
Caranga
Barzana
Pola de Lena
Moreda
Pol
Barbeitos
A Fonsagrada
Negueira de Muñiz
Embalse de Salime
Pola de Somiedo
Páramo
Campomanes
Somiedo
Peña Ubiña
2417
Pajares
Puerto Pajares
Paravadella
Castroverde
San Antolín de Ibias
Ventanueva
Vallado
El Puerto
Baleira
Romeán
Puerto de Leitariegos
Degaña
1521
Villaseca de Laciana
Villablino
San Emiliano
Sena de Luna
Peñarrubla
O Corgo
Sobrado
Navia de Suarna
Ibias
Miravalles
1966
Palacios del Sil
Puerto de la Magdalena
1434
Murias de Paredes
Embalse de Barrios de Luna
Los Barrios de Luna
La Pola de Gordón
Carrocera
Salce
Baralla
Becerreá
Liber
Sierra de Ancares
Ancares
Candín
Salientes
Catoute
2117
Páramo del Sil
Omañas
Soto y Amío
Neira
Sarria
As Nogais
Triacastela
Samos
Fabero
Riello
Canales
Rioseco de Tapia
Noceda
Igüeña
Pedrafita
Balboa
Vega de Espinareda
Toreno
Embalse de Villameca
Folgoso de la Ribera
Villagotón
Quintana del Castillo
Cimanes del Tejar
San Andrés del Rabanedo
Porto de Pedrafita
1110
Vega de Valcarce
Trabadelo
Cubillos del Sil
Embalse de Bárcena
Seoane
Cruz de Incio
Bóveda
Villafranca del Bierzo
Cacabelos
Congosto
Bembibre
Torre del Bierzo
Carrizo de la Ribera
Valverde de la Virgen
Villadecanes
Corullón
Ponferrada
Molinaseca
Puerto del Manzanal
1230
Combarros
Villamejil
Villadangos del Páramo
Turcia
Benavides de Órbigo
Santa Marina del Rey
Folgoso do Courel
Pobra do Brollón
BASÍLICA DE LA ENCINA
CASTILLO DEL TEMPLE
Toral de los Vados
Priaranza del Bierzo
San Esteban de Valdueza
Foncebadón
Montes de León
Monforte de Lemos
Quiroga
San Clodio
Robledo
Borrenes
Santa Colomba de Somoza
Astorga
San Justo de la Vega
Villarejo de Órbigo
Valdevimbre
Sil
Vilamartín de Valdeorras
Rubiá
O Barco
Peñalba de Santiago
Val de San Lorenzo
Riego de la Vega
San Cristóbal de la Polantera
Santa María del Páramo
Castro Caldelas
A Rúa
Petín
Puente de Domingo Flórez
Quintanilla de Somoza
Pobra de Trives
Larouco
Casaio
Sa. do Eixe
Teleño
2185
Destriana
Palacios de la Valduerna
La Bañeza
Villamañán
Leboreiro
Manzaneda
Lentellais
Prada
Tabuyo del Monte
Santa Elena de Jamuz
Laguna de Negrillos
O Bolo
Embalse de Prada
A Veiga
Peña Trevinca
2124
Iruela
Cabrera
Truchas
Manzaneda
Chandrexa de Queixa
Raigada
1583
Peña Negra
Ropuerelos del Páramo
Emb. de Chandrexa
Sierra Cabrera
Eria
Castrocabón
Quintana del Marco
Nogarejas
Castrocontrigo
Pozuelo del Páramo
Serra de Queixa
Lago de Sanabria
Viana do Bolo
Villarino de Conso
San Martín de Castañeda
Lago de Sanabria
Galende
Donado
Alija del Infantado
Alcubilla de Nogales
Villaquejida
Santibáñez de Vidriales
Emb. de las Portas
La Sanabria
Campo de Becerros
Pías
Laza
A Gudiña
Lubián
Puebla de Sanabria
Palacios de Sanabria
San Pedro de Ceque
Moreles de Rey
Mombuey
Manganeses de la Polvorosa
Castrelo do Val
Villavella
Portilla de la Canda
1262
Canda
Portilla del Padornelo
1360
Pedralba de la Pradería
Em. de Cernadilla
Rionegro del Puente
Camarzana de Tera
Tera
Santa Cristina de la Polvorosa
SANTA CRISTINA DE LA POLVOROSA
Ríos
San Cristovo
Monterrey
Hermisende
Manzanal de Arriba
Otero de O Bodas
Villanueva de las Peras
Mózar
Verín
Vilardevós
Soutochao
Portelo
Villardeciervos
Ferreras de Arriba
Morales de Valverde
Sierra de la Culebra
Montezinho
França
Figueruela de Arriba
Ferreras de Abajo
Portillo de Sazadón
820
Mahide
Vinhais
Bragança
Riofrío de Aliste
Tábara
Faramontanos de Tábara
Aliste
Bercianos de Aliste
Riego del Camino
142
149
A8
E70
A63
A66
A64
AP66
AP71
A6
A52
A75
233
135
133
114
140
170
227
43°
42°

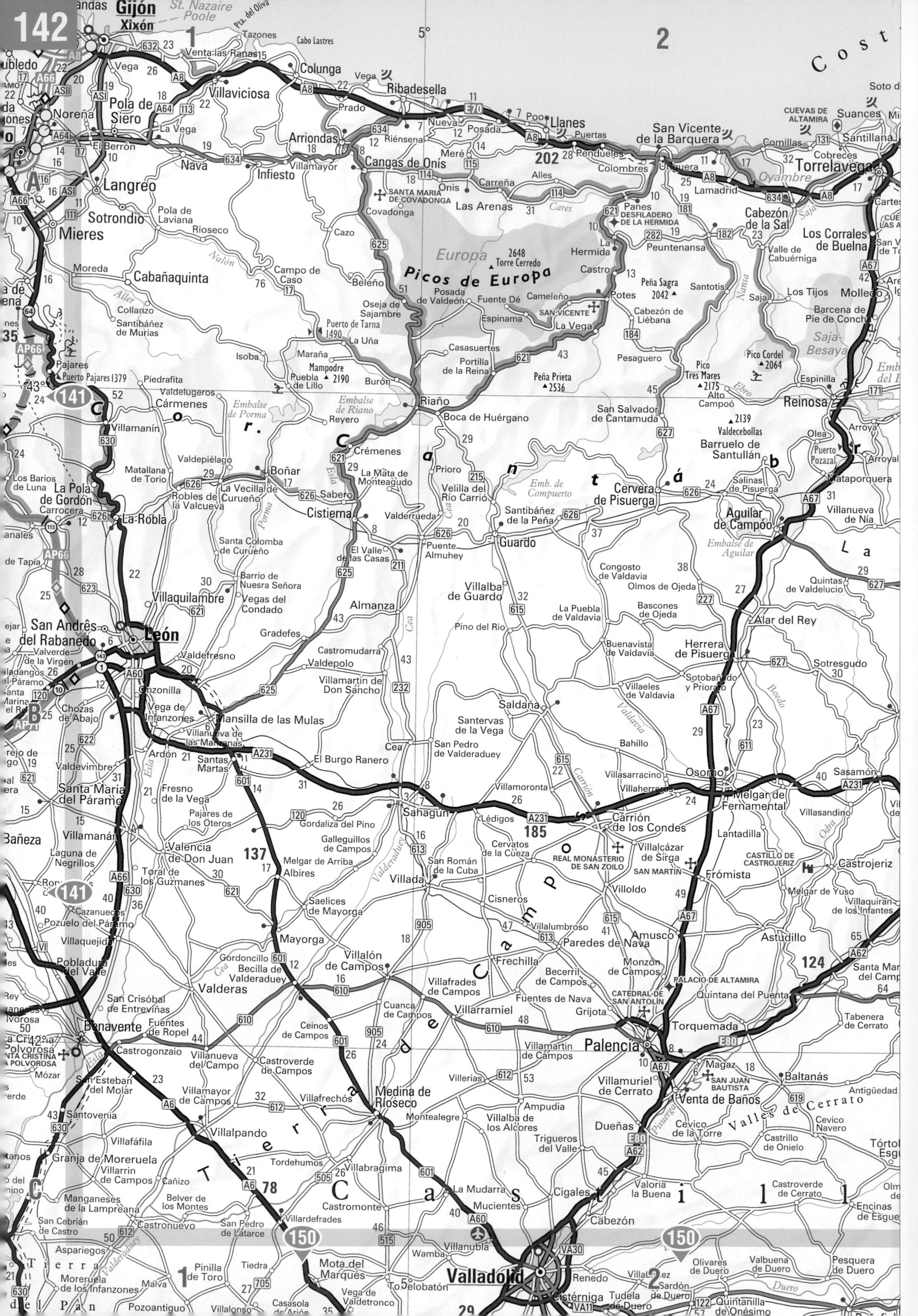

Gijón
Xixón
St. Nazaire - Poole
Tazones
Cabo Lastres
Villaviciosa
Colunga
Ribadesella
Llanes
San Vicente de la Barquera
Comillas
Santillana
Suances
CUEVAS DE ALTAMIRA
Torrelavega
Pola de Siero
Noreña
Arriondas
Cangas de Onís
Infiesto
Nava
Langreo
Mieres
Sotrondio
Pola de Laviana
Cabañaquinta
SANTA MARIA DE COVADONGA
Covadonga
Las Arenas
Panes
DESFILADERO DE LA HERMIDA
Cabezón de la Sal
Los Corrales de Buelna
Picos de Europa
2648 Torre Cerredo
Posada de Valdeón
Fuente Dé
Potes
SAN VICENTE
Peña Sagra 2042
Puerto de Tarna 1490
Mampodre 2190
Peña Prieta 2536
Pico Cordel 2064
Pico Tres Mares 2175
Puerto Pajares 1379
Riaño
Embalse de Riano
Boca de Huérgano
Reinosa
Alto Campoó
Cervera de Pisuerga
Aguilar de Campóo
Embalse de Aguilar
La Pola de Gordón
La Robla
Boñar
Cistierna
Guardo
Villamanín
Villaquilambre
León
San Andrés del Rabanedo
Mansilla de las Mulas
Almanza
Saldaña
Herrera de Pisuerga
Alar del Rey
Sahagún
Carrión de los Condes
REAL MONASTERIO DE SAN ZOILO
Osorno
Melgar de Fernamental
Frómista
Castrojeriz
Santa María del Páramo
Valencia de Don Juan
Mayorga
Villalón de Campos
Paredes de Nava
Astudillo
Benavente
Valderas
Palencia
Villarramiel
Torquemada
PALACIO DE ALTAMIRA
CATEDRAL DE SAN ANTOLÍN
Medina de Rioseco
Venta de Baños
SAN JUAN BAUTISTA
Baltanás
Dueñas
Villalpando
Valladolid
Cigales
Tierra de Campos
Tierra del Pan
Cordillera Cantábrica
Cerrato
Valles de Cerrato
Castilla
1
2
A
B
C
141
150

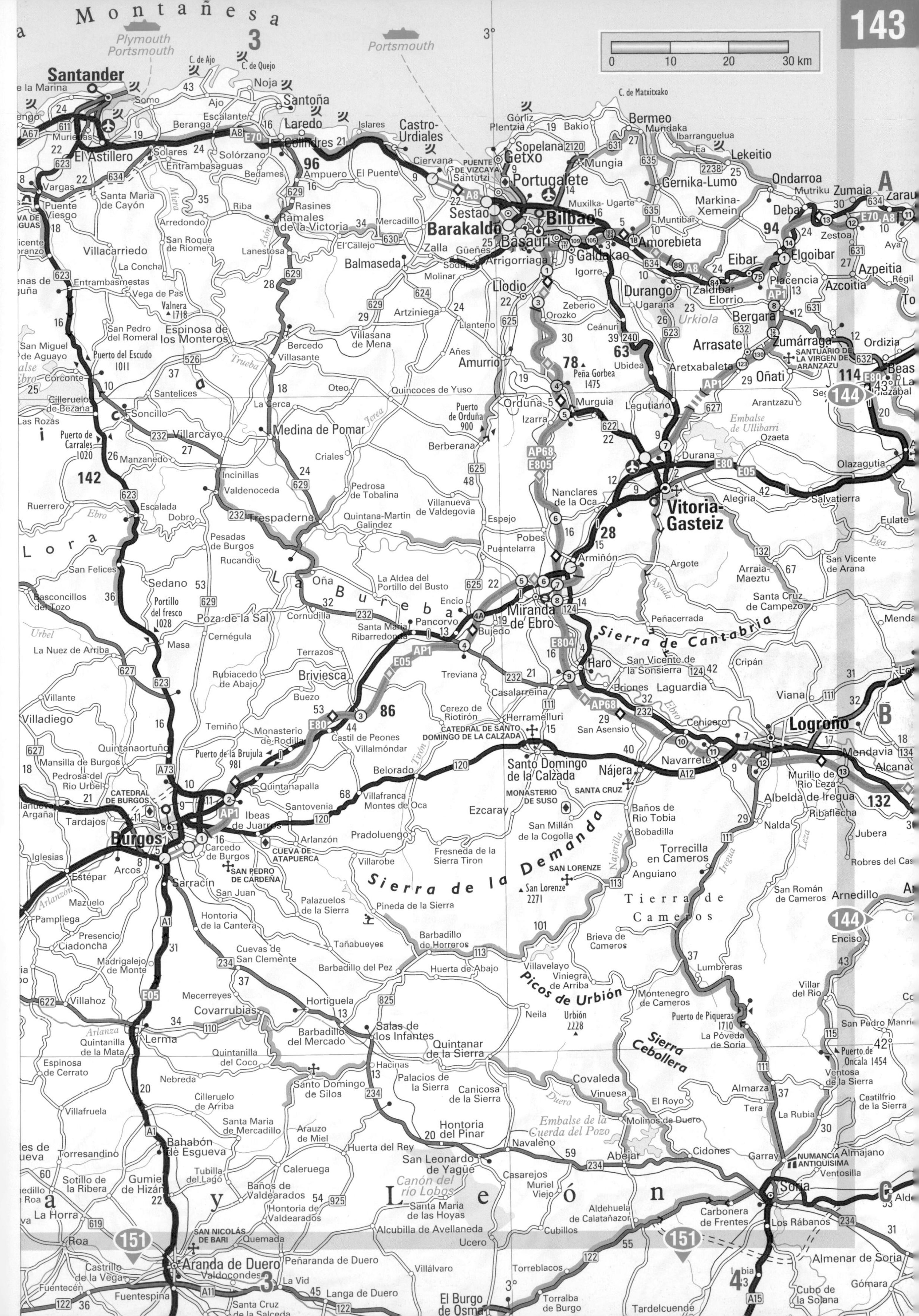

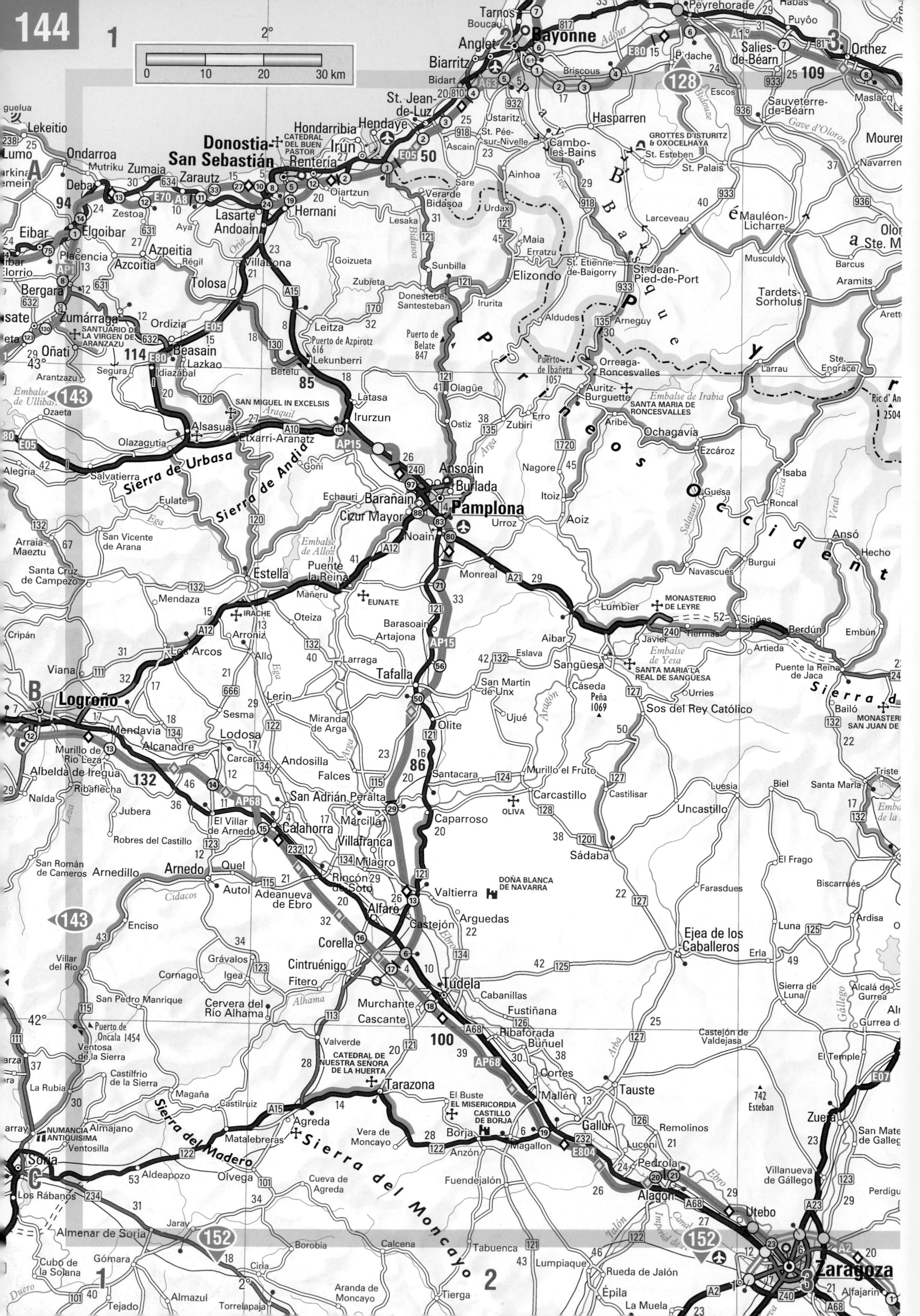

0
10
20
30 km
Bayonne
Anglet
Biarritz
Bidart
Tarnos
Boucau
Peyrehorade
Puyôo
Orthez
Salies-de-Béarn
Bidache
Briscous
Hasparren
St. Jean-de-Luz
Hendaye
Hondarribia
Irún
Donostia-San Sebastián
CATEDRAL DEL BUEN PASTOR
Rentería
Oiartzun
Hernani
Lasarte
Andoain
Zarautz
Zumaia
Mutriku
Ondarroa
Lekeitio
Deba
Zestoa
Elgoibar
Eibar
Azpeitia
Azcoitia
Placencia
Bergara
Zumárraga
Oñati
SANTUARIO DE LA VIRGEN DE ARANZAZU
Beasain
Lazkao
Ordizia
Tolosa
Villabona
Goizueta
Leitza
Puerto de Azpirotz
Lekunberri
Betelu
Idiazábal
Segura
Arantzazu
Alsasua
SAN MIGUEL IN EXCELSIS
Etxarri-Aranatz
Olazagutia
Salvatierra
Alegria
Sierra de Urbasa
Sierra de Andia
Irurzun
Latasa
Ustaritz
St. Pée-sur-Nivelle
Ascain
Sare
Ainhoa
Cambo-les-Bains
GROTTES D'ISTURITZ & OXOCELHAYA
St. Esteben
St. Palais
Mauléon-Licharre
Larceveau
St. Jean-Pied-de-Port
St. Etienne-de-Baigorry
Elizondo
Erratzu
Maia
Urdax
Verarde Bidasoa
Lesaka
Sunbilla
Donestebe-Santesteban
Zubieta
Irurita
Puerto de Belate 847
Aldudes
Arneguy
Orreaga-Roncesvalles
Auritz-Burguette
Embalse de Irabia
SANTA MARIA DE RONCESVALLES
Puerto de Ibañeta 1057
Olagüe
Zubiri
Erro
Ostiz
Aribe
Ochagavía
Ezcároz
Isaba
Roncal
Guesa
Larrau
Ste. Engrâce
Tardets-Sorholus
Aramits
Barcus
Musculdy
Sauveterre-de-Béarn
Navarrenx
Moure
Pirineos Occidentales
Pays Basque
Ansoain
Burlada
Pamplona
Barañain
Cizur Mayor
Echauri
Noain
Urroz
Aoiz
Itoiz
Nagore
Goñi
Eulate
San Vicente de Arana
Arraia-Maeztu
Santa Cruz de Campezo
Estella
Puente la Reina
Mañeru
EUNATE
Monreal
Lumbier
MONASTERIO DE LEYRE
Navascués
Burgui
Ansó
Hecho
Javier
Embalse de Yesa
Sigües
Berdún
Embún
Artieda
Puente la Reina de Jaca
Sierra de
Mendaza
IRACHE
Arroniz
Oteiza
Barasoain
Artajona
Larraga
Tafalla
Allo
Los Arcos
Viana
Logroño
Cripán
Lerin
Sesma
Miranda de Arga
Eslava
Sangüesa
SANTA MARIA LA REAL DE SANGUESA
Urries
Sos del Rey Católico
San Martin de Unx
Ujué
Cáseda
Peña 1069
Olite
Mendavia
Lodosa
Alcanadre
Murillo de Rio Leza
Albelda de Iregua
Ribafiecha
Nalda
Carcar
Andosilla
Falces
Santacara
Murillo el Fruto
Carcastillo
Castilisar
Luesia
Biel
Santa Maria
Bailó
MONASTERIO SAN JUAN DE
Triste
OLIVA
Uncastillo
Sádaba
El Frago
Biscarrués
Farasdues
Ardisa
Luna
San Adrián
Peralta
Marcilla
Caparroso
El Villar de Arnedo
Calahorra
Jubera
Robres del Castillo
Villafranca
Milagro
San Román de Cameros
Arnedillo
Arnedo
Quel
Autol
Adeanueva de Ebro
Rincón de Soto
Valtierra
DOÑA BLANCA DE NAVARRA
Alfaro
Castejón
Arguedas
Cidacos
Enciso
Corella
Cintruénigo
Fitero
Grávalos
Igea
Cornago
Villar del Rio
Ejea de los Caballeros
Erla
Sierra de Luna
Tudela
Cabanillas
Fustiñana
Ribaforada
Buñuel
Murchante
Cascante
Cervera del Río Alhama
San Pedro Manrique
Puerto de Oncala 1454
Ventosa de la Sierra
Valverde
CATEDRAL DE NUESTRA SEÑORA DE LA HUERTA
Tarazona
Castilfrio de la Sierra
La Rubia
Magaña
Castilruiz
Agreda
Vera de Moncayo
El Buste
EL MISERICORDIA
CASTILLO DE BORJA
Borja
Cortes
Mallén
Tauste
Gallur
Castejón de Valdejasa
El Temple
742 Esteban
Zuera
Remolinos
Luceni
Pedrola
Alagón
Utebo
Zaragoza
Alfajarín
San Mateo de Gállego
Villanueva de Gállego
Perdiguera
Alcalá de Gurrea
Gurrea de
NUMANCIA ANTIQUISIMA
Almajano
Ventosilla
Soria
Matalebreras
Sierra del Madero
Sierra del Moncayo
Anzón
Magallon
Olvega
Aldeapozo
Los Rábanos
Cueva de Agreda
Fuendejalón
Almenar de Soria
Jaray
Gómara
Cubo de la Solana
Borobia
Ciria
Calcena
Tabuenca
Lumpiaque
Rueda de Jalón
Épila
La Muela
Aranda de Moncayo
Tierga
Almazul
Torrelapaja
Tejado
Duero
Ebro
Arga
Aragón
Alhama
Jalón
Arba
Gállego
Canal Imperial de Aragón

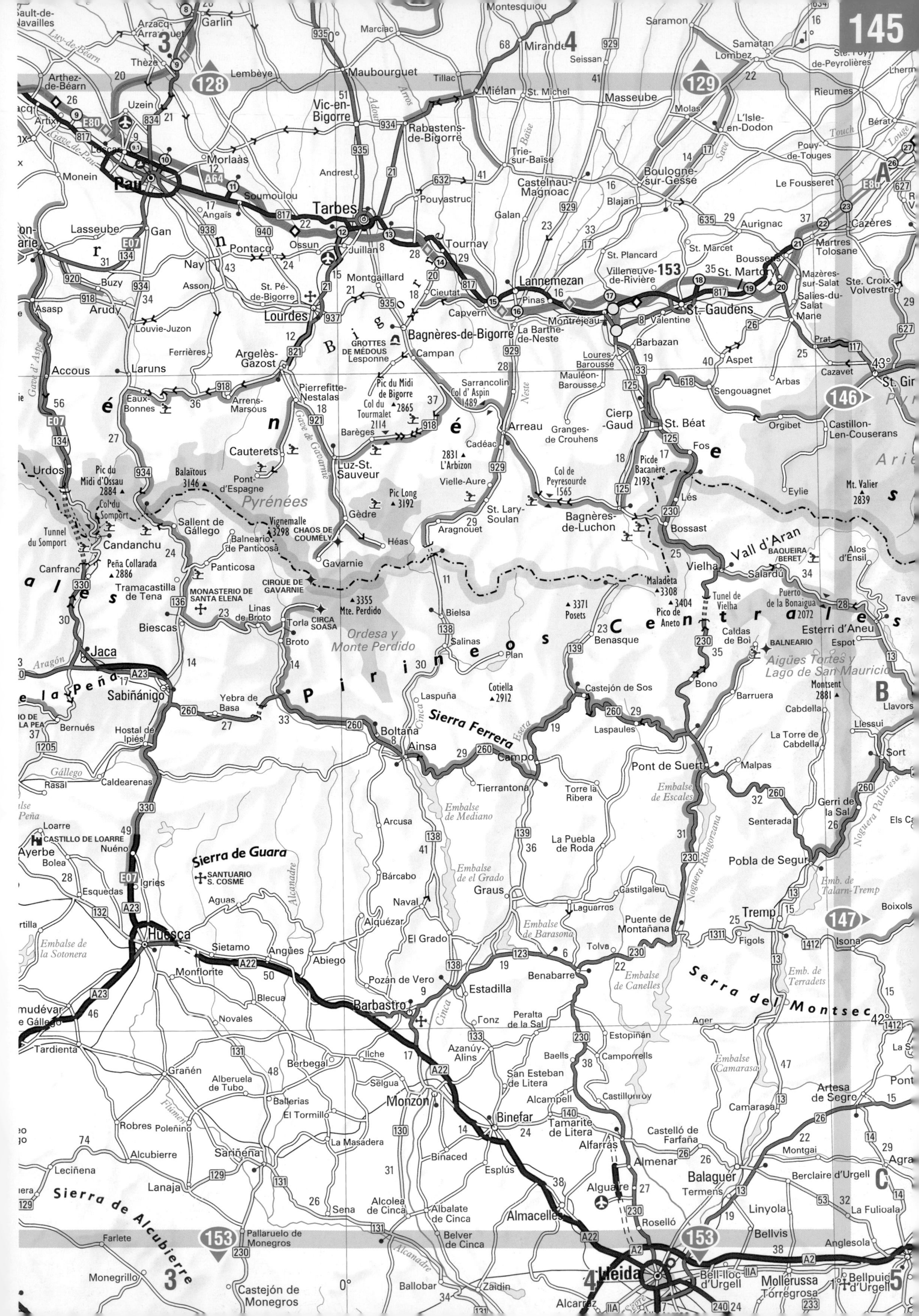
Pau
Tarbes
Lourdes
Vic-en-Bigorre
Maubourguet
Rabastens-de-Bigorre
Morlaàs
Soumoulou
Ossun
Juillan
Tournay
Lannemezan
Montréjeau
St.-Gaudens
Valentine
Castelnau-Magnoac
Trie-sur-Baïse
Mirande
Masseube
Boulogne-sur-Gesse
L'Isle-en-Dodon
Aurignac
Martres Tolosane
Cazères
Le Fousseret
St. Martory
Salies-du-Salat
Mane
Aspet
Barbazan
Bagnères-de-Bigorre
La Barthe-de-Neste
Argelès-Gazost
Pierrefitte-Nestalas
Luz-St. Sauveur
Cauterets
Gèdre
Gavarnie
Arreau
St. Lary-Soulan
Bagnères-de-Luchon
Cierp-Gaud
St. Béat
Fos
Bossòst
Vielha
Vall d'Aran
Salardú
Laruns
Eaux-Bonnes
Arudy
Oloron-Ste-Marie
Accous
Urdos
Col du Somport
Tunnel du Somport
Candanchu
Canfranc
Jaca
Sabiñánigo
Biescas
Sallent de Gállego
Panticosa
Torla
Broto
Ordesa y Monte Perdido
Mte. Perdido 3355
Vignemalle 3298
Pic du Midi d'Ossau 2884
Balaïtous 3146
Pic du Midi de Bigorre 2865
Col du Tourmalet 2114
Col d'Aspin 1489
Col de Peyresourde 1565
Pic Long 3192
Pyrénées
Pirineos Centrales
Maladeta 3308
Pico de Aneto 3404
Posets 3371
Benasque
Bielsa
Salinas
Plan
Cotiella 2912
Sierra Ferrera
Boltaña
Ainsa
Campo
Castejón de Sos
Laspaules
Pont de Suert
Caldas de Boì
Aigües Tortes y Lago de San Mauricio
Esterri d'Aneu
Sort
Gerri de la Sal
Senterada
Pobla de Segur
Tremp
Isona
Serra del Montsec
Sierra de Guara
Huesca
Ayerbe
Nueno
Sietamo
Angüés
Abiego
Barbastro
Estadilla
Graus
Benabarre
Monzón
Binéfar
Tamarite de Litera
Alfarràs
Almenar
Balaguer
Artesa de Segre
Camarasa
Linyola
Bellvís
Almacelles
Alguaire
Lleida
Mollerussa
Bellpuig d'Urgell
Tàrrega
Anglesola
Sariñena
Grañén
Tardienta
Sierra de Alcubierre
Alcubierre
Lanaja
Alcolea de Cinca
Fraga
Castejón de Monegros
Monegrillo
Ballobar
Zaidín
Belver de Cinca
Alcarràs
128
129
146
147
153
A
B
C
3
4
5
43°
42°
0°

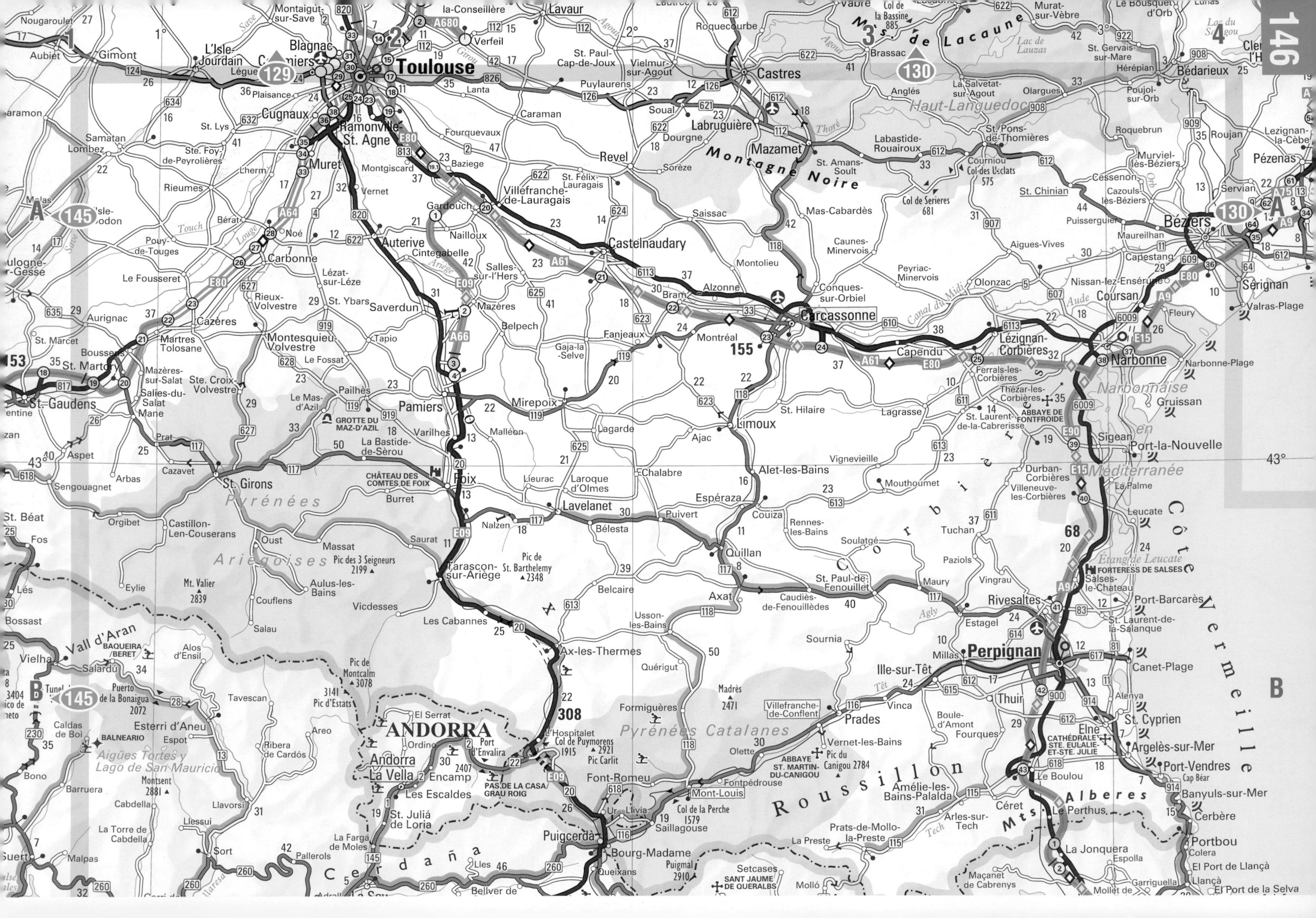
Toulouse
Carcassonne
Narbonne
Perpignan
Béziers
Castres
Mazamet
Castelnaudary
Limoux
Pamiers
Foix
St. Girons
St. Gaudens
Muret
Montagne Noire
Côte Vermeille
Méditerranée
Pyrénées
Pyrénées Catalanes
Roussillon
Mts. Albères
Haut-Languedoc
Mts. de Lacaune
ANDORRA
Andorra La Vella
Puigcerdà
Prades
Ille-sur-Têt
Rivesaltes
Thuir
Elne
Argelès-sur-Mer
Port-Vendres
Banyuls-sur-Mer
Cerbère
Portbou
Le Perthus
La Jonquera
Céret
Amélie-les-Bains-Palalda
Quillan
Axat
Lavelanet
Mirepoix
Tarascon-sur-Ariège
Ax-les-Thermes
Font-Romeu
Mont-Louis
Bourg-Madame
Revel
Lavaur
Gimont
Lézignan-Corbières
Sigean
Port-la-Nouvelle
Leucate
Gruissan
Coursan
Sérignan
Pézenas
Bédarieux
Vall d'Aran
Vielha
Cerdaña

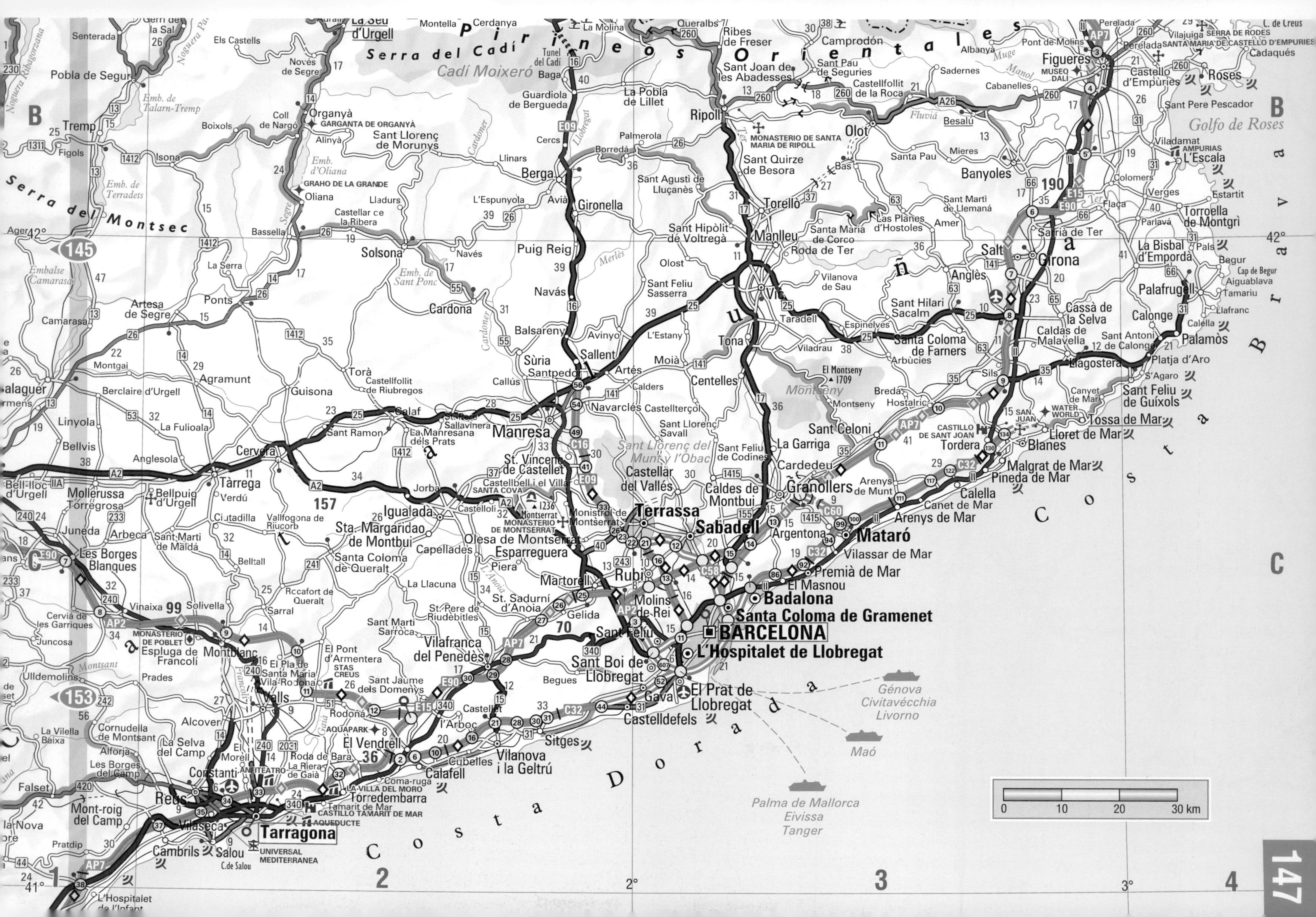

Pirineos Orientales
Serra del Cadí
Cadí Moixeró
Serra del Montsec
Golfo de Roses
Costa Brava
Costa Dorada
BARCELONA
L'Hospitalet de Llobregat
Santa Coloma de Gramenet
Badalona
Mataró
Sabadell
Terrassa
Girona
Figueres
Tarragona
Reus
Manresa
Vic
Granollers
Igualada
Tàrrega
Cervera
Solsona
Berga
Ripoll
Olot
Banyoles
Palafrugell
Palamós
Blanes
Lloret de Mar
Tossa de Mar
Sant Feliu de Guíxols
Calella
Arenys de Mar
El Prat de Llobregat
Castelldefels
Sitges
Vilanova i la Geltrú
Vilafranca del Penedès
El Vendrell
Valls
Montblanc
Salou
Cambrils
Mont-roig del Camp
Tremp
Organyà
La Seu d'Urgell
Roses
Cadaqués
L'Escala
Torroella de Montgrí
La Bisbal d'Empordà
Mollerussa
Les Borges Blanques
El Montseny 1709
Montserrat 1236
Palma de Mallorca
Eivissa
Tanger
Gènova
Civitavècchia
Livorno
Maó
0
10
20
30 km
42°
41°
2°
3°
B
C
1
2
3
4

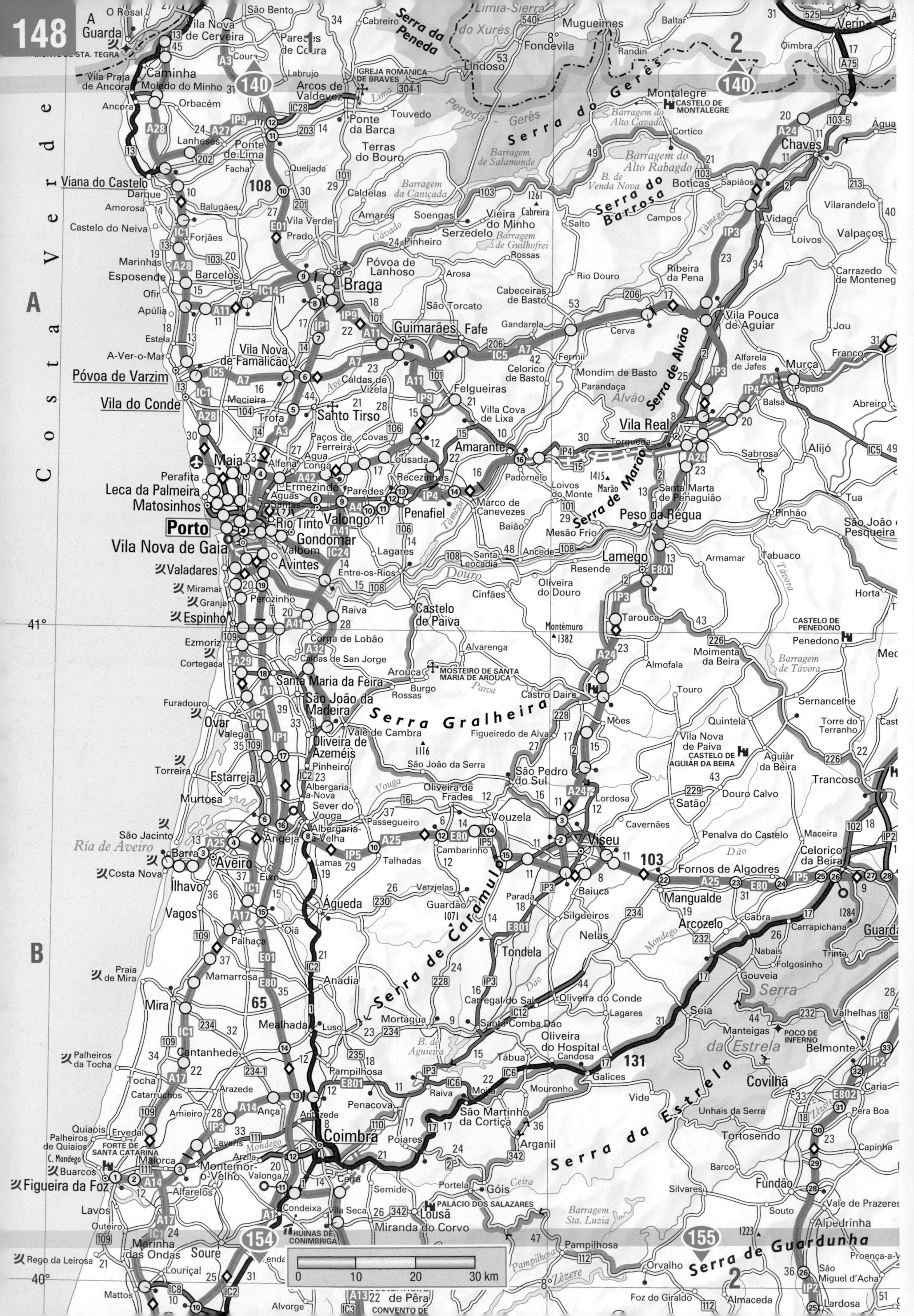

Costa Verde
A Guarda
Monte de Sta. Tegra
O Rosal
Vila Nova de Cerveira
São Bento
Paredes de Coura
Cabreiro
Serra da Peneda
Limia-Sierra do Xurés
Mugueimes
Fondevila
Lindoso
Baltar
Randin
Oimbra
Verín
Caminha
Vila Praia de Ancora
Moledo do Minho
Labrujo
Igreja Romanica de Braves
Arcos de Valdevez
Lima
Montalegre
Castelo de Montalegre
Ancora
Orbacém
Touvedo
Ponte da Barca
Peneda - Gerês
Serra do Gerês
Barragem do Alto Cavado
Cortico
Chaves
Água
Lanheses
Ponte de Lima
Terras do Bouro
Barragem de Salamonde
Barragem do Alto Rabagdo
Facha
Queljada
Viana do Castelo
Darque
Amorosa
Castelo do Neiva
Balugães
Caldelas
Barragem da Caniçada
Amares
Vieira do Minho
Cabreira
Salto
B. de Venda Nova
Serra do Barrosa
Boticas
Sapiãos
Vilarandelo
Campos
Tâmega
Vidago
Vila Verde
Prado
Soengas
Serzedelo
Barragem de Gulhofrei
Rossas
Loivos
Valpaços
Forjães
Pinheiro
Cávado
Marinhas
Esposende
Barcelos
Póvoa de Lanhoso
Arosa
Rio Douro
Ribeira da Pena
Carrazedo de Monteneg
Ofir
Apúlia
Braga
São Torcato
Cabeceiras de Basto
Estela
Guimarães
Fafe
Gandarela
Cerva
Vila Pouca de Aguiar
Jou
A-Ver-o-Mar
Vila Nova de Famalicão
Celorico de Basto
Fermil
Mondim de Basto
Serra de Alvão
Alfarela de Jafes
Franco
Murça
Póvoa de Varzim
Caldas de Vizela
Felgueiras
Parandaça
Alvão
Populo
Vila do Conde
Macieira
Trofa
Santo Tirso
Villa Cova de Lixa
Balsa
Abreiro
Vila Real
Paços de Ferreira
Covas
Amarante
Torgueda
Sabrosa
Alijó
Maia
Alfena
Agua Longa
Lousada
Padornelo
Perafita
Leca da Palmeira
Matosinhos
Ermezinde
Aguas Santas
Paredes
Recezinhos
Loivos do Monte
Marão
Serra de Marão
Santa Marta de Penaguião
Tua
Porto
Rio Tinto
Valongo
Penafiel
Tâmega
Marco de Canevezes
Baião
Mesão Frio
Peso da Régua
Pinhão
São João da Pesqueira
Vila Nova de Gaia
Gondomar
Valbom
Lagares
Santa Leocadia
Ancede
Lamego
Armamar
Tabuaco
Valadares
Avintes
Entre-os-Rios
Douro
Resende
Távora
Miramar
Granja
Perozinho
Cinfães
Oliveira do Douro
Horta
Espinho
Raiva
Castelo de Paiva
Montèmuro
Tarouca
Castelo de Penedono
Penedono
Ezmoriz
Corga de Lobão
Moimenta da Beira
Barragem de Távora
Cortegaca
Caldas de San Jorge
Alvarenga
Almofala
Arouca
Mosteiro de Santa Maria de Arouca
Santa Maria da Feira
Burgo
Rossas
Paiva
Castro Daire
Touro
Furadouro
São João da Madeira
Serra Gralheira
Sernancelhe
Ovar
Valega
Vale de Cambra
Oliveira de Azeméis
Figueiredo de Alva
Mões
Quintela
Torre do Terranho
Vila Nova de Paiva
Castelo de Aguiar da Beira
Aguiar da Beira
Torreira
Estarreja
Pinheiro
São João da Serra
São Pedro do Sul
Trancoso
Murtosa
Albergaria-a-Nova
Vouga
Oliveira de Frades
Lordosa
Douro Calvo
Satão
Sever do Vouga
Passegueiro
Vouzela
Cavernães
São Jacinto
Ría de Áveiro
Barra
Aveiro
Angeja
Albergaria-a-Velha
Cambarinho
Viseu
Penalva do Castelo
Maceira
Celorico da Beira
Costa Nova
Ílhavo
Lamas
Talhadas
Eixo
Fornos de Algodres
Mangualde
Vagos
Águeda
Varzjelas
Guardão
Serra de Caramulo
Parada
Baiuca
Silgueiros
Arcozelo
Cabra
Carrapichana
Guarda
Palhaça
Oiã
Tondela
Nelas
Mondego
Nabais
Folgosinho
Trinta
Praia de Mira
Mamarrosa
Anadia
Gouveia
Serra da Estrela
Mira
Mealhada
Luso
Mortágua
Carregal do Sal
Oliveira do Conde
Santa Comba Dão
Lagares
Seia
Manteigas
Poço de Inferno
Valhelhas
Palheiros da Tocha
Cantanhede
B. de Aguieira
Oliveira do Hospital
Candosa
Tábua
Belmonte
Tocha
Arazede
Pampilhosa
Galices
Covilhã
Caria
Catarruchos
Penacova
Raiva
Moita
Mouronho
Vide
Amieiro
Anca
Antuzede
São Martinho da Cortiça
Unhais da Serra
Pera Boa
Quiaios
Palheiros de Quiaios
Ervedal
Coimbra
Poiares
Arganil
Tortosendo
Forte de Santa Catarina
C. Mondego
Lavaris
Maiorca
Montemor-o-Velho
Arzila
Capinha
Buarcos
Figueira da Foz
Alfarelos
Valonga
Ceira
Semide
Portela
Góis
Barco
Fundão
Silvares
Lavos
Condeixa
Vila Seca
Lousã
Palácio dos Salazares
Barragem Sta. Luzia
Vale de Prazeres
Souto
Alpedrinha
Outeiro
Marinha das Ondas
Soure
Ruinas de Conimbriga
Miranda do Corvo
Pampilhosa
Serra de Guardunha
Proença-a-V
Rego da Leirosa
Louriçal
Orvalho
São Miguel d'Acha
Mattos
Alvorge
de Pêra
Convento de
Foz do Giraldo
Almaceda
Lardosa
Zêzere
0 10 20 30 km

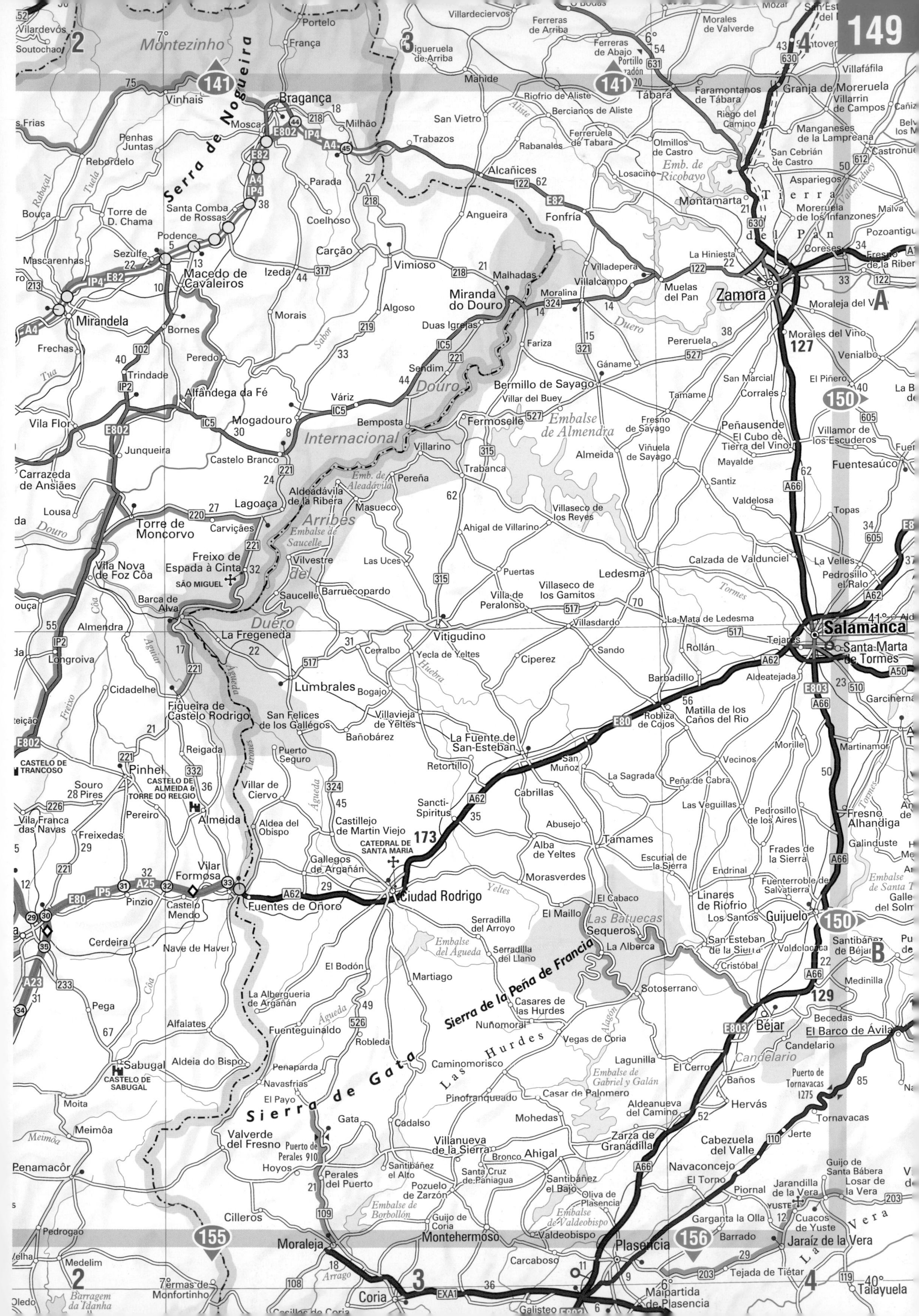

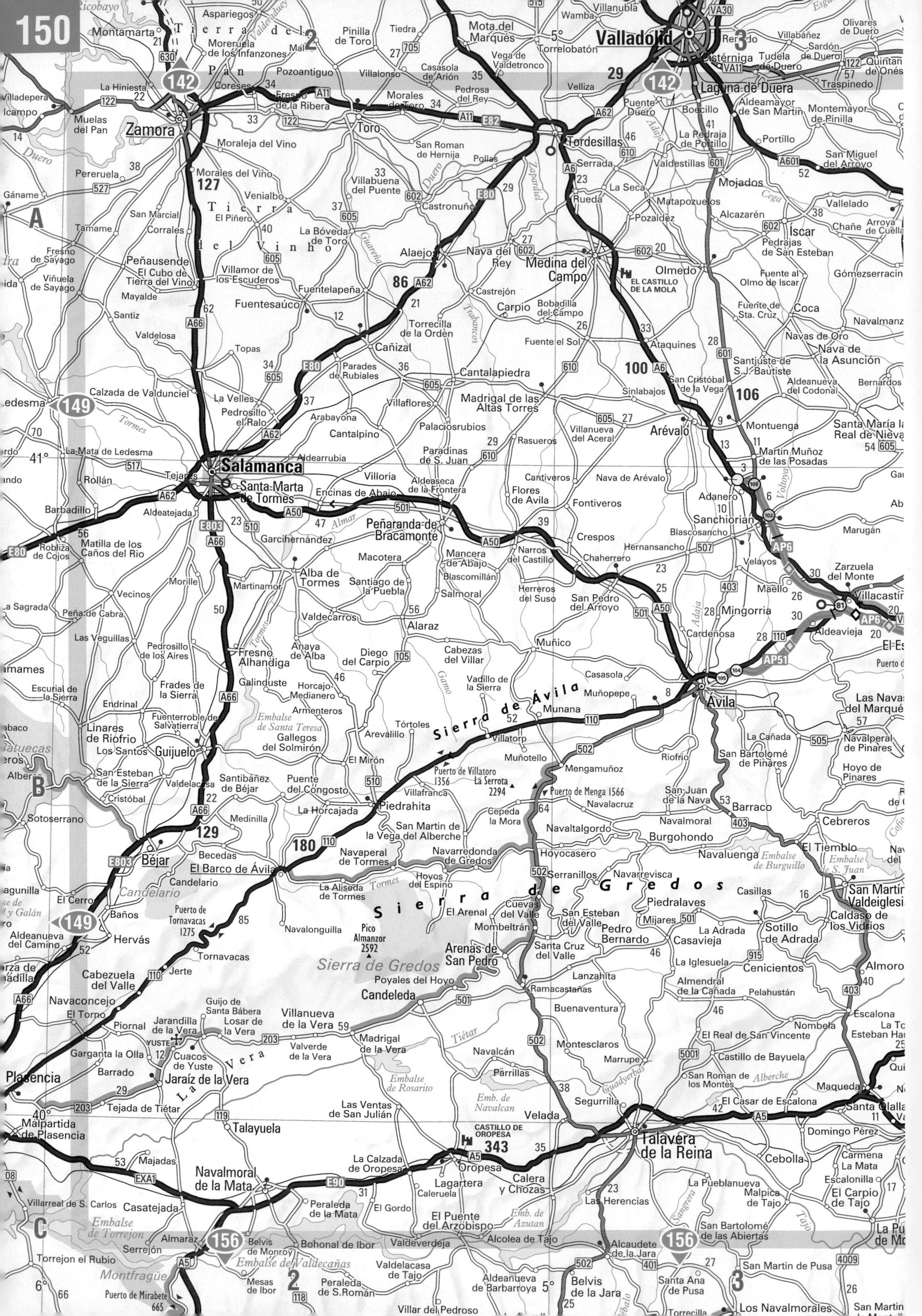
Ricobayo
Montamarta
Aspariegos
Tierra del Pan
Moreruela de los Infanzones
Pinilla de Toro
Tiedra
Mota del Marqués
Wamba
Villanubla
Valladolid
Olivares de Duero
Villabáñez
Sardón de Duero
Tudela de Duero
Quintanilla de Onésimo
Traspinedo
Cistérniga
Laguna de Duera
La Hiniesta
Coreses
Pozoantiguo
Villalonso
Casasola de Arión
Vega de Valdetronco
Torrelobatón
Velliza
Fresno de la Ribera
Morales de Toro
Pedrosa del Rey
Villadepera
Muelas del Pan
Zamora
Toro
Tordesillas
Puente Duero
Boecillo
Aldeamayor de San Martín
Montemayor de Pinilla
La Pedraja de Portillo
Portillo
San Miguel del Arroyo
Moraleja del Vino
San Román de Hornija
Pollos
Duero
Pereruela
Morales del Vino
Villabuena del Puente
Serrada
Valdestillas
Mojados
Gáname
Tierra del Vino
Venialbo
Castronuño
La Seca
Rueda
Matapozuelos
Vallelado
San Marcial
El Piñero
Pozaldez
Alcazarén
Arroyo de Cuéllar
Tamame
Corrales
La Bóveda de Toro
Íscar
Chañe
Pedrajas de San Esteban
Fresno de Sayago
Peñausende
El Cubo de Tierra del Vino
Alaejos
Nava del Rey
Medina del Campo
Olmedo
Viñuela de Sayago
Villamor de los Escuderos
Fuente al Olmo de Íscar
Gómezserracín
Mayalde
EL CASTILLO DE LA MOLA
Fuentelapeña
Castrejón
Carpio
Bobadilla del Campo
Fuente de Sta. Cruz
Coca
Santiz
Fuentesaúco
Torrecilla de la Orden
Navalmanzano
Valdelosa
Fuente el Sol
Ataquines
Navas de Oro
Nava de la Asunción
Topas
Cañizal
Parades de Rubiales
Cantalapiedra
Santiuste de S.J. Bautiste
Bernardos
Ledesma
Calzada de Valdunciel
La Velles
Pedrosillo el Ralo
Arabayona
Villaflores
Madrigal de las Altas Torres
Sinlabajos
San Cristóbal de la Vega
Aldeanueva del Codonal
Tormes
Cantalpino
Palaciosrubios
Villanueva del Aceral
Arévalo
Montuenga
Santa María la Real de Nieva
La Mata de Ledesma
Paradinas de S. Juan
Rasueros
Martín Muñoz de las Posadas
Aldearrubia
Salamanca
Rollán
Tejares
Santa Marta de Tormes
Villoria
Aldeaseca de la Frontera
Cantiveros
Nava de Arévalo
Flores de Ávila
Adanero
Barbadillo
Aldeatejada
Encinas de Abajo
Fontiveros
Sanchidrián
Peñaranda de Bracamonte
Blascosancho
Marugán
Almar
Robliza de Cojos
Matilla de los Caños del Río
Garcihernández
Macotera
Crespos
Hernansancho
Mancera de Abajo
Narros del Castillo
Chaherrero
Velayos
Zarzuela del Monte
Alba de Tormes
Santiago de la Puebla
Blascomillán
Maello
Villacastín
Morille
Martinamor
Salmoral
Herreros del Suso
San Pedro del Arroyo
Mingorria
La Sagrada
Vecinos
Peña de Cabra
Valdecarros
Alaraz
Cardeñosa
Aldeavieja
Las Veguillas
Pedrosillo de los Aires
Muñico
Fresno Alhándiga
Anaya de Alba
Diego del Carpio
Cabezas del Villar
Casasola
Escurial de la Sierra
Frades de la Sierra
Galinduste
Horcajo-Medianero
Vadillo de la Sierra
Muñopepe
Ávila
Las Navas del Marqués
Endrinal
Sierra de Ávila
Armenteros
Munana
Fuenterroble de Salvatierra
Embalse de Santa Teresa
Tórtoles
Linares de Riofrío
Gallegos del Solmirón
Arevalillo
Villatoro
La Cañada
Navalperal de Pinares
Los Santos
Guijuelo
Muñotello
Riofrío
San Bartolomé de Pinares
El Mirón
Mengamuñoz
Hoyo de Pinares
Puerto de Villatoro 1356
La Serrota 2294
San Esteban de la Sierra
Valdelacasa
Santibáñez de Béjar
Puente del Congosto
Puerto de Menga 1566
San Juan de la Nava
Cristóbal
Villafranca
Piedrahita
Navalacruz
Barraco
Sotoserrano
La Horcajada
Cepeda la Mora
Navalmoral
Cebreros
Medinilla
San Martín de la Vega del Alberche
Navaltalgordo
Burgohondo
Béjar
Becedas
Navaperal de Tormes
Navarredonda de Gredos
Hoyocasero
Navaluenga
Embalse de Burguillo
El Tiemblo
Candelario
El Barco de Ávila
Hoyos del Espino
Serranillos
Navarrevisca
Embalse de S. Juan
La Aliseda de Tormes
Sierra de Gredos
Casillas
San Martín de Valdeiglesias
El Cerro
Piedralaves
Baños
Puerto de Tornavacas 1275
El Arenal
Cuevas del Valle
San Esteban del Valle
Mijares
Caldaso de los Vidrios
Aldeanueva del Camino
Hervás
Navalonguilla
Pico Almanzor 2592
Mombeltrán
Pedro Bernardo
La Adrada
Sotillo de Adrada
Santa Cruz del Valle
Casavieja
Tornavacas
Arenas de San Pedro
La Iglesuela
Cenicientos
Almorox
Cabezuela del Valle
Jerte
Poyales del Hoyo
Lanzahíta
Almendral de la Cañada
Candeleda
Ramacastañas
Pelahustán
Navaconcejo
El Torno
Guijo de Santa Bábera
Buenaventura
Escalona
Villanueva de la Vera
Piornal
Jarandilla de la Vera
Losar de la Vera
Nombela
Madrigal de la Vera
El Real de San Vincente
YUSTE
Garganta la Olla
Cuacos de Yuste
Valverde de la Vera
Tiétar
Montesclaros
Navalcán
Castillo de Bayuela
La Vera
Marrupe
Plasencia
Barrado
Jaraíz de la Vera
Parrillas
Embalse de Rosarito
San Román de los Montes
Alberche
Guadyerbas
Maqueda
Segurrilla
Emb. de Navalcán
El Casar de Escalona
Malpartida de Plasencia
Tejada de Tiétar
Las Ventas de San Julián
Velada
Santa Olalla
Talayuela
CASTILLO DE OROPESA
Talavera de la Reina
Domingo Pérez
Majadas
La Calzada de Oropesa
Oropesa
Calera y Chozas
Cebolla
Carmena
La Mata
Navalmoral de la Mata
Lagartera
Caleruela
La Pueblanueva
Escalonilla
El Carpio de Tajo
Malpica de Tajo
Villarreal de S. Carlos
Casatejada
Peraleda de la Mata
El Gordo
Las Herencias
Sangrera
Embalse de Torrejón
El Puente del Arzobispo
Emb. de Azután
Tajo
Almaraz
Belvís de Monroy
Bohonal de Ibor
Valdeverdeja
Alcolea de Tajo
Alcaudete de la Jara
San Bartolomé de las Abiertas
Serrejón
Torrejón el Rubio
Embalse de Valdecañas
Valdelacasa de Tajo
San Martín de Pusa
Monfragüe
Mesas de Ibor
Peraleda de S.Román
Aldeanueva de Barbarroya
Belvís de la Jara
Santa Ana de Pusa
Puerto de Mirabete 665
Villar del Pedroso
Los Navalmorales
Torrecilla
San Martín
A
B
C
2
3
41°
40°
5°
6°
142
149
156
E80
E82
E90
E803
A5
A6
A11
A50
A62
A66
AP6
AP51
A601
EXA1
VA30
VA11

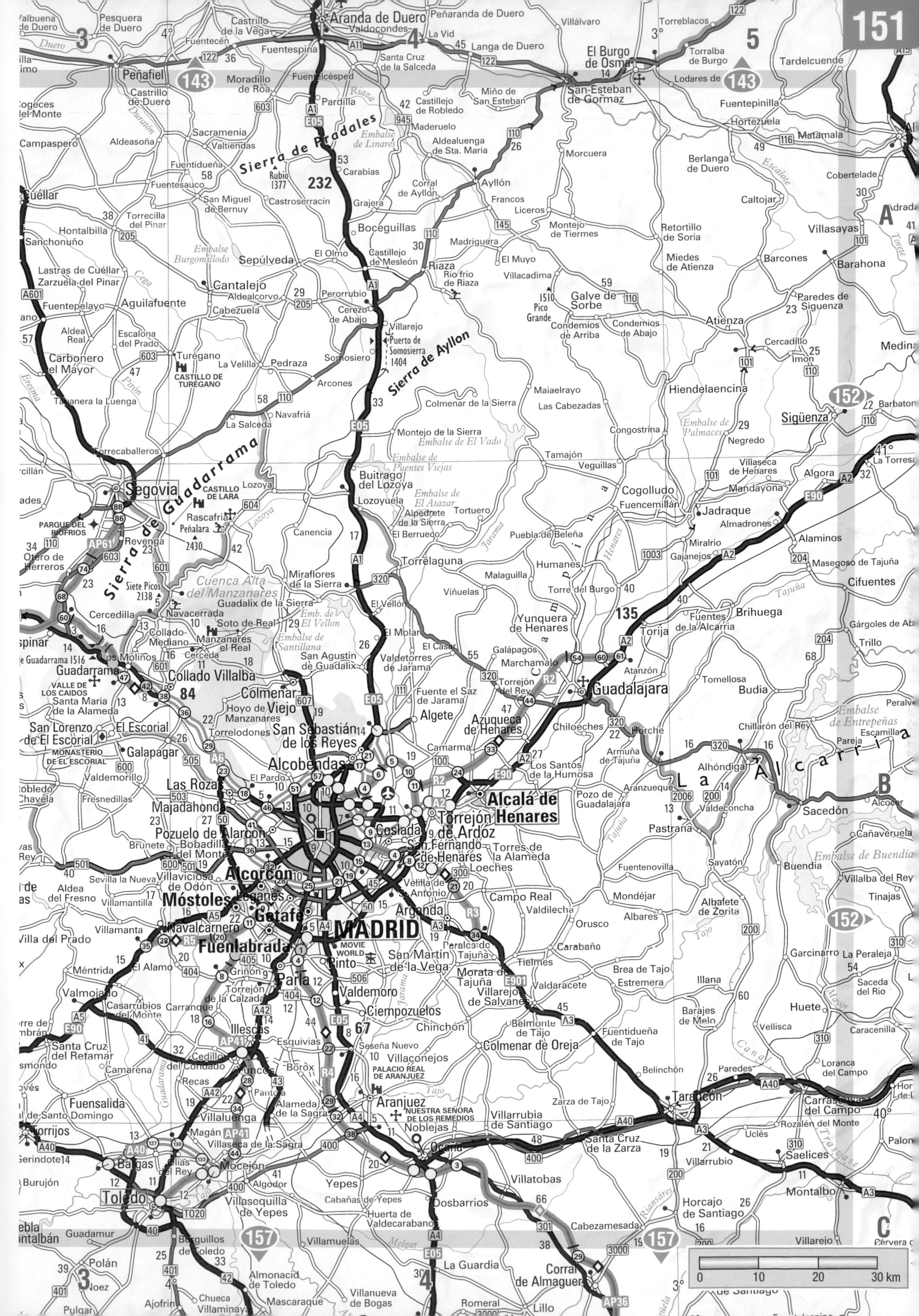
Aranda de Duero
Peñaranda de Duero
Pesquera de Duero
Castrillo de la Vega
Valdocondes
La Vid
Langa de Duero
Villálvaro
Torreblacos
Torralba de Burgo
El Burgo de Osma
Tardelcuende
Peñafiel
Fuentecén
Fuentespina
Santa Cruz de la Salceda
Moradillo de Roa
Fuentelcésped
Miño de San Esteban
San Esteban de Gormaz
Lodares de Osma
Castrillo de Duero
Pardilla
Castillejo de Robledo
Fuentepinilla
Cogeces del Monte
Maderuelo
Hortezuela
Matamala
Campaspero
Aldeasoña
Sacramenia
Valtiendas
Embalse de Linares
Aldealuenga de Sta. Maria
Morcuera
Berlanga de Duero
Sierra de Pradales
Rubio 1377
Carabias
Fuentidueña
Fuentesauco
Castroserracin
Corral de Ayllón
Ayllón
Cobertelade
Cuéllar
San Miguel de Bernuy
Grajera
Francos
Liceros
Caltojar
Torrecilla del Pinar
Hontalbilla
Boceguillas
Montejo de Tiermes
Retortillo de Soria
Villasayas
Sanchonuño
Embalse Burgomillodo
Sepúlveda
El Olmo
Castillejo de Mesleón
Riaza
Madriguera
El Muyo
Miedes de Atienza
Barcones
Barahona
Lastras de Cuéllar
Zarzuela del Pinar
Cantalejo
Aldealcorvo
Perorrubio
Rio frio de Riaza
Villacadima
Galve de Sorbe
Paredes de Sigüenza
Fuentepelayo
Aguilafuente
Cabezuela
Cerezo de Abajo
1510 Pico Grande
Condemios de Arriba
Condemios de Abajo
Atienza
Aldea Real
Escalona del Prado
Villarejo
Puerto de Somosierra 1404
Cercadillo
Imon
Medina
Carbonero el Mayor
Turégano
Castillo de Turégano
La Velilla
Pedraza
Somosierra
Sierra de Ayllon
Arcones
Maiaelrayo
Hiendelaencina
Las Cabezadas
Tabanera la Luenga
Navafriá
Colmenar de la Sierra
Sigüenza
Barbatona
La Salceda
Montejo de la Sierra
Embalse de El Vado
Congostrina
Embalse de Palmaces
Negredo
Sierra de Guadarrama
Torrecaballeros
Tamajón
Veguillas
Villaseca de Henares
Algora
La Torresa
Embalse de Puentes Viejas
Buitrago del Lozoya
Cogolludo
Mandayona
Segovia
Castillo de Lara
Lozoya
Lozoyuela
Embalse de El Atazar
Alpedrete de la Sierra
Tortuero
Fuencemillán
Jadraque
Almadrones
Parque del Riofrío
Rascafría
Peñalara
Canencia
El Berrueco
Puebla de Beleña
Miralrio
Alaminos
Revenga
2430
Otero de Herreros
Gajanejos
Torrelaguna
Humanes
Masegoso de Tajuña
Cuenca Alta del Manzanares
Miraflores de la Sierra
Malaguilla
Cifuentes
Siete Picos 2138
Viñuelas
Torre del Burgo
Guadalix de la Sierra
Emb. de El Vellon
El Vellón
Cercedilla
Navacerrada
Soto de Real
Yunquera de Henares
Torija
Fuentes de la Alcarria
Brihuega
Gárgoles de Abajo
Collado-Mediano
Manzanares el Real
Embalse de Santillana
El Molar
Trillo
Guadarrama 1516
Los Molinos
Cerceda
San Agustín de Guadalix
Valdetorres de Jarama
El Casar
Galápagos
Marchamalo
Atanzón
Tomellosa
Guadarrama
Valle de los Caidos
Collado Villalba
Colmenar Viejo
Fuente el Saz de Jarama
Torrejón del Rey
Guadalajara
Budia
Santa Maria de la Alameda
Hoyo de Manzanares
Algete
Azuqueca de Henares
Chiloeches
Horche
Embalse de Entrepeñas
Peralveche
San Lorenzo de El Escorial
El Escorial
Torrelodones
San Sebastián de los Reyes
Camarma
Armuña de Tajuña
Chillarón del Rey
Escamilla
Pareja
Monasterio de El Escorial
Galapagar
Alcobendas
Los Santos de la Humosa
Aranzueque
Alhóndiga
La Alcarria
Robledo de Chavela
Valdemorillo
El Pardo
Las Rozas
Alcalá de Henares
Pozo de Guadalajara
Valdeconcha
Sacedón
Alcocer
Fresnedillas
Majadahonda
Torrejón de Ardoz
Coslada
Pastrana
Cañaveruela
Pozuelo de Alarcón
Brunete
Bobadilla del Monte
San Fernando de Henares
Torres de la Alameda
Loeches
Embalse de Buendía
Buendía
Sayatón
Fuentenovilla
Sevilla la Nueva
Villaviciosa de Odón
Alcorcón
Velilla de S. Antonio
Villalba del Rey
Aldea del Fresno
Villamantilla
Móstoles
Leganés
Campo Real
Mondéjar
Albalate de Zorita
Tinajas
Getafe
Arganda
Valdilecha
Albares
Villamanta
Navalcarnero
Orusco
Villa del Prado
Fuenlabrada
MADRID
Movie World
Pinto
San Martín de la Vega
Peralejo de Tajuña
Carabaña
Tielmes
Garcinarro
La Peraleja
Méntrida
El Alamo
Griñón
Parla
Morata de Tajuña
Brea de Tajo
Illana
Saceda del Rio
Valmojado
Torrejón de la Calzada
Valdemoro
Villarejo de Salvanés
Valdaracete
Estremera
Casarrubios del Monte
Carranque
Ciempozuelos
Huete
Chinchón
Belmonte de Tajo
Fuentidueña de Tajo
Barajes de Melo
Vellisca
Caracenilla
Illescas
Esquivias
Seseña Nuevo
Santa Cruz del Retamar
Cedillo del Condado
Villaconejos
Colmenar de Oreja
Camarena
Borox
Palacio Real de Aranjuez
Yuncos
Belinchón
Loranca del Campo
Paredes
Recas
Pantoja
Tarancón
Fuensalida
Alameda de la Sagra
Aranjuez
Nuestra Señora de los Remedios
Zarza de Tajo
Carrascosa del Campo
Villaluenga
Villarrubia de Santiago
Torrijos
Magán
Noblejas
Villaseca de la Sagra
Santa Cruz de la Zarza
Rozalén del Monte
Uclés
Gerindote
Bargas
Olías del Rey
Mocejón
Ocaña
Villarrubio
Saelices
Burujón
Algodor
Yepes
Villatobas
Montalbo
Toledo
Villasequilla de Yepes
Cabañas de Yepes
Dosbarrios
Horcajo de Santiago
Huerta de Valdecarabanos
Cabezamesada
Puebla de Montalbán
Guadamur
Burguillos de Toledo
Villamuelas
Villarejo
Cervera del Llano
Polán
Cobisa
La Guardia
Corral de Almaguer
Almonacid de Toledo
Villanueva de Bogas
Chueca
Villaminaya
Mascaraque
Ajofrín
Pulgar
Romeral
Lillo
0
10
20
30 km

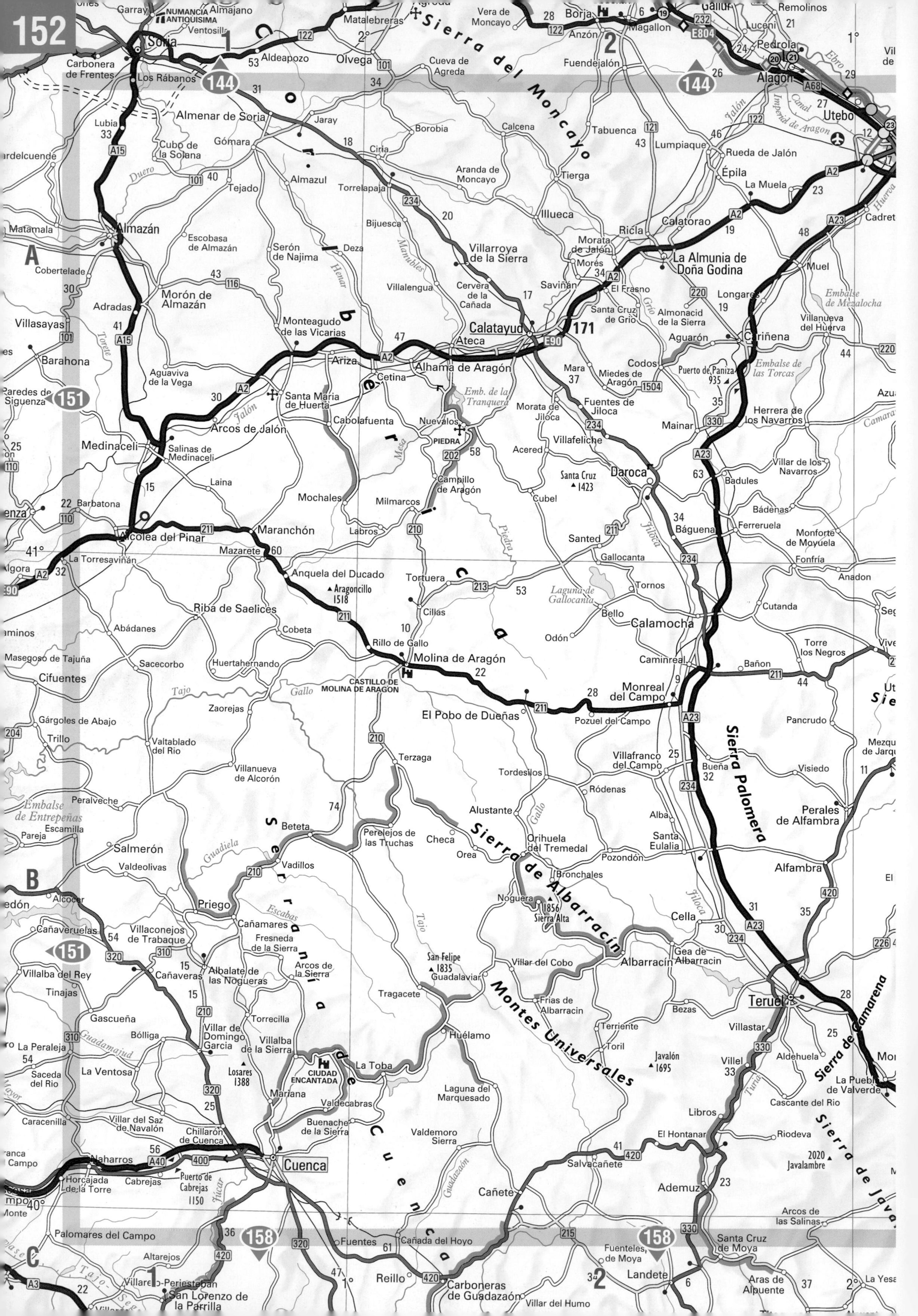

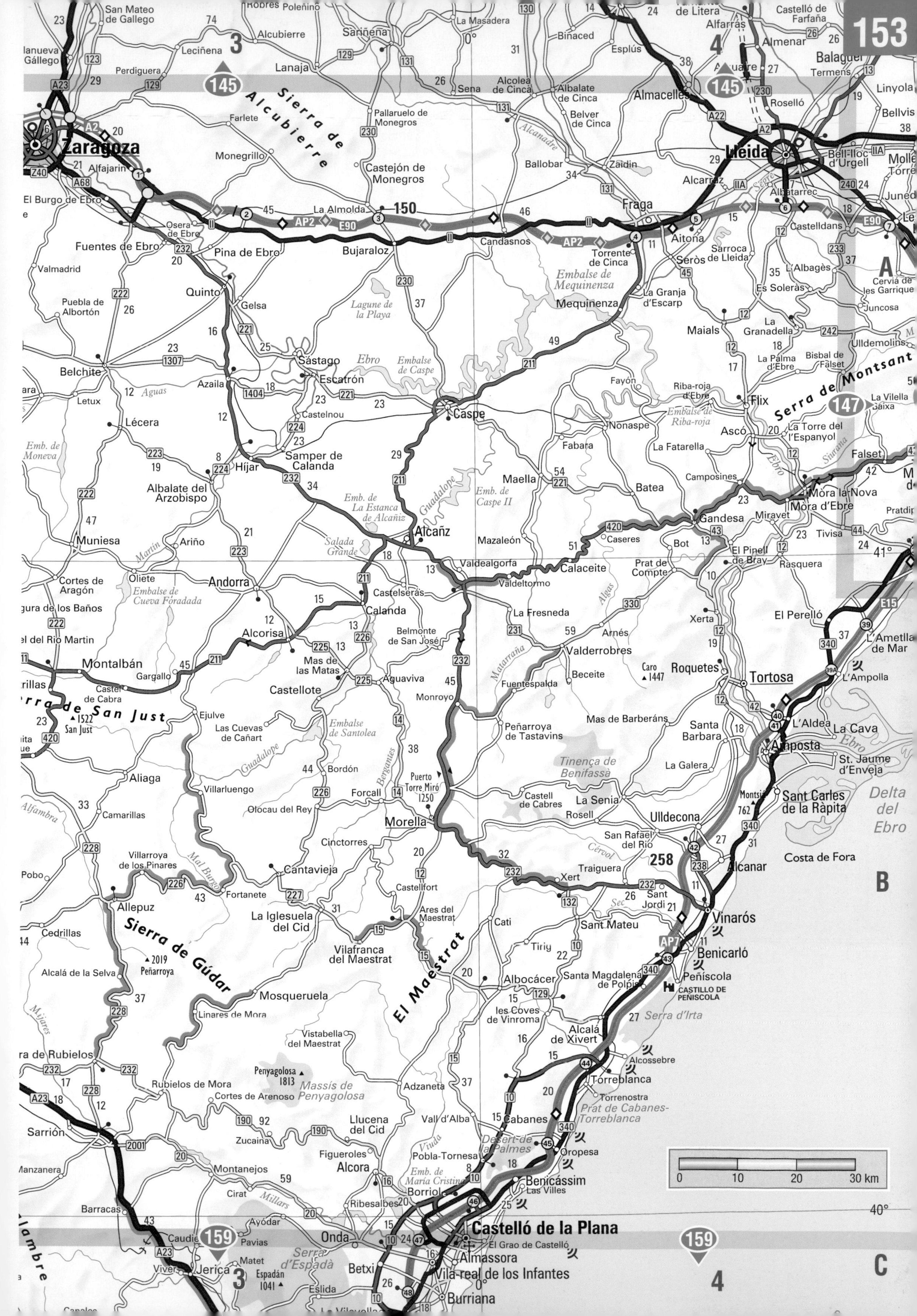
San Mateo de Gallego
Zuera
Leciñena
Alcubierre
Sariñena
Lanaja
La Masadera
Binaced
Esplús
Alfarràs
Almenar
Castelló de Farfaña
Balaguer
Termens
Linyola
Bellvis
Perdiguera
Sierra de Alcubierre
Sena
Alcolea de Cinca
Albalate de Cinca
Belver de Cinca
Almacelles
Alguaire
Roselló
Farlete
Pallaruelo de Monegros
Zaragoza
Monegrillo
Castejón de Monegros
Ballobar
Zaidín
Lleida
Bell-lloc d'Urgell
Mollerussa
Torrefarrera
Alfajarín
Alcarràs
Albatàrrec
Juneda
El Burgo de Ebro
La Almolda
Fraga
Osera de Ebro
Candasnos
Aitona
Castelldans
Fuentes de Ebro
Pina de Ebro
Bujaraloz
Torrente de Cinca
Seròs
Sarroca de Lleida
L'Albagès
Valmadrid
Embalse de Mequinenza
Cervià de les Garrigues
Quinto
La Granja d'Escarp
Es Soleràs
Puebla de Albortón
Gelsa
Lagune de la Playa
Mequinenza
Juncosa
Maials
La Granadella
Belchite
Sástago
Ebro
Embalse de Caspe
Escatrón
La Palma d'Ebre
Bisbal de Falset
Ulldemolins
Serra de Montsant
Letux
Azaila
Aguas
Fayón
Riba-roja d'Ebre
Flix
La Vilella Baixa
Lécera
Castelnou
Caspe
Nonaspe
Embalse de Riba-roja
Ascó
La Torre de l'Espanyol
Emb. de Moneva
Samper de Calanda
Fabara
La Fatarella
Falset
Híjar
Maella
Batea
Camposines
Móra la Nova
Móra d'Ebre
Albalate del Arzobispo
Emb. de La Estanca de Alcañiz
Guadalope
Emb. de Caspe II
Gandesa
Miravet
Pratdip
Muniesa
Ariño
Alcañiz
Mazaleón
Caseres
Bot
Tivisa
El Pinell de Bray
Rasquera
Salada Grande
Valdealgorfa
Calaceite
Prat de Comte
Cortes de Aragón
Oliete
Andorra
Valdeltormo
Embalse de Cueva Foradada
Castelserás
La Fresneda
Calanda
Xerta
El Perelló
Segura de los Baños
Alcorisa
Belmonte de San José
Arnés
L'Ametlla de Mar
Vivel del Río Martín
Montalbán
Mas de las Matas
Valderrobres
Roquetes
Tortosa
Gargallo
Castellote
Aguaviva
Beceite
Caro 1447
L'Ampolla
Castel de Cabra
Sierra de San Just
Monroyo
Fuentespalda
Mas de Barberáns
L'Aldea
La Cava
Ejulve
Peñarroya de Tastavins
Santa Barbara
Amposta
Las Cuevas de Cañart
Embalse de Santolea
1522 San Just
St. Jaume d'Enveja
Tinença de Benifassà
Aliaga
Bordón
La Galera
Puerto Torre Miró 1250
Villarluengo
Forcall
Castell de Cabres
La Senia
Montsià 762
Sant Carles de la Ràpita
Delta del Ebro
Olocau del Rey
Rosell
Alfambra
Camarillas
Morella
Ulldecona
Cinctorres
San Rafael del Río
Villarroya de los Pinares
Alcanar
Costa de Fora
Mal Burgo
Cantavieja
Cérvol
Traiguera
Pobo
Xert
Fortanete
Castellfort
Sant Jordi
Allepuz
Vinaròs
La Iglesuela del Cid
Ares del Maestrat
Cati
Sant Mateu
Cedrillas
Sierra de Gúdar
Vilafranca del Maestrat
El Maestrat
Benicarló
Tírig
2019 Peñarroya
Alcalá de la Selva
Santa Magdalena de Polpís
Peñíscola
Albocácer
Castillo de Peñíscola
Mosqueruela
Linares de Mora
les Coves de Vinromà
Serra d'Irta
Mijares
Alcalà de Xivert
Vistabella del Maestrat
Mora de Rubielos
Penyagolosa 1813
Alcossebre
Torreblanca
Massís de Penyagolosa
Adzaneta
Rubielos de Mora
Torrenostra
Cortes de Arenoso
Prat de Cabanes-Torreblanca
Sarrión
Llucena del Cid
Vall d'Alba
Cabanes
Zucaina
Desert de les Palmes
Oropesa
Manzanera
Figueroles
Pobla-Tornesa
Montanejos
Alcora
Emb. de María Cristina
Benicàssim
Las Villes
Cirat
Millars
Borriol
Barracas
Ribesalbes
Ayódar
Castelló de la Plana
Caudiel
Onda
El Grao de Castelló
Pavias
Serra d'Espadà
Almassora
Matet
Viver
Jérica
Espadán 1041
Betxi
Vila-real de los Infantes
Eslida
Burriana
0 10 20 30 km
40°
41°
A
B
C
3
4
145
147
150
159
258

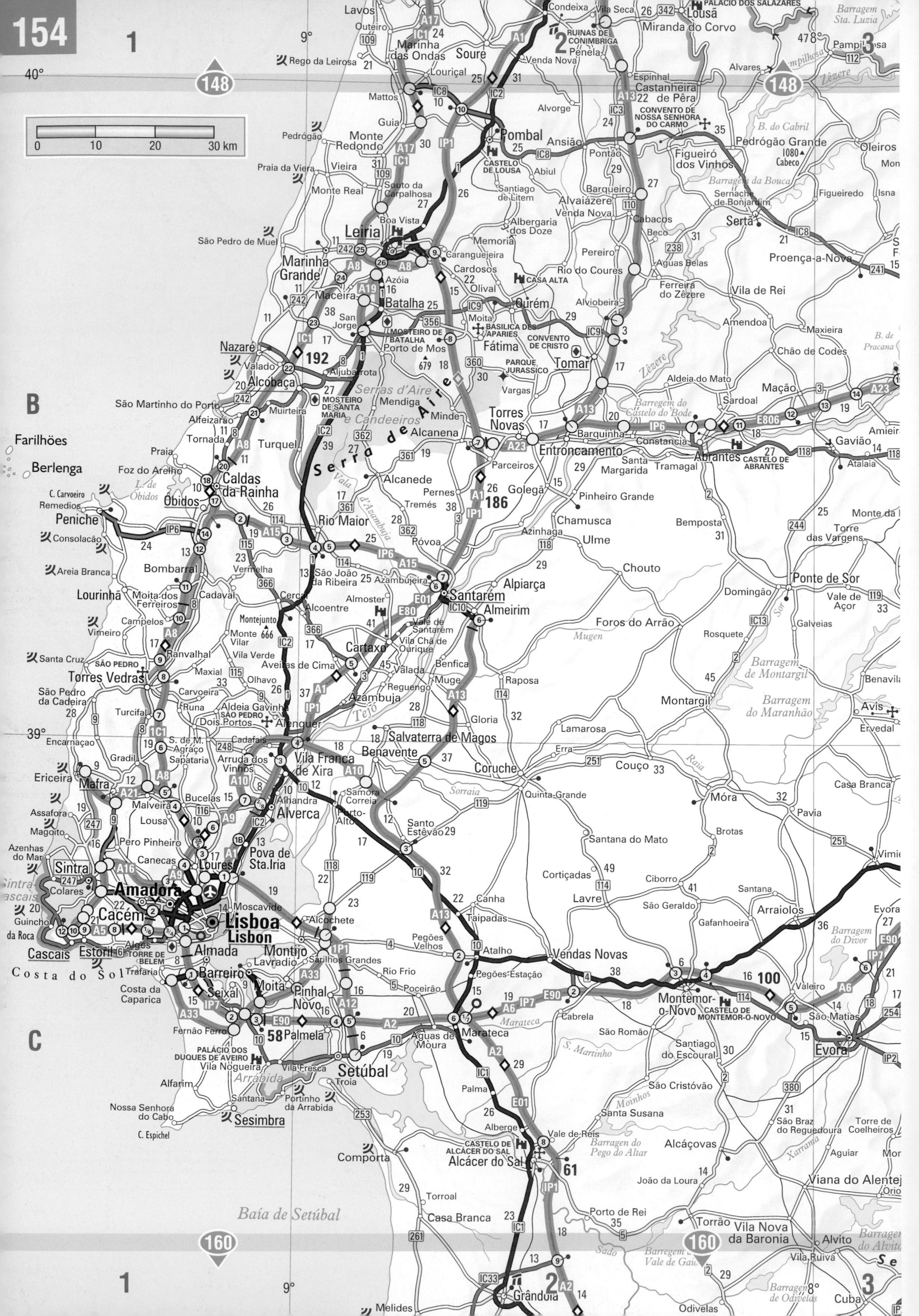

1
2
3
B
C
40°
39°
9°
148
160
0
10
20
30 km
Lavos
Outeiro
Marinha das Ondas
Soure
Condeixa
Vila Seca
Lousã
PALÁCIO DOS SALAZARES
Miranda do Corvo
RUÍNAS DE CONIMBRIGA
Penela
Venda Nova
Rego da Leirosa
Louriçal
Espinhal
Castanheira de Pêra
Barragem Sta. Luzia
Pampilhosa
Alvares
Zêzere
Mattos
Guia
Pedrógão
Monte Redondo
Alvorge
Pombal
Ansião
CONVENTO DE NOSSA SENHORA DO CARMO
B. do Cabril
Pedrógão Grande
Oleiros
1080 Cabeço
Praia da Viera
Vieira
CASTELO DE LOUSA
Abiul
Pontão
Figueiró dos Vinhos
Monte Real
Souto da Carpalhosa
Santiago de Litem
Barqueiro
Barragem da Bouca
Sernache de Bonjardim
Figueiredo
Isna
Alvaiázere
Venda Nova
Cabaços
Sertã
Boa Vista
Albergaria dos Doze
São Pedro de Muel
Leiria
Memória
Beco
Pereiro
Caranguejeira
Marinha Grande
Cardosos
Rio do Coures
Águas Belas
Proença-a-Nova
Olival
CASA ALTA
Azóia
Maceira
Batalha
Ourém
Alviobeira
Ferreira do Zêzere
Vila de Rei
San Jorge
Moita
BASÍLICA DAS APARIES
CONVENTO DE CRISTO
Amendoa
Maxieira
B. de Pracana
MOSTEIRO DE BATALHA
Porto de Mos
Fátima
Tomar
Chão de Codes
Nazaré
192
679
PARQUE JURÁSSICO
Valado
Aljubarrota
Alcobaça
Serras d'Aire
Vargas
Aldeia do Mato
Mação
MOSTEIRO DE SANTA MARIA
Mendiga
Serra de Aire
Sardoal
Barregem do Castelo do Bode
São Martinho do Porto
Muirteira
Minde
Torres Novas
Alfeizarão
e Candeeiros
Alcanena
Barquinha
Constância
Amieira
Farilhões
Tornada
Turquel
Entroncamento
Abrantes
CASTELO DE ABRANTES
Gavião
Atalaia
Praia
Berlenga
Foz do Arelho
Parceiros
Santa Margarida
Tramagal
Caldas da Rainha
Alcanede
L. de Óbidos
C. Carvoeiro
Remedios
Óbidos
Pernes
Golegã
Pinheiro Grande
186
Tremés
Peniche
Rio Maior
Chamusca
Bemposta
Monte da Pedra
Consolação
Azinhaga
Ulme
Torre das Vargens
Póvoa
Areia Branca
Bombarral
Vermelha
São João da Ribeira
Azambujeira
Chouto
Ponte de Sor
Alpiarça
Lourinhã
Moita dos Ferreiros
Cadaval
Cercal
Santarém
Almeirim
Domingão
Vale de Açor
Alcoentre
Almoster
Montejunto
666
Vale de Santarém
Campelos
Foros do Arrão
Galveias
Vimeiro
Monte Vilar
Vila Chã de Ourique
Mugen
Rosquete
Cartaxo
Ranvalhal
Vila Verde
Santa Cruz
SÃO PEDRO
Aveiras de Cima
Benfica
Barragem de Montargil
Benavila
Maxial
Valada
Raposa
Torres Vedras
Olhavo
Reguengo
Muge
São Pedro da Cadeira
Carvoeira
Aldeia Gavinha
Azambuja
Montargil
Barragem do Maranhão
Avis
Runa
Turcifal
SÃO PEDRO
Dois Portos
Alenquer
Tejo
Gloria
Ervedal
Encarnaçao
S. de M. Agraço
Sapataria
Cadafais
Lamarosa
Salvaterra de Magos
Benavente
Gradil
Arruda dos Vinhos
Vila Franca de Xira
Erra
Coruche
Couço
Raia
Ericeira
Mafra
Samora Correia
Alhandra
Quinta Grande
Casa Branca
Sorraia
Móra
Bucelas
Malveira
Alverca
Porto Alto
Pavia
Assafora
Magoito
Lousa
Santo Estêvão
Brotas
Santana do Mato
Pero Pinheiro
Pova de Sta. Iria
Azenhas do Mar
Canecas
Loures
Vimieiro
Sintra
Sintra-Cascais
Colares
Amadora
Corticadas
Ciborro
Santana
Canha
Lavre
São Geraldo
Arraiolos
Cacém
Guincho
Moscavide
Taipadas
Gafanhoeira
Évora
Lisboa
Lisbon
Alcochete
Barragem do Divor
Cabo da Roca
Cascais
Estoril
Algés
TORRE DE BELÉM
Almada
Montijo
Pegões Velhos
Atalho
Vendas Novas
Lavradio
Sarilhos Grandes
Costa do Sol
Trafaria
Barreiro
Rio Frio
Pegões-Estação
100
Moita
Seixal
Poceirão
Valeiro
Costa da Caparica
Pinhal Novo
Montemor-o-Novo
CASTELO DE MONTEMOR-O-NOVO
Cabrela
São Matias
Marateca
Fernão Ferro
Palmela
58
São Romão
Santiago do Escoural
PALÁCIO DOS DUQUES DE AVEIRO
Águas de Moura
S. Martinho
Vila Nogueira
Vila Fresca
Setúbal
Arrábida
Troia
Alfarim
São Cristóvão
Palma
Santana
Portinho da Arrábida
Moinhos
Nossa Senhora do Cabo
Sesimbra
Santa Susana
São Braz do Regueduora
Torre de Coelheiros
C. Espichel
Alberge
Vale de Reis
Barragen do Pego do Altar
Alcáçovas
Comporta
CASTELO DE ALCÁCER DO SAL
Alcácer do Sal
61
Xarrama
Aguiar
João da Loura
Viana do Alentejo
Torroal
Baía de Setúbal
Casa Branca
Porto de Rei
Torrão
Vila Nova da Baronia
Alvito
Sado
Barregem de Vale de Gaio
Vila Ruiva
Barragem de Odivelas
Grândola
Cuba
Melides
Odivelas
A1
A2
A6
A8
A9
A10
A12
A13
A15
A16
A17
A19
A21
A23
A33
A5
IC1
IC2
IC3
IC8
IC9
IC10
IC13
IC33
IP1
IP2
IP6
IP7
E01
E80
E90
E806

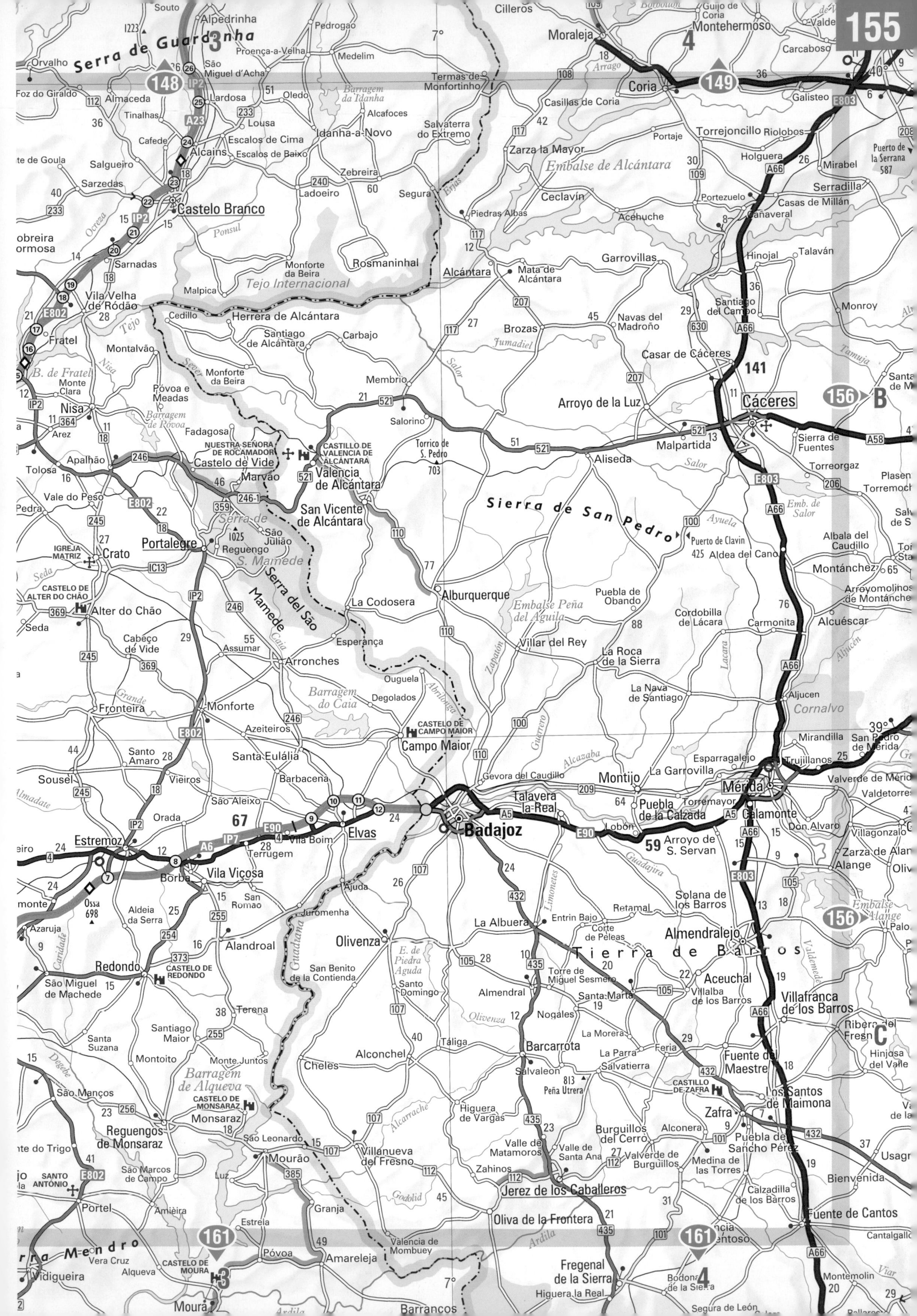
Serra de Guardunha
Alpedrinha
Pedrogão
Proença-a-Velha
Medelim
Orvalho
São Miguel d'Acha
Foz do Giraldo
Almaceda
Lardosa
Oledo
Barragem da Idanha
Termas de Monfortinho
Moraleja
Cilleros
Montehermoso
Carcaboso
Coria
Casillas de Coria
Galisteo
Tinalhas
Lousa
Alcafoces
Cafede
Escalos de Cima
Idanha-a-Novo
Salvaterra do Extremo
Zarza la Mayor
Torrejoncillo
Riolobos
Portaje
Alcains
Escalos de Baixo
Salgueiro
Zebreira
Embalse de Alcántara
Holguera
Mirabel
Puerto de la Serrana
Sarzedas
Ladoeiro
Segura
Ceclavín
Portezuelo
Serradilla
Casas de Millán
Castelo Branco
Piedras Albas
Acehuche
Cañaveral
Ponsul
Garrovillas
Hinojal
Talaván
Sarnadas
Monforte da Beira
Rosmaninhal
Alcántara
Mata de Alcántara
Tejo Internacional
Malpica
Vila Velha de Ródão
Cedillo
Herrera de Alcántara
Navas del Madroño
Santiago del Campo
Monroy
Fratel
Santiago de Alcántara
Carbajo
Brozas
Montalvão
Casar de Cáceres
B. de Fratel
Monte Clara
Monforte da Beira
Membrio
Póvoa e Meadas
Nisa
Salorino
Arroyo de la Luz
Cáceres
Barragem de Póvoa
Fadagosa
Arez
Nuestra Señora de Rocamador
Castillo de Valencia de Alcántara
Torrico de S. Pedro
Malpartida
Sierra de Fuentes
Apalhão
Castelo de Vide
Aliseda
Tolosa
Marvão
Valencia de Alcántara
Torreorgaz
Vale do Peso
Sierra de San Pedro
San Vicente de Alcántara
Portalegre
Reguengo
São Julião
Puerto de Clavin
Aldea del Cano
Albala del Caudillo
Igreja Matriz
Crato
S. Mamede
Serra del São Mamede
Montánchez
Castelo de Alter do Chão
Alter do Chão
La Codosera
Alburquerque
Embalse Peña del Águila
Puebla de Obando
Cordobilla de Lácara
Carmonita
Alcuéscar
Arroyomolinos de Montánchez
Seda
Cabeço de Vide
Assumar
Esperança
Villar del Rey
La Roca de la Sierra
Arronches
Ouguela
La Nava de Santiago
Aljucen
Cornalvo
Barragem do Caia
Degolados
Fronteira
Monforte
Castelo de Campo Maior
Azeiteiros
Campo Maior
Mirandilla
San Pedro de Mérida
Santo Amaro
Santa Eulália
Esparragalejo
Trujillanos
Sousel
Vieiros
Barbacena
Gevora del Caudillo
Montijo
La Garrovilla
Mérida
Valverde de Mérida
Valdetorres
São Aleixo
Talavera la Real
Puebla de la Calzada
Torremayor
Calamonte
Orada
Elvas
Badajoz
Lobón
Don Álvaro
Villagonzalo
Estremoz
Vila Boim
Terrugem
Arroyo de S. Servan
Zarza de Alange
Alange
Borba
Vila Viçosa
Ossa
San Romão
Ajuda
Solana de los Barros
Aldeia da Serra
Juromenha
Retamal
Embalse Alange
Azaruja
La Albuera
Entrin Bajo
Corte de Peleas
Almendralejo
Alandroal
Olivenza
Tierra de Barros
Redondo
Castelo de Redondo
E. de Piedra Aguda
San Benito de la Contienda
Torre de Miguel Sesmero
Aceuchal
São Miguel de Machede
Santo Domingo
Almendral
Santa Marta
Villalba de los Barros
Villafranca de los Barros
Terena
Nogales
Santiago Maior
La Morera
Santa Suzana
Táliga
Barcarrota
Montoito
Monte Juntos
Alconchel
La Parra
Feria
Fuente del Maestre
Cheles
Salvaleón
Salvatierra
Barragem de Alqueva
Peña Utrera
Castillo de Zafra
Los Santos de Maimona
São Manços
Castelo de Monsaraz
Monsaraz
Higuera de Vargas
Zafra
Reguengos de Monsaraz
São Leonardo
Burguillos del Cerro
Alconera
Puebla de Sancho Pérez
Villanueva del Fresno
Valle de Matamoros
Valle de Santa Ana
Valverde de Burguillos
Medina de las Torres
Mourão
São Marcos de Campo
Zahinos
Bienvenida
Santo António
Luz
Calzadilla de los Barros
Jerez de los Caballeros
Portel
Amieira
Granja
Oliva de la Frontera
Fuente de Cantos
Estrela
Valencia de Mombuey
Cantalgallo
Vera Cruz
Castelo de Moura
Póvoa
Amareleja
Fregenal de la Sierra
Vidigueira
Alqueva
Bodonal de la Sierra
Montemolín
Moura
Barrancos
Higuera la Real
Segura de León
Guadiana
Ardila
Tejo
Salor

Trujillo
Jaraicejo
Miajadas
Don Benito
Villanueva de la Serena
Guadalupe
MONASTERIO DE GUADALUPE
Sierra de Guadalupe
Logrosán
Cañamero
Herrera del Duque
Castilblanco
Helechosa
Embalse de Cíjara
Embalse de García Sola
Navalvillar de Pela
Orellana
Talarrubias
Embalse de Orellana
Puebla de Alcocer
Siruela
Campanario
Castuera
La Serena
Embalse de La Serena
Cabeza del Buey
Almadén
Chillón
Zalamea de la Serena
Quintana de la Serena
Guareña
Sierra del Pedrosa
Belalcázar
Hinojosa del Duque
Los Pedroches
Pozoblanco
Peñarroya-Pueblonuevo
Fuente Obejuna
Azuaga
Llerena
Sierra de los Santos
Espiel
Villaviciosa de Córdoba
Sierra Norte de Sevilla
Sierra de Hornachuelos
Cazalla de la Sierra
Constantina
Hornachuelos
Almodóvar del Río
Córdoba
Monesterio
Guadalcanal
Alanís
Usagre
Hornachos
Valencia de las Torres
Montánchez
Alcuéscar
Almoharín
Madroñera
Zorita
Madrigalejo
Villanueva de Córdoba
Alcaracejos
Agudo
Fuenlabrada de los Montes
Belvis de la Jara
Alcaudete de la Jara
150
155
162

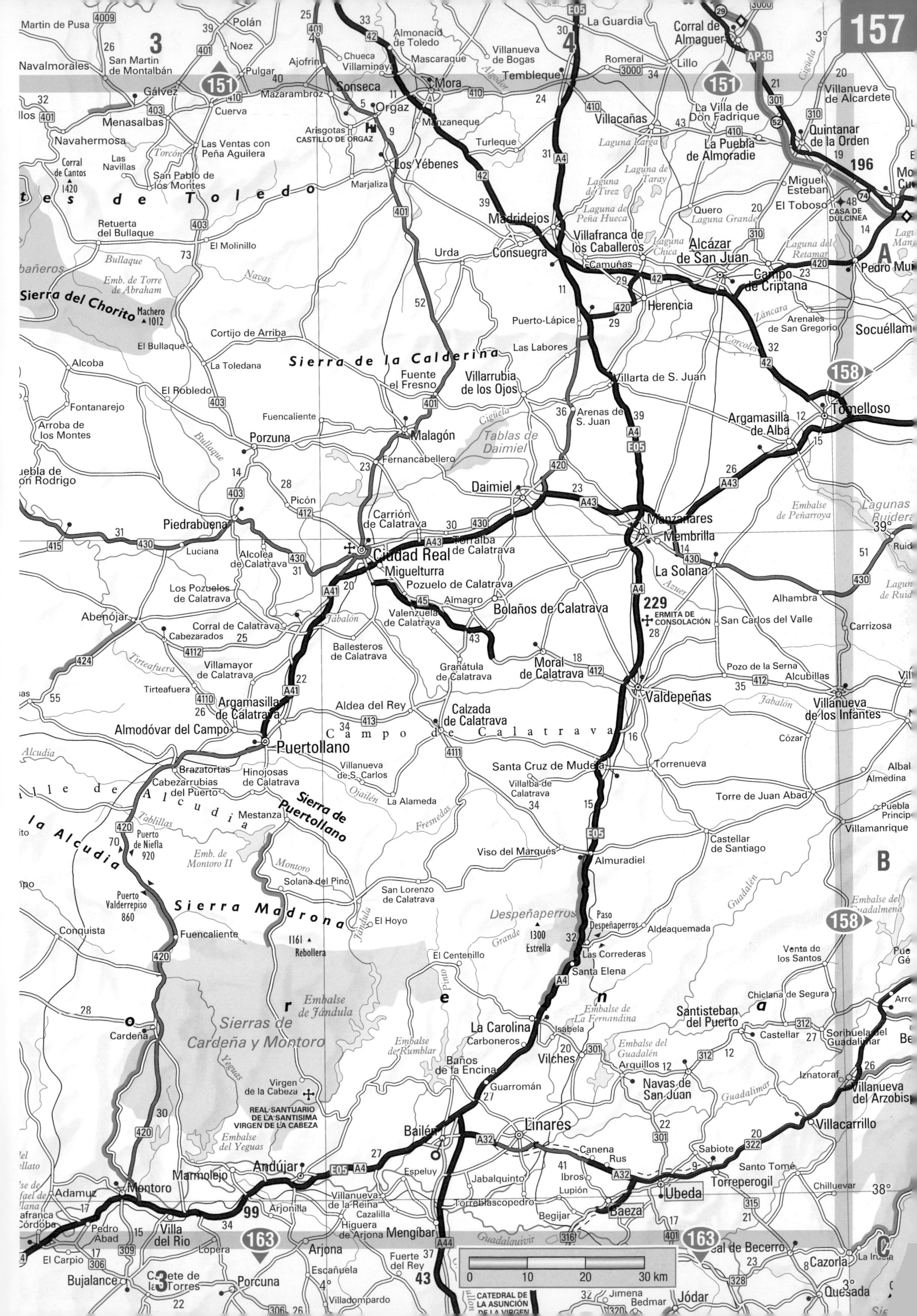
Martin de Pusa
Polán
Almonacid de Toledo
La Guardia
Corral de Almaguer
Navalmorales
San Martin de Montalbán
Noez
Pulgar
Chueca
Villaminaya
Mascaraque
Villanueva de Bogas
Romeral
Lillo
Ajofrín
Tembleque
Gálvez
Mazarambroz
Sonseca
Mora
Orgaz
Villanueva de Alcardete
Cuerva
Menasalbas
La Villa de Don Fadrique
Arisgotas
CASTILLO DE ORGAZ
Manzaneque
Villacañas
Quintanar de la Orden
Navahermosa
Las Ventas con Peña Aguilera
Turleque
Laguna Larga
La Puebla de Almoradie
Corral de Cantos
Las Navillas
San Pablo de los Montes
Los Yébenes
Laguna de Taray
Miguel Esteban
Marjaliza
Laguna de Tirez
Quero
Laguna Grande
El Toboso
CASA DE DULCINEA
Montes de Toledo
Madridejos
Laguna de Peña Hueca
Retuerta del Bullaque
Villafranca de los Caballeros
Laguna Chica
Alcázar de San Juan
Laguna del Retamar
El Molinillo
Urda
Consuegra
Camuñas
Pedro Muñoz
Bullaque
Emb. de Torre de Abraham
Navas
Campo de Criptana
Herencia
Sierra del Chorito
Machero 1012
Puerto-Lápice
Záncara
Arenales de San Gregorio
Socuéllamos
Cortijo de Arriba
Las Labores
Corcoles
El Bullaque
Sierra de la Calderina
Alcoba
La Toledana
Fuente el Fresno
Villarrubia de los Ojos
Villarta de S. Juan
Tomelloso
El Robledo
Fontanarejo
Fuencaliente
Arenas de S. Juan
Argamasilla de Alba
Arroba de los Montes
Malagón
Cigüela
Tablas de Daimiel
Porzuna
Fernancabellero
Puebla de Don Rodrigo
Daimiel
Picón
Embalse de Peñarroya
Lagunas de Ruidera
Carrión de Calatrava
Manzanares
Piedrabuena
Torralba de Calatrava
Membrilla
Luciana
Alcolea de Calatrava
Ciudad Real
Miguelturra
La Solana
Los Pozuelos de Calatrava
Pozuelo de Calatrava
Azuer
Alhambra
Almagro
Bolaños de Calatrava
Abenójar
Valenzuela de Calatrava
ERMITA DE CONSOLACIÓN
San Carlos del Valle
Carrizosa
Corral de Calatrava
Jabalón
Cabezarados
Ballesteros de Calatrava
Tirteafuera
Villamayor de Calatrava
Granátula de Calatrava
Moral de Calatrava
Pozo de la Serna
Alcubillas
Valdepeñas
Argamasilla de Calatrava
Aldea del Rey
Calzada de Calatrava
Villanueva de los Infantes
Almodóvar del Campo
Campo de Calatrava
Puertollano
Cózar
Alcudia
Brazatortas
Hinojosas de Calatrava
Villanueva de S. Carlos
Santa Cruz de Mudela
Torrenueva
Almedina
Cabezarrubias del Puerto
Valle de Alcudia
Ojailén
La Alameda
Villalba de Calatrava
Torre de Juan Abad
Puebla del Príncipe
Mestanza
Sierra de Puertollano
Fresnedas
Villamanrique
Tablillas
Puerto de Niefla 920
Emb. de Montoro II
Castellar de Santiago
Viso del Marqués
Almuradiel
Montoro
Solana del Pino
San Lorenzo de Calatrava
Guadalén
Puerto Valderrepiso 860
Sierra Madrona
Despeñaperros
Paso Despeñaperros
El Hoyo
Conquista
Fuencaliente
1300 Estrella
Aldeaquemada
1161 Rebollera
Grande
El Centenillo
Las Correderas
Venta de los Santos
Santa Elena
Sierra Morena
Embalse de Jándula
Chiclana de Segura
Embalse de La Fernandina
Santisteban del Puerto
Sierras de Cardeña y Montoro
Cardeña
La Carolina
Carboneros
Isabela
Castellar
Sorihuela del Guadalimar
Embalse del Rumblar
Embalse del Guadalén
Baños de la Encina
Vilches
Arquillos
Yeguas
Virgen de la Cabeza
REAL SANTUARIO DE LA SANTISIMA VIRGEN DE LA CABEZA
Guarromán
Navas de San Juan
Guadalimar
Iznatoraf
Villanueva del Arzobispo
Villacarrillo
Embalse del Yeguas
Bailén
Linares
Canena
Sabiote
Rus
Marmolejo
Andújar
Espeluy
Ibros
Santo Tomé
Chilluevar
Adamuz
Jabalquinto
Úbeda
Torreperogil
Lupión
Villanueva de la Reina
Torreblascopedro
Cazalilla
Begíjar
Baeza
Arjonilla
Pedro Abad
Villa del Río
Higuera de Arjona
Mengíbar
Guadalquivir
Lopera
Arjona
Real de Becerro
Cazorla
La Iruela
El Carpio
Fuerte del Rey
Bujalance
Cañete de las Torres
Porcuna
Escañuela
Villardompardo
CATEDRAL DE LA ASUNCIÓN DE LA VIRGEN
Jimena
Bedmar
Jódar
Quesada
0 10 20 30 km

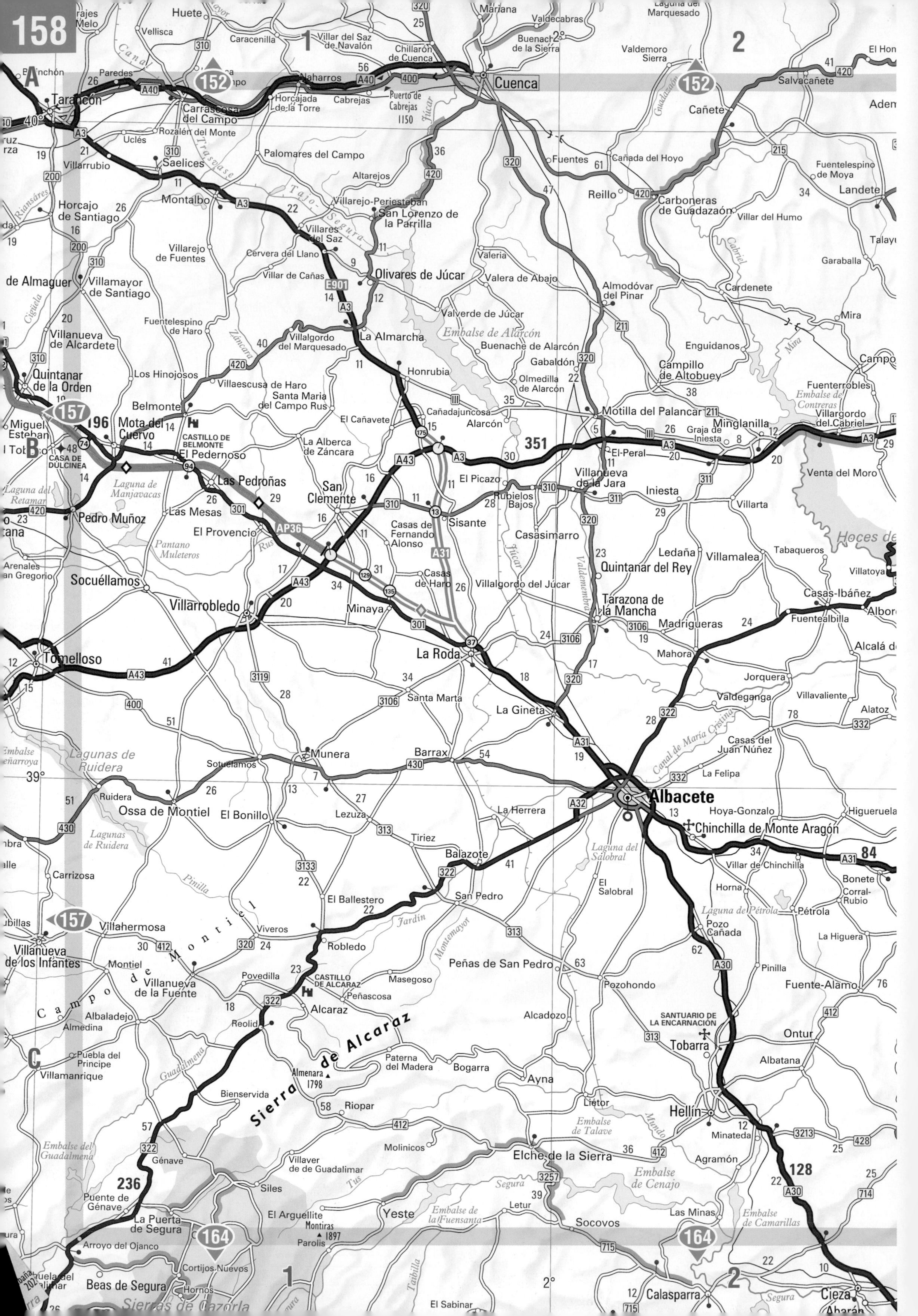

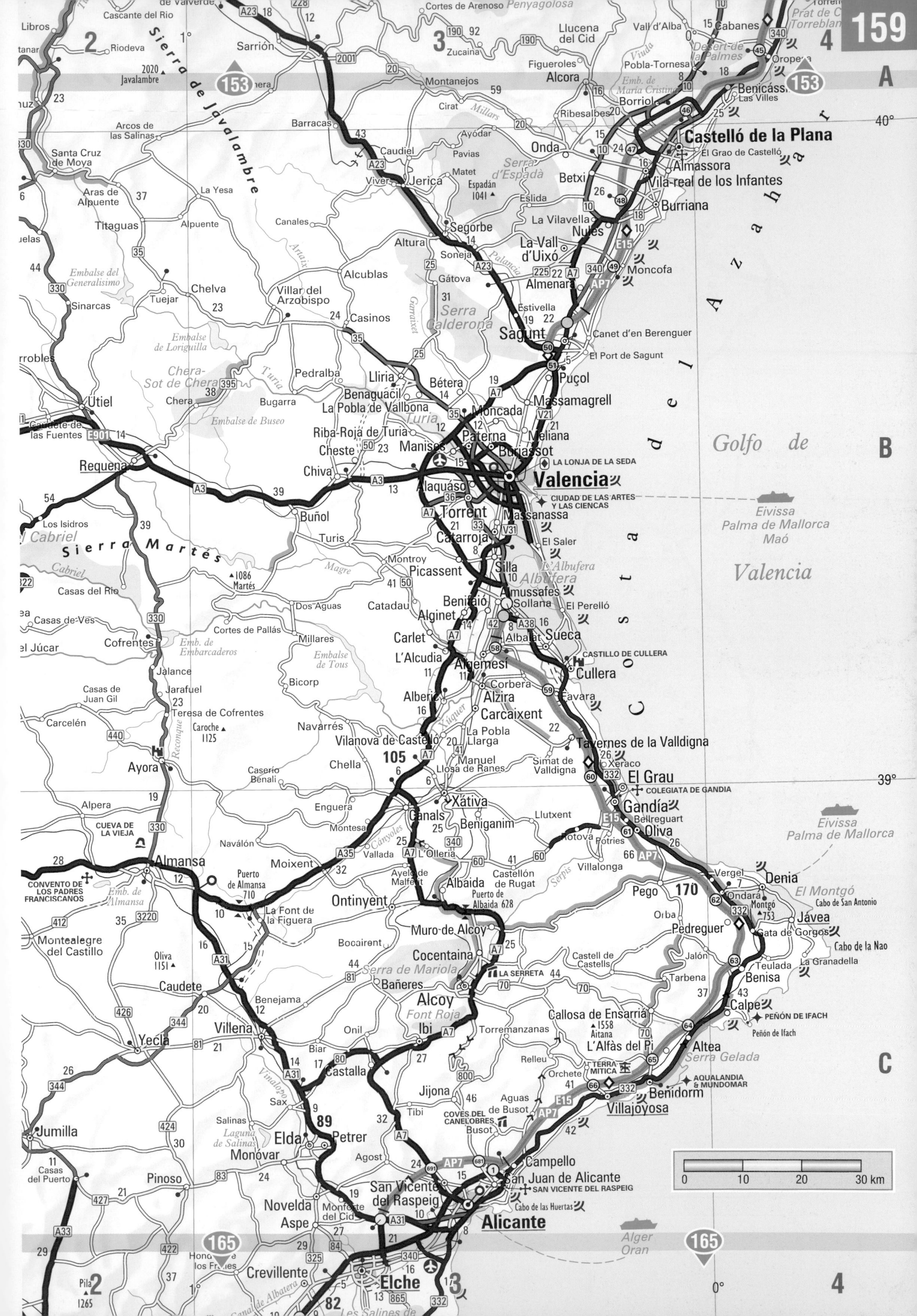
Castelló de la Plana
Valencia
Golfo de Valencia
Costa del Azahar
Sagunt
Torrent
Xàtiva
Gandía
Alcoy
Benidorm
Alicante
Elche
Requena
Utiel
Almansa
Villena
Elda
Yecla
Jumilla
Denia
Jávea
Calpe
Villajoyosa
Sierra de Javalambre
Sierra Martés
Eivissa
Palma de Mallorca
Maó
Alger
Oran
LA LONJA DE LA SEDA
CIUDAD DE LAS ARTES Y LAS CIENCIAS
CASTILLO DE CULLERA
COLEGIATA DE GANDIA
PEÑÓN DE IFACH
TERRA MITICA
AQUALANDIA & MUNDOMAR
CUEVA DE LA VIEJA
CONVENTO DE LOS PADRES FRANCISCANOS
LA SERRETA
SAN VICENTE DEL RASPEIG
COVES DEL CANELOBRES
0 10 20 30 km
153
165

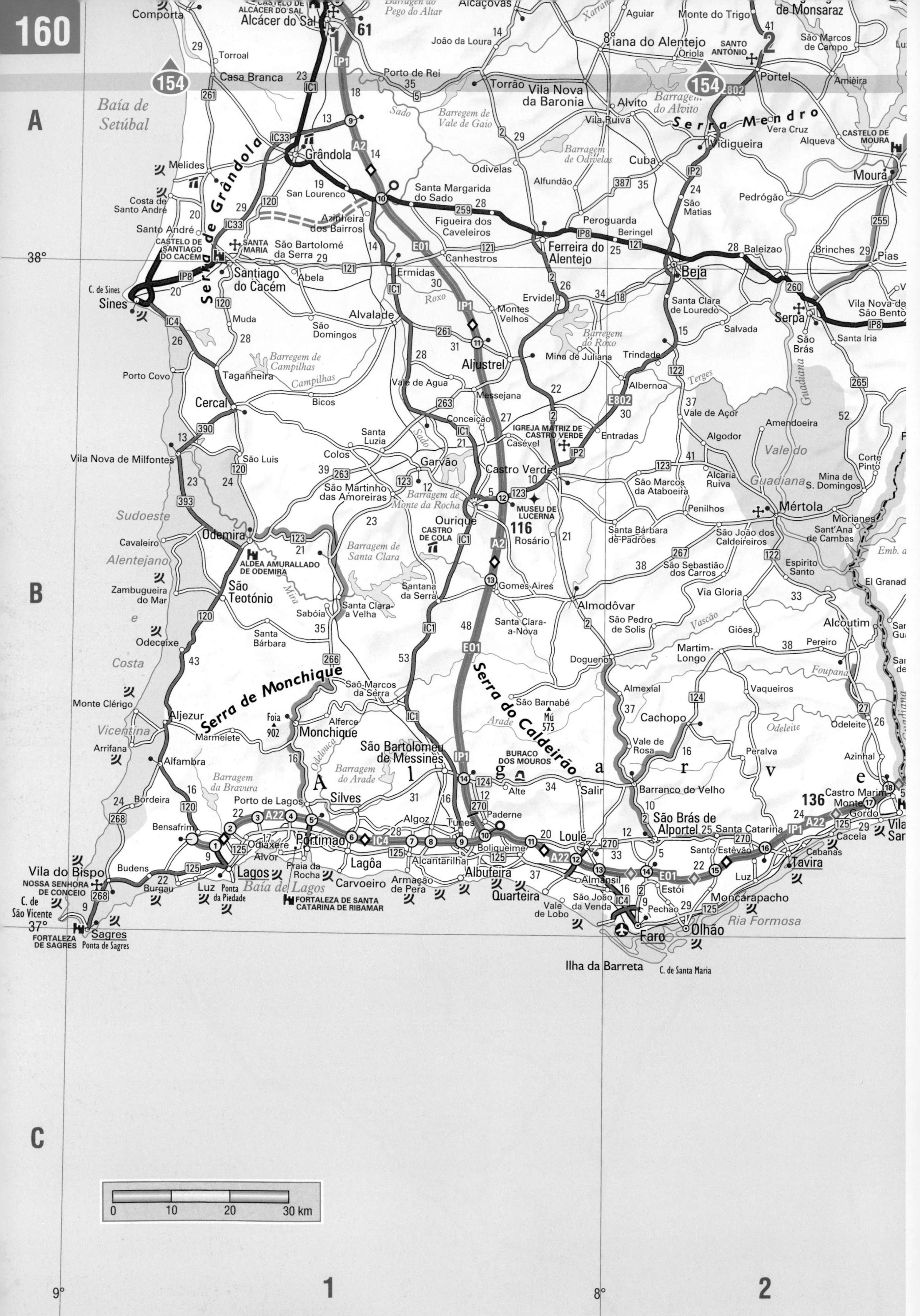
160
Comporta
Alcácer do Sal
Alcáçovas
Aguiar
Monte do Trigo
de Monsaraz
João da Loura
Viana do Alentejo
Oriola
Portel
São Marcos de Campo
Amieira
Torroal
Casa Branca
Porto de Rei
Torrão
Vila Nova da Baronia
Alvito
Barragem do Alvito
Baía de Setúbal
Barregem de Vale de Gaio
Vila Ruiva
Serra Mendro
Vera Cruz
Alqueva
Castelo de Moura
Grândola
Vidigueira
Melides
Serra de Grândola
Odivelas
Barragem de Odivelas
Cuba
Moura
Costa de Santo André
San Lourenço
Santa Margarida do Sado
Alfundão
São Matias
Pedrógão
Santo André
Azinheira dos Bairros
Figueira dos Caveleiros
Peroguarda
Beringel
Castelo de Santiago do Cacém
Santa Maria
São Bartolomé da Serra
Canhestros
Ferreira do Alentejo
Baleizao
Brinches
Pias
Sines
C. de Sines
Santiago do Cacém
Abela
Ermidas
Beja
Vila Nova de São Bento
Ervidel
Montes Velhos
Santa Clara de Louredo
Serpa
Muda
Alvalade
São Domingos
Barregem do Roxo
Salvada
São Brás
Santa Iria
Barragem de Campilhas
Aljustrel
Mina de Juliana
Trindade
Porto Covo
Taganheira
Vale de Agua
Albernoa
Messejana
Bicos
Cercal
Conceição
Igreja Matriz de Castro Verde
Entradas
Vale de Açor
Amendoeira
Santa Luzia
Casével
Algodor
Vale do Guadiana
Vila Nova de Milfontes
São Luis
Colos
Garvão
Castro Verde
São Marcos da Ataboeira
Alcaria Ruiva
Corte Pinto
Mina de S. Domingos
São Martinho das Amoreiras
Barragem de Monte da Rocha
Museu de Lucerna
Penilhos
Mértola
Sudoeste
Ourique
Rosário
Santa Bárbara de Padrões
São João dos Caldeireiros
Morianes
Sant'Ana de Cambas
Cavaleiro
Odemira
Castro de Cola
Barragem de Santa Clara
Espirito Santo
Alentejano
Aldea Amurallado de Odemira
São Sebastião dos Carros
Zambugueira do Mar
São Teotónio
Santana da Serra
Gomes Aires
Via Gloria
El Granad
Santa Clara-a Velha
Sabóia
Almodôvar
São Pedro de Solis
Alcoutim
Odeceixe
Santa Bárbara
Santa Clara-a-Nova
Gióes
Pereiro
Costa
Dogueno
Martim-Longo
Foupana
Serra de Monchique
São Marcos da Serra
Serra do Caldeirão
Almexial
Vaqueiros
Monte Clérigo
São Barnabé
Aljezur
Foia 902
Alferce
Mú 575
Cachopo
Odeleite
Vicentina
Marmelete
Monchique
Vale de Rosa
Arrifana
São Bartolomeu de Messines
Buraco dos Mouros
Peralva
Azinhal
Alfambra
Barragem da Bravura
Barragem do Arade
Algarve
Alte
Salir
Barranco do Velho
Castro Marim
Bordeira
Porto de Lagos
Silves
Paderne
Monte Gordo
Bensafrim
Algoz
Tunes
São Brás de Alportel
Santa Catarina
Cacela
Odiaxere
Portimão
Boliqueime
Loulé
Santo Estêvão
Cabanas
Vila do Bispo
Alvor
Lagôa
Alcantarilha
Tavira
Nossa Senhora de Conceio
Budens
Lagos
Praia da Rocha
Albufeira
Almansil
Burgau
Luz
Ponta da Piedade
Baía de Lagos
Carvoeiro
Armação de Pera
Quarteira
Estói
Moncarapacho
C. de São Vicente
Fortaleza de Santa Catarina de Ribamar
Vale de Lobo
São João da Venda
Pechão
Ria Formosa
Sagres
Fortaleza de Sagres
Ponta de Sagres
Faro
Olhão
Ilha da Barreta
C. de Santa Maria
0
10
20
30 km

Mourão
Villanueva del Fresno
Valle de Matamoros
Valle de Santa Ana
Zahinos
Jerez de los Caballeros
Valverde de Burguillos
Medina de las Torres
Puebla de Sancho Pérez
Calzadilla de los Barros
Bienvenida
Usagre
Llerena
Villagarcia de las Torres
Berlanga
Granja
Oliva de la Frontera
Valencia de Mombuey
Amareleja
Póvoa
Estrela
Valencia del Ventoso
Fuente de Cantos
Cantalgallo
Ahillones
Casas de Reina
Trasierra
Fregenal de la Sierra
Higuera la Real
Bodonal de la Sierra
Montemolín
Fuente del Arco
Barrancos
Safara
Santo Amado
Encinasola
Segura de León
Calera de León
Pallares
Puebla del Maestre
Guadalcanal
Monesterio
Cumbres Mayores
Cumbres de S. Bartolomé
Fuentes de León
Cabeza la Vaca
Tentudía
Cañaveral de León
St. Aleixo
Sobral da Adica
Picos de Aroche
La Contienda
Sierra de Aracena y Picas de Aroche
Hinojales
Arroyomolinos de León
Hoya de Santa María
Embalse de El Pintado
Rosal de la Frontera
Vila Verde de Ficalho
La Nava
Valdelarco
Galaroza
Cala
El Real de la Jara
Sierra Norte de Sevilla
Aroche
Cortegana
Jabugo
Aracena
Embalse de Aracena
Santa Olalla
Almadén de la Plata
Santa Maria de Consolación
Cazalla
Sierra de Aracena
Almonaster la Real
Alájar
Corteconcepción
Puerto Moral
Higuera de la Sierra
Zufre
El Pedroso
Santa Barbara de Casa
San Telmo
Campofrío
Embalse de la Minilla
Embalse de Cala
El Ronquillo
Cabezas Rubias
El Cerro de Andévalo
Nerva
Valdeflores
La Aulaga
Castilblanco de los Arroyos
Villanueva Río y Minas
El Campillo
Zalamea la Real
Minas de Riotinto
El Castillo de las Guardas
El Madroño
El Alamo
Calañas
Las Herrerias
Puebla de Guzmán
Tharsis
Valverde del Camino
Berrocal
El Garrobo
Las Pajanosas
Cantillana
Villaverde del Río
Burguillos
Brenes
Alosno
Guillena
Gerena
El Almendro
Aznalcóllar
Alcalá del Río
Villanueva de los Castillejos
La Rinconada
La Algaba
Ciudad Antiquisima de Italica
Isla Mágica
Paterna del Campo
Santiponce
Camas
San Bartolomé de la Torre
Beas
Dolmen de Soto
La Palma del Condado
Villalba del Alcor
Escacena del Campo
Olivares
Sevilla
Seville
El Viso del Alcor
Trigueros
Castillo de Niebla
Gibraleón
Tariquejas
Niebla
Villarrasa
Manzanilla
Sanlúcar la Mayor
Castilleja
Emb. de Piedras
Carrión
Benacazón
Bormujos
Bollullos
Alcalá de Guadaíra
Alcazar de Alcala de Guadaira
Villablanca
Bonares
Lucena
Rociana del Condado
Bollullos par del Condado
Pilas
Mairena del Aljarafe
Gelves
Dos Hermanas
Aljaraque
Lepe
Cartaya
Monasterio de Santa Clara
Hinojos
Aznalcázar
La Puebla del Río
Coria del Río
La Redondela
El Rompido
Huelva
Moguer
Almonte
Villamanrique de la Condesa
Ayamonte
La Antillas
Monasterio de Santa Maria de la Rabida
Palos de la Frontera
Utrera
Isla Cristina
Isla Canela
Vila Real de Santo António
Punta Umbria
Isla de Saltes
Mazagón
Los Palacios y Villafranca
Villafranco del Guadalquivir
El Rocío
Entorno de Doñana
Queipo
Golfo de Cádiz
Parque Nacional de Doñana
Madre de las Marismas
Torre de la Higuera
Las Cabezas de San Juan
Costa de la Luz
Lebrija
Las Palmas de Gran Canaria
Santa Cruz de Tenerife
Trebujena
El Cuervo
Sanlúcar de Barrameda
Bonanza
Chipiona
Arcos de la Frontera
Jerez de la Frontera
La Barca de la Florida
Embalse de Guadalcacín
Rota
Laguna de Medina
El Puerto de Santa María
Arrecife
Las Palmas de Gran Canaria
Santa Cruz de Tenerife
Santa Cruz de la Palma
Bahía de Cádiz
Puerto Real
Cádiz
Paterna de Rivera
Medina Sidonia
Chiclana de la Frontera
San Fernando

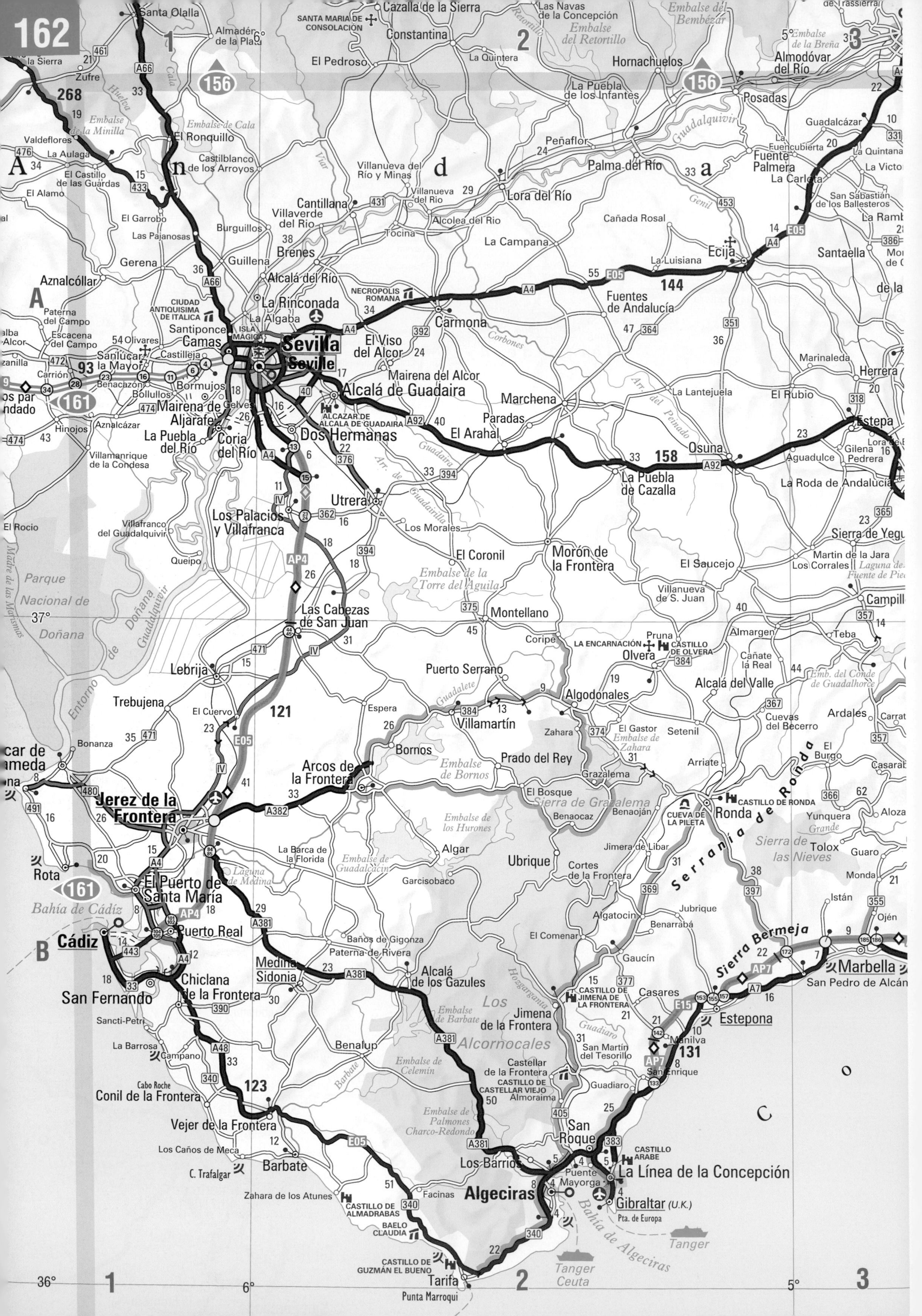
Santa Olalla
Almadén de la Plata
Cazalla de la Sierra
Santa María de Consolación
Constantina
Las Navas de la Concepción
Embalse del Retortillo
Embalse del Bembézar
Almodóvar del Río
Embalse de la Breña
El Pedroso
La Quintera
Hornachuelos
Zufre
La Puebla de los Infantes
Posadas
Guadalcázar
Embalse de la Minilla
Embalse de Cala
El Ronquillo
Valdeflores
La Aulaga
Peñaflor
Guadalquivir
La Fuencubierta
Fuente Palmera
La Carlota
La Quintana
La Victoria
El Castillo de las Guardas
Castilblanco de los Arroyos
Villanueva del Río y Minas
Palma del Río
El Alamo
Cantillana
Villanueva del Río
Lora del Río
San Sebastián de los Ballesteros
Villaverde del Río
Alcolea del Río
Cañada Rosal
La Rambla
El Garrobo
Burguillos
Tocina
Las Pajanosas
Brenes
La Campana
Ecija
Santaella
Gerena
Guillena
La Luisiana
Aznalcóllar
Alcalá del Río
Necrópolis Romana
Fuentes de Andalucía
Ciudad Antiquisima de Italica
La Rinconada
La Algaba
Carmona
Paterna del Campo
Escacena del Campo
Olivares
Santiponce
Isla Mágica
Camas
Sevilla
Seville
El Viso del Alcor
Marinaleda
Herrera
Sanlúcar la Mayor
Castilleja
Carrión
Benacazón
Bormujos
Bollullos
Mairena del Alcor
Alcalá de Guadaira
La Lantejuela
El Rubio
Mairena de Aljarafe
Gelves
Marchena
Alcázar de Alcalá de Guadaira
Paradas
Estepa
Hinojos
Aznalcázar
La Puebla del Río
Coria del Río
Dos Hermanas
El Arahal
Osuna
Gilena
Pedrera
Aguadulce
Villamanrique de la Condesa
La Puebla de Cazalla
La Roda de Andalucía
Utrera
El Rocío
Villafranco del Guadalquivir
Los Palacios y Villafranca
Los Morales
Sierra de Yeguas
Madre de las Marismas
Queipo
El Coronil
Morón de la Frontera
El Saucejo
Martín de la Jara
Los Corrales
Parque Nacional de Doñana
Entorno de Doñana
Embalse de la Torre del Aguila
Villanueva de S. Juan
Campillos
Las Cabezas de San Juan
Montellano
Almargen
Teba
Coripe
La Encarnación
Pruna
Castillo de Olvera
Olvera
Cañete la Real
Lebrija
Puerto Serrano
Emb. del Conde de Guadalhorce
Guadalete
Alcalá del Valle
Trebujena
Algodonales
El Cuervo
Espera
Villamartín
Zahara
El Gastor
Embalse de Zahara
Setenil
Cuevas del Becerro
Ardales
Bonanza
Bornos
Prado del Rey
El Burgo
Embalse de Bornos
Arriate
Grazalema
Arcos de la Frontera
Jerez de la Frontera
El Bosque
Sierra de Grazalema
Benaocaz
Benaoján
Cueva de la Pileta
Castillo de Ronda
Ronda
Serranía de Ronda
Yunquera
Embalse de los Hurones
Jimera de Líbar
Sierra de las Nieves
Tolox
Rota
La Barca de la Florida
Embalse de Guadalcacín
Algar
Ubrique
Cortes de la Frontera
Laguna de Medina
El Puerto de Santa María
Garcisobaco
Bahía de Cádiz
Algatocín
Jubrique
Istán
Benarrabá
Cádiz
Puerto Real
Baños de Gigonza
El Comenar
Sierra Bermeja
Ojén
Paterna de Rivera
Medina Sidonia
Gaucín
Marbella
Chiclana de la Frontera
Alcalá de los Gazules
San Pedro de Alcántara
San Fernando
Los Alcornocales
Embalse de Barbate
Castillo de Jimena de la Frontera
Casares
Jimena de la Frontera
Sancti-Petri
Estepona
La Barrosa
Benalup
San Martín del Tesorillo
Manilva
Campano
Embalse de Celemín
Castellar de la Frontera
San Enrique
Castillo de Castellar Viejo
Almoraima
Guadiaro
Cabo Roche
Conil de la Frontera
Embalse de Palmones
Charco-Redondo
San Roque
Vejer de la Frontera
Los Caños de Meca
Castillo Árabe
Barbate
C. Trafalgar
Los Barrios
La Línea de la Concepción
Puente Mayorga
Algeciras
Gibraltar (U.K.)
Pta. de Europa
Zahara de los Atunes
Facinas
Castillo de Almadrabas
Baelo Claudia
Bahía de Algeciras
Tanger
Castillo de Guzmán el Bueno
Tarifa
Tanger Ceuta
Punta Marroquí
36°
6°
5°
37°

Córdoba
El Carpio
Bujalance
Cañete de las Torres
Porcuna
Arjona
Escañuela
Villardompardo
Fuerte del Rey
Jaén
CATEDRAL DE LA ASUNCIÓN DE LA VIRGEN
Jimena
Bedmar
Jódar
Torres-Cabrera
La Campiña
Higuera de Calatrava
Torredonjimeno
Valenzuela
Jamilena
Torre del Campo
Mancha Real
Torres
Albanchez de Ubeda
Sierra Mágina
Pegalajar
Belmez de la Moraleda
Mágina 2163
Larva
Cabra del Santo Cristo
Solera
Santiago de Calatrava
Martos
La Guardia de Jaén
Fernán Núñez
Espejo
Castro del Río
Montemayor
Noguerones
Albedín
Los Villares
Cambil
Huelma
Andalucía
Montilla
Nueva Carteya
Baena
Alcaudete
Fuensanta de Martos
Valdepeñas de Jaén
Carchelejo
Arbuniel
Alicún de Ortega
Alamedilla
Doña Mencía
Luque
Zuheros
Campillo de Arenas
Montejícar
Villanueva de las Torres
Guadahortuna
Aguilar de la Frontera
Monturque
Cabra
Sierras Subbéticas
Zagrilla
Fuente-Tójar
La Rábita
Priego de Córdoba
Alcalá la Real
Castillo de Locubín
Noalejo
Puerto Carretero 1040
Montillana
Frailes
Santa Ana
Campotéjar
Torre Cardela
Domingo Pérez
Pedro-Martínez
Moriles
Navas del Selpillar
CASTILLO DEL MORAL
Carcabuey
Almedinilla
Benalúa de las Villas
Dehesas Viejas
Piñar
Moreda
Huélago
Puente-Genil
Lucena
Zambra
Rute
Las Navas
Colomera
Puerto del Zegri 1080
Iznalloz
Bogarre
NUESTRA SEÑORA DE ARACELI
El Higuera
Montefrío
Moclín
Sierra Arana
OLMAS VIVIENDAS DES CUEVAS
Diezma
Purullena
Badolatosa
Casariche
Benamejí
Estepa
Encinas Reales
Algarinejo
Íllora
Pinos Puente
1940 Orduña
Cogollos-Vega
Sierra de Huétor
Iznájar
Embalse de Iznájar
Palenciana
Cuevas de S. Marcos
Cuevas Bajas
Tocón
Villanueva de Mesía
Fuente Vaqueros
Albolote
Atarfe
Alfacar
Puerto de la Mora 1429
Cogollos de Guadix
Embalse de Quentar
Lugros
Alameda
Fuente del Conde
Huétor Tájar
Chauchina
Granada
ALHAMBRA
Villanueva de Tapia
Loja
Moraleda de Zafayona
Santa Fe
Armilla
Güéjar-Sierra
Jeres del Marquesado
Villanueva de Algaidas
Salar
ALCAZABA DE LOJA
Chimeneas
Las Gabias
La Zubia
Ogíjares
Alhendín
Sierra Nevada
3479 Mulhacén
3392 La Veleta
Mollina
Humilladero
Archidona
Ventas de Huelma
Dílar
Puerto del Suspiro del Moro 865
Bobadilla
Santa Cruz de Alhama
Cacín
Agrón
Padul
Antequera
Villanueva del Trabuco
Puerto de los Alazores 1040
Alhama de Granada
Dúrcal
Nigüelas
Capileira
Trevelez
Bérchules
Embalse de Guadalhorce
Puerto de las Pedrizas 780
Villanueva del Rosario
Alfarnate
Zafarraya
Arenas del Rey
Jayena
Fornes
Pampaneira
Pitres
Cádiar
Villanueva de la Concepción
Ventas de Zafarraya
Játar
Restábal
Lanjarón
Cañar
Busquistar
Valle de Abdalajís
Riogordo
Periana
Sierra de Almijara
Albuñuelas
Pinos del Valle
Órgiva
Torviscón
Colmenar
Canillas de Aceituno
Sedella
Casabermeja
Viñuela
Guajar-Faragüit
Albondón
Montes de Málaga
Benamargosa
Archez
Cómpeta
1832 Navachica
Vélez de Benaudalla
Álora
Puerto del León 960
Almachar
Arenas
Sayalonga
Ítrabo
Molvízar
Lújar
Albuñol
Pizarra
Almogía
Benamocarra
Algarrobo
Frigiliana
Olivar
Torrox
Vélez-Málaga
Motril
Gualchos
La Mamola
La Rábita
Castell de Ferro
Cártama
Campanillas
Torre del Mar
Nerja
CUEVAS DE NERJA
Almuñécar
Salobreña
Torrenueva
Cabo Sacratif
Calahonda
Alhaurín de la Torre
El Palo
Rincón de la Victoria
Coín
Málaga
Churriana
Alhaurín el Grande
Torremolinos
Mijas
Benalmádena
Carbajal
Fuengirola
Punta de Calaburras
Calahonda
Melilla
Melilla Al Hoceima
Costa del Sol
0 10 20 30 km

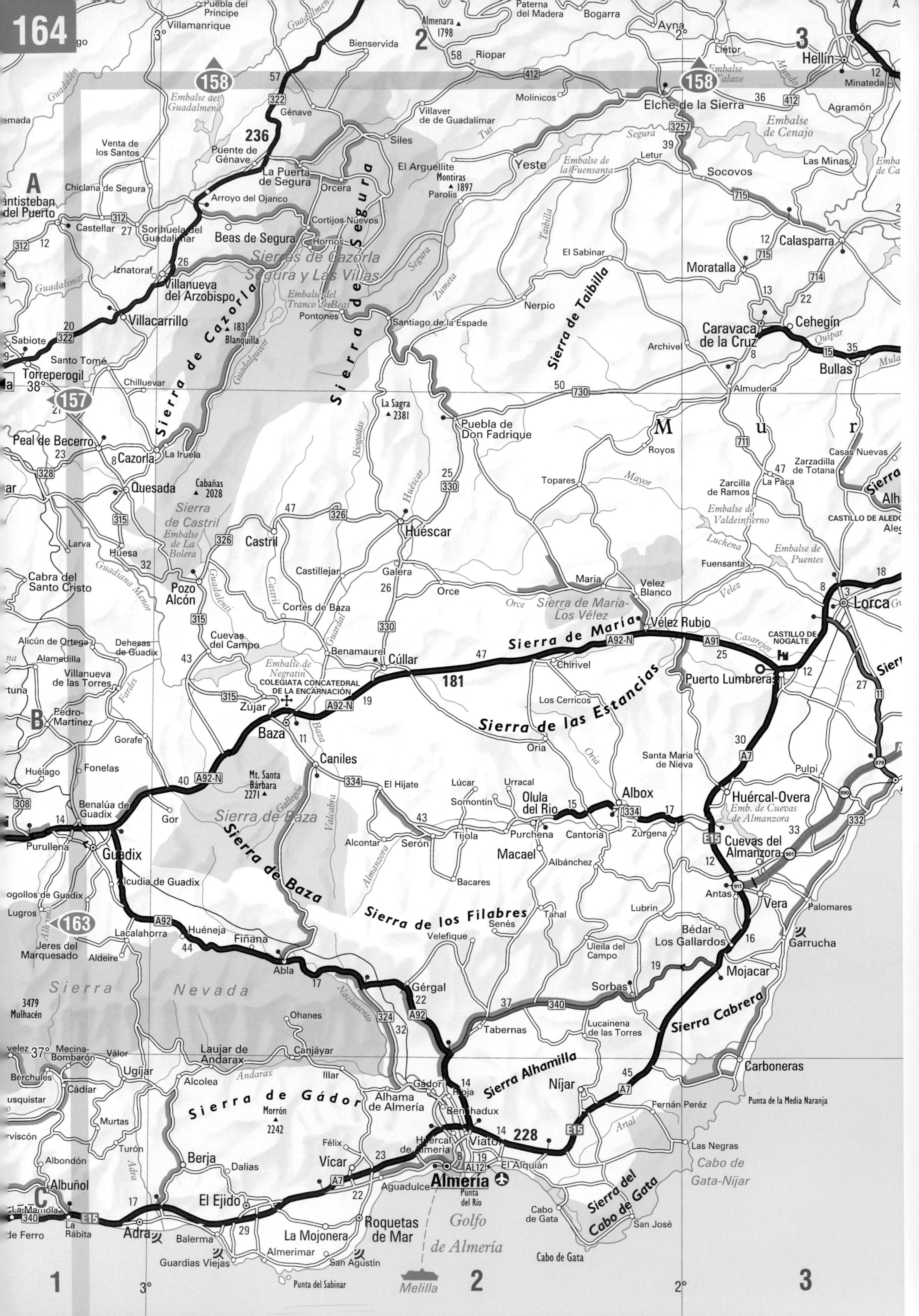
Puebla del Príncipe
Villamanrique
Guadalmena
Bienservida
Almenara 1798
Riopar
Paterna del Madera
Bogarra
Ayna
Liétor
Hellín
Minateda
Agramón
158
Embalse del Guadalmena
Génave
236
Villaver de de Guadalimar
Molinicos
Elche de la Sierra
Embalse de Cenajo
Venta de los Santos
Puente de Génave
Siles
La Puerta de Segura
El Arguellite
Montiras 1897
Parolis
Yeste
Embalse de la Fuensanta
Letur
Socovos
Las Minas
Chiclana de Segura
Orcera
Arroyo del Ojanco
Santisteban del Puerto
Castellar
Sorihuela del Guadalimar
Beas de Segura
Cortijos Nuevos
Hornos
Sierras de Cazorla Segura y Las Villas
El Sabinar
Calasparra
Moratalla
Iznatoraf
Villanueva del Arzobispo
Embalse del Tranco de Beas
Pontones
Santiago de la Espade
Nerpio
Cehegín
Caravaca de la Cruz
Villacarrillo
Sierra de Cazorla
1831 Blanquilla
Sierra de Segura
Sierra de Taibilla
Archivel
Bullas
Sabiote
Santo Tomé
Torreperogil
157
Chilluevar
La Sagra 2381
Almudena
Puebla de Don Fadrique
Peal de Becerro
Cazorla
La Iruela
Royos
Casas Nuevas
Zarzadilla de Totana
Quesada
Cabañas 2028
Topares
Zarcilla de Ramos
La Paca
Sierra de Castril
Embalse de La Bolera
Castril
Huéscar
Embalse de Valdeinfierno
CASTILLO DE ALEDO
Larva
Hüesa
Guadiana Menor
Castillejar
Galera
Fuensanta
Embalse de Puentes
Cabra del Santo Cristo
Pozo Alcón
Orce
Maria
Velez Blanco
Cortes de Baza
Sierra de María-Los Vélez
Lorca
Vélez Rubio
Alicún de Ortega
Dehesas de Guadix
Cuevas del Campo
CASTILLO DE NOGALTE
Alamedilla
Benamaurel
Cúllar
Sierra de María
Chirivel
Villanueva de las Torres
Embalse de Negratín
COLEGIATA CONCATEDRAL DE LA ENCARNACIÓN
181
Puerto Lumbreras
Zújar
Los Cerricos
Pedro-Martinez
Baza
Sierra de las Estancias
Gorafe
Oria
Caniles
Santa Maria de Nieva
Huélago
Fonelas
Mt. Santa Bárbara 2271
Pulpi
El Hijate
Lúcar
Urracal
Albox
Somontin
Olula del Rio
Huércal-Overa
Benalúa de Guadix
Gor
Sierra de Baza
Emb. de Cuevas de Almanzora
Purullena
Guadix
Alcontar
Serón
Tíjola
Purchena
Cantoria
Zurgena
Cuevas del Almanzora
Macael
Albánchez
Alcudia de Guadix
Bacares
Antas
Vera
Palomares
Sierra de los Filabres
Lubrin
Lugros
163
Lacalahorra
Huéneja
Senés
Tahal
Bédar
Los Gallardos
Garrucha
Jeres del Marquesado
Aldeire
Fiñana
Velefique
Uleila del Campo
Abla
Mojacar
Sierra Nevada
Gérgal
Sorbas
3479 Mulhacén
Ohanes
Tabernas
Lucainena de las Torres
Sierra Cabrera
Mecina-Bombarón
Válor
Laujar de Andarax
Canjáyar
Carboneras
Bérchules
Ugíjar
Cádiar
Alcolea
Illar
Gádor
Rioja
Sierra Alhamilla
Níjar
Sierra de Gádor
Alhama de Almería
Benahadux
Fernán Peréz
Punta de la Media Naranja
Murtas
Morrón 2242
Viator
228
Félix
Huércal de Almería
Turón
Berja
Dalias
Vícar
Las Negras
Albondón
El Alquián
Cabo de Gata-Nijar
Albuñol
Aguadulce
Almería
Punta del Río
Sierra del Cabo de Gata
La Mamola
El Ejido
Cabo de Gata
Adra
Roquetas de Mar
Golfo de Almería
San José
La Rábita
Balerma
La Mojonera
Almerimar
Guardias Viejas
San Agustín
Punta del Sabinar
Melilla
1
2
3

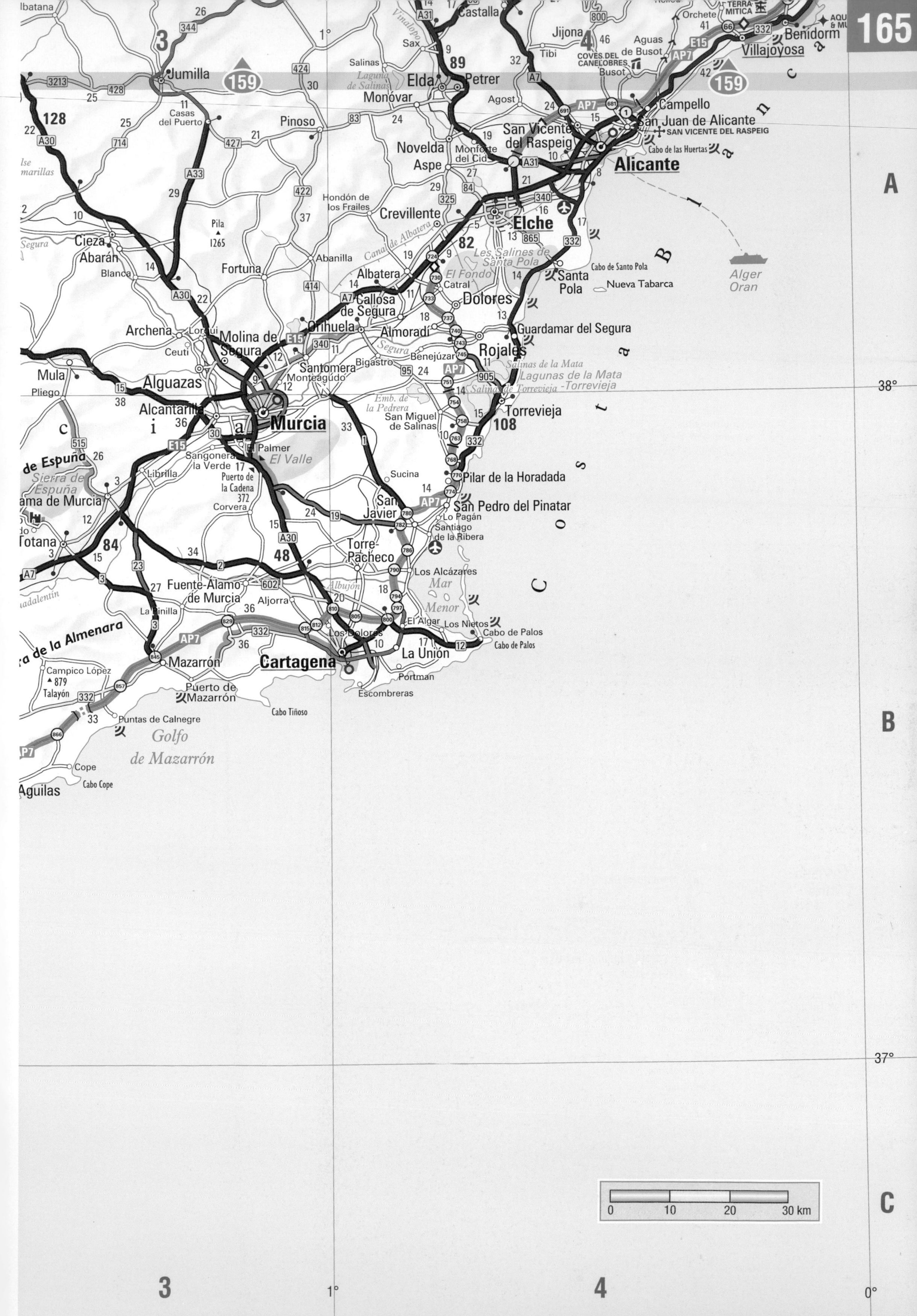
Jumilla
Cieza
Abarán
Fortuna
Archena
Molina de Segura
Alguazas
Alcantarilla
Murcia
Mula
Totana
Fuente-Álamo de Murcia
Mazarrón
Cartagena
La Unión
Torre-Pacheco
San Javier
San Pedro del Pinatar
Pilar de la Horadada
Torrevieja
Guardamar del Segura
Rojales
Dolores
Orihuela
Callosa de Segura
Almoradí
Santomera
Albatera
Crevillente
Elche
Santa Pola
Alicante
San Vicente del Raspeig
San Juan de Alicante
Campello
Novelda
Aspe
Elda
Petrer
Monóvar
Pinoso
Jijona
Villajoyosa
Benidorm
Castalla
Mar Menor
Golfo de Mazarrón
Costa Blanca
Cabo de Palos
Cabo Tiñoso
Nueva Tabarca
Alger
Oran
Aguilas
38°
37°
0 10 20 30 km
A
B
C
3
4
1°
0°

1 2° 2

A

40°

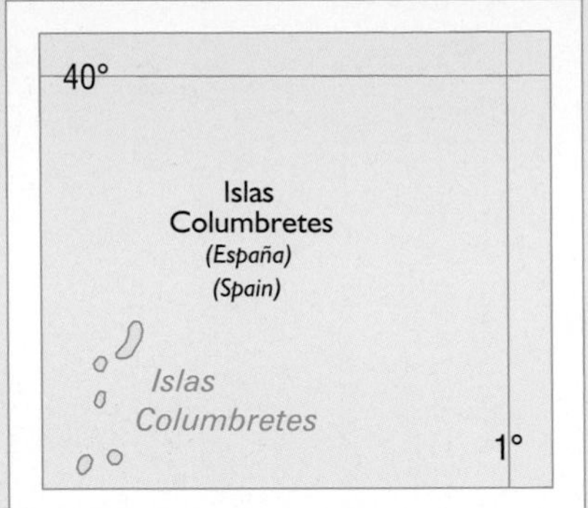

ISLAS
BALEARES

BALEARIC
ISLANDS

B

39°

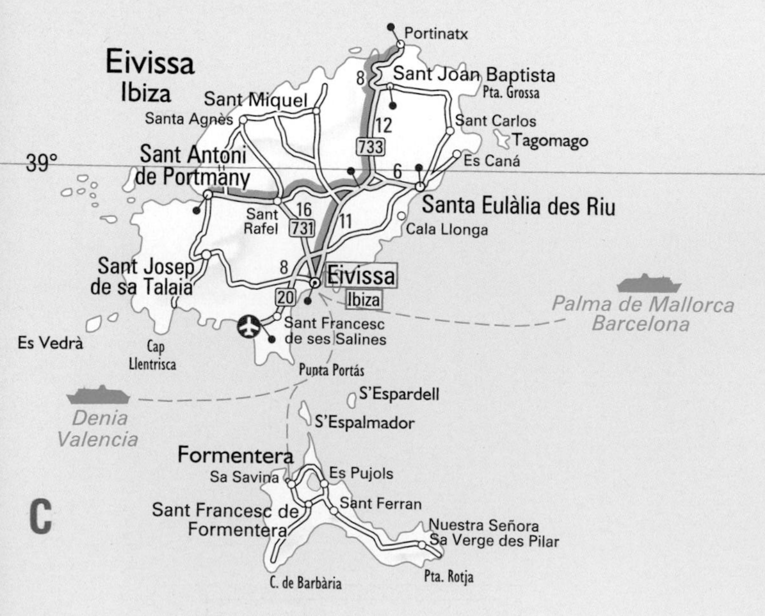

C

1 2° 2

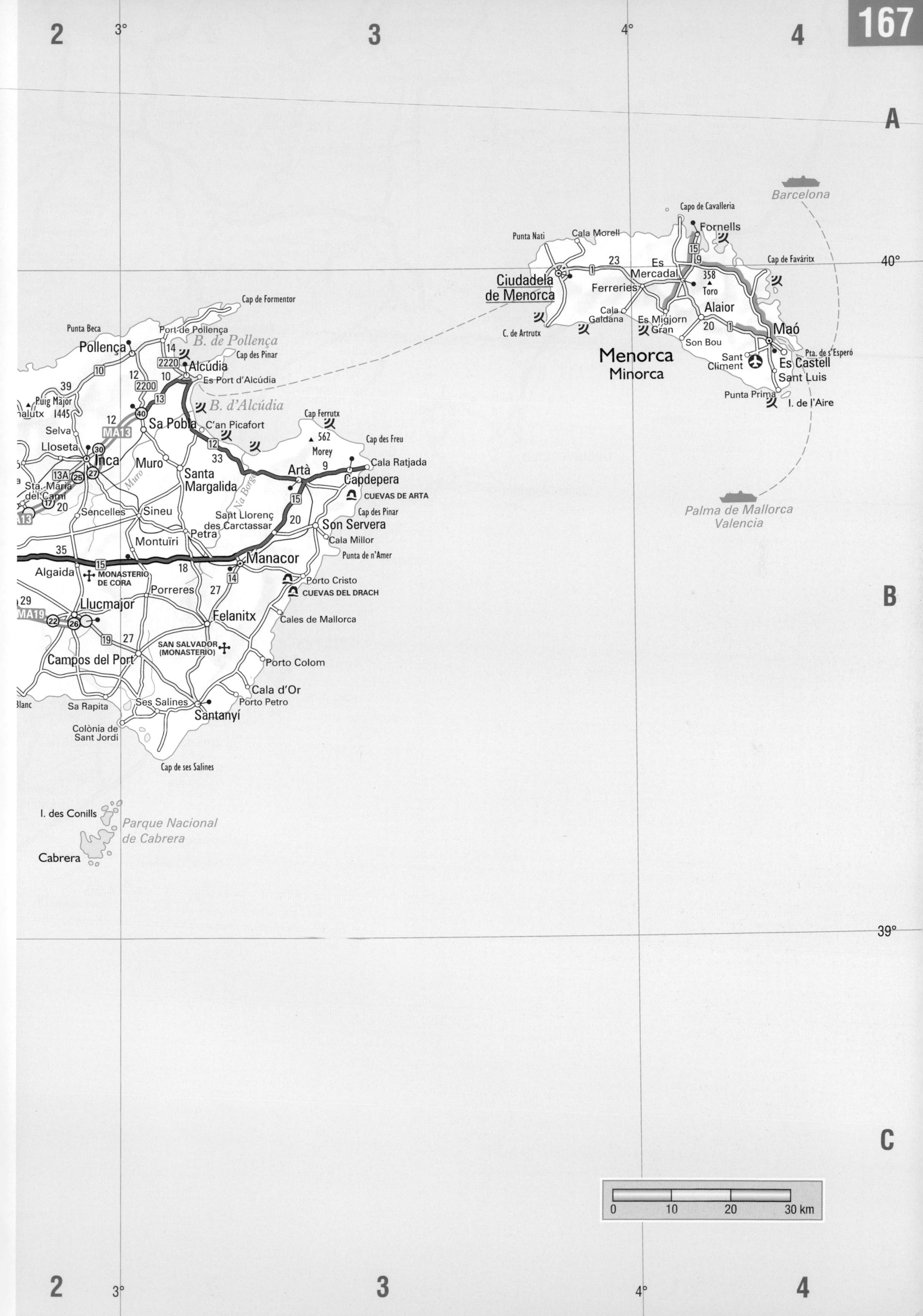

Barcelona
Capo de Cavalleria
Fornells
Punta Nati
Cala Morell
Cap de Favàritx
Ciudadela de Menorca
Es Mercadal
Ferreries
Toro
Alaior
Cala Galdana
Es Migjorn Gran
C. de Artrutx
Maó
Son Bou
Menorca
Minorca
Sant Climent
Es Castell
Pta. de s'Esperó
Sant Luis
Punta Prima
I. de l'Aire
Cap de Formentor
Punta Beca
Port de Pollença
B. de Pollença
Pollença
Alcúdia
Cap des Pinar
Es Port d'Alcúdia
Puig Major 1445
B. d'Alcúdia
Selva
Sa Pobla
C'an Picafort
Cap Ferrutx
Lloseta
Inca
Muro
Morey
Cap des Freu
Cala Ratjada
Santa Margalida
Artà
Capdepera
CUEVAS DE ARTA
Sta. Maria del Camí
Sencelles
Sineu
Sant Llorenç des Carctassar
Cap des Pinar
Son Servera
Petra
Cala Millor
Montuïri
Punta de n'Amer
Manacor
Algaida
MONASTERIO DE CORA
Porreres
Porto Cristo
CUEVAS DEL DRACH
Llucmajor
Felanitx
Cales de Mallorca
SAN SALVADOR (MONASTERIO)
Campos del Port
Porto Colom
Cala d'Or
Porto Petro
Sa Rapita
Ses Salines
Santanyí
Colònia de Sant Jordi
Cap de ses Salines
I. des Conills
Parque Nacional de Cabrera
Cabrera
Palma de Mallorca
Valencia
0 10 20 30 km

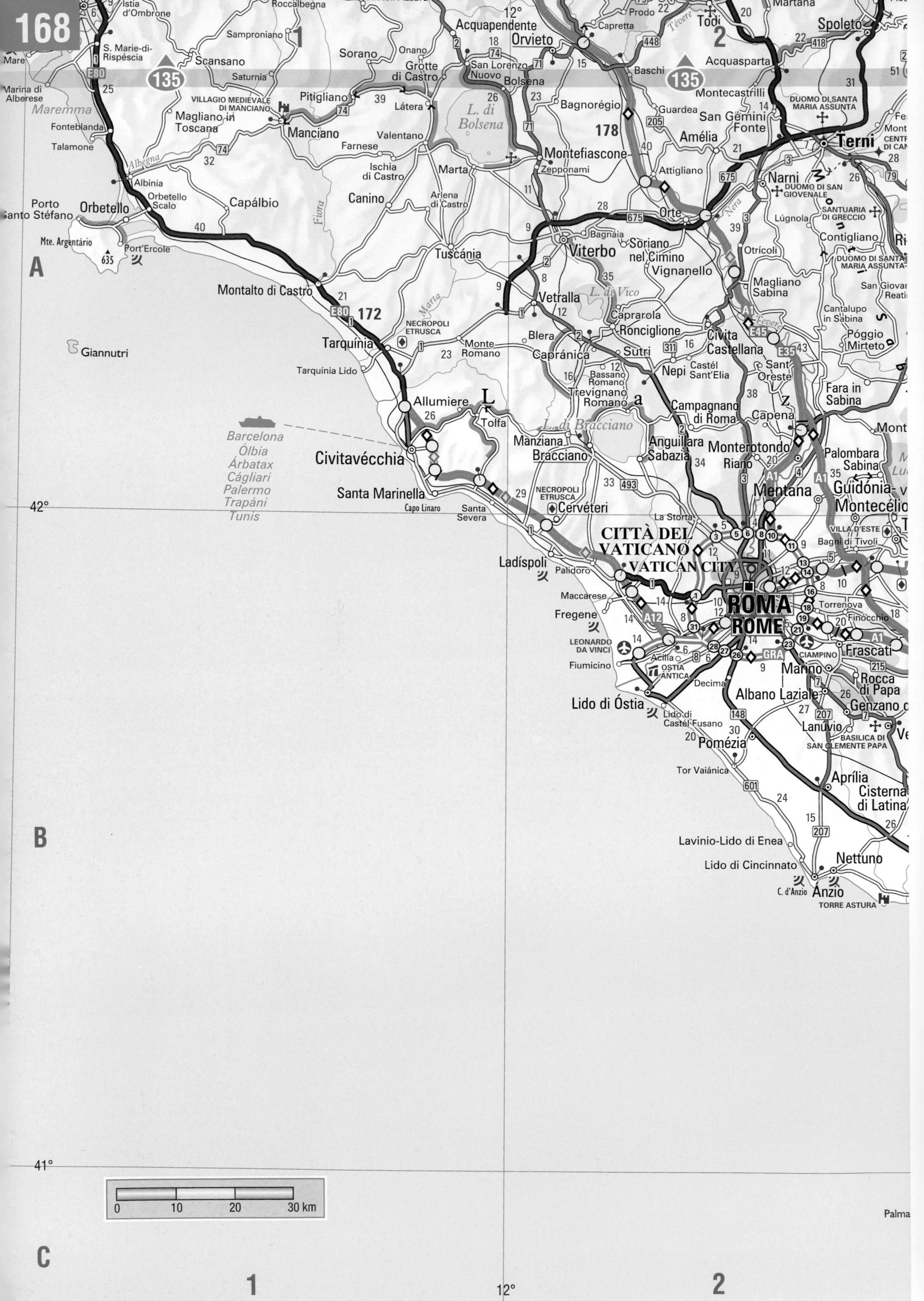
Roccalbegna
Acquapendente
Orvieto
Todi
Spoleto
Scansano
Sorano
Pitigliano
Manciano
Bolsena
L. di Bolsena
Bagnorégio
Montefiascone
Terni
Narni
Amélia
Orbetello
Porto Santo Stéfano
Mte. Argentário
Port'Ercole
Capálbio
Canino
Tuscánia
Viterbo
Orte
Montalto di Castro
Tarquínia
Giannutri
Vetralla
Civita Castellana
Ronciglione
Sutri
Nepi
Allumiere
Tolfa
Civitavécchia
Barcelona
Ólbia
Árbatax
Cágliari
Palermo
Trapáni
Tunis
L. di Bracciano
Bracciano
Anguillara Sabazia
Monterotondo
Mentana
Guidónia-Montecélio
Santa Marinella
Cerveteri
Ladíspoli
CITTÀ DEL VATICANO
VATICAN CITY
ROMA
ROME
Fiumicino
Lido di Óstia
Frascati
Marino
Albano Laziale
Pomézia
Aprília
Cisterna di Latina
Anzio
Nettuno
Lavinio-Lido di Enea
Lido di Cincinnato
Tor Vaiánica
0 10 20 30 km
42°
41°
12°
A
B
C
1
2

Giulianova
Roseto degli Abruzzi
Téramo
Notaresco
Civitella di Tronto
Mosciano Sant'Angelo
Campli
Acquasanta Terme
Valle Castellana
Cattedrale di San Bernardo
Gran Sasso e Monti della Laga
Accúmoli
Amatrice
Cáscia
Monteleone di Spoleto
Leonessa
Montório al Vomano
Pineto
Silvi Marina
Atri
Città Sant'Angelo
Montesilvano
Pescara
Francavilla al Mare
Spoltore
Penne
Pianella
Chieti
Chieti Scalo
Ortona
Lido Riccio
Miglianico
San Vito Chietino
Fossacésia
Lanciano
Castèl Frentano
Guardiagrele
Casalbordino
Paglieta
Atessa
Cásoli
Bomba
Gissi
Cupello
Gran Sasso d'Itália
Corno Grande 2912
Isola del Gr. Sasso d'Itália
Castiglione Messer Raimondo
Tossicía
Campotosto
Montereale
Borbona
Posta
Cantalice
Laghi Riatini
Terminillo
Terme di Antrodoco
Antrodoco
Cittaducale
Rieti
Pízzoli
Preturo
L'Aquila
Pagánica
Castél del Monte
Barisciano
San Demétrio né Vestini
Tornimparte
Castiglione
Fiamignano
Fiumata
Rocca Sinibalda
Póggio Moiano
Castél di Tora
Borgorose
Vigliano
Appennino Abruzzese
Rocca di Mezzo
Capestrano
Navelli
Alanno
Scafa
Manoppello
Catignano
Pópoli
Caramánico Terme
Prátola Peligna
Sulmona
Mte. Amaro 2793
Maiella
Mte. Velino 2487
Sirente Velino
Castelvecchio Subéquo
Ovíndoli
Magliano de'Marsi
Celano
Raiano
Carsóli
Tagliacozzo
Ársoli
Scúrcola Marsicana
Avezzano
Pescina
Corcumello
Orvínio
Licenza
Monti Lucrétili
Vicovaro
Tívoli
Villa Adriana
Sacro Speco
Subiaco
Ciciliano
Capistrello
M. Tarino 1959
Monti Simbruini
Trasacco
Luco dei Marsi
Gióia dei Marsi
Piana del Fúcino
Anversa d'Abruzzi
Villalago
Scanno
Palena
Lama dei Peligni
Colledimezzo
Villa Santa Maria
Pescocostanzo
Carúnchio
Castiglione Messer Marino
Roccaraso
Roccaraso-Aremogna
Mte. Greco 2283
Villetta Barrea
Alfedena
Pescasséroli
Pso. del Diávolo 1400
Abruzzo
Capracotta
Agnone
Trivento
Castèl di Sangro
Carovilli
Bagnoli dei Trigno
Duomo di Sant'Agapitus
Palestrina
San Vito Romano
Genazzano
Píglio
Civitella Roveto
Trevi nel Lázio
Collelongo
Balsorano-Nuovo
Fiuggi
Guarcino
Città Greca & Romana
Valmontone
Artena
Colleferro
Anagni
Villagio Medievale di Anagni
Alatri
Véroli
Santa Maria Maggiore
Ferentino
Sora
Isola del Liri
Abbazia di Casamari
Arpino
San Donato Val di Comino
Atina
San Biágio Saracinisco
Colli a Volturno
Isérnia
Carpinone
Frosolone
Roma
Velletri
Cori
Villagio Medievale di Norma
Norma
Carpineto Romano
Supino
Frosinone
Monte San Giovanni Campano
Arce
Ceprano
Roccasecca
M. Cáiro 1669
Aquino
Cassino
Abbazia di Montecassino
Sant'Elia Fiumerapido
Cervaro
Venafro
Monti Lepini
Sermoneta
M. Semprevisa 1536
Roccagorga
Ceccano
Sezze
Castro dei Volsci
Pontecorvo
Pico
Capriati a Volturno
Letino
Monti del Matese
Mte. Miletto 2050
Pástena
Macchiagódena
Bojano
Guardiarégia
Latina
Agro Pontino
Priverno
Abbazia di Fossanova
Amaseno
Sonnino
Pontínia
Monti Ausoni
M. delle Fate 1090
Lénola
Fondi
Espéria
Monti Aurunci
1533 Mte Petrella
San Giorgio a Liri
Ausónia
Castelforte
Terme di Súio
Mignano Monte Lungo
Pratella
Pso. di Miralago 1102
Piedimonte Matese
Cusano Mutri
Alife
Vairano Scalo
Matese
Circeo
Sabáudia
Terracina
Lido di Fondi
Sperlonga
Itri
Minturno
Fórmia
Gaeta
Sessa Aurunca
Roccamonfina
Teano
Pietravairano
Dragoni
Pietramelara
Alvignano
Pignataro Maggiore
Guárdia Sanframondi
Cerreto Sannita
Telese Terme
Amorosi
Solopaca
Mte. Circeo 541
Acropoli
San Felice Circeo
C. Circeo
Báia Domizia
Carínola
Sparanise
Piana di Monte Verna
Caiazzo
Taburno-Camposáuro
Mondragone
Cápua
Caserta
Reggia di Caserta
Sant'Ágata dei Goti
M. Taburno 1394
Cancello ed Arnone
Santa Maria Cápua Vétere
Maddaloni
Castél Volturno
Marcianise
Golfo di Gaeta
Casal di Principe
Aversa
Acerra
Cicciano
Pineta Grande
Caivano
Afragola
Marigliano
Nola
Giugliano in Campania
Casória
Marano
Sant'Anastasia
Ottaviano
Lido di Lícola
Pozzuoli
Bácoli
Napoli Naples
Pórtici
Ercolano
Vesúvio 1281
Herculanum
Pompei
Ísole Ponziane
Zannone
Ponza
Ventoténe
Próscida

1
2
3
A
B
C
15°
14°
41°
42°
169
222
186
98
Castelvecchio Subéquo
Ovíndoli
Celano
Pópoli
Caramánico Terme
Prátola Peligna
Mte. Amaro 2793
Raiano
Sulmona
Maiella
Guardiagrele
Frentano
Paglieta
Casalbordino
Pta. della Penna
Vasto
Cásoli
Atessa
Bomba
Lama dei Peligni
Avezzano
Pescina
Anversa d'Abruzzi
Colledimezzo
Palena
Villa Santa Maria
Cupello
Gissi
San Salvo
San Salvo Marina
Térmoli
Campomarino
Montenero di Bisáccia
Guglionesi
Luco dei Marsi
Trasacco
Gióia dei Marsi
Piana del Fucino
Villalago
Scanno
Pescocostanzo
Civitella Roveto
Collelongo
Pescasséroli
Pso. del Diávolo 1400
Roccaraso
Roccaraso-Aremogna
Mte. Greco 2283
Villetta Barrea
Carúnchio
Castiglione Messer Marino
Montefalcone nel Sánnio
Palata
Portocannone
San Martino in Pénsilis
Balsorano-Nuovo
Capracotta
Castelmáuro
Guarcino
Abruzzo
Alfedena
Castèl di Sangro
Agnone
Trivento
L. di Guardialfiera
Larino
Serracapriola
Alatri
Véroli
Sora
Isola del Liri
San Donato Val di Comino
Carovilli
Bagnoli dei Trigno
Casacalenda
Abbazia di Casamari
Frosinone
Arpino
Monte San Giovanni Campano
Atina
San Biágio Saracinisco
Isérnia
Petrella Tifernina
Santa Croce di Magliano
Sant'Elia a Pianisi
Matrice
Ceprano
Arce
Roccasecca
M. Cáiro 1669
Colli a Volturno
Carpinone
Frosolone
Campobasso
Baranello
L. di Occhito
Celenza Valfortore
Volturara Appula
Castro dei Volsci
Aquino
Cassino
Sant'Elia Fiumerapido
Abbazia di Montecassino
Cervaro
Venafro
Pástena
Macchiagódena
Vinchiaturo
Monti d. Sánnio
Ielsi
Gambatesa
Amaseno
Pontecorvo
Pico
Capriati a Volturno
Mte. Miletto 2050
Monti del Matese
Bojano
Guardiarégia
Saepinum Antica
Cercemaggiore
Ríccia
Lénola
Letino
Matese
Mignano Monte Lungo
San Giórgio a Liri
Ausónia
Pratella
Pso. di Miralago 1102
Piedimonte Matese
Sepino
Colle Sannita
Sella Canala 805
Baselice
San Bartolomeo in Galdo
Fondi
Espéria
Monti Aurunci
1533 Mte Petrella
Castelforte
Terme di Súio
Vairano Scalo
Alife
Cusano Mutri
Morcone
Roseto Valfortore
Montefalcone di Val Fortore
Lido di Fondi
Roccamonfina
Pietravairano
Gióia Sannitica
Cerreto Sannita
San Marco dei Cavoti
Castelfranco in Miscano
Itri
Minturno
Sessa Aurunca
Teano
Dragoni
Pietramelara
Alvignano
Guárdia Sanframondi
Pontelandolfo
Sperlonga
Fórmia
Gaeta
Báia Domizia
Pignataro Maggiore
Amorosi
Telese Terme
Pesco Sannita
Buonalbergo
Carínola
Sparanise
Piana di Monte Verna
Caiazzo
Solopaca
Taburno-Foglianise
Paduli
Ariano Irpino
Mondragone
Cápua
Reggia di Caserta
Caserta
Camposáuro
Sant'Ágata dei Goti
M. Taburno 1394
Benevento
Montesárchio
Grottaminarda
Golfo di Gaeta
Cancello ed Arnone
Santa Maria Cápua Vétere
Maddaloni
Cervinara
San Giórgio del Sánnio
Mirabella Eclano
Castél Volturno
Marcianise
Arienzo
Altavilla Irpina
Montemilleto
Casal di Principe
Pineta Grande
Aversa
Caivano
Acerra
Cicciano
M. Avella 1598
Baiano
Partenio
Pratola Serra
Gesualdo
Paternópoli
Torella dei Lombardi
Ponza
Giugliano in Campania
Casória
Afrágola
Marigliano
Nola
Avellino
Atripalda
Marano
Sant'Anastasia
Contrada
Lido di Lícola
Palma Campánia
Volturara Irpina
Montella
Pozzuoli
Nápoli
Naples
Vesúvio 1281
Herculanum
Ottaviano
Sarno
Solofra
Monti Picentini
Bagnoli Irpino
Bácoli
Pórtici
Ercolano
Pompei
Mercato S. Severino
Ventoténe
Casamicciola Terme
Prócida
Torre del Greco
Nocera Inferiore
Baronissi
le Croci di Acerno 843
Acerno
Forío
Torre Annunziata
Pagani
Íschia
Golfo di Nápoli
Castellammare di Stábia
Gragnano
Cava de Tirreni
Salerno
Montecorvino Rovella
Cágliari
Vico Equense
1443 M. S. Angelo
Vietri sul Mare
Sorrento
Meta
Positano
Amalfi
Praiano
Pontecagnano
Éboli
Massa Lubrense
Marina d. Cantone
Battipáglia
Golfo di Salerno
Capri
Anacapri
Grotta Azzurra
Villa Jovis
Altavilla Silentina
Palermo
Tunis
Messina
Paestum
Catánia
Strómboli
Ginostra
Panarea
Lípari
Vulcano
Milazzo
Agrópoli
Ogliastro Cilento
0 10 20 30 km
San Marco
Castellabate
Punta Licosa
Ogliastro Marina
Montecórice
Póllica
Acciaroli

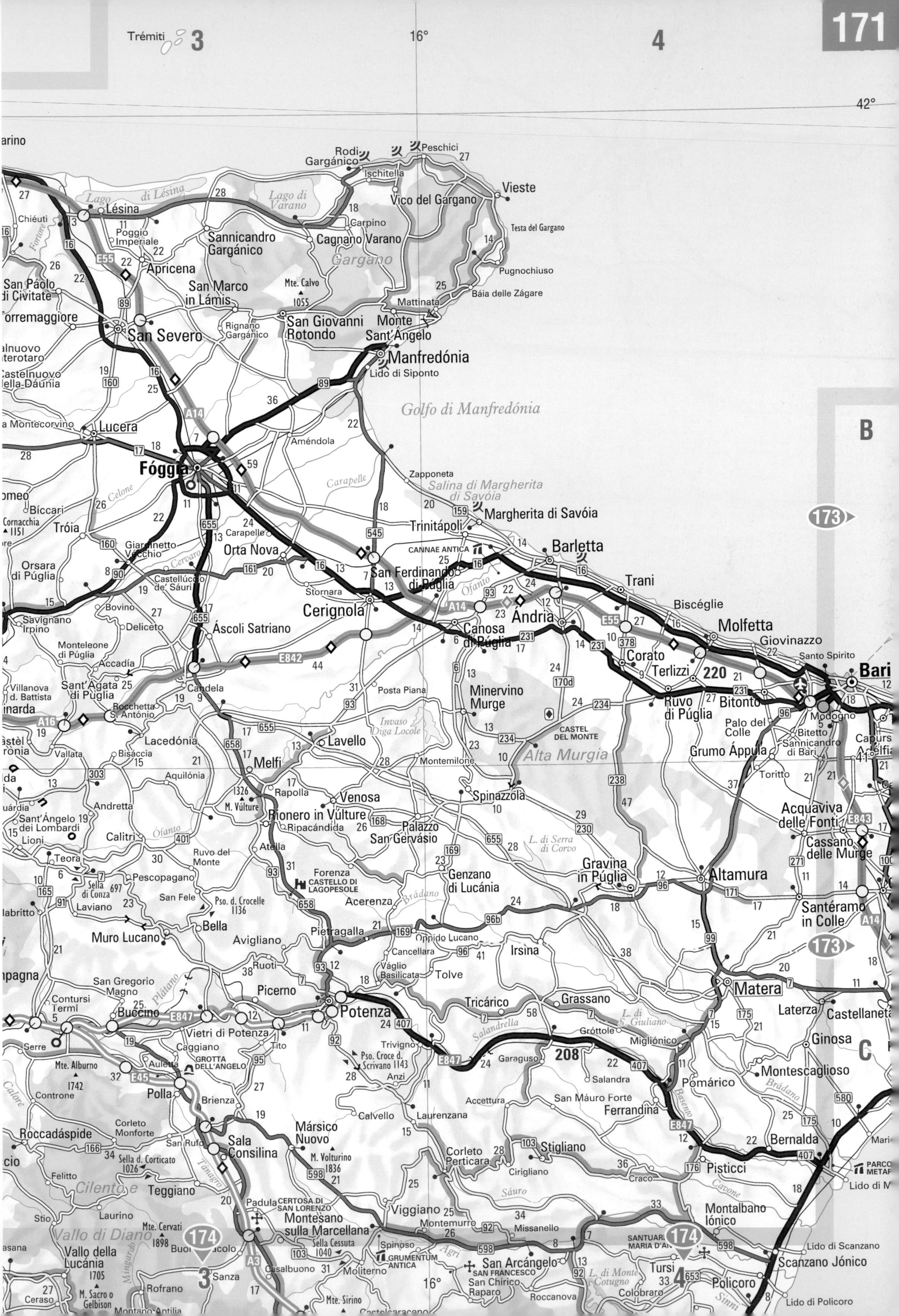

Trémiti 3
16°
4
42°
B
C

Rodi Gargánico
Peschici
Ischitella
Vieste
Lago di Lésina
Lésina
Lago di Varano
Carpino
Vico del Gargano
Testa del Gargano
Chiéuti
Poggio Imperiale
Sannicandro Gargánico
Cagnano Varano
Gargano
Pugnochiuso
Apricena
San Páolo di Civitate
San Marco in Lámis
Mte. Calvo 1055
Báia delle Zágare
Mattinata
Torremaggiore
San Severo
Rignano Gargánico
San Giovanni Rotondo
Monte Sant'Ángelo
Castelnuovo della Dáunia
Manfredónia
Lido di Siponto
Golfo di Manfredónia
Lucera
Améndola
Fóggia
Zapponeta
Salina di Margherita di Savóia
Carapelle
Margherita di Savóia
Bíccari
Tróia
Cornacchia 1151
Trinitápoli
Giardinetto Vécchio
Carapelle
Orta Nova
CANNAE ANTICA
Barletta
Orsara di Púglia
Castellúccio de' Sáuri
San Ferdinando di Púglia
Trani
Stornara
Ofanto
Bovino
Deliceto
Cerignola
Ándria
Bisceglie
Molfetta
Giovinazzo
Santo Spirito
Savignano Irpino
Monteleone di Púglia
Áscoli Satriano
Canosa di Púglia
Corato
Terlizzi
Bari
Accadía
Villanova d. Battista
Sant'Ágata di Púglia
Candela
Posta Piana
Minervino Murge
Ruvo di Púglia
Bitonto
Modugno
Palo del Colle
Bitetto
Sannicandro di Bari
Rocchetta S. António
Invaso Diga Locone
CASTEL DEL MONTE
Alta Murgia
Grumo Áppula
Lacedónia
Lavello
Vallata
Bisáccia
Melfi
Montemilone
Toritto
Aquilónia
Rapolla
Venosa
Spinazzola
M. Vúlture 1326
Rionero in Vúlture
Acquaviva delle Fonti
Andretta
Sant'Ángelo dei Lombardi
Ripacándida
Palazzo San Gervásio
Lioni
Calitri
Ófanto
Cassano delle Murge
Atella
L. di Serra di Corvo
Teora
Ruvo del Monte
Gravina in Púglia
Altamura
Pescopagano
Forenza
CASTELLO DI LAGOPESOLE
Genzano di Lucánia
Sella di Conza 697
San Fele
Pso. d. Crocelle 1136
Acerenza
Bradano
Santéramo in Colle
Laviano
Bella
Muro Lucano
Pietragalla
Avigliano
Oppido Lucano
Cancellara
Irsina
San Gregorio Magno
Ruoti
Váglio Basilicata
Tolve
Matera
Contursi Termi
Picerno
Buccino
Plátano
Potenza
Tricárico
Grassano
L. di S. Giuliano
Laterza
Castellaneta
Serre
Vietri di Potenza
Tito
Grottole
Miglionico
Ginosa
Caggiano
Trivigno
GROTTA DELL'ANGELO
Pso. Croce d. Scrivano 1143
Salandrella
Garaguso
Salandra
Montescaglioso
Mte. Alburno 1742
Auletta
Anzi
Pomárico
Polla
Controne
Brienza
Accettura
San Máuro Forte
Basento
Calore
Corleto Monforte
Calvello
Laurenzana
Ferrandina
Roccadáspide
Sala Consilina
Mársico Nuovo
Bernalda
San Rufo
M. Volturino 1836
Corleto Perticara
Stigliano
Sella d. Corticato 1026
Cirigliano
Pisticci
PARCO METAP
Felitto
Cilento e
Teggiano
Tánagro
Sáuro
Craco
Lido di M
Cavone
Padula
CERTOSA DI SAN LORENZO
Montesano sulla Marcellana
Viggiano
Montalbano Iónico
Stio
Laurino
Vallo di Diano
Mte. Cervati 1898
Montemurro
Missanello
Vallo della Lucánia
Sella Cessuta 1040
Spinoso
GRUMENTUM ANTICA
Agri
San Arcángelo
SAN FRANCESCO
SANTUARIO MARIA D'A
Lido di Scanzano
Scanzano Jónico
Mingardo
Mte. Lucánia 1705
Sanza
Casalbuono
Moliterno
San Chírico Raparo
L. di Monte Cotugno
Tursi
Policoro
Ceraso
M. Sacro o Gelbison
Rofrano
Mte. Sirino
Roccanova
Colobraro
Sinni
Lido di Policoro
Montano Antilia

173
173
174 3
174 4

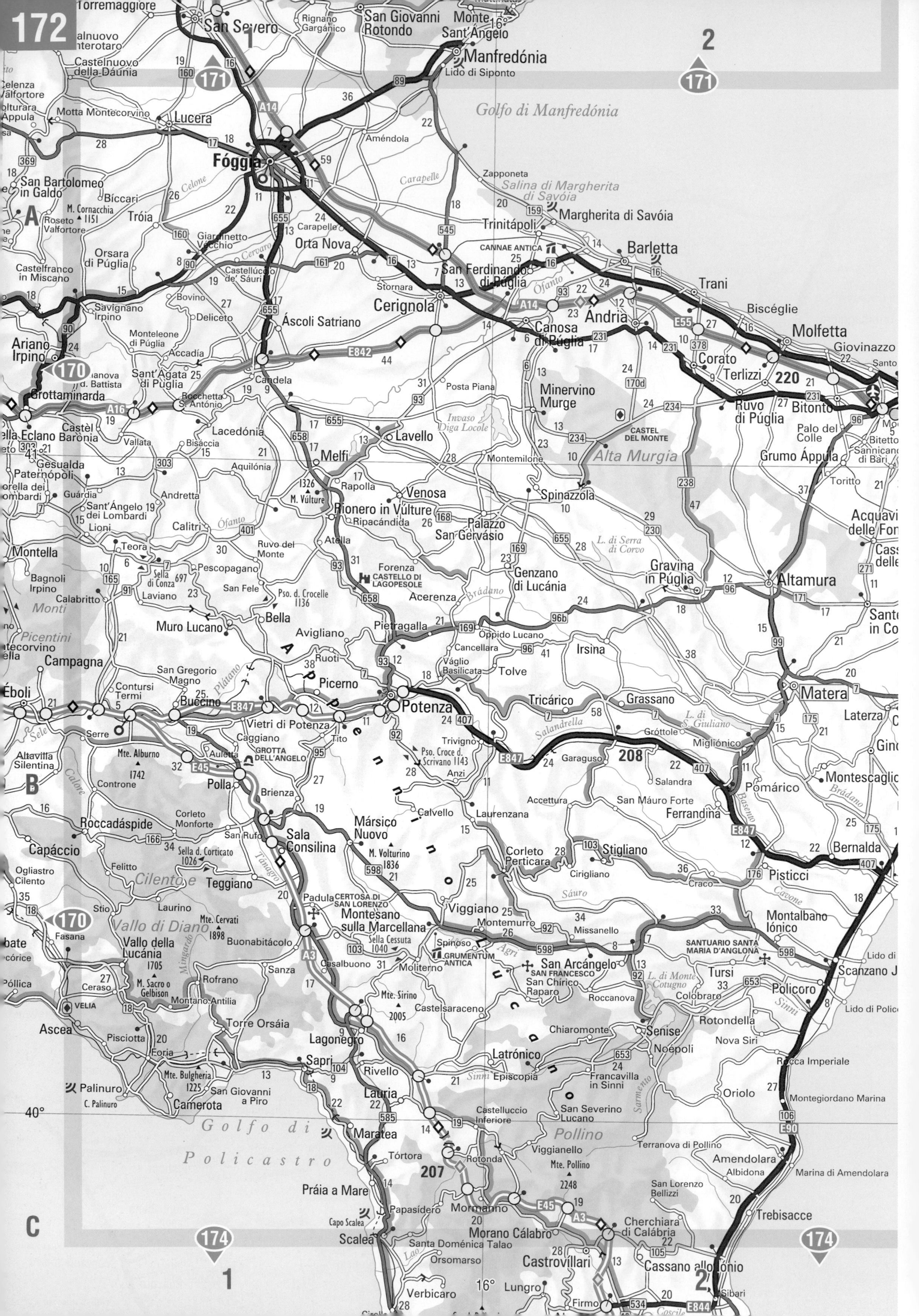

Torremaggiore
San Severo
Rignano Gargánico
San Giovanni Rotondo
Monte Sant'Angelo
Manfredónia
Lido di Siponto
Castelnuovo della Dáunia
Motta Montecorvino
Lucera
Golfo di Manfredónia
Fóggia
Améndola
Zapponeta
Salina di Margherita di Savóia
Margherita di Savóia
Carapelle
San Bartolomeo in Galdo
Bíccari
M. Cornacchia 1151
Roseto Valfortore
Tróia
Celone
Giardinetto Vécchio
Orta Nova
Trinitápoli
Cannae Antica
Barletta
Orsara di Púglia
Castelfranco in Miscano
Castelluccio de' Sáuri
Cervaro
San Ferdinando di Púglia
Stornara
Trani
Bovino
Deliceto
Savignano Irpino
Cerignola
Áscoli Satriano
Ofanto
Ándria
Bisceglie
Molfetta
Giovinazzo
Santo
Canosa di Púglia
Corato
Terlizzi
Ruvo di Púglia
Bitonto
Ariano Irpino
Monteleone di Púglia
Accadía
Sant'Ágata di Púglia
Candela
Grottaminarda
Rocchetta S. António
Posta Piana
Minervino Murge
Castel del Monte
Palo del Colle
Bitetto
Sannicandro di Bari
Invaso Diga Locone
Lacedónia
Castel Baronia
Eclano
Vallata
Bisáccia
Lavello
Gesualdo
Paternópoli
Aquilónia
Melfi
Montemilone
Alta Murgia
Grumo Áppula
Toritto
Guárdia Lombardi
Sant'Ángelo dei Lombardi
Lioni
Andretta
Calitri
Ófanto
M. Vúlture 1326
Rapolla
Venosa
Rionero in Vúlture
Ripacándida
Spinazzola
Palazzo San Gervásio
Atella
Acquaviva delle Fonti
Montella
Teora
Ruvo del Monte
L. di Serra di Corvo
Sella di Conza 697
Pescopagano
Forenza
Castello di Lagopesole
Genzano di Lucánia
Gravina in Púglia
Altamura
Bagnoli Irpino
Laviano
San Fele
Pso. d. Crocelle 1136
Acerenza
Bradano
Calabritto
Monti Picentini
Muro Lucano
Bella
Avigliano
Pietragalla
Oppido Lucano
Irsina
Campagna
San Gregorio Magno
Ruoti
Cancellara
Vaglio Basilicata
Tolve
Matera
Éboli
Contursi Terme
Buccino
Plátano
Picerno
Potenza
Tricárico
Grassano
L. di S. Giuliano
Laterza
Sele
Serre
Vietri di Potenza
Caggiano
Tito
Trivigno
Gróttole
Miglionico
Altavilla Silentina
Mte. Alburno 1742
Auletta
Grotta dell'Angelo
Pso. Croce d. Scrivano 1143
Anzi
Garaguso
Salandra
Calore
Controne
Polla
Brienza
Accettura
San Máuro Forte
Ferrandina
Pomárico
Montescaglioso
Roccadáspide
Corleto Monforte
Calvello
Laurenzana
Basento
Appennino Lucano
Capáccio
San Rufo
Sala Consilina
Mársico Nuovo
M. Volturino 1836
Corleto Perticara
Stigliano
Bernalda
Sella d. Corticato 1026
Ogliastro Cilento
Felitto
Tánagro
Cirigliano
Pisticci
Cilento e Vallo di Diano
Teggiano
Sáuro
Craco
Cavone
Padula
Certosa di San Lorenzo
Montesano sulla Marcellana
Viggiano
Stio
Laurino
Montemurro
Missanello
Montalbano Iónico
Mte. Cervati 1898
Buonabitácolo
Sella Cessuta 1040
Spinoso
Grumentum Antica
Agri
Santuario Santa Maria d'Anglona
Fasana
Vallo della Lucánia
Casalbuono
Moliterno
San Arcángelo
San Francesco
San Chírico Raparo
L. di Monte Cotugno
Tursi
Policoro
Lido di Policoro
Scanzano Jonico
Mingardo
Sanza
Roccanova
Colobraro
Sinni
Ceraso
M. Sacro o Gelbison
Rofrano
Mte. Sirino 2005
Castelsaraceno
Velia
Montano Antilia
Torre Orsáia
Senise
Rotondella
Ascea
Pisciotta
Lagonegro
Chiaromonte
Nova Siri
Noépoli
Foria
Sapri
Latrónico
Rocca Imperiale
Mte. Bulgheria 1225
Palinuro
C. Palinuro
San Giovanni a Piro
Camerota
Rivello
Episcopia
Francavilla in Sinni
Oriolo
Lauria
Castelluccio Inferiore
San Severino Lucano
Sarmento
Montegiordano Marina
40°
Golfo di Policastro
Maratea
Pollino
Tórtora
Rotonda
Viggianello
Terranova di Pollino
Amendolara
Albidona
Marina di Amendolara
Mte. Pollino 2248
Práia a Mare
San Lorenzo Bellizzi
Papasídero
Mormanno
Trebisacce
Capo Scalea
Scalea
Morano Cálabro
Cherchiara di Calábria
Santa Doménica Talao
Lao
Orsomarso
Castrovillari
Cassano allo Iónio
16°
Lungro
Verbicaro
Firmo
Sibari
Coscile

0 10 20 30 km
Dubrovnik Bar
Durrës
Kerkyra Igoumenitsa Patra
Bari
Triggiano
Mola di Bari
Capurso
Noicáttaro
Adélfia
Rutigliano
Polignano a Mare
Monópoli
Casamássima
Conversano
Turi
GROTTA DI CASTELLANA
Castellana Grotte
PARCO ARCHEOLOGICO DI EGNAZIA
Savelletri
Sammichele di Bari
Putignano
Fasano
Torre Canne
Gióia del Colle
Noci
Rosa Marina
Villanova
Alberobello
Locorotondo
Ostuni
Torre Guaceto
Cisternino
Carovigno
Martina Franca
Móttola
Crispiano
Céglie Messápica
San Vito dei Normanni
Bríndisi
Kerkyra Igoumenitsa Sami Patra
Castellaneta
Palagiano
Massafra
Villa Castelli
Francavilla Fontana
Canale Reale
Montemésola
Grottáglie
Mesagne
Latiano
Oria
San Pietro Vernótico
Casa l'Abate
Lido Azzurro
Castellaneta Marina
Táranto
Cellino
S. Marco
Torchiarolo
ABBAZIA SANTA MARIA DI CERRATE
Torre Santa Susanna
S. Dónaci
Squinzano
Monteparano
Fragagnano
Chéradi
San Giórgio Iónico
Érchie
Guagnano
Trepuzzi
Marina di Ginosa
Talsano
Sava
San Pancrázio Salentino
Surbo
San Cataldo
PARCO ARCHEOLOGICO METAPONTO
Lizzano
Manduria
Sálice Salentino
Campi Salentina
Lecce
Lido di Metaponto
Pulsano
Torricella
Avetrana
Véglie
Monteroni di Lecce
Vérnole
San Foca
Lido Silvana
Marúggio
Leverano
Léquile
San Cesário di Lecce
Melendugno
Torre dell'Orso
Scanzano Iónico
Golfo di Táranto
Porto Cesáreo
Copertino
Calimera
Martano
Soleto
Galatina
Nardò
Galátone
Otranto
C. d'Otranto
Santa Maria al Bagno
Cutrofiano
Maglie
Uggiano la Chiesa
Gallípoli
Alézio
Collepasso
Poggiardo
Sant'Andrea
Parábita
Nociglia
Santa Cesárea Terme
Casarano
Diso
Castro
GROTTA DI ROMANELLI & ZINZULUSA
Taviano
Ruffano
Miggiano
Rácale
Taurisano
Tricase
Ugento
Presicce
Alessano
Marina di Nováglie
Gagliano del Capo
Castrignano del Capo
C. Santa Maria di Léuca
Marina di Léuca

Golfo di Táranto
Golfo di Policastro
Táranto
San Giorgio Iónico
Grottáglie
Montescaglioso
Pomárico
Ferrandina
Bernalda
Pisticci
Montalbano Iónico
Scanzano Jónico
Policoro
Tursi
Senise
Latrónico
Lagonegro
Lauria
Maratea
Sapri
Praia a Mare
Scalea
Castrovillari
Morano Cálabro
Cassano allo Iónio
Trebisacce
Corigliano Cálabro
Rossano
Acri
Bisignano
Cosenza
Rende
Páola
San Giovanni in Fiore
Cirò Marina
Sala Consilina
Polla
Teggiano
Vallo della Lucánia
Camerota
Sila Greca
Sila Grande
La Sila
Pollino
Mte. Pollino 2248
Vallo di Diano
Cilento e
Lido di Metaponto
PARCO ARCHEOLOGICO METAPONTO
Mandúria
Sava
Lizzano
Pulsano
Cariati
Crosia
Strongoli
Cetraro
Fuscaldo
San Lúcido
Belvedere Maríttimo
Diamante
Viggiano
Moliterno
Stigliano
San Arcángelo
Trebisacce
Spezzano Albanese
Altomonte
Roggiano Gravina
San Marco Argentano
Montalto Uffugo
Luzzi
Camigliatello Silano
Spezzano della Sila
40°
16°
17°

Crotone
C. Colonna
Ísola di Capo Rizzuto
C. Rizzuto
Cutro
Botricello
Santa Severina
Roccabernarda
Scandale
Cotronei
Petília Policastro
M. Femminamorta
Mesoraca
Petronà
Sila Píccola
Calábria
Villaggio Mancuso
Rogliano
Parenti
Scigliano
Soveria Mannelli
Cóschi
Carlópoli
Taverna
Sersale
Crópani
Catanzaro
Catanzaro Marina
Lido di Squillace
Squillace
Pta. d. Staletti
Soverato
Golfo di Squillace
Chiaravalle Centrale
Olivadi
Bórgia
Girifalco
Máida
Curinga
Filadélfia
Tiriolo
Nicastro
Sambiase
Decollatura
Platania
Serrastretta
Pso. di Acquabona
Lago
Amantea
Aiello Cálabro
Nocera Terinese
Gizzeria
Capo Súvero
Gizzeria Lido
Sant'Eufemia Lamezia
Golfo di Sant'Eufémia
Nápoli
Strómboli
Pizzo
Briático
Vibo Valéntia
Tropea
C. Vaticano
M. Poro
Ióppolo
Nicótera
Mileto
Soriano Cálabro
Simbário
Santuario di Santa Maria nel Bosco
Serra San Bruno
M. Pecoraro
Badolato
Guardavalle
Mongiana
Pso. di Pietra Spada
Stilo
Pta. Stilo
Monasterace Marina
Marchesale
Cropane Micone
Dinami
Laureana di Borrello
Fabrizia
Pso. Croce Ferrata
Rosarno
Gióia Táuro
Golfo di Gióia
Salerno
Polístena
Cinquefrondí
Caulónia
Capo Barbi
Palmi
Taurianova
Cittanova
Seminara
Mámmola
Grotteria
Gioiosa Iónica
Roccella Iónica
Marina di Gioiosa Iónica
Siderno
Locri
Locri Antica
Gerace
Plati
Óppido Mamertina
Bagnara Cálabra
Scilla
Sant'Eufémia d'Aspromonte
Delianuova
Aspromonte
Montalto (M. Cocuzza)
Villa San Giovanni
Laganadi
Gambárie
Sella Entrata
Réggio di Calábria
San Luca
Careri
Ardore
Bovalino Marina
Bianco
Cardeto
Amendolea
Bagaladi
Staiti
Montebello Iónico
Bova
Bova Marina
Brancaleone Marina
C. Spartivento
Mélito di Porto Salvo
Lazzaro
Pta. di Péllaro
Str. di Messina
Torre Faro
Spartà
Mortelle
Golfo di Milazzo
Villafranca Tirrena
Spadafora
Messina
Rometta
Santa Lucia
Castroreale
M. Poverello
Scaletta Zanclea
Mandanici
Antillo
Alì Terme
Roccalumera
Santa Teresa di Riva
Taormina
Giardini Naxos
Appennino Calabro
Gozo
San Dimitri Pt
Victoria (Rabat)
Mgarr
Comino
Pozzallo
Mellieħa
San Pawl il-Bahar
Mosta
Sliema
Valletta
Birkirkara
Rabat
Paola
MALTA
Birżebbuġa
Benghisa Pt
Filfla
14° 30'
36°
39°
38°
16°
17°
0 10 20 30 km
B
C
D
1
2
3

1
2
A
B
C
13°
14°
38°
37°
Cágliari
Tunis
Ústica
Nápoli
Génova
Salerno
Civitavécchia
Cágliari
Civitavécchia
Pantelleria
Tunis
Linosa
Lampedusa
Golfo di Castellammare
Golfo di Términi Imerese
Palermo
Trápani
Marsala
Agrigento
Isola delle Fémmine
C. Gallo
Mondello
C. San Vito
San Vito lo Capo
Terrasini
Capaci
Carini
Monreale
Montelepre
Bagheria
Ficarazzi
Altofonte
Casteldáccia
Misilmeri
Trabia
Términi Imerese
Campofelice di Roccella
M. Spáragio 1110
Scopello
Pizzolungo
Érice
Valdérice
Balestrate
Partinico
Castellammare del Golfo
Alcamo
San Cipirello
San Giuseppe Jato
Piana degli Albanesi
Bolognetta
Marineo
Cáccamo
Favignana
Paceco
Fulgatore
Rilievo
Stagnone
Calatafimi
TEMPIO GRECO DI SEGESTA
Vita
Camporeale
L. Poma
Villafrati
Ciminna
Cerda
Collesano
CASE ROMANA
Salemi
Gibellina Nuova
Roccamena
Mezzojuso
Rca. Busambra 1613
Montemaggiore Belsito
Vicari
Roccapalumba
Caltavuturo
Polizzi Generosa
Matarocco
Santa Ninfa
Corleone
Pll. Imbriaca 718
Ália
Salaparuta
Partanna
Campofiorito
Prizzi
Lercara Friddi
Pla. d. Scavo 566
Valledolmo
Strasatti
L. della Trinità
Délia
Santa Margherita di Belice
Bisacquino
Castelvetrano
Sambuca di Sicília
Chiusa Sclàfani
Palazzo Adriano
Vallelunga Pratameno
Resuttano
Villalba
Mazara del Vallo
Campobello di Mazara
Pll. Misilbesi 295
Menfi
L. Aráncio
San Carlo
Bivona
Santo Stéfano Quisquina
Cammarata
M. Cammarata 1578
Mussomeli
Marianópoli
Granitola-Torretta
C. Granitola
CITTÀ GRECA DI SELINUNTE
Marinella
Caltabellotta
Búrgio
Alessándria della Rocca
CASTELLO DI CHIAROMONTE
Santa Caterina Villarmosa
C. S. Marco
Sciacca
Ribera
Cianciana
Casteltérmini
Campofranco
San Biágio Plátani
Cattólica Eraclea
Raffadali
Aragona
Montedoro
Serradifalco
Racalmuto
Montallegro
HERACLEA MINOA
Siciliana
Canicattì
Délia
Castrofilippo
Favara
Naro
Porto Empédocle
AGRIGENTO
Camastra
Campobello di Licata
Palma di Montechiaro
Licata
Val di Mazara
Sicilia
0
10
20
30 km

Lípari
Canneto
Vulcano
Salerno
Golfo di Milazzo
Capo di Milazzo
Milazzo
Villafranca Tirrena
Spadafora
Messina
Rometta
Réggio di Calábria
Torre Faro
Scilla
Capo Calavá
Golfo di Patti
Gioiosa Marea
C. d'Orlando
Brolo
Naso
Patti
Barcellona-Pozzo di Gotto
Falcone
Santa Lucia del Mela
Castroreale
CITTÀ DI TYNDARIS
San Piero Patti
Mazzarrà S. Andrea
Monti Peloritani
M. Poverello
Sant'Ágata Militello
Cefalù
Santo Stéfano di Camastra
Caronia
Alcara il Fusi
San Fratello
Longi
Tortorici
Ucria
Floresta
Montalbano Elicona
Novara di Sicília
Mandanici
Scaletta Zanclea
Ali Terme
Roccalumera
Antillo
Santa Teresa di Riva
Tusa
Castelbuono
Mistretta
Monti Nébrodi
Nébrodi
M. Soro
Plla Fémmina Morta 1524
Plla. d Zoppo 1264
Plla. Mandrazzi 1125
Francavilla di Sicília
Santa Doménica Vittória
Randazzo
Castiglione di Sicília
Linguaglossa
Taormina
Giardini Naxos
Pzo. Carbonara
Madonie
Geraci Sículo
Colle del Contrasto 1107
Capizzi
L. di Áncipa
Cesarò
Passopisciaro
Petralia Sottana
Gangi
Cerami
Troina
Maletto
Etna
Piedimonte Etneo
Fiumefreddo di Sicília
Máscali
Riposto
Pella. Madonnuzza 1147
Sperlinga
Bronte
CASTELLO DI ADRANO
ETNA
Giarre
Alimena
Nicosia
Gagliano Castelferrato
L. di Pozzillo
Simeto
Salso
Zafferana Etnea
Sicilia
Regalbuto
Adrano
Plla di Recattivo 832
Leonforte
Ássoro
Agira
Centúripe
Biancavilla
Nicolosi
Acireale
Napoli
Villarosa
Calascibetta
Santa Maria di Licodia
Trecastagni
Aci Catena
Enna
Pergusa
Catenanuova
Paternò
Belpasso
Aci Castello
Caltanissetta
Valguarnera Caropepe
Plla Grottacalda 647
Castel di Iúdica
Raddusa
Misterbianco
Catánia
Gerbini
Pietraperzia
Aidone
Gornalunga
Golfo di Catánia
Ramacca
Piazza Armerina
Lago di Lentini
Barrafranca
VILLA ROMANA DEL CASALE
Palagonía
Mirabella Imbáccari
Scordia
Riesi
Mazzarino
San Michele di Ganzaria
Lentini
Militello in Val di Catánia
Caltagirone
Mineo
Villasmundo
Capo S. Croce
Augusta
Grammichele
Francofonte
Golfo di Augusta
Butera
Melilli
Priolo Gargallo
Niscemi
Vizzini
Licodía Eubéa
Buccheri
Sortino
Monti Iblei
Anapo
Falconara
M. Lauro 986
Ferla
Solarino
Siracusa
San Pietro
Monterosso Almo
Florídia
Gela
Maroglio
Acate
Giarratana
Palazzolo Acréide
Chiaramonte Gulfi
Canicattini Bagni
C. Murro di Porco
Golfo di Gela
Vittória
Cómiso
Cassíbile
Ragusa
Noto
Avola
Golfo di Noto
Scoglitti
Módica
Irminio
Tellaro
ELORO ANTICA
Santa Croce Camerina
Rosolini
C. Scarámia
Scicli
Íspica
Marina di Ragusa
Donnalucata
Marzamemi
Sampieri
Pozzallo
Pachino
C. Passero
Portopalo di C. Passero
Valletta
15°
37°

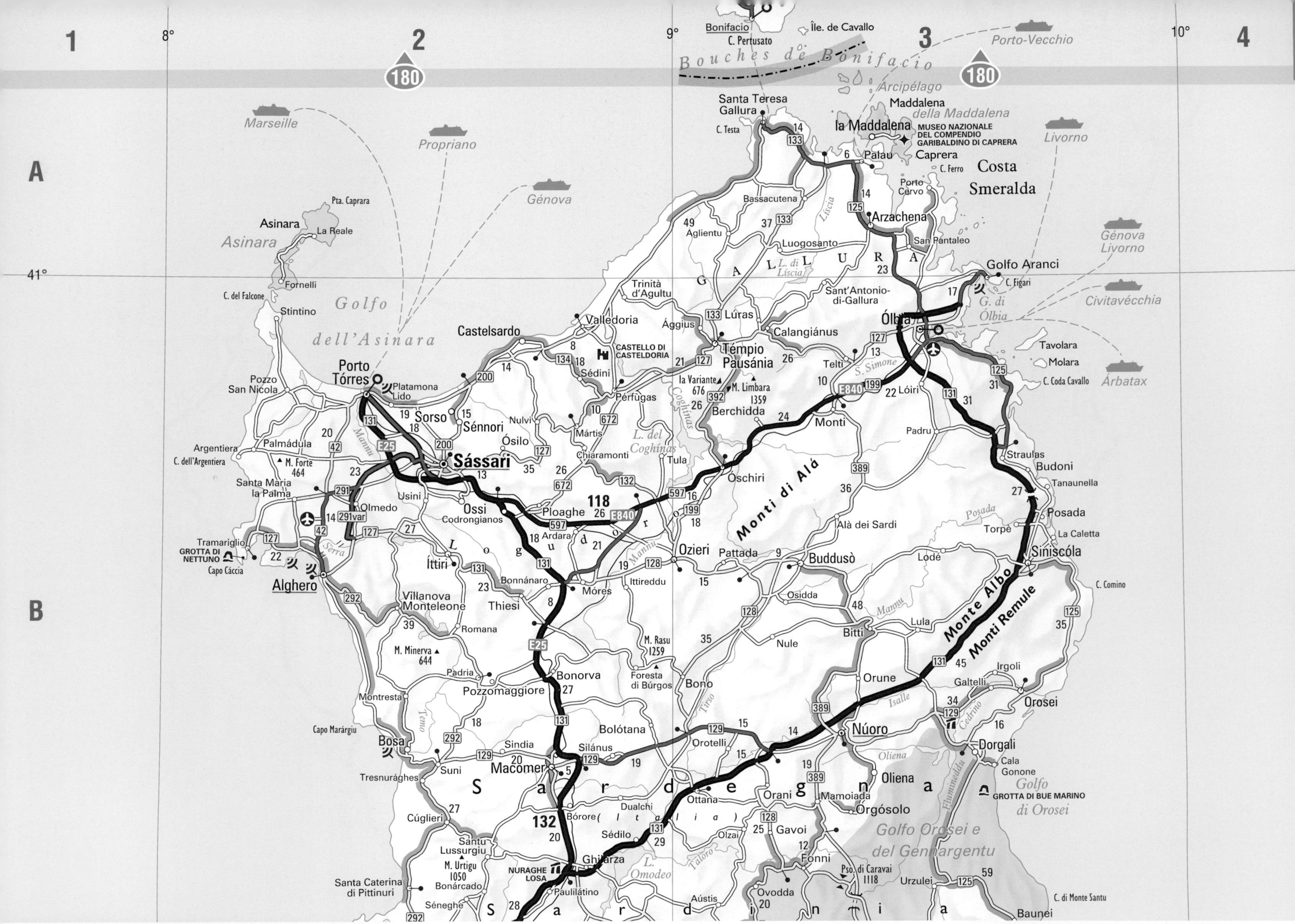

1 8° 2 9° 3 10° 4

180 180

Bonifacio
C. Pertusato
Île. de Cavallo
Porto-Vecchio
Bouches de Bonifacio
Arcipélago
Maddalena
della Maddalena
Santa Teresa Gallura
C. Testa
la Maddalena
MUSEO NAZIONALE DEL COMPENDIO GARIBALDINO DI CAPRERA
Caprera
C. Ferro
Palau
Costa Smeralda
Porto Cervo
Livorno
Marseille
Propriano
Génova
A
Pta. Caprara
Asinara
La Reale
Asinara
Bassacutena
Arzachena
San Pantaleo
Génova Livorno
Aglientu
Luogosanto
Liscia
G A L L U R A
L. di Liscia
41°
Fornelli
C. del Falcone
Stintino
Golfo dell'Asinara
Trinità d'Agultu
Golfo Aranci
C. Figari
Sant'Antonio-di-Gallura
G. di Ólbia
Civitavécchia
Valledoria
Ággius
Lúras
Ólbia
Castelsardo
Calangiánus
Tavolara
Molara
CASTELLO DI CASTELDORIA
Témpio Pausánia
Sédini
Telti
S. Simone
C. Coda Cavallo
Árbatax
Pozzo San Nicola
Porto Tórres
Platamona Lido
la Variante 676
M. Limbara 1359
Pérfugas
Coghinas
Lóiri
Berchidda
Sorso
Sénnori
Nulvi
Mártis
Monti
Padru
Argentiera
C. dell'Argentiera
Palmádula
Mannu
Ósilo
L. del Coghinas
Sássari
Chiaramonti
Tula
Straulas
Budoni
M. Forte 464
Oschiri
Tanaunella
Santa Maria la Palma
Usini
Monti di Alá
Olmedo
Ossi
Codrongianos
Ploaghe
Alà dei Sardi
Posada
Torpè
La Caletta
Tramariglio
GROTTA DI NETTUNO
Capo Cáccia
Serra
Ardara
L o g u d o r o
Íttiri
Ozieri
Pattada
Budduşò
Lodè
Siniscóla
Alghero
Bonnánaro
Móres
Mannu
Ittireddu
C. Comino
Villanova Monteleone
Thiesi
Osidda
Monte Albo
B
Romana
M. Rasu 1259
Nule
Bitti
Lula
Monti Remule
M. Minerva 644
Padria
Bonorva
Foresta di Búrgos
Bono
Orune
Irgoli
Galtellì
Montresta
Pozzomaggiore
Tirso
Orosei
Isalle
Cedrino
Capo Marárgiu
Temo
Bolótana
Orotelli
Núoro
Dorgali
Bosa
Sindia
Silánus
Oliena
Cala Gonone
Tresnurághes
Suni
Macomer
S a r d e g n a
Ottana
Orani
Mamoiada
Golfo di Orosei
GROTTA DI BUE MARINO
Flumineddu
Cúglieri
Dualchi
Orgósolo
Bórore
(I t a l i a)
Santu Lussurgiu
Sédilo
Olzai
Gavoi
Golfo Orosei e del Gennargentu
M. Urtigu 1050
NURAGHE LOSA
Ghilarza
L. Omodeo
Táloro
Fonni
Pso. di Caravai 1118
Santa Caterina di Pittinuri
Bonárcado
Paulilátino
Ovodda
Urzulei
C. di Monte Santu
Séneghe
Aústis
Baunei

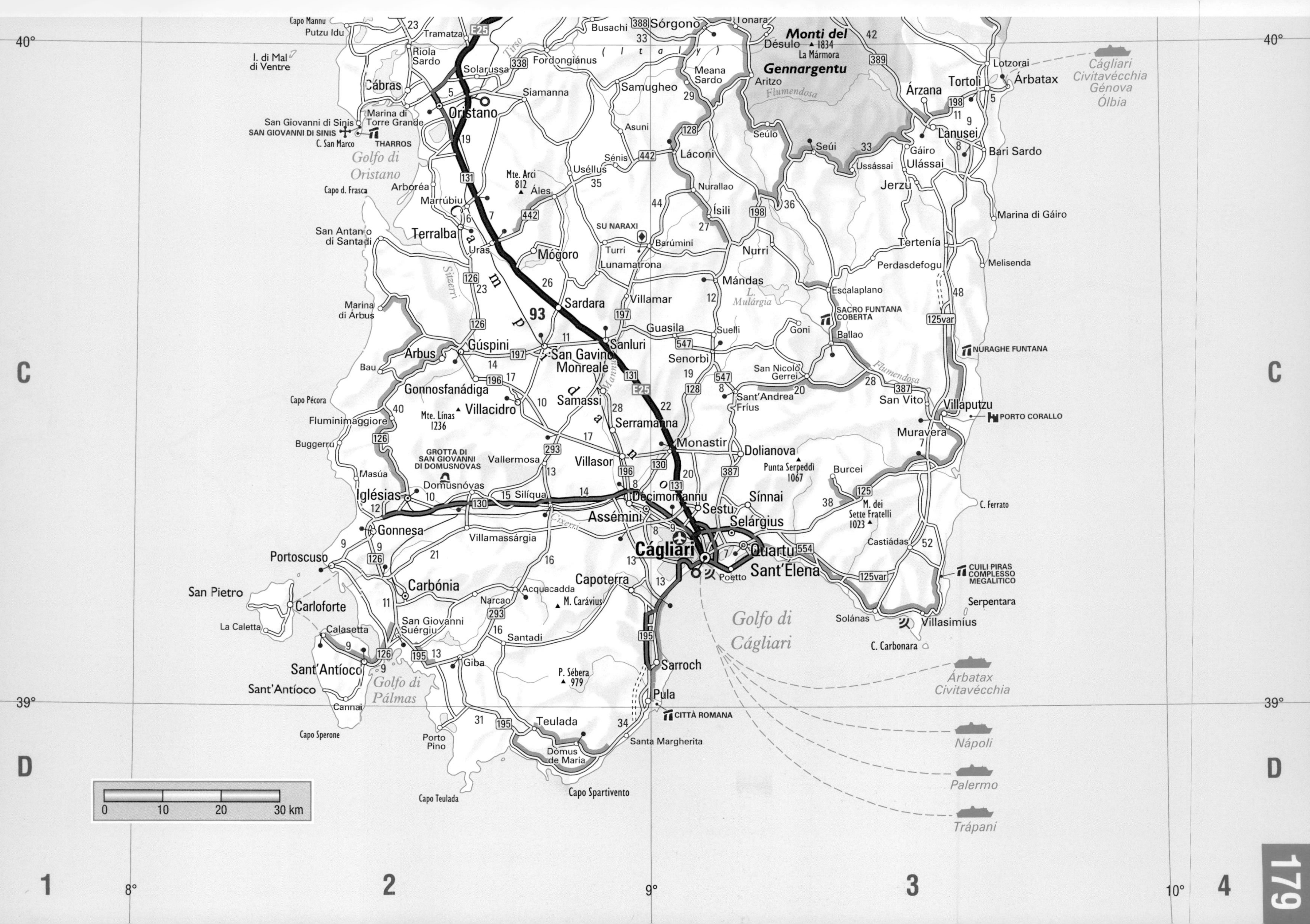

Capo Mannu
Putzu Idu
I. di Mal di Ventre
Tramatza
Riola Sardo
Solarussa
Busachi
Sórgono
Tonara
Fordongiánus
I t a l y
Cábras
Oristano
Siamanna
Samugheo
Meana Sardo
Monti del Gennargentu
Désulo
La Mármora 1834
Aritzo
Flumendosa
Lotzorai
Tortolì
Árbatax
Árzana
Cágliari Civitavécchia Génova Ólbia
Marina di Torre Grande
San Giovanni di Sinis
SAN GIOVANNI DI SINIS
C. San Marco
THARROS
Golfo di Oristano
Capo d. Frasca
Arboréa
Marrúbiu
Terralba
Uras
San Antanio di Santadi
Mte. Arci 812
Áles
Usellus
Sénis
Asuni
Láconi
Seúlo
Seúi
Ussássai
Gáiro
Ulássai
Lanusei
Bari Sardo
Jerzu
Nurallao
Ísili
Marina di Gáiro
SU NARAXI
Barúmini
Turri
Lunamatrona
Mógoro
Nurri
Tertenía
Perdasdefogu
Melisenda
Sitzerri
Mándas
L. Mulárgia
Escalaplano
SACRO FUNTANA COBERTA
Ballao
Marina di Árbus
Sardara
Villamar
Campidano
Guasila
Suelli
Goni
NURAGHE FUNTANA
Arbus
Gúspini
San Gavino Monreale
Sanluri
Senorbì
San Nicolò Gerrei
Bau
Gonnosfanádiga
Samassi
Mannu
Sant'Andrea Frius
San Vito
Villaputzu
PORTO CORALLO
Capo Pécora
Fluminimaggiore
Mte. Linas 1236
Villacidro
Serramanna
Monastir
Dolianova
Muravera
Buggerru
GROTTA DI SAN GIOVANNI DI DOMUSNOVAS
Vallermosa
Villasor
Punta Serpeddì 1067
Burcei
Masúa
Domusnóvas
Iglésias
Siliqua
Decimomannu
Sínnai
M. dei Sette Fratelli 1023
C. Ferrato
Assémini
Sestu
Selárgius
Gonnesa
Villamassárgia
Cixerri
Cágliari
Quartu Sant'Elena
Castiádas
Portoscuso
Carbónia
Capoterra
Poetto
CUILI PIRAS COMPLESSO MEGALITICO
San Pietro
Carloforte
Acquacadda
Narcao
M. Carávius
Serpentara
La Caletta
Calasetta
San Giovanni Suérgiu
Santadi
Golfo di Cágliari
Solánas
Villasimíus
C. Carbonara
Sant'Antíoco
Giba
Sarroch
Árbatax Civitavécchia
Golfo di Pálmas
P. Sébera 979
Pula
CITTÀ ROMANA
Cannai
Teulada
Capo Sperone
Porto Pino
Domus de Maria
Santa Margherita
Nápoli
Palermo
Trápani
Capo Teulada
Capo Spartivento
E25
93
131
125var
0 10 20 30 km
40°
39°
8°
9°
10°
C
D
1
2
3
4

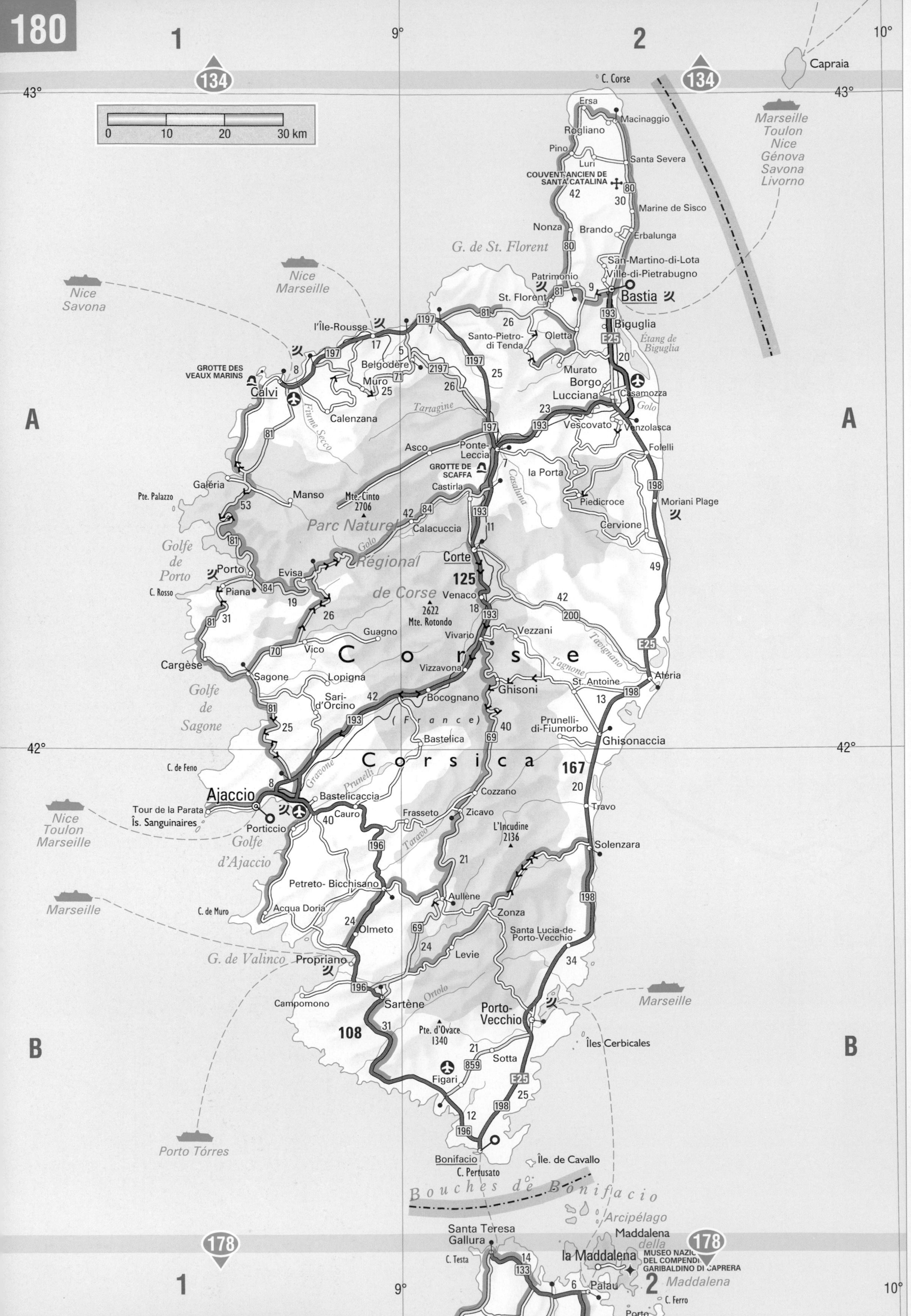
1
2
9°
10°
43°
42°
A
B
134
178
0
10
20
30 km
Capraia
C. Corse
Marseille
Toulon
Nice
Génova
Savona
Livorno
Ersa
Macinaggio
Rogliano
Pino
Luri
Santa Severa
COUVENT ANCIEN DE SANTA CATALINA
Marine de Sisco
Nonza
Brando
Erbalunga
G. de St. Florent
San-Martino-di-Lota
Ville-di-Pietrabugno
Patrimonio
St. Florent
Bastia
Biguglia
Étang de Biguglia
Santo-Pietro-di Tenda
Oletta
Murato
Borgo
Lucciana
Casamozza
Golo
Vescovato
Venzolasca
Folelli
Nice
Savona
Nice
Marseille
l'Île-Rousse
Belgodère
Muro
GROTTE DES VEAUX MARINS
Calvi
Calenzana
Fiume Secco
Tartagine
Asco
Ponte-Leccia
GROTTE DE SCAFFA
la Porta
Castirla
Casaluna
Piedicroce
Moriani Plage
Cervione
Galéria
Pte. Palazzo
Manso
Mte. Cinto
2706
Parc Naturel
Régional
de Corse
Calacuccia
Golfe de Porto
Porto
Evisa
C. Rosso
Piana
Corte
Venaco
2622
Mte. Rotondo
Vivario
Vezzani
Tavignano
Cargèse
Guagno
Vico
Corse
Vizzavona
Tagnone
Aléria
Sagone
Lopigna
St. Antoine
Ghisoni
Golfe de Sagone
Sari-d'Orcino
Bocognano
(France)
Prunelli-di-Fiumorbo
Ghisonaccia
Bastelica
Corsica
C. de Feno
Gravone
Prunelli
Ajaccio
Bastelicaccia
Cozzano
Travo
Tour de la Parata
Îs. Sanguinaires
Porticcio
Cauro
Frasseto
Zicavo
Nice
Toulon
Marseille
Golfe d'Ajaccio
Taravo
L'Incudine
2136
Solenzara
Petreto-Bicchisano
Aullène
Marseille
C. de Muro
Acqua Doria
Zonza
Olmeto
Santa Lucia-de-Porto-Vecchio
Levie
G. de Valinco
Propriano
Marseille
Campomono
Sartène
Ortolo
Porto-Vecchio
Pte. d'Ovace
1340
Îles Cerbicales
Sotta
Figari
Porto Tórres
Bonifacio
C. Pertusato
Île. de Cavallo
Bouches de Bonifacio
Arcipélago
della
Maddalena
Santa Teresa
Gallura
C. Testa
la Maddalena
MUSEO NAZI... DEL COMPENDI... GARIBALDINO DI CAPRERA
Palau
C. Ferro
Porto

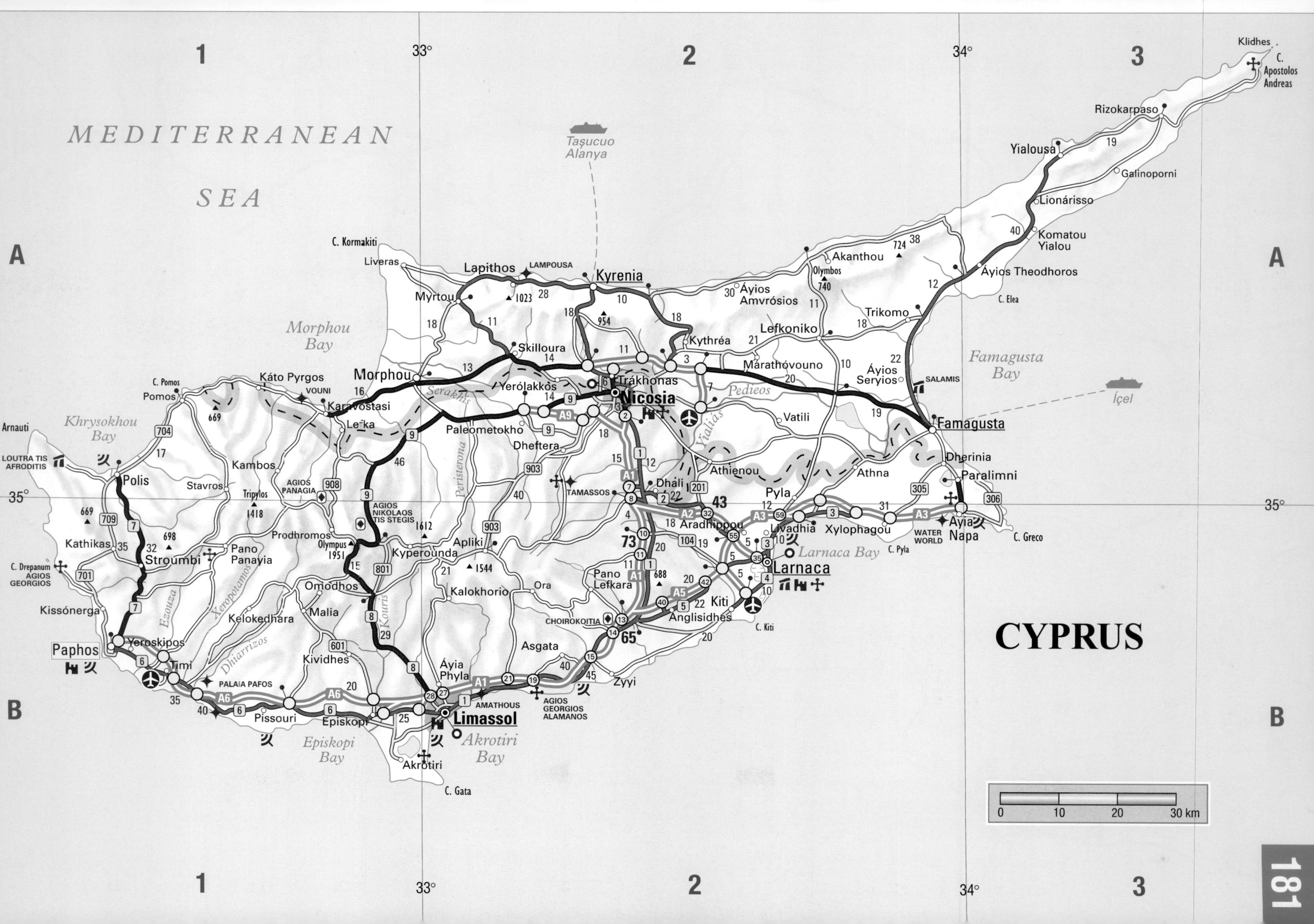
CYPRUS
MEDITERRANEAN SEA
Morphou Bay
Khrysokhou Bay
Famagusta Bay
Larnaca Bay
Akrotiri Bay
Episkopi Bay
Taşucuo Alanya
İçel
Nicosia
Kyrenia
Famagusta
Larnaca
Limassol
Paphos
Morphou
Polis
Pomos
C. Pomos
C. Arnauti
LOUTRA TIS AFRODITIS
C. Drepanum AGIOS GEORGIOS
Kathikas
Kissónerga
Yeroskipos
Timi
PALAIA PAFOS
Pissouri
Episkopi
Akrotiri
C. Gata
AMATHOUS
AGIOS GEORGIOS ALAMANOS
Zyyi
Asgata
CHOIROKOITIA
Anglisidhes
Kiti
C. Kiti
Pano Lefkara
Kalokhorio
Ora
Kyperounda
Olympus 1951
Prodhromos
Pano Panayia
Stroumbi
Kambos
Stavros
Tripylos 1418
AGIOS NIKOLAOS TIS STEGIS
AGIOS PANAGIA
Omodhos
Malia
Kelokedhara
Kividhes
Áyia Phyla
Apliki
Dheftera
Paleometokho
Yerólakkos
Skilloura
Lefka
Karavostasi
VOUNI
Káto Pyrgos
TAMASSOS
Dhali
Aradhippou
Livadhia
Xylophagou
Áyia Napa
WATER WORLD
C. Pyla
C. Greco
Paralimni
Dherinia
Athna
Pyla
Athienou
Vatili
Trákhonas
Kythréa
Márathóvouno
Lefkoniko
Áyios Seryios
SALAMIS
Trikomo
Áyios Amvrósios
Akanthou
Olymbos 740
Áyios Theodhoros
C. Elea
Komatou Yialou
Lionárisso
Yialousa
Galinoporni
Rizokarpaso
Klidhes
C. Apostolos Andreas
Lapithos
LAMPOUSA
Myrtou
Liveras
C. Kormakiti
Pedieos
Yialias
Serakhis
Peristerona
Kouris
Xeropotamos
Ezouza
Dhiarrizos
33°
34°
35°
1
2
3
A
B
0
10
20
30 km

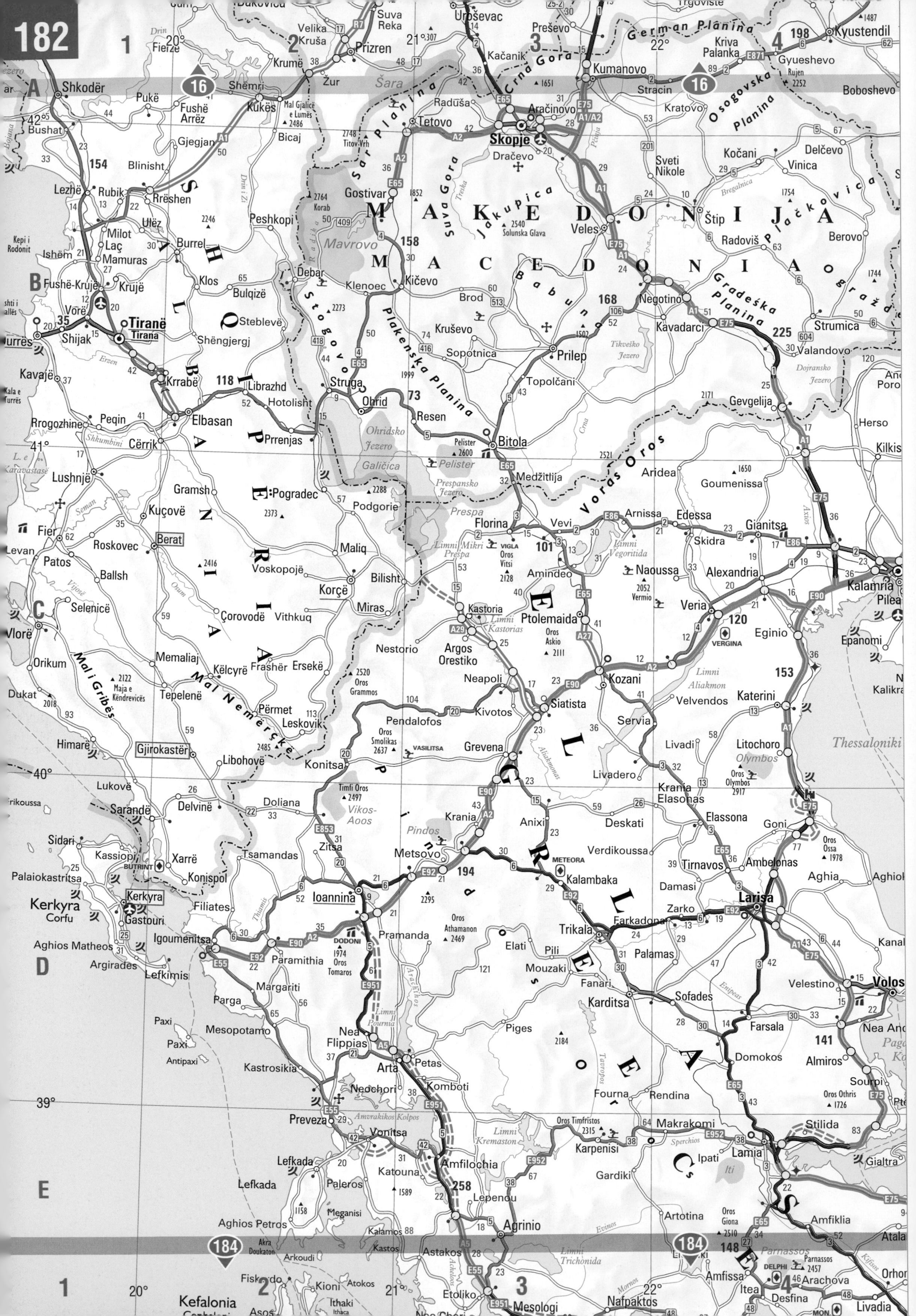
Shkodër
Pukë
Fushë Arrëz
Kukës
Prizren
Suva Reka
Uroševac
Preševo
Kumanovo
Kriva Palanka
Kyustendil
Gyueshevo
Boboshevo
German Planina
Osogovska Planina
Crna Gora
Šar Planina
Tetovo
Skopje
Aračinovo
Dračevo
Kratovo
Sveti Nikole
Kočani
Delčevo
Vinica
Lezhë
Rubik
Rrëshen
Milot
Laç
Mamuras
Burrel
Peshkopi
Gostivar
Mavrovo
Debar
Kičevo
Klenoec
Veles
Štip
Radoviš
Berovo
Jakupica
Suva Gora
Plačkovica
Ogražden
M A K E D O N I J A
M A C E D O N I A
Babuna
Brod
Kruševo
Sopotnica
Prilep
Negotino
Kavadarci
Gradeška Planina
Strumica
Valandovo
Gevgelija
Fushë-Krujë
Krujë
Vorë
Tiranë
Tirana
Durrës
Shijak
Kavajë
Krrabë
Librazhd
Hotolisht
Elbasan
Peqin
Rrogozhine
Cërrik
Lushnjë
Bulqizë
Steblevë
Shëngjergj
Stogovo
Plakenska Planina
Struga
Ohrid
Resen
Ohridsko Jezero
Prrenjas
Bitola
Pelister
Galičica
Prespansko Jezero
Topolčani
Medžitlija
Voras Oros
Aridea
Goumenissa
Edessa
Gianitsa
Skidra
Arnissa
Pogradec
Podgorie
Gramsh
Kuçovë
Fier
Patos
Roskovec
Berat
Ballsh
Maliq
Bilisht
Korçë
Voskopojë
Miras
Çorovodë
Vithkuq
Florina
Vevi
Amindeo
Naoussa
Alexandria
Veria
Kalamria
Pilea
Kastoria
Ptolemaida
Argos Orestiko
Nestorio
Vergina
Eginio
Epanomi
Kozani
Siatista
Neapoli
Kivotos
Servia
Velvendos
Katerini
Selenicë
Vlorë
Orikum
Mal i Gribës
Memaliaj
Këlcyrë
Frashër
Ersekë
Tepelenë
Mal Nemërçkë
Përmet
Leskovik
Pendalofos
Grevena
Litochoro
Olymbos
Thessaloniki
Dukat
Himarë
Gjirokastër
Libohovë
Konitsa
Livadi
Livadero
Krania Elassonas
Elassona
Lukovë
Sarandë
Delvinë
Doliana
Vikos-Aoos
Pindos
Krania
Anixi
Deskati
Goni
Ambelonas
Tirnavos
Aghia
Sidari
Kassiopi
Butrint
Xarrë
Konispol
Tsamandas
Zitsa
Metsovo
Meteora
Kalambaka
Verdikoussa
Damasi
Larisa
Kerkyra
Corfu
Gastouri
Filiates
Ioannina
Pramanda
Dodoni
Trikala
Farkadona
Zarko
Igoumenitsa
Paramithia
Elati
Pili
Palamas
Velestino
Volos
Aghios Matheos
Argirades
Lefkimis
Margariti
Mouzaki
Fanari
Karditsa
Sofades
Farsala
Parga
Paxi
Antipaxi
Mesopotamo
Nea Flippias
Piges
Domokos
Almiros
Sourpi
Kastrosikia
Arta
Petas
Neochori
Komboti
Fourna
Rendina
Preveza
Vonitsa
Makrakomi
Karpenisi
Stilida
Lamia
Lefkada
Katouna
Amfilochia
Gardiki
Ipati
Paleros
Meganisi
Lepenou
Artotina
Amfiklia
Aghios Petros
Agrinio
Kalamos
Kastos
Astakos
Arkoudi
Atokos
Kefalonia
Kioni
Ithaki
Etoliko
Mesologi
Nafpaktos
Amfissa
Delphi
Arachova
Itea
Desfina
Livadia
Gialtra
Parnassos
S T E R E A   E L L A D A
Thessalia
E L L A S
S H Q I P Ë R I A

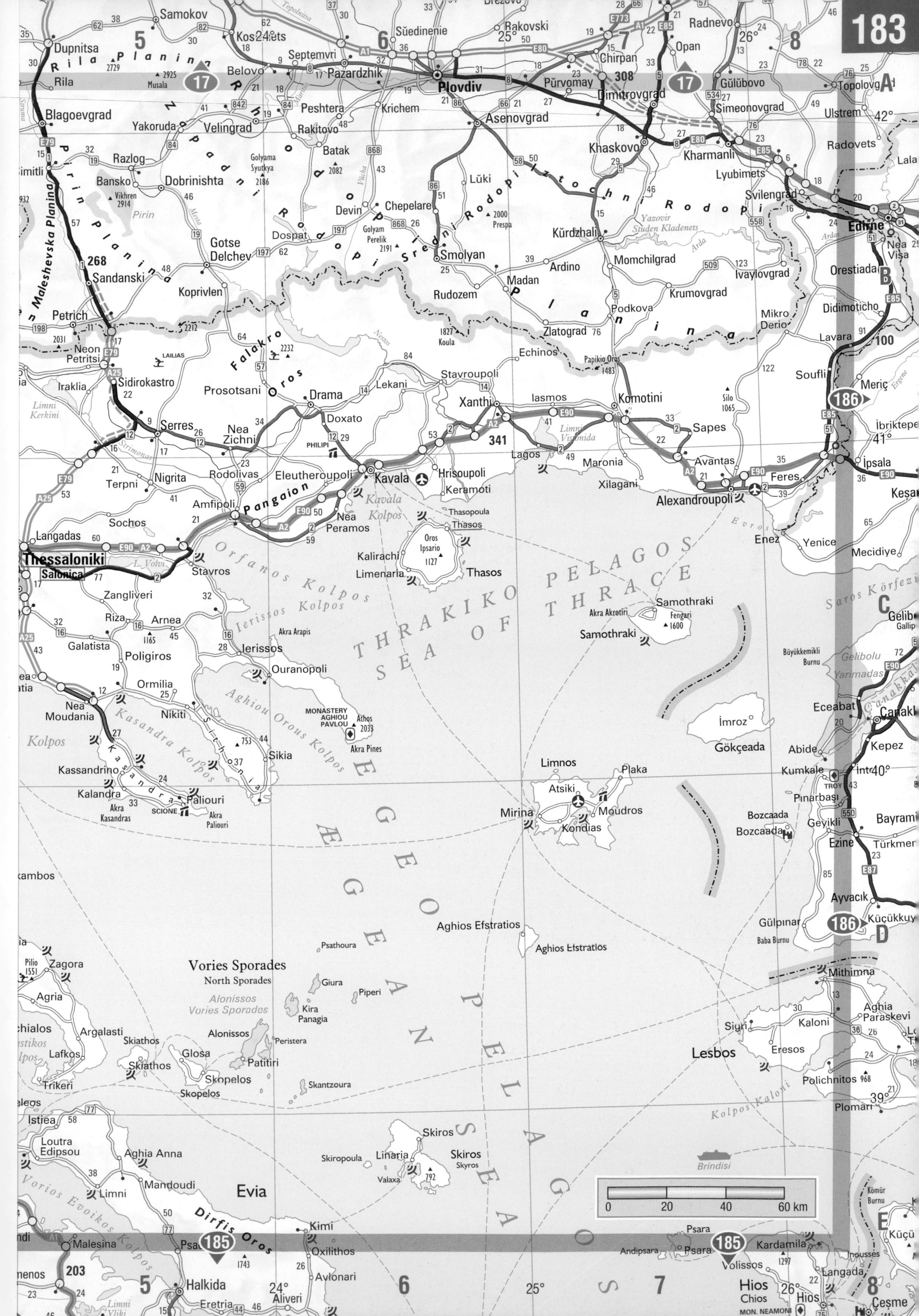
Samokov
Dupnitsa
Rila Planina
Rila
Musala
Blagoevgrad
Yakoruda
Velingrad
Razlog
Bansko
Dobrinishta
Pirin Planina
Maleshevska Planina
Gotse Delchev
Sandanski
Petrich
Kostenets
Septemvri
Pazardzhik
Belovo
Peshtera
Rakitovo
Batak
Plovdiv
Krichem
Asenovgrad
Sŭedinenie
Rakovski
Chirpan
Radnevo
Opan
Pŭrvomay
Dimitrovgrad
Gŭlŭbovo
Topolovgrad
Simeonovgrad
Khaskovo
Kharmanli
Lyubimets
Svilengrad
Ulstrem
Radovets
Edirne
Zapadni Rhodopi
Iztochni Rodopi
Sredni Rodopi
Rodopi Planina
Lŭki
Chepelare
Devin
Dospat
Smolyan
Rudozem
Madan
Ardino
Kŭrdzhali
Momchilgrad
Krumovgrad
Ivaylovgrad
Podkova
Zlatograd
Yazovir Studen Kladenets
Koprivlen
Neon Petritsi
Iraklia
Sidirokastro
Prosotsani
Falakro Oros
Drama
Doxato
Serres
Nea Zichni
Nigrita
Terpni
Rodolivas
Eleutheroupoli
Kavala
Hrisoupoli
Keramoti
Amfipoli
Pangaion
Nea Peramos
Sochos
Langadas
Thessaloniki
Salonica
Stavros
Lekani
Stavroupoli
Echinos
Xanthi
Iasmos
Komotini
Lagos
Maroniá
Sapes
Avantas
Xilagani
Alexandroupoli
Feres
Orestiada
Didimoticho
Mikro Derio
Soufli
Lavara
Meriç
İpsala
Keşan
Enez
Yenice
Mecidiye
Thasos
Limenaria
Kalirachi
Thasopoula
Orfanos Kolpos
Ierissos Kolpos
Thrakiko Pelagos
Sea of Thrace
Samothraki
Saros Körfezi
Zangliveri
Riza
Arnea
Galatista
Poligiros
Ierissos
Ouranopoli
Ormilia
Nea Moudania
Nikiti
Sithonia
Kassandra
Kassandrino
Kalandra
Paliouri
Sikia
Athos
Akra Pines
Aghiou Orous Kolpos
Kasandra Kolpos
Limnos
Mirina
Moudros
Kondias
Atsiki
Plaka
İmroz
Gökçeada
Eceabat
Çanakkale
Kepez
Kumkale
Troy
Bozcaada
Ezine
Bayramiç
Ayvacık
Gülpınar
Aghios Efstratios
Psathoura
Vories Sporades
North Sporades
Alonissos
Skiathos
Skopelos
Glosa
Patitiri
Skantzoura
Lesbos
Mithimna
Kaloni
Sigri
Eresos
Polichnitos
Plomari
Kolpos Kaloni
Istiea
Loutra Edipsou
Aghia Anna
Limni
Mandoudi
Evia
Dirfis Oros
Kimi
Oxilithos
Avlonari
Halkida
Eretria
Aliveri
Skiros
Linaria
Skiropoula
Aegean Sea
Psara
Andipsara
Volissos
Kardamila
Hios
Chios
Langada
Çeşme
0 20 40 60 km

Aghios Petros
Meganisi
Lepenou
Agrinio
Astakos
Kastos
Akra Doukaton
Arkoudi
Fiskardo
Kioni
Ithaki
Ithaca
Kefalonia
Cephalonia
Asos
Sami
Lixouri
Argostoli
Ainos
1628 Ainos Oros
Poros
Skala
Akra Mounta
Etoliko
Mesologi
Neo Chori
Oxia
Limni Trichonida
Evinos
Artotina
Lidoriki
Nafpaktos
Antirio
Patra
Patras
Patraikos Kolpos
Akra Papas
Vrakneika
Kato Achaia
Oros Giona 2510
Amfiklia
Atalandi
Males
Parnassos
Parnassos 2457
Delphi
Arachova
Amfissa
Itea
Desfina
Orhomenos
Livadia
Mon. Osiou Louka
Galaxidi
Elikonos 1748
Vaghia
Egio
Korinthiakos Kolpos
Gulf of Corinth
Domvena
Erithres
Vilia
Egosthena
Derveni
Xilokastro
Perachora
Loutraki
Kiato
Kalavrita
Goura
2376 Killini
Korinthos
Corinth
Aghio Theodori
2224 Erimanthos
Akra Skinari
Korithi
Volimes
Katastari
Zakynthos
Zante
Argasion
Keri
Kyllini
Lechena
Pinios
Aghia Triada
Gastouni
Amaliada
Lambia
Ladonas
Kandila
Nemea
Chiliomodi
Mycenae
Mikines
Sofikon
Langadia
Menalo 1980
Vitina
Dimitsana
Argos
Tirins
Ligourio
Epidavros
Nea Epidavros
Nafplio
Pirgos
Olympia
Katakolo
Epitalio
Krestena
Alphios
Tripoli
Achladokambos
Zacharo
Andritsena
Vasses
Megalopoli
Kiparissiakos Kolpos
Parallo Astros
Argolikos Kolpos
Kranidi
Ermioni
Portokhi
Spetses
Kalo Nero
Kiparissia
Strofades
Meligales
Messini
Kastorio
Parnonas Oros
Leonidio
Taygetos Oros
Filiatra
Gargaliani
Proti
Chora
Sparti
Sparta
Mistras
Kalamata
Geraki
Petalidi
Longa
Pilos
Mithoni
Sapienza
Skhiza
Koroni
Kardamili
Krokees
Vlachiotis
Molai
Githio
Messiniakos Kolpos
Monemvasia
Areopoli
Diros
Lakonikos Kolpos
Kotronas
Neapoli
Elafónisos
Vathia
Akra Tenaro
Akra Malea
Aghia Pelagia
Potamos
Kythira
Cerigo
Akra Kapelo
IONIO PELAGOS
IONION SEA
Pori
Potamos
0 20 40 60 km
38°
37°
36°
35°
21°
22°
23°
A
B
C
D
1
2
3
4
182
203
148
215
244
201

Dirfis Oros
Psachna
Kimi
Oxilithos
Avlonari
Halkida
Eretria
Aliveri
Evia
Notios Evoikos Kolpos
Thiva
Thebes
Skala Oropou
Almiropotamos
Nea Stira
Stira
Ochi Oros
Karistos
Kavo Doro
Parnitha
Marathonas
Mandra
Acharnes
Kiffisia
Nea Makri
Rafina
Elefsina
ATHINA
ATHENS
Megalonisos
Pireas
Piraeus
Glifada
Markopoulo
Keratea
Lavrio
Sounio
Akra Suonio
Salamina
Salamis
Egina
Egina
APHEA
Saronikos Kolpos
Methana
Poros
Galatas
Hydra
Aghios Georgios
Kea
Giaros
Andros
Gavrio
Paliaopoli
Ormos
Tinos
Panormos
Kiklades
Cyclades
Syros
Ano Siros
Ermoupoli
Kithnos
Driopida
Mykonos
Mikonos
Tragonhsi
Htapodia
DILOS
Rinia
Dilos
Serifos
Naxos
Koronos
Naoussa
Paros
Filotio
Marpisa
Antiparos
Despotiko
Donousa
MIRTOO PELAGOS
MIRTOO SEA
Kamares
Sifnos
Apolonia
Kastraki
Koufonisi
Schinousa
Keros
Amorgos
Iraklia
Katapola
Levitha
Kinaros
Liadi
Velopoula
Falkonera
Kimolos
Antimilos
Poliegos
Milos
Adamas
Karavia
Ios
Sikinos
Folegandros
Anidros
Astipalea
Ofidousa
Thirasia
Thira
Santorini
Anafi
Pachia
Makra
Hristiana
Psara
Andipsara
Kardamila
Volissos
Hios
Chios
MON. NEAMONI
Langada
Mesta
Akra Mesta
Pirgi
Nenita
Akra Oura
Inousses
Çeşme
Urla
Alaçati
Seferihisar
Mordoğar
Küçükbahçe
Akdağ
Venézia
Karlovasi
Marathokambos
Fourni
Armenistis
Melissa Oros
Aghios Kirikos
Ikaria
CHORA
Patmos
Sirna
Sofrana
Karavonisia
KRITIKO PELAGOS
SEA OF CRETE
Hamili
Dibounia
Antikythira
Kolpos Kissamos
Akra Spatha
Akra Vouxa
Kolpos Chanion
Chersonisos Akrotiri
Kasteli
Platanos
Chania
Souda
Ormos Almyrou
Kriti
Crete
Avgo
Dia
Lakki
Kandanos
Omalos
Lekva Oros
Samaria
Paleochora
Chora Sfakion
Vamos
Rethimno
Perama
Psiloritis Oros
Spili
Iraklio
Heraklion
KNOSSOS
Limenas Chersonisou
Archanes
Kastelli
Aghios Mironas
Malia
Neapoli
Elouda
LATO
Aghios Nikolaos
Akra Aghios Ioannis
Kolpos Mirabello
Dionisades
Akra Sideros
Elasa
Vai
Sitia
Palekastro
Akra Plaka
ZAKROS
Chandra
Tzermiado
Dikti Oros
Males
Ierapetra
Aghia Galini
Timbaki
PHAESTOS
Mires
Pirgos
Viannos
Paximadia
Matala
Achentrias
Kolpos Mesara
Akra Lithino
Gavdopoula
Gavdos
Gaidouronisi

Elkhovo
Bolyarovo
Topolovgrad
Simeonovgrad
Zvezdets
Tsarevo
Akhtopol
Malko Türnovo
Ulstrem
Rezovo
Kharmanli
Radovets
Kofçaz
Dereköy
Lyubimets
Lalapaşa
Yoğuntaş
Kayalıköy Barajı
İğneada Burnu
İğneada
Demirköy
Svilengrad
Süloğlu
Mahya Dağı
Kladenets
Hasköy
Kırklareli
Edirne
Kavaklı
Pınarhisar
Kıyıköy
Nea Visa
Ivaylovgrad
Orestiada
Havsa
Vize
Krumovgrad
Yıldız Dağları
Mikro Derio
Didimoticho
Kicasalih
Babaeski
Lüleburgaz
Ahmetbey
Saray
Safaalan
Karacaköy
Lavara
Pehlivanköy
Beyazköy
Kapaklı
Duru Gölü
Durusu
Uzunköprü
Büyükkarıştıran
Çerkezköy
Soufli
Hayrabolu
Sinekli
Meriç
Ulaş
Çatalca
Sarıyer
Beykoz
Muratlı
Çorlu
Silo
Sapes
Seymen
Kozyürük
Silivri
Beyoğlu
Üsküdar
İbriktepe
Avantas
Thrace
Büyükçekmece
İpsala
İnecik
Tekirdağ
Maramaraereğlisi
Feres
Yeşilköy
İSTANBUL
Alexandroupoli
Malkara
Barbaros
Keşan
Kumbağ
Kızıl Adalar
Kartal
Evros
Ballı
Işıklar Dağı
Marmara Denizi
Sea of Marmara
Enez
Yenice
Mecidiye
Mürefte
Saraylar
Yalova
Kavakköy
Şarköy
Marmara
Çınarcık
Saros Körfezi
Boz Burun
Türkeli
Armutlu
Bolayır
Kapı Dağı
Orhangazi
Gelibolu
Gallipoli
Paşalimanı
Karabiğa
Yeniköy Plajı
Gemlik Körfezi
Büyükkemikli Burnu
Erdek
Bandırma
Zeytinbağı
Gemlik
Çardak
Mudanya
Lapseki
Balıklıçeşme
Demirtaş
Gelibolu Yarimadası
Çanakkale Boğazı
Nilüfer
Umurbey
Kuş Gölü
Karacabey
Eceabat
Çanakkale
Biga
Sarıköy
Kuşcenneti
Bursa
İmroz
Ulubat Gölü
Uludağ
Gökçeada
Abide
Kepez
Çan
Gönen
Kumkale
İntepe
Kirazlı
Manyas
Mustafakemalpaşa
TROY
Etili
Yenice
Göbel
Pınarbaşı
Çaltılıbük
Bozcaada
Geyikli
Bayramiç
Hamdibey
Susurluk
Devecikonağı
Orhaneli
Ilıca
Ezine
Türkmenli
Evciler
Kalkım
Şamlı
Kaz Dağı
Balya
Büyükorhan
Kepsut
Durak
Ayvacık
Altınoluk
Güre
Edremit
Balıkesir
Karaman
Harmancık
Gülpınar
Küçükkuyu
Havran
Gökçeyazı
İvrindi
Dursunbey
Baba Burnu
Edremit Körfezi
Kireç
Gökçedağ
Burhaniye
Pamukçu
Gömeç
Korucu
Yağcılar
Mithimna
Ayvalık
Madra Dağı
Sarıbeyler
Savaştepe
Bigadiç
Küçükköy
Alaçam Dağları
Emet
Aghia Paraskevi
Sigri
Kaloni
Göçbeyli
Alacaatlı
Sındırgı
Caygören Barajı
Eresos
Loutropoli Thermis
Altınova
Soma
Bergama
Gelembe
Simav Dağları
Mitilini
Lesbos
Polichnitos
Kınık
Kırkağaç
Simav
Dikili
Kratigos
Plomari
Zeytindağ
Demirci
Yarbasan
Çandarlı
Çandarlı Körfezi
Yunt Dağı
Süleymanlı
Akhisar
Brindisi
Gördes
Yeniköy
Aslan Burnu
Yenifoça
Aliağa
Saruhanlı
Selendi
Köprübaşı
Kömür Burnu
Karaburun
Muradiye
Gölmarmara
Borlu
Foça
Gediz
Manisa
Marmara Gölü
Demirköprü Barajı
Gökçeören
Güre
Kardamila
Küçükbahçe
Akdağ
Menemen
Sipil Dağı
Karataş
İzmir Körfezi
Inousses
Mordoğan
Sasalli
Ahmetli
Hios
Chios
Langada
Turgutlu
Salihli
Kula
İZMİR
Kemalpaşa
Ahmetler
Çeşme
Urla
Buca
Armutlu
Boz Dağlar
Yeşilyurt
Eşme
Balçova
Alaşehir
Alaçatı
Ödemiş
Kiraz
Nenita
Ayrancılar
Bayındır
Pirgi
Sarıgöl

4
5
6
7
30°
31°
32°
42°
41°
40°
39°
A
B
C
D
0
20
40
60 km
Sinop
Boğazı
Cide
Kurucaşile
Amasra
Bartin
Ovacuma
Zonguldak
Kozlu
Çaycuma
Safranbolu
Ereğli
Devrek
Karabük
Şile
Ağva
Kefken
Pazarbaşi Burnu
Kandıra
Kaynarca
Karasu
Akçakoca
Teke
Akçaova
Kocaali
Ömerli Baraji
Yığılca
Yedigöller
Mengen
Eskipazar
Ferizli
Söğütlu
Gümüşova
Düzce
Bolu Dağları
Gerede
Çerkeş
Hereke
Kocaeli
İzmit
Körfez
Hendek
Sakarya
Bolu
Gebze
Gölcük
Karamürsel
Akyazı
Kel Tepe
Camlıdere
Soğuksu
Kızılcahamam
Boyalıca
Pamukova
Geyve
Mudurnu
Kapıorman Dağları
İznik Gölü
İznik
Taraklı
Seben
Yazıca
Göynük
Dedeler
Avdan Dağı
Osmaneli
Yenişehir
Vezirhan
Gölpazarı
Nallıhan
Beypazarı
Güdül
Çağa
Bilecik
Çayırhan
Ayaş
İnegöl
Kurşunlu
Inhisar
Sarıcakaya
Mihalgazi
Söğüt
Pazaryeri
Dinek
Sariyar Baraji
Sincan
ANKARA
Tahtaköprü
Bozüyük
Sündiken Dağları
Mihalıççık
Sarıoba
Muttalip
Ağapınar
Bozan
Domaniç
İnönü
Eskişehir
Alpu
Porsuk
Tunçbilek
Hamidiye
Dümerek
Polatlı
Oyaca
Seyitömer
Sabuncu
Kaymaz
Tavşanlı
Seyitgazi
Mahmudiye
Sivrihisar
Haymana
Kütahya
Çiftelerr
Günyüzü
Örencik
Kırka
Gulçayır
Çakmak
Yenice
Çavdarhisar
Han
Aykirikçi
Sinanlı
Altıntaş
İhsaniye
Emirdağ
Çeltik
Saraycık
Bayat
Gediz
Murat Dağı
Başkomutan
Kemerkaya
Sülüklü
Yeniceoba
Abide
Dumlupınar
İscehisar
Emir Dağları
Yunak
Banaz
Düzağac
Uşak
Sincanlı
Afyon
Çobanlar
Bolvadin
Kızılkuyu
Ahat
Ahır Dağı
Eber Gölü
Cihanbeyli
Akarca
Hocalar
Çay
Sultandağı
Karacaören
Sivaslı
Sandıklı
Şuhut
Akşehir Gölü
Tuzlukçu
Atlantı
Ulubey
Çatma Dağı
Banaz
Akşehir
Ilgın
Karahallı
Çivril
Işıklı
Kumdanlı
Kumalar Dağı
Haydarlı
Karaadilli
Yalvaç
Argıthanı
Sarayönü
Kadınhanı
Kızılören
TÜRKİYE
189
23

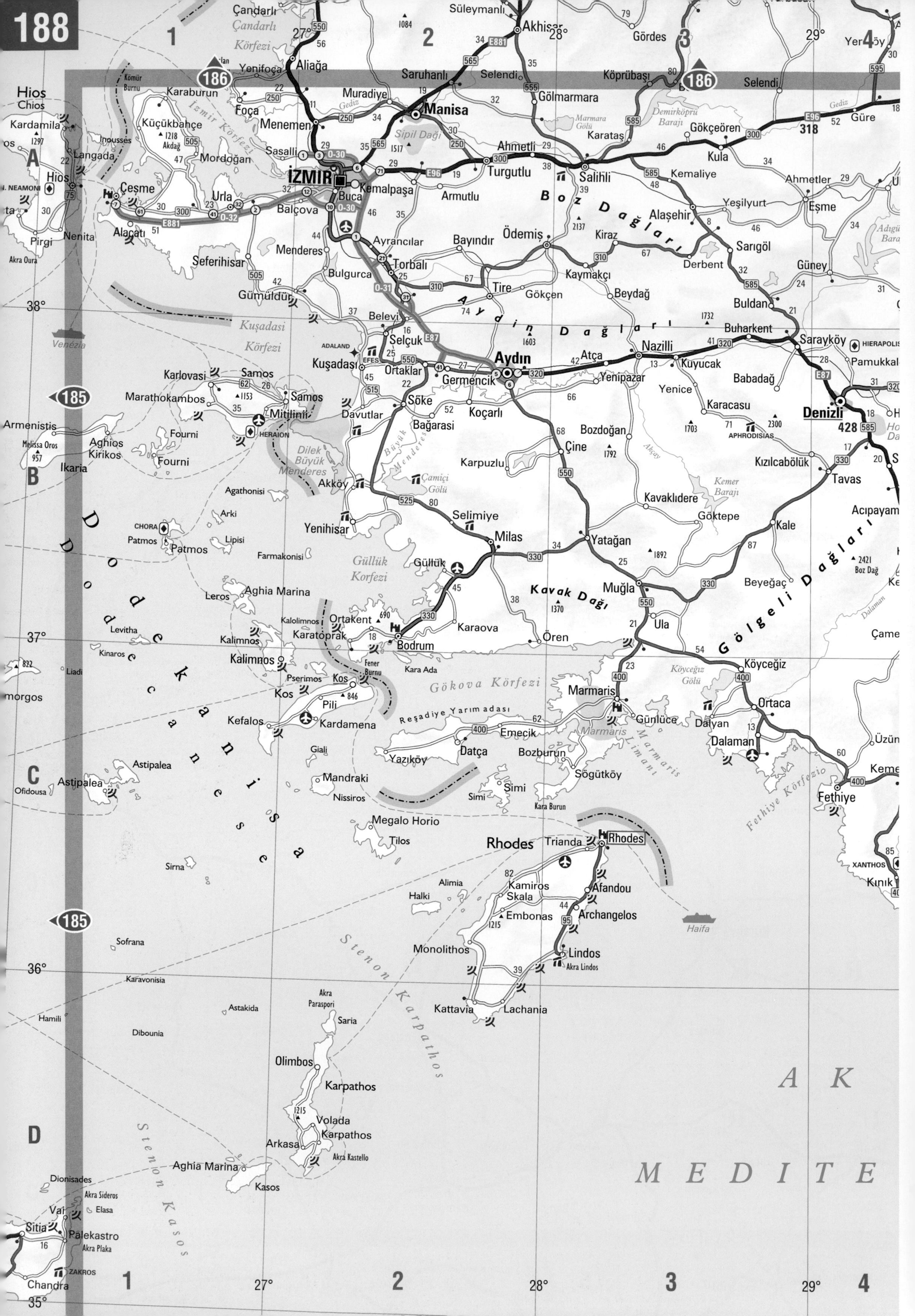
1
2
3
4
A
B
C
D
27°
28°
29°
38°
37°
36°
35°
186
185
Çandarlı
Çandarlı Körfezi
Aliağa
Süleymanlı
Akhisar
Gördes
Yenifoça
Kömür Burnu
Karaburun
Foça
Menemen
Muradiye
Manisa
Saruhanlı
Selendi
Gölmarmara
Marmara Gölü
Köprübaşı
Demirköprü Barajı
Gökçeören
Selendi
Güre
Kula
Karataş
Salihli
Ahmetli
Turgutlu
Sipil Dağı
Hios
Chios
Kardamila
Inousses
Küçükbahçe
Akdağ
Mordoğan
Langada
İzmir Körfezi
Sasalli
İZMIR
Kemalpaşa
Buca
Balçova
Armutlu
Hios
N. NEAMONI
Çeşme
Urla
Alaçatı
Pirgi
Nenita
Akra Oura
Seferihisar
Menderes
Ayrancılar
Torbalı
Bayındır
Ödemiş
Boz Dağları
Alaşehir
Kemaliye
Yeşilyurt
Eşme
Ahmetler
Sarıgöl
Derbent
Kiraz
Kaymakçı
Beydağ
Güney
Buldan
Bulgurca
Gümüldür
Tire
Gökçen
Aydın Dağları
Buharkent
Sarayköy
HIERAPOLIS
Pamukkale
Kuşadası
Kuşadası Körfezi
Venézia
ADALAND
Selçuk
EFES
Belevi
Kuşadası
Ortaklar
Germencik
Aydın
Atça
Nazilli
Kuyucak
Yenipazar
Babadağ
Denizli
Karlovasi
Samos
Marathokambos
Mitilinii
HERAION
Davutlar
Söke
Koçarlı
Bağarasi
Yenice
Karacasu
APHRODISIAS
Armenistis
Melissa Oros
Aghios Kirikos
Fourni
Ikaria
Dilek Büyük Menderes
Büyük Menderes
Akköy
Karpuzlu
Çamiçi Gölü
Bozdoğan
Çine
Kızılcabölük
Tavas
Kemer Barajı
Agathonisi
Arki
CHORA
Patmos
Lipisi
Farmakonisi
Yenihisar
Selimiye
Milas
Kavaklıdere
Göktepe
Acıpayam
Kale
Yatağan
Güllük Körfezi
Güllük
Muğla
Beyeğaç
Boz Dağ
Gölgeli Dağları
Kavak Dağı
Dodekanisa
Dodecanese
Leros
Aghia Marina
Levitha
Kalolimnos
Ortakent
Karatoprak
Bodrum
Karaova
Ören
Ula
Kalimnos
Kinaros
Liadi
Amorgos
Fener Burnu
Kara Ada
Pserimos
Kos
Pili
Kardamena
Kefalos
Gökova Körfezi
Köyceğiz
Köyceğiz Gölü
Marmaris
Ortaca
Reşadiye Yarımadası
Emecik
Günlüce
Dalyan
Dalaman
Giali
Yazıköy
Datça
Bozburun
Marmaris Limanı
Söğütköy
Astipalea
Ofidousa
Mandraki
Nissiros
Simi
Kara Burun
Fethiye
Fethiye Körfezi
Üzümlü
Kemer
Megalo Horio
Tilos
Sirna
Rhodes
Trianda
XANTHOS
Kınık
Alimia
Halki
Kamiros Skala
Afandou
Embonas
Archangelos
Haifa
Monolithos
Lindos
Akra Lindos
Sofrana
Stenon Karpathos
Karavonisia
Kattavia
Lachania
Astakida
Akra Paraspori
Saria
Hamili
Dibounia
Olimbos
Karpathos
Volada
Arkasa
Akra Kastello
Stenon Kasos
Aghia Marina
Kasos
Dionisades
Akra Sideros
Vai
Elasa
Sitia
Palekastro
Akra Plaka
ZAKROS
Chandra
AK
MEDITE

Uşak
Afyon
Bolvadin
Çay
Sandıklı
Şuhut
Akşehir
Ilgın
Konya
Dinar
Burdur
Isparta
Eğridir
Beyşehir
Seydişehir
Antalya
Manavgat
Alanya
Gazipaşa
Kemer
Finike
Kaş
Kalkan
Korkuteli
Elmalı
Serik
Akseki
Bozkır
Kızılören
Sarayönü
Kadınhanı
Yalvaç
Şarkikaraağaç
Gelendost
Uluborlu
Senirkent
Keçiborlu
Bucak
Ağlasun
Tefenni
Gölhisar
Çivril
Sivaslı
Banaz
Sultandağı
Argıthanı
Doğanhisar
Hüyük
Taşkent
Hadım
Gündoğmuş
Kumluca
Kale
Kemerkaya
Çobanlar
Emir Dağları
Ahır Dağı
Kumalar Dağı
Barla Dağı
Söğüt Dağı
Katrancı Dağı
Bey Dağları
Ak Dağları
Beyşehir Gölü
Eğirdir Gölü
Burdur Gölü
Akşehir Gölü
Köprülü Kanyon
Olimpos-Beydağları
Antalya Körfezi
Finike Körfezi
D E N İ Z
R R A N E A N S E A
0 20 40 60 km
30°
31°
32°
36°
37°
38°
35°
A
B
C
D
4
5
6
7

1
24°
2
23°
3
22°
4
21°
5
20°
6
66°30'
ARCTIC CIRCLE
A
Straumnes
Horn
Ísafjarðardjúp
Drangajökull
925
Bolungarvík
Suðureyri
Ísafjörður
Unaðsdalur
Flateyri
Súðavík
Ögur
Munaðarnes
Árnes
66°
Þingeyri
101
Glámа
152
920
Sjónfríð
Arnarfjörður
Hrafnseyri
Selárdalur
Bíldudalur
Tálknafjörður
Patreksfjörður
Ásgarður
Bjargtangar
Brjánslækur
B
35
Hólmavík
Drangsnes
89
24
22
21
Reykhólar
Ospakseyri
92
Saurbær
Breiðafjörður
48
Skarð
Staðarfell
Búðardalur
34
Borðeyri
10
Stykkishólmur
65°
Hellissandur
Öndverðarnes
Grundarfjörður
Ólafsvík
Snæfellsjökull
69
45
17
24
11
34
25
Kolbeinsstaðir
Hellnar
42
48
Faxaflói
Borgarnes
39
Varmaland
34
Hvítá
Reykholt
Húsafell
Hvanneyri
67
28
Borgarfjörður
Saurbær
15
Akranes
26
13
Þingvellir
Þingvellir
32
9
Mosfellsbær
Reykjavík
Kópavogur
Hafnarfjörður
22
29
31
38
Þingvallavatn
Keflavík
20
23
Njarðvík
Hafnir
13
60
Grindavík
Reykjanes
Þorlákshöfn
Hveragerði
23
11
33
Eyrarbakki
Stokkseyri
Selfoss
19
Húnaflói
Skagaströnd
Hrun
112
Skagafjörður
Hvammur
46
Sauðarkrókur
Tjörn
Blönduós
Blanda
53
Varmahlíð
387
Hvammstangi
88
Laugarbakki
Goðdalir
Blöndulón
Héraðsvötn
Eiríksjökull
1675
Langjökull
Hvítárvatn
Siglufjörður
Hofsós
58
25
17
Hólar
Geysir
43
Laugarvatn
34
35
Reykholt
Flúðir
17
Laugarás
49
20
18
60
Hekla
1481
Þjórsá
15
Hella
20
Hvolsvöllur
Þykkvibær
Mýrdals-
jökull
Eyjafjallajökull
1666
Holt
Landeyjahöfn
140
Vestmannaeyjar
Heimaey
Dyrhólaey
Vík
Surtsey
0
20
40
60 km
C
D
64°
63°
Í
I

ARCTIC CIRCLE
Grímsey
Raufarhöfn
Kópasker
Öxarfjörður
Svalbarð
Þórshöfn
Fontur
Bakkaflói
Digranes
Bakkafjörður
Vopnafjörður
Ólafsfjörður
Dalvík
Hauganes
Grenivík
Björg
Húsavík
Laxamýri
Asbygri
Skjálfandi
Laugar
Reykjahlíð
Mývatn
Grímsstaðir
Akureyri
Hrafnagil
Saurbær
Mýri
Bláfjall
Möðrudalur
Ódáðahraun
Herðubreið
Húsey
Sleðbrjótur
Bakkagerði
Glettinganes
Egilsstaðir
Seyðisfjörður
Neskaupstaður
Eskifjörður
Hallormsstaður
Reyðarfjörður
Valþjofsstaður
Fáskrúðsfjörður
Stöðvarfjörður
Breiðdalsvík
Berufjörður
Djúpivogur
Trölladyngja
Hofsjökull
ICELAND
Snæfell
Vatnajökull
Tórshavn
Hirtshals
Nesjahverfi
Höfn
Stokksnes
Þórisvatn
Gerði
LAKAGIGAR
Hvannadalshnúkur
Skaftafell
Skeiðarársandur
Ingólfshöfði
Búland
Kirkjubæjarklaustur
Langholt

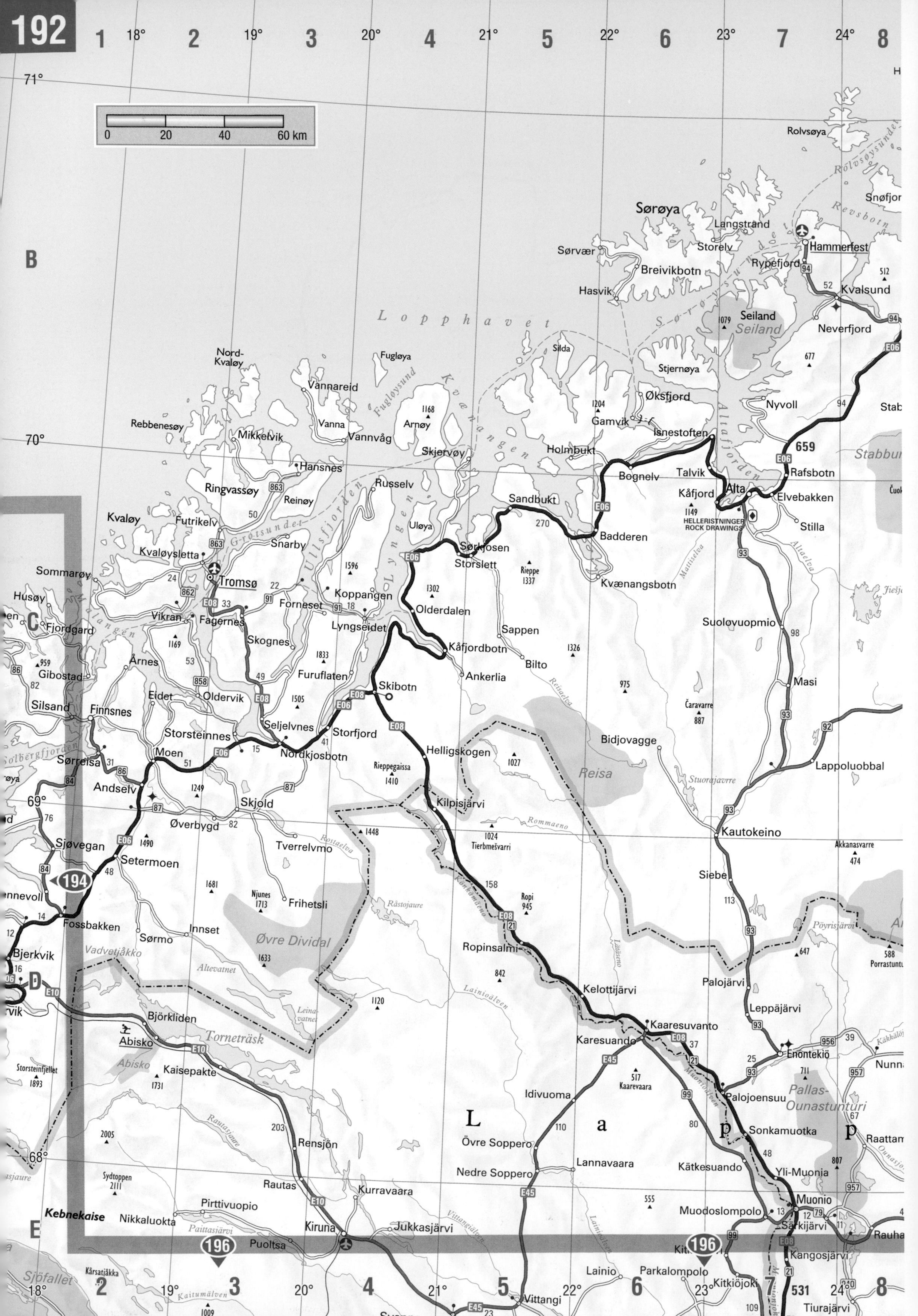

Lopphavet
Sørøya
Hammerfest
Seiland
Alta
Tromsø
Kvaløya
Ringvassøy
Lyngen
Kvænangen
Altafjorden
Kautokeino
Reisa
Øvre Dividal
Torneträsk
Abisko
Kiruna
Kebnekaise
Lapp
Pallas-Ounastunturi
Enontekiö
Karesuando
Kaaresuvanto
Muonio
Kilpisjärvi
Skibotn
Finnsnes
Setermoen
Bjerkvik
Vittangi
HELLERISTNINGER ROCK DRAWINGS

194
196
196

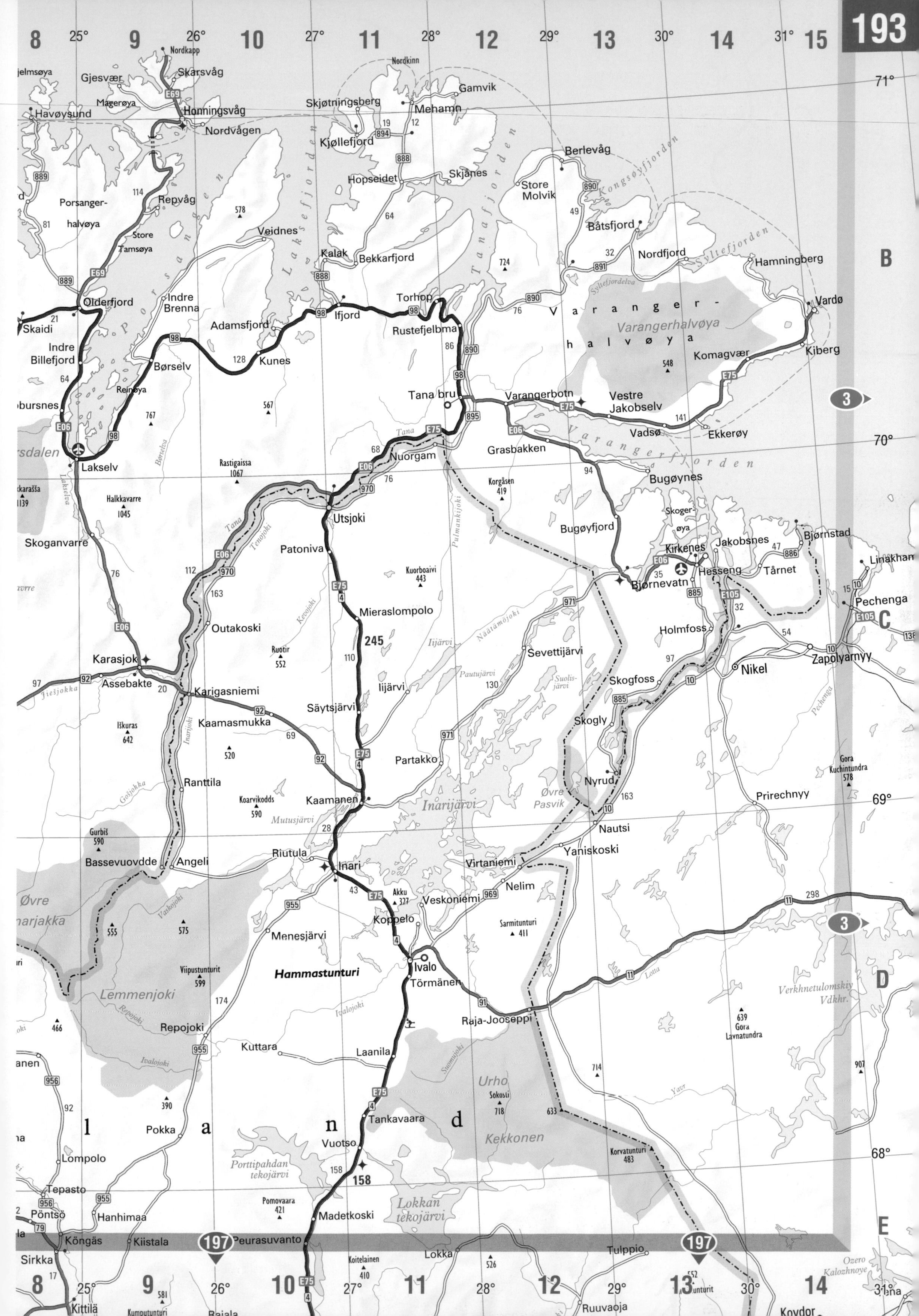

Nordkapp
Skarsvåg
Gjesvær
Magerøya
Honningsvåg
Havøysund
Nordvågen
Nordkinn
Gamvik
Mehamn
Skjøtningsberg
Kjøllefjord
Berlevåg
Hopseidet
Skjånes
Store Molvik
Båtsfjord
Nordfjord
Hamningberg
Porsanger-halvøya
Repvåg
Store Tamsøya
Veidnes
Kalak
Bekkarfjord
Olderfjord
Indre Brenna
Torhop
Ifjord
Rustefjelbma
Vardø
Varanger-halvøya
Varangerhalvøya
Komagvær
Kiberg
Skaidi
Indre Billefjord
Adamsfjord
Kunes
Børselv
Reinøya
Tana bru
Varangerbotn
Vestre Jakobselv
Vadsø
Ekkerøy
Lakselv
Nuorgam
Grasbakken
Varangerfjorden
Bugøynes
Rastigaissa 1067
Korgåsen 419
Halkkavarre 1045
Utsjoki
Skogerøya
Bugøyfjord
Bjørnstad
Skoganvarre
Patoniva
Kirkenes
Jakobsnes
Tårnet
Linakhamari
Hesseng
Bjørnevatn
Kuorboaivi 443
Pechenga
Mieraslompolo
Holmfoss
Outakoski
Sevettijärvi
Zapolyarnyy
Nikel
Karasjok
Assebakte
Ruotir 552
Skogfoss
Karigasniemi
Iijärvi
Säytsjärvi
Kaamasmukka
Skogly
Iškuras 642
Partakko
Gora Kuchintundra 578
Nyrud
Ranttila
Kaamanen
Koarvikodds 590
Inarijärvi
Øvre Pasvik
Prirechnyy
Mutusjärvi
Gurbiš 590
Nautsi
Yaniskoski
Bassevuovdde
Angeli
Riutula
Inari
Virtaniemi
Nelim
Veskoniemi
Akku 327
Øvre Anarjakka
Koppelo
Sarmitunturi 411
Menesjärvi
Ivalo
Hammastunturi
Viipustunturit 599
Törmänen
Lemmenjoki
Verkhnetulomskiy Vdkhr.
Raja-Jooseppi
Repojoki
Gora Lavnatundra 639
Kuttara
Laanila
Urho Kekkonen
Sokosti 718
Pokka
Tankavaara
Lompolo
Vuotso
Korvatunturi 483
Porttipahdan tekojärvi
Tepasto
Pomovaara 421
Pöntsö
Hanhimaa
Madetkoski
Lokkan tekojärvi
Köngäs
Kiistala
Peurasuvanto
Sirkka
Lokka
Tulppio
Koitelainen 410
Kittilä
Ruuvaoja
Kovdor
Ozero Kalozhnoye
Finland

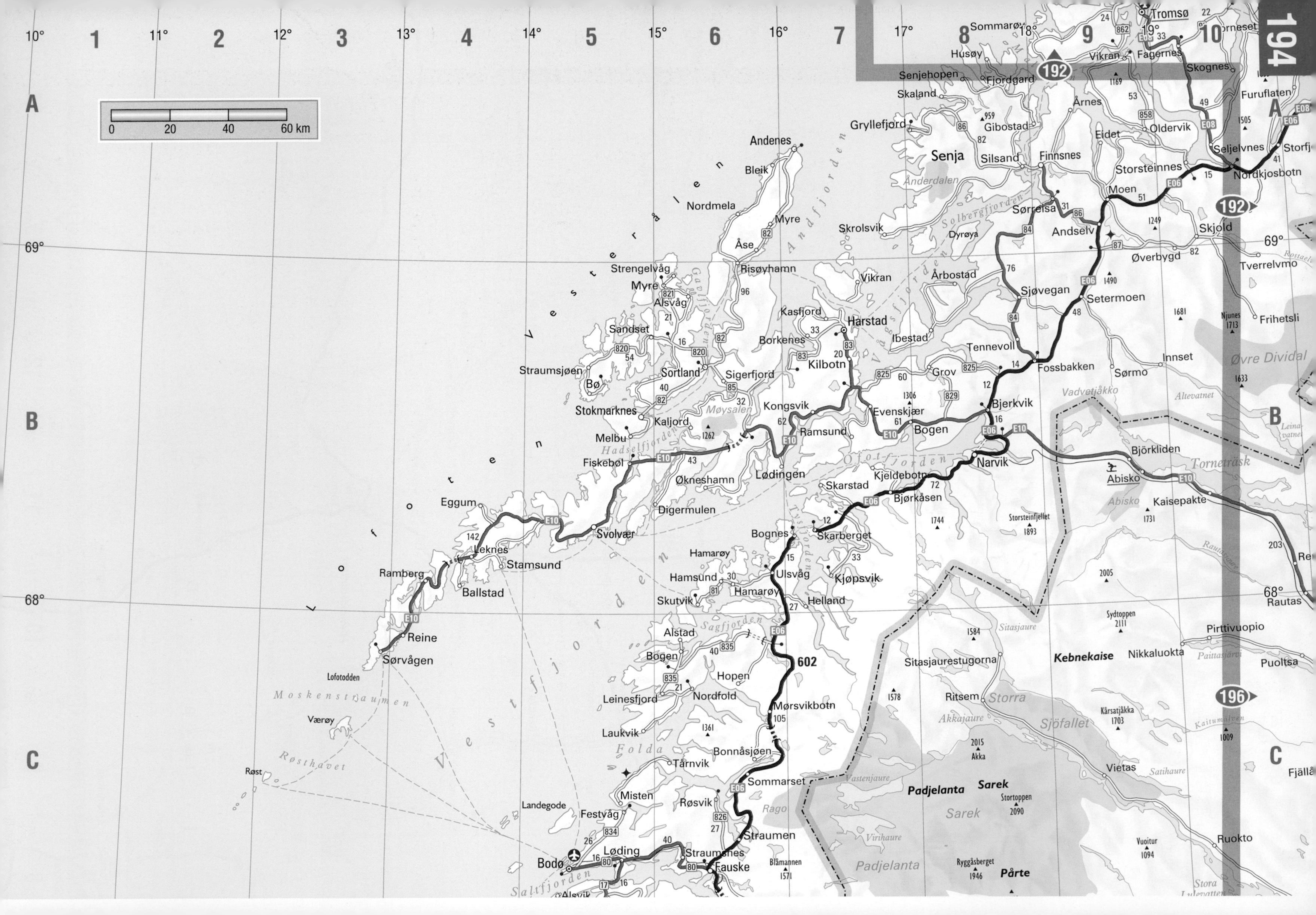
0 20 40 60 km
Tromsø
Vikran
Fagernes
Skognes
Sommarøy
Husøy
Senjehopen
Fjordgard
Skaland
Gryllefjord
Senja
Gibostad
Silsand
Finnsnes
Årnes
Eidet
Oldervik
Storsteinnes
Seljelvnes
Nordkjosbotn
Furuflaten
Moen
Sørreisa
Andselv
Skjold
Øverbygd
Tverrelvmo
Frihetsli
Dyrøya
Skrolsvik
Andenes
Bleik
Nordmela
Myre
Åse
Risøyhamn
Andfjorden
Vesterålen
Strengelvåg
Alsvåg
Sandset
Straumsjøen
Bø
Sortland
Sigerfjord
Stokmarknes
Kaljord
Melbu
Møysalen
Hadselfjorden
Gavlfjorden
Fiskebøl
Vikran
Årbostad
Ibestad
Kasfjord
Harstad
Borkenes
Kilbotn
Kongsvik
Evenskjær
Bogen
Ramsund
Lødingen
Øksneshamn
Digermulen
Tennevoll
Sjøvegan
Setermoen
Fossbakken
Grov
Bjerkvik
Sørmo
Innset
Øvre Dividal
Vadvetjåkko
Altevatnet
Narvik
Ofotfjorden
Kjeldebotn
Skarstad
Bjørkåsen
Bjørkliden
Abisko
Torneträsk
Kaisepakte
Lofoten
Eggum
Svolvær
Leknes
Stamsund
Ramberg
Ballstad
Reine
Sørvågen
Lofotodden
Moskenstraumen
Værøy
Røsthavet
Røst
Vestfjorden
Bognes
Skarberget
Tysfjorden
Hamarøy
Ulsvåg
Kjøpsvik
Hamsund
Skutvik
Helland
Alstad
Sagfjorden
Bogen
Leinesfjord
Nordfold
Hopen
602
Mørsvikbotn
Laukvik
Folda
Bonnåsjøen
Tårnvik
Sommarset
Misten
Landegode
Festvåg
Røsvik
Rago
Straumen
Bodø
Løding
Straumsnes
Fauske
Saltfjorden
Alsvik
Blåmannen 1571
Storsteinfjellet 1893
Sitasjaure
Sitasjaurestugorna
Ritsem
Storra Sjöfallet
Akkajaure
Akka
Vastenjaure
Padjelanta
Sarek
Stortoppen 2090
Ryggåsberget 1946
Pårte
Virihaure
Kebnekaise
Sydtoppen 2111
Nikkaluokta
Paittasjärvi
Pirttivuopio
Puoltsa
Kårsatjåkka 1703
Vietas
Satihaure
Kaitumälven
Vuoitur 1094
Ruokto
Stora Lulevatten
Rautas
Fjällå
Leinavatnet
Rostaelv
Njunes 1713
192
196
E06
E08
E10
A
B
C
1
2
3
4
5
6
7
8
9
10
10°
11°
12°
13°
14°
15°
16°
17°
18°
19°
68°
69°

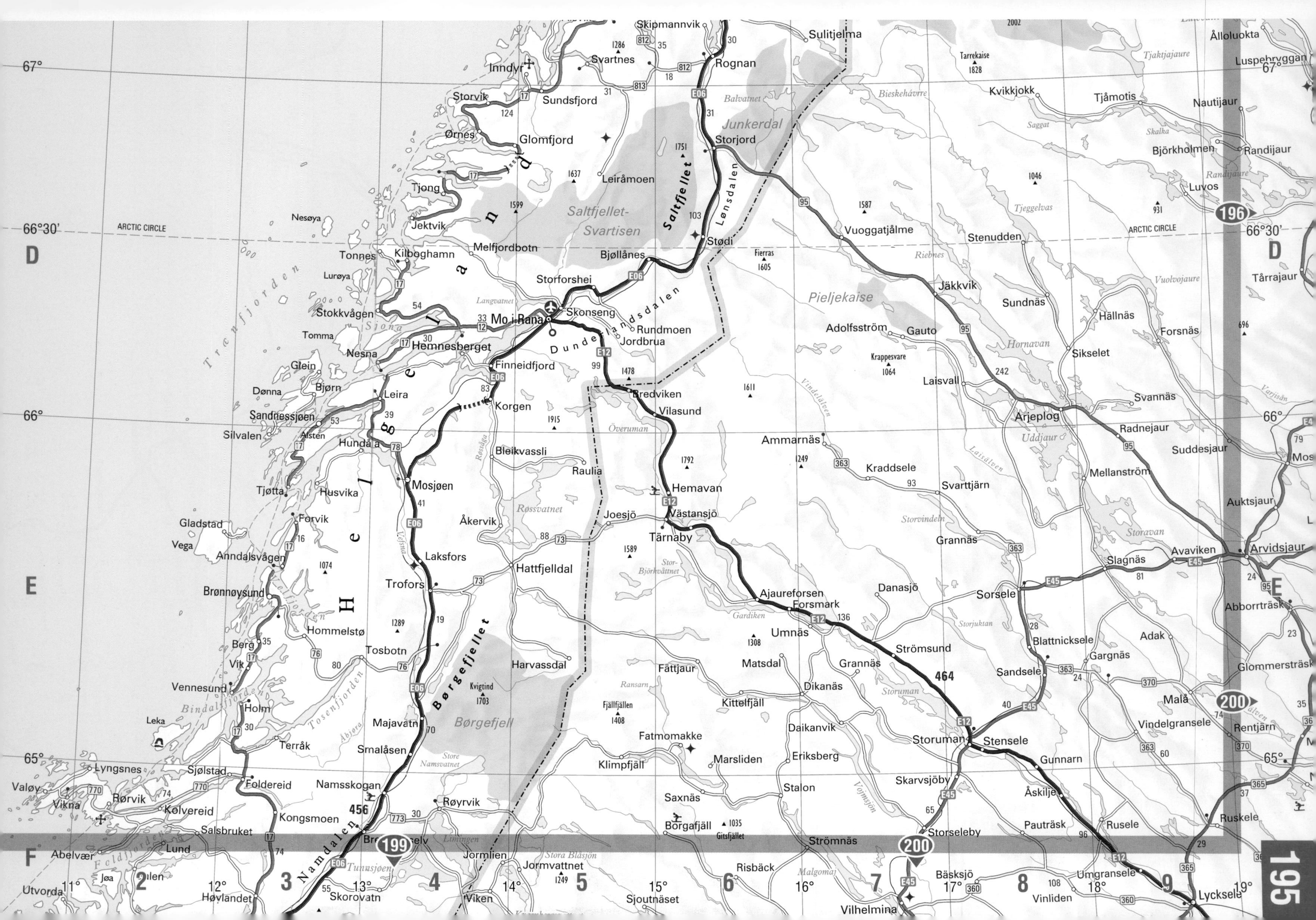
Helgeland
Saltfjellet
Saltfjellet-Svartisen
Junkerdal
Lønsdalen
Dunderlandsdalen
Børgefjellet
Børgefjell
Namdalen
Pieljekaise
ARCTIC CIRCLE
Inndyr
Sundsfjord
Svartnes
Skipmannvik
Rognan
Storjord
Stødi
Sulitjelma
Storvik
Glomfjord
Ørnes
Tjong
Jektvik
Kilboghamn
Tonnes
Melfjordbotn
Storforshei
Bjøllånes
Leiråmoen
Skonseng
Rundmoen
Jordbrua
Mo i Rana
Hemnesberget
Finneidfjord
Korgen
Bleikvassli
Raulia
Nesna
Leira
Stokkvågen
Lurøya
Nesøya
Tomma
Hundåla
Husvika
Mosjøen
Laksfors
Trofors
Åkervik
Hattfjelldal
Harvassdal
Sandnessjøen
Silvalen
Dønna
Tjøtta
Forvik
Alsten
Bjørn
Glein
Hommelstø
Tosbotn
Majavatn
Smalåsen
Namsskogan
Kongsmoen
Terråk
Brønnøysund
Berg
Vik
Holm
Vennesund
Gladstad
Vega
Anndalsvågen
Foldereid
Sjølstad
Salsbruket
Kolvereid
Lund
Rørvik
Vikna
Lyngsnes
Leka
Abelvær
Valøy
Utvorda
Jøa
Høylandet
Skorovatn
Røyrvik
Jormlien
Jormvattnet
Viken
Bredviken
Vilasund
Hemavan
Västansjö
Tärnaby
Joesjö
Fättjaur
Fatmomakke
Klimpfjäll
Saxnäs
Borgafjäll
Sjoutnäset
Marsliden
Risbäck
Kittelfjäll
Matsdal
Umnäs
Ajaureforsen
Forsmark
Dikanäs
Daikanvik
Eriksberg
Stalon
Strömnäs
Vilhelmina
Ammarnäs
Kraddsele
Svarttjärn
Grannäs
Danasjö
Strömsund
Storuman
Stensele
Skarvsjöby
Storseleby
Bäcksjö
Sorsele
Sandsele
Blattnicksele
Gunnarn
Åskilje
Pauträsk
Vinliden
Umgransele
Ruselse
Gargnäs
Slagnäs
Mellanström
Adak
Vindelgransele
Malå
Rentjärn
Abborrträsk
Glommersträsk
Arvidsjaur
Auktsjaur
Avaviken
Ruskele
Lycksele
Adolfsström
Gauto
Laisvall
Jäkkvik
Vuoggatjålme
Stenudden
Sundnäs
Arjeplog
Hällnäs
Sikselet
Svannäs
Radnejaur
Suddesjaur
Forsnäs
Luvos
Björkholmen
Tjåmotis
Kvikkjokk
Nautijaur
Randijaur
Ålloluokta
Tårrajaur
Uddjaur
Hornavan
Storavan
Vojmsjön
Malgomaj
Stora Blåsjön
Tunnsjøen
Vefsna
Røssvatnet
Tosenfjorden
Bindalsfjorden
Foldafjorden
Trænfjorden
Langvatnet
Kvigtind 1703
Krappesvare 1064
Tarrekaise 1828
Fierras 1605
Fjällfjällen 1408
Gitsfjället 1035
D
E
F
67°
66°30'
66°
65°
11°
12°
13°
14°
15°
16°
17°
18°
19°
196
199
200
456
464

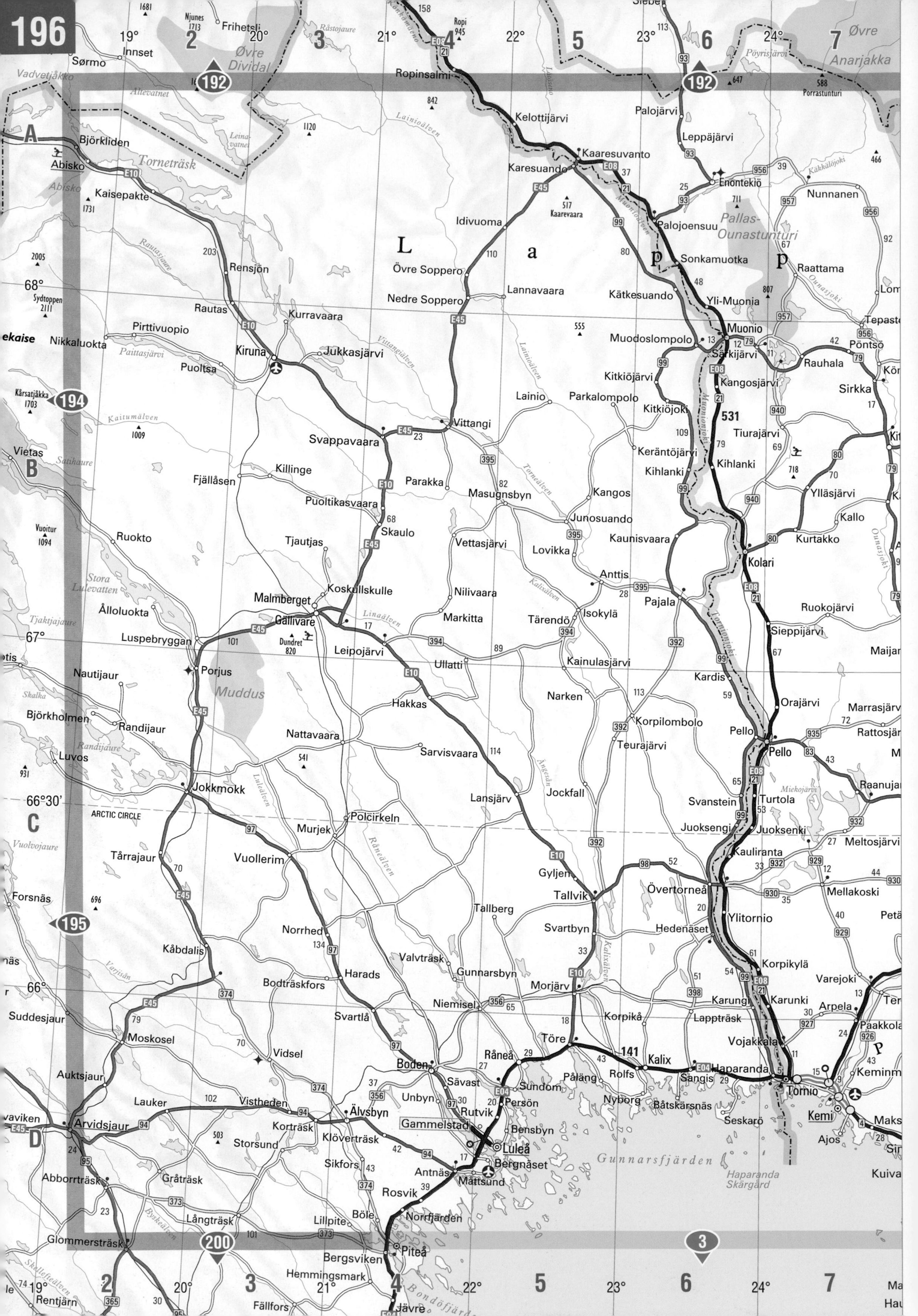

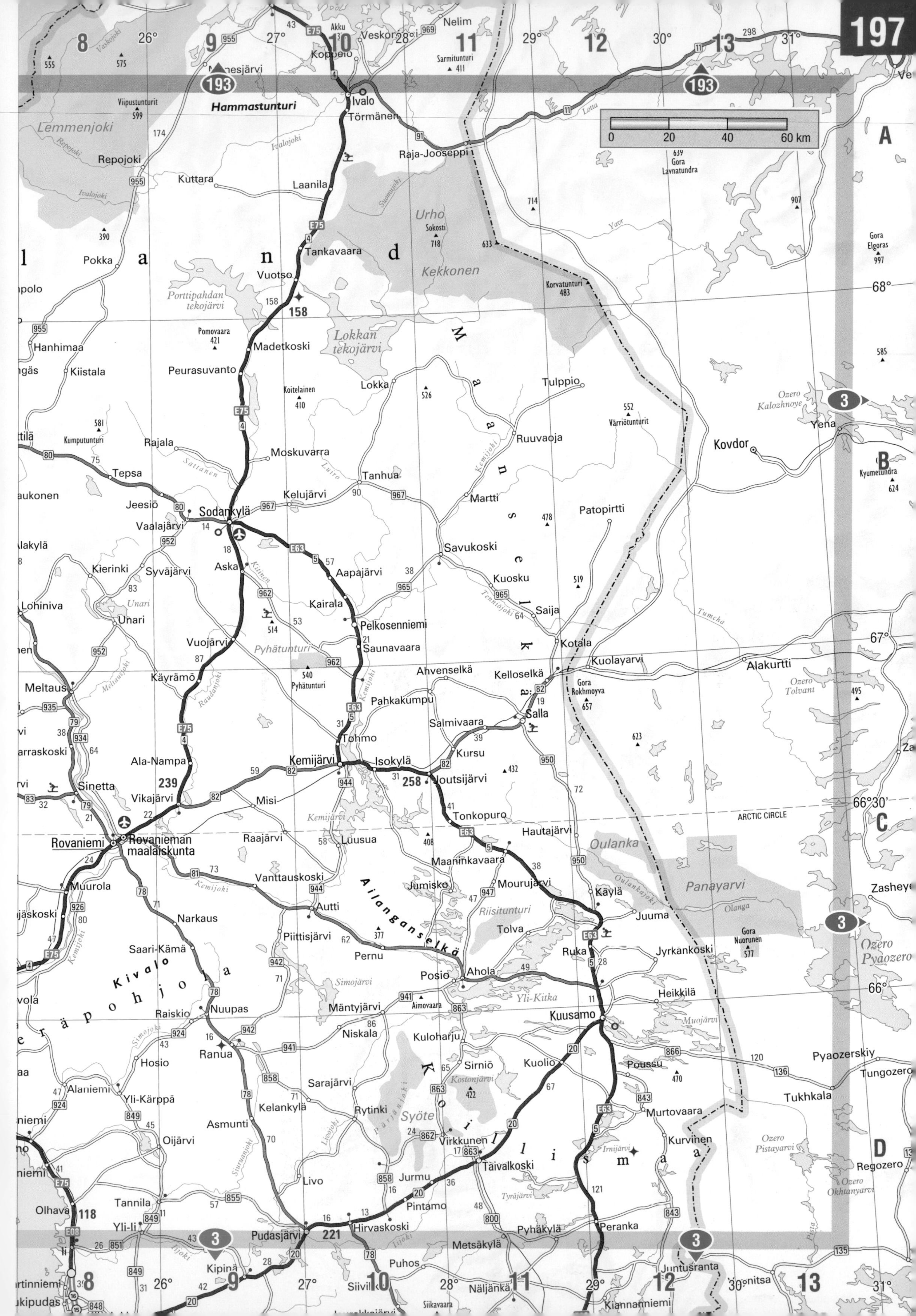

Hammastunturi
Lemmenjoki
Repojoki
Kuttara
Ivalo
Törmänen
Raja-Jooseppi
Laanila
Urho
Sokosti
Kekkonen
Tankavaara
Vuotso
Porttipahdan tekojärvi
Lokkan tekojärvi
Pokka
Madetkoski
Peurasuvanto
Hanhimaa
Kiistala
Lokka
Tulppio
Ruuvaoja
Kovdor
Yena
Ozero Kalozhnoye
Moskuvarra
Rajala
Tepsa
Tanhua
Martti
Patopirtti
Kelujärvi
Sodankylä
Jeesiö
Vaalajärvi
Savukoski
Kuosku
Saija
Aska
Kierinki
Syväjärvi
Aapajärvi
Kairala
Pelkosenniemi
Saunavaara
Unari
Lohiniva
Vuojärvi
Pyhätunturi
Kotala
Kuolayarvi
Alakurtti
Kelloselkä
Ahvenselkä
Käyrämö
Meltaus
Pahkakumpu
Salla
Salmivaara
Kursu
Tohmo
Kemijärvi
Isokylä
Joutsijärvi
Ala-Nampa
Sinetta
Vikajärvi
Misi
Tonkopuro
Hautajärvi
ARCTIC CIRCLE
Rovaniemi
Rovaniemen maalaiskunta
Raajärvi
Luusua
Oulanka
Panayarvi
Maaninkavaara
Muurola
Vanttauskoski
Jumisko
Mourujärvi
Käylä
Juuma
Narkaus
Autti
Ailangantselkä
Riisitunturi
Tolva
Piittisjärvi
Pernu
Ruka
Jyrkankoski
Saari-Kämä
Kivalo
Posio
Ahola
Heikkilä
Raiskio
Nuupas
Mäntyjärvi
Kuusamo
Niskala
Kuloharju
Ranua
Hosio
Sirniö
Kuolio
Poussu
Pyaozerskiy
Tungozero
Tukhkala
Alaniemi
Yli-Kärppä
Sarajärvi
Kelankylä
Rytinki
Syöte
Murtovaara
Asmunti
Oijärvi
Virkkunen
Kurvinen
Taivalkoski
Regozero
Livo
Jurmu
Pintamo
Tannila
Olhava
Yli-Ii
Pudasjärvi
Hirvaskoski
Pyhäkylä
Peranka
Metsäkylä
Kipinä
Puhos
Juntusranta
Siivikko
Näljänkä
Kiannanniemi
0 20 40 60 km

1
2
3
4
5
6
5°
6°
7°
8°
9°
65°
64°
63°
62°
A
B
C
D
0
20
40
60 km
N O R S K E H A V E T
N O R W E G I A N
S E A
Harsvik
Ratvika
Lysøysund
Frohavet
Nes
Botn
Uthaug
Brekstad
Frøya
Sistranda
Titran
Hitra
Fillan
Agdenes
Årn
Sandstad
Veidholmen
Lensvik
Dyrnes
Smøla
Forsnes
Heim
Snillfjord
Trondheimsleia
Edøy
Aure
Kyrksæterøra
Gullstein
Orkanger
Tustna
Aresvika
Vinje
Kristiansund
Bremsnes
Hennset
Storås
Halsa
Løkken
Åsskard
Rindal
Meldal
Hustadvika
Hustad
Averøya
Mo
Bud
Eide
Tingvoll
Surnadalsøra
Elnesvågen
Kvenna
Batnfjordsøra
Rennebu
Gossa
Todal
Troll-heimen
Nordøyane
Molde
Hjelset
Eidsvåg
Otterøya
Sunndalsøra
Storli
Vestnes
Åfarnes
Romsdalsfjorden
Brattvåg
Eresfjord
Isfjorden
Lønset
Oppdal
Søvik
Tomra
Åndalsnes
Gjøra
Ålesund
Sjøholt
Voll
Tresfjord
Sørøyane
Spjelkavik
Eikesdal
Hareid
Sykkylven
Stordal
Drivstua
Storfjorden
Dovrefjell-Sunndalsfjella
Ulsteinvik
Festøy
Stranda
Verma
Stadhavet
Vartdal
Sylte
Romsdalen
Larsnes
Ørsta
Pyttegga 1999
Lesjaskog
Dovrefjell
Leikanger
Eidsdal
Hjerkinn
Volda
Tafjord
Folkestad
Sildegapet
Selje
Åheim
Storfjorden
Hellesylt
Reinheimen
Lora
Fokstua
Dovre
Folldal
Raudeberg
Djupvasshytta
Nyseter
Dombås
Måløy
Totland
Stårheim
Hornindal
Grotli
Pollfoss
Bremangerlandet
Stryn
Videseter
Dovre
Bremanger
Isane
Nordfjordeid
Innvik
Bismo
Vågåvatn
Vågåmo
Kalvåg
Ålfotbreen
Lodalskåpa 2083
Sotaseter
Rondslottet
Midtgulen
Svelgen
Sandane
Olden
Lom
Lalm
Otta
Rondane
Hovden
Byrkjelo
Hyen
Bøverdal
Randsverk
Sjoa
Florø
Eikefjord
Nørdstedalsseter
Glittertind 2470
Kvam
Jostedalsbreen
Skei
Jostedal
Stavang
Naustdal
Vinstra
Stongfjorden
Moskog
Skjolden
Leirvassbu
Jotunheimen
Skåbu
Gjendesheim
Dalseter
46
47
155
185

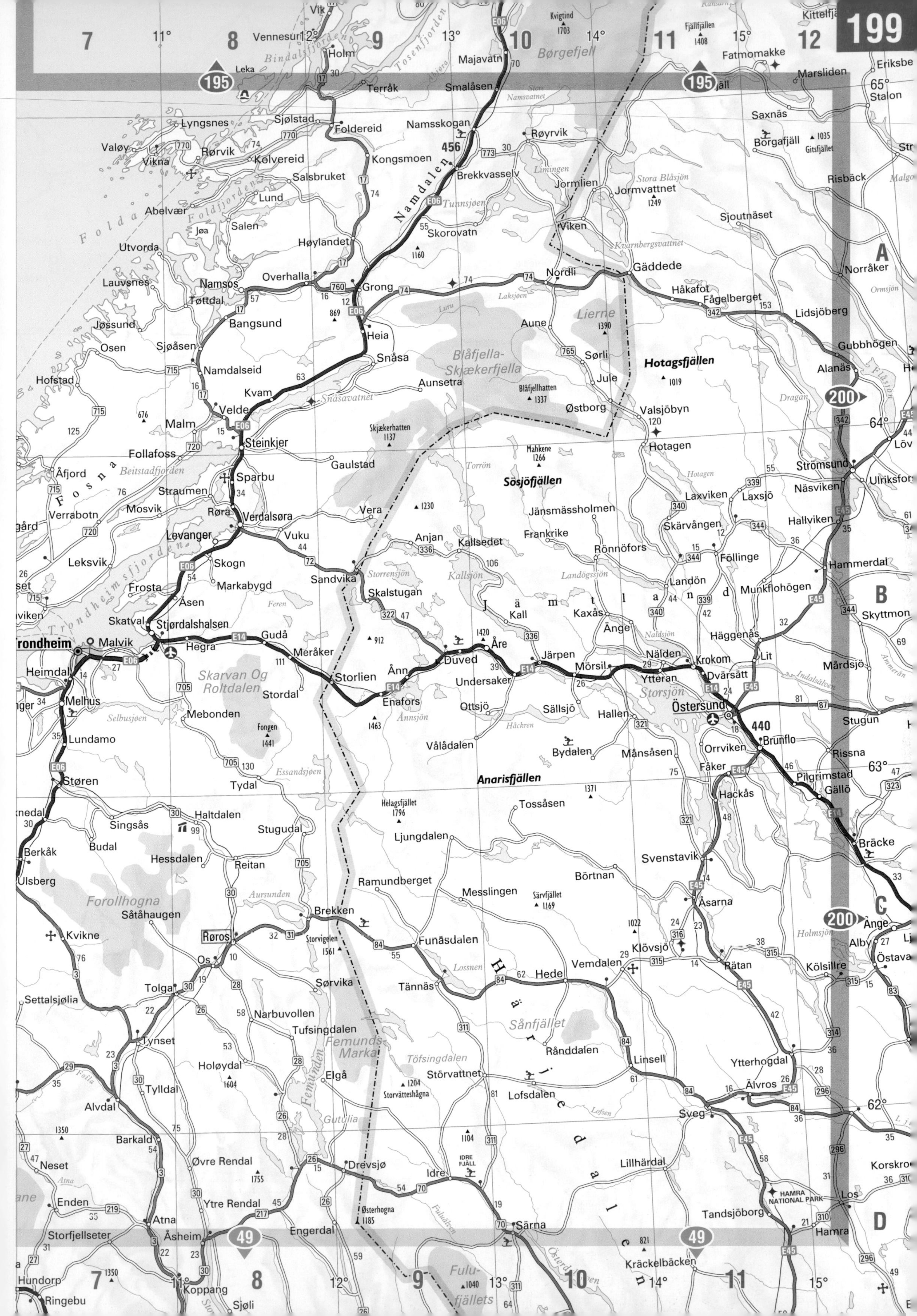

Storuman
Stensele
Vilhelmina
Lycksele
Umeå
Vännäs
Dorotea
Åsele
Strömsund
Junsele
Sollefteå
Kramfors
Härnösand
Örnsköldsvik
Sundsvall
Timrå
Hudiksvall
Ljusdal
Bräcke
Ånge
Holmsund
Nordmaling
Bjurholm
Ångermanland
Västerbotten
Medelpad
Hälsingland
0 20 40 60 km

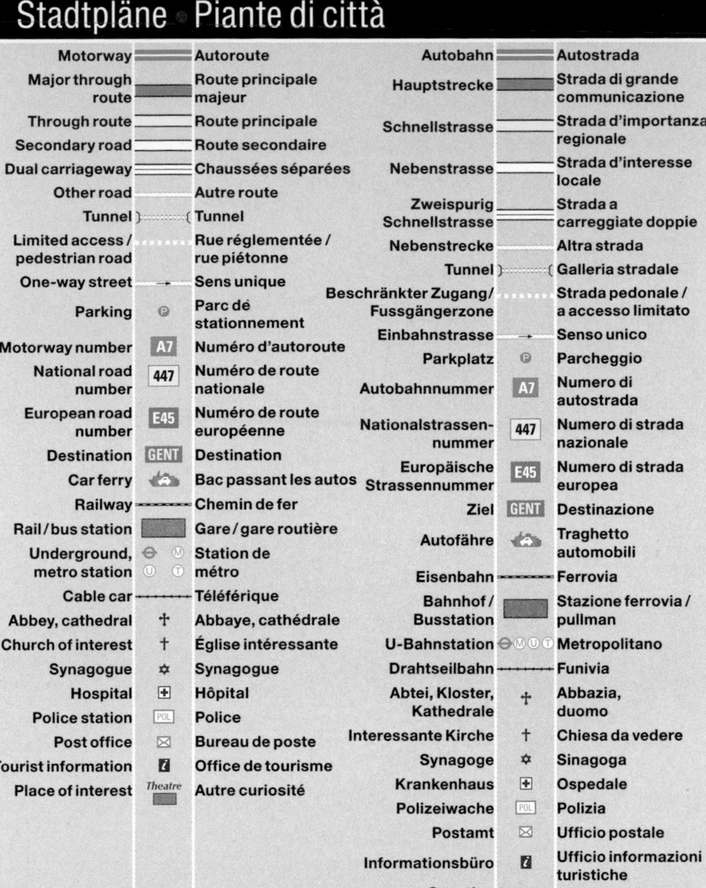
City plans • Plans de villes
Stadtpläne • Piante di città
Motorway – Autoroute
Major through route – Route principale majeur
Through route – Route principale
Secondary road – Route secondaire
Dual carriageway – Chaussées séparées
Other road – Autre route
Tunnel – Tunnel
Limited access / pedestrian road – Rue réglementée / rue piétonne
One-way street – Sens unique
Parking – Parc dé stationnement
Motorway number A7 Numéro d'autoroute
National road number 447 Numéro de route nationale
European road number E45 Numéro de route européenne
Destination GENT Destination
Car ferry – Bac passant les autos
Railway – Chemin de fer
Rail / bus station – Gare / gare routière
Underground, metro station – Station de métro
Cable car – Téléférique
Abbey, cathedral – Abbaye, cathédrale
Church of interest – Église intéressante
Synagogue – Synagogue
Hospital – Hôpital
Police station POL Police
Post office – Bureau de poste
Tourist information – Office de tourisme
Place of interest Theatre Autre curiosité
Autobahn – Autostrada
Hauptstrecke – Strada di grande communicazione
Schnellstrasse – Strada d'importanza regionale
Nebenstrasse – Strada d'interesse locale
Zweispurig Schnellstrasse – Strada a carreggiate doppie
Nebenstrecke – Altra strada
Tunnel – Galleria stradale
Beschränkter Zugang/ Fussgängerzone – Strada pedonale / a accesso limitato
Einbahnstrasse – Senso unico
Parkplatz – Parcheggio
Autobahnnummer A7 Numero di autostrada
Nationalstrassen-nummer 447 Numero di strada nazionale
Europäische Strassennummer E45 Numero di strada europea
Ziel GENT Destinazione
Autofähre – Traghetto automobili
Eisenbahn – Ferrovia
Bahnhof / Busstation – Stazione ferrovia / pullman
U-Bahnstation – Metropolitano
Drahtseilbahn – Funivia
Abtei, Kloster, Kathedrale – Abbazia, duomo
Interessante Kirche – Chiesa da vedere
Synagoge – Sinagoga
Krankenhaus – Ospedale
Polizeiwache POL Polizia
Postamt – Ufficio postale
Informationsbüro – Ufficio informazioni turistiche
Sonstige Sehenswürdigkeit Theatre Luogo da vedere

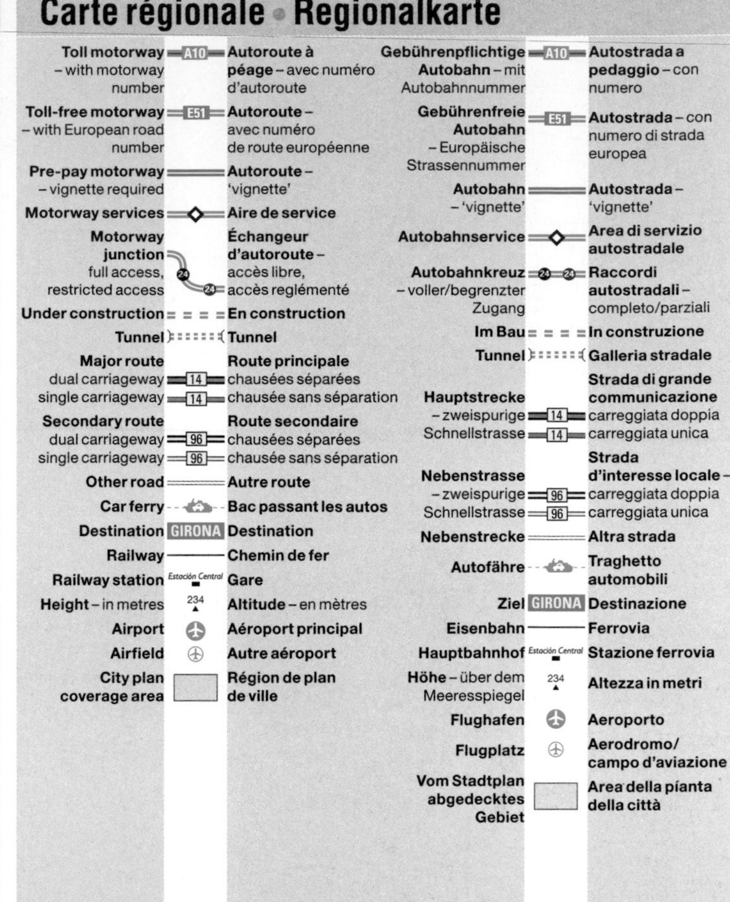
Approach maps • Agglomérations
Carte régionale • Regionalkarte
Toll motorway – with motorway number A10 Autoroute à péage – avec numéro d'autoroute
Toll-free motorway – with European road number E51 Autoroute – avec numéro de route européenne
Pre-pay motorway – vignette required – Autoroute – 'vignette'
Motorway services – Aire de service
Motorway junction full access, restricted access – Échangeur d'autoroute – accès libre, accès reglémenté
Under construction – En construction
Tunnel – Tunnel
Major route dual carriageway, single carriageway 14 Route principale chausées séparées, chausée sans séparation
Secondary route dual carriageway, single carriageway 96 Route secondaire chausées séparées, chausée sans séparation
Other road – Autre route
Car ferry – Bac passant les autos
Destination GIRONA Destination
Railway – Chemin de fer
Railway station Estación Central Gare
Height – in metres 234 Altitude – en mètres
Airport – Aéroport principal
Airfield – Autre aéroport
City plan coverage area – Région de plan de ville
Gebührenpflichtige Autobahn – mit Autobahnnummer A10 Autostrada a pedaggio – con numero
Gebührenfreie Autobahn – Europäische Strassennummer E51 Autostrada – con numero di strada europea
Autobahn – 'vignette' – Autostrada – 'vignette'
Autobahnservice – Area di servizio autostradale
Autobahnkreuz – voller/begrenzter Zugang – Raccordi autostradali – completo/parziali
Im Bau – In construzione
Tunnel – Galleria stradale
Hauptstrecke – zweispurige, Schnellstrasse 14 Strada di grande communicazione – carreggiata doppia, carreggiata unica
Nebenstrasse – zweispurige, Schnellstrasse 96 Strada d'interesse locale – carreggiata doppia, carreggiata unica
Nebenstrecke – Altra strada
Autofähre – Traghetto automobili
Ziel GIRONA Destinazione
Eisenbahn – Ferrovia
Hauptbahnhof Estación Central Stazione ferrovia
Höhe – über dem Meeresspiegel 234 Altezza in metri
Flughafen – Aeroporto
Flugplatz – Aerodromo/ campo d'aviazione
Vom Stadtplan abgedecktes Gebiet – Area della pianta della città

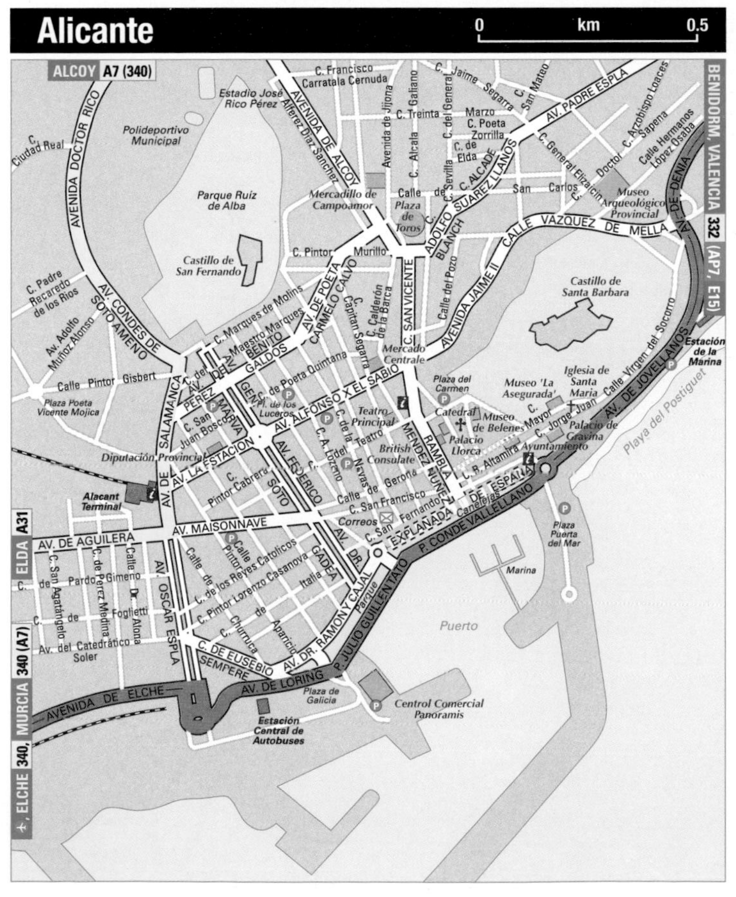
Alicante
0 km 0.5
ALCOY A7 (340)
BENIDORM, VALENCIA 332 (AP7, E15)
ELDA A31
MURCIA 340 (A7)
ELCHE 340
Parque Ruiz de Alba
Castillo de San Fernando
Castillo de Santa Bárbara
Mercado Central
Puerto
Marina
Playa del Postiguet
Estación Central de Autobuses
Centrol Comercial Panoramis
AVENIDA DE ELCHE
AV. DE LORING
AV. MAISONNAVE
AV. DE AGUILERA
AVENIDA DOCTOR RICO
CALLE VAZQUEZ DE MELLA
AV. DE JOVELLANOS
AV. PADRE ESPLA

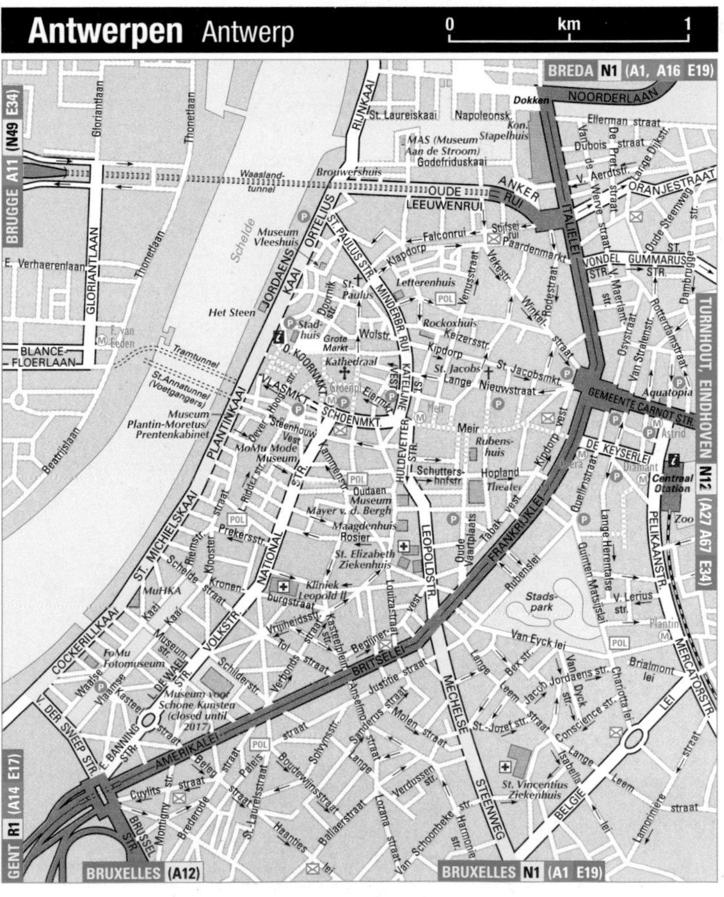
Antwerpen Antwerp
0 km 1
BREDA N1 (A1, A16 E19)
BRUGGE A11 (N49 E34)
TURNHOUT, EINDHOVEN N12 (A27 A67 E34)
GENT R1 (A14 E17)
BRUXELLES (A12)
BRUXELLES N1 (A1 E19)
Scheldt
Waasland-tunnel
Het Steen
Grote Markt
Kathedraal
Museum Plantin-Moretus/ Prentenkabinet
MAS (Museum Aan de Stroom)
Centraal Station
Stadspark
ITALIËLEI
FRANKRIJKLEI
AMERIKALEI
BRITSELEI
LEOPOLDSTR.
NOORDERLAAN
GEMEENTE CARNOT STR.

Amsterdam

0 km 2

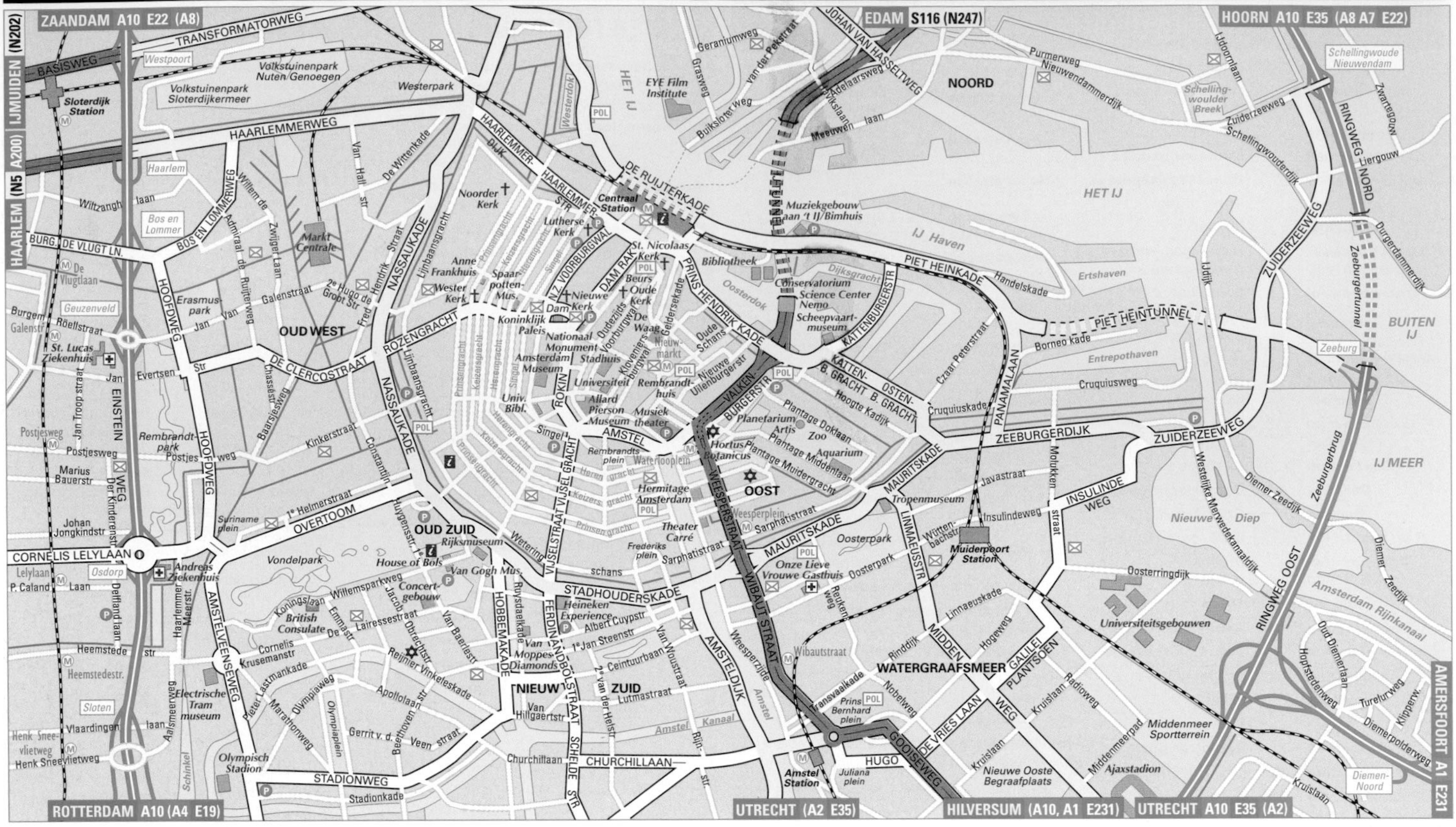

ZAANDAM A10 E22 (A8)
EDAM S116 (N247)
HOORN A10 E35 (A8 A7 E22)
IJMUIDEN (N202)
HAARLEM (N5 A200)
AMERSFOORT A1 E231
ROTTERDAM A10 (A4 E19)
UTRECHT (A2 E35)
HILVERSUM (A10, A1 E231)
UTRECHT A10 E35 (A2)

NOORD
HET IJ
OUD WEST
OUD ZUID
OOST
NIEUW ZUID
WATERGRAAFSMEER
BUITEN IJ
IJ MEER
Centraal Station
Sloterdijk Station
Muiderpoort Station
Amstel Station
Rijksmuseum
Van Gogh Mus.
Vondelpark
Westerpark
Oosterpark
Hortus Botanicus
Artis Zoo
Tropenmuseum
Muziekgebouw aan 't IJ/Bimhuis
Universiteitsgebouwen
Nieuwe Ooste Begraafplaats
Ajaxstadion
Olympisch Stadion

Amsterdam

0 km 5

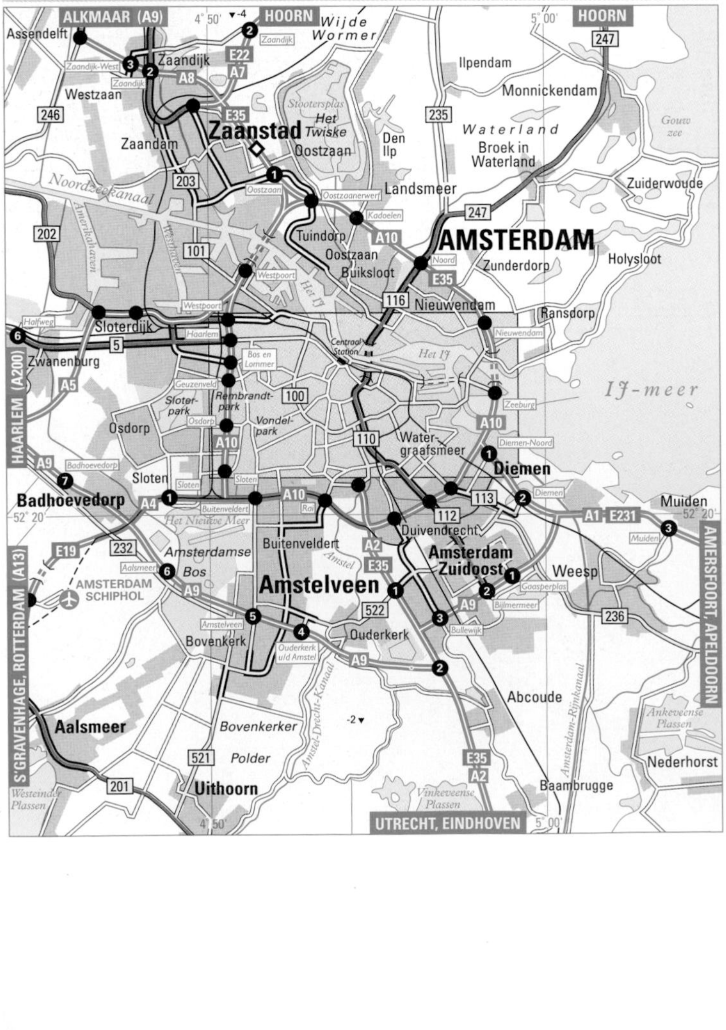

ALKMAAR (A9)
HOORN
HAARLEM (A200)
S'GRAVENHAGE, ROTTERDAM (A13)
AMERSFOORT, APELDOORN
UTRECHT, EINDHOVEN

AMSTERDAM
Zaanstad
Amstelveen
Amsterdam Zuidoost
Diemen
Badhoevedorp
Aalsmeer
Uithoorn
Zaandam
Assendelft
Westzaan
Landsmeer
Monnickendam
Broek in Waterland
Ilpendam
Zuiderwoude
Holysloot
Ransdorp
Sloterdijk
Zwanenburg
Osdorp
Sloten
Buitenveldert
Duivendrecht
Weesp
Muiden
Ouderkerk
Bovenkerk
Abcoude
Baambrugge
Nederhorst
AMSTERDAM SCHIPHOL
IJ-meer
Waterland

Athina Athens

0 km 5

THIVA (3) KORINTHOS (A8)
ACHARNES, LAMIA (A1)
KIFFISIA
ATHINA E. VENIZELOS RAFINA
LAVRIO

ATHINA
Pireas
Kalithea
Glifada
Vouliagmeni
Kalamaki
Peristeri
Kolonos
Neapoli
Marousi
Halandri
Aghia Paraskevi
Zografou
Kessariani
Vironas
Ilioupoli
Argiroupoli
Alimos
Elliniko
Voula
Vari
Varkiza
Aghia Marina
Peania
Glyka Nera
Saronikos Kolpos
Iraklio, Chania, Kithnos, Kos, Mykonos, Milos, Naxos, Paros, Rhodes, Samos

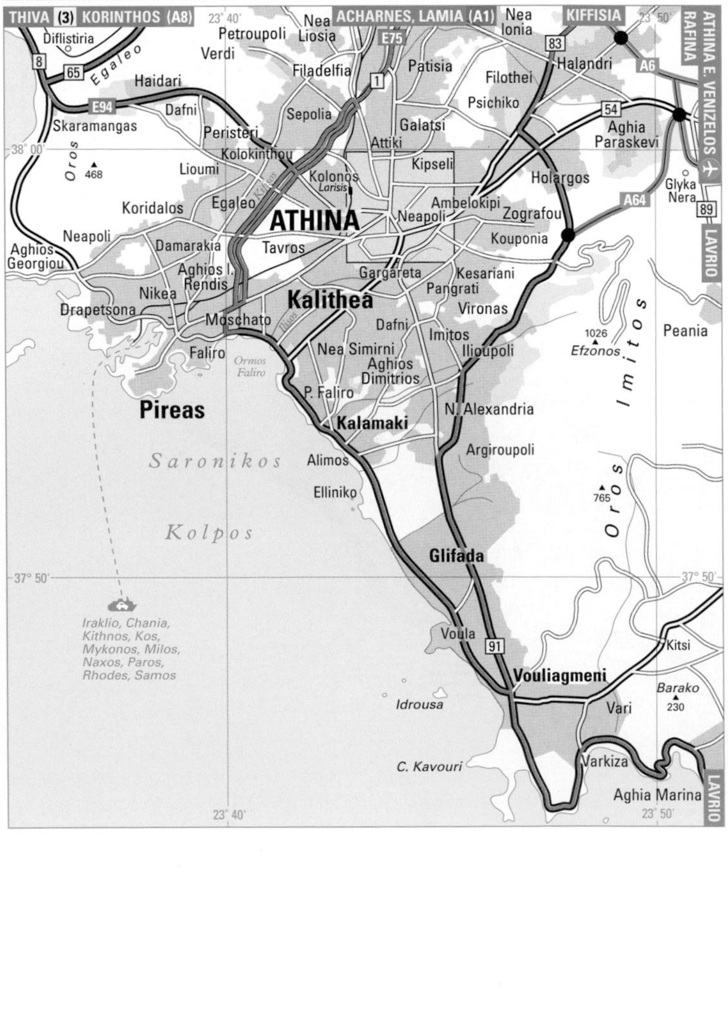

Athina Athens

0 km 1

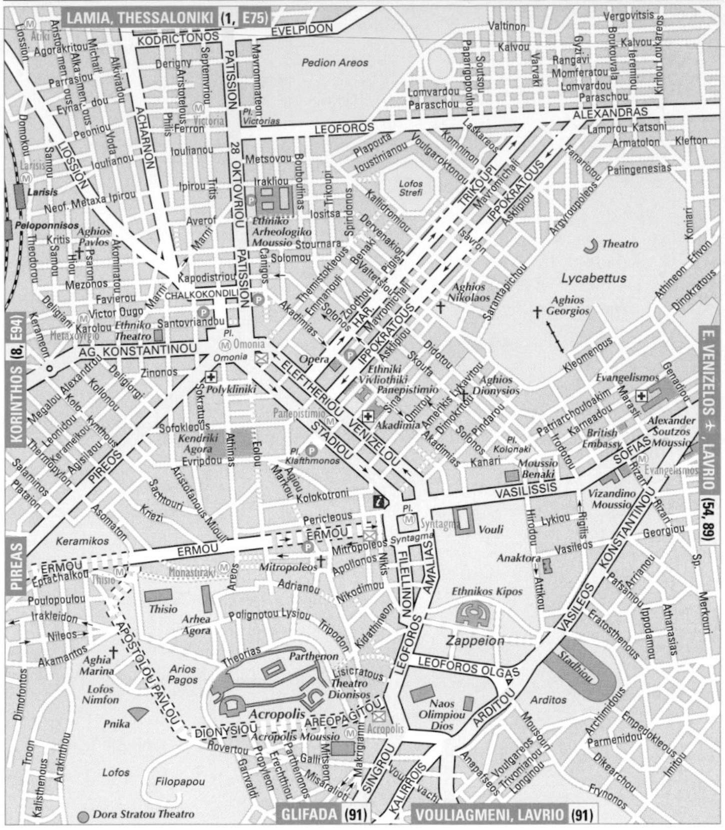

LAMIA, THESSALONIKI (1, E75)

E. VENIZELOS ✈, LAVRIO (54, 89)

KORINTHOS (8, E94)

PIREAS

GLIFADA (91)

VOULIAGMENI, LAVRIO (91)

Basel

0 km 0.5

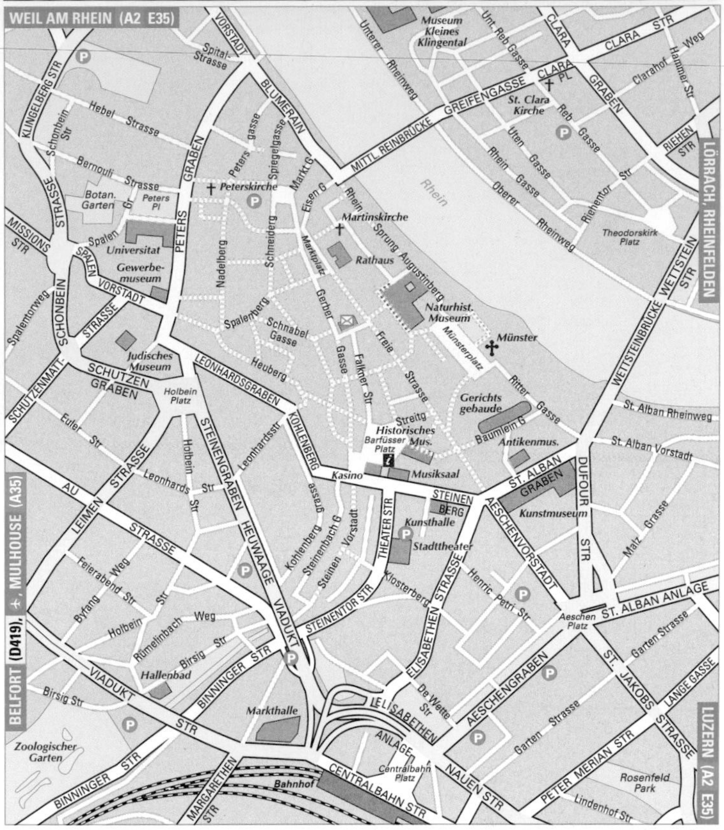

WEIL AM RHEIN (A2 E35)

LÖRRACH, RHEINFELDEN

BELFORT (D419), ✈ MULHOUSE (A35)

LUZERN (A2 E35)

Barcelona

0 km 5

TERRASSA, MANRESA | GIRONA | TERRASSA, MANRESA (C16) | GIRONA, FIGUERES (AP7)

MATARÓ (C32)

LLEIDA (AP2) VALENCIA

VILANOVA I LA GELTRÚ TARRAGONA (AP7)

Barcelona

0 km 1

(C58, C33)

MATARÓ (C32)

LLEIDA (AP7, AP2 E90)

MATARÓ (C32), GIRONA (C33, AP7 E90), MANRESA (C58, C16)

✈ TARRAGONA (C32, AP7)

LLEIDA (AP7, AP2 E90), VALENCIA (C32, AP7 E15)

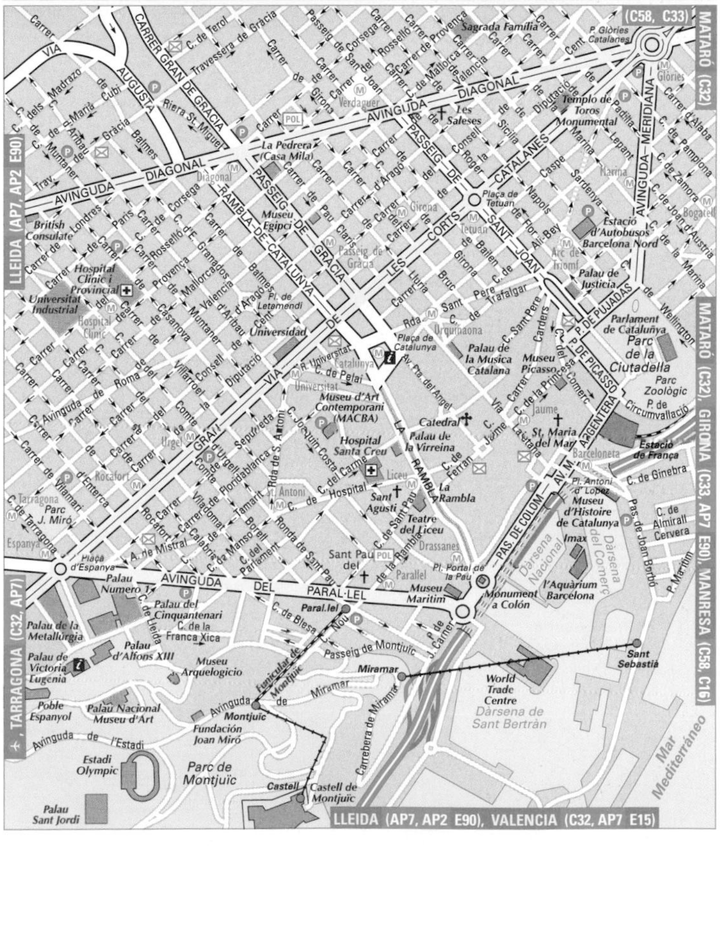

Berlin

0 km 5

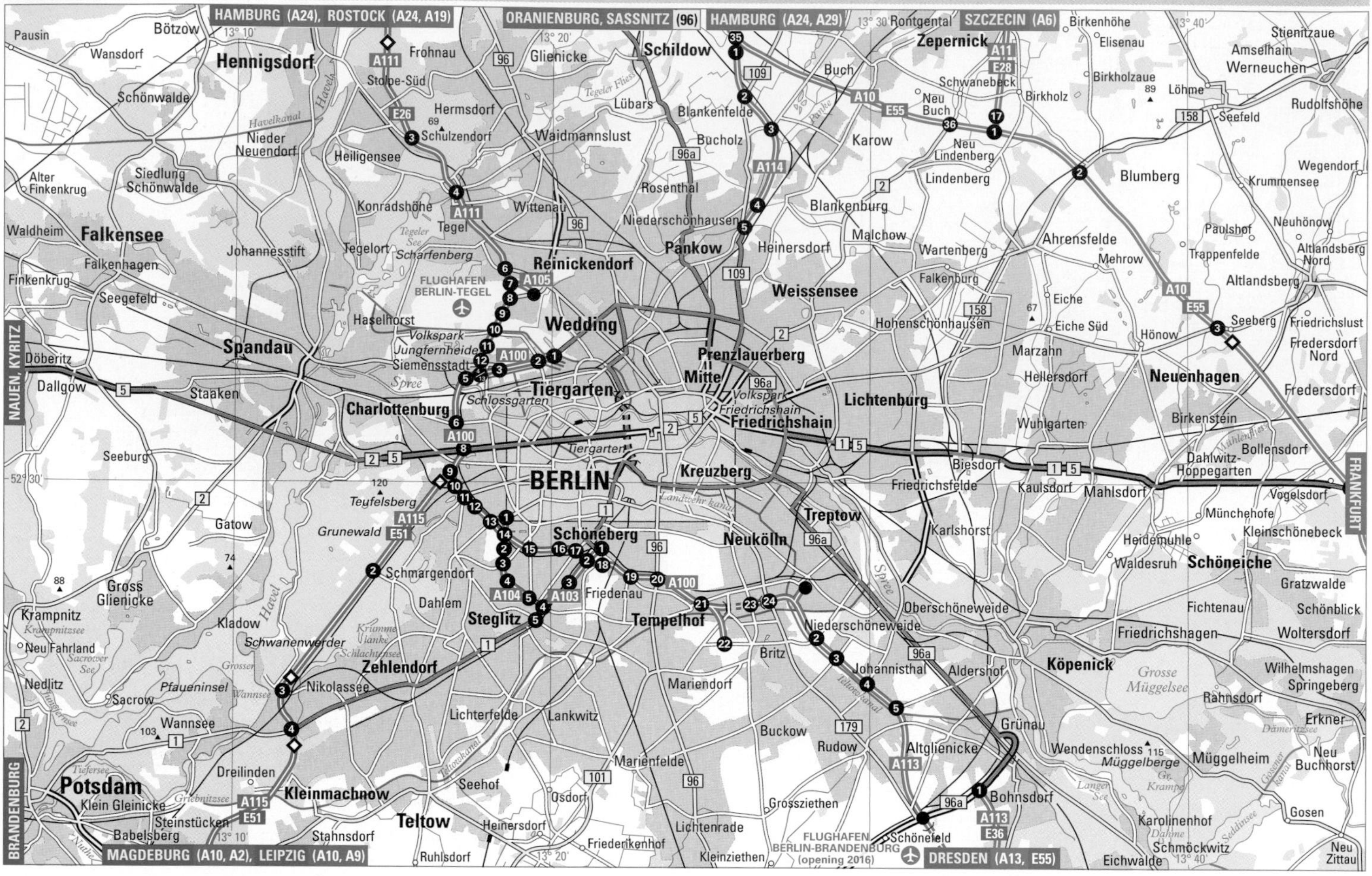

HAMBURG (A24), ROSTOCK (A24, A19)
ORANIENBURG, SASSNITZ (96)
HAMBURG (A24, A29)
SZCZECIN (A6)
NAUEN, KYRITZ
FRANKFURT
BRANDENBURG
MAGDEBURG (A10, A2), LEIPZIG (A10, A9)
DRESDEN (A13, E55)

Pausin
Bötzow
Wansdorf
Hennigsdorf
Schönwalde
Frohnau
Stolpe-Süd
Hermsdorf
Schulzendorf
Glienicke
Schildow
Lübars
Waidmannslust
Blankenfelde
Buch
Zepernick
Schwanebeck
Birkenhöhe
Elisenau
Stienitzaue
Amselhain
Werneuchen
Birkholzaue
Birkholz
Löhme
Seefeld
Rudolfshöhe
Neu Buch
Karow
Neu Lindenberg
Lindenberg
Blumberg
Wegendorf
Krummensee
Nieder Neuendorf
Heiligensee
Bucholz
Rosenthal
Siedlung Schönwalde
Alter Finkenkrug
Konradshöhe
Tegel
Wittenau
Niederschönhausen
Blankenburg
Malchow
Waldheim
Falkensee
Johannesstift
Tegelort
Scharfenberg
Reinickendorf
Pankow
Heinersdorf
Wartenberg
Ahrensfelde
Mehrow
Paulshof
Trappenfelde
Neuhönow
Altlandsberg Nord
Altlandsberg
Falkenhagen
Finkenkrug
Seegefeld
FLUGHAFEN BERLIN-TEGEL
Weissensee
Falkenburg
Eiche
Eiche Süd
Hönow
Seeberg
Friedrichslust
Fredersdorf Nord
Haselhorst
Wedding
Hohenschönhausen
Volkspark Jungfernheide
Siemensstadt
Spandau
Döberitz
Dallgow
Staaken
Spree
Schlossgarten
Tiergarten
Prenzlauerberg
Mitte
Volkspark Friedrichshain
Friedrichshain
Lichtenburg
Marzahn
Hellersdorf
Neuenhagen
Fredersdorf
Charlottenburg
Wuhlgarten
Birkenstein
Bollensdorf
Dahlwitz-Hoppegarten
Seeburg
Tiergarten
BERLIN
Kreuzberg
Biesdorf
Friedrichsfelde
Kaulsdorf
Mahlsdorf
Vogelsdorf
Teufelsberg
Gatow
Grunewald
Landwehrkanal
Treptow
Karlshorst
Münchehofe
Kleinschönebeck
Schöneberg
Neukölln
Heidemühle
Waldesruh
Schöneiche
Gross Glienicke
Schmargendorf
Dahlem
Friedenau
Tempelhof
Oberschöneweide
Niederschöneweide
Gratzwalde
Schönblick
Fichtenau
Woltersdorf
Krampnitz
Kladow
Steglitz
Friedrichshagen
Neu Fahrland
Schwanenwerder
Britz
Johannisthal
Aldershof
Köpenick
Grosse Müggelsee
Wilhelmshagen
Springeberg
Rahnsdorf
Nedlitz
Sacrow
Pfaueninsel
Zehlendorf
Nikolassee
Mariendorf
Wannsee
Lichterfelde
Lankwitz
Buckow
Rudow
Grünau
Erkner
Wendenschloss
Müggelberge
Müggelheim
Neu Buchhorst
Potsdam
Klein Gleinicke
Dreilinden
Kleinmachnow
Marienfelde
Seehof
Osdorf
Altglienicke
Bohnsdorf
Gosen
Steinstücken
Babelsberg
Stahnsdorf
Teltow
Heinersdorf
Lichtenrade
Grossziethen
Karolinenhof
Schmöckwitz
Ruhlsdorf
Friederikenhof
Kleinziethen
FLUGHAFEN BERLIN-BRANDENBURG (opening 2016)
Schönefeld
Eichwalde
Neu Zittau

Berlin

0 km 1

ORANIENBURG 96 E251
ORANIENBURG (96 E251)
BERNAU 2
FRANKFURT 1 5
NAUEN 2 5
POTSDAM (A100 A115 E51 1)
TREPTOW (96a)
POTSDAM 1 (A103)
LUCKAU 96
BERLIN-BRANDENBURG 179

Kaiserin-Augusta-Allee
Turmstrasse
Alt-Moabit
Tiergarten
Charlottenburg
Levetzowstrasse
Hauptbahnhof Lehrter Bahnhof
Invalidenstr.
Bundeskanzleramt
Bellevue
Schloss Bellevue
Haus der Kulturen der Welt
Reichstag
Unter den Linden
Brandenburger Tor
Strasse des 17. Juni
Bismarckstrasse
Otto-Suhr-Allee
Technische Universität
Tiergarten
Holocaust Mahnmal
Sony Center
Potsdamer Platz
Philharmonie
Kulturforum
Neue Nationalgalerie
Leipziger Strasse
Friedrichstrasse
Mitte
Alexanderplatz
Hackescher Markt
Pergamonmus.
Neues Mus.
Altes Mus.
Dom
Staatsoper
Konzerthaus Berlin
Deutscher und Französischer Dom
Checkpoint Charlie
Kantstrasse
Zoologischer Garten
Kaiser Wilhelm Kirche
Europa-Center
Kurfürstendamm
Tauentzien
Kleiststrasse
Lützowufer
Reichpietschufer
Schöneberger Ufer
Anhalter Bf.
Martin-Gropius-Bau
Topographie des Terrors
Tempodrom
Hallesches Ufer
Tempelhofer Ufer
Gitschiner Strasse
Skalitzer Str.
Kreuzberg
Jüdisches Museum
Deutsches Technikmuseum Berlin
Lietzenburger Strasse
Wilmersdorf
Hohenzollerndamm
Bundesallee
Potsdamer Str.
Yorckstrasse
Gneisenaustrasse
Mehringdamm
Grunewaldstrasse
Berliner Str.
Bayerischer Platz
Urbanstrasse
Hasenheide
Südstern
Kottbusser Str.

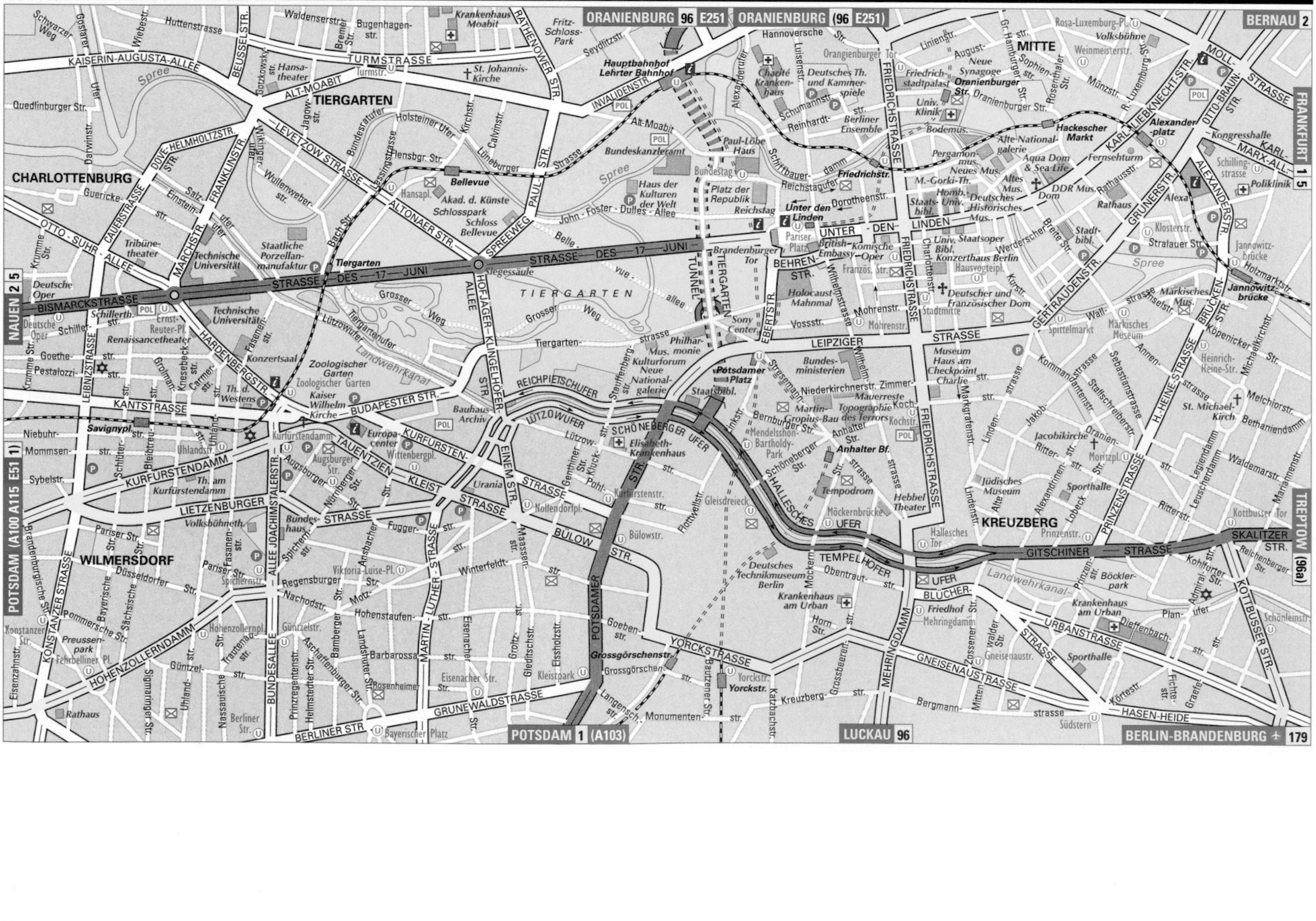

Beograd Belgrade

0 km 1

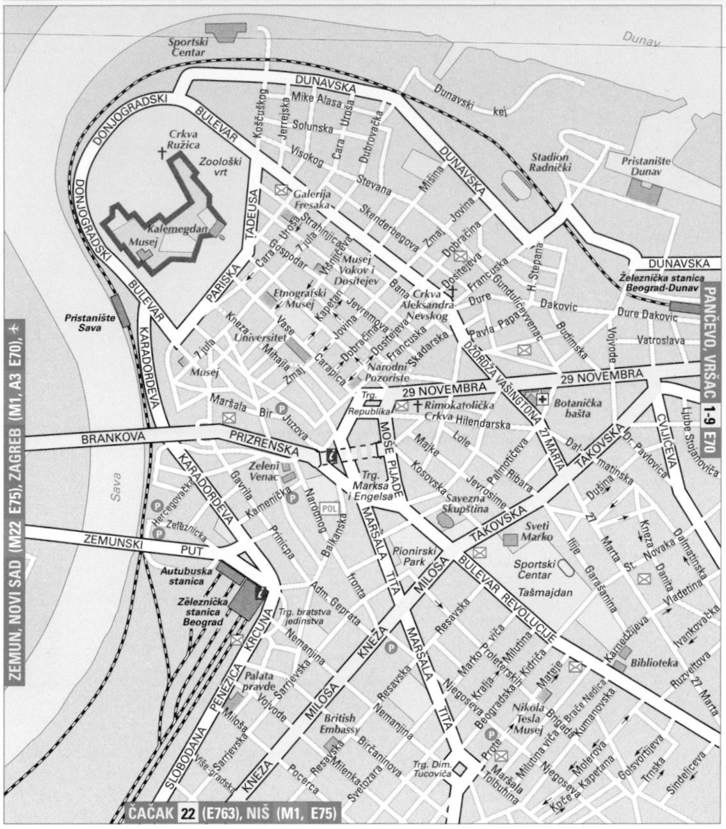

ZEMUN, NOVI SAD (M22 E75), ZAGREB (M1, A3 E70)

PANČEVO, VRŠAC 1-9 E70

ČAČAK 22 (E763), NIŠ (M1, E75)

Bruxelles Brussels

0 km 5

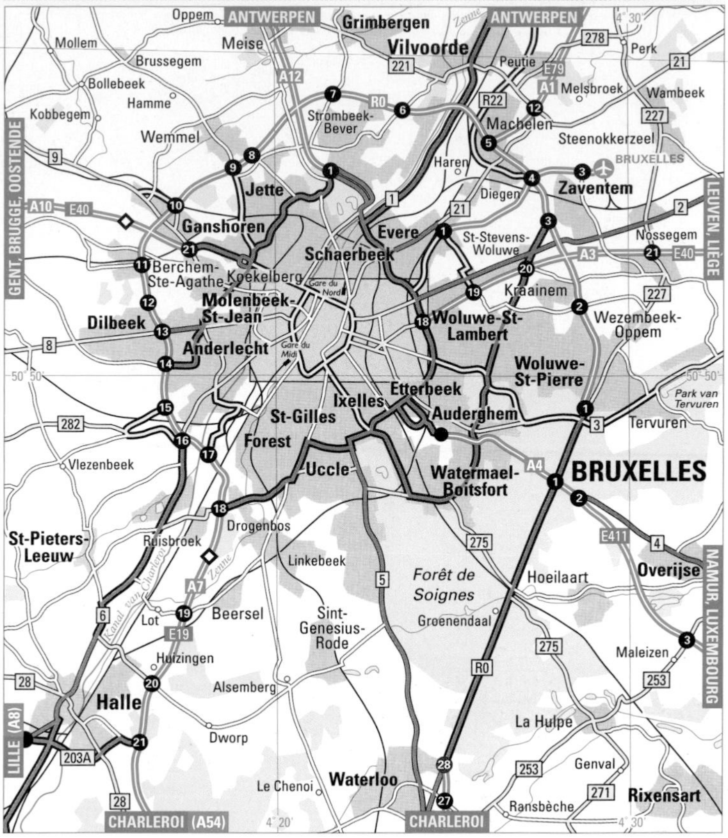

ANTWERPEN

GENT, BRUGGE, OOSTENDE

LEUVEN, LIÈGE

NAMUR, LUXEMBOURG

LILLE (A8)

CHARLEROI (A54)

CHARLEROI

Bordeaux

0 km 5

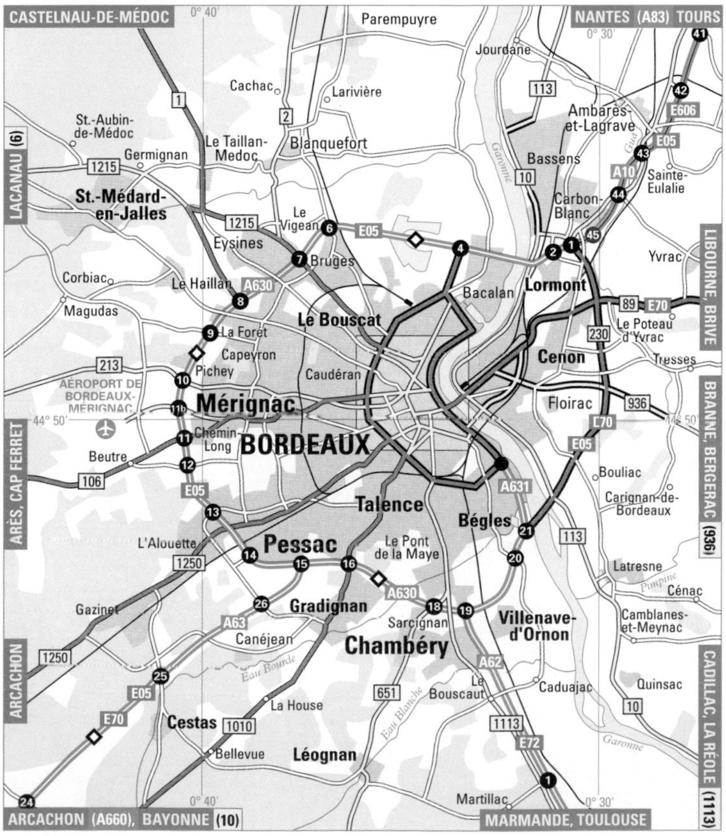

CASTELNAU-DE-MÉDOC

NANTES (A83) TOURS

LACANAU (6)

LIBOURNE, BRIVE

BRANNE, BERGERAC (936)

ARÈS, CAP FERRET

ARCACHON

CADILLAC, LA RÉOLE (1113)

ARCACHON (A660), BAYONNE (10)

MARMANDE, TOULOUSE

Bordeaux

0 km 1

LACANAU (D6) SAINTES, POITIERS (A10 E05)

LA ROCHELLE (A10, A610, E05)

PÉRIGUEUX, CLERMONT FERRAND, N89 E70

CAP FERRET D106

TOULOUSE (A630, A62 E72)

ARCACHON D1250 BAYONNE (N10 E05 E70)

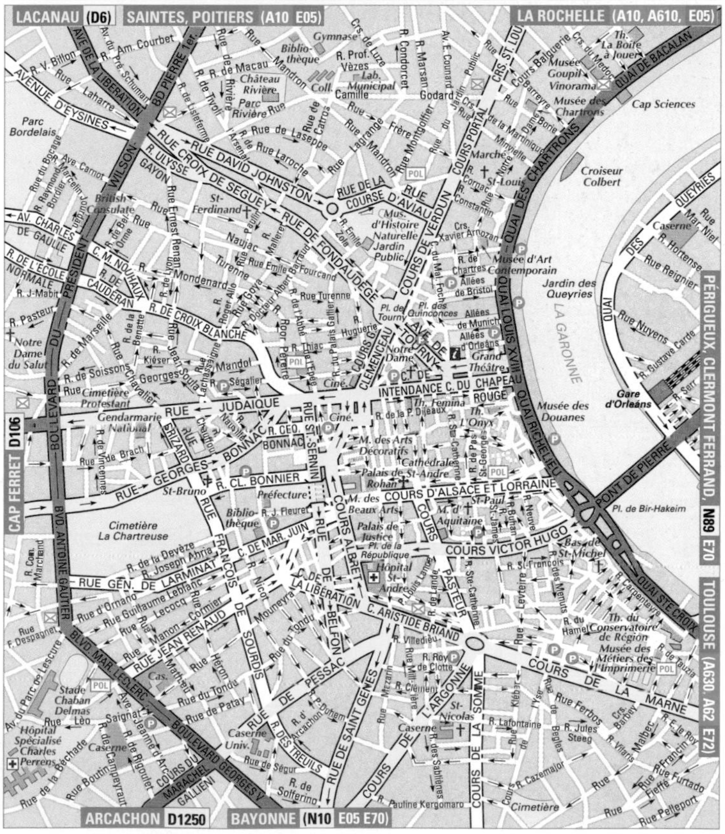

Bruxelles Brussels

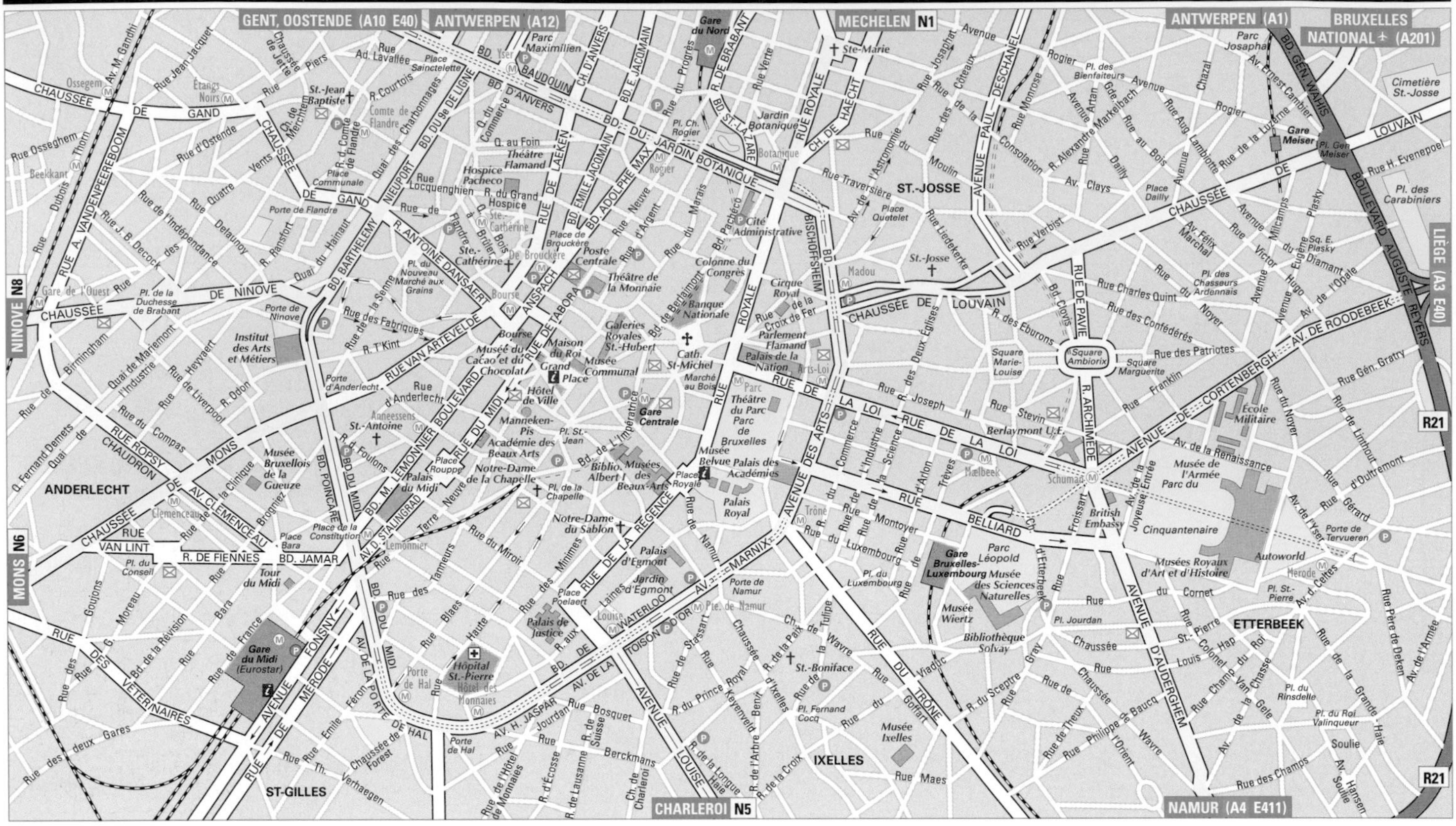

0 km 1

GENT, OOSTENDE (A10 E40)
ANTWERPEN (A12)
MECHELEN N1
ANTWERPEN (A1)
BRUXELLES NATIONAL (A201)
LIÈGE (A3 E40)
R21
NAMUR (A4 E411)
CHARLEROI N5
MONS N6
NINOVE N8

Budapest

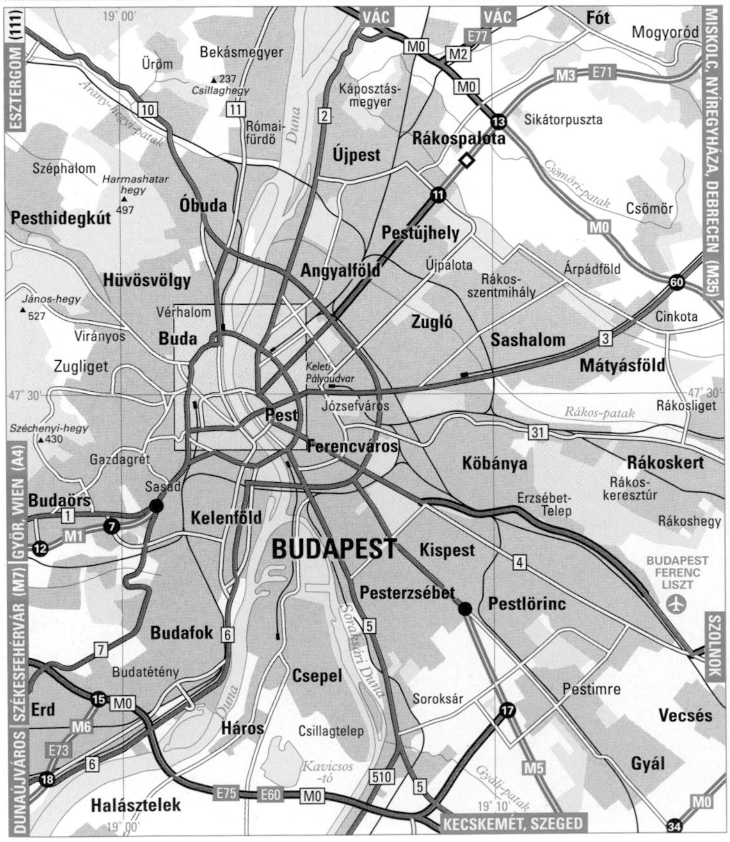

0 km 5

VÁC
MISKOLC, NYÍREGYHÁZA, DEBRECEN (M35)
SZOLNOK
KECSKEMÉT, SZEGED
DUNAÚJVÁROS, SZÉKESFEHÉRVÁR (M7), GYŐR, WIEN (A4)
ESZTERGOM (111)

Budapest

0 km 1

ESZTERGOM 11
VÁC 2, ZVOLEN (66) E77
GYÖNGYÖS (M3 E71)
GÖDÖLLŐ 3
SZOLNOK 4 E60, KECSKEMÉT (M5 E75)
BAJA 51
PÉCS (6 E73)
PÉCS (6 E73)
GYŐR (M1 E60 E75), SZÉKESFEHÉRVÁR (M7 E66 E71)

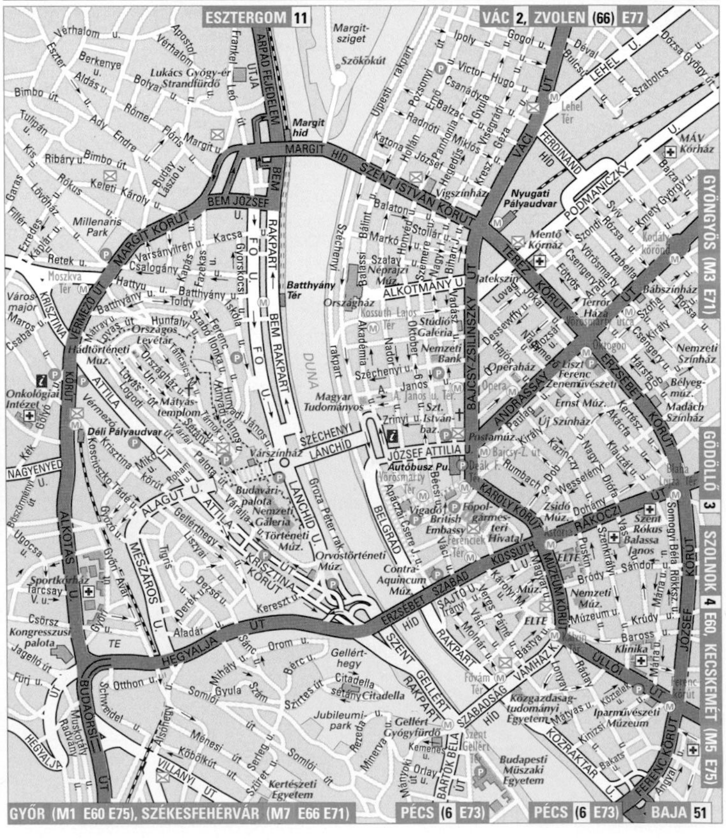

Dublin

0 km 5

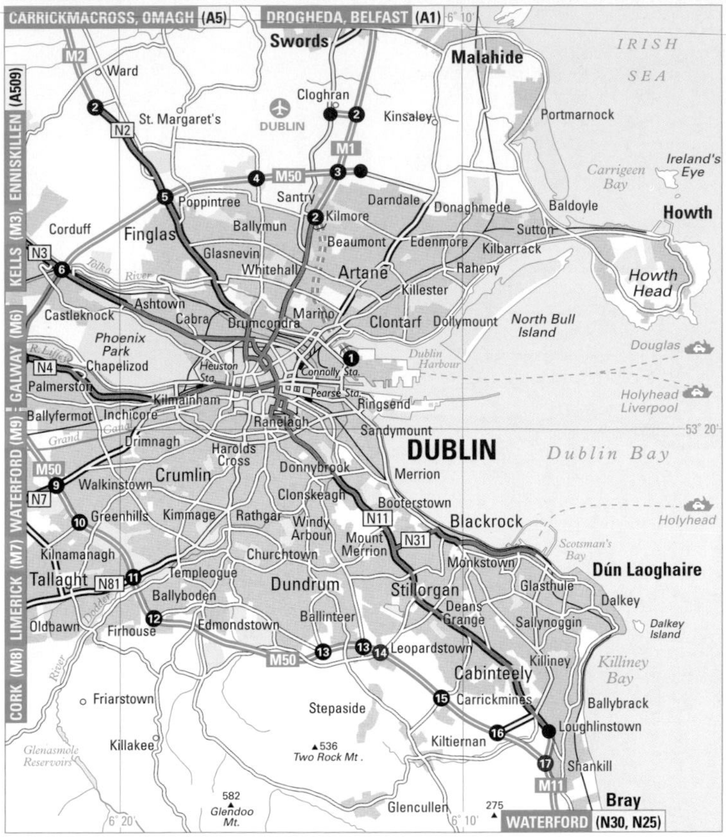

CARRICKMACROSS, OMAGH (A5) — DROGHEDA, BELFAST (A1)

KELLS (M3), ENNISKILLEN (A509) — GALWAY (M6) — WATERFORD (M9) — LIMERICK (M7) — CORK (M8)

WATERFORD (N30, N25)

Dublin

0 km 0.5

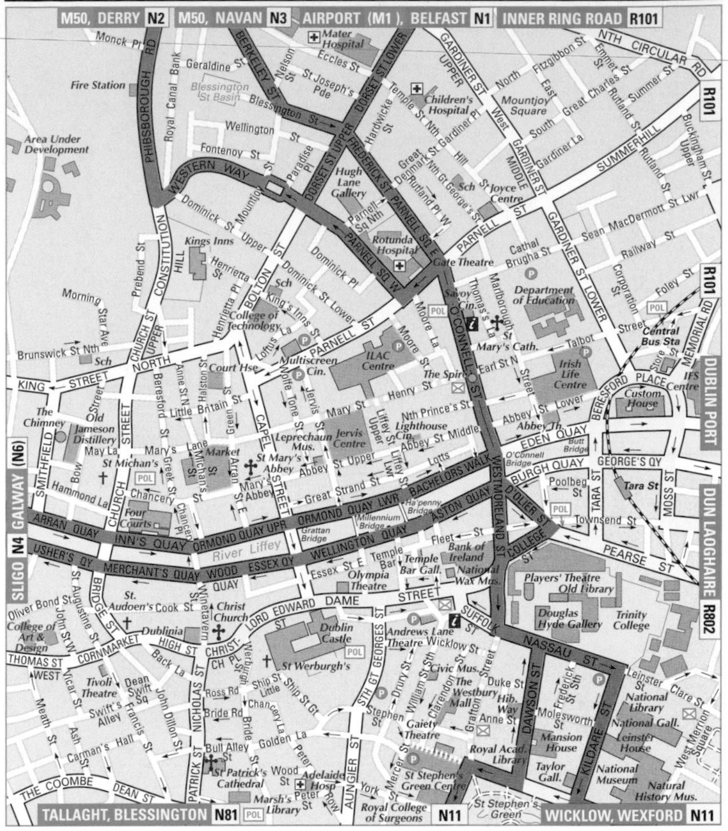

M50, DERRY N2 — M50, NAVAN N3 — AIRPORT (M1), BELFAST N1 — INNER RING ROAD R101

GALWAY (N6) — SLIGO N4

R101 — DUBLIN PORT — DUN LAOGHAIRE R802

TALLAGHT, BLESSINGTON N81 — N11 — WICKLOW, WEXFORD N11

Düsseldorf

0 km 0.5

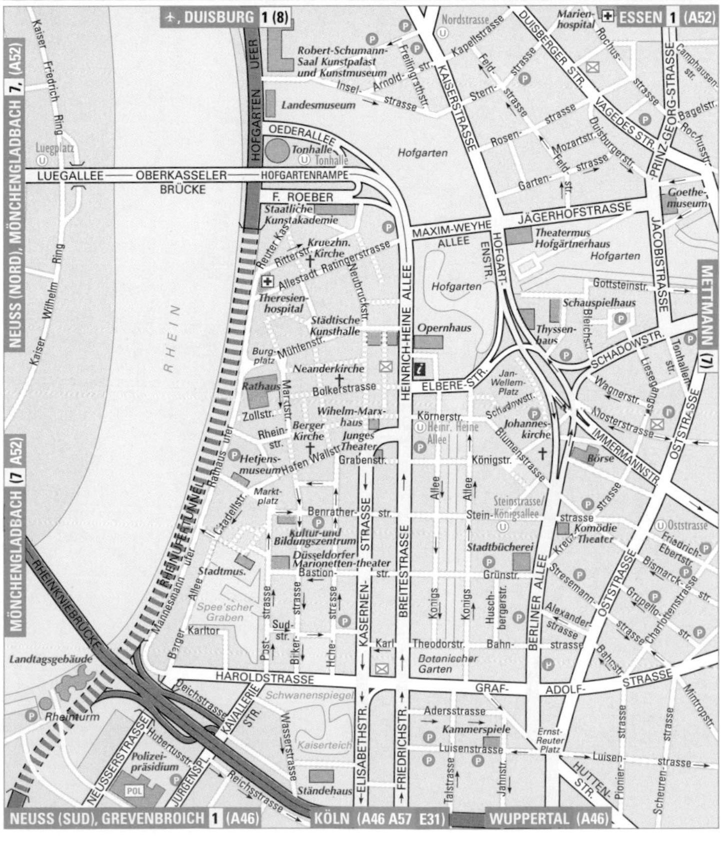

DUISBURG 1 (8) — ESSEN 1 (A52)

MÖNCHENGLADBACH 7, (A52) — NEUSS (NORD), MÖNCHENGLADBACH (7 A52)

METTMANN (7)

NEUSS (SUD), GREVENBROICH 1 (A46) — KÖLN (A46 A57 E31) — WUPPERTAL (A46)

Edinburgh

0 km 0.5

LEITH A900 — BERWICK UPON TWEED A1 — GALASHIELS & JEDBURGH A7 (A68)

FORTH ROAD BRIDGE & PERTH A90 (M90) — GLASGOW A8 (M8)

CARLISLE A702 (A74M) — LOANHEAD (A701)

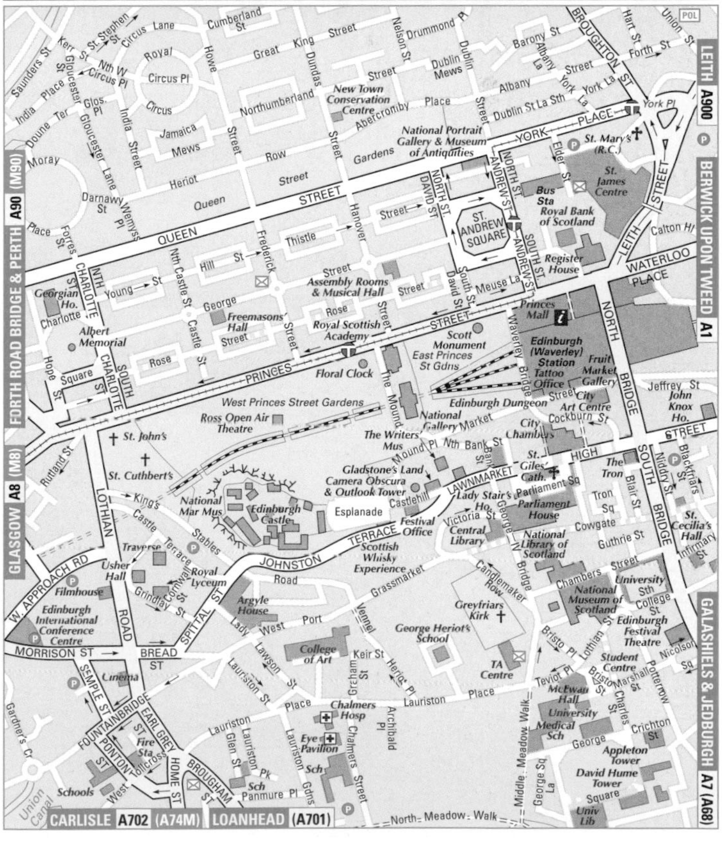

For **Cologne** see page 212

For **Copenhagen** see page 212

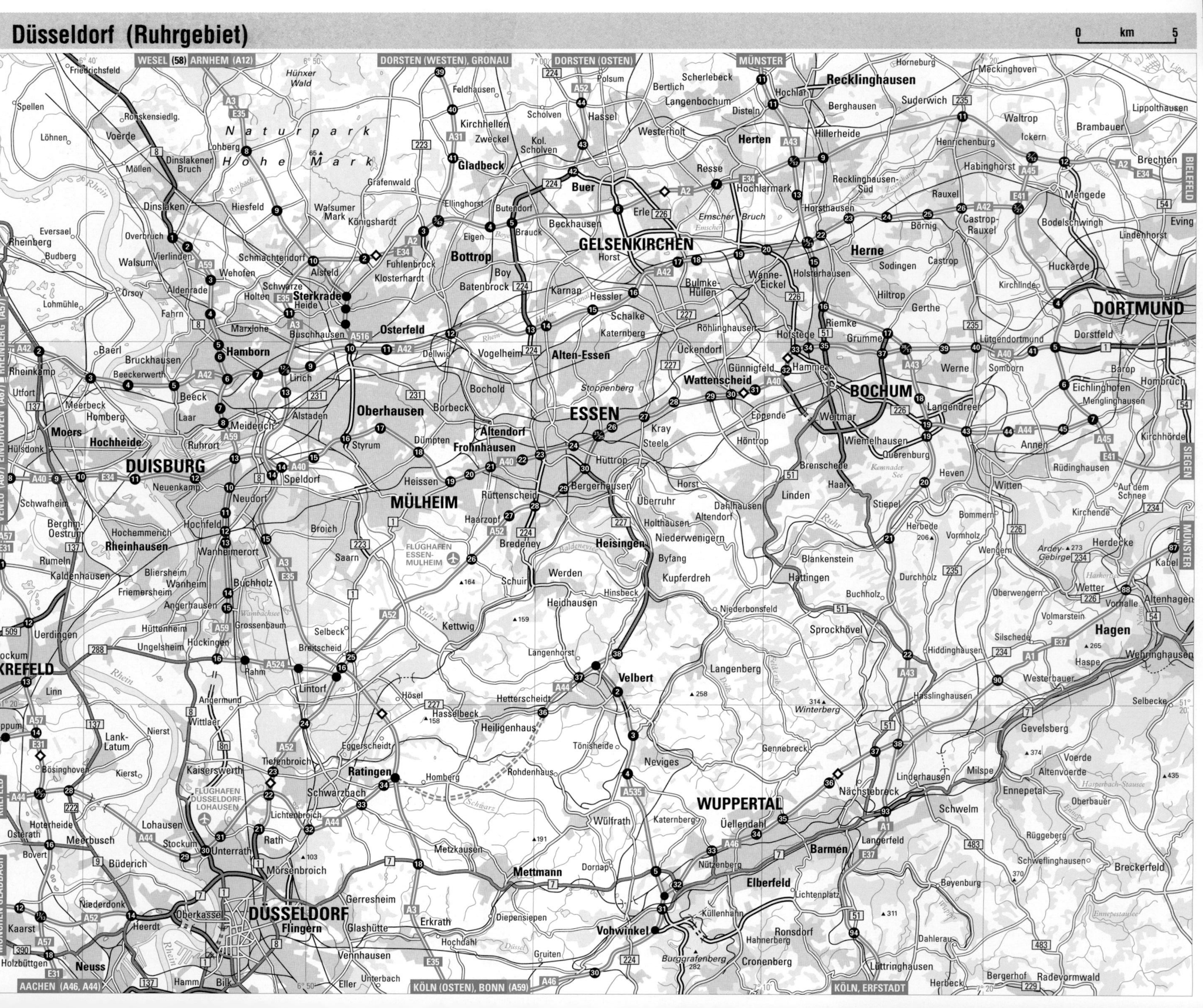
Düsseldorf (Ruhrgebiet)
DORTMUND
BOCHUM
ESSEN
GELSENKIRCHEN
Recklinghausen
Herne
Herten
Bottrop
Oberhausen
MÜLHEIM
DUISBURG
Hagen
WUPPERTAL
Velbert
Ratingen
Mettmann
DÜSSELDORF
Neuss
KREFELD
Moers
Dinslaken
Gladbeck
Wattenscheid
Barmen
Elberfeld
Vohwinkel
FLUGHAFEN ESSEN-MÜLHEIM
FLUGHAFEN DÜSSELDORF-LOHAUSEN
BIELEFELD
SIEGEN
MÜNSTER
WESEL
ARNHEM (A12)
DORSTEN (WESTEN), GRONAU
DORSTEN (OSTEN)
KÖLN, ERFSTADT
KÖLN (OSTEN), BONN (A59)
AACHEN (A46, A44)
MÖNCHEN GLADBACH
KREFELD
VENLO (A67) EINDHOVEN (A67)
RHEINBERG (A57)
km

Firenze Florence

0 km 1

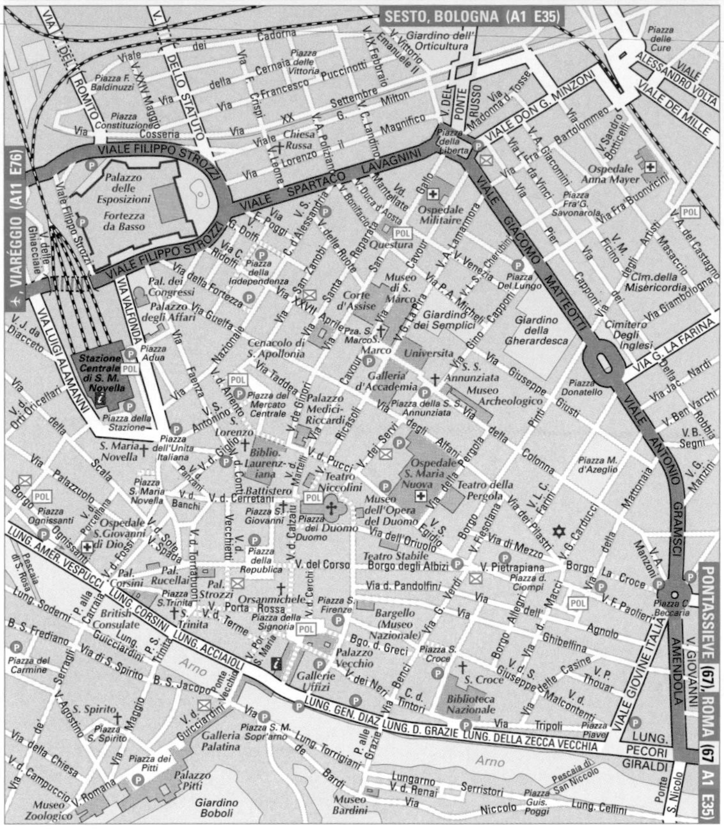

SESTO, BOLOGNA (A1 E35)

✈, VIAREGGIO (A11 E76)

PONTASSIEVE (67), ROMA (67 A1 E35)

Frankfurt

0 km 0,5

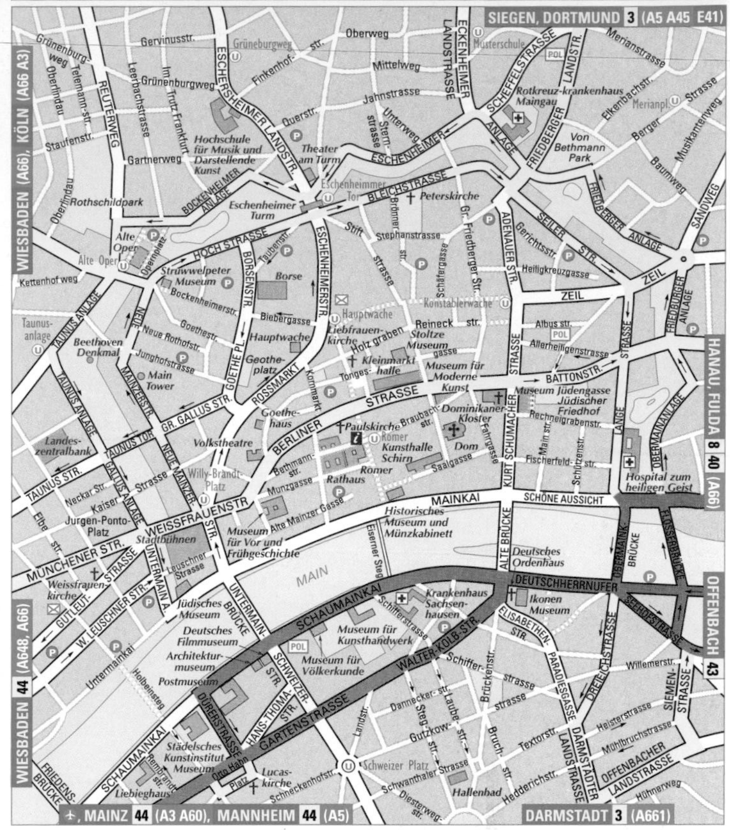

SIEGEN, DORTMUND 3 (A5 A45 E41)

WIESBADEN (A66), KÖLN (A66 A3)

HANAU, FULDA 8 40 (A66)

OFFENBACH 43

WIESBADEN 44 (A648, A66)

✈, MAINZ 44 (A3 A60), MANNHEIM 44 (A5)

DARMSTADT 3 (A661)

Genève Geneva

0 km 1

LAUSANNE 1 (A1, E25)

✈, ST-GENIS-POUILLY 984

THONON-LES-BAINS (5) BONNEVILLE (205)

ANNECY 1 (201)

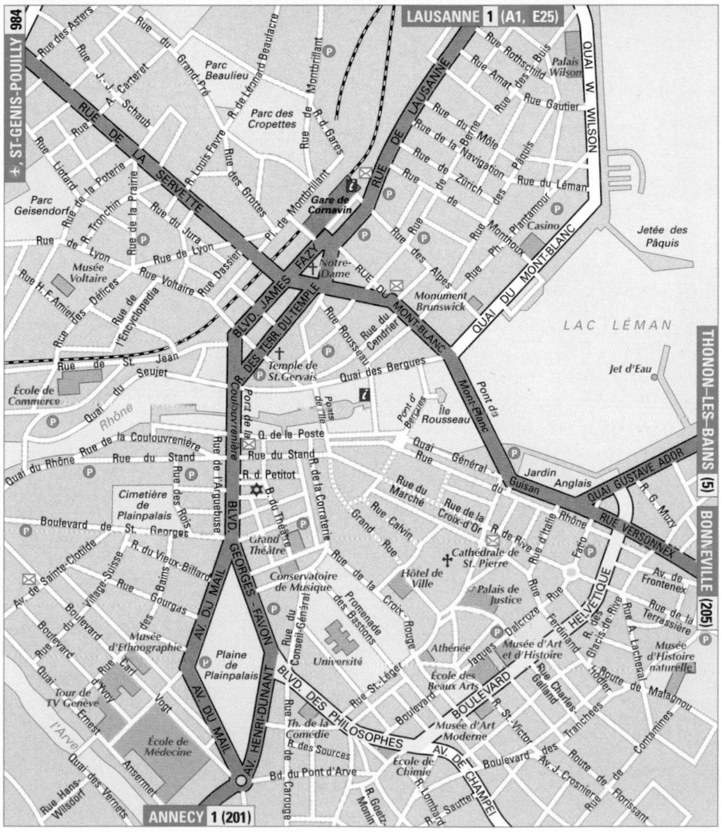

Génova Genoa

0 km 1

SAVONA 1, MILANO (A7 E62), ✈

LA SPEZIA 1, FIRENZE (A12 E80, A11 E76)

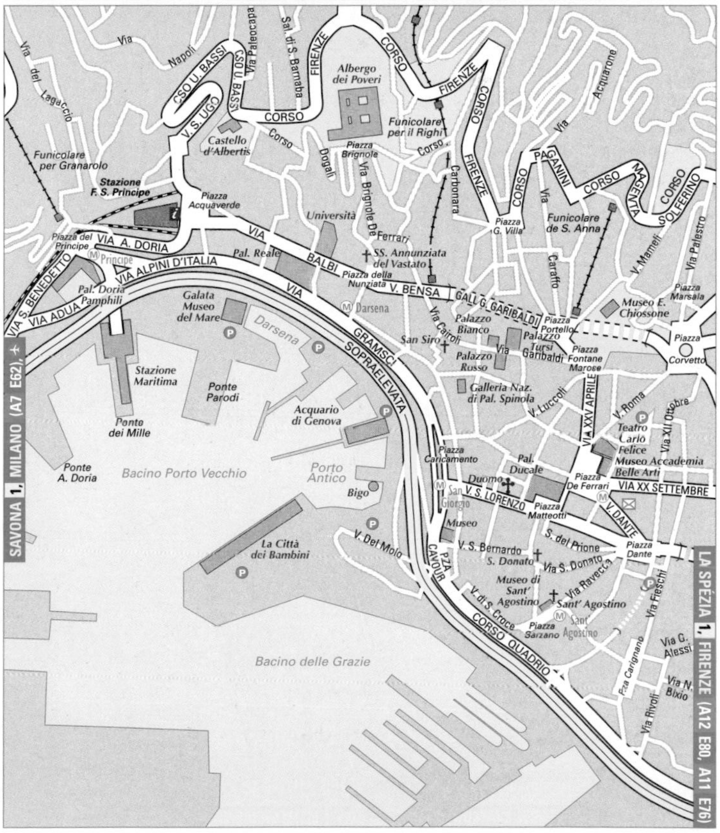

Granada

0 km 0,5

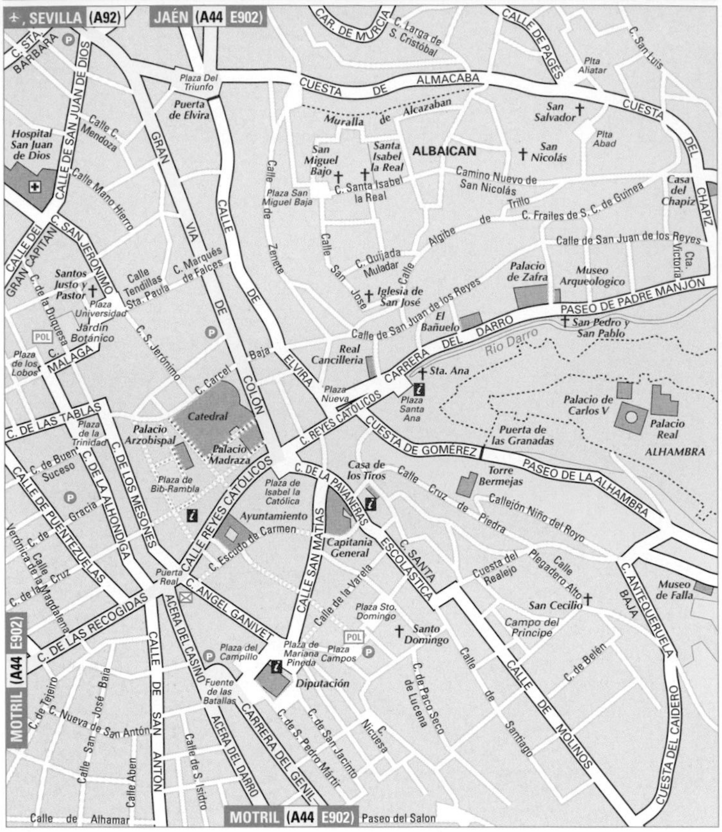

Göteborg Gothenburg

0 km 1

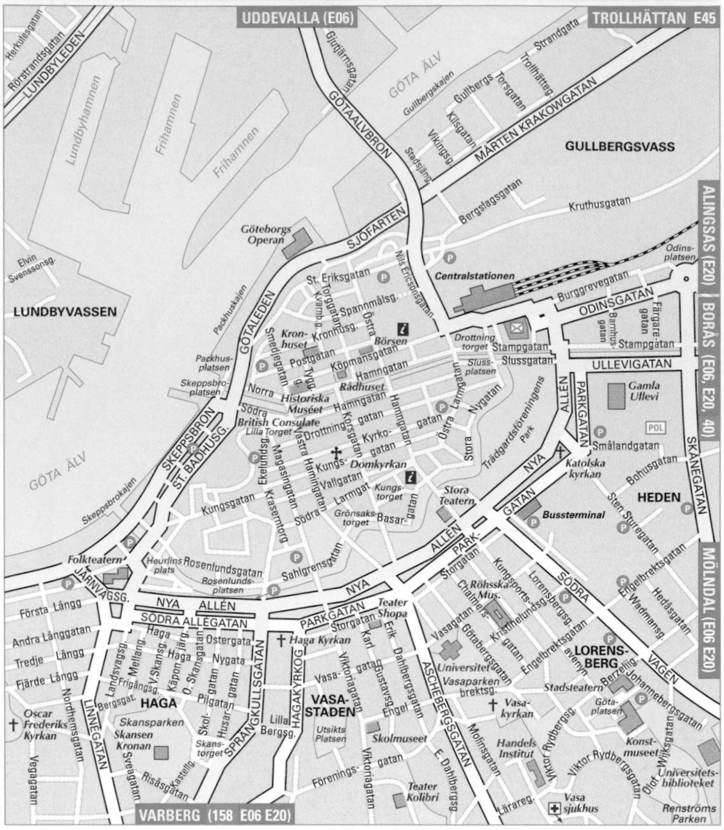

Hamburg

0 km 5

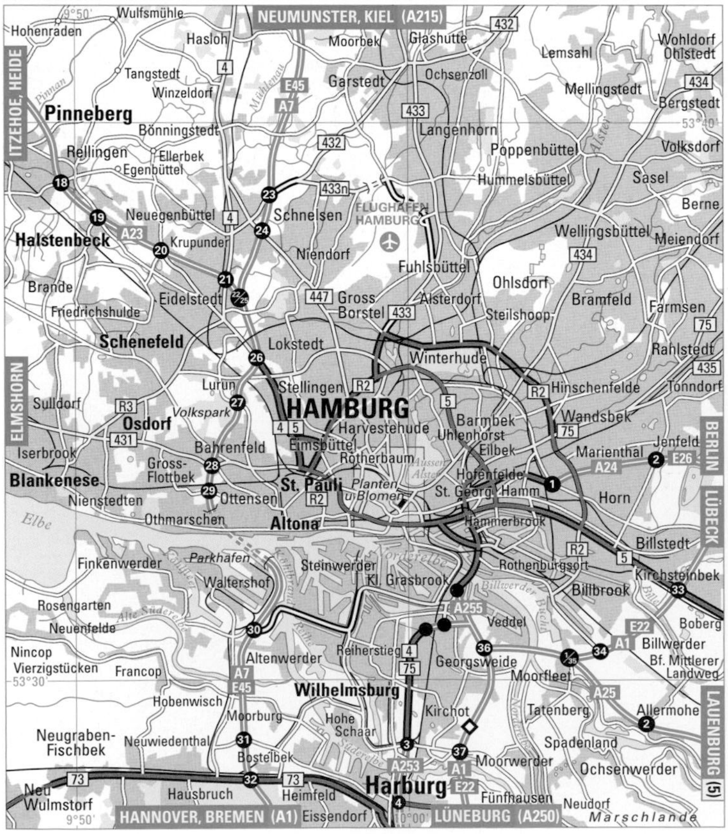

Hamburg

0 km 1

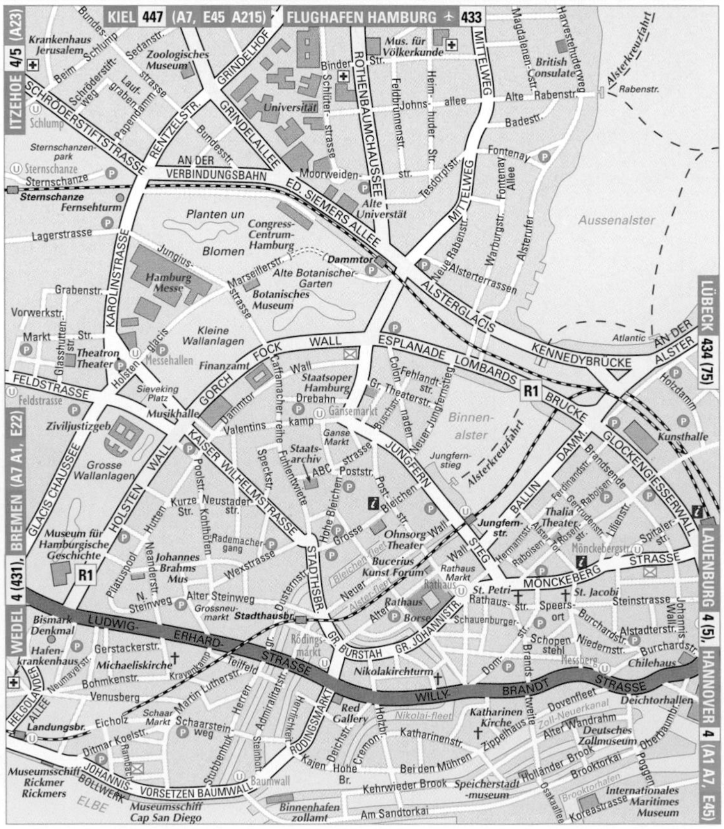

Helsinki

0 km 1

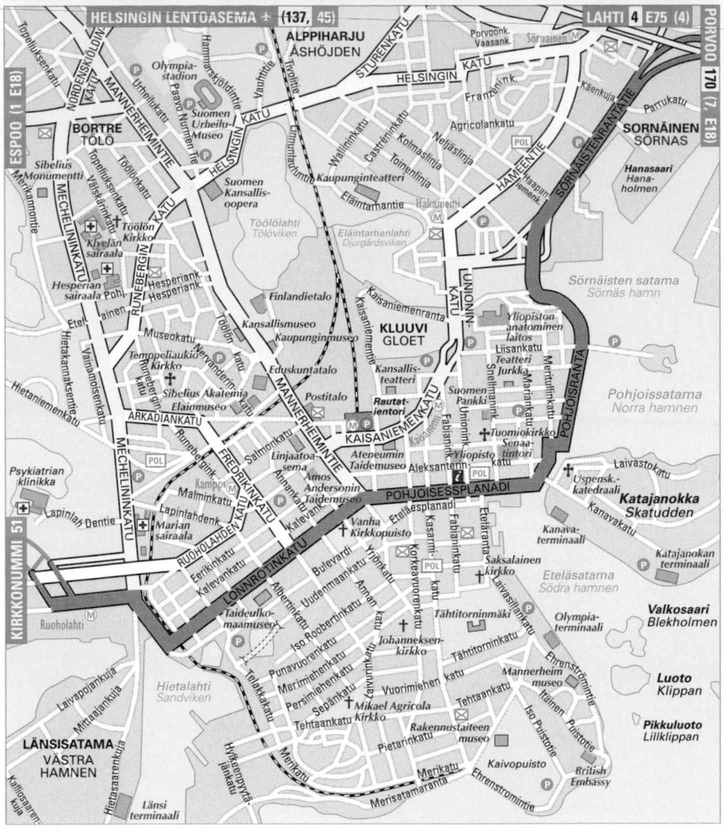

İstanbul

0 km 5

Helsinki

0 km 10

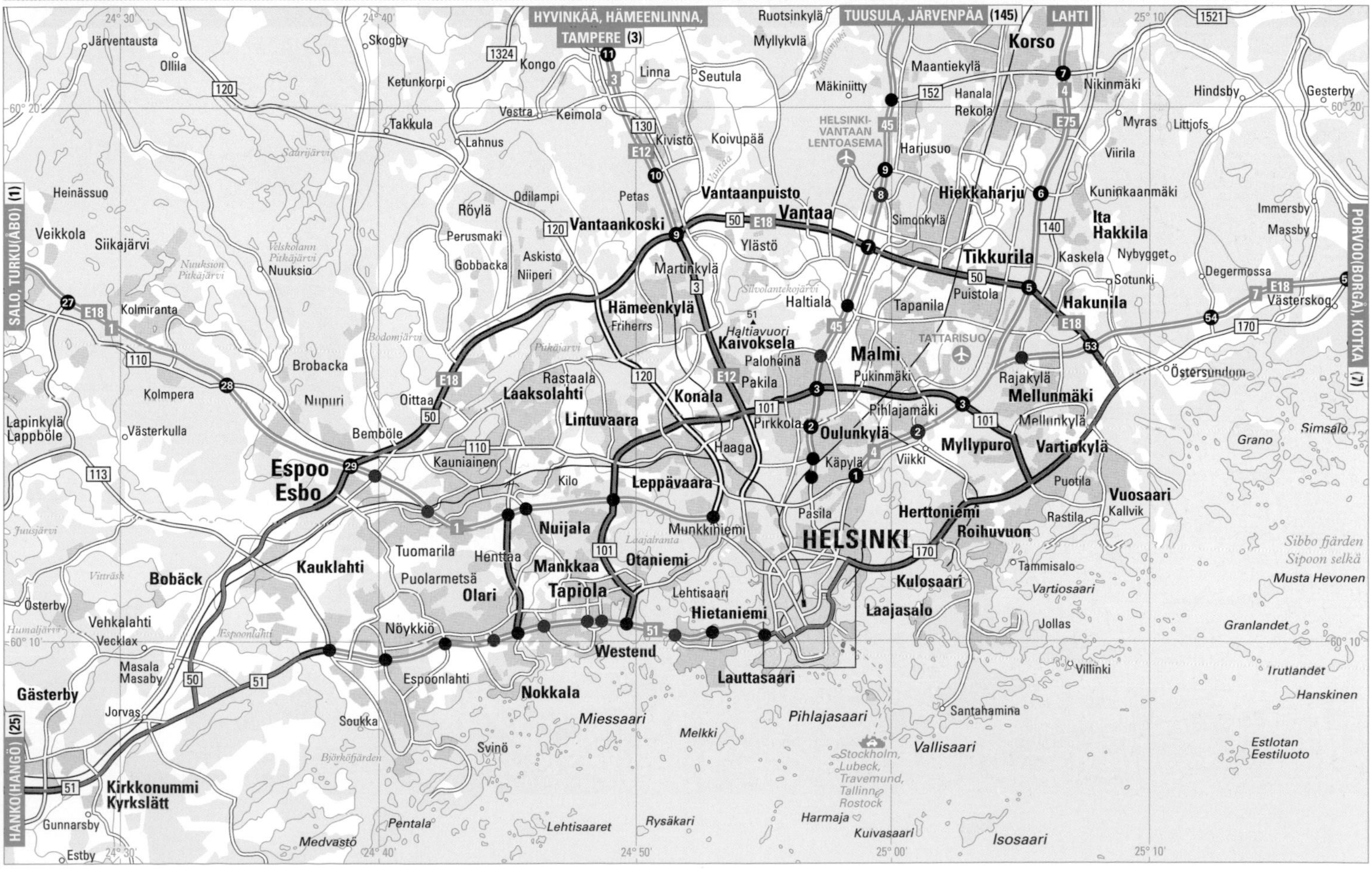

København Copenhagen

0 km 5

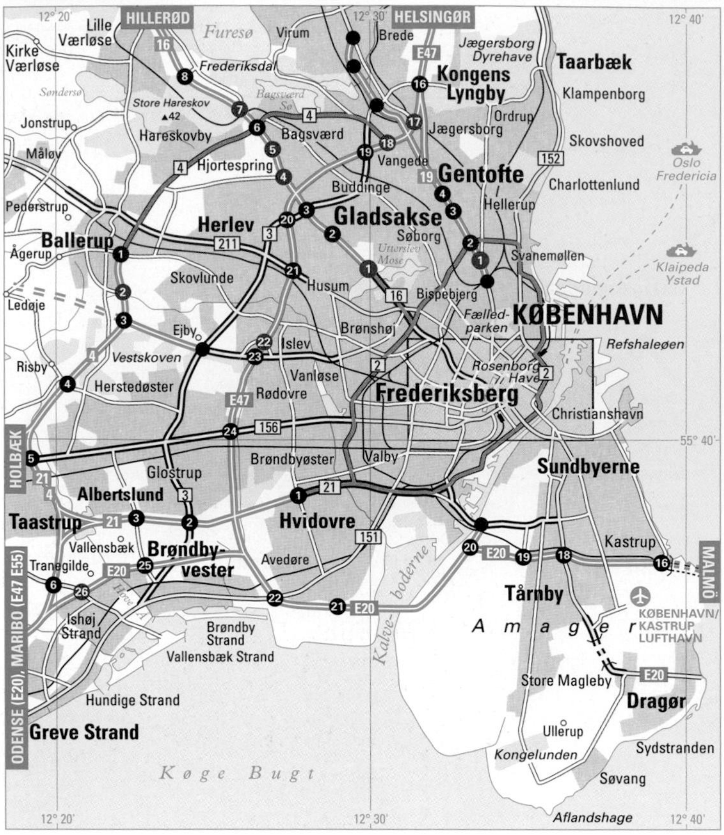

HILLERØD 16 · HELSINGØR E47 · HOLBÆK 21 · ODENSE (E20), MARIBO (E47 E55) · MALMÖ

KØBENHAVN · Frederiksberg · Gentofte · Gladsakse · Herlev · Ballerup · Kongens Lyngby · Taarbæk · Albertslund · Taastrup · Brøndby-vester · Hvidovre · Sundbyerne · Tårnby · Dragør · Amager · Greve Strand · Køge Bugt

Köln Cologne

0 km 1

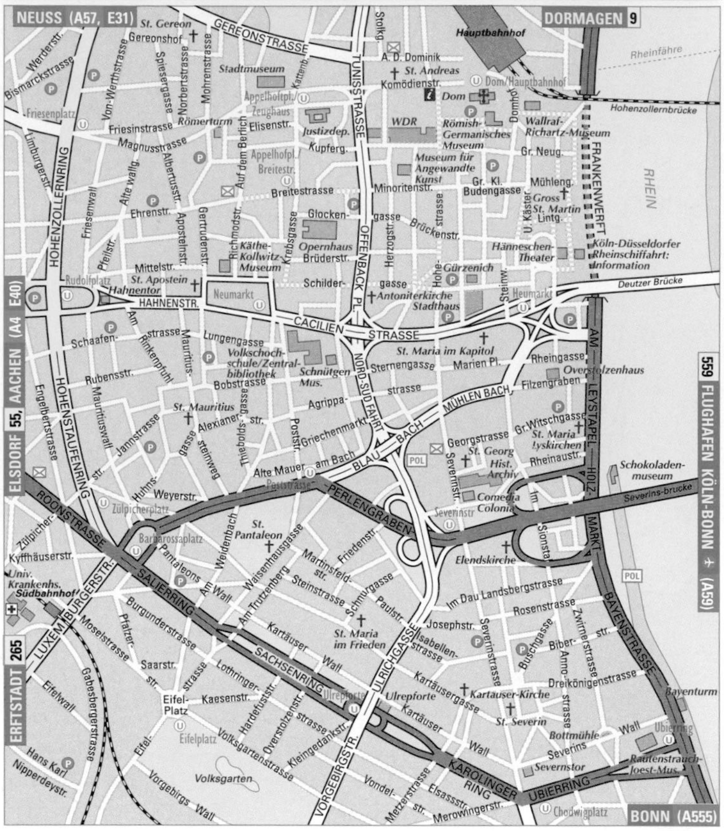

NEUSS (A57, E31) · DORMAGEN 9 · 559 FLUGHAFEN KÖLN-BONN (A59) · BONN (A555) · ERFTSTADT 265 · ELSDORF 55, AACHEN (A4 E40)

RHEIN · Hauptbahnhof · Dom

København Copenhagen

0 km 1

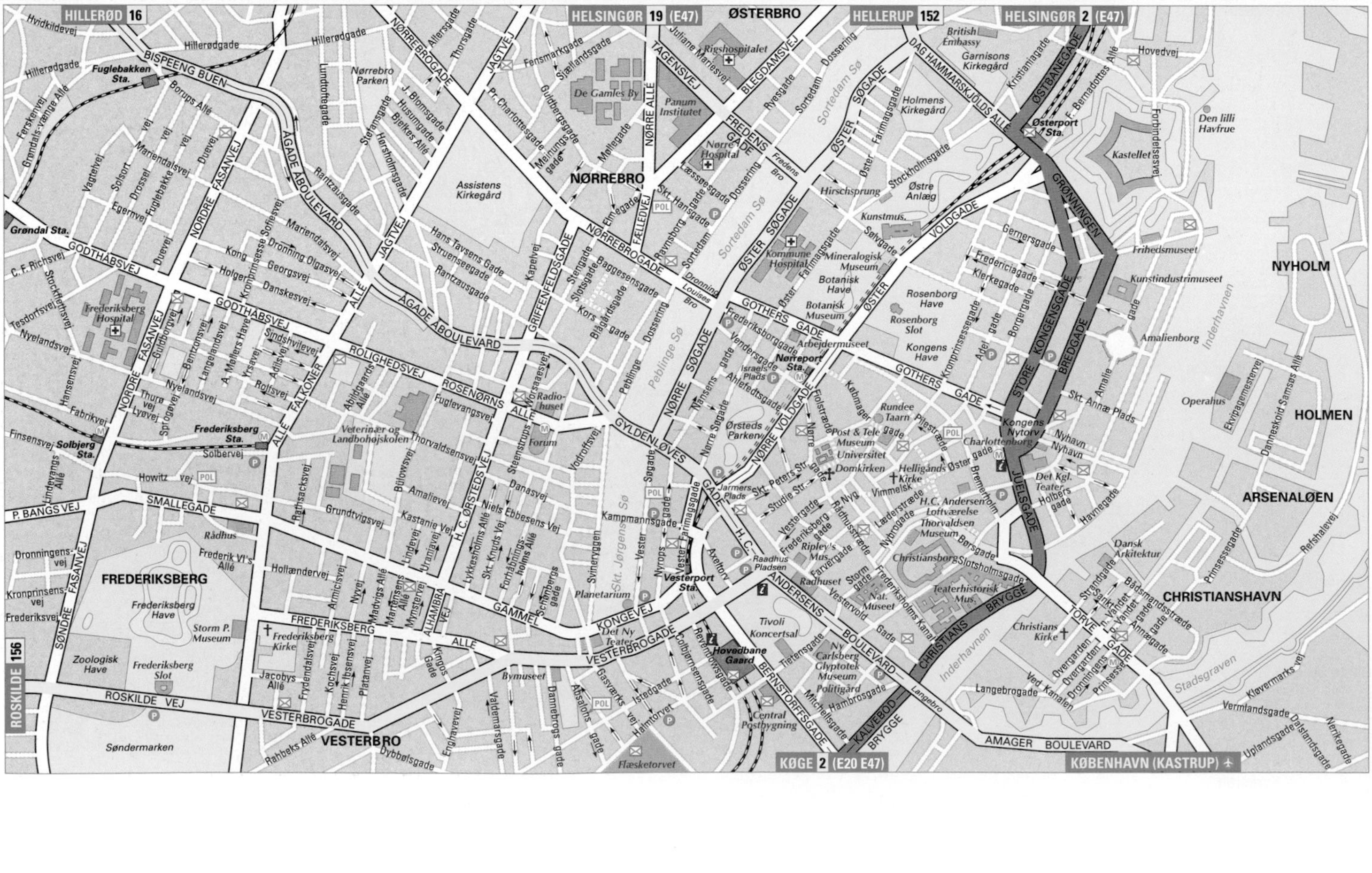

HILLERØD 16 · HELSINGØR 19 (E47) · HELLERUP 152 · HELSINGØR 2 (E47) · ROSKILDE 156 · KØGE 2 (E20 E47) · KØBENHAVN (KASTRUP)

ØSTERBRO · NØRREBRO · FREDERIKSBERG · VESTERBRO · NYHOLM · HOLMEN · ARSENALØEN · CHRISTIANSHAVN

Lisboa Lisbon

0 km 5

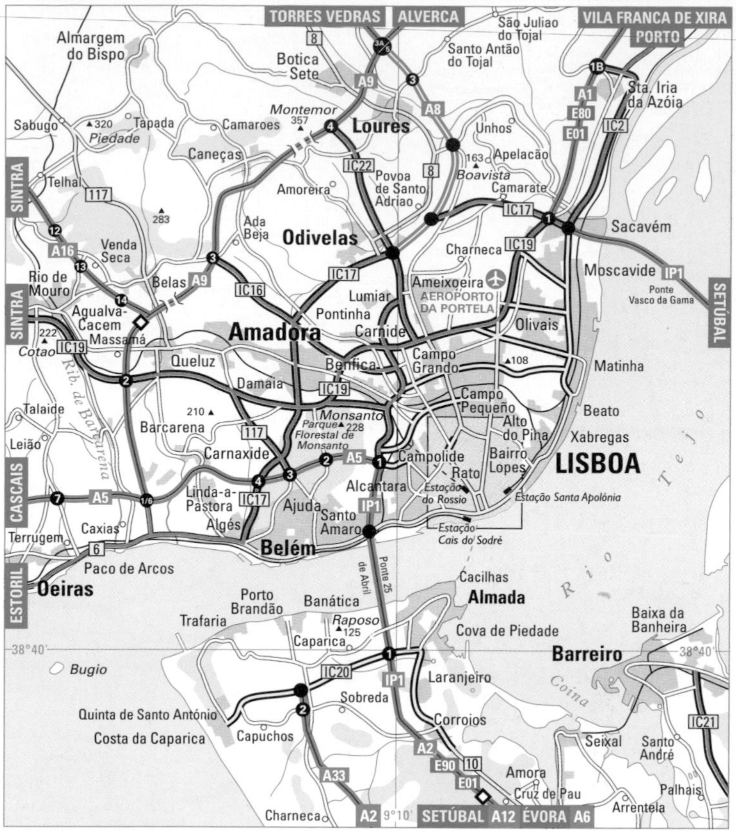

Lisboa Lisbon

0 km 1

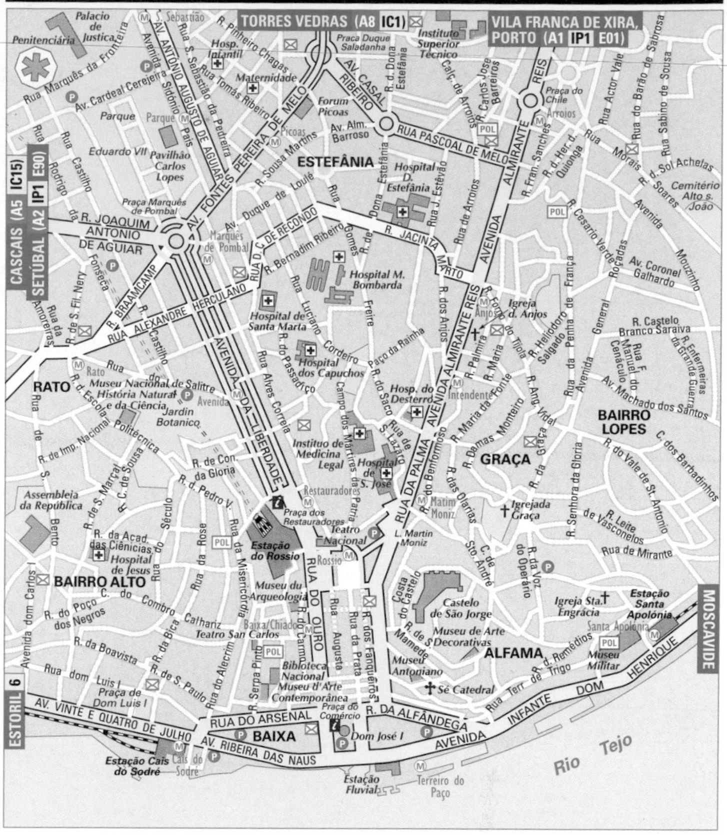

London

0 km 2

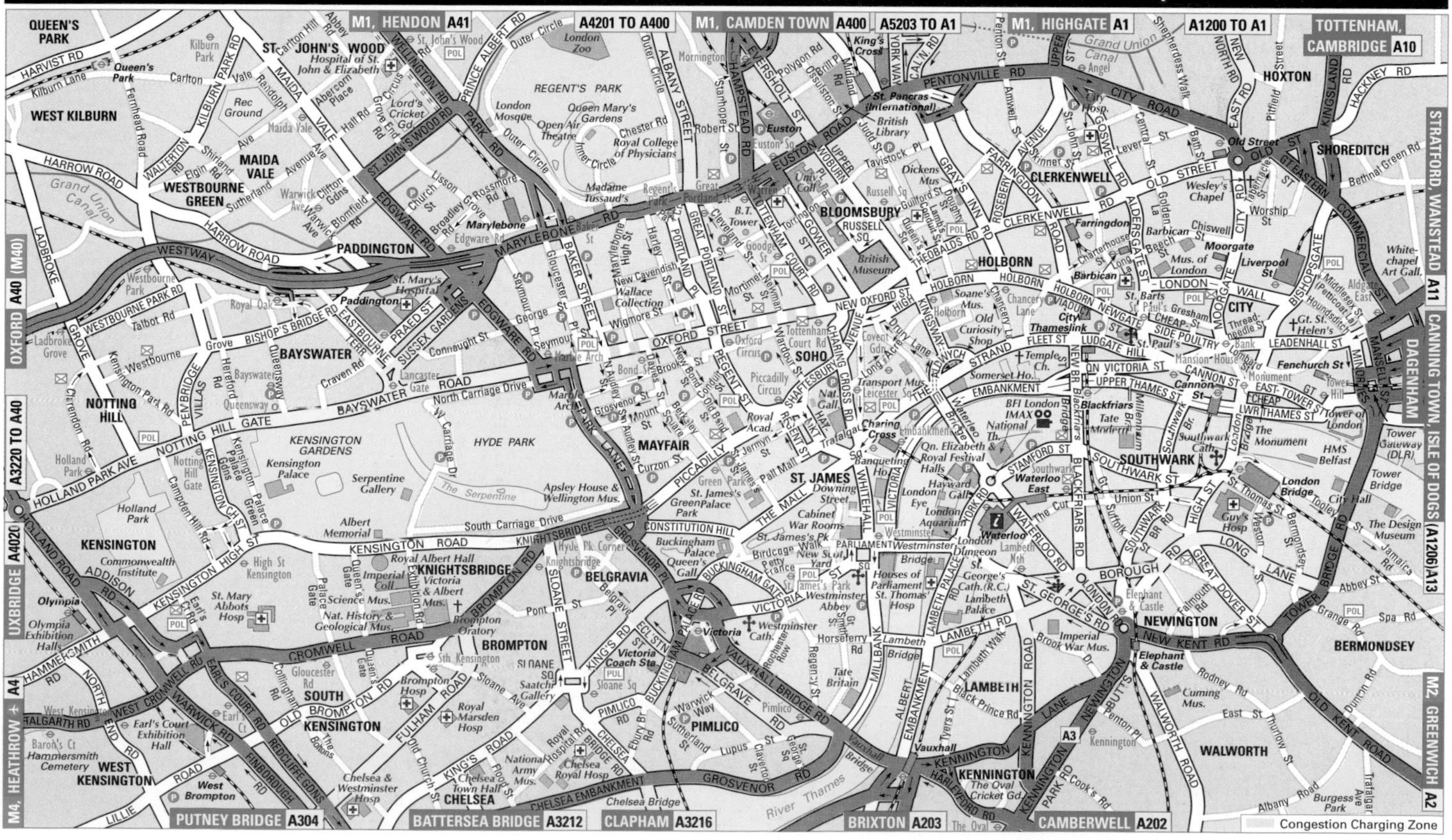

Congestion Charging Zone

London

0 km 10

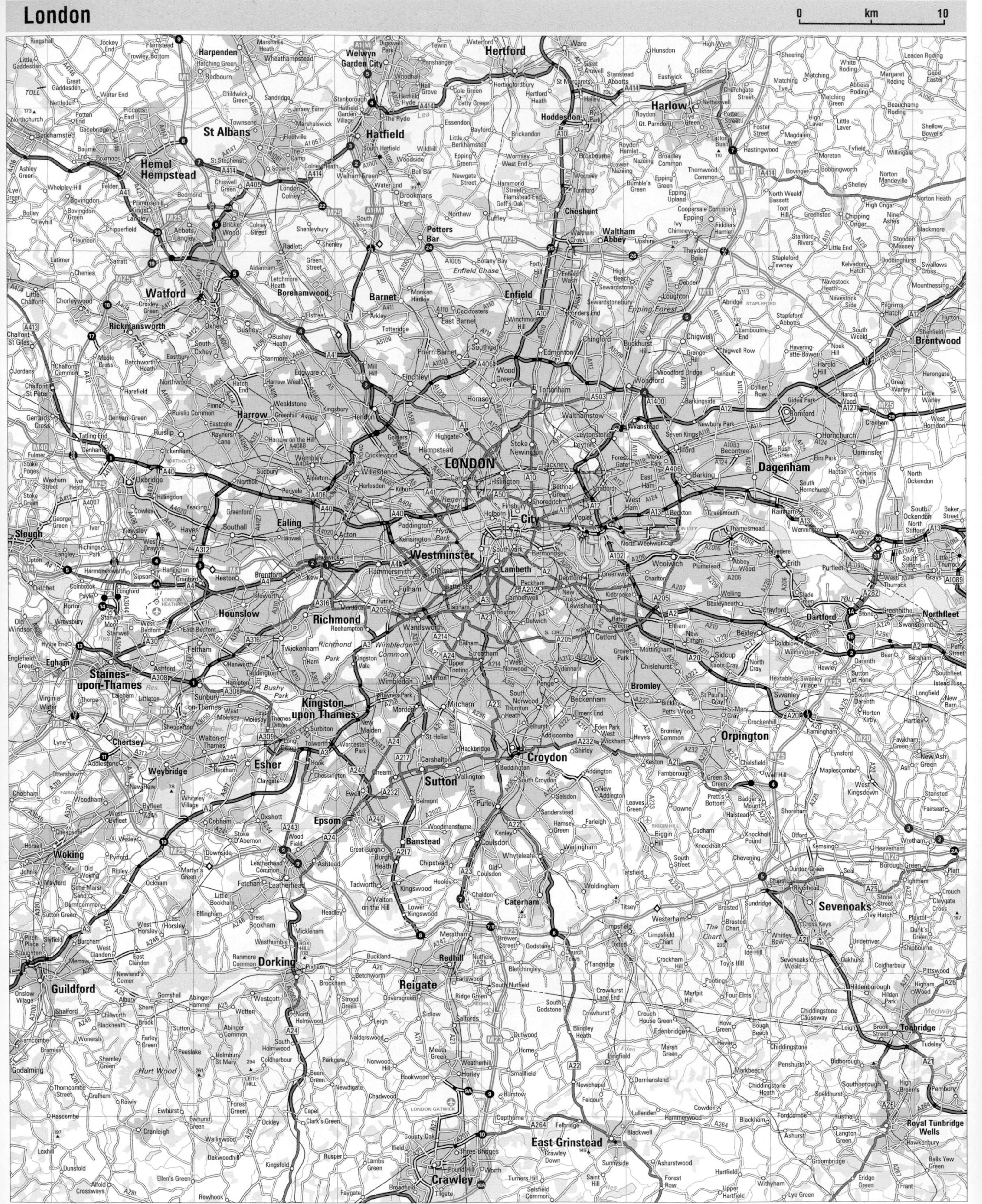

Lyon

0 km 5

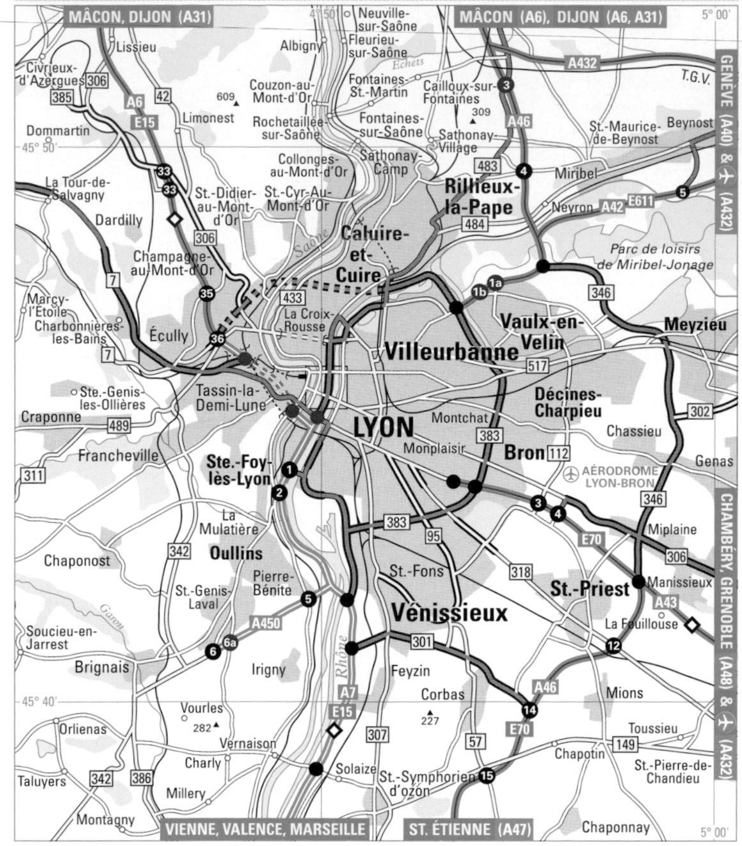

MÂCON, DIJON (A31)
MÂCON (A6), DIJON (A6, A31)
GENÈVE (A40) & ✈ (A432)
CHAMBÉRY, GRENOBLE (A48) & ✈ (A432)
VIENNE, VALENCE, MARSEILLE
ST. ÉTIENNE (A47)

Lissieu
Civrieux-d'Azergues
Dommartin
Albigny
Neuville-sur-Saône
Fleurieu-sur-Saône
Couzon-au-Mont-d'Or
Fontaines-St.-Martin
Cailloux-sur-Fontaines
Limonest
Rochetaillée-sur-Saône
Fontaines-sur-Saône
Sathonay-Village
Sathonay-Camp
St.-Maurice-de-Beynost
Beynost
La Tour-de-Salvagny
Collonges-au-Mont-d'Or
St.-Didier-au-Mont-d'Or
St.-Cyr-au-Mont-d'Or
Rillieux-la-Pape
Miribel
Neyron
Dardilly
Caluire-et-Cuire
Champagne-au-Mont-d'Or
Parc de loisirs de Miribel-Jonage
Marcy-l'Etoile
Charbonnières-les-Bains
Écully
La Croix-Rousse
Villeurbanne
Vaulx-en-Velin
Meyzieu
Ste.-Genis-les-Ollières
Tassin-la-Demi-Lune
Craponne
LYON
Montchat
Décines-Charpieu
Chassieu
Francheville
Monplaisir
Bron
Genas
Ste.-Foy-lès-Lyon
AÉRODROME LYON-BRON
La Mulatière
Oullins
Miplaine
Chaponost
Pierre-Bénite
St.-Fons
St.-Priest
Manissieux
St.-Genis-Laval
Vénissieux
La Fouillouse
Soucieu-en-Jarrest
Brignais
Irigny
Feyzin
Corbas
Mions
Vourles
Vernaison
Toussieu
Orliénas
Charly
Solaize
St.-Symphorien-d'ozon
Chapotin
St.-Pierre-de-Chandieu
Taluyers
Millery
Montagny
Chaponnay

Lyon

0 km 1

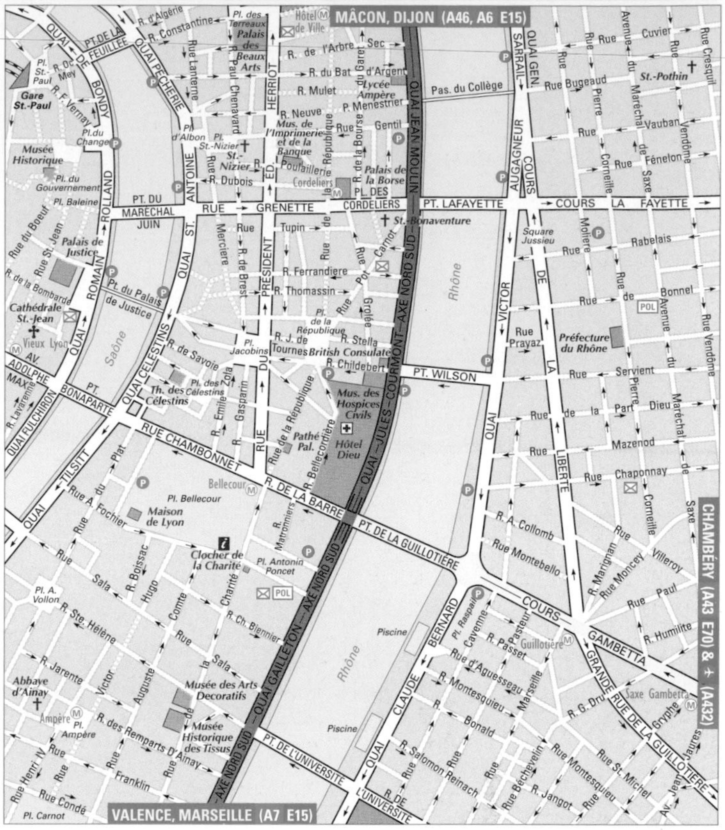

MÂCON, DIJON (A46, A6 E15)
VALENCE, MARSEILLE (A7 E15)
CHAMBÉRY (A43 E70) & ✈ (A432)

Gare St.-Paul
Musée Historique
Pl. du Gouvernement
Palais de Justice
Cathédrale St.-Jean
Vieux Lyon
Hôtel de Ville
Palais des Beaux Arts
Lycée Ampère
Mus. de l'Imprimerie et de la Banque
Palais de la Bourse
Pl. des Cordeliers
St.-Bonaventure
St.-Nizier
Th. des Célestins
Pl. des Jacobins
Mus. des Hospices Civils
Hôtel Dieu
Pl. Bellecour
Maison de Lyon
Clocher de la Charité
Pl. Antonin Poncet
Abbaye d'Ainay
Pl. Ampère
Musée des Arts Décoratifs
Musée Historique des Tissus
Pl. Carnot
Rhône
Saône
Square Jussieu
Préfecture du Rhône
St.-Pothin
Guillotière
Saxe Gambetta
Cours Lafayette
Cours Gambetta
Quai Jules-Courmont
Quai Claude Bernard
Cours de la Liberté

Luxembourg

0 km 0.5

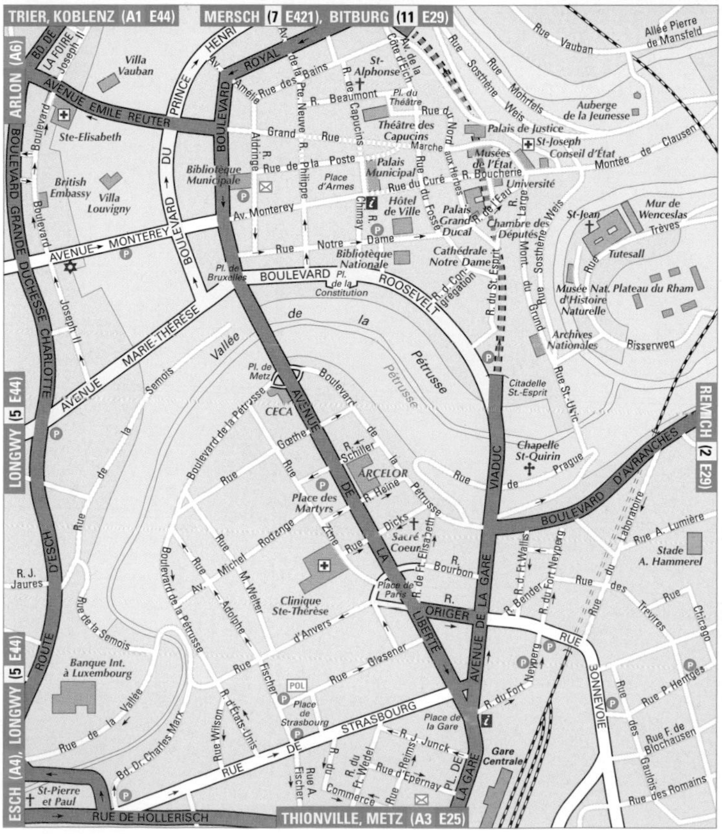

TRIER, KOBLENZ (A1 E44)
MERSCH (7 E421), BITBURG (11 E29)
ARLON (A6)
LONGWY (5 E44)
ESCH (A4), LONGWY (5 E44)
THIONVILLE, METZ (A3 E25)
REMICH (2 E29)

Villa Vauban
Ste-Elisabeth
British Embassy
Villa Louvigny
Bibliothèque Municipale
Palais Municipal
Hôtel de Ville
Palais Grand Ducal
Théâtre des Capucins
Palais de Justice
Conseil d'État
Musées de l'État
Auberge de la Jeunesse
Chambre des Députés
Cathédrale Notre Dame
Bibliothèque Nationale
St-Jean
Mur de Wenceslas
Tutesall
Musée Nat. d'Histoire Naturelle
Plateau du Rham
Archives Nationales
Citadelle St.-Esprit
Chapelle St-Quirin
Pétrusse
CECA
ARCELOR
Place des Martyrs
Sacré Coeur
Clinique Ste-Thérèse
Banque Int. à Luxembourg
Gare Centrale
St-Pierre et Paul
Stade A. Hammerel
Boulevard Royal
Avenue Emile Reuter
Boulevard Grande Duchesse Charlotte
Avenue Marie-Thérèse
Boulevard Roosevelt
Avenue de la Liberté
Avenue de la Gare
Boulevard d'Avranches
Route d'Esch
Rue de Hollerich

Madrid

0 km 5

COLMENAR VIEJO
BURGOS, SANTANDER (N623)
BILBAO (AP1, AP68)
VALLADOLID (AP6, N601)
A CORUÑA (AP6, A6)
GUADALAJARA, ZARAGOZA
ALBACETE A31, VALENCIA
TALAVERA, BADAJOZ
PARLA, TOLEDO
ARANJUEZ, GRANADA (A44)

El Pardo
El Encinar de los Reyes
AEROPUERTO DE MADRID-BARAJAS
Portilleros de las Rozas
Fuencarral
Hortaleza
Barajas
Aravaca
Tetuán
Chamartín
Canillas
La Estación
Ciudad Fin de Semana
Pozuelo de Alarcón
Universidad
Ciudad Lineal
Canillejas
San Cristobal
Humera
Chamberí
Ventas
Pueblo Nuevo
Coslada
Casa de Campo
Salamanca
MADRID
Vicálvaro
Estación Príncipe Pío
Retiro
Moratalaz
Latina
Estación de Atocha
Arganzuela
Campamento
Carabanchel Bajo
Legazpi
Mediodía
Ventorro del Cano
Palomeras
Cuatro Vientos
Usera
Vallecas
Carabanchel Alto
Entrevías
Mercamadrid
Villaverde
La Fortuna
Villaverde Bajo
Canteras de Vallecas
Alcorcón
Cumbres de Vallecas
Leganés
Salmedina
Perales del Río
Getafe
Manzanares
Fuenlabrada

Madrid

0 km 1

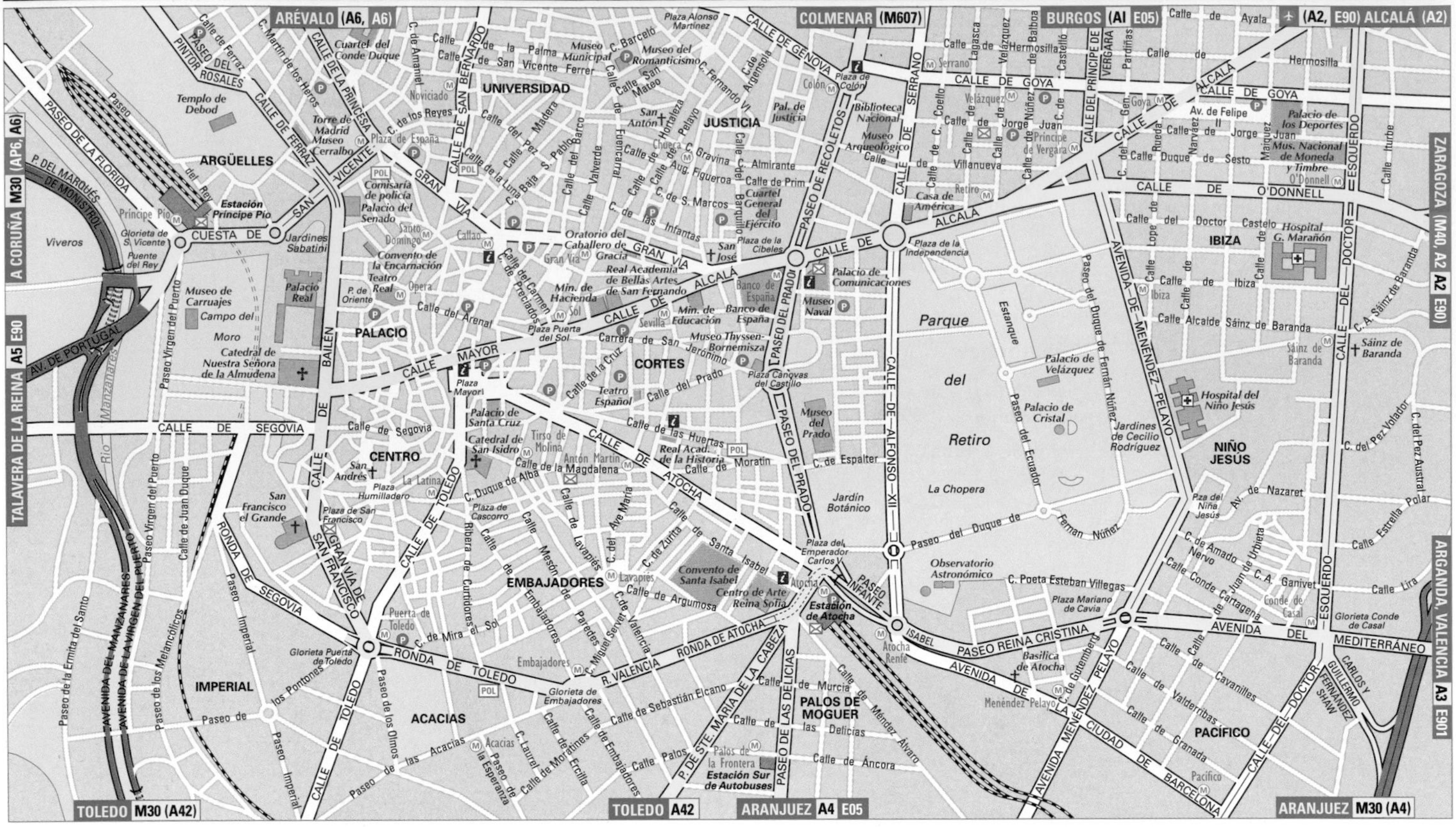

Málaga

0 km 0.5

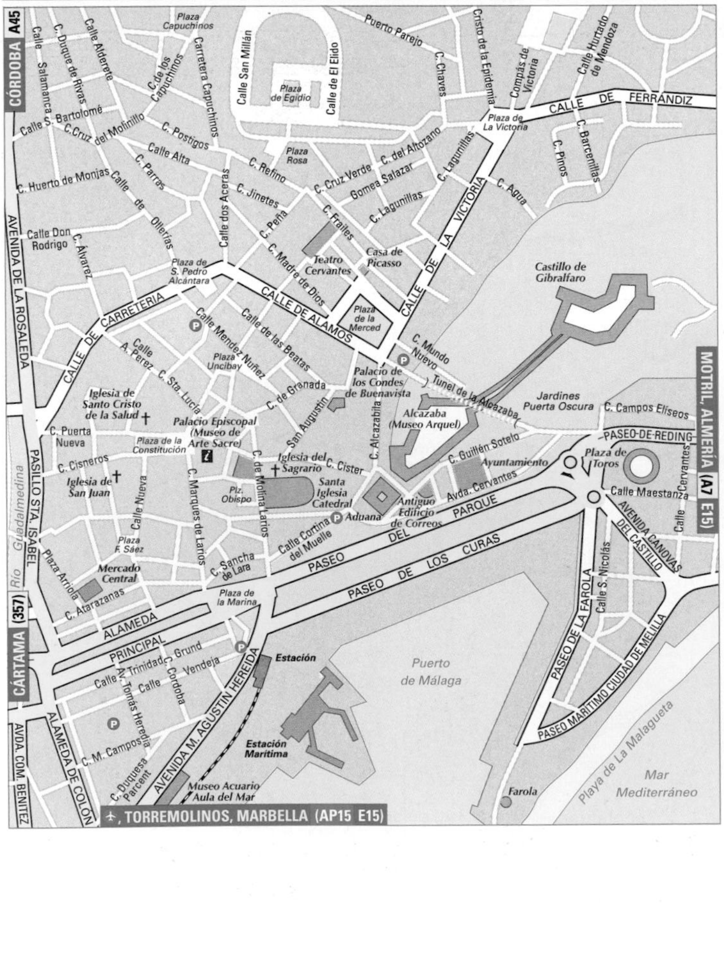

Marseille Marseilles

0 km 0.5

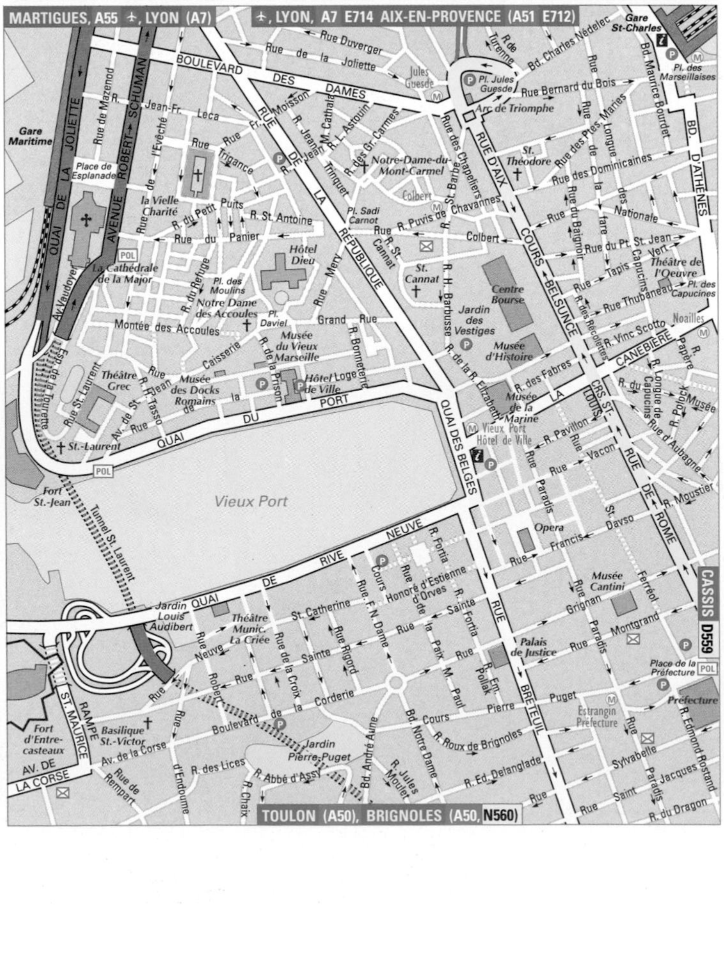

Milano

0 km 5

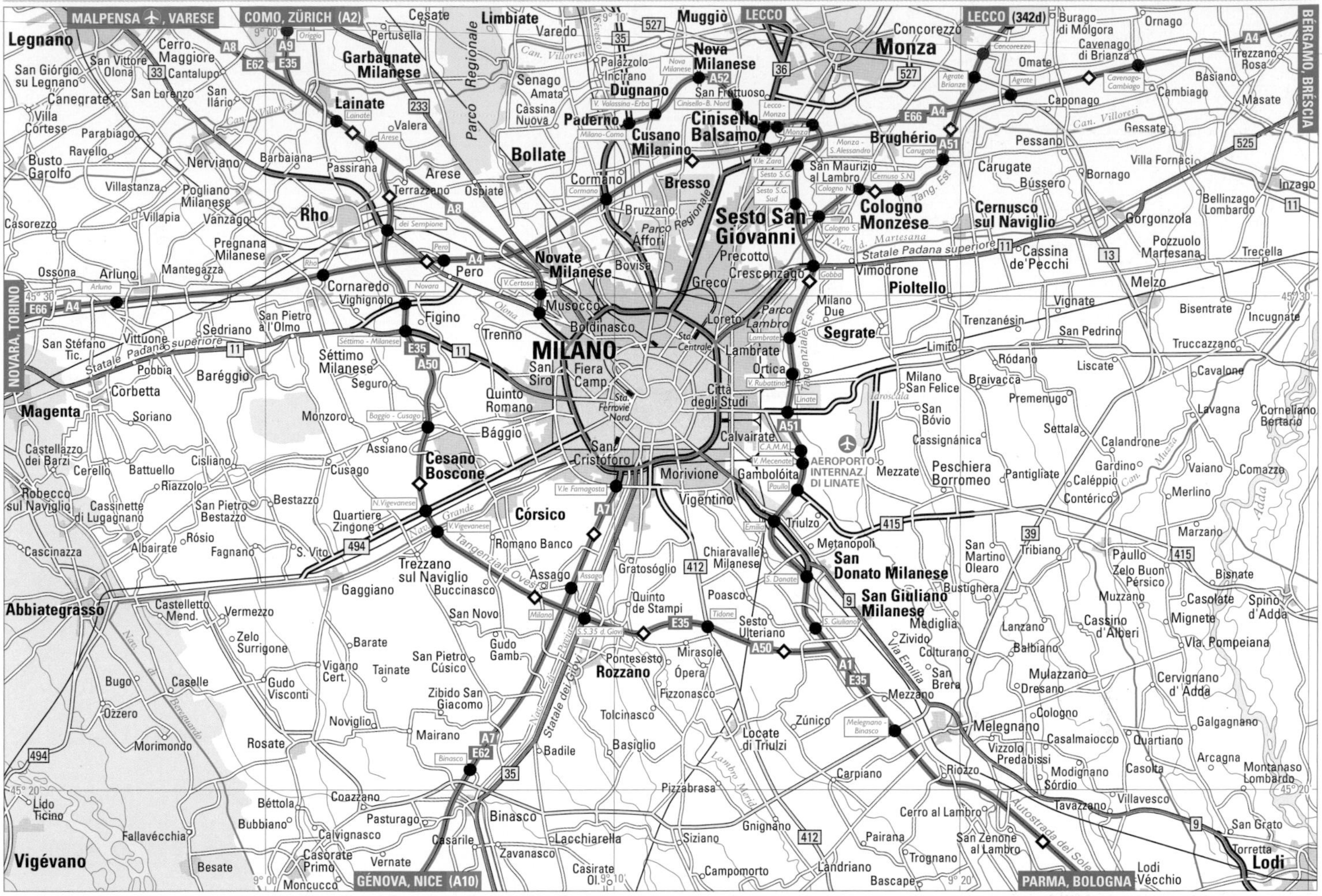

MALPENSA, VARESE · COMO, ZÜRICH (A2) · LECCO · LECCO (342d) · BÉRGAMO, BRESCIA · NOVARA, TORINO · GÉNOVA, NICE (A10) · PARMA, BOLOGNA

Milano Milan

0 km 1

MALPENSA, VARESE (A8) · VARESE 233 · COMO 35 MONZA (36) · BÉRGAMO 11 (525) · SAN SIRO, MAGENTA 11 · LINATE, BRESCIA · ABBIATEGRASSO 494 · GÉNOVA (A7 E62) · PAVIA 35 · LODI 9 PARMA (A51, A1)

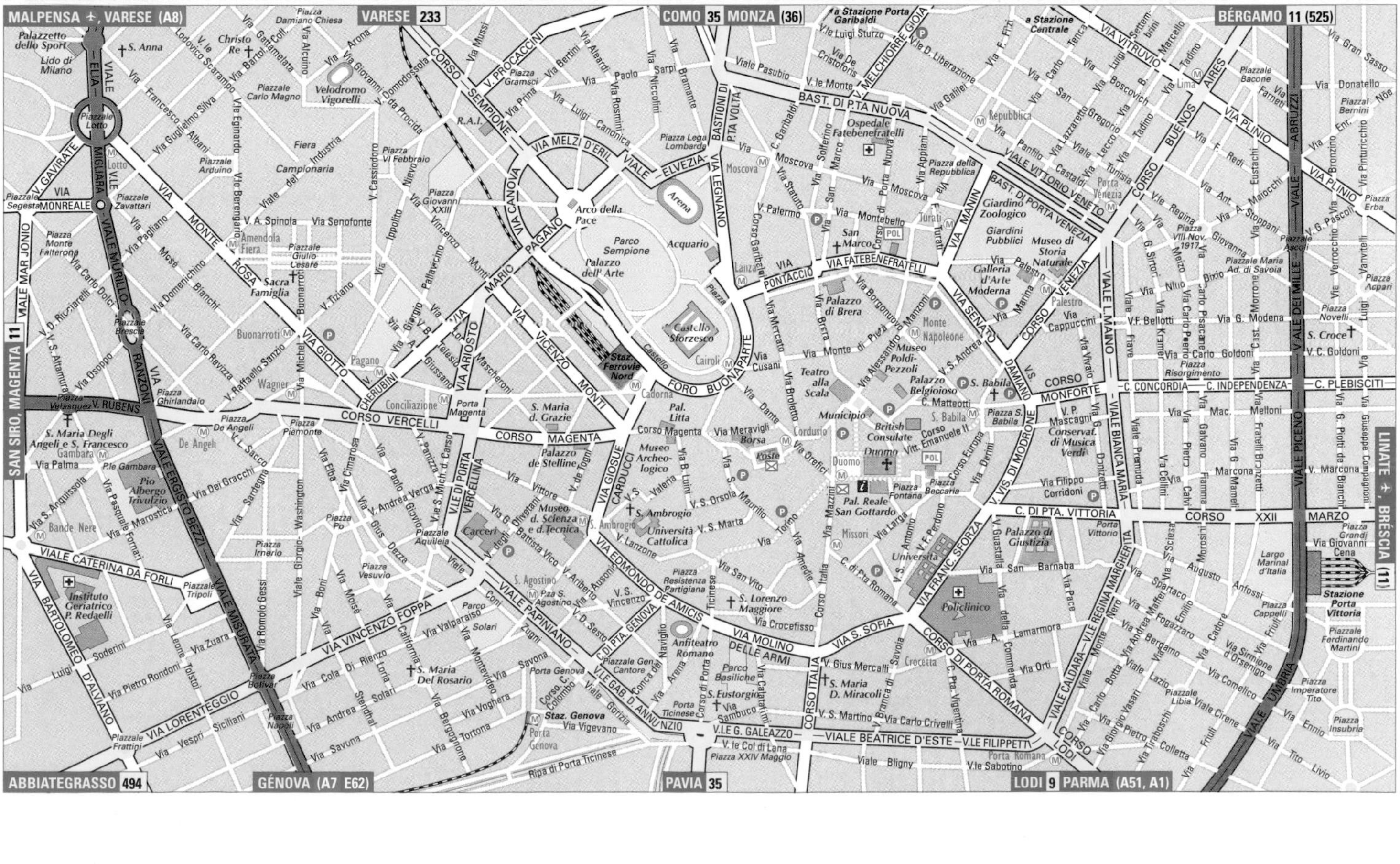

Moskva Moscow

0 km 5

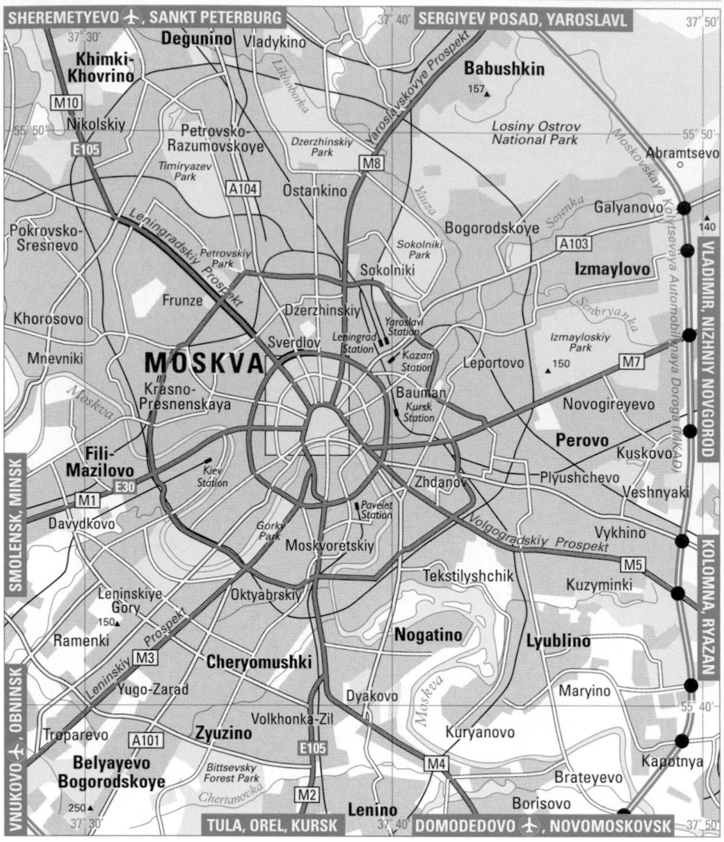

SHEREMETYEVO, SANKT PETERBURG
SERGIYEV POSAD, YAROSLAVL
VLADIMIR, NIZHNIY NOVGOROD
KOLOMNA, RYAZAN
TULA, OREL, KURSK
DOMODEDOVO, NOVOMOSKOVSK
VNUKOVO, OBNINSK
SMOLENSK, MINSK

Degunino
Vladykino
Khimki-Khovrino
Babushkin
Losiny Ostrov National Park
Nikolskiy
Petrovsko-Razumovskoye
Timiryazev Park
Dzerzhinskiy Park
Abramtsevo
Ostankino
Galyanovo
Pokrovsko-Sresnevo
Bogorodskoye
Leningradskiy Prospekt
Petrovskiy Park
Sokolniki Park
Sokolniki
Izmaylovo
Frunze
Dzerzhinskiy
Yaroslavl Station
Leningrad Station
Kazan Station
Khorosovo
Sverdlov
Izmayloskiy Park
Mnevniki
MOSKVA
Leportovo
Krasno-Presnenskaya
Bauman
Kursk Station
Novogireyevo
Fili-Mazilovo
Kiev Station
Perovo
Kuskovo
Zhdanov
Plyushchevo
Veshnyaki
Davydkovo
Paveletz Station
Gorky Park
Moskvoretskiy
Volgogradskiy Prospekt
Vykhino
Tekstilyshchik
Kuzyminki
Leninskiye Gory
Oktyabrskiy
Ramenki
Nogatino
Lyublino
Leninskiy Prospekt
Cheryomushki
Yugo-Zarad
Dyakovo
Maryino
Troparevo
Volkhonka-Zil
Zyuzino
Kuryanovo
Belyayevo Bogorodskoye
Bittsevsky Forest Park
Kapotnya
Brateyevo
Lenino
Borisovo

Moskva

0 km 1

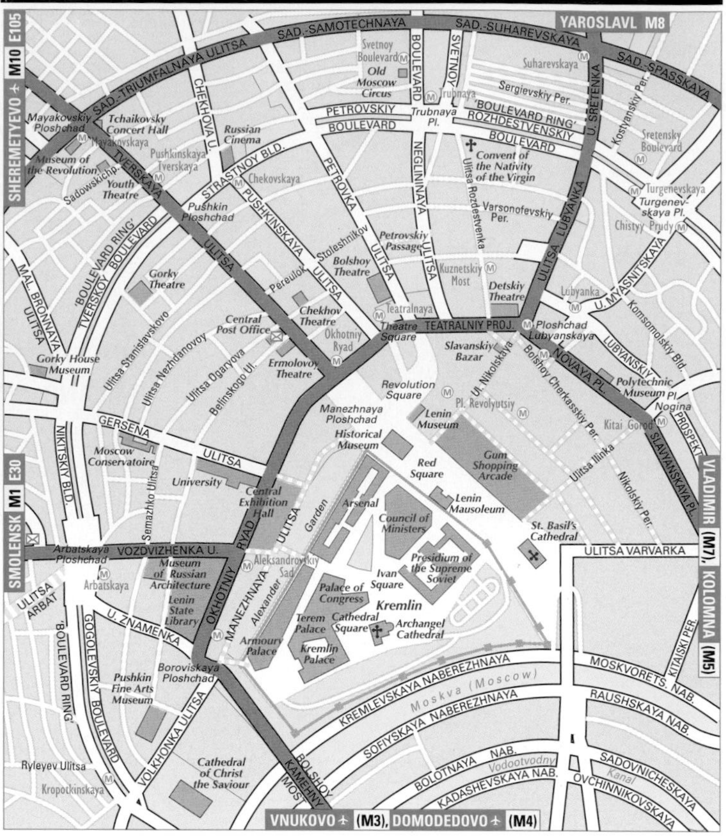

YAROSLAVL M8
SHEREMETYEVO M10 E105
SMOLENSK M1 E30
VLADIMIR (M7), KOLOMNA (M5)
VNUKOVO (M3), DOMODEDOVO (M4)

Sad.-Samotechnaya
Sad.-Suharevskaya
Sad.-Spasskaya
Sad.-Triumfalnaya Ulitsa
Svetnoy Boulevard
Old Moscow Circus
Suharevskaya
Sergievskiy Per.
Mayakovskiy Ploshchad
Tchaikovsky Concert Hall
Russian Cinema
Petrovskiy Boulevard
Trubnaya Pl.
'Boulevard Ring' Rozhdestvenskiy Boulevard
Sretensky Boulevard
Museum of the Revolution
Youth Theatre
Pushkinskaya
Tverskaya
Convent of the Nativity of the Virgin
Chekhovskaya
Turgenevskaya
Pushkin Ploshchad
Varsonofevskiy Per.
Chistyy Prudy
Petrovskiy Passage
Gorky Theatre
Bolshoy Theatre
Kuznetsky Most
Detskiy Theatre
Lubyanka
Central Post Office
Chekhov Theatre
Teatralnaya
Theatre Square
Teatralniy Proj.
Ploshchad Lubyanskaya
Polytechnic Museum
Gorky House Museum
Ermolova Theatre
Okhotniy Ryad
Slavanskiy Bazar
Revolution Square
Pl. Revolyutsiy
Kitai Gorod
Nogina
Manezhnaya Ploshchad
Lenin Museum
Historical Museum
Moscow Conservatoire
University
Red Square
Gum Shopping Arcade
Central Exhibition Hall
Arsenal
Lenin Mausoleum
Council of Ministers
St. Basil's Cathedral
Ulitsa Varvarka
Arbatskaya Ploshchad
Vozdvizhenka U.
Museum of Russian Architecture
Aleksandrovskiy Sad
Presidium of the Supreme Soviet
Palace of Congress
Ivan Square
Lenin State Library
Kremlin
Terem Palace
Cathedral Square
Archangel Cathedral
Armoury Palace
Kremlin Palace
Borovitskaya Ploshchad
Moskvorets. Nab.
Raushskaya Nab.
Kremlevskaya Naberezhnaya
Pushkin Fine Arts Museum
Sofiyskaya Naberezhnaya
Sadovnicheskaya Nab.
Ryleyev Ulitsa
Kropotkinskaya
Cathedral of Christ the Saviour
Bolotnaya Nab.
Kadashevskaya Nab.
Ovchinnikovskaya

München Munich

0 km 5

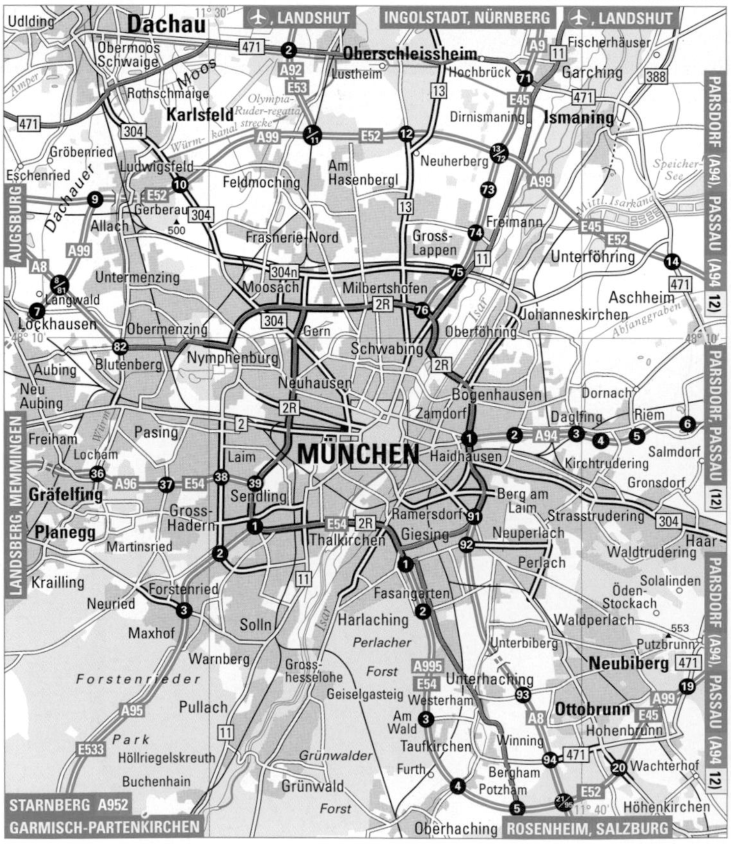

LANDSHUT
INGOLSTADT, NÜRNBERG
PARSDORF (A94), PASSAU (A94)
PARSDORF PASSAU
STARNBERG A952
GARMISCH-PARTENKIRCHEN
ROSENHEIM, SALZBURG
LANDSBERG, MEMMINGEN
AUGSBURG

Udlding
Dachau
Fischerhäuser
Obermoos Schwaige
Oberschleissheim
Lustheim
Hochbrück
Garching
Rothschmaige
Karlsfeld
Olympia-Ruder-regatta-strecke
Dirnismaning
Ismaning
Gröbenried
Eschenried
Neuherberg
Ludwigsfeld
Feldmoching
Am Hasenbergl
Speicher-See
Gerberau
Allach
Freimann
Fasanerie-Nord
Gross-Lappen
Unterföhring
Untermenzing
Aschheim
Langwald
Moosach
Milbertshofen
Lockhausen
Obermenzing
Johanneskirchen
Oberföhring
Schwabing
Aubing
Blutenburg
Nymphenburg
Neu Aubing
Neuhausen
Bogenhausen
Dornach
Zamdorf
Daglfing
Riem
Freiham
Pasing
Lochham
Laim
MÜNCHEN
Haidhausen
Salmdorf
Kirchtrudering
Gräfelfing
Gronsdorf
Sendling
Berg am Laim
Gross-Hadern
Ramersdorf
Strasstrudering
Planegg
Thalkirchen
Giesing
Neuperlach
Haar
Martinsried
Waldtrudering
Perlach
Krailling
Forstenried
Solalinden
Neuried
Fasangarten
Öden-Stockach
Maxhof
Solln
Harlaching
Waldperlach
Perlacher Forst
Unterbiberg
Putzbrunn
Warnberg
Gross-hesselohe
Neubiberg
Forstenrieder Park
Geiselgasteig
Unterhaching
Pullach
Westerham
Ottobrunn
Am Wald
Hohenbrunn
Höllriegelskreuth
Taufkirchen
Winning
Wachterhof
Buchenhain
Grünwalder Forst
Furth
Bergham
Potzham
Grünwald
Höhenkirchen
Oberhaching

München Munich

0 km 1

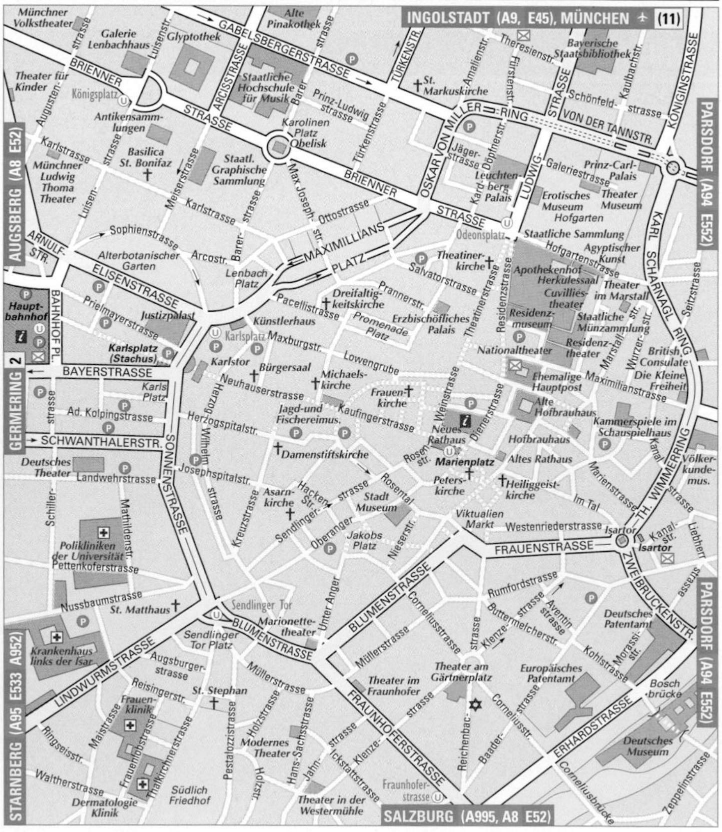

INGOLSTADT (A9, E45), MÜNCHEN (11)
PARSDORF (A94 E52)
AUGSBERG (A8 E52)
GERMERING 2
STARNBERG (A95 E533 A952)
SALZBURG (A995, A8 E52)
PARSDORF (A94 E52)

Münchner Volkstheater
Alte Pinakothek
Galerie Lenbachhaus
Glyptothek
Gabelsbergerstrasse
Theresienstr.
Bayerische Staatsbibliothek
Theater für Kinder
Königsplatz
Brienner Strasse
Staatliche Hochschule für Musik
Prinz-Ludwig strasse
St. Markuskirche
Schönfeld strasse
Antikensammlungen
Karolinen Platz Obelisk
Von der Tannstr.
Basilica St. Bonifaz
Staatl. Graphische Sammlung
Jägerstrasse
Prinz-Carl-Palais
Münchner Ludwig Thoma Theater
Galeriestrasse
Leuchtenberg Palais
Erotisches Museum
Theater Museum
Hofgarten
Sophienstrasse
Maximilians Platz
Odeonsplatz
Staatliche Sammlung Ägyptischer Kunst
Alterbotanischer Garten
Arcostr.
Lenbach Platz
Theatinerkirche
Salvatorstrasse
Apothekenhof Herkulessaal
Theater im Marstall
Elisenstrasse
Haupt-bahnhof
Dreifaltigkeitskirche
Pacellistrasse
Prannerstr.
Cuvilliés-theater
Residenz-museum
Staatliche Münzsammlung
Justizpalast
Künstlerhaus
Promenade Platz
Erzbischöfliches Palais
Nationaltheater
Residenz-theater
British Consulate
Karlsplatz (Stachus)
Maxburgstr.
Karlstor
Bürgersaal
Lowengrube
Ehemalige Hauptpost
Die Kleine Freiheit
Bayerstrasse
Neuhauserstrasse
Michaelskirche
Frauenkirche
Maximilianstrasse
Alte Hofbrauhaus
Ad. Kolpingstrasse
Herzogspitalstr.
Jagd-und Fischereimus.
Kaufingerstrasse
Kammerspiele im Schauspielhaus
Neues Rathaus
Schwanthalerstr.
Damenstiftskirche
Marienplatz
Hofbrauhaus
Altes Rathaus
Deutsches Theater
Landwehrstrasse
Josephspitalstr.
Peterskirche
Heiliggeist-kirche
Völkerkunde-mus.
Asamkirche
Stadt Museum
Viktualien Markt
Westenriederstrasse
Isartor
Polikliniken der Universität Pettenkoferstrasse
Jakobs Platz
Frauenstrasse
Nussbaumstrasse
St. Matthaus
Sendlinger Tor
Marionette-theater
Rumfordstrasse
Deutsches Patentamt
Krankenhaus links der Isar
Sendlinger Tor Platz
Blumenstrasse
Zweibrückenstr.
Augsburgerstrasse
Müllerstrasse
Theater im Fraunhofer
Theater am Gärtnerplatz
Europäisches Patentamt
Lindwurmstrasse
St. Stephan
Frauenklinik
Modernes Theater
Fraunhoferstrasse
Erhardtstrasse
Bosch-brücke
Deutsches Museum
Dermatologie Klinik
Südlich Friedhof
Theater in der Westermühle

Nápoli Naples

0 km 5

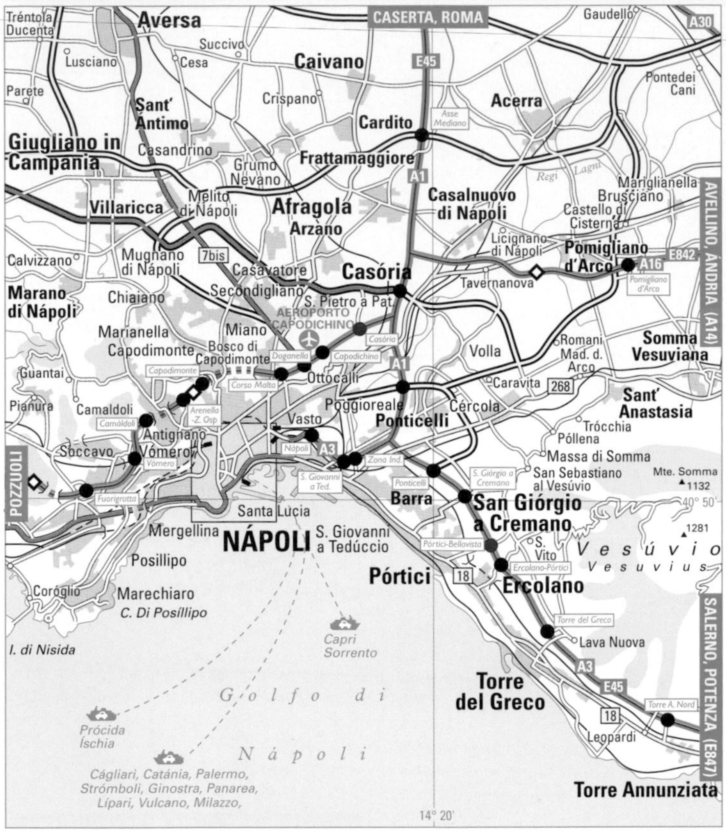

Nápoli Naples

0 km 1

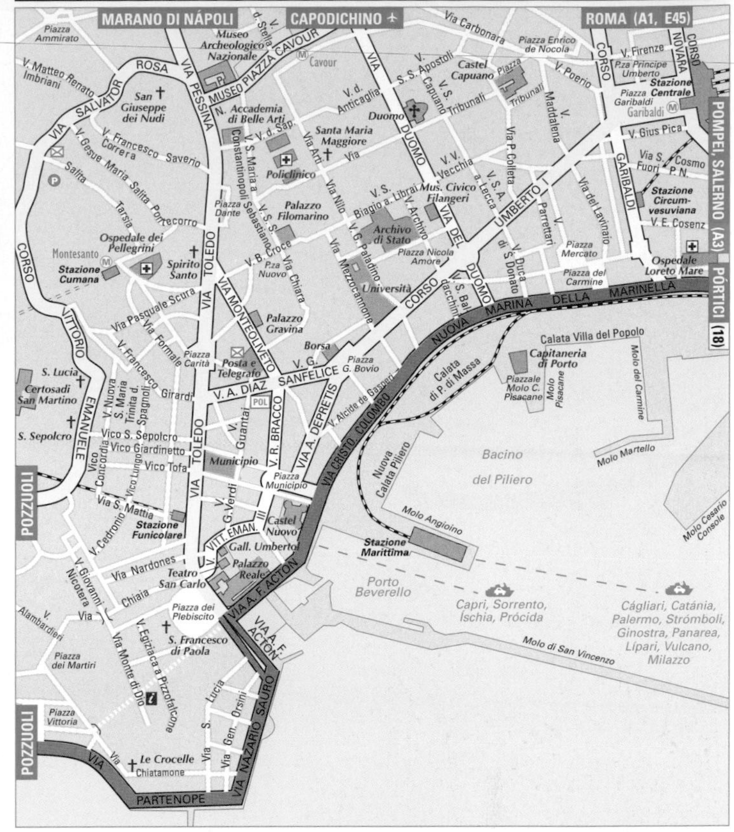

Oslo

0 km 5

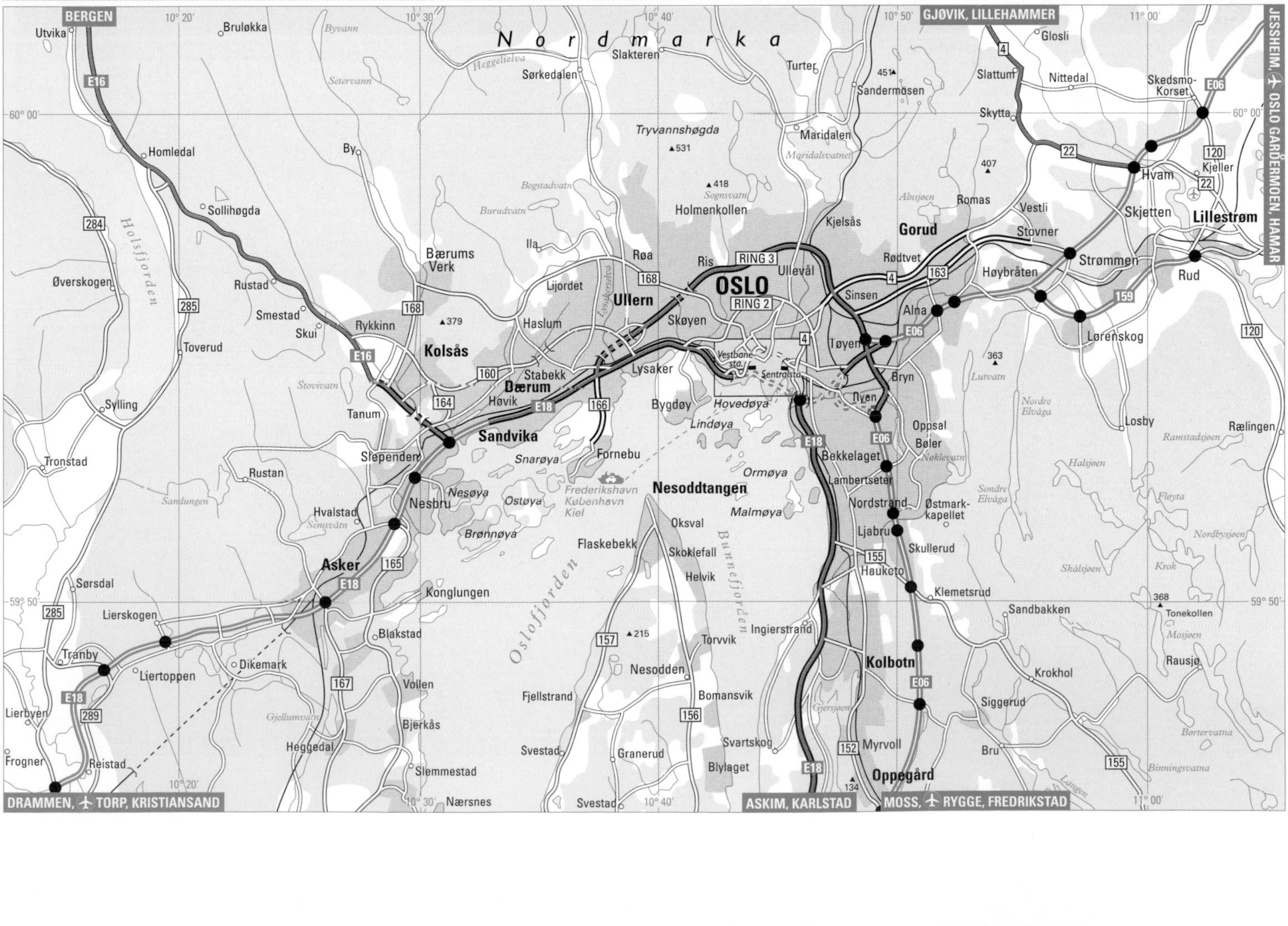

Oslo

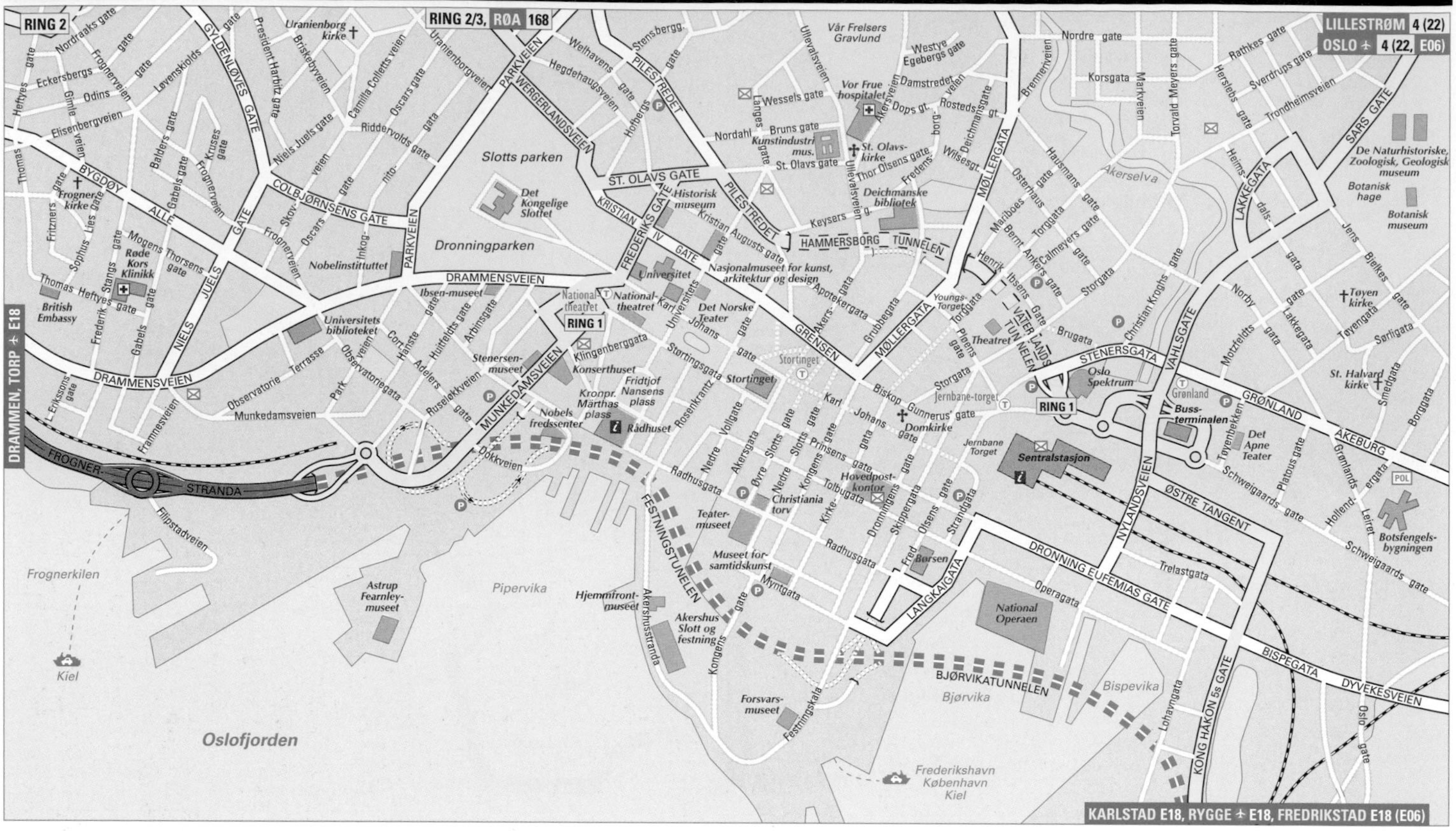
0 km 0.5
RING 2
RING 2/3, RØA 168
LILLESTRØM 4 (22)
OSLO ✈ 4 (22, E06)
DRAMMEN, TORP ✈ E18
KARLSTAD E18, RYGGE ✈ E18, FREDRIKSTAD E18 (E06)
RING 1
Uranienborg kirke
Vår Frelsers Gravlund
Slotts parken
Det Kongelige Slottet
Dronningparken
DRAMMENSVEIEN
BYGDØY ALLÉ
Frogner kirke
Røde Kors Klinikk
British Embassy
Universitets biblioteket
Nobelinstituttet
Ibsen-museet
Nationaltheatret
Universitet
Historisk museum
Nasjonalmuseet for kunst, arkitektur og design
Deichmanske bibliotek
HAMMERSBORG TUNNELEN
Stortinget
Nobels fredssenter
Rådhuset
Konserthuset
Stenersen-museet
Det Norske Teater
Domkirke
Sentralstasjon
Oslo Spektrum
Buss-terminalen
Det Åpne Teater
Grønland
Teater-museet
Christiania torv
Hovedpost-kontor
Børsen
National Operaen
Museet for samtidskunst
Akershus Slott og festning
Hjemmefront-museet
Forsvars-museet
Astrup Fearnley-museet
Pipervika
Frognerkilen
Kiel
Oslofjorden
Bjørvika
Bispevika
BJØRVIKATUNNELEN
FESTNINGSTUNELEN
FROGNER-STRANDA
Frederikshavn København Kiel
De Naturhistoriske, Zoologisk, Geologisk museum
Botanisk hage
Botanisk museum
Tøyen kirke
St. Halvard kirke
Botsfengels-bygningen
Akerselva
KONG HAKON 5s GATE
DRONNING EUFEMIAS GATE
BISPEGATA
DYVEKESVEIEN
ØSTRE TANGENT
GRØNLAND
ÅKEBERG
NYLANDSVEIEN
VAHLSGATE
STENERSGATA
MØLLERGATA
GRENSEN
KARL JOHANS GATE
MUNKEDAMSVEIEN
PARKVEIEN
PILESTREDET
ST. OLAVS GATE
LAKKEGATA
SARS GATE

Paris

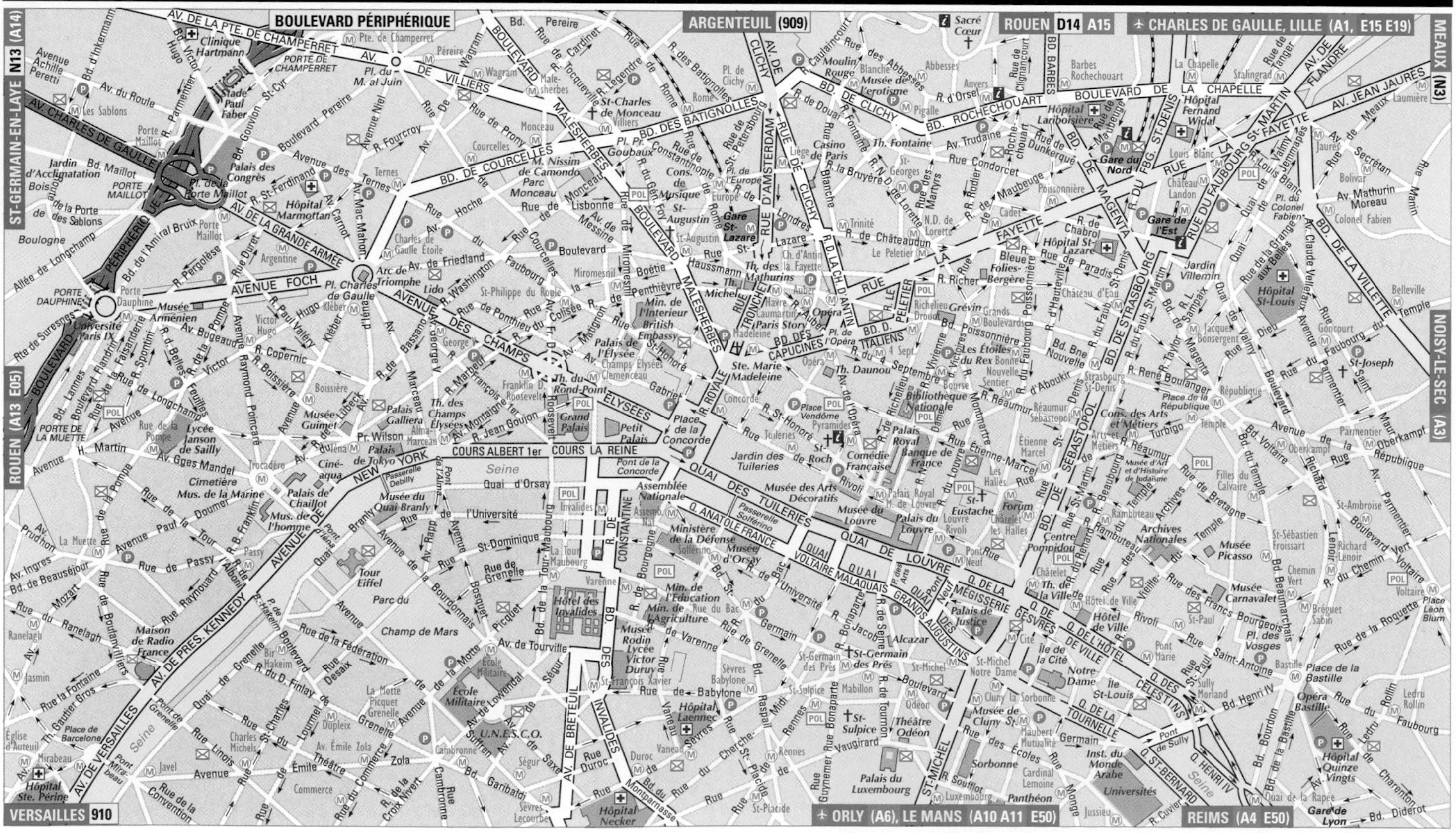
0 km 1
BOULEVARD PÉRIPHÉRIQUE
ARGENTEUIL (909)
ROUEN D14 A15
✈ CHARLES DE GAULLE, LILLE (A1, E15 E19)
MEAUX (N3)
NOISY-LE-SEC (A3)
ST-GERMAIN-EN-LAYE N13 (A14)
ROUEN (A13 E05)
VERSAILLES 910
✈ ORLY (A6), LE MANS (A10 A11 E50)
REIMS (A4 E50)
AV. CHARLES DE GAULLE
AVENUE FOCH
Arc de Triomphe
AVENUE DES CHAMPS ÉLYSÉES
Palais des Congrès
Sacré Cœur
Moulin Rouge
Gare St-Lazare
Gare du Nord
Gare de l'Est
Opéra
Place de la Concorde
Jardin des Tuileries
Musée du Louvre
Musée d'Orsay
Musée des Arts Décoratifs
Palais Royal
Centre Pompidou
Forum des Halles
Hôtel de Ville
Île de la Cité
Notre Dame
Palais de Justice
Île St-Louis
Musée Picasso
Archives Nationales
Place des Vosges
Place de la Bastille
Opéra Bastille
Hôpital Quinze Vingts
Gare de Lyon
Tour Eiffel
Champ de Mars
Palais de Chaillot
Trocadéro
Hôtel des Invalides
École Militaire
U.N.E.S.C.O.
Musée Rodin
Palais du Luxembourg
Sorbonne
Panthéon
Institut du Monde Arabe
Maison de Radio France
Grand Palais
Petit Palais
Assemblée Nationale
Seine
COURS ALBERT 1er
COURS LA REINE
QUAI DES TUILERIES
QUAI DU LOUVRE
BD. ST-GERMAIN
BD. ST-MICHEL
BD. DE SÉBASTOPOL
BD. DE MAGENTA
BD. HAUSSMANN
BD. DE CLICHY
BD. DE COURCELLES
BD. DES BATIGNOLLES
BOULEVARD DE LA CHAPELLE
AV. JEAN JAURÈS
AV. DE PRES. KENNEDY
AV. DE VERSAILLES
AV. DE BRETEUIL
BD. DES INVALIDES
RUE DE RIVOLI
RUE LA FAYETTE
Hôpital St-Louis
Hôpital Necker
Hôpital Laennec
Hôpital Lariboisière

Paris

0 km 5

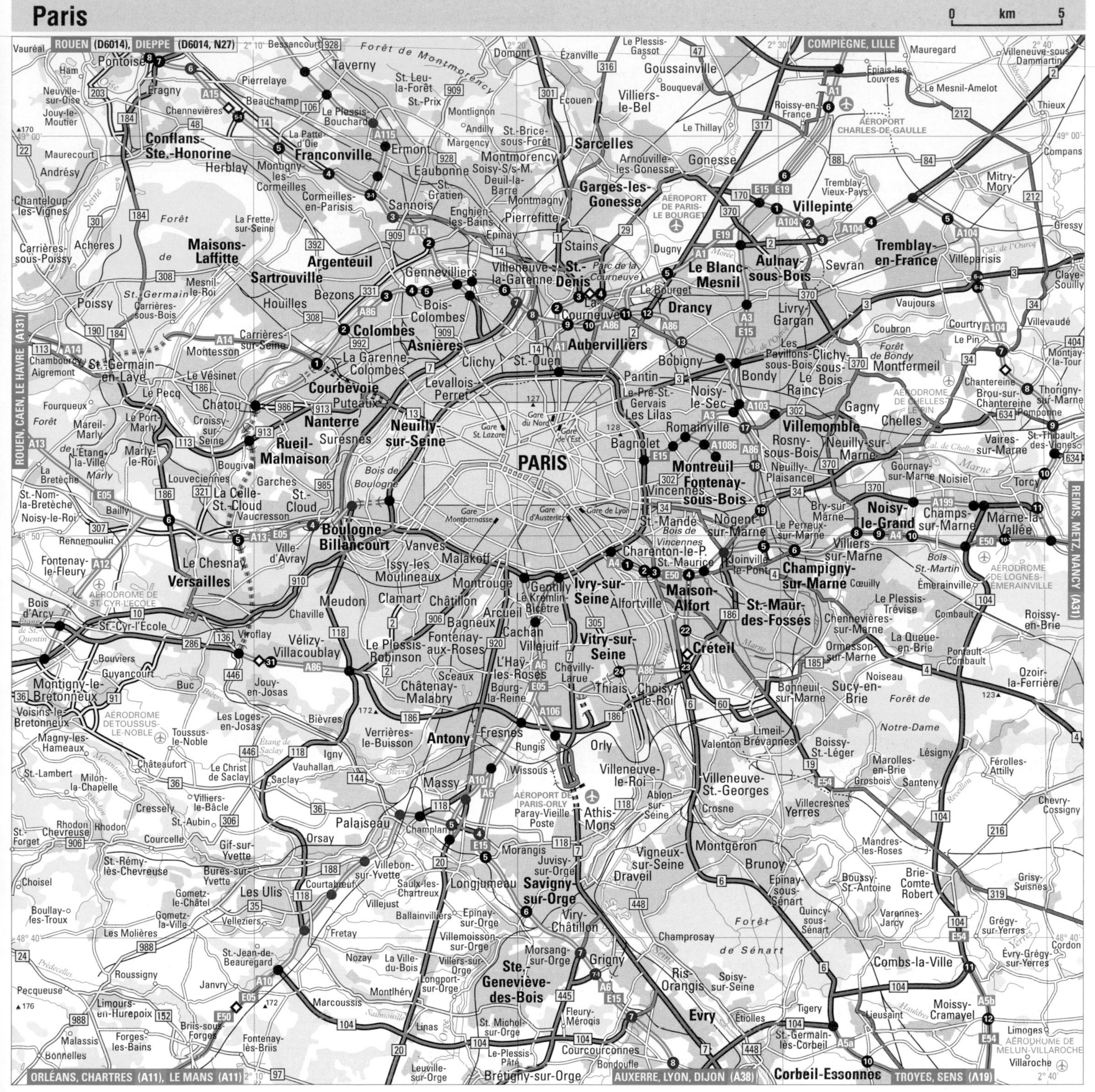
ROUEN (D6014), DIEPPE (D6014, N27)
COMPIÈGNE, LILLE
ROUEN, CAEN, LE HAVRE (A13)
REIMS, METZ, NANCY (A31)
ORLÉANS, CHARTRES (A11), LE MANS (A11)
AUXERRE, LYON, DIJON (A38)
TROYES, SENS (A19)
PARIS
Pontoise
Taverny
Conflans-Ste.-Honorine
Franconville
Ermont
Sarcelles
Garges-lès-Gonesse
Gonesse
Villepinte
Aulnay-sous-Bois
Tremblay-en-France
Sevran
Le Blanc-Mesnil
Drancy
Maisons-Laffitte
Sartrouville
Argenteuil
Colombes
Asnières
Courbevoie
Nanterre
Rueil-Malmaison
Neuilly-sur-Seine
St.-Denis
Aubervilliers
St.-Germain-en-Laye
Bobigny
Bondy
Montfermeil
Villemomble
Montreuil
Fontenay-sous-Bois
Noisy-le-Grand
Champigny-sur-Marne
St.-Maur-des-Fossés
Maison-Alfort
Créteil
Vitry-sur-Seine
Ivry-sur-Seine
Boulogne-Billancourt
Versailles
Antony
Massy
Palaiseau
Les Ulis
Savigny-sur-Orge
Ste.-Geneviève-des-Bois
Evry
Corbeil-Essonnes
AÉROPORT CHARLES-DE-GAULLE
AÉROPORT DE PARIS-LE BOURGET
AÉROPORT DE PARIS-ORLY

Praha Prague

0 km 5

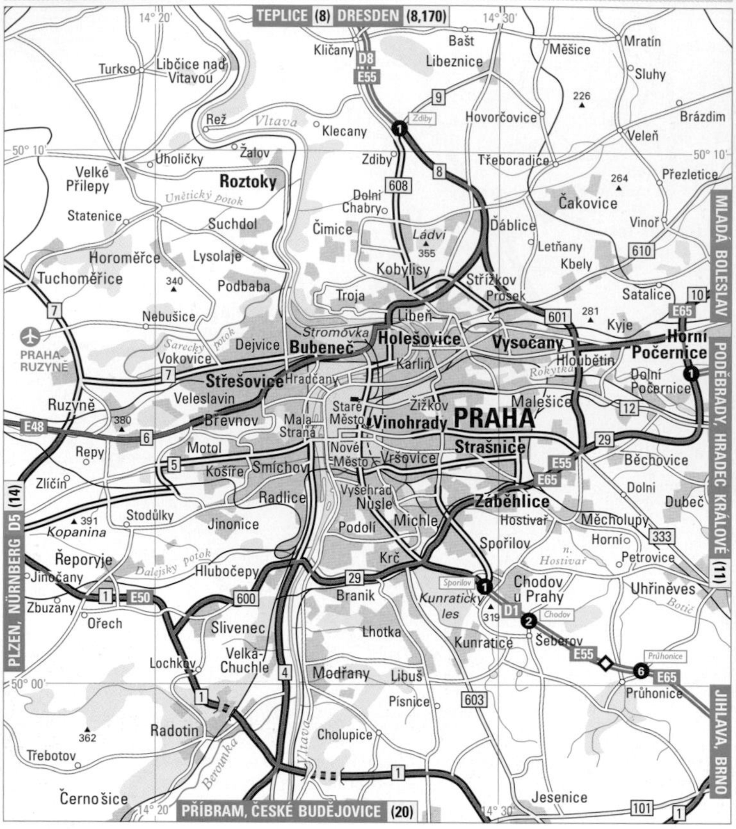

Praha Prague

0 km 1

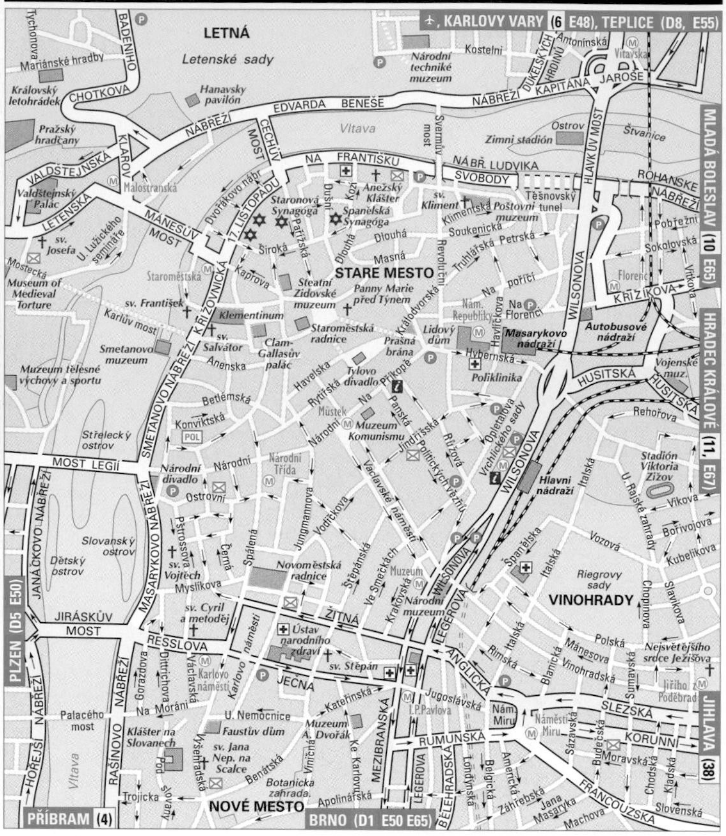

Rotterdam

0 km 1

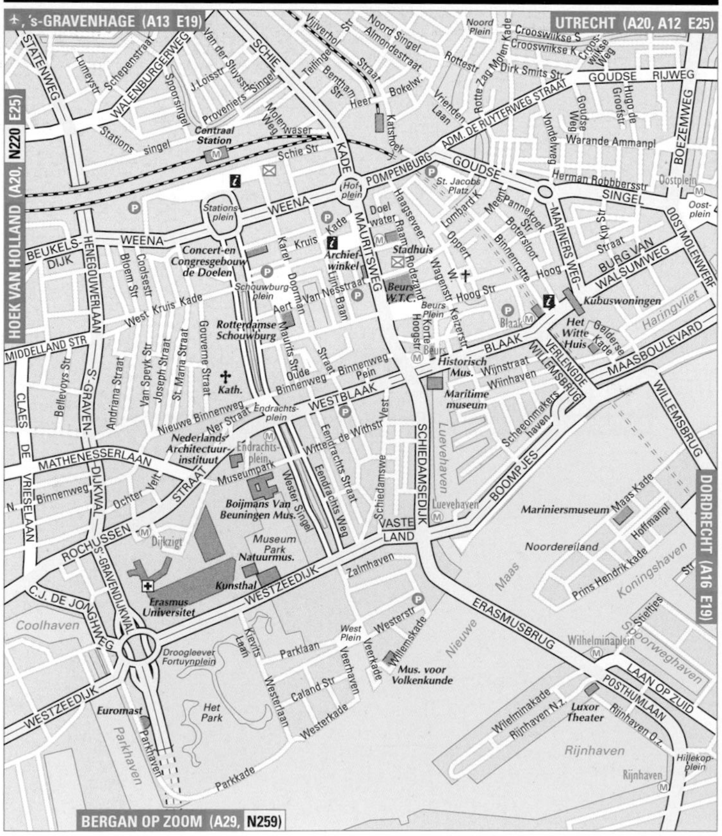

Sankt-Peterburg St. Petersburg

0 km 5

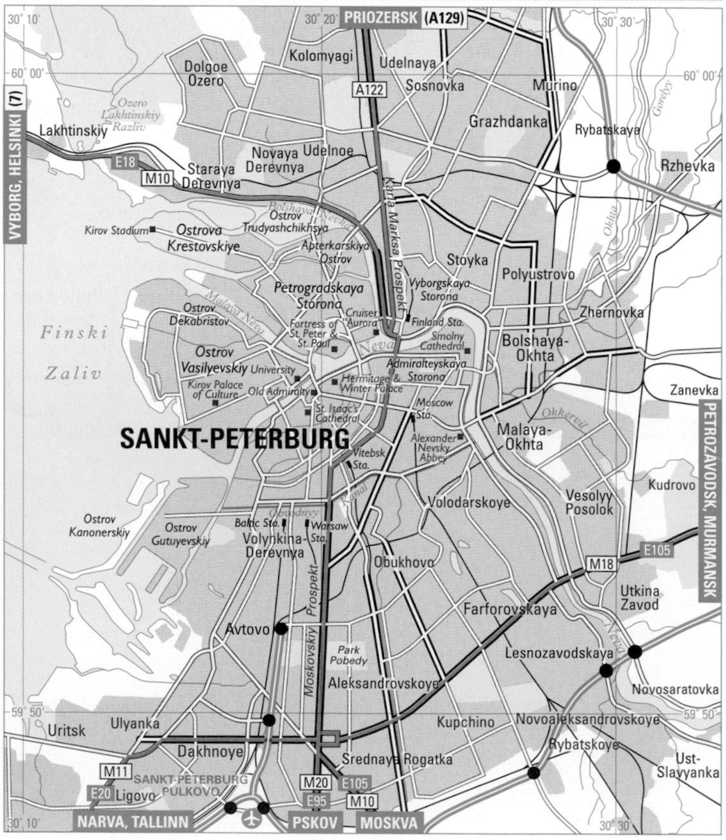

Roma Rome

0 km 5

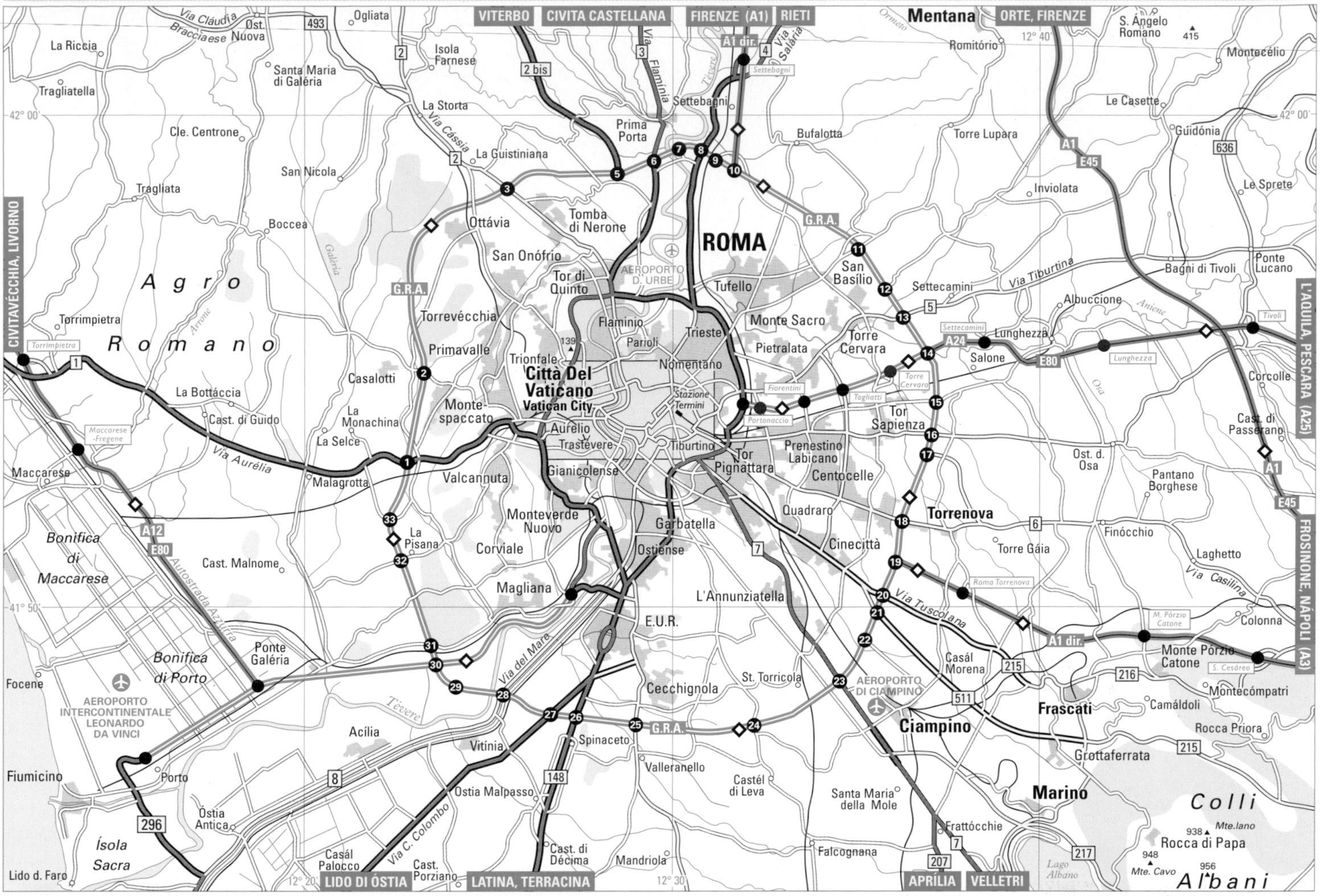

VITERBO | CIVITA CASTELLANA | FIRENZE (A1) | RIETI | ORTE, FIRENZE | L'AQUILA, PESCARA (A25) | FROSINONE, NAPOLI (A3) | VELLETRI | APRÍLIA | LATINA, TERRACINA | LIDO DI ÓSTIA | CIVITAVÉCCHIA, LIVORNO

Roma Rome

0 km 1

TERNI (3) | VITERBO (2) | FIRENZE 4 (A1 dir, A1 E35) | FROSINONE 6 (A1 E45) | LATINA 148 | 'LEONARDO DA VINCI' (A12) | CIVITAVÉCCHIA 1 (A12 E80)

Restricted Zones (ZTL)

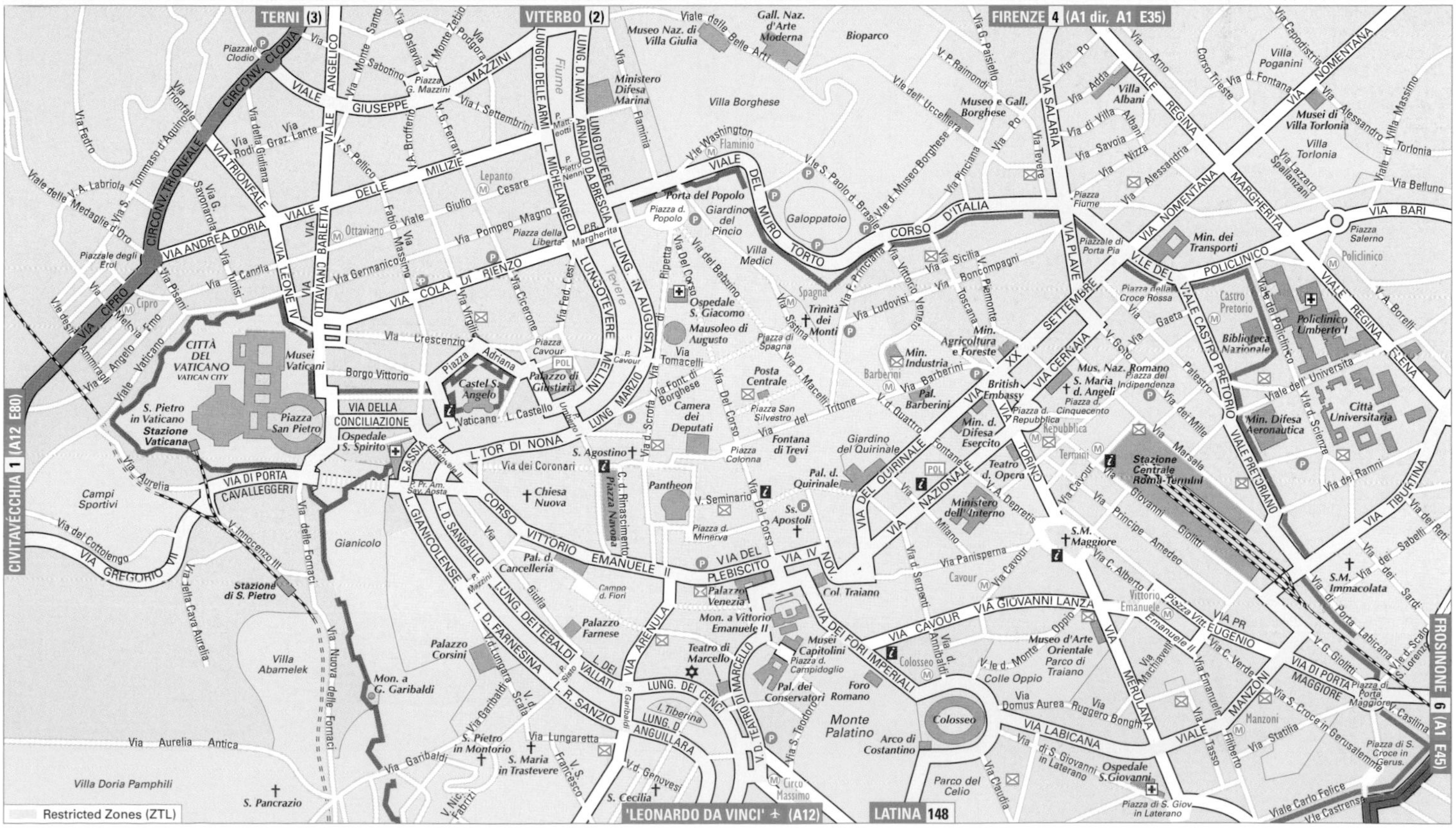

Sevilla Seville

0 km 0.5

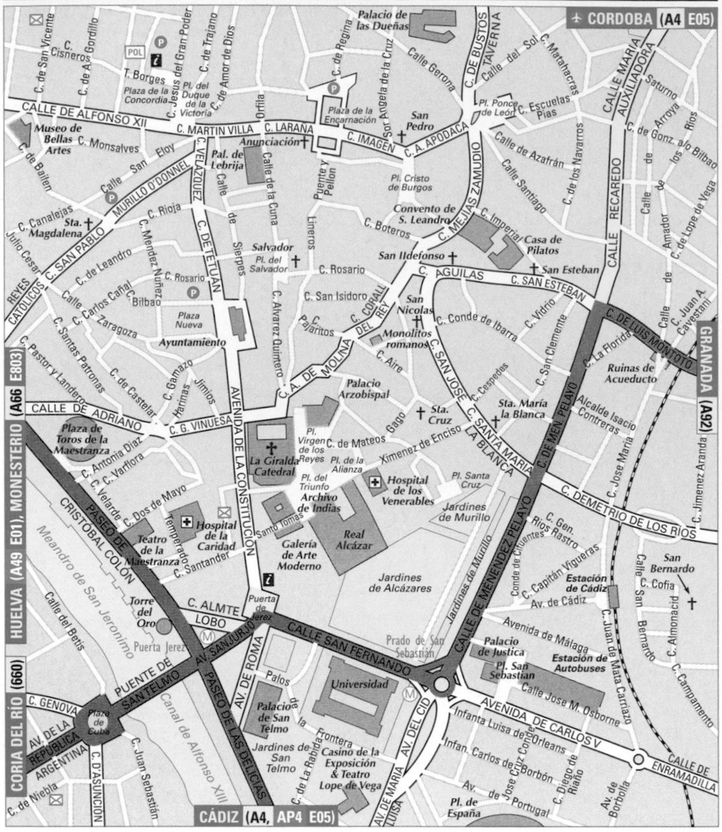

CORDOBA (A4 E05)

GRANADA (A92)

CÁDIZ (A4, AP4 E05)

CORIA DEL RÍO (660) HUELVA (A49 E01), MONESTERIO (A66 E803)

Stuttgart

0 km 0.5

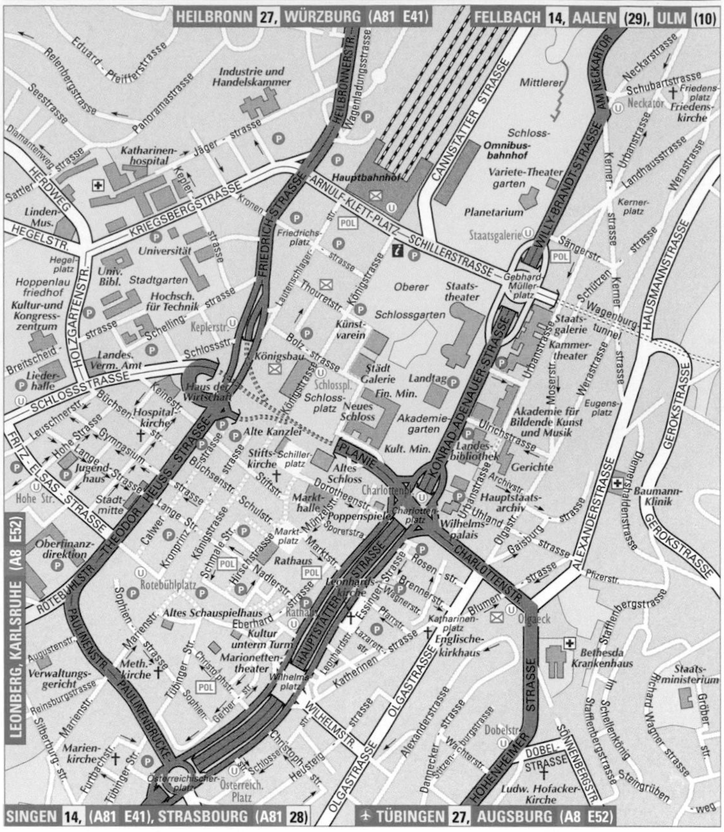

HEILBRONN 27, WÜRZBURG (A81 E41)

FELLBACH 14, AALEN (29), ULM (10)

SINGEN 14, (A81 E41), STRASBOURG (A81 28)

TÜBINGEN 27, AUGSBURG (A8 E52)

LEONBERG, KARLSRUHE (A8 E52)

Strasbourg

0 km 5

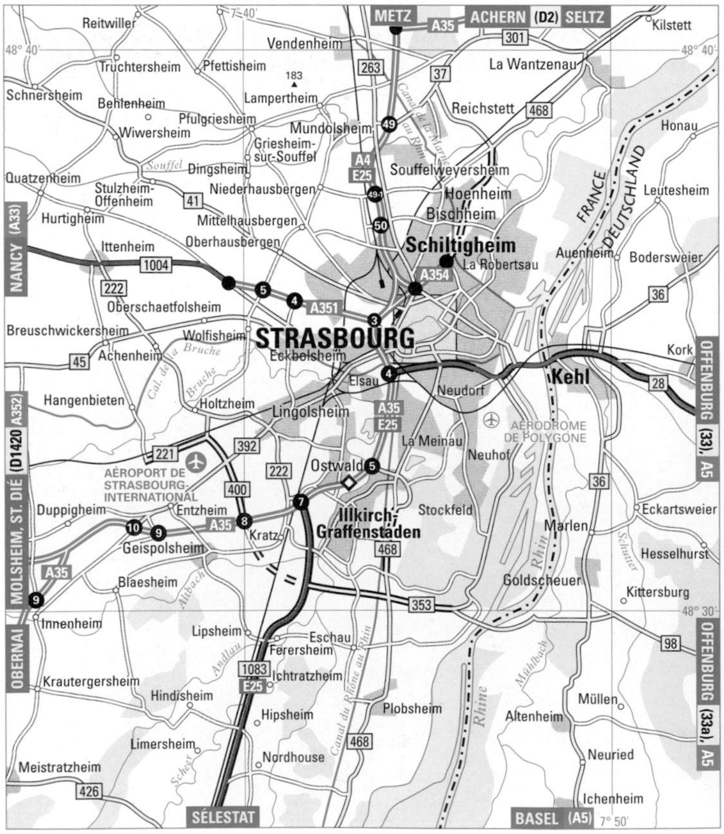

METZ A35 ACHERN (D2) SELTZ

NANCY (A33)

OFFENBURG (28) (33), A5

MOLSHEIM, ST. DIÉ (D1420 A352)

OBERNAI

OFFENBURG (33a), A5

SÉLESTAT

BASEL (A5)

Strasbourg

0 km 0.5

METZ A4 E25 BISCHHEIM A350

SÉLESTAT, MULHOUSE A35

KEHL (28), OFFENBURG (28 A5)

SAVERNE, NANCY (A351 D1004, N4)

MOLSHEIM (A35 A352)

ERSTEIN, SÉLESTAT (A35 D1083)

KEHL (28)

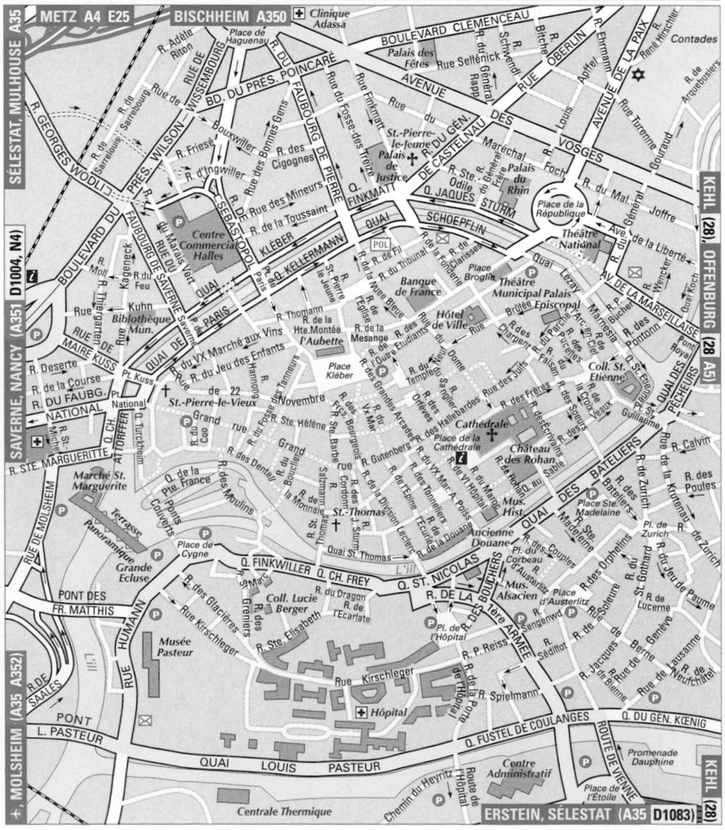

Stockholm

0 km 5

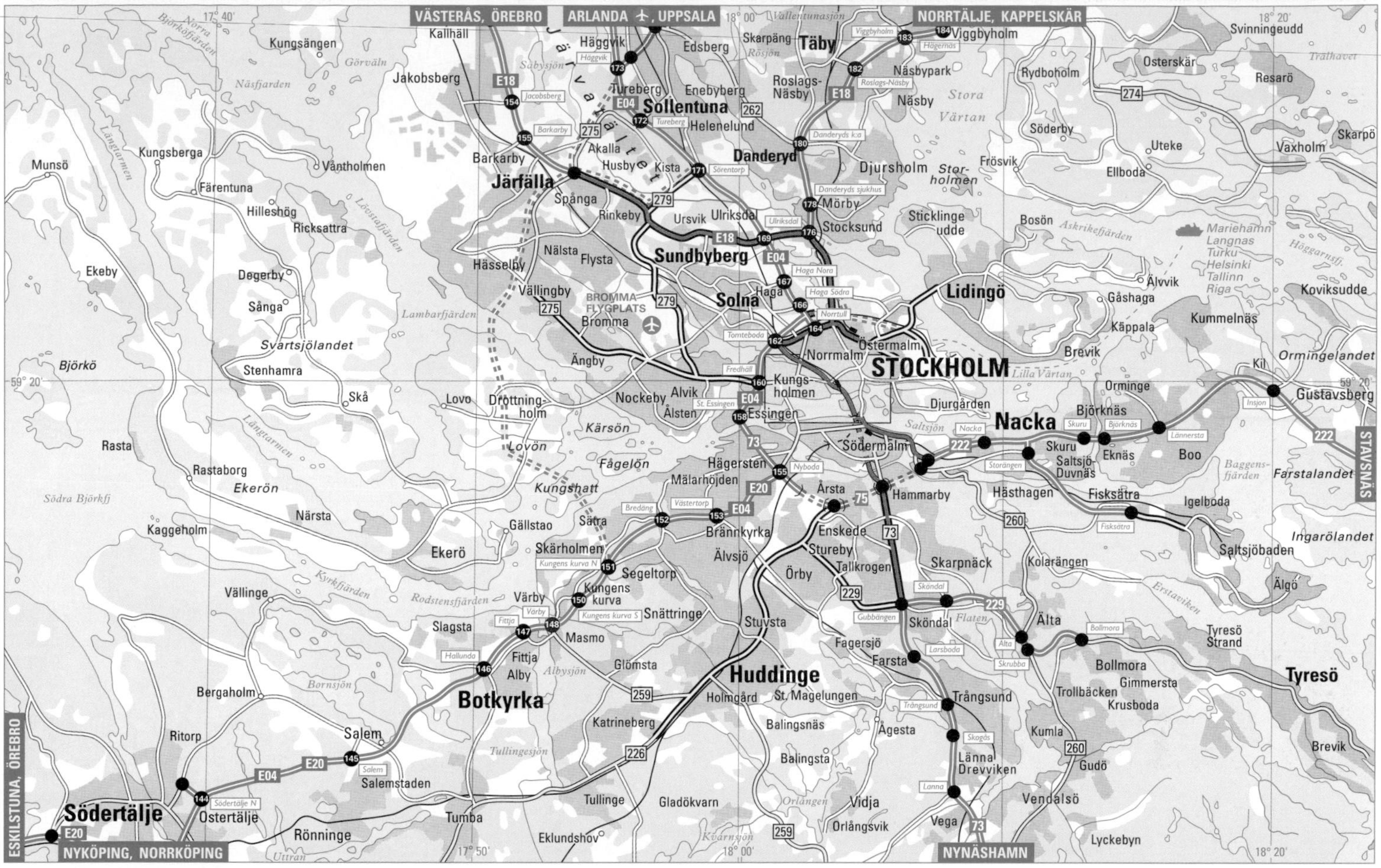

VÄSTERÅS, ÖREBRO
ARLANDA, UPPSALA
NORRTÄLJE, KAPPELSKÄR
STAVSNÄS
NYNÄSHAMN
NYKÖPING, NORRKÖPING
ESKILSTUNA, ÖREBRO

Kallhäll
Kungsängen
Jakobsberg
Häggvik
Täby
Viggbyholm
Sollentuna
Edsberg
Skarpäng
Roslags-Näsby
Näsbypark
Näsby
Enebyberg
Helenelund
Tureberg
Svinningeudd
Österskär
Rydboholm
Resarö
Barkarby
Järfälla
Akalla
Husby
Kista
Danderyd
Djursholm
Stora Värtan
Frösvik
Söderby
Uteke
Ellboda
Vaxholm
Skarpö
Munsö
Kungsberga
Vantholmen
Färentuna
Hilleshög
Ricksattra
Spånga
Rinkeby
Ursvik
Ulriksdal
Mörby
Stocksund
Sticklinge udde
Bosön
Ekeby
Degerby
Sånga
Hässelby
Nälsta
Flysta
Sundbyberg
Vällingby
Bromma Flygplats
Bromma
Solna
Haga
Lidingö
Ålvvik
Gåshaga
Käppala
Kummelnäs
Koviksudde
Svartsjölandet
Björkö
Stenhamra
Ängby
Norrmalm
Östermalm
STOCKHOLM
Brevik
Kil
Ormingelandet
Skå
Lovo
Drottningholm
Nockeby
Alvik
Ålsten
Kungsholmen
Essingen
Djurgården
Nacka
Björknäs
Orminge
Gustavsberg
Rasta
Kärsön
Lovön
Fågelön
Södermalm
Skuru
Saltsjö-Duvnäs
Eknäs
Boo
Rastaborg
Ekerön
Kungshatt
Hägersten
Mälarhöjden
Årsta
Hammarby
Hästhagen
Fisksätra
Igelboda
Farstalandet
Kaggeholm
Närsta
Gällstao
Sätra
Ekerö
Skärholmen
Bränkyrka
Älvsjö
Enskede
Stureby
Tallkrogen
Skarpnäck
Kolarängen
Saltsjöbaden
Ingarölandet
Vällinge
Segeltorp
Örby
Älgö
Slagsta
Värby
Kungens kurva
Snättringe
Stuvsta
Sköndal
Älta
Tyresö Strand
Masmo
Fittja
Alby
Glömsta
Fagersjö
Farsta
Bollmora
Gimmersta
Tyresö
Bergaholm
Botkyrka
Huddinge
Holmgård
St. Magelungen
Trångsund
Trollbäcken
Krusboda
Ritorp
Salem
Katrineberg
Balingsnäs
Ågesta
Kumla
Brevik
Balingsta
Länna
Drevviken
Gudö
Södertälje
Östertälje
Salemstaden
Tullinge
Gladökvarn
Vidja
Vendelsö
Rönninge
Tumba
Eklundshov
Orlångsvik
Vega
Lyckebyn

Stockholm

0 km 1

VÄSTERÅS (E04, E18)
UPPSALA (E04), NORRTÄLJE E04, (E18)
SÖDERTÄLJE 275 (E4, E20)
NYNÄSHAMN 73 (73)
GUSTAVSBERG 222 (222)

STADSHAGEN
KUNGSHOLMEN
NORRMALM
ÖSTERMALM
MARIEBERG
RIDDARHOLMEN
GAMLA STAN
SKEPPSHOLMEN
LÅNGHOLMEN
SÖDERMALM
Karlbergs Slott
Karlbergssjön
Sankt Görans sjukhus
Barnklinik
Kronobergs parken
Polishuset
Rådhuset
Stockholm Central
City Terminalen
Kulturhuset
Klara kyrka
Konserthuset
Observatorielunden
Sabbatsbergs sjukhus
Strindbergsmuseet
Johanneskyrkan
Humlegården
Kungliga Biblioteket
Hedvig Eleonora kyrka
Historiska museet
Armémuseum
Hallwylska museet
Dramatiska teatern
Berzelii Park
Kungsträdgården
Operan
Medelhavsmuseet
Riksdagshuset
Medeltidsmuseum
Kungliga Slottet
Livrustkammaren
Kungliga Myntkabinettet
Storkyrkan
Tyska kyrkan
Riddarholmskyrkan
Nationalmuseum
Östasiatiska museet
Moderna museet/Arkitektur-och design centrum
Nordiska museet
Junibacken
Vasamuseet
Kastellholmen
Stadshuset
Rålambshovsparken
Friluftsteater
Riddarfjärden
Mälaren
Strömmen
Saltsjön
Ladugårdslandsviken
Nybroviken
Långholmskanalen
Klarastrandsleden
Drottningholmsvägen
Västerbron
Centralbron
Skeppsbron
Slussen
Katarinavägen
Valhallavägen
Birger Jarlsgatan
Kungsgatan
Sveavägen

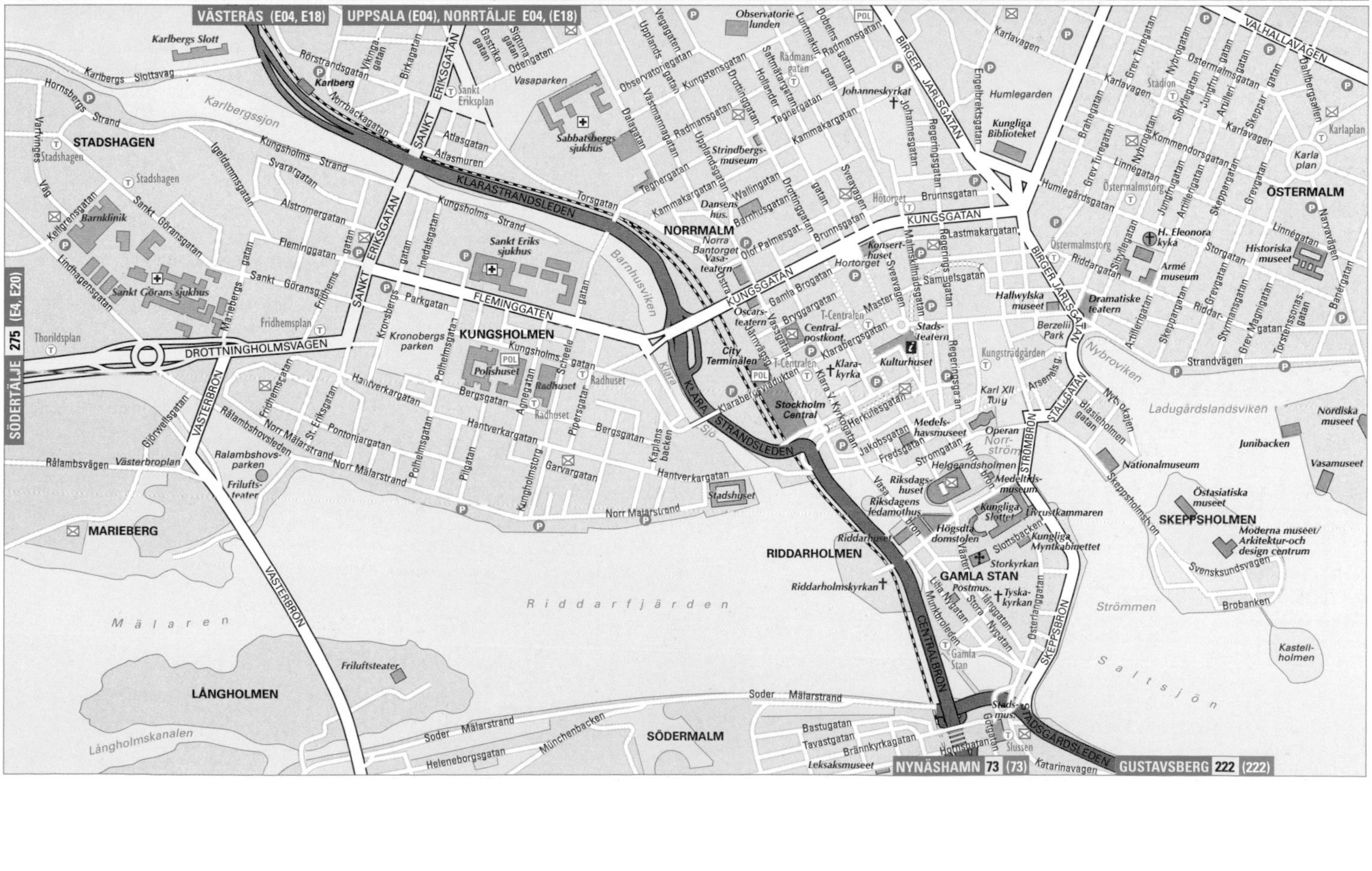

Torino Turin

0 km 5

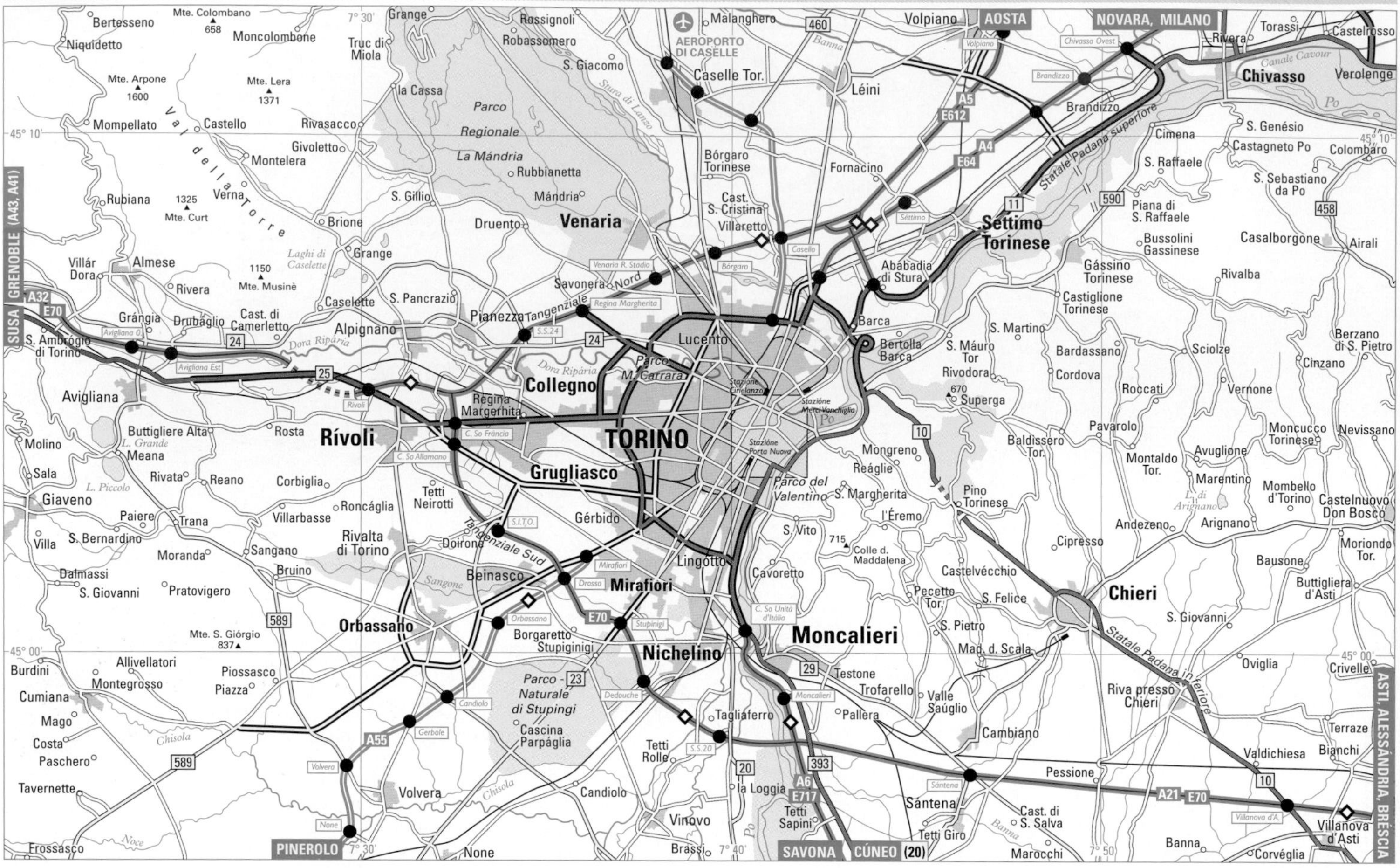

AOSTA

NOVARA, MILANO

SUSA, GRENOBLE (A43, A41)

ASTI, ALESSÁNDRIA, BRÉSCIA

PINEROLO

SAVONA

CÚNEO (20)

Venézia Venice

0 km 0.5

MESTRE, PÁDOVA (A4 E70)

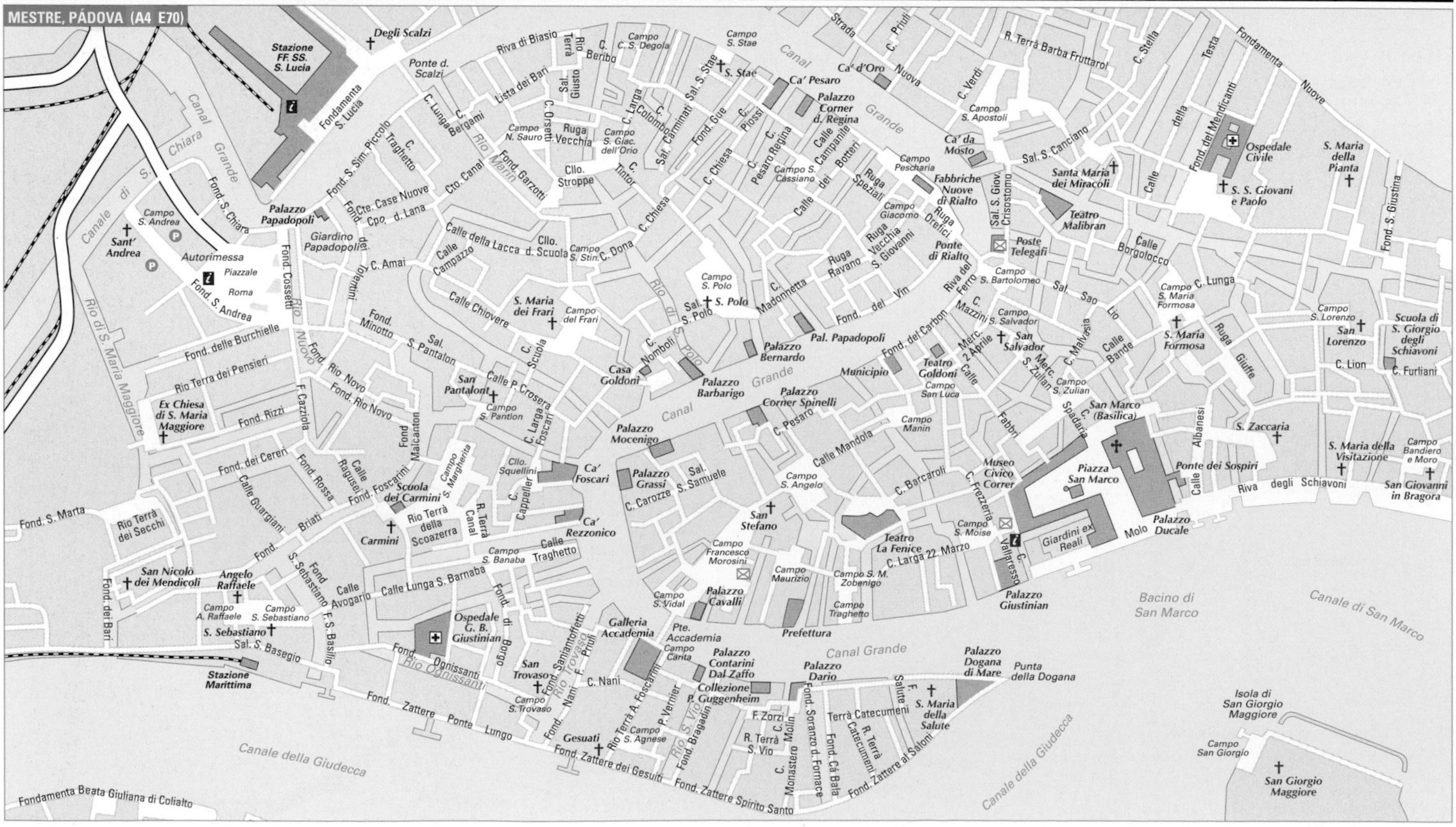

Torino Turin

0 km 1

Wien Vienna

0 km 5

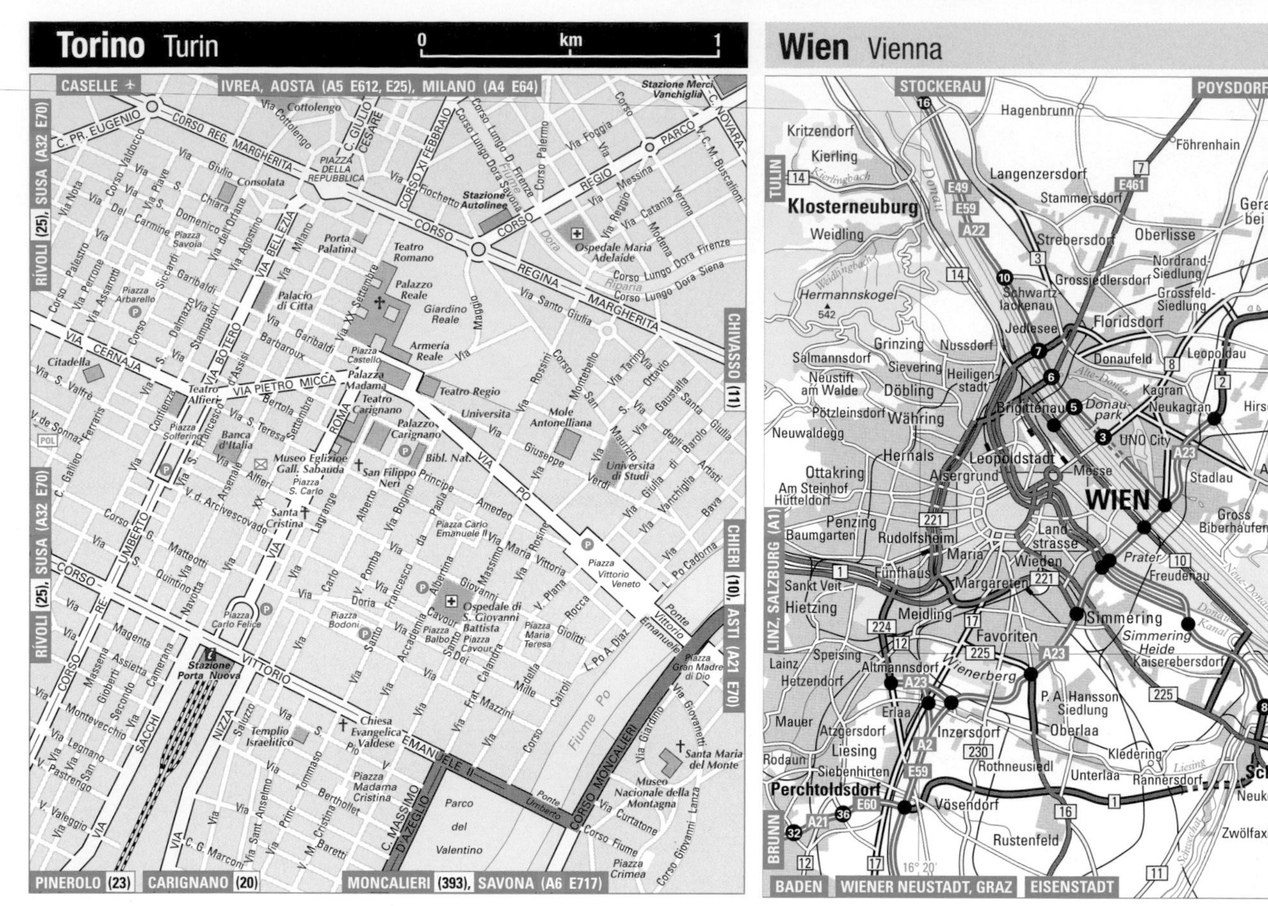

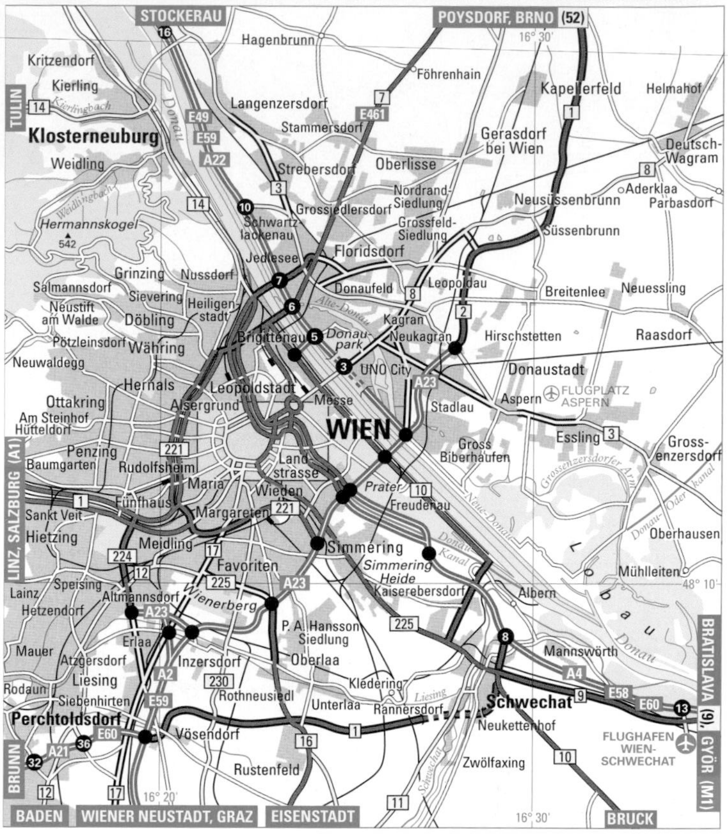

Warszawa Warsaw

0 km 5

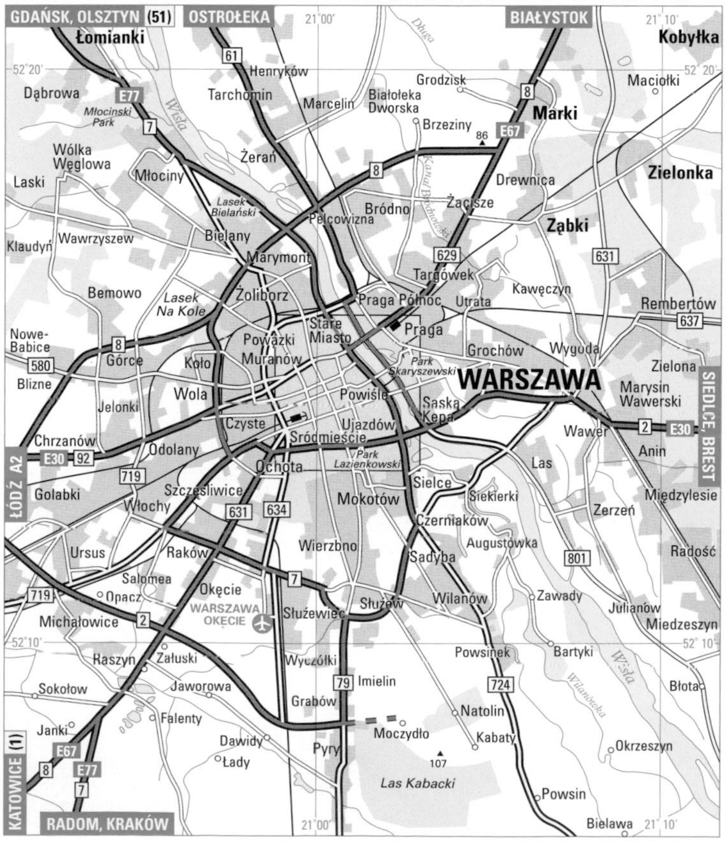

GDAŃSK, OLSZTYN (51)
OSTROŁĘKA
BIAŁYSTOK
SIEDLCE, BREST
ŁÓDŹ A2
KATOWICE (1)
RADOM, KRAKÓW
WARSZAWA
Łomianki
Kobyłka
Marki
Zielonka
Ząbki
Rembertów
Wawer
Piaseczno
WARSZAWA OKĘCIE

Warszawa Warsaw

0 km 1

GDAŃSK 7 E77
OSTROŁĘKA 61
BIAŁYSTOK 629 (8 E67)
WŁOCŁAWEK 634 (7, 62) ŁOWICZ, KONIN 629 (2 E30)
ŁÓDŹ 2 (A2), KRAKÓW 2 (8, 7, E77)
BREST 2 E30
OKĘCIE 634
GÓRA KALWARIA 7 (79)
NOWE MIASTO
STARE MIASTO
PRAGA
POWIŚLE
ŚRÓDMIEŚCIE
UJAZDÓW
WISŁA

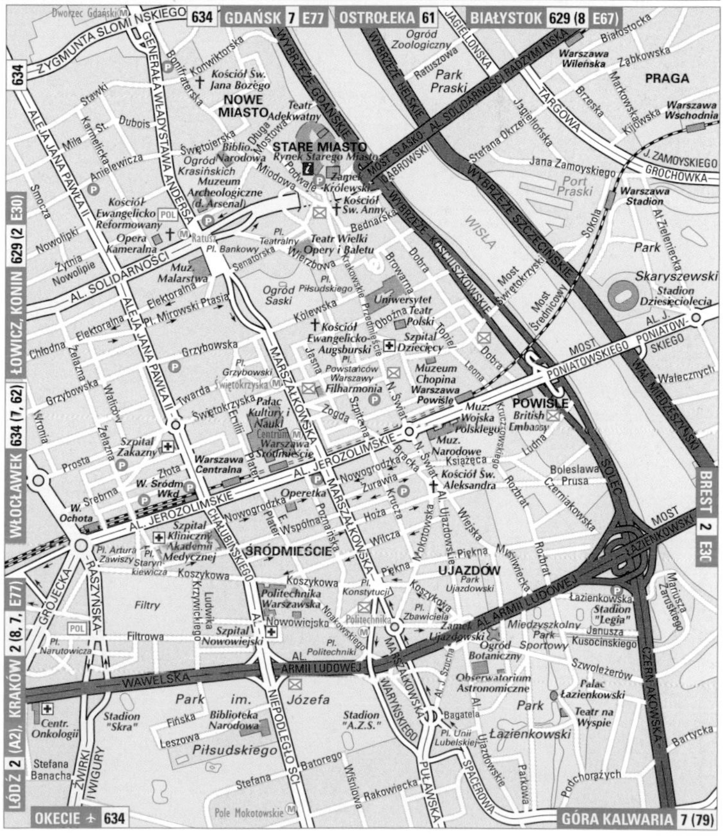

Wien Vienna

0 km 1

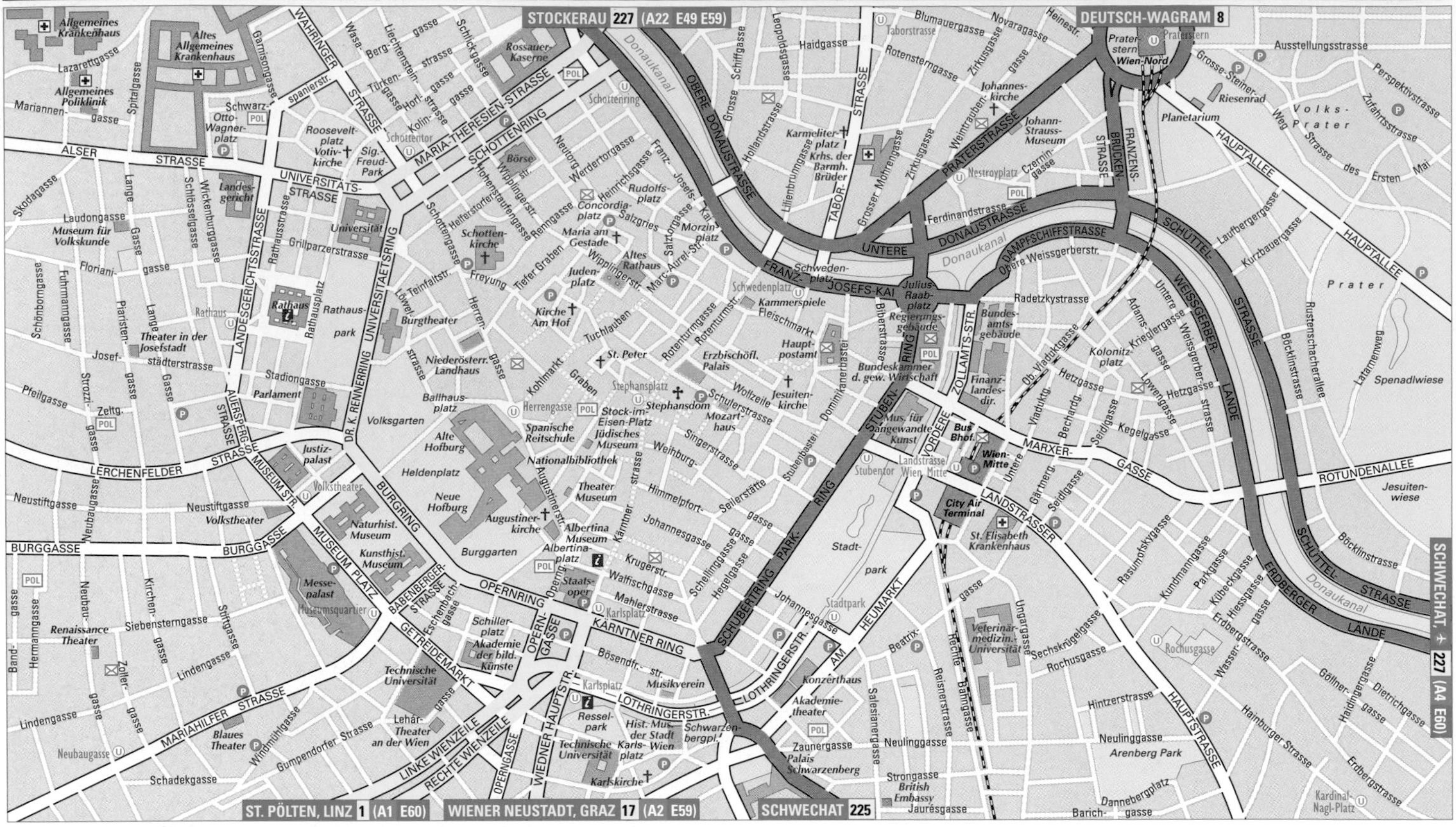

STOCKERAU 227 (A22 E49 E59)

DEUTSCH-WAGRAM 8

SCHWECHAT ✈ 227 (A4 E60)

ST. PÖLTEN, LINZ 1 (A1 E60)

WIENER NEUSTADT, GRAZ 17 (A2 E59)

SCHWECHAT 225

Zagreb

0 km 0.5

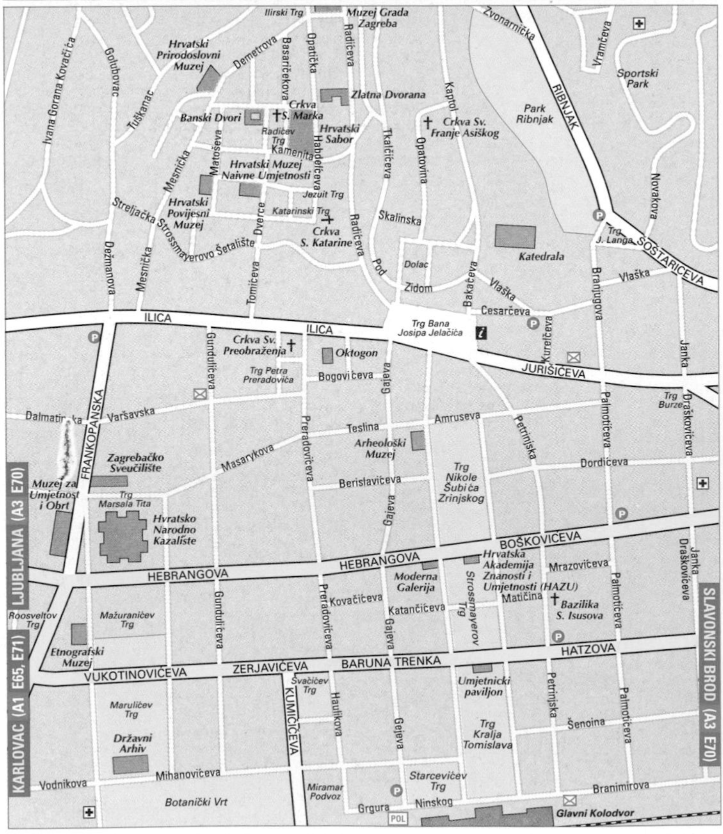

LJUBLJANA (A3 E70)

KARLOVAC (A1 E65, E71)

SLAVONSKI BROD (A3 E70)

Zürich

0 km 0.5

BASEL (A1, A3 E60)

BÜLACH (A1b)

WINTERTHUR (A1, E60)

UITIKON

BADEN (3)

CHUR (A3 A13)

CHUR (A3 A13)

RAPPERSWIL 17

WATTWIL 52 (8)

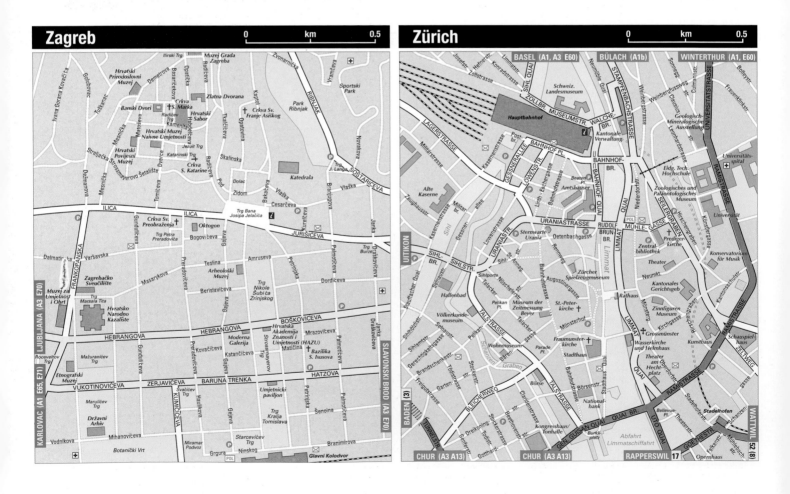

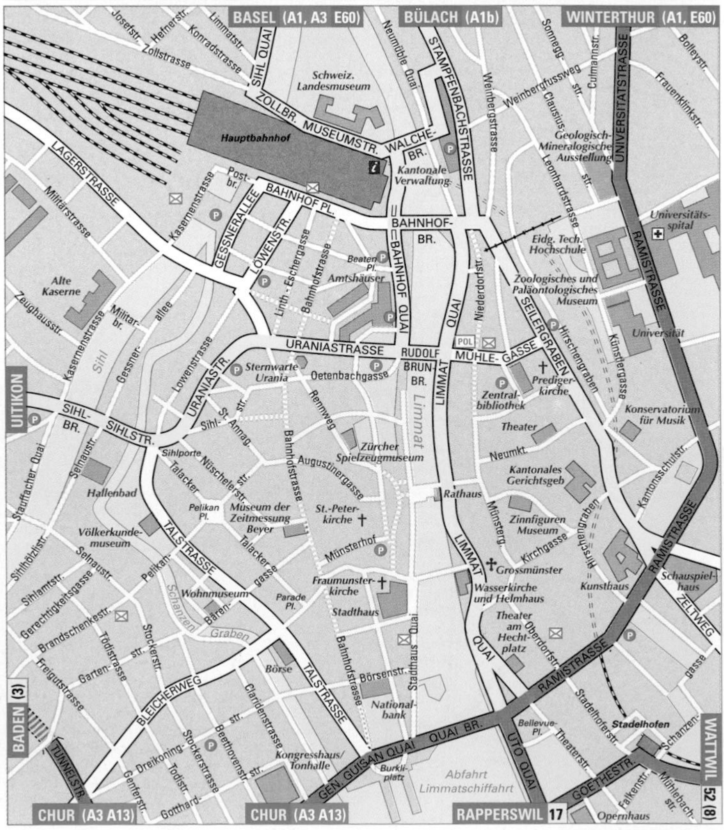

A	Austria	Autriche	Österreich	Austria
AL	Albania	Albanie	Albanien	Albania
AND	Andorra	Andorre	Andorra	Andorra
B	Belgium	Belgique	Belgien	Belgio
BG	Bulgaria	Bulgarie	Bulgarien	Bulgaria
BIH	Bosnia-Herzegovin	Bosnia-Herzegovine	Bosnien-Herzegowina	Bosnia-Herzogovina
BY	Belarus	Belarus	Weissrussland	Bielorussia
CH	Switzerland	Suisse	Schweiz	Svizzera
CY	Cyprus	Chypre	Zypern	Cipro
CZ	Czech Republic	République Tchèque	Tschechische Republik	Repubblica Ceca
D	Germany	Allemagne	Deutschland	Germania
DK	Denmark	Danemark	Dänemark	Danimarca
E	Spain	Espagne	Spanien	Spagna
EST	Estonia	Estonie	Estland	Estonia
F	France	France	Frankreich	Francia
FIN	Finland	Finlande	Finnland	Finlandia
FL	Liechtenstein	Liechtenstein	Liechtenstein	Liechtenstein
FO	Faeroe Islands	Îles Féroé	Färoër-Inseln	Isole Faroe
GB	United Kingdom	Royaume Uni	Grossbritannien und Nordirland	Regno Unito
GBZ	Gibraltar	Gibraltar	Gibraltar	Gibilterra
GR	Greece	Grèce	Greichenland	Grecia
H	Hungary	Hongrie	Ungarn	Ungheria
HR	Croatia	Croatie	Kroatien	Croazia

I	Italy	Italie	Italien	Italia
IRL	Ireland	Irlande	Irland	Irlanda
IS	Iceland	Islande	Island	Islanda
KOS	Kosovo	Kosovo	Kosovo	Kosovo
L	Luxembourg	Luxembourg	Luxemburg	Lussemburgo
LT	Lithuania	Lituanie	Litauen	Lituania
LV	Latvia	Lettonie	Lettland	Lettonia
M	Malta	Malte	Malta	Malta
MC	Monaco	Monaco	Monaco	Monaco
MD	Moldova	Moldavie	Moldawien	Moldavia
MK	Macedonia	Macédoine	Makedonien	Macedonia
MNE	Montenegro	Monténégro	Montenegro	Montenegro
N	Norway	Norvège	Norwegen	Norvegia
NL	Netherlands	Pays-Bas	Niederlande	Paesi Bassi
P	Portugal	Portugal	Portugal	Portogallo
PL	Poland	Pologne	Polen	Polonia
RO	Romania	Roumanie	Rumanien	Romania
RSM	San Marino	Saint-Marin	San Marino	San Marino
RUS	Russia	Russie	Russland	Russia
S	Sweden	Suède	Schweden	Svezia
SK	Slovak Republic	République Slovaque	Slowak Republik	Repubblica Slovacca
SLO	Slovenia	Slovénie	Slowenien	Slovenia
SRB	Serbia	Serbie	Serbien	Serbia
TR	Turkey	Turquie	Türkei	Turchia
UA	Ukraine	Ukraine	Ukraine	Ucraina

A

Aabenraa DK 64 A2
Aabybro DK 58 A2
Aach D 107 B4
Aachen D 80 B2
Aalborg DK 58 A2
Aalen D 94 C2
Aalestrup DK 58 B2
Aalsmeer NL 70 B1
Aalst B 79 B4
Aalten NL 71 C3
Aalter B 79 A3
Äänekoski FIN 8 A4
Aapajärvi FIN 197 B10
Ağapınar TR 187 C5
Aarau CH 106 B3
Aarberg CH 106 B2
Aarburg CH 106 B2
Aardenburg NL 79 A3
Aars DK 58 B2
Aarschot B 79 B4
Aarup DK 59 C3
Aba H 112 B2
Abádanes E 152 B1
Abades E 151 B3
Abadin E 141 A3
Abádszalók H 113 B4
Abaliget H 125 A4
Abana TR 23 A8
A Baña E 140 B2
Abanilla E 165 A3
Abano Terme I 121 B4
Abarán E 165 A3
Abasár H 113 B4
Abbadia San Salvatore I 135 C4
Abbaue D 74 A2
Abbehausen D 72 A1
Abbekäs S 66 A2
Abbeville F 90 A1
Abbey IRL 28 A3
Abbeydorney IRL 29 B2
Abbeyfeale IRL 29 B2
Abbeyleix IRL 30 B1
Abbey Town GB 36 B3
Abbiategrasso I 120 B1
Abborrträsk S 196 D2
Abbots Bromley GB 40 C2
Abbotsbury GB 43 B4
Abda H 111 B4
Abejar E 143 C4
Abela P 160 B1
Abelvær N 199 A8
Abenberg D 94 B2
Abenójar E 157 B3
Abensberg D 95 C3
Aberaeron GB 39 B2
Abercarn GB 39 C3
Aberchirder GB 33 D4
Aberdare GB 39 C3
Aberdaron GB 38 B2
Aberdeen GB 33 D4
Aberdulais GB 39 C3
Aberdyfi GB 39 B2
Aberfeldy GB 35 B4
Aberffraw GB 38 A2
Aberfoyle GB 34 B3
Abergavenny GB 39 C3
Abergele GB 38 A3
Abergynolwyn GB 38 B3
Aberporth GB 39 B2
Abersoch GB 38 B2
Abertillery GB 39 C3
Abertura E 156 A2
Aberystwyth GB 39 B2
Abetone I 135 A3
Abfaltersbach A 109 C3
Abide
Çanakkale TR 186 B1
Kütahya TR 187 D4
Abiego E 145 B3
Abild DK 64 B1
Abingdon-on-Thames GB 44 B2
Abington GB 36 A3
Abisko S 194 B9
Abiul P 154 B2
Abla E 164 B2
Ablis F 90 C1
A Bola E 140 B3
Abondance F 118 A3
Abony H 113 B4
Aboyne GB 33 D4
Abrantes P 154 B2
Abreiro P 148 A2
Abreschviller F 92 C3
Abrest F 117 A3
Abriès F 119 C3
Abrud RO 17 B5
Absdorf A 97 C3
Abtenau A 109 B4
Abtsgmünd D 94 C1
Abusejo E 149 B3
Åby
Kronoberg S 62 A2
Östergötland S 56 B2
Åbyggeby S 51 B4
Åbytorp S 55 A6
A Cañiza E 140 B2
A Capela E 140 A2
Acate I 177 B3
Accadia I 171 B3
Accéglio I 132 A2
Accettura I 172 B2
Acciaroli I 170 C3
Accous F 145 A3
Accrington GB 40 B1
Accúmoli I 169 A3
Acedera E 156 A2
Acehuche E 155 B4
Acered E 152 A2
Acerenza I 172 B1
Acerno I 170 C3
Acerra I 170 C2
Aceuchal E 155 C4
Acharacle GB 34 B2
Acharnes GR 185 A4
Achavanich GB 32 C3
Achene B 79 B5
Achenkirch A 108 B2
Achensee A 108 B2
Achenthal A 108 B2
Achentrias GR 185 E6
Achern D 93 C4
Acheux-en-Amienois F 90 A2
Achiltibuie GB 32 C1
Achim D 72 A2
Achladokambos GR 184 B3
Achnasheen GB 32 D1
Achnashellach GB 32 D1
Achosnich GB 34 B1
Aci Castello I 177 B4
Aci Catena I 177 B4
Acilia I 168 B2
Acıpayam TR 189 B4
Acireale I 177 B4
Acle GB 41 C5
A Coruña E 140 A2
Acquacadda I 179 C2
Acqua Doria F 180 B1
Acquanegra sul Chiese I 121 B3
Acquapendente I 168 A1
Acquasanta Terme I 136 C2
Acquasparta I 168 A2
Acquaviva I 135 B4
Acquaviva delle Fonti I 171 C4
Acquaviva Picena I 136 C2
Acquigny F 89 A5
Acqui Terme I 119 C5
Acri I 174 B2
Acs H 112 B2
Acsa H 112 B3
Ácsteszér H 112 B1
Acy-en-Multien F 90 B2
Ada SRB 126 B2
Adak S 195 E9
Ådalsbruk N 48 B3
Adamas GR 185 C5
Adamsfjord N 193 B10
Adamuz E 157 B3
Adana TR 23 C8
Ádánd H 112 C2
Adanero E 150 B3
Adare IRL 29 B3
Adaševci SRB 125 B5
Adeanueva de Ebro E 144 B2
Adelboden CH 106 C2
Adelebsen D 82 A1
Adélfia I 173 A2
Adelmannsfelden D 94 C2
Adelsheim D 94 B1
Adelsö S 57 A3
Ademuz E 152 B2
Adenau D 80 B2
Adendorf D 72 A3
Adinkerke B 78 A2
Adjud RO 17 B7
Adliswil CH 107 B3
Admont A 110 B1
Ådneram N 52 A2
Adolfsström S 195 D7
Adony H 112 B2
Adorf
Hessen D 81 A4
Sachsen D 83 B4
Adra E 164 C1
Adradas E 152 A1
Adrall E 147 B2
Adrano I 177 B3
Ádria I 121 B5
Adrigole IRL 29 C2
Adwick le Street GB 40 B2
Adzaneta E 153 B3
Aesch CH 106 B2
A Estrada E 140 B2
Afandou GR 188 C3
Åfarnes N 198 C4
Affing D 94 C2
Affoltern CH 106 B3
Affric Lodge GB 32 D1
Åfjord N 199 B7
Aflenz Kurort A 110 B2
A Fonsagrada E 141 A3
Afragóla I 170 C2
Afritz A 109 C4
Afyon TR 187 D5
Ágasegyháza H 112 C3
Agay F 132 B2
Agazzano I 120 C2
Agde F 130 B2
Agdenes N 198 B6
Agen F 129 B3
Ager E 145 C4
Agerbæk DK 59 C1
Agerskov DK 64 A2
Agger DK 58 B1
Aggersund DK 58 A2
Ággius I 178 B3
Aggsbach Dorf A 97 C3
Aggsbach Markt A 97 C3
Aggtelek H 99 C4
Aghalee GB 27 B4
Aghia GR 182 D4
Aghia Anna GR 183 E5
Aghia Galini GR 185 D5
Aghia Marina GR 188 D1
Aghia Paraskevi GR 186 C1
Aghia Pelagia GR 184 C3
Aghia Triada GR 184 B2
Aghiokambos GR 182 D4
Aghios Efstratios GR 183 D6
Aghios Kirikos GR 185 B7
Aghios Matheos GR 182 D1
Aghios Mironas GR 185 D6
Aghios Nikolaos GR 185 D6
Aghios Petros GR 182 E2
Aghio Theodori GR 184 B4
Agiči BIH 124 C2
Agira I 177 B3
Aglientu I 178 A3
Agnières F 118 C2
Agno CH 120 B1
Agnone I 170 B2
Agolada E 140 B2
Agon Coutainville F 88 A2
Ágordo I 121 A5
Agost E 165 A4
Agramón E 158 C2
Agramunt E 147 C2
Agreda E 144 C2
Agria GR 183 D5
Agrigento I 176 B2
Agrinio GR 182 E3
Agrón E 163 A4
Agrópoli I 170 C2
Aguadulce
Almería E 164 C2
Sevilla E 162 A3
Agualada E 140 A2
Agua Longa P 148 A1
A Guarda E 140 C2
Aguarón E 152 A2
Aguas E 145 B3
Aguas Belas P 154 B2
Aguas de Busot E 159 C3
Aguas de Moura P 154 C2
Águas Frias P 148 A2
Aguas Santas P 148 A1
Aguaviva E 153 B3
Aguaviva de la Vega E 152 A1
A Gudiña E 141 B3
Agudo E 156 B3
Águeda P 148 B1
Aguessac F 130 A2
Agugliano I 136 B2
Aguiar P 154 C3
Aguiàr da Beira P 148 B2
Aguilafuente E 151 A3
Aguilar de Campóo E 142 B2
Aguilar de la Frontera E 163 A3
Aguilas E 164 B3
Agunnaryd S 60 C4
Ahat TR 187 D4
Ahaus D 71 B3
Åheim N 198 C2
Ahigal E 149 B3
Ahigal de Villarino E 149 A3
Ahillones E 156 B2
Ahlbeck
Mecklenburg-Vorpommern D 66 C3
Mecklenburg-Vorpommern D 74 A3
Ahlen D 81 A3
Ahlhorn D 71 B5
Ahmetbey TR 186 A2
Ahmetler TR 188 A4
Ahmetli TR 188 A2
Ahoghill GB 27 B4
Ahola FIN 197 C11
Ahrensbök D 65 B3
Ahrensburg D 72 A3
Ahrenshoop D 66 B1
Ahun F 116 A2
Åhus S 63 C2
Ahvenselkä FIN 197 C11
Aibar E 144 B2
Aich D 95 C4
Aicha D 96 C1
Aichach D 94 C3
Aidone I 177 B3
Aiello Cálabro I 175 B2
Aigen im Mühlkreis A 96 C1
Aigle CH 119 A3
Aignan F 128 C3
Aignay-le-Duc F 104 B3
Aigre F 115 C4
Aigrefeuille-d'Aunis F 114 B3
Aigrefeuille-sur-Maine F 101 B4
Aiguablava E 147 C4
Aiguebelle F 118 B3
Aigueperse F 116 A3
Aigues-Mortes F 131 B3
Aigues-Vives F 130 B1
Aiguilles F 119 C3
Aiguillon F 129 B3
Aigurande F 103 C3
Ailefroide F 118 C3
Aillant-sur-Tholon F 104 B2

Ailly-sur-Noye F 90 B2
Ailly-sur-Somme F 90 B2
Aimargues F 131 B3
Aime F 118 B3
Ainaži LV 8 D4
Ainet A 109 C3
Ainhoa F 144 A2
Ainsa E 145 B4
Airaines F 90 B1
Aird GB 34 B2
Aird Asaig Tairbeart GB 31 B2
Airdrie GB 35 C4
Aire-sur-l'Adour F 128 C2
Aire-sur-la-Lys F 78 B2
Airole I 133 B3
Airolo CH 107 C3
Airvault F 102 C1
Aisey-sur-Seine F 104 B3
Aïssey F 105 B5
Aisy-sur-Armançon F 104 B3
Aiterhofen D 95 C4
Aith
Orkney GB 33 B4
Shetland GB 33 A5
Aitona E 153 A4
Aitrach D 107 B5
Aiud RO 17 B5
Aix-en-Othe F 104 A2
Aix-en-Provence F 131 B4
Aixe-sur-Vienne F 115 C5
Aix-les-Bains F 118 B2
Aizenay F 114 B2
Aizkraukle LV 8 D4
Aizpute LV 8 D2
Ajac F 146 A3
Ajaccio F 180 B1
Ajain F 116 A1
Ajaureforsen S 195 E6
Ajdovščina SLO 122 B2
Ajka H 111 B4
Ajo E 143 A3
Ajofrin E 157 A4
Ajos FIN 196 D7
Ajuda P 155 C3
Akanthou CY 181 A2
Akarca TR 189 A4
Akasztó H 112 C3
Akçakoca TR 187 A6
Akçaova TR 187 A4
Akçay TR 189 C4
Aken D 83 A4
Åkerby S 51 B4
Åkernes N 52 B3
Åkersberga S 57 A4
Åkers styckebruk S 56 A3
Åkervik N 195 E4
Akhisar TR 186 D2
Åkirkeby DK 67 A3
Akköy TR 188 B2
Akkrum NL 70 A2
Akören TR 189 B7
Åkra N 52 A2
Akranes IS 190 C3
Åkrehamn N 52 A1
Akrotiri CY 181 B1
Aksaray TR 23 B8
Akşehir TR 189 A6
Akseki TR 189 B6
Aksla N 46 A3
Aksu TR 189 C5
Aktsyabrski BY 13 B8
Akureyri IS 191 B7
Åkvåg N 53 B5
Akyazı TR 187 B5
Ål N 47 B5
Ala I 121 B4
Alaca TR 23 A8
Alacaatlı TR 186 C3
Alaçam TR 23 A8
Alaçatı TR 188 A1
Alàdei Sardi I 178 B3
Ala di Stura I 119 B4
Alaejos E 150 A2
Alagna Valsésia I 119 B4
Alagón E 144 C2
Alaior E 167 B4
Alájar E 161 B3
Alakurtti RUS 197 C13
Alakylä FIN 196 B7
Alameda E 163 A3
Alameda de la Sagra E 151 B4
Alamedilla E 163 A4
Alamillo E 156 B3
Alaminos E 151 B5
Ala-Nampa FIN 197 C9
Alanäs S 199 A12
Alandroal P 155 C3
Alange E 156 B1
Alaniemi FIN 197 D8
Alanís E 156 B2
Alanno I 169 A3
Ålansbro S 200 D3
Alanya TR 189 C7
Alap H 112 C2
Alaquáso E 159 B3
Alaraz E 150 B2
Alarcón E 158 B1
Alar del Rey E 142 B2
Alaró E 167 B2
Alaşehir TR 188 A3
Alássio I 133 A4
Ağlasun TR 189 B5
Alatoz E 158 B2
Alatri I 169 B3
Alavus FIN 8 A3
Alba
E 152 B2
I 119 C5
Alba Adriática I 136 C2
Albacete E 158 C2
Alba de Tormes E 150 B2
Alba de Yeltes E 149 B3
Albaida E 159 C3
Alba-Iulia RO 17 B5
Albæk DK 58 A3
Albaladejo E 158 C1
Albala del Caudillo E 156 A1
Albalat E 159 B3
Albalate de Cinca E 145 C4
Albalate del Arzobispo E 153 A3
Albalate de las Nogueras E 152 B1
Albalete de Zorita E 151 B5
Alban F 130 B1
Albánchez E 164 B2
Albanchez de Ubeda E 163 A4
Albano Laziale I 168 B2
Albanyà E 147 B3
Albaredo d'Adige I 121 B4
Albares E 151 B4
Albarracín E 152 B2
Albatana E 158 C2
Albatarrec E 153 A4
Albatera E 165 A4
Albbruck D 106 B3
Albedin E 163 A3
Albelda de Iregua E 143 B4
Albenga I 133 A4
Albens F 118 B2
Ålberga
Södermanland S 56 A2
Södermanland S 56 B2
Albergaria-a-Nova P 148 B1
Albergaria-a-Velha P 148 B1
Albergaria dos Doze P 154 B2
Alberge P 154 C2
Alberic E 159 B3
Albernoa P 160 B2
Alberobello I 173 B3
Alberoni I 122 B1
Albersdorf D 64 B2
Albersloh D 81 A3
Albert F 90 A2
Albertirsa H 112 B3
Albertville F 118 B3
Alberuela de Tubo E 145 C3
Albi F 130 B1
Albidona I 174 B2
Albínia I 168 A1
Albino I 120 B2
Albinshof D 66 C2
Albires E 142 B1
Albisola Marina I 133 A4
Albocácer E 153 B4
Albolote E 163 A4
Albondón E 164 C1
Alborea E 158 B2
Albox E 164 B2
Albrechtice nad Vitavou CZ 96 B2
Albstadt D 107 A4
Albufeira P 160 B1
Albuñol E 164 C1
Albuñuelas E 163 B4
Alburquerque E 155 B3
Alby
Öland S 63 B4
Västernorrland S 200 D1
Alcácer do Sal P 154 C2
Alcáçovas P 154 C2
Alcadozo E 158 C2
Alcafoces P 155 B3
Alcains P 155 B3
Alcaláde Guadaira E 162 A2
Alcaláde Gurrea E 144 B3
Alcaláde Henares E 151 B4
Alcaláde la Selva E 153 B3
Alcaládel Júcar E 158 B2
Alcaláde los Gazules E 162 B2
Alcaládel Río E 162 A2
Alcaládel Valle E 162 B2
Alcaláde Xivert E 153 B4
Alcalála Real E 163 A4
Álcamo I 176 B1
Alcampell E 145 C4
Alcanadre E 144 B1
Alcanar E 153 B4
Alcanede P 154 B2
Alcanena P 154 B2
Alcañices E 149 A3
Alcántara E 155 B4
Alcantarilha P 160 B1
Alcantarilla E 165 B3
Alcañiz E 153 A3
Alcaracejos E 156 B3
Alcara il Fusi I 177 A3
Alcaraz E 158 C1
Alcaria Ruiva P 160 B2
Alcarraz E 153 A4
Alcaudete E 163 A3
Alcaudete de la Jara E 150 C3
Alcázar de San Juan E 157 A4
Alcazarén E 150 A3
Alcester GB 44 A2
Alcoba E 157 A3
Alcobaça P 154 B1
Alcobendas E 151 B4
Alcocer E 151 B5
Alcochete P 154 C2
Alcoentre P 154 B2
Alcolea
Almería E 164 C2
Córdoba E 156 C3
Alcolea de Calatrava E 157 B3
Alcolea de Cinca E 145 C4
Alcolea del Pinar E 152 A1
Alcolea del Rio E 162 A2
Alcolea de Tajo E 150 C2
Alcollarin E 156 A2
Alconchel E 155 C3
Alconera E 155 C4
Alcontar E 164 B2
Alcora E 153 B3
Alcorcón E 151 B4
Alcorisa E 153 B3
Alcossebre E 153 B4
Alcoutim P 160 B2
Alcover E 147 C2
Alcoy E 159 C3
Alcsútdoboz H 112 B2
Alcubierre E 145 C3
Alcubilla de Avellaneda E 143 C3
Alcubilla de Nogales E 141 B5
Alcubillas E 157 B4
Alcublas E 159 B3
Alcúdia E 167 B3
Alcudia de Guadix E 164 B1
Alcuéscar E 155 B4
Aldbrough GB 41 B3
Aldeacentenera E 156 A2
Aldeadávila de la Ribera E 149 A3
Aldea del Cano E 155 B4
Aldea del Fresno E 151 B3
Aldea del Obispo E 149 B3
Aldea del Rey E 157 B4
Aldea de Trujillo E 156 A2
Aldealcorvo E 151 A4
Aldealuenga de Santa Maria E 151 A4
Aldeamayor de San Martin E 150 A3
Aldeanueva de Barbarroya E 150 C2
Aldeanueva del Camino E 149 B4
Aldeanueva del Codonal E 150 A3
Aldeanueva de San Bartolomé E 156 A2
Aldeapozo E 144 C1
Aldeaquemada E 157 B4
Aldea Real E 151 A3
Aldearrubia E 150 A2
Aldeaseca de la Frontera E 150 B2
Aldeasoña E 151 A3
Aldeatejada E 150 B2
Aldeavieja E 150 B3
Aldeburgh GB 45 A5
Aldehuela E 152 B2
Aldehuela de Calatañazor E 143 C4
Aldeia da Serra P 155 C3
Aldeia do Bispo P 149 B3
Aldeia do Mato P 154 B2
Aldeia Gavinha P 154 B1
Aldeire E 164 B1
Aldenhoven D 80 B2
Aldersbach D 95 C5
Aldershot GB 44 B3
Aldudes F 144 A2
Åled S 60 C2
Aledo E 165 B3
Alegria E 143 B4
Aleksandrovac SRB 127 C3
Aleksandrów Kujawski PL 76 B3
Aleksandrów Łódźki PL 86 A3
Aleksa Šantić SRB 126 B1
Ålem S 62 B4
Alençon F 89 B4
Alenquer P 154 B1
Alenya F 146 B3
Aléria F 180 A2
Alès F 131 A3
Áles I 179 C2
Alessándria I 120 C1
Alessándria della Rocca I 176 B2
Alessano I 173 C4
Ålesund N 198 C3
Alet-les-Bains F 146 B3
Alexandria
GB 34 C3
Alexandria *continued*
GR 182 C4
RO 17 D6
Alexandroupoli GR 183 C7
Aleyrac F 131 A3
Alézio I 173 B4
Alfacar E 163 A4
Alfaiates P 149 B3
Alfajarin E 153 A3
Alfambra
E 152 B2
P 160 B1
Alfândega da Fé P 149 A3
Alfarela de Jafes P 148 A2
Alfarelos P 148 B1
Alfarim P 154 C1
Alfarnate E 163 B3
Alfaro E 144 B2
Alfarrás E 145 C4
Alfaz del Pi E 159 C3
Alfedena I 169 B4
Alfeizarão P 154 B1
Alfeld
Bayern D 95 B3
Niedersachsen D 72 C2
Alfena P 148 A1
Alferce P 160 B1
Alfhausen D 71 B4
Alfonsine I 135 A5
Alford
Aberdeenshire GB 33 D4
Lincolnshire GB 41 B4
Alforja E 147 C1
Alfoz E 141 A3
Alfreton GB 40 B2
Alfta S 50 A3
Alfundão P 160 A1
Algaida E 167 B2
Algar E 162 B2
Älgarås S 55 B5
Ålgård N 52 B1
Algarinejo E 163 A3
Algarrobo E 163 B3
Algatocin E 162 B2
Algeciras E 162 B2
Algemesí E 159 B3
Algés P 154 C1
Algete E 151 B4
Alghero I 178 B2
Älghult S 62 A3
Alginet E 159 B3
Algodonales E 162 B2
Algodor
E 151 C4
P 160 B2
Algora E 151 B5
Algoso P 149 A3
Algoz P 160 B1
Älgsjö S 200 B3
Alguaire E 145 C4
Alguazas E 165 A3
Algutsrum S 63 B4
Algyö H 126 A2
Alhama de Almería E 164 C2
Alhama de Aragón E 152 A2
Alhama de Granada E 163 B4
Alhama de Murcia E 165 B3
Alhambra E 157 B4
Alhandra P 154 C1
Alhaurin de la Torre E 163 B3
Alhaurín el Grande E 163 B3
Alhendin E 163 A4
Alhóndiga E 151 B5
Alia E 156 A2
Ália I 176 B2
Aliağa TR 186 D1
Aliaga E 153 B3
Alibunar SRB 127 B2
Alicante E 165 A4
Alicún de Ortega E 164 B1
Alife I 170 B2
Alija del Infantado E 141 B5
Alijó P 148 A2
Alimena I 177 B3
Alingsås S 60 B2
Alinyà E 147 B2
Aliseda E 155 B4
Ali Terme I 177 A4
Aliveri GR 185 A5
Alixan F 117 C5
Aljaraque E 161 B2
Aljezur P 160 B1
Aljorra E 165 B3
Aljubarrota P 154 B2
Aljucen E 155 B4
Aljustrel P 160 B1
Alken B 79 B5
Alkmaar NL 70 B1
Alkoven A 96 C2
Allaines F 103 A3
Allaire F 101 B3
Allanche F 116 B2
Alland A 111 A3
Allariz E 140 B3
Allassac F 129 A4
Allauch F 131 B4
Alleen N 52 B3
Allègre F 117 B3
Allemont F 118 B3
Allendale Town GB 37 B4
Allendorf D 81 B4
Allentsteig A 97 C3
Allepuz E 153 B3
Allersberg D 95 B3
Allershausen D 95 C3
Alles E 142 A2
Allevard F 118 B3
Allgunnen S 62 A3
Allihies IRL 29 C1
Allingåbro DK 58 B3
Allmannsdorf D 107 B4
Allo E 144 B1
Alloa GB 35 B4
Allogny F 103 B4
Ålloluokta S 196 B2
Allones
Eure et Loire F 90 C1
Maine-et-Loire F 102 B2
Allonnes F 102 B2
Allons F 128 B2
Allos F 132 A2
Allstedt D 82 A3
Alltwalis GB 39 C2
Allumiere I 168 A1
Almaceda P 155 B3
Almacelles E 145 C4
Almachar E 163 B3
Almada P 154 C1
Almadén E 156 B3
Almadén de la Plata E 161 B3
Almadenejos E 156 B3
Almadrones E 151 B5
Almagro E 157 B4
Almajano E 144 C1
Almansa E 159 C2
Almansil P 160 B1
Almanza E 142 B1
Almaraz E 150 C2
Almargen E 162 B2
Almarza E 143 C4
Almásfüzitő H 112 B2
Almassora E 159 B3
Almazán E 152 A1
Almazul E 152 A1
Alme D 81 A4
Almedina E 158 C1
Almedinilla E 163 A3
Almeida
E 149 A3
P 149 B3
Almeirim P 154 B2
Almelo NL 71 B3
Almenar E 145 C4
Almenara E 159 B3
Almenar de Soria E 152 A1
Almendra P 149 B2
Almendral E 155 C4
Almendral de la Cañada E 150 B3
Almendralejo E 155 C4
Almenno San Bartolomeo I 120 B2
Almere NL 70 B2
Almería E 164 C2
Almerimar E 164 C2
Almese I 119 B4
Almexial P 160 B2
Älmhult S 63 B2
Almiropotamos GR 185 A5
Almiros GR 182 D4
Almodôvar P 160 B1
Almodóvar del Campo E 157 B3
Almodóvar del Pinar E 158 B2
Almodóvar del Río E 162 A2
Almofala P 148 B2
Almogia E 163 B3
Almoharin E 156 A1
Almonacid de la Sierra E 152 A2
Almonacid de Toledo E 157 A4
Almonaster la Real E 161 B3
Almondsbury GB 43 A4
Almonte E 161 B3
Almoradí E 165 A4
Almoraima E 162 B2
Almorox E 150 B3
Almoster P 154 B2
Almsele S 200 B3
Älmsta S 51 C5
Almudena E 164 A3
Almudévar E 145 B3
Almuñécar E 163 B4
Almunge S 51 C5
Almuradiel E 157 B4
Almussafes E 159 B3
Almvik S 62 A4
Alness GB 32 D2
Alnmouth GB 37 A5
Alnwick GB 37 A5
Åloppe S 51 C4
Álora E 163 B3
Alos d'Ensil E 146 B2
Alosno E 161 B2
Alozaina E 162 B3
Alpbach A 108 B2
Alpedrete de la Sierra E 151 B4
Alpedrinha P 148 B2
Alpen D 80 A2
Alpera E 159 C2
Alphen aan de Rijn NL 70 B1
Alpiarça P 154 B2
Alpignano I 119 B4
Alpirsbach D 93 C4
Alpu TR 187 C5
Alpuente E 159 B2
Alqueva P 160 A2
Alquézar E 145 B4
Als DK 58 B3
Alsasua E 144 B1
Alsdorf D 80 B2
Alselv DK 59 C1
Alsfeld D 81 B5
Alsike S 57 A3
Alskog S 57 C4
Alsleben D 83 A3
Alsónémedi H 112 B3
Alsótold H 112 B3
Alsóújlak H 111 B3
Alstad N 194 C6
Alstätte D 71 B3
Alsterbro S 62 B3
Alstermo S 62 B3
Alston GB 37 B4
Alsvåg N 194 B6
Alsvik N 194 C5
Alta N 192 C7
Älta S 57 A4
Altamura I 172 B2
Altarejos E 158 B1
Altaussee A 109 B4
Altavilla Irpina I 170 B2
Altavilla Silentina I 170 C3
Altdöbern D 84 A2
Altdorf
CH 107 C3
D 95 C4
Altdorf bei Nürnberg D 95 B3
Alte P 160 B1
Altea E 159 C3
Altedo I 121 C4
Altena D 81 A3
Altenau D 82 A2
Altenberg D 84 B1
Altenberge D 71 B4
Altenbruch D 64 C1
Altenburg D 83 B4
Altenfelden A 96 C1
Altengronau D 82 B1
Altenheim D 93 C3
Altenhundem D 81 A4
Altenkirchen
Mecklenburg-Vorpommern D 66 B2
Radom D 81 B3
Altenkunstadt D 82 B3
Altenmarkt
A 110 B1
D 109 A3
Altenmarkt im Pongall A 109 B4
Altensteig D 93 C4
Altentreptow D 74 A2
Altenwalde D 64 C1
Alten-weddingen D 73 B4
Alter do Chão P 155 B3
Altfraunhofen D 95 C4
Altheim
A 109 A4
D 94 B1
Althofen A 110 C1
Altınoluk TR 186 C1
Altınova TR 186 C1
Altıntaş TR 187 C5
Altınyaka TR 189 C5
Altınyayla TR 189 B4
Altkirch F 106 B2
Altlandsberg D 74 B2
Altlewin D 74 B3
Altmannstein D 95 C3
Altmorschen D 82 A1
Altmunster A 109 B4
Altnaharra GB 32 C2
Alto Campoó E 142 A2
Altofonte I 176 A2
Altomonte I 174 B2
Alton
Hampshire GB 44 B3
Staffordshire GB 40 C2
Altopáscio I 135 B3
Altötting D 109 A3
Altreichenau D 96 C1
Alt Ruppin D 74 B1
Altshausen D 107 B4
Altstätten CH 107 B4
Altura E 159 B3
Altusried D 107 B5
Alūksne LV 8 D5
Alunda S 51 B5
Alustante E 152 B2
Alva GB 35 B4
Alvaiázere P 154 B2
Alvalade P 160 B1
Älvängen S 60 B2
Alvarenga P 148 B1
Alvares P 154 A2
Alvdal N 199 C7
Älvdalen S 49 A6
Alverca P 154 C1
Alversund N 46 B2
Alvesta S 62 B2
Alvignac F 129 B4
Alvignano I 170 B2
Ålvik N 46 B3
Alvik S 50 B1

Alvimare F 89 A4
Alviobeira P 154 B2
Alvito P 160 A2
Älvkarleby S 51 B4
Älvkarleöbruk S 51 B4
Alvor P 160 B1
Alvorge P 154 B2
Alvøy N 46 B2
Älvros S 199 C11
Alvsbacka S 55 A4
Älvsbyn S 196 D4
Älvsered S 60 B2
Alwernia PL 86 B3
Alwinton GB 37 A4
Alyth GB 35 B4
Alytus LT 13 A6
Alzénau D 93 A5
Alzey D 93 B4
Alzira E 159 B3
Alzonne F 146 A3
Amadora P 154 C1
Åmål S 55 A3
Amalfi I 170 C2
Amaliada GR 184 B2
Amance F 105 B5
Amancey F 105 B5
Amándola I 136 C2
Amantea I 175 B2
Amarante P 148 A1
Amareleja P 161 A2
Amares P 148 A1
Amaseno I 169 B3
Amasra TR 187 A7
Amatrice I 169 A3
Amay B 79 B5
Ambarnyy RUS 3 D13
Ambazac F 115 C5
Ambelonas GR 182 D4
Amberg D 95 B3
Ambérieu-en-Bugey
F 118 B2
Ambérieux-en-Dombes
F 117 A4
Ambert F 117 B3
Ambés F 128 A2
Ambjörby S 49 B5
Ambjörnarp S 60 B3
Amble GB 37 A5
Ambleside GB 36 B4
Ambleteuse F 78 B1
Amboise F 102 B2
Ambrières-les-Vallées
F 88 B3
Amden CH 107 B4
Amel B 80 B2
Amélia I 168 A2
Amélie-les-Bains-
Palalda F 146 B3
Amelinghausen D 72 A3
Amendoa P 154 B2
Amendoeira P 160 B2
Améndola I 171 B3
Amendolara I 174 B2
Amer E 147 B3
A Merca E 140 B3
Amerongen NL 70 B2
Amersfoort NL 70 B2
Amersham GB 44 B3
Amesbury GB 44 B2
Amfiklia GR 182 E4
Amfilochia GR 182 E3
Amfipoli GR 183 C5
Amfissa GR 184 A3
Amièira P 155 C3
Amieira P 154 B3
Amieiro P 148 B1
Amiens F 90 B2
Amindeo GR 182 C3
Åminne S 60 B3
Åmli N 53 B4
Amlwch GB 38 A2
Ammanford GB 39 C3
Ammarnäs S 195 E7
Åmmeberg S 55 B5
Amorbach D 94 B1
Amorebieta E 143 A4
Amorgos GR 185 C6
Amorosa P 148 A1
Amorosi I 170 B2
Åmot
Buskerud N 48 C1
Telemark N 53 A3
S 50 B3
Åmotfors S 54 A3
Åmotsdal N 53 A4
Amou F 128 C2
Ampezzo I 122 A1
Ampfing D 95 C4
Ampflwang A 109 A4
Amplepuis F 117 B4
Amposta E 153 B4
Ampthill GB 44 A3
Ampudia E 142 C2
Ampuero E 143 A3
Amriswil CH 107 B4
Åmsele S 200 B5
Amstelveen NL 70 B1
Amsterdam NL 70 B1
Amstetten A 110 A1
Amtzell D 107 B4
Amulree GB 35 B4
Amurrio E 143 A4
Amusco E 142 B2
Anacapri I 170 C2
Anadia P 148 B1
Anadon E 152 B2
Anafi GR 185 C6
Anagni I 169 B3
Anamur TR 23 C7
Ananyiv UA 17 B8
Anascaul IRL 29 B1
Ånäset S 2 D7
Åna-Sira N 52 B2
Anastażewo PL 76 B3
Anaya de Alba E 150 B2
Ança P 148 B1
Ancaster GB 40 C3
Ancede P 148 A1
Ancenis F 101 B4
Ancerville F 91 C5
Anchuras E 156 A3
Ancona I 136 B2
Ancora P 148 A1
Ancrum GB 35 C5
Ancy-le-Franc F 104 B3
Andalo I 121 A3
Åndalsnes N 198 C4
Andance F 117 B4
Andau A 111 B4
Andebu N 53 A6
Andeer CH 107 C4
Andelfingen CH 107 B3
Andelot-Blanchville
F 105 A4
Andelot-en-Montagne
F 105 C4
Andenes N 194 A7
Andenne B 79 B5
Anderlues B 79 B4
Andermatt CH 107 C3
Andernach D 80 B3
Andernos-les-Bains
F 128 B1
Anderslöv S 66 A2
Anderstorp S 60 B3
Andijk NL 70 B2
Andoain E 144 A1
Andocs H 112 C1
Andolsheim F 106 A2
Andorra E 153 B3
Andorra La Vella
AND 146 B2
Andosilla E 144 B2
Andover GB 44 B2
Andratx E 166 B2
Andreapol RUS 9 D8
Andreas GB 36 B2
Andréspol PL 86 A3
Andrest F 145 A4
Andretta I 172 B1
Andrezieux-Bouthéon
F 117 B4
Ándria I 171 B4
Andrijevica MNE 16 D3
Andritsena GR 184 B2
Andros GR 185 B5
Andrychów PL 99 B3
Andselv N 194 A9
Andújar E 157 B3
Anduze F 131 A2
Åneby N 48 B2
Aneby S 62 A2
Añes E 143 A3
Anet F 90 C1
Anfo I 121 B3
Ang S 62 A2
Anga S 57 C4
Angaïs F 145 A3
Änge S 199 B11
Ånge S 200 D1
Angeja P 148 B1
Ängelholm S 61 C2
Angeli FIN 193 D9
Ängelsberg S 50 C3
Anger A 110 B2
Angera I 120 B1
Angermünde D 74 A3
Angern A 97 C4
Angers F 102 B1
Angerville F 90 C2
Anghiari I 135 B5
Angle GB 39 C1
Anglès E 147 C3
Anglés F 130 B1
Angles F 114 B2
Anglesola E 147 C2
Angles sur l'Anglin
F 115 B4
Anglet F 128 C1
Anglisidhes CY 181 B2
Anglure F 91 C3
Angoulême F 115 C4
Angoulins F 114 B2
Angsö S 56 A2
Angueira P 149 A3
Angües E 145 B3
Anguiano E 143 B4
Anguillara Sabazia
I 168 A2
Anguillara Véneta
I 121 B4
Anhée B 79 B4
Anholt DK 60 C1
Aniane F 130 B2
Aniche F 78 B3
Ånimskog S 54 B3
Anina RO 16 C4
Anixi GR 182 D3
Anizy-le-Château F 91 B3
Anjalankoski FIN 8 B5
Anjan S 199 B9
Ankara TR 187 C7
Ankaran SLO 122 B2
Ankarsrum S 62 A4
Ankerlia N 192 C4
Anklam D 66 C2
Ankum D 71 B4
Anlauftal A 109 B4
Anlezy F 104 C2
Ånn S 199 B9
Annaberg A 110 B2
Annaberg-Buchholz
D 83 B5
Annaberg im Lammertal
A 109 B4
Annaburg D 83 A5
Annahütte D 84 A1
Annalong GB 27 B5
Annan GB 36 B3
Anndalsvågen N 195 E3
Anneberg
Halland S 60 B2
Jönköping S 62 A2
Annecy F 118 B3
Annelund S 60 B3
Annemasse F 118 A3
Annenskiy Most
RUS 9 B10
Annerstad S 60 C3
Annestown IRL 30 B1
Annevoie-Rouillon
B 79 B4
Annonay F 117 B4
Annot F 132 B2
Annweiler D 93 B3
Ano Poroia GR 183 B5
Añora E 156 B3
Ano Siros GR 185 B5
Anould F 106 A1
Anquela del Ducado
E 152 B1
Anröchte D 81 A4
Ans DK 59 B2
Ansager DK 59 C1
Ansbach D 94 B2
Anse F 117 B4
Anseroeul B 79 B3
Ansfelden A 110 A1
Ansião P 154 B2
Ansó E 144 B3
Ansoain E 144 B2
Anstruther GB 35 B5
Antalya TR 189 C5
Antas E 164 B3
Antegnate I 120 B2
Antequera E 163 A3
Anterselva di Mezzo
I 108 C3
Antibes F 132 B3
Antigüedad E 142 C2
Antillo I 177 B4
Antirio GR 184 A2
Antnäs S 196 D4
An t-Ob GB 31 B1
Antoing B 79 B3
Antonin PL 86 A1
Antrain F 88 B2
Antrim GB 27 B4
Antrodoco I 169 A3
Antronapiana I 119 A5
Anttis S 196 B5
Antuzede P 148 B1
Antwerp = Antwerpen
B 79 A4
Antwerpen = Antwerp
B 79 A4
Anversa d'Abruzzi
I 169 B3
Anvin F 78 B2
Anzat-le-Luguet F 116 B3
Anzi I 172 B1
Änzio I 168 B2
Anzola d'Emilia I 135 A4
Anzón E 144 C2
Aoiz E 144 B2
Aosta I 119 B4
Apalhão P 155 B3
Apátfalva H 126 A2
Apatin SRB 125 B5
Apatity RUS 3 C13
Apc H 112 B3
Apécchio I 136 B1
Apeldoorn NL 70 B2
Apen D 71 A4
Apenburg D 73 B4
Apensen D 72 A2
A Peroxa E 140 B3
Apiro I 136 B2
Apliki CY 181 B2
Apolda D 82 A3
Apolonia GR 185 C5
A Pontenova E 141 A3
Apostag H 112 C2
Äppelbo S 49 B6
Appennino I 136 C2
Appenzell CH 107 B4
Appiano I 108 C2
Appingedam NL 71 A3
Appleby-in-
Westmorland GB 37 B4
Applecross GB 31 B3
Appledore GB 42 A2
Appoigny F 104 B2
Apremont-la-Forêt
F 92 C1
Aprica I 120 A3
Apricena I 171 B3
Aprigliano I 174 B2
Aprília I 168 B2
Apt F 131 B4
Apúlia P 148 A1
Aquiléia I 122 B2
Aquilónia I 172 B1
Aquino I 169 B3
Ar S 57 C4
Arabayona E 150 A2
Arabba I 108 C2
Araç TR 23 A7
Aracena E 161 B3
Arachova GR 184 A3
Aračinovo MK 182 A3
Arad RO 126 A3
Aradac SRB 126 B2
Aradhippou CY 181 B2
Aragnouet F 145 B4
Aragona I 176 B2
Aramits F 144 A3
Aramon F 131 B3
Aranda de Duero E 143 C3
Aranda de Moncayo
E 152 A2
Arandjelovac SRB 127 C2
Aranjuez E 151 B4
Arantzazu E 143 B4
Aranzueque E 151 B4
Aras de Alpuente
E 159 B2
Arauzo de Miel E 143 C3
Arazede P 148 B1
Arbas F 145 B4
Årbatax I 179 C3
Arbeca E 147 C1
Arberg D 94 B2
Arbesbach A 96 C2
Arboga S 56 A1
Arbois F 105 C4
Arbon CH 107 B4
Arboréa I 179 C2
Arbório I 119 B5
Årbostad N 194 B8
Arbrå S 50 A3
Arbroath GB 35 B5
Arbùcies E 147 C3
Arbuniel E 163 A4
Arbus I 179 C2
Arcachon F 128 B1
Arce I 169 B3
Arcen NL 80 A2
Arc-en-Barrois F 105 B3
Arces-Dilo F 104 A2
Arc-et-Senans F 105 B4
Arcévia I 136 B1
Arcey F 106 B1
Archanes GR 185 D6
Archangelos GR 188 C3
Archena E 165 A3
Archez E 163 B4
Archiac F 115 C3
Archidona E 163 A3
Archiestown GB 32 D3
Archivel E 164 A3
Arcidosso I 135 C4
Arcille I 135 C4
Arcis-sur-Aube F 91 C4
Arc-lès-Gray F 105 B4
Arco I 121 B3
Arcones E 151 A4
Arcos E 143 B3
Arcos de Jalón E 152 A1
Arcos de la Frontera
E 162 B2
Arcos de la Sierra
E 152 B1
Arcos de las Salinas
E 159 B2
Arcos de Valdevez
P 148 A1
Arcozelo P 148 B2
Arc-sur-Tille F 105 B4
Arcusa E 145 B4
Arcy-sur-Cure F 104 B2
Ardagh IRL 29 B2
Årdal N 52 A2
Ardala S 55 B4
Ardales E 162 B3
Årdalstangen N 47 A4
Ardara
I 178 B2
IRL 26 B2
Ardarroch GB 31 B3
Ardbeg GB 34 C1
Ardcharnich GB 32 D1
Ardchyle GB 34 B3
Ardee IRL 27 C4
Arden DK 58 B2
Ardentes F 103 C3
Ardenza I 134 B3
Ardersier GB 32 D2
Ardes F 116 B3
Ardessie GB 32 D1
Ardez CH 107 C5
Ardfert IRL 29 B2
Ardgay GB 32 D2
Ardglass GB 27 B5
Ardgroom IRL 29 C2
Ardhasig GB 31 B2
Ardino BG 183 B7
Ardisa E 144 B3
Ardkearagh IRL 29 C1
Ardlui GB 34 B3
Ardlussa GB 34 B2
Ardón E 142 B1
Ardooie B 78 B3
Ardore I 175 C2
Ardre S 57 C4
Ardres F 78 B1
Ardrishaig GB 34 B2
Ardrossan GB 34 C3
Are N 52 A1
Åre S 199 B10
Areia Branca P 154 B1
Aremark N 54 A2
Arenales de San
Gregorio E 157 A4
Arenas E 163 B3
Arenas de Iguña E 142 A2
Arenas del Rey E 163 B4
Arenas de San Juan
E 157 A4
Arenas de San Pedro
E 150 B2
Arendal N 53 B4
Arendonk B 79 A5
Arengosse F 128 B2
Arentorp S 55 B3
Arenys de Mar E 147 C3
Arenys de Munt E 147 C3
Arenzano I 133 A4
Areo E 146 B2
Areopoli GR 184 C3
Ares E 140 A2
Arès F 128 B1
Ares del Maestrat
E 153 B3
Aresvika N 198 B5
Arette F 144 A3
Aretxabaleta E 143 A4
Arevalillo E 150 B2
Arévalo E 150 A3
Arez P 155 B3
Arezzo I 135 B4
Arfeuilles F 117 A3
Argalasti GR 183 D5
Argallón E 156 B2
Argamasilla de Alba
E 157 A4
Argamasilla de
Calatrava E 157 B3
Arganda E 151 B4
Arganil P 148 B1
Argasion GR 184 B1
Argegno I 120 B2
Argelès-Gazost F 145 A3
Argelès-sur-Mer F 146 B4
Argenta I 121 C4
Argentan F 89 B3
Argentat F 116 B1
Argentera I 132 A2
Argenteuil F 90 C2
Argenthal D 93 B3
Argentiera I 178 B2
Argentona E 147 C3
Argenton-Château
F 102 C1
Argenton-sur-Creuse
F 103 C3
Argentré F 102 A1
Argentré-du-Plessis
F 101 A4
Argent-sur-Sauldre
F 103 B4
Argirades GR 182 D1
Argithani TR 189 A6
Argos GR 184 B3
Argos Orestiko GR 182 C3
Argostoli GR 184 A1
Argote E 143 B4
Arguedas E 144 B2
Argueil F 90 B1
Arholma S 51 C6
Århus DK 59 B3
Ariano Irpino I 170 B3
Ariano nel Polésine
I 121 C5
Aribe E 144 B2
Aridea GR 182 C4
Arienzo I 170 B2
Arild S 61 C2
Arileod GB 34 B1
Arinagour GB 34 B1
Ariño E 153 A3
Arinthod F 118 A2
Arisaig GB 34 B2
Arisgotas E 157 A4
Aritzo I 179 C3
Ariza E 152 A1
Årjäng S 54 A3
Arjeplog S 195 D8
Arjona E 157 C3
Arjonilla E 157 C3
Arkasa GR 188 D2
Arkelstorp S 63 B2
Arklow IRL 30 B2
Arkösund S 56 B2
Ärla S 56 A2
Arlanc F 117 B3
Arlanzón E 143 B3
Arlebosc F 117 B4
Arlena di Castro I 168 A1
Arles F 131 B3
Arles-sur-Tech F 146 B3
Arló H 113 A4
Arlon B 92 B1
Armação de Pera
P 160 B1
Armadale
Highland GB 31 B3
West Lothian GB 35 C4
Armagh GB 27 B4
Armamar P 148 A2
Armenistis GR 185 B7
Armeno I 119 B5
Armenteros E 150 B2
Armentières F 78 B2
Armilla E 163 A4
Armiñón E 143 B4
Armoy GB 27 A4
Armuña de Tajuña
E 151 B4
Armutlu
Bursa TR 186 B3
İzmir TR 188 A2
Arnac-Pompadour
F 115 C5
Arnafjord N 46 A3
Arnage F 102 B2
Arnas F 117 A4
Årnäs S 55 B4
Arnay-le-Duc F 104 B3
Arnborg DK 59 B2
Arnbruck D 95 B4
Arnea GR 183 C5
Arneberg
Hedmark N 48 A2
Hedmark N 49 B4
Arneburg D 73 B5
Arnedillo E 144 B1
Arnedo E 144 B1
Arneguy F 144 A2
Arnés E 153 B4
Árnes IS 190 A4
Årnes
Akershus N 48 B3
Troms N 194 A9
Arnfels A 110 C2
Arnhem NL 70 C2
Arnissa GR 182 C3
Arno S 56 B3
Arnold GB 40 B2
Arnoldstein A 109 C4
Arnsberg D 81 A4
Arnschwang D 95 B4
Arnsdorf D 84 A1
Årnset N 198 B6
Arnside GB 37 B4
Arnstadt D 82 B2
Arnstein D 94 B1
Arnstorf D 95 C4
Arnum DK 59 C1
Aroche E 161 B3
Ároktő H 113 B4
Arolla CH 119 A4
Arolsen D 81 A5
Arona I 119 B5
Äros N 54 A1
Arosa
CH 107 C4
P 148 A1
Ærøskøbing DK 65 B3
Årøsund DK 59 C2
Arouca P 148 B1
Årøysund N 54 A1
Arpajon F 90 C2
Arpajon-sur-Cère
F 116 C2
Arpela FIN 196 C7
Arpino I 169 B3
Arquata del Tronto
I 136 C2
Arques F 78 B2
Arques-la-Bataille F 89 A5
Arquillos E 157 B4
Arraia-Maeztu E 143 B4
Arraiolos P 154 C2
Arrancourt F 92 C2
Arras F 78 B2
Arrasate E 143 A4
Årre DK 59 C1
Arreau F 145 B4
Arredondo E 143 A3
Arrens-Marsous F 145 B3
Arriate E 162 B2
Arrifana P 160 B1
Arrigorriaga E 143 A4
Arriondas E 142 A1
Arroba de los Montes
E 157 A3
Arrochar GB 34 B3
Arromanches-les-Bains
F 88 A3
Arronches P 155 B3
Arroniz E 144 B1
Arrou F 103 A3
Arroya E 142 B2
Arroya de Cuéllar
E 150 A3
Arroyal E 142 B2
Arroyo de la Luz E 155 B4
Arroyo del Ojanco
E 164 A2
Arroyo de San Servan
E 155 C4
Arroyomolinos de León
E 161 A3
Arroyomolinos de
Montánchez E 156 A1
Arruda dos Vinhos
P 154 C1
Arsac F 128 B2
Ars-en-Ré F 114 B2
Arsiè I 121 B4
Arsiero I 121 B4
Årslev DK 59 C3
Ärsoli I 169 A3
Ars-sur-Moselle F 92 B2
Årsunda S 50 B3
Artà E 167 B3
Arta GR 182 D3
Artajona E 144 B2
Artegna I 122 A2
Arteixo E 140 A2
Artemare F 118 B2
Arten I 121 A4
Artena I 169 B2

Artenay F 103 A3
Artern D 82 A3
Artés E 147 C2
Artesa de Segre E 147 C2
Arth CH 107 B3
Arthez-de-Béarn F 145 A3
Arthon-en-Retz F 101 B4
Arthurstown IRL 30 B2
Artieda E 144 B3
Artix F 145 A3
Artotina GR 182 E4
Artsyz UA 17 B8
Artziniega E 143 A3
A Rúa E 141 B3
Arudy F 145 A3
Arundel GB 44 C3
Arveyres F 128 B2
Arvidsjaur S 196 D2
Arvieux F 118 C3
Arvika S 54 A3
Åryd
Blekinge S 63 B3
Kronoberg S 62 B2
Arzachena I 178 A3
Arzacq-Arraziguet F 128 C2
Árzana I 179 C3
Arzano F 100 B2
Aržano HR 138 B2
Arzberg D 95 A4
Arzignano I 121 B4
Arzila P 148 B1
Arzl im Pitztal A 108 B1
Arzúa E 140 B2
As B 80 A1
Aš CZ 83 B4
Ås N 54 A1
Åsa S 60 B2
Asaa DK 58 A3
Aşağıçiğil TR 189 A6
Ašanja SRB 127 C2
Åsarna S 199 C11
Åsarøy N 52 A2
Åsarp S 55 B4
Asasp F 145 A3
Åsbro S 55 A6
Åsby S 60 B2
Åsby S 62 A3
Asbygri IS 191 A9
Ascain F 144 A2
Ascea I 172 B1
Ascha D 95 B4
Aschach an der Donau A 96 C2
Aschaffenburg D 93 B5
Aschbach Markt A 110 A1
Ascheberg
Nordrhein-Westfalen D 81 A3
Schleswig-Holstein D 65 B3
Aschendorf D 71 A4
Aschersleben D 82 A3
Asciano I 135 B4
Ascó E 153 A4
Asco F 180 A2
Áscoli Piceno I 136 C2
Áscoli Satriano I 171 B3
Ascona CH 120 A1
Ascot GB 44 B3
Ascoux F 103 A4
Åse N 194 A6
Åseda S 62 A3
Åsele S 200 B3
Åsen
N 199 B8
S 49 A5
Asendorf D 72 B2
Asenovgrad BG 183 A6
Åsensbruk S 54 B3
Åseral N 52 B3
Asfeld F 91 B4
Åsgårdstrand N 54 A1
Ásgarður IS 190 B1
Asgate CY 181 B2
Ash
Kent GB 45 B5
Surrey GB 44 B3
Åshammar S 50 B3
Ashbourne
GB 40 B2
IRL 30 A2
Ashburton GB 43 B3
Ashby-de-la-Zouch GB 40 C2
Ashchurch GB 44 B1
Åsheim N 199 D8
Ashford GB 45 B4
Ashington GB 37 A5
Ashley GB 38 B4
Ashmyany BY 13 A6
Ashton Under Lyne GB 40 B1
Ashwell GB 44 A3
Asiago I 121 B4
Asipovichy BY 13 B8
Aska FIN 197 B9
Askam-in-Furness GB 36 B3
Askeaton IRL 29 B3
Asker N 48 C2
Askersund S 55 B5
Åskilje S 200 B3
Askim N 54 A2
Askland N 53 B4
Äsköping S 56 A2
Askvoll N 46 A2
Åsljunga S 61 C3
Asmunti FIN 197 D9
Asnæs DK 61 D1
As Neves E 140 B2
As Nogaís E 141 B3
Ásola I 120 B3
Asolo I 121 B4
Asos GR 184 A1
Asotthalom H 126 A1
Aspach A 109 A4
Aspang Markt A 111 B3
Aspariegos E 149 A4
Asparn an der Zaya A 97 C4
Aspatria GB 36 B3
Aspberg S 55 A4
Aspe E 165 A4
Aspet F 145 A4
Äspö S 63 B3
As Pontes de García Rodríguez E 140 A3
Aspres-sur-Buëch F 132 A1
Aspsele S 200 C4
Assafora P 154 C1
Asse B 79 B4
Assebakte N 193 C9
Assel D 72 A2
Asselborn L 92 A1
Assémini I 179 C2
Assen NL 71 B3
Assenede B 79 A3
Assens
Aarhus Amt. DK 58 B3
Fyns Amt. DK 59 C2
Assesse B 79 B5
Assisi I 136 B1
Åsskard N 198 B5
Assling D 108 B3
Asso I 120 B2
Asson F 145 A3
Ássoro I 177 B3
Assumar P 155 B3
Åsta N 48 A3
Astaffort F 129 B3
Astakos GR 184 A2
Asten NL 80 A1
Asti I 119 C5
Astipalea GR 188 C1
Astorga E 141 B4
Åstorp S 61 C2
Åsträsk S 200 B5
Astudillo E 142 B2
Asuni I 179 C2
Asványráró H 111 B4
Aszód H 112 B3
Aszófő H 111 C4
Atabey TR 189 B5
Atalaia P 154 B3
Atalandi GR 182 E4
Atalho P 154 C2
Átány H 113 B4
Atanzón E 151 B4
Ataquines E 150 A3
Atarfe E 163 A4
Atça TR 188 B3
Ateca E 152 A2
A Teixeira E 141 B3
Atella I 172 B1
Atessa I 169 A4
Ath B 79 B3
Athboy IRL 30 A2
Athea IRL 29 B2
Athenry IRL 28 A3
Athens = Athina GR 185 B4
Atherstone GB 40 C2
Athienou CY 181 A2
Athies F 90 B2
Athies-sous-Laon F 91 B3
Athina = Athens GR 185 B4
Athleague IRL 28 A3
Athlone IRL 28 A4
Athna CY 181 A2
Athy IRL 30 B2
Atienza E 151 A5
Atina I 169 B3
Atkár H 113 B3
Atlantı TR 189 A7
Atna N 199 D7
Åtorp S 55 A5
Atrå N 47 C5
Ätran S 60 B2
Atri I 169 A3
Atripalda I 170 C2
Atsiki GR 183 D7
Attendorn D 81 A3
Attichy F 90 B3
Attigliano I 168 A2
Attigny F 91 B4
Attleborough GB 41 C5
Åtvidaberg S 56 B1
Atzendorf D 73 C4
Au
Steiermark A 110 B2
Vorarlberg A 107 B4
Bayern D 95 C3
Bayern D 108 B2
Aub D 94 B2
Aubagne F 132 B1
Aubange B 92 B1
Aubel B 80 B1
Aubenas F 117 C4
Aubenton F 91 B4
Auberive F 105 B4
Aubeterre-sur-Dronne F 128 A3
Aubiet F 129 C3
Aubigné F 115 B3
Aubigny F 114 B2
Aubigny-au-Bac F 78 B3
Aubigny-en-Artois F 78 B2
Aubigny-sur-Nère F 103 B4
Aubin F 130 A1
Aubonne CH 105 C5
Aubrac F 116 C2
Aubusson F 116 B2
Auch F 129 C3
Auchencairn GB 36 B3
Auchinleck GB 36 A2
Auchterarder GB 35 B4
Auchtermuchty GB 35 B4
Auchtertyre GB 31 B3
Auchy-au-Bois F 78 B2
Audenge F 128 B1
Auderville F 88 A2
Audierne F 100 A1
Audincourt F 106 B1
Audlem GB 38 B4
Audruicq F 78 B2
Audun-le-Roman F 92 B1
Audun-le-Tiche F 92 B1
Aue
Nordrhein-Westfalen D 81 A4
Sachsen D 83 B4
Auerbach
Bayern D 95 B3
Sachsen D 83 B4
Auffach A 108 B3
Augher GB 27 B3
Aughnacloy GB 27 B4
Aughrim IRL 30 B2
Augignac F 115 C4
Augsburg D 94 C2
Augusta I 177 B4
Augusten-borg DK 64 B2
Augustfehn D 71 A4
Augustów PL 12 B5
Aukrug D 64 B2
Auktsjaur S 196 D2
Auldearn GB 32 D3
Aulendorf D 107 B4
Auletta I 172 B1
Aulla I 134 A2
Aullène F 180 B2
Aulnay F 115 B3
Aulnoye-Aymeries F 79 B3
Ault F 90 A1
Aultbea GB 31 B3
Aulum DK 59 B1
Aulus-les-Bains F 146 B2
Auma D 83 B3
Aumale F 90 B1
Aumetz F 92 B1
Aumont-Aubrac F 116 C3
Aunay-en-Bazois F 104 B2
Aunay-sur-Odon F 88 A3
Aune N 199 A10
Auneau F 90 C1
Auneuil F 90 B1
Auning DK 58 B3
Aunsetra N 199 A9
Aups F 132 B2
Aura D 82 B1
Auray F 100 B3
Aurdal N 47 B6
Aure N 198 B5
Aurich D 71 A4
Aurignac F 145 A4
Aurillac F 116 C2
Auriol F 132 B1
Auritz-Burguette E 144 B2
Aurlandsvangen N 47 B4
Auronzo di Cadore I 109 C3
Auros F 128 B2
Auroux F 117 C3
Aurskog N 48 C3
Aursmoen N 48 C3
Ausónia I 169 B3
Ausservillgraton A 109 C3
Austad N 52 B3
Austbygda N 47 B5
Aústis I 178 B3
Austmarka N 49 B4
Austre Moland N 53 B4
Austre Vikebygd N 52 A1
Austrheim N 46 B1
Auterive F 146 A2
Autheuil-Authouillet F 89 A5
Authon F 132 A2
Authon-du-Perche F 102 A2
Autol E 144 B2
Autreville F 92 C1
Autrey-lès-Gray F 105 B4
Autti FIN 197 C10
Autun F 104 C3
Auty-le-Châtel F 103 B4
Auvelais B 79 B4
Auvillar F 129 B3
Auxerre F 104 B2
Auxi-le-Château F 78 B2
Auxon F 104 A2
Auxonne F 105 B4
Auxy F 104 C3
Auzances F 116 A2
Auzon F 117 B3
Ağva TR 187 A4
Availles-Limouzine F 115 B4
Avaldsnes N 52 A1
Avallon F 104 B2
Avantas GR 183 C7
Avaviken S 195 E9
Avebury GB 44 B2
A Veiga E 141 B3
Aveiras de Cima P 154 B2
Aveiro P 148 B1
Avelgem B 79 B3
Avellino I 170 C2
Avenches CH 106 C2
A-Ver-o-Mar P 148 A1
Aversa I 170 C2
Avesnes-le-Comte F 78 B2
Avesnes-sur-Helpe F 91 A3
Avesta S 50 B3
Avetrana I 173 B3
Avezzano I 169 A3
Avià E 147 B2
Aviano I 122 A1
Aviemore GB 32 D3
Avigliana I 119 B4
Avigliano I 172 B1
Avignon F 131 B3
Ávila E 150 B3
Avilés E 141 A5
Avilley F 105 B5
Avintes P 148 A1
Avinyo E 147 C2
Àvio I 121 B3
Avioth F 92 B1
Avis P 154 B3
Avize F 91 C4
Avlonari GR 185 A5
Ávola I 177 C4
Avon F 90 C2
Avonmouth GB 43 A4
Avord F 103 B4
Avranches F 88 B2
Avril F 92 B1
Avrillé F 102 B1
Avtovac BIH 139 B4
Awans B 79 B5
Axams A 108 B2
Axat F 146 B3
Axbridge GB 43 A4
Axel NL 79 A3
Ax-les-Thermes F 146 B2
Axmarby S 51 B4
Axmarsbruk S 51 A4
Axminster GB 43 B3
Axvall S 55 B4
Ay F 91 B4
Aya E 144 A1
Ayamonte E 161 B2
Ayancık TR 23 A8
Ayaş TR 187 B7
Aydın TR 188 B2
Ayelo de Malferit E 159 C3
Ayer CH 119 A4
Ayerbe E 144 B3
Ayette F 78 B2
Ayia Napa CY 181 B2
Áyia Phyla CY 181 B2
Áyios Amvrósios CY 181 A2
Áyios Seryios CY 181 A2
Áyios Theodhoros CY 181 A3
Aykırikçi TR 187 C5
Aylesbury GB 44 B3
Ayllón E 151 A4
Aylsham GB 41 C5
Ayna E 158 C1
Ayódar E 159 B3
Ayora E 159 B2
Ayr GB 36 A2
Ayrancı TR 23 C7
Ayrancılar TR 188 A2
Ayron F 115 B4
Aysgarth GB 37 B4
Ayton GB 35 C5
Aytos BG 17 D7
Ayvacık TR 186 C1
Ayvalık TR 186 C1
Aywaille B 80 B1
Azaila E 153 A3
Azambuja P 154 B2
Azambujeira P 154 B2
Azanja SRB 127 C2
Azannes-et-Soumazannes F 92 B1
Azanúy-Alins E 145 C4
Azaruja P 155 C3
Azay-le-Ferron F 115 B5
Azay-le-Rideau F 102 B2
Azcoitia E 143 A4
Azé F 117 A4
Azeiteiros P 155 B3
Azenhas do Mar P 154 C1
Azinhaga P 154 B2
Azinhal P 160 B2
Azinheira dos Bairros P 160 A1
Aznalcázar E 161 B3
Aznalcóllar E 161 B3
Azóia P 154 B2
Azpeitia E 144 A1
Azuaga E 156 B2
Azuara E 153 A3
Azuqueca de Henares E 151 B4
Azur F 128 C1
Azzano Décimo I 122 B1

B

Baad A 107 B5
Baamonde E 140 A3
Baar CH 107 B3
Bağarasi TR 188 B2
Baarle-Nassau B 79 A4
Baarn NL 70 B2
Babadağ TR 188 B3
Babadag RO 17 C8
Babaeski TR 186 A2
Babayevo RUS 9 C9
Babenhausen
Bayern D 107 A5
Hessen D 93 B4
Babiak PL 76 B3
Babice PL 86 B3
Babigoszcz PL 75 A3
Babimost PL 75 B4
Babina Greda HR 125 B4
Babócsa H 124 A3
Bábolma H 112 B1
Baborów PL 86 B1
Baboszewo PL 77 B5
Babót H 111 B4
Babruysk BY 13 B8
Babsk PL 87 A4
Bac GB 31 A2
Bač SRB 125 B5
Bacares E 164 B2
Bacău RO 17 B7
Baccarat F 92 C2
Bacharach D 93 A3
Backa S 50 B2
Bačka Palanka SRB 126 B1
Backaryd S 63 B3
Bačka Topola SRB 126 B1
Backe S 200 C2
Bäckebo S 62 B4
Bäckefors S 54 B3
Bäckhammar S 55 A5
Bački Breg SRB 125 B4
Bački-Brestovac SRB 126 B1
Bački Monoštor SRB 125 B4
Bački Petrovac SRB 126 B1
Bački Sokolac SRB 126 B1
Backnang D 94 C1
Bačko Gradište SRB 126 B2
Bačko Novo Selo SRB 125 B5
Bačko Petrovo Selo SRB 126 B2
Bácoli I 170 C2
Bacqueville-en-Caux F 89 A5
Bácsalmás H 126 A1
Bácsbokod H 125 A5
Bad Abbach D 95 C4
Badacsonytomaj H 111 C4
Bad Aibling D 108 B3
Badajoz E 155 C4
Badalona E 147 C3
Badalucco I 133 B3
Bad Aussee A 109 B4
Bad Bederkesa D 72 A1
Bad Bentheim D 71 B4
Bad Bergzabern D 93 B3
Bad Berka D 82 B3
Bad Berleburg D 81 A4
Bad Berneck D 95 A3
Bad Bevensen D 73 A3
Bad Bibra D 82 A3
Bad Birnbach D 95 C5
Bad Blankenburg D 82 B3
Bad Bleiberg A 109 C4
Bad Brambach D 83 B4
Bad Bramstedt D 64 C2
Bad Breisig D 80 B3
Bad Brückenau D 82 B1
Bad Buchau D 107 A4
Bad Camberg D 81 B4
Badderen N 192 C6
Bad Doberan D 65 B4
Bad Driburg D 81 A5
Bad Düben D 83 A4
Bad Dürkheim D 93 B4
Bad Dürrenberg D 83 A4
Bad Dürrheim D 107 A3
Bad Elster D 83 B4
Bad Ems D 81 B3
Baden
A 111 A3
CH 106 B3
Bádenas E 152 A2
Baden-Baden D 93 C4
Bad Endorf D 109 B3
Badenweiler D 106 B2
Baderna HR 122 B2
Bad Essen D 71 B5
Bad Fischau A 111 B3
Bad Frankenhausen D 82 A3
Bad Freienwalde D 74 B3
Bad Friedrichshall D 93 B5
Bad Füssing D 96 C1
Bad Gandersheim D 82 A2
Bad Gastein A 109 B4
Bad Gleichenberg A 110 C2
Bad Goisern A 109 B4
Bad Gottleuba D 84 B1
Bad Grund D 82 A2
Bad Hall A 110 A1
Bad Harzburg D 82 A2
Bad Herrenalb D 93 C4
Bad Hersfeld D 82 B1
Bad Hofgastein A 109 B4
Bad Homburg D 81 B4
Bad Honnef D 80 B3
Bad Hönningen D 80 B3
Badia Calavena I 121 B4
Badia Polésine I 121 B4
Badia Pratáglia I 135 B4
Badia Tedalda I 135 B5
Bad Iburg D 71 B5
Bad Innerlaterns A 107 B4
Bad Ischl A 109 B4
Bad Karlshafen D 81 A5
Bad Kemmeriboden CH 106 C2
Bądki PL 69 B3
Bad Kissingen D 82 B2
Bad Kleinen D 65 C4
Bad Kohlgrub D 108 B2
Bad König D 93 B5
Bad Königshofen D 82 B2
Bad Köstritz D 83 B4
Badkowo PL 76 B3
Bad Kreuzen A 110 A1
Bad Kreuznach D 93 B3
Bad Krozingen D 106 B2
Bad Laasphe D 81 B4
Bad Langensalza D 82 A2
Bad Lauchstädt D 83 A3
Bad Lausick D 83 A4
Bad Lauterberg D 82 A2
Bad Leonfelden A 96 C2
Bad Liebenwerda D 83 A5
Bad Liebenzell D 93 C4
Bad Lippspringe D 81 A4
Badljevina HR 124 B3
Bad Meinberg D 81 A4
Bad Mergentheim D 94 B1
Bad Mitterndorf A 109 B4
Bad Münder D 72 B2
Bad Münstereifel D 80 B2
Bad Muskau D 84 A2
Bad Nauheim D 81 B4
Bad Nenndorf D 72 B2
Bad Neuenahr-Ahrweiler D 80 B3
Bad Neustadt D 82 B2
Bad Oeynhausen D 72 B1
Badolato I 175 C2
Badolatosa E 163 A3
Bad Oldesloe D 65 C3
Badonviller F 92 C2
Bad Orb D 81 B5
Badovinci SRB 127 C1
Bad Peterstal D 93 C4
Bad Pyrmont D 72 C2
Bad Radkersburg A 110 C2
Bad Ragaz CH 107 C4
Bad Rappenau D 93 B5
Bad Reichenhall D 109 B3
Bad Saarow-Pieskow D 74 B3
Bad Sachsa D 82 A2
Bad Säckingen D 106 B2
Bad Salzdetfurth D 72 B3
Bad Salzig D 81 B3
Bad Salzuflen D 72 B1
Bad Salzungen D 82 B2
Bad Sankt Leonhard A 110 C1
Bad Sassendorf D 81 A4
Bad Schandau D 84 B2
Bad Schmiedeberg D 83 A4
Bad Schönborn D 93 B4
Bad Schussenried D 107 A4
Bad Schwalbach D 81 B4
Bad Schwartau D 65 C3
Bad Segeberg D 64 C3
Bad Soden D 81 B4
Bad Soden-Salmünster D 81 B5
Bad Sooden-Allendorf D 82 A1
Bad Sulza D 83 A3
Bad Sülze D 66 B1
Bad Tatzmannsdorf A 111 B3
Bad Tennstedt D 82 A2
Bad Tölz D 108 B2
Badules E 152 A2
Bad Urach D 94 C1
Bad Vellach A 110 C1
Bad Vilbel D 81 B4
Bad Vöslau A 111 B3
Bad Waldsee D 107 B4
Bad Wiessee D 108 B2
Bad Wildungen D 81 A5
Bad Wilsnack D 73 B4
Bad Windsheim D 94 B2
Bad Wörishafen D 108 A1
Bad Wurzach D 107 B4
Bad Zwesten D 81 A5
Bad Zwischenahn D 71 A5
Baells E 145 C4
Baena E 163 A3
Baesweiler D 80 B2
Baeza E 157 C4
Baflo NL 71 A3
Baga E 147 B2
Bagaladi I 175 C1

Bagenkop DK 65 B3
Baggetorp S 56 A2
Bagh a Chaisteil GB 31 C1
Bagheria I 176 A2
Bagn N 47 B6
Bagnacavallo I 135 A4
Bagnáia I 168 A2
Bagnara Cálabra I 175 C1
Bagnasco I 133 A4
Bagnères-de-Bigorre
F 145 A4
Bagnères-de-Luchon
F 145 B4
Bagni del Màsino I 120 A2
Bagni di Lucca I 134 A3
Bagni di Rabbi I 121 A3
Bagni di Tivoli I 168 B2
Bagno di Romagna
I 135 B4
Bagnoles-de-l'Orne
F 89 B3
Bagnoli dei Trigno
I 170 B2
Bagnoli di Sopra I 121 B4
Bagnoli Irpino I 170 C3
Bagnolo Mella I 120 B3
Bagnols-en-Forêt
F 132 B2
Bagnols-sur-Cèze
F 131 A3
Bagnorégio I 168 A2
Bagolino I 121 B3
Bagrationovsk RUS 12 A4
Bagrdan SRB 127 C3
Báguena E 152 A2
Bahabón de Esgueva
E 143 C3
Bahillo E 142 B2
Báia delle Zágare
I 171 B4
Báia Domizia I 169 B3
Baia Mare RO 17 B5
Baiano I 170 C2
Baião P 148 A1
Baiersbronn D 93 C4
Baiersdorf D 94 B3
Baignes-Ste Radegonde
F 115 C3
Baigneux-les-Juifs
F 104 B3
Baildon GB 40 B2
Bailén E 157 B4
Băileşti RO 17 C5
Baileux B 91 A4
Bailieborough IRL 27 C4
Bailleul F 78 B2
Baillonville B 79 B5
Bailó E 144 B3
Bain-de-Bretagne
F 101 B4
Bains F 117 B3
Bains-les-Bains F 105 A5
Bainton GB 40 B3
Baio E 140 A2
Baiona E 140 B2
Bais F 89 B3
Baiso I 134 A3
Baiuca P 148 B2
Baja H 125 A4
Bajánsenye H 111 C3
Bajina Bašta SRB 127 D1
Bajmok SRB 126 B1
Bajna H 112 B2
Bajovo Polje MNE 139 B4
Bajša SRB 126 B1
Bak H 111 C3
Bakar HR 123 B3
Bakewell GB 40 B2
Bakio E 143 A4
Bakka N 47 C6
Bakkafjörður IS 191 A11
Bakkagerði IS 191 B12
Bække DK 59 C2
Bakken N 48 B3
Baklan TR 189 B4
Bækmarksbro DK 58 B1
Bakonybél H 111 B4
Bakonycsernye H 112 B2
Bakonyjákó H 111 B4
Bakonyszentkirály
H 111 B4
Bakonyszombathely
H 112 B1
Bakov nad Jizerou
CZ 84 B2
Bąkowiec PL 87 A5
Baks H 113 C4
Baksa H 125 B4
Bakum D 71 B5
Bala GB 38 B3
Bâlâ TR 23 B7
Balaguer E 145 C4
Balassagyarmat H 112 A3
Balástya H 113 C4
Balatonakali H 111 C4
Balatonalmádi H 112 B2
Balatonboglár H 111 C4
Balatonbozsok H 112 C2
Balatonederics H 111 C4
Balatonfenyves H 111 C4
Balatonföldvár H 112 C1
Balatonfüred H 112 C1
Balatonfűzfő H 112 B2
Balatonkenese H 112 B2
Balatonkiliti H 112 C2
Balatonlelle H 111 C4
Balatonszabadi H 112 C2
Balatonszemes H 111 C4
Balatonszentgyörgy
H 111 C4
Balazote E 158 C1
Balbeggie GB 35 B4
Balbigny F 117 B4
Balboa E 141 B4
Balbriggan IRL 30 A2
Balchik BG 17 D8
Balçova TR 188 A2
Baldock GB 44 B3
Bale HR 122 B2
Baleira E 141 A3
Baleizao P 160 A2
Balen B 79 A5
Balerma E 164 C2
Balestrand N 46 A3
Balestrate I 176 A2
Balfour GB 33 B4
Bälganet S 63 B3
Balıkesir TR 186 C2
Balıklıçeşme TR 186 B2
Bälinge S 51 C4
Balingen D 107 A3
Balingsta S 56 A3
Balintore GB 32 D3
Balizac F 128 B2
Balk NL 70 B2
Balkbrug NL 71 B3
Balla IRL 28 A2
Ballachulish GB 34 B2
Ballaghaderreen
IRL 26 C2
Ballancourt-sur-
Essonne F 90 C2
Ballantrae GB 36 A2
Ballao I 179 C3
Ballasalla GB 36 B2
Ballater GB 32 D3
Ballen DK 59 C3
Ballenstedt D 82 A3
Ballerias E 145 C3
Balleroy F 88 A3
Ballerup DK 61 D2
Ballesteros de Calatrava
E 157 B4
Ballı TR 186 B2
Ballina IRL 26 B1
Ballinalack IRL 30 A1
Ballinamore IRL 26 B3
Ballinascarty IRL 29 C3
Ballinasloe IRL 28 A3
Ballindine IRL 28 A3
Balling DK 58 B1
Ballingarry
Limerick IRL 29 B3
Tipperary IRL 30 B1
Ballingeary IRL 29 C2
Ballinhassig IRL 29 C3
Ballinluig GB 35 B4
Ballino I 121 B3
Ballinrobe IRL 28 A2
Ballinskelligs IRL 29 C1
Ballinspittle IRL 29 C3
Ballintra IRL 26 B2
Ballivor IRL 30 A2
Ballobar E 153 A4
Ballon
F 102 A2
IRL 30 B2
Ballószög H 112 C3
Ballsh AL 182 C1
Ballstad N 194 B4
Ballum DK 64 A1
Ballybay IRL 27 B4
Ballybofey IRL 26 B3
Ballybunion IRL 29 B2
Ballycanew IRL 30 B2
Ballycarry GB 27 B5
Ballycastle
GB 27 A4
IRL 26 B1
Ballyclare GB 27 B5
Ballyconneely IRL 28 A1
Ballycotton IRL 29 C3
Ballycroy IRL 26 B1
Ballydehob IRL 29 C2
Ballyferriter IRL 29 B1
Ballygawley GB 27 B3
Ballygowan GB 27 B5
Ballyhaunis IRL 28 A3
Ballyheige IRL 29 B2
Ballyjamesduff IRL 27 C3
Ballylanders IRL 29 B3
Ballylynan IRL 30 B1
Ballymahon IRL 28 A4
Ballymena GB 27 B4
Ballymoe IRL 28 A3
Ballymoney GB 27 A4
Ballymore IRL 28 A4
Ballymote IRL 26 B2
Ballynacorra IRL 29 C3
Ballynagore IRL 30 A1
Ballynahinch GB 27 B5
Ballynure GB 27 B5
Ballyragget IRL 30 B1
Ballysadare IRL 26 B2
Ballyshannon IRL 26 B2
Ballyvaughan IRL 28 A2
Ballyvourney IRL 29 C2
Ballywalter GB 27 B5
Balmaclellan GB 36 A2
Balmaseda E 143 A3
Balmazújváros H 113 B5
Balme I 119 B4
Balmedie GB 33 D4
Balmuccia I 119 B5
Balna-paling GB 32 D2
Balneario de Panticosa
E 145 B3
Balotaszállás H 126 A1
Balsa P 148 A2
Balsareny E 147 C2
Balsorano-Nuovo I 169 B3
Bålsta S 57 A3
Balsthal CH 106 B2
Balta UA 17 A8
Baltanás E 142 C2
Baltar E 140 C3
Baltasound GB 33 A6
Bălţi MD 17 B7
Baltimore IRL 29 C2
Baltinglass IRL 30 B2
Baltiysk RUS 69 A4
Baltów PL 87 A5
Balugães P 148 A1
Bælum DK 58 B3
Balve D 81 A3
Balvi LV 8 D5
Balvicar GB 34 B2
Balya TR 186 C2
Balzo I 136 C2
Bamberg D 94 B2
Bamburgh GB 37 A5
Banatska Palanka
SRB 127 C3
Banatski Brestovac
SRB 127 C2
Banatski Despotovac
SRB 126 B2
Banatski Dvor SRB 126 B2
Banatski-Karlovac
SRB 127 B3
Banatsko Arandjelovo
SRB 126 A2
Banatsko-Novo Selo
SRB 127 C2
Banaz TR 187 D4
Banbridge GB 27 B4
Banbury GB 44 A2
Banchory GB 33 D4
Bande
B 79 B5
E 140 B3
Bandholm DK 65 B4
Bandırma TR 186 B2
Bandol F 132 B1
Bandon IRL 29 C3
Bañeres E 159 C3
Banff GB 33 D4
Bangor
F 100 B2
Down GB 27 B5
Gwynedd GB 38 A2
IRL 26 B1
Bangsund N 199 A8
Banie PL 74 A3
Banja Koviljača
SRB 127 C1
Banjaloka SLO 123 B3
Banja Luka BIH 124 C3
Banjani SRB 127 C1
Banja Vručica BIH 125 C3
Banka SK 98 C1
Bankekind S 56 B1
Bankend GB 36 A3
Bankeryd S 62 A2
Bankfoot GB 35 B4
Banloc RO 126 B3
Bannalec F 100 B2
Bannes F 91 C3
Bannockburn GB 35 B4
Bañobárez E 149 B3
Bañon E 152 B2
Banon F 132 A1
Baños E 149 B4
Baños de Gigonza
E 162 B2
Baños de la Encina
E 157 B4
Baños de Molgas
E 140 B3
Baños de Rio Tobia
E 143 B4
Baños de Valdearados
E 143 C3
Bánov CZ 98 C1
Banova Jaruga HR 124 B2
Bánovce nad Bebravou
SK 98 C2
Banovići BIH 139 A4
Banoviči Selo BIH 139 A4
Bánréve H 99 C4
Bansin D 66 C3
Banská Belá SK 98 C2
Banská Bystrica SK 99 C3
Banská Štiavnica
SK 98 C2
Bansko BG 183 B5
Banstead GB 44 B3
Banteer IRL 29 B3
Bantheville F 91 B5
Bantry IRL 29 C2
Bantzenheim F 106 B2
Banyalbufar E 166 B2
Banyoles E 147 B3
Banyuls-sur-Mer F 146 B4
Bapaume F 90 A2
Bar
MNE 16 D3
UA 13 D7
Barabhas GB 31 A2
Barači BIH 138 A2
Baracs H 112 C2
Baracska H 112 B2
Barahona E 151 A5
Barajes de Melo E 151 B5
Barakaldo E 143 A4
Baralla E 141 B3
Barañain E 144 B2
Baranavichy BY 13 B7
Báránd H 113 B5
Baranda SRB 127 B2
Baranello I 170 B2
Baranów Sandomierski
PL 87 B5
Baraqueville F 130 A1
Barasoain E 144 B2
Barbacena P 155 C3
Barbadás E 140 B3
Barbadillo E 149 B4
Barbadillo de Herreros
E 143 B3
Barbadillo del Mercado
E 143 B3
Barbadillo del Pez
E 143 B3
Barban HR 123 B3
Barbarano Vicento
I 121 B4
Barbariga HR 122 C2
Barbaros TR 186 B2
Barbastro E 145 B4
Barbate E 162 B2
Barbatona E 152 A1
Barbâtre F 114 B1
Barbazan F 145 A4
Barbeitos E 141 A3
Barbentane F 131 B3
Barberino di Mugello
I 135 A4
Barbezieux-St Hilaire
F 115 C3
Barbonne-Fayel F 91 C3
Barbotan-les-Thermes
F 128 C2
Barby D 73 C4
Bárcabo E 145 B4
Barca de Alva P 149 A3
Barcarrota E 155 C4
Barcellona-Pozzo di
Gotto I 177 A4
Barcelona E 147 C3
Barcelonette F 132 A2
Barcelos P 148 A1
Bárcena del Monasterio
E 141 A4
Barcena de Pie de
Concha E 142 A2
Barchfeld D 82 B2
Barcin PL 76 B2
Barcino PL 68 A1
Bárcis I 122 A1
Barco P 148 B2
Barcones E 151 A5
Barcs H 124 B3
Barcus F 144 A3
Bardejov SK 12 D4
Bårdesø DK 59 C3
Bardi I 120 C2
Bardney GB 40 B3
Bardo PL 85 B4
Bardolino I 121 B3
Bardonécchia I 118 B3
Bardoňovo SK 112 A2
Barèges F 145 B4
Barenstein D 83 B5
Barentin F 89 A4
Barenton F 88 B3
Barevo BIH 138 A3
Barfleur F 88 A2
Barga I 134 A3
Bargas E 151 C3
Barge I 119 C4
Bargemon F 132 B2
Barghe I 120 B3
Bargoed GB 39 C3
Bargrennan GB 36 A2
Bargteheide D 64 C3
Barham GB 45 B5
Bari I 173 A2
Barič Draga HR 137 A4
Barilović HR 123 B4
Bari Sardo I 179 C3
Barisciano I 169 A3
Barjac F 131 A3
Barjols F 132 B1
Barjon F 105 B3
Bårkåker N 54 A1
Barkald N 199 D7
Barkowo
Dolnośląskie PL 85 A4
Pomorskie PL 68 B2
Bârlad RO 17 B7
Bar-le-Duc F 91 C5
Barles F 132 A2
Barletta I 171 B4
Barlinek PL 75 B4
Barmouth GB 38 B2
Barmstedt D 64 C2
Barnard Castle GB 37 B5
Barnarp S 62 A2
Bärnau D 95 B4
Bärnbach A 110 B2
Barneberg D 73 B4
Barnenitz D 74 B1
Barnet GB 44 B3
Barnetby le Wold
GB 40 B3
Barneveld NL 70 B2
Barneville-Carteret
F 88 A2
Barnoldswick GB 40 B1
Barnowko PL 75 B3
Barnsley GB 40 B2
Barnstädt D 83 A3
Barnstaple GB 42 A2
Barnstorf D 72 B1
Barntrup D 72 C2
Baron F 90 B2
Baronissi I 170 C2
Barqueiro P 154 B2
Barquinha P 154 B2
Barr
F 93 C3
GB 36 A2
Barra P 148 B1
Barracas E 159 A3
Barraco E 150 B3
Barrado E 150 B2
Barrafranca I 177 B3
Barranco do Velho
P 160 B2
Barrancos P 161 A3
Barrax E 158 B1
Barrbaar D 94 C2
Barre-des-Cevennes
F 130 A2
Barreiro P 154 C1
Barreiros E 141 A3
Barrême F 132 B2
Barret-le-Bas F 132 A1
Barrhead GB 34 C3
Barrhill GB 36 A2
Barrio de Nuesra
Señora E 142 B1
Barrowford GB 40 B1
Barrow-in-Furness
GB 36 B3
Barrow upon Humber
GB 40 B3
Barruecopardo E 149 A3
Barruelo de Santullán
E 142 B2
Barruera E 145 B4
Barry GB 39 C3
Bårse DK 65 A4
Barsinghausen D 72 B2
Barssel D 71 A4
Bar-sur-Aube F 104 A3
Bar-sur-Seine F 104 A3
Barth D 66 B1
Bartholomä D 94 C1
Bartin TR 187 A7
Barton upon Humber
GB 40 B3
Barúmini I 179 C2
Baruth D 74 B2
Barvaux B 80 B1
Barver D 72 B1
Barwatd PL 99 B3
Barwice PL 68 B1
Barysaw BY 13 A8
Barzana E 141 A5
Bârzava RO 16 B4
Bárzio I 120 B2
Bas E 147 B3
Bašaid SRB 126 B2
Basaluzzo I 120 C1
Basarabeasca MD 17 B8
Basauri E 143 A4
Baschi I 168 A2
Baschurch GB 38 B4
Basconcillos del Tozo
E 143 B3
Bascones de Ojeda
E 142 B2
Basécles B 79 B3
Basel CH 106 B2
Basélice I 170 B2
Basildon GB 45 B4
Basingstoke GB 44 B2
Baška
CZ 98 B2
HR 123 C3
Baška Voda HR 138 B2
Bäsksjö S 200 B3
Baslow GB 40 B2
Başmakçı TR 189 B5
Basovizza I 122 B2
Bassacutena I 178 A3
Bassano del Grappa
I 121 B4
Bassano Romano I 168 A2
Bassecourt CH 106 B2
Bassella E 147 B2
Bassevuovdde N 193 D9
Bassou F 104 B2
Bassoues F 128 C3
Bassum D 72 B1
Båstad S 61 C2
Bastardo I 136 C1
Bastelica F 180 A2
Bastelicaccia F 180 B1
Bastia
F 180 A2
I 136 B1
Bastogne B 92 A1
Baston GB 40 C3
Bastuträsk S 200 B6
Bata H 125 A4
Batajnica SRB 127 C2
Batak BG 183 B6
Batalha P 154 B2
Bátaszék H 125 A4
Batea E 153 A4
Batelov CZ 97 B3
Bath GB 43 A4
Bathgate GB 35 C4
Batida H 126 A2
Batignano I 135 C4
Batina HR 125 B4
Bátka SK 99 C4
Batković BIH 125 C5
Batley GB 40 B2
Batnfjordsøra N 198 C4
Batočina SRB 127 C3
Bátonyterenye H 113 B3
Batrina HR 125 B3
Båtsfjord N 193 B13
Båtskärsnäs S 196 D6
Battaglia Terme I 121 B4
Bätterkinden CH 106 B2
Battice B 80 B1
Battipáglia I 170 C2
Battle GB 45 C4
Battonya H 126 A3
Batuša SRB 127 C3
Bátya H 112 C2
Bau I 179 C2
Baud F 100 B2
Baudour B 79 B3
Baugé F 102 B1
Baugy F 103 B4
Bauma CH 107 B3
Baume-les-Dames
F 105 B5
Baumholder D 93 B3
Baunatal D 81 A5
Baunei I 178 B3
Bauska LV 8 D4
Bautzen D 84 A2
Bavanište SRB 127 C2
Bavay F 79 B3
Bavilliers F 106 B1
Bavorov CZ 96 B2
Bawdsey GB 45 A5
Bawinkel D 71 B4
Bawtry GB 40 B2
Bayat TR 187 D5
Bayel F 105 A3
Bayeux F 88 A3
Bayındır TR 188 A2
Bayon F 92 C2
Bayonne F 128 C1
Bayons F 132 A2
Bayramiç TR 186 C1
Bayreuth D 95 B3
Bayrischzell D 108 B3
Baza E 164 B2
Bazas F 128 B2
Baziege F 146 A2
Bazoches-les-
Gallerandes F 103 A4
Bazoches-sur-Hoëne
F 89 B4
Bazzano I 135 A4
Beaconsfield GB 44 B3
Beade E 140 B2
Beadnell GB 37 A5
Beaminster GB 43 B4
Bearsden GB 34 C3
Beas E 161 B3
Beasain E 144 A1
Beas de Segura E 164 A2
Beattock GB 36 A3
Beaubery F 117 A4
Beaucaire F 131 B3
Beaufort
F 118 B3
IRL 29 B2
Beaufort-en Vallée
F 102 B1
Beaugency F 103 B3
Beaujeu
Alpes-de-Haute-Provence F 132 A2
Rhône F 117 A4
Beaulac F 128 B2
Beaulieu
F 103 B4
GB 44 C2
Beaulieu-sous-la-Roche
F 114 B2
Beaulieu-sur-Dordogne
F 129 B4
Beaulieu-sur-Mer F 133 B3
Beaulon F 104 C2
Beauly GB 32 D2
Beaumaris GB 38 A2
Beaumesnil F 89 A4
Beaumetz-lès-Loges
F 78 B2
Beaumont
B 79 B4
F 129 B3
Beaumont-de-Lomagne
F 129 C3
Beaumont-du-Gâtinais
F 103 A4
Beaumont-en-Argonne
F 91 B5
Beaumont-Hague F 88 A2
Beaumont-la-Ronce
F 102 B2
Beaumont-le-Roger
F 89 A4
Beaumont-sur-Oise
F 90 B2
Beaumont-sur-Sarthe
F 102 A2
Beaune F 105 B3
Beaune-la-Rolande
F 103 A4
Beaupréau F 101 B5
Beauraing B 91 A4
Beaurepaire F 117 B5

Beaurepaire-en-Bresse F 105 C4
Beaurières F 132 A1
Beauvais F 90 B2
Beauval F 90 A2
Beauville F 129 B3
Beauvoir-sur-Mer F 114 B1
Beauvoir-sur-Niort F 114 B3
Beba Veche RO 126 A2
Bebertal D 73 B4
Bebington GB 38 A3
Bebra D 82 B1
Bebrina HR 125 B3
Beccles GB 45 A5
Becedas E 150 B2
Beceite E 153 B4
Bečej SRB 126 B2
Becerreá E 141 B3
Becerril de Campos E 142 B2
Bécherel F 101 A4
Bechhofen D 94 B2
Bechyně CZ 96 B2
Becilla de Valderaduey E 142 B1
Beckfoot GB 36 B3
Beckingham GB 40 B3
Beckum D 81 A4
Beco P 154 B2
Bécon-les-Granits F 102 B1
Bečov nad Teplou CZ 83 B4
Becsehely H 111 C3
Bedale GB 37 B5
Bedames E 143 A3
Bédar E 164 B3
Bédarieux F 130 B2
Bédarrides F 131 A3
Bedburg D 80 B2
Beddgelert GB 38 A2
Beddingestrand S 66 A2
Bédée F 101 A4
Bedegkér H 112 C2
Beden TR 189 C7
Bedford GB 44 A3
Będków PL 87 A3
Bedlington GB 37 A5
Bedlno PL 77 B4
Bedmar E 163 A4
Bédoin F 131 A4
Bedónia I 134 A2
Bedretto CH 107 C3
Bedsted DK 58 B1
Bedum NL 71 A3
Bedwas GB 39 C3
Bedworth GB 40 C2
Będzin PL 86 B3
Beekbergen NL 70 B2
Beek en Donk NL 80 A1
Beelen D 71 C5
Beelitz D 74 B1
Beer GB 43 B3
Beerfelde D 74 B3
Beerfelden D 93 B4
Beernem B 78 A3
Beeskow D 74 B3
Beetsterzwaag NL 70 A3
Beetzendorf D 73 B4
Beflelay CH 106 B2
Begaljica SRB 127 C2
Bégard F 100 A2
Begejci SRB 126 B2
Begijar E 157 C4
Begijnendijk B 79 A4
Begndal N 48 B1
Begues E 147 C2
Beguildy GB 39 B3
Begur E 147 C4
Beho B 80 B1
Behringen D 82 A2
Beilen NL 71 B3
Beilngries D 95 B3
Beine-Nauroy F 91 B4
Beinwil CH 106 B3
Beiseförth D 82 A1
Beith GB 34 C3
Beitostølen N 47 A5
Beiuş RO 16 B5
Beja P 160 A2
Béjar E 149 B4
Bekçiler TR 189 C4
Békés H 113 C5
Békéscsaba H 113 C5
Bekilli TR 189 A4
Bekkarfjord N 193 B11
Bela SK 98 B2
Bélâbre F 115 B5
Bela Crkva SRB 127 C3
Belalcázar E 156 B2
Belánad Radbuzou CZ 95 B4
Belanovica SRB 127 C2
Bélapátfalva H 113 A4
Bělápod Bezdězem CZ 84 B2
Belcaire F 146 B2
Bełchatów PL 86 A3
Belchite E 153 A3
Bělčice CZ 96 B1
Belcoo GB 26 B3
Belecke D 81 A4
Beled H 111 B4
Belej HR 123 C3
Beleño E 142 A1
Bélesta F 146 B2
Belevi TR 188 A2
Belfast GB 27 B5
Belford GB 37 A5
Belfort F 106 B1
Belgentier F 132 B1
Belgern D 83 A5
Belgioioso I 120 B2
Belgodère F 180 A2
Belgooly IRL 29 C3
Belgrade = Beograd SRB 127 C2
Belhade F 128 B2
Belica HR 124 A2
Beli Manastir HR 125 B4
Belin-Bèliet F 128 B2
Belinchón E 151 B4
Belišće HR 125 B4
Bělkovice-Lašťany CZ 98 B1
Bella I 172 B1
Bellac F 115 B5
Bellágio I 120 B2
Bellananagh IRL 27 C3
Bellano I 120 A2
Bellária I 136 A1
Bellavary IRL 26 C1
Belleau F 90 B3
Belleek GB 26 B2
Bellegarde
Gard F 131 B3
Loiret F 103 B4
Bellegarde-en-Diois F 132 A1
Bellegarde-en-Marche F 116 B2
Bellegarde-sur-Valserine F 118 A2
Belle-Isle-en-Terre F 100 A2
Bellême F 89 B4
Bellenaves F 116 A3
Bellentre F 118 B3
Bellevaux F 118 A3
Bellevesvre F 105 C4
Belleville F 117 A4
Belleville-sur-Vie F 114 B2
Bellevue-la-Montagne F 117 B3
Belley F 118 B2
Bellheim D 93 B4
Bellinge DK 59 C3
Bellingham GB 37 A4
Bellinzago Novarese I 120 B1
Bellinzona CH 120 A2
Bell-lloc d'Urgell E 153 A4
Bello E 152 B2
Bellpuig d'Urgell E 147 C2
Bellreguart E 159 C3
Bellsbank GB 36 A2
Belltall E 147 C2
Belluno I 121 A5
Bellver de Cerdanya E 146 B2
Bellvis E 147 C1
Bélmez E 156 B2
Belmez de la Moraleda E 163 A4
Belmont GB 33 A6
Belmont-de-la-Loire F 117 A4
Belmonte
Asturias E 141 A4
Cuenca E 158 B1
P 148 B2
Belmonte de San José E 153 B3
Belmonte de Tajo E 151 B4
Belmont-sur-Rance F 130 B1
Belmullet IRL 26 B1
Belobreşca RO 127 C3
Beloeil B 79 B3
Belogradchik BG 16 D5
Belokorovichi UA 13 C8
Belorado E 143 B3
Belotič SRB 127 C1
Bělotín CZ 98 B1
Belovo BG 183 A6
Belozersk RUS 9 C10
Belp CH 106 C2
Belpasso I 177 B3
Belpech F 146 A2
Belper GB 40 B2
Belsay GB 37 A5
Belsk Duzy PL 87 A4
Beltinci SLO 111 C3
Beltra IRL 26 C1
Belturbet IRL 27 B3
Beluša SK 98 B2
Belvedere Marittimo I 174 B1
Belver de Cinca E 153 A4
Belver de los Montes E 142 C1
Belvès F 129 B3
Belvezet F 130 A2
Belvis de la Jara E 150 C3
Belvis de Monroy E 150 C2
Belyy RUS 9 E8
Belz F 100 B2
Bełżec PL 13 C5
Belzig D 73 B5
Bembibre E 141 B4
Bembridge GB 44 C2
Bemmel NL 80 A1
Bemposta
Bragança P 149 A3
Santarém P 154 B2
Benabarre E 145 B4
Benacazón E 161 B3
Benaguacil E 159 B3
Benahadux E 164 C2
Benalmádena E 163 B3
Benalúa de Guadix E 164 B1
Benalúa de las Villas E 163 A4
Benalup E 162 B2
Benamargosa E 163 B3
Benamaurel E 164 B2
Benameji E 163 A3
Benamocarra E 163 B3
Benaocaz E 162 B2
Benaoján E 162 B2
Benarrabá E 162 B2
Benasque E 145 B4
Benátky nad Jizerou CZ 84 B2
Benavente
E 142 B1
P 154 C2
Benavides de Órbigo E 141 B5
Benavila P 154 B3
Bendorf D 81 B3
Benedikt SLO 110 C2
Benejama E 159 C3
Benejúzar E 165 A4
Benešov CZ 96 B2
Bénestroff F 92 C2
Benet F 114 B3
Bene Vagienna I 133 A3
Bénévent-l'Abbaye F 116 A1
Benevento I 170 B2
Benfeld F 93 C3
Benfica P 154 B2
Bengtsfors S 54 A3
Bengtsheden S 50 B2
Beničanci HR 125 B4
Benicarló E 153 B4
Benicássim E 153 B4
Benidorm E 159 C3
Benifaió E 159 B3
Beniganim E 159 C3
Benington GB 41 B4
Benisa E 159 C4
Benkovac HR 137 A4
Benllech GB 38 A2
Benneckenstein D 82 A2
Bénodet F 100 B1
Benquerencia de la Serena E 156 B2
Bensafrim P 160 B1
Bensbyn S 196 D5
Bensdorf D 73 B5
Benshausen D 82 B2
Bensheim D 93 B4
Bentley GB 44 B3
Bentwisch D 65 B5
Beočin SRB 126 B1
Beograd = Belgrade SRB 127 C2
Beragh GB 27 B3
Beranga E 143 A3
Berat AL 182 C1
Bérat F 146 A2
Beratzhausen D 95 B3
Bérbaltavár H 111 B3
Berbegal E 145 C3
Berbenno di Valtellina I 120 A2
Berberana E 143 B3
Bercedo E 143 A3
Bercel H 112 B3
Bercenay-le-Hayer F 91 C3
Berceto I 134 A2
Berchem B 79 B3
Berchidda I 178 B3
Berching D 95 B3
Berchtesgaden D 109 B4
Bérchules E 163 B4
Bercianos de Aliste E 149 A3
Berck F 78 B1
Berclaire d'Urgell E 147 C1
Berdoias E 140 A1
Berducedo E 141 A4
Berdún E 144 B3
Berdychiv UA 13 D8
Bere Alston GB 42 B2
Bereguardo I 120 B2
Berehommen N 53 A3
Berehove UA 16 A5
Berek BIH 124 B3
Beremend H 125 B4
Bere Regis GB 43 B4
Berestechko UA 13 C6
Berettyóújfalu H 113 B5
Berezhany UA 13 D6
Berezivka UA 17 B9
Berezna UA 13 C9
Berg
D 95 B3
N 195 E3
S 56 B2
Berga
Sachsen-Anhalt D 82 A3
Berga *continued*
Thüringen D 83 B4
E 147 B2
S 62 A4
Bergama TR 186 C2
Bérgamo I 120 B2
Bergara E 143 A4
Bergby S 51 B4
Berge
Brandenburg D 74 B1
Niedersachsen D 71 B4
Telemark N 53 A4
Telemark N 53 A3
Bergeforsen S 200 D3
Bergen
Mecklenburg-Vorpommern D 66 B2
Niedersachsen D 72 B2
Niedersachsen D 73 B3
N 46 B2
NL 70 B1
Bergen op Zoom NL 79 A4
Bergerac F 129 B3
Bergères-lés-Vertus F 91 C4
Bergeyk NL 79 A5
Berghausen D 93 C4
Bergheim D 80 B2
Berghem S 60 B2
Berg im Gau D 95 C3
Bergisch Gladbach D 80 B3
Bergkamen D 81 A3
Bergkvara S 63 B4
Berglern D 95 C3
Bergnäset S 196 D5
Bergneustadt D 81 A3
Bergsäng S 49 B5
Bergshamra S 57 A4
Bergsjö S 200 E3
Bergs slussar S 56 B1
Bergsviken S 196 D4
Bergtheim D 94 B2
Bergues F 78 B2
Bergum NL 70 A2
Bergün Bravuogn CH 107 C4
Bergwitz D 83 A4
Berhida H 112 B2
Beringel P 160 A2
Beringen B 79 A5
Berja E 164 C2
Berkåk N 199 C7
Berkeley GB 43 A4
Berkenthin D 65 C3
Berkhamsted GB 44 B3
Berkheim D 107 A5
Berkhof D 72 B2
Berkovići BIH 139 B4
Berkovitsa BG 17 D5
Berlanga E 156 B2
Berlanga de Duero E 151 A5
Berlevåg N 193 B13
Berlikum NL 70 A2
Berlin D 74 B2
Berlstedt D 82 A3
Bermeo E 143 A4
Bermillo de Sayago E 149 A3
Bern CH 106 C2
Bernalda I 174 A2
Bernardos E 150 A3
Bernartice
Jihočeský CZ 96 B2
Vychodočeský CZ 85 B3
Bernau
Baden-Württemberg D 106 B3
Bayern D 109 B3
Brandenburg D 74 B2
Bernaville F 90 A2
Bernay F 89 A4
Bernburg D 83 A3
Berndorf A 111 B3
Berne D 72 A1
Bernecebarati H 112 A2
Bernhardsthal A 97 C4
Bernkastel-Kues D 92 B3
Bernolakovo SK 111 A4
Bernsdorf D 84 A2
Bernstadt D 84 A2
Bernstein A 111 B3
Bernués E 145 B3
Beromünster CH 106 B3
Beroun CZ 96 B2
Berovo MK 182 B4
Berre-l'Etang F 131 B4
Berriedale GB 32 C3
Berriew GB 39 B3
Berrocal E 161 B3
Bersenbrück D 71 B4
Bershad' UA 13 D8
Bertamiráns E 140 B2
Berthåga S 51 C4
Berthelming F 92 C2
Bertincourt F 90 A2
Bertinoro I 135 A5
Bertogne B 92 A1
Bertrix B 91 B5
Berufjörður IS 191 C11
Berville-sur-Mer F 89 A4
Berwick-upon-Tweed GB 37 A4
Berzasca RO 16 C4
Berzence H 124 A3
Berzocana E 156 A2
Besalú E 147 B3
Besançon F 105 B5
Besenfeld D 93 C4
Besenyötelek H 113 B4
Besenyszög H 113 B4
Beshenkovichi BY 13 A8
Besigheim D 93 C5
Běšiny CZ 96 B1
Beška SRB 126 B2
Beşkonak TR 189 B6
Besle F 101 B4
Besnyö H 112 B2
Bessais-le-Fromental F 103 C4
Bessan F 130 B2
Besse-en-Chandesse F 116 B2
Bessèges F 131 A3
Bessé-sur-Braye F 102 B2
Bessines-sur-Gartempe F 115 B5
Best NL 79 A5
Bestorp S 56 B1
Betanzos E 140 A2
Betelu E 144 A2
Bétera E 159 B3
Beteta E 152 B1
Béthenville F 91 B4
Bethesda GB 38 A2
Béthune F 78 B2
Beton-Bazoches F 90 C3
Bettembourg L 92 B2
Betterdorf L 92 B2
Bettna S 56 B2
Béttola I 120 C2
Bettona I 136 B1
Bettyhill GB 32 C2
Betws-y-Coed GB 38 A3
Betxi E 159 B3
Betz F 90 B2
Betzdorf D 81 B3
Beuil F 132 A2
Beulah GB 39 B3
Beuzeville F 89 A4
Bevagna I 136 C1
Bevens-bruk S 56 A1
Beveren B 79 A4
Beverley GB 40 B3
Bevern D 81 A5
Beverstedt D 72 A1
Beverungen D 81 A5
Beverwijk NL 70 B1
Bex CH 119 A4
Bexhill GB 45 C4
Beyazköy TR 186 A2
Beychevelle F 128 A2
Beydağ TR 188 A3
Beyeğaç TR 188 B3
Beykoz TR 186 A4
Beynat F 129 A4
Beyoğlu TR 186 A4
Beypazarı TR 187 B6
Beyşehir TR 189 B6
Bezas E 152 B2
Bezau A 107 B4
Bezdan SRB 125 B4
Bèze F 105 B4
Bezenet F 116 A2
Bezhetsk RUS 9 D10
Béziers F 130 B2
Bezzecca I 121 B3
Biadki PL 85 A5
Biała
Łódzkie PL 77 C4
Opolskie PL 85 B5
Białaczów PL 87 A4
Biała Podlaska PL 13 B5
Biała Rawska PL 87 A4
Biale Błota PL 76 A2
Białobłoty PL 76 B2
Białobrzegi PL 87 A4
Białogard PL 67 C4
Białośliwie PL 76 A2
Białowąs PL 68 B1
Biały Bór PL 68 B1
Białystok PL 13 B5
Biancavilla I 177 B3
Bianco I 175 C2
Biandrate I 119 B5
Biar E 159 C3
Biarritz F 144 A2
Bias F 128 B1
Biasca CH 120 A1
Biatorbágy H 112 B2
Bibbiena I 135 B4
Bibbona I 134 B3
Biberach
Baden-Württemberg D 93 C4
Baden-Württemberg D 107 A4
Bibinje HR 137 A4
Bibione I 122 B2
Biblis D 93 B4
Bibury GB 44 B2
Bicaj AL 182 B2
Biccari I 171 B3
Bicester GB 44 B2
Bichl D 108 B2
Bichlbach A 108 B1
Bicorp E 159 B3
Bicos P 160 B1
Bicske H 112 B2
Bidache F 128 C1
Bidart F 144 A2
Biddinghuizen NL 70 B2
Biddulph GB 40 B1
Bideford GB 42 A2
Bidford-on-Avon GB 44 A2
Bidjovagge N 192 C6
Bie S 56 A2
Bieber D 81 B5
Biebersdorf D 74 C2
Biedenkopf D 81 B4
Biel
CH 106 B2
E 144 B3
Bielany Wroclawskie PL 85 A4
Bielawa PL 85 B4
Bielawy PL 77 B4
Bielefeld D 72 B1
Biella I 119 B5
Bielsa E 145 B4
Bielsk PL 77 B4
Bielsko-Biała PL 99 B3
Bielsk Podlaski PL 13 B5
Bienenbuttel D 72 A3
Bieniow PL 84 A3
Bienservida E 158 C1
Bienvenida E 156 B1
Bierdzany PL 86 B2
Bierné F 102 B1
Biersted DK 58 A2
Bierun PL 86 B3
Bierutów PL 85 A5
Bierwart B 79 B5
Bierzwina PL 75 A4
Bierzwnik PL 75 A4
Biescas E 145 B3
Biesenthal D 74 B2
Biesiekierz PL 67 B5
Bietigheim-Bissingen D 93 C5
Bièvre B 91 B5
Bieżuń PL 77 B4
Biga TR 186 B2
Bigadiç TR 186 C3
Biganos F 128 B2
Bigas P 148 B2
Bigastro E 165 A4
Bigbury GB 42 B3
Biggar GB 36 A3
Biggin Hill GB 45 B4
Biggleswade GB 44 A3
Bignasco CH 119 A5
Biguglia F 180 A2
Bihać BIH 124 C1
Biharnagybajom H 113 B5
Bijeljani BIH 139 B4
Bijeljina BIH 125 C5
Bijuesca E 152 A2
Bilaj HR 137 A4
Bila Tserkva UA 13 D9
Bilbao E 143 A4
Bilcza PL 87 B4
Bildudalur IS 190 B2
Bileća BIH 139 C4
Bilecik TR 187 B4
Biled RO 126 B2
Biłgoraj PL 12 C5
Bilhorod-Dnistrovskyy UA 17 B9
Bilina CZ 84 B1
Bilisht AL 182 C2
Bilje HR 125 B4
Billdal S 60 B1
Billerbeck D 71 C4
Billericay GB 45 B4
Billesholm S 61 C2
Billingborough GB 40 C3
Billinge S 61 D3
Billingham GB 37 B5
Billinghay GB 41 B3
Billingsfors S 54 B3
Billingshurst GB 44 B3
Billom F 116 B3
Billsta S 200 C4
Billund DK 59 C2
Bílovec CZ 98 B2
Bilstein D 81 A4
Bilthoven NL 70 B2
Bilto N 192 C5
Bilzen B 80 B1
Bíňa SK 112 B2
Binaced E 145 C4
Binasco I 120 B2
Binbrook GB 41 B3
Binche B 79 B4
Bindlach D 95 B3
Bindslev DK 58 A3
Binefar E 145 C4
Bingen D 93 B3
Bingham GB 40 C3
Bingley GB 40 B2
Bingsjö S 50 A2
Binic F 100 A3
Binz D 66 B2
Biograd na Moru HR 137 B4
Bionaz I 119 B4
Bioska SRB 127 D1
Birda RO 126 B3
Birdlip GB 44 B1
Biri N 48 B2
Birkeland N 53 B4
Birkenfeld
Baden-Württemberg D 93 C4
Rheinland-Pfalz D 92 B3
Birkenhead GB 38 A3
Birkerød DK 61 D2
Birkfeld A 110 B2
Birkirkara M 175 C3
Birmingham GB 40 C2

Birr IRL 28 A4
Birresborn D 80 B2
Birstein D 81 B5
Biržai LT 8 D4
Birzebbugia M 175 C3
Bisáccia I 172 A1
Bisacquino I 176 B2
Bisbal de Falset E 153 A4
Biscarosse F 128 B1
Biscarosse Plage
F 128 B1
Biscarrués E 144 B3
Bisceglie I 171 B4
Bischheim F 93 C3
Bischofsheim D 82 B1
Bischofshofen A 109 B4
Bischofswerda D 84 A2
Bischofswiesen D 109 B3
Bischofszell CH 107 B4
Bischwiller F 93 C3
Bisenti I 169 A3
Bishop Auckland
GB 37 B5
Bishop's Castle GB 39 B4
Bishops Lydeard
GB 43 A3
Bishop's Stortford
GB 45 B4
Bishop's Waltham
GB 44 C2
Bisignano I 174 B2
Bisingen D 93 C4
Biskupice-Oławskie
PL 85 A5
Biskupiec PL 69 B4
Bismark D 73 B4
Bismo N 198 D5
Bispgården S 200 C2
Bispingen D 72 A2
Bissen L 92 B2
Bissendorf D 71 B5
Bisserup DK 65 A4
Bistango I 119 C5
Bistarac Donje BIH 139 A4
Bistrica BIH 124 C3
Bistrica ob Sotli
SLO 123 A4
Bistrița RO 17 B6
Bitburg D 92 B2
Bitche F 93 B3
Bitetto I 171 B4
Bitola MK 182 B3
Bitonto I 171 B4
Bitschwiller F 106 B2
Bitterfeld D 83 A4
Bitti I 178 B3
Biville-sur-Mer F 89 A5
Bivona I 176 B2
Biwer L 92 B2
Bizeljsko SLO 123 A4
Bizovac HR 125 B4
Bjåen N 52 A3
Bjärnum S 61 C3
Bjärred S 61 D3
Bjästa S 200 C4
Bjelland
Vest-Agder N 52 B2
Vest-Agder N 52 B3
Bjelovar HR 124 B2
Bjerkreim N 52 B2
Bjerkvik N 194 B8
Bjerreby DK 65 B3
Bjerregrav DK 58 B2
Bjerringbro DK 59 B2
Bjøberg N 47 B5
Bjøllånes N 195 D5
Björbo S 50 B1
Bjordal N 46 A2
Björg IS 191 B8
Bjørkåsen N 194 B7
Björke
Gävleborg S 51 B4
Östergötland S 56 B1
Bjørkelangen N 48 C3
Björketorp S 60 B2
Björkholmen S 196 C2
Björkliden S 194 B9
Björklinge S 51 B4
Björko S 51 C6
Björkö S 60 B1
Björköby S 62 A2
Björkvik S 56 B2
Bjørn N 195 D3
Björna S 200 C4
Björneborg S 55 A5
Björnerod S 54 A2
Bjørnevatn N 193 C13
Björnlunda S 56 A3
Bjørnstad N 193 C14
Björsäter S 56 B2
Bjurberget S 49 B4
Bjurholm S 200 C5
Bjursås S 50 B2
Bjurtjärn S 55 A5
Bjuv S 61 C2
Blachownia PL 86 B2
Blackburn GB 38 A4
Blackpool GB 38 A3
Blackstad S 62 A4
Blackwater IRL 30 B2
Blackwaterfoot GB 34 C2
Blacy F 91 C4
Bladåker S 51 B5
Blaenau Ffestiniog
GB 38 B3
Blaenavon GB 39 C3
Blaengarw GB 39 C3
Blagaj
BIH 124 B2
BIH 139 B3
Blagdon GB 43 A4
Blagnac F 129 C4
Blagoevgrad BG 183 A5
Blaichach D 107 B5
Blain F 101 B4
Blainville-sur-l'Eau
F 92 C2
Blair Atholl GB 35 B4
Blairgowrie GB 35 B4
Blajan F 145 A4
Blakeney GB 39 C4
Blakstad N 53 B4
Blâmont F 92 C2
Blanca E 165 A3
Blancos E 140 C3
Blandford Forum
GB 43 B4
Blanes E 147 C3
Blangy-sur-Bresle F 90 B1
Blankaholm S 62 A4
Blankenberge B 78 A3
Blankenburg D 82 A2
Blankenfelde D 74 B2
Blankenhain D 82 B3
Blankenheim D 80 B2
Blanquefort F 128 B2
Blansko CZ 97 B4
Blanzac F 115 C4
Blanzy F 104 C3
Blaricum NL 70 B2
Blarney IRL 29 C3
Blascomillán E 150 B2
Blascosancho E 150 B3
Błaszki PL 86 A2
Blatná CZ 96 B1
Blatné SK 111 A4
Blatnice CZ 98 C1
Blatnika BIH 139 A3
Blato HR 138 C2
Blato na Cetini HR 138 B2
Blatten CH 119 A4
Blattnicksele S 195 E8
Blatzheim D 80 B2
Blaubeuren D 94 C1
Blaufelden D 94 B1
Blaustein D 94 C1
Blaydon GB 37 B5
Blaye F 128 A2
Blaye-les-Mines F 130 A1
Blázquez E 156 B2
Bleckede D 73 A3
Blecua E 145 B3
Bled SLO 123 A3
Bleiburg A 110 C1
Bleichenbach D 81 B5
Bleicherode D 82 A2
Bleik N 194 A6
Bleikvassli N 195 E4
Bléneau F 104 B1
Blentarp S 61 D3
Blera I 168 A2
Blérancourt F 90 B3
Bléré F 102 B2
Blesle F 116 B3
Blessington IRL 30 A2
Blet F 103 C4
Bletchley GB 44 B3
Bletterans F 105 C4
Blidö S 57 A4
Blidsberg S 60 B3
Blieskastel D 92 B3
Bligny-sur-Ouche
F 104 B3
Blikstorp S 55 B5
Blinisht AL 182 B1
Blinja HR 124 B2
Blizanówek PL 76 C3
Bliżyn PL 87 A4
Blois F 103 B3
Blokhus DK 58 A2
Blokzijl NL 70 B2
Blombacka S 55 A4
Blomberg D 72 C2
Blomskog S 54 A3
Blomstermåla S 62 B4
Blomvåg N 46 B1
Blönduós IS 190 B5
Błonie PL 77 B5
Blonville-sur-Mer F 89 A4
Blötberget S 50 B2
Blovice CZ 96 B1
Bloxham GB 44 A2
Blšany CZ 83 B5
Bludenz A 107 B4
Bludov CZ 97 B4
Blumberg D 107 B3
Blyberg S 49 A6
Blyth
Northumberland
GB 37 A5
Nottinghamshire
GB 40 B2
Blyth Bridge GB 35 C4
Blythburgh GB 45 A5
Blythe Bridge GB 40 C1
Bø
Nordland N 194 B5
Telemark N 53 A5
Boal E 141 A4
Boan MNE 139 C5
Boario Terme I 120 B3
Boat of Garten GB 32 D3
Boa Vista P 154 B2
Boğazkale TR 23 A8
Boğazlıyan TR 23 B8
Boba H 111 B4
Bobadilla
Logroño E 143 B4
Málaga E 163 A3
Bobadilla del Campo
E 150 A2
Bobadilla del Monte
E 151 B4
Bóbbio I 120 C2
Bóbbio Pellice I 119 C4
Bobigny F 90 C2
Bobingen D 94 C2
Böblingen D 93 C5
Bobolice PL 68 B1
Boboras E 140 B2
Boboshevo BG 182 A4
Bobowa PL 99 B4
Bobrová CZ 97 B4
Bobrovitsa UA 13 C9
Bobrowice PL 75 C4
Bobrówko PL 75 B4
Boca de Huérgano
E 142 B2
Bocairent E 159 C3
Bočar SRB 126 B2
Bocchigliero I 174 B2
Boceguillas E 151 A4
Bochnia PL 99 B4
Bocholt
B 80 A1
D 80 A2
Bochov CZ 83 B5
Bochum D 80 A3
Bockara S 62 A4
Bockenem D 72 B3
Bockfliess A 97 C4
Bockhorn D 71 A5
Bočna SLO 123 A3
Bocognano F 180 A2
Boconád H 113 B4
Bőcs H 113 A4
Boczów PL 75 B3
Boda S 50 A2
Böda S 62 A5
Boda
Stockholm S 51 B5
Värmland S 55 A4
Västernorrland S 200 D2
Bodafors S 62 A2
Boda Glasbruk S 63 B3
Bodajk H 112 B2
Boddam
Aberdeenshire
GB 33 D5
Shetland GB 33 B5
Boddin D 73 A4
Bödefeld-Freiheit D 81 A4
Boden S 196 D4
Bodenmais D 95 B5
Bodenteich D 73 B3
Bodenwerder D 72 C2
Bodiam GB 45 B4
Bodinnick GB 42 B2
Bodio CH 120 A1
Bodjani SRB 125 B5
Bodmin GB 42 B2
Bodø N 194 C5
Bodonal de la Sierra
E 161 A3
Bodrum TR 188 B2
Bodstedt D 66 B1
Bodträskfors S 196 C3
Bodzanów PL 77 B5
Bodzanowice PL 86 B2
Bodzechów PL 87 B5
Bodzentyn PL 87 B4
Boecillo E 150 A3
Boëge F 118 A3
Boën F 117 B3
Bogács H 113 B4
Bogadmindszent H 125 B4
Bogajo E 149 B3
Bogarra E 158 C1
Bogarre E 163 A4
Bogatić SRB 127 C1
Bogatynia PL 84 B2
Bogda RO 126 B3
Bogdaniec PL 75 B4
Boge S 57 C4
Bogen
D 95 C4
Nordland N 194 B7
Nordland N 194 C6
S 49 B4
Bogense DK 59 C3
Bognanco Fonti I 119 A5
Bognelv N 192 B6
Bognes N 194 B7
Bogno CH 120 A2
Bognor Regis GB 44 C3
Bogoria PL 87 B5
Bograngen S 49 B4
Boguchwaly PL 69 B5
Bogumiłowice PL 86 A3
Boguslav UA 13 D9
Boguszów-Gorce
PL 85 B4
Bogyiszló H 112 C2
Bohain-en-Vermandois
F 91 B3
Böheimkirchen A 110 A2
Bohinjska Bistrica
SLO 122 A2
Böhlen D 83 A4
Böhmenkirch D 94 C1
Bohmte D 71 B5
Bohonal de Ibor E 150 C2
Böhönye H 124 A3
Bohumin CZ 98 B2
Boiro E 140 B2
Bois-d'Amont F 105 C5
Boisseron F 131 B3
Boitzenburg D 74 A2
Boixols E 147 B2
Boizenburg D 73 A3
Bojadła PL 75 C4
Bojano I 170 B2
Bojanowo PL 85 A4
Bøjden DK 64 A3
Bojkovice CZ 98 B1
Bojná SK 98 C2
Bojnice SK 98 C2
Boka SRB 126 B2
Böklund D 64 B2
Bokod H 112 B2
Böksholm S 62 A2
Boksitogorsk RUS 9 C8
Bol HR 138 B2
Bolaños de Calatrava
E 157 B4
Bolayır TR 186 B1
Bolbec F 89 A4
Bölcske H 112 C2
Bolderslev DK 64 B2
Boldog H 112 B3
Boldva H 113 A4
Böle S 196 D4
Bolea E 145 B3
Bolekhiv UA 13 D5
Bolesławiec PL 84 A3
Boleszkowice PL 74 B3
Bolewice PL 75 B5
Bólgheri I 134 B3
Bolhrad UA 17 C8
Boliden S 200 B6
Bolimów PL 77 B5
Boliqueime P 160 B1
Boljevci SRB 127 C2
Boljkovci SRB 127 C2
Bolków PL 85 B4
Bollebygd S 60 B2
Bollène F 131 A3
Bólliga E 152 B1
Bollnäs S 50 A3
Bollstabruk S 200 D3
Bollullos E 161 B3
Bollullos par del
Condado E 161 B3
Bologna I 135 A4
Bologne F 105 A4
Bolognetta I 176 B2
Bolognola I 136 C2
Bologoye RUS 9 D9
Bolótana I 178 B2
Bolsena I 168 A1
Bolshaya Vradiyevka
UA 17 B9
Bolsover GB 40 B2
Bolstad S 54 B3
Bolsward NL 70 A2
Boltaña E 145 B4
Boltenhagen D 65 C4
Boltigen CH 106 C2
Bolton GB 38 A4
Bolu TR 187 B6
Bolungarvík IS 190 A2
Bolvadin TR 187 D6
Bóly H 125 B4
Bolzaneto I 133 A4
Bolzano I 108 C2
Bomba I 169 A4
Bombarral P 154 B1
Bömenzien D 73 B4
Bomlitz D 72 B2
Bømlo N 52 A1
Bøn N 48 B3
Bona F 104 B2
Bonaduz CH 107 C4
Bonanza E 161 C3
Boñar E 142 B1
Bonarbridge GB 32 D2
Bonárcado I 178 B2
Bonares E 161 B3
Bonäs S 50 A1
Bonassola I 134 A2
Bonawe GB 34 B2
Bondal N 53 A4
Bondeno I 121 C4
Bondorf D 93 C4
Bondstorp S 60 B3
Bon-Encontre F 129 B3
Bo'ness GB 35 B4
Bonete E 158 C2
Bonifacio F 180 B2
Bonigen CH 106 C2
Bonin PL 67 B5
Bonn D 80 B3
Bonnánaro I 178 B2
Bonnåsjøen N 194 C6
Bonnat F 116 A1
Bonndorf D 106 B3
Bonnétable F 102 A2
Bonnétage F 106 B1
Bonneuil-les-Eaux F 90 B2
Bonneuil-Matours
F 115 B4
Bonneval F 103 A3
Bonneval-sur-Arc
F 119 B4
Bonneville F 118 A3
Bonnières-sur-Seine
F 90 B1
Bonnieux F 131 B4
Bönnigheim D 93 B5
Bonnyrigg GB 35 C4
Bonny-sur-Loire F 103 B4
Bono
E 145 B4
I 178 B3
Bonorva I 178 B2
Bønsnes N 48 B2
Bonyhád H 125 A4
Boom B 79 A4
Boos F 89 A5
Boostedt D 64 B3
Bootle
Cumbria GB 36 B3
Merseyside GB 38 A3
Bopfingen D 94 C2
Boppard D 81 B3
Boqueixón E 140 B2
Bor
CZ 95 B4
S 62 A2
SRB 16 C5
TR 23 C8
Boran-sur-Oise F 90 B2
Borås S 60 B2
Borba P 155 C3
Borbona I 169 A3
Borča SRB 127 C2
Borci BIH 139 B4
Borculo NL 71 B3
Bordány H 126 A1
Bordeaux F 128 B2
Bordeira P 160 B1
Bordesholm D 64 B3
Borðeyri IS 190 B4
Bordighera I 133 B3
Bording DK 59 B2
Bordón E 153 B3
Bore I 120 C2
Borehamwood GB 44 B3
Borek Strzeliński PL 85 B5
Borek Wielkopolski
PL 76 C2
Boreland GB 36 A3
Borello I 135 A5
Borensberg S 56 B1
Borgafjäll S 199 A12
Borgarnes IS 190 C4
Borgentreich D 81 A5
Börger D 71 B4
Borger NL 71 B3
Borggård S 56 B1
Borghamn S 55 B5
Borghetta di Vara I 134 A2
Borghetto d'Arróscia
I 133 A3
Borghetto Santo Spirito
I 133 A4
Borgholm S 62 B4
Borghorst D 71 B4
Bórgia I 175 C2
Borgloon B 79 B5
Børglum DK 58 A2
Borgo F 180 A2
Borgo alla Collina I 135 B4
Borgo a Mozzano I 134 B3
Borgoforte I 121 B3
Borgofranco d'Ivrea
I 119 B4
Borgomanero I 119 B5
Borgomasino I 119 B4
Borgonovo Val Tidone
I 120 B2
Borgo Pace I 135 B5
Borgorose I 169 A3
Borgo San Dalmazzo
I 133 A3
Borgo San Lorenzo
I 135 B4
Borgosésia I 119 B5
Borgo Val di Taro I 134 A2
Borgo Valsugana I 121 A4
Borgo Vercelli I 119 B5
Borgstena S 60 B3
Borgue GB 36 B2
Borgund N 47 A4
Borgvik S 55 A3
Borja E 144 C2
Bork D 80 A3
Borken D 80 A2
Borkenes N 194 D7
Børkop DK 59 C2
Borkowice PL 87 A4
Borkowo PL 77 B5
Borkum D 71 A3
Borlänge S 50 B2
Borlu TR 186 D3
Bormes-les-Mimosas
F 132 B2
Bórmio I 107 C5
Bormujos E 161 B3
Borna D 83 A4
Borne NL 71 B3
Bornes P 149 A2
Borne Sulinowo PL 68 B1
Bornheim D 80 B2
Bornhöved D 64 B3
Börnicke D 74 B1
Bornos E 162 B2
Borobia E 152 A2
Borodino RUS 9 E9
Borohrádek CZ 85 B4
Boronów PL 86 B2
Bórore I 178 B2
Borosźow PL 86 B2
Borota H 126 A1
Boroughbridge GB 40 A2
Borovany CZ 96 C2
Borovichi RUS 9 C8
Borovnica SLO 123 B3
Borovo HR 125 B4
Borovsk RUS 9 E10
Borovy CZ 96 B1
Borowa PL 85 A5
Borox E 151 B4
Borrby S 66 A3
Borre
DK 65 B5
N 54 A1
Borredá E 147 B2
Borrenes E 141 B4
Borriol E 159 A3
Borris
DK 59 C1
IRL 30 B2
Borris-in-Ossory
IRL 28 B4
Borrisokane IRL 28 B3
Borrisoleigh IRL 28 B4
Borrowdale GB 36 B3
Børrud N 49 C4
Borşa RO 17 B6
Borsdorf D 83 A4
Børselv N 193 B9
Borsfa H 111 C3
Borský Mikuláš SK 98 C1
Borsodivánka H 113 B4
Borsodnádasd H 113 A4
Börte N 53 A3
Borth GB 39 B2
Bort-les-Orgues F 116 B2
Börtnan S 199 C10
Børtnes N 47 B6
Boruja Kościelne
PL 75 B5
Borup DK 61 D1
Boryslav UA 13 D5
Boryspil UA 13 C9
Boryszyn PL 75 B4
Borzęciczki PL 85 A5
Borzęcin PL 77 B5
Borzonasca I 134 A2
Borzyszkowy PL 68 A2
Borzytuchom PL 68 A2
Bosa I 178 B2
Bošáca SK 98 C1
Bosanci HR 123 B4
Bosanska Dubica
BIH 124 B2
Bosanska Gradiška
BIH 124 B3
Bosanska Kostajnica
BIH 124 B2
Bosanska Krupa
BIH 124 C2
Bosanski Brod BIH 125 B3
Bosanski Novi BIH 124 B2
Bosanski Petrovac
BIH 124 C2
Bosanski Šamac
BIH 125 B4
Bosansko Grahovo
BIH 138 A2
Bošany SK 98 C2
Bösárkány H 111 B4
Bosau D 65 B3
Bósca H 112 C3
Boscastle GB 42 B2
Bosco I 120 C1
Bosco Chiesanuova
I 121 B4
Bösdorf D 65 B3
Bösel D 71 A4
Bosham GB 44 C3
Bösingfeld D 72 B2
Bosjön S 49 C5
Boskoop NL 70 B1
Boskovice CZ 97 B4
Bošnjaci HR 125 B4
Bošnjane SRB 127 D3
Bossast E 145 B4
Bossolasco I 133 A4
Boštanj SLO 123 A4
Boston GB 41 C3
Bostrak N 53 A4
Böszénfa H 125 A3
Bot E 153 A4
Botajica BIH 125 C4
Bøte By DK 65 B4
Bothel GB 36 B3
Boticas P 148 A2
Botilsäter S 55 A4
Botngård N 198 B6
Botoš SRB 126 B2
Botoşani RO 17 B7
Botricello I 175 C2
Botsmark S 200 B6
Bottendorf D 81 A4
Bottesford GB 40 C3
Bottnaryd S 60 B3
Bottrop D 80 A2
Botunje SRB 127 C3
Bötzingen D 106 A2
Bouaye F 101 B4
Bouça P 149 A2
Boucau F 128 C1
Bouchain F 78 B3
Bouchoir F 90 B2
Boudreville F 105 B3
Boudry CH 106 C1
Bouesse F 103 C3
Bouguenais F 101 B4
Bouhy F 104 B2
Bouillargues F 131 B3
Bouillon B 91 B5
Bouilly F 104 A2

Bouin F 114 B2
Boulay-Moselle F 92 B2
Boulazac F 129 A3
Boule-d'Amont F 146 B3
Bouligny F 92 B1
Boulogne-sur-Gesse F 145 A4
Boulogne-sur-Mer F 78 B1
Bouloire F 102 B2
Bouquemaison F 78 B2
Bourbon-Lancy F 104 C2
Bourbon-l'Archambault F 104 C2
Bourbonne-les-Bains F 105 B4
Bourbourg F 78 B2
Bourbriac F 100 A2
Bourcefranc-le-Chapus F 114 C2
Bourdeaux F 131 A4
Bouresse F 115 B4
Bourg F 128 A2
Bourg-Achard F 89 A4
Bourganeuf F 116 B1
Bourg-Argental F 117 B4
Bourg-de-Péage F 117 B5
Bourg-de-Thizy F 117 A4
Bourg-de-Visa F 129 B3
Bourg-en-Bresse F 118 A2
Bourges F 103 B4
Bourg-et-Comin F 91 B3
Bourg-Lastic F 116 B2
Bourg-Madame F 146 B2
Bourgneuf-en-Retz F 114 A2
Bourgogne F 91 B4
Bourgoin-Jallieu F 118 B2
Bourg-St Andéol F 131 A3
Bourg-St Maurice F 119 B3
Bourgtheroulde F 89 A4
Bourgueil F 102 B2
Bourmont F 105 A4
Bourne GB 40 C3
Bournemouth GB 43 B5
Bourneville F 89 A4
Bournezeau F 114 B2
Bourran F 129 B3
Bourret F 129 C4
Bourron-Marlotte F 90 C2
Bourton-on-The-Water GB 44 B2
Boussac F 116 A2
Boussens F 145 A4
Boutersem B 79 B4
Bouttencourt F 90 B1
Bouvières F 131 A4
Bouvron F 101 B4
Bouxwiller F 93 C3
Bouzas E 140 B2
Bouzonville F 92 B2
Bova I 175 D1
Bovalino Marina I 175 C2
Bovallstrand S 54 B2
Bova Marina I 175 D1
Bovec SLO 122 A2
Bóveda E 141 B3
Bóvegno I 120 B3
Bovenau D 64 B2
Bovenden D 82 A1
Bøverdal N 198 D5
Boves F 90 B2
Bóves I 133 A3
Bovey Tracey GB 43 B3
Bovino I 171 B3
Bøvlingbjerg DK 58 B1
Bovolenta I 121 B4
Bovolone I 121 B4
Bowes GB 37 B5
Bowmore GB 34 C1
Bowness-on-Windermere GB 36 B4
Box GB 43 A4
Boxberg
Baden-Württemberg D 94 B1
Sachsen D 84 A2
Boxholm S 55 B6
Boxmeer NL 80 A1
Boxtel NL 79 A5
Boyabat TR 23 A8
Boyalıca TR 187 B4
Boyle IRL 26 C2
Bozan TR 187 C6
Božava HR 137 A3
Bozburun TR 188 C3
Bozcaada TR 186 C1
Bozdoğan TR 188 B3
Bożepole Wielkie PL 68 A2
Boževac SRB 127 C3
Božice CZ 97 C4
Boží Dar CZ 83 B4
Bozkır TR 189 B7
Bozouls F 130 A1
Bozova TR 189 B5
Bozüyük TR 187 C5
Bòzzolo I 121 B3
Bra I 119 C4
Braås S 62 A3
Brabrand DK 59 B3
Bracadale GB 31 B2
Bracciano I 168 A2
Bracieux F 103 B3
Bräcke S 199 C12
Brackenheim D 93 B5
Brackley GB 44 A2
Bracklin IRL 27 C4
Bracknell GB 44 B3
Brackwede D 72 C1
Braco GB 35 B4
Brad RO 16 B5
Bradford GB 40 B2
Bradford on Avon GB 43 A4
Bradina BIH 139 B4
Brådland N 52 B2
Brædstrup DK 59 C2
Brae GB 33 A5
Braemar GB 32 D3
Braemore GB 32 D1
Braga P 148 A1
Bragança P 149 A3
Brăila RO 17 C7
Braine F 91 B3
Braine-le-Comte B 79 B4
Braintree GB 45 B4
Braives B 79 B5
Brake D 72 A1
Brakel
B 79 B3
D 81 A5
Bräkne-Hoby S 63 B3
Brålanda S 54 B3
Bralin PL 86 A1
Brallo di Pregola I 120 C2
Bram F 146 A3
Bramafan F 132 B2
Bramberg am Wildkogel A 109 B3
Bramdrupdam DK 59 C2
Bramming DK 59 C1
Brampton GB 37 B4
Bramsche D 71 B4
Branca I 136 B1
Brancaleone Marina I 175 D2
Brancaster GB 41 C4
Brand
Nieder Östereich A 96 C3
Vorarlberg A 107 B4
Brandbu N 48 B2
Brande DK 59 C2
Brande-Hornerkirchen D 64 C2
Brandenberg A 108 B2
Brandenburg D 73 B5
Brand-Erbisdorf D 83 B5
Brandis D 83 A4
Brando F 180 A2
Brandomil E 140 A2
Brandon GB 45 A4
Brandshagen D 66 B2
Brandval N 49 B4
Brandýs nad Labem CZ 84 B2
Branice PL 98 A1
Braničevo SRB 127 C3
Braniewo PL 69 A4
Branik SLO 122 B2
Brankovina SRB 127 C1
Branky CZ 98 B1
Branne F 128 B2
Brannenburg-Degerndorf D 108 B3
Brantôme F 115 C4
Branzi I 120 A2
Bras d'Asse F 132 B2
Braskereidfoss N 48 B3
Braslaw BY 13 A7
Braşov RO 17 C6
Brasparts F 100 A2
Brassac F 130 B1
Brassac-les-Mines F 116 B3
Brasschaat B 79 A4
Brastad S 54 B2
Břasy CZ 96 B1
Brąszewice PL 86 A2
Bratislava SK 111 A4
Brattfors S 55 A5
Brattvåg N 198 C3
Bratunac BIH 127 C1
Braubach D 81 B3
Braunau A 95 C5
Braunfels D 81 B4
Braunlage D 82 A2
Braunsbedra D 83 A3
Braunschweig D 73 B3
Bray IRL 30 A2
Bray Dunes F 78 A2
Bray-sur-Seine F 90 C3
Bray-sur-Somme F 90 B2
Brazatortas E 157 B3
Brazey-en-Plaine F 105 B4
Brbinj HR 137 A4
Brčko BIH 125 C4
Brdani SRB 127 D2
Brdów PL 76 B3
Brea de Tajo E 151 B4
Brécey F 88 B2
Brechen D 81 B4
Brechin GB 35 B5
Brecht B 79 A4
Brecketfeld D 80 A3
Břeclav CZ 97 C4
Brecon GB 39 C3
Brécy F 103 B4
Breda
E 147 C3
NL 79 A4
Bredaryd S 60 B3
Bredbyn S 200 C4
Breddin D 73 B5
Bredebro DK 64 A1
Bredelar D 81 A4
Bredenfelde D 74 A2
Bredsjö S 50 C1
Bredstedt D 64 B1
Bredsten DK 59 C2
Bredträsk S 200 C4
Bredviken S 195 D5
Bree B 80 A1
Bregana HR 123 B4
Breganze I 121 B4
Bregenz A 107 B4
Bréhal F 88 B2
Brehna D 83 A4
Breiðdalsvík IS 191 C11
Breidenbach F 93 B3
Breil-sur-Roya F 133 B3
Breisach D 106 A2
Breitenbach
CH 106 B2
D 81 B5
Breitenberg D 96 C1
Breitenfelde D 73 A3
Breitengussbach D 94 B2
Breivikbotn N 192 B6
Brejning DK 59 C2
Brekke N 46 A2
Brekken N 199 C8
Brekkestø N 53 B4
Brekkvasselv N 199 A10
Brekstad N 198 B6
Breland N 53 B3
Bremanger N 198 D1
Bremen D 72 A1
Bremerhaven D 72 A1
Bremervörde D 72 A2
Bremgarten CH 106 B3
Bremsnes N 198 B4
Brem-sur-Mer F 114 B2
Brenderup DK 59 C2
Brenes E 162 A2
Brengova SLO 110 C2
Brenna PL 98 B2
Breno I 120 B3
Brénod F 118 A2
Brensbach D 93 B4
Brentwood GB 45 B4
Brescello I 121 C3
Bréscia I 120 B3
Breskens NL 79 A3
Bresles F 90 B2
Bresnica SRB 127 D2
Bressana I 120 B2
Bressanone I 108 C2
Bressuire F 102 C1
Brest
BY 13 B5
F 100 A1
HR 122 B2
Brestač SRB 127 C1
Brestanica SLO 123 A4
Brestova HR 123 B3
Brestovac HR 125 B3
Bretenoux F 129 B4
Breteuil
Eure F 89 B4
Oise F 90 B2
Brétigny-sur-Orge F 90 C2
Bretten D 93 B4
Bretteville-sur-Laize F 89 A3
Brettheim D 94 B2
Breuil-Cervinia I 119 B4
Breukelen NL 70 B2
Brevik
N 53 A5
Stockholm S 57 A4
Västra Götaland S 55 B5
Breza BIH 139 A4
Brežice SLO 123 B4
Bréziers F 132 A2
Breznica HR 124 A2
Breznica Našička HR 125 B4
Březnice CZ 96 B1
Brezno SK 99 C3
Brezolles F 89 B5
Březovánad Svitavou CZ 97 B4
Brezovápod Bradlom SK 98 C1
Brezovica
SK 99 B4
SLO 123 A3
Brezovo Polje Selo BIH 125 C4
Briançon F 118 C3
Brianconnet F 132 B2
Briare F 103 B4
Briatexte F 129 C4
Briático I 175 C2
Briaucourt F 105 A4
Bribir HR 123 B3
Bricquebec F 88 A2
Bridgend
Argyll & Bute GB 34 C1
Bridgend GB 39 C3
Bridge of Cally GB 35 B4
Bridge of Don GB 33 D4
Bridge of Earn GB 35 B4
Bridge of Orchy GB 34 B3
Bridgnorth GB 39 B4
Bridgwater GB 43 A4
Břidličná CZ 98 B1
Bridlington GB 41 A3
Bridport GB 43 B4
Briec F 100 A1
Brie-Comte-Robert F 90 C2
Brienne-le-Château F 91 C4
Brienon-sur-Armançon F 104 B2
Brienz CH 106 C3
Brienza I 172 B1
Briesen D 74 B3
Brieskow Finkenheerd D 74 B3
Brietlingen D 72 A3
Brieva de Cameros E 143 B4
Briey F 92 B1
Brig CH 119 A5
Brigg GB 40 B3
Brighouse GB 40 B2
Brightlingsea GB 45 B5
Brighton GB 44 C3
Brignogan-Plage F 100 A1
Brignoles F 132 B2
Brigstock GB 40 C3
Brihuega E 151 B5
Brijuni HR 122 C2
Brillon-en-Barrois F 91 C5
Brilon D 81 A4
Brimnes N 46 B3
Brinches P 160 A2
Brindisi I 173 B3
Brinje HR 123 B4
Brinon-sur-Beuvron F 104 B2
Brinon-sur-Sauldre F 103 B4
Brinyan GB 33 B3
Brión E 140 B2
Briones E 143 B4
Brionne F 89 A4
Brioude F 117 B3
Brioux-sur-Boutonne F 115 B3
Briouze F 89 B3
Briscous F 144 A2
Brisighella I 135 A4
Brissac-Quincé F 102 B1
Brissago CH 120 A1
Bristol GB 43 A4
Brive-la-Gaillarde F 129 A4
Briviesca E 143 B3
Brixham GB 43 B3
Brixlegg A 108 B2
Brjánslækur IS 190 B2
Brka BIH 125 C4
Brnaze HR 138 B2
Brněnec CZ 97 B4
Brno CZ 97 B4
Bro S 57 A3
Broadclyst GB 43 B3
Broadford
GB 31 B3
IRL 28 B3
Broad Haven GB 39 C1
Broadstairs GB 45 B5
Broadstone GB 43 B4
Broadway GB 44 A2
Broager DK 64 B2
Broaryd S 60 B3
Broby S 61 C4
Brobyværk DK 59 C3
Bročanac BIH 138 B3
Brocas F 128 B2
Brock D 71 B4
Brockel D 72 A2
Brockenhurst GB 44 C2
Broczyno PL 75 A5
Brod MK 182 B3
Brodalen S 54 B2
Broddbo S 50 C3
Brodek u Přerova CZ 98 B1
Broden-bach D 80 B3
Brodick GB 34 C2
Brod na Kupi HR 123 B3
Brodnica PL 69 B4
Brodnica Graniczna PL 68 A3
Brodowe Łąki PL 77 A6
Brody
Lubuskie PL 75 B4
Lubuskie PL 84 A2
Mazowieckie PL 77 B5
UA 13 C6
Broglie F 89 B4
Brójce PL 75 B4
Brokind S 56 B1
Brolo I 177 A3
Brome D 73 B3
Bromley GB 45 B4
Bromölla S 63 B2
Bromont-Lamothe F 116 B2
Brömsebro S 63 B3
Bromsgrove GB 44 A1
Bromyard GB 39 B4
Bronchales E 152 B2
Bronco E 149 B3
Brønderslev DK 58 A2
Broni I 120 B2
Brønnøysund N 195 E3
Brøns DK 59 C1
Bronte I 177 B3
Bronzani Mejdan BIH 124 C2
Bronzolo I 121 A4
Broons F 101 A3
Broquies F 130 A1
Brora GB 32 C3
Brørup DK 59 C2
Brösarp S 63 C2
Brossac F 115 C3
Brostrud N 47 B5
Brotas P 154 C2
Brötjärna S 50 B2
Broto E 145 B3
Brottby S 57 A4
Brøttum N 48 A2
Brou F 103 A3
Brouage F 114 C2
Brough GB 37 B4
Broughshane GB 27 B4
Broughton GB 35 C4
Broughton-in-Furness GB 36 B3
Broumov CZ 85 B4
Broût-Vernet F 116 A3
Brouvelieures F 106 A1
Brouwershaven NL 79 A3
Brovary UA 13 C9
Brovst DK 58 A2
Brownhills GB 40 C2
Brozas E 155 B4
Brozzo I 120 B3
Brtnice CZ 97 B3
Brtonigla HR 122 B2
Bruay-la-Buissière F 78 B2
Bruchhausen-Vilsen D 72 B2
Bruchsal D 93 B4
Bruck D 95 B4
Brück D 74 B1
Bruck an der Grossglocknerstrasse A 109 B3
Bruck an der Leitha A 111 A3
Bruck an der Mur A 110 B2
Brückl A 110 C1
Bruckmühl D 108 B2
Brue-Auriac F 132 B1
Brüel D 65 C4
Bruen CH 107 C3
Bruère-Allichamps F 103 C4
Bruff IRL 29 B3
Bruflat N 47 B6
Brugg CH 106 B3
Brugge B 78 A3
Brüggen D 80 A2
Brühl D 80 B2
Bruinisse NL 79 A4
Brûlon F 102 B1
Brumano I 120 B2
Brumath F 93 C3
Brummen NL 70 B3
Brumov-Bylnice CZ 98 B2
Brumunddal N 48 B2
Brunau D 73 B4
Brunehamel F 91 B4
Brünen D 80 A2
Brunete E 151 B3
Brunflo S 199 B11
Brunico I 108 C2
Brunkeberg N 53 A4
Brunn D 74 A2
Brunnen CH 107 C3
Brunsbüttel D 64 C2
Brunssum NL 80 B1
Bruntál CZ 98 B1
Brušane HR 137 A4
Brusasco I 119 B5
Brusio CH 120 A3
Brusno SK 99 C3
Brusque F 130 B1
Brussels = Bruxelles B 79 B4
Brusson I 119 B4
Brüssow D 74 A3
Brusy PL 68 B2
Bruton GB 43 A4
Bruvno HR 138 A1
Bruvoll N 48 B3
Bruxelles = Brussels B 79 B4
Bruyères F 106 A1
Bruz F 101 A4
Bruzaholm S 62 A3
Brwinów PL 77 B5
Brynamman GB 39 C3
Bryncrug GB 39 B2
Bryne N 52 B1
Brynmawr GB 39 C3
Bryrup DK 59 B2
Brzeg PL 85 B5
Brzeg Dolny PL 85 A4
Brześć Kujawski PL 76 B3
Brzesko PL 99 B4
Brzeszcze PL 99 B3
Brzezie PL 68 B1
Brzeziny
Łódzkie PL 87 A3
Wielkopolskie PL 86 A2
Brzeźnica PL 84 A3
Brzeźnica Nowa PL 86 A3
Brzeżno PL 75 A4
Brzotin SK 99 C4
Brzozie Lubawskie PL 69 B4
Bua S 60 B2
Buarcos P 148 B1
Buaveg N 52 A1
Bubbio I 119 C5
Bubry F 100 B2
Buca TR 188 A2
Bucak TR 189 B5
Bučany SK 98 C1
Buccheri I 177 B3
Buccino I 172 B1
Bucelas P 154 C1
Buch
Bayern D 94 C2
Bayern D 95 C4
Buchach UA 13 D6
Bucharest = Bucureşti RO 17 C7
Buchbach D 95 C4
Buchboden A 107 B4
Buchen D 94 B1
Büchen D 73 A3
Buchenberg D 107 B5
Buchères F 104 A3
Buchholz D 72 A2
Buchloe D 108 A1
Buchlovice CZ 98 B1
Buchlyvie GB 34 B3
Bucholz D 73 A5
Buchs CH 107 B4
Buchy F 89 A5
Bückeburg D 72 B2
Buckfastleigh GB 42 B3
Buckhaven GB 35 B4
Buckie GB 33 D4
Buckingham GB 44 A3
Buckley GB 38 A3
Bückwitz D 73 B5
Bučovice CZ 97 B5
Bucsa H 113 B5
Bucureşti = Bucharest RO 17 C7
Bucy-lés-Pierreport F 91 B3
Buczek PL 86 A3
Bud N 198 C3
Budakalasz H 112 B3
Budakeszi H 112 B2
Budal N 199 C7
Budaörs H 112 B2
Budapest H 112 B3
Búðardalur IS 190 B4
Budča SK 99 C3
Buddusò I 178 B3
Bude GB 42 B2
Budeč CZ 97 B3
Büdelsdorf D 64 B2
Budens P 160 B1
Budia E 151 B5
Budimlić-Japra BIH 124 C2
Büdingen D 81 B5
Budinšćina HR 124 A2
Budišov CZ 98 B1
Budleigh Salterton GB 43 B3
Budmerice SK 98 C1
Budoni I 178 B3
Búdrio I 135 A4
Budva MNE 16 D3
Budyněnad Ohří CZ 84 B2
Budziszewice PL 87 A3
Budzyń PL 76 B1
Bue N 52 B1
Bueña E 152 B2
Buenache de Alarcón E 158 B1
Buenache de la Sierra E 152 B2
Buenaventura E 150 B3
Buenavista de Valdavia E 142 B2
Buendia E 151 B5
Bueu E 140 B2
Buezo E 143 B3
Bugac H 112 C3
Bugarra E 159 B3
Bugeat F 116 B1
Buggerru I 179 C2
Bugojno BIH 138 A3
Bugøyfjord N 193 C13
Bugøynes N 193 C13
Bugyi H 112 B3
Buharkent TR 188 B3
Bühl
Baden-Württemberg D 93 C4
Bayern D 107 B5
Bühlertal D 93 C4
Bühlertann D 94 B1
Buia I 122 A2
Builth Wells GB 39 B3
Buin N 47 B6
Buis-les-Baronnies F 131 A4
Buitenpost NL 70 A3
Buitrago del Lozoya E 151 B4
Bujalance E 157 C3
Bujaraloz E 153 A3
Buje HR 122 B2
Bujedo E 143 B3
Bük H 111 B3
Buk PL 75 B5
Bükkösd H 125 A3
Bükkzsérc H 113 B4
Bukovci SLO 124 A1
Bukowiec PL 75 B5
Bukowina Tatrzańska PL 99 B4
Bukownica PL 86 A2
Bukowno PL 86 B3

Bülach CH 107 B3
Búland IS 191 D7
Buldan TR 188 A3
Bulgari BG 17 D7
Bulgnéville F 105 A4
Bulgurca TR 188 A2
Bülkau D 64 C1
Bulken N 46 B3
Bulkowo PL 77 B5
Bullas E 164 A3
Bulle CH 106 C2
Büllingen B 80 B2
Bullmark S 200 B6
Bulqizë AL 182 B2
Buna BIH 139 B3
Bunahowen IRL 26 B1
Bunbeg IRL 26 A2
Bunclody IRL 30 B2
Buncrana IRL 27 A3
Bunde D 71 A4
Bünde D 72 B1
Bundoran IRL 26 B2
Bunessan GB 34 B1
Bungay GB 45 A5
Bunge S 57 C5
Bunić HR 123 C4
Bunmahon IRL 30 B1
Bunnyconnellan IRL 26 B1
Buño E 140 A2
Buñol E 159 B3
Bunratty IRL 29 B3
Bunsbeek B 79 B4
Buñuel E 144 C2
Bunyola E 166 B2
Buonabitácolo I 172 B1
Buonalbergo I 170 B2
Buonconvento I 135 B4
Buonvicino I 174 B1
Burano I 122 B1
Burbach D 81 B4
Burcei I 179 C3
Burdons-sur-Rognon
F 105 A4
Burdur TR 189 B5
Bureå S 2 D7
Burela E 141 A3
Büren D 81 A4
Büren an der Aare
CH 106 B2
Burford GB 44 B2
Burg
Cottbus D 84 A2
Magdeburg D 73 B4
Schleswig-Holstein
D 64 C2
Burgas BG 17 D7
Burgau
A 111 B3
D 94 C2
P 160 B1
Burg auf Fehmarn D 65 B4
Burgbernheim D 94 B2
Burgdorf
CH 106 B2
D 72 B3
Burgebrach D 94 B2
Bürgel D 83 B3
Burgess Hill GB 44 C3
Burghaslach D 94 B2
Burghausen D 109 A3
Burghead GB 32 D3
Burgheim D 94 C3
Burgh le Marsh GB 41 B4
Búrgio I 176 B2
Burgkirchen D 109 A3
Burgkunstadt D 82 B3
Burglengenfeld D 95 B4
Burgo P 148 B1
Burgoberbach D 94 B2
Burgohondo E 150 B3
Burgos E 143 B3
Burgsinn D 82 B1
Burgstädt D 83 B4
Burgstall D 73 B4
Burg Stargard D 74 A2
Burgsvik S 57 C4
Burgui E 144 B3
Burguillos E 162 A2
Burguillos del Cerro
E 155 C4
Burguillos de Toledo
E 151 C4
Burhaniye TR 186 C1
Burhave D 71 A5
Burie F 114 C3
Burjassot E 159 B3
Burk D 94 B2
Burkhardtsdorf D 83 B4
Burlada E 144 B2
Burladingen D 107 A4
Burlage D 71 A4
Burness GB 33 B4
Burnham GB 44 B3
Burnham Market
GB 41 C4
Burnham-on-Crouch
GB 45 B4
Burnham-on-Sea
GB 43 A4
Burniston GB 40 A3
Burnley GB 40 B1
Burntisland GB 35 B4
Burón E 142 A1
Buronzo I 119 B5
Burovac SRB 127 C3
Burow D 74 A2
Burravoe GB 33 A5
Burrel AL 182 B2
Burret F 146 B2
Burriana E 159 B3
Burry Port GB 39 C2
Bürs A 107 B4
Bursa TR 186 B4
Burseryd S 60 B3
Bürstadt D 93 B4
Burton GB 37 B4
Burton Agnes GB 41 A3
Burton Bradstock
GB 43 B4
Burton Latimer GB 44 A3
Burton upon Stather
GB 40 B3
Burton upon Trent
GB 40 C2
Burträsk S 200 B6
Burujón E 151 C3
Burwell GB 45 A4
Burwick GB 33 C4
Bury GB 40 B1
Bury St Edmunds
GB 45 A4
Burzenin PL 86 A2
Busachi I 179 B2
Busalla I 134 A1
Busana I 134 A3
Busano I 119 B4
Busca I 133 A3
Busch D 73 B4
Buševec HR 124 B2
Bushat AL 182 B1
Bushey GB 44 B3
Bushmills GB 27 A4
Bušince SK 112 A3
Buskhyttan S 56 B2
Busko-Zdrój PL 87 B4
Busot E 159 C3
Busovača BIH 139 A3
Busquistar E 163 B4
Bussang F 106 B1
Busseto I 120 C3
Bussière-Badil F 115 C4
Bussière-Poitevine
F 115 B4
Bussolengo I 121 B3
Bussoleno I 119 B4
Bussum NL 70 B2
Busto Arsízio I 120 B1
Büsum D 64 B1
Butera I 177 B3
Butgenbach B 80 B2
Butler's Bridge IRL 27 B3
Butryny PL 77 A5
Bütschwil CH 107 B4
Buttermere GB 36 B3
Buttevant IRL 29 B3
Buttle S 57 C4
Buttstädt D 82 A3
Butzbach D 81 B4
Bützfleth D 72 A2
Bützow D 65 C4
Buxières-les-Mines
F 104 C1
Buxtehude D 72 A2
Buxton GB 40 B2
Buxy F 104 C3
Büyükçekmece
TR 186 A3
Büyükkariştiran
TR 186 A2
Büyükorhan TR 186 C3
Buzançais F 103 C3
Buzancy F 91 B4
Buzău RO 17 C7
Buzet HR 122 B2
Buziaş RO 126 B3
Buzsák H 111 C4
Buzy F 145 A3
By S 50 B3
Byala BG 17 D6
Byaroza BY 13 B6
Byczyna PL 86 A2
Bydalen S 199 B10
Bydgoszcz PL 76 A3
Bygdin N 47 A5
Bygdsiljum S 200 B6
Bygland N 53 B3
Byglandsfjord N 53 B3
Bygstad N 46 A2
Bykhaw BY 13 B9
Bykle N 52 A3
Bylderup-Bov DK 64 B2
Byrkjedal N 52 B2
Byrkjelo N 198 D3
Byrum DK 58 A3
Byšice CZ 84 B2
Byske S 2 D7
Býškovice CZ 98 B1
Bysław PL 76 A2
Bystré CZ 97 B4
Bystřice CZ 96 B2
Bystrice CZ 98 B2
Bystřice nad
Pernštejnem CZ 97 B4
Bystřice pod Hostýnem
CZ 98 B1
Bystrzyca Kłodzka
PL 85 B4
Bytča SK 98 B2
Bytnica PL 75 B4
Bytom PL 86 B2
Bytom Odrzański
PL 85 A3
Bytów PL 68 A2
Byxelkrok S 62 A5
Bzenec CZ 98 C1
Bzince SK 98 C1

C

Çağa TR 187 B7
Cabacos P 154 B2
Cabaj-Čápor SK 98 C2
Cabana E 140 A2
Cabanac-et-Villagrains
F 128 B2
Cabañaquinta E 142 A1
Cabanas P 160 B2
Cabañas del Castillo
E 156 A2
Cabañas de Yepes
E 151 C4
Cabanelles E 147 B3
Cabanes E 153 B4
Cabanillas E 144 B2
Čabar HR 123 B3
Cabasse F 132 B2
Cabdella E 146 B2
Cabeceiras de Basto
P 148 A1
Cabeço de Vide P 155 B3
Cabella Ligure I 120 C2
Cabeza del Buey E 156 B2
Cabeza la Vaca E 161 A3
Cabezamesada E 151 C4
Cabezarados E 157 B3
Cabezarrubias del
Puerto E 157 B3
Cabezas del Villar
E 150 B2
Cabezas Rubias E 161 B2
Cabezón E 142 C2
Cabezón de la Sal
E 142 A2
Cabezón de Liébana
E 142 A2
Cabezuela E 151 A4
Cabezuela del Valle
E 149 B4
Cabo de Gata E 164 C2
Cabo de Palos E 165 B4
Cabolafuenta E 152 A1
Cabourg F 89 A3
Cabra
E 163 A3
P 148 B2
Cabrach GB 32 D3
Cabra del Santo Cristo
E 163 A4
Cábras I 179 C2
Cabreiro P 140 C2
Cabreiros E 140 A3
Cabrejas E 152 B1
Cabrela P 154 C2
Cabrillas E 149 B3
Cabuna HR 125 B3
Cacabelos E 141 B4
Čačak SRB 127 D2
Cáccamo I 176 B2
Caccuri I 174 B2
Cacela P 160 B2
Cacém P 154 C1
Cáceres E 155 B4
Cachafeiro E 140 B2
Cachopo P 160 B2
Čachtice SK 98 C1
Cacin E 163 A4
Čačinci HR 125 B3
Cadafais P 154 C1
Cadalen F 129 C5
Cadalso E 149 B3
Cadaqués E 147 B4
Cadaval P 154 B1
Cadavedo E 141 A4
Čadavica BIH 138 A2
Čadca SK 98 B2
Cadéac F 145 B4
Cadelbosco di Sopra
I 121 C3
Cadenazzo CH 120 A1
Cadenberge D 64 C2
Cadenet F 131 B4
Cadeuil F 114 C3
Cádiar E 164 C1
Cadillac F 128 B2
Cádiz E 162 B1
Čadjavica HR 125 B3
Cadouin F 129 B3
Cadours F 129 C4
Cadrete E 152 A3
Caen F 89 A3
Caerleon GB 39 C4
Caernarfon GB 38 A2
Caerphilly GB 39 C3
Caersws GB 39 B3
Cafede P 155 B3
Caggiano I 172 B1
Cagli I 136 B1
Cágliari I 179 C3
Čaglin HR 125 B3
Cagnano Varano I 171 B3
Cagnes-sur-Mer F 132 B3
Caher IRL 29 B4
Caherciveen IRL 29 C1
Caherdaniel IRL 29 C1
Cahors F 129 B4
Cahul MD 17 C8
Caiazzo I 170 B2
Caion E 140 A2
Cairndow GB 34 B3
Cairnryan GB 36 B1
Cairo Montenotte I 133 A4
Caister-on-Sea GB 41 C5
Caistor GB 41 B3
Caivano I 170 C2
Cajarc F 129 B4
Čajniče BIH 139 B5
Çakırlar TR 189 C5
Çakmak TR 187 C6
Čakovec HR 124 A2
Çal TR 189 A4
Cala E 161 B3
Calabritto I 172 B1
Calaceite E 153 B4
Calacuccia F 180 A2
Cala d'Or E 167 B3
Calaf E 147 C2
Calafat RO 17 C5
Calafell E 147 C2
Cala Galdana E 167 B3
Cala Gonone I 178 B3
Calahonda
Granada E 163 B4
Málaga E 163 B3
Calahorra E 144 B2
Calais F 78 B1
Cala Llonga E 166 C1
Calalzo di Cadore I 109 C3
Cala Millor E 167 B3
Calamocha E 152 B2
Calamonte E 155 C4
Cala Morell E 167 A3
Calanais GB 31 A2
Calañas E 161 B3
Calanda E 153 B3
Calangiánus I 178 B3
Călăraşi RO 17 C7
Cala Ratjada E 167 B3
Calascibetta I 177 B3
Calasetta I 179 C2
Calasparra E 164 A3
Calatafimi I 176 B1
Calatayud E 152 A2
Calatorao E 152 A2
Calau D 84 A1
Calbe D 73 C4
Calcena E 152 A2
Calcinelli I 136 B1
Calco I 120 B2
Caldarola I 136 B2
Caldaro sulla strada del
Vino I 121 A4
Caldas da Rainha
P 154 B1
Caldas de Bo i E 145 B4
Caldas de Malavella
E 147 C3
Caldas de Reis E 140 B2
Caldas de San Jorge
P 148 B1
Caldas de Vizela P 148 A1
Caldaso de los Vidrios
E 150 B3
Caldbeck GB 36 B3
Caldearenas E 145 B3
Caldelas P 148 A1
Calders E 147 C2
Caldes de Montbui
E 147 C3
Caldicot GB 39 C4
Caldirola I 120 C2
Caledon GB 27 B4
Calella
Barcelona E 147 C3
Girona E 147 C4
Calenzana F 180 A1
Calera de León E 161 A3
Calera y Chozas E 150 C3
Caleruega E 143 C3
Caleruela E 150 C2
Cales de Mallorca
E 167 B3
Calestano I 134 A3
Calfsound GB 33 B4
Calgary GB 34 B1
Calimera I 173 B4
Calitri I 172 B1
Calizzano I 133 A4
Callac F 100 A2
Callan IRL 30 B1
Callander GB 35 B3
Callas F 132 B2
Calliano
Piemonte I 119 B5
Trentino Alto Adige
I 121 B4
Callington GB 42 B2
Callosa de Ensarriá
E 159 C3
Callosa de Segura
E 165 A4
Callús E 147 C2
Čalma SRB 127 B1
Calmbach D 93 C4
Calne GB 43 A5
Calolziocorte I 120 B2
Calonge E 147 C4
Čalovec SK 112 B1
Calpe E 159 C4
Caltabellotta I 176 B2
Caltagirone I 177 B3
Caltanissetta I 177 B3
Caltavuturo I 176 B2
Çaltılıbük TR 186 C3
Caltojar E 151 A5
Caluire-et-Cuire F 117 B4
Caluso I 119 B4
Calvello I 172 B1
Calvi F 180 A1
Calviá E 166 B2
Calvinet F 116 C2
Calvisson F 131 B3
Calvörde D 73 B4
Calw D 93 C4
Calzada de Calatrava
E 157 B4
Calzada de Valdunciel
E 150 A2
Calzadilla de los Barros
E 155 C4
Cam GB 43 A4
Camaiore I 134 B3
Camarasa E 145 C4
Camarena E 151 B3
Camarès F 130 B1
Camaret-sur-Aigues
F 131 A3
Camaret-sur-Mer F 100 A1
Camarillas E 153 B3
Camariñas E 140 A1
Camarma E 151 B4
Camarzana de Tera
E 141 B4
Camas E 162 A1
Camastra I 176 B2
Cambados E 140 B2
Cambarinho P 148 B1
Camberley GB 44 B3
Cambil E 163 A4
Cambligeu F 78 B2
Cambo-les-Bains F 144 A2
Camborne GB 42 B1
Cambrai F 78 B3
Cambre E 140 A2
Cambridge GB 45 A4
Cambrils E 147 C2
Cambs D 65 C4
Camburg D 83 A3
Camden GB 44 B3
Cameleño E 142 A2
Camelford GB 42 B2
Çameli TR 189 B4
Camelle E 140 A1
Camerano I 136 B2
Camerino I 136 B2
Camerota I 172 B1
Camigliatello Silano
I 174 B2
Caminha P 148 A1
Caminomorisco E 149 B3
Camineal E 152 B2
Camisano Vicentino
I 121 B4
Camlıdere TR 187 B7
Cammarata I 176 B2
Camogli I 134 A2
Camors F 100 B3
Camp IRL 29 B2
Campagna I 172 B1
Campagnano di Roma
I 168 A2
Campagnático I 135 C4
Campan F 145 A4
Campana I 174 B2
Campanario E 156 B2
Campanillas E 163 B3
Campano E 162 B1
Campaspero E 151 A3
Campbeltown GB 34 C2
Campello E 165 A4
Campelos P 154 B1
Campi Bisénzio I 135 B4
Campico López E 165 B3
Campíglia Maríttima
I 134 B3
Campillo de Altobuey
E 158 B2
Campillo de Aragón
E 152 A2
Campillo de Arenas
E 163 A4
Campillo de Llerena
E 156 B2
Campillos E 162 A3
Câmpina RO 17 C6
Campi Salentina I 173 B4
Campli I 136 C2
Campo E 145 B4
Campobasso I 170 B2
Campobello di Licata
I 176 B2
Campobello di Mazara
I 176 B1
Campo da Feira E 140 A3
Campodársego I 121 B4
Campo de Bacerros
E 141 B3
Campo de Caso E 142 A1
Campo de Criptana
E 157 A4
Campodolcino I 120 A2
Campofelice di Roccella
I 176 B2
Campofiorito I 176 B2
Campofórmido I 122 A2
Campofranco I 176 B2
Campofrio E 161 B3
Campogalliano I 121 C3
Campo Ligure I 133 A4
Campolongo I 109 C3
Campo Lugar E 156 A2
Campo Maior P 155 B3
Campomanes E 141 A5
Campomarino I 170 B3
Campo Molino I 133 A3
Campomono F 180 B1
Campo Real E 151 B4
Camporeale I 176 B2
Camporeggiano I 136 B1
Camporrells E 145 C4
Camporrobles E 158 B2
Campos P 148 A2
Camposa P 148 A1
Camposampiero I 121 B4
Camposanto I 121 C4
Campos del Port E 167 B3
Camposines E 153 A4
Campotéjar E 163 A4
Campotosto I 169 A3
Campo Túres I 108 C2
Camprodón E 147 B3
Campsegret F 129 B3
Camrose GB 39 C1
Camuñas E 157 A4
Çamyolu TR 189 C7
Çan TR 186 B2
Cana I 135 C4
Cañada del Hoyo
E 158 B2
Cañadajuncosa E 158 B1
Cañada Rosal E 162 A2
Čanak HR 123 C4
Çanakkale TR 186 B1
Canale I 119 C4
Canales
Asturias E 141 B5
Castellón de la Plana
E 159 B3
Canals E 159 C3
Canal San Bovo I 121 A4
Cañamares E 152 B1
Cañamero E 156 A2
Cañar E 163 B4
Cañate la Real E 162 B2
Cañaveral E 155 B4
Cañaveral de León
E 161 A3
Cañaveras E 152 B1
Cañaveruelas E 151 B5
Canazei I 108 C2
Cancale F 88 B2
Cancellara I 172 B1
Cancello ed Arnone
I 170 B2
Cancon F 129 B3
Canda E 141 B4
Candamil E 140 A3
Candanchu E 145 B3
Çandarlı TR 186 D1
Candas E 141 A5
Candasnos E 153 A4
Candé F 101 B4
Candela I 172 A1
Candelario E 150 B2
Candeleda E 150 B2
Cándia Lomellina I 120 B1
Candide Casamazzagno
I 109 C3
Candin E 141 B4
Candosa P 148 B2
Canecas P 154 C1
Canelli I 119 C5
Canena E 157 B4
Canencia E 151 B4
Canero E 141 A4
Canet F 130 B2
Canet de Mar E 147 C3
Canet d'en Berenguer
E 159 B3
Cañete E 158 A2
Cañete de las Torres
E 163 A3
Canet-Plage F 146 B4
Canfranc E 145 B3
Cangas
Lugo E 141 A3
Pontevedra E 140 B2
Cangas de Narcea
E 141 A4
Cangas de Onís E 142 A1
Canha P 154 C2
Canhestros P 160 A1
Canicattì I 176 B2
Canicattini Bagni I 177 B4
Canicosa de la Sierra
E 143 C3
Caniles E 164 B2
Canillas de Aceituno
E 163 B3
Canino I 168 A1
Canisy F 88 A2
Cañizal E 150 A2
Cañizo E 142 C1
Canjáyar E 164 C2
Çankırı TR 23 A7
Cannai I 179 C2
Cannara I 136 B1
Cánnero Riviera I 120 A1
Cannes F 132 B3
Canneto
Sicilia I 177 A3
Toscana I 135 B3
Canneto sull'Oglio
I 120 B3
Cannich GB 32 D2
Cannóbio I 120 A1
Cannock GB 40 C1
Canonbie GB 36 A4
Canosa di Púglia I 171 B4
Can Pastilla E 166 B2
C'an Picafort E 167 B3
Cantalapiedra E 150 A2
Cantalejo E 151 A4
Cantalgallo E 161 A3
Cantalice I 169 A2
Cantalpino E 150 A2

Cantalupo in Sabina I 168 A2
Cantanhede P 148 B1
Cantavieja E 153 B3
Čantavir SRB 126 B1
Canterbury GB 45 B5
Cantiano I 136 B1
Cantillana E 162 A2
Cantiveros E 150 B3
Cantoria E 164 B2
Cantù I 120 B2
Canvey GB 45 B4
Cany-Barville F 89 A4
Canyet de Mar E 147 C3
Caol GB 34 B2
Cáorle I 122 B1
Caorso I 120 B2
Capáccio I 172 B1
Capaci I 176 A2
Capálbio I 168 A1
Capánnori I 134 B3
Caparde BIH 139 A4
Caparroso E 144 B2
Capbreton F 128 C1
Capdenac-Gare F 116 C2
Capdepera E 167 B3
Cap-de-Pin F 128 B2
Capel Curig GB 38 A3
Capellades E 147 C2
Capena I 168 A2
Capendu F 146 A3
Capestang F 130 B2
Capestrano I 169 A3
Cap Ferret F 128 B1
Capileira E 163 B4
Capinha P 148 B2
Ca'Pisani I 122 C1
Capistrello I 169 B3
Capizzi I 177 B3
Čaplje BIH 124 C2
Čapljina BIH 139 B3
Capo di Ponte I 120 A3
Caposile I 122 B1
Capoterra I 179 C2
Cappamore IRL 29 B3
Cappeln D 71 B5
Cappoquin IRL 29 B4
Capracotta I 169 B4
Capránica I 168 A2
Caprarola I 168 A2
Capretta I 135 C5
Capri I 170 C2
Capriati a Volturno I 170 B2
Caprino Veronese I 121 B3
Captieux F 128 B2
Cápua I 170 B2
Capurso I 173 A2
Capvern F 145 A4
Carabaña E 151 B4
Carabias E 151 A4
Caracal RO 17 C6
Caracenilla E 152 B1
Caráglio I 133 A3
Caraman F 146 A2
Caramánico Terme I 169 A4
Caranga E 141 A4
Caranguejeira P 154 B2
Caransebeş RO 16 C5
Carantec F 100 A2
Carapelle I 171 B3
Carasco I 134 A2
Carate Brianza I 120 B2
Caravaca de la Cruz E 164 A3
Caravággio I 120 B2
Carbajal E 163 B3
Carbajo E 155 B3
Carballeda E 140 B3
Carballeda de Avia E 140 B2
Carballo E 140 A2
Carbis Bay GB 42 B1
Carbon-Blanc F 128 B2
Carbonera de Frentes E 143 C4
Carboneras E 164 C3
Carboneras de Guadazaón E 158 B2
Carbonero el Mayor E 151 A3
Carboneros E 157 B4
Carbónia I 179 C2
Carbonin I 108 C3
Carbonne F 146 A2
Carbost
Highland GB 31 B2
Highland GB 31 B2
Carcaboso E 149 B3
Carcabuey E 163 A3
Carcaixent E 159 B3
Carcans F 128 A1
Carcans-Plage F 128 A1
Carção P 149 A3
Carcar E 144 B2
Cárcare I 133 A4
Carcassonne F 146 A3
Carcastillo E 144 B2
Carcedo de Burgos E 143 B3
Carcelén E 159 B2
Carcès F 132 B2
Carchelejo E 163 A4
Çardak
Çanakkale TR 186 B1
Denizli TR 189 B4
Cardedeu E 147 C3
Cardeña E 157 B3
Cardenete E 158 B2
Cardeñosa E 150 B3
Cardeto I 175 C1
Cardiff GB 39 C3
Cardigan GB 39 B2
Cardona E 147 C2
Cardosos P 154 B2
Carei RO 16 B5
Carentan F 88 A2
Carentoir F 101 B3
Careri I 175 C2
Carevdar HR 124 A2
Cargèse F 180 A1
Carhaix-Plouguer F 100 A2
Caria P 148 B2
Cariati I 174 B2
Carignan F 91 B5
Carignano I 119 C4
Cariñena E 152 A2
Carini I 176 A2
Cariño E 140 A3
Carínola I 170 B1
Carisbrooke GB 44 C2
Carlabhagh GB 31 A2
Carlepont F 90 B3
Carlet E 159 B3
Carlingford IRL 27 B4
Carlisle GB 36 B4
Carloforte I 179 C2
Carlópoli I 175 B2
Carlow
D 65 C3
I RL 30 B2
Carlton GB 40 C2
Carluke GB 35 C4
Carmagnola I 119 C4
Carmarthen GB 39 C2
Carmaux F 130 A1
Carmena E 150 C3
Cármenes E 142 B1
Carmine I 133 A3
Carmona E 162 A2
Carmonita E 155 B4
Carmyllie GB 35 B5
Carnac F 100 B2
Carndonagh IRL 27 A3
Carnew IRL 30 B2
Carnforth GB 37 B4
Cárnia I 122 A2
Carnlough GB 27 B5
Carno GB 39 B3
Carnon Plage F 131 B2
Carnota E 140 B1
Carnoustie GB 35 B5
Carnwath GB 35 C4
Carolei I 174 B2
Carolinensiel D 71 A4
Carolles F 88 B2
Carona I 120 A2
Caronía I 177 A3
Carovigno I 173 B3
Carovilli I 170 B2
Carpaneto Piacentino I 120 C2
Carpegna I 135 B5
Carpenédolo I 121 B3
Carpentras F 131 A4
Carpi I 121 C3
Carpignano Sésia I 119 B5
Carpineti I 134 A3
Carpineto Romano I 169 B3
Cărpiniş RO 126 B2
Carpino I 171 B3
Carpinone I 170 B2
Carpio E 150 A2
Carquefou F 101 B4
Carqueiranne F 132 B2
Carral E 140 A2
Carranque E 151 B4
Carrapichana P 148 B2
Carrara I 134 A3
Carraroe IRL 28 A2
Carrascalejo E 156 A2
Carrascosa del Campo E 151 B5
Carratraca E 162 B3
Carrazeda de Ansiães P 148 A2
Carrazedo de Montenegro P 148 A2
Carrbridge GB 32 D3
Carregal do Sal P 148 B1
Carreña E 142 A2
Carrick IRL 26 B2
Carrickart IRL 26 A3
Carrickfergus GB 27 B5
Carrickmacross IRL 27 C4
Carrick-on-Shannon IRL 26 C2
Carrick-on-Suir IRL 30 B1
Carrigallen IRL 27 C3
Carrión E 161 B3
Carrión de Calatrava E 157 A4
Carrión de los Condes E 142 B2
Carrizo de la Ribera E 141 B5
Carrizosa E 157 B5
Carro F 131 B4
Carrocera E 142 B1
Carros F 133 B3
Carrouge CH 106 C1
Carrouges F 89 B3
Carrù I 133 A3
Carryduff GB 27 B5
Carry-le-Rouet F 131 B4
Carsóli I 169 A3
Carsphairn GB 36 A2
Cartagena E 165 B4
Cártama E 163 B3
Cartaxo P 154 B2
Cartaya E 161 B2
Carteret F 88 A2
Cartes E 142 A2
Carúnchio I 170 B2
Carviçães P 149 A3
Carvin F 78 B2
Carvoeira P 154 B1
Carvoeiro P 160 B1
Casabermeja E 163 B3
Casa Branca
Portalegre P 154 C3
Setúbal P 154 C2
Casacalenda I 170 B2
Casa Castalda I 136 B1
Casaio E 141 B4
Casa l'Abate I 173 B4
Casalarreina E 143 B4
Casalbordino I 169 A4
Casalborgone I 119 B4
Casalbuono I 174 A1
Casalbuttano ed Uniti I 120 B2
Casàl di Principe I 170 B2
Casalécchio di Reno I 135 A4
Casale Monferrato I 119 B5
Casalina I 136 C1
Casalmaggiore I 121 C3
Casalnuovo Monterotaro I 170 B3
Casaloldo I 121 B3
Casalpusterlengo I 120 B2
Casamássima I 173 B2
Casamicciola Terme I 170 C1
Casamozza F 180 A2
Casarabonela E 162 B3
Casarano I 173 B4
Casar de Cáceres E 155 B4
Casar de Palomero E 149 B3
Casarejos E 143 C3
Casares E 162 B2
Casares de las Hurdes E 149 B3
Casariche E 163 A3
Casarrubios del Monte E 151 B3
Casas de Don Pedro E 156 A2
Casas de Fernando Alonso E 158 B1
Casas de Haro E 158 B1
Casas de Juan Gil E 159 B2
Casas del Juan Núñez E 158 B2
Casas del Puerto E 159 C2
Casas del Rio E 159 B2
Casas de Millán E 155 B4
Casas de Reina E 156 B2
Casas de Ves E 159 B2
Casas-Ibáñez E 158 B2
Casasimarro E 158 B1
Casas Nuevas E 164 B3
Casasola E 150 B3
Casasola de Arión E 150 A2
Casasuertes E 142 A2
Casatejada E 150 C2
Casavieja E 150 B3
Casazza I 120 B2
Cascais P 154 C1
Cascante E 144 C2
Cascante del Rio E 152 B2
Cáscia I 169 A3
Casciana Terme I 134 B3
Cáscina I 134 B3
Cáseda E 144 B2
Casekow D 74 A3
Casella I 134 A2
Caselle Torinese I 119 B4
Casemurate I 135 A5
Casenove I 136 C1
Caseres E 153 A4
Caserío Benali E 159 B3
Caserta I 170 B2
Casével P 160 B1
Cashel IRL 29 B4
Casillas E 150 B3
Casillas de Coria E 155 B4
Casina I 134 A3
Casinos E 159 B3
Čáslav CZ 97 B3
Cásola Valsénio I 135 A4
Cásole d'Elsa I 135 B4
Cásoli I 169 A4
Casória I 170 C2
Caspe E 153 A3
Cassàde la Selva E 147 C3
Cassagnas F 130 A2
Cassagnes-Bégonhès F 130 A1
Cassano allo Iónio I 174 B2
Cassano d'Adda I 120 B2
Cassano delle Murge I 171 C4
Cassano Magnago I 120 B1
Cassano Spinola I 120 C1
Cassel F 78 B2
Cassíbile I 177 C4
Cassine I 119 C5
Cassino I 169 B3
Cassis F 132 B1
Cassolnovo I 120 B1
Cassuéjouls F 116 C2
Častá SK 98 C1
Castagnaro I 121 B4
Castagneto Carducci I 134 B3
Castagnola CH 120 A1
Castalla E 159 C3
Castañar de Ibor E 156 A2
Castanheira de Pêra P 154 A2
Cástano Primo I 120 B1
Castasegna CH 120 A2
Castéggio I 120 B2
Casteição P 148 B2
Castejón E 144 B2
Castejón de Monegros E 153 A3
Castejón de Sos E 145 B4
Castejón de Valdejasa E 144 C3
Castèl Baronia I 172 A1
Castel Bolognese I 135 A4
Castelbuono I 177 B3
Casteldáccia I 176 A2
Castel d'Aiano I 135 A3
Castel d'Ario I 121 B3
Castel de Cabra E 153 B3
Casteldelfino I 132 A3
Castél del Monte I 169 A3
Castel del Piano I 135 C4
Castel di Iúdica I 177 B3
Castel di Rio I 135 A4
Castèl di Sangro I 169 B4
Castél di Tora I 169 A2
Castelfidardo I 136 B2
Castelfiorentino I 135 B3
Castelforte I 169 B3
Castelfranco Emília I 121 C4
Castelfranco in Miscano I 170 B3
Castelfranco Véneto I 121 B4
Castèl Frentano I 169 A4
Casteljaloux F 128 B3
Castellabate I 170 C2
Castellammare del Golfo I 176 A1
Castellammare di Stábia I 170 C2
Castellamonte I 119 B4
Castellana Grotte I 173 B3
Castellane F 132 B2
Castellaneta I 173 B2
Castellaneta Marina I 173 B2
Castellar E 157 B4
Castellarano I 135 A3
Castellar de la Frontera E 162 B2
Castellar de la Ribera E 147 B2
Castellar del Vallés E 147 C3
Castellar de Santiago E 157 B4
Castell Arquato I 120 C2
Castell'Azzara I 135 C4
Castellbell i Villar E 147 C2
Castelldans E 153 A4
Castell de Cabres E 153 B4
Castell de Castells E 159 C3
Castelldefels E 147 C2
Castell de Ferro E 163 B4
Castelleone I 120 B2
Castellet E 147 C2
Castelletto di Brenzone I 121 B3
Castellfollit de la Roca E 147 B3
Castellfollit de Riubregos E 147 C2
Castellfort E 153 B3
Castellina in Chianti I 135 B4
Castellina Marittima I 134 B3
Castellóde Farfaña E 145 C4
Castellóde la Plana E 159 B3
Castello d'Empùries E 147 B4
Castello di Fiemme I 121 A4
Castelloli E 147 C2
Castellón de Rugat E 159 C3
Castellote E 153 B3
Castello Tesino I 121 A4
Castellterçol E 147 C3
Castellúcchio I 121 B3
Castellúccio de'Sáuri I 171 B3
Castelluccio Inferiore I 174 B1
Castelmassa I 121 B4
Castelmáuro I 170 B2
Castelmoron-sur-Lot F 129 B3
Castelnaudary F 146 A2
Castelnau-de-Médoc F 128 A2
Castelnau-de-Montmirail F 129 C4
Castelnau-Magnoac F 145 A4
Castelnau-Montratier F 129 B4
Castelnou E 153 A3
Castelnovo ne'Monti I 134 A3
Castelnuovo Berardenga I 135 B4
Castelnuovo della Dáunia I 170 B3
Castelnuovo di Garfagnana I 134 A3
Castelnuovo di Val di Cécina I 135 B3
Castelnuovo Don Bosco I 119 B4
Castelnuovo Scrivia I 120 C1
Castelo Branco
Bragança P 149 A3
Castelo Branco P 155 B3
Castelo de Paiva P 148 A1
Castelo de Vide P 155 B3
Castelo do Neiva P 148 A1
Castelo Mendo P 149 B3
Castelraimondo I 136 B2
Castel San Gimignano I 135 B4
Castèl San Giovanni I 120 B2
Castèl San Pietro Terme I 135 A4
Castelsantángelo I 136 C2
Castél Sant'Elia I 168 A2
Castelsaraceno I 174 A1
Castelsardo I 178 B2
Castelsarrasin F 129 B4
Castelserás E 153 B3
Casteltérmini I 176 B2
Castelvecchio Subéquo I 169 A3
Castelvetrano I 176 B1
Castél Volturno I 170 B1
Castenédolo I 120 B3
Castets F 128 C1
Castiádas I 179 C3
Castiglioncello I 134 B3
Castiglione I 169 A3
Castiglione Chiavarese I 134 A2
Castiglione d'Adda I 120 B2
Castiglione dei Pepoli I 135 A4
Castiglione del Lago I 135 B5
Castiglione della Pescáia I 135 C3
Castiglione delle Stiviere I 121 B3
Castiglione di Sicília I 177 B4
Castiglione d'Órcia I 135 B4
Castiglione Messer Marino I 170 B2
Castiglione Messer Raimondo I 169 A3
Castiglion Fibocchi I 135 B4
Castiglion Fiorentino I 135 B4
Castilblanco E 156 A2
Castilblanco de los Arroyos E 161 B4
Castil de Peones E 143 B3
Castilfrío de la Sierra E 144 C1
Castilgaleu E 145 B4
Castilisar E 144 B2
Castilleja E 161 B3
Castillejar E 164 B2
Castillejo de Martin Viejo E 149 B3
Castillejo de Mesleón E 151 A4
Castillejo de Robledo E 151 A4
Castillo de Bayuela E 150 B3
Castillo de Locubín E 163 A4
Castillonès F 129 B3
Castillon-la-Bataille F 128 B2
Castillon-Len-Couserans F 146 B2
Castillonroy E 145 C4
Castilruiz E 144 C1
Castione CH 120 A2
Castions di Strada I 122 B2
Castirla F 180 A2
Castlebar IRL 28 A2
Castlebellingham IRL 27 C4
Castleblaney IRL 27 B4
Castlebridge IRL 30 B2
Castle Cary GB 43 A4
Castlecomer IRL 30 B1
Castlederg GB 27 B3
Castledermot IRL 30 B2
Castle Douglas GB 36 B3
Castleford GB 40 B2
Castleisland IRL 29 B2
Castlemaine IRL 29 B2
Castlemartyr IRL 29 C3
Castlepollard IRL 30 A1
Castlerea IRL 28 A3
Castleton GB 40 B2
Castletown
Highland GB 32 C3
I sle of Man GB 36 B2
Castletown Bearhaven IRL 29 C2
Castletownroche IRL 29 B3
Castlewellan GB 27 B5
Casto I 120 B3
Castrejón E 150 A2
Castrelo del Valle E 141 B3
Castres F 130 B1
Castricum NL 70 B1
Castries F 131 B2
Castrignano del Capo I 173 C4
Castril E 164 B2
Castrillo de Duero E 151 A4
Castrillo de la Vega E 143 C3
Castrillo de Onielo E 142 C2
Castro
E 142 A2
I 173 B4
Castrocabón E 141 B5
Castro-Caldelas E 141 B3
Castrocaro Terme I 135 A4
Castrocontrigo E 141 B4
Castro Daire P 148 B2
Castro dei Volsci I 169 B3
Castro del Río E 163 A3
Castro de Rey E 141 A3
Castrofilippo I 176 B2
Castrogonzaio E 142 B1
Castrojeriz E 142 B2
Castro Laboreiro P 140 B2
Castro Marim P 160 B2
Castromonte E 142 C1
Castromudarra E 142 B1
Castronuevo E 142 C1
Castronuño E 150 A2
Castropol E 141 A3
Castroreale I 177 A4
Castroserracin E 151 A4
Castro-Urdiales E 143 A3
Castroverde E 141 A3
Castro Verde P 160 B1
Castroverde de Campos E 142 C1
Castroverde de Cerrato E 142 C2
Castrovíllari I 174 B2
Castuera E 156 B2
Catadau E 159 B3
Cataéggio I 120 A2
Çatalca TR 186 A3
Catallar TR 189 C5
Çatalzeytin TR 23 A8
Catánia I 177 B4
Catanzaro I 175 C2
Catanzaro Marina I 175 C2
Catarroja E 159 B3
Catarruchos P 148 B1
Catcleugh GB 37 A4
Catenanuova I 177 B3
Caterham GB 44 B3
Cati E 153 B4
Čatići BIH 139 A4
Catignano I 169 A3
Catillon F 91 A3
Catoira E 140 B2
Caton GB 37 B4
Catral E 165 A4
Catterick GB 37 B5
Cattólica I 136 B1
Cattólica Eraclea I 176 B2
Catton GB 37 B4
Caudebec-en-Caux F 89 A4
Caudete E 159 C3
Caudete de las Fuentes E 159 B2
Caudiel E 159 B3
Caudiès-de-Fenouillèdes F 146 B3
Caudry F 91 A3
Caulkerbush GB 36 B3
Caulnes F 101 A3
Caulónia I 175 C2
Caumont-l'Evente F 88 A3
Caunes-Minervois F 146 A3
Cauro F 180 B1
Caussade F 129 B4

Causse-de-la-Selle F 130 B2
Cauterets F 145 B3
Cava de Tirreni I 170 C2
Cavaglia I 119 B5
Cavaillon F 131 B4
Cavalaire-sur-Mer F 132 B2
Cavaleiro P 160 B1
Cavalese I 121 A4
Cavallermaggiore I 119 C4
Cavallino I 122 B1
Cavan IRL 27 C3
Cavárzere I 121 B5
Çavdarhisar TR 187 C4
Çavdır TR 189 B4
Cavernães P 148 B2
Cavezzo I 121 C4
Cavignac F 128 A2
Čavle HR 123 B3
Cavo I 134 C3
Cavour I 119 C4
Cawdor GB 32 D3
Çay TR 187 D6
Çaycuma TR 187 A7
Cayeux-sur-Mer F 78 B1
Cayiralan TR 23 B8
Çayırhan TR 187 B6
Caylus F 129 B4
Cayres F 117 C3
Cazalilla E 157 C4
Cazalla de la Sierra E 156 C2
Cazals F 129 B4
Cazanuecos E 142 B1
Cazaubon F 128 C2
Cazaux F 128 B1
Cazavet F 146 A2
Cazères F 146 A2
Cazin BIH 124 C1
Cazis CH 107 C4
Čazma HR 124 B2
Cazo E 142 A1
Cazorla E 164 B2
Cazouls-lès-Béziers F 130 B2
Cea
- *León* E 142 B1
- *Orense* E 140 B3
Ceánuri E 143 A4
Ceauce F 88 B3
Cebolla E 150 C3
Čebovce SK 112 A3
Cebreros E 150 B3
Čečava BIH 125 C3
Ceccano I 169 B3
Cece H 112 C2
Cecenowo PL 68 A2
Čechtice CZ 96 B3
Čechtin CZ 97 B3
Cécina I 134 B3
Ceclavín E 155 B4
Cedégolo I 120 A3
Cedeira E 140 A2
Cedillo E 155 B3
Cedillo del Condado E 151 B4
Cedrillas E 153 B3
Cedynia PL 74 B3
Cée E 140 B1
Cefalù I 177 A3
Céggia I 122 B1
Cegléd H 113 B3
Ceglédbercel H 112 B3
Céglie Messápica I 173 B3
Cehegín E 164 A3
Ceilhes-et-Rocozels F 130 B2
Ceinos de Campos E 142 B1
Ceira P 148 B1
Čejč CZ 97 C4
Cekcyn PL 76 A3
Cela BIH 124 C2
Čelákovice CZ 84 B2
Celano I 169 A3
Celanova E 140 B3
Celbridge IRL 30 A2
Čelebič BIH 138 B2
Celenza Valfortore I 170 B2
Čelić BIH 125 C4
Čelinac BIH 124 C3
Celje SLO 123 A4
Cella E 152 B2
Celldömölk H 111 B4
Celle D 72 B3
Celle Ligure I 133 A4
Celles B 79 B4
Celles-sur-Belle F 115 B3
Cellino San Marco I 173 B3
Celorico da Beira P 148 B2
Celorico de Basto P 148 A1
Çeltik TR 187 C6
Çeltikçi TR 189 B5
Cemaes GB 38 A2
Cembra I 121 A4
Čemerno BIH 139 B4
Cenad RO 126 A2
Cencenighe Agordino I 121 A4
Cenei RO 126 B2
Ceneselli I 121 B4
Cenicero E 143 B4
Cenicientos E 150 B3
Censeau F 105 C5
Čenta SRB 126 B2
Centallo I 133 A3
Centelles E 147 C3
Cento I 121 C4
Centúripe I 177 B3
Cepeda la Mora E 150 B2
Cépet F 129 C4
Čepin HR 125 B4
Čepinski Martinci HR 125 B4
Cepovan SLO 122 A2
Ceprano I 169 B3
Čeralije HR 125 B3
Cerami I 177 B3
Cerano I 120 B1
Cérans Foulletourte F 102 B2
Ceraso I 172 B1
Cerbaia I 135 B4
Cerbère F 146 B4
Cercadillo E 151 A5
Cercal
- *Lisboa* P 154 B1
- *Setúbal* P 160 B1
Čerčany CZ 96 B2
Cerceda E 151 B4
Cercedilla E 151 B3
Cercemaggiore I 170 B2
Cercs E 147 B2
Cercy-la-Tour F 104 C2
Cerda I 176 B2
Cerdedo E 140 B2
Cerdeira P 149 B2
Cerdon F 103 B4
Cerea I 121 B4
Ceres
- GB 35 B5
- I 119 B4
Cerese I 121 B3
Ceresole-Reale I 119 B4
Cereste F 132 B1
Céret F 146 B3
Cerezo de Abajo E 151 A4
Cerezo de Riotirón E 143 B3
Cerfontaine B 79 B4
Cergy F 90 B2
Cerignola I 171 B3
Cérilly F 103 C4
Cerisiers F 104 A2
Cerizay F 114 B3
Çerkeş TR 23 A7
Çerkezköy TR 186 A3
Cerkije SLO 123 A3
Cerknica SLO 123 B3
Cerkno SLO 122 A2
Cerkwica PL 67 B4
Cerna HR 125 B4
Černá Hora CZ 97 B4
Cernavodă RO 17 C8
Cernay F 106 B2
Cerne Abbas GB 43 B4
Cernégula E 143 B3
Cernik HR 124 B3
Cernóbbio I 120 B2
Černošin CZ 95 B4
Cernovice CZ 96 B2
Cérons F 128 B2
Cerovlje HR 123 B3
Cerovo SK 99 C3
Cerqueto I 135 C5
Cerralbo E 149 B3
Cerreto d'Esi I 136 B1
Cerreto Sannita I 170 B2
Cerrigydrudion GB 38 A3
Cërrik AL 182 B1
Cerro Muriano E 156 B3
Certaldo I 135 B4
Certosa di Pésio I 133 A3
Cerva P 148 A2
Cervaro I 169 B3
Cervatos de la Cueza E 142 B2
Červena Řečice CZ 97 B3
Červená-Skala SK 99 C4
Cervená Voda CZ 97 A4
Cerveny Kostelec CZ 85 B4
Cervera E 147 C2
Cervera de la Cañada E 152 A2
Cervera del Llano E 158 B1
Cervera del Río Alhama E 144 B2
Cervera de Pisuerga E 142 B2
Cervéteri I 168 B2
Cérvia I 135 A5
Cerviáde les Garriques E 147 C1
Cervignano del Friuli I 122 B2
Cervinara I 170 B2
Cervione F 180 A2
Cervo E 141 A3
Cervon F 104 B2
Cesana Torinese I 119 C3
Cesarica HR 137 A4
Cesarò I 177 B3
Cesena I 135 A5
Cesenático I 135 A5
Cēsis LV 8 D4
Česká Belá CZ 97 B3
Česká Kamenice CZ 84 B2
Česká Lípa CZ 84 B2
Česká Skalice CZ 85 B4
Česká Třebová CZ 97 B4
České Budějovice CZ 96 C2
České Velenice CZ 96 C2
Český Brod CZ 96 A2
Český Dub CZ 84 B2
Český Krumlov CZ 96 C2
Český Těšin CZ 98 B2
Češljeva Bara SRB 127 C3
Çeşme TR 188 A1
Cessenon F 130 B2
Cesson-Sévigné F 101 A4
Cestas F 128 B2
Čestobrodica SRB 127 D2
Cesuras E 140 A2
Cetina E 152 A2
Cetin Grad HR 123 B4
Cetinje MNE 16 D3
Cetraro I 174 B1
Ceuti E 165 A3
Ceva I 133 A4
Cevico de la Torre E 142 C2
Cevico Navero E 142 C2
Cevins F 118 B3
Cévio CH 119 A5
Cevizli TR 189 B6
Cewice PL 68 A2
Ceylan TR 189 C4
Ceyrat F 116 B3
Ceyzériat F 118 A2
Chaam NL 79 A4
Chabanais F 115 C4
Chabeuil F 117 C5
Chabielice PL 86 A3
Chablis F 104 B2
Châbons F 118 B2
Chabówka PL 99 B3
Chabreloche F 117 B3
Chabris F 103 B3
Chagford GB 42 B3
Chagny F 105 C3
Chagoda RUS 9 C9
Chaherrero E 150 B3
Chailland F 88 B3
Chaillé-les-Marais F 114 B2
Chailles F 103 B3
Chailley F 104 A2
Chalabre F 146 B3
Chalais F 128 A3
Chalamont F 118 B2
Châlette-sur-Loing F 103 A4
Chalindrey F 105 B4
Challacombe GB 42 A3
Challans F 114 B2
Challes-les-Eaux F 118 B2
Chalmazel F 117 B3
Chalmoux F 104 C2
Chalonnes-sur-Loire F 102 B1
Châlons-en-Champagne F 91 C4
Chalon-sur-Saône F 105 C3
Chalupy PL 69 A3
Châlus F 115 C4
Cham
- CH 106 B3
- D 95 B4
Chamberet F 116 B1
Chambéry F 118 B2
Chambilly F 117 A4
Chambley F 92 B1
Chambly F 90 B2
Chambois F 89 B4
Chambon-sur-Lac F 116 B2
Chambon-sur-Voueize F 116 A2
Chambord F 103 B3
Chamborigaud F 131 A2
Chamboulive F 116 B1
Chamerau D 95 B4
Chamonix-Mont Blanc F 119 B3
Chamoux-sur-Gelon F 118 B3
Champagnac-le-Vieux F 117 B3
Champagney F 106 B1
Champagnole F 105 C4
Champagny-Mouton F 115 B4
Champaubert F 91 C3
Champdeniers-St Denis F 114 B3
Champdieu F 117 B4
Champdôtre F 105 B4
Champeix F 116 B3
Champéry CH 119 A3
Champigne F 102 B1
Champignelles F 104 B2
Champigny-sur-Veude F 102 B2
Champlitte-et-le-Prelot F 105 B4
Champoluc I 119 B4
Champoly F 117 B3
Champorcher I 119 B4
Champrond-en-Gâtine F 89 B5
Champs-sur-Tarentaine F 116 B2
Champs-sur-Yonne F 104 B2
Champtoceaux F 101 B4
Chamrousse F 118 B2
Chamusca P 154 B2
Chanac F 130 A2
Chanaleilles F 117 C3
Chandler's Ford GB 44 C2
Chandra GR 185 D7
Chandrexa de Queixa E 141 B3
Chañe E 150 A3
Changy F 117 A3
Chania GR 185 D5
Channes F 104 B3
Chantada E 140 B3
Chantelle F 116 A3
Chantenay-St Imbert F 104 C2
Chanteuges F 117 B3
Chantilly F 90 B2
Chantonnay F 114 B2
Chão de Codes P 154 B2
Chaource F 104 A3
Chapa E 140 B2
Chapareillan F 118 B2
Chapel en le Frith GB 40 B2
Chapelle Royale F 103 A3
Chapelle-St Laurent F 102 C1
Charbonnat F 104 C3
Chard GB 43 B4
Charenton-du-Cher F 103 C4
Charlbury GB 44 B2
Charleroi B 79 B4
Charlestown
- GB 42 B2
- IRL 26 C2
Charlestown of Aberlour GB 32 D3
Charleville IRL 29 B3
Charleville-Mézières F 91 B4
Charlieu F 117 A4
Charlottenberg S 49 C4
Charlton Kings GB 44 B1
Charly F 90 C3
Charmes F 92 C2
Charmes-sur-Rhône F 117 C4
Charmey CH 106 C2
Charminster GB 43 B4
Charmont-en-Beauce F 103 A4
Charny F 104 B2
Charolles F 117 A4
Chârost F 103 C4
Charquemont F 106 B1
Charrin F 104 C2
Charroux F 115 B4
Chartres F 90 C1
Charzykow PL 68 B2
Chasseneuil-sur-Bonnieure F 115 C4
Chassigny F 105 B4
Château-Arnoux F 132 A2
Châteaubernard F 115 C3
Châteaubourg F 101 A4
Châteaubriant F 101 B4
Château-Chinon F 104 B2
Château-d'Oex CH 106 C2
Château-d'Olonne F 114 B2
Château-du-Loir F 102 B2
Châteaudun F 103 A3
Châteaugiron F 101 A4
Château-Gontier F 102 B1
Château-Landon F 103 A4
Château-la-Vallière F 102 B2
Château-l'Evêque F 129 A3
Châteaulin F 100 A1
Châteaumeillant F 103 C4
Châteauneuf
- *Nièvre* F 104 B2
- *Saône-et-Loire* F 117 A4
Châteauneuf-de-Randon F 117 C3
Châteauneuf-d'Ille-et-Vilaine F 88 B2
Châteauneuf-du-Faou F 100 A2
Châteauneuf-du-Pape F 131 A3
Châteauneuf-en-Thymerais F 89 B5
Châteauneuf la-Forêt F 116 B1
Châteauneuf-le-Rouge F 132 B1
Châteauneuf-sur-Charente F 115 C3
Châteauneuf-sur-Cher F 103 C4
Châteauneuf-sur-Loire F 103 B4
Châteauneuf-sur-Sarthe F 102 B1
Châteauponsac F 115 B5
Château-Porcien F 91 B4
Châteauredon F 132 A2
Châteaurenard
- *Bouches du Rhône* F 131 B3
- *Loiret* F 104 B1
Château-Renault F 102 B2
Châteauroux F 103 C3
Châteauroux-les-Alpes F 118 C3
Château-Salins F 92 C2
Château-Thierry F 91 B3
Châteauvillain F 105 A3
Châtel F 119 A3
Châtelaillon-Plage F 114 B2
Châtelaudren F 100 A3
Châtel-Censoir F 104 B2
Châtel-de-Neuvre F 116 A3
Châtelet B 79 B4
Châtelguyon F 116 B3
Châtellerault F 115 B4
Châtel-Montagne F 117 A3
Châtel-St Denis CH 106 C1
Châtel-sur-Moselle F 92 C2
Châtelus-Malvaleix F 116 A2
Châtenois F 105 A4
Châtenois-les-Forges F 106 B1
Chatham GB 45 B4
Châtillon I 119 B4
Châtillon-Coligny F 103 B4
Châtillon-en-Bazois F 104 B2
Châtillon-en-Diois F 118 C2
Châtillon-sur Chalaronne F 117 A4
Châtillon-sur-Indre F 103 C3
Châtillon-sur-Loire F 103 B4
Châtillon-sur-Marne F 91 B3
Châtillon-sur-Seine F 104 B3
Châtres F 91 C3
Chatteris GB 45 A4
Chatton GB 37 A5
Chauchina E 163 A4
Chaudes-Aigues F 116 C3
Chaudrey F 91 C4
Chauffailles F 117 A4
Chaulnes F 90 B2
Chaument Gistoux B 79 B4
Chaumergy F 105 C4
Chaumont F 105 A4
Chaumont-en-Vexin F 90 B1
Chaumont-Porcien F 91 B4
Chaumont-sur-Aire F 91 C5
Chaumont-sur-Loire F 103 B3
Chaunay F 115 B4
Chauny F 90 B3
Chaussin F 105 C4
Chauvigny F 115 B4
Chavagnes-en-Paillers F 114 B2
Chavanges F 91 C4
Chaves P 148 A2
Chavignon F 91 B3
Chazelles-sur-Lyon F 117 B4
Chazey-Bons F 118 B2
Cheadle
- *Greater Manchester* GB 40 B1
- *Staffordshire* GB 40 C2
Cheb CZ 83 B4
Chebsara RUS 9 C11
Checa E 152 B2
Chęciny PL 87 B4
Cheddar GB 43 A4
Cheddleton GB 40 B1
Chef-Boutonne F 115 B3
Cheles E 155 C3
Chella E 159 B3
Chelles F 90 C2
Chełm PL 13 C5
Chełmno
- *Kujawsko-Pomorskie* PL 76 A3
- *Wielkopolskie* PL 76 B3
Chelmsford GB 45 B4
Chelmuzhi RUS 9 A9
Chełmża PL 76 A3
Cheltenham GB 44 B1
Chelva E 159 B2
Chémery F 103 B3
Chemery-sur-Bar F 91 B4
Chemillé F 102 B1
Chemin F 105 C4
Chemnitz D 83 B4
Chénerailles F 116 A2
Cheniménil F 105 A5
Chenonceaux F 103 B3
Chenôve F 105 B3
Chepelare BG 183 B6
Chepstow GB 39 C4
Chera E 159 B3
Cherasco I 119 C4
Cherbonnières F 115 C3
Cherbourg F 88 A2
Cherchiara di Calábria I 174 B2
Cherepovets RUS 9 C10
Chernihiv UA 13 C9
Chernivtsi UA 17 A6
Chernobyl = Chornobyl UA 13 C9
Chernyakhovsk RUS 12 A4
Chéroy F 104 A1
Cherven BY 13 B8
Chervonohrad UA 13 C6
Cherykaw BY 13 B9
Chesham GB 44 B3
Cheshunt GB 44 B3
Chessy-lès-Pres F 104 A2
Cheste E 159 B3
Chester GB 38 A4
Chesterfield GB 40 B2
Chester-le-Street GB 37 B5
Chevagnes F 104 C2
Chevanceaux F 115 C3
Chevillon F 91 C5
Chevilly F 103 A3
Chew Magna GB 43 A4
Chézery-Forens F 118 A2
Chialamberto I 119 B4
Chiampo I 121 B4
Chianale I 119 C4
Chianciano Terme I 135 B4
Chiaramonte Gulfi I 177 B3
Chiaramonti I 178 B2
Chiaravalle I 136 B2
Chiaravalle Centrale I 175 C2
Chiaréggio I 120 A2
Chiari I 120 B2
Chiaromonte I 174 A2
Chiasso CH 120 B2
Chiávari I 134 A2
Chiavenna I 120 A2
Chiché F 102 C1
Chichester GB 44 C3
Chiclana de la Frontera E 162 B1
Chiclana de Segura E 164 A1
Chiddingfold GB 44 B3
Chieri I 119 B4
Chiesa in Valmalenco I 120 A2
Chieti I 169 A4
Chieti Scalo I 169 A4
Chiéuti I 171 B3
Chigwell GB 45 B4
Chiliomodi GR 184 B3
Chillarón de Cuenca E 152 B1
Chillarón del Rey E 151 B5
Chilleurs-aux-Bois F 103 A4
Chillón E 156 B3
Chilluevar E 164 B1
Chiloeches E 151 B4
Chimay B 91 A4
Chimeneas E 163 A4
Chinchilla de Monte Aragón E 158 C2
Chinchón E 151 B4
Chingford GB 45 B4
Chinon F 102 B2
Chióggia I 122 B1
Chiomonte I 119 B3
Chipiona E 161 C3
Chippenham GB 43 A4
Chipping Campden GB 44 A2
Chipping Norton GB 44 B2
Chipping Ongar GB 45 B4
Chipping Sodbury GB 43 A4
Chirac F 130 A2
Chirbury GB 39 B3
Chirens F 118 B2
Chirivel E 164 B2
Chirk GB 38 B3
Chirnside GB 35 C5
Chişinău = Khisinev MD 17 B8
Chişineu Criş RO 113 C5
Chissey-en-Morvan F 104 B3
Chiusa I 108 C2
Chiusa di Pésio I 133 A3
Chiusaforte I 122 A2
Chiusa Sclàfani I 176 B2
Chiusi I 135 B4
Chiva E 159 B3
Chivasso I 119 B4
Chlewiska PL 87 A4
Chludowo PL 75 B5
Chlumec nad Cidlinou CZ 84 B3
Chlum u Třeboně CZ 96 C2
Chmielnik PL 87 B4
Chobienia PL 85 A4
Chobienice PL 75 B4
Choceň CZ 97 A4
Choceń PL 77 B4
Chochołow PL 99 B3
Chocianów PL 85 A3
Chociw PL 86 A3
Chociwel PL 75 A4

Choczewo PL 68 A2
Chodaków PL 77 B5
Chodecz PL 77 B4
Chodov CZ 83 B4
Chodzież PL 75 B5
Chojna PL 74 B3
Chojnice PL 68 B2
Chojno
Kujawsko-Pomorskie PL 77 B4
Wielkopolskie PL 75 B5
Chojnów PL 85 A3
Cholet F 114 A3
Chomérac F 117 C4
Chomutov CZ 83 B5
Chop UA 12 D5
Chora GR 184 B2
Chora Sfakion GR 185 D5
Chorges F 132 A2
Chorley GB 38 A4
Chornobyl = Chernobyl UA 13 C9
Chortkiv UA 13 D6
Chorzele PL 77 A5
Chorzew PL 86 A2
Chorzów PL 86 B2
Choszczno PL 75 A4
Chotěboř CZ 97 B3
Chouilly F 91 B4
Chouto P 154 B2
Chouzy-sur-Cisse F 103 B3
Chozas de Abajo E 142 B1
Chrast CZ 97 B3
Chrást CZ 96 B1
Chrastava CZ 84 B2
Chřibská CZ 84 B2
Christchurch GB 44 C2
Christiansfeld DK 59 C2
Chroberz PL 87 B4
Chropyně CZ 98 B1
Chrudim CZ 97 B3
Chrzanów PL 86 B3
Chtelnica SK 98 C1
Chudovo RUS 9 C7
Chueca E 157 A4
Chulmleigh GB 42 B3
Chur CH 107 C4
Church Stretton GB 39 B4
Churriana E 163 B3
Churwalden CH 107 C4
Chvalšiny CZ 96 C2
Chwaszczyno PL 69 A3
Chynava CZ 96 A2
Chýnov CZ 96 B2
Ciacova RO 126 B3
Ciadîr-Lunga MD 17 B8
Ciadoncha E 143 B3
Cianciana I 176 B2
Ciano d'Enza I 134 A3
Ciążen PL 76 B2
Cibakhaza H 113 C4
Ciborro P 154 C2
Cicagna I 134 A2
Cicciano I 170 C2
Ciciliano I 169 B2
Cicognolo I 120 B3
Cidadelhe P 149 B2
Cide TR 23 A7
Cidones E 143 C4
Ciechanów
Dolnośląskie PL 85 A4
Mazowieckie PL 77 B5
Ciechocinek PL 76 B3
Cielądz PL 87 A4
Ciemnik PL 75 A4
Ciempozuelos E 151 B4
Ciepielów PL 87 A5
Čierny Balog SK 99 C3
Cierp-Gaud F 145 B4
Cierpice PL 76 B3
Ciervana E 143 A3
Cierznie PL 68 B2
Cieslé PL 77 B5
Cieszyn PL 98 B2
Cieutat F 145 A4
Cieza E 165 A3
Cifer SK 98 C1
Çifteler TR 187 C6
Cifuentes E 151 B5
Cigales E 142 C2
Cigliano I 119 B5
Cihanbeyli TR 23 B7
Cillas E 152 B2
Cilleros E 149 B3
Cilleruelo de Arriba E 143 C3
Cilleruelo de Bezana E 143 B3
Cimalmotto CH 119 A5
Cimanes del Tejar E 141 B5
Ciminna I 176 B2
Cimişlia MD 17 B8
Cimoláis I 122 A1
Cîmpulung RO 17 C6
Çınarcık TR 186 B4
Cinctorres E 153 B3
Cinderford GB 39 C4
Çine TR 188 B3
Činěves CZ 84 B3
Ciney B 79 B5
Cinfães P 148 A1
Cingia de Botti I 120 B3
Cingoli I 136 B2
Cinigiano I 135 C4
Cinobaňa SK 99 C3
Cinq-Mars-la-Pile F 102 B2
Cinquefrondi I 175 C2
Cintegabelle F 146 A2
Cintruénigo E 144 B2
Ciółkowo PL 77 B4
Ciperez E 149 B3
Cirat E 153 B3
Cirella I 174 B1
Cirencester GB 44 B2
Cirey-sur-Vezouze F 92 C2
Ciria E 152 A2
Ciriè I 119 B4
Cirigliano I 174 A2
Cirò I 174 B3
Cirò Marina I 174 B3
Ciry-le-Noble F 104 C3
Cislău RO 17 C7
Cismon del Grappa I 121 B4
Cisneros E 142 B2
Cissac-Médoc F 128 A2
Čista CZ 96 A1
Cisterna di Latina I 169 B2
Cistérniga E 150 A3
Cisternino I 173 B3
Cistierna E 142 B1
Čitluk BIH 139 B3
Cítov CZ 84 B2
Cittadella I 121 B4
Cittàdella Pieve I 135 C5
Cittádel Vaticano = Vatican City I 168 B2
Cittàdi Castello I 135 B5
Cittaducale I 169 A2
Cittanova I 175 C2
Città Sant'Angelo I 169 A4
Ciudadela de Menorca E 167 B3
Ciudad Real E 157 B4
Ciudad Rodrigo E 149 B3
Ciutadilla E 147 C2
Cividale del Friuli I 122 A2
Cívita I 169 A3
Cívita Castellana I 168 A2
Civitanova Alta I 136 B2
Civitanova Marche I 136 B2
Civitavécchia I 168 A1
Civitella di Romagna I 135 A4
Civitella di Tronto I 136 C2
Civitella Roveto I 169 B3
Civray F 115 B4
Çivril TR 189 A4
Cizur Mayor E 144 B2
Clabhach GB 34 B1
Clachan GB 31 B2
Clachan na Luib GB 31 B1
Clacton-on-Sea GB 45 B5
Cladich GB 34 B2
Claggan GB 34 B2
Clairvaux-les-Lacs F 105 C4
Clamecy F 104 B2
Claonaig GB 34 C2
Clarecastle IRL 28 B3
Claregalway IRL 28 A3
Claremorris IRL 28 A2
Clarinbridge IRL 28 A3
Clashmore
GB 32 D2
IRL 29 B4
Claudy GB 27 B3
Clausthal-Zellerfeld D 82 A2
Cláut I 122 A1
Clay Cross GB 40 B2
Claye-Souilly F 90 C2
Cléder F 100 A1
Cleethorpes GB 41 B3
Clefmont F 105 A4
Cléguérec F 100 A2
Clelles F 118 C2
Clenze D 73 B3
Cleobury Mortimer GB 39 B4
Cléon-d'Andran F 117 C4
Cléré-les-Pins F 102 B2
Clères F 89 A5
Clermont F 90 B2
Clermont-en-Argonne F 91 B5
Clermont-Ferrand F 116 B3
Clermont-l'Hérault F 130 B2
Clerval F 105 B5
Clervaux L 92 A2
Cléry-St André F 103 B3
Cles I 121 A4
Clevedon GB 43 A4
Cleveleys GB 38 A3
Cley GB 41 C5
Clifden IRL 28 A1
Clifford GB 39 B3
Clisson F 101 B4
Clitheroe GB 40 B1
Clogh IRL 30 B1
Cloghan
Donegal IRL 26 B3
Offaly IRL 28 A4
Clogheen IRL 29 B4
Clogher GB 27 B3
Cloghjordan IRL 28 B3
Clohars-Carnoët F 100 B2
Clonakilty IRL 29 C3
Clonaslee IRL 30 A1
Clondalkin IRL 30 A2
Clones IRL 27 B3
Clonmany IRL 27 A3
Clonmel IRL 29 B4
Clonmellon IRL 30 A1
Clonord IRL 30 A1
Clonroche IRL 30 B2
Cloone IRL 26 C3
Cloppenburg D 71 B5
Closeburn GB 36 A3
Clough GB 27 B5
Clova GB 35 B4
Clovelly GB 42 B2
Clowne GB 40 B2
Cloyes-sur-le-Loir F 103 B3
Cloyne IRL 29 C3
Cluis F 103 C3
Cluj-Napoca RO 17 B5
Clun GB 39 B3
Clunes GB 34 B3
Cluny F 117 A4
Cluses F 118 A3
Clusone I 120 B2
Clydach GB 39 C3
Clydebank GB 34 C3
Coachford IRL 29 C3
Coagh GB 27 B4
Coalisland GB 27 B4
Coalville GB 40 C2
Coaña E 141 A4
Çobanlar TR 187 D5
Cobas E 140 A2
Cobertelade E 151 A5
Cobeta E 152 B1
Cóbh IRL 29 C3
Cobreces E 142 A2
Coburg D 82 B2
Coca E 150 A3
Cocentaina E 159 C3
Cochem D 80 B3
Cockburnspath GB 35 C5
Cockermouth GB 36 B3
Codigoro I 121 C5
Codogno I 120 B2
Codos E 152 A2
Codróipo I 122 B1
Codrongianos I 178 B2
Coelhoso P 149 A3
Coesfeld D 71 C4
Coevorden NL 71 B3
Cofrentes E 159 B2
Cogeces del Monte E 150 A3
Coggeshall GB 45 B4
Cognac F 115 C3
Cogne I 119 B4
Cognin F 118 B2
Cogolin F 132 B2
Cogollos de Guadix E 164 B1
Cogollos-Vega E 163 A4
Cogolludo E 151 B4
Coimbra P 148 B1
Coín E 163 B3
Coirós E 140 A2
Čoka SRB 126 B2
Col SLO 123 B3
Colares P 154 C1
Cölbe D 81 B4
Colbitz D 73 B4
Colchester GB 45 B4
Coldingham GB 35 C5
Colditz D 83 A4
Coldstream GB 35 C5
Colebrooke GB 43 B3
Colera E 146 B4
Coleraine GB 27 A4
Colfiorito I 136 B1
Cólico I 120 A2
Coligny F 118 A2
Colindres E 143 A3
Collado-Mediano E 151 B3
Collado Villalba E 151 B4
Collagna I 134 A3
Collanzo E 142 A1
Collat F 117 B3
Coll de Nargó E 147 B2
Collécchio I 120 C3
Colledimezzo I 169 B4
Colle di Val d'Elsa I 135 B4
Colleferro I 169 B3
Colle Isarco I 108 C2
Collelongo I 169 B3
Collepasso I 173 B4
Collepepe I 136 C1
Collesalvetti I 134 B3
Colle Sannita I 170 B2
Collesano I 176 B2
Colli a Volturno I 169 B4
Collin GB 36 A3
Collinée F 101 A3
Collingham
Nottinghamshire GB 40 B2
West Yorkshire GB 40 B3
Collinghorst D 71 A4
Cóllio I 120 B3
Collobrières F 132 B2
Collon IRL 27 C4
Collooney IRL 26 B2
Colmar F 106 A2
Colmars F 132 A2
Colmenar E 163 B3
Colmenar de la Sierra E 151 A4
Colmenar de Oreja E 151 B4
Colmenar Viejo E 151 B4
Colmonel GB 36 A2
Colne GB 40 B1
Colobraro I 174 A2
Cologna Véneta I 121 B4
Cologne = Köln D 80 B2
Cologne F 129 C3
Cologne al Serio I 120 B2
Colombey-les-Belles F 92 C1
Colombey-les-deux-Églises F 105 A3
Colombres E 142 A2
Colomera E 163 A4
Colomers E 147 B3
Colomiers F 129 C4
Colònia de Sant Jordi E 167 B3
Colorno I 120 C3
Colos P 160 B1
Cölpin D 74 A2
Colpy GB 33 D4
Colsterworth GB 40 C3
Coltishall GB 41 C5
Colunga E 142 A1
Colwell GB 37 A4
Colwyn Bay GB 38 A3
Colyford GB 43 B3
Comácchio I 121 C5
Coma-ruga E 147 C2
Combarros E 141 B4
Combeaufontaine F 105 B4
Comber GB 27 B5
Comblain-au-Pont B 80 B1
Combloux F 118 B3
Combourg F 88 B2
Combronde F 116 B3
Comeglians I 109 C3
Comillas E 142 A2
Comines F 78 B3
Cómiso I 177 C3
Comloşu Mare RO 126 B2
Commensacq F 128 B2
Commentry F 116 A2
Commerau D 84 A2
Commercy F 92 C1
Como I 120 B2
Cómpeta E 163 B4
Compiègne F 90 B2
Comporta P 154 C2
Comps-sur-Artuby F 132 B2
Comrat MD 17 B8
Comrie GB 35 B4
Comunanza I 136 C2
Cona
Emilia Romagna I 121 C4
Veneto I 121 B5
Concarneau F 100 B2
Conceição P 160 B1
Conches-en-Ouche F 89 B4
Concordia Sagittária I 122 B1
Concordia sulla Sécchia I 121 C3
Concots F 129 B4
Condat F 116 B2
Condé-en-Brie F 91 C3
Condeixa P 148 B1
Condemios de Abajo E 151 A4
Condemios de Arriba E 151 A4
Condé-sur-l'Escaut F 79 B3
Conde-sur-Marne F 91 B4
Condé-sur-Noireau F 88 B3
Condino I 121 B3
Condom F 129 C3
Condove I 119 B4
Condrieu F 117 B4
Conegliano I 122 B1
Conflans-sur-Lanterne F 105 B5
Confolens F 115 B4
Conforto E 141 A3
Cong IRL 28 A2
Congleton GB 40 B1
Congosto E 141 B4
Congosto de Valdavia E 142 B2
Congostrina E 151 A4
Conil de la Frontera E 162 B1
Coningsby GB 41 B3
Coniston GB 36 B3
Conlie F 102 A1
Conliège F 105 C4
Conna IRL 29 B3
Connah's Quay GB 38 A3
Connantre F 91 C3
Connaugh IRL 28 B3
Connaux F 131 A3
Connel GB 34 B2
Connerré F 102 A2
Cononbridge GB 32 D2
Čonoplja SRB 126 B1
Conques F 116 C2
Conques-sur-Orbiel F 146 A3
Conquista E 157 B3
Conquista de la Sierra E 156 A2
Consándolo I 121 C4
Consélice I 135 A4
Conselve I 121 B4
Consenvoye F 91 B5
Consett GB 37 B5
Consolacão P 154 B1
Constancia P 154 B2
Constanco E 140 A2
Constanța RO 17 C8
Constanti E 147 C2
Constantina E 162 A2
Consuegra E 157 A4
Consuma I 135 B4
Contarina I 122 B1
Contay F 90 B2
Conthey CH 119 A4
Contigliano I 168 A2
Contis-Plage F 128 B1
Contrada I 170 C2
Contres F 103 B3
Contrexéville F 105 A4
Controne I 172 B1
Contursi Termi I 172 B1
Conty F 90 B2
Conversano I 173 B3
Conwy GB 38 A3
Cookstown GB 27 B4
Coole F 91 C4
Coolgreany IRL 30 B2
Cooneen GB 27 B3
Cootehill IRL 27 B3
Cope E 165 B3
Copenhagen = København DK 61 D2
Copertino I 173 B4
Copparo I 121 C4
Coppenbrugge D 72 B2
Corabia RO 17 D6
Córaci I 175 B2
Coralići BIH 124 C1
Corato I 171 B4
Coray F 100 A2
Corbeil-Essonnes F 90 C2
Corbeny F 91 B3
Corbera E 159 B3
Corbie F 90 B2
Corbigny F 104 B2
Corbion B 91 B4
Corbridge GB 37 B4
Corby GB 40 C3
Corconte E 143 A3
Corcubión E 140 B1
Corcumello I 169 A3
Cordenòns I 122 B1
Cordes-sur-Ciel F 129 B4
Córdoba E 156 C3
Cordobilla de Lácara E 155 B4
Cordovado I 122 B1
Corella E 144 B2
Coreses E 150 A2
Corfe Castle GB 43 B4
Corga de Lobão P 148 B1
Cori I 169 B2
Coria E 155 B4
Coria del Río E 162 A1
Corigliano Cálabro I 174 B2
Corinaldo I 136 B1
Corinth = Korinthos GR 184 B3
Cório I 119 B4
Coripe E 162 B2
Cork IRL 29 C3
Corlay F 100 A2
Corleone I 176 B2
Corleto Monforte I 172 B1
Corleto Perticara I 174 A2
Çorlu TR 186 A2
Cormainville F 103 A3
Cormatin F 104 C3
Cormeilles F 89 A4
Cormery F 102 B2
Cormòns I 122 B2
Cormoz F 118 A2
Cornago E 144 B1
Cornberg D 82 A1
Cornellana E 141 A4
Corneşti MD 17 B8
Corníglio I 134 A3
Cornimont F 106 B1
Corniolo I 135 B4
Cornuda I 121 B5
Cornudella de Montsant E 147 C1
Cornudilla E 143 B3
Cornus F 130 B2
Çorovodë AL 182 C2
Corpach GB 34 B2
Corps F 118 C2
Corps Nuds F 101 B4
Corral de Almaguer E 157 A4
Corral de Ayllon E 151 A4
Corral de Calatrava E 157 B3
Corrales E 149 A4
Corral-Rubio E 158 C2
Corran GB 34 B2
Corredoiras E 140 A2
Corréggio I 121 C3
Corrèze F 116 B1
Corridónia I 136 B2
Corris GB 38 B3
Corrubedo E 140 B1
Córsico I 120 B2
Corsock GB 36 A3
Corte F 180 A2
Corteconceptión E 161 B3
Corte de Peleas E 155 C4
Cortegaca P 148 B1
Cortegada E 140 B2
Cortegana E 161 B3
Cortemaggiore I 120 B2
Cortemilia I 133 A4
Corte Pinto P 160 B2
Cortes E 144 C2
Cortes de Aragón E 153 B3
Cortes de Arenoso E 153 B3
Cortes de Baza E 164 B2
Cortes de la Frontera E 162 B2
Cortes de Pallás E 159 B3
Cortiçadas P 154 C2
Cortico P 148 A2
Cortijo de Arriba E 157 A3
Cortijos Nuevos E 164 A2
Cortina d'Ampezzo I 108 C3
Corton GB 41 C5
Cortona I 135 B4
Coruche P 154 C2
Corullón E 141 B4
Çorum TR 23 A8
Corvara in Badia I 108 C2
Corvera E 165 B3
Corwen GB 38 B3
Cosenza I 174 B2
Cosham GB 44 C2
Coslada E 151 B4
Cosne-Cours-sur-Loire F 104 B1
Cosne d'Allier F 103 C4
Cospeito E 140 A3
Cossato I 119 B5
Cossaye F 104 C2
Cossé-le-Vivien F 101 B5
Cossonay CH 105 C5
Costa da Caparica P 154 C1
Costa de Santo André P 160 A1
Costalpino I 135 B4
Costa Nova P 148 B1
Costaros F 117 C3
Costeşti RO 17 C6
Costigliole d'Asti I 119 C5
Costigliole Saluzzo I 133 A3
Coswig
Sachsen D 83 A5
Sachsen-Anhalt D 83 A4
Cotherstone GB 37 B5
Cotronei I 175 B2
Cottbus D 84 A2
Cottenham GB 45 A4
Cottingham GB 40 B3
Coublanc F 105 B4
Couches F 104 C3
Couço P 154 C2
Coucouron F 117 C3
Coucy-le-Château-Auffrique F 90 B3
Couëron F 101 B4
Couflens F 146 B2
Couhé F 115 B4
Couiza F 146 B3
Coulags GB 31 B3
Coulanges F 104 C2
Coulanges-la-Vineuse F 104 B2
Coulanges-sur-Yonne F 104 B2
Couleuvre F 104 C1
Coulmier-le-Sec F 104 B3
Coulommiers F 90 C3
Coulonges-sur-l'Autize F 114 B3
Coulounieix-Chamiers F 129 A3
Coulport GB 34 B3
Coupar Angus GB 35 B4
Coupéville F 91 C4
Couptrain F 89 B3
Coura P 140 C2
Courcelles B 79 B4
Courcelles-Chaussy F 92 B2
Courchevel F 118 B3
Cour-Cheverny F 103 B3
Courcôme F 115 C4
Courçon F 114 B3
Cour-et-Buis F 117 B4
Courgenay CH 106 B2
Courmayeur I 119 B3
Courniou F 130 B1
Cournon-d'Auvergne F 116 B3
Cournonterral F 130 B2
Courpière F 117 B3
Coursan F 130 B2
Courseulles-sur-Mer F 89 A3
Cours-la-Ville F 117 A4
Courson-les-Carrières F 104 B2
Courtalain F 103 A3
Courtenay F 104 A2
Courtomer F 89 B4
Courville
Eure-et-Loire F 89 B5

Courville *continued*
Marne F 91 B3
Coussac-Bonneval
F 115 C5
Coutances F 88 A2
Couterne F 89 B3
Coutras F 128 A2
Couvet CH 106 C1
Couvin B 91 A4
Couzon F 104 C2
Covadonga E 142 A1
Covaleda E 143 C4
Covarrubias E 143 B3
Covas P 148 A1
Cove GB 31 B3
Coventry GB 44 A2
Coverack GB 42 B1
Covigliáio I 135 A4
Covilhã P 148 B2
Cowbridge GB 39 C3
Cowdenbeath GB 35 B4
Cowes GB 44 C2
Cox F 129 C4
Cózar E 157 B4
Cozes F 114 C3
Cozzano F 180 B2
Craco I 174 A2
Cracow = Kraków
PL 99 A3
Craibstone GB 33 D4
Craighouse GB 34 C2
Craignure GB 34 B2
Crail GB 35 B5
Crailsheim D 94 B2
Craiova RO 17 C5
Cramlington GB 37 A5
Cranleigh GB 44 B3
Craon F 101 B5
Craonne F 91 B3
Craponne F 117 B4
Craponne-sur-Arzon
F 117 B3
Crathie GB 32 D3
Crato P 155 B3
Craughwell IRL 28 A3
Craven Arms GB 39 B4
Crawford GB 36 A3
Crawinkel D 82 B2
Crawley GB 44 B3
Creag Ghoraidh GB 31 B1
Crecente E 140 B2
Crèches-sur-Saône
F 117 A4
Crécy-en-Ponthieu
F 78 B1
Crécy-la-Chapelle F 90 C2
Crécy-sur-Serre F 91 B3
Crediton GB 43 B3
Creeslough IRL 26 A3
Creetown GB 36 B2
Creeve GB 27 B4
Creglingen D 94 B2
Creil F 90 B2
Creissels F 130 A2
Crema I 120 B2
Cremeaux F 117 B3
Crémenes E 142 B1
Crémieu F 118 B2
Cremlingen D 73 B3
Cremona I 120 B3
Creney F 91 C4
Črenšovci SLO 111 C3
Créon F 128 B2
Crepaja SRB 127 B2
Crépey F 92 C1
Crépy F 91 B3
Crépy-en-Valois F 90 B2
Cres HR 123 C3
Crescentino I 119 B5
Crespino I 121 C4
Crespos E 150 B3
Cressage GB 39 B4
Cressensac F 129 A4
Cressia F 105 C4
Crest F 117 C5
Cresta CH 107 C4
Créteil F 90 C2
Creully F 88 A3
Creussen D 95 B3
Creutzwald F 92 B2
Creuzburg D 82 A2
Crevalcore I 121 C4
Crèvecoeur-le-Grand
F 90 B2
Crevillente E 165 A4
Crévola d'Ossola I 119 A5
Crewe GB 38 A4
Crewkerne GB 43 B4
Criales E 143 B3
Crianlarich GB 34 B3
Criccieth GB 38 B2
Crickhowell GB 39 C3
Cricklade GB 44 B2
Crieff GB 35 B4
Criel-sur-Mer F 90 A1
Crikvenica HR 123 B3
Crillon F 90 B1
Crimmitschau D 83 B4
Crimond GB 33 D5
Crinitz D 84 A1
Cripán E 143 B4
Criquetot-l'Esneval
F 89 A4
Crispiano I 173 B3
Crissolo I 119 C4
Cristóbal E 149 B4
Crivitz D 73 A4
Črna SLO 110 C1
Crna Bara
Srbija SRB 127 C1
Vojvodina SRB 126 B2
Crnac HR 125 B3
Crnča SRB 127 C1
Crni Lug
BIH 138 A2
HR 123 B3
Črni Vrh SLO 123 B3
Crnjelovo Donje
BIH 125 C5
Črnomelj SLO 123 B4
Crocketford GB 36 A3
Crocq F 116 B2
Crodo I 119 A5
Croglin GB 37 B4
Crolly IRL 26 A2
Cromarty GB 32 D2
Cromer GB 41 C5
Cronat F 104 C2
Crookhaven IRL 29 C2
Crookstown IRL 29 C3
Croom IRL 29 B3
Cropalati I 174 B2
Crópani I 175 C2
Crosbost GB 31 A2
Crosby GB 38 A3
Crosía I 174 B2
Crossakiel IRL 27 C3
Cross-Hands GB 39 C2
Crosshaven IRL 29 C3
Crosshill GB 36 A2
Crossmolina IRL 26 B1
Crotone I 175 B3
Crottendorf D 83 B4
Crouy F 90 B3
Crowborough GB 45 B4
Crowland GB 41 C3
Crowthorne GB 44 B3
Croyde GB 42 A2
Croydon GB 44 B3
Crozon F 100 A1
Cruas F 117 C4
Cruceni RO 126 A3
Crúcoli I 174 B3
Cruden Bay GB 33 D5
Crudgington GB 38 B4
Cruis F 132 A1
Crumlin GB 27 B4
Cruseilles F 118 A3
Crusheen IRL 28 B3
Cruz de Incio E 141 B3
Crvenka SRB 126 B1
Črveny Kamen SK 98 B2
Csabacsüd H 113 C4
Csabrendek H 111 B4
Csákánydoroszló
H 111 C3
Csákvár H 112 B2
Csanádapáca H 113 C4
Csanádpalota H 126 A2
Csány H 113 B3
Csanytelek H 113 C4
Csapod H 111 B3
Császár H 112 B2
Császártöltés H 112 C3
Csávoly H 125 A5
Csemö H 113 B3
Csengöd H 112 C3
Csépa H 113 C4
Csepreg H 111 B3
Cserkeszölö H 113 C4
Csernely H 113 A4
Csesztreg H 111 C3
Csökmö H 113 B5
Csököly H 124 A3
Csokonyavisonta
H 124 A3
Csólyospálos H 113 C3
Csongrád H 113 C4
Csopak H 112 C1
Csorna H 111 B4
Csorvás H 113 C4
Csurgo H 124 A3
Cuacos de Yuste E 150 B2
Cualedro E 140 C3
Cuanca de Campos
E 142 B1
Cuba P 160 A2
Cubel E 152 A2
Cubelles E 147 C2
Cubillos E 143 C4
Cubillos del Sil E 141 B4
Cubjac F 129 A3
Cubo de la Solana
E 152 A1
Çubuk TR 23 A7
Cuckfield GB 44 B3
Cucuron F 131 B4
Cudillero E 141 A4
Cuéllar E 151 A3
Cuenca E 152 B1
Cuers F 132 B2
Cuerva E 157 A3
Cueva de Agreda
E 144 C2
Cuevas Bajas E 163 A3
Cuevas del Almanzora
E 164 B3
Cuevas del Becerro
E 162 B2
Cuevas del Campo
E 164 B2
Cuevas del Valle E 150 B2
Cuevas de San
Clemente E 143 B3
Cuevas de San Marcos
E 163 A3
Cuges-les-Pins F 132 B1
Cúglieri I 178 B2
Cugnaux F 129 C4
Cuijk NL 80 A1
Cuinzier F 117 A4
Cuiseaux F 105 C4
Cuisery F 105 C4
Culan F 103 C4
Culemborg NL 79 A5
Cúllar E 164 B2
Cullaville GB 27 B4
Cullera E 159 B3
Cullivoe GB 33 A5
Cullompton GB 43 B3
Cully CH 106 C1
Culoz F 118 B2
Cults GB 33 D4
Cumbernauld GB 35 C4
Cumbres de San
Bartolomé E 161 A3
Cumbres Mayores
E 161 A3
Cumiana I 119 C4
Čumić SRB 127 C2
Cumnock GB 36 A2
Çumra TR 23 C7
Cúneo I 133 A3
Cunlhat F 117 B3
Čunski HR 123 C3
Cuntis E 140 B2
Cuorgnè I 119 B4
Cupar GB 35 B4
Cupello I 170 A2
Cupra Maríttima I 136 B2
Cupramontana I 136 B2
Čuprija SRB 127 D3
Curinga I 175 C2
Currelos E 140 B3
Currie GB 35 C4
Curtea de Argeş RO 17 C6
Curtici RO 126 A3
Curtis E 140 A2
Curtis Santa Eulalia
E 140 A2
Čurug SRB 126 B2
Cusano Mutri I 170 B2
Cushendall GB 27 A4
Cusset F 117 A3
Cussy-les-Forges
F 104 B3
Custines F 92 C2
Cutanda E 152 B2
Cutro I 175 B2
Cutrofiano I 173 B4
Cuts F 90 B3
Cuvilly F 90 B2
Cuxhaven D 64 C1
Cvikov CZ 84 B2
Cwmbran GB 39 C3
Cybinka PL 75 B3
Czacz PL 75 B5
Czajków PL 86 A2
Czaplinek PL 75 A5
Czarlin PL 69 A3
Czarna-Dąbrówka
PL 68 A2
Czarna Woda PL 68 B3
Czarnca PL 87 B3
Czarne PL 68 B1
Czarnków PL 75 B5
Czarnowo PL 76 A3
Czarnozyly PL 86 A2
Czarny Bór PL 85 B4
Czarny-Dunajec PL 99 B3
Czarny Las PL 86 A1
Czchow PL 99 B4
Czechowice-Dziedzice
PL 98 B2
Czempiń PL 75 B5
Czermno PL 87 A4
Czernichow PL 99 B3
Czerniejewo PL 76 B2
Czernikowo PL 76 B3
Czersk PL 68 B2
Czerwieńsk PL 75 B4
Czerwionka-Leszczyny
PL 86 B2
Częstochowa PL 86 B3
Czeszewo PL 76 B2
Człopa PL 75 A5
Człuchów PL 68 B2
Czołpino PL 68 A2

D

Dağ TR 189 B5
Daaden D 81 B3
Dabas H 112 B3
Dąbie PL 76 B3
Dąbki PL 67 B5
Dabo F 92 C3
Dabrowa PL 76 B2
Dąbrowa Górnicza
PL 86 B3
Dąbrowa Tarnowska
PL 87 B4
Dąbrowice PL 77 B4
Dabrowno PL 77 A5
Dachau D 108 A2
Dačice CZ 97 B3
Daday TR 23 A7
Dagali N 47 B5
Dägebüll D 64 B1
Dagmersellen CH 106 B2
Dahlen D 83 A4
Dahlenburg D 73 A3
Dahme D 83 A5
Dahn D 93 B3
Dähre D 73 B3
Daikanvik S 195 E7
Dail bho Dheas GB 31 A2
Dailly GB 36 A2
Daimiel E 157 A4
Daingean IRL 30 A1
Đakovica KOS 16 D4
Đakovo HR 125 B4
Dal
Akershus N 48 B3
Telemark N 47 C5
Dalaas A 107 B5
Dalabrog GB 31 B1
Dala-Floda S 50 B1
Dala-Husby S 50 B2
Dala-Järna S 50 B1
Dalaman TR 188 C3
Dalarö S 57 A4
Dalbeattie GB 36 B3
Dalby
DK 59 C3
Skåne S 61 D3
Uppsala S 57 A3
Värmland S 49 B4
Dale
Pembrokeshire
GB 39 C1
Shetland GB 33 A5
Hordaland N 46 B2
Sogn og Fjordane
N 46 A2
Dalen
Akershus N 48 C3
Telemark N 53 A4
Daleszyce PL 87 B4
Dalhalvaig GB 32 C3
Dalheim L 92 B2
Dalhem S 57 C4
Dalias E 164 C2
Dalj HR 125 B4
Dalkeith GB 35 C4
Dalkey IRL 30 A2
Dalmally GB 34 B3
Dalmellington GB 36 A2
Dalmose DK 65 A4
Daløy N 46 A1
Dalry
Dumfries & Galloway
GB 34 C3
North Ayrshire GB 36 A2
Dalrymple GB 36 A2
Dalseter N 47 A6
Dalsjöfors S 60 B3
Dalskog S 54 B3
Dals Långed S 54 B3
Dals Rostock S 54 B3
Dalston GB 36 B4
Dalstorp S 60 B3
Dalton-in-Furness
GB 36 B3
Daluis F 132 A2
Dalum
D 71 B4
S 60 B3
Dalvík IS 191 B7
Dalwhinnie GB 32 E2
Dalyan TR 188 C3
Damasi GR 182 D4
Damasławek PL 76 B2
Damazan F 129 B3
Damgan F 101 B3
Dammarie-les-Lys F 90 C2
Dammartin-en-Goële
F 90 B2
Damme D 71 B5
Damnica PL 68 A2
Dampierre F 105 B4
Dampierre-sur-Salon
F 105 B4
Damüls A 107 B4
Damville F 89 B5
Damvillers F 92 B1
Damwoude NL 70 A2
Danasjö S 195 E7
Danbury GB 45 B4
Dångebo S 63 B3
Dangers F 89 D5
Dangé-St Romain
F 102 C2
Dangeul F 89 B4
Danilovgrad MNE 16 D3
Danischenhagen D 64 B3
Daniszyn PL 85 A5
Danjoutin F 106 B1
Dannas S 60 B3
Dannemarie F 106 B2
Dannemora S 51 B4
Dannenberg D 73 A4
Dánszentmiklós H 112 B3
Dány H 112 B3
Daoulas F 100 A1
Darabani RO 17 A7
Darány H 125 B3
Darda HR 125 B4
Dardesheim D 73 C3
Darfeld D 71 B4
Darfo I 120 B3
Dargiń PL 68 A1
Dargun D 66 C1
Darlington GB 37 B5
Darłowo PL 68 A1
Darmstadt D 93 B4
Darney F 105 A5
Daroca E 152 A2
Darque P 148 A1
Darragh IRL 28 B2
Dartford GB 45 B4
Dartington GB 43 B3
Dartmouth GB 43 B3
Darton GB 40 B2
Daruvar HR 124 B3
Darvas H 113 B5
Darvel GB 36 A2
Darwen GB 38 A4
Dassel D 82 A1
Dassow D 65 C3
Datça TR 188 C2
Datteln D 80 A3
Dattenfeld D 81 B3
Daugard DK 59 C2
Daugavpils LV 8 E5
Daumeray F 102 B1
Daun D 80 B2
Daventry GB 44 A2
Davle CZ 96 B2
Davor HR 124 B3
Davos CH 107 C4
Davutlar TR 188 B2
Davyd Haradok BY 13 B7
Dawlish GB 43 B3
Dax F 128 C1
Dazkırı TR 189 B4
Deal GB 45 B5
Deauville F 89 A4
Deba E 143 A4
Debar MK 182 B2
Dębe PL 77 B5
Dębica PL 87 B5
Dębnica Kaszubska
PL 68 A2
Dębno PL 74 B3
Dębołęka PL 86 A2
Dębowa Łaka PL 69 B4
Debrc SRB 127 C1
Debrecen H 113 B5
Debrznica PL 75 B4
Debrzno PL 68 B2
Debstedt D 72 A1
Decazeville F 130 A1
Dechtice SK 98 C1
Decima I 168 B2
Decimomannu I 179 C2
Děčín CZ 84 B2
Decize F 104 C2
De Cocksdorp NL 70 A1
Decollatura I 175 B2
Decs H 125 A4
Deddington GB 44 B2
Dedeler TR 187 B5
Dedelow D 74 A2
Dedemli TR 189 B7
Dedemsvaart NL 71 B3
Dédestapolcsány
H 113 A4
Dedovichi RUS 9 D6
Deeping St Nicholas
GB 41 C3
Dég H 112 C2
Degaña E 141 B4
Degeberga S 61 D4
Degerby FIN 51 B7
Degerfors S 55 A5
Degerhamn S 63 B4
Degernes N 54 A2
Deggendorf D 95 C4
Deggingen D 94 C1
Dego I 133 A4
Degolados P 155 B3
De Haan B 78 A3
Dehesas de Guadix
E 164 B1
Dehesas Viejas E 163 A4
Deia E 166 B2
Deining D 95 B3
Deinze B 79 B3
Déiva Marina I 134 A2
Dej RO 17 B5
Deje S 55 A4
De Koog NL 70 A1
Delabole GB 42 B2
Delary S 61 C3
Delbrück D 81 A4
Delčevo MK 182 B4
Delden NL 71 B3
Deleitosa E 156 A2
Delekovec HR 124 A2
Delémont CH 106 B2
Delft NL 70 B1
Delfzijl NL 71 A3
Délia I 176 B2
Delianuova I 175 C1
Deliblato SRB 127 C3
Delice TR 23 B7
Deliceto I 171 B3
Delitzsch D 83 A4
Dellach A 109 C4
Delle F 106 B2
Delme F 92 C2
Delmen-horst D 72 A1
Delnice HR 123 B3
Delsbo S 200 E2
Delvin IRL 30 A1
Delvinë AL 182 D2
Demandice SK 112 A2
Demen D 73 A4
Demidov RUS 13 A9
Demigny F 105 C3
Demirci TR 186 C3
Demirköy TR 186 A2
Demirtaş TR 186 B4
Demmin D 66 C2
Demonte I 133 A3
Demyansk RUS 9 D8
Denain F 78 B3
Denbigh GB 38 A3
Den Burg NL 70 A1
Dender-monde B 79 A4
Denekamp NL 71 B4
Den Ham NL 71 B3
Den Helder NL 70 B1
Denholm GB 35 C5
Denia E 159 C4
Denizli TR 188 B4
Denkendorf D 95 C3
Denklingen D 81 B3
Denny GB 35 B4
Den Oever NL 70 B2
Denta RO 126 B3
Déols F 103 C3
De Panne B 78 A2
Derbent TR 188 A3
Derby GB 40 C2
Derecske H 113 B5
Dereköy TR 186 A2
Derenberg D 82 A2
Derinkuyu TR 23 B8
Dermbach D 82 B2
Dermulo I 121 A4
Deronje SRB 125 B5
Derrygonnelly GB 26 B3
Derrylin GB 27 B3
Derry/Londonderry
GB 27 B3
Dersingham GB 41 C4
Deruta I 136 C1
Dervaig GB 34 B1
Derval F 101 B4
Derveni GR 184 A3
Derventa BIH 125 C3
Dervock GB 27 A4
Desana I 119 B5
Descartes F 102 C2
Desenzano del Garda
I 121 B3
Deset N 48 A3
Deševa BIH 139 B4
Desfina GR 184 A3
Desimirovac SRB 127 C2
Désio I 120 B2
Deskati GR 182 D3
Deskle SLO 122 A2
Desná CZ 84 B3
Dešov CZ 97 C3
Despotovac SRB 127 C3
Despotovo SRB 126 B1
Dessau D 83 A4
Deštná CZ 96 B2
Destriana E 141 B4
Désulo I 179 B3
Desvres F 78 B1
Deszk H 126 A2
Deta RO 126 B3
Detmold D 72 C1
Dětřichov CZ 98 B1
Dettelbach D 94 B2
Dettingen
Baden-Württemberg
D 94 C1
Baden-Württemberg
D 107 B4
Dettwiller F 93 C3
Detva SK 99 C3
Deurne NL 80 A1
Deutschkreutz A 111 B3
Deutschlandsberg
A 110 C2
Deutsch Wagram
A 111 A3
Deva RO 16 C5
Dévaványa H 113 B4
Devecikonağı TR 186 C3
Devecser H 111 B4
Develi TR 23 B8
Deventer NL 70 B3
Devil's Bridge GB 39 B3
Devin BG 183 B6
Devinska Nova Ves
SK 111 A3
Devizes GB 43 A5
Devonport GB 42 B2
Devrek TR 187 A6
Devrekâni TR 23 A7
Đevrske HR 137 B4
De Wijk NL 71 B3
Dewsbury GB 40 B2
Deza E 152 A1
Dežanovac HR 124 B3
Dezzo I 120 B3
Dhali CY 181 A2
Dheftera CY 181 A2
Dherinia CY 181 A2
Diamante I 174 B1
Dianalund DK 61 D1
Diano d'Alba I 119 C5
Diano Marina I 133 B4
Dicomano I 135 B4
Didcot GB 44 B2
Didimoticho GR 186 A1
Die F 118 C2
Diebling F 92 B2
Dieburg D 93 B4
Diego del Carpio E 150 B2
Diekirch L 92 B2
Diélette F 88 A2
Diémoz F 118 B2
Dienten am Hochkönig
A 109 B3
Diepenbeck B 79 B5
Diepholz D 71 B5
Dieppe F 89 A5

Dierberg D 74 A1
Dierdorf D 81 B3
Dieren NL 70 B3
Dierhagen D 66 B1
Diesdorf D 73 B3
Diessen D 108 B2
Diest B 79 B5
Dietenheim D 94 C2
Dietfurt D 95 B3
Dietikon CH 106 B3
Dietzenbach D 93 A4
Dieue-sur-Meuse F 92 B1
Dieulefit F 131 A4
Dieulouard F 92 C2
Dieuze F 92 C2
Diever NL 71 B3
Diez D 81 B4
Diezma E 163 A4
Differdange L 92 B1
Digermulen N 194 B6
Dignac F 115 C4
Dignano I 122 A1
Digne-les-Bains F 132 A2
Digny F 89 B5
Digoin F 104 C2
Dijon F 105 B4
Dikanäs S 195 E7
Dikili TR 186 C1
Diksmuide B 78 A2
Dilar E 163 A4
Dillenburg D 81 B4
Dillingen
Bayern D 94 C2
Saarland D 92 B2
Dilsen B 80 A1
Dimaro I 121 A3
Dimitrovgrad BG 183 A7
Dimitsana GR 184 B3
Dinami I 175 C2
Dinan F 101 A3
Dinant B 79 B4
Dinar TR 189 A5
Dinard F 101 A3
Dinek TR 187 C6
Dingden D 80 A2
Dingelstädt D 82 A2
Dingle
IRL 29 B1
S 54 B2
Dingolfing D 95 C4
Dingtuna S 56 A2
Dingwall GB 32 D2
Dinkelsbühl D 94 B2
Dinkelscherben D 94 C2
Dinklage D 71 B5
Dinslaken D 80 A2
Dinxperlo NL 80 A2
Diö S 63 B2
Diósgyör H 113 A4
Diósjeno H 112 B3
Diou F 104 C2
Dippen GB 34 C2
Dipperz D 82 B1
Dippoldiswalde D 84 B1
Dirdal N 52 B2
Dirksland NL 79 A4
Dirlewang D 108 B1
Dischingen D 94 C2
Disentis CH 107 C3
Diso I 173 B4
Diss GB 45 A5
Dissen D 71 B5
Distington GB 36 B3
Ditzingen D 93 C5
Ditzum D 71 A4
Divača SLO 122 B2
Dives-sur-Mer F 89 A3
Divín SK 99 C3
Divion F 78 B2
Divišov CZ 96 B2
Divonne les Bains
F 118 A3
Dixmont F 104 A2
Dizy-le-Gros F 91 B4
Djúpivogur IS 191 C11
Djupvasshytta N 198 C4
Djura S 50 B1
Djurås S 50 B2
Djurmo S 50 B2
Djursdala S 62 A3
Dlouhá Loucka CZ 98 B1
Długowola PL 87 A5
Dmitrov RUS 9 D10
Dno RUS 9 D6
Doade E 141 B3
Doğanhisar TR 189 A6
Dobanovci SRB 127 C2
Dobbertin D 73 A5
Dobbiaco I 108 C3
Dobczyce PL 99 B4
Dobele LV 8 D3
Döbeln D 83 A5
Doberlug-Kirchhain
D 83 A5
Dobern D 84 A2
Dobersberg A 97 C3
Dobiegniew PL 75 B4
Dobieszyn PL 87 A5
Doboj BIH 125 C4
Dobošnica BIH 125 C4
Doboz H 113 C5
Dobrá CZ 98 B2
Dobra
Wielkopolskie PL 76 C3
Dobra *continued*
Zachodnio-Pomorskie
PL 74 A3
Zachodnio-Pomorskie
PL 75 A4
Dobrá Niva SK 99 C3
Dobřany CZ 96 B1
Dobre PL 76 B3
Dobre Miasto PL 69 B5
Dobreta-Turnu-Severin
RO 16 C5
Dobri H 111 C3
Dobrica SRB 126 B2
Dobrich BG 17 D7
Dobrinishta BG 183 B5
Dobříš CZ 96 B2
Dobro E 143 B3
Dobrodzień PL 86 B2
Döbrököz H 112 C2
Dobromierz PL 85 B4
Dobrosołowo PL 76 B3
Dobroszyce PL 85 A5
Dobrovnik SLO 111 C3
Dobrush BY 13 B9
Dobruška CZ 85 B4
Dobrzany PL 75 A4
Dobrzen Wielki PL 86 B1
Dobrzyca
Wielkopolskie PL 75 A5
Wielkopolskie PL 85 A5
Zachodnio-Pomorskie
PL 67 B4
Dobrzyńnad Wisłą
PL 77 B4
Dobšiná SK 99 C4
Dobwalls GB 42 B2
Dochamps B 80 B1
Docking GB 41 C4
Docksta S 200 C4
Doddington GB 37 A4
Döderhult S 62 A4
Doesburg NL 70 B3
Doetinchem NL 71 C3
Dogliani I 133 A3
Dogueno P 160 B2
Doische B 91 A4
Dois Portos P 154 B1
Dojč SK 98 C1
Dokka N 48 B2
Dokkedal DK 58 B3
Dokkum NL 70 A2
Dokležovje SLO 111 C3
Doksy CZ 84 B2
Dokuz TR 189 A7
Dolancourt F 104 A3
Dolceácqua I 133 B3
Dol-de-Bretagne F 88 B2
Dole F 105 B4
Dølemo N 53 B4
Dolenja vas SLO 123 B3
Dolenjske Toplice
SLO 123 B4
Dolfor GB 39 B3
Dolgarrog GB 38 A3
Dolgellau GB 38 B3
Doliana GR 182 D2
Dolianova I 179 C3
Dolice PL 75 A4
Doljani HR 138 A2
Döllach im Mölltal
A 109 C3
Dolle D 73 B4
Dollnstein D 94 C3
Dollot F 104 A2
Döllstadt D 82 A2
Dolná Strehová SK 99 C3
Dolné Saliby SK 111 A4
Dolni Benešov CZ 98 B2
Dolni Bousov CZ 84 B3
Dolni Kounice CZ 97 B4
Dolni Kralovice CZ 97 B3
Dolni Újezd CZ 97 B4
Dolni Žandov CZ 95 A4
Dolný Kubín SK 99 B3
Dolo I 121 B5
Dolores E 165 A4
Dolovo SRB 127 C2
Dölsach A 109 C3
Dolsk PL 76 B2
Dolwyddelan GB 38 A3
Domaljevac BIH 125 B4
Domaniç TR 187 C4
Domaniža SK 98 B2
Domanovići BIH 139 B3
Domašov CZ 85 B5
Domaszék H 126 A1
Domaszków PL 85 B4
Domaszowice PL 86 A1
Domat-Ems CH 107 C4
Domažlice CZ 95 B4
Dombås N 198 C6
Dombasle-sur-Meurthe
F 92 C2
Dombegyház H 126 A3
Dombóvár H 112 C2
Domène F 118 B2
Domérat F 116 A2
Domfessel F 92 C3
Domfront F 88 B3
Domfront-en-
Champagne F 102 A2
Domingão P 154 B2
Domingo Pérez
Granada E 163 A4
Toledo E 150 C3
Dömitz D 73 A4
Dommartin F 91 C4
Dommartin-le-Franc
F 91 C4
Domme F 129 B4
Dommitzsch D 83 A4
Domodóssola I 119 A5
Domokos GR 182 D4
Domoszló H 113 B4
Dompaire F 105 A5
Dompierre-du-Chemin
F 88 B2
Dompierre-sur-Besbre
F 104 C2
Dompierre-sur-Mer
F 114 B2
Domrémy-la-Pucelle
F 92 C1
Dömsöd H 112 B3
Domsure F 118 A2
Dómus de Maria I 179 D2
Domusnóvas I 179 C2
Domvena GR 184 A3
Domžale SLO 123 A3
Donado E 141 B4
Donaghadee GB 27 B5
Don Alvaro E 155 C4
Doña Mencía E 163 A3
Donaueschingen D 106 B3
Donauwörth D 94 C2
Don Benito E 156 B2
Doncaster GB 40 B2
Donegal IRL 26 B2
Donestebe-Santesteban
E 144 A2
Donges F 101 B3
Dongo I 120 A2
Donington GB 41 C3
Doniños E 140 A2
Donja Bebrina HR 125 B4
Donja Brela HR 138 B2
Donja Dubica BIH 125 B4
Donja Dubrava HR 124 A2
Donja Kupčina HR 123 B4
Donja Šatornja
SRB 127 C2
Donja Stubica HR 124 B1
Donje Brišnik BIH 138 B3
Donje Stative HR 123 B4
Donji-Andrijevci
HR 125 B4
Donji Kazanci BIH 138 B2
Donji Koričáni BIH 138 A3
Donji Lapac HR 124 C1
Donji Malovan BIH 138 B3
Donji Miholjac HR 125 B4
Donji Mosti HR 124 A2
Donji Poloj HR 123 B4
Donji-Rujani BIH 138 B2
Donji Srb HR 138 A2
Donji Svilaj BIH 125 B4
Donji Tovarnik
SRB 127 C1
Donji Vakuf BIH 138 A3
Donnalucata I 177 C3
Donnemarie-Dontilly
F 90 C3
Donnersbach A 110 B1
Donnersbachwald
A 109 B5
Donnerskirchen A 111 B3
Donorático I 134 B3
Donostia-San Sebastián
E 144 A2
Donovaly SK 99 C3
Donzenac F 129 A4
Donzère F 131 A3
Donzy F 104 B2
Doonbeg IRL 29 B2
Doorn NL 70 B2
Dor E 140 A1
Dorchester GB 43 B4
Dørdal N 53 B5
Dordrecht NL 79 A4
Dörenthe D 71 B4
Dores GB 32 D2
Dorfen D 95 C4
Dorfgastein A 109 B4
Dorfmark D 72 B2
Dorf Mecklenburg D 65 C4
Dorgali I 178 B3
Dorking GB 44 B3
Dormagen D 80 A2
Dormánd H 113 B4
Dormans F 91 B3
Dornava SLO 124 A1
Dornbirn A 107 B4
Dornburg D 83 A3
Dorndorf D 82 B2
Dornecy F 104 B2
Dornes F 104 C2
Dornhan D 93 C4
Dornie GB 31 B3
Dornoch GB 32 D2
Dornum D 71 A4
Dorog H 112 B2
Dorohoi RO 17 B7
Dorotea S 200 B2
Dorotowo PL 69 B5
Dörpen D 71 B4
Dorsten D 80 A2
Dortan F 118 A2
Dortmund D 80 A3
Doruchów PL 86 A2
Dorum D 64 C1
Dörverden D 72 B2
Dörzbach D 94 B1
Dos Aguas E 159 B3
Dosbarrios E 151 C4
Döşemealtı TR 189 B5
Dos Hermanas E 162 A2
Dospat BG 183 B6
Dos-Torres E 156 B3
Dötlingen D 72 B1
Dottignies B 78 B3
Döttingen CH 106 B3
Douai F 78 B3
Douarnenez F 100 A1
Douchy F 104 B2
Douchy-les-Mines F 78 B3
Doucier F 105 C4
Doudeville F 89 A4
Doué-la-Fontaine
F 102 B1
Douglas
Isle of Man GB 36 B2
South Lanarkshire
GB 36 A3
Doulaincourt-Saucourt
F 91 C5
Doulevant-le-Château
F 91 C4
Doullens F 90 A2
Dounby GB 33 B3
Doune GB 35 B3
Dounreay GB 32 C3
Dour B 79 B3
Dourdan F 90 C2
Dourgne F 146 A3
Dournazac F 115 C4
Douro Calvo P 148 B2
Douvaine F 118 A3
Douvres-la-Délivrande
F 89 A3
Douzy F 91 B5
Dover GB 45 B5
Dovje SLO 109 C4
Dovre N 198 D6
Downham Market
GB 41 C4
Downhill GB 27 A4
Downpatrick GB 27 B5
Dowra IRL 26 B2
Doxato GR 183 B6
Doyet F 116 A2
Dozule F 89 A3
Drača SRB 127 C2
Dračevo
BIH 139 C4
MK 182 B3
Drachten NL 70 A3
Draga SLO 123 B3
Drăgăşani RO 17 C6
Dragatuš SLO 123 B4
Dragichyn BY 13 B6
Draginja SRB 127 C1
Dragocvet SRB 127 D3
Dragolovci BIH 125 C3
Dragoni I 170 B2
Dragør DK 61 D2
Dragotina HR 124 B2
Dragotinja BIH 124 B2
Dragozetići HR 123 B3
Draguignan F 132 B2
Drahnsdorf D 74 C2
Drahonice CZ 96 B2
Drahovce SK 98 C1
Drama GR 183 B6
Drammen N 54 A1
Drangedal N 53 A5
Drangsnes IS 190 B4
Dransfeld D 82 A1
Dranske D 66 B2
Draperstown GB 27 B4
Drassburg A 111 B3
Drávaszabolcs H 125 B4
Dravograd SLO 110 C2
Drawno PL 75 A4
Drawsko Pomorskie
PL 75 A4
Drayton GB 41 C5
Drązdżewo PL 77 A6
Draženov CZ 95 B4
Draževac SRB 127 C2
Dražice HR 123 B3
Drebkau D 84 A2
Dreieich D 93 A4
Dreisen D 93 B4
Drenovci HR 125 C4
Drensteinfurt D 81 A3
Dresden D 84 A1
Dretyń PL 68 A1
Dreux F 89 B5
Dřevohostice CZ 98 B1
Drevsjø N 199 D9
Drewitz D 73 B5
Drezdenko PL 75 B4
Drežnica HR 123 B4
Drežnik-Grad HR 123 C4
Drietona SK 98 C1
Driffield GB 40 A3
Drimnin GB 34 B2
Drimoleague IRL 29 C2
Dringenberg D 81 A5
Drinić BIH 138 A2
Drinjača BIH 139 A5
Drinovci BIH 138 B3
Driopida GR 185 B5
Drivstua N 198 C6
Drlače SRB 127 C1
Drnholec CZ 97 C4
Drniš HR 138 B2
Drnje HR 124 A2
Drnovice CZ 97 B4
Dro I 121 B3
Drøbak N 54 A1
Drobin PL 77 B5
Drochia MD 17 A7
Drochtersen D 64 C2
Drogheda IRL 30 A2
Drohobych UA 13 D5
Droitwich Spa GB 44 A1
Drołtowice PL 85 A5
Dromahair IRL 26 B2
Dromcolliher IRL 29 B3
Dromore
Down GB 27 B4
Tyrone GB 27 B3
Dromore West IRL 26 B2
Dronero I 133 A3
Dronfield GB 40 B2
Drongan GB 36 A2
Dronninglund DK 58 A3
Dronrijp NL 70 A2
Dronten NL 70 B2
Drosendorf A 97 C3
Drösing A 97 C4
Drottningholm S 57 A3
Droué F 103 A3
Drulingen F 92 C3
Drumbeg GB 32 C1
Drumcliff IRL 26 B2
Drumgask GB 32 D2
Drumkeeran IRL 26 B2
Drummore GB 36 B2
Drumnadrochit GB 32 D2
Drumquin GB 27 B3
Drumshanbo IRL 26 B2
Drumsna IRL 26 C2
Drunen NL 79 A5
Druskininkai LT 13 A5
Druten NL 80 A1
Druya BY 13 A7
Družetići SRB 127 C2
Drvar BIH 138 A2
Drvenik HR 138 B3
Drwalew PL 77 C6
Drymen GB 34 B3
Drynoch GB 31 B2
Drzewce PL 76 B2
Drzewiany PL 68 B1
Drzewica PL 87 A4
Dualchi I 178 B2
Duas Igrejas P 149 A3
Dub SRB 127 D1
Dubá CZ 84 B2
Dubăsari MD 17 B8
Duben D 74 C2
Dübendorf CH 107 B3
Dubi CZ 84 B1
Dubica HR 124 B2
Dublin IRL 30 A2
Dubna RUS 9 D10
Dubňany CZ 98 C1
Dubnica nad Váhom
SK 98 C2
Dubnik SK 112 B2
Dubno UA 13 C6
Dubodiel SK 98 C2
Dubona SRB 127 C2
Dubovac SRB 127 C3
Dubovic BIH 124 C2
Dubranec HR 124 B1
Dubrava HR 124 B2
Dubrave BIH 125 C4
Dubravica
HR 123 B4
SRB 127 C3
Dubrovnik HR 139 C4
Dubrovytsya UA 13 C7
Ducey F 88 B2
Duchcov CZ 84 B1
Ducherow D 74 A2
Dučina SRB 127 C2
Duclair F 89 A4
Dudar H 112 B1
Duddington GB 40 C3
Duderstadt D 82 A2
Dudeştii Vechi RO 126 A2
Dudley GB 40 C1
Dueñas E 142 C2
Duesund N 46 B2
Dueville I 121 B4
Duffel B 79 A4
Duffield GB 40 C2
Dufftown GB 32 D3
Duga Resa HR 123 B4
Dugi Rat HR 138 B2
Dugny-sur-Meuse F 92 B1
Dugopolje HR 138 B2
Dugo Selo HR 124 B2
Duino I 122 B2
Duisburg D 80 A2
Dukat AL 182 C1
Dukovany CZ 97 B4
Duleek IRL 30 A2
Dülken D 80 A2
Dülmen D 80 A3
Dulovo BG 17 D7
Dulpetorpet N 49 B4
Dulverton GB 43 A3
Dumbarton GB 34 C3
Dümerek TR 187 C6
Dumfries GB 36 A3
Dumlupınar TR 187 D4
Dümpelfeld D 80 B2
Dunaalmás H 112 B2
Dunabogdány H 112 B3
Dunafalva H 125 A4
Dunaföldvár H 112 C2
Dunaharaszti H 112 B3
Dunajská Streda
SK 111 B4
Dunakeszi H 112 B3
Dunakiliti H 111 B4
Dunakömlöd H 112 C2
Dunapataj H 112 C2
Dunaszekcsö H 125 A4
Dunaszentgyorgy
H 112 C2
Dunatetétlen H 112 C3
Dunaújváros H 112 C2
Dunavecse H 112 C2
Dunbar GB 35 B5
Dunbeath GB 32 C3
Dunblane GB 35 B4
Dunboyne IRL 30 A2
Dundalk IRL 27 B4
Dundee GB 35 B5
Dundrennan GB 36 B3
Dundrum GB 27 B5
Dunfanaghy IRL 26 A3
Dunfermline GB 35 B4
Dungannon GB 27 B4
Dungarvan IRL 29 B4
Dungiven GB 27 B4
Dunglow IRL 26 B2
Dungourney IRL 29 C3
Duninowo PL 68 A1
Dunkeld GB 35 B4
Dunker S 56 A2
Dunkerque = Dunkirk
F 78 A2
Dunkineely IRL 26 B2
Dunkirk = Dunkerque
F 78 A2
Dun Laoghaire IRL 30 A2
Dunlavin IRL 30 A2
Dunleer IRL 27 C4
Dun-le-Palestel F 116 A1
Dun-les-Places F 104 B3
Dunlop GB 36 A2
Dunloy GB 27 A4
Dunmanway IRL 29 C2
Dunmore IRL 28 A3
Dunmore East IRL 30 B2
Dunmurry GB 27 B4
Dunnet GB 32 C3
Dunningen D 107 A3
Dunoon GB 34 C3
Duns GB 35 C5
Dunscore GB 36 A3
Dunsford GB 43 B3
Dunshaughlin IRL 30 A2
Dunstable GB 44 B3
Dunster GB 43 A3
Dun-sur-Auron F 103 C4
Dun-sur-Meuse F 91 B5
Dunvegan GB 31 B2
Duplek SLO 110 C2
Dupnitsa BG 17 D5
Durağan TR 23 A8
Durach D 107 B5
Durak TR 186 C3
Durana E 143 B4
Durance F 128 B3
Durango E 143 A4
Durankulak BG 17 D8
Duras F 128 B3
Durban-Corbières
F 146 B3
Dürbheim D 107 A3
Durbuy B 79 B5
Dúrcal E 163 B4
Đurdjenovac HR 125 B4
Đurdjevac HR 124 A3
Đurdjevik BIH 139 A4
Düren D 80 B2
Durham GB 37 B5
Đurinci SRB 127 C2
Durlach D 93 C4
Đurmanec HR 124 A1
Durness GB 32 C2
Dürnkrut A 97 C4
Dürrboden CH 107 C4
Dürrenboden CH 107 C3
Durrës AL 182 B1
Durrow IRL 30 B1
Durrus IRL 29 C2
Dursunbey TR 186 C3
Durtal F 102 B1
Durup DK 58 B1
Durusu TR 186 A3
Dusina BIH 139 B3
Dusnok H 112 C2
Dusocin PL 69 B3
Düsseldorf D 80 A2
Dusslingen D 93 C5
Duszniki PL 75 B5
Duszniki-Zdrój PL 85 B4
Dutovlje SLO 122 B2
Duvebo S 55 B5
Duved S 199 B9
Düzağac TR 187 D5
Düzce TR 187 B6
Dvärsätt S 199 B11
Dvor HR 124 B2
Dvorce CZ 98 B1
Dvorníky SK 98 C1
Dvory nad Žitavou
SK 112 B2
Dvůr Královénad Labem
CZ 85 B3
Dybvad DK 58 A3
Dyce GB 33 D4
Dygowo PL 67 B4
Dykehead GB 35 B4
Dymchurch GB 45 B5
Dymer UA 13 C9
Dyrnes N 198 B4
Dywity PL 69 B5
Džanići BIH 139 B3
Dziadowa Kłoda PL 86 A1
Działdowo PL 77 A5

Działoszyce PL 87 B4
Działoszyn PL 86 A2
Dziemiany PL 68 A2
Dzierzążnia PL 77 B5
Dzierzgoń PL 69 B4
Dzierzgowo PL 77 A5
Dzierżoniów PL 85 B4
Dzisna BY 13 A8
Dziwnów PL 67 B3
Dźwierzuty PL 77 A5
Dzyarzhynsk BY 13 B7
Dzyatlava BY 13 B6

E

Ea E 143 A4
Eaglesfield GB 36 A3
Ealing GB 44 B3
Eardisley GB 39 B3
Earls Barton GB 44 A3
Earl Shilton GB 40 C2
Earlston GB 35 C5
Easington GB 41 B4
Easky IRL 26 B2
Eastbourne GB 45 C4
East Calder GB 35 C4
East Dereham GB 41 C4
Easter Skeld GB 33 A5
East Grinstead GB 45 B4
East Ilsley GB 44 B2
East Kilbride GB 36 A2
Eastleigh GB 44 C2
East Linton GB 35 C5
East Markham GB 40 B3
Easton GB 43 B4
East Wittering GB 44 C3
Eaton Socon GB 44 A3
Eaux-Bonnes F 145 B3
Eauze F 128 C3
Ebberup DK 59 C2
Ebbs A 108 B3
Ebbw Vale GB 39 C3
Ebeleben D 82 A2
Ebeltoft DK 59 B3
Ebene Reichenau
A 109 C4
Eben im Pongau A 109 B4
Ebensee A 109 B4
Ebensfeld D 94 A2
Eberbach D 93 B4
Ebergötzen D 82 A2
Ebermann-Stadt D 94 B3
Ebern D 82 B2
Eberndorf A 110 C1
Ebersbach D 84 A2
Ebersberg D 108 A2
Ebersdorf
Bayern D 82 B3
Niedersachsen D 72 A2
Eberstein A 110 C1
Eberswalde D 74 B2
Ebnat-Kappel CH 107 B4
Éboli I 170 C3
Ebrach D 94 B2
Ebreichsdorf A 111 B3
Ebreuil F 116 A3
Ebstorf D 72 A3
Ecclefechan GB 36 A3
Eccleshall GB 40 C1
Eceabat TR 186 B1
Echallens CH 106 C1
Echauri E 144 B2
Echinos GR 183 B7
Echiré F 114 B3
Échirolles F 118 B2
Echourgnac F 128 A3
Echt NL 80 A1
Echte D 82 A2
Echternach L 92 B2
Ecija E 162 A2
Ečka SRB 126 B2
Eckartsberga D 82 A3
Eckelshausen D 81 B4
Eckental D 94 B3
Eckernförde D 64 B2
Eckerö FIN 51 B6
Eckington GB 40 B2
Éclaron F 91 C4
Écommoy F 102 B2
Écouché F 89 B3
Ecouis F 90 B1
Ecséd H 113 B3
Ecsegfalva H 113 B4
Écueillé F 103 B3
Ed S 54 B2
Eda S 49 C4
Eda glasbruk S 49 C4
Edam NL 70 B2
Edane S 55 A3
Edderton GB 32 D2
Ede NL 70 B2
Edebäck S 49 B5
Edebo S 51 B5
Edelény H 99 C4
Edelschrott A 110 B2
Edemissen D 72 B3
Edenbridge GB 45 B4
Edenderry IRL 30 A1
Edenkoben D 93 B4
Edesheim D 93 B4
Edessa GR 182 C4
Edewecht D 71 A4
Edgeworthstown
IRL 30 A1
Edinburgh GB 35 C4
Edineţ MD 17 A7
Edirne TR 186 A1
Edland N 52 A3
Edolo I 120 A3
Edøy N 198 B5
Edremit TR 186 C1
Edsbro S 51 C5
Edsbruk S 56 B2
Edsbyn S 50 A2
Edsele S 200 C2
Edsleskog S 54 A3
Edsvalla S 55 A4
Eekloo B 79 A3
Eemshaven NL 71 A3
Eerbeek NL 70 B3
Eersel NL 79 A5
Eferding A 96 C2
Effiat F 116 A3
Efteløt N 53 A5
Egeln D 73 C4
Eger H 113 B4
Egerbakta H 113 B4
Egernsund DK 64 B2
Egersund N 52 B2
Egerszólát H 113 B4
Egervár H 111 C3
Egg
A 107 B4
D 107 A5
Eggby S 55 B4
Eggedal N 47 B6
Eggenburg A 97 C3
Eggenfelden D 95 C4
Eggesin D 74 A3
Eggum N 194 B4
Egham GB 44 B3
Éghezée B 79 B4
Egiertowo PL 68 A3
Egilsstaðir IS 191 B11
Egina GR 185 B4
Eginio GR 182 C4
Egio GR 184 A3
Égletons F 116 B2
Egling D 108 B2
Eglinton GB 27 A3
Eglisau CH 107 B3
Égliseneuve-
d'Entraigues F 116 B2
Eglofs D 107 B4
Egmond aan Zee NL 70 B1
Egna I 121 A4
Egosthena GR 184 A4
Egremont GB 36 B3
Egtved DK 59 C2
Eguilles F 131 B4
Eguilly-sous-Bois
F 104 A3
Éguzon-Chantôme
F 103 C3
Egyek H 113 B4
Egyházasrádóc H 111 B3
Ehekirchen D 94 C3
Ehingen D 94 C1
Ehra-Lessien D 73 B3
Ehrang D 92 B2
Ehrenfriedersdorf D 83 B4
Ehrenhain D 83 B4
Ehrenhausen A 110 C2
Ehringshausen D 81 B4
Ehrwald A 108 B1
Eibar E 143 A4
Eibelstadt D 94 B2
Eibenstock D 83 B4
Eibergen NL 71 B3
Eibiswald A 110 C2
Eichenbarleben D 73 B4
Eichendorf D 95 C4
Eichstätt D 95 C3
Eickelborn D 81 A4
Eide
Hordaland N 46 B3
Møre og Romsdal
N 198 C4
Eidet N 194 A9
Eidfjord N 46 B4
Eidsberg N 54 A2
Eidsbugarden N 47 A5
Eidsdal N 198 C4
Eidsfoss N 53 A6
Eidskog N 49 B4
Eidsvåg
Hordaland N 46 B2
Møre og Romsdal
N 198 C5
Eidsvoll N 48 B3
Eikefjord N 46 A2
Eikelandsosen N 46 B2
Eiken N 52 B3
Eikesdal N 198 C5
Eikstrand N 53 A5
Eilenburg D 83 A4
Eilsleben D 73 B4
Eina N 48 B2
Einbeck D 82 A1
Eindhoven NL 79 A5
Einsiedeln CH 107 B3
Einville-au-Jard F 92 C2
Eisenach D 82 B2
Eisenberg
Rheinland-Pfalz D 93 B4
Thüringen D 83 B3
Eisenerz A 110 B1
Eisenhüttenstadt D 74 B3
Eisenkappel A 110 C1
Eisenstadt A 111 B3
Eisentratten A 109 C4
Eisfeld D 82 B2
Eisleben D 82 A3
Eislingen D 94 C1
Eitensheim D 95 C3
Eiterfeld D 82 B1
Eitorf D 80 B3
Eivindvik N 46 B2
Eivissa = Ibiza E 166 C1
Eixo P 148 B1
Ejby DK 59 C2
Ejea de los Caballeros
E 144 B2
Ejstrupholm DK 59 C2
Ejulve E 153 B3
Eke B 79 B3
Ekeby
Gotland S 57 C4
Skåne S 61 D2
Uppsala S 51 B5
Ekeby-Almby S 56 A1
Ekenäs S 55 B4
Ekenässjön S 62 A3
Ekerö S 57 A3
Eket S 61 C3
Eketorp S 63 B4
Ekevik S 56 B2
Ekkerøy N 193 B14
Ekshärad S 49 B5
Eksingedal N 46 B2
Eksjö S 62 A2
Eksta S 57 C4
Ekträsk S 200 B5
El Alamo
Madrid E 151 B4
Sevilla E 161 B3
El Algar E 165 B4
El Almendro E 161 B2
El Alquián E 164 C2
Élancourt F 90 C1
El Arahal E 162 A2
El Arenal E 150 B2
El Arguellite E 164 A2
Elassona GR 182 D4
El Astillero E 143 A3
Elati GR 182 D3
Żelazno PL 85 B4
El Ballestero E 158 C1
El Barco de Ávila
E 150 B2
Elbasan AL 182 B2
El Berrón E 142 A1
El Berrueco E 151 B4
Elbeuf F 89 A4
Elbingerode D 82 A2
Elbląg PL 69 A4
El Bodón E 149 B3
El Bonillo E 158 C1
El Bosque E 162 B2
El Bullaque E 157 A3
Elburg NL 70 B2
El Burgo E 162 B3
El Burgo de Ebro
E 153 A3
El Burgo de Osma
E 151 A4
El Burgo Ranero E 142 B1
El Buste E 144 C2
El Cabaco E 149 B3
El Callejo E 143 A3
El Campillo E 161 B3
El Campillo de la Jara
E 156 A2
El Cañavete E 158 B1
El Carpio E 157 C3
El Carpio de Tajo
E 150 C3
El Casar E 151 B4
El Casar de Escalona
E 150 B3
El Castillo de las
Guardas E 161 B3
El Centenillo E 157 B4
El Cerro E 149 B4
El Cerro de Andévalo
E 161 B3
Elche E 165 A4
Elche de la Sierra
E 158 C1
Elchingen D 94 C2
El Comenar E 162 B2
El Coronil E 162 A2
El Crucero E 141 A4
El Cubo de Tierra del
Vino E 149 A4
El Cuervo E 162 B1
Elda E 159 C3
Eldena D 73 A4
Eldingen D 72 B3
Elefsina GR 185 A4
El Ejido E 164 C2
Elek H 113 C5
Elemir SRB 126 B2
El Escorial E 151 B3
El Espinar E 151 B3
Eleutheroupoli GR 183 C6
El Frago E 144 B3
El Franco E 141 A4
El Frasno E 152 A2
Elgå N 199 C8
El Garrobo E 161 B3
El Gastor E 162 B2
Elgin GB 32 D3
Elgoibar E 143 A4
Elgol GB 31 B2
El Gordo E 150 C2
El Grado E 145 B4
El Granado E 161 B2
El Grao de Castelló
E 159 B4
El Grau E 159 C3
Elgshøa N 49 A4
El Higuera E 163 A3
El Hijate E 164 B2
El Hontanar E 152 B2
El Hoyo E 157 B4
Elie GB 35 B5
Elizondo E 144 A2
Ełk PL 12 B5
Elkhovo BG 17 D7
Ellenberg D 94 B2
Ellesmere GB 38 B4
Ellesmere Port GB 38 A4
Ellezelles B 79 B3
Ellingen D 94 B2
Ellmau A 109 B3
Ellon GB 33 D4
Ellös S 54 B2
Ellrich D 82 A2
Ellwangen D 94 C2
Elm
CH 107 C4
D 72 A2
Elmadağ TR 23 B7
El Madroño E 161 B3
El Maillo E 149 B3
Elmalı TR 189 C4
El Masnou E 147 C3
El Mirón E 150 B2
El Molar E 151 B4
El Molinillo E 157 A3
El Morell E 147 C2
Elmshorn D 64 C2
Elmstein D 93 B3
El Muyo E 151 A4
Elne F 146 B3
Elnesvågen N 198 C4
El Olmo E 151 A4
Elorrio E 143 A4
Elöszállás H 112 C2
Elouda GR 185 D6
Éloyes F 105 A5
El Palo E 163 B3
El Pardo E 151 B4
El Payo E 149 B3
El Pedernoso E 158 B1
El Pedroso E 162 A2
El Peral E 158 B2
El Perelló
Tarragona E 153 B4
Valencia E 159 B3
Elphin GB 32 C1
El Picazo E 158 B1
El Pinell de Bray E 153 A4
El Piñero E 150 A2
El Pla de Santa Maria
E 147 C2
El Pobo E 153 B3
El Pobo de Dueñas
E 152 B2
El Pont d'Armentera
E 147 C2
El Port de la Selva
E 147 B4
El Port de Llançà
E 146 B4
El Port de Sagunt
E 159 B3
El Prat de Llobregat
E 147 C3
El Provencio E 158 B1
El Puente E 143 A3
El Puente del Arzobispo
E 150 C2
El Puerto E 141 A4
El Puerto de Santa María
E 162 B1
El Real de la Jara
E 161 B3
El Real de San Vincente
E 150 B3
El Robledo E 157 A3
El Rocío E 161 B3
El Rompido E 161 B2
El Ronquillo E 161 B3
El Royo E 143 C4
El Rubio E 162 A3
El Sabinar E 164 A2
El Saler E 159 B3
El Salobral E 158 C2
El Saucejo E 162 A2
Els Castells E 147 B2
Elsdorf D 80 B2
Elsenfeld D 93 B5
El Serrat AND 146 B2
Elsfleth D 72 A1
Elspeet NL 70 B2
Elst NL 70 C2
Elstead GB 44 B3
Elster D 83 A4
Elsterberg D 83 B4
Elsterwerda D 83 A5
Elstra D 84 A2
El Temple E 144 C3
El Tiemblo E 150 B3
Eltmann D 94 B2
El Toboso E 157 A5
El Tormillo E 145 C3
El Torno E 149 B4
Eltville D 93 A4
El Valle de las Casas
E 142 B1
Elvas P 155 C3
Elvebakken N 192 C7
El Vellón E 151 B4
Elven F 101 B3
El Vendrell E 147 C2
Elverum N 48 B3
El Villar de Arnedo
E 144 B1
Elvington GB 40 B3
El Viso E 156 B3
El Viso del Alcor E 162 A2
Elxleben D 82 A2
Ely GB 45 A4
Elzach D 106 A3
Elze D 72 B2
Emådalen S 50 A1
Embleton GB 37 A5
Embonas GR 188 C2
Embrun F 132 A2
Embún E 144 B3
Emden D 71 A4
Emecik TR 188 C2
Emet TR 186 C4
Emirdağ TR 187 C6
Emlichheim D 71 B3
Emmaboda S 63 B3
Emmaljunga S 61 C3
Emmeloord NL 70 B2
Emmen
CH 106 B3
NL 71 B3
Emmendingen D 106 A2
Emmer-Compascuum
NL 71 B4
Emmerich D 80 A2
Emmern D 72 B2
Emöd H 113 B4
Émpoli I 135 B3
Emsbüren D 71 B4
Emsdetten D 71 B4
Emsfors S 62 A4
Emskirchen D 94 B2
Emstek D 71 B5
Emsworth GB 44 C3
Emyvale IRL 27 B4
Enafors S 199 B9
Enånger S 51 A4
Encamp AND 146 B2
Encarnaçao P 154 C1
Encinas de Abajo
E 150 B2
Encinas de Esgueva
E 142 C2
Encinasola E 161 A3
Encinas Reales E 163 A3
Encio E 143 B3
Enciso E 144 B1
Enden N 199 D7
Endingen D 106 A2
Endrinal E 149 B4
Endröd H 113 C4
Enebakk N 54 A2
Eneryda S 63 B2
Enese H 111 B4
Enez TR 183 C8
Enfield IRL 30 A2
Eng A 108 B2
Engelberg CH 106 C3
Engelhartszell A 96 C1
Engelskirchen D 80 B3
Engen D 107 B3
Enger N 48 B2
Engerdal N 199 D8
Engerneset N 49 A4
Enge-sande D 64 B1
Engesvang DK 59 B2
Enghien B 79 B4
Engstingen D 94 C1
Engter D 71 B5
Enguera E 159 C3
Enguidanos E 158 B2
Enkenbach D 93 B3
Enkhuizen NL 70 B2
Enklinge FIN 51 B7
Enköping S 56 A3
Enna I 177 B3
Ennezat F 116 B3
Ennigerloh D 81 A4
Enningdal N 54 B2
Ennis IRL 28 B3
Enniscorthy IRL 30 B2
Enniskean IRL 29 C3
Enniskillen GB 27 B3
Ennistimon IRL 28 B2
Enns A 110 A1
Eno FIN 9 A7
Enontekiö FIN 196 A6
Ens NL 70 B2
Enschede NL 71 B3
Ensdorf D 95 B3
Ensisheim F 106 B2
Enstaberga S 56 B2
Enstone GB 44 B2
Entlebuch CH 106 B3
Entrácque I 133 A3
Entradas P 160 B1
Entrains-sur-Nohain
F 104 B2
Entrambasaguas E 143 A3
Entrambasmestas
E 143 A3
Entraygues-sur-Truyère
F 116 C2
Entre-os-Rios P 148 A1
Entrevaux F 132 B2
Entrin Bajo E 155 C4
Entroncamento P 154 B2
Entzheim F 93 C3
Envermeu F 89 A5
Enviken S 50 B2
Enying H 112 C2
Enzingerboden A 109 B3
Enzklösterle D 93 C4
Épagny F 90 B3
Epalinges CH 106 C1
Epannes F 114 B3
Epanomi GR 182 C4
Epe
D 71 B4
NL 70 B2
Épernay F 91 B3
Épernon F 90 C1
Epfig F 93 C3
Epierre F 118 B3
Épila E 152 A2
Épinac F 104 C3
Épinal F 105 A5
Episcopia I 174 A2
Episkopi CY 181 B1
Epitalio GR 184 B2
Epoisses F 104 B3
Eppenbrunn D 93 B3
Eppendorf D 83 B5
Epping GB 45 B4
Eppingen D 93 B4
Epsom GB 44 B3
Epworth GB 40 B3
Eraclea I 122 B1
Eraclea Mare I 122 B1
Erba I 120 B2
Erbach
Baden-Württemberg
D 94 C1
Hessen D 93 B4
Erbalunga F 180 A2
Erbendorf D 95 B4
Érchie I 173 B3
Ercolano I 170 C2
Ercsi H 112 B2
Érd H 112 B2
Erdek TR 186 B2
Erdemli TR 23 C8
Erdevik SRB 126 B1
Erding D 95 C3
Erdőtelek H 113 B4
Erdut HR 125 B5
Erdweg D 95 C3
Ereğli
Konya TR 23 C8
Zonguldak TR 187 A6
Erenkaya TR 189 B7
Eresfjord N 198 C5
Eresos GR 183 D7
Eretria GR 185 A4
Erfde D 64 B2
Erfjord N 52 A2
Erfstadt D 80 B2
Erfurt D 82 B3
Ērgli LV 8 D4
Ergoldsbach D 95 C4
Eriboll GB 32 C2
Érice I 176 A1
Ericeira P 154 C1
Eğridir TR 189 B5
Eriksberg S 195 E6
Eriksmåla S 62 B3
Eringsboda S 63 B3
Eriswil CH 106 B2
Erithres GR 185 A4
Erkelenz D 80 A2
Erkner D 74 B2
Erkrath D 80 A2
Erla E 144 B3
Erlangen D 94 B3
Erli I 133 A4
Erlsbach A 109 C3
Ermelo NL 70 B2
Ermenak TR 23 C7
Ermenonville F 90 B2
Ermezinde P 148 A1
Ermidas P 160 A1
Ermioni GR 184 B4
Ermoupoli GR 185 B5
Ermsleben D 82 A3
Erndtebrück D 81 B4
Ernée F 88 B3
Ernestinovo HR 125 B4
Ernstbrunn A 97 C4
Erolzheim D 107 A5
Erquelinnes B 79 B4
Erquy F 101 A3
Erra P 154 C2
Erratzu E 144 A2
Errindlev DK 65 B4
Erro E 144 B2
Ersa F 180 A2
Érsekcsanád H 125 A4
Ersekë AL 182 C2
Érsekvadkert H 112 B3
Ersmark S 200 C6
Erstein F 93 C3
Erstfeld CH 107 C3
Ertebølle DK 58 B2
Ertingen D 107 A4
Ervedal
Coimbra P 148 B1
Portalegre P 154 B3
Ervenik HR 138 A1
Ervidel P 160 B1
Ervy-le-Châtel F 104 A2
Erwitte D 81 A4
Erxleben D 73 B4
Erzsébet H 125 A4
Esbjerg DK 59 C1
Esbly F 90 C2
Escacena del Campo
E 161 B3
Escairón E 140 B3
Escalada E 143 B3
Escalante E 143 A3
Escalaplano I 179 C3
Escalona E 150 B3

Escalona del Prado E 151 A3
Escalonilla E 150 C3
Escalos de Baixo P 155 B3
Escalos de Cima P 155 B3
Escamilla E 152 B1
Es Caná E 166 B1
Escañuela E 157 C3
Es Castell E 167 B4
Escatrón E 153 A3
Eschach D 107 B4
Eschau D 94 B1
Eschede D 72 B3
Eschenau D 95 B3
Eschenbach D 95 B3
Eschenz CH 107 B3
Eschershausen D 72 C2
Esch-sur-Alzette L 92 B1
Esch-sur-Sûre L 92 B1
Eschwege D 82 A2
Eschweiler D 80 B2
Escobasa de Almazán E 152 A1
Escoeuilles F 78 B1
Escombreras E 165 B4
Escos F 144 A2
Escource F 128 B1
Escragnolles F 132 B2
Escrick GB 40 B2
Escurial E 156 A2
Escurial de la Sierra E 149 B4
Esens D 71 A4
Esgos E 140 B3
Esher GB 44 B3
Eskdalemuir GB 36 A3
Eskifjörður IS 191 B12
Eskilhem S 57 C4
Eskilsäter S 55 B4
Eskilstrup DK 65 B4
Eskilstuna S 56 A2
Eskipazar TR 187 B7
Eskişehir TR 187 C5
Eslarn D 95 B4
Eslava E 144 B2
Eslida E 159 B3
Eslohe D 81 A4
Eslöv S 61 D3
Eşme TR 188 A3
Es Mercadal E 167 B4
Es Migjorn Gran E 167 B4
Espa N 48 B3
Espalion F 130 A1
Esparragalejo E 155 C4
Esparragosa del Caudillo E 156 B2
Esparragossa de la Serena E 156 B2
Esparreguera E 147 C2
Esparron F 132 B1
Espe N 46 B3
Espedal N 52 B2
Espejo
Alava E 143 B3
Córdoba E 163 A3
Espeland N 46 B2
Espelkamp D 72 B1
Espeluche F 131 A3
Espeluy E 157 B4
Espera E 162 B2
Esperança P 155 B3
Espéraza F 146 B3
Espéria I 169 B3
Espevær N 52 A1
Espiel E 156 B2
Espinama E 142 A2
Espiñaredo E 140 A3
Espinasses F 132 A2
Espinelves E 147 C3
Espinhal P 154 A2
Espinho P 148 A1
Espinilla E 142 A2
Espinosa de Cerrato E 143 C3
Espinosa de los Monteros E 143 A3
Espinoso del Rey E 156 A3
Espirito Santo P 160 B2
Espluga de Francolí E 147 C2
Esplús E 145 C4
Espolla E 146 B3
Espoo FIN 8 B4
Esporles E 166 B2
Es Port d'Alcúdia E 167 B3
Esposende P 148 A1
Espot E 146 B2
Es Pujols E 166 C1
Esquedas E 145 B3
Esquivias E 151 B4
Essay F 89 B4
Essen
B 79 A4
Niedersachsen D 71 B4
Nordrhein-Westfalen D 80 A3
Essenbach D 95 C4
Essertaux F 90 B2
Essingen D 94 C2
Esslingen D 94 C1
Es Soleràs E 153 A4
Essoyes F 104 A3
Estacas E 140 B2
Estadilla E 145 B4
Estagel F 146 B3
Estaires F 78 B2
Estang F 128 C2
Estarreja P 148 B1
Estartit E 147 B4
Estavayer-le-Lac CH 106 C1
Este I 121 B4
Esteiro E 140 A2
Estela P 148 A1
Estella E 144 B1
Estellencs E 166 B2
Estepa E 162 A3
Estépar E 143 B3
Estepona E 162 B2
Esternay F 91 C3
Esterri d'Aneu E 146 B2
Esterwegen D 71 B4
Estissac F 104 A2
Estivadas E 140 B3
Estivareilles F 116 A2
Estivella E 159 B3
Estói P 160 B2
Estopiñán E 145 C4
Estoril P 154 C1
Estoublon F 132 B2
Estrée-Blanche F 78 B2
Estrées-St Denis F 90 B2
Estrela P 155 C3
Estremera E 151 B4
Estremoz P 155 C3
Estuna S 51 C5
Esyres F 102 B2
Esztergom H 112 B2
Etables-sur-Mer F 100 A3
Étain F 92 B1
Étalans F 105 B5
Étalle B 92 B1
Étampes F 90 C2
Etang-sur-Arroux F 104 C3
Étaples F 78 B1
Etauliers F 128 A2
Etili TR 186 C1
Etna N 48 B1
Etne N 52 A1
Etoges F 91 C3
Etoliko GR 184 A2
Eton GB 44 B3
Etréaupont F 91 B3
Étréchy F 90 C2
Étrépagny F 90 B1
Étretat F 89 A4
Étroeungt F 91 A3
Étroubles I 119 B4
Ettal D 108 B2
Ettelbruck L 92 B2
Etten NL 79 A4
Ettenheim D 106 A2
Ettington GB 44 A2
Ettlingen D 93 C4
Ettringen D 108 A1
Etuz F 105 B4
Etxarri-Aranatz E 144 B1
Etyek H 112 B2
Eu F 90 A1
Euerdorf D 82 B2
Eulate E 144 B1
Eupen B 80 B2
Europoort NL 79 A4
Euskirchen D 80 B2
Eutin D 65 B3
Evanger N 46 B3
Évaux-les-Bains F 116 A2
Evciler
Afyon TR 189 A4
Çanakkale TR 186 C1
Evenskjær N 194 B7
Evenstad N 48 A3
Evercreech GB 43 A4
Evergem B 79 A3
Everöd S 61 D4
Eversberg D 81 A4
Everswinkel D 71 C4
Evertsberg S 49 A5
Evesham GB 44 A2
Évian-les-Bains F 118 A3
Evisa F 180 A1
Evje N 53 B3
Evolène CH 119 A4
Évora P 154 C3
Evoramonte P 155 C3
Evran F 101 A4
Evrecy F 89 A3
Évreux F 89 A5
Évron F 102 A1
Évry F 90 C2
Ewell GB 44 B3
Ewersbach D 81 B4
Excideuil F 115 C5
Exeter GB 43 B3
Exmes F 89 B4
Exminster GB 43 B3
Exmouth GB 43 B3
Eydehamn N 53 B4
Eye
Peterborough GB 41 C3
Suffolk GB 45 A5
Eyemouth GB 35 C5
Eyguians F 132 A1
Eyguières F 131 B4
Eygurande F 116 B2
Eylie F 145 B4
Eymet F 129 B3
Eymoutiers F 116 B1
Eynsham GB 44 B2
Eyrarbakki IS 190 D4
Eystrup D 72 B2
Ezaro E 140 B1
Ezcaray E 143 B4
Ezcároz E 144 B2
Ezine TR 186 C1
Ezmoriz P 148 B1

F

Fabara E 153 A4
Fábbrico I 121 C3
Fåberg N 48 A2
Fabero E 141 B4
Fábiánsebestyén H 113 C4
Fåborg DK 64 A3
Fabrègues F 130 B2
Fabriano I 136 B1
Fabrizia I 175 C2
Facha P 148 A1
Facinas E 162 B2
Fačkov SK 98 B2
Fadagosa P 155 B3
Fadd H 112 C2
Faédis I 122 A2
Faenza I 135 A4
Fafe P 148 A1
Fagagna I 122 A2
Făgăras RO 17 C6
Fågelberget S 199 A11
Fågelfors S 62 A3
Fågelmara S 63 B3
Fågelsta S 55 B6
Fagerås S 55 A4
Fagerheim N 47 B4
Fagerhøy N 48 A1
Fagerhult S 62 A3
Fagerlund N 48 B2
Fagernes
Oppland N 47 B6
Troms N 192 C3
Fagersanna S 55 B5
Fagersta S 50 B2
Fåglavik S 55 B4
Fagnano Castello I 174 B2
Fagnières F 91 C4
Faido CH 107 C3
Fains-Véel F 91 C5
Fairford GB 44 B2
Fairlie GB 34 C3
Fajsz H 112 C2
Fakenham GB 41 C4
Fåker S 199 B11
Fakse DK 65 A5
Fakse Ladeplads DK 65 A5
Falaise F 89 B3
Falcade I 121 A4
Falcarragh IRL 26 A2
Falces E 144 B2
Fălciu RO 17 B8
Falconara I 177 B3
Falconara Maríttima I 136 B2
Falcone I 177 A4
Faldingworth GB 40 B3
Falerum S 56 B2
Fălești MD 17 B7
Falkenberg
Bayern D 95 B4
Bayern D 95 C4
Brandenburg D 83 A5
S 60 C2
Falkensee D 74 B2
Falkenstein
Bayern D 95 B4
Sachsen D 83 B4
Falkenthal D 74 B2
Falkirk GB 35 B4
Falkland GB 35 B4
Falköping S 55 B4
Fall D 108 B2
Falla S 56 B1
Fallingbostel D 72 B2
Falmouth GB 42 B1
Falset E 147 C1
Fălticeni RO 17 B7
Falun S 50 B2
Famagusta CY 181 A2
Fammestad N 46 B2
Fana N 46 B2
Fanano I 135 A3
Fanari GR 182 D3
Fanjeaux F 146 A3
Fano I 136 B2
Fântânele RO 126 A3
Fara in Sabina I 168 A2
Faramontanos de Tábara E 149 A4
Fara Novarese I 119 B5
Farasdues E 144 B2
Fårbo S 62 A4
Fareham GB 44 C2
Färentuna S 57 A3
Färgelanda S 54 B2
Färila S 200 E1
Faringdon GB 44 B2
Faringe S 51 C5
Farini I 120 C2
Fariza E 149 A3
Färjestaden S 63 B4
Farkadona GR 182 D4
Farkasfa H 111 C3
Farlete E 153 A3
Färlöv S 61 C4
Farmos H 113 B3
Farnă SK 112 B2
Färnäs S 50 B1
Farnborough GB 44 B3
Farnese I 168 A1
Farnham GB 44 B3
Farnroda D 82 B2
Faro P 160 B2
Fåro S 57 C5
Fårösund S 57 C5
Farra d'Alpago I 122 A1
Farranfore IRL 29 B2
Farre DK 59 B2
Farsala GR 182 D4
Farsø DK 58 B2
Farsund N 52 B2
Farum DK 61 D2
Fårup DK 58 B2
Fasana I 172 B1
Fasano I 173 B3
Fáskrúðsfjörður IS 191 C11
Fassberg D 72 B3
Fastiv UA 13 C8
Fastnäs S 49 B5
Fátima P 154 B2
Fatmomakke S 195 E6
Fättjaur S 195 E6
Faucogney-et-la-Mer F 105 B5
Fauguerolles F 128 B3
Faulenrost D 74 A1
Faulquemont F 92 B2
Fauquembergues F 78 B2
Fauske N 194 C6
Fauville-en-Caux F 89 A4
Fauvillers B 92 B1
Fåvang N 48 A2
Favara
E 159 B3
I 176 B2
Faverges F 118 B3
Faverney F 105 B5
Faversham GB 45 B4
Favignana I 176 B1
Fawley GB 44 C2
Fay-aux-Loges F 103 B4
Fayence F 132 B2
Fayet F 130 B1
Fayl-Billot F 105 B4
Fayón E 153 A4
Fearn GB 32 D3
Fécamp F 89 A4
Feda N 52 B2
Fedje N 46 B1
Feeny GB 27 B3
Fegen S 60 B3
Fegyvernek H 113 B4
Fehrbellin D 74 B1
Fehring A 111 C3
Feichten A 108 B1
Feiring N 48 B3
Feistritz im Rosental A 110 C1
Feketić SRB 126 B1
Felanitx E 167 B3
Feld am See A 109 C4
Feldbach A 110 C2
Feldberg D 74 A2
Feldkirch A 107 B4
Feldkirchen in Kärnten A 109 C5
Feldkirchen-Westerham D 108 B2
Felgueiras P 148 A1
Felitto I 172 B1
Félix E 164 C2
Felixstowe GB 45 B5
Felizzano I 119 C5
Felletin F 116 B2
Fellingsbro S 56 A1
Felnac RO 126 A3
Felnémet H 113 B4
Felpéc H 111 B4
Fels am Wagram A 97 C3
Felsberg D 81 A5
Felsönyék H 112 C2
Felsöszentiván H 126 A1
Felsöszentmárton H 125 B3
Felsözsolca H 113 A4
Felsted DK 64 B2
Feltre I 121 A4
Femsjö S 60 C3
Fenagh IRL 26 B3
Fene E 140 A2
Fenestrelle I 119 B4
Fénétrange F 92 C3
Feneu F 102 B1
Fengersfors S 54 B3
Fenit IRL 29 B2
Fensmark DK 65 A4
Fenwick GB 36 A2
Feolin Ferry GB 34 C1
Ferbane IRL 28 A4
Ferdinandovac HR 124 A3
Ferdinandshof D 74 A2
Fère-Champenoise F 91 C3
Fère-en-Tardenois F 91 B3
Ferentillo I 168 A2
Ferentino I 169 B3
Feres GR 183 C8
Feria E 155 C4
Feričanci HR 125 B3
Ferizli TR 187 B5
Ferla I 177 B3
Ferlach A 110 C1
Ferleiten A 109 B3
Fermil P 148 A2
Fermo I 136 B2
Fermoselle E 149 A3
Fermoy IRL 29 B3
Fernancabellero E 157 A4
Fernán Nuñéz E 163 A3
Fernán Peréz E 164 C2
Fernão Ferro P 154 C1
Fernay-Voltaire F 118 A3
Ferndown GB 43 B5
Ferness GB 32 D3
Fernhurst GB 44 B3
Ferns IRL 30 B2
Ferpécle CH 119 A4
Ferrals-les-Corbières F 146 A3
Ferrandina I 172 B2
Ferrara I 121 C4
Ferrara di Monte Baldo I 121 B3
Ferreira E 141 A3
Ferreira do Alentejo P 160 A1
Ferreira do Zêzere P 154 B2
Ferreras de Abajo E 141 C4
Ferreras de Arriba E 141 C4
Ferreries E 167 B4
Ferreruela E 152 A2
Ferreruela de Tabara E 149 A3
Ferret CH 119 B4
Ferrette F 106 B2
Ferriere I 120 C2
Ferrière-la-Grande F 79 B3
Ferrières
Hautes-Pyrénées F 145 A3
Loiret F 103 A4
Oise F 90 B2
Ferrières-sur-Sichon F 117 A3
Ferrol E 140 A2
Ferryhill GB 37 B5
Fertörakos H 111 B3
Fertöszentmiklós H 111 B3
Ferwerd NL 70 A2
Festieux F 91 B3
Festøy N 198 C3
Festvåg N 194 C5
Fetești RO 17 C7
Fethard
Tipperary IRL 29 B4
Wexford IRL 30 B2
Fethiye TR 188 C4
Fetsund N 48 C3
Fettercairn GB 35 B5
Feucht D 95 B3
Feuchtwangen D 94 B2
Feudingen D 81 B4
Feuges F 91 C4
Feuquières F 90 B1
Feurs F 117 B4
Fevik N 53 B4
Ffestiniog GB 38 B3
Fiamignano I 169 A3
Fiano I 119 B4
Ficarazzi I 176 A2
Ficarolo I 121 C4
Fichtelberg D 95 A3
Ficulle I 135 C5
Fidenza I 120 C3
Fidjeland N 52 B2
Fieberbrunn A 109 B3
Fier AL 182 C1
Fiera di Primiero I 121 A4
Fiesch CH 119 A5
Fiesso Umbertiano I 121 C4
Figari F 180 B2
Figeac F 116 C2
Figeholm S 62 A4
Figgjo N 52 B1
Figline Valdarno I 135 B4
Figols E 145 B4
Figueira da Foz P 148 B1
Figueira de Castelo Rodrigo P 149 B3
Figueira dos Caveleiros P 160 A1
Figueiredo P 154 B3
Figueiredo de Alva P 148 B2
Figueiródos Vinhos P 154 B2
Figueres E 147 B3
Figueroles E 153 B3
Figueruela de Arriba E 141 C4
Filadélfia I 175 C2
Fil'akovo SK 99 C3
Filderstadt D 94 C1
Filey GB 41 A3
Filiași RO 17 C5
Filiates GR 182 D2
Filiatra GR 184 B2
Filipstad S 55 A5
Filisur CH 107 C4
Fillan N 198 B5
Filotio GR 185 B6
Filottrano I 136 B2
Filskov DK 59 C2
Filton GB 43 A4
Filtvet N 54 A1
Filzmoos A 109 B4
Finale Emília I 121 C4
Finale Lígure I 133 A4
Fiñana E 164 B2
Finby FIN 51 B7
Fincham GB 41 C4
Finchingfield GB 45 B4
Findhorn GB 32 D3
Findochty GB 33 D4
Finike TR 189 C5
Finkenberg A 108 B2
Finnea IRL 27 C3
Finneidfjord N 195 D4
Finnerödja S 55 B5
Finnskog N 49 B4
Finnsnes N 194 A9
Finntorp S 54 A3
Finócchio I 168 B2
Finsjö S 62 A4
Finsland N 52 B3
Finspång S 56 B1
Finsterwalde D 84 A1
Finsterwolde NL 71 A4
Finstown GB 33 B3
Fintona GB 27 B3
Fionnphort GB 34 B1
Fiorenzuola d'Arda I 120 C2
Firenze = Florence I 135 B4
Firenzuola I 135 A4
Firmi F 130 A1
Firminy F 117 B4
Firmo I 174 B2
Fischamend Markt A 111 A3
Fischbach
A 110 B2
D 93 B3
Fischbeck D 73 B5
Fischen D 107 B5
Fishbourne GB 44 C2
Fishguard GB 39 C2
Fiskardo GR 184 A1
Fiskebäckskil S 54 B2
Fiskebøl N 194 B5
Fismes F 91 B3
Fisterra E 140 B1
Fitero E 144 B2
Fitjar N 46 C2
Fiuggi I 169 B3
Fiumata I 169 A3
Fiumefreddo Brúzio I 174 B2
Fiumefreddo di Sicília I 177 B4
Fiumicino I 168 B2
Fivemiletown GB 27 B3
Fivizzano I 134 A3
Fjälkinge S 63 B2
Fjällåsen S 196 B3
Fjällbacka S 54 B2
Fjæra N 46 C3
Fjärdhundra S 56 A2
Fjellerup DK 58 B3
Fjerritslev DK 58 A2
Fjordgard N 194 A8
Fjugesta S 55 A5
Flå N 47 B6
Flåbygd N 53 A4
Flaça E 147 B3
Flace F 117 A4
Fladungen D 82 B2
Flaine F 118 A3
Flaka FIN 51 B7
Flåm N 46 B4
Flamatt CH 106 C2
Flamborough GB 41 A3
Flammersfeld D 81 B3
Flassans-sur-Issole F 132 B2
Flatdal N 53 A4
Flatebø N 46 B3
Flateby N 48 C3
Flateland N 52 A3
Flateyri IS 190 A2
Flatøydegard N 47 B6
Flatråker N 46 C2
Flattach A 109 C4
Flatvarp S 62 A4
Flauenskjold DK 58 A3
Flavigny-sur-Moselle F 92 C2
Flavy-le-Martel F 90 B3
Flawil CH 107 B4
Flayosc F 132 B2
Flechtingen D 73 B4
Fleckeby D 64 B2
Fleet GB 44 B3
Fleetmark D 73 B4
Fleetwood GB 38 A3
Flehingen D 93 B4
Flekke N 46 A2
Flekkefjord N 52 B2
Flen S 56 A2
Flensburg D 64 B2
Fleringe S 57 C4
Flerohopp S 62 B3
Flers F 88 B3
Flesberg N 47 C6
Fleurance F 129 C3
Fleuré F 115 B4
Fleurier CH 105 C5
Fleurus B 79 B4
Fleury
Hérault F 130 B2
Yonne F 104 B2

Fleury-les-Aubrais
F 103 B3
Fleury-sur-Andelle
F 89 A5
Fleury-sur-Orne F 89 A3
Flieden D 81 B5
Flimby GB 36 B3
Flims CH 107 C4
Flines-lèz-Raches F 78 B3
Flint GB 38 A3
Flirey F 92 C1
Flirsch A 108 B1
Flisa N 49 B4
Flisby S 62 A2
Fliseryd S 62 A4
Flix E 153 A4
Flixecourt F 90 A2
Flize F 91 B4
Flobecq B 79 B3
Floby S 55 B4
Floda S 60 B2
Flodden GB 37 A4
Flogny-la-Chapelle
F 104 B2
Flöha D 83 B5
Flonheim D 93 B4
Florac F 130 A2
Floreffe B 79 B4
Florence = Firenze
I 135 B4
Florennes B 79 B4
Florensac F 130 B2
Florentin F 129 C5
Florenville B 91 B5
Flores de Avila E 150 B2
Floresta I 177 B3
Floreşti MD 17 B8
Florídia I 177 B4
Florina GR 182 C3
Florø N 46 A2
Flörsheim D 93 A4
Floss D 95 B4
Fluberg N 48 B2
Flúðir IS 190 C5
Flühli CH 106 C3
Flumet F 118 B3
Fluminimaggiore I 179 C2
Flums CH 107 B4
Flyeryd S 63 B3
Flygsfors S 62 B3
Foča BIH 139 B4
Foça TR 186 D1
Fochabers GB 32 D3
Focşani RO 17 C7
Foel GB 38 B3
Foeni RO 126 B2
Fogdö S 56 A2
Fóggia I 171 B3
Foglianise I 170 B2
Föglö FIN 51 B7
Fohnsdorf A 110 B1
Foiano della Chiana
I 135 B4
Foix F 146 B2
Fojnica
BIH 139 B3
BIH 139 B4
Fokstua N 198 C6
Földeák H 126 A2
Foldereid N 199 A9
Főldes H 113 B5
Folegandros GR 185 C5
Folelli F 180 A2
Folgaria I 121 B4
Folgosinho P 148 B2
Folgoso de la Ribera
E 141 B4
Folgoso do Courel
E 141 B3
Foligno I 136 C1
Folkärna S 50 B3
Folkestad N 198 C3
Folkestone GB 45 B5
Follafoss N 199 B8
Folldal N 198 C6
Follebu N 48 A2
Follina I 121 B5
Föllinge S 199 B11
Follónica I 135 C3
Fölsbyn S 54 A3
Foncebadón E 141 B4
Foncine-le-Bas F 105 C5
Fondevila E 140 C2
Fondi I 169 B3
Fondo I 121 A4
Fonelas E 164 B1
Fonfría
Teruel E 152 B2
Zamora E 149 A3
Fonn N 46 A3
Fonnes N 46 B1
Fonni I 178 B3
Fontaine F 91 C4
Fontainebleau F 90 C2
Fontaine de Vaucluse
F 131 B4
Fontaine-Française
F 105 B4
Fontaine-le-Dun F 89 A4
Fontan F 133 A3
Fontanarejo E 157 A3
Fontane I 133 A3
Fontanélice I 135 A4
Fontanières F 116 A2
Fontanosas E 157 B3
Fontebianda I 168 A1
Fontenay-le-Comte
F 114 B3
Fontenay-Trésigny
F 90 C2
Fontevrault-l'Abbaye
F 102 B2
Fontiveros E 150 B3
Fontoy F 92 B1
Fontpédrouse F 146 B3
Font-Romeu F 146 B3
Fontstown IRL 30 A2
Fonyód H 111 C4
Fonz E 145 B4
Fonzaso I 121 A4
Fóppolo I 120 A2
Föra S 62 A4
Forbach
D 93 C4
F 92 B2
Forcall E 153 B3
Forcalquier F 132 B1
Forcarei E 140 B2
Forchheim D 94 B3
Forchtenau A 111 B3
Forchtenberg D 94 B1
Ford GB 34 B2
Førde
Hordaland N 52 A1
Sogn og Fjordane
N 46 A2
Förderstedt D 83 A3
Førdesfjorden N 52 A1
Fordham GB 45 A4
Fordingbridge GB 44 C2
Fordon PL 76 A3
Fordongiánus I 179 C2
Forenza I 172 B1
Foresta di Búrgos
I 178 B2
Forfar GB 35 B5
Forges-les-Eaux F 90 B1
Foria I 172 B1
Forío I 170 C1
Forjães P 148 A1
Førland N 52 B3
Forlì I 135 A5
Forlimpopoli I 135 A5
Formazza I 119 A5
Formby GB 38 A3
Formerie F 90 B1
Fórmia I 169 B3
Formígine I 135 A3
Formigliana I 119 B5
Formiguères F 146 B3
Fornalutx E 166 B2
Fornåsa S 56 B1
Fornelli I 178 B2
Fornells E 167 A4
Fornelos de Montes
E 140 B2
Fornes E 163 B4
Forneset N 192 C3
Forni Avoltri I 109 C3
Forni di Sopra I 122 A1
Forni di Sotto I 122 A1
Forno
Piemonte I 119 B4
Piemonte I 119 B5
Forno Alpi-Gráie I 119 B4
Forno di Zoldo I 121 A5
Fornos de Algodres
P 148 B2
Fornovo di Taro I 120 C3
Foros do Arrão P 154 B2
Forráskút H 126 A1
Forres GB 32 D3
Forriolo E 140 B3
Fors S 50 B3
Forsand N 52 B2
Forsbacka S 51 B3
Forserum S 62 A2
Forshaga S 55 A4
Forsheda S 60 B3
Forsinain GB 32 C3
Førslev DK 65 A4
Förslöv S 61 C2
Forsmark
Uppsala S 51 B5
Västerbotten S 195 E6
Forsmo S 200 C3
Forsnäs S 195 D9
Forsnes N 198 B5
Forssa FIN 8 B3
Forssjöbruk S 56 B2
Forst D 84 A2
Forsvik S 55 B5
Fortanete E 153 B3
Fort Augustus GB 32 D2
Forte dei Marmi I 134 B3
Fortezza I 108 C2
Forth GB 35 C4
Fort-Mahon-Plage F 78 B1
Fortrie GB 33 D4
Fortrose GB 32 D2
Fortun N 47 A4
Fortuna E 165 A3
Fortuneswell GB 43 B4
Fort William GB 34 B2
Forvik N 195 E3
Fos F 145 B4
Fosdinovo I 134 A3
Foss N 47 B6
Fossacésia I 169 A4
Fossano I 133 A3
Fossato di Vico I 136 B1
Fossbakken N 194 B8
Fosse-la-Ville B 79 B4
Fossombrone I 136 B1
Fos-sur-Mer F 131 B3
Fot H 112 B3
Fouchères F 104 A3
Fouesnant F 100 B1
Foug F 92 C1
Fougères F 88 B2
Fougerolles F 105 B5
Foulain F 105 A4
Fountainhall GB 35 C5
Fouras F 114 C2
Fourchambault F 104 B2
Fourmies F 91 A4
Fourna GR 182 D3
Fournels F 116 C3
Fourni GR 188 B1
Fournols F 117 B3
Fourques F 146 B3
Fourquevaux F 146 A2
Fours F 104 C2
Fowey GB 42 B2
Foxdale GB 36 B2
Foxford IRL 26 C1
Foyers GB 32 D2
Foynes IRL 29 B2
Foz E 141 A3
Foza I 121 B4
Foz do Arelho P 154 B1
Foz do Giraldo P 155 B3
Frabosa Soprana I 133 A3
Frades de la Sierra
E 149 B4
Fraga E 153 A4
Fragagnano I 173 B3
Frailes E 163 A4
Fraire B 79 B4
Fraize F 106 A1
Framlingham GB 45 A5
Frammersbach D 94 A1
Framnes N 54 A1
França P 141 C4
Francaltroff F 92 C2
Francavilla al Mare
I 169 A4
Francavilla di Sicilia
I 177 B4
Francavilla Fontana
I 173 B3
Francavilla in Sinni
I 174 A2
Francescas F 129 B3
Franco P 148 A2
Francofonte I 177 B3
Francos E 151 A4
Frändefors S 54 B3
Franeker NL 70 A2
Frangy F 118 A2
Frankenau D 81 A4
Frankenberg
Hessen D 81 A4
Sachsen D 83 B5
Frankenburg A 109 A4
Frankenfels A 110 B2
Frankenmarkt A 109 B4
Frankenthal D 93 B4
Frankfurt
Brandenburg D 74 B3
Hessen D 81 B4
Frankrike S 199 B10
Fränsta S 200 D2
Františkovy Lázně
CZ 83 B4
Franzburg D 66 B1
Frascati I 168 B2
Frasdorf D 109 B3
Fraserburgh GB 33 D4
Frashër AL 182 C2
Frasne F 105 C5
Frasnes-lez-Anvaing
B 79 B3
Frasseto F 180 B2
Frastanz A 107 B4
Fratel P 155 B3
Fratta Todina I 135 C5
Frauenau D 96 C1
Frauenfeld CH 107 B3
Frauenkirchen A 111 B3
Frauenstein D 83 B5
Frauental A 110 C2
Frayssinet F 129 B4
Frayssinet-le-Gélat
F 129 B4
Frechas P 149 A2
Frechen D 80 B2
Frechilla E 142 B2
Freckenhorst D 71 C4
Fredeburg D 81 A4
Fredelsloh D 82 A1
Fredeng N 48 B2
Fredensborg DK 61 D2
Fredericia DK 59 C2
Frederiks DK 59 B2
Frederikshavn DK 58 A3
Frederikssund DK 61 D2
Frederiksværk DK 61 D2
Fredrika S 200 B4
Fredriksberg S 50 B1
Fredriksdal S 62 A2
Fredrikstad N 54 A1
Fregenal de la Sierra
E 161 A3
Fregene I 168 B2
Freiberg D 83 B5
Freiburg
Baden-Württemberg
D 106 B2
Niedersachsen D 64 C2
Freienhagen D 81 A5
Freienhufen D 84 A1
Freiensteinau D 81 B5
Freihung D 95 B3
Freilassing D 109 B3
Freisen D 92 B3
Freising D 95 C3
Freistadt A 96 C2
Freital D 84 A1
Freixedas P 149 B2
Freixo de Espada à
Cinta P 149 A3
Fréjus F 132 B2
Fremdingen D 94 C2
Frenštát pod
Radhoštěm CZ 98 B2
Freren D 71 B4
Freshford IRL 30 B1
Freshwater GB 44 C2
Fresnay-sur-Sarthe
F 89 B4
Fresneda de la Sierra
E 152 B1
Fresneda de la Sierra
Tiron E 143 B3
Fresnedillas E 151 B3
Fresnes-en-Woevre
F 92 B1
Fresne-St Mamès
F 105 B4
Fresno Alhandiga
E 150 B2
Fresno de la Ribera
E 150 A2
Fresno de la Vega
E 142 B1
Fresno de Sayago
E 149 A4
Fresnoy-Folny F 90 B1
Fresnoy-le-Grand F 91 B3
Fressenville F 90 A1
Fresvik N 46 A3
Fréteval F 103 B3
Fretigney F 105 B4
Freudenberg
Baden-Württemberg
D 94 B1
Nordrhein-Westfalen
D 81 B3
Freudenstadt D 93 C4
Freux B 92 B1
Frévent F 78 B2
Freyburg D 83 A3
Freyenstein D 73 A5
Freyming-Merlebach
F 92 B2
Freystadt D 95 B3
Freyung D 96 C1
Frias de Albarracin
E 152 B2
Fribourg CH 106 C2
Frick CH 106 B3
Fridafors S 63 B2
Fridaythorpe GB 40 A3
Friedberg
A 111 B3
Bayern D 94 C2
Hessen D 81 B4
Friedeburg D 71 A4
Friedewald D 82 B1
Friedland
Brandenburg D 74 B3
Mecklenburg-
Vorpommern D 74 A2
Niedersachsen D 82 A1
Friedrichroda D 82 B2
Friedrichsdorf D 81 B4
Friedrichshafen D 107 B4
Friedrichskoog D 64 B1
Friedrichstadt D 64 B2
Friedrichswalde D 74 A2
Friesach A 110 C1
Friesack D 73 B5
Friesenheim D 93 C3
Friesoythe D 71 A4
Friggesund S 200 E2
Frigiliana E 163 B4
Frihetsli N 192 D3
Frillesås S 60 B2
Frinnaryd S 62 A2
Frinton-on-Sea GB 45 B5
Friockheim GB 35 B5
Friol E 140 A3
Fristad S 60 B2
Fritsla S 60 B2
Fritzlar D 81 A5
Frizington GB 36 B3
Frödinge S 62 A4
Froges F 118 B2
Frohburg D 83 A4
Frohnhausen D 81 B4
Frohnleiten A 110 B2
Froissy F 90 B2
Frombork PL 69 A4
Frome GB 43 A4
Frómista E 142 B2
Fröndenberg D 81 A3
Fronsac F 128 B2
Front I 119 B4
Fronteira P 155 B3
Frontenay-Rohan-Rohan
F 114 B3
Frontenhausen D 95 C4
Frontignan F 130 B2
Fronton F 129 C4
Fröseke S 62 B3
Frosinone I 169 B3
Frosolone I 170 B2
Frosta N 199 B7
Frøstrup DK 58 A1
Frosunda S 57 A4
Frouard F 92 C2
Frövi S 56 A1
Frøyset N 46 B2
Fruges F 78 B2
Frutigen CH 106 C2
Frýdek-Místek CZ 98 B2
Frýdlant CZ 84 B3
Frydlant nad Ostravicí
CZ 98 B2
Frygnowo PL 77 A5
Fryšták CZ 98 B1
Fucécchio I 135 B3
Fuencaliente
Ciudad Real E 157 A4
Ciudad Real E 157 B3
Fuencemillán E 151 B4
Fuendejalón E 144 C2
Fuengirola E 163 B3
Fuenlabrada E 151 B4
Fuenlabrada de los
Montes E 156 A3
Fuensalida E 151 B3
Fuensanta E 164 B3
Fuensanta de Martos
E 163 A4
Fuente-Alamo E 158 C2
Fuente-Álamo de Murcia
E 165 B3
Fuentealbilla E 158 B2
Fuente al Olmo de Iscar
E 150 A3
Fuentecén E 151 A4
Fuente Dé E 142 A2
Fuente de Cantos
E 155 C4
Fuente del Arco E 156 B2
Fuente del Conde
E 163 A3
Fuente del Maestre
E 155 C4
Fuente de Santa Cruz
E 150 A3
Fuente el Fresno E 157 A4
Fuente el Saz de Jarama
E 151 B4
Fuente el Sol E 150 A3
Fuenteguinaldo E 149 B3
Fuentelapeña E 150 A2
Fuentelcésped E 151 A4
Fuentelespino de Haro
E 158 B1
Fuentelespino de Moya
E 158 B2
Fuentenovilla E 151 B4
Fuente Obejuna E 156 B2
Fuente Palmera E 162 A2
Fuentepelayo E 151 A3
Fuentepinilla E 151 A5
Fuenterroble de
Salvatierra E 150 B2
Fuenterrobles E 158 B2
Fuentes E 158 B1
Fuentesauco E 151 A3
Fuentesaúco E 150 A2
Fuentes de Andalucía
E 162 A2
Fuentes de Ebro E 153 A3
Fuentes de Jiloca
E 152 A2
Fuentes de la Alcarria
E 151 B5
Fuentes de León E 161 A3
Fuentes de Nava E 142 B2
Fuentes de Oñoro
E 149 B3
Fuentes de Ropel
E 142 B1
Fuentespalda E 153 B4
Fuentespina E 151 A4
Fuente-Tójar E 163 A3
Fuente Vaqueros E 163 A4
Fuentidueña E 151 A4
Fuentidueña de Tajo
E 151 B4
Fuerte del Rey E 157 C4
Fügen A 108 B2
Fuglebjerg DK 65 A4
Fuglevik N 54 A1
Fuhrberg D 72 B2
Fulda D 82 B1
Fulgatore I 176 B1
Fully CH 119 A4
Fulnek CZ 98 B1
Fülöpszállás H 112 C3
Fulpmes A 108 B2
Fulunäs S 49 A5
Fumay F 91 B4
Fumel F 129 B3
Funäsdalen S 199 C9
Fundão P 148 B2
Funzie GB 33 A6
Furadouro P 148 B1
Fure N 46 A2
Fürstenau D 71 B4
Furstenau D 81 A5
Fürstenberg D 74 A2
Fürstenfeld A 111 B3
Fürstenfeldbruck
D 108 A2
Fürstenstein D 96 C1
Fürstenwalde D 74 B3
Fürstenwerder D 74 A2
Fürstenzell D 96 C1
Furta H 113 B5
Fürth
Bayern D 94 B2
Hessen D 93 B4
Furth im Wald D 95 B4
Furtwangen D 106 A3
Furuby S 62 B3
Furudal S 50 A2
Furuflaten N 192 C4
Furulund S 61 D3
Furusjö S 60 B3
Fusa N 46 B2
Fuscaldo I 174 B2
Fusch an der
Grossglocknerstrasse
A 109 B3
Fushë Arrëz AL 182 A2
Fushë-Krujë AL 182 B1
Fusina I 122 B1
Fusio CH 107 C3
Füssen D 108 B1
Fustiñana E 144 B2
Futog SRB 126 B1
Futrikelv N 192 C3
Füzesabony H 113 B4
Füzesgyarmat H 113 B5
Fužine HR 123 B3
Fyllinge S 61 C2
Fynshav DK 64 B2
Fyresdal N 53 A4

G

Gaaldorf A 110 B1
Gabaldón E 158 B2
Gabarret F 128 C2
Gabčíkovo SK 111 B4
Gąbin PL 77 B4
Gabriac F 130 A1
Gabrovo BG 17 D6
Gaby I 119 B4
Gacé F 89 B4
Gacko BIH 139 B4
Gäddede S 199 A11
Gadebusch D 65 C4
Gadmen CH 106 C3
Gádor E 164 C2
Gádoros H 113 C4
Gael F 101 A3
Găeşti RO 17 C6
Gaeta I 169 B3
Gafanhoeira P 154 C2
Gaflenz A 110 B1
Gagarin RUS 9 E9
Gaggenau D 93 C4
Gagliano Castelferrato
I 177 B3
Gagliano del Capo
I 173 C4
Gagnet S 50 B2
Gaibanella I 121 C4
Gaildorf D 94 B1
Gaillac F 129 C4
Gaillefontaine F 90 B1
Gaillon F 89 A5
Gainsborough GB 40 B3
Gairloch GB 31 B3
Gairlochy GB 34 B3
Gáiro I 179 C3
Gaj
HR 124 B3
SRB 127 C3
Gaja-la-Selve F 146 A2
Gajanejos E 151 B5
Gajary SK 97 C4
Gajdobra SRB 126 B1
Galan F 145 A4
Galanta SK 111 A4
Galapagar E 151 B3
Galápagos E 151 B4
Galaroza E 161 B3
Galashiels GB 35 C5
Galatas GR 185 B4
Galaţi RO 17 C8
Galatina I 173 B4
Galatista GR 183 C5
Galátone I 173 B4
Galaxidi GR 184 A3
Galdakao E 143 A4
Galeata I 135 B4
Galende E 141 B4
Galera E 164 B2
Galéria F 180 A1
Galgamácsa H 112 B3
Galgate GB 38 A4
Galgon F 128 B2
Galices P 148 B2
Galinduste E 150 B2
Galinoporni CY 181 A3
Galisteo E 155 B4
Galków PL 87 A3
Gallarate I 120 B1
Gallardon F 90 C1
Gallegos de Argañán
E 149 B3
Gallegos del Solmirón
E 150 B2
Galleguillos de Campos
E 142 B1
Galleno I 135 B3
Galliate I 120 B1
Gallicano I 134 A3
Gállio I 121 B4
Gallipoli = Gelibolu
TR 186 B1
Gallípoli I 173 B3
Gällivare S 196 B3
Gallizien A 110 C1
Gallneukirchen A 96 C2
Gällö S 199 C12

Gallocanta E 152 B2
Gällstad S 60 B3
Gallur E 144 C2
Galmisdale GB 31 C2
Galmpton GB 43 B3
Galston GB 36 A2
Galta N 52 A1
Galtelli I 178 B3
Galten DK 59 B2
Galtür A 107 C5
Galve de Sorbe E 151 A4
Galveias P 154 B2
Gálvez E 157 A3
Galway IRL 28 A2
Gamaches F 90 B1
Gámbara I 120 B3
Gambárie I 175 C1
Gambassi Terme I 135 B3
Gambatesa I 170 B2
Gambolò I 120 B1
Gaming A 110 B2
Gamla Uppsala S 51 C4
Gamleby S 62 A4
Gamlingay GB 44 A3
Gammelgarn S 57 C4
Gammelstad S 196 D5
Gammertingen D 107 A4
Gams CH 107 B4
Gamvik
Finnmark N 192 B6
Finnmark N 193 A12
Gan F 145 A3
Gáname E 149 A3
Ganda di Martello I 108 C1
Gandarela P 148 A1
Ganddal N 52 B1
Ganderkesee D 72 A1
Gandesa E 153 A4
Gandía E 159 C3
Gandino I 120 B2
Gandrup DK 58 A3
Ganges F 130 B2
Gånghester S 60 B3
Gangi I 177 B3
Gangkofen D 95 C4
Gannat F 116 A3
Gannay-sur-Loire
F 104 C2
Gänserdorf A 97 C4
Ganzlin D 73 A5
Gap F 132 A2
Gara H 125 A5
Garaballa E 158 B2
Garaguso I 172 B2
Garbayuela E 156 A2
Garbhallt GB 34 B2
Garbsen D 72 B2
Garching D 109 A3
Garciaz E 156 A2
Garcihernández E 150 B2
Garcillán E 151 B3
Garcinarro E 151 B5
Garcisobaco E 162 B2
Garda I 121 B3
Gardanne F 131 B4
Gärdås S 49 B5
Gårdby S 63 B4
Gardeja PL 69 B3
Gardelegen D 73 B4
Gardermoen N 48 B3
Gardiki GR 182 E3
Garding D 64 B1
Gardone Riviera I 121 B3
Gardone Val Trómpia
I 120 B3
Gárdony H 112 B2
Gardouch F 146 A2
Gårdsjö S 55 B5
Gårdskär S 51 B4
Gards Köpinge S 63 C2
Garein F 128 B2
Garelochhead GB 34 B3
Garéoult F 132 B2
Garešnica HR 124 B2
Garéssio I 133 A4
Garforth GB 40 B2
Gargaliani GR 184 B2
Gargaligas E 156 A2
Gargallo E 153 B3
Garganta la Olla E 150 B2
Gargantiel E 156 B3
Gargellen A 107 C4
Gargilesse-Dampierre
F 103 C3
Gargnano I 121 B3
Gargnäs S 195 E8
Gárgoles de Abajo
E 152 B1
Gargrave GB 40 B1
Garitz D 73 C5
Garlasco I 120 B1
Garlieston GB 36 B2
Garlin F 128 C2
Garlitos E 156 B2
Garmisch-Partenkirchen
D 108 B2
Garnat-sur-Engièvre
F 104 C2
Garpenberg S 50 B3
Garphyttan S 55 A5
Garray E 143 C4
Garrel D 71 B5
Garriguella E 146 B4
Garrison GB 26 B2
Garrovillas E 155 B4
Garrucha E 164 B3
Gars-am-Kamp A 97 C3
Garsås S 50 B1
Garsdale Head GB 37 B4
Gärsnäs S 63 C2
Garstang GB 38 A4
Gartow D 73 A4
Gartz D 74 A3
Gærum DK 58 A3
Garvagh GB 27 B4
Garvão P 160 B1
Garve GB 32 D2
Garwolin PL 12 C4
Garz D 66 B2
Garzyn PL 85 A4
Gąsawa PL 76 B2
Gåsborn S 49 C6
Gaschurn A 107 C5
Gascueña E 152 B1
Gasny F 90 B1
Gąsocin PL 77 B5
Gastes F 128 B1
Gastouni GR 184 B2
Gastouri GR 182 D1
Gata
E 149 B3
HR 138 B2
Gata de Gorgos E 159 C4
Gătaia RO 126 B3
Gatchina RUS 9 C7
Gatehouse of Fleet
GB 36 B2
Gátér H 113 C3
Gateshead GB 37 B5
Gátova E 159 B3
Gattendorf A 111 A3
Gatteo a Mare I 136 A1
Gattinara I 119 B5
Gattorna I 134 A2
Gaucín E 162 B2
Gaulstad N 199 B9
Gaupne N 47 A4
Gautefall N 53 A4
Gauting D 108 A2
Gauto S 195 D7
Gava E 147 C3
Gavardo I 121 B3
Gavarnie F 145 B3
Gávavencsello H 113 A5
Gavi I 120 C1
Gavião P 154 B3
Gavirate I 120 B1
Gävle S 51 B4
Gavoi I 178 B3
Gavorrano I 135 C3
Gavray F 88 B2
Gavrio GR 185 B5
Gävunda S 49 B6
Gaweinstal A 97 C4
Gaworzyce PL 85 A3
Gawroniec PL 75 A5
Gaydon GB 44 A2
Gayton GB 41 C4
Gazipaşa TR 189 C7
Gazoldo degli Ippoliti
I 121 B3
Gazzuolo I 121 B3
Gbelce SK 112 B2
Gdańsk PL 69 A3
Gdinj HR 138 B2
Gdov RUS 8 C5
Gdów PL 99 B4
Gdynia PL 69 A3
Gea de Albarracin
E 152 B2
Geary GB 31 B2
Géaudot F 91 C4
Geaune F 128 C2
Gebesee D 82 A2
Gebiz TR 189 B5
Gebze TR 187 B4
Géderlak H 112 C2
Gedern D 81 B5
Gedinne B 91 B4
Gediz TR 187 D4
Gèdre F 145 B4
Gedser DK 65 B4
Gedsted DK 58 B2
Geel B 79 A4
Geesthacht D 72 A3
Geetbets B 79 B5
Gefell D 83 B3
Gehrden D 72 B2
Gehren D 82 B3
Geilenkirchen D 80 B2
Geilo N 47 B5
Geinsheim D 93 B4
Geisa D 82 B1
Geiselhöring D 95 C4
Geiselwind D 94 B2
Geisenfeld D 95 C3
Geisenhausen D 95 C4
Geisenheim D 93 B4
Geising D 84 B1
Geisingen D 107 B3
Geislingen D 94 C1
Geistthal A 110 B2
Geiterygghytta N 47 B4
Geithain D 83 A4
Geithus N 48 C1
Gela I 177 B3
Geldermalsen NL 79 A5
Geldern D 80 A2
Geldrop NL 80 A1
Geleen NL 80 B1
Gelembe TR 186 C2
Gelendost TR 189 A6
Gelibolu = Gallipoli
TR 186 B1
Gelida E 147 C2
Gelnhausen D 81 B5
Gelnica SK 99 C4
Gelsa E 153 A3
Gelse H 111 C3
Gelsenkirchen D 80 A3
Gelsted DK 59 C2
Geltendorf D 108 A2
Gelterkinden CH 106 B2
Gelting D 64 B2
Gelu RO 126 A3
Gelves E 162 A1
Gembloux B 79 B4
Gemeaux F 105 B4
Gémenos F 132 B1
Gemerská Poloma
SK 99 C4
Gemerská Ves SK 99 C4
Gemert NL 80 A1
Gemla S 62 B2
Gemlik TR 186 B4
Gemmenich B 80 B1
Gemona del Friuli I 122 A2
Gémozac F 114 C3
Gemund D 80 B2
Gemünden
Bayern D 94 A1
Hessen D 81 B4
Rheinland-Pfalz D 93 B3
Genappe B 79 B4
Génave E 164 A2
Genazzano I 169 B2
Gençay F 115 B4
Gencsapáti H 111 B3
Gendringen NL 80 A2
Genelard F 104 C3
Genemuiden NL 70 B3
Generalski Stol HR 123 B4
Geneva = Genève
CH 118 A3
Genevad S 61 C3
Genève = Geneva
CH 118 A3
Genevriéres F 105 B4
Gengenbach D 93 C4
Genillé F 103 B3
Genk B 80 B1
Genlis F 105 B4
Gennep NL 80 A1
Genner DK 64 A2
Gennes F 102 B1
Genoa = Génova I 134 A1
Genola I 133 A3
Génova = Genoa I 134 A1
Genowefa PL 76 B3
Gensingen D 93 B3
Gent = Ghent B 79 A3
Genthin D 73 B5
Gentioux F 116 B1
Genzano di Lucánia
I 172 B2
Genzano di Roma I 168 B2
Georgenthal D 82 B2
Georgsmarienhütte
D 71 B5
Gera D 83 B4
Geraards-bergen B 79 B3
Gerace I 175 C2
Geraci Siculo I 177 B3
Geraki GR 184 C3
Gérardmer F 106 A1
Geras A 97 C3
Gerbéviller F 92 C2
Gerbini I 177 B3
Gerbstedt D 83 A3
Gerði IS 191 C9
Gerede TR 187 B7
Gerena E 161 B3
Geretsried D 108 B2
Gérgal E 164 B2
Gergy F 105 C3
Gerindote E 150 C3
Gerjen H 112 C2
Gerlos A 108 B3
Germay F 92 C1
Germencik TR 188 B2
Germering D 108 A2
Germersheim D 93 B4
Gernika-Lumo E 143 A4
Gernrode D 82 A3
Gernsbach D 93 C4
Gernsheim D 93 B4
Geroda D 82 B1
Gerola Alta I 120 A2
Geroldsgrun D 83 B3
Gerolsbach D 95 C3
Gerolstein D 80 B2
Gerolzhofen D 94 B2
Gerovo HR 123 B3
Gerpinnes B 79 B4
Gerrards Cross GB 44 B3
Gerri de la Sal E 147 B2
Gersfeld D 82 B1
Gerstetten D 94 C2
Gersthofen D 94 C2
Gerstungen D 82 B2
Gerswalde D 74 A2
Gerzat F 116 B3
Gerze TR 23 A8
Gerzen D 95 C4
Gescher D 71 C4
Geseke D 81 A4
Geslau D 94 B2
Gespunsart F 91 B4
Gesté F 101 B4
Gestorf D 72 B2
Gesualda I 170 C3
Gesunda S 50 B1
Gesztely H 113 A4
Geta FIN 51 B6
Getafe E 151 B4
Getinge S 60 C2
Getxo E 143 A4
Geversdorf D 64 C2
Gevgelija MK 182 B4
Gevora del Caudillo
E 155 C4
Gevrey-Chambertin
F 105 B3
Gex F 118 A3
Gey D 80 B2
Geyikli TR 186 C1
Geysir IS 190 C5
Geyve TR 187 B5
Gföhl A 97 C3
Ghedi I 120 B3
Ghent = Gent B 79 A3
Gheorgheni RO 17 B6
Ghigo I 119 C4
Ghilarza I 178 B2
Ghisonaccia F 180 A2
Ghisoni F 180 A2
Gialtra GR 182 E4
Gianitsa GR 182 C4
Giardinetto Vécchio
I 171 B3
Giardini Naxos I 177 B4
Giarratana I 177 B3
Giarre I 177 B4
Giat F 116 B2
Giaveno I 119 B4
Giazza I 121 B4
Giba I 179 C2
Gibellina Nuova I 176 B1
Gibostad N 194 A9
Gibraleón E 161 B3
Gibraltar GBZ 162 B2
Gic H 111 B4
Gideå S 200 C5
Gideåkroken S 200 B3
Gidle PL 86 B3
Giebelstadt D 94 B1
Gieboldehausen D 82 A2
Gielniów PL 87 A4
Gielow D 74 A1
Gien F 103 B4
Giengen D 94 C2
Giens F 132 B2
Giera RO 126 B2
Gieselwerder D 81 A5
Giessen D 81 B4
Gieten NL 71 A3
Giethoorn NL 70 B3
Giffaumont-
Champaubert F 91 C4
Gifford GB 35 C5
Gifhorn D 73 B3
Gige H 125 A3
Gignac F 130 B2
Gijón = Xixón E 142 A1
Gilena E 162 A3
Gilford GB 27 B4
Gillberga S 55 A3
Gilleleje DK 61 C2
Gilley F 105 B5
Gilley-sur-Loire F 104 C2
Gillingham
Dorset GB 43 A4
Medway GB 45 B4
Gilocourt F 90 B2
Gilserberg D 81 B5
Gilsland GB 37 B4
Gilze NL 79 A4
Gimåt S 200 C4
Gimo S 51 B5
Gimont F 129 C3
Ginasservis F 132 B1
Gingelom B 79 B5
Gingst D 66 B2
Ginosa I 171 C4
Ginzling A 108 B2
Giões P 160 B2
Gióia dei Marsi I 169 B3
Gióia del Colle I 173 B2
Gióia Sannitica I 170 B2
Gióia Táuro I 175 C1
Gioiosa Iónica I 175 C2
Gioiosa Marea I 177 A3
Giosla GB 31 A2
Giovinazzo I 171 B4
Girifalco I 175 C2
Giromagny F 106 B1
Girona E 147 C3
Gironcourt-sur-Vraine
F 92 C1
Gironella E 147 B2
Gironville-sous-les-
Côtes F 92 C1
Girvan GB 36 A2
Gislaved S 60 B3
Gislev DK 59 C3
Gisors F 90 B1
Gissi I 170 A2
Gistad S 56 B1
Gistel B 78 A2
Gistrup DK 58 B3
Giswil CH 106 C3
Githio GR 184 C3
Giugliano in Campania
I 170 C2
Giulianova I 136 C2
Giulvăz RO 126 B2
Giurgiu RO 17 D6
Give DK 59 C2
Givet F 91 A4
Givors F 117 B4
Givry
B 79 B4
F 104 C3
Givry-en-Argonne F 91 C4
Givskud DK 59 C2
Giźalki PL 76 B2
Gizeux F 102 B2
Giżycko PL 12 A4
Gizzeria I 175 C2
Gizzeria Lido I 175 C2
Gjedved DK 59 C2
Gjegjan AL 182 B2
Gjendesheim N 47 A5
Gjerde N 46 B3
Gjerlev DK 58 B3
Gjermundshamn N 46 B2
Gjerrild DK 58 B3
Gjerstad N 53 B5
Gjesås N 49 B4
Gjesvær N 193 A9
Gjirokastër AL 182 C2
Gjøfjell N 54 A1
Gjøl DK 58 A2
Gjøra N 198 C6
Gjøvik N 48 B2
Gladbeck D 80 A2
Gladenbach D 81 B4
Gladstad N 195 E2
Glamis GB 35 B4
Glamoč BIH 138 A2
Glamsbjerg DK 59 C3
Gland CH 105 C5
Glandorf D 71 B4
Glanegg A 110 C1
Glanshammar S 56 A1
Glarus CH 107 B4
Glasgow GB 35 C3
Glashütte
Bayern D 108 B2
Sachsen D 84 B1
Glastonbury GB 43 A4
Glatzau A 110 C2
Glauchau D 83 B4
Glava S 54 A3
Glavatičevo BIH 139 B4
Glavičice BIH 127 C1
Gŭlŭbovo BG 183 A7
Glein
A 110 B1
N 195 D3
Gleinstätten A 110 C2
Gleisdorf A 110 B2
Glenamoy IRL 26 B1
Glenarm GB 27 B5
Glenavy GB 27 B4
Glenbarr GB 34 C2
Glenbeigh IRL 29 B2
Glenbrittle GB 31 B2
Glencoe GB 34 B2
Glencolumbkille IRL 26 B2
Glendalough IRL 30 A2
Glenealy IRL 30 B2
Glenelg GB 31 B3
Glenfinnan GB 34 B2
Glengarriff IRL 29 C2
Glenluce GB 36 B2
Glennamaddy IRL 28 A3
Glenrothes GB 35 B4
Glenties IRL 26 B2
Glesborg DK 58 B3
Glesien D 83 A4
Gletsch CH 106 C3
Glewitz D 66 B1
Glifada GR 185 B4
Glimåkra S 63 B2
Glin IRL 29 B2
Glina HR 124 B2
Glinde D 72 A3
Glinojeck PL 77 B5
Glinsk IRL 28 A2
Gliwice PL 86 B2
Glödnitz A 109 C5
Gloggnitz A 110 B2
Głogoczów PL 99 B3
Glogonj SRB 127 C2
Glogovac SRB 127 C3
Głogów PL 85 A4
Głogówek PL 86 B1
Glomel F 100 A2
Glomfjord N 195 D4
Glommen S 60 C2
Glommersträsk S 196 D2
Glonn D 108 B2
Glorenza I 108 C1
Gloria P 154 B2
Glosa GR 183 D5
Glossop GB 40 B2
Gloucester GB 39 C4
Głowaczów PL 87 A5
Główczyce PL 68 A2
Glöwen D 73 B5
Głowno PL 77 C4
Gložan SRB 126 B1
Głubczyce PL 86 B1
Głuchołazy PL 85 B5
Głuchów PL 87 A4
Głuchowo PL 75 B5
Glücksburg D 64 B2
Glückstadt D 64 C2
Glumina BIH 139 A5
Glumsø DK 65 A4
Glušci SRB 127 C1
Glusk BY 13 B8
Głuszyca PL 85 B4
Glyngøre DK 58 B1
Glyn Neath GB 39 C3
Gmünd
Karnten A 109 C4
Nieder Östereich A 96 C2
Gmund D 108 B2
Gmunden A 109 B4
Gnarp S 200 D3
Gnarrenburg D 72 A2
Gnesau A 109 C4
Gnesta S 56 A3
Gnięchowice PL 85 A4
Gniew PL 69 B3
Gniewkowo PL 76 B3
Gniezno PL 76 B2
Gnoien D 66 C1
Gnojnice BIH 139 B3
Gnojno PL 87 B4
Gnosall GB 40 C1
Gnosjö S 60 B3
Göbel TR 186 B3
Göçbeyli TR 186 C2
Goch D 80 A2
Gochsheim D 94 A2
Göd H 112 B3
Godalming GB 44 B3
Godby FIN 51 B6
Goðdalir IS 190 B6
Goddelsheim D 81 A4
Gódega di Sant'Urbano
I 122 B1
Godegård S 56 B1
Godelheim D 81 A5
Goderville F 89 A4
Godiasco I 120 C2
Godič SLO 123 A3
Godkowo PL 69 A4
Godmanchester GB 44 A3
Gödöllö H 112 B3
Gödre H 125 A3
Godshill GB 44 C2
Godzikowice PL 85 B5
Godziszewo PL 69 A3
Goes NL 79 A3
Goetzenbrück F 93 C3
Góglio I 119 A5
Gogolin PL 86 B2
Göhren D 66 B2
Goirle NL 79 A5
Góis P 148 B1
Góito I 121 B3
Goizueta E 144 A2
Gojna Gora SRB 127 D2
Gójsk PL 77 B4
Gökçedağ TR 186 C3
Gökçen TR 188 A2
Gökçeören TR 188 A3
Gökçeyazı TR 186 C2
Göktepe TR 188 B3
Gol N 47 B5
Gola
HR 124 A3
N 48 A1
Gołańcz PL 76 B2
Gölbaşı TR 23 B7
Gölby FIN 51 B6
Gölcük
Kocaeli TR 187 B4
Niğde TR 23 B8
Golčův Jenikov CZ 97 B3
Gołczewo PL 67 C3
Goldach CH 107 B4
Goldbach D 93 A5
Goldbeck D 73 B4
Goldberg D 73 A5
Goldelund D 64 B2
Goldenstedt D 72 B1
Gołębiewo PL 69 A3
Golegã P 154 B2
Goleniów PL 75 A3
Golfo Aranci I 178 B3
Gölhisar TR 189 B4
Golina PL 76 B3
Gölle H 112 C2
Göllersdorf A 97 C4
Golling an der Salzach
A 109 B4
Gölmarmara TR 186 D2
Golnice PL 84 A3
Golnik SLO 123 A3
Gölova TR 189 C5
Gölpazarı TR 187 B5
Gols A 111 B3
Golspie GB 32 D3
Golssen D 74 C2
Golub-Dobrzyń PL 77 A4
Golubinci SRB 127 C2
Goluchów PL 86 A1
Golymin-Ośrodek
PL 77 B5
Golzow D 73 B5
Gomagoi I 108 C1
Gómara E 152 A1
Gomaringen D 93 C5
Gömbe TR 189 C4
Gömeç TR 186 C1
Gomel = Homyel BY 13 B9
Gomes Aires P 160 B1
Gómezserracin E 150 A3
Gommern D 73 B4
Gomulin PL 86 A3
Gonäs S 50 B2
Goncelin F 118 B2
Gończyce PL 87 A5
Gondomar
E 140 B2
P 148 A1
Gondrecourt-le-Château
F 92 C1
Gondrin F 128 C3

Gönen
Balıkesir TR 186 B2
Isparta TR 189 B5
Gonfaron F 132 B2
Goñi E 144 B2
Goni
GR 182 D4
I 179 C3
Gonnesa I 179 C2
Gonnosfanádiga I 179 C2
Gönyü H 111 B4
Gonzaga I 121 C3
Goodrich GB 39 C4
Goodwick GB 39 B1
Gooik B 79 B4
Goole GB 40 B3
Goor NL 71 B3
Göpfritz an der Wild
A 97 C3
Goppenstein CH 119 A4
Göppingen D 94 C1
Gor E 164 B2
Góra
Dolnośląskie PL 85 A4
Mazowieckie PL 77 B5
Gorafe E 164 B1
Gorawino PL 67 C4
Goražde BIH 139 B4
Gőrbeháza H 113 B5
Gordaliza del Pino
E 142 B1
Gördes TR 186 D3
Gørding DK 59 C1
Górdola CH 120 A1
Gordon GB 35 C5
Gordoncillo E 142 B1
Gorebridge GB 35 C4
Gorenja Vas SLO 123 A3
Gorenje Jelenje
HR 123 B3
Gorey
GB 88 A1
IRL 30 B2
Gorgonzola I 120 B2
Gorica HR 137 A4
Gorican HR 124 A2
Gorinchem NL 79 A4
Goring GB 44 B2
Goritsy RUS 9 D10
Göritz D 74 A2
Gorízia I 122 B2
Górki PL 77 B4
Gorleben D 73 A4
Gorleston-on-sea
GB 41 C5
Gørlev DK 61 D1
Görlitz D 84 A2
Górliz E 143 A4
Görmin D 66 C2
Górna Grupa PL 69 B3
Gorna Oryakhovitsa
BG 17 D6
Gornja Gorevnica
SRB 127 D2
Gornja Ploča HR 137 A4
Gornja Radgona
SLO 110 C2
Gornja Sabanta
SRB 127 D3
Gornja Trešnjevica
SRB 127 C2
Gornja Tuzla BIH 125 C4
Gornje Polje MNE 139 C4
Gornje Ratkovo
BIH 124 C2
Gornji Grad SLO 123 A3
Gornji Humac HR 138 B2
Gornji Jasenjani
BIH 139 B3
Gornji Kamengrad
BIH 124 C2
Gornji Kneginec
HR 124 A2
Gornji Kosinj HR 123 C4
Gornji Milanovac
SRB 127 C2
Gornji Podgradci
BIH 124 B3
Gornji Ravno BIH 138 B3
Gornji Sjenicak HR 124 B1
Gornji Vakuf BIH 138 B3
Górno PL 87 B4
Görömböly H 113 A4
Górowo Iławeckie
PL 69 A5
Gorran Haven GB 42 B2
Gorredijk NL 70 A3
Gorron F 88 B3
Gorseinon GB 39 C2
Gort IRL 28 A3
Gortin GB 27 B3
Görzke D 73 B5
Gorzkowice PL 86 A3
Górzno
Kujawsko-Pomorskie
PL 77 A4
Zachodnio-Pomorskie
PL 75 A4
Gorzów Śląski PL 86 A2
Gorzów Wielkopolski
PL 75 B4
Górzyca PL 74 B3
Gorzyce PL 98 B2
Górzyn PL 84 A2
Gorzyń PL 75 B4
Gorzyno PL 68 A2
Gosaldo I 121 A4
Gosau A 109 B4
Gosberton GB 41 C3
Gościcino PL 68 A3
Gościęcin PL 86 B2
Gościm PL 75 B4
Gościno PL 67 B4
Gosdorf A 110 C2
Gosforth GB 36 B3
Goslar D 82 A2
Goslice PL 77 B4
Gospič HR 137 A4
Gosport GB 44 C2
Gössäter S 55 B4
Gossau CH 107 B4
Goss Ilsede D 72 B3
Gössnitz D 83 B4
Gössweinstein D 95 B3
Gostivar MK 182 B2
Gostkow PL 77 C4
Göstling an der Ybbs
A 110 B1
Gostomia PL 75 A5
Gostycyn PL 76 A2
Gostyń PL 85 A5
Gostynin PL 77 B4
Goszczyn PL 87 A4
Göta S 54 B3
Göteborg = Gothenburg
S 60 B1
Götene S 55 B4
Gotha D 82 B2
Gothem S 57 C4
Gothenburg = Göteborg
S 60 B1
Gotse Delchev BG 183 B5
Gottersdorf D 95 C4
Göttingen D 82 A1
Gottne S 200 C4
Götzis A 107 B4
Gouarec F 100 A2
Gouda NL 70 B1
Goudhurst GB 45 B4
Goumenissa GR 182 C4
Goura GR 184 B3
Gourdon F 129 B4
Gourgançon F 91 C4
Gourin F 100 A2
Gournay-en-Bray F 90 B1
Gourock GB 34 C3
Gouveia P 148 B2
Gouvy B 80 B1
Gouzeacourt F 90 A3
Gouzon F 116 A2
Govedari HR 138 C3
Govérnolo I 121 B3
Gowarczów PL 87 A4
Gowerton GB 39 C2
Gowidlino PL 68 A2
Gowran IRL 30 B1
Goyatz D 74 B3
Göynük
TR 187 B5
Antalya TR 189 C5
Gozdnica PL 84 A3
Gozdowo PL 77 B4
Gozee B 79 B4
Graal-Müritz D 65 B5
Grabenstätt D 109 B3
Grabhair GB 31 A2
Gråbo S 60 B2
Grabovac
HR 138 B2
SRB 127 C2
Grabovci SRB 127 C1
Grabow D 73 A4
Grabów PL 77 B4
Grabow nad Pilicą
PL 87 A5
Grabów nad Prosną
PL 86 A2
Grabowno PL 76 A2
Grabs CH 107 B4
Gračac HR 138 A1
Gračanica BIH 125 C4
Graçay F 103 B3
Grad SLO 111 C3
Gradac
BIH 139 C4
HR 138 B3
MNE 139 B5
Gradačac BIH 125 C4
Gradec HR 124 B2
Gradefes E 142 B1
Grades A 110 C1
Gradil P 154 C1
Gradina
HR 124 B3
MNE 139 B5
Gradisca d'Isonzo
I 122 B2
Gradište HR 125 B4
Grado
E 141 A4
I 122 B2
Grafenau D 96 C1
Gräfenberg D 95 B3
Gräfenhainichen D 83 A4
Grafenschlag A 97 C3
Grafenstein A 110 C1
Gräfenthal D 82 B3
Grafentonna D 82 A2
Grafenwöhr D 95 B3
Grafing D 108 A2
Grafling D 95 C4
Gräfsnäs S 54 B3
Gragnano I 170 C2
Grahovo SLO 122 A2
Graiguenamanagh
IRL 30 B2
Grain GB 45 B4
Grainau D 108 B2
Graja de Iniesta E 158 B2
Grajera E 151 A4
Gram DK 59 C2
Gramais A 108 B1
Gramat F 129 B4
Gramatneusiedl A 111 A3
Grambow D 74 A3
Grammichele I 177 B3
Gramsh AL 182 C2
Gramzow D 74 A3
Gran N 48 B2
Granada E 163 A4
Granard IRL 27 C3
Grañas E 140 A3
Granátula de Calatrava
E 157 B4
Grancey-le-Château
F 105 B4
Grandas de Salime
E 141 A4
Grandcamp-Maisy F 88 A2
Grand-Champ F 100 B3
Grand Couronne F 89 A5
Grand-Fougeray F 101 B4
Grândola P 160 A1
Grandpré F 91 B4
Grandrieu
B 79 B4
F 117 C3
Grandson CH 106 C1
Grandvillars F 106 B1
Grandvilliers F 90 B1
Grañén E 145 C3
Grangärde S 50 B1
Grange IRL 26 B2
Grangemouth GB 35 B4
Grange-over-Sands
GB 36 B4
Grängesberg S 50 B1
Granges-de Crouhens
F 145 B4
Granges-sur-Vologne
F 106 A1
Gräningen D 73 B5
Granitola-Torretta I 176 B1
Granja
Évora P 155 C3
Porto P 148 A1
Granja de Moreruela
E 142 C1
Granja de Torrehermosa
E 156 B2
Gränna S 55 B5
Grannäs
Västerbotten S 195 E7
Västerbotten S 195 E8
Granö S 200 B5
Granollers E 147 C3
Granowiec PL 85 A5
Granowo PL 75 B5
Gransee D 74 A2
Gransherad N 53 A5
Grantham GB 40 C3
Grantown-on-Spey
GB 32 D3
Grantshouse GB 35 C5
Granville F 88 B2
Granvin N 46 B3
Grærup Strand DK 59 C1
Gräsås S 60 C2
Grasbakken N 193 B12
Grasberg D 72 A2
Grasmere GB 36 B3
Gräsmyr S 200 C5
Grasö S 51 B5
Grassano I 172 B2
Grassau D 109 B3
Grasse F 132 B2
Grassington GB 40 A2
Græsted DK 61 C2
Gråsten DK 64 B2
Grästorp S 54 B3
Gratkorn A 110 B2
Gråträsk S 196 D2
Gratwein A 110 B2
Graulhet F 129 C4
Graus E 145 B4
Grávalos E 144 B2
Gravberget N 49 B4
Grave NL 80 A1
Gravedona I 120 A2
Gravelines F 78 A2
Gravellona Toce I 119 B5
Gravendal S 50 B1
Gravens DK 59 C2
Gravesend GB 45 B4
Graveson F 131 B3
Gravina in Púglia I 172 B2
Gray F 105 B4
Grayrigg GB 37 B4
Grays GB 45 B4
Grayshott GB 44 B3
Graz A 110 B2
Grazalema E 162 B2
Grążawy PL 69 B4
Grazzano Visconti
I 120 C2
Greåker N 54 A2
Great Dunmow GB 45 B4
Great Malvern GB 39 B4
Great Torrington
GB 42 B2
Great Waltham GB 45 B4
Great Yarmouth GB 41 C5
Grebbestad S 54 B2
Grebenstein D 81 A5
Grębocice PL 85 A4
Grębocin PL 76 A3
Greding D 95 B3
Gredstedbro DK 59 C1
Greencastle IRL 27 A3
Greenhead GB 37 B4
Greenisland GB 27 B5
Greenlaw GB 35 C5
Greenock GB 34 C3
Greenway GB 39 C2
Greenwich GB 45 B4
Grefrath D 80 A2
Greifenburg A 109 C4
Greiffenberg D 74 A2
Greifswald D 66 B2
Grein A 110 A1
Greipstad N 53 B3
Greiz D 83 B4
Grenaa DK 58 B3
Grenade F 129 C4
Grenade-sur-l'Adour
F 128 C2
Grenchen CH 106 B2
Grendi N 53 B3
Grenivík IS 191 B7
Grenoble F 118 B2
Gréoux-les-Bains
F 132 B1
Gresenhorst D 66 B1
Gressoney-la-Trinité
I 119 B4
Gressoney-St.-Jean
I 119 B4
Gressthal D 82 B2
Gressvik N 54 A1
Gresten A 110 B2
Gretna GB 36 B3
Greussen D 82 A2
Greve in Chianti I 135 B4
Greven
Mecklenburg-Vorpommern D 73 A3
Nordrhein-Westfalen
D 71 B4
Grevena GR 182 C3
Grevenbroich D 80 A2
Grevenbrück D 81 A4
Grevenmacher L 92 B2
Grevesmühlen D 65 C4
Grevestrand DK 61 D2
Grevie S 61 C2
Greystoke GB 36 B4
Greystones IRL 30 A2
Grez-Doiceau B 79 B4
Grèzec F 129 B4
Grez-en-Bouère F 102 B1
Grezzana I 121 B4
Grgar SLO 122 A2
Grgurevci SRB 127 B1
Gries A 108 B2
Griesbach D 96 C1
Griesheim D 93 B4
Gries in Sellrain A 108 B2
Grieskirchen A 109 A4
Griffen A 110 C1
Grignan F 131 A3
Grignano I 122 B2
Grigno I 121 A4
Grignols F 128 B2
Grignon F 118 B3
Grijota E 142 B2
Grijpskerk NL 71 A3
Grillby S 56 A3
Grimaud F 132 B2
Grimbergen B 79 B4
Grimma D 83 A4
Grimmen D 66 B2
Grimmialp CH 106 C2
Grimsås S 60 B3
Grimsby GB 41 B3
Grimslöv S 62 B2
Grímsstaðir IS 191 B9
Grimstad N 53 B4
Grimstorp S 62 A2
Grindavík IS 190 D3
Grindelwald CH 106 C3
Grindheim N 52 B3
Grindsted DK 59 C1
Griñón E 151 B4
Gripenberg S 62 A2
Gripsholm S 56 A3
Grisolles F 129 C4
Grisslehamn S 51 B5
Gritley GB 33 C4
Grizebeck GB 36 B3
Grndina BIH 124 C2
Gröbming A 109 B4
Gröbzig D 83 A3
Grocka SRB 127 C2
Gröditz D 83 A5
Gródki PL 77 A5
Grodków PL 85 B5
Grodziec PL 76 B3
Grodzisk Mazowiecki
PL 77 B5
Groenlo NL 71 B3
Groesbeek NL 80 A1
Grohote HR 138 B2
Groitzsch D 83 A4
Groix F 100 B2
Grójec PL 77 C5
Grom PL 77 A5
Gromiljca BIH 139 B4
Grömitz D 65 B3
Gromnik PL 99 B4
Gromo I 120 B2
Gronau
Niedersachsen D 72 B2
Gronau *continued*
Nordrhein-Westfalen
D 71 B4
Grønbjerg DK 59 B1
Grönenbach D 107 B5
Grong N 199 A9
Grönhögen S 63 B4
Groningen
D 73 C4
NL 71 A3
Grønnestrand DK 58 A2
Grono CH 120 A2
Grönskåra S 62 A3
Grootegast NL 71 A3
Gropello Cairoli I 120 B1
Grorud N 48 C2
Grósio I 120 A3
Grošnica SRB 127 D2
Grossalmerode D 82 A1
Grossarl A 109 B4
Gross Beeren D 74 B2
Gross Berkel D 72 B2
Grossbodungen D 82 A2
Gross-botwar D 94 C1
Grossburgwedel D 72 B2
Grosschönau D 84 B2
Gross-Dölln D 74 A2
Grossenbrode D 65 B4
Grossenehrich D 82 A2
Grossengottern D 82 A2
Grossenhain D 83 A5
Grossenkneten D 71 B5
Grossenlüder D 81 B5
Grossensee D 72 A3
Grossenzersdorf A 111 A3
Grosseto I 135 C4
Gross-Gerau D 93 B4
Grossgerungs A 96 C2
Grossglobnitz A 97 C3
Grosshabersdorf D 94 B2
Grossharras A 97 C4
Grosshartmansdorf
D 83 B5
Grosshöchstetten
CH 106 C2
Gross Kreutz D 74 B1
Grosskrut A 97 C4
Gross Lafferde D 72 B3
Gross Leutheb D 74 B3
Grosslohra D 82 A2
Grossmehring D 95 C3
Gross Muckrow D 74 B3
Gross Oesingen D 72 B3
Grossostheim D 93 B5
Grosspertholz A 96 C2
Grosspetersdorf A 111 B3
Grosspostwitz D 84 A2
Grossraming A 110 B1
Grossräschen D 84 A2
Gross Reken D 80 A3
Grossrinderfeld D 94 B1
Grossröhrsdorf D 84 A2
Gross Sarau D 65 C3
Gross Särchen D 84 A2
Grossschirma D 83 B5
Gross Schönebeck
D 74 B2
Grossschweinbarth
A 97 C4
Grosssiegharts A 97 C3
Grosssölk A 109 B4
Gross Umstadt D 93 B4
Grosswarasdorf A 111 B3
Gross Warnow D 73 A4
Gross-Weikersdorf
A 97 C3
Gross-Welle D 73 A5
Grosswilfersdorf A 110 B2
Gross Wokern D 65 C5
Grostenquin F 92 C2
Grosuplje SLO 123 B3
Grotli N 198 C4
Grötlingbo S 57 C4
Grottáglie I 173 B3
Grottaminarda I 170 B3
Grottammare I 136 C2
Grotte di Castro I 168 A1
Grotteria I 175 C2
Gróttole I 172 B2
Grouw NL 70 A2
Grov N 194 B8
Grova N 53 A4
Grove E 140 B2
Grua N 48 B2
Grube D 65 B4
Grubišno Polje HR 124 B3
Grude BIH 138 B3
Grudusk PL 77 A5
Grudziądz PL 69 B3
Grue N 49 B4
Gruissan F 130 B2
Grullos E 141 A4
Grumo Áppula I 171 B4
Grums S 55 A4
Grünau im Almtal
A 109 B4
Grünberg D 81 B4
Grünburg A 110 B1
Grundarfjörður IS 190 C2
Gründau D 81 B5
Gründelhardt D 94 B1
Grundforsen S 49 A4
Grundlsee A 109 B4
Grundsund S 54 B2
Grunewald D 84 A1
Grungedal N 53 A3
Grunow D 74 B3
Grünstadt D 93 B4
Gruvberget S 50 A3
Gruyères CH 106 C2
Gruža SRB 127 D2
Grybów PL 99 B4
Grycksbo S 50 B2
Gryfice PL 67 C4
Gryfino PL 74 A3
Gryfów Śląski PL 84 A3
Gryllefjord N 194 A8
Grymyr N 48 B2
Gryt S 56 B2
Grytgöl S 56 B1
Grythyttan S 55 A5
Grytnäs S 57 B3
Grzmiąca PL 68 B1
Grzybno PL 74 A3
Grzywna PL 76 A3
Gschnitz A 108 B2
Gschwend D 94 C1
Gstaad CH 106 C2
Gsteig CH 119 A4
Guadahortuna E 163 A4
Guadalajara E 151 B4
Guadalaviar E 152 B2
Guadalcanal E 156 B2
Guadalcázar E 162 A3
Guadalix de la Sierra
E 151 B4
Guadálmez E 156 B3
Guadalupe E 156 A2
Guadamur E 151 C3
Guadarrama E 151 B3
Guadiaro E 162 B2
Guadix E 164 B1
Guagnano I 173 B3
Guagno F 180 A1
Guajar-Faragüit E 163 B4
Gualchos E 163 B4
Gualdo Tadino I 136 B1
Gualtieri I 121 C3
Guarcino I 169 B3
Guarda P 149 B2
Guardamar del Segura
E 165 A4
Guardão P 148 B1
Guardavalle I 175 C2
Guardea I 168 A2
Guárdia I 172 B1
Guardiagrele I 169 A4
Guardiarégia I 170 B2
Guárdia Sanframondi
I 170 B2
Guardias Viejas E 164 C2
Guardiola de Bergueda
E 147 B2
Guardo E 142 B2
Guareña E 156 B1
Guaro E 162 B3
Guarromán E 157 B4
Guasila I 179 C3
Guastalla I 121 C3
Gubbhögen S 199 A12
Gúbbio I 136 B1
Guben D 74 C3
Gubin PL 74 C3
Gudå N 199 B8
Gudavac BIH 124 C2
Guddal N 46 A2
Güderup DK 64 B2
Gudhem S 55 B4
Gudhjem DK 67 A3
Gudovac HR 124 B2
Gudow D 73 A3
Güdül TR 187 B7
Gudvangen N 46 B3
Guebwiller F 106 B2
Guéjar-Sierra E 163 A4
Guéméné-Penfao
F 101 B4
Guéméné-sur-Scorff
F 100 A2
Güeñes E 143 A3
Guer F 101 B3
Guérande F 101 B3
Guéret F 116 A1
Guérigny F 104 B2
Guesa E 144 B2
Gueugnon F 104 C3
Guglionesi I 170 B2
Gühlen Glienicke D 74 A1
Guia P 154 B2
Guichen F 101 B4
Guidizzolo I 121 B3
Guidónia-Montecelio
I 168 B2
Guiglia I 135 A3
Guignes F 90 C2
Guijo E 156 B3
Guijo de Coria E 149 B3
Guijo de Santa Bábera
E 150 B2
Guijuelo E 150 B2
Guildford GB 44 B3
Guillaumes F 132 A2
Guillena E 162 A1
Guillestre F 118 C3
Guillos F 128 B2
Guilsfield GB 38 B3
Guilvinec F 100 B1
Guimarães P 148 A1
Guincho P 154 C1
Guînes F 78 B1
Guingamp F 100 A2
Guipavas F 100 A1
Guisborough GB 37 B5

Guiscard F 90 B3
Guiscriff F 100 A2
Guise F 91 B3
Guisona E 147 C2
Guitiriz E 140 A3
Guîtres F 128 A2
Gujan-Mestras F 128 B1
Gulbene LV 8 D5
Gulçayır TR 187 C6
Guldborg DK 65 B4
Gullabo S 63 B3
Gullane GB 35 B5
Gullbrå N 46 B3
Gullbrandstorp S 61 C2
Gulleråsen S 50 A2
Gullhaug N 53 A6
Gullringen S 62 A3
Gullspång S 55 B5
Gullstein N 198 B5
Güllük TR 188 B2
Gülnar TR 23 C7
Gülpınar TR 186 C1
Gülşehir TR 23 B8
Gulsvik N 48 B1
Gumiel de Hizán E 143 C3
Gummersbach D 81 A3
Gümüldür TR 188 A2
Gümüşhaciköy TR 23 A8
Gümüşova TR 187 B5
Gundelfingen D 94 C2
Gundel-fingen D 106 A2
Gundelsheim D 93 B5
Gunderschoffen F 93 C3
Gundertshausen A 109 A3
Gundinci HR 125 B4
Gündoğmuş TR 189 C7
Güney
Burdur TR 189 B4
Denizli TR 188 A4
Gunja HR 125 C4
Günlüce TR 188 C3
Gunnarn S 195 E8
Gunnarsbyn S 196 C4
Gunnarskog S 49 C4
Gunnebo S 62 A4
Gunnislake GB 42 B2
Günselsdorf A 111 B3
Guntersblum D 93 B4
Guntersdorf A 97 C4
Guntin E 140 B3
Günyüzü TR 187 C6
Günzburg D 94 C2
Gunzenhausen D 94 B2
Güre
Balıkesir TR 186 C1
Uşak TR 186 D4
Gurk A 110 C1
Gurrea de Gállego
E 144 B3
Gürsu TR 186 B4
Gušće HR 124 B2
Gusev RUS 12 A5
Gúspini I 179 C2
Gusselby S 56 A1
Güssing A 111 B3
Gusswerk A 110 B2
Gustav Adolf S 49 B5
Gustavsberg S 57 A4
Gustavsfors S 54 A3
Güstrow D 65 C5
Gusum S 56 B2
Gutcher GB 33 A5
Gutenstein A 110 B2
Gütersloh D 81 A4
Guttannen CH 106 C3
Guttaring A 110 C1
Guttau D 84 A2
Güttingen CH 107 B4
Gützkow D 66 C2
Guzów PL 77 B5
Gvardeysk RUS 12 A4
Gvarv N 53 A5
Gvozd MNE 139 C5
Gvozdansko HR 124 B2
Gwda Wielka PL 68 B1
Gwennap GB 42 B1
Gy F 105 B4
Gyál H 112 B3
Gyarmat H 111 B4
Gyékényes H 124 A3
Gyé-sur-Seine F 104 A3
Gyljen S 196 C5
Gylling DK 59 C3
Gyoma H 113 C4
Gyömöre H 111 B4
Gyömrö H 112 B3
Gyón H 112 B3
Gyöngyfa H 125 B3
Gyöngyös H 113 B3
Gyöngyöspata H 113 B3
Gyönk H 112 C2
Györ H 111 B4
Györszemere H 111 B4
Gypsera CH 106 C2
Gysinge S 51 B3
Gyttorp S 55 A5
Gyula H 113 C5
Gyulafirátót H 112 B1
Gyulaj H 112 C2

H

Haacht B 79 B4
Haag
Nieder Östereich
A 110 A1
Ober Östereich A 109 A4
D 108 A3
Haaksbergen NL 71 B3
Haamstede NL 79 A3
Haan D 80 A3
Haapajärvi FIN 3 E9
Haapsalu EST 8 C3
Haarlem NL 70 B1
Habas F 128 C2
Habay B 92 B1
Habo S 62 A2
Håbol S 54 B3
Habry CZ 97 B3
Habsheim F 106 B2
Hachenburg D 81 B3
Hacıbektaş TR 23 B8
Hacılar TR 23 B8
Hacinas E 143 C3
Hackås S 199 C11
Hacketstown IRL 30 B2
Hackthorpe GB 37 B4
Hadamar D 81 B4
Hädanberg S 200 C4
Haddington GB 35 C5
Hadersdorf am Kamp
A 97 C3
Haderslev DK 59 C2
Haderup DK 59 B1
Hadım TR 23 C7
Hadleigh
Essex GB 45 B4
Suffolk GB 45 A4
Hadlow GB 45 B4
Hadmersleben D 73 B4
Hadsten DK 59 B3
Hadsund DK 58 B3
Hadžići BIH 139 B4
Hafnarfjörður IS 190 C4
Hafnir IS 190 D3
Hafslo N 47 A4
Haganj HR 124 B2
Hagby S 63 B4
Hage D 71 A4
Hægebostad N 52 B3
Hægeland N 53 B3
Hagen
Niedersachsen D 72 A1
Nordrhein-Westfalen
D 80 A3
Hagenbach D 93 B4
Hagenow D 73 A4
Hagetmau F 128 C2
Hagfors S 49 B5
Häggenås S 199 B11
Hagondange F 92 B2
Hagsta S 51 B4
Haguenau F 93 C3
Hahnbach D 95 B3
Hahnslätten D 81 B4
Hahót H 111 C3
Haiger D 81 B4
Haigerloch D 93 C4
Hailsham GB 45 C4
Hainburg A 111 A3
Hainfeld A 110 A2
Hainichen D 83 B5
Hajdúböszörmény
H 113 B5
Hajdučica SRB 126 B2
Hajdúdorogo H 113 B5
Hajdúnánás H 113 B5
Hajdúszoboszló H 113 B5
Hajnáčka SK 113 A3
Hajnówka PL 13 B5
Hajós H 112 C3
Håkafot S 199 A11
Hakkas S 196 C4
Håksberg S 50 B2
Halaszi H 111 B4
Halberstadt D 82 A3
Halberton GB 43 B3
Hald Ege DK 58 B2
Haldem D 71 B5
Halden N 54 A2
Haldensleben D 73 B4
Halenbeck D 73 A5
Halesowen GB 40 C1
Halesworth GB 45 A5
Halfing D 109 B3
Halhjem N 46 B2
Håliden S 49 B5
Halifax GB 40 B2
Häljelöt S 56 B2
Halkida GR 185 A4
Halkirk GB 32 C3
Hall S 57 C4
Hälla S 200 C3
Hallabro S 63 B3
Hällabrottet S 56 A1
Halland GB 45 C4
Hällaryd S 63 B2
Hallaryd S 61 C3
Hällberga S 56 A2
Hällbybrunn S 56 A2
Halle
B 79 B4
Nordrhein-Westfalen
D 72 B1
Sachsen-Anhalt D 83 A3
Hålleberga S 62 B3
Hällefors S 55 A5
Hälleforsnäs S 56 A2
Hallein A 109 B4
Hällekis S 55 B4
Hallen S 199 B11
Hållen S 51 B4
Hallenberg D 81 A4
Hällestad S 56 B1
Hällevadsholm S 54 B2
Hällevik S 63 B2
Hälleviksstrand S 54 B2
Hallingby N 48 B2
Hallingeberg S 62 A4
Hallingen N 47 B6
Hall in Tirol A 108 B2
Hällnäs S 195 D9
Hållnäs S 51 B4
Hällnäs S 200 B5
Hallormsstaður
IS 191 B11
Hallsberg S 56 A1
Hållsta S 56 A2
Hallstahammar S 56 A2
Hallstatt A 109 B4
Hallstavik S 51 B5
Halltorp S 63 B4
Halluin F 78 B3
Hallviken S 199 B12
Hallworthy GB 42 B2
Halmstad S 61 C2
Hals DK 58 A3
Halsa N 198 B5
Halstead GB 45 B4
Haltdalen N 199 C8
Haltern D 80 A3
Haltwhistle GB 37 B4
Halvarsgårdarna S 50 B2
Halver D 80 A3
Halvrimmen DK 58 A2
Ham F 90 B3
Hamar N 48 B3
Hamarhaug N 46 B2
Hamarøy N 194 B6
Hambach F 92 B3
Hambergen D 72 A1
Hambergsund S 54 B2
Hambledon GB 44 C2
Hambuhren D 72 B2
Hamburg D 72 A3
Hamdibey TR 186 C2
Hamdorf D 64 B2
Hämeenlinna FIN 8 B4
Hameln = Hamlin D 72 B2
Hamersleben D 73 B4
Hamidiye TR 187 C5
Hamilton GB 36 A2
Hamina FIN 8 B5
Hamlagrø N 46 B3
Hamlin = Hameln D 72 B2
Hamm D 81 A3
Hammar S 55 B5
Hammarland FIN 51 B6
Hammarö S 55 A4
Hammarstrand S 200 C2
Hamme B 79 A4
Hammel DK 59 B2
Hammelburg D 82 B1
Hammelspring D 74 A2
Hammenhög S 66 A3
Hammerdal S 199 B12
Hammerfest N 192 B7
Hammershøj DK 58 B2
Hammerum DK 59 B2
Hamminkeln D 80 A2
Hamnavoe GB 33 A5
Hamneda S 60 C3
Hamningberg N 193 B14
Hamoir B 80 B1
Hamont B 80 A1
Hámor H 113 A4
Hamra
Gävleborg S 199 D12
Gotland S 57 D4
Hamrångefjärden S 51 B4
Hamstreet GB 45 B4
Hamsund N 194 B6
Han TR 187 C5
Hanaskog S 61 C4
Hanau D 81 B4
Händelöp S 62 A4
Handlová SK 98 C2
Hanerau-Hademarschen
D 64 B2
Hånger S 60 B3
Hanhimaa FIN 197 B8
Hanken S 55 B5
Hankensbüttel D 73 B3
Han Knežica BIH 124 B2
Hanko FIN 8 C3
Hannover D 72 B2
Hannut B 79 B5
Han Pijesak BIH 139 A4
Hansnes N 192 C3
Hanstedt D 72 A3
Hanstholm DK 58 A1
Hantsavichy BY 13 B7
Hanušovice CZ 85 B4
Haparanda S 196 D7
Haradok BY 13 A8
Harads S 196 C4
Häradsbäck S 63 B2
Häradsbygden S 50 B2
Harbo S 51 B4
Harboør DK 58 B1
Harburg
Bayern D 94 C2
Hamburg D 72 A2
Hårby DK 59 C3
Harc H 112 C2
Hardegarijp NL 70 A2
Hardegsen D 82 A1
Hardelot Plage F 78 B1
Hardenbeck D 74 A2
Hardenberg NL 71 B3
Harderwijk NL 70 B2
Hardheim D 94 B1
Hardt D 106 A3
Hareid N 198 C3
Haren
D 71 B4
NL 71 A3
Harestua N 48 B2
Harfleur F 89 A4
Harg S 51 B5
Hargicourt F 90 B3
Hargnies F 91 A4
Hargshamn S 51 B5
Härja S 55 B4
Harkány H 125 B4
Härkeberga S 56 A3
Harkebrügge D 71 A4
Harlech GB 38 B2
Harleston GB 45 A5
Hårlev DK 65 A5
Harlingen NL 70 A2
Harlösa S 61 D3
Harlow GB 45 B4
Harmancık TR 186 C4
Harmånger S 200 E3
Härnevi S 56 A3
Härnösand S 200 D3
Haro E 143 B4
Haroldswick GB 33 A6
Háromfa H 124 A3
Haroué F 92 C2
Harpenden GB 44 B3
Harplinge S 60 C2
Harpstedt D 72 B1
Harrogate GB 40 A2
Harrow GB 44 B3
Härryda S 60 B2
Harsefeld D 72 A2
Harsewinkel D 71 C5
Hârşova 17 C7
Harstad N 194 B7
Harsum D 72 B2
Harsvik N 199 A7
Harta H 112 C3
Hartberg A 110 B2
Hartburn GB 37 A5
Hartennes F 90 B3
Hartest GB 45 A4
Hartha D 83 A4
Hartland GB 42 B2
Hartlepool GB 37 B5
Hartmanice CZ 96 B1
Hartmannsdorf A 110 B2
Harvassdal N 195 E5
Harwell GB 44 B2
Harwich GB 45 B5
Harzgerode D 82 A3
Häselgehr A 108 B1
Haselünne D 71 B4
Hasköy TR 186 A1
Haslach D 106 A3
Haslach an der Mühl
A 96 C2
Hasle DK 67 A3
Haslemere GB 44 B3
Haslev DK 65 A4
Hasloch D 94 B1
Hasparren F 144 A2
Hassela S 200 D2
Hasselfelde D 82 A2
Hasselfors S 55 A5
Hasselt
B 79 B5
NL 70 B3
Hassfurt D 94 A2
Hassleben D 74 A2
Hässleholm S 61 C3
Hasslö S 63 B3
Hassloch D 93 B4
Hästbo S 51 B4
Hastersboda FIN 51 B7
Hästholmen S 55 B5
Hastière-Lavaux B 79 B4
Hastigrow GB 32 C3
Hastings GB 45 C4
Hästveda S 61 C3
Hasvik N 192 B6
Hatfield
Hertfordshire GB 44 B3
South Yorkshire GB 40 B3
Hatherleigh GB 42 B2
Hathersage GB 40 B2
Hatlestrand N 46 B2
Hattem NL 70 B3
Hatten
D 71 A5
F 93 C3
Hattfjelldal N 195 E4
Hatting DK 59 C2
Hattingen D 80 A3
Hattstadt F 106 A2
Hattstedt D 64 B2
Hatvan H 112 B3
Hatvik N 46 B2
Hau D 80 A2
Haudainville F 92 B1
Hauganes IS 191 B7
Haugastøl N 47 B4
Hauge N 52 B2
Haugesund N 52 A1
Haughom N 52 B2
Haugsdal N 46 B2
Haugsdorf A 97 C4
Haukedal N 46 A3
Haukeland N 46 B2
Haukeligrend N 52 A3
Haukeliseter N 52 A3
Haukipudas FIN 3 D9
Haulerwijk NL 71 A3
Haunersdorf D 95 C4
Haus N 46 B2
Hausach D 106 A3
Hausham D 108 B2
Hausmannstätten
A 110 C2
Hausvik N 52 B2
Hautajärvi FIN 197 C12
Hautefort F 129 A4
Hauterives F 117 B5
Hauteville-Lompnès
F 118 B2
Haut-Fays B 91 A5
Hautmont F 79 B3
Hautrage B 79 B3
Hauzenberg D 96 C1
Havant GB 44 C3
Havdhem S 57 C4
Havdrup DK 61 D2
Havelange B 79 B5
Havelberg D 73 B5
Havelte NL 70 B3
Haverfordwest GB 39 C2
Haverhill GB 45 A4
Havering GB 45 B4
Håverud S 54 B3
Havířov CZ 98 B2
Havixbeck D 71 C4
Havlíčkův Brod CZ 97 B3
Havndal DK 58 B3
Havneby DK 64 A1
Havnebyen DK 61 D1
Havnsø DK 61 D1
Havøysund N 193 A8
Havran TR 186 C2
Havrebjerg DK 61 D1
Havsa TR 186 A1
Havstenssund S 54 B2
Havza TR 23 A8
Hawes GB 37 B4
Hawick GB 35 C5
Hawkhurst GB 45 B4
Hawkinge GB 45 B5
Haxey GB 40 B3
Hayange F 92 B2
Haydarlı TR 189 A5
Haydon Bridge GB 37 B4
Hayle GB 42 B1
Haymana TR 187 C7
Hay-on-Wye GB 39 B3
Hayrabolu TR 186 A2
Haysyn UA 13 D8
Hayvoron UA 13 D8
Haywards Heath GB 44 C3
Hazebrouck F 78 B2
Hazlov CZ 83 B4
Heacham GB 41 C4
Headcorn GB 45 B4
Headford IRL 28 A2
Heanor GB 40 B2
Héas F 145 B4
Heathfield GB 45 C4
Hebden Bridge GB 40 B1
Heberg S 60 C2
Heby S 51 C3
Hechingen D 93 C4
Hechlingen D 94 C2
Hecho E 144 B3
Hechtel B 79 A5
Hechthausen D 72 A2
Heckelberg D 74 B2
Heckington GB 41 C3
Hecklingen D 82 A3
Hed S 56 A1
Hedalen N 48 B1
Hedared S 60 B2
Heddal N 53 A5
Hédé F 101 A4
Hede S 199 C10
Hedekas S 54 B2
Hedemora S 50 B2
Hedenäset S 196 C6
Hedensted DK 59 C2
Hedersleben D 82 A3
Hedesunda S 51 B4
Hedge End GB 44 C2
Hedon GB 41 B3
Heede D 71 B4
Heek D 71 B4
Heemstede NL 70 B1
Heerde NL 70 B3
Heerenveen NL 70 B2
Heerhugowaard NL 70 B1
Heerlen NL 80 B1
Heeze NL 80 A1
Heggenes N 47 A6
Hegra N 199 B8
Hegyeshalom H 111 B4
Hegyközség H 111 B3
Heia N 199 A9
Heide D 64 B2
Heidelberg D 93 B4
Heiden D 80 A2
Heidenau D 84 B1
Heidenheim D 94 C2
Heidenreichstein A 97 C3
Heikendorf D 64 B3
Heikkilä FIN 197 C12
Heilam GB 32 C2
Heiland N 53 B4
Heilbad Heiligenstadt
D 82 A2
Heilbronn D 93 B5
Heiligenblut A 109 B3
Heiligendamn D 65 B4
Heiligendorf D 73 B3
Heiligengrabe D 73 A5
Heiligenhafen D 65 B3
Heiligenhaus D 80 A2
Heiligenkreuz A 111 C3
Heiligenstadt D 94 B3
Heiloo NL 70 B1
Heilsbronn D 94 B2
Heim N 198 B6
Heimburg D 82 A2
Heimdal N 199 B7
Heinerscheid L 92 A2
Heinersdorf D 74 B3
Heining D 96 C1
Heiningen D 94 C1
Heinola FIN 8 B5
Heinsberg D 80 A2
Heist-op-den-Berg
B 79 A4
Hejde S 57 C4
Hejdeby S 57 C4
Hejls DK 59 C2
Hejnice CZ 84 B3
Hel PL 69 A3
Helchteren B 79 A5
Heldburg D 82 B2
Heldrungen D 82 A3
Helechosa E 156 A3
Helensburgh GB 34 B3
Helfenberg A 96 C2
Helgen N 53 A5
Helgeroa N 53 B5
Hella
IS 190 D5
N 46 A3
Helland N 194 B7
Hellas S 55 B3
Helle N 52 B2
Helleland N 52 B2
Hellendoorn NL 71 B3
Hellenthal D 80 B2
Hellesøy N 46 B1
Hellesylt N 198 C3
Hellevoetsluis NL 79 A4
Helligskogen N 192 C4
Hellín E 158 C2
Hellissandur IS 190 C2
Hellnar IS 190 C2
Hellum DK 58 A3
Hellvi S 57 C4
Hellvik N 52 B1
Helm-brechts D 83 B3
Helmond NL 80 A1
Helmsdale GB 32 C3
Helmsley GB 37 B5
Helmstedt D 73 B3
Hel'pa SK 99 C3
Helsa D 82 A1
Helsby GB 38 A4
Helsingborg S 61 C2
Helsinge DK 61 C2
Helsingør DK 61 C2
Helsinki FIN 8 B4
Helston GB 42 B1
Hemau D 95 B3
Hemavan S 195 E6
Hemel Hempstead
GB 44 B3
Hemer D 81 A3
Héming F 92 C2
Hemmet DK 59 C1
Hemmingstedt D 64 B2
Hemmoor D 64 C2
Hemnes N 54 A2
Hemnesberget N 195 D4
Hemse S 57 C4
Hemsedal N 47 B5
Hemslingen D 72 A2
Hemsworth GB 40 B2
Hen N 48 B2
Henån S 54 B2
Hendaye F 144 A2
Hendek TR 187 B5
Hendungen D 82 B2
Henfield GB 44 C3
Hengelo
Gelderland NL 71 B3
Overijssel NL 71 B3
Hengersberg D 95 C5
Hengoed GB 39 C3
Hénin-Beaumont F 78 B2
Henley-on-Thames
GB 44 B3
Hennan S 200 D1
Henneberg D 82 B2
Hennebont F 100 B2
Henne Strand DK 59 C1
Hennigsdorf D 74 B2
Hennset N 198 B5
Hennstedt
Schleswig-Holstein
D 64 B2
Schleswig-Holstein
D 64 B2
Henrichemont F 103 B4
Henryków PL 85 B5
Henrykowo PL 69 A5
Hensås N 47 A5
Henstedt-Ulzburg D 64 C2
Heppenheim D 93 B4
Herad
Buskerud N 47 B6
Vest-Agder N 52 B2
Heradsbygd N 48 B3

Heraklion = Iraklio GR 185 D6
Herálec CZ 97 B4
Herand N 46 B3
Herbault F 103 B3
Herbern D 81 A3
Herbertstown IRL 29 B3
Herbeumont B 91 B5
Herbignac F 101 B3
Herbisse F 91 C4
Herbitzheim F 92 B3
Herbolzheim D 106 A2
Herborn D 81 B4
Herbrechtingen D 94 C2
Herby PL 86 B2
Herceg-Novi MNE 16 D3
Hercegovać HR 124 B3
Hercegszántó H 125 B4
Herchen D 80 B3
Heréd H 112 B3
Hereford GB 39 B4
Herefoss N 53 B4
Hereke TR 187 B4
Herencia E 157 A4
Herend H 111 B4
Herent B 79 B4
Herentals B 79 A4
Hérépian F 130 B2
Herfølge DK 61 D2
Herford D 72 B1
Herguijuela E 156 A2
Héric F 101 B4
Héricourt F 106 B1
Héricourt-en-Caux F 89 A4
Hérimoncourt F 106 B1
Heringsdorf D 65 B4
Herisau CH 107 B4
Hérisson F 103 C4
Herk-de-Stad B 79 B5
Herlufmagle DK 65 A4
Hermagor A 109 C4
Hermannsburg D 72 B3
Hermansverk N 46 A3
Heřmanův Městec CZ 97 B3
Herment F 116 B2
Hermeskeil D 92 B2
Hermisende E 141 C4
Hermonville F 91 B3
Hermsdorf D 83 B3
Hernani E 144 A2
Hernansancho E 150 B3
Herne D 80 A3
Herne Bay GB 45 B5
Hernes N 48 B3
Herning DK 59 B1
Herøya N 53 A5
Herramelluri E 143 B3
Herräng S 51 B5
Herre N 53 A5
Herrenberg D 93 C4
Herrera E 162 A3
Herrera de Alcántara E 155 B3
Herrera del Duque E 156 A2
Herrera de los Navarros E 152 A2
Herrera de Pisuerga E 142 B2
Herreros del Suso E 150 B2
Herrestad S 54 B2
Herrhamra S 57 B3
Herritslev DK 65 B4
Herrlisheim F 93 C3
Herrljunga S 55 B4
Herrnhut D 84 A2
Herrsching D 108 A2
Hersbruck D 95 B3
Hersby S 57 A4
Herscheid D 81 A3
Herselt B 79 A4
Herso GR 182 B4
Herstal B 80 B1
Herstmonceux GB 45 C4
Herten D 80 A3
Hertford GB 44 B3
Hervás E 149 B4
Hervik N 52 A1
Herxheim D 93 B4
Herzberg
Brandenburg D 74 B1
Brandenburg D 83 A5
Niedersachsen D 82 A2
Herzebrock D 81 A4
Herzfelde D 74 B2
Herzlake D 71 B4
Herzogenaurach D 94 B2
Herzogenbuchsee CH 106 B2
Herzogenburg A 110 A2
Herzsprung D 73 A5
Hesby N 52 A1
Hesdin F 78 B2
Hesel D 71 A4
Heskestad N 52 B2
Hessdalen N 199 C8
Hesselager DK 65 A3
Hesseng N 193 C13
Hessisch Lichtenau D 82 A1
Hessisch-Oldendorf D 72 B2
Hestra S 60 B3
Heswall GB 38 A3
Hetlevik N 46 B2
Hettange-Grande F 92 B2
Hetton-le-Hole GB 37 B5
Hettstedt D 82 A3
Heuchin F 78 B2
Heudicourt-sous-les-Côtes F 92 C1
Heunezel F 105 A5
Heuqueville F 89 A4
Heves H 113 B4
Héviz H 111 C4
Hexham GB 37 B4
Heysham GB 36 B4
Heytesbury GB 43 A4
Hidas H 125 A4
Hieflau A 110 B1
Hiendelaencina E 151 A5
Hiersac F 115 C4
High Bentham GB 37 B4
Highclere GB 44 B2
High Hesket GB 37 B4
Highley GB 39 B4
High Wycombe GB 44 B3
Higuera de Arjona E 157 C4
Higuera de Calatrava E 163 A3
Higuera de la Serena E 156 B2
Higuera de la Sierra E 161 B3
Higuera de Vargas E 155 C4
Higuera la Real E 161 A3
Higuers de Llerena E 156 B1
Higueruela E 158 C2
Híjar E 153 A3
Hilchenbach D 81 A4
Hildburghausen D 82 B2
Hilden D 80 A2
Hilders D 82 B1
Hildesheim D 72 B2
Hilgay GB 41 C4
Hillared S 60 B3
Hille D 72 B1
Hillegom NL 70 B1
Hillerød DK 61 D2
Hillerstorp S 60 B3
Hillesheim D 80 B2
Hillestad N 53 A6
Hillmersdorf D 83 A5
Hillsborough GB 27 B4
Hillswick GB 33 A5
Hilpoltstein D 95 B3
Hiltpoltstein D 94 B3
Hilvarenbeek NL 79 A5
Hilversum NL 70 B2
Himarë AL 182 C1
Himbergen D 73 A3
Himesháza H 125 A4
Himmelberg A 109 C5
Himmelpforten D 72 A2
Himód H 111 B4
Hinckley GB 40 C2
Hindås S 60 B2
Hindelang D 108 B1
Hindelbank CH 106 B2
Hinderavåg N 52 A1
Hindhead GB 44 B3
Hinjosa del Valle E 156 B1
Hinnerup DK 59 B3
Hinneryd S 61 C3
Hinojal E 155 B4
Hinojales E 161 B3
Hinojos E 161 B3
Hinojosa del Duque E 156 B2
Hinojosas de Calatrava E 157 B3
Hinterhornbach A 108 B1
Hinterriss A 108 B2
Hintersee
A 109 B4
D 74 A3
Hinterstoder A 110 B1
Hintertux A 108 B2
Hinterweidenthal D 93 B3
Hinwil CH 107 B3
Hios GR 185 A7
Hippolytushoef NL 70 B1
Hirschaid D 94 B2
Hirschau D 95 B3
Hirschfeld D 83 A5
Hirschhorn D 93 B4
Hirsingue F 106 B2
Hirson F 91 B4
Hirtshals DK 58 A2
Hirvaskoski FIN 197 D10
Hirzenhain D 81 B5
Hisarcık TR 186 C4
Hishult S 61 C3
Hissjön S 200 C6
Hitchin GB 44 B3
Hitra N 198 B5
Hittarp S 61 C2
Hittisau A 107 B4
Hittun N 46 A1
Hitzacker D 73 A4
Hjallerup DK 58 A3
Hjällstad S 49 B5
Hjältevad S 62 A3
Hjärnarp S 61 C2
Hjartdal N 53 A4
Hjellestad N 46 B2
Hjelmeland N 52 A2
Hjelset N 198 C4
Hjerkinn N 198 C6
Hjerm DK 58 B1
Hjerpsted DK 64 A1
Hjerting DK 59 C1
Hjo S 55 B5
Hjordkær DK 64 A2
Hjørring DK 58 A2
Hjorted S 62 A4
Hjortkvarn S 56 B1
Hjortnäs S 50 B1
Hjortsberga S 62 B2
Hjukse N 53 A5
Hjuksebø N 53 A5
Hjulsjö S 55 A5
Hliník nad Hronom SK 98 C2
Hlinsko CZ 97 B3
Hlío IS 191 A10
Hlohovec SK 98 C1
Hlubokánad Vltavou CZ 96 B2
Hlučín CZ 98 B2
Hlyboka UA 17 A6
Hlybokaye BY 13 A7
Hniezdne SK 99 B4
Hnilec SK 99 C4
Hnúšťa SK 99 C3
Hobol H 125 A3
Hobro DK 58 B2
Hobscheid L 92 B1
Hocalar TR 189 A4
Hochdonn D 64 B2
Hochdorf CH 106 B3
Hochfelden F 93 C3
Hochspeyer D 93 B3
Höchstadt D 94 B2
Höchstädt D 94 C2
Hochstenbach D 81 B3
Höchst im Odenwald D 93 B5
Höckendorf D 83 B5
Hockenheim D 93 B4
Hoddesdon GB 44 B3
Hodejov SK 99 C3
Hodenhagen D 72 B2
Hodkovice CZ 84 B3
Hódmezövásárhely H 113 C4
Hodnet GB 38 B4
Hodonín CZ 98 C1
Hodslavice CZ 98 B2
Hoedekenskerke NL 79 A3
Hoegaarden B 79 B4
Hoek van Holland NL 79 A4
Hoenderlo NL 70 B2
Hof
D 83 B3
N 53 A6
Hofbieber D 82 B1
Hoff GB 37 B4
Hofgeismar D 81 A5
Hofheim
Bayern D 82 B2
Hessen D 93 A4
Hofkirchen im Mühlkreis A 96 C1
Höfn IS 191 C10
Hofors S 50 B3
Hofsós IS 190 B6
Hofstad N 199 A7
Höganäs S 61 C2
Högbo S 51 B3
Hogdal S 54 A2
Högebru N 46 A4
Högfors S 50 C2
Högklint S 57 C4
Högsäter S 54 B3
Högsby S 62 A4
Högsjö S 56 A1
Hogstad S 55 B6
Högyész H 112 C2
Hohenau A 97 C4
Hohenberg A 110 B2
Hohenbucko D 83 A5
Hohenburg D 95 B3
Hohendorf D 66 B1
Hohenems A 107 B4
Hohenhameln D 72 B3
Hohenhausen D 72 B1
Hohenkirchen D 71 A4
Hohenlinden D 108 A2
Hohenlockstedt D 64 C2
Hohenmölsen D 83 A4
Hohennauen D 73 B5
Hohen Neuendorf D 74 B2
Hohenseeden D 73 B5
Hohentauern A 110 B1
Hohentengen D 106 B3
Hohenwepel D 81 A5
Hohenwestedt D 64 B2
Hohenwutzen D 74 B3
Hohenzieritz D 74 A2
Hohn D 64 B2
Hohne D 72 B3
Hohnstorf D 73 A3
Højer DK 64 B1
Højslev Stby DK 58 B2
Hok S 62 A2
Hökerum S 60 B3
Hökhuvud S 51 B5
Hokksund N 53 A5
Hökön S 63 B2
Hol N 47 B5
Hólar IS 190 B6
Holašovice CZ 96 C2
Holbæk
Aarhus Amt. DK 58 B3
Vestsjællands Amt. DK 61 D1
Holbeach GB 41 C4
Holdenstedt D 73 B3
Holdhus N 46 B2
Holdorf D 71 B5
Holeby DK 65 B4
Hølen N 54 A1
Hølervasseter N 47 B6
Holešov CZ 98 B1
Holguera E 155 B4
Holič SK 98 C1
Holice
CZ 97 A3
SK 111 B4
Höljes S 49 B4
Hollabrunn A 97 C4
Hollandstoun GB 33 B4
Høllen N 53 B3
Hollfeld D 95 B3
Hollókő H 112 B3
Hollstadt D 82 B2
Hollum NL 70 A2
Höllviksnäs S 66 A1
Holm N 195 E3
Hólmavík IS 190 B4
Holmbukt N 192 B5
Holmedal S 54 A2
Holmegil N 54 A2
Holmen N 48 B2
Holme-on-Spalding-Moor GB 40 B3
Holmes Chapel GB 38 A4
Holmestrand N 54 A1
Holmfirth GB 40 B2
Holmfoss N 193 C14
Holmsbu N 54 A1
Holmsjö S 63 B3
Holmsund S 200 C6
Holmsveden S 50 A3
Holmudden S 57 C5
Hölö S 57 A3
Holøydal N 199 C8
Holsbybrunn S 62 A3
Holseter N 48 A1
Holsljunga S 60 B2
Holstebro DK 59 B1
Holsted DK 59 C1
Holsworthy GB 42 B2
Holt
D 64 B2
Norfolk GB 41 C5
Wrexham GB 38 A4
I S 190 D6
N 53 B4
Holten NL 71 B3
Holtwick D 71 B4
Holum N 52 B3
Holwerd NL 70 A2
Holycross IRL 29 B4
Holyhead GB 38 A2
Holýšov CZ 95 B5
Holywell GB 38 A3
Holywood GB 27 B5
Holzdorf D 83 A5
Holzhausen D 72 B1
Holzheim D 94 C2
Holzkirchen D 108 B2
Holzminden D 81 A5
Holzthaleben D 82 A2
Homberg
Hessen D 81 A5
Hessen D 81 B5
Homburg D 93 B3
Hommelstø N 195 E3
Hommersåk N 52 B1
Homokmegy H 112 C3
Homokszentgyörgy H 124 A3
Homyel = Gomel BY 13 B9
Honaz TR 188 B4
Hondarribia E 144 A2
Hondón de los Frailes E 165 A4
Hondschoote F 78 B2
Hönebach D 82 B1
Hønefoss N 48 B2
Honfleur F 89 A4
Høng DK 61 D1
Honiton GB 43 B3
Hönningen D 80 B2
Honningsvåg N 193 B9
Hönö S 60 B1
Honrubia E 158 B1
Hontalbilla E 151 A3
Hontheim D 92 A2
Hontianske-Nemce SK 98 C2
Hontoria de la Cantera E 143 B3
Hontoria del Pinar E 143 C3
Hontoria de Valdearados E 143 C3
Hoofddorp NL 70 B1
Hoogerheide NL 79 A4
Hoogeveen NL 71 B3
Hoogezand-Sappemeer NL 71 A3
Hoogkarspel NL 70 B2
Hoogkerk NL 71 A3
Hoogstede D 71 B3
Hoogstraten B 79 A4
Hook GB 44 B3
Hooksiel D 71 A5
Höör S 61 D3
Hoorn NL 70 B2
Hope GB 38 A3
Hopen N 194 C6
Hope under Dinmore GB 39 B4
Hopfgarten A 108 B3
Hopfgarten in Defereggen A 109 C3
Hopseidet N 193 B11
Hopsten D 71 B4
Hoptrup DK 59 C2
Hora Svatého Sebestiána CZ 83 B5
Horaždóvice CZ 96 B1
Horb am Neckar D 93 C4
Horbelev DK 65 B5
Hørby DK 58 A3
Hörby S 61 D3
Horcajada de la Torre E 158 A1
Horcajo de los Montes E 156 A3
Horcajo de Santiago E 151 C4
Horcajo-Medianero E 150 B2
Horche E 151 B4
Horda S 62 A2
Hordabø N 46 B1
Hordalia N 52 A2
Hordvik N 46 B2
Hořesedly CZ 83 B5
Horezu RO 17 C6
Horgen CH 107 B3
Horgoš SRB 126 A1
Horia RO 126 A3
Hořice CZ 84 B3
Horjul SLO 123 A3
Horka D 84 A2
Hörken S 50 B1
Horki BY 13 A9
Hörle S 60 B4
Horn
A 97 C3
D 81 A4
N 48 B2
S 62 A3
Horna E 158 C2
Hornachos E 156 B1
Hornachuelos E 162 A2
Horná Mariková SK 98 B2
Hornanes N 46 C2
Horná Streda SK 98 C1
Horná Štrubna SK 98 C2
Horná Súča SK 98 C1
Hornbæk
Aarhus Amt. DK 58 B2
Frederiksværk DK 61 C2
Hornberg D 106 A3
Hornburg D 73 B3
Horncastle GB 41 B3
Horndal S 50 B3
Horndean GB 44 C2
Horne
Fyns Amt. DK 64 A3
Ribe Amt. DK 59 C1
Hörnebo S 55 B5
Horneburg D 72 A2
Hörnefors S 200 C5
Horní Bečva CZ 98 B2
Horni Benešov CZ 98 B1
Horni Cerekev CZ 97 B3
Horní Jiřetín CZ 83 B5
Horní Lomná CZ 98 B2
Horni Maršov CZ 85 B3
Hornindal N 198 D3
Hørning DK 59 B3
Hörningsholm S 57 A3
Horní Planá CZ 96 C2
Horni Slavkov CZ 83 B4
Horni Vltavice CZ 96 C1
Hornnes N 53 B3
Horno D 84 A2
Hornos E 164 A2
Hornoy-le-Bourg F 90 B1
Hornsea GB 41 B3
Hornsjø N 48 A2
Hornslet DK 59 B3
Hornstein A 111 B3
Hörnum D 64 B1
Hornum DK 58 B2
Horný Tisovnik SK 99 C3
Horodenka UA 13 D6
Horodnya UA 13 C9
Horodok
Khmelnytskyy UA 13 D7
Lviv UA 13 D5
Horokhiv UA 13 C6
Horovice CZ 96 B1
Horred S 60 B2
Hörröd S 61 D4
Hörsching A 110 A1
Horsens DK 59 C2
Horsham GB 44 B3
Hørsholm DK 61 D2
Horslunde DK 65 B4
Horšovský Týn CZ 95 B4
Horst NL 80 A2
Horstel D 71 B4
Horsten D 71 A4
Horstmar D 71 B4
Hort H 113 B3
Horta P 148 A2
Horten N 54 A1
Hortezuela E 151 A5
Hortiguela E 143 B3
Hortobágy H 113 B5
Horton in Ribblesdale GB 37 B4
Hørve DK 61 D1
Hörvik S 63 B2
Horwich GB 38 A4
Hosanger N 46 B2
Hösbach D 93 A5
Hosena D 84 A2
Hosenfeld D 81 B5
Hosingen L 92 A2
Hosio FIN 197 D8
Hospental CH 107 C3
Hospital IRL 29 B3
Hossegor F 128 C1
Hosszuhetény H 125 A4
Hostal de Ipiés E 145 B3
Hoštálkova CZ 98 B1
Hostalric E 147 C3
Hostens F 128 B2
Hostěradice CZ 97 C4
Hostinné CZ 85 B3
Hostomice CZ 96 B2
Hostouň CZ 95 B4
Hotagen S 199 B11
Hoting S 200 B2
Hotolisht AL 182 B2
Hotton B 79 B5
Houdain F 78 B2
Houdan F 90 C1
Houdelaincourt F 92 C1
Houeillès F 128 B3
Houffalize B 92 A1
Houghton-le-Spring GB 37 B5
Houlberg DK 59 B2
Houlgate F 89 A3
Hounslow GB 44 B3
Hourtin F 128 A1
Hourtin-Plage F 128 A1
Houthalen B 79 A5
Houyet B 79 B4
Hov
DK 59 C3
N 48 B2
Hova S 55 B5
Høvåg N 53 B4
Hovborg DK 59 C1
Hovda N 47 B6
Hovden N 52 A3
Hove GB 44 C3
Hovedgård DK 59 C2
Hovelhof D 81 A4
Hoven DK 59 C1
Hovet N 47 B5
Hovingham GB 40 A3
Hovmantorp S 62 B3
Hovsta S 56 A1
Howden GB 40 B3
Howe D 72 A3
Höxter D 81 A5
Hoya D 72 B2
Hoya de Santa Maria E 161 B3
Hoya-Gonzalo E 158 C2
Høyanger N 46 A3
Hoyerswerda D 84 A2
Høyjord N 53 A6
Hoylake GB 38 A3
Høylandet N 199 A9
Hoym D 82 A3
Høymyr N 47 C6
Hoyocasero E 150 B3
Hoyo de Manzanares E 151 B4
Hoyo de Pinares E 150 B3
Hoyos E 149 B3
Hoyos del Espino E 150 B2
Hrabusiče SK 99 C4
Hradec Králové CZ 85 B3
Hradec nad Moravicí CZ 98 B1
Hrádek CZ 97 C4
Hrádek nad Nisou CZ 84 B2
Hradište SK 98 C2
Hrafnagil IS 191 B7
Hrafnseyri IS 190 B2
Hranice
Severomoravsky CZ 98 B1
Západočeský CZ 83 B4
Hranovnica SK 99 C4
Hrasnica BIH 139 B4
Hrastnik SLO 123 A4
Hřensko CZ 84 B2
Hriňová SK 99 C3
Hrisoupoli GR 183 C6
Hrochov CZ 97 B4
Hrochův Tynec CZ 97 B3
Hrodna BY 13 B5
Hrodzyanka BY 13 B8
Hronov CZ 85 B4
Hronský Beňadik SK 98 C2
Hrotovice CZ 97 B4
Hrtkovci SRB 127 C1
Hrun IS 190 A5
Hrušov SK 112 A3
Hrušovany nad Jevišovkou CZ 97 C4
Hřuštin SK 99 B3
Hrvaćani BIH 124 C3
Hrvace HR 138 B2
Hrymayliv UA 13 D7
Huben A 109 C3
Hückel-hoven D 80 A2
Hückeswagen D 80 A3
Hucknall GB 40 B2

Hucqueliers F 78 B1
Huddersfield GB 40 B2
Huddinge S 57 A3
Huddunge S 51 B3
Hude D 72 A1
Hudiksvall S 200 E3
Huélago E 163 A4
Huélamo E 152 B2
Huelgoat F 100 A2
Huelma E 163 A4
Huelva E 161 B3
Huéneja E 164 B2
Huércal de Almeria E 164 C2
Huércal-Overa E 164 B3
Huerta de Abajo E 143 B3
Huerta del Rey E 143 C3
Huerta de Valdecarabanos E 151 C4
Huertahernando E 152 B1
Huesa E 164 B1
Huesca E 145 B3
Huéscar E 164 B2
Huete E 151 B5
Huétor Tájar E 163 A3
Hüfingen D 106 B3
Hufthamar N 46 B2
Hugh Town GB 42 B1
Huglfing D 108 B2
Huissen NL 70 C2
Huittinen FIN 8 B3
Huizen NL 70 B2
Hulín CZ 98 B1
Hüls D 80 A2
Hulsig DK 58 A3
Hulst NL 79 A4
Hult S 62 A3
Hulta S 56 B2
Hulteby S 55 A5
Hulterstad S 63 B4
Hultsfred S 62 A3
Humanes E 151 B4
Humberston GB 41 B3
Humble DK 65 B3
Humenné SK 12 D4
Humilladero E 163 A3
Humlebæk DK 61 D2
Humlum DK 58 B1
Hummelsta S 56 A2
Humpolec CZ 97 B3
Humshaugh GB 37 A4
Hundåla N 195 E3
Hundested DK 61 D1
Hundorp N 48 A1
Hundvåg N 52 A1
Hundvin N 46 B2
Hunedoara RO 17 C5
Hünfeld D 82 B1
Hungen D 81 B4
Hungerford GB 44 B2
Hunndalen N 48 B2
Hunnebostrand S 54 B2
Hunstanton GB 41 C4
Huntingdon GB 44 A3
Huntley GB 39 C4
Huntly GB 33 D4
Hünxe D 80 A2
Hurbanovo SK 112 B2
Hürbel D 107 A4
Hurdal N 48 B3
Hurezani RO 17 C5
Hurlford GB 36 A2
Hurstbourne Tarrant GB 44 B2
Hurstpierpoint GB 44 C3
Hürth D 80 B2
Hurum N 47 A5
Hurup DK 58 B1
Húsafell IS 190 C5
Húsavík IS 191 A8
Husbands Bosworth GB 44 A2
Husby
D 64 B2
DK 59 B1
Husey IS 191 B11
Huşi RO 17 B8
Husina BIH 139 A4
Husinec CZ 96 B1
Husinish GB 31 B1
Huskvarna S 62 A2
Husnes N 46 C2
Husøy N 194 A8
Hustad N 198 C4
Hüsten D 81 A3
Hustopeče CZ 97 C4
Hustopeče nad Bečvou CZ 98 B1
Husum
D 64 B2
S 200 C5
Husvika N 195 E3
Huta PL 75 B5
Hutovo BIH 139 C3
Hüttenberg A 110 C1
Hüttlingen D 94 C2
Huttoft GB 41 B4
Hutton Cranswick GB 40 B3
Hüttschlag A 109 B4
Huttwil CH 106 B2
Huy B 79 B5
Hüyük TR 189 B6
Hval N 48 B2
Hvåle N 47 B6
Hvaler N 54 A2
Hvalpsund DK 58 B2
Hvammstangi IS 190 B5
Hvammur IS 190 B6
Hvanneyri IS 190 C4
Hvar HR 138 B2
Hvarnes N 53 A5
Hveragerði IS 190 D4
Hvidbjerg DK 58 B1
Hvide Sande DK 59 C1
Hvittingfoss N 53 A6
Hvolsvöllur IS 190 D5
Hybe SK 99 B3
Hycklinge S 62 A3
Hydra GR 185 B4
Hyen N 198 D2
Hyères F 132 B2
Hyères Plage F 132 B2
Hylestad N 52 A3
Hylke DK 59 C2
Hyllestad N 46 A2
Hyllstofta S 61 C3
Hyltebruk S 60 B3
Hynnekleiv N 53 B4
Hythe
Hampshire GB 44 C2
Kent GB 45 B5
Hyvinkää FIN 8 B4

I

Iam RO 127 B3
Iaşi RO 17 B7
Iasmos GR 183 B7
Ibahernando E 156 A2
Ibarranguelua E 143 A4
Ibbenbüren D 71 B4
Ibeas de Juarros E 143 B3
Ibestad N 194 B8
Ibi E 159 C3
Ibiza = Eivissa E 166 C1
İbradı TR 189 B6
İbriktepe TR 186 A1
Ibros E 157 B4
Ibstock GB 40 C2
İçel TR 23 C8
Ichenhausen D 94 C2
Ichtegem B 78 A3
Ichtershausen D 82 B2
Idanha-a-Novo P 155 B3
Idar-Oberstein D 93 B3
Idd N 54 A2
Idiazábal E 144 B1
Idivuoma S 196 A4
Idkerberget S 50 B2
Idön S 51 B5
Idre S 199 D9
Idrija SLO 123 A3
Idritsa RUS 9 D6
Idstein D 81 B4
Idvor SRB 126 B2
Iecca Mare RO 126 B2
Ielsi I 170 B2
Ieper = Ypres B 78 B2
Ierapetra GR 185 D6
Ierissos GR 183 C5
Ifjord N 193 B11
Ig SLO 123 B3
Igal H 112 C1
Igea E 144 B1
Igea Marina I 136 A1
Igelfors S 56 B1
Igersheim D 94 B1
Iggesund S 200 E3
Iglesias E 143 B3
Iglésias I 179 C2
Igls A 108 B2
Igny-Comblizy F 91 B3
Igorre E 143 A4
Igoumenitsa GR 182 D2
Igries E 145 B3
Igualada E 147 C2
Igüeña E 141 B4
Iguerande F 117 A4
Iharosberény H 124 A3
Ihl'any SK 99 B4
Ihlienworth D 64 C1
Ihringen D 106 A2
Ihrlerstein D 95 C3
İhsaniye TR 187 C5
Ii FIN 197 D8
Iijärvi FIN 193 C11
Iisalmi FIN 3 E10
IJmuiden NL 70 B1
IJsselmuiden NL 70 B2
IJzendijke NL 79 A3
Ikast DK 59 B2
Ikervár H 111 B3
Ilandža SRB 126 B2
Ilanz CH 107 C4
Ilava SK 98 C2
Iława PL 69 B4
il Castagno I 135 B3
Ilche E 145 C4
Ilchester GB 43 B4
Ilfeld D 82 A2
Ilfracombe GB 42 A2
Ilgaz TR 23 A7
Ilgın TR 189 A6
Ílhavo P 148 B1
Ilıca TR 186 C2
Ilidža BIH 139 B4
Ilijaš BIH 139 B4
Ilirska Bistrica SLO 123 B3
Ilkeston GB 40 C2
Ilkley GB 40 B2
Illana E 151 B5
Illano E 141 A4
Illar E 164 C2
Illas E 141 A5
Illats F 128 B2
Illertissen D 94 C2
Illescas E 151 B4
Ille-sur-Têt F 146 B3
Illfurth F 106 B2
Illichivsk UA 17 B9
Illiers-Combray F 89 B5
Illkirch-Graffenstaden F 93 C3
Illmersdorf D 74 C2
Illmitz A 111 B3
Íllora E 163 A4
Illueca E 152 A2
Ilmajoki FIN 8 A3
Ilmenau D 82 B2
Ilminster GB 43 B4
Ilok HR 126 B1
Ilomantsi FIN 9 A7
Iłow PL 77 B5
Iłowa PL 84 A3
Iłowo-Osada PL 77 A5
Ilsenburg D 82 A2
Ilshofen D 94 B1
Ilz A 110 B2
Iłża PL 87 A5
Imatra FIN 9 B6
Imielin PL 86 B3
Imingen N 47 B5
Immeln S 63 B2
Immenhausen D 81 A5
Immenstadt D 107 B5
Immingham GB 41 B3
Ímola I 135 A4
Imon E 151 A5
Imotski HR 138 B3
Impéria I 133 B4
Imphy F 104 C2
İmroz TR 183 C7
Imsland N 52 A1
Imst A 108 B1
Inagh IRL 28 B2
Inari FIN 193 D10
Inca E 167 B2
Inchnadamph GB 32 C2
Incinillas E 143 B3
Indal S 200 D3
Indjija SRB 127 B2
Indre Arna N 46 B2
Indre Billefjord N 193 B9
Indre Brenna N 193 B9
İğneada TR 186 A2
İnebolu TR 23 A7
İnecik TR 186 B2
İnegöl TR 187 B4
Inerthal CH 107 B3
Infiesto E 142 A1
Ingatorp S 62 A3
Ingedal N 54 A2
Ingelheim D 93 B4
Ingelmunster B 78 B3
Ingelstad S 62 B2
Ingleton GB 37 B4
Ingolfsland N 47 C5
Ingolstadt D 95 C3
Ingrandes
Maine-et-Loire F 101 B5
Vienne F 102 C2
Ingwiller F 93 C3
Inhisar TR 187 B5
Iniesta E 158 B2
Inishannon IRL 29 C3
Inishcrone IRL 26 B1
Inke H 124 A3
Inndyr N 195 C5
Innellan GB 34 C3
Innerleithen GB 35 C4
Innermessan GB 36 B2
Innertkirchen CH 106 C3
Innervillgraten A 109 C3
Innsbruck A 108 B2
Innset N 194 B9
Innvik N 198 D3
İnönü TR 187 C5
Inowłódz PL 87 A4
Inowrocław PL 76 B3
Ins CH 106 B2
Insch GB 33 D4
Insjön S 50 B2
Ińsko PL 75 A4
Instow GB 42 A2
İntepe TR 186 B1
Interlaken CH 106 C2
Intragna CH 120 A1
Introbio I 120 B2
Inverallochy GB 33 D5
Inveran
GB 32 D2
IRL 28 A2
Inveraray GB 34 B2
Inverbervie GB 35 B5
Invergarry GB 32 D2
Invergordon GB 32 D2
Invergowrie GB 35 B4
Inverkeilor GB 35 B5
Inverkeithing GB 35 B4
Invermoriston GB 32 D2
Inverness GB 32 D2
Inveruno I 120 B1
Inverurie GB 33 D4
Ioannina GR 182 D2
Iolanda di Savoia I 121 C4
Ion Corvin RO 17 C7
Ióppolo I 175 C1
Ios GR 185 C6
Ipati GR 182 E4
İpsala TR 186 B1
Ipswich GB 45 A5
Iraklia GR 183 B5
Iraklio = Heraklion GR 185 D6
Irdning A 110 B1
Iregszemcse H 112 C2
Irgoli I 178 B3
Irig SRB 127 B1
Ironbridge GB 39 B4
Irpin UA 13 C9
Irrel D 92 B2
Irsina I 172 B2
Irsta S 56 A2
Irthlingborough GB 44 A3
Iruela E 141 B4
Irún E 144 A2
Irurita E 144 A2
Irurzun E 144 B2
Irvine GB 36 A2
Irvinestown GB 27 B3
Isaba E 144 B3
Isabela E 157 B4
Ísafjörður IS 190 A2
Isane N 198 D2
Isaszeg H 112 B3
Isbister GB 33 A5
Íscar E 150 A3
İscehisar TR 187 D5
Ischgl A 107 B5
Íschia I 170 C1
Ischia di Castro I 168 A1
Ischitella I 171 B3
Isdes F 103 B4
Ise N 54 A2
Iselle I 119 A5
Iseltwald CH 106 C2
Isen D 108 A3
Isenbüttel D 73 B3
Iseo I 120 B3
Iserlohn D 81 A3
Isérnia I 170 B2
Isfjorden N 198 C4
Ishëm AL 182 B1
Isigny-sur-Mer F 88 A2
Işıklı TR 189 A4
Ísili I 179 C3
İskilip TR 23 A8
Isla Canela E 161 B2
Isla Cristina E 161 B2
Islares E 143 A3
Isleham GB 45 A4
Isle of Whithorn GB 36 B2
Ismaning D 108 A2
Isna P 154 B3
Isnestoften N 192 B6
Isny D 107 B5
Isoba E 142 A1
Isokylä
FIN 197 C10
S 196 B5
Isola F 132 A3
Isola d'Asti I 119 C5
Isola del Gran Sasso d'Itália I 169 A3
Ísola della Scala I 121 B4
Isola delle Fémmine I 176 A2
Ísola del Liri I 169 B3
Ísola di Capo Rizzuto I 175 C3
Isona E 147 B2
Ispagnac F 130 A2
Isparta TR 189 B5
Isperikh BG 17 D7
Íspica I 177 C3
Isselburg D 80 A2
Issigeac F 129 B3
Issogne I 119 B4
Issoire F 116 B3
Issoncourt F 91 C5
Issoudun F 103 C4
Issum D 80 A2
Is-sur-Tille F 105 B4
Issy-l'Evêque F 104 C2
Istán E 162 B3
İstanbul TR 186 A3
Istebna PL 98 B2
Ístia d'Ombrone I 135 C4
Istiea GR 183 E5
Istres F 131 B3
Istvándi H 125 A3
Itea GR 184 A3
Ithaki GR 184 A1
Itoiz E 144 B2
Ítrabo E 163 B4
Itri I 169 B3
Ittireddu I 178 B2
Íttiri I 178 B2
Itzehoe D 64 C2
Ivalo FIN 193 D11
Iván H 111 B3
Ivanava BY 13 B6
Ivančice CZ 97 B4
Ivančna Gorica SLO 123 B3
Iváncsa H 112 B2
Ivanec HR 124 A2
Ivanić Grad HR 124 B2
Ivanjska BIH 124 C3
Ivanka SK 98 C2
Ivankovo HR 125 B4
Ivano-Frankivsk UA 13 D6
Ivanovice na Hané CZ 98 B1
Ivanska HR 124 B2
Ivatsevichy BY 13 B6
Ivaylovgrad BG 183 B8
Iveland N 53 B3
Ivoz Ramet B 79 B5
Ivrea I 119 B4
İvrindi TR 186 C2
Ivry-en-Montagne F 104 B3
Ivry-la-Bataille F 90 C1
Ivybridge GB 42 B3
Iwaniska PL 87 B5
Iwiny PL 85 A3
Iwuy F 78 B3
Ixworth GB 45 A4
Izarra E 143 B4
Izbica Kujawska PL 76 B3
Izbište SRB 127 B3
Izeda P 149 A3
Izegem B 78 B3
Izernore F 118 A2
Izmayil UA 17 C8
İzmir TR 188 A2
İzmit = Kocaeli TR 187 B4
Iznájar E 163 A3
Iznalloz E 163 A4
Iznatoraf E 164 A1
İznik TR 187 B4
Izola SLO 122 B2
Izsák H 112 C3
Izsófalva H 99 C4
Izyaslav UA 13 C7

J

Jabalquinto E 157 B4
Jablanac HR 123 C3
Jablanica BIH 139 B3
Jablonec nad Jizerou CZ 84 B3
Jablonec nad Nisou CZ 84 B3
Jablonica SK 98 C1
Jablonka PL 99 B3
Jabłonna PL 77 B5
Jablonnénad Orlicí CZ 97 A4
Jablonne Podještědi CZ 84 B2
Jablonov nad Turňou SK 99 C4
Jabłonowo Pomorskie PL 69 B4
Jablúnka CZ 98 B1
Jablunkov CZ 98 B2
Jabučje SRB 127 C2
Jabugo E 161 B3
Jabuka SRB 127 C2
Jabukovac HR 124 B2
Jaca E 145 B3
Jáchymov CZ 83 B4
Jacobidrebber D 72 B1
Jade D 71 A5
Jäderfors S 50 B3
Jädraås S 50 B3
Jadraque E 151 B5
Jaén E 163 A4
Jagare BIH 124 C3
Jagel D 64 B2
Jagenbach A 96 C3
Jægerspris DK 61 D1
Jagodina SRB 127 D3
Jagodnjak HR 125 B4
Jagodzin PL 84 A3
Jagstheim D 94 B2
Jagstzell D 94 B2
Jahodna SK 111 A4
Jajce BIH 138 A3
Ják H 111 B3
Jakabszálbs H 112 C3
Jäkkvik S 195 D8
Jakobsnes N 193 C14
Jakovlje HR 124 B1
Jakšic HR 125 B3
Jakubany SK 99 B4
Jalance E 159 B2
Jalasjärvi FIN 8 A3
Jalhay B 80 B1
Jaligny-sur-Besbre F 117 A3
Jallais F 102 B1
Jalón E 159 C3
Jâlons F 91 C4
Jamena SRB 125 C5
Jamilena E 163 A4
Jämjö S 63 B3
Jamnička Kiselica HR 124 B1
Jamno PL 67 B5
Jamoigne B 92 B1
Jämsä FIN 8 B4
Jämshög S 63 B2
Jamu Mare RO 126 B3
Janakkala FIN 8 B4
Jandelsbrunn D 96 C1
Jänickendorf D 74 B2
Janikowo PL 76 B3
Janja BIH 125 C5
Janjina HR 138 C3
Janki
Łódzkie PL 86 A3
Mazowieckie PL 77 B5
Jankov CZ 96 B2
Jankowo Dolne PL 76 B2
Jánoshalma H 126 A1
Jánosháza H 111 B4
Jánoshida H 113 B4
Jánossomorja H 111 B4
Janovice nad Uhlavou CZ 96 B1
Janów PL 86 B3
Janowiec Wielkopolski PL 76 B2
Janowo PL 77 A5
Jänsmässholmen S 199 B10
Janville F 103 A3
Janzé F 101 B4
Jarabá SK 99 C3
Jaraczewo PL 76 C2
Jarafuel E 159 B2
Jaraicejo E 156 A2
Jaraíz de la Vera E 150 B2
Jarak SRB 127 C1
Jarandilla de la Vera E 150 B2
Jaray E 152 A1
Järbo S 50 B3
Jard-sur-Mer F 114 B2
Jaren N 48 B2
Jargeau F 103 B4
Jarkovac SRB 126 B2
Järlåsa S 51 C4
Jarmen D 66 C2
Järna S 57 A3
Jarnac F 115 C3
Järnäs S 200 C5
Järnforsen S 62 A3
Jarny F 92 B1
Jarocin PL 76 C2
Jaroměř CZ 85 B3
Jaroměřice nad Rokytnou CZ 97 B3
Jaroslav CZ 97 A4
Jaroslavice CZ 97 C4
Jarosław PL 12 C5
Jaroslawiec PL 68 A1
Jarošov nad Nežarkou CZ 96 B3
Järpås S 55 B3
Järpen S 199 B10
Jarrow GB 37 B5
Järso FIN 51 B6
Järvenpää FIN 8 B4
Jarvorník CZ 85 B4
Järvsö S 200 E2
Jarzé F 102 B1
Jaša Tomic SRB 126 B2
Jasenak HR 123 B4
Jasenica BIH 124 C2
Jasenice HR 137 A4
Jasenovac HR 124 B2
Jasenovo SRB 127 C3
Jasień PL 84 A3
Jasienica PL 84 A2
Jasło PL 12 D4
Jásova SK 112 B2
Jasseron F 118 A2
Jastarnia PL 69 A3
Jastrebarsko HR 123 B4
Jastrowie PL 68 B1
Jastrzębia-Góra PL 68 A3
Jastrzębie Zdrój PL 98 B2
Jászals-Lószentgyörgy H 113 B4
Jászapáti H 113 B4
Jászárokszállás H 113 B3
Jászberény H 113 B3
Jászdózsa H 113 B4
Jászfényszaru H 113 B3
Jászjakóhalma H 113 B4
Jászkarajenö H 113 B4
Jászkisér H 113 B4
Jászladány H 113 B4
Jászszentlászló H 113 C3
Jásztelek H 113 B4
Játar E 163 B4
Jättendal S 200 E3
Jatznick D 74 A2
Jaun CH 106 C2
Jausiers F 132 A2
Jávea E 159 C4
Jävenitz D 73 B4
Javerlhac F 115 C4
Javier E 144 B2
Javorani BIH 124 C3
Javorina SK 99 B4
Javron F 89 B3
Jawor PL 85 A4
Jaworzno PL 86 B3
Jaworzyna Śl. PL 85 B4
Jayena E 163 B4
Jażow PL 84 A2
Jebel RO 126 B3
Jebjerg DK 58 B2
Jedburgh GB 35 C5
Jedlinsk PL 87 A5
Jedlnia PL 87 A5
Jedlnia Letnisko PL 87 A5
Jednorożec PL 77 A6
Jedovnice CZ 97 B4
Jędrychow PL 69 B4
Jędrzejów PL 87 B4
Jedwabno PL 77 A5
Jeesiö FIN 197 B9
Jegłownik PL 69 A4
Jegun F 129 C3
Jēkabpils LV 8 D4
Jektevik N 46 C2
Jektvik N 195 D4
Jelcz-Laskowice PL 85 A5
Jelenec SK 98 C2
Jelenia Góra PL 85 B3
Jelgava LV 8 D3
Jelka SK 111 A4

Jelling DK 59 C2
Jels DK 59 C2
Jelsa
HR 138 B2
N 52 A2
Jelšava SK 99 C4
Jemgum D 71 A4
Jemnice CZ 97 B3
Jena D 82 B3
Jenaz CH 107 C4
Jenbach A 108 B2
Jenikow PL 75 A4
Jennersdorf A 111 C3
Jenny S 62 A4
Jerchel D 73 B4
Jeres del Marquesado
E 164 B1
Jerez de la Frontera
E 162 B1
Jerez de los Caballeros
E 155 C4
Jerica E 159 B3
Jerichow D 73 B5
Jerka PL 75 B5
Jermenovci SRB 126 B3
Jerslev DK 58 A3
Jerte E 150 B2
Jerup DK 58 A3
Jerxheim D 73 B3
Jerzmanowice PL 87 B3
Jerzu I 179 C3
Jerzwałd PL 69 B4
Jesberg D 81 B5
Jesenice
Středočeský CZ 83 B5
Středočeský CZ 96 B2
SLO 109 C5
Jeseník CZ 85 B5
Jesenké SK 99 C4
Jesi I 136 B2
Jésolo I 122 B1
Jessen D 83 A4
Jessenitz D 73 A4
Jessheim N 48 B3
Jessnitz D 83 A4
Jesteburg D 72 A2
Jeumont F 79 B4
Jeven-stedt D 64 B2
Jever D 71 A4
Jevičko CZ 97 B4
Jevišovice CZ 97 C3
Jevnaker N 48 B2
Jezerane HR 123 B4
Jezero
BIH 138 A3
HR 123 B4
Jezów PL 87 A3
Jičín CZ 84 B3
Jičiněves CZ 84 B3
Jihlava CZ 97 B3
Jijona E 159 C3
Jilemnice CZ 84 B3
Jilové CZ 84 B2
Jilovéu Prahy CZ 96 B2
Jimbolia RO 126 B2
Jimena E 163 A4
Jimena de la Frontera
E 162 B2
Jimera de Libar E 162 B2
Jimramov CZ 97 B4
Jince CZ 96 B1
Jindřichovice CZ 83 B4
Jindřichův Hradec
CZ 96 B3
Jirkov CZ 83 B5
Jistebnice CZ 96 B2
Joachimsthal D 74 B2
João da Loura P 154 C2
Jobbágyi H 112 B3
Jochberg A 109 B3
Jockfall S 196 C5
Jódar E 163 A4
Jodoigne B 79 B4
Joensuu FIN 9 A6
Joesjö S 195 E5
Joeuf F 92 B1
Jõgeva EST 8 C5
Johanngeorgenstadt
D 83 B4
Johannishus S 63 B3
Johanniskirchen D 95 C4
Johansfors S 63 B3
John o'Groats GB 32 C3
Johnshaven GB 35 B5
Johnstone GB 34 C3
Johnstown IRL 30 B1
Jõhvi EST 8 C5
Joigny F 104 B2
Joinville F 91 C5
Jokkmokk S 196 C2
Jöllenbeck D 72 B1
Jomala FIN 51 B6
Jönåker S 56 B2
Jonava LT 13 A6
Jonchery-sur-Vesle
F 91 B3
Jondal N 46 B3
Jondalen N 53 A5
Joniškis LT 8 D3
Jönköping S 62 A2
Jonkowo PL 69 B5
Jønnbu N 53 A5
Jonsberg S 56 B2
Jonsered S 60 B2
Jonstorp S 61 C2
Jonzac F 114 C3
Jorba E 147 C2
Jordanów PL 99 B3
Jordanowo PL 75 B4
Jordanów Śląski PL 85 B4
Jordbro S 57 A4
Jordbrua N 195 D5
Jördenstorf D 66 C1
Jordet N 49 A4
Jordøse DK 59 C3
Jork D 72 A2
Jörlanda S 60 B1
Jormlien S 199 A10
Jormvattnet S 199 A11
Jörn S 200 A6
Jørpeland N 52 A2
Jorquera E 158 B2
Jošan HR 123 C4
Jošavka BIH 124 C3
Josipdol HR 123 B4
Josipovac HR 125 B4
Jössefors S 54 A3
Josselin F 101 B3
Jøssund N 199 A7
Jostedal N 47 A4
Jósvafő H 99 C4
Jou P 148 A2
Jouarre F 90 C3
Joué-lès-Tours F 102 B2
Joué-sur-Erdre F 101 B4
Joure NL 70 B2
Joutseno FIN 9 B6
Joutsijärvi FIN 197 C10
Joux-la-Ville F 104 B2
Jouy F 90 C1
Jouy-le-Châtel F 90 C3
Jouy-le-Potier F 103 B3
Joyeuse F 131 A3
Joze F 116 B3
Juankoski FIN 8 A6
Juan-les-Pins F 132 B3
Jübek D 64 B2
Jubera E 144 B1
Jubrique E 162 B2
Jüchsen D 82 B2
Judaberg N 52 A1
Judenburg A 110 B1
Juelsminde DK 59 C3
Jugon-les-Lacs F 101 A3
Juillac F 129 A4
Juillan F 145 A4
Juist D 71 A4
Jukkasjärvi S 196 B3
Jule N 199 A10
Julianadorp NL 70 B1
Julianstown IRL 30 A2
Jülich D 80 B2
Jullouville F 88 B2
Jumeaux F 117 B3
Jumièges F 89 A4
Jumilhac-le-Grand
F 115 C5
Jumilla E 159 C2
Jumisko FIN 197 C11
Juncosa E 153 A4
Juneda E 147 C1
Jung S 55 B4
Jungingen D 93 C5
Junglingster L 92 B2
Juniville F 91 B4
Junosuando S 196 B5
Junqueira P 149 A2
Junsele S 200 C2
Juoksengi S 196 C6
Juoksenki FIN 196 C6
Juprelle B 80 B1
Jurata PL 69 A3
Jurbarkas LT 12 A5
Jurjevo HR 123 C3
Jūrmala LV 8 D3
Jurmu FIN 197 D10
Juromenha P 155 C3
Jursla S 56 B2
Jussac F 116 C2
Jussey F 105 B4
Jussy F 90 B3
Juta H 125 A3
Jüterbog D 74 C2
Juuka FIN 3 E11
Juuma FIN 197 C12
Juvigny le Tertre F 88 B2
Juvigny-sous-Andaine
F 89 B3
Juzennecourt F 105 A3
Jyderup DK 61 D1
Jyrkänkoski FIN 197 C12
Jyväskylä FIN 8 A4

K

Kaamanen FIN 193 C11
Kaamasmukka
FIN 193 C10
Kaaresuvanto FIN 192 D6
Kaarssen D 73 A4
Kaatscheuvel NL 79 A5
Kaba H 113 B5
Kåbdalis S 196 C3
Kačarevo SRB 127 C2
Kács H 113 B4
Kadan CZ 83 B5
Kadarkút H 125 A3
Kadınhanı TR 189 A7
Kaduy RUS 9 C10
Kåfalla S 56 A1
Kåfjord N 192 C7
Kåfjordbotn N 192 C4
Kågeröd S 61 D3
Kahl D 93 A5
Kahla D 82 B3
Kainach bei Voitsberg
A 110 B2
Kaindorf A 110 B2
Kainulasjärvi S 196 C5
Kairala FIN 197 B10
Kaisepakte S 192 D3
Kaisersesch D 80 B3
Kaiserslautern D 93 B3
Kaisheim D 94 C2
Kajaani FIN 3 D10
Kajárpéc H 111 B4
Kajdacs H 112 C2
Kakanj BIH 139 A4
Kakasd H 125 A4
Kaklik TR 189 B4
Kakolewo PL 85 A4
Kál H 113 B4
Kalajoki FIN 3 D8
Kalak N 193 B11
Kalamata GR 184 B3
Kalambaka GR 182 D3
Kalamria GR 182 C4
Kalandra GR 183 D5
Kälarne S 200 D2
Kalavrita GR 184 A3
Kalbe D 73 B4
Kalce SLO 123 B3
Káld H 111 B4
Kale
Antalya TR 189 C4
Denizli TR 188 B3
Kalecik TR 23 A7
Kalefeld D 82 A2
Kalesija BIH 139 A4
Kalety PL 86 B2
Kalevala RUS 3 D12
Kalhovd N 47 B5
Kalí HR 137 A4
Kalimnos GR 188 C2
Kaliningrad RUS 69 A5
Kalinkavichy BY 13 B8
Kalinovac HR 124 A3
Kalinovik BIH 139 B4
Kalinovo SK 99 C3
Kalirachi GR 183 C6
Kaliska
Pomorskie PL 68 A3
Pomorskie PL 68 B3
Kalisko PL 86 A3
Kalisz PL 86 A2
Kalisz Pomorski PL 75 A4
Kaljord N 194 B6
Kalkan TR 189 C4
Kalkar D 80 A2
Kalkım TR 186 C2
Kall
D 80 B2
S 199 B10
Källby S 55 B4
Kållered S 60 B2
Kållerstad S 60 B3
Kallinge S 63 B3
Kallmünz D 95 B3
Kallo FIN 196 B7
Kallsedet S 199 B9
Källvik S 56 B3
Kalmar S 63 B4
Kalmthout B 79 A4
Kalná SK 112 A2
Kalocsa H 112 C2
Kalokhorio CY 181 B2
Kalo Nero GR 184 B2
Kaloni GR 186 C1
Káloz H 112 C2
Kals A 109 B3
Kalsdorf A 110 C2
Kaltbrunn CH 107 B4
Kaltenbach A 108 B2
Kaltenkirchen D 64 C2
Kaltennordheim D 82 B2
Kalundborg DK 61 D1
Kalush UA 13 D6
Kalv S 60 B3
Kalvåg N 198 D1
Kalvehave DK 65 A5
Kalwang A 110 B1
Kalwaria-Zebrzydowska
PL 99 B3
Kalyazin RUS 9 D10
Kam H 111 B3
Kaman TR 23 B7
Kamares GR 185 C5
Kambos CY 181 A1
Kamen D 81 A3
Kamenice CZ 97 B3
Kamenice nad Lipou
CZ 96 B3
Kameničná SK 112 B2
Kamenný Most SK 112 B2
Kamenny Ujezd CZ 96 C2
Kamenska HR 124 B3
Kamensko HR 138 B2
Kamenz D 84 A2
Kamičak BIH 124 C2
Kamień PL 87 A4
Kamieniec Ząbk PL 85 B4
Kamienka SK 99 B4
Kamień Krajeński
PL 76 A2
Kamienna Góra PL 85 B4
Kamień Pomorski
PL 67 C3
Kamieńsk PL 86 A3
Kamiros Skala GR 188 C2
Kamnik SLO 123 A3
Kampen NL 70 B2
Kampinos PL 77 B5
Kamp-Lintfort D 80 A2
Kampor HR 123 C3
Kamyanets-Podil's'kyy
UA 13 D7
Kamyanka-Buz'ka
UA 13 C6
Kamýk nad Vltavou
CZ 96 B2
Kanal SLO 122 A2
Kanalia GR 182 D4
Kandalaksha RUS 3 C13
Kandanos GR 185 D4
Kandel D 93 B4
Kandern D 106 B2
Kandersteg CH 106 C2
Kandila GR 184 B3
Kandıra TR 187 A5
Kandyty PL 69 A5
Kanfanar HR 122 B2
Kangasala FIN 8 B4
Kangos S 196 B5
Kangosjärvi FIN 196 B6
Kaniów PL 75 C3
Kanjiža SRB 126 A2
Kankaanpää FIN 8 B3
Kannus FIN 3 E8
Kanturk IRL 29 B3
Kapaklı TR 186 A2
Kapellen
A 110 B2
B 79 A4
Kapellskär S 57 A5
Kapfenberg A 110 B2
Kapfenstein A 110 C2
Kaplice CZ 96 C2
Kapljuh BIH 124 C2
Kápolna H 113 B4
Kápolnásnyék H 112 B2
Kaposfő H 125 A3
Kaposfüred H 125 A3
Kaposszekcsö H 125 A4
Kaposvár H 125 A3
Kapp N 48 B2
Kappel D 93 C3
Kappeln D 64 B2
Kappelshamn S 57 C4
Kappl A 107 B5
Kappstad S 55 A4
Kaprun A 109 B3
Kaptol HR 125 B3
Kapuvár H 111 B4
Karaadilli TR 189 A5
Karabiğa TR 186 B2
Karabük TR 187 A7
Karaburun TR 186 D1
Karacabey TR 186 B3
Karacaköy TR 186 A3
Karacaören TR 189 A5
Karacasu TR 188 B3
Karácsond H 113 B4
Karád H 112 C1
Karahallı TR 189 A4
Karaisali TR 23 C8
Karaman
Balıkesir TR 186 C3
Karaman TR 23 C7
Karamanlı TR 189 B4
Karamürsel TR 187 B4
Karan SRB 127 D1
Karancslapujto H 113 A3
Karaova TR 188 B2
Karapınar TR 23 C7
Karasjok N 193 C9
Karasu TR 187 A5
Karataş
Adana TR 23 C8
Manisa TR 188 A3
Karatoprak TR 188 B2
Karavostasi CY 181 A1
Karbenning S 50 B3
Kårberg S 55 B5
Kårböle S 199 D12
Karby
D 64 B2
DK 58 B1
Kårby S 62 A4
Karby S 57 A4
Karcag H 113 B4
Karczów PL 86 B1
Karczowiska PL 85 A4
Kardamena GR 188 C2
Kardamila GR 185 A7
Kardamili GR 184 C3
Kardašova Rečice
CZ 96 B2
Kardis S 196 C6
Karditsa GR 182 D3
Kärdla EST 8 C3
Kardoskút H 113 C4
Karesuando S 192 D6
Kargı TR 23 A8
Kargopol RUS 9 B11
Kargowa PL 75 B4
Karigasniemi FIN 193 C9
Karise DK 65 A5
Karistos GR 185 A5
Karkkila FIN 8 B4
Karlholmsbruk S 51 B4
Karlino PL 67 B4
Karlobag HR 137 A4
Karlovac HR 123 B4
Karlovasi GR 188 B1
Karlovčic SRB 127 C2
Karlovice CZ 85 B5
Karlovo BG 17 D6
Karlovy Vary CZ 83 B4
Karłowice PL 86 B1
Karlsborg S 55 B5
Karlshamn S 63 B2
Karlshöfen D 72 A2
Karlshus N 54 A1
Karlskoga S 55 A5
Karlskrona S 63 B3
Karlsrud N 47 B5
Karlsruhe D 93 B4
Karlstad S 55 A4
Karlstadt D 94 B1
Karlstetten A 110 A2
Karlstift A 96 C2
Karlstorp S 62 A3
Karmacs H 111 C4
Karmin PL 85 A5
Kärna S 60 B1
Karnobat BG 17 D7
Karojba HR 122 B2
Karow D 73 A5
Karpacz PL 85 B3
Karpathos GR 188 D2
Karpenisi GR 182 E3
Karpuzlu TR 188 B2
Kärrbo S 56 A2
Karrebaeksminde
DK 65 A4
Karshult S 60 B3
Karsin PL 68 B2
Kårsta S 57 A4
Karstädt D 73 A4
Kartal TR 186 B4
Kartitsch A 109 C3
Kartuzy PL 68 A3
Karungi S 196 C6
Karunki FIN 196 C7
Karup DK 59 B2
Karviná CZ 98 B2
Kås DK 58 A2
Kaş TR 189 C4
Kasaba TR 189 C4
Kašava CZ 98 B1
Kåseberga S 66 A3
Kasejovice CZ 96 B1
Kasfjord N 194 B7
Kashin RUS 9 D10
Kašina HR 124 B2
Kasina-Wielka PL 99 B4
Kaskinen FIN 8 A2
Kašperské Hory CZ 96 B1
Kassandrino GR 183 C5
Kassel D 81 A5
Kassiopi GR 182 D1
Kastamonu TR 23 A7
Kastav HR 123 B3
Kasteli GR 185 D4
Kastellaun D 93 A3
Kastelli GR 185 D6
Kaštel-Stari HR 138 B2
Kaštel Zegarski
HR 138 A1
Kasterlee B 79 A4
Kastl D 95 B3
Kastlösa S 63 B4
Kastorf D 65 C3
Kastoria GR 182 C3
Kastorio GR 184 B3
Kastraki GR 185 C6
Kastrosikia GR 182 D2
Kastsyukovichy
BY 13 B10
Kaszaper H 113 C4
Katakolo GR 184 B2
Katapola GR 185 C6
Katastari GR 184 B1
Katerbow D 74 B1
Katerini GR 182 C4
Kathikas CY 181 B1
Kätkesuando S 196 A6
Katlenburg-Lindau
D 82 A2
Kato Achaia GR 184 A2
Káto Pyrgos CY 181 A1
Katouna GR 182 E3
Katovice CZ 96 B1
Katowice PL 86 B3
Katrineberg S 50 A3
Katrineholm S 56 B2
Kattarp S 61 C2
Kattavia GR 188 D2
Katthammarsvik S 57 C4
Kattilstorp S 55 B4
Katwijk NL 70 B1
Katymár H 125 A5
Kąty Wrocławskie
PL 85 A4
Katzenelnbogen D 81 B3
Katzhütte D 82 B3
Kaub D 93 A3
Kaufbeuren D 108 B1
Kauhajoki FIN 8 A3
Kauhava FIN 8 A3
Kaukonen FIN 196 B7
Kauliranta FIN 196 C6
Kaulsdorf D 82 B3
Kaunas LT 13 A5
Kaunisvaara S 196 B6
Kaupanger N 47 A4
Kautokeino N 192 C7
Kautzen A 97 C3
Kavadarci MK 182 B4
Kavajë AL 182 B1
Kavakköy TR 186 B1
Kavaklı TR 186 A2
Kavaklıdere TR 188 B3
Kavala GR 183 C6
Kavarna BG 17 D8
Kävlinge S 61 D3
Kawcze PL 68 A1
Kaxås S 199 B10
Kaxholmen S 62 A2
Käylä FIN 197 C12
Kaymakçı TR 188 A3
Kaymaz TR 187 C6
Kaynarca TR 187 A5
Käyrämö FIN 197 C9
Kayseri TR 23 B8
Kaysersberg F 106 A2
Kazanlŭk BG 17 D6
Kazár H 113 A3
Kazimierza Wielka
PL 87 B4
Kazincbarcika H 113 A4
Kaźmierz PL 75 B5
Kcynia PL 76 A2
Kdyně CZ 95 B5
Kea GR 185 B5
Keadew IRL 26 B2
Keady GB 27 B4
Kecel H 112 C3
Keçiborlu TR 189 B5
Kecskemét H 113 C3
Kėdainiai LT 13 A5
Kędzierzyn-Koźle
PL 86 B2
Keel IRL 28 A1
Keenagh IRL 28 A4
Keerbergen B 79 A4
Kefalos GR 188 C1
Kefken TR 187 A5
Keflavík IS 190 C3
Kegworth GB 40 C2
Kehl D 93 C3
Kehrigk D 74 B2
Keighley GB 40 B2
Keila EST 8 C4
Keillmore GB 34 C2
Keiss GB 32 C3
Keith GB 33 D4
Kelankylä FIN 197 D10
Kelberg D 80 B2
Kelbra D 82 A3
Kelč CZ 98 B1
Kelchsau A 108 B3
Këlcyrë AL 182 C2
Keld GB 37 B4
Kelebia H 126 A1
Kelekçi TR 188 B4
Kelemér H 99 C4
Keles TR 186 C4
Kelheim D 95 C3
Kell D 92 B2
Kellas GB 32 D3
Kellinghusen D 64 C2
Kelloselkä FIN 197 C11
Kells
GB 27 B4
IRL 27 C4
Kelmis B 80 B2
Kelokedhara CY 181 B1
Kelottijärvi FIN 192 D6
Kelsall GB 38 A4
Kelso GB 35 C5
Kelsterbach D 93 A4
Keltneyburn GB 35 B3
Kelujärvi FIN 197 B10
Kemaliye TR 188 A3
Kemalpaşa TR 188 A2
Kematen A 108 B2
Kemberg D 83 A4
Kemer
Antalya TR 189 C5
Burdur TR 189 B5
Muğla TR 189 C4
Kemerkaya TR 187 D6
Kemeten A 111 B3
Kemi FIN 196 D7
Kemijärvi FIN 197 C10
Keminmaa FIN 196 D7
Kemnath D 95 B3
Kemnay GB 33 D4
Kemnitz
Brandenburg D 74 B1
Mecklenburg-Vorpommern D 66 B2
Kempen D 80 A2
Kempsey GB 39 B4
Kempten D 107 B5
Kemptthal CH 107 B3
Kendal GB 37 B4
Kenderes H 113 B4
Kengyel H 113 B4
Kenilworth GB 44 A2
Kenmare IRL 29 C2
Kenmore GB 35 B4
Kennacraig GB 34 C2
Kenyeri H 111 B4
Kenzingen D 106 A2
Kepez TR 186 B1
Kępice PL 68 A1
Kępno PL 86 A2
Kepsut TR 186 C3
Keramoti GR 183 C6
Keräntöjärvi S 196 B6
Keratea GR 185 B4
Kerava FIN 8 B4
Kerecsend H 113 B4
Kerekegyhaza H 112 C3
Kerepestarcsa H 112 B3
Keri GR 184 B1
Kérien F 100 A2
Kerkafalva H 111 C3
Kerken D 80 A2
Kerkrade NL 80 B2
Kerkyra GR 182 D1
Kerlouan F 100 A1

Kernascléden F 100 A2
Kernhof A 110 B2
Kerns CH 106 C3
Kerpen D 80 B2
Kerrysdale GB 31 B3
Kerta H 111 B4
Kerteminde DK 59 C3
Kerzers CH 106 C2
Keşan TR 186 B1
Kesgrave GB 45 A5
Kesh GB 26 B3
Keskin TR 23 B7
Kesselfall A 109 B3
Kestenga RUS 3 D12
Keswick GB 36 B3
Keszthely H 111 C4
Kétegyháza H 113 C5
Kéthely H 111 C4
Kętrzyn PL 12 A4
Kettering GB 44 A3
Kettlewell GB 40 A1
Kęty PL 99 B3
Ketzin D 74 B1
Keula D 82 A2
Keuruu FIN 8 A4
Kevelaer D 80 A2
Kevermes H 113 C5
Kevi SRB 126 B1
Keyingham GB 41 B3
Keynsham GB 43 A4
Kežmarok SK 99 B4
Kharmanli BG 183 B7
Khaskovo BG 183 B7
Khimki RUS 9 E10
Khisinev = Chişinău
MD 17 B8
Khmelnik UA 13 D7
Khmelnytskyy UA 13 D7
Khodoriv UA 13 D6
Kholm RUS 9 D7
Khotyn UA 13 D7
Khoyniki BY 13 C8
Khust UA 17 A5
Khvoynaya RUS 9 C9
Kiato GR 184 A3
Kibæk DK 59 B1
Kiberg N 193 B14
Kicasalih TR 186 A1
Kičevo MK 182 B2
Kidderminster GB 39 B4
Kidlington GB 44 B2
Kidsgrove GB 40 B1
Kidwelly GB 39 C2
Kiefersfelden D 108 B3
Kiel D 64 B3
Kielce PL 87 B4
Kiełczygłów PL 86 A3
Kielder GB 37 A4
Kiełpino PL 68 A3
Kielpiny PL 77 A4
Kierinki FIN 197 B8
Kiernozia PL 77 B4
Kierspe D 81 A3
Kietrz PL 86 B2
Kietz D 74 B3
Kiev = Kyyiv UA 13 C9
Kiezmark PL 69 A3
Kiffisia GR 185 A4
Kifino Selo BIH 139 B4
Kihlanki
FIN 196 B6
S 196 B6
Kiistala FIN 197 B8
Kije PL 87 B4
Kijevo HR 138 B2
Kikallen N 46 B2
Kikinda SRB 126 B2
Kil
N 53 B5
Örebro S 55 A6
Värmland S 55 A4
Kila S 55 A3
Kilafors S 50 A3
Kilbaha IRL 29 B2
Kilbeggan IRL 30 A1
Kilberry GB 34 C2
Kilbirnie GB 34 C3
Kilboghamn N 195 D4
Kilbotn N 194 B7
Kilb Rabenstein A 110 A2
Kilchattan GB 34 C2
Kilchoan GB 34 B1
Kilcock IRL 30 A2
Kilconnell IRL 28 A3
Kilcormac IRL 28 A4
Kilcreggan GB 34 C3
Kilcullen IRL 30 A2
Kilcurry IRL 27 B4
Kildare IRL 30 A2
Kildinstroy RUS 3 B13
Kildonan GB 32 C3
Kildorrery IRL 29 B3
Kilegrend N 53 A4
Kilen N 53 A4
Kilgarvan IRL 29 C2
Kiliya UA 17 C8
Kilkee IRL 29 B2
Kilkeel GB 27 B4
Kilkelly IRL 26 C2
Kilkenny IRL 30 B1
Kilkieran IRL 28 A2
Kilkinlea IRL 29 B2
Kilkis GR 182 B4
Killadysert IRL 29 B2
Killala IRL 26 B1
Killaloe IRL 28 B3
Killarney IRL 29 B2
Killashandra IRL 27 B3
Killashee IRL 28 A4
Killearn GB 34 B3
Killeberg S 61 C4
Killeigh IRL 30 A1
Killenaule IRL 29 B4
Killimor IRL 28 A3
Killin GB 34 B3
Killinaboy IRL 28 B2
Killinge S 196 B3
Killinick IRL 30 B2
Killorglin IRL 29 B2
Killucan IRL 30 A1
Killybegs IRL 26 B2
Killyleagh GB 27 B5
Kilmacrenan IRL 26 A3
Kilmacthomas IRL 30 B1
Kilmaine IRL 28 A2
Kilmallock IRL 29 B3
Kilmarnock GB 36 A2
Kilmartin GB 34 B2
Kilmaurs GB 36 A2
Kilmeadan IRL 30 B1
Kilmeedy IRL 29 B3
Kilmelford GB 34 B2
Kilmore Quay IRL 30 B2
Kilmuir GB 32 D2
Kilnaleck IRL 27 C3
Kilninver GB 34 B2
Kilpisjärvi FIN 192 C4
Kilrea GB 27 B4
Kilrush IRL 29 B2
Kilsmo S 56 A1
Kilsyth GB 35 C3
Kiltoom IRL 28 A3
Kilwinning GB 36 A2
Kimasozero RUS 3 D12
Kimi GR 185 A5
Kimolos GR 185 C5
Kimovsk RUS 9 E10
Kimratshofen D 107 B5
Kimry RUS 9 D10
Kimstad S 56 B1
Kinbrace GB 32 C3
Kincardine GB 35 B4
Kincraig GB 32 D3
Kindberg A 110 B2
Kindelbruck D 82 A3
Kingarrow IRL 26 B2
Kingisepp RUS 9 C6
Kingsbridge GB 43 B3
Kingsclere GB 44 B2
Kingscourt IRL 27 C4
King's Lynn GB 41 C4
Kingsteignton GB 43 B3
Kingston
Greater London
GB 44 B3
Moray GB 32 D3
Kingston Bagpuize
GB 44 B2
Kingston upon Hull
GB 40 B3
Kingswear GB 43 B3
Kingswood GB 43 A4
Kington GB 39 B3
Kingussie GB 32 D2
Kınık
Antalya TR 188 C4
İzmir TR 186 C2
Kinloch
Highland GB 31 B2
Highland GB 32 C2
Kinlochbervie GB 32 C1
Kinlochewe GB 32 D1
Kinlochleven GB 34 B3
Kinlochmoidart GB 34 B2
Kinloch Rannoch
GB 35 B3
Kinloss GB 32 D3
Kinlough IRL 26 B2
Kinn N 48 B2
Kinna S 60 B2
Kinnared S 60 B3
Kinnarp S 55 B4
Kinnegad IRL 30 A1
Kinne-Kleva S 55 B4
Kinnitty IRL 28 A4
Kinrooi B 80 A1
Kinross GB 35 B4
Kinsale IRL 29 C3
Kinsarvik N 46 B3
Kintarvie GB 31 A2
Kintore GB 33 D4
Kinvarra IRL 28 A3
Kioni GR 184 A1
Kiparissia GR 184 B2
Kipfenburg D 95 C3
Kippen GB 35 B3
Kiraz TR 188 A3
Kirazlı TR 186 B1
Kirberg D 81 B4
Kirchbach in Steiermark
A 110 C2
Kirchberg
CH 106 B2
Baden-Württemberg
D 94 B1
Rheinland-Pfalz D 93 B3
Kirchberg am Wechsel
A 110 B2
Kirchberg an der Pielach
A 110 A2
Kirchberg in Tirol
A 109 B3
Kirchbichl A 108 B3
Kirchdorf
Bayern D 96 C1
Mecklenburg-Vorpommern D 65 C4
Niedersachsen D 72 B1
Kirchdorf an der Krems
A 109 B5
Kirchdorf in Tirol A 109 B3
Kirchenlamitz D 83 B3
Kirchenthumbach D 95 B3
Kirchhain D 81 B4
Kirchheim
Baden-Württemberg
D 94 C1
Bayern D 108 A1
Hessen D 81 B5
Kirchheimbolanden
D 93 B4
Kirchhundem D 81 A4
Kirchlintein D 72 B2
Kirchschlag A 111 B3
Kirchweidach D 109 A3
Kirchzarten D 106 B2
Kircubbin GB 27 B5
Kireç TR 186 C3
Kırıkkale TR 23 B7
Kirillov RUS 9 C11
Kirishi RUS 9 C8
Kırka TR 187 C5
Kırkağaç TR 186 C2
Kirkbean GB 36 B3
Kirkbride GB 36 B3
Kirkby GB 38 A4
Kirkby Lonsdale GB 37 B4
Kirkby Malzeard GB 40 A2
Kirkbymoorside GB 37 B6
Kirkby Stephen GB 37 B4
Kirkcaldy GB 35 B4
Kirkcolm GB 36 B1
Kirkconnel GB 36 A2
Kirkcowan GB 36 B2
Kirkcudbright GB 36 B2
Kirkehamn N 52 B2
Kirke Hyllinge DK 61 D1
Kirkenær N 49 B4
Kirkenes N 193 C14
Kirkham GB 38 A4
Kirkintilloch GB 35 C3
Kirkjubæjarklaustur
IS 191 D7
Kirkkonummi FIN 8 B4
Kırklareli TR 186 A2
Kirkmichael GB 35 B4
Kirk Michael GB 36 B2
Kirkoswald GB 36 A2
Kirkpatrick Fleming
GB 36 A3
Kirkton of Glenisla
GB 35 B4
Kirkwall GB 33 C4
Kirkwhelpington GB 37 A5
Kirn D 93 B3
Kirovsk RUS 3 C13
Kirriemuir GB 35 B5
Kırşehir TR 23 B8
Kirton GB 41 C3
Kirton in Lindsey
GB 40 B3
Kirtorf D 81 B5
Kiruna S 196 B3
Kisa S 62 A3
Kisač SRB 126 B1
Kisbér H 112 B2
Kiseljak BIH 139 B4
Kisielice PL 69 B4
Kisköre H 113 B4
Kiskőrös H 112 C3
Kiskunfélegyháza
H 113 C3
Kiskunhalas H 112 C3
Kiskunlacháza H 112 B2
Kiskunmajsa H 113 C3
Kisláng H 112 C2
Kisslegg D 107 B4
Kissolt H 112 C3
Kissónerga CY 181 B1
Kist D 94 B1
Kistanje HR 138 B1
Kistelek H 113 C3
Kisterenye H 113 A3
Kisújszállás H 113 B4
Kisvárda H 16 A5
Kisvejke H 112 C2
Kiszkowo PL 76 B2
Kiszombor H 126 A2
Kitee FIN 9 A7
Kithnos GR 185 B5
Kiti CY 181 B2
Kitkiöjärvi S 196 B6
Kitkiöjoki S 196 B6
Kittelfjäll S 195 E6
Kittendorf D 74 A1
Kittilä FIN 196 B7
Kittlitz D 84 A2
Kittsee A 111 A4
Kitzbühel A 109 B3
Kitzingen D 94 B2
Kiuruvesi FIN 3 E10
Kivertsi UA 13 C6
Kividhes CY 181 B1
Kivik S 63 C2
Kivotos GR 182 C3
Kıyıköy TR 186 A3
Kızılcabölük TR 188 B4
Kızılcadağ TR 189 B4
Kızılcahamam TR 23 A7
Kızılırmak TR 23 A7
Kızılkaya TR 189 B5
Kızılkuyu TR 187 D6
Kızılören
Afyon TR 189 A5
Konya TR 189 B7
Kjeldebotn N 194 B7
Kjellerup DK 59 B2
Kjellmyra N 49 B4
Kjøllefjord N 193 B11
Kjopmannskjaer N 54 A1
Kjøpsvik N 194 B7
Kl'ačno SK 98 C2
Kladanj BIH 139 A4
Kläden D 73 B4
Klädesholmen S 60 B1
Kladnice HR 138 B2
Kladno CZ 84 B2
Kladruby CZ 95 B4
Klagenfurt A 110 C1
Klågerup S 61 D3
Klagstorp S 66 A2
Klaipėda LT 8 E2
Klaistow D 74 B1
Klaksvík FO 4 A3
Klana HR 123 B3
Klanac HR 123 C4
Klanjec HR 123 A4
Klardorf D 95 B4
Klarup DK 58 A3
Klašnice BIH 124 C3
Klässbol S 55 A3
Klášterec nad Ohří
CZ 83 B5
Kláštor pod Znievom
SK 98 C2
Klatovy CZ 96 B1
Klaus an der Pyhrnbahn
A 110 B1
Klazienaveen NL 71 B3
Kłecko PL 76 B2
Kleczew PL 76 B3
Klein Plasten D 74 A1
Klein Sankt Paul A 110 C1
Kleinsölk A 109 B4
Kleinzell A 110 B2
Klejtrup DK 58 B2
Klek SRB 126 B2
Klemensker DK 67 A3
Klenak SRB 127 C1
Klenci pod Cerchovem
CZ 95 B4
Klenica PL 75 C4
Klenje SRB 127 C1
Klenoec MK 182 B2
Klenovec SK 99 C3
Klenovica HR 123 B3
Klenovnik HR 124 A2
Kleppe N 52 B1
Kleppestø N 46 B2
Kleptow D 74 A2
Kleszewo PL 77 B6
Kleve D 80 A2
Klevshult S 60 B4
Klewki PL 77 A5
Kličevac SRB 127 C3
Kliening A 110 C1
Klietz D 73 B5
Klikuszowa PL 99 B3
Klimkovice CZ 98 B2
Klimontów PL 87 B5
Klimovichi BY 13 B9
Klimpfjäll S 195 E5
Klin RUS 9 D10
Klinča Sela HR 123 B4
Klingenbach A 111 B3
Klingenberg D 93 B5
Klingenmunster D 93 B4
Klingenthal D 83 B4
Klinken D 73 A4
Klintehamn S 57 C4
Kliny PL 87 A4
Kliplev DK 64 B2
Klippan S 61 C3
Klis HR 138 B2
Klitmøller DK 58 A1
Klitten S 49 A6
Klixbüll D 64 B1
Kljajićevo SRB 126 B1
Ključ BIH 138 A2
Klobouky CZ 97 C4
Kłobuck PL 86 B2
Klockestrand S 200 D3
Kłodawa
Lubuskie PL 75 B4
Wielkopolskie PL 76 B3
Kłodzko PL 85 B4
Kløfta N 48 B3
Klokkarvik N 46 B2
Klokkerholm DK 58 A3
Klokočov SK 98 B2
Kłomnice PL 86 B3
Klonowa PL 86 A2
Kloosterzande NL 79 A4
Kłopot PL 74 B3
Klos AL 182 B2
Kloštar Ivanić HR 124 B2
Kloster
D 66 B2
DK 59 B1
Klösterle A 107 B5
Klostermansfeld D 82 A3
Klosterneuburg A 97 C4
Klosters CH 107 C4
Kloten CH 107 B3
Klötze D 73 B4
Klöverträsk S 196 D4
Klövsjö S 199 C11
Kluczbork PL 86 B2
Kluczewo PL 75 A5
Kluisbergen B 79 B3
Klundert NL 79 A4
Klutz D 65 C4
Klwów PL 87 A4
Klyetsk BY 13 B7
Knaben N 52 B2
Knaften S 200 B4
Knapstad N 54 A2
Knäred S 61 C3
Knaresborough GB 40 A2
Knarvik N 46 B2
Knebel DK 59 B3
Knebworth GB 44 B3
Knesebeck D 73 B3
Knesselare B 78 A3
Knežak SLO 123 B3
Kneževi Vinogradi
HR 125 B4
Kneževo HR 125 B4
Knić SRB 127 D2
Knighton GB 39 B3
Knin HR 138 A2
Knislinge S 61 C4
Knittelfeld A 110 B1
Knivsta S 57 A3
Knock IRL 28 A3
Knocktopher IRL 30 B1
Knokke-Heist B 78 A3
Knowle GB 44 A2
Knurów PL 86 B2
Knutby S 51 C5
Knutsford GB 38 A4
Kobarid SLO 122 A2
København =
Copenhagen DK 61 D2
Kobenz A 110 B1
Kobersdorf A 111 B3
Kobiernice PL 99 B3
Kobierzyce PL 85 B4
Kobilje SLO 111 C3
Kobiór PL 86 B2
Koblenz
CH 106 B3
D 81 B3
Kobryn BY 13 B6
Kobylanka PL 75 A3
Kobylin PL 85 A5
Kobylniki PL 77 B5
Kocaali TR 187 A5
Kocaaliler TR 189 B5
Kocaeli = İzmit TR 187 B4
Kočani MK 182 B4
Koçarlı TR 188 B2
Koceljevo SRB 127 C1
Kočerin BIH 138 B3
Kočevje SLO 123 B3
Kočevska Reka
SLO 123 B3
Kochel am see D 108 B2
Kocs H 112 B2
Kocsér H 113 B3
Kocsola H 112 C2
Koczala PL 68 B2
Kodal N 53 A6
Kode S 60 B1
Kodersdorf D 84 A2
Kodrab PL 86 A3
Koekelare B 78 A2
Kofçaz TR 186 A2
Köflach A 110 B2
Køge DK 61 D2
Kohlberg D 95 B4
Kohtla-Järve EST 8 C5
Köinge S 60 B2
Kojetín CZ 98 B1
Kökar FIN 51 C7
Kokava SK 99 C3
Kokkola FIN 3 E8
Kokori BIH 124 C3
Kokoski PL 69 A3
Koksijde B 78 A2
Kola
BIH 124 C3
RUS 3 B13
Köla S 54 A3
Kołacin PL 87 A3
Kolari FIN 196 B6
Kolárovo SK 112 B1
Kolašin MNE 16 D3
Kolbäck S 56 A2
Kolbacz PL 75 A3
Kolbeinsstaðir IS 190 C3
Kolbermoor D 108 B3
Kolbnitz A 109 C4
Kolbotn N 54 A1
Kolbu N 48 B2
Kolby Kås DK 59 C3
Kolczewo PL 67 C3
Kolczyglowy PL 68 A2
Kolding DK 59 C2
Kölesd H 112 C2
Kolgrov N 46 A1
Kolín CZ 97 A3
Kolind DK 59 B3
Kolinec CZ 96 B1
Koljane HR 138 B2
Kølkær DK 59 B2
Kölleda D 82 A3
Kollum NL 70 A3
Köln = Cologne D 80 B2
Koło PL 76 B3
Kołobrzeg PL 67 B4
Kolochau D 83 A5
Kolomyya UA 13 D6
Kolonowskie PL 86 B2
Koloveč CZ 95 B5
Kolpino RUS 9 C7
Kolrep D 73 A5
Kölsillre S 199 C12
Kolsko PL 75 C4
Kolsva S 56 A1
Kolta SK 112 A2
Kolunič BIH 138 A2
Koluszki PL 87 A3
Kolut SRB 125 B4
Kolvereid N 199 A8
Kølvrå DK 59 B2
Komadi H 113 B5
Komagvær N 193 B14
Komarica BIH 125 C3
Komárno SK 112 B2
Komárom H 112 B2
Komatou Yialou
CY 181 A3
Komboti GR 182 D3
Komen SLO 122 B2
Komin HR 138 B3
Komiža HR 138 B2
Komjáti H 99 C4
Komjatice SK 112 A2
Komletinci HR 125 B4
Komló H 125 A4
Kömlo H 113 B4
Komoča SK 112 B2
Komorniki PL 75 B5
Komorzno PL 86 A2
Komotini GR 183 B7
Konak SRB 126 B2
Konakovo RUS 9 D10
Konarzyny PL 68 B2
Kondias GR 183 D7
Kondopaga RUS 9 A9
Kondorfa H 111 C3
Kondoros H 113 C4
Konevo RUS 9 A11
Køng DK 65 A4
Konga S 63 B3
Köngäs FIN 196 B7
Kongerslev DK 58 B3
Kongsberg N 53 A5
Kongshamn N 53 B4
Kongsmark DK 64 A1
Kongsmoen N 199 A9
Kongsvik N 194 B7
Kongsvinger N 48 B3
Konice CZ 97 B4
Konie PL 77 C5
Koniecpol PL 86 B3
Königsberg D 82 B2
Königsbronn D 94 C2
Königsbruck D 84 A1
Königsbrunn D 94 C2
Konigsdorf D 108 B2
Königsee D 82 B3
Königshorst D 74 B1
Königslutter D 73 B3
Königssee D 109 B3
Königstein
Hessen D 81 B4
Sachsen D 84 B2
Königstetten A 97 C4
Königswartha D 84 A2
Konigswiesen A 96 C2
Königswinter D 80 B3
Königs Wusterhausen
D 74 B2
Konin PL 76 B3
Konispol AL 182 D2
Konitsa GR 182 C2
Köniz CH 106 C2
Konjevići BIH 139 A5
Konjevrate HR 138 B2
Konjic BIH 139 B3
Konjščina HR 124 A2
Könnern D 83 A3
Konnerud N 53 A6
Konopiska PL 86 B2
Konotop PL 75 C4
Końskie PL 87 A4
Konsmo N 52 B3
Konstancin-Jeziorna
PL 77 B6
Konstantynów Łódźki
PL 86 A3
Konstanz D 107 B4
Kontich B 79 A4
Kontiolahti FIN 9 A6
Konya TR 189 B7
Konz D 92 B2
Kópasker IS 191 A9
Kópavogur IS 190 C4
Kopčany SK 98 C1
Koper SLO 122 B2
Kopervik N 52 A1
Kópháza H 111 B3
Kopice PL 85 B5
Kopidlno CZ 84 B3
Köping S 56 A1
Köpingebro S 66 A2
Köpingsvik S 62 B4
Köpmanholmen S 200 C4
Koppang N 48 A3
Koppangen N 192 C4
Kopparberg S 50 C1
Koppelo FIN 193 D11
Koppom S 54 A3
Koprivlen BG 183 B5
Koprivna BIH 125 C4
Koprivnica HR 124 A2
Kopřivnice CZ 98 B2
Köprübaşı TR 186 D3
Koprzywnica PL 87 B5
Kopstal L 92 B2
Kopychyntsi UA 13 D6
Kopytkowo PL 69 B3
Korbach D 81 A4

Körbecke D 81 A4
Korçë AL 182 C2
Korčula HR 138 C3
Korczyców PL 75 B3
Korenita SRB 127 C1
Korets UA 13 C7
Korfantów PL 85 B5
Körfez TR 187 B4
Korgen N 195 D4
Korinth DK 64 A3
Korinthos = Corinth GR 184 B3
Korita
BIH 138 A2
HR 139 C3
Korithi GR 184 B1
Korkuteli TR 189 B5
Körmend H 111 B3
Korne PL 68 A2
Korneuburg A 97 C4
Kornevo RUS 69 A5
Kórnik PL 76 B2
Kornsjø N 54 B2
Környe H 112 B2
Koromačno HR 123 C3
Koroni GR 184 C2
Koronos GR 185 B6
Koronowo PL 76 A2
Körösladány H 113 C5
Köröstarcsa H 113 C5
Korosten UA 13 C8
Korostyshev UA 13 C8
Korpikå S 196 D6
Korpikylä FIN 196 C6
Korpilombolo S 196 C6
Korsberga
Jönköping S 62 A3
Skaraborg S 55 B5
Korshavn N 54 A1
Korskrogen S 200 E1
Korsnäs S 50 B2
Korsør DK 65 A4
Korsun Shevchenkovskiy UA 13 D9
Korträsk S 196 D3
Kortrijk B 78 B3
Korucu TR 186 C2
Koryčany CZ 98 B1
Korzeńsko PL 85 A4
Korzybie PL 68 A1
Kos GR 188 C2
Kosakowo PL 69 A3
Kosanica MNE 139 B5
Kösching D 95 C3
Kościan PL 75 B5
Kościelec PL 76 B3
Kościerzyna PL 68 A2
Koserow D 66 B2
Košetice CZ 97 B3
Košice SK 12 D4
Kosjerić SRB 127 D1
Koška HR 125 B4
Koskullskulle S 196 B3
Kosovska Mitrovica KOS 16 D4
Kosta S 62 B3
Kostajnica HR 124 B2
Kostajnik SRB 127 C1
Kostanjevica SLO 123 B4
Kostelec nad Černými Lesy CZ 96 B2
Kostelec na Hané CZ 97 B5
Kostice CZ 84 B1
Kostkowo PL 68 A3
Kostojevići SRB 127 C1
Kostolac SRB 127 C3
Kostomłoty PL 85 A4
Kostopil UA 13 C7
Kostów PL 86 A2
Kostrzyn
Lubuskie PL 74 B3
Wielkopolskie PL 76 B2
Koszalin PL 67 B5
Koszęcin PL 86 B2
Kőszeg H 111 B3
Koszwaly PL 69 A3
Koszyce PL 87 B4
Kot SLO 123 B4
Kotala FIN 197 B11
Kötelek H 113 B4
Köthen D 83 A3
Kotka FIN 8 B5
Kotomierz PL 76 A3
Kotor MNE 16 D3
Kotoriba HR 124 A2
Kotorsko BIH 125 C4
Kotor Varoš BIH 124 C3
Kotovsk UA 17 B8
Kotronas GR 184 C3
Kötschach A 109 C3
Kötzting D 95 B4
Koudum NL 70 B2
Kouřim CZ 96 A2
Kout na Šumave CZ 95 B5
Kouvola FIN 8 B5
Kovačevac SRB 127 C2
Kovačica SRB 126 B2
Kovdor RUS 197 B13
Kovel' UA 13 C6
Kovilj SRB 126 B2
Kovin SRB 127 C2
Kowal PL 77 B4
Kowalewo Pomorskie PL 69 B3
Kowalów PL 75 B3
Kowary PL 85 B3
Köyceğiz TR 188 C3
Kozani GR 182 C3
Kozarac
BIH 124 C2
HR 124 B1
Kozárovce SK 98 C2
Kozelets UA 13 C9
Kozica HR 138 B3
Koziegłowy PL 86 B3
Kozienice PL 87 A5
Kozina SLO 122 B2
Kozje SLO 123 A4
Kozlu TR 187 A6
Kozluk BIH 139 A5
Koźmin PL 85 A5
Koźminek PL 86 A2
Kozolupy CZ 96 B1
Kożuchów PL 84 A3
Kožuhe BIH 125 C4
Kozyatyn UA 13 D8
Kozyürük TR 186 A1
Kräckelbräken S 49 A6
Krackow D 74 A3
Kraddsele S 195 E7
Krąg PL 68 A1
Kragenæs DK 65 B4
Kragerø N 53 B5
Krągi PL 68 B1
Kragujevac SRB 127 C2
Kraiburg D 109 A3
Krajenka PL 68 B1
Krajišnik SRB 126 B2
Krajková CZ 83 B4
Krajné SK 98 C1
Krajnik Dolny PL 74 A3
Krakača BIH 124 B1
Kräklingbo S 57 C4
Kraków = Cracow PL 99 A3
Krakow am See D 73 A5
Králíky CZ 85 B4
Kraljevica HR 123 B3
Kraljevo SRB 16 D4
Kral'ovany SK 99 B3
Král'ov Brod SK 111 A4
Kralovice CZ 96 B1
Kralupy nad Vltavou CZ 84 B2
Králův Dvůr CZ 96 B2
Kramfors S 200 D3
Kramsach A 108 B2
Kramsk PL 76 B3
Kråmvik N 53 A4
Kranenburg D 80 A2
Krania GR 182 D3
Krania Elasonas GR 182 D4
Kranichfeld D 82 B3
Kranidi GR 184 B4
Kranj SLO 123 A3
Kranjska Gora SLO 109 C4
Krapanj HR 138 B1
Krapina HR 124 A1
Krapje HR 124 B2
Krapkowice PL 86 B1
Kraselov CZ 96 B1
Krašić HR 123 B4
Krāslava LV 8 E5
Kraslice CZ 83 B4
Krasna PL 87 A4
Krasna Lipa CZ 84 B2
Krasne PL 77 B5
Kraśnik PL 12 C5
Krašnja SLO 123 A3
Krásno SK 98 B2
Krásnohorské Podhradie SK 99 C4
Krasno Polje HR 123 C4
Krasnozavodsk RUS 9 D11
Krasnystaw PL 13 C5
Krasnyy RUS 13 A9
Krasnyy Kholm RUS 9 C10
Krasocin PL 87 B4
Kraszewice PL 86 A2
Kraszkowice PL 86 A2
Kratigos GR 186 C1
Kratovo MK 182 A4
Kraubath A 110 B1
Krausnick D 74 B2
Krautheim D 94 B1
Kravaře CZ 84 B2
Kraváre CZ 98 B2
Kravarsko HR 124 B2
Kraznějov CZ 96 B1
Krčedin SRB 126 B2
Kŭrdzhali BG 183 B7
Krefeld D 80 A2
Kregme DK 61 D2
Krembz D 73 A4
Kremenets UA 13 C6
Kremmen D 74 B2
Kremna SRB 127 D1
Kremnica SK 98 C2
Krempe D 64 C2
Krems A 97 C3
Kremsbrücke A 109 C4
Kremsmünster A 110 A1
Křemže CZ 96 C2
Křenov CZ 97 B4
Krepa PL 76 C3
Krępa Krajeńska PL 75 A5
Krepsko PL 68 B1
Kreševo BIH 139 B4
Kressbronn D 107 B4
Krestena GR 184 B2
Kretinga LT 8 E2
Krettsy RUS 9 C8
Kreuth D 108 B2
Kreuzau D 80 B2
Kreuzlingen CH 107 B4
Kreuztal D 81 B3
Krewelin D 74 B2
Krezluk BIH 138 A3
Krichem BG 183 A6
Krieglach A 110 B2
Kriegsfeld D 93 B3
Kriens CH 106 B3
Krimml A 108 B3
Krimpen aan de IJssel NL 79 A4
Křinec CZ 84 B3
Kristdala S 62 A4
Kristiansand N 53 B4
Kristianstad S 61 C4
Kristiansund N 198 B4
Kristiinankaupunki FIN 8 A2
Kristinefors S 49 B4
Kristinehamn S 55 A5
Kriváň SK 99 C3
Kriva Palanka MK 182 A4
Křivokát CZ 96 A1
Kriź HR 124 B2
Křižanov CZ 97 B4
Križevci HR 124 A2
Krk HR 123 B3
Krka SLO 123 B3
Krnjača SRB 127 C2
Krnjak HR 123 B4
Krnjeuša BIH 124 C2
Krnjevo SRB 127 C3
Krnov CZ 98 A1
Krobia PL 85 A4
Kroczyce PL 86 B3
Krøderen N 48 B1
Krokees GR 184 C3
Krokek S 56 B2
Krokom S 199 B11
Krokowa PL 68 A3
Krokstad-elva N 53 A5
Kroksund N 54 A2
Kroměříž CZ 98 B1
Krommenie NL 70 B1
Krompachy SK 99 C4
Kronach D 82 B3
Kronshagen D 64 B3
Kronshtadt RUS 9 C6
Kröpelin D 65 B4
Kropp D 64 B2
Kroppenstedt D 73 C4
Kropstädt D 74 C1
Krościenko nad Dunajcem PL 99 B4
Kröslin D 66 B2
Krośnice PL 85 A5
Krośniewice PL 77 B4
Krosno PL 12 D4
Krosno Odrzańskie PL 75 B4
Krostitz D 83 A4
Krotoszyn PL 85 A5
Krottendorf A 110 B2
Krouna CZ 97 B4
Krowiarki PL 86 B2
Krrabë AL 182 B1
Kršan HR 123 B3
Krško SLO 123 B4
Krstac MNE 139 B4
Krstur SRB 126 A2
Křtiny CZ 97 B4
Kruft D 80 B3
Kruishoutem B 79 B3
Krujë AL 182 B1
Krulyewshchyna BY 13 A7
Krumbach
A 111 B3
D 94 C2
Krumovgrad BG 183 B7
Krün D 108 B2
Krupá CZ 84 B1
Krupa na Vrbasu BIH 124 C3
Krupanj SRB 127 C1
Krupina SK 99 C3
Krupka CZ 84 B1
Krupki BY 13 A8
Kruså DK 64 B2
Krušćica BIH 139 A3
Kruševac SRB 16 D4
Kruševo MK 182 B3
Kruszwica PL 76 B3
Kruszyn PL 77 B4
Krychaw BY 13 B9
Krynica PL 99 B4
Krynica Morska PL 69 A4
Krzęcin PL 75 A4
Krzelów PL 85 A4
Krzepice PL 86 B2
Krzepielów PL 85 A4
Krzeszowice PL 86 B3
Krzeszyce PL 75 B4
Krzynowlaga Mała PL 77 A5
Krzywiń PL 75 C5
Krzyżanowice PL 98 B2
Krzyżowa PL 99 B3
Krzyż Wielkopolski PL 75 B5
Ksiaz Wielkopolski PL 87 B4
Książ Wielkopolski PL 76 B2
Kłębowiec PL 75 A5
Kübekháza H 126 A2
Küblis CH 107 C4
Kuchary PL 86 A1
Kuchl A 109 B4
Kucice PL 77 B5
Kuciste HR 138 C3
Kuçovë AL 182 C1
Küçükbahçe TR 188 A1
Küçükköy TR 186 C1
Küçükkuyu TR 186 C1
Kucura SRB 126 B1
Kuczbork-Osada PL 77 A5
Kuddby S 56 B2
Kudowa-Zdrój PL 85 B4
Kufstein A 108 B3
Kuggeboda S 63 B3
Kuggörana S 200 E3
Kühbach D 95 C3
Kuhmo FIN 3 D11
Kuhmoinen FIN 8 B4
Kuhnsdorf A 110 C1
Kuhstedt D 72 A1
Kuinre NL 70 B2
Kuivaniemi FIN 197 D8
Kuivastu EST 8 C3
Kukës AL 182 A2
Kuklin PL 77 A5
Kukljica HR 137 A4
Kukujevci SRB 127 B1
Kula
Srbija SRB 127 C3
Vojvodina SRB 126 B1
TR 188 A3
Kuldīga LV 8 D2
Kulen Vakuf BIH 124 C2
Kulina BIH 125 C4
Kullstedt D 82 A2
Kulmain D 95 B3
Kulmbach D 82 B3
Kuloharju FIN 197 D11
Kulu TR 23 B7
Kumachevo RUS 69 A5
Kumafşarı TR 189 B4
Kumane SRB 126 B2
Kumanovo MK 182 A3
Kumbağ TR 186 B2
Kumdanlı TR 189 A5
Kumkale TR 186 C1
Kumla S 56 A1
Kumlakyrkby S 50 C3
Kumlinge FIN 51 B7
Kumluca TR 189 C5
Kumrovec HR 123 A4
Kunadacs H 112 C3
Kunágota H 113 C5
Kunbaja H 126 A1
Kunda EST 8 C5
Kundl A 108 B2
Kunes N 193 B10
Kunfehértó H 126 A1
Kungälv S 60 B1
Kungsängen S 57 A3
Kungsäter S 60 B2
Kungsbacka S 60 B2
Kungsgården S 50 B3
Kungshamn S 54 B2
Kungs-Husby S 56 A3
Kungsör S 56 A2
Kunhegyes H 113 B4
Kunmadaras H 113 B4
Kunovice CZ 98 B1
Kunów PL 87 B5
Kunowo
Wielkopolskie PL 76 C2
Zachodnio-Pomorskie PL 74 A3
Kunštát CZ 97 B4
Kunszállás H 113 C3
Kunszentmárton H 113 C4
Kunszentmiklós H 112 B3
Kunžak CZ 97 B3
Künzelsau D 94 B1
Kuolayarvi RUS 197 C12
Kuolio FIN 197 D11
Kuopio FIN 8 A5
Kuosku FIN 197 B11
Kup
H 111 B4
PL 86 B1
Kupferzell D 94 B1
Kupinec HR 123 B4
Kupinečki Kraljevac HR 124 B1
Kupinovo SRB 127 C2
Kupirovo HR 138 A2
Kupjak HR 123 B3
Kuppenheim D 93 C4
Kupres BIH 138 B3
Küps D 82 B3
Kurd H 112 C2
Küre TR 23 A7
Kuressaare EST 8 C3
Kurikka FIN 8 A3
Kuřim CZ 97 B4
Kuřivody CZ 84 B2
Kurki PL 77 A5
Kurort Oberwiesenthal D 83 B4
Kurort Schmalkalden D 82 B2
Kurort Stolberg D 82 A2
Kurort Wippra D 82 A3
Kurów PL 12 C5
Kurowice PL 86 A3
Kurravaara S 196 B3
Kursu FIN 197 C11
Kurşunlu
Bursa TR 187 B4
Çankırı TR 23 A7
Kurtakko FIN 196 B7
Kürten D 80 A3
Kurucaşile TR 187 A7
Kurvinen FIN 197 D12
Kurzelów PL 87 B3
Kusadak SRB 127 C2
Kuşadası TR 188 B2
Kusel D 93 B3
Kusey D 73 B4
Küsnacht CH 106 B3
Kütahya TR 187 C4
Kutenholz D 72 A2
Kutina HR 124 B2
Kutjevo HR 125 B3
Kutná Hora CZ 97 B3
Kutno PL 77 B4
Kuttara FIN 193 D10
Küttingen CH 106 B3
Kúty SK 98 C1
Kuusamo FIN 197 D12
Kuusankoski FIN 8 B5
Kuvshinovo RUS 9 D9
Kuyucak TR 188 B3
Kuzmin SRB 127 B1
Kuźnia Raciborska PL 86 B2
Kuźnica Czarnkowska PL 75 B5
Kuźnica Żelichowska PL 75 B5
Kvaløysletta N 192 C2
Kvalsund N 192 B7
Kvam
Nord-Trøndelag N 199 A8
Oppland N 198 D6
Kvamsøy N 46 A3
Kvænangsbotn N 192 C6
Kvanndal N 46 B3
Kvänum S 55 B4
Kværndrup DK 59 C3
Kvås N 52 B3
Kvasice CZ 98 B1
Kvelde N 53 A5
Kvenna N 198 C5
Kvernaland N 52 B1
Kvibille S 60 C2
Kvicksund S 56 A2
Kvidinge S 61 C3
Kvikkjokk S 195 D8
Kvikne
Hedmark N 199 C7
Oppland N 47 A6
Kvilda CZ 96 B1
Kville S 54 B2
Kvillsfors S 62 A3
Kvinesdal N 52 B2
Kvinlog N 52 B2
Kvinnherad N 46 C3
Kvissel DK 58 A3
Kvissleby S 200 D3
Kviteseid N 53 A4
Kvitsøy N 52 A1
Kwakowo PL 68 A2
Kwidzyn PL 69 B3
Kwilcz PL 75 B5
Kyjov CZ 98 C1
Kyleakin GB 31 B3
Kyle of Lochalsh GB 31 B3
Kylerhea GB 31 B3
Kylestrome GB 32 C1
Kyllburg D 92 A2
Kyllini GR 184 B2
Kynšperk nad Ohří CZ 83 B4
Kyperounda CY 181 B1
Kyrenia CY 181 A2
Kyritz D 73 B5
Kyrkesund S 60 A1
Kyrkhult S 63 B2
Kyrksæterøra N 198 B6
Kysucké Nové Mesto SK 98 B2
Kythira GR 184 C3
Kythréa CY 181 A2
Kyustendil BG 16 D5
Kyyiv = Kiev UA 13 C9
Kyyjärvi FIN 8 A4

L

Laa an der Thaya A 97 C4
La Adrada E 150 B3
Laage D 65 C5
La Alameda E 157 B4
La Alberca E 149 B3
La Alberca de Záncara E 158 B1
La Albergueria de Argañán E 149 B3
La Albuera E 155 C4
La Aldea del Portillo del Busto E 143 B3
La Algaba E 162 A1
La Aliseda de Tormes E 150 B2
La Almarcha E 158 B1
La Almolda E 153 A3
La Almunia de Doña Godina E 152 A2
Laanila FIN 193 D11
La Antillas E 161 B2
La Arena E 141 A4
Laatzen D 72 B2
La Aulaga E 161 B3
La Balme-de-Sillingy F 118 B3
Laban IRL 28 A3
La Bañeza E 141 B5
La Barca de la Florida E 162 B2
La Barre-de-Monts F 114 B1
La Barre-en-Ouche F 89 B4
La Barrosa E 162 B1
La Barthe-de-Neste F 145 A4
La Bassée F 78 B2
La Bastide-de-Sèrou F 146 A2
La Bastide-des-Jourdans F 132 B1
Labastide-Murat F 129 B4
La Bastide-Puylaurent F 117 C3
Labastide-Rouairoux F 130 B1
Labastide-St Pierre F 129 C4
La Bathie F 118 B3
Lábatlan H 112 B2
La Baule-Escoublac F 101 B3
La Bazoche-Gouet F 102 A2
La Bégude-de-Mazenc F 131 A3
Labenne F 128 C1
La Bernerie-en-Retz F 114 A1
Labin HR 123 B3
La Bisbal d'Empordà E 147 C4
Łabiszyn PL 76 B2
Lablachère F 131 A3
Lábod H 124 A3
Laboe D 64 B3
La Boissière F 89 A4
Labouheyre F 128 B2
La Bourboule F 116 B2
La Bóveda de Toro E 150 A2
Łabowa PL 99 B4
La Brède F 128 B2
La Bresse F 106 A1
La Bridoire F 118 B2
La Brillanne F 132 B1
Labrit F 128 B2
Labros E 152 A2
La Bruffière F 114 A2
Labruguière F 130 B1
Labrujo P 148 A1
L'Absie F 114 B3
La Bussière F 103 B4
Laç AL 182 B1
La Caillère F 114 B3
Lacalahorra E 164 B1
La Caletta
Cágliari I 179 C2
Núoro I 178 B3
La Calmette F 131 B3
La Calzada de Oropesa E 150 C2
La Campana E 162 A2
La Cañada E 150 B3
Lacanau F 128 B1
Lacanau-Océan F 128 A1
Lacanche F 104 B3
La Canourgue F 130 A2
La Capelle F 91 B3
Lacapelle-Marival F 129 B4
Laćarak SRB 127 B1
La Cardanchosa E 156 B2
La Caridad E 141 A4
La Carlota E 162 A3
La Carolina E 157 B4
Lacaune F 130 B1
La Cava E 153 B4
La Cavalerie F 130 A2
Laceby GB 41 B3
Lacedónia I 172 A1
La Celle-en-Moravan F 104 B3
La Celle-St Avant F 102 B2
La Cerca E 143 B3
Láces I 108 C1
La Chaise-Dieu F 117 B3
La Chaize-Giraud F 114 B2
La Chaize-le-Vicomte F 114 B2
La Chambre F 118 B3
Lachania GR 188 D2
La Chapelaude F 116 A2
La Chapelle-d'Angillon F 103 B4
La Chapelle-en-Aalgaudémar F 118 C3
La Chapelle-en-Vercors F 118 C2
La Chapelle-Glain F 101 B4
La Chapelle-la-Reine F 90 C2

La Chapelle-Laurent F 116 B3
La Chapelle-St Luc F 91 C4
La Chapelle-sur-Erdre F 101 B4
La Chapelle-Vicomtesse F 103 B3
La Charce F 132 A1
La Charité-sur-Loire F 104 B2
La Chartre-sur-le-Loir F 102 B2
La Châtaigneraie F 114 B3
La Châtre F 103 C3
La Chaussée-sur-Marne F 91 C4
La Chaux-de-Fonds CH 106 B1
Lachen CH 107 B3
Lachendorf D 72 B3
La Cheppe F 91 B4
La Chèze F 101 A3
Lachowice PL 99 B3
La Ciotat F 132 B1
Łąck PL 77 B4
Läckeby S 62 B4
Läckö S 55 B4
La Clayette F 117 A4
La Clusaz F 118 B3
Lacock GB 43 A4
La Codosera E 155 B3
La Concha E 143 A3
La Condamine-Châtelard F 132 A2
Láconi I 179 C3
La Contienda E 161 A3
La Coquille F 115 C4
La Coronada E 156 B2
La Côte-St André F 118 B2
La Cotinière F 114 C2
La Courtine F 116 B2
Lacq F 145 A3
La Crau F 132 B2
La Crèche F 115 B3
La Croix F 102 B2
Lacroix-Barrez F 116 C2
Lacroix-St Ouen F 90 B2
Lacroix-sur-Meuse F 92 C1
La Croix-Valmer F 132 B2
La Cumbre E 156 A2
Łącznik PL 86 B1
Lad H 125 A3
Ladbergen D 71 B4
Lądek-Zdrój PL 85 B4
Ladelund D 64 B2
Ladendorf A 97 C4
Ladignac-le-Long F 115 C5
Ladíspoli I 168 B2
Ladoeiro P 155 B3
Ladon F 103 B4
La Douze F 129 A3
Ladushkin RUS 69 A5
Ladybank GB 35 B4
Laer D 71 B4
La Espina E 141 A4
La Estrella E 156 A2
La Farga de Moles E 146 B2
La Fatarella E 153 A4
La Felipa E 158 B2
La Fère F 90 B3
La Ferrière
I ndre-et-Loire F 102 B2
Vendée F 114 B2
La Ferrière-en-Parthenay F 115 B3
La-Ferté-Alais F 90 C2
La Ferté-Bernard F 102 A2
La Ferté-Frênel F 89 B4
La Ferté-Gaucher F 90 C3
La Ferté-Imbault F 103 B3
La Ferté-Macé F 89 B3
La Ferté-Milon F 90 B3
La Ferté-sous-Jouarre F 90 C3
La Ferté-St-Aubin F 103 B3
La Ferté-St-Cyr F 103 B3
La Ferté-Vidame F 89 B4
La Ferté Villeneuil F 103 B3
La Feuillie F 90 B1
Lafkos GR 183 D5
La Flèche F 102 B1
La Flotte F 114 B2
Lafnitz A 111 B3
La Font de la Figuera E 159 C3
La Fouillade F 130 A1
Lafrançaise F 129 B4
La Fregeneda E 149 B3
La Fresneda E 153 B4
La Fuencubierta E 162 A3
La Fuente de San Esteban E 149 B3
La Fulioala E 147 C2
La Gacilly F 101 B3
La Galera E 153 B4
Lagan S 60 C3
Laganadi I 175 C1
Lagarde F 146 A2
La Garde-Freinet F 132 B2
Lagares
Coimbra P 148 B2
Porto P 148 A1
La Garnache F 114 B2
Lagaro I 135 A4
La Garriga E 147 C3
La Garrovilla E 155 C4
Lagartera E 150 C2
La Gaubretière F 114 B2
Lågbol S 51 B5
Lage D 72 C1
Lägerdorf D 64 C2
Lagg GB 34 C2
Laggan GB 32 D2
Laggartorp S 55 A5
Łagiewniki PL 85 B4
La Gineta E 158 B1
Láglio I 120 B2
Lagnieu F 118 B2
Lagny-sur-Marne F 90 C2
Lago
Calabria I 175 B2
Veneto I 121 B5
Lagôa P 160 B1
Lagoaça P 149 A3
Lagonegro I 174 A1
Lagos
GR 183 B7
P 160 B1
Lagosanto I 121 C5
Łagów
Lubuskie PL 75 B4
Świętokrzyskie PL 87 B5
La Granadella
Alicante E 159 C4
Lleida E 153 A4
La Grand-Combe F 131 A3
La Grande-Croix F 117 B4
La Grande-Motte F 131 B3
La Granja d'Escarp E 153 A4
La Granjuela E 156 B2
Lagrasse F 146 A3
La Grave F 118 B3
La Gravelle F 101 A4
Laguardia E 143 B4
La Guardia E 151 C4
La Guardia de Jaén E 163 A4
Laguarres E 145 B4
Laguenne F 116 B1
Laguépie F 129 B4
La Guerche-de-Bretagne F 101 B4
La Guerche-sur-l'Aubois F 104 C1
La Guérinière F 114 B1
Laguiole F 116 C2
Laguna de Duera E 150 A3
Laguna del Marquesado E 152 B2
Laguna de Negrillos E 142 B1
Lagundo I 108 C2
Lagunilla E 149 B3
La Haba E 156 B2
Laharie F 128 B1
La Haye-du-Puits F 88 A2
La Haye-Pesnel F 88 B2
Lahden D 71 B4
La Herlière F 78 B2
La Hermida E 142 A2
La Herrera E 158 C1
Laheycourt F 91 C5
La Higuera E 158 C2
La Hiniesta E 149 A4
Lahnstein D 81 B3
Laholm S 61 C3
La Horcajada E 150 B2
La Horra E 143 C3
Lahr D 93 C3
Lahti FIN 8 B4
La Hulpe B 79 B4
La Hutte F 89 B4
Laichingen D 94 C1
L'Aigle F 89 B4
La Iglesuela E 150 B3
La Iglesuela del Cid E 153 B3
Laignes F 104 B3
Laiguéglia I 133 B4
L'Aiguillon-sur-Mer F 114 B2
Laimbach am Ostrong A 97 C3
Laina E 152 A1
Lainio S 196 B5
Lairg GB 32 C2
La Iruela E 164 B2
Laissac F 130 A1
Laisvall S 195 D8
Láives I 121 A4
La Javie F 132 A2
Lajkovac SRB 127 C2
La Jonchère-St Maurice F 116 A1
La Jonquera E 146 B3
Lajoskomárom H 112 C2
Lajosmizse H 112 B3
Lak H 99 C4
Lakenheath GB 45 A4
Lakitelek H 113 C4
Lakki GR 185 D4
Lakolk DK 64 A1
Łąkorz PL 69 B4
Lakšárska Nová Ves SK 98 C1
Lakselv N 193 B8
Laksfors N 195 E4
Laktaši BIH 124 C3
La Lantejuela E 162 A2
Lalapaşa TR 186 A1
L'Albagès E 153 A4
Lalbenque F 129 B4
L'Alcudia E 159 B3
L'Aldea E 153 B4
Lalín E 140 B2
Lalinde F 129 B3
La Línea de la Concepción E 162 B2
Lalizolle F 116 A3
La Llacuna E 147 C2
Lalley F 118 C2
Lalling D 95 C5
Lalm N 198 D6
La Londe-les-Maures F 132 B2
La Loupe F 89 B5
La Louvière B 79 B4
L'Alpe-d'Huez F 118 B3
La Luisiana E 162 A2
Laluque F 128 C1
Lam D 95 B5
La Machine F 104 C2
la Maddalena I 178 A3
Lama dei Peligni I 169 A4
Lamadrid E 142 A2
Lamagistére F 129 B3
La Mailleraye-sur-Seine F 89 A4
La Malène F 130 A2
Lama Mocogno I 135 A3
La Mamola E 163 B4
La Manresana dels Prats E 147 C2
Lamarche F 105 A4
Lamarche-sur-Saône F 105 B4
Lamargelle F 105 B3
Lamarosa P 154 B2
Lamarque F 128 A2
Lamas P 148 B1
La Masadera E 145 C3
Lamas de Moaro P 140 B2
Lamastre F 117 C4
La Mata E 150 C3
La Mata de Ledesma E 149 A4
La Mata de Monteagudo E 142 B1
Lambach A 109 A4
Lamballe F 101 A3
Lamberhurst GB 45 B4
Lambesc F 131 B4
Lambia GR 184 B2
Lambley GB 37 B4
Lambourn GB 44 B2
Lamego P 148 A2
La Meilleraye-de-Bretagne F 101 B4
La Ménitré F 102 B1
L'Ametlla de Mar E 153 B4
Lamia GR 182 E4
Lammhult S 62 A2
La Mojonera E 164 C2
La Mole F 132 B2
La Molina E 147 B2
La Monnerie-le-Montel F 117 B3
La Morera E 155 C4
La Mothe-Achard F 114 B2
Lamothe-Cassel F 129 B4
Lamothe-Montravel F 128 B3
La Mothe-St Héray F 115 B3
Lamotte-Beuvron F 103 B4
La Motte-Chalançon F 131 A4
La Motte-du-Caire F 132 A2
La Motte-Servolex F 118 B2
Lampertheim D 93 B4
Lampeter GB 39 B2
L'Ampolla E 153 B4
Lamprechtshausen A 109 B3
Lamsfeld D 74 C3
Lamspringe D 72 C3
Lamstedt D 72 A2
La Mudarra E 142 C2
La Muela E 152 A2
La Mure F 118 C2
Lamure-sur-Azergues F 117 A4
Lana I 108 C2
Lanaja E 145 C3
Lanarce F 117 C3
Lanark GB 36 A3
La Nava E 161 B3
La Nava de Ricomalillo E 156 A3
La Nava de Santiago E 155 B4
Lancaster GB 37 B4
Lanchester GB 37 B5
Lanciano I 169 A4
Lancing GB 44 C3
Lançon-Provence F 131 B4
Lancova Vas SLO 124 A1
Landau
Bayern D 95 C4
Rheinland-Pfalz D 93 B4
Landeck A 108 B1
Landen B 79 B5
Landerneau F 100 A1
Landeryd S 60 B3
Landesbergen D 72 B2
Landete E 158 B2
Landévant F 100 B2
Landévennec F 100 A1
Landeyjahöfn 190 D5
Landivisiau F 100 A1
Landivy F 88 B2
Landl A 108 B3
Landön S 199 B11
Landos F 117 C3
Landouzy-le-Ville F 91 B4
Landquart CH 107 C4
Landrecies F 91 A3
Landreville F 104 A3
Landriano I 120 B2
Landsberg D 108 A1
Lands-berg D 83 A4
Landsbro S 62 A2
Landscheid D 92 B2
Landshut D 95 C4
Landskrona S 61 D2
Landstuhl D 93 B3
Lanesborough IRL 28 A4
Lanester F 100 B2
Lanestosa E 143 A3
La Neuve-Lyre F 89 B4
La Neuveville CH 106 B2
Langå DK 59 B2
Langada GR 185 A7
Langadas GR 183 C5
Langa de Duero E 151 A4
Langadia GR 184 B3
Langangen N 53 A5
Långared S 60 A2
Långaröd S 61 D3
Långaryd S 60 B3
Långås S 60 C2
Långasjö S 63 B3
Langau A 97 C3
Langeac F 117 B3
Langeais F 102 B2
Langedijk NL 70 B1
Langeln D 73 C3
Langelsheim D 72 C3
Langemark-Poelkapelle B 78 B2
Langen
Hessen D 93 B4
Niedersachsen D 72 A1
Langenau D 94 C2
Langenberg D 81 A4
Langenbruck CH 106 B2
Langenburg D 94 B1
Längenfeld A 108 B1
Langenfeld D 80 A2
Langenhorn D 64 B1
Langenlois A 97 C3
Langenlonsheim D 93 B3
Langennaudorf D 83 A5
Langenneufnach D 94 C2
Langenthal CH 106 B2
Langenzenn D 94 B2
Langeoog D 71 A4
Langeskov DK 59 C3
Langesund N 53 A5
Langewiesen D 82 B2
Långflon S 49 A4
Langförden D 71 B5
Langhagen D 73 A5
Länghem S 60 B3
Langhirano I 120 C3
Langholm GB 36 A4
Langholt IS 191 D7
Långlöt S 62 B4
Langnau CH 106 C2
Langø DK 65 B4
Langogne F 117 C3
Langon F 128 B2
Langquaid D 95 C4
Långrådna S 56 B2
Langreo E 142 A1
Langres F 105 B4
Långsele S 200 C3
Långserud S 54 A3
Langset N 48 B3
Långshyttan S 50 B3
Langstrand N 192 B7
Långträsk S 196 D3
Langueux F 101 A3
Languidic F 100 B2
Längvik S 57 A4
Langwarden D 71 A5
Langwathby GB 37 B4
Langwedel D 72 B2
Langweid D 94 C2
Langwies CH 107 C4
Lanheses P 148 A1
Lanięta PL 77 B4
Lanildut F 100 A1
Lanjarón E 163 B4
Lanmeur F 100 A2
Lanna
Jönköping S 60 B3
Örebro S 55 A5
Lännaholm S 51 C4
Lannavaara S 196 A4
Lannéanou F 100 A2
Lannemezan F 145 A4
Lanneuville-sur-Meuse F 91 B5
Lannilis F 100 A1
Lannion F 100 A2
La Nocle-Maulaix F 104 C2
Lanouaille F 115 C5
Lansjärv S 196 C5
Lanškroun CZ 97 B4
Lanslebourg-Mont-Cenis F 119 B3
Lanta F 129 C4
Lantadilla E 142 B2
Lanton F 128 B1
Lantosque F 133 B3
La Nuez de Arriba E 143 B3
Lanusei I 179 C3
Lanúvio I 168 B2
Lanvollon F 100 A3
Lánycsók H 125 A4
Lanz D 73 A4
Lanza E 140 A2
Lanzada E 140 B2
Lanzahita E 150 B3
Lanžhot CZ 97 C4
Lanzo Torinese I 119 B4
Laole SRB 127 C3
Laon F 91 B3
Laons F 89 B5
La Paca E 164 B3
La Pacaudière F 117 A3
Lapalisse F 117 A3
La Palma d'Ebre E 153 A4
La Palma del Condado E 161 B3
La Palme F 146 B4
La Palmyre F 114 C2
La Parra E 155 C4
Łapczyna Wola PL 87 B3
La Pedraja de Portillo E 150 A3
La Peraleja E 152 B1
La Petit-Pierre F 93 C3
Lapeyrade F 128 B2
Lapeyrouse F 116 A2
Lapford GB 42 B3
La Pinilla E 165 B3
Lapithos CY 181 A2
La Plagne F 118 B3
La Plaza E 141 A4
Laplume F 129 B3
La Pobla de Lillet E 147 B2
La Pobla de Vallbona E 159 B3
La Pobla Llarga E 159 B3
La Pola de Gordón E 142 B1
la Porta F 180 A2
La Pouëze F 102 B1
Lapoutroie F 106 A2
La Póveda de Soria E 143 B4
Lapovo SRB 127 C3
Läppe S 56 A1
Lappeenranta FIN 8 B6
Lappoluobbal N 192 C7
Lappträsk S 196 C6
La Preste F 146 B3
La Primaube F 130 A1
Lapseki TR 186 B1
Lapua FIN 8 A3
La Puebla de Almoradie E 157 A4
La Puebla de Cazalla E 162 A2
La Puebla de los Infantes E 162 A2
La Puebla del Río E 162 A1
La Puebla de Montalbán E 150 C3
La Puebla de Roda E 145 B4
La Puebla de Valdavia E 142 B2
La Puebla de Valverde E 152 B3
La Pueblanueva E 150 C3
La Puerta de Segura E 164 A2
La Punt CH 107 C4
L'Àquila I 169 A3
La Quintana E 162 A3
La Quintera E 162 A2
La Rábita
Granada E 164 C1
Jaén E 163 A3
Laracha E 140 A2
Laragh IRL 30 A2
Laragne-Montéglin F 132 A1
La Rambla E 163 A3
l'Arboç E 147 C2
L'Arbresle F 117 B4
Lärbro S 57 C4
Larceveau F 144 A2
Larche
Alpes-de-Haute-Provence F 132 A2
Corrèze F 129 A4
Lårdal N 53 A4
Lærdalsøyri N 47 A4
Lardosa P 155 B3
La Reale I 178 A2
Laredo E 143 A3
La Redondela E 161 B2
La Réole F 128 B2
Largentière F 131 A3
L'Argentière-la-Bessée F 118 C3
Largs GB 34 C3
Lari I 134 B3
La Riera E 141 A4
La Riera de Gaià E 147 C2
La Rinconada E 162 A1
Lariño E 140 B1
Larino I 170 B2
Larisa GR 182 D4
La Rivière-Thibouville F 89 A4
Larkhall GB 36 A3
Larkollen N 54 A1
Larmor-Plage F 100 B2
Larnaca CY 181 B2
Larne GB 27 B5
La Robla E 142 B1
La Roca de la Sierra E 155 B4
La Roche CH 106 C2
La Rochebeaucourt-Argentine F 115 C4
La Roche-Bernard F 101 B3
La Roche-Canillac F 116 B1
La Roche-Chalais F 128 A3
La Roche Derrien F 100 A2
La Roche-des-Arnauds F 132 A1
La Roche-en-Ardenne B 80 B1
La Roche-en-Brénil F 104 B3
La Rochefoucauld F 115 C4
La Roche-Guyon F 90 B1
La Rochelle F 114 B2
La Roche-Posay F 115 B4
La Roche-sur-Foron F 118 A3
La Roche-sur-Yon F 114 B2
Larochette L 92 B2
La Rochette F 131 A4
La Roda
Albacete E 158 B1
Oviedo E 141 A4
La Roda de Andalucía E 162 A3
Laroquebrou F 116 C2
La Roquebrussanne F 132 B1
Laroque d'Olmes F 146 B2
La Roque-Gageac F 129 B4
La Roque-Ste Marguerite F 130 A2
Laroque-Timbaut F 129 B3
Larouco E 141 B3
Larraga E 144 B2
Larrau F 144 A3
Larrazet F 129 C4
Larsnes N 198 C2
La Rubia E 143 C4
Laruns F 145 A3
Larva E 164 B1
Larvik N 53 A6
La Sagrada E 149 B3
La Salceda E 151 A4
Lasalle F 131 A2
La Salle F 118 C3
la Salute di Livenza I 122 B1
La Salvetat-Peyralés F 130 A1
La Salvetat-sur-Agout F 130 B1
Las Arenas E 142 A2
La Sarraz CH 105 C5
Lasarte E 144 A1
Låsby DK 59 B2
Las Cabezadas E 151 A4
Las Cabezas de San Juan E 162 B2
Las Correderas E 157 B4
Las Cuevas de Cañart E 153 B3
La Seca E 150 A3
La Selva del Camp E 147 C2
La Senia E 153 B4
La Serra E 147 C2
La Seu d'Urgell E 146 B2
La Seyne-sur-Mer F 132 B1
Las Gabias E 163 A4
Las Herencias E 150 C3
Las Herrerias E 161 B2
Łasin PL 69 B4
Lask PL 86 A3
Laska PL 68 B2
Łaskarzow PL 87 A5
Laško SLO 123 A4
Laskowice PL 76 A3
Las Labores E 157 A4
Las Mesas E 158 B1
Las Minas E 164 A3
Las Navas E 163 A3
Las Navas de la Concepción E 156 C2
Las Navas del Marqués E 150 B3
Las Navillas E 157 A3
Las Negras E 164 C3

La Solana E 157 B4
La Souterraine F 116 A1
Las Pajanosas E 161 B3
Laspaules E 145 B4
Las Pedroñas E 158 B1
La Spézia I 134 A2
Las Planes d'Hostoles E 147 B3
Laspuña E 145 B4
Las Rozas
Cantabria E 142 B2
Madrid E 151 B4
Lassan D 66 C2
Lassay-les-Châteaux F 89 B3
Lasseube F 145 A3
Lassigny F 90 B2
La Storta I 168 B2
Lastovo HR 138 C2
Lastras de Cuéllar E 151 A3
Lästringe S 56 B3
Lastrup D 71 B4
Las Uces E 149 A3
La Suze-sur-Sarthe F 102 B2
Las Veguillas E 149 B4
Las Ventas con Peña Aguilera E 157 A3
Las Ventas de San Julián E 150 B2
Las Villes E 153 B4
Latasa E 144 B2
Látera I 168 A1
Laterza I 171 C4
La Teste F 128 B1
Lathen D 71 B4
Latheron GB 32 C3
La Thuile I 119 B3
Latiano I 173 B3
Latina I 169 B2
Latisana I 122 B2
Látky SK 99 C3
La Toba E 152 B2
La Toledana E 157 A3
La Torre de Cabdella E 146 B1
La Torre de Esteban Hambrán E 151 B3
La Torre del l'Espanyol E 153 A4
La Torresaviñán E 152 B1
La Tour d'Aigues F 132 B1
La Tour de Peilz CH 106 C1
La Tour-du-Pin F 118 B2
La Tranche-sur-Mer F 114 B2
La Tremblade F 114 C2
La Trimouille F 115 B5
La Trinité F 100 B2
La Trinité-Porhoët F 101 A3
Latrónico I 174 A2
Latronquière F 116 C2
Latterbach CH 106 C2
La Turballe F 101 B3
Laubach D 81 B4
Laubert F 117 C3
Laucha D 83 A3
Lauchhammer D 84 A1
Lauchheim D 94 C2
Lauda-Königshofen D 94 B1
Laudal N 52 B3
Lauder GB 35 C5
Lauenau D 72 B2
Lauenburg D 73 A3
Lauf D 95 B3
Laufach D 94 A1
Laufen
CH 106 B2
D 109 B3
Lauffen D 93 B5
Laugar IS 191 B8
Laugarás IS 190 C5
Laugarbakki IS 190 B5
Laugarvatn IS 190 C5
Laugharne GB 39 C2
Lauingen D 94 C2
Laujar de Andarax E 164 C2
Laukaa FIN 8 A4
Lauker S 196 D2
Laukvik N 194 C5
La Uña E 142 A1
Launceston GB 42 B2
La Unión E 165 B4
Launois-sur-Vence F 91 B4
Laupheim D 94 C1
Lauragh IRL 29 C2
Laureana di Borrello I 175 C2
Laurencekirk GB 35 B5
Laurencetown IRL 28 A3
Laurenzana I 172 B1
Lauria I 174 A1
Laurière F 116 A1
Laurieston GB 36 B2
Laurino I 172 B1
Lausanne CH 106 C1
Laussonne F 117 C4
Lauta D 84 A2
Lautenthal D 82 A2
Lauterach A 107 B4
Lauterbach D 81 B5
Lauterbrunnen CH 106 C2
Lauterecken D 93 B3
Lauterhofen D 95 B3
Lautrec F 130 B1
Lauvsnes N 199 A7
Lauvvlk N 52 B2
Lauzerte F 129 B4
Lauzès F 129 B4
Lauzun F 129 B3
Lavagna I 134 A2
Laval F 102 A1
La Vall d'Uixó E 159 B3
Lavamünd A 110 C1
Lavara GR 186 A1
Lavardac F 129 B3
Lavaris P 148 B1
Lavarone I 121 B4
Lavau F 104 B1
Lavaur F 129 C4
La Vecilla de Curueño E 142 B1
La Vega
Asturias E 141 A5
Asturias E 142 A1
Cantabria E 142 A2
Lavelanet F 146 B2
La Velilla E 151 A4
La Velles E 150 A2
Lavello I 172 A1
Lavelsloh D 72 B1
Lavenham GB 45 A4
Laveno I 120 B1
La Ventosa E 152 B1
Lavezzola I 135 A4
Laviano I 172 B1
La Victoria E 162 A3
La Vid E 151 A4
Lavik N 46 A2
La Vilavella E 159 B3
La Vilella Baixa E 147 C1
La Villa de Don Fadrique E 157 A4
Lavilledieu F 131 A3
La Villedieu F 115 B3
La Ville Dieu-du-Temple F 129 B4
Lavinio-Lido di Enea I 168 B2
Lav is I 121 A4
Lavit F 129 C3
Lavoncourt F 105 B4
Lavos P 148 B1
La Voulte-sur-Rhône F 117 C4
Lavoûte-Chilhac F 117 B3
Lavradio P 154 C1
Lavre P 154 C2
Lavrio GR 185 B5
La Wantzenau F 93 C3
Lawers GB 35 B3
Ławy PL 75 B3
Laxå S 55 B5
Laxamýri IS 191 B8
Laxe E 140 A2
Laxey GB 36 B2
Laxford Bridge GB 32 C1
Laxhall S 55 B4
Laxsjö S 199 B11
Laxtjarn S 49 B6
Laxvik S 61 C2
Laxviken S 199 B11
La Yesa E 159 B3
Laza E 141 B3
Lazarevac SRB 127 C2
Lazarevo SRB 126 B2
Lazise I 121 B3
Łaziska Grn. PL 86 B2
Lazkao E 144 A1
Lázně Bělohrad CZ 84 B3
Lázně Bohdaneč CZ 97 A3
Lázně Kynžvart CZ 95 A4
Lazonby GB 37 B4
La Zubia E 163 A4
Łazy PL 67 B5
Lazzaro I 175 D1
Lea GB 40 B3
Leadburn GB 35 C4
Leadhills GB 36 A3
Leap IRL 29 C2
Leatherhead GB 44 B3
Łeba PL 68 A2
Lebach D 92 B2
Le Barp F 128 B2
Le Bar-sur-Loup F 132 B2
Le Béage F 117 C4
Le Beausset F 132 B1
Lebekke B 79 A4
Lébény H 111 B4
Le Bessat F 117 B4
Le Blanc F 115 B5
Le Bleymard F 130 A2
Łebno PL 68 A3
Leboreiro E 140 B3
Lębork PL 68 A2
Le Boullay-Mivoye F 89 B5
Le Boulou F 146 B3
Le Bourg F 129 B4
Le Bourg-d'Oisans F 118 B3
Le Bourget-du-Lac F 118 B2
Le Bourgneuf-la-Forêt F 101 A5
Le Bousquet d'Orb F 130 B2
Le Brassus CH 105 C5
Le Breuil F 117 A3
Le Breuil-en-Auge F 89 A4
Lebrija E 162 B1
Lebring A 110 C2
Le Brusquet F 132 A2
Le Bry CH 106 C2
Le Bugue F 129 B3
Le Buisson F 129 B3
Lebus D 74 B3
Lebusa D 83 A5
Leca da Palmeira P 148 A1
Le Caloy F 128 C2
Le Cap d'Agde F 130 B2
Le Cateau Cambrésis F 91 A3
Le Caylar F 130 B2
Le Cayrol F 116 C2
Lecce I 173 B4
Lecco I 120 B2
Lécera E 153 A3
Lećevica HR 138 B2
Lech A 107 B5
Le Chambon-Feugerolles F 117 B4
Le Chambon-sur-Lignon F 117 B4
Le Château d'Oléron F 114 C2
Le Châtelard F 118 B3
Le Châtelet F 103 C4
Le Chatelet-en-Brie F 90 C2
Lechbruck D 108 B1
Lechena GR 184 B2
Le Chesne F 91 B4
Le Cheylard F 117 C4
Lechlade GB 44 B2
Lechovice CZ 97 C4
Leciñena E 145 C3
Leck D 64 B1
Le Collet-de-Deze F 131 A2
Le Conquet F 100 A1
Le Creusot F 104 C3
Le Croisic F 101 B3
Le Crotoy F 78 B1
Lectoure F 129 C3
Łęczyca
Łódzkie PL 77 B4
Zachodnio-Pomorskie PL 75 A4
Ledaña E 158 B2
Ledbury GB 39 B4
Lede B 79 B3
Ledečnad Sazavou CZ 97 B3
Ledenice CZ 96 C2
Le Deschaux F 105 C4
Ledesma E 149 A3
Lédignan F 131 B3
Lédigos E 142 B2
Ledmore GB 32 C2
Lednice CZ 97 C4
Lednicke-Rovné SK 98 B2
Le Donjon F 117 A3
Le Dorat F 115 B5
Lędyczek PL 68 B1
Lędziny PL 86 B3
Leeds GB 40 B2
Leek
GB 40 B1
NL 71 A3
Leenaun IRL 28 A2
Leens NL 71 A3
Leer D 71 A4
Leerdam NL 79 A5
Leerhafe D 71 A4
Leese D 72 B2
Leeuwarden NL 70 A2
Leezen D 64 C3
Le Faou F 100 A1
Le Faoüet F 100 A2
Lefka CY 181 A1
Lefkada GR 182 E2
Lefkimis GR 182 D2
Lefkoniko CY 181 A2
Le Folgoet F 100 A1
Le Fossat F 146 A2
Le Fousseret F 146 A2
Le Fugeret F 132 A2
Leganés E 151 B4
Legau D 107 B5
Le Gault-Soigny F 91 C3
Legbąd PL 68 B2
Legé F 114 B2
Lège-Cap-Ferret F 128 B1
Legionowo PL 77 B5
Léglise B 92 B1
Legnago I 121 B4
Legnano I 120 B1
Legnaro I 121 B4
Legnica PL 85 A4
Łęgowo PL 69 A3
Legrad HR 124 A2
Le Grand-Bornand F 118 B3
Le-Grand-Bourg F 116 A1
Le Grand-Lucé F 102 B2
Le Grand-Pressigny F 102 C2
Le Grand-Quevilly F 89 A5
Le Grau-du-Roi F 131 B3
Léguevin F 129 C4
Legutiano E 143 B4
Le Havre F 89 A4
Lehesten D 82 B3
Lehnice SK 111 A4
Lehnin D 74 B1
Le Hohwald F 93 C3
Le Houga F 128 C2
Lehrberg D 94 B2
Lehre D 73 B3
Lehrte D 72 B2
Lehsen D 73 A4
Leibnitz A 110 C2
Leicester GB 40 C2
Leiden NL 70 B1
Leidschendam NL 70 B1
Leigh GB 38 A4
Leighlinbridge IRL 30 B2
Leighton Buzzard GB 44 B3
Leignon B 79 B5
Leikanger N 198 C2
Leimen D 93 B4
Leinefelde D 82 A2
Leinesfjord N 194 C6
Leintwardine GB 39 B4
Leipojärvi S 196 B4
Leipzig D 83 A4
Leira
Nordland N 195 D4
Oppland N 47 B6
Leiråmoen N 195 D5
Leiria P 154 B2
Leirvassbu N 47 A5
Leirvik
Hordaland N 52 A1
Sogn og Fjordane N 46 A2
Leisach A 109 C3
Leisnig D 83 A4
Leiston GB 45 A5
Leitholm GB 35 C5
Leitrim IRL 26 C2
Leitza E 144 A2
Leitzkau D 73 B4
Lejkowo PL 68 A1
Lekani GR 183 B6
Łękawa PL 86 A3
Łekawica PL 99 B3
Lekeitio E 143 A4
Lekenik HR 124 B2
Lekeryd S 62 A2
Leknes N 194 B4
Łęknica PL 84 A2
Leksand S 50 B1
Leksvik N 199 B7
Lekunberri E 144 A2
Lekvattnet S 49 B4
Le Lardin-St Lazare F 129 A4
Le Lauzet-Ubaye F 132 A2
Le Lavandou F 132 B2
Le Lion-d'Angers F 102 B1
Lelkowo PL 69 A5
Le Locle CH 106 B1
Le Loroux-Bottereau F 101 B4
Le Louroux-Béconnais F 101 B5
Lelów PL 86 B3
Le Luc F 132 B2
Le Lude F 102 B2
Lelystad NL 70 B2
Lem
Ringkøbing DK 59 B1
Viborg Amt. DK 58 B1
Le Malzieu-Ville F 116 C3
Le Mans F 102 A2
Le Mas-d'Azil F 146 A2
Le Massegros F 130 A2
Le Mayet-de-Montagne F 117 A3
Le May-sur-Evre F 101 B5
Lembach F 93 B3
Lemberg F 93 B3
Lembèye F 145 A3
Lemelerveld NL 71 B3
Le Mêle-sur-Sarthe F 89 B4
Le Ménil F 105 A5
Le Merlerault F 89 B4
Le Mesnil-sur-Oger F 91 C4
Lemförde D 71 B5
Lemgo D 72 B1
Le Miroir F 105 C4
Lemland FIN 51 B7
Lemmer NL 70 B2
Le Molay-Littry F 88 A3
Le Monastier-sur-Gazeille F 117 C3
Le Monêtier-les-Bains F 118 C3
Le Mont-Dore F 116 B2
Le Montet F 116 A3
Le Mont-St Michel F 88 B2
Lempdes F 116 B3
Le Muret F 128 B2
Le Muy F 132 B2
Lemvig DK 58 B1
Lemwerder D 72 A1
Lena N 48 B2
Lenart SLO 110 C2
Lenartovce SK 99 C4
Lenauheim RO 126 B2
Lencloître F 102 C2
Lend A 109 B4
Lendalfoot GB 36 A2
Lendava SLO 111 C3
Lendery RUS 3 E12
Lendinara I 121 B4
Lendorf A 109 C4
Lendum DK 58 A3
Le Neubourg F 89 A4
Lengefeld D 83 B5
Lengerich
Niedersachsen D 71 B4
Nordrhein-Westfalen D 71 B4
Lenggries D 108 B2
Lengyeltóti H 111 C4
Lenhovda S 62 B3
Lenk CH 106 C2
Lennartsfors S 54 A2
Lennestadt D 81 A4
Lennoxtown GB 35 C3
Leno I 120 B3
Lénola I 169 B3
Le Nouvion-en-Thiérache F 91 A3
Lens
B 79 B3
F 78 B2
Lensahn D 65 B3
Lens Lestang F 117 B5
Lensvik N 198 B6
Lentellais E 141 B3
Lentföhrden D 64 C2
Lenti H 111 C3
Lentini I 177 B3
Lenungshammar S 54 A3
Lenzburg CH 106 B3
Lenzen D 73 A4
Lenzerheide CH 107 C4
Leoben A 110 B2
Leogang A 109 B3
Leominster GB 39 B4
León E 142 B1
Léon F 128 C1
Leonberg D 93 C5
Léoncel F 118 C2
Leonding A 96 C2
Leonessa I 169 A2
Leonforte I 177 B3
Leonidio GR 184 B3
Leopoldsburg B 79 A5
Leopoldsdorf im Marchfeld A 111 A3
Leopoldshagen D 74 A2
Leova MD 17 B8
Le Palais F 100 B2
Le Parcq F 78 B2
Lepe E 161 B2
Le Péage-de-Roussillon F 117 B4
Le Pellerin F 101 B4
Lepenou GR 182 E3
Le Perthus F 146 B3
Le Pertuis F 117 B4
Le Petit-Bornand F 118 B3
Lephin GB 31 B2
L'Epine F 132 A1
Le Poët F 132 A1
Lepoglava HR 124 A2
Le Poirè-sur-Vie F 114 B2
Le Pont CH 105 C5
Le Pont-de-Montvert F 130 A2
Le Porge F 128 B1
Le Porge-Océan F 128 B1
Le Portel F 78 B1
Le Pouldu F 100 B2
Le Pouliguen F 101 B3
Leppäjärvi FIN 192 D7
Leppävirta FIN 8 A5
Leppin D 73 B4
le Prese I 120 A3
Lepsény H 112 C2
Le Puy-en-Velay F 117 B3
Le Puy-Ste Réparade F 131 B4
Le Quesnoy F 79 B3
Léquile I 173 B4
Le Rayol F 132 B2
Lercara Friddi I 176 B2
Lerdal S 54 B2
Leré F 103 B4
Lérici I 134 A2
Lerin E 144 B2
Lerma E 143 B3
Lerm-et-Musset F 128 B2
Lermoos A 108 B1
Le Roeulx B 79 B4
Le Rouget F 116 C2
Lérouville F 92 C1
Le Rozier F 130 A2
Lerum S 60 B2
Le Russey F 106 B1
Lervik N 54 A1
Lerwick GB 33 A5
Lés E 145 B4
Les Abrets F 118 B2
Les Aix-d'Angillon F 103 B4
Lesaka E 144 A2
Les Ancizes-Comps F 116 B2
Les Andelys F 90 B1
Les Arcs
Savoie F 119 B3
Var F 132 B2
Les-Aubiers F 102 C1
Les Baux-de-Provence F 131 B3
Les Bézards F 103 B4
Les Bois CH 106 B1
Les Bordes F 103 B4
Les Borges Blanques E 147 C1
Les Borges del Camp E 147 C2
Les Brunettes F 104 C2
Lesbury GB 37 A5
Les Cabannes F 146 B2
L'Escala E 147 B4
Lescar F 145 A3
L'Escarène F 133 B3
Lesce SLO 123 A3
Lescheraines F 118 B3
Lesconil F 100 B1
Les Contamines-Montjoie F 118 B3
les Coves de Vinroma E 153 B4
Les Déserts F 118 B2
Les Deux-Alpes F 118 C3
Les Diablerets CH 119 A4
Lesdins F 90 B3
Les Echelles F 118 B2
Le Sel-de-Bretagne F 101 B4
Le Sentier CH 105 C5
Les Escaldes AND 146 B2
Les Essarts F 114 B2
Les Estables F 117 C4
Les Eyzies-de-Tayac F 129 B4
Les Gets F 118 A3
Les Grandes-Ventes F 89 A5
Les Haudères CH 119 A4
Les Herbiers F 114 B2
Les Hôpitaux-Neufs F 105 C5
Lesično SLO 123 A4
Lésina I 171 B3
Lesjaskog N 198 C5
Lesjöfors S 49 C6
Leskovac SRB 16 D4
Leskova Dolina SLO 123 B3
Leskovec
CZ 98 B1
SLO 123 B4
Leskovice CZ 97 B3
Leskovik AL 182 C2
Leslie GB 35 B4
Les Lucs-sur-Boulogne F 114 B2
Les Mages F 131 A3
Lesmahagow GB 36 A3
Les Mazures F 91 B4
Les Mées F 132 A1
Lesmont F 91 C4
Les Mureaux F 90 C1
Leśna PL 84 A3
Lesneven F 100 A1
Leśnica PL 86 B2
Lešnica SRB 127 C1
Leśniów Wielkoplski PL 75 C4
Lesnoye RUS 9 C9
Les Omergues F 132 A1
Les Ormes-sur-Voulzie F 90 C3
Les Orres F 132 A2
Le Souquet F 128 C1
Lesparre-Médoc F 128 A2
l'Espérance F 91 B3
l'Esperou F 130 A2
Les Pieux F 88 A2
Lesponne F 145 A4
Les Ponts-de-Cé F 102 B1
Les Ponts-de-Martel CH 106 C1
Les Praz F 119 B3
L'Espunyola E 147 B2
Les Riceys F 104 B3
Les Roches F 117 B4
Les Rosaires F 101 A3
Les Rosiers F 102 B1
Les Rousses F 105 C5
Les Sables-d'Olonne F 114 B2
Lessach A 109 B4
Lessay F 88 A2
Lessebo S 62 B3
Les Settons F 104 B3
Lessines B 79 B3
L'Estany E 147 C3
Les Ternes F 116 B2
Lesterps F 115 B4
Les Thilliers en-Vexin F 90 B1
Les Touches F 101 B4
Les Trois Moûtiers F 102 B2
Les Vans F 131 A3
Les Verrières CH 105 C5
Les Vignes F 130 A2
Leswalt GB 36 B1
Leszno
Mazowieckie PL 77 B5
Wielkopolskie PL 85 A4
Leszno Górne PL 84 A3
Letchworth GB 44 B3
Le Teil F 131 A3
Le Teilleul F 88 B3
Le Temple-de-Bretagne F 101 B4
Letenye H 111 C3
Le Theil F 89 B4
Le Thillot F 106 B1
Letino I 170 B2
Letohrad CZ 97 A4

Le Touquet-Paris-Plage F 78 B1
Le Touvet F 118 B2
Letovice CZ 97 B4
Le Translay F 90 B1
Le Tréport F 90 A1
Letschin D 74 B3
Letterfrack IRL 28 A2
Letterkenny IRL 26 B3
Lettermacaward IRL 26 B2
Lettoch GB 32 D3
Letur E 164 A2
Letux E 153 A3
Letzlingen D 73 B4
Leucate F 146 B4
Leuchars GB 35 B5
Leuglay F 105 B3
Leuk CH 119 A4
Leukerbad CH 119 A4
Leumrabhagh GB 31 A2
Leuna D 83 A4
Leusden NL 70 B2
Leutenberg D 82 B3
Leuterschach D 108 B1
Leutershausen D 94 B2
Leutkirch D 107 B5
Leuven B 79 B4
Leuze-en-Hainaut B 79 B3
Le Val F 132 B2
Le Val-André F 101 A3
Le Val-d'Ajol F 105 B5
Levan AL 182 C1
Levanger N 199 B8
Levanjska Varoš
HR 125 B4
Lévanto I 134 A2
Levaré F 88 B3
Levata I 120 B3
Leveld N 47 B5
Leven
East Yorkshire GB 41 B3
Fife GB 35 B5
Leverano I 173 B3
Le Verdon-sur-Mer
F 114 C2
Leverkusen D 80 A2
Levern D 72 B1
Le Vernet F 132 A2
Levet F 103 C4
Levice SK 112 A2
Lévico Terme I 121 A4
Levie F 180 B2
Levier F 105 C5
Le Vigan F 130 B2
Lévignen F 90 B2
le Ville I 135 B5
Levinovac HR 124 B3
Le Vivier-sur-Mer F 88 B2
Levoča SK 99 B4
Levroux F 103 C3
Lewes GB 45 C4
Lewin Brzeski PL 85 B5
Lewisham GB 44 B3
Leyburn GB 37 B5
Leyland GB 38 A4
Leysdown-on-Sea
GB 45 B4
Leysin CH 119 A4
Lezajsk PL 12 C5
Lézardrieux F 100 A2
Lézat-sur-Léze F 146 A2
Lezay F 115 B3
Lezhë AL 182 B1
Lézignan-Corbières
F 130 B1
Lezignan-la-Cèbe
F 130 B2
Ležimir SRB 126 B1
Lézinnes F 104 B3
Lezoux F 117 B3
Lezuza E 158 C1
Lhenice CZ 96 C2
Lherm F 146 A2
Lhommaizé F 115 B4
L'Hospitalet F 146 B2
L'Hospitalet de l'Infant
E 147 D1
L'Hospitalet de
Llobregat E 147 C3
L'Hospitalet-du-Larzac
F 130 B2
Lhuître F 91 C4
Liancourt F 90 B2
Liart F 91 B4
Liatorp S 63 B2
Liatrie GB 32 D2
Libáň CZ 84 B3
Libceves CZ 84 B1
Liběchov CZ 84 B2
Liber E 141 B3
Liberec CZ 84 B3
Libiąż PL 86 B3
Libina CZ 98 B1
Libochovice CZ 84 B2
Libohovë AL 182 C2
Libourne F 128 B2
Libramont B 92 B1
Librazhd AL 182 B2
Librilla E 165 B3
Libros E 152 B2
Licata I 176 B2
Licciana Nardi I 134 A3
Licenza I 169 A2
Liceros E 151 A4
Lich D 81 B4
Lichères-près-
Aigremont F 104 B2
Lichfield GB 40 C2
Lichtenau
A 97 C3
D 81 A4
Lichtenberg D 83 B3
Lichtenfels D 82 B3
Lichtensteig CH 107 B4
Lichtenstein D 83 B4
Lichtenvoorde NL 71 C3
Lichtervelde B 78 A3
Lička Jesenica HR 123 B4
Lickershamn S 57 C4
Lički Osik HR 123 C4
Ličko Lešce HR 123 C4
Licodía Eubéa I 177 B3
Licques F 78 B1
Lida BY 13 B6
Lidar N 47 A6
Lidečko CZ 98 B2
Liden S 200 D2
Lidhult S 60 C3
Lidköping S 55 B4
Lido I 122 B1
Lido Azzurro I 173 B3
Lido degli Estensi
I 122 C1
Lido degli Scacchi
I 122 C1
Lido della Nazioni
I 122 C1
Lido di Camaiore I 134 B3
Lido di Casalbordino
I 169 A4
Lido di Castél Fusano
I 168 B2
Lido di Cincinnato
I 168 B2
Lido di Classe I 135 A5
Lido di Fermo I 136 B2
Lido di Fondi I 169 B3
Lido di Jésolo I 122 B1
Lido di Licola I 170 C2
Lido di Metaponto
I 174 A2
Lido di Óstia I 168 B2
Lido di Policoro I 174 A2
Lido di Pomposa I 122 C1
Lido di Savio I 135 A5
Lido di Scanzano I 174 A2
Lido di Siponto I 171 B3
Lido di Squillace I 175 C2
Lido di Volano I 122 C1
Lido Riccio I 169 A4
Lidoriki GR 184 A3
Lido Silvana I 173 B3
Lidsjöberg S 199 A12
Lidzbark PL 77 A4
Lidzbark Warmiński
PL 69 A5
Liebenau
A 96 C2
D 72 B2
Liebenwalde D 74 B2
Lieberose D 74 C3
Liebling RO 126 B3
Lieboch A 110 C2
Liège B 80 B1
Lieksa FIN 3 E12
Lienen D 71 B4
Lienz A 109 C3
Liepāja LV 8 D2
Lier B 79 A4
Lierbyen N 54 A1
Liernais F 104 B3
Liesing A 109 C3
Liestal CH 106 B2
Liétor E 158 C2
Lieurac F 146 B2
Lieurey F 89 A4
Liévin F 78 B2
Liezen A 110 B1
Liffol-le-Grand F 92 C1
Lifford IRL 27 B3
Liffré F 101 A4
Ligardes F 129 B3
Lignano Sabbiadoro
I 122 B2
Ligne F 101 B4
Lignières F 103 C4
Ligny-en-Barrois F 92 C1
Ligny-le-Châtel F 104 B2
Ligoła Polska PL 85 A5
Ligourio GR 184 B4
Ligowo PL 77 B4
Ligueil F 102 B2
Likavka SK 99 B3
Likenäs S 49 B5
Likhoslavl RUS 9 D9
Lild Strand DK 58 A1
L'Île-Bouchard F 102 B2
l'Île-Rousse F 180 A1
Lilienfeld A 110 A2
Lilienthal D 72 A1
Lilla Edet S 54 B3
Lilla Tjärby S 61 C3
Lille
B 79 A4
F 78 B3
Lillebonne F 89 A4
Lillehammer N 48 A2
Lillerød DK 61 D2
Lillers F 78 B2
Lillesand N 53 B4
Lillestrøm N 48 C3
Lillhärdal S 199 D11
Lillkyrka S 56 A3
Lillo E 157 A4
Lillögda S 200 B3
Lillpite S 196 D4
Lima S 49 B5
Limanowa PL 99 B4
Limassol CY 181 B2
Limavady GB 27 A4
Limbach-Oberfrohna
D 83 B4
Limbaži LV 8 D4
Limbourg B 80 B1
Limburg D 81 B4
Lime DK 58 B3
Limedsforsen S 49 B5
Limenaria GR 183 C6
Limenas Chersonisou
GR 185 D6
Limerick IRL 29 B3
Limes I 121 B3
Limésy F 89 A4
Limmared S 60 B3
Limni GR 183 E5
Limoges F 115 C5
Limogne-en-Quercy
F 129 B4
Limoise F 104 C2
Limone Piemonte I 133 A3
Limone sul Garda I 121 B3
Limons F 117 B3
Limours F 90 C2
Limoux F 146 A3
Linares E 157 B4
Linares de Mora E 153 B3
Linares de Riofrio
E 149 B4
Linaria GR 183 E6
Linas de Broto E 145 B3
Lincoln GB 40 B3
Lind DK 59 B1
Lindås N 46 B2
Lindau D 107 B4
Lindberget N 48 A3
Lindelse DK 65 B3
Lindenberg D 74 B3
Lindenberg im Allgäu
D 107 B4
Lindern D 71 B4
Linderöd S 61 D3
Lindesberg S 56 A1
Lindesnäs S 50 B1
Lindesnes N 52 C3
Lindholmen S 57 A4
Lindknud DK 59 C2
Lindlar D 80 A3
Lindö S 56 B2
Lindome S 60 B2
Lindos GR 188 C3
Lindoso P 148 A1
Lindow D 74 B1
Lindsdal S 62 B4
Lindshammar S 62 A3
Lindstedt D 73 B4
Lindved DK 59 C2
Líně CZ 96 B1
Lingbo S 50 A3
Lingen D 71 B4
Linghed S 50 B2
Linghem S 56 B1
Linguaglossa I 177 B4
Linia PL 68 A2
Linie PL 74 A3
Liniewo PL 68 A3
Linkenheim D 93 B4
Linköping S 56 B1
Linksness GB 33 C3
Linlithgow GB 35 C4
Linneryd S 63 B3
Linnes Hammarby
S 51 C4
Linnich D 80 B2
Linsell S 199 C10
Linslade GB 44 B3
Linthal CH 107 C4
Linyola E 147 C1
Linz
A 96 C2
D 80 B3
Liomseter N 47 A6
Lionárisso CY 181 A3
Lioni I 172 B1
Lion-sur-Mer F 89 A3
Lipany SK 99 B4
Lipar SRB 126 B1
Lípari I 177 A3
Lipcani MD 17 A7
Liperi FIN 9 A6
Liphook GB 44 B3
Lipiany PL 75 A3
Lipik HR 124 B3
Lipka PL 68 B2
Lipki Wielkie PL 75 B4
Lipnica PL 68 B2
Lipnica Murowana
PL 99 B4
Lipnik PL 87 B5
Lipník nad Bečvou
CZ 98 B1
Lipno
Kujawsko-Pomorskie
PL 77 B4
Łódzkie PL 86 A2
Liposthey F 128 B2
Lipovac HR 125 B5
Lipovec CZ 97 B4
Lipovets UA 13 D8
Lipovljani HR 124 B2
Lipowiec PL 77 A6
Lipowina PL 69 A4
Lippborg D 81 A4
Lippó H 125 B4
Lippoldsberg D 81 A5
Lippstadt D 81 A4
Lipsko PL 87 A5
Liptál CZ 98 B1
Liptovská-Lúžna
SK 99 C3
Liptovská Osada
SK 99 C3
Liptovská-Teplička
SK 99 C4
Liptovský Hrádok
SK 99 B3
Liptovský Milkuláš
SK 99 B3
Lipusz PL 68 A2
Lipůvka CZ 97 B4
Liré F 101 B4
Lisac BIH 139 A3
Lisbellaw GB 27 B3
Lisboa = Lisbon P 154 C1
Lisbon = Lisboa P 154 C1
Lisburn GB 27 B4
Liscannor IRL 28 B2
Lisdoonvarna IRL 28 A2
Lisewo PL 69 B3
Lisia Góra PL 87 B5
Lisięcice PL 86 B1
Lisieux F 89 A4
Lisjö S 56 A2
Liskeard GB 42 B2
L'Isle CH 105 C5
L'Isle-Adam F 90 B2
L'Isle-de-Noé F 129 C3
L'Isle-en-Dodon F 145 A4
L'Isle-Jourdain
Gers F 129 C4
Vienne F 115 B4
L'Isle-sur-la-Sorgue
F 131 B4
L'Isle-sur-le Doubs
F 105 B5
L'Isle-sur-Serein F 104 B3
Lisle-sur-Tarn F 129 C4
Lismore IRL 29 B4
Lisnaskea GB 27 B3
Lišov CZ 96 B2
Lisów
Lubuskie PL 74 B3
Śląskie PL 86 B2
Lisse NL 70 B1
Lissycasey IRL 28 B2
List D 64 A1
Listerby S 63 B3
Listowel IRL 29 B2
Listrac-Médoc F 128 A2
Liszki PL 99 A3
Liszkowo PL 76 A2
Lit S 199 B11
Litava SK 99 C3
Litcham GB 41 C4
Lit-et-Mixe F 128 B1
Litija SLO 123 A3
Litke H 112 A3
Litlabø N 52 A1
Litochoro GR 182 C4
Litoměřice CZ 84 B2
Litomyšl CZ 97 B4
Litovel CZ 98 B1
Litschau A 96 C3
Littlehampton GB 44 C3
Littleport GB 45 A4
Littleton IRL 29 B4
Little Walsingham
GB 41 C4
Litvinov CZ 83 B5
Livadero GR 182 C3
Livadhia CY 181 B2
Livadi GR 182 C4
Livadia GR 184 A3
Livarot F 89 B4
Liveras CY 181 A1
Livernon F 129 B4
Liverovici MNE 139 C5
Liverpool GB 38 A4
Livigno I 107 C5
Livingston GB 35 C4
Livno BIH 138 B2
Livo FIN 197 D9
Livold SLO 123 B3
Livorno I 134 B3
Livorno Ferraris I 119 B5
Livron-sur-Drôme
F 117 C4
Livry-Louvercy F 91 B4
Lixheim F 92 C3
Lixouri GR 184 A1
Lizard GB 42 C1
Lizy-sur-Ourcq F 90 B3
Lizzano I 173 B3
Lizzano in Belvedere
I 135 A3
Ljig SRB 127 C2
Ljørdalen N 49 A4
Ljosland N 52 B3
Ljubija BIH 124 C2
Ljubinje BIH 139 C4
Ljubljana SLO 123 A3
Ljubno ob Savinji
SLO 123 A3
Ljubovija SRB 127 C1
Ljubuški BIH 138 B3
Ljugarn S 57 C4
Ljung S 60 B3
Ljunga S 56 B2
Ljungaverk S 200 D2
Ljungby S 60 C3
Ljungbyhed S 61 C3
Ljungbyholm S 63 B4
Ljungdalen S 199 C9
Ljungsarp S 60 B3
Ljungsbro S 56 B1
Ljungskile S 54 B2
Ljusdal S 200 E2
Ljusfallshammar S 56 B1
Ljusne S 51 A4
Ljusterö S 57 A4
Ljutomer SLO 111 C3
Lŭki BG 183 B6
Lladurs E 147 B2
Llafranc E 147 C4
Llagostera E 147 C3
Llanaelhaiarn GB 38 B2
Llanarth GB 39 B2
Llanbedr GB 38 B2
Llanbedrog GB 38 B2
Llanberis GB 38 A2
Llanbister GB 39 B3
Llanbrynmair GB 39 B3
Llançà E 146 B4
Llandeilo GB 39 C3
Llandissilio GB 39 C2
Llandovery GB 39 C3
Llandrillo GB 38 B3
Llandrindod Wells
GB 39 B3
Llandudec F 100 A1
Llandudno GB 38 A3
Llandysul GB 39 B2
Llanelli GB 39 C2
Llanerchymedd GB 38 A2
Llanes E 142 A2
Llanfair Caereinion
GB 38 B3
Llanfairfechan GB 38 A3
Llanfyllin GB 38 B3
Llangadog GB 39 C3
Llangefni GB 38 A2
Llangollen GB 38 B3
Llangrannog GB 39 B2
Llangurig GB 39 B3
Llanidloes GB 39 B3
Llanilar GB 39 B2
Llanrhystud GB 39 B2
Llanrwst GB 38 A3
Llansannan GB 38 A3
Llansawel GB 39 B2
Llanstephan GB 39 C2
Llanteno E 143 A3
Llanthony GB 39 C3
Llantrisant GB 39 C3
Llantwit-Major GB 39 C3
Llanuwchllyn GB 38 B3
Llanwddyn GB 38 B3
Llanwrda GB 39 C3
Llanwrtyd Wells GB 39 B3
Llanybydder GB 39 B2
Llanymynech GB 38 B3
Llavorsi E 146 B2
Lleida E 153 A4
Llera E 156 B1
Llerena E 156 B1
Lles E 146 B2
Llessui E 146 B2
Llinars E 147 B2
Lliria E 159 B3
Llivia E 146 B2
Llodio E 143 A4
Lloret de Mar E 147 C3
Llosa de Ranes E 159 B3
Lloseta E 167 B2
Llucena del Cid E 153 B3
Llucmajor E 167 B2
Llutxent E 159 C3
Llwyngwril GB 38 B2
Llyswen GB 39 B3
Lnáře CZ 96 B1
Lniano PL 76 A3
Loanhead GB 35 C4
Loano I 133 A4
Loarre E 145 B3
Löbau D 84 A2
Löbejün D 83 A3
Löberöd S 61 D3
Łobez PL 75 A4
Löbnitz D 66 B1
Lobón E 155 C4
Loburg D 73 B5
Łobżenica PL 76 A2
Locana I 119 B4
Locarno CH 120 A1
Loccum D 72 B2
Loče SLO 123 A4
Lochailort GB 34 B2
Lochaline GB 34 B2
Lochans GB 36 B1
Locharbriggs GB 36 A3
Lochau A 107 B4
Loch Baghasdail
GB 31 B1
Lochcarron GB 31 B3
Lochearnhead GB 34 B3
Lochem NL 71 B3
Loches F 102 B2
Lochgelly GB 35 B4
Lochgilphead GB 34 B2
Lochgoilhead GB 34 B3
Lochinver GB 32 C1
Loch nam Madadh
GB 31 B1
Lochranza GB 34 C2
Ločika SRB 127 D3
Lockenhaus A 111 B3
Lockerbie GB 36 A3
Löcknitz D 74 A3
Locmaria F 100 B2
Locmariaquer F 100 B3
Locminé F 100 B3
Locorotondo I 173 B3
Locquirec F 100 A2
Locri I 175 C2
Locronan F 100 A1
Loctudy F 100 B1
Lodares de Osma
E 151 A5
Lodé I 178 B3
Lodeinoye Pole RUS 9 B8
Lodève F 130 B2
Lodi I 120 B2
Løding N 194 C5
Lødingen N 194 B6
Lodosa E 144 B1
Lödöse S 54 B3
Łódź PL 86 A3
Loeches E 151 B4
Løfallstrand N 46 B3
Lofer A 109 B3
Lofsdalen S 199 C10
Loftahammar S 62 A4
Lofthus N 46 B3
Loftus GB 37 B6
Loga N 52 B2
Logatec SLO 123 B3
Lögdeå S 200 C5
Lograto I 120 B3
Logroño E 143 B4
Logrosán E 156 A2
Løgstør DK 58 B2
Løgumgårde DK 64 A1
Løgumkloster DK 64 A1
Lohals DK 65 A3
Lohiniva FIN 197 B8
Lohja FIN 8 B4
Löhlbach D 81 A4
Lohmen
Mecklenburg-Vorpommern D 65 C5
Sachsen D 84 B2
Löhnberg D 81 B4
Lohne D 71 B5
Löhne D 72 B1
Lohr D 94 B1
Lohra D 81 B4
Lohsa D 84 A2
Loiano I 135 A4
Loimaa FIN 8 B3
Lóiri I 178 B3
Loitz D 66 C2
Loivos P 148 A2
Loivos do Monte P 148 A2
Loja E 163 A3
Lojanice SRB 127 C1
Lojsta S 57 C4
Løjt Kirkeby DK 64 A2
Lok SK 112 A2
Lokca SK 99 B3
Løken N 54 A2
Lokeren B 79 A3
Loket CZ 83 B4
Lokka FIN 197 B10
Løkken
DK 58 A2
N 198 B6
Loknya RUS 9 D7
Lökosháza H 113 C5
Lokve SRB 126 B3
Lollar D 81 B4
L'Olleria E 159 C3
Lölling-Graben A 110 C1
Lom
BG 17 D5
N 198 D5
SK 99 C3
Lombez F 146 A1
Lomello I 120 B1
Łomianki PL 77 B5
Lomma S 61 D3
Lommaryd S 62 A2
Lommatzsch D 83 A5
Lommel B 79 A5
Lommersum D 80 B2
Lomnice CZ 97 B4
Lomnice nad Lužnici
CZ 96 B2
Lomnice-nad Popelkou
CZ 84 B3
Lompolo FIN 196 A7
Łomza PL 12 B5
Lönashult S 63 B2
Lønborg DK 59 C1
Londerzeel B 79 A4
Londinières F 89 A5
London GB 44 B3
Lonevåg N 46 B2
Longa GR 184 C2
Longare I 121 B4
Longares E 152 A2
Longarone I 122 A1
Longastrino I 135 A5
Long Bennington
GB 40 C3
Longbenton GB 37 A5
Longchamp-sur-Aujon
F 105 A3
Longchaumois F 118 A2
Long Eaton GB 40 C2
Longeau F 105 B4
Longecourt-en-Plaine
F 105 B4
Longeville-les-St Avold
F 92 B2

Longeville-sur-Mer F 114 B2
Longford IRL 28 A4
Longframlington GB 37 A5
Longhope GB 33 C3
Longhorsley GB 37 A5
Longhoughton GB 37 A5
Longi I 177 A3
Long Melford GB 45 A4
Longny-au-Perche F 89 B4
Longobucco I 174 B2
Long Preston GB 40 A1
Longré F 115 B3
Longridge GB 38 A4
Longroiva P 149 B2
Long Sutton GB 41 C4
Longtown
Cumbria GB 36 A4
Herefordshire GB 39 C4
Longueau F 90 B2
Longué-Jumelles F 102 B1
Longuyon F 92 B1
Longvic F 105 B4
Longvilly B 92 A1
Longwy F 92 B1
Lonigo I 121 B4
Löningen D 71 B4
Lonja HR 124 B2
Lönneberga S 62 A3
Lönsboda S 63 B2
Lønset N 198 C6
Lons-le-Saunier F 105 C4
Lønstrup DK 58 A2
Looe GB 42 B2
Loone-Plage F 78 A2
Loon op Zand NL 79 A5
Loosdorf A 110 A2
Lo Pagán E 165 B4
Lopar HR 123 C3
Lopare BIH 125 C4
Lopera E 157 C3
Lopigna F 180 A1
Loppersum NL 71 A3
Łopuszna PL 99 B4
Łopuszno PL 87 B4
Lor F 91 B4
Lora N 198 C5
Lora de Estepa E 162 A3
Lora del Río E 162 A2
Loranca del Campo E 151 B5
Lörby S 63 B2
Lorca E 164 B3
Lorch D 93 A3
Lørenfallet N 48 B3
Lørenskog N 48 C2
Loreo I 122 B1
Loreto I 136 B2
Lorgues F 132 B2
Lorica I 174 B2
Lorient F 100 B2
Lorignac F 114 C3
Lörinci H 112 B3
Loriol-sur-Drôme F 117 C4
Lormes F 104 B2
Loro Ciuffenna I 135 B4
Lorqui E 165 A3
Lörrach D 106 B2
Lorrez-le-Bocage F 103 A4
Lorris F 103 B4
Lorup D 71 B4
Łoś PL 77 C5
Los S 199 D12
Losacino E 149 A3
Los Alcázares E 165 B4
Los Arcos E 144 B1
Losar de la Vera E 150 B2
Los Barios de Luna E 141 B5
Los Barrios E 162 B2
Los Caños de Meca E 162 B1
Los Cerricos E 164 B2
Los Corrales E 162 A3
Los Corrales de Buelna E 142 A2
Los Dolores E 165 B3
Losenstein A 110 B1
Los Gallardos E 164 B3
Losheim
Nordrhein-Westfalen D 80 B2
Saarland D 92 B2
Los Hinojosos E 158 B1
Los Isidros E 159 B2
Los Molinos E 151 B3
Los Morales E 162 A2
Los Navalmorales E 156 A3
Los Navalucillos E 156 A3
Losne F 105 B4
Los Nietos E 165 B4
Løsning DK 59 C2
Los Palacios y Villafranca E 162 A2
Los Pozuelos de Calatrava E 157 B3
Los Rábanos E 143 C4
Los Santos E 149 B4
Los Santos de la Humosa E 151 B4
Los Santos de Maimona E 155 C4
Lossburg D 93 C4
Losse F 128 B2
Losser NL 71 B4
Lossiemouth GB 32 D3
Lössnitz D 83 B4
Loštice CZ 97 B4
Los Tijos E 142 A2
Lostwithiel GB 42 B2
Los Villares E 163 A4
Los Yébenes E 157 A4
Løten N 48 B3
Lotorp S 56 B1
Lottefors S 50 A3
Löttorp S 62 A5
Lotyń PL 68 B1
Lotzorai I 179 C3
Louargat F 100 A2
Loudéac F 101 A3
Loudun F 102 B2
Loué F 102 B1
Loughborough GB 40 C2
Loughbrickland GB 27 B4
Loughrea IRL 28 A3
Louhans F 105 C4
Louisburgh IRL 28 A2
Loukhi RUS 3 C13
Loulay F 114 B3
Loulé P 160 B1
Louny CZ 84 B1
Lourdes F 145 A3
Lourenzá E 141 A3
Loures P 154 C1
Loures-Barousse F 145 A4
Louriçal P 154 A2
Lourinhã P 154 B1
Lourmarin F 131 B4
Loury F 103 B4
Lousa
Bragança P 149 A2
Castelo Branco P 155 B3
Lousã P 148 B1
Lousa P 154 C1
Lousada
E 140 B3
P 148 A1
Louth GB 41 B3
Loutra Edipsou GR 183 E5
Loutraki GR 184 B3
Loutropoli Thermis GR 186 C1
Louverné F 102 A1
Louvie-Juzon F 145 A3
Louviers F 89 A5
Louvigné-du-Désert F 88 B2
Louvois F 91 B4
Lova I 121 B5
Lovasberény H 112 B2
Lövåsen S 49 C5
Lovászpatona H 111 B4
Lövberga S 200 C1
Lovech BG 17 D6
Lövenich D 80 A2
Lóvere I 120 B3
Lövestad S 61 D3
Loviisa FIN 8 B5
Lovikka S 196 B5
Lovinobaňa SK 99 C3
Loviste HR 138 B3
Lovke HR 123 B3
Lovnäs S 49 A5
Lövö H 111 B3
Lovosice CZ 84 B2
Lovozero RUS 3 C14
Lovran HR 123 B3
Lovreć HR 138 B2
Lovrenc na Pohorju SLO 110 C2
Lovrin RO 126 B2
Lövstabruk S 51 B4
Löwenberg D 74 B2
Löwenstein D 94 B1
Lowestoft GB 41 C5
Lowick GB 37 A5
Łowicz PL 77 B4
Loxstedt D 72 A1
Loyew BY 13 C9
Lož SLO 123 B3
Loza CZ 96 B1
Łozina PL 85 A5
Loznica SRB 127 C1
Lozničko Polje SRB 127 C1
Lozorno SK 111 A4
Lozovik SRB 127 C3
Lozoya E 151 B4
Lozoyuela E 151 B4
Lozzo di Cadore I 109 C3
Luanco E 141 A5
Luarca E 141 A4
Lubaczów PL 13 C5
Lubań PL 84 A3
Lubanie PL 76 B3
Lubanów PL 86 A3
Lubars D 73 B5
Lubasz PL 75 B5
Lubawa PL 69 B4
Lubawka PL 85 B4
Lübbecke D 72 B1
Lübben D 74 C2
Lübbenau D 84 A1
Lubczyna PL 74 A3
Lübeck D 65 C3
Lubenec CZ 83 B5
Lubersac F 115 C5
Lübesse D 73 A4
Lubia E 152 A1
Lubian E 141 B4
Lubiatowo PL 75 A4
Lubichowo PL 69 B3
Lubicz Dolny PL 76 A3
Lubień PL 99 B3
Lubienia PL 87 A5
Lubień Kujawski PL 77 B4
Lubieszewo PL 75 A4
Lubin
Dolnośląskie PL 85 A4
Zachodnio-Pomorskie PL 67 C3
Lublin PL 12 C5
Lubliniec PL 86 B2
Lubmin D 66 B2
Lubniewice PL 75 B4
Lubochnia PL 87 A4
Lubomierz
Dolnośląskie PL 84 A3
Małopolskie PL 99 B4
Lubomino PL 69 A5
Luboń PL 76 B1
L'ubotín SK 99 B4
Lubowidz PL 77 A4
Łubowo
Wielkopolskie PL 76 B2
Zachodnio-Pomorskie PL 68 B1
Lubraniec PL 76 B3
Lubrin E 164 B2
Lubrza PL 85 B5
Lubsko PL 84 A2
Lübtheen D 73 A4
Lubuczewo PL 68 A2
Luby CZ 83 B4
Lübz D 73 A5
Luc F 117 C3
Lucainena de las Torres E 164 B2
Lucan IRL 30 A2
Lučani SRB 127 D2
Lúcar E 164 B2
Luçay-le-Mâle F 103 B3
Lucca I 134 B3
Lucciana F 180 A2
Lucé F 90 C1
Luče SLO 123 A3
Lucena
Córdoba E 163 A3
Huelva E 161 B3
Lucenay-les-Aix F 104 C2
Lucenay-l'Evêque F 104 B3
Luc-en-Diois F 118 C2
Lučenec SK 99 C3
Luceni E 144 C2
Lucens CH 106 C1
Lucera I 171 B3
Luceram F 133 B3
Lüchow D 73 B4
Luciana E 157 B3
Lucignano I 135 B4
Lucija SLO 122 B2
Lucka D 83 A4
Luckau D 84 A1
Luckenwalde D 74 B2
Lückstedt D 73 B4
Luco dei Marsi I 169 B3
Luçon F 114 B2
Luc-sur-Mer F 89 A3
Ludanice SK 98 C2
Ludbreg HR 124 A2
Lüdenscheid D 81 A3
Lüderitz D 73 B4
Lüdersdorf D 65 C3
Ludgershall GB 44 B2
Ludgo S 56 B3
Lüdinghausen D 80 A3
Ludlow GB 39 B4
Ludomy PL 75 B5
Ludvika S 50 B2
Ludweiler Warndt D 92 B2
Ludwigsburg D 94 C1
Ludwigsfelde D 74 B2
Ludwigshafen D 93 B4
Ludwigslust D 73 A4
Ludwigsstadt D 82 B3
Ludza LV 8 D5
Luesia E 144 B2
Luftkurort Arendsee D 73 B4
Lug
BIH 139 C4
HR 125 B4
Luga RUS 9 C6
Lugagnano Val d'Arda I 120 C2
Lugano CH 120 A1
Lugau D 83 B4
Lugnas S 55 B4
Lúgnola I 168 A2
Lugny F 105 C3
Lugo
E 140 A3
I 135 A4
Lugoj RO 16 C4
Lugones E 141 A5
Lugros E 163 A4
Luhačovice CZ 98 B1
Luhe D 95 B4
Luino I 120 B1
Luintra E 140 B3
Lújar E 163 B4
Luka nad Jihlavou CZ 97 B3
Lukavac BIH 125 C4
Lukavika BIH 125 C4
Lukovë AL 182 D1
Lukovica SLO 123 A3
Lukovit BG 17 D6
Lukovo HR 123 C3
Lukovo Šugorje HR 137 A4
Łuków PL 12 C5
Łukowice Brzeskie PL 85 B5
Luksefjell N 53 A5
Łukta PL 69 B5
Lula I 178 B3
Luleå S 196 D5
Lüleburgaz TR 186 A2
Lumbarda HR 138 C3
Lumbier E 144 B2
Lumbrales E 149 B3
Lumbreras E 143 B4
Lumbres F 78 B2
Lummelunda S 57 C4
Lummen B 79 B5
Lumparland FIN 51 B7
Lumpiaque E 152 A2
Lumsås DK 61 D1
Lumsden GB 33 D4
Lumsheden S 50 B3
Lun HR 123 C3
Luna E 144 B3
Lunamatrona I 179 C2
Lunano I 136 B1
Lunas F 130 B2
Lund
N 199 A8
Skåne S 61 D3
Västra Götaland S 54 A3
Lundamo N 199 B7
Lunde
DK 59 C1
Sogn og Fjordane N 46 A3
Sogn og Fjordane N 46 A3
Telemark N 53 A5
S 200 D3
Lundebyvollen N 49 B4
Lunden D 64 B2
Lunderseter N 49 B4
Lunderskov DK 59 C2
Lundsberg S 55 A5
Lüneburg D 72 A3
Lunel F 131 B3
Lünen D 81 A3
Lunéville F 92 C2
Lungern CH 106 C3
Lungro I 174 B2
Luninyets BY 13 B7
Lünne D 71 B4
Lunner N 48 B2
Lunteren NL 70 B2
Lunz am See A 110 B2
Luogosanto I 178 A3
Łupawa PL 68 A2
Lupión E 157 B4
Lupoglav HR 123 B3
Luppa D 83 A4
Luque E 163 A3
Lurago d'Erba I 120 B2
Lúras I 178 B3
Lurcy-Lévis F 104 C1
Lure F 105 B5
Lurgan GB 27 B4
Luri F 180 A2
Lury-sur-Arnon F 103 B4
Lušci Palanka BIH 124 C2
Lusévera I 122 A2
Lushnjë AL 182 C1
Lusignan F 115 B4
Lusigny-sur-Barse F 104 A3
Lusnić BIH 138 B2
Luso P 148 B1
Lusówko PL 75 B5
Luspebryggan S 196 B2
Luss GB 34 B3
Lussac F 128 B2
Lussac-les-Châteaux F 115 B4
Lussac-les-Eglises F 115 B5
Lussan F 131 A3
Lüssow D 65 C5
Lustenau A 107 B4
Luštěnice CZ 84 B2
Luster N 47 A4
Lutago I 108 C2
Lutherstadt Wittenberg D 83 A4
Lütjenburg D 65 B3
Lutnes N 49 A4
Lutocin PL 77 B4
Lutomiersk PL 86 A3
Luton GB 44 B3
Lutry CH 106 C1
Lutsk UA 13 C6
Lutter am Barenberge D 72 C3
Lutterworth GB 40 C2
Lututów PL 86 A2
Lützen D 83 A4
Lutzow D 73 A4
Luusua FIN 197 C10
Luvos S 196 C1
Luxembourg L 92 B2
Luxeuil-les-Bains F 105 B5
Luxey F 128 B2
Luz
Évora P 155 C3
Faro P 160 B1
Luz *continued*
Faro P 160 B2
Luzarches F 90 B2
Luže CZ 97 B4
Luzech F 129 B4
Luzern CH 106 B3
Luzino PL 68 A3
Luz-St Sauveur F 145 B3
Luzy F 104 C2
Luzzi I 174 B2
L'viv UA 13 D6
Lwówek PL 75 B5
Lwówek Śląski PL 84 A3
Lyakhavichy BY 13 B7
Lybster GB 32 C3
Lychen D 74 A2
Lychkova RUS 9 D8
Lyckeby S 63 B3
Lycksele S 200 B4
Lydd GB 45 C4
Lydford GB 42 B2
Lydney GB 39 C4
Lyepyel BY 13 A8
Lygna N 48 B2
Lykkja N 47 B5
Lykling N 52 A1
Lyme Regis GB 43 B4
Lymington GB 44 C2
Lympne GB 45 B5
Lyndhurst GB 44 C2
Lyneham GB 43 A5
Lyness GB 33 C3
Lyngdal
Buskerud N 47 C6
Vest-Agder N 52 B3
Lyngør N 53 B5
Lyngsa DK 58 A3
Lyngseidet N 192 C4
Lyngsnes N 199 A8
Lynmouth GB 42 A3
Lynton GB 42 A3
Lyntupy BY 13 A7
Lyon F 117 B4
Lyons-la-Forêt F 90 B1
Lyozna BY 13 A9
Lyrestad S 55 B5
Lysánad Labem CZ 84 B2
Lysápod Makytou SK 98 B2
Lysebotn N 52 A2
Lysekil S 54 B2
Lysice CZ 97 B4
Lysomice PL 76 A3
Lysøysund N 198 B6
Lyss CH 106 B2
Lystrup DK 59 B3
Lysvik S 49 B5
Łyszkowice PL 77 C4
Lytham St Anne's GB 38 A3
Lyuban RUS 9 C7
Lyubertsy RUS 9 E10
Lyubimets BG 183 B8
Lyuboml' UA 13 C6
Lyubytino RUS 9 C8

M

Maaninkavaara FIN 197 C11
Maarheeze NL 80 A1
Maaseik B 80 A1
Maastricht NL 80 B1
Mablethorpe GB 41 B4
Mably F 117 A4
Macael E 164 B2
Maçanet de Cabrenys E 146 B3
Mação P 154 B2
Macau F 128 A2
Maccagno-Agra I 120 A1
Maccarese I 168 B2
Macchiagódena I 170 B2
Macclesfield GB 40 B1
Macduff GB 33 D4
Maceda E 140 B3
Macedo de Cavaleiros P 149 A3
Maceira
Guarda P 148 B2
Leiria P 154 B2
Macelj HR 124 A1
Macerata I 136 B2
Macerata Féltria I 136 B1
Machault F 91 B4
Machecoul F 114 B2
Mchowo PL 77 A5
Machrihanish GB 34 C2
Machynlleth GB 39 B3
Macieira P 148 A1
Maciejowice PL 87 A5
Macinaggio F 180 A2
Mackenrode D 82 A2
Mačkovci SLO 111 C3
Macomer I 178 B2
Macon B 91 A4
Mâcon F 117 A4
Macotera E 150 B2
Macroom IRL 29 C3
Macugnaga I 119 B4
Madan BG 183 B6
Madängsholm S 55 B4
Madaras H 126 A1
Maddaloni I 170 B2
Made NL 79 A4
Madeley GB 38 B4
Maderuelo E 151 A4
Madetkoski FIN 197 B9
Madley GB 39 B4
Madocsa H 112 C2
Madona LV 8 D5
Madonna di Campiglio I 121 A3
Madrid E 151 B4
Madridejos E 157 A4
Madrigal de las Altas Torres E 150 A2
Madrigal de la Vera E 150 B2
Madrigalejo E 156 A2
Madrigalejo de Monte E 143 B3
Madriguera E 151 A4
Madrigueras E 158 B2
Madroñera E 156 A2
Maël-Carhaix F 100 A2
Maella E 153 A4
Maello E 150 B3
Maesteg GB 39 C3
Mafra P 154 C1
Magacela E 156 B2
Magallon E 144 C2
Magaluf E 166 B2
Magán E 151 C4
Magaña E 144 C1
Magasa I 121 B3
Magaz E 142 C2
Magdeburg D 73 B4
Magenta I 120 B1
Magescq F 128 C1
Maghera GB 27 B4
Magherafelt GB 27 B4
Maghull GB 38 A4
Magilligan GB 27 A4
Magione I 135 B5
Magioto P 154 C1
Maglaj BIH 125 C4
Maglehem S 63 C2
Magliano de'Marsi I 169 A3
Magliano in Toscana I 168 A1
Magliano Sabina I 168 A2
Maglić SRB 126 B1
Máglie I 173 B4
Maglód H 112 B3
Magnac-Bourg F 115 C5
Magnac-Laval F 115 B5
Magnieres F 92 C2
Magnor N 49 C4
Magnuszew PL 87 A5
Magny-Cours F 104 C2
Magny-en-Vexin F 90 B1
Mágocs H 125 A4
Maguilla E 156 B2
Maguiresbridge GB 27 B3
Magyarbóly H 125 B4
Magyarkeszi H 112 C2
Magyarszék H 125 A4
Mahide E 141 C4
Mahilyow BY 13 B9
Mahmudiye TR 187 C5
Mahora E 158 B2
Mahovo HR 124 B2
Mähring D 95 B4
Maia
E 144 A2
P 148 A1
Maiaelrayo E 151 A4
Maials E 153 A4
Maîche F 106 B1
Máida I 175 C2
Maiden Bradley GB 43 A4
Maidenhead GB 44 B3
Maiden Newton GB 43 B4
Maidstone GB 45 B4
Maienfeld CH 107 B4
Maignelay Montigny F 90 B2
Maijanen FIN 197 B8
Maillezais F 114 B3
Mailly-le-Camp F 91 C4
Mailly-le-Château F 104 B2
Mainar E 152 A2
Mainbernheim D 94 B2
Mainburg D 95 C3
Mainhardt D 94 B1
Maintal D 81 B4
Maintenon F 90 C1
Mainvilliers F 90 C1
Mainz D 93 A4
Maiorca P 148 B1
Mairena de Aljarafe E 162 A1
Mairena del Alcor E 162 A2
Maisach D 108 A2
Maishofen A 109 B3
Maison-Rouge F 90 C3
Maissau A 97 C3
Maisse F 90 C2
Maizières-lès-Vic F 92 C2
Maja HR 124 B2
Majadahonda E 151 B4
Majadas E 150 C2
Majavatn N 195 E4
Majs H 125 B4
Majšperk SLO 123 A4
Makarska HR 138 B3
Makkum NL 70 A2
Maklár H 113 B4

Makó H 126 A2
Makoszyce PL 85 B5
Makov SK 98 B2
Mąkowarsko PL 76 A2
Maków Mazowiecki PL 77 B6
Maków Podhalański PL 99 B3
Makrakomi GR 182 E4
Maksniemi FIN 196 D7
Malá S 195 E9
Mala Bosna SRB 126 A1
Malacky SK 97 C5
Maladzyechna BY 13 A7
Málaga E 163 B3
Malagón E 157 A4
Malaguilla E 151 B4
Malahide IRL 30 A2
Mala Kladuša BIH 124 B1
Mala Krsna SRB 127 C3
Malalbergo I 121 C4
Malá Lehota SK 98 C2
Malanów PL 76 C3
Mala Pijace SRB 126 A1
Mala Subotica HR 124 A2
Malaucène F 131 A4
Malaunay F 89 A5
Malaya Vishera RUS 9 C8
Malborghetto I 109 C4
Malbork PL 69 A4
Malborn D 92 B2
Malbuisson F 105 C5
Malcésine I 121 B3
Malchin D 74 A1
Malching D 96 C1
Malchow D 73 A5
Malcocinado E 156 B2
Malczyce PL 85 A4
Maldegem B 79 A3
Maldon GB 45 B4
Małdyty PL 69 B4
Malè I 121 A3
Malemort F 129 A4
Malente D 65 B3
Måløerås S 62 B3
Males GR 185 D6
Malesherbes F 90 C2
Malesina GR 183 E5
Malestroit F 101 B3
Maletto I 177 B3
Malexander S 56 B1
Malgrat de Mar E 147 C3
Malhadas P 149 A3
Malia
CY 181 B1
GR 185 D6
Malicorne-sur-Sarthe F 102 B1
Malijai F 132 A2
Malildjoš SRB 126 B1
Målilla S 62 A3
Mali Lošinj HR 137 A3
Malin IRL 27 A3
Málinec SK 99 C3
Malingsbo S 50 C2
Maliniec PL 76 B3
Malinska HR 123 B3
Maliq AL 182 C2
Maljevac HR 123 B4
Malkara TR 186 B1
Małki PL 69 B4
Malko Tŭrnovo BG 17 D7
Mallaig GB 34 A2
Mallaranny IRL 28 A2
Mallemort F 131 B4
Mallén E 144 C2
Malléon F 146 A2
Mallersdorf-Pfaffenberg D 95 C4
Málles Venosta I 108 C1
Malling DK 59 B3
Mallnitz A 109 C4
Mallow IRL 29 B3
Mallwyd GB 38 B3
Malm N 199 A8
Malmbäck S 62 A2
Malmberget S 196 B3
Malmby S 56 A3
Malmédy B 80 B2
Malmesbury GB 43 A4
Malmköping S 56 A2
Malmö S 61 D3
Malmon S 54 B2
Malmslätt S 56 B1
Malnate I 120 B1
Malo I 121 B4
Małogoszcz PL 87 B4
Maloja CH 120 A2
Małomice PL 84 A3
Måløy N 198 D2
Malpartida E 155 B4
Malpartida de la Serena E 156 B2
Malpartida de Plasencia E 150 C1
Malpas
E 145 B4
GB 38 A4
Malpica P 155 B3
Malpica de Bergantiños E 140 A2
Malpica de Tajo E 150 C3
Malsch D 93 C4
Malšice CZ 96 B2
Malta A 109 C4
Maltat F 104 C2
Maltby GB 40 B2
Malung S 49 B5
Malungsfors S 49 B5
Maluszów PL 75 B4
Maluszyn PL 87 B3
Malva E 142 C1
Malvaglia CH 120 A1
Malveira P 154 C1
Malvik N 199 B7
Malyn UA 13 C8
Mamarrosa P 148 B1
Mamer L 92 B2
Mamers F 89 B4
Mamirolle F 105 B5
Mammendorf D 108 A2
Mámmola I 175 C2
Mamoiada I 178 B3
Mamonovo RUS 69 A4
Mamuras AL 182 B1
Maña SK 112 A2
Manacor E 167 B3
Manavgat TR 189 C6
Mancera de Abajo E 150 B2
Mancha Real E 163 A4
Manchester GB 40 B1
Manching D 95 C3
Manchita E 156 B1
Manciano I 168 A1
Manciet F 128 C3
Mandal N 52 B3
Mandanici I 177 A4
Mándas I 179 C3
Mandatoríccio I 174 B2
Mandayona E 151 B5
Mandelieu-la-Napoule F 132 B2
Mandello del Lário I 120 B2
Mandelsloh D 72 B2
Manderfeld B 80 B2
Manderscheid D 80 B2
Mandino Selo BIH 138 B3
Mandoudi GR 183 E5
Mandra GR 185 A4
Mandraki GR 188 C2
Mandúria I 173 B3
Mane
Alpes-de-Haute-Provence F 132 B1
Haute-Garonne F 145 A4
Manérbio I 120 B3
Mañeru E 144 B2
Manetin CZ 96 B1
Manfredónia I 171 B3
Mangalia RO 17 D8
Manganeses de la Lampreana E 149 A4
Manganeses de la Polvorosa E 141 B5
Mangen N 48 C3
Manger N 46 B2
Mangiennes F 92 B1
Mangotsfield GB 43 A4
Mångsbodarna S 49 A5
Mangualde P 148 B2
Maniago I 122 A1
Manilva E 162 B2
Manisa TR 186 D2
Manises E 159 B3
Mank A 110 A2
Månkarbo S 51 B4
Manlleu E 147 C3
Manna DK 58 A2
Männedorf CH 107 B3
Mannersdorf am Leithagebirge A 111 B3
Mannheim D 93 B4
Manningtree GB 45 B5
Manoppello I 169 A4
Manorbier GB 39 C2
Manorhamilton IRL 26 B2
Manosque F 132 B1
Manowo PL 67 B5
Manresa E 147 C2
Månsarp S 62 A2
Månsåsen S 199 B11
Manschnow D 74 B3
Mansfeld D 82 A3
Mansfield GB 40 B2
Mansilla de Burgos E 143 B3
Mansilla de las Mulas E 142 B1
Manskog S 55 A3
Mansle F 115 C4
Manso F 180 A1
Manteigas P 148 B2
Mantel D 95 B4
Mantes-la-Jolie F 90 C1
Mantes-la-Ville F 90 C1
Manthelan F 102 B2
Mantorp S 56 B1
Mántova I 121 B3
Mänttä FIN 8 A4
Mäntyjärvi FIN 197 C10
Manuel E 159 B3
Manyas TR 186 B2
Manzanal de Arriba E 141 B4
Manzanares E 157 A4
Manzanares el Real E 151 B4
Manzaneda
León E 141 B4
Orense E 141 B3
Manzanedo E 143 B3
Manzaneque E 157 A4
Manzanera E 153 B3
Manzanilla E 161 B3
Manzat F 116 B2
Manziana I 168 A2
Manziat F 117 A4
Maó E 167 B4
Maoča BIH 125 C4
Maqueda E 150 B3
Mara E 152 A2
Maramaraereğlisi TR 186 B2
Maraña E 142 A1
Maranchón E 152 A1
Maranello I 135 A3
Marano I 170 C2
Marano Lagunare I 122 B2
Marans F 114 B2
Maratea I 174 B1
Marateca P 154 C2
Marathokambos GR 188 B1
Marathonas GR 185 A4
Marathóvouno CY 181 A2
Marazion GB 42 B1
Marbach
Baden-Württemberg D 94 C1
Hessen D 82 B1
F 92 C2
Marbäck S 60 B3
Mårbacka S 55 A4
Marbella E 162 B3
Marboz F 118 A2
Marburg D 81 B4
Marcali H 111 C4
Marčana HR 122 C2
Marcaria I 121 B3
Marcelová SK 112 B2
Marcenat F 116 B2
March GB 41 C4
Marchamalo E 151 B4
Marchaux F 105 B5
Marche-en-Famenne B 79 B5
Marchegg A 111 A3
Marchena E 162 A2
Marchenoir F 103 B3
Marcheprime F 128 B2
Marciac F 128 C3
Marciana Marina I 134 C3
Marcianise I 170 B2
Marcigny F 117 A4
Marcilla E 144 B2
Marcillac-la-Croisille F 116 B2
Marcillac-Vallon F 130 A1
Marcillat-en-Combraille F 116 A2
Marcille-sur-Seine F 91 C3
Marcilloles F 118 B2
Marcilly-le-Hayer F 91 C3
Marcinkowice PL 75 A5
Marciszów PL 85 B4
Marck F 78 B1
Marckolsheim F 106 A2
Marco de Canevezes P 148 A1
Mårdsele S 200 B5
Mårdsjö S 200 C1
Mareham le Fen GB 41 B3
Marek S 62 A3
Marennes F 114 C2
Maresquel F 78 B1
Mareuil F 115 C4
Mareuil-en-Brie F 91 C3
Mareuil-sur-Arnon F 103 C4
Mareuil-sur-Lay F 114 B2
Mareuil-sur-Ourcq F 90 B3
Margam GB 39 C3
Margariti GR 182 D2
Margate GB 45 B5
Margaux F 128 A2
Margerie-Hancourt F 91 C4
Margès F 117 B5
Margherita di Savóia I 171 B4
Margita SRB 126 B3
Margone I 119 B4
Margonin PL 76 B2
Marguerittes F 131 B3
Margut F 91 B5
Maria E 164 B2
Mariager DK 58 B2
Mariana E 152 B1
Maria Neustift A 110 B1
Mariannelund S 62 A3
Marianópoli I 176 B2
Mariánské Lázně CZ 95 B4
Mariapfarr A 109 B4
Maria Saal A 110 C1
Mariazell A 110 B2
Maribo DK 65 B4
Maribor SLO 110 C2
Marieberg S 56 A1
Mariefred S 56 A3
Mariehamn FIN 51 B6
Marieholm S 61 D3
Mariembourg B 91 A4
Marienbaum D 80 A2
Marienberg D 83 B5
Marienheide D 81 A3
Mariental D 73 B3
Mariestad S 55 B4
Marieux F 90 A2
Marigliano I 170 C2
Marignane F 131 B4
Marigny
Jura F 105 C4
Manche F 88 A2
Marigny-le-Châtel F 91 C3
Marija Bistrica HR 124 A2
Marijampolė LT 13 A5
Marín E 140 B2
Marina HR 138 B2
Marina del Cantone I 170 C2
Marina di Acquappesa I 174 B1
Marina di Alberese I 168 A1
Marina di Amendolara I 174 B2
Marina di Árbus I 179 C2
Marina di Campo I 134 C3
Marina di Carrara I 134 A3
Marina di Castagneto-Donorático I 134 B3
Marina di Cécina I 134 B3
Marina di Gáiro I 179 C3
Marina di Ginosa I 173 B2
Marina di Gioiosa Iónica I 175 C2
Marina di Grosseto I 135 C3
Marina di Léuca I 173 C4
Marina di Massa I 134 A3
Marina di Noväglie I 173 C4
Marina di Pisa I 134 B3
Marina di Ragusa I 177 C3
Marina di Ravenna I 135 A5
Marina di Torre Grande I 179 C2
Marinaleda E 162 A3
Marina Romea I 135 A5
Marine de Sisco F 180 A2
Marinella I 176 B1
Marinella di Sarzana I 134 A3
Marineo I 176 B2
Marines F 90 B1
Maringues F 116 B3
Marinha das Ondas P 154 A2
Marinha Grande P 154 B2
Marinhas P 148 A1
Marino I 168 B2
Marjaliza E 157 A4
Markabygd N 199 B8
Markaryd S 61 C3
Markdorf D 107 B4
Markelo NL 71 B3
Market Deeping GB 40 C3
Market Drayton GB 38 B4
Market Harborough GB 40 C3
Markethill GB 27 B4
Market Rasen GB 40 B3
Market Warsop GB 40 B2
Market Weighton GB 40 B3
Markgröningen D 93 C5
Markhausen D 71 B4
Marki PL 77 B6
Markina-Xemein E 143 A4
Markinch GB 35 B4
Märkische Buchholz D 74 B2
Markitta S 196 B4
Markkleeberg D 83 A4
Marklohe D 72 B2
Marknesse NL 70 B2
Markneukirchen D 83 B4
Markopoulo GR 185 B4
Markovac
Srbija SRB 127 C3
Vojvodina SRB 126 B3
Markowice PL 86 B2
Markranstädt D 83 A4
Marksuhl D 82 B2
Markt Allhau A 111 B3
Markt Bibart D 94 B2
Marktbreit D 94 B2
Markt Erlbach D 94 B2
Markt-heidenfeld D 94 B1
Markt Indersdorf D 95 C3
Marktl D 95 C4
Marktleuthen D 83 B3
Marktoberdorf D 108 B1
Marktredwitz D 95 A4
Markt Rettenbach D 108 B1
Markt Schwaben D 108 A2
Markt-Übelbach A 110 B2
Markusica HR 125 B4
Markušovce SK 99 C4
Marl D 80 A3
Marlborough
Devon GB 42 B3
Wiltshire GB 44 B2
Marle F 91 B3
Marlieux F 117 A5
Marlow
D 66 B1
GB 44 B3
Marma S 51 B4
Marmagne F 104 C3
Marmande F 128 B3
Marmara TR 186 B2
Marmaris TR 188 C3
Marmelete P 160 B1
Marmolejo E 157 B3
Marmoutier F 93 C3
Marnay F 105 B4
Marne D 64 C2
Marnheim D 93 B4
Marnitz D 73 A4
Maroldsweisach D 82 B2
Marolles-les-Braults F 89 B4
Maromme F 89 A5
Marone I 120 B3
Maronia GR 183 C7
Maroslele H 126 A2
Maróstica I 121 B4
Marotta I 136 B2
Marpisa GR 185 B6
Marquion F 78 B3
Marquise F 78 B1
Marradi I 135 A4
Marrasjärvi FIN 197 C8
Marraskoski FIN 197 C8
Marratxi E 166 B2
Marrúbiu I 179 C2
Marrum NL 70 A2
Marrupe E 150 B3
Marsac F 129 C5
Marsac-en-Livradois F 117 B3
Marságlia I 120 C2
Marsala I 176 B1
Marsberg D 81 A4
Marsciano I 135 C5
Marseillan F 130 B2
Marseille = Marseilles F 131 B4
Marseille en Beauvaisis F 90 B1
Marseilles = Marseille F 131 B4
Mársico Nuovo I 172 B1
Marske-by-the-Sea GB 37 B5
Mars-la-Tours F 92 B1
Marsliden S 195 E6
Marson F 91 C4
Märsta S 57 A3
Marstal DK 65 B3
Marstrand S 60 B1
Marta I 168 A1
Martano I 173 B4
Martel F 129 B4
Martelange B 92 B1
Martfeld D 72 B2
Martfű H 113 B4
Martham GB 41 C5
Marthon F 115 C4
Martiago E 149 B3
Martigné-Briand F 102 B1
Martigné-Ferchaud F 101 B4
Martigne-sur-Mayenne F 102 A1
Martigny CH 119 A4
Martigny-les-Bains F 105 A4
Martigues F 131 B4
Martim-Longo P 160 B2
Martin SK 98 B2
Martina CH 108 C1
Martina Franca I 173 B3
Martinamor E 150 B2
Martin de la Jara E 162 A3
Martinengo I 120 B2
Martin Muñoz de las Posadas E 150 A3
Martinsberg A 97 C3
Martinšćica HR 123 C3
Martinshöhe D 93 B3
Martinsicuro I 136 C2
Martinszell D 107 B5
Mártis I 178 B2
Martofte DK 59 C3
Martonvásár H 112 B2
Martorell E 147 C2
Martos E 163 A4
Martres Tolosane F 146 A1
Martti FIN 197 B11
Marugán E 150 B3
Marúggio I 173 B3
Marvão P 155 B3
Marvejols F 130 A2
Marville F 92 B1
Marwałd PL 77 A4
Marykirk GB 35 B5
Marypark GB 32 D3
Maryport GB 36 B3
Marytavy GB 42 B2
Marzabotto I 135 A4
Marzahna D 74 C1
Marzahne D 73 B5
Marzamemi I 177 C4
Marzocca I 136 B2
Masa E 143 B3
Mas-Cabardès F 146 A3
Máscali I 177 B4
Mascaraque E 157 A4
Mascarenhas P 149 A2
Mascioni I 169 A3
Mas de Barberáns E 153 B4
Mas de las Matas E 153 B3
Masegoso E 158 C1
Masegoso de Tajuña E 151 B5
Masera I 119 A5
Masevaux F 106 B1
Masfjorden N 46 B2
Masham GB 37 B5
Masi N 192 C7
Maside E 140 B2
Maslacq F 144 A3
Maslinica HR 138 B2
Maşloc RO 126 B3
Maslovare BIH 138 A3
Masone I 133 A4
Massa I 134 A3
Massa Fiscáglia I 121 C5
Massafra I 173 B3
Massa Lombarda I 135 A4
Massa Lubrense I 170 C2
Massamagrell E 159 B3
Massa Maríttima I 135 B3
Massa Martana I 136 C1
Massanassa E 159 B3
Massarosa I 134 B3
Massat F 146 B2
Massay F 103 B3
Massbach D 82 B2
Masseret F 116 B1
Masseube F 145 A4
Massiac F 116 B3
Massignac F 115 C4
Massing D 95 C4
Massmechelen B 80 B1
Masterud N 49 B4
Mästocka S 61 C3
Masty BY 13 B6
Masúa I 179 C2
Masueco E 149 A3
Masugnsbyn S 196 B5
Mašun SLO 123 B3
Maszewo
Lubuskie PL 75 B3
Zachodnio-Pomorskie PL 75 A4
Mata de Alcántara E 155 B4
Matala GR 185 E5
Matalebreras E 144 C1
Matallana de Torio E 142 B1
Matamala E 151 A5
Mataporquera E 142 B2
Matapozuelos E 150 A3
Mataró E 147 C3
Matarocco I 176 B1
Matélica I 136 B2
Matera I 172 B2
Mátészalka H 16 B5
Matet E 159 B3
Matfors S 200 D3
Matha F 115 C3
Mathay F 106 B1
Matignon F 101 A3
Matilla de los Caños del Rio E 149 B4
Matlock GB 40 B2
Matosinhos P 148 A1
Matour F 117 A4
Mátrafüred H 113 B3
Mátraterenye H 113 A3
Matre
Hordaland N 46 B2
Hordaland N 52 A1
Matrei am Brenner A 108 B2
Matrei in Osttirol A 109 B3
Matrice I 170 B2
Matsdal S 195 E6
Mattarello I 121 A4
Mattersburg A 111 B3
Mattighofen A 109 A4
Mattinata I 171 B4
Mattos P 154 B2
Mattsee A 109 B4
Mattsmyra S 50 A2
Måttsund S 196 D5
Matulji HR 123 B3
Maubert-Fontaine F 91 B4
Maubeuge F 79 B3
Maubourguet F 145 A4
Mauchline GB 36 A2
Maud GB 33 D4
Mauer-kirchen A 109 A4
Mauern D 95 C3
Mauguio F 131 B3
Maulbronn D 93 C4
Maule F 90 C1
Mauléon F 114 B3
Mauléon-Barousse F 145 B4
Mauléon-Licharre F 144 A3
Maulévrier F 114 A3
Maum IRL 28 A2
Maurach A 108 B2
Maure-de-Bretagne F 101 B4
Maureilhan F 130 B2
Măureni RO 126 B3
Mauriac F 116 B2
Mauron F 101 A3
Maurs F 116 C2
Maury F 146 B3
Maussane-les-Alpilles F 131 B3
Mautern A 97 C3
Mauterndorf A 109 B4
Mautern im Steiermark A 110 B1
Mauthausen A 110 A1
Mauthen A 109 C3
Mauvezin F 129 C3

Mauzé-sur-le-Mignon F 114 B3
Maxent F 101 B3
Maxey-sur-Vaise F 92 C1
Maxial P 154 B1
Maxieira P 154 B2
Maxwellheugh GB 35 C5
Mayalde E 149 A4
Maybole GB 36 A2
Mayen D 80 B3
Mayenne F 88 B3
Mayet F 102 B2
Mayorga E 142 B1
Mayres F 117 C4
Mayrhofen A 108 B2
Mazagón E 161 B3
Mazaleón E 153 A4
Mazamet F 130 B1
Mazan F 131 A4
Mazara del Vallo I 176 B1
Mazarambroz E 157 A3
Mazarete E 152 B1
Mazaricos E 140 B2
Mazarrón E 165 B3
Mažeikiai LT 8 D3
Mazères F 146 A2
Mazères-sur-Salat F 145 A4
Mazières-en-Gâtine F 115 B3
Mazin HR 138 A1
Mazuelo E 143 B3
Mazyr BY 13 B8
Mazzarino I 177 B3
Mazzarrà Sant'Andrea I 177 A4
Mazzo di Valtellina I 120 A3
Mdzewo PL 77 B5
Mealabost GB 31 A2
Mealhada P 148 B1
Méan B 79 B5
Meana Sardo I 179 C3
Meaulne F 103 C4
Meaux F 90 C2
Mebonden N 199 B8
Mecerreyes E 143 B3
Mechelen B 79 A4
Mechernich D 80 B2
Mechnica PL 86 B2
Mechowo PL 67 C4
Mechterstädt D 82 B2
Mecidiye TR 186 B1
Mecikal PL 68 B2
Mecina-Bombarón E 164 C1
Mecitözü TR 23 A8
Meckenbeuren D 107 B4
Meckenheim
Rheinland-Pfalz D 80 B3
Rheinland-Pfalz D 93 B4
Meckesheim D 93 B4
Mecseknádasd H 125 A4
Meda
I 120 B2
P 149 B2
Medak HR 137 A4
Mede I 120 B1
Medebach D 81 A4
Medelim P 155 A3
Medemblik NL 70 B2
Medena Selista BIH 138 A2
Medesano I 120 C3
Medevi S 55 B5
Medgidia RO 17 C8
Medgyesháza H 113 C5
Medhamn S 55 A4
Mediaş RO 17 B6
Medicina I 135 A4
Medinaceli E 152 A1
Medina de las Torres E 155 C4
Medina del Campo E 150 A3
Medina de Pomar E 143 B3
Medina de Rioseco E 142 C1
Medina Sidonia E 162 B2
Medinilla E 150 B2
Medja SRB 126 B2
Medjedja BIH 139 B5
Medulin HR 122 C2
Meduno I 122 A1
Medveda SRB 127 C3
Medvedov SK 111 B4
Medvezhyegorsk RUS 9 A9
Medvide HR 137 A4
Medvode SLO 123 A3
Medzev SK 99 C4
Medzitlija MK 182 C3
Meerane D 83 B4
Meerle B 79 A4
Meersburg D 107 B4
Meeuwen B 79 A5
Megalo Horio GR 188 C2
Megalopoli GR 184 B3
Megara GR 185 A4
Megève F 118 B3
Meggenhofen A 109 A4
Megra RUS 9 B10
Megyaszó H 113 A5
Mehamn N 193 A11
Mehedeby S 51 B4
Méhkerék H 113 C5
Mehun-sur-Yèvre F 103 B4
Meigle GB 35 B4
Meijel NL 80 A1
Meilen CH 107 B3
Meilhan F 128 C2
Meimôa P 149 B2
Meina I 119 B5
Meine D 73 B3
Meinersen D 72 B3
Meinerzhagen D 81 A3
Meiningen D 82 B2
Meira E 141 A3
Meiringen CH 106 C3
Meisenheim D 93 B3
Meissen D 83 A5
Meitingen D 94 C2
Meix-devant-Virton B 92 B1
Męka PL 86 A2
Meka Gruda BIH 139 B4
Mel I 121 A5
Melbu N 194 B5
Melč CZ 98 B1
Meldal N 198 B6
Méldola I 135 A5
Meldorf D 64 B2
Melegnano I 120 B2
Melenci SRB 126 B2
Melendugno I 173 B4
Melfi I 172 B1
Melfjordbotn N 195 D4
Melgaço P 140 B2
Melgar de Arriba E 142 B1
Melgar de Fernamental E 142 B2
Melgar de Yuso E 142 B2
Melhus N 199 B7
Meliana E 159 B3
Melide
CH 120 B1
E 140 B2
Melides P 160 A1
Meligales GR 184 B2
Melilli I 177 B4
Melinovac HR 124 C1
Melisenda I 179 C3
Melisey F 105 B5
Mélito di Porto Salvo I 175 D1
Melk A 110 A2
Melksham GB 43 A4
Mellakoski FIN 196 C7
Mellanström S 195 E9
Mellbystrand S 61 C2
Melle
B 79 A3
D 71 B5
F 115 B3
Mellendorf D 72 B2
Mellerud S 54 B3
Mellieha M 175 C3
Mellösa S 56 A2
Mellrichstadt D 82 B2
Mělnické Vtelno CZ 84 B2
Mělník CZ 84 B2
Melón E 140 B2
Melrose GB 35 C5
Mels CH 107 B4
Melsungen D 82 A1
Meltaus FIN 197 C8
Meltham GB 40 B2
Melton Mowbray GB 40 C3
Meltosjärvi FIN 196 C7
Melun F 90 C2
Melvaig GB 31 B3
Melvich GB 32 C3
Mélykút H 126 A1
Melzo I 120 B2
Memaliaj AL 182 C1
Membrilla E 157 B4
Membrio E 155 B3
Memer F 129 B4
Memmelsdorf D 94 B2
Memmingen D 107 B5
Memoria P 154 B2
Menággio I 120 A2
Menai Bridge GB 38 A2
Menasalbas E 157 A3
Menat F 116 A2
Mendavia E 144 B1
Mendaza E 144 B1
Mende F 130 A2
Menden D 81 A3
Menderes TR 188 A2
Mendig D 80 B3
Mendiga P 154 B2
Mendrisio CH 120 B1
Ménéac F 101 A3
Menemen TR 188 A2
Menen B 78 B3
Menesjärvi FIN 193 D10
Menetou-Salon F 103 B4
Menfi I 176 B1
Ménfőcsanak H 111 B4
Mengamuñoz E 150 B3
Mengen
D 107 A4
TR 187 B7
Mengeš SLO 123 A3
Mengibar E 157 C4
Mengkofen D 95 C4
Menou F 104 B2
Mens F 118 C2
Menslage D 71 B4
Mensträsk S 200 A5
Mentana I 168 A2
Menton F 133 B3
Méntrida E 151 B3
Méobecq F 115 B5
Méounes-les-Montrieux F 132 B1
Meppel NL 70 B3
Meppen D 71 B4
Mequinenza E 153 A4
Mer F 103 B3
Mera
Coruña E 140 A2
Coruña E 140 A3
Meråker N 199 B8
Merano I 108 C2
Merate I 120 B2
Mercadillo E 143 A3
Mercatale I 135 B5
Mercatino Conca I 136 B1
Mercato San Severino I 170 C2
Mercato Saraceno I 135 B5
Merching D 108 A1
Merchtem B 79 B4
Merdrignac F 101 A3
Merdžanići BIH 139 B3
Meré E 142 A2
Mere GB 43 A4
Meréville F 90 C2
Merfeld D 80 A3
Méribel F 118 B3
Méribel Motraret F 118 B3
Meriç TR 186 A1
Mérida E 155 C4
Mérignac F 128 B2
Měřín CZ 97 B3
Mering D 94 C2
Merkendorf D 94 B2
Merklin CZ 96 B1
Merksplas B 79 A4
Merlånna S 56 A2
Merlimont Plage F 78 B1
Mern DK 65 A5
Mernye H 111 C4
Mersch L 92 B2
Merseburg D 83 A3
Mers-les-Bains F 90 A1
Merthyr Tydfil GB 39 C3
Mertingen D 94 C2
Mértola P 160 B2
Méru F 90 B2
Merufe P 140 B2
Mervans F 105 C4
Merville F 78 B2
Méry-sur-Seine F 91 C3
Merzen D 71 B4
Merzifon TR 23 A8
Merzig D 92 B2
Mesagne I 173 B3
Mesão Frio P 148 A2
Mesas de Ibor E 156 A2
Meschede D 81 A4
Meschers-sur-Gironde F 114 C3
Meslay-du-Maine F 102 B1
Mesna N 48 A2
Mesnalien N 48 A2
Mesocco CH 120 A2
Mésola I 122 C1
Mesologi GR 184 A2
Mesopotamo GR 182 D2
Mesoraca I 175 B2
Messac F 101 B4
Messancy B 92 B1
Messdorf D 73 B4
Messei F 88 B3
Messejana P 160 B1
Messelt N 48 A3
Messina I 177 A4
Messingen D 71 B4
Messini GR 184 B3
Messkirch D 107 B4
Messlingen S 199 C9
Messtetten D 107 A3
Mesta GR 185 A6
Mestanza E 157 B3
Městec Králové CZ 84 B3
Mestlin D 73 A4
Město Albrechtice CZ 85 B5
Město Libavá CZ 98 B1
Město Touškov CZ 96 B1
Mestre I 122 B1
Mesvres F 104 C3
Mesztegnyő H 111 C4
Meta I 170 C2
Metajna HR 137 A4
Metelen D 71 B4
Methana GR 185 B4
Methlick GB 33 D4
Methven GB 35 B4
Methwold GB 41 C4
Metković HR 139 B3
Metlika SLO 123 B4
Metnitz A 110 C1
Metsäkylä FIN 197 D11
Metslawier NL 70 A3
Metsovo GR 182 D3
Metten D 95 C4
Mettendorf D 92 B2
Mettet B 79 B4
Mettingen D 71 B4
Mettlach D 92 B2
Mettlen CH 106 C2
Mettmann D 80 A2
Metz F 92 B2
Metzervisse F 92 B2
Metzingen D 94 C1
Meulan F 90 B1
Meung-sur-Loire F 103 B3
Meuselwitz D 83 A4
Meuzac F 115 C5
Mevagissey GB 42 B2
Mexborough GB 40 B2
Meximieux F 118 B2
Mey GB 32 C3
Meyenburg D 73 A5
Meyerhöfen D 71 B5
Meylan F 118 B2
Meymac F 116 B2
Meyrargues F 132 B1
Meyrueis F 130 A2
Meyssac F 129 A4
Meysse F 117 C4
Meyzieu F 117 B4
Mèze F 130 B2
Mézériat F 117 A5
Mežica SLO 110 C1
Mézidon-Canon F 89 A3
Mézières-en-Brenne F 115 B5
Mézières-sur-Issoire F 115 B4
Mézilhac F 117 C4
Mézilles F 104 B2
Mézin F 128 B3
Mezőberény H 113 C5
Mezőcsát H 113 B4
Mezőfalva H 112 C2
Mezőhegyes H 126 A2
Mezőkeresztes H 113 B4
Mezőkomárom H 112 C2
Mezőkövácsháza H 113 C4
Mezőkövesd H 113 B4
Mezőörs H 111 B4
Mézos F 128 B1
Mezőszilas H 112 C2
Mezőtúr H 113 B4
Mezquita de Jarque E 153 B3
Mezzano
Emilia Romagna I 135 A5
Trentino Alto Adige I 121 A4
Mezzojuso I 176 B2
Mezzoldo I 120 A2
Mezzolombardo I 121 A4
Mgarr M 175 C3
Miajadas E 156 A2
Miały PL 75 B5
Mianowice PL 68 A2
Miasteczko Krajeńskie PL 76 A2
Miasteczko Śl. PL 86 B2
Miastko PL 68 A1
Michalovce SK 12 D4
Michałowice PL 87 B3
Michelau D 94 B2
Michelbach D 94 B2
Micheldorf A 110 B1
Michelhausen A 110 A2
Michelsneukirchen D 95 B4
Michelstadt D 93 B5
Michendorf D 74 B2
Mickleover GB 40 C2
Midbea GB 33 B4
Middelburg NL 79 A3
Middelfart DK 59 C2
Middelharnis NL 79 A4
Middelkerke B 78 A2
Middelstum NL 71 A3
Middlesbrough GB 37 B5
Middleton Cheney GB 44 A2
Middleton-in-Teesdale GB 37 B4
Middletown GB 27 B4
Middlewich GB 38 A4
Middlezoy GB 43 A4
Midhurst GB 44 C3
Midleton IRL 29 C3
Midlum D 64 C1
Midsomer Norton GB 43 A4
Midtgulen N 198 D2
Midtskogberget N 49 A4
Midwolda NL 71 A4
Mid Yell GB 33 A5
Miechów PL 87 B4
Miedes de Aragón E 152 A2
Miedes de Atienza E 151 A4
Międzybodzie Bielskie PL 99 B3
Międzybórz PL 85 A5
Międzychód PL 75 B4
Międzylesie PL 85 B4
Międzyrzec Podlaski PL 12 C5
Międzyrzecz PL 75 B4
Międzywodzie PL 67 B3
Międzyzdroje PL 67 C3
Miejska Górka PL 85 A4
Miélan F 145 A4
Mielec PL 87 B5
Mielęcin PL 75 A3
Mielno
Warmińsko-Mazurskie PL 77 A5
Zachodnio-Pomorskie PL 67 B5
Miengo E 143 A3
Mieraslompolo FIN 193 C11
Miercurea Ciuc RO 17 B6
Mieres
Asturias E 141 A5
Girona E 147 B3
Mieroszów PL 85 B4
Mierzyn PL 86 A3
Miesau D 93 B3
Miesbach D 108 B2
Mieścisko PL 76 B2
Mieste D 73 B4
Miesterhorst D 73 B4
Mieszków PL 76 B2
Mieszkowice PL 74 B3
Mietków PL 85 B4
Migennes F 104 B2
Miggiano I 173 C4
Migliánico I 169 A4
Migliarino I 121 C4
Migliónico I 172 B2
Mignano Monte Lungo I 169 B3
Migné F 115 B5
Miguel Esteban E 157 A4
Miguelturra E 157 B4
Mihajlovac SRB 127 C2
Miháld H 111 C4
Mihalgazi TR 187 B5
Mihaliççık TR 187 C6
Mihályi H 111 B4
Mihla D 82 A2
Mihohnić HR 123 B3
Miholjsko HR 123 B4
Mihovljan HR 124 A1
Mijares E 150 B3
Mijas E 163 B3
Mike H 124 A3
Mikines GR 184 B3
Mikkeli FIN 8 B5
Mikkelvik N 192 B3
Mikleuš HR 125 B3
Mikołajki Pomorskie PL 69 B4
Mikołów PL 86 B2
Mikonos GR 185 B6
Mikorzyn PL 86 A2
Mikro Derio GR 183 B8
Mikstat PL 86 A1
Mikulášovice CZ 84 B2
Mikulov CZ 97 C4
Mikulovice CZ 85 B5
Milagro E 144 B2
Miłakowo PL 69 A5
Milan = Milano I 120 B2
Miland N 47 C5
Milano = Milan I 120 B2
Milano Marittima I 135 A5
Milas TR 188 B2
Milazzo I 177 A4
Mildenhall GB 45 A4
Milejewo PL 69 A4
Milelín CZ 85 B3
Miletić SRB 125 B5
Miletićevo SRB 126 B3
Mileto I 175 C2
Milevsko CZ 96 B2
Milford IRL 26 A3
Milford Haven GB 39 C1
Milford on Sea GB 44 C2
Milhão P 149 A3
Milići BIH 139 A5
Miličin CZ 96 B2
Milicz PL 85 A5
Milín CZ 96 B2
Militello in Val di Catánia I 177 B3
Miljevina BIH 139 B4
Milkowice PL 85 A4
Millançay F 103 B3
Millares E 159 B3
Millas F 146 B3
Millau F 130 A2
Millesimo I 133 A4
Millevaches F 116 B2
Millom GB 36 B3
Millport GB 34 C3
Millstatt A 109 C4
Millstreet
Cork IRL 29 B2
Waterford IRL 29 B4
Milltown
Galway IRL 28 A3
Kerry IRL 29 B1
Milltown Malbay IRL 28 B2
Milly-la-Forêt F 90 C2
Milmarcos E 152 A2
Milmersdorf D 74 A2
Milna HR 138 B2
Milnthorpe GB 37 B4
Milogórze PL 69 A5
Miłomłyn PL 69 B4
Milos GR 185 C5
Miloševo SRB 127 C3
Miłosław PL 76 B2
Milot AL 182 B1
Milówka PL 99 B3
Miltach D 95 B4
Miltenberg D 94 B1
Milton Keynes GB 44 A3
Miltzow D 66 B2
Milverton GB 43 A3
Milzyn PL 76 B3
Mimice HR 138 B2
Mimizan F 128 B1
Mimizan-Plage F 128 B1
Mimoň CZ 84 B2
Mina de Juliana P 160 B1
Mina de São Domingos P 160 B2
Minas de Riotinto E 161 B3
Minateda E 158 C2
Minaya E 158 B1
Minde P 154 B2
Mindelheim D 108 A1
Mindelstetten D 95 C3
Minden D 72 B1
Mindszent H 113 C4
Minehead GB 43 A3
Mineo I 177 B3
Minerbe I 121 B4
Minérbio I 121 C4
Minervino Murge I 171 B4
Minglanilla E 158 B2
Mingorria E 150 B3
Minnesund N 48 B3
Miño E 140 A2
Miño de San Esteban E 151 A4
Minsen D 71 A4
Minsk BY 13 B7
Mińsk Mazowiecki PL 12 B4
Minsterley GB 39 B4
Mintlaw GB 33 D4
Minturno I 169 B3
Mionica
BIH 125 C4
SRB 127 C2
Mios F 128 B2
Mira
E 158 B2
I 121 B5
P 148 B1
Mirabel E 155 B4
Mirabel-aux-Baronnies F 131 A4
Mirabella Eclano I 170 B3
Mirabella Imbáccari I 177 B3
Mirabello I 121 C4
Miradoux F 129 B3
Miraflores de la Sierra E 151 B4
Miralrio E 151 B5
Miramar P 148 A1
Miramare I 136 A1
Miramas F 131 B3
Mirambeau F 114 C3
Miramont-de-Guyenne F 129 B3
Miranda de Arga E 144 B2
Miranda de Ebro E 143 B4
Miranda do Corvo P 148 B1
Miranda do Douro P 149 A3
Mirande F 129 C3
Mirandela P 149 A2
Mirandilla E 155 C4
Mirándola I 121 C4
Miranje HR 137 A4
Mirano I 121 B5
Miras AL 182 C2
Miravet E 153 A4
Miré F 102 B1
Mirebeau F 102 C2
Mirebeau-sur-Bèze F 105 B4
Mirecourt F 105 A5
Mirepoix F 146 A2
Mires GR 185 D5
Miribel F 117 B4
Miričina BIH 125 C4
Mirina GR 183 D7
Mirna SLO 123 B4
Miroslav CZ 97 C4
Mirosławice PL 85 B4
Mirosławiec PL 75 A5
Mirošov CZ 96 B1
Mirotice CZ 96 B2
Mirovice CZ 96 B2
Mirow D 74 A1
Mirsk PL 84 B3
Mirzec PL 87 A5
Misi FIN 197 C9
Misilmeri I 176 A2
Miske H 112 C3
Miskolc H 113 A4
Mislinja SLO 110 C2
Missanello I 174 A2
Missillac F 101 B3
Mistelbach
A 97 C4
D 95 B3
Misten N 194 C5
Misterbianco I 177 B4
Misterhult S 62 A4
Mistretta I 177 B3
Misurina I 109 C3
Mitchelstown IRL 29 B3
Mithimna GR 186 C1
Mithoni GR 184 C2
Mitilini GR 186 C1
Mitilinii GR 188 B1
Mittelberg
Tirol A 108 C1
Vorarlberg A 107 B5
Mittenwald D 108 B2
Mittenwalde D 74 B2
Mitterback A 110 B2

Mitterdorf im Mürztal A 110 B2
Mitter-Kleinarl A 109 B4
Mittersheim F 92 C2
Mittersill A 109 B3
Mitterskirchen D 95 C4
Mitterteich D 95 B4
Mitton F 128 B2
Mittweida D 83 B4
Mitwitz D 82 B3
Mizhhir'ya UA 13 D5
Mjällby S 63 B2
Mjåvatn N 53 B4
Mjöbäck S 60 B2
Mjölby S 56 B1
Mjølfjell N 46 B3
Mjøndalen N 53 A6
Mjørlund N 48 B2
Mladá Boleslav CZ 84 B2
Mladá Vožice CZ 96 B2
Mladé Buky CZ 85 B3
Mladenovac SRB 127 C2
Mladenovo SRB 126 B1
Mladikovine BIH 139 A3
Mława PL 77 A5
Mlinište BIH 138 A2
Młodzieszyn PL 77 B5
Młogoszyn PL 77 B4
Młynary PL 69 A4
Mnichóvice CZ 96 B2
Mnichovo Hradiště CZ 84 B2
Mniów PL 87 A4
Mnisek nad Hnilcom SK 99 C4
Mníšek pod Brdy CZ 96 B2
Mniszek PL 87 A4
Mniszków PL 87 A4
Mo
Hedmark N 48 B3
Hordaland N 46 B2
Møre og Romsdal N 198 C5
Telemark N 53 A3
Gävleborg S 51 A3
Västra Götaland S 54 B2
Moaña E 140 B2
Moate IRL 28 A4
Mocejón E 151 C4
Močenok SK 111 A4
Mochales E 152 A1
Mochowo PL 77 B4
Mochy PL 75 B5
Mockern D 73 B4
Mockfjärd S 50 B1
Möckmühl D 94 B1
Mockrehna D 83 A4
Moclin E 163 A4
Mocsa H 112 B2
Möcsény H 125 A4
Modane F 118 B3
Modbury GB 42 B3
Módena I 121 C3
Módica I 177 C3
Modigliana I 135 A4
Modlin PL 77 B5
Mödling A 111 A3
Modliszewice PL 87 A4
Modliszewko PL 76 B2
Modogno I 171 B4
Modra SK 98 C1
Modran BIH 125 C3
Modriča BIH 125 C4
Möðrudalur IS 191 B10
Modrý Kamen SK 99 C3
Moëlan-sur-Mer F 100 B2
Moelfre GB 38 A2
Moelv N 48 B2
Moen N 194 A9
Moena I 121 A4
Moerbeke B 79 A3
Moers D 80 A2
Móes P 148 B2
Moffat GB 36 A3
Mogadouro P 149 A3
Mogata S 56 B2
Móggio Udinese I 122 A2
Mogielnica PL 87 A4
Mogilany PL 99 B3
Mogilno PL 76 B2
Mogliano I 136 B2
Mogliano Véneto I 122 B1
Mogor E 140 B2
Mógoro I 179 C2
Moguer E 161 B3
Mohács H 125 B4
Moheda S 62 A2
Mohedas E 149 B3
Mohedas de la Jara E 156 A2
Mohelnice CZ 97 B4
Mohill IRL 26 C3
Möhlin CH 106 B2
Moholm S 55 B5
Mohorn D 83 A5
Mohyliv-Podil's'kyy UA 13 D7
Moi N 52 B2
Moià E 147 C3
Móie I 136 B2
Moimenta da Beira P 148 B2
Mo i Rana N 195 D5
Moirans F 118 B2
Moirans-en-Montagne F 118 A2
Moisaküla EST 8 C4
Moisdon-la-Rivière F 101 B4
Moissac F 129 B4
Moita
Coimbra P 148 B1
Guarda P 149 B2
Santarém P 154 B2
Setúbal P 154 C1
Moita dos Ferreiros P 154 B1
Moixent E 159 C3
Mojacar E 164 B3
Mojados E 150 A3
Mojmírovce SK 112 A2
Mojtin SK 98 C2
Möklinta S 50 B3
Mokošica HR 139 C4
Mokronog SLO 123 B4
Mokro Polje HR 138 A2
Mokrzyska PL 99 A4
Møkster N 46 B2
Mol
B 79 A5
SRB 126 B2
Mola di Bari I 173 A3
Molai GR 184 C3
Molare I 133 A4
Molaretto I 119 B4
Molas F 145 A4
Molassano I 134 A1
Molbergen D 71 B4
Mold GB 38 A3
Molde N 198 C4
Møldrup DK 58 B2
Moledo do Minho P 148 A1
Molfetta I 171 B4
Molfsee D 64 B3
Moliden S 200 C4
Molières F 129 B4
Molina de Aragón E 152 B2
Molina de Segura E 165 A3
Molinar E 143 A3
Molinaseca E 141 B4
Molinella I 121 C4
Molinet F 104 C2
Molinicos E 158 C1
Molini di Tures I 108 C2
Molinos de Duero E 143 C4
Molins de Rei E 147 C3
Moliterno I 174 A1
Molkom S 55 A4
Möllbrücke A 109 C4
Mölle S 61 C2
Molledo E 142 A2
Möllenbeck D 74 A2
Mollerussa E 147 C1
Mollet de Perelada E 146 B3
Mollina E 163 A3
Mölln D 73 A3
Molló E 146 B3
Mollösund S 54 B2
Mölltorp S 55 B5
Mölnbo S 56 A3
Mölndal S 60 B2
Mölnlycke S 60 B2
Molompize F 116 B3
Moloy F 105 B3
Molsheim F 93 C3
Moltzow D 73 A5
Molve HR 124 A3
Molveno I 121 A3
Molvizar E 163 B4
Molzbichl A 109 C4
Mombaróccio I 136 B1
Mombeltrán E 150 B2
Mombris D 93 A5
Mombuey E 141 B4
Momchilgrad BG 183 B7
Mommark DK 64 B3
Momo I 119 B5
Monaghan IRL 27 B4
Monar Lodge GB 32 D2
Monasterace Marina I 175 C2
Monasterevin IRL 30 A1
Monasterio de Rodilla E 143 B3
Monastir I 179 C3
Monbahus F 129 B3
Monbazillac F 129 B3
Moncada E 159 B3
Moncalieri I 119 B4
Moncalvo I 119 B5
Monção P 140 B2
Moncarapacho P 160 B2
Moncel-sur-Seille F 92 C2
Monchegorsk RUS 3 C13
Mönchengladbach = Munchen-Gladbach D 80 A2
Mónchio della Corti I 134 A3
Monchique P 160 B1
Monclar-de-Quercy F 129 C4
Moncofa E 159 B3
Moncontour F 101 A3
Moncoutant F 114 B3
Monda E 162 B3
Mondariz E 140 B2
Mondavio I 136 B1
Mondéjar E 151 B4
Mondello I 176 A2
Mondim de Basto P 148 A2
Mondolfo I 136 B2
Mondoñedo E 141 A3
Mondorf-les-Bains L 92 B2
Mondoubleau F 102 B2
Mondovì I 133 A3
Mondragon F 131 A3
Mondragone I 170 B1
Mondsee A 109 B4
Monéglia I 134 A2
Monegrillo E 153 A3
Monein F 145 A3
Monemvasia GR 184 C4
Mónesi I 133 A3
Monesiglio I 133 A4
Monesterio E 161 A3
Monestier-de-Clermont F 118 C2
Monestiés F 130 A1
Monéteau F 104 B2
Moneygall IRL 28 B4
Moneymore GB 27 B4
Monfalcone I 122 B2
Monfero E 140 A2
Monflanquin F 129 B3
Monflorite E 145 B3
Monforte P 155 B3
Monforte da Beira
E 155 B3
P 155 B3
Monforte d'Alba I 133 A3
Monforte del Cid E 165 A4
Monforte de Lemos E 140 B3
Monforte de Moyuela E 152 A2
Monghidoro I 135 A4
Mongiana I 175 C2
Monguelfo I 108 C3
Monheim D 94 C2
Moniaive GB 36 A3
Monifieth GB 35 B5
Monikie GB 35 B5
Monistrol-d'Allier F 117 C3
Monistrol de Montserrat E 147 C2
Monistrol-sur-Loire F 117 B4
Mönkebude D 74 A2
Monkton GB 36 A2
Monmouth GB 39 C4
Monnaie F 102 B2
Monnerville F 90 C2
Monnickendam NL 70 B2
Monolithos GR 188 C2
Monópoli I 173 B3
Monor H 112 B3
Monóvar E 159 C3
Monpazier F 129 B3
Monreal
D 80 B3
E 144 B2
Monreal del Campo E 152 B2
Monreale I 176 A2
Monroy E 155 B4
Monroyo E 153 B3
Mons B 79 B3
Monsaraz P 155 C3
Monschau D 80 B2
Monségur F 128 B3
Monsélice I 121 B4
Mønshaug N 46 B3
Monster NL 70 B1
Mönsterås S 62 A4
Monsummano Terme I 135 B3
Montabaur D 81 B3
Montafia I 119 C5
Montagnac F 130 B2
Montagnana I 121 B4
Montaigu F 114 B2
Montaigu-de-Quercy F 129 B4
Montaiguët-en-Forez F 117 A3
Montaigut F 116 A2
Montaigut-sur-Save F 129 C4
Montainville F 90 C1
Montalbán E 153 B3
Montalbán de Córdoba E 163 A3
Montalbano Elicona I 177 A4
Montalbano Iónico I 174 A2
Montalbo E 158 B1
Montalcino I 135 B4
Montaldo di Cósola I 120 C2
Montalegre P 148 A2
Montalieu-Vercieu F 118 B2
Montalivet-les-Bains F 114 C2
Montallegro I 176 B2
Montalto delle Marche I 136 C2
Montalto di Castro I 168 A1
Montalto Pavese I 120 C2
Montalto Uffugo I 174 B2
Montalvão P 155 B3
Montamarta E 149 A4
Montana BG 17 D5
Montana-Vermala CH 119 A4
Montánchez E 156 A1
Montanejos E 153 B3
Montano Antilia I 172 B1
Montans F 129 C4
Montargil P 154 B2
Montargis F 103 B4
Montastruc-la-Conseillère F 129 C4
Montauban F 129 B4
Montauban-de-Bretagne F 101 A3
Montbard F 104 B3
Montbarrey F 105 B4
Montbazens F 130 A1
Montbazon F 102 B2
Montbéliard F 106 B1
Montbenoit F 105 C5
Montbeugny F 104 C2
Montblanc E 147 C2
Montbozon F 105 B5
Montbrison F 117 B4
Montbron F 115 C4
Montbrun-les-Bains F 131 A4
Montceau-les-Mines F 104 C3
Montcenis F 104 C3
Montchanin F 104 C3
Montcornet F 91 B4
Montcuq F 129 B4
Montdardier F 130 B2
Mont-de-Marsan F 128 C2
Montdidier F 90 B2
Monteagudo E 165 A3
Monteagudo de las Vicarias E 152 A1
Montealegre E 142 C2
Montealegre del Castillo E 159 C2
Montebello Iónico I 175 D1
Montebello Vicentino I 121 B4
Montebelluna I 121 B5
Montebourg F 88 A2
Montebruno I 134 A2
Monte-Carlo MC 133 B3
Montecarotto I 136 B2
Montecassiano I 136 B2
Montecastrilli I 168 A2
Montecatini Terme I 135 B3
Montécchio I 136 B1
Montécchio Emilia I 121 C3
Montécchio Maggiore I 121 B4
Montech F 129 C4
Montechiaro d'Asti I 119 B5
Monte Clara P 155 B3
Monte Clérigo P 160 B1
Montecórice I 170 C2
Montecorvino Rovella I 170 C2
Monte da Pedra P 155 B3
Monte de Goula P 155 B3
Montederramo E 141 B3
Montedoro I 176 B2
Monte do Trigo P 155 C3
Montefalco I 136 C1
Montefalcone di Val Fortore I 170 B3
Montefalcone nel Sánnio I 170 B2
Montefano I 136 B2
Montefiascone I 168 A2
Montefiorino I 134 A3
Montefortino I 136 C2
Montefranco I 168 A2
Montefrío E 163 A4
Montegiordano Marina I 174 A2
Montegiórgio I 136 B2
Monte Gordo P 160 B2
Montegranaro I 136 B2
Montehermoso E 149 B3
Montejicar E 163 A4
Montejo de la Sierra E 151 A4
Montejo de Tiermes E 151 A4
Monte Juntos P 155 C3
Montel-de-Gelat F 116 B2
Monteleone di Púglia I 171 B3
Monteleone di Spoleto I 169 A2
Monteleone d'Orvieto I 135 C5
Montelepre I 176 A2
Montelibretti I 168 A2
Montelier F 117 C5
Montélimar F 131 A3
Montella
E 146 B2
I 170 C3
Montellano E 162 A2
Montelupo Fiorentino I 135 B4
Montemaggiore Belsito I 176 B2
Montemagno I 119 C5
Montemayor E 163 A3
Montemayor de Pinilla E 150 A3
Montemésola I 173 B3
Montemilleto I 170 B2
Montemilone I 172 A1
Montemolin E 161 A3
Montemónaco I 136 C2
Montemor-o-Novo P 154 C2
Montemor-o-Velho P 148 B1
Montemurro I 174 A1
Montendre F 128 A2
Montenegro de Cameros E 143 B4
Montenero di Bisáccia I 170 B2
Monteneuf F 101 B3
Monteparano I 173 B3
Montepescali I 135 C4
Montepiano I 135 A4
Monte Porzio I 136 B2
Montepulciano I 135 B4
Monte Real P 154 B2
Montereale I 169 A3
Montereale Valcellina I 122 A1
Montereau-Faut-Yonne F 90 C2
Monte Redondo P 154 B2
Monterénzio I 135 A4
Monte Romano I 168 A1
Monteroni d'Arbia I 135 B4
Monteroni di Lecce I 173 B4
Monterosso al Mare I 134 A2
Monterosso Almo I 177 B3
Monterosso Grana I 133 A3
Monterotondo I 168 A2
Monterotondo Maríttimo I 135 B3
Monterrey E 141 C3
Monterroso E 140 B3
Monterrubio de la Serena E 156 B2
Monterubbiano I 136 B2
Montesa E 159 C3
Montesalgueiro E 140 A2
Monte San Giovanni Campano I 169 B3
Montesano sulla Marcellana I 174 A1
Monte San Savino I 135 B4
Monte Sant'Ángelo I 171 B3
Montesárchio I 170 B2
Montescaglioso I 171 C4
Montesclaros E 150 B3
Montesilvano I 169 A4
Montespértoli I 135 B4
Montesquieu-Volvestre F 146 A2
Montesquiou F 129 C3
Montestruc-sur-Gers F 129 C3
Montes Velhos P 160 B1
Montevarchi I 135 B4
Montevéglio I 135 A4
Monte Vilar P 154 B1
Montfaucon F 101 B4
Montfaucon-d'Argonne F 91 B5
Montfaucon-en-Velay F 117 B4
Montferrat
Isère F 118 B2
Var F 132 B2
Montfort-en-Chalosse F 128 C2
Montfort-l'Amaury F 90 C1
Montfort-le-Gesnois F 102 A2
Montfort-sur-Meu F 101 A4
Montfort-sur-Risle F 89 A4
Montgai E 147 C1
Montgaillard F 145 A4
Montgenèvre F 118 C3
Montgiscard F 146 A2
Montgomery GB 39 B3
Montguyon F 128 A2
Monthermé F 91 B4
Monthey CH 119 A3
Monthois F 91 B4
Monthureux-sur-Saône F 105 A4
Monti I 178 B3
Monticelli d'Ongina I 120 B2
Montichiari I 120 B3
Monticiano I 135 B4
Montiel E 158 C1
Montier-en-Der F 91 C4
Montieri I 135 B4
Montiglio I 119 B5
Montignac F 129 A4
Montigny-le-Roi F 105 B4
Montigny-lès-Metz F 92 B2
Montigny-sur-Aube F 105 B3
Montijo
E 155 C4
Montijo *continued*
P 154 C2
Montilla E 163 A3
Montillana E 163 A4
Montilly F 104 C2
Montivilliers F 89 A4
Montjaux F 130 A1
Montjean-sur-Loire F 102 B1
Montlhéry F 90 C2
Montlieu-la-Garde F 128 A2
Mont-Louis F 146 B3
Montlouis-sur-Loire F 102 B2
Montluçon F 116 A2
Montluel F 117 B5
Montmarault F 116 A2
Montmartin-sur-Mer F 88 B2
Montmédy F 92 B1
Montmélian F 118 B3
Montmeyan F 132 B2
Montmeyran F 117 C4
Montmirail
Marne F 91 C3
Sarthe F 102 A2
Montmiral F 118 B2
Montmirat F 131 B3
Montmirey-le-Château F 105 B4
Montmoreau-St Cybard F 115 C4
Montmorency F 90 C2
Montmorillon F 115 B4
Montmort-Lucy F 91 C3
Montoir-de-Bretagne F 101 B3
Montoire-sur-le-Loir F 102 B2
Montoito P 155 C3
Montolieu F 146 A3
Montório al Vomano I 169 A3
Montoro E 157 B3
Montpellier F 131 B2
Montpezat-de-Quercy F 129 B4
Montpezat-sous-Bouzon F 117 C4
Montpon-Ménestérol F 128 A3
Montpont-en-Bresse F 105 C4
Montréal
Aude F 146 A3
Gers F 128 C3
Montredon-Labessonnié F 130 B1
Montréjeau F 145 A4
Montrésor F 103 B3
Montresta I 178 B2
Montret F 105 C4
Montreuil
Pas de Calais F 78 B1
Seine St Denis F 90 C2
Montreuil-aux-Lions F 90 B3
Montreuil-Bellay F 102 B1
Montreux CH 106 C1
Montrevault F 101 B4
Montrevel-en-Bresse F 118 A2
Montrichard F 103 B3
Montricoux F 129 B4
Mont-roig del Camp E 147 C1
Montrond-les-Bains F 117 B4
Montrose GB 35 B5
Montroy E 159 B3
Montsalvy F 116 C2
Montsauche-les-Settons F 104 B3
Montseny E 147 C3
Montsoreau F 102 B2
Mont-sous-Vaudrey F 105 C4
Monts-sur-Guesnes F 102 C2
Mont-St Aignan F 89 A5
Mont-St Vincent F 104 C3
Montsûrs F 102 A1
Montuenga E 150 A3
Montuïri E 167 B3
Monturque E 163 A3
Monza I 120 B2
Monzón E 145 C4
Monzón de Campos E 142 B2
Moorbad Lobenstein D 83 B3
Moordorf D 71 A4
Moorslede B 78 B3
Moos D 107 B3
Moosburg D 95 C3
Moosburg im Kärnten A 110 C1
Mór H 112 B2
Mora E 157 A4
Móra P 154 C2
Mora S 50 A1
Moraby S 50 B2
Móra d'Ebre E 153 A4
Mora de Rubielos E 153 B3
Moradillo de Roa E 151 A4
Morąg PL 69 B4

Mórahalom H 126 A1
Moraime E 140 A1
Morais P 149 A3
Mòra la Nova E 153 A4
Moral de Calatrava E 157 B4
Moraleda de Zafayona E 163 A4
Moraleja E 149 B3
Moraleja del Vino E 150 A2
Morales del Vino E 150 A2
Morales de Toro E 150 A2
Morales de Valverde E 141 C5
Moralina E 149 A3
Morano Cálabro I 174 B2
Mörarp S 61 C2
Morasverdes E 149 B3
Morata de Jalón E 152 A2
Morata de Jiloca E 152 A2
Morata de Tajuña E 151 B4
Moratalla E 164 A3
Moravče SLO 123 A3
Moravec CZ 97 B4
Moraviţa RO 126 B3
Morávka CZ 98 B2
Moravská Třebová CZ 97 B4
Moravské Budějovice CZ 97 B3
Moravské Lieskové SK 98 C1
Moravske Toplice SLO 111 C3
Moravský-Beroun CZ 98 B1
Moravský Krumlov CZ 97 B4
Moravský Svätý Ján SK 98 C1
Morawica PL 87 B4
Morawin PL 86 A2
Morbach D 92 B3
Morbegno I 120 A2
Morbier F 105 C5
Mörbisch am See A 111 B3
Mörbylånga S 63 B4
Morcenx F 128 B2
Morciano di Romagna I 136 B1
Morcone I 170 B2
Morcuera E 151 A4
Mordelles F 101 A4
Mordoğan TR 188 A1
Moréac F 100 B3
Morebattle GB 35 C5
Morecambe GB 36 B4
Moreda
Granada E 163 A4
Oviedo E 142 A1
Morée F 103 B3
Moreles de Rey E 141 B5
Morella E 153 B3
Moreruela de los Infanzones E 149 A4
Morés E 152 A2
Móres I 178 B2
Morestel F 118 B2
Moretonhampstead GB 43 B3
Moreton-in-Marsh GB 44 B2
Moret-sur-Loing F 90 C2
Moretta I 119 C4
Moreuil F 90 B2
Morez F 105 C5
Mörfelden D 93 B4
Morgat F 100 A1
Morges CH 105 C5
Morgex I 119 B4
Morgongåva S 51 C3
Morhange F 92 C2
Morhet B 92 B1
Mori I 121 B3
Morialmé B 79 B4
Morianes P 160 B2
Moriani Plage F 180 A2
Mórichida H 111 B4
Moriles E 163 A3
Morille E 150 B2
Moringen D 82 A1
Morjärv S 196 C5
Morkarla S 51 B4
Mørke DK 59 B3
Mørkøv DK 61 D1
Morkovice-Slížany CZ 98 B1
Morlaàs F 145 A3
Morlaix F 100 A2
Morley F 91 C5
Mörlunda S 62 A3
Mormanno I 174 B1
Mormant F 90 C2
Mornant F 117 B4
Mornay-Berry F 103 B4
Morón de Almazán E 152 A1
Morón de la Frontera E 162 A2
Morović SRB 125 B5
Morozzo I 133 A3
Morpeth GB 37 A5
Morphou CY 181 A1
Mörrum S 63 B2
Morsbach D 81 B3
Mörsch D 93 C4
Mörsil S 199 B10
Morsum D 64 B1
Mørsvikbotn N 194 C6
Mortagne-au-Perche F 89 B4
Mortagne-sur-Gironde F 114 C3
Mortagne-sur-Sèvre F 114 B3
Mortágua P 148 B1
Mortain F 88 B3
Mortara I 120 B1
Morteau F 105 B5
Mortegliano I 122 B2
Mortelle I 177 A4
Mortemart F 115 B4
Mortimer's Cross GB 39 B4
Mortrée F 89 B4
Mörtschach A 109 C3
Mortsel B 79 A4
Morud DK 59 C3
Morwenstow GB 42 B2
Moryń PL 74 B3
Morzeszczyn PL 69 B3
Morzewo PL 69 B4
Morzine F 118 A3
Mosbach D 93 B5
Mosbjerg DK 58 A3
Mosby N 53 B3
Mosca P 149 A3
Moscavide P 154 C1
Moščenica HR 124 B2
Mošćenice HR 123 B3
Moščenicka Draga HR 123 B3
Mosciano Sant'Ángelo I 136 C2
Mościsko PL 85 B4
Moscow = Moskva RUS 9 E10
Mosina PL 75 B5
Mosjøen N 195 E4
Moskog N 46 A3
Moskorzew PL 87 B3
Moskosel S 196 D2
Moskuvarra FIN 197 B9
Moskva = Moscow RUS 9 E10
Moslavina Podravska HR 125 B3
Moşniţa Nouă RO 126 B3
Moso in Passíria I 108 C2
Mosonmagyaróvár H 111 B4
Mošorin SRB 126 B2
Mošovce SK 98 C2
Mosqueruela E 153 B3
Moss N 54 A1
Mossfellsbær IS 190 C4
Mössingen D 93 C5
Møsstrand N 47 C5
Most CZ 83 B5
Mosta M 175 C3
Mostar BIH 139 B3
Mosterhamn N 52 A1
Mostki PL 75 B4
Most na Soči SLO 122 A2
Móstoles E 151 B4
Mostová SK 111 A4
Mostowo PL 68 A1
Mostuéjouls F 130 A2
Mosty PL 75 A3
Mostys'ka UA 13 D5
Mosvik N 199 B7
Mota del Cuervo E 158 B1
Mota del Marqués E 150 A2
Motala S 55 B6
Motherwell GB 35 C4
Möthlow D 74 B1
Motilla del Palancar E 158 B2
Motnik SLO 123 A3
Motovun HR 122 B2
Motril E 163 B4
Motta I 121 B4
Motta di Livenza I 122 B1
Motta Montecorvino I 170 B3
Motta Visconti I 120 B1
Mottisfont GB 44 B2
Móttola I 173 B3
Mou DK 58 B3
Mouchard F 105 C4
Moudon CH 106 C1
Moudros GR 183 D7
Mougins F 132 B2
Mouilleron en-Pareds F 114 B3
Mouliherne F 102 B2
Moulinet F 133 B3
Moulins F 104 C2
Moulins-Engilbert F 104 C2
Moulins-la-Marche F 89 B4
Moulismes F 115 B4
Moult F 89 A3
Mountain Ash GB 39 C3
Mountbellew IRL 28 A3
Mountfield GB 27 B3
Mountmellick IRL 30 A1
Mountrath IRL 30 A1
Mountsorrel GB 40 C2
Moura P 160 A2
Mourão P 155 C3
Mourenx F 145 A3
Mouriés F 131 B3
Mourmelon-le-Grand F 91 B4
Mouronho P 148 B1
Mourujärvi FIN 197 C11
Mouscron B 78 B3
Mousehole GB 42 B1
Moussac F 131 B3
Moussey F 92 C2
Mousteru F 100 A2
Moustey F 128 B2
Moustiers-Ste Marie F 132 B2
Mouthe F 105 C5
Mouthier-Haute-Pierre F 105 B5
Mouthoumet F 146 B3
Moutier CH 106 B2
Moûtiers F 118 B3
Moutiers-les-Mauxfaits F 114 B2
Mouy F 90 B2
Mouzaki GR 182 D3
Mouzon F 91 B5
Møvik N 46 B2
Moville IRL 27 A3
Moy
Highland GB 32 D2
Tyrone GB 27 B4
Moycullen IRL 28 A2
Moyenmoutier F 92 C2
Moyenvic F 92 C2
Moylough IRL 28 A3
Mózar E 141 C5
Mozhaysk RUS 9 E10
Mozirje SLO 123 A3
Mözs H 112 C2
Mozzanica I 120 B2
Mramorak SRB 127 C2
Mrčajevci SRB 127 D2
Mrkonjić Grad BIH 138 A3
Mrkopalj HR 123 B3
Mrocza PL 76 A2
Mroczeń PL 86 A1
Mroczno PL 69 B4
Mrzezyno PL 67 B4
Mšec CZ 84 B1
Mšeno CZ 84 B2
Mstów PL 86 B3
Mstsislaw BY 13 A9
Mszana Dolna PL 99 B4
Mszczonów PL 77 C5
Muć HR 138 B2
Múccia I 136 B2
Much D 80 B3
Mücheln D 83 A3
Much Marcle GB 39 C4
Muchów PL 85 A4
Much Wenlock GB 39 B4
Mucientes E 142 C2
Muckross IRL 29 B2
Mucur TR 23 B8
Muda P 160 B1
Mudanya TR 186 B3
Mudau D 93 B5
Müden D 72 B3
Mudersbach D 81 B3
Mudurnu TR 187 B6
Muel E 152 A2
Muelas del Pan E 149 A4
Muess D 73 A4
Muff IRL 27 A3
Mugardos E 140 A2
Muge P 154 B2
Mügeln
Sachsen D 83 A5
Sachsen-Anhalt D 83 A5
Múggia I 122 B2
Mugnano I 135 B5
Mugron F 128 C2
Mugueimes E 140 C3
Muhi H 113 B4
Mühlacker D 93 C4
Mühlbach am Hochkönig A 109 B4
Mühlberg
Brandenburg D 83 A5
Thüringen D 82 B2
Mühldorf
A 109 C4
D 95 C4
Muhleberg CH 106 C2
Mühleim D 107 A3
Muhlen-Eichsen D 65 C4
Mühlhausen
Bayern D 94 B2
Thüringen D 82 A2
Mühltroff D 83 B3
Muhos FIN 3 D10
Muhr A 109 B4
Muine Bheag IRL 30 B2
Muirkirk GB 36 A2
Muir of Ord GB 32 D2
Muirteira P 154 B1
Mukacheve UA 12 D5
Muker GB 37 B4
Mula E 165 A3
Muğla TR 188 B3
Mulben GB 32 D3
Mulegns CH 107 C4
Mules I 108 C2
Mülheim D 80 A2
Mulhouse F 106 B2
Muljava SLO 123 B3
Mullanys Cross IRL 26 B2
Müllheim D 106 B2
Mullhyttan S 55 A5
Mullinavat IRL 30 B1
Mullingar IRL 30 A1
Mullion GB 42 B1
Müllrose D 74 B3
Mullsjö S 60 B3
Mulseryd S 60 B3
Munaðarnes IS 190 A4
Munana E 150 B2
Muñás E 141 A4
Münchberg D 83 B3
Müncheberg D 74 B3
München = Munich D 108 A2
Munchen-Gladbach = Mönchengladbach D 80 A2
Münchhausen D 81 B4
Mundaka E 143 A4
Münden D 82 A1
Munderfing A 109 A4
Munderkingen D 107 A4
Mundesley GB 41 C5
Munera E 158 B1
Mungia E 143 A4
Munich = München D 108 A2
Muñico E 150 B2
Muniesa E 153 A3
Munka-Ljungby S 61 C2
Munkebo DK 59 C3
Munkedal S 54 B2
Munkflohögen S 199 B11
Munkfors S 49 C5
Munktorp S 56 A2
Münnerstadt D 82 B2
Muñopepe E 150 B3
Muñotello E 150 B2
Münsingen
CH 106 C2
D 94 C1
Munsö S 57 A3
Münster
CH 106 C3
Hessen D 93 B4
Munster D 72 B3
Münster D 71 C4
Munster F 106 A2
Muntibar E 143 A4
Münzkirchen A 96 C1
Muodoslompolo S 196 B6
Muonio FIN 196 B6
Muotathal CH 107 C3
Muradiye TR 186 D2
Murakeresztúr H 124 A2
Murán SK 99 C4
Murano I 122 B1
Muras E 140 A3
Murat F 116 B2
Muratlı TR 186 A2
Murato F 180 A2
Murat-sur-Vèbre F 130 B1
Murau A 109 B5
Muravera I 179 C3
Murazzano I 133 A4
Murça P 148 A2
Murchante E 144 B2
Murchin D 66 C2
Murcia E 165 B3
Murczyn PL 76 B2
Mur-de-Barrez F 116 C2
Mur-de-Bretagne F 100 A2
Mur-de-Sologne F 103 B3
Mureck A 110 C2
Mürefte TR 186 B2
Muret F 146 A2
Murg CH 107 B4
Murguia E 143 B4
Muri CH 106 B3
Murias de Paredes E 141 B4
Muriedas E 143 A3
Muriel Viejo E 143 C4
Murillo de Rio Leza E 143 B4
Murillo el Fruto E 144 B2
Murjek S 196 C3
Murlaggan GB 34 B2
Murmansk RUS 3 B13
Murmashi RUS 3 B13
Murnau D 108 B2
Muro
E 167 B3
F 180 A1
Muro de Alcoy E 159 C3
Murol F 116 B2
Muro Lucano I 172 B1
Muron F 114 B3
Muros E 140 B1
Muros de Nalón E 141 A4
Murowana Goślina PL 76 B2
Mürren CH 106 C2
Murrhardt D 94 C1
Murska Sobota SLO 111 C3
Mursko Središce HR 111 C3
Murtas E 164 C1
Murten CH 106 C2
Murter HR 137 B4
Murtiçi TR 189 C6
Murtosa P 148 B1
Murtovaara FIN 197 D12
Murvica HR 137 A4
Murviel-lès-Béziers F 130 B2
Mürzsteg A 110 B2
Murzynowo PL 75 B4
Mürzzuschlag A 110 B2
Musculdy F 144 A3
Muskö S 57 A4
Mušov CZ 97 C4
Musselburgh GB 35 C4
Musselkanaal NL 71 B4
Mussidan F 129 A3
Mussomeli I 176 B2
Musson B 92 B1
Mussy-sur-Seine F 104 B3
Mustafakemalpaşa TR 186 B3
Muszaki PL 77 A5
Muszyna PL 99 B4
Mut TR 23 C7
Muta SLO 110 C2
Muthill GB 35 B4
Mutné SK 99 B3
Mutriku E 143 A4
Muttalip TR 187 C5
Mutterbergalm A 108 B2
Muurola FIN 197 C8
Muxía E 140 A1
Muxilka-Ugarte E 143 A4
Muzillac F 101 B3
Mužla SK 112 B2
Muzzano del Turgnano I 122 B2
Mybster GB 32 C3
Myckelgensjö S 200 C3
Myennes F 104 B1
Myjava SK 98 C1
Myking N 46 B2
Mykland N 53 B4
Myra N 53 B5
Myrdal N 46 B4
Myre
Nordland N 194 A6
Nordland N 194 B6
Myresjö S 62 A2
Mýri IS 191 B8
Myrtou CY 181 A2
Mysen N 54 A2
Mysłakowice PL 85 B3
Myślenice PL 99 B3
Myślibórz PL 75 B3
Mysłowice PL 86 B3
Myszków PL 86 B3
Mytishchi RUS 9 E10
Mýtna SK 99 C3
Mýtne Ludany SK 112 A2
Mýto CZ 96 B1

N

Nå N 46 B3
Naaldwijk NL 79 A4
Naantali FIN 8 B2
Naas IRL 30 A2
Nabais P 148 B2
Nabbelund S 62 A5
Nabburg D 95 B4
Načeradec CZ 96 B2
Náchod CZ 85 B4
Nacław PL 68 A1
Nadarzyce PL 75 A5
Nadarzyn PL 77 B5
Nádasd H 111 C3
Nădlac RO 126 A2
Nádudvar H 113 B5
Nadvirna UA 13 D6
Näfels CH 107 B4
Nafpaktos GR 184 A2
Nafplio GR 184 B3
Nagel D 95 B3
Nagele NL 70 B2
Naggen S 200 D2
Nagłowice PL 87 B4
Nagold D 93 C4
Nagore E 144 B2
Nagyatád H 124 A3
Nagybajom H 124 A3
Nagybaracska H 125 A4
Nagybátony H 113 B3
Nagyberény H 112 C2
Nagybörzsöny H 112 B2
Nagycenk H 111 B3
Nagycserkesz H 113 B5
Nagydorog H 112 C2
Nagyfüged H 113 B4
Nagyhersány H 125 B4
Nagyigmánd H 112 B2
Nagyiván H 113 B4
Nagykanizsa H 111 C3
Nagykáta H 113 B3
Nagykonyi H 112 C2
Nagykörös H 113 B3
Nagykörü H 113 B4
Nagylóc H 112 A3
Nagymágocs H 113 C4
Nagymányok H 125 A4
Nagymaros H 112 B2
Nagyoroszi H 112 A3
Nagyrábé H 113 B5
Nagyréde H 113 B3
Nagyszékely H 112 C2
Nagyszénás H 113 C4
Nagyszokoly H 112 C2
Nagytöke H 113 C4
Nagyvázsony H 111 C4
Nagyvenyim H 112 C2
Naharros E 152 B1
Nahe D 64 C3
Naila D 83 B3
Nailloux F 146 A2
Nailsworth GB 43 A4
Naintré F 115 B4
Nairn GB 32 D3
Najac F 129 B4
Nájera E 143 B4
Nak H 112 C2
Nakksjø N 53 A5
Nakło nad Notecią PL 76 A2
Nakskov DK 65 B4
Nalda E 143 B4
Nälden S 199 B11
Nálepkovo SK 99 C4
Nalliers F 114 B2
Nallıhan TR 187 B6
Nalzen F 146 B2
Nalžouské Hory CZ 96 B1
Namdalseid N 199 A8
Náměšť nad Oslavou CZ 97 B4
Námestovo SK 99 B3
Namnå N 49 B4
Namsos N 199 A8
Namsskogan N 199 A10
Namur B 79 B4
Namysłów PL 86 A1
Nançay F 103 B4
Nanclares de la Oca E 143 B4
Nancy F 92 C2
Nangis F 90 C3
Nannestad N 48 B3
Nant F 130 A2
Nanterre F 90 C2
Nantes F 101 B4
Nanteuil-le-Haudouin F 90 B2
Nantiat F 115 B5
Nantua F 118 A2
Nantwich GB 38 A4
Naoussa
Cyclades GR 185 B6
I mathia GR 182 C4
Napajedla CZ 98 B1
Napiwoda PL 77 A5
Naples = Nápoli I 170 C2
Nápoli = Naples I 170 C2
Nar S 57 C4
Nara N 46 A1
Naraval E 141 A4
Narberth GB 39 C2
Nærbø N 52 B1
Narbonne F 130 B1
Narbonne-Plage F 130 B2
Narbuvollen N 199 C8
Narcao I 179 C2
Nardò I 173 B4
Narkaus FIN 197 C9
Narken S 196 C5
Narmo N 48 B3
Narni I 168 A2
Naro I 176 B2
Naro Fominsk RUS 9 E10
Narón E 140 A2
Narros del Castillo E 150 B2
Narta HR 124 B2
Naruszewo PL 77 B5
Narva EST 8 C6
Narvik N 194 B8
Narzole I 133 A3
Näs FIN 51 B7
Nås S 50 B1
Näs S 57 C4
Näsåker S 200 C2
Năsăud RO 17 B6
Nasavrky CZ 97 B3
Nasbinals F 116 C3
Næsbjerg DK 59 C1
Näshull S 62 A3
Našice HR 125 B4
Nasielsk PL 77 B5
Naso I 177 A3
Nassau D 81 B3
Nassenfels D 95 C3
Nassenheide D 74 B2
Nassereith A 108 B1
Nässjö S 62 A2
Nastätten D 81 B3
Næstved DK 65 A4
Näsum S 63 B2
Näsviken S 199 B12
Natalinci SRB 127 C2
Naters CH 119 A5
Nater-Stetten D 108 A2
Nattavaara S 196 C3
Natters A 108 B2
Nattheim D 94 C2
Nättraby S 63 B3
Naturno I 108 C1
Naucelle F 130 A1
Nauders A 108 C1
Nauen D 74 B1
Naul IRL 30 A2
Naumburg D 83 A3
Naundorf D 83 B5
Naunhof D 83 A4
Naustdal N 46 A2
Nautijaur S 196 C2
Nautsi RUS 193 D13
Nava E 142 A1
Navacerrada E 151 B3
Navaconcejo E 149 B4
Nava de Arévalo E 150 B3
Nava de la Asunción E 150 A3
Nava del Rey E 150 A2

Navafriá E 151 A4
Navahermosa E 157 A3
Navahrudak BY 13 B6
Naval E 145 B4
Navalacruz E 150 B3
Navalcán E 150 B2
Navalcarnero E 151 B3
Navaleno E 143 C3
Navalmanzano E 151 A3
Navalmoral E 150 B3
Navalmoral de la Mata E 150 C2
Naválón E 159 C3
Navalonguilla E 150 B2
Navalperal de Pinares E 150 B3
Navalpino E 157 A3
Navaltalgordo E 150 B3
Navaltoril E 156 A3
Navaluenga E 150 B3
Navalvillar de Pela E 156 A2
Navan IRL 30 A2
Navaperal de Tormes E 150 B2
Navapolatsk BY 13 A8
Navarclés E 147 C2
Navarredonda de Gredos E 150 B2
Navarrenx F 144 A3
Navarrés E 159 B3
Navarrete E 143 B4
Navarrevisca E 150 B3
Navás E 147 C2
Navascués E 144 B2
Navas del Madroño E 155 B4
Navas del Rey E 151 B3
Navas del Sepillar E 163 A3
Navas de Oro E 150 A3
Navas de San Juan E 157 B4
Navasfrias E 149 B3
Nave I 120 B3
Nave de Haver P 149 B3
Nävekvarn S 56 B2
Navelli I 169 A3
Navenby GB 40 B3
Näverkärret S 56 A1
Naverstad S 54 B2
Navés E 147 C2
Navezuelas E 156 A2
Navia E 141 A4
Navia de Suarna E 141 B4
Navilly F 105 C4
Năvodari RO 17 C8
Naxos GR 185 B6
Nay F 145 A3
Nazaré P 154 B1
Nazarje SLO 123 A3
Nazilli TR 188 B3
Nazza D 82 A2
Nea Anchialos GR 182 D4
Nea Epidavros GR 184 B4
Nea Flippias GR 182 D2
Nea Kalikratia GR 183 C5
Nea Makri GR 185 A4
Nea Moudania GR 183 C5
Neap GB 33 A5
Nea Peramos GR 183 C6
Neapoli
Kozani GR 182 C3
Kriti GR 185 D6
Lakonia GR 184 C4
Nea Stira GR 185 A5
Neath GB 39 C3
Nea Visa GR 186 A1
Nea Zichni GR 183 B5
Nebljusi HR 124 C1
Neblo SLO 122 A2
Nebolchy RUS 9 C8
Nebra D 82 A3
Nebreda E 143 C3
Nechanice CZ 84 B3
Neckargemünd D 93 B4
Neckarsulm D 94 B1
Neda E 140 A2
Neded SK 112 A1
Nedelišće HR 124 A2
Nederweert NL 80 A1
Nedreberg N 48 B3
Nedre Gärdsjö S 50 B2
Nedre Soppero S 196 A4
Nedstrand N 52 A1
Nedvědice CZ 97 B4
Nędza PL 86 B2
Neede NL 71 B3
Needham Market GB 45 A5
Needingworth GB 44 A3
Neermoor D 71 A4
Neeroeteren B 80 A1
Neerpelt B 79 A5
Neesen D 72 B1
Neetze D 73 A3
Nefyn GB 38 B2
Negotin SRB 16 C5
Negotino MK 182 B4
Negrar I 121 B3
Negredo E 151 A5
Negreira E 140 B2
Nègrepelisse F 129 B4
Negru Vodă RO 17 D8
Negueira de Muñiz E 141 A4
Neheim D 81 A3
Neila E 143 B4
Néive I 119 C5
Nejdek CZ 83 B4
Nekla PL 76 B2
Neksø DK 67 A4
Nelas P 148 B2
Nelaug N 53 B4
Nelidovo RUS 9 D8
Nelim FIN 193 D12
Nellingen D 94 C1
Nelson GB 40 B1
Neman RUS 12 A5
Nemea GR 184 B3
Nemesgörzsöny H 111 B4
Nemeskér H 111 B3
Nemesnádudvar H 125 A5
Nemesszalók H 111 B4
Németkér H 112 C2
Nemours F 103 A4
Nemška Loka SLO 123 B4
Nemšová SK 98 C2
Nenagh IRL 28 B3
Nenince SK 112 A3
Nenita GR 185 A7
Nenzing A 107 B4
Neochori GR 182 D3
Neo Chori GR 184 A2
Neon Petritsi GR 183 B5
Nepi I 168 A2
Nepomuk CZ 96 B1
Nérac F 129 B3
Neratovice CZ 84 B2
Nerchau D 83 A4
Néré F 115 C3
Neresheim D 94 C2
Nereto I 136 C2
Nerezine HR 123 C3
Nerežišća HR 138 B2
Neringa LT 12 A4
Néris-les Bains F 116 A2
Nerito I 169 A3
Nerja E 163 B4
Néronde F 117 B4
Nérondes F 103 C4
Nerpio E 164 A2
Nersingen D 94 C2
Nerva E 161 B3
Nervesa della Battáglia I 121 B5
Nervi I 134 A2
Nes
Buskerud N 48 B1
Hedmark N 48 B2
NL 70 A2
Sogn og Fjordane N 46 A3
Sør-Trøndelag N 198 B6
Nesbyen N 47 B6
Neset N 199 D7
Nesflaten N 52 A2
Nesjahverfi IS 191 C10
Neskaupstaður IS 191 B12
Nesland N 53 A3
Neslandsvatn N 53 B5
Nesle F 90 B2
Nesna N 195 D4
Nesoddtangen N 48 C2
Nesovice CZ 98 B1
Nesselwang D 108 B1
Nesslau CH 107 B4
Nessmersiel D 71 A4
Nesso I 120 B2
Nesterov UA 13 C5
Nestorio GR 182 C3
Nesttun N 46 B2
Nesvady SK 112 B2
Nesvatnstemmen N 53 B4
Nether Stowey GB 43 A3
Netland N 52 B2
Netolice CZ 96 B2
Netphen D 81 B4
Netstal CH 107 B4
Nettancourt F 91 C4
Nettetal D 80 A2
Nettlingen D 72 B3
Nettuno I 168 B2
Neualbenreuth D 95 B4
Neubeckum D 81 A4
Neubrandenburg D 74 A2
Neubruchhausen D 72 B1
Neubukow D 65 B4
Neuburg D 94 C3
Neuchâtel CH 106 C1
Neu Darchau D 73 A3
Neudau A 111 B3
Neudietendorf D 82 B2
Neudorf D 93 B4
Neuenbürg D 93 C4
Neuenburg D 71 A4
Neuendorf D 66 B2
Neuenhagen D 74 B2
Neuenhaus D 71 B3
Neuenkirchen
Niedersachsen D 71 B5
Niedersachsen D 72 A2
Nordrhein-Westfalen D 71 B4
Nordrhein-Westfalen D 81 B3
Neuenrade D 81 A3
Neuenwalde D 64 C1
Neuerburg D 92 A2
Neufahrn
Bayern D 95 C3
Bayern D 95 C4
Neuf-Brisach F 106 A2
Neufchâteau
B 92 B1
F 92 C1
Neufchâtel-en-Bray F 90 B1
Neufchâtel-sur-Aisne F 91 B4
Neuflize F 91 B4
Neugersdorf D 84 B2
Neuhardenberg D 74 B3
Neuharlingersiel D 71 A4
Neuhaus
Bayern D 95 B3
Bayern D 96 C1
Niedersachsen D 64 C2
Niedersachsen D 73 A3
Niedersachsen D 81 A5
Neuhaus a Rennweg D 82 B3
Neuhausen
CH 107 B3
D 83 B5
Neuhausen ob Eck D 107 B3
Neuhof
Bayern D 94 B2
Hessen D 82 B1
Neuhofen an der Krems A 110 A1
Neuillé-Pont-Pierre F 102 B2
Neuilly-en-Thelle F 90 B2
Neuilly-le-Réal F 104 C2
Neuilly-l'Évêque F 105 B4
Neuilly-St Front F 90 B3
Neu-Isenburg D 93 A4
Neukalen D 66 C1
Neu Kaliss D 73 A4
Neukirch D 84 A2
Neukirchen
A 109 A4
Hessen D 81 B5
Schleswig-Holstein D 64 B1
Neukirchen am Grossvenediger A 109 B3
Neukirchen bei Heiligen Blut D 95 B4
Neukloster D 65 C4
Neulengbach A 110 A2
Neulise F 117 B4
Neu Lübbenau D 74 B2
Neum BIH 139 C3
Neumagen D 92 B2
Neumarkt D 95 B3
Neumarkt am Wallersee A 109 B4
Neumarkt im Hausruckkreis A 109 A4
Neumarkt im Mühlkreis A 96 C2
Neumarkt im Steiermark A 110 B1
Neumarkt Sankt Veit D 95 C4
Neumünster D 64 B2
Neunburg vorm Wald D 95 B4
Neung-sur-Beuvron F 103 B3
Neunkirch
Luzern CH 106 B3
Schaffhausen CH 107 B3
Neunkirchen
A 111 B3
Nordrhein-Westfalen D 80 B3
Saarland D 92 B3
Neunkirchen am Brand D 94 B3
Neuötting D 95 C4
Neupetershain D 84 A2
Neuravensburg D 107 B4
Neureut D 93 B4
Neuruppin D 74 B1
Neusäss D 94 C2
Neusiedl A 111 B3
Neuss D 80 A2
Neussargues-Moissac F 116 B2
Neustadt
Bayern D 94 B2
Bayern D 95 B4
Bayern D 95 C3
Brandenburg D 73 B5
Hessen D 81 B5
Niedersachsen D 72 B2
Rheinland-Pfalz D 93 B4
Sachsen D 84 A2
Schleswig-Holstein D 65 B3
Thüringen D 82 B3
Thüringen D 83 B3
Neustadt-Glewe D 73 A4
Neustift im Stubaital A 108 B2
Neustrelitz D 74 A2
Neutal A 111 B3
Neutrebbin D 74 B3
Neu-Ulm D 94 C2
Neuves-Maisons F 92 C2
Neuvic
Corrèze F 116 B2
Dordogne F 129 A3
Neuville-aux-Bois F 103 A4
Neuville-de-Poitou F 115 B4
Neuville-les-Dames F 117 A5
Neuville-sur-Saône F 117 B4
Neuvy-le-Roi F 102 B2
Neuvy-Santour F 104 A2
Neuvy-St Sépulchre F 103 C3
Neuvy-sur-Barangeon F 103 B4
Neuwied D 80 B3
Neuzelle D 74 B3
Névache F 118 B3
Neveklov CZ 96 B2
Nevel RUS 9 D6
Neverfjord N 192 B7
Nevers F 104 C2
Nevesinje BIH 139 B4
Névez F 100 B2
Nevlunghavn N 53 B5
Nevşehir TR 23 B8
New Abbey GB 36 B3
New Aberdour GB 33 D4
New Alresford GB 44 B2
Newark-on-Trent GB 40 B3
Newbiggin-by-the-Sea GB 37 A5
Newbliss IRL 27 B3
Newborough GB 38 A2
Newbridge IRL 30 A2
Newbridge on Wye GB 39 B3
Newburgh
Aberdeenshire GB 33 D4
Fife GB 35 B4
Newbury GB 44 B2
Newby Bridge GB 36 B4
Newcastle GB 27 B5
Newcastle Emlyn GB 39 B2
Newcastleton GB 37 A4
Newcastle-under-Lyme GB 40 B1
Newcastle upon Tyne GB 37 B5
Newcastle West IRL 29 B2
Newchurch GB 39 B3
New Costessey GB 41 C5
New Cumnock GB 36 A2
Newent GB 39 C4
New Galloway GB 36 A2
Newham GB 45 B4
Newhaven GB 45 C4
Newington GB 45 B5
Newinn IRL 29 B4
Newlyn GB 42 B1
Newmachar GB 33 D4
Newmarket
Suffolk GB 45 A4
Western Isles GB 31 A2
IRL 29 B3
Newmarket-on-Fergus IRL 28 B3
New Mills GB 40 B2
New Milton GB 44 C2
New Pitsligo GB 33 D4
Newport
I sle of Wight GB 44 C2
Newport GB 39 C4
Pembrokeshire GB 39 B2
Telford & Wrekin GB 38 B4
Mayo IRL 28 A2
Tipperary IRL 29 B3
Newport-on-Tay GB 35 B5
Newport Pagnell GB 44 A3
Newquay GB 42 B1
New Quay GB 39 B2
New Radnor GB 39 B3
New Romney GB 45 C4
New Ross IRL 30 B2
Newry GB 27 B4
New Scone GB 35 B4
Newton Abbot GB 43 B3
Newton Arlosh GB 36 B3
Newton Aycliffe GB 37 B5
Newton Ferrers GB 42 B2
Newtonhill GB 33 D4
Newtonmore GB 32 D2
Newton Stewart GB 36 B2
Newtown
Herefordshire GB 39 B4
Powys GB 39 B3
Newtownabbey GB 27 B5
Newtownards GB 27 B5
Newtownbutler GB 27 B3
Newtown Cunningham IRL 27 B3
Newtownhamilton GB 27 B4
Newtownmountkennedy IRL 30 A2
Newtown St Boswells GB 35 C5
Newtown Sands IRL 29 B2
Newtownstewart GB 27 B3
Nexon F 115 C5
Neyland GB 39 C2
Nibbiano I 120 C2
Nibe DK 58 B2
Nicastro I 175 C2
Niccone I 135 B5
Nice F 133 B3
Nickelsdorf A 111 B4
Nicolosi I 177 B4
Nicosia
CY 181 A2
I 177 B3
Nicótera I 175 C1
Nidda D 81 B5
Niğde TR 23 C8
Nidzica PL 77 A5
Niebla E 161 B3
Nieborów PL 77 B5
Niebüll D 64 B1
Niechanowo PL 76 B2
Niechorze PL 67 B4
Niedalino PL 67 B5
Niederaula D 82 B1
Niederbipp CH 106 B2
Niederbronn-les-Bains F 93 C3
Niederfischbach D 81 B3
Niedergörsdorf D 74 C1
Niederkrüchten D 80 A2
Niederndorf A 108 B3
Nieder-Olm D 93 B4
Niedersachswerfen D 82 A2
Niederstetten D 94 B1
Niederurnen CH 107 B4
Niederwölz A 110 B1
Niedoradz PL 85 A3
Niedzica PL 99 B4
Niegosławice PL 85 A3
Nieheim D 81 A5
Niemcza PL 85 B4
Niemegk D 74 B1
Niemisel S 196 C5
Niemodlin PL 85 B5
Nienburg
Niedersachsen D 72 B2
Sachsen-Anhalt D 83 A3
Niepołomice PL 99 A4
Nierstein D 93 B4
Niesky D 84 A2
Niestronno PL 76 B2
Nieświń PL 87 A4
Nieszawa PL 76 B3
Nieul-le-Dolent F 114 B2
Nieul-sur-Mer F 114 B2
Nieuw-Amsterdam NL 71 B3
Nieuw-Buinen NL 71 B3
Nieuwegein NL 70 B2
Nieuwe Niedorp NL 70 B1
Nieuwe-Pekela NL 71 A3
Nieuwerkerken B 79 B5
Nieuwe-schans NL 71 A4
Nieuwolda NL 71 A3
Nieuwpoort B 78 A2
Nieuw-Weerdinge NL 71 B3
Nigrita GR 183 C5
Nigüelas E 163 B4
Níjar E 164 C2
Nijemci HR 125 B5
Nijkerk NL 70 B2
Nijlen B 79 A4
Nijmegen NL 80 A1
Nijverdal NL 71 B3
Nikel RUS 193 C14
Nikinci SRB 127 C1
Nikiti GR 183 C5
Nikitsch A 111 B3
Nikkaluokta S 196 B2
Nikla H 111 C4
Niklasdorf A 110 B2
Nikšić MNE 139 C4
Nilivaara S 196 B4
Nîmes F 131 B3
Nimis I 122 A2
Nimtofte DK 58 B3
Nin HR 137 A4
Nindorf D 64 B2
Ninemilehouse IRL 30 B1
Ninove B 79 B4
Niort F 114 B3
Niš SRB 16 D4
Nisa P 155 B3
Niscemi I 177 B3
Niskala FIN 197 D10
Nissafors S 60 B3
Nissan-lez-Ensérune F 130 B2
Nissedal N 53 A4
Nissumby DK 58 B1
Nisterud N 53 A5
Niton GB 44 C2
Nitra SK 98 C2
Nitrianske-Pravno SK 98 C2
Nitrianske Rudno SK 98 C2
Nitry F 104 B2
Nittedal N 48 B2
Nittenau D 95 B4
Nittendorf D 95 B3
Nivala FIN 3 E9
Nivelles B 79 B4
Nivnice CZ 98 C1
Nižná SK 99 B3
Nižná Boca SK 99 C3
Nižne Repaše SK 99 B4
Nizza Monferrato I 119 C5
Njarðvík IS 190 D3
Njegŭsevo SRB 126 B1
Njivice HR 123 B3
Njurundabommen S 200 D3
Njutånger S 200 E3
Noailles F 90 B2
Noain E 144 B2
Noale I 121 B5
Noalejo E 163 A4
Noblejas E 151 C4
Noceda E 141 B4
Nocera Inferiore I 170 C2
Nocera Terinese I 175 B2
Nocera Umbra I 136 B1
Noceto I 120 C3
Noci I 173 B3
Nociglia I 173 B4
Nodeland N 53 B3
Nödinge S 60 B2
Nods F 105 B5
Noé F 146 A2
Noépoli I 174 A2
Noeux-les-Mines F 78 B2
Noez E 157 A3
Nogales E 155 C4
Nogara I 121 B4
Nogarejas E 141 B4
Nogaro F 128 C2
Nogent F 105 A4
Nogent l'Artaud F 90 C3
Nogent-le-Roi F 90 C1
Nogent-le-Rotrou F 89 B4
Nogent-sur-Seine F 91 C3
Nogent-sur-Vernisson F 103 B4
Nogersund S 63 B2
Noguera E 152 B2
Noguerones E 163 A3
Nohfelden D 92 B3
Nohn D 80 B2
Noia E 140 B2
Noicáttaro I 173 A2
Noirétable F 117 B3
Noirmoutier-en-l'Île F 114 A1
Noja E 143 A3
Nojewo PL 75 B5
Nokia FIN 8 B3
Nol S 60 B2
Nola I 170 C2
Nolay F 104 C3
Noli I 133 A4
Nolnyra S 51 B4
Nombela E 150 B3
Nomeny F 92 C2
Nomexy F 92 C2
Nonancourt F 89 B5
Nonant-le-Pin F 89 B4
Nonántola I 121 C4
Nonaspe E 153 A4
None I 119 C4
Nontron F 115 C4
Nonza F 180 A2
Noordhorn NL 71 A3
Noordwijk NL 70 B1
Noordwijkerhout NL 70 B1
Noordwolde NL 70 B3
Noppikoski S 50 A1
Nora S 55 A6
Nørager DK 58 B2
Norberg S 50 B2
Norboda S 51 B5
Nórcia I 136 C2
Nordagutu N 53 A5
Nordanås S 200 B4
Nordausques F 78 B2
Nordborg DK 64 A2
Nordby
Aarhus Amt. DK 59 C3
Ribe Amt. DK 59 C1
Norddeich D 71 A4
Norddorf D 64 B1
Norden D 71 A4
Nordenham D 72 A1
Norderhov N 48 B2
Norderney D 71 A4
Norderstapel D 64 B2
Norderstedt D 64 C3
Nordfjord N 193 B14
Nordfjordeid N 198 D3
Nordfold N 194 C6
Nordhalben D 82 B3
Nordhausen D 82 A2
Nordheim vor der Rhön D 82 B2
Nordholz D 64 C1
Nordhorn D 71 B4
Nordingrå S 200 D4
Nordkjosbotn N 192 C3
Nordli N 199 A10
Nördlingen D 94 C2
Nordmaling S 200 C5
Nordmark S 49 C6
Nordmela N 194 A6
Nord-Odal N 48 B3
Nordre Osen N 48 A3
Nordsinni N 48 B1
Nørdstedalsseter N 198 D4
Nordstemmen D 72 B2
Nordvågen N 193 B10
Nordwalde D 71 B4
Noreña E 142 A1
Noresund N 48 B1
Norg NL 71 A3
Norheimsund N 46 B3
Norie S 63 B2
Norma I 169 B2
Nornäs S 49 A5
Norrahammar S 62 A2
Norråker S 200 B1
Norrala S 51 A3
Norra Vi S 62 A3
Nørre Aaby DK 59 C2

Nørre Alslev DK 65 B4
Nørre Lyndelse DK 59 C3
Nørre Nebel DK 59 C1
Norrent-Fontes F 78 B2
Nørre Snede DK 59 C2
Nørresundby DK 58 A2
Nørre Vorupør DK 58 B1
Norrfjärden S 196 D4
Norrhed S 196 C3
Norrhult Klavreström S 62 A3
Norrköping S 56 B2
Norrskedika S 51 B5
Norrsundet S 51 B4
Norrtälje S 57 A4
Nors DK 58 A1
Norsbron S 55 A4
Norsholm S 56 B1
Norsjö S 200 B5
Nörten-Hardenberg D 82 A1
Northallerton GB 37 B5
Northampton GB 44 A3
North Berwick GB 35 B5
North Charlton GB 37 A5
Northeim D 82 A2
Northfleet GB 45 B4
North Frodingham GB 40 B3
North Kessock GB 32 D2
Northleach GB 44 B2
North Molton GB 42 A3
North Petherton GB 43 A3
Northpunds GB 33 B5
North Somercotes GB 41 B4
North Tawton GB 42 B3
North Thoresby GB 41 B3
North Walsham GB 41 C5
Northwich GB 38 A4
Norton GB 40 A3
Nortorf D 64 B2
Nort-sur-Erdre F 101 B4
Nörvenich D 80 B2
Norwich GB 41 C5
Norwick GB 33 A6
Nøsen N 47 B5
Nossa Senhora do Cabo P 154 C1
Nossebro S 55 B3
Nössemark S 54 A2
Nossen D 83 A5
Notaresco I 169 A3
Noto I 177 C4
Notodden N 53 A5
Nottingham GB 40 C2
Nottuln D 71 C4
Nouan-le-Fuzelier F 103 B4
Nouans-les-Fontaines F 103 B3
Nougaroulet F 129 C3
Nouvion F 78 B1
Nouzonville F 91 B4
Nova H 111 C3
Nová Baňa SK 98 C2
Nová Bystrica SK 99 B3
Nová Bystřice CZ 97 B3
Nova Crnja SRB 126 B2
Novaféltria I 135 B5
Nova Gorica SLO 122 B2
Nova Gradiška HR 124 B3
Nováky SK 98 C2
Novalaise F 118 B2
Novales E 145 B3
Nova Levante I 108 C2
Novalja HR 137 A3
Nová Paka CZ 84 B3
Nova Pazova SRB 127 C2
Nová Pec CZ 96 C1
Novara I 120 B1
Novara di Sicília I 177 A4
Nova Siri I 174 A2
Novate Mezzola I 120 A2
Nova Topola BIH 124 B3
Novaya Ladoga RUS 9 B8
Nova Zagora BG 17 D6
Nové Hrady CZ 96 C2
Novelda E 165 A4
Novellara I 121 C3
Nové Město SK 98 C1
Nové Město nad Metují CZ 85 B4
Nové Město na Moravě CZ 97 B4
Nové Město pod Smrkem CZ 84 B3
Nové Mitrovice CZ 96 B1
Noventa di Piave I 122 B1
Noventa Vicentina I 121 B4
Novés E 151 B3
Noves F 131 B3
Nové Sady SK 98 C1
Novés de Segre E 147 B2
Nové Strašeci CZ 84 B1
Nové Zámky SK 112 B2
Novgorod RUS 9 C7
Novi Bečej SRB 126 B2
Novi di Módena I 121 C3
Novigrad
Istarska HR 122 B2
Zadarsko-Kninska HR 137 A4
Novigrad Podravski HR 124 A2
Novi Kneževac SRB 126 A2
Novi Lígure I 120 C1
Noville B 92 A1
Novi Marof HR 124 A2
Novion-Porcien F 91 B4
Novi Pazar
BG 17 D7
SRB 16 D4
Novi Sad SRB 126 B1
Novi Slankamen SRB 126 B2
Novi Travnik BIH 139 A3
Novi Vinodolski HR 123 B3
Novohrad-Volynskyy UA 13 C7
Novo Mesto SLO 123 B4
Novo Miloševo SRB 126 B2
Novorzhev RUS 9 D6
Novo Selo BIH 125 B3
Novoselytsya UA 17 A7
Novosokolniki RUS 9 D6
Novoveská Huta SK 99 C4
Novovolynsk UA 13 C6
Novska HR 124 B2
Nový Bor CZ 84 B2
Nový Bydžov CZ 84 B3
Novy-Chevrières F 91 B4
Novy Dwór Mazowiecki PL 77 B5
Nový-Hrozenkov CZ 98 B2
Nový Jičín CZ 98 B2
Novy Knin CZ 96 B2
Nowa Cerekwia PL 86 B1
Nowa Dęba PL 87 B5
Nowa Karczma PL 68 A3
Nowa Kościoł PL 85 A3
Nowa Ruda PL 85 B4
Nowa Słupia PL 87 B5
Nowa Sól PL 85 A3
Nowa Wieś PL 69 B4
Nowa-Wieś Wielka PL 76 B3
Nowe PL 69 B3
Nowe Brzesko PL 87 B4
Nowe Grudze PL 77 B4
Nowe Kiejkuty PL 77 A6
Nowe Miasteczko PL 85 A3
Nowe Miasto
Mazowieckie PL 77 B5
Mazowieckie PL 87 A4
Nowe Miasto Lubawskie PL 69 B4
Nowe Miasto nad Wartą PL 76 B2
Nowe Skalmierzyce PL 86 A2
Nowe Warpno PL 74 A3
Nowica PL 69 A4
Nowogard PL 75 A4
Nowogród Bobrzanski PL 84 A3
Nowogrodziec PL 84 A3
Nowosolna PL 86 A3
Nowy Dwór Gdański PL 69 A4
Nowy Korczyn PL 87 B4
Nowy Sącz PL 99 B4
Nowy Staw PL 69 A4
Nowy Targ PL 99 B4
Nowy Tomyśl PL 75 B5
Nowy Wiśnicz PL 99 B4
Noyalo F 101 B3
Noyal-Pontivy F 100 A3
Noyant F 102 B2
Noyelles-sur-Mer F 78 B1
Noyen-sur-Sarthe F 102 B1
Noyers F 104 B2
Noyers-sur-Cher F 103 B3
Noyers-sur-Jabron F 132 A1
Noyon F 90 B2
Nozay F 101 B4
Nuaillé F 102 B1
Nuaillé-d'Aunis F 114 B3
Nuars F 104 B2
Nubledo E 141 A5
Nuéno E 145 B3
Nuestra Señora Sa Verge des Pilar E 166 C1
Nueva E 142 A2
Nueva Carteya E 163 A3
Nuevalos E 152 A2
Nuits F 104 B3
Nuits-St Georges F 105 B3
Nule I 178 B3
Nules E 159 B3
Nulvi I 178 B2
Numana I 136 B2
Numansdorp NL 79 A4
Nümbrecht D 81 B3
Nunchritz D 83 A5
Nuneaton GB 40 C2
Nunnanen FIN 196 A7
N Unnaryd S 60 B3
Nuñomoral E 149 B3
Nunspeet NL 70 B2
Nuorgam FIN 193 B11
Núoro I 178 B3
Nurallao I 179 C3
Nuremberg = Nürnberg D 94 B3
Nurmes FIN 3 E11
Nürnberg = Nuremberg D 94 B3
Nurri I 179 C3
Nürtingen D 94 C1
Nus I 119 B4
Nusnäs S 50 B1
Nusplingen D 107 A3
Nuštar HR 125 B4
Nuupas FIN 197 C9
Nyåker S 200 C5
Nyáregyháza H 112 B3
Nyarlörinc H 113 C3
Nyasvizh BY 13 B7
Nybble S 55 A5
Nybergsund N 49 A4
Nybøl DK 64 B2
Nyborg
DK 59 C3
S 196 D6
Nybro S 62 B3
Nybster GB 32 C3
Nyby DK 65 B5
Nye S 62 A3
Nyékládháza H 113 B4
Nyergesujfalu H 112 B2
Nyhammar S 50 B1
Nyhyttan S 55 A5
Nyirád H 111 B4
Nyirbátor H 16 B5
Nyiregyháza H 16 B4
Nyker DK 67 A3
Nykil S 56 B1
Nykirke N 48 B2
Nykøbing
Falster DK 65 B4
Vestsjællands Amt. DK 61 D1
Nykøbing Mors DK 58 B1
Nyköping S 56 B3
Nykroppa S 55 A5
Nykvarn S 56 A3
Nykyrke S 55 B5
Nyland S 200 C3
Nylars DK 67 A3
Nymburk CZ 84 B3
Nynäshamn S 57 B3
Nyon CH 118 A3
Nyons F 131 A4
Nýřany CZ 96 B1
Nýrsko CZ 95 B5
Nyrud N 193 C13
Nysa PL 85 B5
Nysäter S 55 A3
Nyseter N 198 C5
Nyskoga S 49 B4
Nysted DK 65 B4
Nystrand N 53 A5
Nyúl H 111 B4
Nyvoll N 192 B7

O

Oadby GB 40 C2
Oakengates GB 38 B4
Oakham GB 40 C3
Oanes N 52 B2
Obalj BIH 139 B4
Oban GB 34 B2
O Barco E 141 B4
Obbola S 200 C6
Obdach A 110 B1
Obejo E 156 B3
Oberammergau D 108 B2
Oberasbach D 94 B2
Oberau D 108 B2
Oberaudorf D 108 B3
Oberbruck F 106 B1
Oberdiessbach CH 106 C2
Oberdorf CH 106 B2
Oberdrauburg A 109 C3
Oberelsbach D 82 B2
Obere Stanz A 110 B2
Ober Grafendorf A 110 A2
Obergünzburg D 108 B1
Obergurgl A 108 C2
Oberhausen D 80 A2
Oberhof D 82 B2
Oberkirch D 93 C4
Oberkirchen D 81 A4
Oberkochen D 94 C2
Obermassfeld-Grimmenthal D 82 B2
Ober-Morlen D 81 B4
Obermünchen D 95 C3
Obernai F 93 C3
Obernberg A 96 C1
Obernburg D 93 B5
Oberndorf D 93 C4
Oberndorf bei Salzburg A 109 B3
Obernkirchen D 72 B2
Oberort A 110 B2
Oberpullendorf A 111 B3
Oberriet CH 107 B4
Oberröblingen D 82 A3
Oberrot D 94 B1
Oberstaufen D 107 B5
Oberstdorf D 107 B5
Obertauern A 109 B4
Obertilliach A 109 C3
Obertraubling D 95 C4
Obertraun A 109 B4
Obertrubach D 95 B3
Obertrum A 109 B4
Oberursel D 81 B4
Obervellach A 109 C4
Oberviechtach D 95 B4
Oberwart A 111 B3
Oberwesel D 93 A3
Oberwinter D 80 B3
Oberwölzstadt A 110 B1
Oberzell D 96 C1
Obice PL 87 B4
Óbidos P 154 B1
Obing D 109 B3
Objat F 129 A4
Objazda PL 68 A2
Öblarn A 109 B5
Obninsk RUS 9 E10
O Bolo E 141 B3
Oborniki PL 75 B5
Oborniki Śląskie PL 85 A4
Obornjača SRB 126 B1
Obrenovac SRB 127 C2
Obrež SRB 127 C1
Obrigheim D 93 B5
Obrov SLO 123 B3
Obrovac
HR 137 A4
SRB 126 B1
Obrovac Sinjski HR 138 B2
Obruk TR 23 B7
Obrzycko PL 75 B5
Obudovac BIH 125 C4
Ocaña E 151 C4
O Carballiño E 140 B2
Occhiobello I 121 C4
Occimiano I 119 B5
Očevlja BIH 139 A4
Ochagavía E 144 B2
Ochiltree GB 36 A2
Ochla PL 84 A3
Ochotnica-Dolna PL 99 B4
Ochotnica-Górna PL 99 B4
Ochsenfurt D 94 B2
Ochsenhausen D 107 A4
Ochtendung D 80 B3
Ochtrup D 71 B4
Ocieka PL 87 B5
Ockelbo S 50 B3
Öckerö S 60 B1
Ocnița MD 17 A7
O Corgo E 141 B3
Očová SK 99 C3
Ócsa H 112 B3
Öcseny H 125 A4
Öcsöd H 113 C4
Octeville F 88 A2
Ocypel PL 69 B3
Ödåkra S 61 C2
Odby DK 58 B1
Odda N 46 B3
Odder DK 59 C3
Ödeborg S 54 B2
Odeceixe P 160 B1
Odechów PL 87 A5
Odeleite P 160 B2
Odemira P 160 B1
Ödemiş TR 188 A2
Ödensbacken S 56 A1
Odense DK 59 C3
Odensjö
Jönköping S 62 A2
Kronoberg S 60 C3
Oderberg D 74 B3
Oderzo I 122 B1
Odesa = Odessa UA 17 B9
Ödeshög S 55 B5
Odessa = Odesa UA 17 B9
Odiáxere P 160 B1
Odie GB 33 B4
Odiham GB 44 B3
Odintsovo RUS 9 E10
Odivelas P 160 A1
Odolanów PL 85 A5
Odón E 152 B2
Odorheiu Secuiesc RO 17 B6
Odrowąz PL 87 A4
Odry CZ 98 B1
Odrzywół PL 87 A4
Ødsted DK 59 C2
Odžaci SRB 126 B1
Odžak BIH 125 B4
Oebisfelde D 73 B3
Oederan D 83 B5
Oeding D 71 C3
Oegstgeest NL 70 B1
Oelde D 81 A4
Oelsnitz D 83 B4
Oer-Erkenschwick D 80 A3
Oerlinghausen D 72 C1
Oettingen D 94 C2
Oetz A 108 B1
Oeventrop D 81 A4
Offanengo I 120 B2
Offenbach D 81 B4
Offenburg D 93 C3
Offida I 136 C2
Offingen D 94 C2
Offranville F 89 A5
Ofir P 148 A1
Ofte N 53 A4
Ofterschwang D 107 B5
Oggiono I 120 B2
Ogihares E 163 A4
Ogliastro Cilento I 170 C3
Ogliastro Marina I 170 C2
Ogmore-by-Sea GB 39 C3
Ogna N 52 B1
Ogre LV 8 D4
Ogrodzieniec PL 86 B3
Ogulin HR 123 B4
Ögur IS 190 A3
Ohanes E 164 B2
Ohey B 79 B5
Ohlstadt D 108 B2
Ohrdorf D 73 B3
Ohrdruf D 82 B2
Ohrid MK 182 B2
Öhringen D 94 B1
Oia E 140 B2
Oiã P 148 B1
Oiartzun E 144 A2
Oijärvi FIN 197 D8
Oilgate IRL 30 B2
Oimbra E 148 A2
Oiselay-et-Grachoux F 105 B4
Oisemont F 90 B1
Oisterwijk NL 79 A5
Öja S 57 C4
Öje S 49 B5
Ojén E 162 B3
Ojrzeń PL 77 B5
Ojuelos Altos E 156 B2
Okalewo PL 77 A4
Okány H 113 C5
Okehampton GB 42 B2
Oklaj HR 138 B2
Økneshamn N 194 B6
Okoč SK 111 B4
Okoličné SK 99 B3
Okonek PL 68 B1
Okonin PL 69 B3
Okřisky CZ 97 B3
Oksa PL 87 B4
Oksbøl DK 59 C1
Oksby DK 59 C1
Øksfjord N 192 B6
Øksna N 48 B3
Okučani HR 124 B3
Okulovka RUS 9 C8
Ólafsfjörður IS 191 A7
Ólafsvík IS 190 C2
ÖLagnö S 57 A4
Olagüe E 144 B2
Oland N 53 B4
Olargues F 130 B1
Oława PL 85 B5
Olazagutia E 144 B1
Olbernhau D 83 B5
Ólbia I 178 B3
Olching D 108 A2
Oldbury GB 43 A4
Oldcastle IRL 27 C3
Old Deer GB 33 D4
Oldeberkoop NL 70 B3
Oldeboorn NL 70 A2
Olden N 198 D3
Oldenbrok D 71 A5
Oldenburg
Niedersachsen D 71 A5
Schleswig-Holstein D 65 B3
Oldenzaal NL 71 B3
Olderdalen N 192 C4
Olderfjord N 193 B9
Oldersum D 71 A4
Oldervik N 192 C2
Oldham GB 40 B1
Oldisleben D 82 A3
Oldmeldrum GB 33 D4
Olea E 142 B2
Oleby S 49 B5
Olechów PL 87 A5
Oledo P 155 B3
Oléggio I 120 B1
Oleiros
Coruña E 140 A2
Coruña E 140 B1
P 154 B3
Oleksandriya UA 13 C7
Olen B 79 A4
Ølen N 52 A1
Olenegorsk RUS 3 B13
Olenino RUS 9 D8
Olesa de Montserrat E 147 C2
Oleśnica PL 85 A5
Olešnice CZ 97 B4
Olesno PL 86 B2
Oletta F 180 A2
Olette F 146 B3
Olevsk UA 13 C7
Olfen D 80 A3
Olgiate Comasco I 120 B1
Olginate I 120 B2
Ølgod DK 59 C1
Olgrinmore GB 32 C3
Olhão P 160 B2
Olhava FIN 197 D8
Olhavo P 154 B1
Oliana E 147 B2
Olias del Rey E 151 C4
Oliena I 178 B3
Oliete E 153 B3
Olimbos GR 188 D2
Olite E 144 B2
Oliva E 159 C3
Oliva de la Frontera E 155 C4
Oliva de Mérida E 156 B1
Oliva de Plasencia E 149 B3
Olivadi I 175 C2
Olival P 154 B2
Olivar E 163 B4
Olivares E 161 B3
Olivares de Duero E 142 C2
Olivares de Júcar E 158 B1
Oliveira de Azeméis P 148 B1
Oliveira de Frades P 148 B1
Oliveira do Conde P 148 B2
Oliveira do Douro P 148 A1
Oliveira do Hospital P 148 B2
Olivenza E 155 C3
Olivet F 103 B3
Olivone CH 107 C3
Öljehult S 63 B3
Olkusz PL 86 B3
Ollerton GB 40 B2
Ollerup DK 65 A3
Olliergues F 117 B3
Ölmbrotorp S 56 A1
Ölme S 55 A4
Olmedilla de Alarcón E 158 B1
Olmedillo de Roa E 143 C3
Olmedo
E 150 A3
I 178 B2
Olmeto F 180 B1
Olmillos de Castro E 149 A3
Olmos de Ojeda E 142 B2
Olney GB 44 A3
Ołobok PL 86 A2
Olocau del Rey E 153 B3
Olofström S 63 B2
Olomouc CZ 98 B1
Olonets RUS 9 B8
Olonne-sur-Mer F 114 B2
Olonzac F 130 B1
Oloron-Ste Marie F 145 A3
Olost E 147 C3
Olot E 147 B3
Olovo BIH 139 A4
Olpe D 81 A3
Olsberg D 81 A4
Olsene B 79 B3
Olserud S 55 A4
Olshammar S 55 B5
Olshanka UA 13 D9
Olszanica PL 85 A3
Olsztyn
Śląskie PL 86 B3
Warmińsko-Mazurskie PL 69 B5
Olsztynek PL 77 A5
Olszyna PL 84 A3
Olszyny PL 77 A6
Oltedal N 52 B2
Olten CH 106 B2
Oltenița RO 17 C7
Olula del Rio E 164 B2
Ølve N 46 B2
Olvega E 144 C2
Olvera E 162 B2
Olympia GR 184 B2
Olzai I 178 B3
Omagh GB 27 B3
Omalos GR 185 D4
Omegna I 119 B5
Omiš HR 138 B2
Omišalj HR 123 B3
Ommen NL 71 B3
Omodhos CY 181 B1
Omoljica SRB 127 C2
On B 79 B5
Oña E 143 B3
Onano I 168 A1
O Näsberg S 49 B5
Oñati E 143 A4
Onda E 159 B3
Ondara E 159 C4
Ondarroa E 143 A4
Onesse-et-Laharie F 128 B1
Onești RO 17 B7
Onhaye B 79 B4
Onich GB 34 B2
Onil E 159 C3
Onis E 142 A2
Önnestad S 61 C4
Onsala S 60 B2
Ontinyent E 159 C3
Ontur E 158 C2
Onzain F 103 B3
Onzonilla E 142 B1
Oostburg NL 79 A3
Oostende B 78 A2
Oosterend NL 70 A2
Oosterhout NL 79 A4
Oosterwolde NL 71 B3
Oosterzele B 79 B3
Oosthuizen NL 70 B2
Oostkamp B 78 A3
Oostmalle B 79 A4
Oost-Vlieland NL 70 A2
Oostvoorne NL 79 A4
Ootmarsum NL 71 B3
Opalenica PL 75 B5
O Páramo E 140 B3
Opařany CZ 96 B2
Opatija HR 123 B3
Opatów
Śląskie PL 86 B2
Świętokrzyskie PL 87 B5
Wielkopolskie PL 86 A2

Opatówek PL 86 A2
Opatowiec PL 87 B4
Opava CZ 98 B1
O Pedrouzo E 140 B2
Opeinde NL 70 A3
Oper Thalkirchdorf
D 107 B5
Opglabbeerk B 80 A1
Opicina I 122 B2
O Pino E 140 B2
Oplotnica SLO 123 A4
Opmeer NL 70 B1
Opochka RUS 9 D6
Opočno CZ 85 B4
Opoczno PL 87 A4
Opole PL 86 B1
Oporów PL 77 B4
O Porriño E 140 B2
Opovo SRB 127 B2
Oppach D 84 A2
Oppdal N 198 C6
Oppeby
Östergötland S 56 B1
Södermanland S 56 B2
Oppedal N 46 A2
Oppegård N 54 A1
Oppenau D 93 C4
Oppenberg A 110 B1
Oppenheim D 93 B4
Óppido Lucano I 172 B1
Óppido Mamertina
I 175 C1
Opponitz A 110 B1
Oppstad N 48 B3
Oprtalj HR 122 B2
Opsaheden S 49 B5
Ópusztaszer H 113 C4
Opuzen HR 138 B3
Ora
CY 181 B2
I 121 A4
Orada P 155 C3
Oradea RO 16 B4
Oradour-sur-Glane
F 115 C5
Oradour-sur-Vayres
F 115 C4
Oragonja SLO 122 B2
Orah BIH 139 C4
Orahova BIH 138 A3
Orahovica HR 125 B3
Orahovo BIH 124 B3
Oraison F 132 B1
Orajärvi FIN 196 C7
Orange F 131 A3
Orani I 178 B3
Oranienbaum D 83 A4
Oranienburg D 74 B2
Oranmore IRL 28 A3
Orašac SRB 127 C2
Orašje BIH 125 B4
Oravská Lesná SK 99 B3
Oravská Polhora
SK 99 B3
Oravské Veselé SK 99 B3
Oravsky-Podzámok
SK 99 B3
Orba E 159 C3
Orbacém P 148 A1
Orbais F 91 C3
Ørbæk DK 59 C3
Orbassano I 119 B4
Orbe CH 105 C5
Orbec F 89 A4
Orbetello I 168 A1
Orbetello Scalo I 168 A1
Orbigny F 103 B3
Ørby DK 59 B3
Örbyhus S 51 B4
Orce E 164 B2
Orcera E 164 A2
Orchamps-Vennes
F 105 B5
Orches F 102 C2
Orchete E 159 C3
Orchies F 78 B3
Orchowo PL 76 B3
Orcières F 118 C3
Ordes E 140 A2
Ordhead GB 33 D4
Ordino AND 146 B2
Ordizia E 144 A1
Orduña E 143 B4
Ore S 50 A2
Orea E 152 B2
Orebić HR 138 C3
Örebro S 56 A1
Öregcsertő H 112 C3
Öregrund S 51 B5
Orehoved DK 65 B4
Orellana E 156 A2
Orellana de la Sierra
E 156 A2
Ören TR 188 B2
Örencik TR 187 C4
Orestiada GR 186 A1
Organyà E 147 B2
Orgaz E 157 A4
Orgelet F 105 C4
Ørgenvika N 48 B1
Orgères-en-Beauce
F 103 A3
Orgibet F 145 B4
Orgnac-l'Aven F 131 A3
Orgon F 131 B4
Orgósolo I 178 B3
Orhaneli TR 186 C3
Orhangazi TR 187 B4
Orhei MD 17 B8
Orhomenos GR 184 A3
Oria E 164 B2
Ória I 173 B3
Origny-Ste Benoite
F 91 B3
Orihuela E 165 A4
Orihuela del Tremedal
E 152 B2
Orikum AL 182 C1
Oriola P 154 C3
Oriolo I 174 A2
Oriovac HR 125 B3
Orissaare EST 8 C3
Oristano I 179 C2
Öriszentpéter H 111 C3
Ørje N 54 A2
Orjiva E 163 B4
Orkanger N 198 B6
Örkelljunga S 61 C3
Örkény H 112 B3
Orlamünde D 82 B3
Orléans F 103 B3
Orlová CZ 98 B2
Orlovat SRB 126 B2
Ormea I 133 A3
Ormelet N 54 A1
Ormemyr N 53 A5
Ormilia GR 183 C5
Ormos GR 185 B5
Ormož SLO 124 A2
Ormskirk GB 38 A4
Ornans F 105 B5
Ornäs S 50 B2
Ørnes N 195 D4
Orneta PL 69 A5
Ørnhøj DK 59 B1
Ornö S 57 A4
Örnsköldsvik S 200 C4
Orolik HR 125 B4
Orom SRB 126 B1
Oron-la-Ville CH 106 C1
Oronsko PL 87 A4
Oropa I 119 B4
Oropesa
Castellón de la Plana
E 153 B4
Toledo E 150 C2
O Rosal E 140 C2
Orosei I 178 B3
Orosháza H 113 C4
Oroslavje HR 124 B1
Oroszlány H 112 B2
Oroszlo H 125 A4
Orotelli I 178 B3
Orozko E 143 A4
Orphir GB 33 C3
Orpington GB 45 B4
Orreaga-Roncesvalles
E 144 A2
Orrefors S 62 B3
Orrviken S 199 B11
Orsa S 50 A1
Orsara di Púglia I 171 B3
Orsay F 90 C2
Orscholz D 92 B2
Orsennes F 103 C3
Orserum S 55 B5
Orsha BY 13 A9
Orsières CH 119 A4
Örsjö S 63 B3
Ørslev DK 65 A4
Örslösa S 55 B3
Orsogna I 169 A4
Orsomarso I 174 B1
Orşova RO 16 C5
Ørsta N 198 C3
Ørsted DK 58 B3
Örsundsbro S 56 A3
Ortaca TR 188 C3
Ortakent TR 188 B2
Ortaklar TR 188 B2
Ortaköy TR 23 B8
Orta Nova I 171 B3
Orte I 168 A2
Ortenburg D 96 C1
Orth A 111 A3
Orthez F 128 C2
Ortigueira E 140 A3
Ortilla E 145 B3
Ortisei I 108 C2
Orţişoara RO 126 B3
Ortnevik N 46 A3
Orton GB 37 B4
Ortona I 169 A4
Ortrand D 84 A1
Orubica HR 124 B3
Ørum DK 58 B2
Orune I 178 B3
Orusco E 151 B4
Orvalho P 155 A3
Orvault F 101 B4
Ørvella N 53 A5
Orvieto I 168 A2
Orvínio I 169 A2
Oryakhovo BG 17 D5
Orzesze PL 86 B2
Orzinuovi I 120 B2
Orzivécchi I 120 B2
Orzysz PL 77 A6
Os
Hedmark N 48 B3
Hedmark N 199 C8
Osann-Monzel D 92 B2
Osbruk S 62 A2
Øsby DK 59 C2
Osby S 61 C3
Oščadnica SK 98 B2
Oschatz D 83 A5
Oschersleben D 73 B4
Óschiri I 178 B3
Osciłowo PL 77 B5
Osdorf D 64 B3
Osečina SRB 127 C1
Osečná CZ 84 B2
Oseja de Sajambre
E 142 A1
Osek CZ 84 B1
Osen N 199 A7
Osera de Ebro E 153 A3
Osidda I 178 B3
Osie PL 69 B3
Osieczna
Pomorskie PL 68 B3
Wielkopolskie PL 75 C5
Osieczno PL 75 A4
Osiek
Kujawsko-Pomorskie
PL 76 B3
Kujawsko-Pomorskie
PL 77 A4
Pomorskie PL 69 B3
Świętokrzyskie PL 87 B5
Osiek nad Notecią
PL 76 A2
Osielsko PL 76 A3
Osijek HR 125 B4
Osilnica SLO 123 B3
Ósilo I 178 B2
Ósimo I 136 B2
Osinja BIH 125 C3
Osintorf BY 13 A9
Osipaonica SRB 127 C3
Osjaków PL 86 A2
Oskamull GB 34 B1
Oskarshamn S 62 A4
Oskarström S 60 C2
Oslany SK 98 C2
Oslavany CZ 97 B4
Ošlje HR 139 C3
Oslo N 48 C2
Øsløs DK 58 A1
Osmancık TR 23 A8
Osmaneli TR 187 B4
Ösmo S 57 B3
Osmolin PL 77 B4
Osnabrück D 71 B5
Ośno Lubuskie PL 75 B3
Osoblaha CZ 85 B5
Osor HR 123 C3
Osorno E 142 B2
Øsoyra N 46 A2
Osøyro N 46 B2
Óspakseyri IS 190 B4
Os Peares E 140 B3
Ospedaletti I 133 B3
Ospitaletto I 120 B3
Oss NL 80 A1
Ossa de Montiel E 158 C1
Ossi I 178 B2
Ossjøen N 47 B5
Ossun F 145 A3
Ostanå S 61 C4
Ostanvik S 50 A2
Ostashkov RUS 9 D8
Östavall S 200 D1
Ostbevern D 71 B4
Østborg N 199 A10
Østby N 49 A4
Osted DK 61 D1
Ostenfeld D 64 B2
Oster UA 13 C9
Øster Assels DK 58 B1
Osterburg D 73 B4
Osterburken D 94 B1
Österbybruk S 51 B4
Osterbyhavn DK 58 A4
Österbymo S 62 A3
Ostercappeln D 71 B5
Österfärnebo S 51 B3
Osterfeld D 83 A3
Österforse S 200 C3
Osterhever D 64 B1
Osterhofen D 95 C5
Osterholz-Scharmbeck
D 72 A1
Øster Hornum DK 58 B2
Øster Hurup DK 58 B3
Østerild DK 58 A1
Øster Jølby DK 58 B1
Österlövsta S 51 B4
Øster-marie DK 67 A4
Ostermiething A 109 A3
Osterode am Harz D 82 A2
Ostersiel D 64 B1
Östersund S 199 B11
Øster Tørslev DK 58 B3
Östervåla S 51 B4
Östervallskog S 54 A2
Østervrå DK 58 A3
Osterwieck D 73 C3
Osterzell D 108 B1
Ostffyasszonyfa H 111 B4
Östfora S 51 C4
Östhammar S 51 B5
Ostheim F 106 A2
Ostheim vor der Rhön
D 82 B2
Osthofen D 93 B4
Ostiano I 120 B3
Ostíglia I 121 B4
Ostiz E 144 B2
Östmark S 49 B4
Östnor S 50 A1
Ostojićevo SRB 126 B2
Ostra I 136 B2
Östra Amtervik S 55 A4
Östraby S 61 D3
Ostrach D 107 B4
Östra Husby S 56 B2
Östra Ljungby S 61 C3
Östra Ryd S 56 B2
Ostrau D 83 A5
Ostrava CZ 98 B2
Østre Halsen N 53 A6
Ostrhauderfehn D 71 A4
Ostritz D 84 A2
Ostróda PL 69 B4
Ostroh UA 13 C7
Ostrołęka PL 12 B4
Ostropole PL 68 B1
Ostroróg PL 75 B5
Ostrošovac BIH 124 C1
Ostrov
CZ 83 B4
RUS 8 D6
Ostrov nad Oslavou
CZ 97 B3
Ostrówek PL 86 A2
Ostrowiec PL 68 A1
Ostrowiec-Świętokrzyski
PL 87 B5
Ostrowite PL 77 A4
Ostrów Mazowiecka
PL 12 B4
Ostrowo PL 76 B3
Ostrów Wielkopolski
PL 86 A1
Ostrožac BIH 139 B3
Ostrzeszów PL 86 A1
Ostseebad
Kühlungsborn D 65 B4
Ostuni I 173 B3
Osuna E 162 A2
Osvětimany CZ 98 B1
Oswestry GB 38 B3
Oświęcim PL 86 B3
Osztopán H 111 C4
Oteiza E 144 B2
Otelec RO 126 B2
Oteo E 143 A3
Oterbekk N 54 A1
Otero de Herreros
E 151 B3
Otero de O Bodas
E 141 C4
Othem S 57 C4
Otley GB 40 B2
Otmuchów PL 85 B5
Otočac HR 123 C4
Otok
Splitsko-Dalmatinska
HR 138 B2
Vukovarsko-Srijemska
HR 125 B4
Otoka BIH 124 C2
Otranto I 173 B4
Otrić HR 138 A2
Otrícoli I 168 A2
Otrokovice CZ 98 B1
Otta N 198 D6
Ottana I 178 B3
Ottaviano I 170 C2
Ottenby S 63 B4
Ottendorf-Okrilla D 84 A1
Ottenhöfen D 93 C4
Ottenschlag A 97 C3
Ottensheim A 96 C2
Otterbach D 93 B3
Otterbäcken S 55 B5
Otterberg D 93 B3
Otterburn GB 37 A4
Otter Ferry GB 34 B2
Otterndorf D 64 C1
Ottersburg D 72 A2
Ottersweier D 93 C4
Otterup DK 59 C3
Ottery St Mary GB 43 B3
Ottignies B 79 B4
Ottmarsheim F 106 B2
Ottobeuren D 107 B5
Öttömös H 126 A1
Ottone I 120 C2
Ottsjö S 199 B10
Ottweiler D 92 B3
Otveşti RO 126 B3
Ötvöskónyi H 124 A3
Otwock PL 12 B4
Ouanne F 104 B2
Ouarville F 90 C1
Oucques F 103 B3
Oud-Beijerland NL 79 A4
Ouddorp NL 79 A3
Oudemirdum NL 70 B2
Oudenaarde B 79 B3
Oudenbosch NL 79 A4
Oudenburg B 78 A3
Oude-Pekela NL 71 A4
Oude-Tonge NL 79 A4
Oudewater NL 70 B1
Oud Gastel NL 79 A4
Oudon F 101 B4
Oue DK 58 B2
Oughterard IRL 28 A2
Ouguela P 155 B3
Ouistreham F 89 A3
Oulainen FIN 3 D9
Oulchy-le-Château
F 91 B3
Oullins F 117 B4
Oulmes F 114 B3
Oulton GB 41 C5
Oulton Broad GB 41 C5
Oulu FIN 3 D9
Oulx I 119 B3
Oundle GB 40 C3
Ouranopoli GR 183 C6
Ourém P 154 B2
Ourense E 140 B3
Ourique P 160 B1
Ourol E 140 A3
Ouroux-en-Morvan
F 104 B2
Ousdale GB 32 C3
Oust F 146 B2
Outakoski FIN 193 C10
Outeiro P 148 B1
Outeiro de Rei E 140 A3
Outes E 140 B2
Outokumpu FIN 9 A6
Outreau F 78 B1
Outwell GB 41 C4
Ouzouer-le-Marché
F 103 B3
Ouzouer-sur-Loire
F 103 B4
Ovada I 133 A4
Ovar P 148 B1
Ovelgönne D 72 A1
Overath D 80 B3
Overbister GB 33 B4
Øverbygd N 192 D3
Overdinkel NL 71 B4
Överenhörna S 56 A3
Overhalla N 199 A8
Overijse B 79 B4
Over-jerstal DK 59 C2
Overlade DK 58 B2
Överlida S 60 B2
Överö FIN 51 B7
Overpelt B 79 A5
Overton GB 38 B4
Övertorneå S 196 C6
Överum S 62 A4
Ovidiopol UA 17 B9
Oviedo E 141 A5
Oviglio I 119 C5
Ovíndoli I 169 A3
Ovodda I 178 B3
Øvre Årdal N 47 A4
Øvrebygd N 52 B2
Øvre Rendal N 199 D8
Øvre Sirdal N 52 B2
Övre Soppero S 196 A4
Övre Ullerud S 55 A4
Ovruch UA 13 C8
Ovtrup DK 59 C1
Owińska PL 76 B1
Oxaback S 60 B2
Oxberg S 49 A6
Oxelösund S 56 B3
Oxenholme GB 37 B4
Oxford GB 44 B2
Oxie S 61 D3
Oxilithos GR 185 A5
Oxted GB 45 B4
Oyaca TR 187 C7
Øye N 47 A5
Øyenkilen N 54 A1
Øyer N 48 A2
Øyeren N 49 B4
Oyfiell N 53 A4
Øygärdslia N 53 B4
Oykel Bridge GB 32 D2
Øymark N 54 A2
Oyonnax F 118 A2
Øyslebø N 52 B3
Øystese N 46 B3
Oyten D 72 A2
Øyuvsbu N 52 A3
Ozaeta E 143 B4
Ozalj HR 123 B4
Ożarów PL 87 B5
Ożarów Maz PL 77 B5
Ožbalt SLO 110 C2
Ózd H 113 A4
Ožďany SK 99 C3
Ozieri I 178 B3
Ozimek PL 86 B2
Ozimica BIH 139 A4
Ozora H 112 C2
Ozorków PL 77 C4
Ozzano Monferrato
I 119 B5

P

Paakkola FIN 196 D7
Paal B 79 A5
Pabianice PL 86 A3
Pacanów PL 87 B5
Paceco I 176 B1
Pachino I 177 C4
Pačir SRB 126 B1
Pack A 110 B2
Paços de Ferreira
P 148 A1
Pacov CZ 96 B3
Pacsa H 111 C4
Pacy-sur-Eure F 89 A5
Paczków PL 85 B5
Padany RUS 3 E13
Padborg DK 64 B2
Padej SRB 126 B2
Padene HR 138 A2
Paderborn D 81 A4
Paderne P 160 B1
Padiham GB 40 B1
Padina SRB 126 B2
Padinska Skela
SRB 127 C2
Padornelo P 148 A1
Pádova I 121 B4
Padragkút H 111 B4
Padria I 178 B2
Padrón E 140 B2
Padru I 178 B3
Padstow GB 42 B2
Padul E 163 A4
Padula I 172 B1
Paduli I 170 B2
Paesana I 119 C4
Paese I 121 B5
Pag HR 137 A4
Pagani I 170 C2
Pagánica I 169 A3
Pagánico I 135 C4
Pagl ieta I 169 A4
Pagny-sur-Moselle
F 92 C2
Páhi H 112 C3
Pahkakumpu FIN 197 C11
Pahl D 108 B2
Paide EST 8 C4
Paignton GB 43 B3
Pailhès F 146 A2
Paimboeuf F 101 B3
Paimpol F 100 A2
Paimpont F 101 A3
Painswick GB 43 A4
Painten D 95 C3
Paisley GB 34 C3
Pajala S 196 B6
Pajares E 141 A5
Pajares de los Oteros
E 142 B1
Pajęczno PL 86 A2
Páka H 111 C3
Pakość PL 76 B3
Pakosławice PL 85 B5
Pakoštane HR 137 B4
Pakrac HR 124 B3
Paks H 112 C2
Palacios de la Sierra
E 143 C3
Palaciòs de la
Valduerna E 141 B5
Palacios del Sil E 141 B4
Palacios de Sanabria
E 141 B4
Palaciosrubios E 150 A2
Palafrugell E 147 C4
Palagiano I 173 B3
Palagonía I 177 B3
Paláia I 135 B3
Palaiokastritsa GR 182 D1
Palaiseau F 90 C2
Palamas GR 182 D4
Palamós E 147 C4
Påläng S 196 D5
Palanga LT 8 E2
Palanzano I 134 A3
Palárikovo SK 112 A2
Palas de Rei E 140 B3
Palata I 170 B2
Palau I 178 A3
Palavas-les-Flots F 131 B2
Palazuelos de la Sierra
E 143 B3
Palazzo Adriano I 176 B2
Palazzo del Pero I 135 B4
Palazzolo Acréide
I 177 B3
Palazzolo sull Oglio
I 120 B2
Palazzo San Gervásio
I 172 B1
Palazzuolo sul Senio
I 135 A4
Paldiski EST 8 C4
Pale BIH 139 B4
Palekastro GR 185 D7
Palena I 169 B4
Palencia E 142 B2
Palenciana E 163 A3
Paleochora GR 185 D4
Paleometokho CY 181 A2
Palermo I 176 A2
Paleros GR 182 E2
Palestrina I 169 B2
Pálfa H 112 C2
Palfau A 110 B1
Palhaça P 148 B1
Palheiros da Tocha
P 148 B1
Palheiros de Quiaios
P 148 B1
Paliaopoli GR 185 B5
Palić SRB 126 A1
Palidoro I 168 B2
Palinuro I 172 B1
Paliouri GR 183 D5
Paliseul B 91 B5
Pallanza I 119 B5
Pallares E 161 A3
Pallaruelo de Monegros
E 153 A3
Pallas Green IRL 29 B3
Pallerols E 146 B2
Palling D 109 A3
Palluau F 114 B2
Palma P 154 C2
Palma Campánia I 170 C2
Palma del Río E 162 A2
Palma de Mallorca
E 166 B2

Palma di Montechiaro I 176 B2
Palmádula I 178 B2
Palmanova I 122 B2
Palma Nova E 166 B2
Palmela P 154 C2
Palmerola E 147 B3
Palmi I 175 C1
Pälmonostora H 113 C3
Palo del Colle I 171 B4
Palojärvi FIN 192 D7
Palojoensuu FIN 196 A6
Palomares E 164 B3
Palomares del Campo E 158 B1
Palomas E 156 B1
Palombara Sabina I 168 A2
Palos de la Frontera E 161 B3
Palotaboszok H 125 A4
Palotás H 112 B3
Pals E 147 C4
Pålsboda S 56 A1
Paluzza I 109 C4
Pamhagen A 111 B3
Pamiers F 146 A2
Pamiętowo PL 76 A2
Pampaneira E 163 B4
Pamparato I 133 A3
Pampilhosa
Aveiro P 148 B1
Coimbra P 148 B2
Pampliega E 143 B3
Pamplona E 144 B2
Pampow D 73 A4
Pamukçu TR 186 C2
Pamukkale TR 188 B4
Pamukova TR 187 B5
Panagyurishte BG 17 D6
Pancalieri I 119 C4
Pančevo SRB 127 C2
Pancey F 91 C5
Pancorvo E 143 B3
Pancrudo E 152 B2
Pandino I 120 B2
Pandrup DK 58 A2
Panenský-Týnec CZ 84 B1
Panes E 142 A2
Panevėžys LT 8 E4
Pangbourne GB 44 B2
Panissières F 117 B4
Panki PL 86 B2
Pannes F 103 A4
Panningen NL 80 A1
Pannonhalma H 111 B4
Pano Lefkara CY 181 B2
Pano Panayia CY 181 B1
Panormos GR 185 B6
Panschwitz-Kuckau D 84 A2
Pansdorf D 65 C3
Pantano de Cíjara E 156 A3
Panticosa E 145 B3
Pantín E 140 A2
Pantoja E 151 B4
Pantón E 140 B3
Panxon E 140 B2
Páola I 174 B2
Paola M 175 C3
Pápa H 111 B4
Papasídero I 174 B1
Pápateszér H 111 B4
Papenburg D 71 A4
Paphos CY 181 B1
Pappenheim D 94 C2
Paprotnia PL 77 B5
Parábita I 173 B4
Paraćin SRB 127 D3
Parád H 113 B4
Parada
Bragança P 149 A3
Viseu P 148 B1
Paradas E 162 A2
Paradela E 140 B3
Parades de Rublales E 150 A2
Paradinas de San Juan E 150 B2
Paradiso di Cevadale I 108 C1
Paradyż PL 87 A4
Parainen FIN 8 B3
Parakhino Paddubye RUS 9 C8
Parakka S 196 B4
Paralimni CY 181 A2
Parallo Astros GR 184 B3
Paramé F 88 B2
Paramithia GR 182 D2
Páramo E 141 A4
Páramo del Sil E 141 B4
Parandaça P 148 A2
Paravadella E 141 A3
Paray-le-Monial F 104 C3
Parceiros P 154 B2
Parcey F 105 B4
Parchim D 73 A4
Parciaki PL 77 A6
Parcice PL 86 A2
Pardilla E 151 A4
Pardubice CZ 97 A3
Paredes
E 151 B5
P 148 A1
Paredes de Coura P 140 C2
Paredes de Nava E 142 B2
Paredes de Siguenza E 151 A5
Pareja E 151 B5
Parennes F 102 A1
Parenti I 175 B2
Parentis-en-Born F 128 B1
Parey D 73 B4
Parfino RUS 9 D7
Parga GR 182 D2
Pargny-sur-Saulx F 91 C4
Pari-Gagné F 117 A4
Parigné-l'Évêque F 102 B2
Parikkala FIN 9 B6
Paris F 90 C2
Parisot F 129 B4
Parkalompolo S 196 B5
Parkano FIN 8 A3
Parknasilla IRL 29 C2
Parla E 151 B4
Parlavá E 147 B4
Parma I 120 C3
Parndorf A 111 B3
Párnica SK 99 B3
Parnu EST 8 C4
Parolis E 164 A2
Paros GR 185 B6
Parrillas E 150 B2
Parsberg D 95 B3
Parstein D 74 B3
Partakko FIN 193 C11
Partanna I 176 B1
Parthenay F 102 C1
Partinico I 176 A2
Partizani SRB 127 C2
Partizánske SK 98 C2
Partney GB 41 B4
Påryd S 63 B3
Parzymiechy PL 86 A2
Paşcani RO 17 B7
Pasewalk D 74 A2
Pašina Voda MNE 139 B5
Påskallavik S 62 A4
Pasłęk PL 69 A4
Pašman HR 137 B4
Passage East IRL 30 B2
Passail A 110 B2
Passais F 88 B3
Passau D 96 C1
Passegueiro P 148 B1
Passignano sul Trasimeno I 135 B5
Passo di Tréia I 136 B2
Passopisciaro I 177 B4
Passow D 74 A3
Passy F 118 B3
Pastavy BY 13 A7
Pástena I 170 B2
Pastrana E 151 B5
Pastrengo I 121 B3
Pasym PL 77 A5
Pásztó H 113 B3
Pata SK 98 C1
Patay F 103 A3
Pateley Bridge GB 40 A2
Paterek PL 76 A2
Paterna E 159 B3
Paterna del Campo E 161 B3
Paterna del Madera E 158 C1
Paterna de Rivera E 162 B2
Paternion A 109 C4
Paternò I 177 B3
Paternópoli I 170 C3
Patersdorf D 95 B4
Paterswolde NL 71 A3
Patitiri GR 183 D5
Patmos GR 188 B1
Patna GB 36 A2
Pątnow PL 76 B3
Patoniva FIN 193 C11
Patopirtti FIN 197 B12
Patos AL 182 C1
Patra = Patras GR 184 A2
Patras = Patra GR 184 A2
Patreksfjörður IS 190 B2
Patrickswell IRL 29 B3
Patrimonio F 180 A2
Patrington GB 41 B3
Pattada I 178 B3
Pattensen
Niedersachsen D 72 A3
Niedersachsen D 72 B2
Patterdale GB 36 B4
Patti I 177 A3
Páty H 112 B2
Pau F 145 A3
Pauillac F 128 A2
Paularo I 109 C4
Paulhaguet F 117 B3
Paulhan F 130 B2
Paulilátino I 178 B2
Paulistrom S 62 A3
Paullo I 120 B2
Paulstown IRL 30 B1
Pausa D 83 B3
Pauträsk S 200 B3
Pavia
I 120 B2
P 154 C2
Pavias E 159 B3
Pavilly F 89 A4
Pāvilosta LV 8 D2
Pavullo nel Frignano I 135 A3
Pawłowice PL 86 A1
Pawlowice PL 98 B2
Paxi GR 182 D2
Payallar TR 189 C6
Payerne CH 106 C1
Paymogo E 161 B2
Payrac F 129 B4
Pazardzhik BG 183 A6
Pazaryeri TR 187 B4
Pazin HR 122 B2
Paziols F 146 B3
Pčelić HR 124 B3
Peal de Becerro E 164 B1
Peasmarsh GB 45 C4
Peć KOS 16 D4
Péccioli I 135 B3
Pécel H 112 B3
Pechao P 160 B2
Pechenga RUS 3 B12
Pechenizhyn UA 13 D6
Pecica RO 126 A3
Pećinci SRB 127 C1
Pecka SRB 127 C1
Peckelsheim D 81 A5
Pečory RUS 8 D5
Pécs H 125 A4
Pécsvárad H 125 A4
Peczniew PL 86 A2
Pedaso I 136 B2
Pedavena I 121 A4
Pedérobba I 121 B4
Pedersker DK 67 A3
Pedescala I 121 B4
Pedrafita E 141 B3
Pedrajas de San Esteban E 150 A3
Pedralba E 159 B3
Pedralba de la Praderia E 141 B4
Pedraza E 151 A4
Pedreguer E 159 C4
Pedrera E 162 A3
Pedro Abad E 157 C3
Pedro Bernardo E 150 B3
Pedroche E 156 B3
Pedrógão P 160 A2
Pedrogao P 149 B2
Pedrógão P 154 B2
Pedrógão Grande P 154 B2
Pedrola E 144 C2
Pedro-Martinez E 164 B1
Pedro Muñoz E 158 B1
Pedrosa del Rey E 150 A2
Pedrosa del Rio Urbel E 143 B3
Pedrosa de Tobalina E 143 B3
Pedrosillo de los Aires E 150 B2
Pedrosillo el Ralo E 150 A2
Pędzewo PL 76 A3
Peebles GB 35 C4
Peel GB 36 B2
Peenemünde D 66 B2
Peer B 79 A5
Pega P 149 B2
Pegalajar E 163 A4
Pegau D 83 A4
Peggau A 110 B2
Pegli I 133 A4
Pegnitz D 95 B3
Pego E 159 C3
Pegões-Estação P 154 C2
Pegões Velhos P 154 C2
Pęgów PL 85 A4
Pegswood GB 37 A5
Peguera E 166 B2
Pehlivanköy TR 186 A1
Peine D 72 B3
Peisey-Nancroix F 118 B3
Peissenberg D 108 B2
Peiting D 108 B1
Peitz D 84 A2
Péjo I 121 A3
Pelagićevo BIH 125 C4
Pelahustán E 150 B3
Pełczyce PL 75 A4
Pelhřimov CZ 97 B3
Pélissanne F 131 B4
Pelkosenniemi FIN 197 B10
Pellegrino Parmense I 120 C2
Pellegrue F 128 B3
Pellérd H 125 A4
Pellestrina I 122 B1
Pellevoisin F 103 C3
Pellizzano I 121 A3
Pello
FIN 196 C7
S 196 C6
Peloche E 156 A2
Pelplin PL 69 B3
Pelussin F 117 B4
Pély H 113 B4
Pembroke GB 39 C2
Pembroke Dock GB 39 C2
Peñacerrada E 143 B4
Penacova P 148 B1
Peña de Cabra E 149 B4
Peñafiel E 151 A3
Penafiel P 148 A1
Peñaflor E 162 A2
Peñalba de Santiago E 141 B4
Peñalsordo E 156 B2
Penalva do Castelo P 148 B2
Penamacôr P 149 B2
Peñaparda E 149 B3
Peñaranda de Bracamonte E 150 B2
Peñaranda de Duero E 143 C3
Peñarroya de Tastavins E 153 B4
Peñarroya-Pueblonuevo E 156 B2
Peñarrubla E 141 B3
Penarth GB 39 C3
Peñascosa E 158 C1
Peñas de San Pedro E 158 C2
Peñausende E 149 A4
Penc H 112 B3
Pencoed GB 39 C3
Pendalofos GR 182 C3
Pendeen GB 42 B1
Pendine GB 39 C2
Pendueles E 142 A2
Penedono P 148 B2
Penela P 154 A2
Pénestin F 101 B3
Penhas Juntas P 149 A2
Peniche P 154 B1
Penicuik GB 35 C4
Penig D 83 B4
Penilhos P 160 B2
Peñíscola E 153 B4
Penistone GB 40 B2
Penkridge GB 40 C1
Penkun D 74 A3
Penmarch F 100 B1
Pennabilli I 135 B5
Penne I 169 A3
Penne-d'Agenais F 129 B3
Pennes I 108 C2
Pennyghael GB 34 B1
Peno RUS 9 D8
Penpont GB 36 A3
Penrhyndeudraeth GB 38 B2
Penrith GB 37 B4
Penryn GB 42 B1
Pentraeth GB 38 A2
Penybontfawr GB 38 B3
Penygroes
Carmarthenshire GB 39 C2
Gwynedd GB 38 A2
Penzance GB 42 B1
Penzberg D 108 B2
Penzlin D 74 A2
Pepinster B 80 B1
Peqin AL 182 B1
Pér H 111 B4
Pera Boa P 148 B2
Perachora GR 184 A3
Perafita P 148 A1
Peraleda de la Mata E 150 C2
Peraleda del Zaucejo E 156 B2
Peraleda de San Román E 156 A2
Perales de Alfambra E 152 B2
Perales del Puerto E 149 B3
Perales de Tajuña E 151 B4
Peralta E 144 B2
Peralta de la Sal E 145 C4
Peralva P 160 B2
Peralveche E 152 B1
Perama GR 185 D5
Peranka FIN 197 D12
Perbál H 112 B2
Perchtoldsdorf A 111 A3
Percy F 88 B2
Perdasdefogu I 179 C3
Perdiguera E 145 C3
Peredo P 149 A3
Peregu Mare RO 126 A2
Pereiro
Faro P 160 B2
Guarda P 149 B2
Santarém P 154 B2
Pereiro de Aguiar E 140 B3
Perelada E 147 B4
Perelejos de las Truchas E 152 B2
Pereña E 149 A3
Pereruela E 149 A4
Pértugas I 178 B2
Perg A 110 A1
Pérgine Valsugana I 121 A4
Pérgola I 136 B1
Pergusa I 177 B3
Periam RO 126 A2
Periana E 163 B3
Périers F 88 A2
Périgueux F 129 A3
Perino I 120 C2
Perjasica HR 123 B4
Perkáta H 112 B2
Perković HR 138 B2
Perleberg D 73 A4
Perlez SRB 126 B2
Përmet AL 182 C2
Pernarec CZ 95 B5
Pernek SK 98 C1
Pernes P 154 B2
Pernes-les-Fontaines F 131 A4
Pernik BG 17 D5
Pernink CZ 83 B4
Pernitz A 110 B2
Pernu FIN 197 C10
Peroguarda P 160 A1
Pérols F 131 B2
Péronne F 90 B2
Péronnes B 79 B4
Pero Pinheiro P 154 C1
Perorrubio E 151 A4
Perosa Argentina I 119 C4
Perozinho P 148 A1
Perpignan F 146 B3
Perranporth GB 42 B1
Perranzabuloe GB 42 B1
Perrecy-les-Forges F 104 C3
Perrero I 119 C4
Perrignier F 118 A3
Perros-Guirec F 100 A2
Persan F 90 B2
Persberg S 55 A5
Persenbeug A 110 A2
Pershore GB 44 A1
Persön S 196 D5
Perstorp S 61 C3
Perth GB 35 B4
Pertisau A 108 B2
Pertoča SLO 111 C3
Pertuis F 131 B4
Perućac SRB 127 D1
Perúgia I 136 B1
Perušić HR 123 C4
Péruwelz B 79 B3
Pervomaysk UA 13 D9
Perwez B 79 B4
Pesadas de Burgos E 143 B3
Pesaguero E 142 A2
Pésaro I 136 B1
Pescantina I 121 B3
Pescara I 169 A4
Pescasséroli I 169 B3
Peschici I 171 B4
Peschiera del Garda I 121 B3
Péscia I 135 B3
Pescina I 169 A3
Pescocostanzo I 169 B4
Pescopagano I 172 B1
Pesco Sannita I 170 B2
Peshkopi AL 182 B2
Peshtera BG 183 A6
Pesmes F 105 B4
Pesnica SLO 110 C2
Peso da Régua P 148 A2
Pesquera de Duero E 142 C2
Pessac F 128 B2
Pestovo RUS 9 C9
Petäjäskoski FIN 197 C8
Petalidi GR 184 C2
Pétange L 92 B1
Petas GR 182 D3
Peteranec HR 124 A2
Peterborough GB 41 C3
Peterculter GB 33 D4
Peterhead GB 33 D5
Peterlee GB 37 B5
Petersfield GB 44 B3
Petershagen
Brandenburg D 74 B2
Brandenburg D 74 B3
Nordrhein-Westfalen D 72 B1
Petershausen D 95 C3
Peterswell IRL 28 A3
Pétervására H 113 A4
Petília Policastro I 175 B2
Petín E 141 B3
Pětipsy CZ 83 B5
Petkus D 74 C2
Petlovac HR 125 B4
Petlovača SRB 127 C1
Petőfiszallás H 113 C3
Petra E 167 B3
Petralia Sottana I 177 B3
Petrčane HR 137 A4
Petrella Tifernina I 170 B2
Petrer E 159 C3
Petreto-Bicchisano F 180 B1
Petrich BG 183 B5
Petrijevci HR 125 B4
Petrinja HR 124 B2
Petrodvorets RUS 9 C6
Pétrola E 158 C2
Petronà I 175 B2
Petronell A 111 A3
Petroşani RO 17 C5
Petrovac SRB 127 C3
Petrovaradin SRB 126 B1
Petrovice
BIH 139 A4
CZ 84 B1
Petrovo RUS 69 A5
Petrozavodsk RUS 9 B9
Pettenbach A 109 B5
Pettigo IRL 26 B3
Petworth GB 44 C3
Peuerbach A 96 C1
Peuntenansa E 142 A2
Peurasuvanto FIN 197 B9
Pevensey Bay GB 45 C4
Peveragno I 133 A3
Pewsey GB 44 B2
Pewsum D 71 A4
Peyrat-le-Château F 116 B1
Peyrehorade F 128 C1
Peyriac-Minervois F 146 A3
Peyrins F 117 B5
Peyrissac F 116 B1
Peyrolles-en-Provence F 132 B1
Peyruis F 132 A1
Pézarches F 90 C2
Pézenas F 130 B2
Pezinok SK 111 A4
Pezuls F 129 B3
Pfaffenhausen D 108 A1
Pfaffenhofen
Bayern D 94 C2
Bayern D 95 C3
Pfaffenhoffen F 93 C3
Pfäffikon CH 107 B3
Pfarrkirchen D 95 C4
Pfeffenhausen D 95 C3
Pfetterhouse F 106 B2
Pforzheim D 93 C4
Pfreimd D 95 B4
Pfronten D 108 B1
Pfullendorf D 107 B4
Pfullingen D 94 C1
Pfunds A 108 C1
Pfungstadt D 93 B4
Pfyn CH 107 B3
Phalsbourg F 92 C3
Philippeville B 79 B4
Philippsreut D 96 C1
Philippsthal D 82 B1
Piacenza I 120 B2
Piacenza d'Adige I 121 B4
Piádena I 120 B3
Piana F 180 A1
Piana Crixia I 133 A4
Piana degli Albanesi I 176 B2
Piana di Monte Verna I 170 B2
Piancastagnáio I 135 C4
Piandelagotti I 134 A3
Pianella
Abruzzi I 169 A4
Toscana I 135 B4
Pianello Val Tidone I 120 C2
Pianoro I 135 A4
Pians A 108 B1
Pías E 141 B4
Pias P 160 A2
Piaseczno PL 77 B6
Piasek PL 74 B3
Piaski PL 69 A4
Piastów PL 77 B5
Piaszcyna PL 68 A2
Piątek PL 77 B4
Piatra Neamţ RO 17 B7
Piazza al Sérchio I 134 A3
Piazza Armerina I 177 B3
Piazza Brembana I 120 B2
Piazze I 135 C4
Piazzola sul Brenta I 121 B4
Picassent E 159 B3
Piccione I 136 B1
Picerno I 172 B1
Picher D 73 A4
Pickering GB 40 A3
Pico I 169 B3
Picón E 157 A3
Picquigny F 90 B2
Piechowice PL 84 B3
Piecnik PL 75 A5
Piedicavallo I 119 B4
Piedicroce F 180 A2
Piedimonte Etneo I 177 B4
Piedimonte Matese I 170 B2
Piedimulera I 119 A5
Piedipaterno I 136 C1
Piedrabuena E 157 A3
Piedraescrita E 156 A3
Piedrafita E 142 A1
Piedrahita E 150 B2
Piedralaves E 150 B3
Piedras Albas E 155 B4
Piedras Blancas E 141 A5
Piegaro I 135 C5
Piekary Śl. PL 86 B2
Piekoszów PL 87 B4
Pieksämäki FIN 8 A5
Pielenhofen D 95 B3
Pielgrzymka PL 85 A3
Pieniężno PL 69 A5
Pieńsk PL 84 A3
Pienza I 135 B4
Piera E 147 C2
Pieranie PL 76 B3
Pierowall GB 33 B4
Pierre-Buffière F 115 C5
Pierrecourt F 105 B4
Pierre-de-Bresse F 105 C4
Pierrefeu-du-Var F 132 B2
Pierrefitte-Nestalas F 145 B3

Pierrefitte-sur-Aire F 92 C1
Pierrefonds F 90 B2
Pierrefontaine-les-Varans F 105 B5
Pierrefort F 116 C2
Pierrelatte F 131 A3
Pierrepont
Aisne F 91 B3
Meurthe-et-Moselle F 92 B1
Piesendorf A 109 B3
Pieštany SK 98 C1
Pieszkowo PL 69 A5
Pieszyce PL 85 B4
Pietarsaari FIN 3 E8
Pietragalla I 172 B1
Pietra Ligure I 133 A4
Pietralunga I 136 B1
Pietramelara I 170 B2
Pietraperzia I 177 B3
Pietrasanta I 134 B3
Pietravairano I 170 B2
Pieve del Cáiro I 120 B1
Pieve di Bono I 121 B3
Pieve di Cadore I 122 A1
Pieve di Cento I 121 C4
Pieve di Soligo I 121 B5
Pieve di Teco I 133 A3
Pievepélago I 134 A3
Pieve Santo Stefano I 135 B5
Pieve Torina I 136 B2
Piges GR 182 D3
Píglio I 169 B3
Pigna I 133 B3
Pignan F 130 B2
Pignataro Maggiore I 170 B2
Piittisjärvi FIN 197 C9
Pijnacker NL 70 B1
Pikalevo RUS 9 C9
Piła PL 75 A5
Pilar de la Horadada E 165 B4
Pilas E 161 B3
Pilastri I 121 C4
Piława Górna PL 85 B4
Piławki PL 69 B4
Pilchowice PL 86 B2
Pilea GR 183 C5
Pilgrimstad S 199 C12
Pili
Dodekanisa GR 188 C2
Trikala GR 182 D3
Pilica PL 86 B3
Pilis H 112 B3
Piliscaba H 112 B2
Pilisszántó H 112 B2
Pilisvörösvár H 112 B2
Pilos GR 184 C2
Pilsting D 95 C4
Pilszcz PL 98 A1
Pilterud N 48 C2
Pilu RO 113 C5
Pina de Ebro E 153 A3
Piñar E 163 A4
Pınarbaşı TR 186 C1
Pınarhisar TR 186 A2
Pinas F 145 A4
Pincehely H 112 C2
Pinchbeck GB 41 C3
Pińczów PL 87 B4
Pineda de la Sierra E 143 B3
Pineda de Mar E 147 C3
Pinerella I 135 A5
Pinerolo I 119 C4
Pineta Grande I 170 C1
Pineto I 169 A4
Piney F 91 C4
Pinggau A 111 B3
Pinhal Novo P 154 C2
Pinhão P 148 A2
Pinheiro
Aveiro P 148 A1
Aveiro P 148 B1
Pinheiro Grande P 154 B2
Pinhel P 149 B2
Pinhoe GB 43 B3
Pinilla E 158 C2
Pinilla de Toro E 150 A2
Pinkafeld A 111 B3
Pinneberg D 72 A2
Pinnow D 74 C3
Pino F 180 A2
Pino del Rio E 142 B2
Pino de Val E 140 B2
Pinofranqueado E 149 B3
Pinols F 117 B3
Piñor E 140 B2
Pinos del Valle E 163 B4
Pinoso E 159 C2
Pinos Puente E 163 A4
Pinsk BY 13 B7
Pintamo FIN 197 D10
Pinto E 151 B4
Pinzano al Tagliamento I 122 A1
Pinzio P 149 B2
Pinzolo I 121 A3
Piòbbico I 136 B1
Piombino I 134 C3
Pionki PL 87 A5
Pionsat F 116 A2
Pióraco I 136 B1
Piornal E 150 B2
Piotrkowice PL 87 B4
Piotrków-Kujawski PL 76 B3
Piotrków Trybunalski PL 86 A3
Piotrowo PL 75 B5
Piove di Sacco I 121 B5
Piovene I 121 B4
Piperskärr S 62 A4
Pipriac F 101 B4
Piraeus = Pireas GR 185 B4
Piran SLO 122 B2
Pireas = Piraeus GR 185 B4
Piré-sur-Seiche F 101 A4
Pirgi GR 185 A6
Pirgos
Ilia GR 184 B2
Kriti GR 185 D6
Piriac-sur-Mer F 101 B3
Piringsdorf A 111 B3
Pirmasens D 93 B3
Pirna D 84 B1
Pirnmill GB 34 C2
Pirot SRB 16 D5
Pirovac HR 137 B4
Pirttivuopio S 196 B2
Pisa I 134 B3
Pisany F 114 C3
Pisarovina HR 124 B1
Pischelsdorf in der Steiermark A 110 B2
Pişchia RO 126 B3
Pisciotta I 172 B1
Písek CZ 96 B2
Pisogne I 120 B3
Pissos F 128 B2
Pissouri CY 181 B1
Pisticci I 174 A2
Pistóia I 135 B3
Piteå S 196 D4
Piteşti RO 17 C6
Pithiviers F 103 A4
Pitigliano I 168 A1
Pitkyaranta RUS 9 B7
Pitlochry GB 35 B4
Pitomača HR 124 B3
Pitres E 163 B4
Pittentrail GB 32 D2
Pitvaros H 126 A2
Pivka SLO 123 B3
Pivnice SRB 126 B1
Piwniczna PL 99 B4
Pizarra E 163 B3
Pizzano I 121 A3
Pizzighettone I 120 B2
Pizzo I 175 C2
Pizzoli I 169 A3
Pizzolungo I 176 A1
Pjätteryd S 61 C4
Plabennec F 100 A1
Placencia E 143 A4
Plaffeien CH 106 C2
Plaisance
Gers F 128 C3
Haute-Garonne F 129 C4
Tarn F 130 B1
Plaka GR 183 D7
Plan E 145 B4
Planá CZ 95 B4
Planánad Lužnici CZ 96 B2
Plaňany CZ 96 A3
Planchez F 104 B3
Plancoët F 101 A3
Plancy-l'Abbaye F 91 C3
Plan-de-Baix F 118 C2
Plandište SRB 126 B3
Plan-d'Orgon F 131 B3
Plánice CZ 96 B1
Planina
SLO 123 A4
SLO 123 B3
Plankenfels D 95 B3
Plasencia E 149 B3
Plasenzuela E 156 A1
Plaški HR 123 B4
Plassen
Buskerud N 47 B4
Hedmark N 49 A4
Plášťovce SK 112 A3
Plasy CZ 96 B1
Platamona Lido I 178 B2
Platania I 175 B2
Platanos GR 185 D4
Platí I 175 C2
Platičevo SRB 127 C1
Platja d'Aro E 147 C4
Plattling D 95 C4
Plau D 73 A5
Plaue
Brandenburg D 73 B5
Thüringen D 82 B2
Plauen D 83 B4
Plavecký Mikuláš SK 98 C1
Plavinas LV 8 D4
Plavna SRB 125 B5
Plavnica SK 99 B4
Plavno HR 138 A2
Playben F 100 A2
Pléaux F 116 B2
Pleine-Fougères F 88 B2
Pleinfeld D 94 B2
Pleinting D 95 C5
Plélan-le-Grand F 101 B3
Plémet F 101 A3
Pléneuf-Val-André F 101 A3
Plentzia E 143 A4
Plérin F 101 A3
Plešivec SK 99 C4
Plessa D 83 A5
Plessé F 101 B4
Plestin-les-Grèves F 100 A2
Pleszew PL 76 C2
Pleternica HR 125 B3
Plettenberg D 81 A3
Pleubian F 100 A2
Pleumartin F 115 B4
Pleumeur-Bodou F 100 A2
Pleurs F 91 C3
Pleven BG 17 D6
Plevnik-Drienové SK 98 B2
Pleyber-Christ F 100 A2
Pliego E 165 B3
Pliešovce SK 99 C3
Plitvička Jezera HR 123 C4
Plitvički Ljeskovac HR 123 C4
Ploaghe I 178 B2
Ploče HR 138 B3
Plochingen D 94 C1
Płock PL 77 B4
Ploemeur F 100 B2
Ploërmel F 101 B3
Ploeuc-sur-Lie F 101 A3
Plogastel St Germain F 100 B1
Plogoff F 100 A1
Ploieşti RO 17 C7
Plomari GR 186 D1
Plombières-les-Bains F 105 B5
Plomin HR 123 B3
Plön D 65 B3
Plonéour-Lanvern F 100 B1
Płonia PL 74 A3
Płoniawy PL 77 B6
Płońsk PL 77 B5
Płoskinia PL 69 A4
Plössberg D 95 B4
Płoty PL 67 C4
Plouagat F 100 A2
Plouaret F 100 A2
Plouarzel F 100 A1
Plouay F 100 B2
Ploubalay F 101 A3
Ploubazlanec F 100 A2
Ploudalmézeau F 100 A1
Ploudiry F 100 A1
Plouescat F 100 A1
Plouézec F 100 A3
Plougasnou F 100 A2
Plougastel-Daoulas F 100 A1
Plougonven F 100 A2
Plougonver F 100 A2
Plougrescant F 100 A2
Plouguenast F 101 A3
Plouguerneau F 100 A1
Plouha F 100 A3
Plouhinec F 100 A1
Plouigneau F 100 A2
Ploumanach F 100 A2
Plounévez-Quintin F 100 A2
Plouray F 100 A2
Plouzévédé F 100 A1
Plovdiv BG 183 A6
Plozévet F 100 B1
Plumbridge GB 27 B3
Pluméliau F 100 B3
Plumlov CZ 97 B5
Plungė LT 8 E2
Pluty PL 69 A5
Pluvigner F 100 B3
Plužine
BIH 139 B4
MNE 139 B4
Płużnica PL 69 B3
Plymouth GB 42 B2
Plymstock GB 42 B2
Płytnica PL 68 B1
Plyusa RUS 9 C6
Plzeň CZ 96 B1
Pniewy PL 75 B5
Pobes E 143 B4
Poběžovice CZ 95 B4
Pobiedziska PL 76 B2
Pobierowo PL 67 B3
Pobla de Segur E 145 B4
Pobladura del Valle E 142 B1
Pobla-Tornesa E 153 B4
Pobra de Trives E 141 B3
Pobra do Brollón E 141 B3
Pobra do Caramiñal E 140 B2
Pobudje BIH 139 A5
Počátky CZ 97 B3
Poceirão P 154 C2
Pöchlarn A 110 A2
Pociecha PL 87 A4
Pockau D 83 B5
Pocking D 96 C1
Pocklington GB 40 B3
Podbořany CZ 83 B5
Podbrdo SLO 122 A2
Podbrezová SK 99 C3
Podčetrtek SLO 123 A4
Poddębice PL 76 C3
Poděbrady CZ 84 B3
Podence P 149 A3
Podensac F 128 B2
Podenzano I 120 C2
Podersdorf am See A 111 B3
Podgaje PL 68 B1
Podgora HR 138 B3
Podgóra PL 87 A5
Podgorač HR 125 B4
Podgorica MNE 16 D3
Podgorie AL 182 C2
Podgrad SLO 123 B3
Podhájska SK 112 A2
Podkova BG 183 B7
Podlapača HR 123 C4
Podlejki PL 69 B5
Podlužany SK 98 C2
Podnovlje BIH 125 C4
Podolie SK 98 C1
Podolínec SK 99 B4
Podolsk RUS 9 E10
Podporozhy RUS 9 B9
Podromanija BIH 139 B4
Podturen HR 111 C3
Podvín CZ 97 C4
Podwilk PL 99 B3
Poetto I 179 C3
Poggendorf D 66 B2
Poggiardo I 173 B4
Poggibonsi I 135 B4
Póggio a Caiano I 135 B4
Poggio Imperiale I 171 B3
Póggio Mirteto I 168 A2
Póggio Moiano I 169 A2
Póggio Renatico I 121 C4
Póggio Rusco I 121 C4
Pöggstall A 97 C3
Pogny F 91 C4
Pogorzela PL 85 A5
Pogorzelice PL 68 A2
Pogradec AL 182 C2
Pogrodzie PL 69 A4
Pohorelá SK 99 C4
Pohořelice CZ 97 C4
Pohronská Polhora SK 99 C3
Poiares P 148 B1
Poio E 140 B2
Poirino I 119 C4
Poisson F 117 A4
Poissons F 91 C5
Poissy F 90 C2
Poitiers F 115 B4
Poix-de-Picardie F 90 B1
Poix-Terron F 91 B4
Pokka FIN 197 A8
Pokój PL 86 B1
Pokupsko HR 124 B1
Pol E 141 A3
Pola RUS 9 D7
Pol a Charra GB 31 B1
Pola de Allande E 141 A4
Pola de Laviana E 142 A1
Pola de Lena E 141 A5
Pola de Siero E 142 A1
Pola de Somiedo E 141 A4
Polaincourt-et-Clairefontaine F 105 B5
Połajewo PL 75 B5
Polán E 151 C3
Polanica-Zdrój PL 85 B4
Połaniec PL 87 B5
Polanów PL 68 A1
Polatlı TR 187 C7
Polatsk BY 13 A8
Polch D 80 B3
Polcirkeln S 196 C4
Pólczno PL 68 A2
Połczyn-Zdrój PL 67 C5
Polegate GB 45 C4
Poleñino E 145 C3
Polesella I 121 C4
Polessk RUS 12 A4
Polgár H 113 B5
Polgárdi H 112 B2
Polhov Gradec SLO 123 A3
Police PL 74 A3
Police nad Metují CZ 85 B4
Polichnitos GR 186 C1
Polička CZ 97 B4
Poličnik HR 137 A4
Policoro I 174 A2
Policzna PL 87 A5
Poligiros GR 183 C5
Polignano a Mare I 173 B3
Poligny F 105 C4
Polis CY 181 A1
Polistena I 175 C2
Polizzi Generosa I 176 B3
Poljana SRB 127 C3
Poljanák HR 123 C4
Poljčane SLO 123 A4
Polje BIH 125 C3
Poljice
BIH 138 A2
BIH 139 A4
Polkowice PL 85 A4
Polla I 172 B1
Pollas E 150 A2
Pöllau A 110 B2
Polleben D 82 A3
Pollença E 167 B3
Pollenfeld D 95 C3
Pollfoss N 198 D4
Póllica I 170 C3
Polminhac F 116 C2
Polná CZ 97 B3
Polna RUS 8 C6
Polne PL 75 A5
Polomka SK 99 C3
Polonne UA 13 C7
Polperro GB 42 B2
Polruan GB 42 B2
Pöls A 110 B1
Polska Cerekiew PL 86 B2
Poltár SK 99 C3
Põltsamaa EST 8 C4
Polyarny RUS 3 B13
Polyarnyye Zori RUS 3 C13
Polzela SLO 123 A4
Pomarance I 135 B3
Pomarez F 128 C2
Pomárico I 172 B2
Pomáz H 112 B3
Pombal P 154 B2
Pomeroy GB 27 B4
Pomézia I 168 B2
Pommard F 105 B3
Pommelsbrunn D 95 B3
Pomonte I 134 C3
Pomorie BG 17 D7
Pomos CY 181 A1
Pompei I 170 C2
Pompey F 92 C2
Pomposa I 122 C1
Poncin F 118 A2
Pondorf D 95 C3
Ponferrada E 141 B4
Poniec PL 85 A4
Ponikva SLO 123 A4
Poniky SK 99 C3
Pons F 114 C3
Ponsacco I 134 B3
Pont I 119 B4
Pont-a-Celles B 79 B4
Pontacq F 145 A3
Pontailler-sur-Saône F 105 B4
Pont-a-Marcq F 78 B3
Pont-à-Mousson F 92 C2
Pontão P 154 B2
Pontardawe GB 39 C3
Pontarddulais GB 39 C2
Pontarion F 116 B1
Pontarlier F 105 C5
Pontassieve I 135 B4
Pontaubault F 88 B2
Pont-Audemer F 89 A4
Pontaumur F 116 B2
Pont-Aven F 100 B2
Pont Canavese I 119 B4
Pontcharra F 118 B3
Pontcharra-sur-Turdine F 117 B4
Pontchâteau F 101 B3
Pont-Croix F 100 A1
Pont-d'Ain F 118 A2
Pont-de-Beauvoisin F 118 B2
Pont-de-Buis-lès-Quimerch F 100 A1
Pont-de-Chéruy F 118 B2
Pont de Dore F 117 B3
Pont-de-Labeaume F 117 C4
Pont-de-l'Arche F 89 A5
Pont de Molins E 147 B3
Pont-de-Roide F 106 B1
Pont-de-Salars F 130 A1
Pont-d'Espagne F 145 B3
Pont de Suert E 145 B4
Pont-de-Vaux F 117 A4
Pont-de-Veyle F 117 A4
Pont d'Ouilly F 89 B3
Pont-du-Château F 116 B3
Pont-du-Navoy F 105 C4
Ponte a Moriano I 134 B3
Ponte Arche I 121 A3
Ponteareas E 140 B2
Pontebba I 109 C4
Ponte Cáffaro I 121 B3
Pontecagnano I 170 C2
Ponte-Caldelas E 140 B2
Ponteceso E 140 A2
Pontecesures E 140 B2
Pontecorvo I 169 B3
Ponte da Barca P 148 A1
Pontedássio I 133 B4
Pontedécimo I 133 A4
Ponte de Lima P 148 A1
Ponte dell'Ólio I 120 C2
Pontedera I 134 B3
Ponte de Sor P 154 B2
Pontedeume E 140 A2
Ponte di Barbarano I 121 B4
Ponte di Legno I 121 A3
Ponte di Nava I 133 A3
Ponte di Piave I 122 B1
Ponte Felcino I 136 B1
Pontefract GB 40 B2
Ponte Gardena I 108 C2
Ponteginori I 135 B3
Pontelagoscuro I 121 C4
Ponteland GB 37 A5
Pontelandolfo I 170 B2
Ponte-Leccia F 180 A2
Pontelongo I 121 B5
Ponte nelle Alpi I 122 A1
Pont-en-Royans F 118 B2
Pontenure I 120 C2
Pontenx-les-Forges F 128 B1
Ponterwyd GB 39 B3
Ponte San Giovanni I 136 B1
Ponte San Pietro I 120 B2
Pontevedra E 140 B2
Pontevico I 120 B3
Pont Farcy F 88 B2
Pontfaverger-Moronvillers F 91 B4
Pontgibaud F 116 B2
Ponticino I 135 B4
Pontigny F 104 B2
Pontijou F 103 B3
Pontinia I 169 B3
Pontinvrea I 133 A4
Pontivy F 100 A3
Pont-l'Abbé F 100 B1
Pont-l'Évêque F 89 A4
Pontlevoy F 103 B3
Pontoise F 90 B2
Pontones E 164 A2
Pontonx-sur-l'Abour F 128 C2
Pontoon IRL 26 C1
Pontorson F 88 B2
Pontrémoli I 134 A2
Pont-Remy F 90 A1
Pontresina CH 107 C4
Pontrhydfendigaid GB 39 B3
Pontrieux F 100 A2
Ponts E 147 C2
Ponts-aux-Dames F 90 C2
Pont Scorff F 100 B2
Pöntsö FIN 196 B7
Pont-Ste Maxence F 90 B2
Pont-St Esprit F 131 A3
Pont-St Mamet F 129 B3
Pont-St Martin
F 101 B4
I 119 B4
Pont-St Vincent F 92 C2
Pont-sur-Yonne F 104 A2
Pontvallain F 102 B2
Pontypool GB 39 C3
Pontypridd GB 39 C3
Ponza I 169 C2
Poo E 142 A2
Poole GB 43 B5
Poolewe GB 31 B3
Poperinge B 78 B2
Pópoli I 169 A3
Popovac SRB 127 D3
Popovača HR 124 B2
Popow PL 77 B4
Poppel B 79 A5
Poppenhausen
Bayern D 82 B2
Hessen D 82 B1
Poppi I 135 B4
Poprad SK 99 B4
Popučke SRB 127 C1
Pópulo P 148 A2
Populónia I 134 C3
Pörböly H 125 A4
Porcuna E 163 A3
Pordenone I 122 B1
Pordic F 100 A3
Poręba PL 86 B3
Poreč HR 122 B2
Pori FIN 8 B2
Porjus S 196 C2
Porkhov RUS 9 D6
Porlezza I 120 A2
Porlock GB 43 A3
Pörnbach D 95 C3
Pornic F 101 B3
Pornichet F 101 B3
Porodin SRB 127 C3
Poronin PL 99 B3
Poros
Attiki GR 185 B4
Kefalonia GR 184 A1
Poroszló H 113 B4
Porozina HR 123 B3
Porquerolles F 132 C2
Porrentruy CH 106 B2
Porreres E 167 B3
Porretta Terme I 135 A3
Porsgrunn N 53 A5
Porspoder F 100 A1
Port-a-Binson F 91 B3
Portacloy IRL 26 B1
Portadown GB 27 B4
Portaferry GB 27 B5
Portaje E 155 B4
Portalegre P 155 B3
Portarlington IRL 30 A1
Port Askaig GB 34 C1
Portavadie GB 34 C2
Portavogie GB 27 B5
Portbail F 88 A2
Port Bannatyne GB 34 C2
Port-Barcarès F 146 B4
Portbou E 146 B4
Port-Camargue F 131 B3
Port Charlotte GB 34 C1
Port d'Andratx E 166 B2
Port-de-Bouc F 131 B3
Port-de-Lanne F 128 C1
Port de Pollença E 167 B3

Port-des-Barques F 114 C2
Port de Sóller E 166 B2
Portegrandi I 122 B1
Portel P 155 C3
Portela P 148 B1
Port Ellen GB 34 C1
Portelo P 141 C4
Portemouro E 140 B2
Port-en-Bessin F 88 A3
Port'Ercole I 168 A1
Port Erin GB 36 B2
Portes-lès-Valence F 117 C4
Portets F 128 B2
Port Eynon GB 39 C2
Portezuelo E 155 B4
Port Glasgow GB 34 C3
Portglenone GB 27 B4
Porthcawl GB 39 C3
Port Henderson GB 31 B3
Porthleven GB 42 B1
Porthmadog GB 38 B2
Porticcio F 180 B1
Portici I 170 C2
Portico di Romagna I 135 A4
Portilla de la Reina E 142 A2
Portillo E 150 A3
Portimao P 160 B1
Portinatx E 166 B1
Portinho da Arrabida P 154 C1
Port Isaac GB 42 B2
Portishead GB 43 A4
Port-Joinville F 114 B1
Portknockie GB 33 D4
Port-la-Nouvelle F 130 B2
Portlaoise IRL 30 A1
Portlethen GB 33 D4
Port Logan GB 36 B2
Port Louis F 100 B2
Portmagne IRL 29 C1
Portmahomack GB 32 D3
Portman E 165 B4
Port Manech F 100 B2
Portnacroish GB 34 B2
Portnahaven GB 34 C1
Port Nan Giuran GB 31 A2
Port-Navalo F 100 B3
Port Nis GB 31 A2
Porto
F 180 A1
P 148 A1
Porto-Alto P 154 C2
Porto Azzurro I 134 C3
Portocannone I 170 B3
Porto Cerésio I 120 B1
Porto Cervo I 178 A3
Porto Cesáreo I 173 B3
Porto Colom E 167 B3
Porto Covo P 160 B1
Porto Cristo E 167 B3
Porto d'Áscoli I 136 C2
Porto de Lagos P 160 B1
Porto de Mos P 154 B2
Porto de Rei P 154 C2
Porto do Son E 140 B2
Porto Empédocle I 176 B2
Portoferráio I 134 C3
Portofino I 134 A2
Porto Garibaldi I 122 C1
Portogruaro I 122 B1
Portokhelion GR 184 B4
Portomaggiore I 121 C4
Portomarin E 140 B3
Porton GB 44 B2
Portonovo E 140 B2
Portopalo di Capo Passero I 177 C4
Porto Petro E 167 B3
Porto Pino I 179 D2
Porto Potenza Picena I 136 B2
Portør N 53 B5
Porto Recanati I 136 B2
Porto San Giórgio I 136 B2
Porto Sant'Elpídio I 136 B2
Porto Santo Stéfano I 168 A1
Portoscuso I 179 C2
Porto Tolle I 122 C1
Porto Tórres I 178 B2
Porto-Vecchio F 180 B2
Portovénere I 134 A2
Portpatrick GB 36 B1
Portreath GB 42 B1
Portree GB 31 B2
Portroe IRL 28 B3
Portrush GB 27 A4
Port St Mary GB 36 B2
Portsall F 100 A1
Portsmouth GB 44 C2
Portsoy GB 33 D4
Port-Ste Marie F 129 B3
Portstewart GB 27 A4
Port-St-Louis-du-Rhône F 131 B3
Port-sur-Saône F 105 B5
Port Talbot GB 39 C3
Portugalete E 143 A4
Portumna IRL 28 A3
Port-Vendres F 146 B4
Port William GB 36 B2
Porvoo FIN 8 B4
Porzuna E 157 A3
Posada
Oviedo E 141 A5
Oviedo E 142 A2
I 178 B3
Posada de Valdeón E 142 A2
Posadas E 162 A2
Poschiavo CH 120 A3
Posedarje HR 137 A4
Posio FIN 197 C11
Positano I 170 C2
Possagno I 121 B4
Posseck D 83 B4
Possesse F 91 C4
Pössneck D 83 B3
Posta I 169 A3
Postal I 108 C2
Posta Piana I 172 A1
Postbauer-Heng D 95 B3
Posterholt NL 80 A2
Postioma I 121 B5
Postira HR 138 B2
Postojna SLO 123 B3
Postoloprty CZ 84 B1
Postomino PL 68 A1
Posušje BIH 138 B3
Potamos
Attiki GR 184 C3
Attiki GR 184 D4
Potegowo PL 68 A2
Potenza I 172 B1
Potenza Picena I 136 B2
Potes E 142 A2
Potigny F 89 B3
Potočari BIH 127 C1
Potoci
BIH 138 A2
BIH 139 B3
Potony H 125 B3
Potries E 159 C3
Potsdam D 74 B2
Potštát CZ 98 B1
Pottenbrunn A 110 A2
Pottendorf A 111 B3
Pottenstein
A 111 B3
D 95 B3
Potters Bar GB 44 B3
Pöttmes D 94 C3
Pöttsching A 111 B3
Potworów PL 87 A4
Pouancé F 101 B4
Pougues-les-Eaux F 104 B2
Pouilly-en-Auxois F 104 B3
Pouilly-sous Charlieu F 117 A4
Pouilly-sur-Loire F 104 B1
Poujol-sur-Orb F 130 B2
Poullaouen F 100 A2
Poulton-le-Fylde GB 38 A4
Poundstock GB 42 B2
Pourcy F 91 B3
Pourrain F 104 B2
Poussu FIN 197 D12
Pouyastruc F 145 A4
Pouy-de-Touges F 146 A2
Pouzauges F 114 B3
Pova de Santa Iria P 154 C1
Považská Bystrica SK 98 B2
Povedilla E 158 C1
Povenets RUS 9 A9
Povlja HR 138 B2
Povljana HR 137 A4
Póvoa
Beja P 161 A2
Santarém P 154 B2
Póvoa de Lanhoso P 148 A1
Póvoa de Varzim P 148 A1
Póvoa e Meadas P 155 B3
Powidz PL 76 B2
Poyales del Hoyo E 150 B2
Poynton GB 40 B1
Poyntz Pass GB 27 B4
Poysdorf A 97 C4
Poza de la Sal E 143 B3
Pozaldez E 150 A3
Pozán de Vero E 145 B4
Pozanti TR 23 C8
Požarevac SRB 127 C3
Požega
HR 125 B3
SRB 127 D2
Poznań PL 76 B1
Pozo Alcón E 164 B2
Pozoantiguo E 150 A2
Pozoblanco E 156 B3
Pozo Cañada E 158 C2
Pozo de Guadalajara E 151 B4
Pozo de la Serna E 157 B4
Pozohondo E 158 C2
Pozondón E 152 B2
Poźrzadło Wielkie PL 75 A4
Pozuel del Campo E 152 B2
Pozuelo de Alarcón E 151 B4
Pozuelo de Calatrava E 157 B4
Pozuelo del Páramo E 142 B1
Pozuelo de Zarzón E 149 B3
Pozzallo I 177 C3
Pozzomaggiore I 178 B2
Pozzo San Nicola I 178 B2
Pozzuoli I 170 C2
Pozzuolo I 135 B4
Prabuty PL 69 B4
Prača BIH 139 B4
Prachatice CZ 96 B1
Prada E 141 B3
Pradelle F 118 C2
Pradelles F 117 C3
Prades
E 147 C1
F 146 B3
Pradła PL 86 B3
Prado
E 142 A1
P 148 A1
Prado del Rey E 162 B2
Pradoluengo E 143 B3
Pragelato I 119 B3
Pragersko SLO 123 A4
Prägraten A 109 B3
Prague = Praha CZ 84 B2
Praha = Prague CZ 84 B2
Prahecq F 115 B3
Praia P 154 B1
Práia a Mare I 174 B1
Praia da Rocha P 160 B1
Praia da Viera P 154 B2
Praia de Mira P 148 B1
Praiano I 170 C2
Pralboino I 120 B3
Pralognan-la-Vanoise F 118 B3
Pramanda GR 182 D3
Pranjani SRB 127 C2
Prapatnica HR 138 B2
Præstø DK 65 A5
Praszka PL 86 A2
Prat F 146 A1
Prata I 135 B3
Prata di Pordenone I 122 B1
Pratau D 83 A4
Prat de Compte E 153 B4
Pratdip E 147 C1
Pratella I 170 B2
Prato I 135 B4
Prátola Peligna I 169 A3
Pratola Serra I 170 C2
Prats-de-Mollo-la-Preste F 146 B3
Prauthoy F 105 B4
Pravia E 141 A4
Praxmar A 108 B2
Prayssac F 129 B4
Prazzo I 132 A3
Prebold SLO 123 A4
Préchac F 128 B2
Précy-sur-Thil F 104 B3
Predáppio I 135 A4
Predazzo I 121 A4
Předin CZ 97 B3
Preding A 110 C2
Predjame SLO 123 B3
Predlitz A 109 B4
Predmeja SLO 122 B2
Predoi I 108 B3
Pré-en-Pail F 89 B3
Prees GB 38 B4
Preetz D 64 B3
Préfailles F 101 B3
Pregarten A 96 C2
Pregrada HR 123 A4
Preignan F 129 C3
Preiļi LV 8 D5
Preitenegg A 110 C1
Prekaja BIH 138 A2
Preko HR 137 A4
Preljina SRB 127 D2
Prelog HR 124 A2
Prelošćica HR 124 B2
Přelouč CZ 97 A3
Prem SLO 123 B3
Premantura HR 122 C2
Prémery F 104 B2
Prémia I 119 A5
Premiàde Mar E 147 C3
Premnitz D 73 B5
Prémont F 91 A3
Prenzlau D 74 A2
Preodac BIH 138 A2
Přerov CZ 98 B1
Prerow D 66 B1
Presencio E 143 B3
Presicce I 173 C4
Presly F 103 B4
Prešov SK 12 D4
Pressac F 115 B4
Pressath D 95 B3
Pressbaum A 111 A3
Prestatyn GB 38 A3
Prestebakke N 54 B2
Presteigne GB 39 B3
Přeštice CZ 96 B1
Preston
Lancashire GB 38 A4
Scottish Borders GB 35 C5
Prestonpans GB 35 C5
Prestwick GB 36 A2
Prettin D 83 A4
Preturo I 169 A3
Pretzchendorf D 83 B5
Pretzier D 73 B4
Pretzsch D 83 A4
Preuilly-sur-Claise F 115 B4
Prevalje SLO 110 C1
Prevenchères F 131 A2
Préveranges F 116 A2
Preveza GR 182 E2
Prevršac HR 124 B2
Prezid HR 123 B3
Priaranza del Bierzo E 141 B4
Priay F 118 A2
Pribeta SK 112 B2
Priboj
BIH 125 C4
SRB 16 D3
Přibor CZ 98 B2
Příbram CZ 96 B2
Pribylina SK 99 B3
Přibyslav CZ 97 B3
Pričević SRB 127 C1
Pridjel BIH 125 C4
Priego E 152 B1
Priego de Córdoba E 163 A3
Priekule LV 8 D2
Prien D 109 B3
Prienai LT 13 A5
Prievidza SK 98 C2
Prigradica HR 138 C2
Prigrevica SRB 125 B5
Prijeboj HR 123 C4
Prijedor BIH 124 C2
Prijepolje SRB 16 D3
Prilep MK 182 B3
Priluka BIH 138 B2
Primda CZ 95 B4
Primel-Trégastel F 100 A2
Primišje HR 123 B4
Primorsk
Kaliningrad RUS 69 A5
Severo-Zapadnyy RUS 9 B6
Primošten HR 138 B1
Primstal D 92 B2
Princes Risborough GB 44 B3
Princetown GB 42 B2
Principina a Mare I 135 C4
Priolo Gargallo I 177 B4
Prioro E 142 B2
Priozersk RUS 9 B7
Prirechnyy RUS 193 C14
Prisoje BIH 138 B3
Priština KOS 16 D4
Pritzerbe D 73 B5
Pritzier D 73 A4
Pritzwalk D 73 A5
Privas F 117 C4
Priverno I 169 B3
Privlaka
Vukovarsko-Srijemska HR 125 B4
Zadarska HR 137 A4
Prizna HR 123 C3
Prizren KOS 16 D4
Prizzi I 176 B2
Prnjavor
BIH 125 C3
HR 124 B1
SRB 127 C1
Proaza E 141 A4
Probstzella D 82 B3
Probus GB 42 B2
Prócchio I 134 C3
Prochowice PL 85 A4
Prócida I 170 C2
Prodhromos CY 181 B1
Prodo I 135 C5
Proença-a-Nova P 154 B3
Proença-a-Velha P 155 A3
Profondeville B 79 B4
Prokuplje SRB 16 D4
Propriano F 180 B1
Prosec CZ 97 B4
Prösen D 83 A5
Prosenjakovci SLO 111 C3
Prosotsani GR 183 B5
Prostějov CZ 98 B1
Prószków PL 86 B1
Proszowice PL 87 B4
Protić BIH 138 A2
Protivanov CZ 97 B4
Protivín CZ 96 B2
Prötzel D 74 B2
Provins F 90 C3
Prozor BIH 139 B3
Prrenjas AL 182 B2
Prudhoe GB 37 B5
Prudnik PL 85 B5
Pruggern A 109 B4
Prügy H 113 A5
Prüm D 80 B2
Pruna E 162 B2
Prunelli-di-Fiumorbo F 180 A2
Prunetta I 135 A3
Pruniers F 103 C4
Prusice PL 85 A4
Pruské SK 98 B2
Pruszce PL 76 A3
Pruszcz Gdański PL 69 A3
Pruszków PL 77 B5
Prutz A 108 B1
Prüzen D 65 C5
Pruzhany BY 13 B6
Pružina SK 98 B2
Pŭrvomay BG 183 A7
Pryzlęg PL 75 B4
Przasnysz PL 77 A5
Przechlewo PL 68 B2
Przecław PL 87 B5
Przedbórz PL 87 A3
Przedecz PL 76 B3
Przejęslav PL 84 A3
Przemków PL 85 A3
Przemocze PL 75 A3
Przemyśl PL 12 D5
Przerąb PL 87 A3
Przewodnik PL 69 B3
Przewodowo Parcele PL 77 B5
Przewóz PL 84 A2
Przezmark PL 69 B4
Przodkowo PL 68 A3
Przybiernów PL 75 A3
Przyborowice PL 77 B5
Przybyszew PL 87 A4
Przybyszów PL 86 A3
Przylęg PL 75 B4
Przysucha PL 87 A4
Przytóczna PL 75 B4
Przytyk PL 87 A4
Przywidz PL 68 A3
Psachna GR 185 A4
Psara GR 185 A6
Psary PL 76 C3
Pskov RUS 8 D6
Pszczew PL 75 B4
Pszczółki PL 69 A3
Pszczyna PL 98 B2
Pszów PL 86 B2
Pteleos GR 182 D4
Ptolemaida GR 182 C3
Ptuj SLO 124 A1
Ptusza PL 68 B1
Puch A 109 B4
Puchberg am Schneeberg A 110 B2
Puchevillers F 90 A2
Puchheim D 108 A2
Púchov SK 98 B2
Pučišća HR 138 B2
Puck PL 69 A3
Puçol E 159 B3
Puconci SLO 111 C3
Pudasjärvi FIN 197 D10
Puderbach D 81 B3
Pudozh RUS 9 B10
Puebla de Albortón E 153 A3
Puebla de Alcocer E 156 B2
Puebla de Beleña E 151 B4
Puebla de Don Fadrique E 164 B2
Puebla de Don Rodrigo E 156 A3
Puebla de Guzmán E 161 B2
Puebla de la Calzada E 155 C4
Puebla de la Reina E 156 B1
Puebla de Lillo E 142 A1
Puebla del Maestre E 161 A3
Puebla del Principe E 158 C1
Puebla de Obando E 155 B4
Puebla de Sanabria E 141 B4
Puebla de Sancho Pérez E 155 C4
Puente Almuhey E 142 B2
Puente de Domingo Flórez E 141 B4
Puente de Génave E 164 A2
Puente del Congosto E 150 B2
Puente de Montañana E 145 B4
Puente Duero E 150 A3
Puente-Genil E 162 A3
Puente la Reina E 144 B2
Puente la Reina de Jaca E 144 B3
Puentelarra E 143 B3
Puente Mayorga E 162 B2
Puente Viesgo E 143 A3
Puertas
Asturias E 142 A2
Salamanca E 149 A3
Puerto de Mazarrón E 165 B3
Puerto de Santa Cruz E 156 A2
Puerto de San Vicente E 156 A2
Puerto-Lápice E 157 A4
Puertollano E 157 B3
Puerto Lumbreras E 164 B3
Puerto Moral E 161 B3
Puerto Real E 162 B1
Puerto Rey E 156 A2
Puerto Seguro E 149 B3
Puerto Serrano E 162 B2
Puget-Sur-Argens F 132 B2
Puget-Théniers F 132 B2
Puget-ville F 132 B2
Pugnochiuso I 171 B4
Puigcerdà E 146 B2
Puigpunyent E 166 B2
Puig Reig E 147 C2
Puillon F 128 C2
Puimichel F 132 B2
Puimoisson F 132 B2
Puiseaux F 103 A4
Puisieux F 90 A2
Puisserguier F 130 B2
Puivert F 146 B3
Pujols F 128 B2
Pukanec SK 98 C2
Pukavik S 63 B2
Pukë AL 182 A1
Pula
HR 122 C2
I 179 C2
Puławy PL 12 C4
Pulborough GB 44 C3
Pulfero I 122 A2
Pulgar E 157 A3
Pulheim D 80 A2
Pulkau A 97 C3
Pulpi E 164 B3
Pulsano I 173 B3
Pulsnitz D 84 A2
Pułtusk PL 77 B6
Pumpsaint GB 39 B3
Punat HR 123 B3
Punta Marina I 135 A5
Punta Prima E 167 B4
Punta Sabbioni I 122 B1
Puntas de Calnegre E 165 B3
Punta Umbria E 161 B3
Puolanka FIN 3 D10
Puoltikasvaara S 196 B4
Puoltsa S 196 B2
Puračić BIH 125 C4
Purbach am Neusiedler See A 111 B3
Purchena E 164 B2
Purfleet GB 45 B4
Purgstall A 110 A2
Purkersdorf A 111 A3
Purmerend NL 70 B1
Purullena E 164 B1
Pushkin RUS 9 C7
Pushkino RUS 9 D10
Püspökladány H 113 B5
Pusté Ulany SK 111 A4
Pustoshka RUS 9 D6
Puszcza Mariańska PL 77 C5
Puszczykowo PL 76 B1
Pusztamagyaród H 111 C3
Pusztamonostor H 113 B3
Pusztaszabolcs H 112 B2
Pusztavám H 112 B2
Putanges-Pont-Ecrepin F 89 B3
Putbus D 66 B2
Putignano I 173 B3
Putlitz D 73 A5
Putnok H 99 C4
Putte B 79 A4
Puttelange-aux-Lacs F 92 B2
Putten NL 70 B2
Puttgarden D 65 B4
Püttlingen D 92 B2
Putzu Idu I 179 B2
Puy-Guillaume F 117 B3
Puylaroque F 129 B4
Puylaurens F 146 A3
Puy-l'Évêque F 129 B4
Puymirol F 129 B3
Puyôo F 128 C2
Puyrolland F 114 B3
Pwllheli GB 38 B2
Pyetrikaw BY 13 B8
Pyhäjärvi FIN 3 E9
Pyhäkylä FIN 197 D11
Pyla CY 181 A2
Pyla-sur-Mer F 128 B1
Pyrzyce PL 75 A3
Pysely CZ 96 B2
Pyskowice PL 86 B2
Pytalovo RUS 8 D5
Pyzdry PL 76 B2

Q

Quakenbrück D 71 B4
Quargnento I 119 C5
Quarré-les-Tombes F 104 B2
Quarteira P 160 B1
Quartu Sant'Élena I 179 C3
Quatre-Champs F 91 B4
Quedlinburg D 82 A3
Queensferry
Edinburgh GB 35 C4
Flintshire GB 38 A3
Queige F 118 B3
Queipo E 161 B3
Queixans E 146 B2
Quel E 144 B1

Quelaines-St-Gault F 102 B1
Queljada P 148 A1
Quemada E 143 C3
Queralbs E 147 B3
Quercianella I 134 B3
Querfurt D 82 A3
Quérigut F 146 B3
Quero
E 157 A4
I 121 B4
Querqueville F 88 A2
Quesada E 164 B1
Questembert F 101 B3
Quettehou F 88 A2
Quevauvillers F 90 B2
Quevy B 79 B4
Quiaois P 148 B1
Quiberon F 100 B2
Quiberville F 89 A4
Quickborn D 64 C2
Quiévrain B 79 B3
Quillan F 146 B3
Quillebeuf F 89 A4
Quimper F 100 A1
Quimperlé F 100 B2
Quincampoix F 89 A5
Quincoces de Yuso
E 143 B3
Quincy F 103 B4
Quinéville F 88 A2
Quingey F 105 B4
Quinson F 132 B2
Quinssaines F 116 A2
Quinta-Grande P 154 C2
Quintana de la Serena
E 156 B2
Quintana del Castillo
E 141 B4
Quintana del Marco
E 141 B5
Quintana del Puenta
E 142 B2
Quintana-Martin Galindez E 143 B3
Quintanaortuño E 143 B3
Quintanapalla E 143 B3
Quintanar de la Orden
E 157 A4
Quintanar de la Sierra
E 143 C3
Quintanar del Rey
E 158 B2
Quintanilla de la Mata
E 143 C3
Quintanilla del Coco
E 143 C3
Quintanilla de Onésimo
E 150 A3
Quintanilla de Somoza
E 141 B4
Quintas de Valdelucio
E 142 B2
Quintela P 148 B2
Quintin F 100 A3
Quinto E 153 A3
Quinzano d'Oglio I 120 B3
Quiroga E 141 B3
Quismondo E 150 B3
Quissac F 131 B2
Quistello I 121 B3

R

Raab A 96 C1
Raabs an der Thaya
A 97 C3
Raahe FIN 3 D9
Raajärvi FIN 197 C9
Raalte NL 71 B3
Raamsdonksveer
NL 79 A4
Raanujarvi FIN 196 C7
Raattama FIN 196 A7
Rab HR 123 C3
Rabac HR 123 B3
Rábade E 140 A3
Rábafüzes H 111 C3
Rábahidvég H 111 B3
Rabanales E 149 A3
Rábapatona H 111 B4
Rabapordány H 111 B4
Rabastens F 129 C4
Rabastens-de-Bigorre
F 145 A4
Rabat = Victoria M 175 C3
Rabat M 175 C3
Rabča SK 99 B3
Rabe SRB 126 A2
Rabi CZ 96 B1
Rabino PL 67 C4
Rabka PL 99 B3
Rabrovo SRB 127 C3
Rača SRB 127 C3
Rácale I 173 C4
Rácalmás H 112 B2
Racalmuto I 176 B2
Racconigi I 119 C4
Rače SLO 123 A4
Rachecourt-sur-Marne
F 91 C5
Raciąż PL 77 B5
Racibórz PL 86 B2
Račinovci HR 125 C4
Ráckeve H 112 B2
Racławice PL 87 B4
Racławice Śląskie
PL 86 B1
Racot PL 75 B5
Råda
Skaraborg S 55 B4
Värmland S 49 B5
Radalj SRB 127 C1
Rădăuţi RO 17 B6
Radda in Chianti I 135 B4
Raddusa I 177 B3
Radeberg D 84 A1
Radebeul D 84 A1
Radeburg D 84 A1
Radeče SLO 123 A4
Radekhiv UA 13 C6
Radenci SLO 111 C3
Radenthein A 109 C4
Radevormwald D 80 A3
Radicófani I 135 C4
Radicóndoli I 135 B4
Radišići BIH 138 B3
Radizel SLO 110 C2
Radków PL 85 B4
Radlje ob Dravi
SLO 110 C2
Radłów PL 87 B4
Radmer an der Stube
A 110 B1
Radnejaur S 195 E9
Radnice CZ 96 B1
Radohova BIH 138 A3
Radojevo SRB 126 B2
Radolfzell D 107 B3
Radom PL 87 A5
Radomice PL 77 B4
Radomin PL 77 A4
Radomsko PL 86 A3
Radomyshl UA 13 C8
Radomyśl Wielki PL 87 B5
Radošina SK 98 C1
Radošovce SK 98 C1
Radoszewice PL 86 A2
Radoszyce PL 87 A4
Radotin CZ 96 B2
Radovets BG 186 A1
Radoviš MK 182 B4
Radovljica SLO 123 A3
Radowo Wielkie PL 75 A4
Radstadt A 109 B4
Radstock GB 43 A4
Raduc HR 137 A4
Raduša MK 182 A3
Radviliškis LT 8 E3
Radzanów
Mazowieckie PL 77 B5
Mazowieckie PL 87 A4
Radziejów PL 76 B3
Radziejowice PL 77 B5
Radzovce SK 113 A3
Radzyń Chełmiński
PL 69 B3
Raeren B 80 B2
Raesfeld D 80 A2
Raffadali I 176 B2
Rafina GR 185 A4
Rafsbotn N 192 B7
Ragachow BY 13 B9
Ragály H 99 C4
Rågeleje DK 61 C2
Raglan GB 39 C4
Ragnitz A 110 C2
Ragusa I 177 C3
Rahden D 72 B1
Råholt N 48 B3
Raiano I 169 A3
Raigada E 141 B3
Rain D 94 C2
Rainbach im Mühlkreis
A 96 C2
Rainham GB 45 B4
Rairiz de Veiga E 140 B3
Raisdorf D 64 B3
Raisio FIN 8 B3
Raiskio FIN 197 D9
Raiva
Aveiro P 148 A1
Coimbra P 148 B1
Raja-Jooseppi
FIN 193 D12
Rajala FIN 197 B9
Rajcza PL 99 B3
Rajec SK 98 B2
Rájec-Jestřebi CZ 97 B4
Rajecké Teplice SK 98 B2
Rajevo Selo HR 125 C4
Rajhrad CZ 97 B4
Rajić HR 124 B3
Rajka H 111 B4
Rakaca H 99 C4
Rakamaz H 113 A5
Rakek SLO 123 B3
Rakhiv UA 17 A6
Rakitna SLO 123 B3
Rakitovo BG 183 B6
Rakkestad N 54 A2
Rákóczifalva H 113 B4
Rakoniewice PL 75 B5
Rakoszyce PL 85 A4
Raková SK 98 B2
Rakovac BIH 125 B3
Rakovica HR 123 C4
Rakovník CZ 96 A1
Rakow D 66 B2
Raków PL 87 B5
Rakvere EST 8 C5
Ralja SRB 127 C2
Rälla S 62 B4
Ramacastañas E 150 B2
Ramacca I 177 B3
Ramales de la Victoria
E 143 A3
Ramberg N 194 B4
Rambervillers F 92 C2
Rambouillet F 90 C1
Rambucourt F 92 C1
Ramdala S 63 B3
Ramerupt F 91 C4
Ramingstein A 109 B4
Ramirás E 140 B2
Ramiswil CH 106 B2
Ramkvilla S 62 A2
Ramme DK 58 B1
Rämmen S 49 B6
Ramnäs S 56 A2
Ramnes N 54 A1
Râmnicu Vâlcea
RO 17 C6
Ramonville-St Agne
F 129 C4
Rampside GB 36 B3
Ramsau D 109 B3
Ramsbeck D 81 A4
Ramsberg S 56 A1
Ramsele S 200 C2
Ramsey
Cambridgeshire
GB 44 A3
I sle of Man GB 36 B2
Ramseycleuch GB 36 A3
Ramsgate GB 45 B5
Ramsjö S 200 D1
Ramstein-Meisenbach
D 93 B3
Ramsund N 194 B7
Ramundberget S 199 C9
Ramvik S 200 D3
Ranalt A 108 B2
Rånäs S 51 C5
Rånåsfoss N 48 B3
Rance B 91 A4
Ránchio I 135 B5
Randaberg N 52 A1
Randalstown GB 27 B4
Randan F 117 A3
Randazzo I 177 B3
Rånddalen S 199 C10
Randegg A 110 A1
Randers DK 58 B3
Randijaur S 196 C2
Randin E 140 C3
Randsverk N 198 D6
Råneå S 196 D5
Rânes F 89 B3
Rångedala S 60 B3
Ranis D 82 B3
Rankweil A 107 B4
Rånnaväg S 60 B3
Ränneslöv S 61 C3
Rannoch Station
GB 34 B3
Ranovac SRB 127 C3
Ransäter S 55 A4
Ransbach-Baumbach
D 81 B3
Ransta S 56 A2
Ranttila FIN 193 C9
Ranua FIN 197 D9
Ranum DK 58 B2
Ranvalhal P 154 B1
Raon-l'Étape F 92 C2
Ráossi I 121 B4
Rapallo I 134 A2
Rapla EST 8 C4
Rapness GB 33 B4
Rapolano Terme I 135 B4
Rapolla I 172 B1
Raposa P 154 B2
Rapperswil CH 107 B3
Raša HR 123 B3
Rasal E 145 B3
Rascafria E 151 B4
Rasdorf D 82 B1
Raseiniai LT 13 A5
Rašica SLO 123 B3
Rasines E 143 A3
Rasquera E 153 A4
Rássina I 135 B4
Rastatt D 93 C4
Rastede D 71 A5
Rastenberg D 82 A3
Rastošnica BIH 125 C4
Rastovac MNE 139 C4
Rasueros E 150 A2
Rasy PL 86 A3
Raszków PL 86 A1
Rätan S 199 C11
Rateče SLO 109 C4
Ratekau D 65 C3
Ratež SLO 123 B4
Rathangan IRL 30 A2
Rathcoole IRL 30 A2
Rathcormack IRL 29 B3
Rathdrum IRL 30 B2
Rathebur D 74 A2
Rathenow D 73 B5
Rathfriland GB 27 B4
Rathkeale IRL 29 B3
Rathmelton IRL 27 A3
Rathmolyon IRL 30 A2
Rathmore IRL 29 B2
Rathmullan IRL 27 A3
Rathnew IRL 30 B2
Rathvilly IRL 30 B2
Ratibořské Hory
CZ 96 B2
Ratingen D 80 A2
Ratková SK 99 C4
Ratkovo SRB 126 B1
Ratne UA 13 C6
Rattelsdorf D 94 A2
Ratten A 110 B2
Rattosjärvi FIN 196 C7
Rattray GB 35 B4
Rättvik S 50 B2
Ratvika N 199 B7
Ratzeburg D 65 C3
Rätzlingen D 73 B4
Raucourt-et-Flaba F 91 B4
Raudeberg N 198 D2
Raufarhöfn IS 191 A10
Raufoss N 48 B2
Rauhala FIN 196 B7
Rauland N 53 A4
Raulhac F 116 C2
Raulia N 195 E5
Rauma FIN 8 B2
Raundal N 46 B3
Raunds GB 44 A3
Rauris A 109 B4
Rautas S 196 B2
Rautavaara FIN 3 E11
Rauville-la-Bigot F 88 A2
Rauzan F 128 B2
Ravanusa I 176 B2
Rava-Rus'ka UA 13 C5
Ravča HR 138 B3
Ravels B 79 A4
Rävemåla S 63 B3
Ravenglass GB 36 B3
Ravenna I 135 A5
Ravensburg D 107 B4
Rävlanda S 60 B2
Ravna Gora HR 123 B3
Ravne na Koroškem
SLO 110 C1
Ravnje SRB 127 C1
Ravno BIH 139 C3
Ravno Selo SRB 126 B1
Rawa Mazowiecka
PL 87 A4
Rawicz PL 85 A4
Rawtenstall GB 40 B1
Rayleigh GB 45 B4
Ražana SRB 127 C1
Ražanac HR 137 A4
Razboj BIH 124 B3
Razes F 115 B5
Razgrad BG 17 D7
Razkrižie SLO 111 C3
Razlog BG 183 B5
Razo E 140 A2
Reading GB 44 B3
Réalmont F 130 B1
Rebais F 90 C3
Reboly RUS 3 E12
Rebordelo P 149 A2
Recanati I 136 B2
Recas E 151 B4
Recco I 134 A2
Recess IRL 28 A2
Recey-sur-Ource F 105 B3
Recezinhos P 148 A1
Rechnitz A 111 B3
Rechytsa BY 13 B9
Recke D 71 B4
Recklinghausen D 80 A3
Recoaro Terme I 121 B4
Recogne B 92 B1
Recoules-Prévinquières
F 130 A1
Recsk H 113 B4
Recz PL 75 A4
Reda PL 69 A3
Redalen N 48 B2
Redange L 92 B1
Redcar GB 37 B5
Redditch GB 44 A2
Redefin D 73 A4
Redhill GB 44 B3
Redics H 111 C3
Redkino RUS 9 D10
Redland GB 33 B3
Redlin D 73 A5
Redon F 101 B3
Redondela E 140 B2
Redondo P 155 C3
Red Point GB 31 B3
Redruth GB 42 B1
Redzikowo PL 68 A2
Reepham GB 41 C5
Rees D 80 A2
Reeth GB 37 B5
Reetz D 73 A4
Reftele S 60 B3
Regalbuto I 177 B3
Regen D 95 C5
Regensburg D 95 B4
Regenstauf D 95 B4
Reggello I 135 B4
Réggio di Calábria
I 175 C1
Reggiolo I 121 C3
Réggio nell'Emilia
I 121 C3
Reghin RO 17 B6
Régil E 144 A1
Regna S 56 B1
Regniéville F 92 C1
Regny F 117 B4
Rego da Leirosa P 154 A2
Regöly H 112 C2
Regueiro E 140 B2
Reguengo
Portalegre P 155 B3
Santarém P 154 B2
Reguengos de Monsaraz
P 155 C3
Rehau D 83 B4
Rehburg D 72 B2
Rehden D 72 B1
Rehna D 65 C4
Reichelsheim D 93 B4
Reichelshofen D 94 B2
Reichenau A 110 B2
Reichenbach
Sachsen D 83 B4
Sachsen D 84 A2
Reichenfels A 110 B1
Reichensachsen D 82 A2
Reichertshofen D 95 C3
Reichshoffen F 93 C3
Reiden CH 106 B2
Reigada
E 141 A4
P 149 B3
Reigate GB 44 B3
Reillanne F 132 B1
Reillo E 158 B2
Reims F 91 B4
Reinach CH 106 B3
Reinbek D 72 A3
Reinberg D 66 B2
Reine N 194 C4
Reinfeld D 65 C3
Reinheim D 93 B4
Reinli N 47 B6
Reinosa E 142 A2
Reinstorf D 65 C4
Reinsvoll N 48 B2
Reisach A 109 C4
Reiss GB 32 C3
Reitan N 199 C8
Reit im Winkl D 109 B3
Rejmyre S 56 B1
Rekavice BIH 124 C3
Rekovac SRB 127 D3
Relleu E 159 C3
Rém H 125 A5
Remagen D 80 B3
Rémalard F 89 B4
Rembercourt-aux-Pots
F 91 C5
Remedios P 154 B1
Remels D 71 A4
Remetea Mare RO 126 B3
Remich L 92 B2
Rémilly F 92 B2
Remiremont F 105 A5
Remolinos E 144 C2
Remoulins F 131 B3
Remscheid D 80 A3
Rémuzat F 131 A4
Rena N 48 A3
Renaison F 117 A3
Renazé F 101 B4
Renchen D 93 C4
Rencurel F 118 B2
Rende I 174 B2
Rendina GR 182 D3
Rendsburg D 64 B2
Renedo E 150 A3
Renens CH 105 C5
Renfrew GB 34 C3
Rengsjö S 50 A3
Reni UA 17 C8
Rennebu N 198 C6
Rennerod D 81 B4
Rennertshofen D 94 C3
Rennes F 101 A4
Rennes-les-Bains
F 146 B3
Rennweg A 109 B4
Rens DK 64 B2
Rensjön S 196 A2
Rentería E 144 A2
Rentjärn S 200 A4
Répcelak H 111 B4
Repojoki FIN 193 D9
Repvåg N 193 B9
Requena E 159 B2
Réquista F 130 A1
Rerik D 65 B4
Resana I 121 B4
Resarö S 57 A4
Reschen = Résia I 108 C1
Resen MK 182 B3
Resende P 148 A2
Résia = Reschen I 108 C1
Reşiţa
RO 16 C4
RO 126 B3
Resko PL 67 C4
Resnik SRB 127 C2
Ressons-sur-Matz F 90 B2
Restábal E 163 B4
Resuttano I 177 B3
Retamal E 155 C4
Retford GB 40 B3
Rethel F 91 B4
Rethem D 72 B2
Rethimno GR 185 D5
Retie B 79 A5
Retiers F 101 B4
Retortillo E 149 B3
Retortillo de Soria
E 151 A4
Retournac F 117 B4
Rétság H 112 B3
Rettenegg A 110 B2
Retuerta del Bullaque
E 157 A3
Retz A 97 C3
Retzbach D 94 B1
Reuden D 73 B5
Reuilly F 103 B4
Reus E 147 C2
Reusel NL 79 A5
Reuterstadt Stavenhagen D 74 A1
Reuth D 95 B4
Reutlingen D 94 C1
Reutte A 108 B1
Reuver NL 80 A2
Revel F 146 A2
Revello I 119 C4
Revenga E 151 B3
Revest-du-Bion F 132 A1
Révfülöp H 111 C4
Revigny-sur-Ornain
F 91 C4
Revin F 91 B4
Řevnice CZ 96 B2
Řevničov CZ 84 B1
Revo I 121 A4
Revsnes N 47 A4
Revúca SK 99 C4
Rewa PL 69 A3
Rewal PL 67 B4
Rexbo S 50 B2
Reyðarfjörður IS 191 B11
Reyero E 142 B1
Reykhólar IS 190 B3
Reykholt
Árnessýsla IS 190 C5
Borgarfjarðarsýsla
I S 190 C4
Reykjahlið IS 191 B9
Reykjavík IS 190 C4
Rezé F 101 B4
Rēzekne LV 8 D5
Rezovo BG 17 E8
Rezzato I 120 B3
Rezzoáglio I 134 A2
Rhade D 72 A2
Rhaunen D 93 B3
Rhayader GB 39 B3
Rheda-Wiedenbrück
D 81 A4
Rhede
Niedersachsen D 71 A4
Nordrhein-Westfalen
D 80 A2
Rheinau D 93 C3
Rheinbach D 80 B2
Rheinberg D 80 A2
Rheine D 71 B4
Rheinfelden D 106 B2
Rheinsberg D 74 A1
Rhêmes-Notre-Dame
I 119 B4
Rhenen NL 70 C2
Rhens D 81 B3
Rheydt D 80 A2
Rhiconich GB 32 C2
Rhinow D 73 B5
Rhiw GB 38 B2
Rho I 120 B2
Rhoden D 81 A5
Rhodes GR 188 C3
Rhondda GB 39 C3
Rhosllanerchrugog
GB 38 A3
Rhosneigr GB 38 A2
Rhossili GB 39 C2
Rhubodach GB 34 C2
Rhuddlan GB 38 A3
Rhyl GB 38 A3
Rhynie GB 33 D4
Riala S 57 A4
Riallé F 101 B4
Riaño E 142 B1
Riano I 168 A2
Rians F 132 B1
Rianxo E 140 B2
Riaza E 151 A4
Riba E 143 A3
Ribadavia E 140 B2
Ribadeo E 141 A3
Riba de Saelices E 152 B1
Ribadesella E 142 A1
Ribaflecha E 143 B4
Ribaforada E 144 C2
Ribare SRB 127 C3
Riba-roja d'Ebre E 153 A4
Riba-Roja de Turia
E 159 B3
Ribe DK 59 C1
Ribeauvillé F 106 A2
Ribécourt-Dreslincourt
F 90 B2
Ribeira da Pena P 148 A2
Ribeira de Piquín
E 141 A3
Ribemont F 91 B3
Ribera I 176 B2
Ribérac F 129 A3
Ribera de Cardós
E 146 B2
Ribera del Fresno
E 156 B1
Ribesalbes E 159 A3
Ribes de Freser E 147 B3
Ribiers F 132 A1
Ribnica
BIH 139 A4
SLO 123 B3

Ribnica na Potorju SLO 110 C2
Ribnik HR 123 B4
Rîbniţa MD 17 B8
Ribnitz-Damgarten D 66 B1
Ribolla I 135 C4
Řicany CZ 97 B4
Říčany CZ 96 B2
Riccia I 170 B2
Riccione I 136 A1
Ricco Del Golfo I 134 A2
Richebourg F 105 A4
Richelieu F 102 B2
Richisau CH 107 B3
Richmond
Greater London GB 44 B3
North Yorkshire GB 37 B5
Richtenberg D 66 B1
Richterswil CH 107 B3
Rickling D 64 B3
Rickmansworth GB 44 B3
Ricla E 152 A2
Riddarhyttan S 50 C2
Ridderkerk NL 79 A4
Riddes CH 119 A4
Ridjica SRB 125 B5
Riec-sur-Bélon F 100 B2
Ried A 109 A4
Riedenburg D 95 C3
Ried im Oberinntal A 108 B1
Riedlingen D 107 A4
Riedstadt D 93 B4
Riegersburg A 110 C2
Riego de la Vega E 141 B5
Riego del Camino E 149 A4
Riello E 141 B5
Riemst B 80 B1
Rienne B 91 B4
Riénsena E 142 A2
Riesa D 83 A5
Riese Pio X I 121 B4
Riesi I 177 B3
Riestedt D 82 A3
Rietberg D 81 A4
Rieti I 169 A2
Rietschen D 84 A2
Rieumes F 146 A2
Rieupeyroux F 130 A1
Rieux-Volvestre F 146 A2
Riez F 132 B2
Rīga LV 8 D4
Riggisberg CH 106 C2
Rignac F 130 A1
Rignano Gargánico I 171 B3
Rigolato I 109 C3
Rigside GB 36 A3
Rigutino I 135 B4
Riihimäki FIN 8 B4
Rijeka HR 123 B3
Rijen NL 79 A4
Rijkevorsel B 79 A4
Rijssen NL 71 B3
Rila BG 183 A5
Rilić BIH 138 B3
Rilievo I 176 B1
Rillé F 102 B2
Rillo de Gallo E 152 B2
Rimavská Baňa SK 99 C3
Rimavská Seč SK 99 C4
Rimavská Sobota SK 99 C4
Rimbo S 57 A4
Rimforsa S 56 B1
Rímini I 136 A1
Rîmnicu Sărat RO 17 C7
Rimogne F 91 B4
Rimpar D 94 B1
Rimske Toplice SLO 123 A4
Rincón de la Victoria E 163 B3
Rincón de Soto E 144 B2
Rindal N 198 B6
Rinde N 46 A3
Ringarum S 56 B2
Ringaskiddy IRL 29 C3
Ringe DK 59 C3
Ringebu N 48 A2
Ringkøbing DK 59 B1
Ringsaker N 48 B2
Ringsted DK 61 D1
Ringwood GB 44 C2
Rinkaby S 63 C2
Rinkabyholm S 63 B4
Rinlo E 141 A3
Rinn A 108 B2
Rinteln D 72 B2
Rio E 140 B3
Riobo E 140 B2
Riodeva E 152 B2
Rio do Coures P 154 B2
Rio Douro P 148 A2
Riofrio E 150 B3
Rio Frio P 154 C2
Riofrio de Aliste E 149 A3
Rio frio de Riaza E 151 A4
Riogordo E 163 B3
Rioja E 164 C2
Riola I 135 A4
Riola Sardo I 179 C2
Riolobos E 155 B4
Riom F 116 B3
Riomaggiore I 134 A2
Rio Maior P 154 B2
Rio Marina I 134 C3
Riom-ès-Montagnes F 116 B2
Rion-des-Landes F 128 C2
Rionegro del Puente E 141 B4
Rionero in Vúlture I 172 B1
Riopar E 158 C1
Riós E 141 C3
Rioseco E 142 A1
Rioseco de Tapia E 141 B5
Rio Tinto P 148 A1
Riotord F 117 B4
Riotorto E 141 A3
Rioz F 105 B5
Ripač BIH 124 C1
Ripacándida I 172 B1
Ripanj SRB 127 C2
Ripatransone I 136 C2
Ripley GB 40 B2
Ripoll E 147 B3
Ripon GB 40 A2
Riposto I 177 B4
Ripsa S 56 B2
Risan MNE 16 D3
Risbäck S 200 B1
Risca GB 39 C3
Rischenau D 81 A5
Riscle F 128 C2
Risebo S 56 B2
Risnes N 46 A2
Rišňovce SK 98 C1
Risør N 53 B5
Risøyhamn N 194 B6
Rissna S 199 B12
Ritsem S 194 C8
Ritterhude D 72 A1
Riutula FIN 193 D10
Riva del Garda I 121 B3
Riva Ligure I 133 B3
Rivanazzano I 120 C2
Rivarolo Canavese I 119 B4
Rivarolo Mantovano I 121 B3
Rive-de-Gier F 117 B4
Rivedoux-Plage F 114 B2
Rivello I 174 A1
Rivergaro I 120 C2
Rives F 118 B2
Rivesaltes F 146 B3
Rivignano I 122 B2
Rivne UA 13 C7
Rivoli I 119 B4
Rivolta d'Adda I 120 B2
Rixheim F 106 B2
Rixo S 54 B2
Riza GR 183 C5
Rizokarpaso CY 181 A3
Rjukan N 47 C5
Rø DK 67 A3
Rö S 57 A4
Roa
E 143 C3
N 48 B2
Roade GB 44 A3
Roager DK 59 C1
Roaldkvam N 52 A2
Roanne F 117 A4
Röbäck S 200 C6
Robakowo PL 69 B3
Róbbio I 120 B1
Röbel D 73 A5
Roberton GB 35 C5
Robertsfors S 200 B6
Robertville B 80 B2
Robin Hood's Bay GB 37 B6
Robleda E 149 B3
Robledillo de Trujillo E 156 A2
Robledo
Albacete E 158 C1
Orense E 141 B4
Robledo de Chavela E 151 B3
Robledo del Buey E 156 A3
Robledo del Mazo E 156 A3
Robledollano E 156 A2
Robles de la Valcueva E 142 B1
Robliza de Cojos E 149 B4
Robres E 145 C3
Robres del Castillo E 144 B1
Rocafort de Queralt E 147 C2
Rocamadour F 129 B4
Roccabernarda I 175 B2
Roccabianca I 120 B3
Roccadáspide I 172 B1
Rocca di Mezzo I 169 A3
Rocca di Papa I 168 B2
Roccagorga I 169 B3
Rocca Imperiale I 174 A2
Roccalbegna I 135 C4
Roccalumera I 177 B4
Roccamena I 176 B2
Roccamonfina I 170 B1
Roccanova I 174 A2
Roccapalumba I 176 B2
Roccapassa I 169 A3
Rocca Priora I 136 B2
Roccaraso I 169 B4
Rocca San Casciano I 135 A4
Roccasecca I 169 B3
Rocca Sinibalda I 169 A2
Roccastrada I 135 B4
Roccatederighi I 135 B4
Roccella Iónica I 175 C2
Rocchetta Sant'António I 172 A1
Rocester GB 40 C2
Rochdale GB 40 B1
Rochechouart F 115 C4
Rochefort
B 79 B5
F 114 C3
Rochefort-en-Terre F 101 B3
Rochefort-Montagne F 116 B2
Rochefort-sur-Nenon F 105 B4
Roche-lez-Beaupré F 105 B5
Rochemaure F 131 A3
Rocheservière F 114 B2
Rochester
Medway GB 45 B4
Northumberland GB 37 A4
Rochlitz D 83 A4
Rociana del Condado E 161 B3
Rockenhausen D 93 B3
Rockhammar S 56 A1
Rockneby S 62 B4
Ročko Polje HR 123 B3
Ročov CZ 84 B1
Rocroi F 91 B4
Rodach D 82 B2
Roda de Bara E 147 C2
Roda de Ter E 147 C3
Rodalben D 93 B3
Rødberg N 47 B5
Rødby DK 65 B4
Rødbyhavn DK 65 B4
Rødding
Sonderjyllands Amt. DK 59 C2
Viborg Amt. DK 58 B1
Rödeby S 63 B3
Rodeiro E 140 B3
Rødekro DK 64 A2
Roden NL 71 A3
Ródenas E 152 B2
Rodenkirchen D 72 A1
Rödental D 82 B3
Rödermark D 93 B4
Rodewisch D 83 B4
Rodez F 130 A1
Rodi Gargánico I 171 B3
Roding D 95 B4
Rödjebro S 51 B4
Rødkærsbro DK 59 B2
Rodolivas GR 183 C5
Rodoñá E 147 C2
Rødvig DK 65 A5
Roermond NL 80 A1
Roesbrugge B 78 B2
Roeschwoog F 93 C4
Roeselare B 78 B3
Roetgen D 80 B2
Roffiac F 116 B3
Röfors S 55 B5
Rofrano I 172 B1
Rogač HR 138 B2
Rogačica SRB 127 C1
Rogalinek PL 76 B1
Rogaška Slatina SLO 123 A4
Rogatec SLO 123 A4
Rogatica BIH 139 B5
Rogatyn UA 13 D6
Rogätz D 73 B4
Roggendorf D 65 C4
Roggiano Gravina I 174 B2
Roghadal GB 31 B2
Rogliano
F 180 A2
I 175 B2
Rognan N 195 C6
Rogne N 47 A6
Rognes F 131 B4
Rogny-les-7-Ecluses F 103 B4
Rogowo PL 76 B2
Rogoznica HR 138 B1
Rogoźnica PL 85 A4
Rogoźno PL 76 B1
Rohan F 101 A3
Röhlingen D 94 C2
Rohožnik SK 98 C1
Rohr D 82 B2
Rohrbach A 96 C1
Rohrbach-lès-Bitche F 92 B3
Rohrberg D 73 B4
Rohr im Gebirge A 110 B2
Röhrnbach D 96 C1
Roisel F 90 B3
Roja LV 8 D3
Rojales E 165 A4
Röjeråsen S 50 B1
Rojewo PL 76 B3
Rokiciny PL 87 A3
Rokietnica PL 75 B5
Rokiškis LT 8 E4
Rokitki PL 85 A3
Rokycany CZ 96 B1
Rolampont F 105 B4
Rold DK 58 B2
Røldal N 52 A2
Rolde NL 71 B3
Rolfs S 196 D6
Rollag N 47 B6
Rollán E 149 B4
Rolle CH 105 C5
Roma = Rome I 168 B2
Roma S 57 C4
Romagnano Sésia I 119 B5
Romagné F 88 B2
Romakloster S 57 C4
Roman RO 17 B7
Romana I 178 B2
Romanèche-Thorins F 117 A4
Romano di Lombardia I 120 B2
Romanshorn CH 107 B4
Romans-sur-Isère F 118 B2
Rombas F 92 B2
Rome = Roma I 168 B2
Romeán E 141 B3
Romenay F 105 C4
Romeral E 157 A4
Römerstein D 94 C1
Rometta I 177 A4
Romford GB 45 B4
Romhány H 112 B3
Römhild D 82 B2
Romilly-sur-Seine F 91 C3
Romont CH 106 C1
Romorantin-Lanthenay F 103 B3
Romrod D 81 B5
Romsey GB 44 C2
Rømskog N 54 A2
Rønbjerg DK 58 B1
Roncal E 144 B3
Ronce-les-Bains F 114 C2
Ronchamp F 106 B1
Ronchi dei Legionari I 122 B2
Ronciglione I 168 A2
Ronco Canavese I 119 B4
Ronco Scrivia I 120 C1
Ronda E 162 B2
Rønde DK 59 B3
Rone S 57 C4
Ronehamn S 57 C4
Rong N 46 B1
Rönnäng S 60 B1
Rønne DK 67 A3
Ronneburg D 83 B4
Ronneby S 63 B3
Rönneshytta S 55 B6
Rönninge S 57 A3
Rönnöfors S 199 B10
Rönö S 56 B2
Ronov nad Doubravou CZ 97 B3
Ronse B 79 B3
Roosendaal NL 79 A4
Roosky IRL 26 C3
Ropczyce PL 87 B5
Ropeid N 52 A2
Ropinsalmi FIN 192 D5
Ropuerelos del Páramo E 141 B5
Roquebilière F 133 A3
Roquebrun F 130 B2
Roquecourbe F 130 B1
Roquefort F 128 B2
Roquemaure F 131 A3
Roquesteron F 132 B3
Roquetas de Mar E 164 C2
Roquetes E 153 B4
Roquevaire F 132 B1
Røra N 199 B8
Rörbäcksnäs S 49 A4
Rørbæk DK 58 B2
Rore BIH 138 A2
Röro S 60 B1
Røros N 199 C8
Rorschach CH 107 B4
Rørvig DK 61 D1
Rørvik N 199 A8
Rörvik S 62 A2
Rosà I 121 B4
Rosal de la Frontera E 161 B2
Rosalina Mare I 122 B1
Rosa Marina I 173 B3
Rosans F 132 A1
Rosário P 160 B1
Rosarno I 175 C1
Rosbach D 81 B3
Rosche D 73 B3
Rościszewo PL 77 B4
Roscoff F 100 A2
Roscommon IRL 28 A3
Roscrea IRL 28 B4
Rosdorf D 82 A1
Rose I 174 B2
Rosegg A 109 C5
Rosehall GB 32 D2
Rosehearty GB 33 D4
Rosel GB 88 A1
Rosell E 153 B4
Roselló E 153 A4
Rosendal N 46 C3
Rosenfeld D 93 C4
Rosenfors S 62 A3
Rosenheim D 108 B3
Rosenow D 74 A2
Rosenthal D 81 A4
Rosersberg S 57 A3
Roses E 147 B4
Roseto degli Abruzzi I 169 A4
Roseto Valfortore I 170 B3
Rosheim F 93 C3
Rosia I 135 B4
Rosice CZ 97 B4
Rosières-en-Santerre F 90 B2
Rosignano Maríttimo I 134 B3
Rosignano Solvay I 134 B3
Roşiori-de-Vede RO 17 C6
Roskhill GB 31 B2
Roskilde DK 61 D2
Roskovec AL 182 C1
Röslau D 83 B3
Roslev DK 58 B1
Rosmaninhal P 155 B3
Rosnowo PL 67 B5
Rosolini I 177 C3
Rosova MNE 139 B5
Rosoy F 104 A2
Rosporden F 100 B2
Rosquete P 154 B2
Rosrath D 80 B3
Rossa CH 120 A2
Rossano I 174 B2
Rossas
Aveiro P 148 B1
Braga P 148 A1
Rossdorf D 82 B2
Rossett GB 38 A4
Rosshaupten D 108 B1
Rossiglione I 133 A4
Rossignol B 92 B1
Rossla D 82 A3
Rosslare IRL 30 B2
Rosslare Harbour IRL 30 B2
Rosslau D 83 A4
Rosslea GB 27 B3
Rossleben D 82 A3
Rossön S 200 C2
Ross-on-Wye GB 39 C4
Rossoszyca PL 86 A2
Rosswein D 83 A5
Röstånga S 61 C3
Roštár SK 99 C4
Rostock D 65 B5
Rostrenen F 100 A2
Røsvik N 194 C6
Rosvik S 196 D4
Rosyth GB 35 B4
Röszke H 126 A2
Rot S 49 A6
Rota E 161 C3
Rota Greca I 174 B2
Rot am See D 94 B2
Rotberget N 49 B4
Rotella I 136 C2
Rotenburg
Hessen D 82 B1
Niedersachsen D 72 A2
Roth
Bayern D 94 B3
Rheinland-Pfalz D 81 B3
Rothbury GB 37 A5
Rothemühl D 74 A2
Röthenbach D 95 B3
Rothenburg D 84 A2
Rothenburg ob der Tauber D 94 B2
Rothéneuf F 88 B2
Rothenklempenow D 74 A3
Rothenstein D 94 C3
Rotherham GB 40 B2
Rothes GB 32 D3
Rothesay GB 34 C2
Rothwell GB 44 A3
Rotnes N 48 B2
Rotonda I 174 B2
Rotondella I 174 A2
Rotova E 159 C3
Rott
Bayern D 108 B1
Bayern D 108 B3
Rottach-Egern D 108 B2
Röttenbach D 94 B3
Rottenbuch D 108 B1
Rottenburg
Baden-Württemberg D 93 C4
Bayern D 95 C4
Rottenmann A 110 B1
Rotterdam NL 79 A4
Rotthalmünster D 96 C1
Rottingdean GB 44 C3
Röttingen D 94 B1
Rottleberode D 82 A2
Rottne S 62 A2
Rottneros S 55 A4
Rottofreno I 120 B2
Rottweil D 107 A3
Rötz D 95 B4
Roubaix F 78 B3
Roudnice nad Labem CZ 84 B2
Roudouallec F 100 A2
Rouen F 89 A5
Rouffach F 106 B2
Rougé F 101 B4
Rougemont F 105 B5
Rougemont le-Château F 106 B1
Rouillac F 115 C3
Rouillé F 115 B4
Roujan F 130 B2
Roulans F 105 B5
Roundwood IRL 30 A2
Rousínov CZ 97 B4
Roussac F 115 B5
Roussennac F 130 A1
Rousses F 130 A2
Roussillon F 117 B4
Rouvroy-sur-Audry F 91 B4
Rouy F 104 B2
Rovaniemen maalaiskunta FIN 197 C8
Rovaniemi FIN 197 C8
Rovato I 120 B2
Rovensko pod Troskami CZ 84 B3
Roverbella I 121 B3
Rovereto I 121 B4
Rövershagen D 65 B5
Roverud N 49 B4
Rovigo I 121 B4
Rovinj HR 122 B2
Rovišce HR 124 B2
Rów PL 74 B3
Rowy PL 68 A2
Royal Leamington Spa GB 44 A2
Royal Tunbridge Wells GB 45 B4
Royan F 114 C2
Royat F 116 B3
Roybon F 118 B2
Roybridge GB 34 B3
Roye F 90 B2
Royère-de-Vassivière F 116 B1
Røykenvik N 48 B2
Royos E 164 B2
Røyrvik N 199 A10
Royston GB 44 A3
Rozadas E 141 A4
Rozalén del Monte E 151 C5
Rózańsko PL 75 B3
Rozay-en-Brie F 90 C2
Roždalovice CZ 84 B3
Rozdilna UA 17 B9
Rozental PL 69 B4
Rozhyshche UA 13 C6
Rožmitál pod Třemšínem CZ 96 B1
Rožňava SK 99 C4
Rožnov pod Radhoštěm CZ 98 B2
Rozoy-sur-Serre F 91 B4
Rozprza PL 86 A3
Roztoky CZ 84 B2
Rozvadov CZ 95 B4
Rozzano I 120 B2
Rrëshen AL 182 B1
Rrogozhine AL 182 B1
Ruanes E 156 A2
Rubbestadneset N 46 C2
Rubi E 147 C3
Rubiá E 141 B4
Rubiacedo de Abajo E 143 B3
Rubielos Bajos E 158 B1
Rubielos de Mora E 153 B3
Rubiera I 121 C3
Rubik AL 182 B1
Rucandio E 143 B3
Rud
Akershus N 48 B3
Buskerud N 48 B2
Ruda
PL 86 A2
S 62 A4
Rudabánya H 99 C4
Ruda Maleniecka PL 87 A4
Ruda Pilczycka PL 87 A4
Ruda Śl. PL 86 B2
Ruddervorde B 78 A3
Ruden A 110 C1
Rudersberg D 94 C1
Rudersdorf A 111 B3
Rüdersdorf D 74 B2
Ruderting D 96 C1
Rüdesheim D 93 B3
Rudkøbing DK 65 B3
Rudmanns A 97 C3
Rudna
CZ 96 A2
PL 85 A4
Rudnik SRB 127 C2
Rudniki
Opolskie PL 86 A2
Śląskie PL 86 B3
Rudno
Dolnośląskie PL 85 A4
Pomorskie PL 69 B3
Rudnya RUS 13 A9
Rudolstadt D 82 B3
Rudowica PL 84 A3
Rudozem BG 183 B6
Rudskoga S 55 A5
Rudston GB 40 A3
Ruds Vedby DK 61 D1
Rudy PL 86 B2

Rue F 78 B1
Rueda E 150 A3
Rueda de Jalón E 152 A2
Ruelle-sur-Touvre F 115 C4
Ruerrero E 143 B3
Ruffano I 173 C4
Ruffec F 115 B4
Rufina I 135 B4
Rugby GB 44 A2
Rugeley GB 40 C2
Ruggstrop S 62 B4
Rugles F 89 B4
Rugozero RUS 3 D13
Rühen D 73 B3
Ruhla D 82 B2
Ruhland D 84 A1
Ruhle D 71 B4
Ruhpolding D 109 B3
Ruhstorf D 96 C1
Ruidera E 158 C1
Ruillé-sur-le-Loir F 102 B2
Ruinen NL 71 B3
Ruiselede B 78 A3
Ruka FIN 197 C12
Rulles B 92 B1
Rülzheim D 93 B4
Rum H 111 B3
Ruma SRB 127 B1
Rumboci BIH 138 B3
Rumburk CZ 84 B2
Rumenka SRB 126 B1
Rumia PL 69 A3
Rumigny F 91 B4
Rumilly F 118 B2
Rumma S 56 B2
Rumney GB 39 C3
Rumont F 91 C5
Runa P 154 B1
Runcorn GB 38 A4
Rundmoen N 195 D5
Rungsted DK 61 D2
Runhällen S 51 B3
Runowo PL 69 A5
Runtuna S 56 B3
Ruokojärvi FIN 196 B7
Ruokolahti FIN 9 B6
Ruokto S 196 B2
Ruoms F 131 A3
Ruoti I 172 B1
Rupa HR 123 B3
Ruppichteroth D 80 B3
Rupt-sur-Moselle F 106 B1
Rus E 157 B4
Ruse BG 17 D7
Ruše SLO 110 C2
Rusele S 200 B4
Ruševo HR 125 B4
Rush IRL 30 A2
Rushden GB 44 A3
Rusiec PL 86 A2
Rusinowo
Zachodnio-Pomorskie PL 67 C4
Zachodnio-Pomorskie PL 75 A5
Ruskele S 200 B4
Ruski Krstur SRB 126 B1
Ruskington GB 40 B3
Rusovce SK 111 A4
Rüsselsheim D 93 B4
Russelv N 192 C4
Russi I 135 A5
Rust A 111 B3
Rustefjelbma N 193 B12
Rustrel F 131 B4
Ruszki PL 77 B5
Ruszów PL 84 A3
Rute E 163 A3
Rüthen D 81 A4
Rutherglen GB 35 C3
Ruthin GB 38 A3
Ruthven GB 32 D2
Ruthwell GB 36 B3
Rüti CH 107 B3
Rutigliano I 173 A3
Rutledal N 46 A2
Rutvik S 196 D5
Ruurlo NL 71 B3
Ruuvaoja FIN 197 B11
Ruvo del Monte I 172 B1
Ruvo di Púglia I 171 B4
Ruynes-en-Margeride F 116 C3
Ružic HR 138 B2
Ružomberok SK 99 B3
Ruzsa H 126 A1
Ry DK 59 B2
Rybany SK 98 C2
Rybina PL 69 A4
Rybnik PL 86 B2
Rychliki PL 69 B4
Rychlocice PL 86 A2
Rychnov nad Kněžnou CZ 85 B4
Rychnowo PL 77 A5
Rychtal PL 86 A1
Rychwał PL 76 B3
Ryczywół PL 87 A5
Ryczywól PL 75 B5
Ryd S 63 B2
Rydaholm S 62 B2
Rydal S 60 B2
Rydbo S 57 A4
Rydboholm S 60 B2
Ryde GB 44 C2
Rydöbruk S 60 C3
Rydsgård S 66 A2
Rydsnäs S 62 A3
Rydultowy PL 86 B2
Rydzyna PL 85 A4
Rye GB 45 C4
Rygge N 54 A1
Ryjewo PL 69 B3
Rykene N 53 B4
Rymań PL 67 C4
Rýmařov CZ 98 B1
Rynarzewo PL 76 A2
Ryomgård DK 59 B3
Rypefjord N 192 B7
Rypin PL 77 A4
Rysjedalsvika N 46 A2
Ryssby S 60 C4
Rytel PL 68 B2
Rytinki FIN 197 D10
Rytro PL 99 B4
Rywociny PL 77 A5
Rzeczenica PL 68 B2
Rzeczniów PL 87 A5
Rzeczyca PL 87 A4
Rzęgnowo PL 77 A5
Rzejowice PL 87 A3
Rzemień PL 87 B5
Rzepin PL 75 B3
Rzesznikowo PL 67 C4
Rzeszów PL 12 C4
Rzgów PL 86 A3
Rzhev RUS 9 D9

S

Saal
Bayern D 82 B2
Bayern D 95 C3
Saalbach A 109 B3
Saalburg D 83 B3
Saales F 92 C3
Saalfeld D 82 B3
Saalfelden am Steinernen Meer A 109 B3
Saanen CH 106 C2
Saarbrücken D 92 B2
Saarburg D 92 B2
Saarijärvi FIN 8 A4
Saari-Kämä FIN 197 C9
Saarlouis D 92 B2
Saas-Fee CH 119 A4
Šabac SRB 127 C1
Sabadell E 147 C3
Sabáudia I 169 B3
Sabbioneta I 121 C3
Sabero E 142 B1
Sabiñánigo E 145 B3
Sabiote E 157 B4
Sables-d'Or-les-Pins F 101 A3
Sablé-sur-Sarthe F 102 B1
Sabóia P 160 B1
Saborsko HR 123 B4
Sæbøvik N 52 A1
Sabres F 128 B2
Sabrosa P 148 A2
Sabugal P 149 B2
Sabuncu TR 187 C5
Sæby DK 58 A3
Săcălaz RO 126 B3
Sacecorbo E 152 B1
Saceda del Rio E 151 B5
Sacedón E 151 B5
Săcele RO 17 C6
Saceruela E 156 B3
Sachsenburg A 109 C4
Sachsenhagen D 72 B2
Sacile I 122 B1
Sacramenia E 151 A4
Sada E 140 A2
Sádaba E 144 B2
Saddell GB 34 C2
Sadernes E 147 B3
Sadki PL 76 A2
Sadkowice PL 87 A4
Sadlinki PL 69 B3
Sadów PL 75 B3
Sadská CZ 84 B2
Saelices E 151 C5
Saelices de Mayorga E 142 B1
Saerbeck D 71 B4
Saeul L 92 B1
Safaalan TR 186 A3
Safara P 161 A2
Säffle S 55 A3
Saffron Walden GB 45 A4
Safranbolu TR 187 A7
Säfsnäs S 50 B1
Şag RO 126 B3
Sagard D 66 B2
S'Agaro E 147 C4
Sågmyra S 50 B2
Sagone F 180 A1
Sagres P 160 C1
Ságújfalu H 113 A3
Sagunt E 159 B3
Sagvåg N 52 A1
Ságvár H 112 C2
Sagy F 105 C4
Sahagún E 142 B1
Šahy SK 112 A2
Saignelégier CH 106 B1
Saignes F 116 B2
Saija FIN 197 B11
Saillagouse F 146 B3
Saillans F 118 C2
Sains Richaumont F 91 B3
St Abb's GB 35 C5
St Affrique F 130 B1
St Agnan F 104 C2
St Agnant F 114 C3
St Agnes GB 42 B1
St Agrève F 117 B4
St Aignan F 103 B3
St Aignan-sur-Roë F 101 B4
St Albans GB 44 B3
St Alban-sur-Limagnole F 117 C3
St Amand-en-Puisaye F 104 B2
St Amand-les-Eaux F 79 B3
St Amand-Longpré F 103 B3
St Amand-Montrond F 103 C4
St Amans F 117 C3
St Amans-Soult F 130 B1
St Amant-Roche-Savine F 117 B3
St Amarin F 106 B1
St Ambroix F 131 A3
St Amé F 106 A1
St Amour F 118 A2
St André-de-Corcy F 117 B4
St André-de-Cubzac F 128 B2
St André-de-l'Eure F 89 B5
St André-de-Roquepertuis F 131 A3
St André-de-Sangonis F 130 B2
St Andre-de-Valborgne F 130 A2
St André-les-Alpes F 132 B2
St Andrews GB 35 B5
St Angel F 116 B2
St Anthème F 117 B3
St Antoine F 180 A2
St Antoine-de-Ficalba F 129 B3
St Antönien CH 107 C4
St Antonin-Noble-Val F 129 B4
St Août F 103 C3
St Armant-Tallende F 116 B3
St Arnoult F 90 C1
St Asaph GB 38 A3
St Astier F 129 A3
St Athan GB 39 C3
St Auban F 132 B2
St Aubin
CH 106 C1
F 105 B4
GB 88 A1
St Aubin-d'Aubigne F 101 A4
St Aubin-du-Cormier F 101 A4
St Aubin-sur-Aire F 92 C1
St Aubin-sur-Mer F 89 A3
St Aulaye F 128 A3
St Austell GB 42 B2
St Avit F 116 B2
St Avold F 92 B2
St Aygulf F 132 B2
St Bauzille-de-Putois F 130 B2
St Béat F 145 B4
St Beauzély F 130 A1
St Bees GB 36 B3
St Benim-d'Azy F 104 C2
St Benoît-du-Sault F 115 B5
St Benoit-en-Woëvre F 92 C1
St Berthevin F 102 A1
St Blaise-la-Roche F 92 C3
St Blazey GB 42 B2
St Blin F 105 A4
St Bonnet F 118 C3
St Bonnet Briance F 115 C5
St Bonnet-de-Joux F 104 C3
St Bonnet-le-Château F 117 B4
St Bonnet-le-Froid F 117 B4
St Brévin-les-Pins F 101 B3
St Briac-sur-Mer F 101 A3
St Brice-en-Coglès F 88 B2
St Brieuc F 101 A3
St Bris-le-Vineux F 104 B2
St Broladre F 88 B2
St Calais F 102 B2
St Cannat F 131 B4
St Cast-le-Guildo F 101 A3
St Céré F 129 B4
St Cergue CH 118 A3
St Cergues F 118 A3
St Cernin F 116 B2
St Chamant F 116 B1
St Chamas F 131 B4
St Chamond F 117 B4
St Chély-d'Apcher F 116 C3
St Chély-d'Aubrac F 116 C2
St Chinian F 130 B1
St Christol F 131 A4
St Christol-lès-Alès F 131 A3
St Christoly-Médoc F 114 C3
St Christophe-du-Ligneron F 114 B2
St Christophe-en-Brionnais F 117 A4
St Ciers-sur-Gironde F 128 A2
St Clair-sur-Epte F 90 B1
St Clar F 129 C3
St Claud F 115 C4
St Claude F 118 A2
St Clears GB 39 C2
St Columb Major GB 42 B2
St Come-d'Olt F 130 A1
St Cosme-en-Vairais F 89 B4
St Cyprien
Dordogne F 129 B4
Pyrenées-Orientales F 146 B4
St Cyr-sur-Loire F 102 B2
St Cyr-sur-Mer F 132 B1
St Cyr-sur-Methon F 117 A4
St David's GB 39 C1
St Denis F 90 C2
St Denis-d'Oléron F 114 B2
St Denis d'Orques F 102 A1
St Didier F 117 A4
St Didier-en-Velay F 117 B4
St Dié F 92 C2
St Dier-d'Auvergne F 117 B3
St Dizier F 91 C4
St Dizier-Leyrenne F 116 A1
St Dogmaels GB 39 B2
Ste Adresse F 89 A4
Ste Anne F 89 B4
Ste Anne-d'Auray F 100 B3
Ste Croix CH 105 C5
Ste Croix-Volvestre F 146 A2
Ste Engrâce F 144 A3
Ste Enimie F 130 A2
St Efflam F 100 A2
Ste Foy-de-Peyrolières F 146 A2
Ste Foy-la-Grande F 128 B3
Ste Foy l'Argentiere F 117 B4
Ste Gauburge-Ste Colombe F 89 B4
Ste Gemme la Plaine F 114 B2
Ste Geneviève F 90 B2
St Égrève F 118 B2
Ste Hélène F 128 B2
Ste Hélène-sur-Isère F 118 B3
Ste Hermine F 114 B2
Ste Jalle F 131 A4
Ste Livrade-sur-Lot F 129 B3
St Eloy-les-Mines F 116 A2
Ste Marie-aux-Mines F 106 A2
Ste Marie-du-Mont F 88 A2
Ste Maure-de-Touraine F 102 B2
Ste Maxime F 132 B2
Ste Ménéhould F 91 B4
Ste Mère-Église F 88 A2
St Emiland F 104 C3
St Émilion F 128 B2
St Enoder GB 42 B2
Sainteny F 88 A2
Ste Ode B 92 A1
Saintes F 114 C3
Ste Savine F 91 C4
Ste Sévère-sur-Indre F 103 C4
Ste Sigolène F 117 B4
St Esteben F 144 A2
St Estèphe F 128 A2
Ste Suzanne F 102 A1
St Étienne F 117 B4
St Etienne-de-Baigorry F 144 A2
St Étienne-de-Cuines F 118 B3
St Etienne-de-Fursac F 116 A1
St Etienne-de-Montluc F 101 B4
St Etienne-de-St Geoirs F 118 B2
St Étienne-de-Tinée F 132 A2
St Étienne-du-Bois F 118 A2
St Étienne-du-Rouvray F 89 A5
St Etienne-les-Orgues F 132 A1
Ste Tulle F 132 B1
St Fargeau F 104 B2
St Félicien F 117 B4
St Felix-de-Sorgues F 130 B1
St Félix-Lauragais F 146 A2
Saintfield GB 27 B5
St Fillans GB 35 B3
St Firmin F 118 C3
St Florent F 180 A2
St Florentin F 104 B2
St Florent-le-Vieil F 101 B4
St Florent-sur-Cher F 103 C4
St Flour F 116 B3
St Flovier F 103 C3
St Fort-sur-le-Né F 115 C3
St Fulgent F 114 B2
St Galmier F 117 B4
St Gaudens F 145 A4
St Gaultier F 115 B5
St Gély-du-Fesc F 130 B2
St Genest-Malifaux F 117 B4
St Gengoux-le-National F 104 C3
St Geniez F 132 A2
St Geniez-d'Olt F 130 A1
St Genis-de-Saintonge F 114 C3
St Genis-Pouilly F 118 A3
St Genix-sur-Guiers F 118 B2
St Georges Buttavent F 88 B3
St Georges-d'Aurac F 117 B3
St Georges-de-Commiers F 118 B2
St Georges-de-Didonne F 114 C3
St Georges-de-Luzençon F 130 A1
St Georges-de Mons F 116 B2
St Georges-de-Reneins F 117 A4
St Georges d'Oléron F 114 C2
St Georges-en-Couzan F 117 B3
St Georges-lès-Baillargeaux F 115 B4
St Georges-sur-Loire F 102 B1
St Georges-sur-Meuse B 79 B5
St Geours-de-Maremne F 128 C1
St Gérand-de-Vaux F 117 A3
St Gérand-le-Puy F 117 A3
St Germain F 105 B5
St Germain-Chassenay F 104 C2
St Germain-de-Calberte F 130 A2
St Germain-de-Confolens F 115 B4
St Germain-de-Joux F 118 A2
St Germain-des-Fossés F 117 A3
St Germain-du-Bois F 105 C4
St Germain-du-Plain F 105 C3
St Germain-du Puy F 103 B4
St Germain-en-Laye F 90 C2
St Germain-Laval F 117 B4
St Germain-Lembron F 116 B3
St Germain-les-Belles F 116 B1
St Germain-Lespinasse F 117 A3
St Germain-l'Herm F 117 B3
St Gervais-d'Auvergne F 116 A2
St Gervais-les-Bains F 118 B3
St Gervais-sur-Mare F 130 B2
St Gildas-de-Rhuys F 100 B3
St Gildas-des-Bois F 101 B3
St Gilles
Gard F 131 B3
Ille-et-Vilaine F 101 A4
St Gilles-Croix-de-Vie F 114 B2
St Gingolph F 119 A3
St Girons
Ariège F 146 B2
Landes F 128 C1
St Girons-Plage F 128 C1
St Gobain F 91 B3
St Gorgon-Main F 105 B5
St Guénolé F 100 B1
St Harmon GB 39 B3
St Helens GB 38 A4
St Helier GB 88 A1
St Herblain F 101 B4
St Hilaire
Allier F 104 C2
Aude F 146 A3
St Hilaire-de-Riez F 114 B2
St Hilaire-des-Loges F 114 B3
St Hilaire-de-Villefranche F 114 C3
St Hilaire-du-Harcouët F 88 B2
St Hilaire-du-Rosier F 118 B2
St Hippolyte
Aveyron F 116 C2
Doubs F 106 B1
St Hippolyte-du-Fort F 130 B2
St Honoré-les-Bains F 104 C2
St Hubert B 92 A1
St Imier CH 106 B2
St Issey GB 42 B2
St Ives
Cambridgeshire GB 44 A3
Cornwall GB 42 B1
St Izaire F 130 B1
St Jacques-de-la-Lande F 101 A4
St Jacut-de-la-Mer F 101 A3
St James F 88 B2
St Jaume d'Enveja E 153 B4
St Jean-Brévelay F 101 B3
St Jean-d'Angély F 114 C3
St Jean-de-Belleville F 118 B3
St Jean-de-Bournay F 118 B2
St Jean-de-Braye F 103 B3
St Jean-de-Côle F 115 C4
St Jean-de-Daye F 88 A2
St Jean de Losne F 105 B4
St Jean-de-Luz F 144 A2
St Jean-de-Maurienne F 118 B3
St Jean-de-Monts F 114 B1
St Jean-d'Illac F 128 B2
St Jean-du-Bruel F 130 A2
St Jean-du-Gard F 131 A2
St Jean-en-Royans F 118 B2
St Jean-la-Riviere F 133 B3
St Jean-Pied-de-Port F 144 A2
St Jean-Poutge F 129 C3
St Jeoire F 118 A3
St Joachim F 101 B3
St Johnstown IRL 27 B3
St Jorioz F 118 B3
St Joris Winge B 79 B4
St Jouin-de-Marnes F 102 C1
St Juéry F 130 B1
St Julien F 118 A2
St Julien-Chapteuil F 117 B4
St Julien-de-Vouvantes F 101 B4
St Julien-du-Sault F 104 A2
St Julien-du-Verdon F 132 B2
St Julien-en-Born F 128 B1
St Julien-en-Genevois F 118 A3
St Julien-l'Ars F 115 B4
St Julien la-Vêtre F 117 B3
St Julien-Mont-Denis F 118 B3
St Julien-sur-Reyssouze F 118 A2
St Junien F 115 C4
St Just
F 131 A3
GB 42 B1
St Just-en-Chaussée F 90 B2
St Just-en-Chevalet F 117 B3
St Justin F 128 C2
St Just-St Rambert F 117 B4
St Keverne GB 42 B1
St Lary-Soulan F 145 B4
St Laurent-d'Aigouze F 131 B3
St Laurent-de-Chamousset F 117 B4
St Laurent-de-Condel F 89 A3
St Laurent-de-la-Cabrerisse F 146 A3

St Laurent-de-la-Salanque F 146 B3
St Laurent-des-Autels F 101 B4
St Laurent-du-Pont F 118 B2
St Laurent-en-Caux F 89 A4
St Laurent-en-Grandvaux F 105 C4
St Laurent-Médoc F 128 A2
St Laurent-sur-Gorre F 115 C4
St Laurent-sur-Mer F 88 A3
St Laurent-sur-Sèvre F 114 B3
St Leger B 92 B1
St Léger-de-Vignes F 104 C2
St Léger-sous-Beuvray F 104 C3
St Léger-sur-Dheune F 104 C3
St Léonard-de-Noblat F 116 B1
St Leonards GB 45 C4
St Lô F 88 A2
St Lon-les-Mines F 128 C1
St Louis F 106 B2
St Loup F 117 A3
St Loup-de-la-Salle F 105 C3
St Loup-sur-Semouse F 105 B5
St Lunaire F 101 A3
St Lupicin F 118 A2
St Lyphard F 101 B3
St Lys F 146 A2
St Macaire F 128 B2
St Maclou F 89 A4
St Maixent-l'École F 115 B3
St Malo F 88 B1
St Mamet-la-Salvetat F 116 C2
St Mandrier-sur-Mer F 132 B1
St Marcel
Drôme F 117 C4
Saône-et-Loire F 105 C3
St Marcellin F 118 B2
St Marcellin sur Loire F 117 B4
St Marcet F 145 A4
St Mards-en-Othe F 104 A2
St Margaret's-at-Cliffe GB 45 B5
St Margaret's Hope GB 33 C4
St Mars-la-Jaille F 101 B4
St Martin-d'Ablois F 91 C3
St Martin-d'Auxigny F 103 B4
St Martin-de-Belleville F 118 B3
St Martin-de-Bossenay F 91 C3
St Martin-de-Crau F 131 B3
St Martin-de-Londres F 130 B2
St Martin-d'Entraunes F 132 A2
St Martin-de-Queyrières F 118 C3
St Martin-de-Ré F 114 B2
St Martin des Besaces F 88 A3
St Martin-d'Estreaux F 117 A3
St Martin-de-Valamas F 117 C4
St Martin-d'Hères F 118 B2
St Martin-du-Frêne F 118 A2
St Martin-en-Bresse F 105 C4
St Martin-en-Haut F 117 B4
St Martin-la-Méanne F 116 B1
St Martin-Osmonville F 90 B1
St Martin-sur-Ouanne F 104 B2
St Martin-Valmeroux F 116 B2
St Martin-Vésubie F 133 A3
St Martory F 145 A4
St Mary's GB 33 C4
St Mathieu F 115 C4
St Mathieu-de-Tréviers F 131 B2
St Maurice CH 119 A3
St Maurice-Navacelles F 130 B2
St Maurice-sur-Moselle F 106 B1
St Mawes GB 42 B1
St Maximin-la-Ste Baume F 132 B1
St Méard-de-Gurçon F 128 B3
St Médard-de-Guizières F 128 A2
St Médard-en-Jalles F 128 B2
St Méen-le-Grand F 101 A3
St Menges F 91 B4
St Merløse DK 61 D1
St Město CZ 85 B4
St M'Hervé F 101 A4
St Michel
Aisne F 91 B4
Gers F 145 A4
St Michel-Chef-Chef F 101 B3
St Michel-de-Castelnau F 128 B2
St Michel-de-Maurienne F 118 B3
St Michel-en-Grève F 100 A2
St Michel-enl'Herm F 114 B2
St Michel-Mont-Mercure F 114 B3
St Mihiel F 92 C1
St Monance GB 35 B5
St Montant F 131 A3
St Moritz CH 107 C4
St Nazaire F 101 B3
St Nazaire-en-Royans F 118 B2
St Nazaire-le-Désert F 131 A4
St Nectaire F 116 B2
St Neots GB 44 A3
St Nicolas-de-Port F 92 C2
St Nicolas-de-Redon F 101 B3
St Nicolas-du-Pélem F 100 A2
St Niklaas B 79 A4
St Omer F 78 B2
St Pair-sur-Mer F 88 B2
St Palais F 144 A2
St Palais-sur-Mer F 114 C2
St Pardoux-la-Rivière F 115 C4
St Paul-Cap-de-Joux F 129 C4
St Paul-de-Fenouillet F 146 B3
St Paul-de-Varax F 118 A2
St Paulien F 117 B3
St Paul-le-Jeune F 131 A3
St Paul-lès-Dax F 128 C1
St Paul-Trois-Châteaux F 131 A3
St Pé-de-Bigorre F 145 A3
St Pée-sur-Nivelle F 144 A2
St Péravy-la-Colombe F 103 B3
St Péray F 117 C4
St Père-en-Retz F 101 B3
St Peter Port GB 88 A1
St Petersburg = Sankt-Peterburg RUS 9 C7
St Philbert-de-Grand-Lieu F 114 A2
St Pierre F 130 B1
St Pierre-d'Albigny F 118 B3
St Pierre-d'Allevard F 118 B3
St Pierre-de-Chartreuse F 118 B2
St Pierre-de-Chignac F 129 A3
St Pierre-de-la-Fage F 130 B2
St Pierre-d'Entremont F 118 B2
St Pierre-d'Oléron F 114 C2
St Pierre-Eglise F 88 A2
St Pierre-en-Port F 89 A4
St Pierre-le-Moûtier F 104 C2
St Pierre Montlimart F 101 B4
St Pierre-Quiberon F 100 B2
St Pierre-sur-Dives F 89 A3
St Pierreville F 117 C4
St Pieters-Leeuw B 79 B4
St Plancard F 145 A4
St Poix F 101 B4
St Pol-de-Léon F 100 A2
St Polgues F 117 B3
St Pol-sur-Ternoise F 78 B2
St Pons-de-Thomières F 130 B1
St Porchaire F 114 C3
St Pourçain-sur-Sioule F 116 A3
St Priest F 117 B4
St Privat F 116 B2
St Quay-Portrieux F 100 A3
St Quentin F 90 B3
St Quentin-la-Poterie F 131 A3
St Quentin-les-Anges F 102 B1
St Rambert-d'Albon F 117 B4
St Rambert-en-Bugey F 118 B2
St Raphaël F 132 B2
St Rémy-de-Provence F 131 B3
St Rémy-du-Val F 89 B4
St Remy-en-Bouzemont F 91 C4
St Renan F 100 A1
St Révérien F 104 B2
St Riquier F 90 A1
St Romain-de-Colbosc F 89 A4
St Rome-de-Cernon F 130 A1
St Rome-de-Tarn F 130 A1
St Sadurní-d'Anoia E 147 C2
St Saëns F 89 A5
St Sampson GB 88 A1
St Samson-la-Poterie F 90 B1
St Saturnin-de-Lenne F 130 A2
St Saturnin-lès-Apt F 131 B4
St Saufieu F 90 B2
St Saulge F 104 B2
St Sauveur
Finistère F 100 A2
Haute-Saône F 105 B5
St Sauveur-de-Montagut F 117 C4
St Sauveur-en-Puisaye F 104 B2
St Sauveur-en-Rue F 117 B4
St Sauveur-Lendelin F 88 A2
St Sauveur-le-Vicomte F 88 A2
St Sauveur-sur-Tinée F 132 A3
St Savin
Gironde F 128 A2
Vienne F 115 B4
St Savinien F 114 C3
St Savournin F 131 B4
St Seine-l'Abbaye F 105 B3
St Sernin-sur-Rance F 130 B1
St Sevan-sur-Mer F 88 B1
St Sever F 128 C2
St Sever-Calvados F 88 B2
St Sorlin-d'Arves F 118 B3
St Soupplets F 90 B2
St Sulpice F 129 C4
St Sulpice-Laurière F 116 A1
St Sulpice-les-Feuilles F 115 B5
St Symphorien F 128 B2
St Symphoriende-Lay F 117 B4
St Symphorien d'Ozon F 117 B4
St Symphoriensur-Coise F 117 B4
St Teath GB 42 B2
St Thégonnec F 100 A2
St Thiébault F 105 A4
St Trivier-de-Courtes F 118 A2
St Trivier sur-Moignans F 117 A4
St Trojan-les-Bains F 114 C2
St Tropez F 132 B2
St Truiden B 79 B5
St Vaast-la-Hougue F 88 A2
St Valérien F 104 A2
St Valery-en-Caux F 89 A4
St Valéry-sur-Somme F 78 B1
St Vallier
Drôme F 117 B4
Saône-et-Loire F 104 C3
St Vallier-de-Thiey F 132 B2
St Varent F 102 C1
St Vaury F 116 A1
St Venant F 78 B2
St Véran F 119 C3
St Vincent I 119 B4
St Vincent-de-Tyrosse F 128 C1
St Vit F 105 B4
St Vith B 80 B2
St Vivien-de-Médoc F 114 C2
St Yan F 117 A4
St Ybars F 146 A2
St Yorre F 117 A3
St Yrieix-la-Perche F 115 C5
Saissac F 146 A3
Saja E 142 A2
Sajan SRB 126 B2
Šajkaš SRB 126 B2
Sajókaza H 99 C4
Sajószentpéter H 113 A4
Sajóvámos H 113 A4
Sakarya TR 187 B5
Šakiai LT 13 A5
Sakskøbing DK 65 B4
Sakule SRB 126 B2
Sala S 50 C3
Šal'a SK 111 A4
Sala Baganza I 120 C3
Sala Consilina I 172 B1
Salakovac SRB 127 C3
Salamanca E 150 B2
Salamina GR 185 B4
Salandra I 172 B2
Salaparuta I 176 B1
Salar E 163 A3
Salardú E 145 B4
Salas E 141 A4
Salas de los Infantes E 143 B3
Salau F 146 B2
Salavaux CH 106 C2
Salbertrand I 119 B3
Salbohed S 50 C3
Salbris F 103 B4
Salbu N 46 A2
Salce E 141 B4
Salching D 95 C4
Salcombe GB 43 B3
Saldaña E 142 B2
Saldus LV 8 D3
Sale I 120 C1
Saleby S 55 B4
Salem D 107 B4
Salemi I 176 B1
Salen
Argyll & Bute GB 34 B2
Highland GB 34 B2
N 199 A8
Sälen S 49 A5
Salernes F 132 B2
Salerno I 170 C2
Salers F 116 B2
Salford GB 40 B1
Salgótarján H 113 A3
Salgueiro P 155 B3
Salhus N 46 B2
Sali HR 137 B4
Sálice Salentino I 173 B3
Salientes E 141 B4
Salies-de-Béarn F 144 A3
Salies-du-Salat F 145 A4
Salignac-Eyvigues F 129 B4
Saligney-sur-Roudon F 104 C2
Salihli TR 188 A3
Salihorsk BY 13 B7
Salinas
Alicante E 159 C3
Huesca E 145 B4
Salinas de Medinaceli E 152 A1
Salinas de Pisuerga E 142 B2
Salindres F 131 A3
Saline di Volterra I 135 B3
Salins-les-Bains F 105 C4
Salir P 160 B1
Salisbury GB 44 B2
Salla
A 110 B1
FIN 197 C11
Sallachy GB 32 C2
Sallanches F 118 B3
Sallent E 147 C2
Sallent de Gállego E 145 B3
Salles F 128 B2
Salles-Curan F 130 A1
Salles-sur-l'Hers F 146 A2
Sallins IRL 30 A2
Sällsjö S 199 B10
Salmerón E 152 B1
Salmiech F 130 A1
Salmivaara FIN 197 C11
Salmoral E 150 B2
Salo FIN 8 B3
Salò I 121 B3
Salobreña E 163 B4
Salon-de-Provence F 131 B4
Salonica = Thessaloniki GR 182 C4
Salonta RO 16 B4
Salorino E 155 B3
Salornay-sur-Guye F 104 C3
Salorno I 121 A4
Salou E 147 C2
Šalovci SLO 111 C3
Salsbruket N 199 A8
Salses-le-Chateau F 146 B3
Salsomaggiore Terme I 120 C2
Salt E 147 C3
Saltaire GB 40 B2
Saltara I 136 B1
Saltash GB 42 B2
Saltburn-by-the-Sea GB 37 B6
Saltcoats GB 34 C3
Saltfleet GB 41 B4
Salto P 148 A2
Saltrød N 53 B4
Saltsjöbaden S 57 A4
Saltvik
FIN 51 B7
S 62 A4
Saludécio I 136 B1
Salussola I 119 B5
Saluzzo I 119 C4
Salvacañete E 152 B2
Salvada P 160 B2
Salvagnac F 129 C4
Salvaleon E 155 C4
Salvaterra de Magos P 154 B2
Salvaterra do Extremo P 155 B4
Salvatierra
Avila E 143 B4
Badajoz E 155 C4
Salvatierra de Santiago E 156 A1
Salviac F 129 B4
Salzburg A 109 B4
Salzgitter D 72 B3
Salzgitter Bad D 72 B3
Salzhausen D 72 A3
Salzhemmendorf D 72 B2
Salzkotten D 81 A4
Salzmünde D 83 A3
Salzwedel D 73 B4
Samadet F 128 C2
Samandıra TR 186 B4
Samassi I 179 C2
Samatan F 146 A1
Sambiase I 175 C2
Sambir UA 13 D5
Samborowo PL 69 B4
Sambuca di Sicília I 176 B2
Samedan CH 107 C4
Samer F 78 B1
Sami GR 184 A1
Şamlı TR 186 C2
Sammichele di Bari I 173 B2
Samnaun CH 107 C5
Samobor HR 123 B4
Samoëns F 118 A3
Samogneux F 92 B1
Samokov BG 17 D5
Samora Correia P 154 C2
Šamorín SK 111 A4
Samos
E 141 B3
GR 188 B1
Samoš SRB 126 B2
Samothraki GR 183 C7
Samper de Calanda E 153 A3
Sampéyre I 133 A3
Sampieri I 177 C3
Sampigny F 92 C1
Samplawa PL 69 B4
Samproniano I 168 A1
Samtens D 66 B2
Samugheo I 179 C2
San Adrián E 144 B2
San Agustín E 164 C2
San Agustin de Guadalix E 151 B4
Sanaigmore GB 34 C1
San Alberto I 135 A5
San Amaro E 140 B2
Sânandrei RO 126 B3
San Andrês del Rabanedo E 142 B1
San Antanio di Santadi I 179 C2
San Antolín de Ibias E 141 A4
San Arcángelo I 174 A2
Sanary-sur-Mer F 132 B1
San Asensio E 143 B4
San Bartoloméde las Abiertas E 150 C3
San Bartoloméde la Torre E 161 B2
San Bartoloméde Pinares E 150 B3
San Bartolomeo in Galdo I 170 B3
San Benedetto del Tronto I 136 C2
San Benedetto in Alpe I 135 B4
San Benedetto Po I 121 B3
San Benito E 156 B3
San Benito de la Contienda E 155 C3
San Biágio Plátani I 176 B2
San Biágio Saracinisco I 169 B3
San Bonifacio I 121 B4
San Calixto E 156 C2
San Cándido I 109 C3
San Carlo
CH 119 A5
I 176 B2
San Carlos del Valle E 157 B4
San Casciano dei Bagni I 135 C4
San Casciano in Val di Pesa I 135 B4
San Cataldo
Puglia I 173 B4
Sicilia I 176 B2
San Cebrián de Castro E 149 A4
Sancergues F 104 B1
Sancerre F 103 B4
San Cesário di Lecce I 173 B4
Sancey-le-Long F 105 B5
Sanchiorian E 150 B3
San Chírico Raparo I 174 A2
Sanchonuño E 151 A3
San Cibrao das Viñas E 140 B3
San Cipirello I 176 B2
San Ciprián E 141 A3
San Clemente E 158 B1
San Clodio E 141 B3
Sancoins F 104 C1
San Colombano al Lambro I 120 B2
San Costanzo I 136 B2
San Crisóbal de Entreviñas E 142 B1
San Cristóbal de la Polantera E 141 B5
San Cristóbal de la Vega E 150 A3
San Cristovo E 141 C3
Sancti-Petri E 162 B1
Sancti-Spiritus E 149 B3
Sand
Hedmark N 48 B3
Rogaland N 52 A2
Sanda S 57 C4
San Damiano d'Asti I 119 C5
San Damiano Macra I 133 A3
Sandane N 198 D3
San Daniele del Friuli I 122 A2
Sandanski BG 183 B5
Sandared S 60 B2
Sandarne S 51 A4
Sandau D 73 B5
Sandbach
D 96 C1
GB 38 A4
Sandbank GB 34 C3
Sandbanks GB 43 B5
Sandbukt N 192 C5
Sandby DK 65 B4
Sande
D 71 A5
Sogn og Fjordane N 46 A2
Vestfold N 54 A1
Sandefjord N 54 A1
Sandeid N 52 A1
San Demétrio Corone I 174 B2
San Demétrio né Vestini I 169 A3
Sandersleben D 82 A3
Sanderstølen N 47 B6
Sandes N 53 B3
Sandesneben D 65 C3
Sandhead GB 36 B2
Sandhem S 60 B3
Sandhorst D 71 A4
Sandhurst GB 44 B3
Sandıklı TR 189 A5
Sandillon F 103 B4
Sandl A 96 C2
Sandnes N 52 B1
Sandness GB 33 A5
Sandnessjøen N 195 D3
Sando E 149 B3
Sandomierz PL 87 B5
San Dónaci I 173 B3
San Donàdi Piave I 122 B1
San Donato Val di Comino I 169 B3
Sándorfalva H 126 A2
Sandown GB 44 C2
Sandøysund N 54 A1
Sandrigo I 121 B4
Sandsele S 195 E8
Sandset N 194 B5
Sandsjöfors S 62 A2
Sandstad N 198 B6
Sandvatn N 52 B2
Sandvig-Allinge DK 67 A3
Sandvika
Akershus N 48 C2
Hedmark N 48 B3
Nord-Trøndelag N 199 B9
Sandviken S 51 B3
Sandvikvåy N 46 C2
Sandwich GB 45 B5
Sandy GB 44 A3
San Emiliano E 141 B5
San Enrique E 162 B2
San Esteban E 141 A4
San Esteban de Gormaz E 151 A4
San Esteban de la Sierra E 149 B4
San Esteban de Litera E 145 C4
San Esteban del Molar E 142 C1
San Esteban del Valle E 150 B3
San Esteban de Valdueza E 141 B4
San Fele I 172 B1
San Felice Circeo I 169 B3

San Felices E . . . 143 B3
San Felices de los Gallégos E . . . 149 B3
San Felice sul Panaro I . . . 121 C4
San Ferdinando di Púglia I . . . 171 B4
San Fernando E . . 162 B1
San Fernando de Henares E . . . 151 B4
San Fili I . . . 174 B2
San Foca I . . . 173 B4
San Fratello I . . . 177 B3
Sangatte F . . . 78 B1
San Gavino Monreale I . . . 179 C2
San Gémini Fonte I . . . 168 A2
Sangerhausen D . . . 82 A3
San Germano Vercellese I . . . 119 B5
San Giácomo
Trentino Alto Adige I . . . 108 C2
Umbria I . . . 136 C1
San Gimignano I . . 135 B4
San Ginésio I . . . 136 B2
Sangineto Lido I . . 174 B1
San Giórgio a Liri I 169 B3
San Giorgio della Richinvelda I . . . 122 A1
San Giórgio del Sánnio I . . . 170 B2
San Giórgio di Lomellina I . . . 120 B1
San Giórgio di Nogaro I . . . 122 B2
San Giorgio di Piano I . . . 121 C4
San Giórgio Iónico I . . . 173 B3
San Giovanni a Piro I . . . 172 B1
San Giovanni Bianco I . . . 120 B2
San Giovanni di Sinis I . . . 179 C2
San Giovanni in Croce I . . . 120 B3
San Giovanni in Fiore I . . . 174 B2
San Giovanni in Persiceto I . . . 121 C4
San Giovanni Reatino I . . . 169 A2
San Giovanni Rotondo I . . . 171 B3
San Giovanni Suérgiu I . . . 179 C2
San Giovanni Valdarno I . . . 135 B4
Sangis S . . . 196 D6
San Giuliano Terme I . . . 134 B3
San Giustino I . . . 135 B5
San Godenzo I . . . 135 B4
Sangonera la Verde E . . . 165 B3
San Gregorio Magno I . . . 172 B1
Sangüesa E . . . 144 B2
Sanguinet F . . . 128 B1
San Guiseppe Jato I . . . 176 B2
Sanica BIH . . . 124 C2
Sanitz D . . . 65 B5
San Javier E . . . 165 B4
San Jorge P . . . 154 B2
San José E . . . 164 C2
San Juan E . . . 143 B3
San Juan de Alicante E . . . 165 A4
San Juan de la Nava E . . . 150 B3
San Justo de la Vega E . . . 141 B4
Sankt Aegyd am Neuwalde A . . . 110 B2
Sankt Andrä A . . . 110 C1
Sankt Andreasberg D . . . 82 A2
Sankt Anna S . . . 56 B2
Sankt Anna am Aigen A . . . 110 C2
Sankt Anton am Arlberg A . . . 107 B5
Sankt Anton an der Jessnitz A . . . 110 B2
Sankt Augustin D . . 80 B3
Sankt Blasien D . . . 106 B3
Sankt Englmar D . . . 95 B4
Sankt Gallen
A . . . 110 B1
CH . . . 107 B4
Sankt Gallenkirch A . . . 107 B4
Sankt Georgen
A . . . 96 C2
D . . . 106 A3
Sankt Georgen am Reith A . . . 110 B1
Sankt Georgen ob Judenburg A . . . 110 B1
Sankt Georgen ob Murau A . . . 109 B5
Sankt Gilgen A . . . 109 B4
Sankt Goar D . . . 81 B3
Sankt Goarshausen D . . . 81 B3
Sankt Ingbert D . . . 92 B3
Sankt Jacob A . . . 109 C5
Sankt Jakob in Defereggen A . . . 109 C3
Sankt Johann am Tauern A . . . 110 B1
Sankt Johann am Wesen A . . . 109 A4
Sankt Johann im Pongau A . . . 109 B4
Sankt Johann in Tirol A . . . 109 B3
Sankt Katharein an der Laming A . . . 110 B2
Sankt Kathrein am Hauenstein A . . . 110 B2
Sankt Lambrecht A 110 B1
Sankt Leonhard am Forst A . . . 110 A2
Sankt Leonhard im Pitztal A . . . 108 B1
Sankt Lorenzen A . 109 C3
Sankt Marein
Steiermark A . . . 110 B2
Steiermark A . . . 110 B2
Sankt Margarethen im Lavanttal A . . . 110 C1
Sankt Margrethen CH . . . 107 B4
Sankt Michael A . . . 110 B2
Sankt Michael im Burgenland A . . . 111 B3
Sankt Michael im Lungau A . . . 109 B4
Sankt Michaelisdonn D . . . 64 C2
Sankt Niklaus CH . . 119 A4
Sankt Nikolai im Sölktal A . . . 109 B5
Sankt Olof S . . . 63 C2
Sankt Oswald D . . . 96 C1
Sankt Paul
A . . . 110 C1
F . . . 132 A2
Sankt Peter D . . . 106 A3
Sankt Peter am Kammersberg A . 110 B1
Sankt-Peterburg = St Petersburg RUS . . . 9 C7
Sankt Peter-Ording D . . . 64 B1
Sankt Pölten A . . . 110 A2
Sankt Radegund A . 110 B2
Sankt Ruprecht an der Raab A . . . 110 B2
Sankt Salvator A . . 110 C1
Sankt Stefan A . . . 110 C1
Sankt Stefan an der Gail A . . . 109 C4
Sankt Stefan im Rosental A . . . 110 C2
Sankt Valentin A . . . 110 A1
Sankt Veit an der Glan A . . . 110 C1
Sankt Veit an der Gölsen A . . . 110 A2
Sankt Veit in Defereggen A . . . 109 C3
Sankt Wendel D . . . 92 B3
Sankt Wolfgang
A . . . 109 B4
D . . . 108 A3
San Lazzaro di Sávena I . . . 135 A4
San Leo I . . . 135 B5
San Leonardo de Yagüe E . . . 143 C3
San Leonardo in Passiria I . . . 108 C2
San Lorenzo al Mare I . . . 133 B3
San Lorenzo a Merse I . . . 135 B4
San Lorenzo Bellizzi I . . . 174 B2
San Lorenzo de Calatrava E . . . 157 B4
San Lorenzo de El Escorial E . . . 151 B3
San Lorenzo de la Parrilla E . . . 158 B1
San Lorenzo di Sebato I . . . 108 C2
San Lorenzo in Campo I . . . 136 B1
San Lorenzo Nuovo I . . . 168 A1
San Lourenco P . . 160 A1
San Luca I . . . 175 C2
Sanlúcar de Barrameda E . . . 161 C3
Sanlúcar de Guadiana E . . . 160 B2
Sanlúcar la Mayor E . . . 161 B3
San Lúcido I . . . 174 B2
Sanluri I . . . 179 C2
San Marcello I . . . 136 B2
San Marcello Pistoiese I . . . 135 A3
San Marcial E . . . 149 A4
San Marco I . . . 170 C2
San Marco Argentano I . . . 174 B2
San Marco dei Cavoti I . . . 170 B2
San Marco in Lámis I . . . 171 B3
San Marino RSM . . 136 B1
San Martin de Castañeda E . . . 141 B4
San Martin de la Vega E . . . 151 B4
San Martin de la Vega del Alberche E . . 150 B2
San Martín del Tesorillo E . . . 162 B2
San Martin de Luiña E . . . 141 A4
San Martin de Montalbán E . . . 157 A3
San Martin de Oscos E . . . 141 A4
San Martin de Pusa E . . . 150 C3
San Martin de Unx E . . . 144 B2
San Martín de Valdeiglesias E . . 150 B3
San Martino di Campagna I . . . 122 A1
San Martino di Castrozza I . . . 121 A4
San-Martino-di-Lota F . . . 180 A2
San Martino in Pénsilis I . . . 170 B3
San Mateo de Gallego E . . . 144 C3
San Máuro Forte I . 172 B2
San Michele all'Adige I . . . 121 A4
San Michele di Ganzaria I . . . 177 B3
San Michele Mondov ì I . . . 133 A3
San Miguel de Aguayo E . . . 142 A2
San Miguel de Bernuy E . . . 151 A4
San Miguel del Arroyo E . . . 150 A3
San Miguel de Salinas E . . . 165 B4
Sânmihaiu Roman RO . . . 126 B3
San Millán de la Cogolla E . . . 143 B4
San Miniato I . . . 135 B3
San Muñoz E . . . 149 B3
Sänna S . . . 55 B5
Sannazzaro de'Burgondi I . . . 120 B1
Sanne D . . . 73 B4
Sannicandro di Bari I . . . 171 B4
Sannicandro Gargánico I . . . 171 B3
San Nicola del'Alto I . . . 174 B2
San Nicolás del Puerto E . . . 156 C2
Sânnicolau Mare RO . . . 126 A2
San Nicolò I . . . 121 C4
San Nicolò Gerrei I . . . 179 C3
Sannidal N . . . 53 B5
Sanniki PL . . . 77 B4
Sanok PL . . . 12 D5
San Pablo de los Montes E . . . 157 A3
San Pancrázio Salentino I . . . 173 B3
San Pantaleo I . . . 178 A3
San Páolo di Civitate I . . . 171 B3
San Pawl il-Bahar M . . . 175 C3
San Pedro
Albacete E . . . 158 C1
Oviedo E . . . 141 A4
San Pedro de Alcántara E . . . 162 B3
San Pedro de Ceque E . . . 141 B4
San Pedro del Arroyo E . . . 150 B3
San Pedro de Latarce E . . . 142 C1
San Pedro del Pinatar E . . . 165 B4
San Pedro del Romeral E . . . 143 A3
San Pedro de Merida E . . . 156 B1
San Pedro de Valderaduey E . . . 142 B2
San Pedro Manrique E . . . 144 B1
San Pellegrino Terme I . . . 120 B2
San Piero a Sieve I 135 B4
San Piero in Bagno I . . . 135 B4
San Piero Patti I . . 177 A3
San Pietro I . . . 177 B3
San Pietro in Casale I . . . 121 C4
San Pietro in Gu I . 121 B4
San Pietro in Palazzi I . . . 134 B3
San Pietro in Volta I . . . 122 B1
San Pietro Vara I . . 134 A2
San Pietro Vernótico I . . . 173 B3
San Polo d'Enza I . 121 C3
Sanquhar GB . . . 36 A3
San Quírico d'Órcia I . . . 135 B4
San Rafael del Rio E . . . 153 B4
San Remo I . . . 133 B3
San Román de Cameros E . . . 143 B4
San Roman de Hernija E . . . 150 A2
San Román de la Cuba E . . . 142 B2
San Roman de los Montes E . . . 150 B3
San Romao P . . . 155 C3
San Roque E . . . 162 B2
San Roque de Riomera E . . . 143 A3
San Rufo I . . . 172 B1
San Sabastián de los Ballesteros E . . . 162 A3
San Salvador de Cantamuda E . . . 142 B2
San Salvo I . . . 170 A2
San Salvo Marina I 170 A2
San Sebastián de los Reyes E . . . 151 B4
San Sebastiano Curone I . . . 120 C2
San Secondo Parmense I . . . 120 C3
Sansepolcro I . . . 135 B5
San Serverino Marche I . . . 136 B2
San Severino Lucano I . . . 174 A2
San Severo I . . . 171 B3
San Silvestre de Guzmán E . . . 161 B2
Sanski Most BIH . 124 C2
San Sosti I . . . 174 B2
San Stéfano di Cadore I . . . 109 C3
San Stino di Livenza I . . . 122 B1
Santa Agnès E . . . 166 B1
Santa Amalia E . . . 156 A1
Santa Ana
Cáceres E . . . 156 A2
Jaén E . . . 163 A4
Santa Ana de Pusa E . . . 150 C3
Santa Barbara E . . 153 B4
Santa Bárbara P . . 160 B1
Santa Barbara de Casa E . . . 161 B2
Santa Bárbara de Padrões P . . . 160 B2
Santacara E . . . 144 B2
Santa Catarina P . . 160 B2
Santa Caterina di Pittinuri I . . . 178 B2
Santa Caterina Villarmosa I . . . 177 B3
Santa Cesárea Terme I . . . 173 B4
Santa Clara-a-Nova P . . . 160 B1
Santa Clara-a-Velha P . . . 160 B1
Santa Clara de Louredo P . . . 160 B2
Santa Coloma de Farners E . . . 147 C3
Santa Coloma de Gramenet E . . . 147 C3
Santa Coloma de Queralt E . . . 147 C2
Santa Colomba de Curueño E . . . 142 B1
Santa Colomba de Somoza E . . . 141 B4
Santa Comba E . . . 140 A2
Santa Comba Dáo P . . . 148 B1
Santa Comba de Rossas P . . . 149 A3
Santa Cristina I . . . 120 B2
Santa Cristina de la Polvorosa E . . . 141 B5
Santa Croce Camerina I . . . 177 C3
Santa Croce di Magliano I . . . 170 B2
Santa Cruz
E . . . 140 A2
P . . . 154 B1
Santa Cruz de Alhama E . . . 163 A4
Santa Cruz de Campezo E . . . 143 B4
Santa Cruz de Grio E . . . 152 A2
Santa Cruz de la Salceda E . . . 151 A4
Santa Cruz de la Sierra E . . . 156 A2
Santa Cruz de la Zarza E . . . 151 C4
Santa Cruz del Retamar E . . . 151 B3
Santa Cruz del Valle E . . . 150 B2
Santa Cruz de Moya E . . . 159 B2
Santa Cruz de Mudela E . . . 157 B4
Santa Cruz de Paniagua E . . . 149 B3
Santadi I . . . 179 C2
Santa Doménica Talao I . . . 174 B1
Santa Doménica Vittória I . . . 177 B3
Santa Elena E . . . 157 B4
Santa Elena de Jamuz E . . . 141 B5
Santaella E . . . 162 A3
Santa Eufemia E . . 156 B3
Santa Eufémia d'Aspromonte I . . 175 C1
Santa Eulalia E . . . 152 B2
Santa Eulália P . . . 155 C3
Santa Eulalia de Oscos E . . . 141 A3
Santa Eulàlia des Riu E . . . 166 C1
Santa Fe E . . . 163 A4
Santa Fiora I . . . 135 C4
Sant'Ágata dei Goti I . . . 170 B2
Sant'Ágata di Ésaro I . . . 174 B1
Sant'Ágata di Puglia I . . . 171 B3
Sant'Agata Feltria I 135 B5
Sant'Ágata Militello I . . . 177 A3
Santa Gertrude I . . 108 C1
Santa Giustina I . . . 121 A5
Sant Agust ìde Lluçanès E . . . 147 B3
Santa Iria P . . . 160 B2
Santa Leocadia P . 148 A1
Santa Lucia del Mela I . . . 177 A4
Santa Lucia-de-Porto-Vecchio F . . . 180 B2
Santa Luzia P . . . 160 B1
Santa Maddalena Vallalta I . . . 108 C3
Santa Magdalena de Polpis E . . . 153 B4
Santa Margalida E. 167 B3
Santa Margarida P 154 B2
Santa Margarida do Sado P . . . 160 A1
Santa Margaridao de Montbui E . . . 147 C2
Santa Margherita I. 179 D2
Santa Margherita di Belice I . . . 176 B2
Santa Margherita Ligure I . . . 134 A2
Santa Maria
CH . . . 108 C1
E . . . 144 B3
Santa Maria al Bagno I . . . 173 B3
Santa Maria Cápua Vétere I . . . 170 B2
Santa Maria da Feira P . . . 148 B1
Santa Maria de Cayón E . . . 143 A3
Santa Maria de Corco E . . . 147 B3
Santa Maria de Huerta E . . . 152 A1
Santa Maria de la Alameda E . . . 151 B3
Santa Maria de las Hoyas E . . . 143 C3
Santa Maria del Camí E . . . 167 B2
Santa Maria del Campo E . . . 143 B3
Santa Maria del Campo Rus E . . . 158 B1
Santa Maria della Versa I . . . 120 C2
Santa Maria del Páramo E . . . 142 B1
Santa Maria del Taro I . . . 134 A2
Santa Maria de Mercadillo E . . . 143 C3
Santa Maria de Nieva E . . . 164 B3
Santa Maria de Trassierra E . . . 156 C3
Santa Maria di Licodia I . . . 177 B3
Santa Maria-di-Rispéscia I . . . 168 A1
Santa Maria la Palma I . . . 178 B2
Santa Maria la Real de Nieva E . . . 150 A3
Santa Maria Maggiore I . . . 119 A5
Santa Maria Ribarredonda E . 143 B3
Santa Marina del Rey E . . . 141 B5
Santa Marinella I . . 168 A1
Santa Marta
Albacete E . . . 158 B1
Badajoz E . . . 155 C4
Santa Marta de Magasca E . . . 156 A1
Santa Marta de Penaguião P . . . 148 A2
Santa Marta de Tormes E . . . 150 B2
Santana
Évora P . . . 154 C2
Setúbal P . . . 154 C1
Sântana RO . . . 126 A3
Santana da Serra P . . . 160 B1
Sant'Ana de Cambas P . . . 160 B2
Santana do Mato P 154 C2
Sant'Anastasia I . . 170 C2
Santander E . . . 143 A3
Sant'Andrea Frius I . . . 179 C3
Sant'Ángelo dei Lombardi I . . . 172 B1
Sant'Angelo in Vado I . . . 136 B1
Sant'Angelo Lodigiano I . . . 120 B2
Santa Ninfa I . . . 176 B1
Sant'Antíoco I . . . 179 C2
Sant Antoni de Calonge E . . . 147 C4
Sant Antoni de Portmany E . . . 166 C1
Sant'Antonio-di-Gallura I . . . 178 B3
Santanyí E . . . 167 B3
Santa Olalla
Huelva E . . . 161 B3
Toledo E . . . 150 B3
Santa Pau E . . . 147 B3
Santa Pola E . . . 165 A4
Santa Ponça E . . . 166 B2
Santarcángelo di Romagna I . . . 136 A1
Santarém P . . . 154 B2
Santa Severa
F . . . 180 A2
I . . . 168 A1
Santa Severina I . . 175 B2
Santas Martas E . . 142 B1
Santa Sofia I . . . 135 B4
Santa Susana P . . . 154 C2
Santa Suzana P . . . 155 C3
Santa Teresa di Riva I . . . 177 B4
Santa Teresa Gallura I . . . 178 A3
Santa Uxía E . . . 140 B2
Santa Valburga I . . 108 C1
Santa Vittória in Matenano I . . . 136 B2
Sant Boi de Llobregat E . . . 147 C3
Sant Carles de la Ràpita E . . . 153 B4
Sant Carlos E . . . 166 B1
Sant'Caterina I . . . 135 C4
Sant Celoni E . . . 147 C3
Sant Climent E . . . 167 B4
Santed E . . . 152 A2
Sant'Egidio alla Vibrata I . . . 136 C2
Sant'Elia a Pianisi I . . . 170 B2
Sant'Elia Fiumerapido I . . . 169 B3
Santelices E . . . 143 A3
San Telmo E . . . 161 B3
Sant'Elpídio a Mare I . . . 136 B2
Santéramo in Colle I . . . 171 C4
Santervas de la Vega E . . . 142 B2
Sant' Eufemia Lamezia . . . 175 C2
Sant Felíu E . . . 147 C3
Sant Feliu de Codines E . . . 147 C3
Sant Feliu de Guíxols E . . . 147 C4
Sant Feliu Sasserra E . . . 147 C3
Sant Ferran E . . . 166 C1
Sant Francesc de Formentera E . . . 166 C1
Sant Francesc de ses Salines E . . . 166 C1
Santhià I . . . 119 B5
Sant Hilari Sacalm E . . . 147 C3
Sant Hipòlit de Voltregà E . . . 147 B3
Santiago de Alcántara E . . . 155 B3
Santiago de Calatrava E . . . 163 A3
Santiago de Compostela E . . . 140 B2
Santiago de la Espade E . . . 164 A2
Santiago de la Puebla E . . . 150 B2
Santiago de la Ribera E . . . 165 B4
Santiago del Campo E . . . 155 B4
Santiago de Litem P . . . 154 B2

Santiago do Cacém P 160 B1
Santiago do Escoural P 154 C2
Santiago Maior P 155 C3
Santibáñez de Béjar E 150 B2
Santibáñez de la Peña E 142 B2
Santibáñez de Murias E 142 A1
Santibáñez de Vidriales E 141 B4
Santibáñez el Alto E 149 B3
Santibáñez el Bajo E 149 B3
Santillana E 142 A2
Santiponce E 162 A1
San Tirso de Abres E 141 A3
Santisteban del Puerto E 157 B4
Santiuste de San Juan Bautiste E 150 A3
Santiz E 149 A4
Sant Jaume dels Domenys E 147 C2
Sant Joan Baptista E 166 B1
Sant Joan de les Abadesses E 147 B3
Sant Jordi E 153 B4
Sant Josep de sa Talaia E 166 C1
Sant Juliáde Loria AND 146 B2
Sant'llario d'Enza I 121 C3
Sant Llorençde Morunys E 147 B2
Sant Llorençdes Carctassar E 167 B3
Sant Llorenç Savall E 147 C3
Sant Luis E 167 B4
Sant Mart ide Llemaná E 147 B3
Sant Marti de Maldá E 147 C2
Sant Marti Sarroca E 147 C2
Sant Mateu E 153 B4
Sant Miquel E 166 B1
Santo Aleixo P 161 A2
Santo Amado P 161 A2
Santo Amaro P 155 C3
Santo André P 160 A1
Santo Domingo E 155 C3
Santo Domingo de la Calzada E 143 B4
Santo Domingo de Silos E 143 C3
Santo Estêvão
Faro P 160 B2
Santarém P 154 C2
Santok PL 75 B4
Santomera E 165 A3
Santoña E 143 A3
Santo-Pietro-di Tenda F 180 A2
Sant'Oreste I 168 A2
Santo Spirito I 171 B4
Santo Stefano d'Aveto I 134 A2
Santo Stéfano di Camastra I 177 A3
Santo Stefano di Magra I 134 A2
Santo Stéfano Quisquina I 176 B2
Santo Tirso P 148 A1
Santotis E 142 A2
Santo Tomé E 164 A1
Santovenia
Burgos E 143 B3
Zamora E 142 C1
Sant Pau de Seguries E 147 B3
Santpedor E 147 C2
Sant Pere de Riudebitlles E 147 C2
Sant Pere Pescador E 147 B4
Sant Pere Sallavinera E 147 C2
Sant Quirze de Besora E 147 B3
Sant Rafel E 166 C1
Sant Ramon E 147 C2
Santu Lussurgiu I 178 B2
Santutzi E 143 A3
Sant Vincençde Castellet E 147 C2
San Valentino alla Muta I 108 C1
San Venanzo I 135 C5
San Vicente de Alcántara E 155 B3
San Vicente de Arana E 144 B1
San Vicente de la Barquera E 142 A2
San Vicente de la Sonsierra E 143 B4
San Vicente de Toranzo E 143 A3
San Vietro E 149 A3
San Vigilio I 108 C2
San Vincente del Raspeig E 165 A4
San Vincenzo I 134 B3
San Vito I 179 C3
San Vito al Tagliamento I 122 B1
San Vito Chietino I 169 A4
San Vito dei Normanni I 173 B3
San Vito di Cadore I 108 C3
San Vito lo Capo I 176 A1
San Vito Romano I 169 B2
Sanxenxo E 140 B2
Sanza I 172 B1
São Aleixo P 155 C3
São Barnabé P 160 B1
São Bartoloméda Serra P 160 A1
São Bartolomeu de Messines P 160 B1
São Bento P 140 C2
São Brás P 160 B2
São Brás de Alportel P 160 B2
São Braz do Reguedoura P 154 C2
São Cristóvão P 154 C2
São Domingos P 160 B1
São Geraldo P 154 C2
São Jacinto P 148 B1
São João da Madeira P 148 B1
São João da Pesqueira P 148 A2
São João da Ribeira P 154 B2
São João da Serra P 148 B1
São João da Venda P 160 B2
São João dos Caldeireiros P 160 B2
São Julião P 155 B3
São Leonardo P 155 C3
São Luis P 160 B1
São Manços P 155 C3
São Marcos da Ataboeira P 160 B2
Saõ Marcos da Serra P 160 B1
São Marcos de Campo P 155 C3
São Martinho da Cortiça P 148 B1
São Martinho das Amoreiras P 160 B1
São Martinho do Porto P 154 B1
São Matias
Beja P 160 A2
Évora P 154 C2
São Miguel d'Acha P 155 A3
São Miguel de Machede P 155 C3
São Pedro da Torre P 140 C2
São Pedro de Cadeira P 154 B1
São Pedro de Muel P 154 B1
São Pedro de Solis P 160 B2
São Pedro do Sul P 148 B1
Saorge F 133 B3
São Romão P 154 C2
São Sebastião dos Carros P 160 B2
São Teotónio P 160 B1
São Torcato P 148 A1
Sapataria P 154 C1
Sapes GR 183 B7
Sapiãos P 148 A2
Sa Pobla E 167 B3
Sappada I 109 C3
Sappen N 192 C5
Sapri I 174 A1
Sarajärvi FIN 197 D10
Sarajevo BIH 139 B4
Saramon F 129 C3
Sarandë AL 182 D2
Saranovo SRB 127 C2
Saraorci SRB 127 C3
Sa Rapita E 167 B3
Saray TR 186 A2
Saraycık TR 187 C4
Sarayköy TR 188 B3
Saraylar TR 186 B2
Sarayönü TR 189 A7
Sarbia PL 75 B5
Sarbinowo
Zachodnio-Pomorskie PL 67 B4
Zachodnio-Pomorskie PL 74 B3
Sárbogárd H 112 C2
Sarcelles F 90 B2
Sarche I 121 A3
Sardara I 179 C2
Sardoal P 154 B2
Sardón de Duero E 150 A3
Sare F 144 A2
S'Arenal E 166 B2
Šarengrad HR 125 B5
Sarentino I 108 C2
Sarezzo I 120 B3
Sargans CH 107 B4
Sári H 112 B3
Sarıbeyler TR 186 C2
Sarıcakaya TR 187 B5
Sari-d'Orcino F 180 A1
Sarıgöl TR 188 A3
Sarıkaya TR 23 B8
Sarıköy TR 186 B2
Sarilhos Grandes P 154 C2
Sariñena E 145 C3
Sarıoba TR 187 C7
Sárisáp H 112 B2
Sariyer TR 186 A4
Sarkad H 113 C5
Sárkeresztes H 112 B2
Sárkeresztúr H 112 B2
Särkijärvi FIN 196 B6
Şarkikaraağaç TR 189 A6
Şarköy TR 186 B2
Sarlat-la-Canéda F 129 B4
Sarliac-sur-l'Isle F 129 A3
Sármellék H 111 C4
Särna S 199 D10
Sarnadas P 155 B3
Sarnano I 136 B2
Sarnen CH 106 C3
Sarnesfield GB 39 B4
Sárnico I 120 B2
Sarno I 170 C2
Sarnonico I 121 A4
Sarnow D 74 A2
Sarny UA 13 C7
Särö S 60 B1
Saronno I 120 B2
Sárosd H 112 B2
Šarovce SK 112 A2
Sarpoil F 117 B3
Sarpsborg N 54 A2
Sarracín E 143 B3
Sarral E 147 C2
Sarralbe F 92 B3
Sarrancolin F 145 B4
Sarras F 117 B4
Sarre I 119 B4
Sarreaus E 140 B3
Sarrebourg F 92 C3
Sarreguemines F 92 B3
Sárrétudvari H 113 B5
Sarre-Union F 92 C3
Sarria E 141 B3
Sarriàde Ter E 147 B3
Sarrión E 153 B3
Sarroca de Lleida E 153 A4
Sarroch I 179 C3
Sarron F 128 C2
Sársina I 135 B5
Særslev DK 59 C3
Sarstedt D 72 B2
Sárszentlörinc H 112 C2
Sárszentmihaly H 112 B2
Sárszentmiklós H 112 C2
Sarteano I 135 C4
Sartène F 180 B1
Sartilly F 88 B2
Sartirana Lomellina I 120 B1
Saruhanlı TR 186 D2
Sárvár H 111 B3
Sarvisvaara S 196 C4
Sarzana I 134 A2
Sarzeau F 101 B3
Sarzedas P 155 B3
Sasalli TR 188 A1
Sasamón E 142 B2
Sa Savina E 166 C1
Sásd H 125 A4
Sasino PL 68 A2
Sássari I 178 B2
Sassello I 133 A4
Sassenberg D 71 C5
Sassetta I 134 B3
Sassnitz D 66 B2
Sassocorvaro I 136 B1
Sasso d'Ombrone I 135 C4
Sassoferrato I 136 B1
Sassoleone I 135 A4
Sasso Marconi I 135 A4
Sassuolo I 135 A3
Sástago E 153 A3
Šaštinske Stráže SK 98 C1
Sas van Gent NL 79 A3
Såtåhaugen N 199 C7
Satão P 148 B2
Såtenäs S 55 B3
Säter S 50 B2
Sätila S 60 B2
Satillieu F 117 B4
Satnica Đakovačka HR 125 B4
Sátoraljaújhely H 16 A4
Satow D 65 C4
Sätra-brunn S 50 C3
Sætre N 54 A1
Satrup D 64 B2
Satteins A 107 B4
Satu Mare RO 17 B5
Saturnia I 168 A1
Saucats F 128 B2
Saucelle E 149 A3
Sauda N 52 A2
Sauðarkrókur IS 190 B6
Saudasjøen N 52 A2
Sauerlach D 108 B2
Saugues F 117 C3
Sauherad N 53 A5
Saujon F 114 C3
Sauland N 53 A4
Saulces Monclin F 91 B4
Saulgau D 107 A4
Saulgrub D 108 B2
Saulieu F 104 B3
Saulnot F 106 B1
Sault F 131 A4
Sault-Brénaz F 118 B2
Sault-de-Navailles F 128 C2
Saulx F 105 B5
Saulxures-sur-Moselotte F 106 B1
Saulzais-le-Potier F 103 C4
Saumos F 128 B1
Saumur F 102 B1
Saunavaara FIN 197 B10
Saundersfoot GB 39 C2
Saurat F 146 B2
Saurbær
Borgarfjarðarsýsla IS 190 C4
Dalasýsla IS 190 B4
Eyjafjarðarsýsla IS 191 B7
Sáuris I 109 C3
Sausset-les-Pins F 131 B4
Sauteyrargues F 131 B2
Sauvagnat F 116 B2
Sauve F 131 B2
Sauveterre-de-Béarn F 144 A3
Sauveterre-de-Guyenne F 128 B2
Sauviat-sur-Vige F 116 B1
Sauxillanges F 117 B3
Sauzet
Drôme F 117 C4
Lot F 129 B4
Sauzé-Vaussais F 115 B4
Sauzon F 100 B2
Sava I 173 B3
Sävar S 200 C6
Sævareid N 46 B2
Savarsin RO 16 B5
Sävast S 196 D4
Savaştepe TR 186 C2
Savci SLO 111 C3
Säve S 60 B1
Savelletri I 173 B3
Savelli I 174 B2
Savenay F 101 B4
Saverdun F 146 A2
Saverne F 93 C3
Savières F 91 C3
Savigliano I 119 C4
Savignac-les-Eglises F 129 A3
Savignano Irpino I 171 B3
Savignano sul Rubicone I 136 A1
Savigny-sur-Braye F 102 B2
Saviñán E 152 A2
Savines-le-lac F 132 A2
Savino Selo SRB 126 B1
Savio I 135 A5
Sävja S 51 C4
Šavnik MNE 139 C5
Savognin CH 107 C4
Savona I 133 A4
Savonlinna FIN 9 B6
Savournon F 132 A1
Sævråsvåg N 46 B2
Sävsjö S 62 A2
Savsjön S 50 C1
Sävsjöström S 62 A3
Savudrija HR 122 B2
Savukoski FIN 197 B11
Sawbridgeworth GB 45 B4
Sawtry GB 44 A3
Sax E 159 C3
Saxdalen S 50 B1
Saxilby GB 40 B3
Saxmundham GB 45 A5
Saxnäs S 195 F6
Saxthorpe GB 41 C5
Sayalonga E 163 B3
Sayatón E 151 B5
Sayda D 83 B5
Säytsjärvi FIN 193 C11
Śazava CZ 97 B3
Sázava CZ 96 B2
Scaër F 100 A2
Scafa I 169 A4
Scalasaig GB 34 B1
Scalby GB 40 A3
Scalea I 174 B1
Scaletta Zanclea I 177 A4
Scalloway GB 33 A5
Scamblesby GB 41 B3
Scandale I 175 B2
Scandiano I 121 C3
Scandicci I 135 B4
Scandolara Ravara I 120 B3
Scanno I 169 B3
Scansano I 168 A1
Scanzano Jónico I 174 A2
Scarborough GB 40 A3
Scardovari I 122 C1
Scardoy GB 32 D2
Scarperia I 135 B4
Scarriff IRL 28 B3
Scey-sur-Saône et St Albin F 105 B4
Schachendorf A 111 B3
Schaffhausen CH 107 B3
Schafstädt D 83 A3
Schafstedt D 64 B2
Schäftlarn D 108 B2
Schagen NL 70 B1
Schalkau D 82 B3
Schangnau CH 106 C2
Schapbach D 93 C4
Scharbeutz D 65 B3
Schärding A 96 C1
Scharnitz A 108 B2
Scharrel D 71 A4
Schattendorf A 111 B3
Scheemda NL 71 A3
Scheessel D 72 A2
Schéggia I 136 B1
Scheibbs A 110 A2
Scheibenberg D 83 B4
Scheidegg D 107 B4
Scheifling A 110 B1
Scheinfeld D 94 B2
Schelklingen D 94 C1
Schenefeld
Schleswig-Holstein D 64 B2
Schleswig-Holstein D 72 A2
Schenklengsfeld D 82 B1
Scherfede D 81 A5
Schermbeck D 80 A2
Scherpenzeel NL 70 B2
Schesslitz D 94 B3
Scheveningen NL 70 B1
Schiedam NL 79 A4
Schieder-Schwalenberg D 72 C2
Schierling D 95 C4
Schiers CH 107 C4
Schildau D 83 A4
Schillingen D 92 B2
Schillingsfürst D 94 B2
Schilpário I 120 A3
Schiltach D 93 C4
Schiltigheim F 93 C3
Schio I 121 B4
Schirmeck F 92 C3
Schirnding D 83 B4
Schkeuditz D 83 A4
Schkölen D 83 A3
Schlabendorf D 84 A1
Schladen D 73 B3
Schladming A 109 B4
Schlangen D 81 A4
Schleiden D 80 B2
Schleiz D 83 B3
Schleswig D 64 B2
Schleusingen D 82 B2
Schlieben D 83 A5
Schliengen D 106 B2
Schliersee D 108 B2
Schlitz D 81 B5
Schloss Neuhans D 81 A4
Schlossvippach D 82 A3
Schlotheim D 82 A2
Schluchsee D 106 B3
Schlüchtern D 81 B5
Schmallenberg D 81 A4
Schmelz D 92 B2
Schmidmühlen D 95 B3
Schmiedeberg D 84 B1
Schmiedefeld D 82 B2
Schmirn A 108 B2
Schmölln
Brandenburg D 74 A3
Sachsen D 83 B4
Schnaittach D 95 B3
Schneeberg D 83 B4
Schneizlreuth D 109 B3
Schneverdingen D 72 A2
Schöder A 109 B5
Schoenburg B 80 B2
Schollene D 73 B5
Schöllkrippen D 81 B5
Schomberg D 107 A3
Schönach D 95 C4
Schönau
Baden-Württemberg D 106 B2
Bayern D 95 C4
Schönbeck D 74 A2
Schönberg
Bayern D 96 C1
Mecklenburg-Vorpommern D 65 C3
Schleswig-Holstein D 65 B3
Schönebeck D 73 B4
Schöneck D 83 B4
Schönecken- D 80 B2
Schönermark D 74 A2
Schönewalde D 83 A5
Schongau D 108 B1
Schöngrabern A 97 C4
Schönhagen D 81 A5
Schönhausen D 73 B5
Schöningen D 73 B3
Schönkirchen D 64 B3
Schönsee D 95 B4
Schöntal D 94 B1
Schönthal D 95 B4
Schonungen D 94 A2
Schönwalde D 65 B3
Schoondijke NL 79 A3
Schoonebeek NL 71 B3
Schoonhoven NL 79 A4
Schopfheim D 106 B2
Schöppenstedt D 73 B3
Schörfling A 109 B4
Schorndorf D 94 C1
Schortens D 71 A4
Schotten D 81 B5
Schramberg D 106 A3
Schraplau D 83 A3
Schrattenberg A 97 C4
Schrecksbach D 81 B5
Schrems A 96 C3
Schrobenhausen D 95 C3
Schröcken A 107 B5
Schrozberg D 94 B1
Schruns A 107 B4
Schüpfheim CH 106 C3
Schüttorf D 71 B4
Schwaan D 65 C5
Schwabach D 94 B3
Schwäbisch Gmünd D 94 C1
Schwäbisch Hall D 94 B1
Schwabmünchen D 108 A1
Schwadorf A 111 A3
Schwagstorf D 71 B4
Schwaigern D 93 B5
Schwalmstadt D 81 B5
Schwanberg A 110 C2
Schwanden CH 107 C4
Schwandorf D 95 B4
Schwanebeck D 73 C4
Schwanenstadt A 109 A4
Schwanewede D 72 A1
Schwanfeld D 94 B2
Schwangau D 108 B1
Schwarmstedt D 72 B2
Schwarza D 82 B2
Schwarzach im Pongau A 109 B4
Schwarzau im Gebirge A 110 B2
Schwarzenau A 97 C3
Schwarzenbach D 83 B3
Schwarzenbach am Wald D 83 B3
Schwarzenbek D 72 A3
Schwarzenberg D 83 B4
Schwarzenburg CH 106 C2
Schwarzenfeld D 95 B4
Schwarz-heide D 84 A1
Schwaz A 108 B2
Schwechat A 111 A3
Schwedt D 74 A3
Schwei D 71 A5
Schweich D 92 B2
Schweighausen D 106 A2
Schweinfurt D 94 A2
Schweinitz D 83 A5
Schweinrich D 74 A1
Schwelm D 80 A3
Schwemsal D 83 A4
Schwendt A 109 B3
Schwenningen D 107 A3
Schwepnitz D 84 A1
Schwerin D 73 A4
Schwerte D 81 A3
Schweskau D 73 B4
Schwetzingen D 93 B4
Schwyz CH 107 B3
Sciacca I 176 B2
Scicli I 177 C3
Ściechów PL 75 B3
Scigliano I 175 B2
Scilla I 175 C1
Ścinawa PL 85 A4
Scionzier F 118 A3
Scoglitti I 177 C3
Scole GB 45 A5
Sconser GB 31 B2
Scopello
Piemonte I 119 B5
Sicilia I 176 A1
Scordia I 177 B3
Scorzè I 121 B5
Scotch Corner GB 37 B5
Scotter GB 40 B3
Scourie GB 32 C1
Scousburgh GB 33 B5
Scrabster GB 32 C3
Screeb IRL 28 A2
Scremerston GB 37 A5
Scritto I 136 B1
Scunthorpe GB 40 B3
Scuol CH 107 C5
Scúrcola Marsicana I 169 A3
Seaford GB 45 C4
Seaham GB 37 B5
Seahouses GB 37 A5
Seascale GB 36 B3
Seaton GB 43 B3
Sebazac-Concourès F 130 A1
Seben TR 187 B6
Sebersdorf A 110 B2
Sebezh RUS 8 D6
Sebnitz D 84 B2
Seborga I 133 B3
Seby S 63 B4
Seč
Vychodočeský CZ 97 B3
Západočeský CZ 96 B1

Sečanj SRB 126 B2
Secemin PL 87 B3
Séchault F 91 B4
Seckau A 110 B1
Seclin F 78 B3
Secondigny F 114 B3
Seda P 155 B3
Sedan F 91 B4
Sedano E 143 B3
Sedbergh GB 37 B4
Sedella E 163 B3
Séderon F 131 A4
Sedgefield GB 37 B5
Sedico I 121 A5
Sédilo I 178 B2
Sédini I 178 B2
Sedlarica HR 124 B3
Sedlčany CZ 96 B2
Sedlec-Prčice CZ 96 B2
Sedlice CZ 96 B1
Sędziejowice PL 86 A3
Sędziszów PL 87 B4
Sędziszów Małapolski PL 87 B5
Seebach F 93 C3
Seeboden A 109 C4
Seefeld
Brandenburg D 74 B2
Niedersachsen D 71 A5
Seefeld in Tirol A 108 B2
Seeg D 108 B1
Seehausen
Sachsen-Anhalt D 73 B4
Sachsen-Anhalt D 73 B4
Seeheim-Jugenheim D 93 B4
Seelbach D 93 C3
Seelow D 74 B3
Seelze D 72 B2
Seerhausen D 83 A5
Sées F 89 B4
Seesen D 82 A2
Seeshaupt D 108 B2
Seewalchen A 109 B4
Seferihisar TR 188 A1
Sefkerin SRB 127 B2
Segård N 48 B2
Segerstad S 55 A4
Segesd H 124 A3
Seglinge FIN 51 B7
Segmon S 55 A4
Segonzac F 115 C3
Segorbe E 159 B3
Segovia E 151 B3
Segré F 101 B5
Segura
E 144 B1
P 155 B3
Segura de León E 161 A3
Segura de los Baños E 152 B3
Ségur-les-Villas F 116 B2
Segurrilla E 150 B3
Sehnde D 72 B2
Seia P 148 B2
Seiches-sur-le-Loir F 102 B1
Seifhennersdorf D 84 B2
Seignelay F 104 B2
Seijo E 140 C2
Seilhac F 116 B1
Seilles B 79 B5
Seim N 46 B2
Seinäjoki FIN 8 A3
Seissan F 145 A4
Seitenstetten Markt A 110 A1
Seixal P 154 C1
Seiz A 110 B1
Seizthal A 110 B1
Sejerslev DK 58 B1
Seksna RUS 9 C11
Selárdalur IS 190 B1
Selárgius I 179 C3
Selb D 83 B4
Selby GB 40 B2
Selca HR 138 B2
Selce HR 123 B3
Selçuk TR 188 B2
Selde DK 58 B2
Selenča SRB 126 B1
Selendi
Manisa TR 186 D2
Manisa TR 186 D3
Selenicë AL 182 C1
Sélestat F 106 A2
Seleuš SRB 126 B2
Selevac SRB 127 C2
Selfoss IS 190 D5
Selgua E 145 C4
Selice SK 112 A1
Seligenstadt D 93 A4
Seligenthal D 82 B2
Selimiye TR 188 B2
Selizharovo RUS 9 D8
Selja S 50 A1
Selje N 198 C2
Seljelvnes N 192 C3
Seljord N 53 A4
Selkirk GB 35 C5
Sellano I 136 C1
Selles-St Denis F 103 B3
Selles-sur-Cher F 103 B3
Sellières F 105 C4
Sellin D 66 B2
Sellye H 125 B3
Selm D 80 A3
Selnica ob Dravi SLO 110 C2
Selongey F 105 B4
Selonnet F 132 A2
Selow D 65 C4
Selsey GB 44 C3
Selsingen D 72 A2
Selters D 81 B3
Seltz F 93 C4
Selva E 167 B2
Selva di Cadore I 108 C3
Selva di Val Gardena I 108 C2
Selvik
Sogn og Fjordane N 46 A2
Vestfold N 54 A1
Selvino I 120 B2
Selyatyn UA 17 B6
Sem N 54 A1
Semeljci HR 125 B4
Semič SLO 123 B4
Semide
F 91 B4
P 148 B1
Semily CZ 84 B3
Seminara I 175 C1
Semlac RO 126 A2
Semlacu Mare RO 126 B3
Semmen-stedt D 73 B3
Šempeter SLO 123 A4
Semriach A 110 B2
Semur-en-Auxois F 104 B3
Sena E 145 C3
Sena de Luna E 141 B5
Senarpont F 90 B1
Sénas F 131 B4
Senćanski Trešnjevac SRB 126 B1
Sencelles E 167 B2
Senčur SLO 123 A3
Senden
Bayern D 94 C2
Nordrhein-Westfalen D 80 A3
Sendenhorst D 81 A3
Sendim P 149 A3
Senec SK 111 A4
Seneffe B 79 B4
Séneghe I 178 B2
Senés E 164 B2
Senez F 132 B2
Senftenberg D 84 A1
Sengouagnet F 145 B4
Sengwarden D 71 A5
Senica SK 98 C1
Senice na Hané CZ 98 B1
Senigállia I 136 B2
Senirkent TR 189 A5
Sénis I 179 C2
Senise I 174 A2
Senj HR 123 C3
Senje SRB 127 D3
Senjehopen N 194 A8
Senjski Rudnik SRB 127 D3
Senlis F 90 B2
Sennan S 60 C2
Sennecey-le-Grand F 105 C3
Sennen GB 42 B1
Senno BY 13 A8
Sénnori I 178 B2
Sennwald CH 107 B4
Sennybridge GB 39 C3
Senohrad SK 99 C3
Senonches F 89 B5
Senones F 92 C2
Senorbì I 179 C3
Senovo SLO 123 A4
Senožeče SLO 123 B3
Senožeti SLO 123 A3
Sens F 104 A2
Sens-de-Bretagne F 101 A4
Senta SRB 126 B2
Senterada E 145 B4
Sentilj SLO 110 C2
Šentjernej SLO 123 B4
Šentjur SLO 123 A4
Senumstad N 53 B4
Seoane E 141 B3
Seon CH 106 B3
Sépeaux F 104 B2
Sépey CH 119 A4
Sepino I 170 B2
Sępólno Krajeńskie PL 76 A2
Seppenrade D 80 A3
Seppois F 106 B2
Septemvri BG 183 A6
Septeuil F 90 C1
Sepúlveda E 151 A4
Sequals I 122 A1
Sequeros E 149 B3
Seraincourt F 91 B4
Seraing B 80 B1
Seravezza I 134 B3
Sered' SK 98 C1
Seredka RUS 8 C6
Şereflikoçhisar TR 23 B7
Seregélyes H 112 B2
Seregno I 120 B2
Sérent F 101 B3
Serfaus A 108 B1
Sergiyev Posad RUS 9 D11
Seriate I 120 B2
Sérifontaine F 90 B1
Serifos GR 185 B5
Sérignan F 130 B2
Serik TR 189 C6
Serina I 120 B2
Serinhisar TR 188 B4
Sermaises F 90 C2
Sermaize-les-Bains F 91 C4
Sérmide I 121 C4
Sermoneta I 169 B2
Sernache de Bonjardim P 154 B2
Sernancelhe P 148 B2
Serock PL 77 B6
Serón E 164 B2
Serón de Najima E 152 A1
Serooskerke NL 79 A3
Seròs E 153 A4
Serpa P 160 B2
Serracapriola I 171 B3
Serrada E 150 A3
Serra de Outes E 140 B2
Serradifalco I 176 B2
Serradilla E 155 B4
Serradilla del Arroyo E 149 B3
Serradilla del Llano E 149 B3
Serramanna I 179 C2
Serramazzoni I 135 A3
Serranillos E 150 B3
Serrapetrona I 136 B2
Serra San Bruno I 175 C2
Serra San Quírico I 136 B2
Serrastretta I 175 B2
Serravalle
Piemonte I 119 B5
Umbria I 136 C2
Serravalle di Chienti I 136 B1
Serravalle Scrívia I 120 C1
Serre I 172 B1
Serrejón E 150 C2
Serres
F 132 A1
GR 183 B5
Serrières F 117 B4
Serrières-de-Briord F 118 B2
Sersale I 175 B2
Sertã P 154 B2
Sertig Dörfli CH 107 C4
Servance F 106 B1
Serverette F 117 C3
Servia GR 182 C4
Servian F 130 B2
Serviers F 131 A3
Servigliano I 136 B2
Serzedelo P 148 A1
Seseña Nuevo E 151 B4
Sesimbra P 154 C1
Seskarö S 196 D6
Seskinore GB 27 B3
Sesma E 144 B1
Sessa Aurunca I 170 B1
Ses Salines E 167 B3
Sesta Godano I 134 A2
Šestanovac HR 138 B2
Sestao E 143 A4
Sestino I 135 B5
Sesto I 109 C3
Sesto Calende I 120 B1
Sesto Fiorentino I 135 B4
Séstola I 135 A3
Sesto San Giovanni I 120 B2
Sestriere I 119 C3
Sestri Levante I 134 A2
Sestroretsk RUS 9 B7
Sestu I 179 C3
Sesvete HR 124 B2
Setcases E 146 B3
Sète F 130 B2
Setenil E 162 B2
Setermoen N 194 B9
Šetonje SRB 127 C3
Setskog N 54 A2
Settalsjølia N 199 C7
Séttimo Torinese I 119 B4
Settimo Vittone I 119 B4
Settle GB 40 A1
Setúbal P 154 C2
Seubersdort D 95 B3
Seùi I 179 C3
Seùlo I 179 C3
Seurre F 105 C4
Sevel DK 58 B1
Sevenoaks GB 45 B4
Sévérac-le-Château F 130 A2
Sever do Vouga P 148 B1
Severin HR 123 B4
Severomorsk RUS 3 B13
Séveso I 120 B2
Ševětin CZ 96 B2
Sevettijärvi FIN 193 C12
Sévigny F 91 B4
Sevilla = Seville E 162 A2
Sevilla la Nueva E 151 B3
Seville = Sevilla E 162 A2
Sevilleja de la Jara E 156 A3
Sevlievo BG 17 D6
Sevnica SLO 123 A4
Sevojno SRB 127 D1
Sevrier F 118 B3
Sexdrega S 60 B3
Seyches F 129 B3
Seyda D 83 A4
Seydişehir TR 189 B6
Seyðisfjörður IS 191 B12
Seyitgazi TR 187 C5
Seyitömer TR 187 C4
Seymen TR 186 A2
Seyne F 132 A2
Seynes F 131 A3
Seyssel F 118 B2
Sežana SLO 122 B2
Sézanne F 91 C3
Sezulfe P 149 A2
Sezze I 169 B3
Sfântu Gheorghe RO 17 C6
Sforzacosta I 136 B2
Sgarasta Mhor GB 31 B1
's-Gravendeel NL 79 A4
's-Gravenhage = The Hague NL 70 B1
's-Gravenzande NL 79 A4
Shaftesbury GB 43 A4
Shaldon GB 43 B3
Shalskiy RUS 9 B9
Shanagolden IRL 29 B2
Shanklin GB 44 C2
Shap GB 37 B4
Sharpness GB 43 A4
Shawbury GB 38 B4
's-Heerenberg NL 80 A2
Sheerness GB 45 B4
Sheffield GB 40 B2
Shefford GB 44 A3
Shëmri AL 182 A2
Shenfield GB 45 B4
Shëngjergj AL 182 B2
Shepetivka UA 13 C7
Shepshed GB 40 C2
Shepton Mallet GB 43 A4
Sherborne GB 43 B4
Shercock IRL 27 C4
Sheringham GB 41 C5
's-Hertogenbosch NL 79 A5
Shiel Bridge GB 32 D1
Shieldaig GB 31 B3
Shijak AL 182 B1
Shillelagh IRL 30 B2
Shimsk RUS 9 C7
Shipston-on-Stour GB 44 A2
Shklow BY 13 A9
Shkodër AL 182 A1
Shoeburyness GB 45 B4
Shoreham-by-Sea GB 44 C3
Shotley Gate GB 45 B5
Shrewsbury GB 38 B4
Shugozero RUS 9 C9
Shumen BG 17 D7
Siabost GB 31 A2
Siamanna I 179 C2
Sianów PL 67 B5
Siatista GR 182 C3
Siauges-St Romain F 117 B3
Šiauliai LT 8 E3
Sibari I 174 B2
Sibbhult S 63 B2
Šibenik HR 138 B1
Sibinj HR 125 B3
Sibiu RO 17 C6
Sibnica SRB 127 C2
Sibsey GB 41 B4
Siculiana I 176 B2
Šid SRB 125 B5
Sidari GR 182 D1
Siddeburen NL 71 A3
Sidensjö S 200 C4
Siderno I 175 C2
Sidirokastro GR 183 B5
Sidmouth GB 43 B3
Sidzina PL 99 B3
Siebe N 192 D7
Siebenlehn D 83 A5
Siedlce PL 12 B5
Siedlice PL 75 A4
Siedlinghausen D 81 A4
Siedlisko PL 75 B5
Siegburg D 80 B3
Siegen D 81 B4
Siegenburg D 95 C3
Sieghartskirchen A 111 A3
Siegsdorf D 109 B3
Siekierki PL 74 B3
Sielpia PL 87 A4
Siemiany PL 69 B4
Siena I 135 B4
Sieniawka PL 84 B2
Sienno PL 87 A5
Sieppijärvi FIN 196 B7
Sieradz PL 86 A2
Sieraków
Śląskie PL 86 B2
Wielkopolskie PL 75 B5
Sierakowice PL 68 A2
Sierck-les-Bains F 92 B2
Sierentz F 106 B2
Sierning A 110 A1
Sierpc PL 77 B4
Sierra de Fuentes E 155 B4
Sierra de Luna E 144 B3
Sierra de Yeguas E 162 A3
Sierre CH 119 A4
Siestrzeń PL 77 B5
Sietamo E 145 B3
Siewierz PL 86 B3
Sigdal N 48 B1
Sigean F 130 B1
Sigerfjord N 194 B6
Sighetu-Marmatiei RO 17 B5
Sighişoara RO 17 B6
Sigillo I 136 B1
Siglufjörður IS 191 A7
Sigmaringen D 107 A4
Signa I 135 B4
Signes F 132 B1
Signy-l'Abbaye F 91 B4
Signy-le-Petit F 91 B4
Sigogne F 115 C3
Sigri GR 183 D7
Sigtuna S 57 A3
Sigueiro E 140 B2
Sigüenza E 151 A5
Sigües E 144 B2
Sigulda LV 8 D4
Siilinjärvi FIN 8 A5
Sikenica SK 112 A2
Sikfors S 196 D4
Sikia GR 183 C5
Sikinos GR 185 C6
Sikkilsdalseter N 47 A6
Siklós H 125 B4
Sikórz PL 77 B4
Sikselet S 195 D8
Silandro I 108 C1
Silánus I 178 B2
Silbaš SRB 126 B1
Silbersted D 64 B2
Şile TR 187 A4
Siles E 164 A2
Silgueiros P 148 B2
Silifke TR 23 C7
Silíqua I 179 C2
Silistra BG 17 C7
Silivri TR 186 A3
Siljan N 53 A5
Siljansnäs S 50 B1
Silkeborg DK 59 B2
Silla E 159 B3
Sillamäe EST 8 C5
Silleda E 140 B2
Sillé-le-Guillaume F 102 A1
Sillenstede D 71 A4
Sillerud S 54 A3
Sillian A 109 C3
Silloth GB 36 B3
Silno PL 68 B2
Silnowo PL 68 B1
Silo HR 123 B3
Sils E 147 C3
Silsand N 194 A8
Silte S 57 C4
Šilute LT 12 A4
Silvalen N 195 E3
Silvaplana CH 107 C4
Silvares P 148 B2
Silvberg S 50 B2
Silverdalen S 62 A3
Silvermines IRL 28 B3
Silverstone GB 44 A2
Silverton GB 43 B3
Silves P 160 B1
Silvi Marina I 169 A4
Simandre F 105 C3
Šimanovci SRB 127 C2
Simard F 105 C4
Simat de Valldigna E 159 B3
Simav TR 186 C3
Simbach
Bayern D 95 C4
Bayern D 95 C5
Simbário I 175 C2
Simeonovgrad BG 183 A7
Simeria RO 17 C5
Simi GR 188 C2
Simićevo SRB 127 C3
Simitli BG 183 B5
Simlångsdalen S 60 C3
Simmerath D 80 B2
Simmerberg D 107 B4
Simmern D 93 B3
Simo FIN 197 D8
Šimonovce SK 99 C4
Simonsbath GB 43 A3
Simonstorp S 56 B2
Simontornya H 112 C2
Simplon CH 119 A5
Simrishamn S 63 C2
Sinaia RO 17 C6
Sinalunga I 135 B4
Sinarcas E 159 B2
Sincan TR 187 C7
Sincanlı TR 187 D5
Sindal DK 58 A3
Sindelfingen D 93 C5
Sindia I 178 B2
Sındırgı TR 186 C3
Sinekli TR 186 A3
Sines P 160 B1
Sinetta FIN 197 C8
Sineu E 167 B3
Singen D 107 B3
Singleton GB 44 C3
Singsås N 199 C7
Siniscóla I 178 B3
Sinj HR 138 B2
Sinlabajos E 150 A3
Sinn D 81 B4
Sinnai I 179 C3
Sinnes N 52 B2
Sinop TR 23 A8
Sins CH 106 B3
Sinsheim D 93 B4
Sint Annaland NL 79 A4
Sint Annaparochie NL 70 A2
Sint Athonis NL 80 A1
Sint Nicolaasga NL 70 B2
Sint Oedenrode NL 79 A5
Sintra P 154 C1
Sinzheim D 93 C4
Sinzig D 80 B3
Siófok H 112 C2
Sion CH 119 A4
Sion Mills GB 27 B3
Siorac-en-Périgord F 129 B3
Šipanska Luka HR 139 C3
Šipovo BIH 138 A3
Sira N 52 B2
Siracusa I 177 B4
Siret RO 17 B7
Sirevåg N 52 B1
Sirig SRB 126 B1
Sirkka FIN 196 B7
Sirmione I 121 B3
Sirniö FIN 197 D11
Sirok H 113 B4
Široké SK 99 C4
Široki Brijeg BIH 139 B3
Sirolo I 136 B2
Siruela E 156 B2
Sisak HR 124 B2
Sisante E 158 B1
Šišljavić HR 123 B4
Sissach CH 106 B2
Sissonne F 91 B3
Sistelo P 140 C2
Sisteron F 132 A1
Sistiana I 122 B2
Sistranda N 198 B5
Sitasjaurestugorna S 194 C8
Sitges E 147 C2
Sitia GR 185 D7
Sittard NL 80 A1
Sittensen D 72 A2
Sittingbourne GB 45 B4
Sitzenroda D 83 A4
Sivac SRB 126 B1
Sivaslı TR 189 A4
Siverić HR 138 B2
Sivrihisar TR 187 C6
Sixt-Fer-á-Cheval F 119 A3
Siziano I 120 B2
Sizun F 100 A1
Sjenica SRB 16 D3
Sjoa N 198 D6
Sjøåsen N 199 A8
Sjöbo S 61 D3
Sjøenden
Hedmark N 48 A3
Hedmark N 48 B3
Sjøholt N 198 C3
Sjøli N 48 A3
Sjølstad N 199 A9
Sjölunda S 56 A1
Sjømarken S 60 B2
Sjørring DK 58 B1
Sjötofta S 60 B3
Sjötorp S 55 B4
Sjoutnäset S 199 A11
Sjøvegan N 194 B8
Sjuntorp S 54 B3
Skåbu N 47 A6
Skafså N 53 A4
Skaftafell IS 191 D9
Skagaströnd IS 190 B5
Skagen DK 58 A3
Skagersvik S 55 B5
Skaiå N 53 B3
Skaidi N 193 B8
Skala GR 184 A1
Skała PL 87 B3
Skaland N 194 A8
Skala Oropou GR 185 A4
Skala-Podilska UA 13 D7
Skalat UA 13 D6
Skalbmierz PL 87 B4
Skålevik N 53 B4
Skalica SK 98 C1
Skalité SK 98 B2
Skällinge S 60 B2
Skalná CZ 83 B4
Skals DK 58 B2
Skælskør DK 65 A4
Skalstugan S 199 B9
Skanderborg DK 59 B2
Skånes-Fagerhult S 61 C3
Skåne-Tranås S 61 D3
Skånevik N 52 A1
Skänninge S 55 B6
Skanör med Falsterbo S 66 A1
Skåpafors S 54 A3
Skąpe PL 75 B4
Skara S 55 B4
Skærbæk DK 64 A1
Skarberget N 194 B7
Skärblacka S 56 B1
Skarð IS 190 B3
Skarda S 200 B4
Skare N 46 C3
Skåre S 55 A4

Skärhamn S 60 B1
Skarnes N 48 B3
Skärplinge S 51 B4
Skarpnatö FIN 51 B6
Skarp Salling DK 58 B2
Skarrild DK 59 C1
Skarstad N 194 B7
Skärstad S 62 A2
Skarsvåg N 193 A9
Skarszewy PL 69 A3
Skårup DK 65 A3
Skärvången S 199 B11
Skarvsjöby S 195 F8
Skaryszew PL 87 A5
Skarżysko-Kamienna PL 87 A4
Skarzysko Ksiazece PL 87 A4
Skatøy N 53 B5
Skattkärr S 55 A4
Skattungbyn S 50 A1
Skatval N 199 B7
Skaulo S 196 B4
Skave DK 59 B1
Skawina PL 99 B3
Skebobruk S 51 C5
Skebokvarn S 56 A2
Skedala S 61 C2
Skedevi S 56 B1
Skedsmokorset N 48 B3
Skee S 54 B2
Skegness GB 41 B4
Skei N 46 A3
Skela SRB 127 C2
Skelani BIH 127 D1
Skellefteå S 2 D7
Skelleftehamn S 2 D7
Skelmersdale GB 38 A4
Skelmorlie GB 34 C3
Skelund DK 58 B3
Skender Vakuf BIH 138 A3
Skene S 60 B2
Skępe PL 77 B4
Skepplanda S 60 B2
Skeppshult S 60 B3
Skerries IRL 30 A2
Ski N 54 A1
Skiathos GR 183 D5
Skibbereen IRL 29 C2
Skibotn N 192 C4
Skidra GR 182 C4
Skien N 53 A5
Skierniewice PL 77 C5
Skillingaryd S 60 B4
Skillinge S 63 C2
Skillingmark S 49 C4
Skilloura CY 181 A2
Skinnardai S 57 A4
Skinnskatteberg S 50 C2
Skipmannvik N 195 C6
Skipness GB 34 C2
Skipsea GB 41 B3
Skipton GB 40 B1
Skiptvet N 54 A2
Skiros GR 183 E6
Skivarp S 66 A2
Skive DK 58 B2
Skjånes N 193 B12
Skjærhalden N 54 A2
Skjeberg N 54 A2
Skjeggedal N 46 B3
Skjeljanger N 46 B1
Skjeljavik N 46 C2
Skjern DK 59 C1
Skjervøy N 192 B4
Skjold
Rogaland N 52 A1
Troms N 192 C3
Skjoldastraumen N 52 A1
Skjolden N 47 A4
Skjønhaug N 54 A2
Skjøtningsberg N 193 A11
Škocjan SLO 123 B4
Skoczów PL 98 B2
Skodborg DK 59 C2
Škofja Loka SLO 123 A3
Škofljica SLO 123 B3
Skog S 51 A3
Skoganvarre N 193 C9
Skogen S 54 A3
Skogfoss N 193 C13
Skoghall S 55 A4
Skogly N 193 C13
Skogn N 199 B8
Skognes N 192 C3
Skogstorp
Halland S 60 C2
Södermanland S 56 A2
Skoki PL 76 B2
Skokloster S 57 A3
Sköldinge S 56 A2
Skole UA 13 D5
Skollenborg N 53 A5
Sköllersta S 56 A1
Skomlin PL 86 A2
Skonseng N 195 D5
Skopelos GR 183 D5
Skopje MK 182 A3
Skoppum N 54 A1
Skórcz PL 69 B3
Skorogoszcz PL 86 B1
Skoroszów PL 85 A5
Skorovatn N 199 A10
Skorped S 200 C3
Skørping DK 58 B2
Skotfoss N 53 A5
Skotniki PL 87 A3
Skotselv N 48 C1
Skotterud N 49 C4
Skottorp S 61 C2
Skovby DK 64 B2
Skövde S 55 B4
Skovsgård DK 58 A2
Skrad HR 123 B3
Skradin HR 138 B1
Skradnik HR 123 B4
Skråmestø N 46 B1
Škrdlovice CZ 97 B3
Skrea S 60 C2
Skreia N 48 B2
Skrolsvik N 194 A7
Skruv S 63 B3
Skrwilno PL 77 A4
Skrydstrup DK 59 C2
Skucani BIH 138 B2
Skudeneshavn N 52 A1
Skui N 48 C2
Skulsk PL 76 B3
Skultorp S 55 B4
Skultuna S 56 A2
Skuodas LT 8 D2
Skurup S 66 A2
Skute N 48 B2
Skuteč CZ 97 B3
Skutskär S 51 B4
Skutvik N 194 B6
Skvyra UA 13 D8
Skwierzyna PL 75 B4
Skýcov SK 98 C2
Skyllberg S 55 B5
Skyttmon S 200 C1
Skyttorp S 51 B4
Sládkovičovo SK 111 A4
Slagelse DK 61 D1
Slagharen NL 71 B3
Slagnäs S 195 E9
Slaidburn GB 40 B1
Slane IRL 30 A2
Slangerup DK 61 D2
Slano HR 139 C3
Slantsy RUS 8 C6
Slaný CZ 84 B2
Slap SLO 122 A2
Šlapanice CZ 97 B4
Slåstad N 48 B3
Slatina
BIH 139 B3
HR 125 B3
RO 17 C6
Slatiňany CZ 97 B3
Slatinice CZ 98 B1
Slättberg S 50 A1
Slattum N 48 C2
Slavičin CZ 98 B1
Slavkov CZ 98 C1
Slavkovica SRB 127 C2
Slavkov u Brna CZ 97 B4
Slavonice CZ 97 C3
Slavonski Brod HR 125 B4
Slavonski Kobas
HR 125 B3
Slavošovce SK 99 C4
Slavskoye RUS 69 A5
Slavuta UA 13 C7
Sława
Lubuskie PL 85 A4
Zachodnio-Pomorskie PL 67 C4
Slawharad BY 13 B9
Sławków PL 86 B3
Sławno
Wielkopolskie PL 76 B2
Zachodnio-Pomorskie PL 68 A1
Sławoborze PL 67 C4
Sl'ažany SK 98 C2
Sleaford GB 40 C3
Sleðbrjótur IS 191 B11
Sledmere GB 40 A3
Sleights GB 37 B6
Slemmestad N 54 A1
Ślesin PL 76 B3
Sliač SK 99 C3
Sliema M 175 C3
Sligo IRL 26 B2
Slite S 57 C4
Slitu N 54 A2
Sliven BG 17 D7
Śliwice PL 68 B3
Slobozia RO 17 C7
Slochteren NL 71 A3
Slöinge S 60 C2
Słomniki PL 87 B4
Slonim BY 13 B6
Słońsk PL 75 B3
Slootdorp NL 70 B1
Slottsbron S 55 A4
Slough GB 44 B3
Slövag N 46 B2
Slovenj Gradec
SLO 110 C2
Slovenska Bistrica
SLO 123 A4
Slovenská L'upča
SK 99 C3
Slovenská-Ves SK 99 B4
Slovenské Darmoty
SK 112 A3
Slovenske Konjice
SLO 123 A4
Słubice PL 74 B3
Sluderno I 108 C1
Sluis NL 78 A3
Šluknov CZ 84 A2
Slunj HR 123 B4
Słupca PL 76 B2
Słupia PL 87 A3
Słupiec PL 85 B4
Słupsk PL 68 A2
Slutsk BY 13 B7
Smålandsstenar S 60 B3
Smalåsen N 195 E4
Smardzewo PL 75 B4
Smarhon BY 13 A7
Smarje SLO 123 A4
Šmarjeta SLO 123 B4
Šmartno SLO 123 A3
Smečno CZ 84 B2
Smedby S 63 B4
Smědec CZ 96 C2
Smederevo SRB 127 C2
Smederevska Palanka
SRB 127 C2
Smedjebacken S 50 B2
Smęgorzów PL 87 B5
Smeland N 53 B4
Smidary CZ 84 B3
Śmigiel PL 75 B5
Smilde NL 71 B3
Smiřice CZ 85 B3
Smithfield GB 36 B4
Śmitowo PL 75 A5
Smögen S 54 B2
Smogulec PL 76 A2
Smołdzino PL 68 A2
Smolenice SK 98 C1
Smolensk RUS 13 A10
Smolník SK 99 C4
Smolyan BG 183 B6
Smuka SLO 123 B3
Smygehamn S 66 A2
Smykow PL 87 A4
Snainton GB 40 A3
Snaith GB 40 B2
Snaptun DK 59 C3
Snarby N 192 C3
Snarum N 48 B1
Snåsa N 199 A9
Snedsted DK 58 B1
Sneek NL 70 A2
Sneem IRL 29 C2
Snejbjerg DK 59 B1
Snillfjord N 198 B6
Šnjegotina BIH 125 C3
Snøde DK 65 A3
Snøfjord N 193 B8
Snogebaek DK 67 A4
Snyatyn UA 13 D6
Soave I 121 B4
Sober E 140 B3
Sobernheim D 93 B3
Soběslav CZ 96 B2
Sobota
Dolnośląskie PL 85 A3
Łódzkie PL 77 B4
Sobotište SK 98 C1
Sobotka CZ 84 B3
Sobótka
Dolnośląskie PL 85 B4
Wielkopolskie PL 86 A1
Sobra HR 139 C3
Sobrado
Coruña E 140 A2
Lugo E 141 B3
Sobral da Adica P 161 A2
Sobral de Monte Agraço
P 154 C1
Sobreira Formosa
P 154 B3
Søby DK 64 B3
Soca SLO 122 A2
Sochaczew PL 77 B5
Sochos GR 183 C5
Socodor RO 113 C5
Socol RO 127 C3
Socovos E 164 A3
Socuéllamos E 158 B1
Sodankylä FIN 197 B9
Soderåkra S 63 B4
Söderala S 51 A3
Söderås S 50 B2
Söderbärke S 50 B2
Söderby-Karl S 51 C5
Söderfors S 51 B4
Söderhamn S 51 A4
Söderköping S 56 B2
Söderö S 56 B1
Södertälje S 57 A3
Södingberg A 110 B2
Södra Finnö S 56 B2
Södra Ny S 55 A4
Södra Råda S 55 A5
Södra Sandby S 61 D3
Södra Vi S 62 A3
Sodražica SLO 123 B3
Sodupe E 143 A3
Soengas P 148 A1
Soest
D 81 A4
NL 70 B2
Sofades GR 182 D4
Sofia = Sofiya BG 17 D5
Sofikon GR 184 B4
Sofiya = Sofia BG 17 D5
Şofronea RO 126 A3
Sögel D 71 B4
Sogliano al Rubicone
I 135 A5
Sogndalsfjøra N 46 A4
Søgne N 53 B3
Sögütköy TR 188 C3
Soham GB 45 A4
Sohland D 84 A2
Sohren D 93 B3
Soignies B 79 B4
Soissons F 90 B3
Söjtör H 111 C3
Sokal' UA 13 C6
Söke TR 188 B2
Sokna N 48 B1
Sokndal N 52 B2
Soknedal N 199 C7
Soko BIH 125 C4
Sokolac BIH 139 B4
Sokółka PL 13 B5
Sokolov CZ 83 B4
Sokołowo PL 76 B3
Sokołów Podlaski
PL 12 B5
Sola N 52 B1
Solana de los Barros
E 155 C4
Solana del Pino E 157 B3
Solánas I 179 C3
Solares E 143 A3
Solarino I 177 B4
Solarussa I 179 C2
Solas GB 31 B1
Solberg S 200 C3
Solberga S 62 A2
Solber-gelva N 53 A6
Solbjørg N 46 B2
Solčany SK 98 C2
Solčava SLO 123 A3
Solda I 108 C1
Sölden A 108 C2
Solec Kujawski PL 76 A3
Soleils F 132 B2
Solenzara F 180 B2
Solera E 163 A4
Solesmes F 79 B3
Soleto I 173 B4
Solgne F 92 C2
Solheim N 46 B2
Solheimsvik N 52 A2
Solignac F 115 C5
Solihull GB 44 A2
Solin HR 138 B2
Solingen D 80 A3
Solivella E 147 C2
Solkan SLO 122 B2
Söll A 108 B3
Sollana E 159 B3
Sollebrunn S 54 B3
Sollefteå S 200 C3
Sollenau A 111 B3
Sollen-tuna S 57 A3
Sóller E 166 B2
Sollerön S 50 B1
Søllested DK 65 B4
Solliès-Pont F 132 B2
Sollihøgda N 48 C2
Solnechnogorsk
RUS 9 D10
Solnice CZ 85 B4
Solofra I 170 C2
Solomiac F 129 C3
Solopaca I 170 B2
Solórzano E 143 A3
Solothurn CH 106 B2
Solre-le-Château F 79 B4
Solsona E 147 C2
Solsvik N 46 B1
Solt H 112 C3
Soltau D 72 B2
Soltsy RUS 9 C7
Soltszentimre H 112 C3
Soltvadkert H 112 C3
Solumsmoen N 48 C1
Solund N 46 A1
Solva GB 39 C1
Sölvesborg S 63 B2
Solymár H 112 B2
Soma TR 186 C2
Somain F 78 B3
Somberek H 125 A4
Sombernon F 104 B3
Sombor SRB 125 B5
Sombreffe B 79 B4
Someren NL 80 A1
Somero FIN 8 B3
Somersham GB 44 A3
Somerton GB 43 A4
Sominy PL 68 A2
Somma Lombardo
I 120 B1
Sommariva del Bosco
I 119 C4
Sommarøy N 192 C2
Sommarset N 194 C6
Sommatino I 176 B2
Sommeilles F 91 C4
Sommen S 55 B5
Sommepy-Tahure F 91 B4
Sömmerda D 82 A3
Sommerfeld D 74 B2
Sommersted DK 59 C2
Sommesous F 91 C4
Somme-Tourbe F 91 B4
Sommières F 131 B3
Sommières-du-Clain
F 115 B4
Somo E 143 A3
Somogyfajsz H 111 C4
Somogyjád H 111 C4
Somogysámson H 111 C4
Somogysárd H 125 A3
Somogyszil H 112 C2
Somogyszob H 124 A3
Somogyvár H 111 C4
Somontin E 164 B2
Somosiero E 151 A4
Somoskőújfalu H 113 A3
Sompolno PL 76 B3
Sompuis F 91 C4
Son N 54 A1
Son Bou E 167 B4
Sonceboz CH 106 B2
Soncillo E 143 B3
Soncino I 120 B2
Sóndalo I 120 A3
Søndeled N 53 B5
Sønder Bjert DK 59 C2
Sønderborg DK 64 B2
Sønderby DK 64 B2
Sønder Felding DK 59 C1
Sønderho DK 59 C1
Sønder Hygum DK 59 C1
Sønder Omme DK 59 C1
Sondershausen D 82 A2
Søndersø DK 59 C3
Søndervig DK 59 B1
Søndre Enningdal
Kappel N 54 B2
Sóndrio I 120 A2
Soneja E 159 B3
Son en Breugel NL 80 A1
Songe N 53 B5
Songeons F 90 B1
Sonkamuotka FIN 196 A6
Sonkovo RUS 9 D10
Sönnarslöv S 61 D4
Sonneberg D 82 B3
Sonnefeld D 82 B3
Sonnewalde D 84 A1
Sonnino I 169 B3
Sonogno CH 120 A1
Sonsbeck D 80 A2
Sonseca E 157 A4
Son Servera E 167 B3
Sønsterud N 49 B4
Sonstorp S 56 B1
Sonta SRB 125 B5
Sontheim D 94 C2
Sonthofen D 107 B5
Sontra D 82 A1
Sopelana E 143 A4
Sopje HR 125 B3
Šoporňa SK 111 A4
Sopot
PL 69 A3
SRB 127 C2
Sopotnica MK 182 B3
Sopron H 111 B3
Šor SRB 127 C1
Sora I 169 B3
Soragna I 120 C3
Söråker S 200 D3
Sorano I 168 A1
Sorbara I 121 C4
Sorbas E 164 B2
Sórbolo I 121 C3
Sörbygden S 200 D2
Sordal N 52 B3
Sordale GB 32 C3
Sore F 128 B2
Sörenberg CH 106 C3
Soresina I 120 B2
Sorèze F 146 A3
Sörforsa S 200 E3
Sorges F 115 C4
Sórgono I 179 B3
Sorgues F 131 A3
Sorgun TR 23 B8
Soria E 143 C4
Soriano Cálabro I 175 C2
Soriano nel Cimino
I 168 A2
Sorihuela del
Guadalimar E 164 A1
Sorisdale GB 34 B1
Sørkjosen N 192 C4
Sørli N 199 A10
Sormás H 111 C3
Sörmjöle S 200 C6
Sørmo N 194 B9
Sornac F 116 B2
Sorø DK 61 D1
Soroca MD 17 A8
Sørreisa N 194 A9
Sorrento I 170 C2
Sorsele S 195 E8
Sörsjön S 49 A5
Sorso I 178 B2
Sort E 146 B2
Sortavala RUS 9 B7
Sortino I 177 B4
Sortland N 194 B6
Sørum N 48 B2
Sørumsand N 48 C3
Sorunda S 57 A3
Sörup D 64 B2
Sørvågen N 194 C3
Sørvær N 192 B6
Sorvik S 50 B2
Sørvika N 199 C8
Sos F 128 B3
Sösdala S 61 C3
Sos del Rey Católico
E 144 B2
Sošice HR 123 B4
Sośnica PL 75 A5
Sośnicowice PL 86 B2
Sośno PL 76 A2
Sosnovyy Bor RUS 9 C6
Sosnowiec PL 86 B3
Sospel F 133 B3
Šoštanj SLO 123 A4
Sotaseter N 198 D4
Sotillo de Adrada
E 150 B3
Sotillo de la Ribera
E 143 C3
Sotin HR 125 B5
Sotkamo FIN 3 D11
Sotobañado y Priorato
E 142 B2
Soto de la Marina
E 143 A3
Soto del Barco E 141 A4
Soto de los Infantes
E 141 A4
Soto de Real E 151 B4
Soto de Ribera E 141 A5
Sotoserrano E 149 B3
Soto y Amío E 141 B5
Sotresgudo E 142 B2
Sotrondio E 142 A1
Sotta F 180 B2
Sottomarina I 122 B1
Sottrum D 72 A2
Sottunga FIN 51 B7
Sotuelamos E 158 B1
Souain F 91 B4
Soual F 146 A3
Soucy F 104 A2
Souda GR 185 D5
Soudron F 91 C4
Souesmes F 103 B4
Soufflenheim F 93 C3
Soufli GR 186 A1
Souillac F 129 B4
Souilly F 91 B5
Soulac-sur-Mer F 114 C2
Soulaines-Dhuys F 91 C4
Soulatgé F 146 B3
Soultz-Haut-Rhin F 106 B2
Soultz-sous-Forêts
F 93 C3
Soumagne B 80 B1
Soumoulou F 145 A3
Souppes-sur-Loing
F 103 A4
Souprosse F 128 C2
Sourdeval F 88 B3
Soure P 154 A2
Sournia F 146 B3
Souro Pires P 149 B2
Sourpi GR 182 D4
Sours F 90 C1
Sousceyrac F 116 C2
Sousel P 155 C3
Soustons F 128 C1
Söğüt
Bilecik TR 187 B5
Burdur TR 189 B4
Soutelo de Montes
E 140 B2
Southam GB 44 A2
Southampton GB 44 C2
Southborough GB 45 B4
South Brent GB 42 B3
South Cave GB 40 B3
Southend GB 34 C2
Southend-on-Sea
GB 45 B4
South Hayling GB 44 C3
South Molton GB 42 A3
South Ockendon
GB 45 B4
South Petherton GB 43 B4
Southport GB 38 A3
South Shields GB 37 B5
South Tawton GB 42 B3
Southwell GB 40 B3
Southwold GB 45 A5
South Woodham Ferrers
GB 45 B4
Söğütlu TR 187 B5
Souto P 148 B2
Soutochao E 141 C3
Souto da Carpalhosa
P 154 B2
Souvigny F 104 C2
Souzay-Champigny
F 102 B1
Soverato I 175 C2
Soveria Mannelli I 175 B2
Sövestad S 66 A2
Sovetsk RUS 12 A4
Sovići BIH 138 B3
Sovicille I 135 B4
Søvik N 198 C3
Sowerby GB 37 B5
Soyaux F 115 C4
Sozopol BG 17 D7
Spa B 80 B1
Spadafora I 177 A4
Spaichingen D 107 A3
Spakenburg NL 70 B2
Spalding GB 41 C3
Spálené Poříčí CZ 96 B1
Spalt D 94 B2
Spangenberg D 82 A1
Spangereid N 52 B3
Spantekow D 74 A2
Sparanise I 170 B2
Sparbu N 199 B8
Sparkær DK 58 B2
Sparkford GB 43 A4
Sparreholm S 56 A2
Sparta = Sparti GR 184 B3
Spartà I 177 A4
Sparti = Sparta GR 184 B3

Spean Bridge GB . . 34 B3
Speicher D . . . 92 B2
Speichersdorf D . . . 95 B3
Speke GB . . . 38 A4
Spello I . . . 136 C1
Spenge D . . . 72 B1
Spennymoor GB . . . 37 B5
Spentrup DK . . . 58 B3
Sperenberg D . . . 74 B2
Sperlinga I . . . 177 B3
Sperlonga I . . . 169 B3
Spetalen N . . . 54 A1
Spetses GR . . . 184 B4
Speyer D . . . 93 B4
Spézet F . . . 100 A2
Spezzano Albanese I . . . 174 B2
Spezzano della Sila I . . . 174 B2
Spiddle IRL . . . 28 A2
Spiegelau D . . . 96 C1
Spiekeroog D . . . 71 A4
Spiez CH . . . 106 C2
Spigno Monferrato I . . . 133 A4
Spijk NL . . . 71 A3
Spijkenisse NL . . . 79 A4
Spilamberto I . . . 135 A4
Spili GR . . . 185 D5
Spilimbergo I . . . 122 A1
Spilsby GB . . . 41 B4
Spinazzola I . . . 172 B2
Spincourt F . . . 92 B1
Spind N . . . 52 B2
Spindleruv-Mlyn CZ 84 B3
Spinoso I . . . 174 A1
Špišjć Bukovica HR . . . 124 B3
Spišská Belá SK . . . 99 B4
Spišská Nová Ves SK . . . 99 C4
Spisská Stará Ves SK . . . 99 B4
Spišské-Hanušovce SK . . . 99 B4
Spišské Podhradie SK . . . 99 C4
Spišské Vlachy SK . 99 C4
Spišský-Štvrtok SK. 99 C4
Spital A . . . 110 B1
Spital am Semmering A . . . 110 B2
Spittal an der Drau A . . . 109 C4
Spittle of Glenshee GB . . . 35 B4
Spitz A . . . 97 C3
Spjald DK . . . 59 B1
Spjærøy N . . . 54 A1
Spjelkavik N . . . 198 C3
Spjutsbygd S . . . 63 B3
Split HR . . . 138 B2
Splügen CH . . . 107 C4
Spodsbjerg DK . . . 65 B3
Spofforth GB . . . 40 B2
Spohle D . . . 71 A5
Spoleto I . . . 136 C1
Spoltore I . . . 169 A4
Spondigna I . . . 108 C1
Sponvika N . . . 54 A2
Spornitz D . . . 73 A4
Spotorno I . . . 133 A4
Spraitbach D . . . 94 C1
Sprakensehl D . . . 72 B3
Spręcowo PL . . . 69 B5
Spremberg D . . . 84 A2
Spresiano I . . . 122 B1
Sprimont B . . . 80 B1
Springe D . . . 72 B2
Sproatley GB . . . 41 B3
Spydeberg N . . . 54 A2
Spytkowice PL . . . 99 B3
Squillace I . . . 175 C2
Squinzano I . . . 173 B4
Sračinec HR . . . 124 A2
Srbac BIH . . . 124 B3
Srbobran SRB . . . 126 B1
Srebrenica BIH . . . 127 C1
Srebrenik BIH . . . 125 C4
Sredets BG . . . 17 D7
Središče SLO . . . 124 A2
Śrem PL . . . 76 B2
Sremska Mitrovica SRB . . . 127 C1
Sremski Karlovci SRB . . . 126 B1
Srní CZ . . . 96 B1
Srnice Gornje BIH . 125 C4
Srock PL . . . 86 A3
Środa Śląska PL . . . 85 A4
Środa Wielkopolski PL . . . 76 B2
Srpska Crnja SRB . 126 B2
Srpski Itebej SRB . 126 B2
Srpski Miletić SRB 125 B5
Staatz A . . . 97 C4
Stabbursnes N . . . 193 B8
Staberdorf D . . . 65 B4
Stabroek B . . . 79 A4
Stachy CZ . . . 96 B1
Staðarfell IS . . . 190 B3
Stade D . . . 72 A2
Staden B . . . 78 B3
Stadl an der Mur A . 109 B4
Stadskanaal NL . . . 71 B3
Stadtallendorf D . . . 81 B5
Stadthagen D . . . 72 B2
Stadtilm D . . . 82 B3
Stadtkyll D . . . 80 B2
Stadtlauringen D . . . 82 B2
Stadtlengsfeld D . . . 82 B2
Stadtlohn D . . . 71 C3
Stadtoldendorf D . . 82 A1
Stadtroda D . . . 83 B3
Stadtsteinach D . . . 82 B3
Stäfa CH . . . 107 B3
Staffanstorp S . . . 61 D3
Staffelstein D . . . 82 B2
Staffin GB . . . 31 B2
Stafford GB . . . 40 C1
Stainach A . . . 110 B1
Staindrop GB . . . 37 B5
Staines-upon-Thames GB . . . 44 B3
Stainville F . . . 91 C5
Stainz A . . . 110 C2
Staithes GB . . . 37 B6
Staíti I . . . 175 D2
Stäket S . . . 57 A3
Stakroge DK . . . 59 C1
Štalcerji SLO . . . 123 B3
Stalden CH . . . 119 A4
Stalham GB . . . 41 C5
Stalheim N . . . 46 B3
Stallarholmen S . . . 56 A3
Ställberg S . . . 50 C1
Ställdalen S . . . 50 C1
Stallhofen A . . . 110 B2
Stalon S . . . 195 F6
Stalowa Wola PL . . . 12 C5
Stamford GB . . . 40 C3
Stamford Bridge GB 40 B3
Stamnes N . . . 46 B2
Stams A . . . 108 B1
Stamsried D . . . 95 B4
Stamsund N . . . 194 B4
Stanford le Hope GB . . . 45 B4
Stånga S . . . 57 C4
Stange N . . . 48 B3
Stanghella I . . . 121 B4
Stanhope GB . . . 37 B4
Stanišić SRB . . . 125 B5
Staňkov CZ . . . 95 B5
Stankovci HR . . . 137 B4
Stanley GB . . . 37 B5
Stans CH . . . 106 C3
Stansted Mountfitchet GB . . . 45 B4
Stanzach A . . . 108 B1
Stapar SRB . . . 125 B5
Staphorst NL . . . 70 B3
Staplehurst GB . . . 45 B4
Stąporków PL . . . 87 A4
Stara Baška HR . . . 123 C3
Starachowice PL . . . 87 A5
Stara Fužina SLO . 122 A2
Stara Kamienica PL 84 B3
Stara Kiszewa PL . . 68 B3
Stará L'ubovnă SK . 99 B4
Stara Moravica SRB . . . 126 B1
Stara Novalja HR . . 137 A3
Stara Pazova SRB . 127 C2
Stará Turá SK . . . 98 C1
Staraya Russa RUS . 9 D7
Stara Zagora BG . . . 17 D6
Stärbsnäs S . . . 51 C6
Starčevo SRB . . . 127 C2
Stare Dłutowo PL . . 77 A4
Staré Hamry CZ . . . 98 B2
Stare Jablonki PL . . 69 B5
Staré Město CZ . . . 98 B1
Stare Pole PL . . . 69 A4
Stare Sedlo CZ . . . 96 B2
Stare Strącze PL . . . 85 A4
Stargard Szczeciński PL . . . 75 A4
Stårheim N . . . 198 D2
Stari Banovci SRB 127 C2
Starigrad
Ličko-Senjska HR . . . 123 C3
Splitsko-Dalmatinska HR . . . 138 B2
Stari Gradac HR . . 124 B3
Starigrad-Paklenica HR . . . 137 A4
Stari Jankovci HR . 125 B4
Stari Majdan BIH . . 124 C2
Stari-Mikanovci HR . . . 125 B4
Staritsa RUS . . . 9 D9
Starkenbach A . . . 108 B1
Starnberg D . . . 108 B2
Starogard PL . . . 75 A4
Starogard Gdański PL . . . 69 B3
Starokonstyantyniv UA . . . 13 D7
Staro Petrovo Selo HR . . . 124 B3
Staro Selo
HR . . . 124 B1
SRB . . . 127 C3
Stary Brzozów PL . . 77 B5
Stary Dzierzgoń PL . 69 B4
Starý Hrozenkov CZ . . . 98 C1
Stary Jaroslaw PL . . 68 A1
Stary Plzenec CZ . . 96 B1
Stary Sącz PL . . . 99 B4
Starý Smokovec SK 99 B4
Staryy Chartoriysk UA . . . 13 C6
Staškov SK . . . 98 B2
Stassfurt D . . . 82 A3
Staszów PL . . . 87 B5
Stathelle N . . . 53 A5
Staufen D . . . 106 B2
Staunton GB . . . 39 C4
Stavang N . . . 46 A2
Stavanger N . . . 52 B1
Stavåsnäs S . . . 49 B4
Stavby S . . . 51 B5
Staveley GB . . . 40 B2
Stavelot B . . . 80 B1
Stavenisse NL . . . 79 A4
Stavern N . . . 53 B6
Stavnäs S . . . 55 A3
Stavoren NL . . . 70 B2
Stavros
CY . . . 181 A1
GR . . . 183 C5
Stavroupoli GR . . . 183 B6
Stavseng N . . . 47 A6
Stavsiø N . . . 48 B2
Stavsnäs S . . . 57 A4
Stawiszyn PL . . . 76 C3
Steane N . . . 53 A4
Steblevë AL . . . 182 B2
Stechelberg CH . . . 106 C2
Štěchovice CZ . . . 96 B2
Stechow D . . . 73 B5
Steckborn CH . . . 107 B3
Stede Broek NL . . . 70 B2
Steeg A . . . 107 B5
Steenbergen NL . . . 79 A4
Steenvoorde F . . . 78 B2
Steenwijk NL . . . 70 B3
Štefanje HR . . . 124 B2
Steffisburg CH . . . 106 C2
Stegaurach D . . . 94 B2
Stege DK . . . 65 B5
Stegelitz D . . . 74 A2
Stegersbach A . . . 111 B3
Stegna PL . . . 69 A4
Steimbke D . . . 72 B2
Stein GB . . . 31 B2
Steinach
A . . . 108 B2
Baden-Württemberg D . . . 106 A3
Bayern D . . . 82 B2
Thüringen D . . . 82 B3
Stein an Rhein CH . 107 B3
Steinau
Bayern D . . . 81 B5
Niedersachsen D . . . 64 C1
Steinbeck D . . . 74 B2
Steinberg am Rofan A . . . 108 B2
Steindorf A . . . 109 C5
Steine N . . . 46 B2
Steinen D . . . 106 B2
Steinfeld
A . . . 109 C4
D . . . 71 B5
Steinfurt D . . . 71 B4
Steingaden D . . . 108 B1
Steinhagen D . . . 72 B1
Steinheid D . . . 82 B3
Steinheim
Bayern D . . . 107 A5
Nordrhein-Westfalen D . . . 81 A5
Steinhöfel D . . . 74 B3
Steinhorst D . . . 72 B3
Steinigtwolmsdorf D . . . 84 A2
Steinkjer N . . . 199 A8
Steinsholt N . . . 53 A5
Stekene B . . . 79 A4
Stelle D . . . 72 A3
Stellendam NL . . . 79 A4
Stenåsa S . . . 63 B4
Stenay F . . . 91 B5
Stenberga S . . . 62 A3
Stendal D . . . 73 B4
Stenhammar S . . . 55 B4
Stenhamra S . . . 57 A3
Stenhousemuir GB . 35 B4
Stenlose DK . . . 61 D2
Stensätra S . . . 50 B3
Stensele S . . . 195 E8
Stenstorp S . . . 55 B4
Stenstrup DK . . . 65 A3
Stenudden S . . . 195 D8
Stenungsund S . . . 54 B2
Štěpánov CZ . . . 98 B1
Stephanskirchen D 108 B3
Stepnica PL . . . 74 A3
Stepojevac SRB . . 127 C2
Stepping DK . . . 59 C2
Sterbfritz D . . . 82 B1
Sternberg D . . . 65 C4
Šternberk CZ . . . 98 B1
Sterup D . . . 64 B2
Stes Maries-de-la-Mer F . . . 131 B3
Stęszew PL . . . 75 B5
Štětí CZ . . . 84 B2
Stevenage GB . . . 44 B3
Stewarton GB . . . 36 A2
Steyerburg D . . . 72 B2
Steyning GB . . . 44 C3
Steyr A . . . 110 A1
Stężyca PL . . . 68 A2
Stezzano I . . . 120 B2
Stia I . . . 135 B4
Stibb Cross GB . . . 42 B2
Sticciano Scalo I . . 135 C4
Stidsvig S . . . 61 C3
Stiens NL . . . 70 A2
Stige DK . . . 59 C3
Stigen S . . . 54 B3
Stigliano I . . . 174 A2
Stigtomta S . . . 56 B2
Stilida GR . . . 182 E4
Stilla N . . . 192 C7
Stillington GB . . . 40 A2
Stilo I . . . 175 C2
Stintino I . . . 178 B2
Stio I . . . 172 B1
Štip MK . . . 182 B4
Stira GR . . . 185 A5
Stirling GB . . . 35 B4
Štítnik SK . . . 99 C4
Štíty CZ . . . 97 B4
Stjärnhov S . . . 56 A3
Stjärnsund S . . . 50 B3
Stjørdalshalsen N . 199 B7
Stobnica PL . . . 87 A3
Stobno PL . . . 75 A5
Stobreč HR . . . 138 B2
Stochov CZ . . . 84 B1
Stockach D . . . 107 B4
Stöckalp CH . . . 106 C3
Stockaryd S . . . 62 A2
Stockbridge GB . . . 44 B2
Stockerau A . . . 97 C4
Stockheim D . . . 82 B3
Stockholm S . . . 57 A4
Stockport GB . . . 40 B1
Stocksbridge GB . . . 40 B2
Stockton-on-Tees GB . . . 37 B5
Stod CZ . . . 96 B1
Stöde S . . . 200 D2
Stødi N . . . 195 D6
Stöðvarfjörður IS . . . 191 C12
Stoer GB . . . 32 C1
Stoholm DK . . . 58 B2
Stoke Ferry GB . . . 41 C4
Stoke Fleming GB . . 43 B3
Stoke Mandeville GB . . . 44 B3
Stoke-on-Trent GB . 40 B1
Stokesley GB . . . 37 B5
Stokke N . . . 54 A1
Stokkemarke DK . . . 65 B4
Stokken N . . . 53 B4
Stokkseyri IS . . . 190 D4
Stokkvågen N . . . 195 D4
Stokmarknes N . . . 194 B5
Štoky CZ . . . 97 B3
Stolac BIH . . . 139 B3
Stølaholmen N . . . 46 A3
Stolberg D . . . 80 B2
Stolin BY . . . 13 C7
Stollberg D . . . 83 B4
Stöllet S . . . 49 B5
Stollhamm D . . . 71 A5
Stolno PL . . . 76 A3
Stolpen D . . . 84 A2
Stolzenau D . . . 72 B2
Stompetoren NL . . . 70 B1
Ston HR . . . 139 C3
Stonařov CZ . . . 97 B3
Stone GB . . . 40 C1
Stonehaven GB . . . 33 E4
Stonehouse GB . . . 36 A3
Stongfjorden N . . . 46 A2
Stonndalen N . . . 47 B4
Stony Stratford GB . 44 A3
Stopnica PL . . . 87 B4
Storå S . . . 56 A1
Storås N . . . 198 B6
Storby FIN . . . 51 B6
Stordal
Møre og Romsdal N . . . 198 C4
Nord-Trøndelag N . 199 B8
Store GB . . . 33 B4
Storebø N . . . 46 B2
Storebro S . . . 62 A3
Store Damme DK . . . 65 B5
Store Heddinge DK . 65 A5
Store Herrestad S . . 66 A2
Store Levene S . . . 55 B3
Storelv N . . . 192 B6
Store Molvik N . . . 193 B12
Støren N . . . 199 B7
Store Skedvi S . . . 50 B2
Store Vika S . . . 57 B3
Storfjellseter N . . . 199 D7
Storfjord N . . . 192 C3
Storfjorden N . . . 198 C3
Storfors S . . . 55 A5
Storforshei N . . . 195 D5
Storhøliseter N . . . 47 A6
Storjord N . . . 195 D6
Storkow
Brandenburg D . . . 74 B2
Mecklenburg-Vorpommern D . . . 74 A3
Storli N . . . 198 C6
Storlien S . . . 199 B9
Stornara I . . . 171 B3
Stornoway GB . . . 31 A2
Storo I . . . 121 B3
Storozhynets UA . . . 17 A6
Storrington GB . . . 44 C3
Storseleby S . . . 200 B2
Storsjön S . . . 50 A3
Storslett N . . . 192 C5
Storsteinnes N . . . 192 C3
Storsund S . . . 196 D3
Storuman S . . . 195 E8
Störvattnet S . . . 199 C9
Storvik
N . . . 195 D4
S . . . 50 B3
Storvreta S . . . 51 C4
Štos SK . . . 99 C4
Stössen D . . . 83 A3
Stotel D . . . 72 A1
Stötten D . . . 108 B1
Stotternheim D . . . 82 A3
Stouby DK . . . 59 C2
Stourbridge GB . . . 40 C1
Stourport-on-Severn GB . . . 39 B4
Støvring DK . . . 58 B2
Stow GB . . . 35 C5
Stowbtsy BY . . . 13 B7
Stowmarket GB . . . 45 A5
Stow-on-the-Wold GB . . . 44 B2
Straach D . . . 73 C5
Strabane GB . . . 27 B3
Strachan GB . . . 33 D4
Strachur GB . . . 34 B2
Stracin MK . . . 182 A4
Strackholt D . . . 71 A4
Stradbally IRL . . . 29 B1
Stradella I . . . 120 B2
Straelen D . . . 80 A2
Stragari SRB . . . 127 C2
Strakonice CZ . . . 96 B1
Strålsnäs S . . . 55 B6
Stralsund D . . . 66 B2
Strand N . . . 48 A3
Stranda N . . . 198 C3
Strandby DK . . . 58 A3
Strandebarm N . . . 46 B3
Strandhill IRL . . . 26 B2
Strandlykkja N . . . 48 B3
Strandvik N . . . 46 B2
Strangford GB . . . 27 B5
Strängnäs S . . . 56 A3
Strångsjö S . . . 56 B2
Stráni CZ . . . 98 C1
Stranice SLO . . . 123 A4
Stranorlar IRL . . . 26 B3
Stranraer GB . . . 36 B1
Strasatti I . . . 176 B1
Strasbourg F . . . 93 C3
Strasburg D . . . 74 A2
Strašice CZ . . . 96 B1
Stråssa S . . . 56 A1
Strassburg A . . . 110 C1
Strass im Steiermark A . . . 110 C2
Strasskirchen D . . . 95 C4
Strasswalchen A . . 109 B4
Stratford-upon-Avon GB . . . 44 A2
Strathaven GB . . . 36 A2
Strathdon GB . . . 32 D3
Strathkanaird GB . . 32 D1
Strathpeffer GB . . . 32 D2
Strathy GB . . . 32 C3
Strathyre GB . . . 34 B3
Stratinska BIH . . . 124 C2
Stratton GB . . . 42 B2
Straubing D . . . 95 C4
Straulas I . . . 178 B3
Straume N . . . 53 A5
Straumen
Nordland N . . . 194 C6
Nord-Trøndelag N . 199 B8
Straumsjøen N . . . 194 B5
Straumsnes N . . . 194 C6
Straupitz D . . . 74 C3
Strausberg D . . . 74 B2
Straussfurt D . . . 82 A3
Strawczyn PL . . . 87 B4
Straža
SLO . . . 123 B4
SRB . . . 127 C3
Stražnad Nezárkou CZ . . . 96 B2
Strážnice CZ . . . 98 C1
Strážný CZ . . . 96 C1
Stráž Pod Ralskem CZ . . . 84 B2
Štrbské Pleso SK . . . 99 B4
Strečno SK . . . 98 B2
Street GB . . . 43 A4
Strehla D . . . 83 A5
Strekov SK . . . 112 B2
Strem A . . . 111 B3
Stremska-Rača SRB . . . 127 C1
Strengberg A . . . 110 A1
Strengelvåg N . . . 194 B6
Stresa I . . . 119 B5
Streufdorf D . . . 82 B2
Strib DK . . . 59 C2
Striberg S . . . 55 A5
Stříbro CZ . . . 95 B4
Strichen GB . . . 33 D4
Strigno I . . . 121 A4
Štrigova HR . . . 111 C3
Strijen NL . . . 79 A4
Strizivojna HR . . . 125 B4
Strmica HR . . . 138 A2
Strmilov CZ . . . 97 B3
Ströhen D . . . 72 B1
Strokestown IRL . . . 28 A3
Stromberg
Nordrhein-Westfalen D . . . 81 A4
Rheinland-Pfalz D . . 93 B3
Stromeferry GB . . . 31 B3
Strömnäs S . . . 200 B2
Stromness GB . . . 33 C3
Strömsberg S . . . 51 B4
Strömsbruk S . . . 200 E3
Strömsfors S . . . 56 B2
Strömsnäsbruk S . . 61 C3
Strömstad S . . . 54 B2
Strömsund
Jämtland S . . . 199 B12
Västerbotten S . . . 195 E7
Stronachlachar GB . 34 B3
Stróngoli I . . . 174 B3
Stronie Śląskie PL . . 85 B4
Strontian GB . . . 34 B2
Stroppiana I . . . 119 B5
Stroud GB . . . 43 A4
Stroumbi CY . . . 181 B1
Stróża PL . . . 99 B3
Strücklingen D . . . 71 A4
Struer DK . . . 58 B1
Struga MK . . . 182 B2
Strugi Krasnyye RUS 9 C6
Strumica MK . . . 182 B4
Strumien PL . . . 98 B2
Struy GB . . . 32 D2
Strużec HR . . . 124 B2
Stryków PL . . . 77 C4
Stryn N . . . 198 D3
Stryy UA . . . 13 D5
Strzałkowo PL . . . 76 B2
Strzegocin PL . . . 77 B5
Strzegom PL . . . 85 B4
Strzegowo PL . . . 77 B5
Strzelce PL . . . 77 B4
Strzelce Krajeńskie PL . . . 75 B4
Strzelce Kurowo PL 75 B4
Strzelce Opolskie PL . . . 86 B2
Strzelin PL . . . 85 B5
Strzelno PL . . . 76 B3
Strzepcz PL . . . 68 A3
Strzybnica PL . . . 86 B2
Strzygi PL . . . 77 A4
Stubbekøbing DK . . 65 B5
Stuben A . . . 107 B5
Stubenberg A . . . 110 B2
Stubline SRB . . . 127 C2
Studená CZ . . . 97 B3
Studenci HR . . . 138 B3
Studenka CZ . . . 98 B2
Studenzen A . . . 110 B2
Studienka SK . . . 98 C1
Studland GB . . . 43 B5
Studley GB . . . 44 A2
Studzienice PL . . . 68 A2
Stuer D . . . 73 A5
Stugudal N . . . 199 C8
Stugun S . . . 200 C1
Stuhr D . . . 72 A1
Stukenbrock D . . . 81 A4
Stülpe D . . . 74 B2
Stupava SK . . . 111 A4
Stupnik HR . . . 124 B1
Stupsk PL . . . 77 A5
Sturkö S . . . 63 B3
Sturminster Newton GB . . . 43 B4
Štúrovo SK . . . 112 B2
Sturton GB . . . 40 B3
Stuttgart D . . . 94 C1
Stvolny CZ . . . 96 A1
Stykkishólmur IS . 190 B3
Styri N . . . 48 B3
Stysö S . . . 60 B1
Suances E . . . 142 A2
Subbiano I . . . 135 B4
Subiaco I . . . 169 B3
Subotica SRB . . . 126 A1
Subotište SRB . . . 127 C1
Sučany SK . . . 98 B2
Suceava RO . . . 17 B7
Sucha-Beskidzka PL . . . 99 B3
Suchacz PL . . . 69 A4
Suchań PL . . . 75 A4
Suchdol nad Lužnice CZ . . . 96 C2
Suchedniów PL . . . 87 A4
Suchorze PL . . . 68 A2
Suchteln D . . . 80 A2
Sucina E . . . 165 B4
Suckow D . . . 73 A4
Sućuraj HR . . . 138 B3
Súðavík IS . . . 190 A3
Sudbury GB . . . 45 A4
Suddesjaur S . . . 195 E10
Suden D . . . 64 B1
Süderbrarup D . . . 64 B2
Süderlügum D . . . 64 B1
Sudoměřice u Bechyně CZ . . . 96 B2
Sudovec HR . . . 124 A2
Suðureyri IS . . . 190 A2
Sueca E . . . 159 B3
Suelli I . . . 179 C3
Sugenheim D . . . 94 B2
Sugères F . . . 117 B3
Sugny B . . . 91 B4
Suhl D . . . 82 B2
Suhlendorf D . . . 73 B3
Suhopolje HR . . . 124 B3
Suho Polje BIH . . . 125 C5
Şuhut TR . . . 189 A5
Šuica BIH . . . 138 B3
Suippes F . . . 91 B4
Sukošan HR . . . 137 A4
Sükösd H . . . 125 A4

Suków PL 87 B4
Šul'a SK 99 C3
Suldalsosen N 52 A2
Suldrup DK 58 B2
Sulechów PL 75 B4
Sulęcin PL 75 B4
Sulęczyno PL 68 A2
Sulejów PL 87 A3
Süleymanlı TR 186 D2
Sulgen CH 107 B4
Sulibórz PL 75 A4
Sulina RO 17 C8
Sulingen D 72 B1
Suliszewo PL 75 A4
Sulitjelma N 195 C7
Sułkowice PL 99 B3
Süller TR 189 A4
Sully-sur-Loire F 103 B4
Sulmierzyce
Łódzkie PL 86 A3
Wielkopolskie PL 85 A5
Sulmona I 169 A3
Süloğlu TR 186 A1
Sułoszowa PL 87 B3
Sulów PL 85 A5
Sulsdorf D 65 B4
Sultandağı TR 189 A6
Sülüklü TR 187 D7
Suluova TR 23 A8
Sulvik S 54 A3
Sülysáp H 112 B3
Sülz D 93 C4
Sulzbach
Baden-Württemberg D 94 B1
Baden-Württemberg D 94 C1
Bayern D 93 B5
Saarland D 92 B3
Sulzbach-Rosenberg D 95 B3
Sülze D 72 B3
Sulzfeld D 82 B2
Sumartin HR 138 B2
Sumburgh GB 33 B5
Sümeg H 111 C4
Sumiswald CH 106 B2
Šumná CZ 97 C3
Šumperk CZ 97 B4
Šumvald CZ 98 B1
Sunbilla E 144 A2
Sünching D 95 C4
Sund
FIN 51 B7
S 54 A2
Sundborn S 50 B2
Sundby DK 58 B1
Sunde N 46 C2
Sunde bru N 53 B5
Sunderland GB 37 B5
Sundern D 81 A4
Sundhultsbrunn S 62 A2
Sundnäs S 195 D8
Sundom S 196 D5
Sunds DK 59 B2
Sundsfjord N 195 D5
Sundsvall S 200 D3
Sungurlu TR 23 A8
Suni I 178 B2
Sunja HR 124 B2
Sunnansjö S 50 B1
Sunnaryd S 60 B3
Sunndalsøra N 198 C5
Sunne S 49 C5
Sunnemo S 49 C5
Sunnersberg S 55 B4
Suolovuopmio N 192 C7
Suomussalmi FIN 3 D11
Suoyarvi RUS 9 A8
Super Sauze F 132 A2
Supetar HR 138 B2
Supetarska Draga HR 123 C3
Supino I 169 B3
Šuplja Stijena MNE 139 B5
Surahammar S 56 A2
Šurany SK 112 A2
Surazh BY 13 A9
Surbo I 173 B4
Surčin SRB 127 C2
Surgères F 114 B3
Surhuisterveen NL 70 A3
Súria E 147 C2
Surin F 115 B4
Surka N 48 B2
Surnadalsøra N 198 C5
Sursee CH 106 B3
Surte S 60 B2
Surwold D 71 B4
Sury-le-Comtal F 117 B4
Susa I 119 B4
Šušara SRB 127 C3
Susch CH 107 C5
Susegana I 122 B1
Süsel D 65 B3
Sušice CZ 96 B1
Šušnjevica HR 123 B3
Sussen D 94 C1
Susurluk TR 186 C3
Susz PL 69 B4
Sütçüler TR 189 B5
Sutivan HR 138 B2
Sutjeska SRB 126 B2
Sutri I 168 A2
Sutton GB 44 B3
Sutton Coldfield GB 40 C2
Sutton-in-Ashfield GB 40 B2
Sutton-on-Sea GB 41 B4
Sutton-on-Trent GB 40 B3
Sutton Scotney GB 44 B2
Sutton Valence GB 45 B4
Suvaja BIH 124 C2
Suvereto I 135 B3
Suwałki PL 12 A5
Suze-la-Rousse F 131 A3
Suzzara I 121 C3
Svabensverk S 50 A2
Svalbarð IS 191 A10
Svalöv S 61 D3
Svanabyn S 200 B2
Svanberga S 51 C5
Svaneke DK 67 A4
Svanesund S 54 B2
Svängsta S 63 B2
Svannäs S 195 D9
Svanskog S 54 A3
Svanstein S 196 C6
Svappavaara S 196 B4
Svärdsjö S 50 B2
Svarstad N 53 A5
Svartå S 55 A5
Svärta S 56 B3
Svartå S 55 A4
Svartbyn S 196 C5
Svärtinge S 56 B2
Svartlå S 196 D4
Svartnäs S 50 B3
Svartnes N 195 C5
Svarttjärn S 195 E7
Svatsum N 48 A1
Svätý Jur SK 111 A4
Svätý Peter SK 112 B2
Svedala S 61 D3
Sveg S 199 C11
Sveindal N 52 B3
Sveio N 52 A1
Svejbæk DK 59 B2
Svelgen N 198 D2
Svelvik N 54 A1
Svendborg DK 65 A3
Svene N 53 A5
Svenljunga S 60 B3
Svennevad S 56 A1
Svenstavik S 199 C11
Svenstrup DK 58 B2
Švermov CZ 84 B2
Sveti Ivan Zabno HR 124 B2
Sveti Ivan Zelina HR 124 B2
Sveti Nikole MK 182 B3
Sveti Rok HR 137 A4
Světlá nad Sázavou CZ 97 B3
Svetlyy RUS 69 A5
Svetvinčenat HR 122 B2
Švica HR 123 C4
Svidník SK 12 D4
Švihov CZ 96 B1
Svilajnac SRB 127 C3
Svilengrad BG 183 B8
Svindal N 54 A2
Svinhult S 62 A3
Svinna SK 98 C2
Svinninge
DK 61 D1
S 57 A4
Sviritsa RUS 9 B8
Svishtov BG 17 D6
Svislach BY 13 B6
Svit SK 99 B4
Svitavy CZ 97 B4
Svodin SK 112 B2
Svolvær N 194 B5
Svortemyr N 46 A2
Svortland N 52 A1
Svratka CZ 97 B4
Svrčinovec SK 98 B2
Svullrya N 49 B4
Svyetlahorsk BY 13 B8
Swadlincote GB 40 C2
Swaffham GB 41 C4
Swanage GB 43 B5
Swanley GB 45 B4
Swanlinbar IRL 26 B3
Swansea GB 39 C3
Swarzędz PL 76 B2
Swatragh GB 27 B4
Świątki PL 69 B5
Świdnica
Dolnośląskie PL 85 B4
Lubuskie PL 84 A3
Świdnik PL 12 C5
Świdwin PL 67 C4
Świebodzice PL 85 B4
Świebodzin PL 75 B4
Świecie PL 76 A3
Świedziebnia PL 77 A4
Świeradów Zdrój PL 84 B3
Świerki PL 85 B4
Swierzawa PL 85 A3
Swierzno PL 67 C3
Swięta PL 74 A3
Swieta Anna PL 86 B3
Świętno PL 75 B5
Swifterbant NL 70 B2
Swindon GB 44 B2
Swineshead GB 41 C3
Swinford IRL 26 C2
Świnoujście PL 66 C3
Swinton GB 35 C5
Swobnica PL 74 A3
Swords IRL 30 A2
Swornegacie PL 68 B2
Sya S 56 B1
Syasstroy RUS 9 B8
Sycewice PL 68 A1
Sychevka RUS 9 E9
Syców PL 86 A1
Sycowice PL 75 B4
Sydnes N 52 A1
Syfteland N 46 B2
Syke D 72 B1
Sykkylven N 198 C3
Sylling N 48 C2
Sylte N 198 C4
Symbister GB 33 A5
Symington GB 36 A3
Symonds Yat GB 39 C4
Sypniewo
Kujawsko-Pomorskie PL 76 A2
Wielkopolskie PL 68 B1
Syserum S 62 A4
Sysslebäck S 49 B4
Syväjärvi FIN 197 B8
Szabadbattyán H 112 B2
Szabadegyháza H 112 B2
Szabadszállás H 112 C3
Szadek PL 86 A2
Szajol H 113 B4
Szakály H 112 C2
Szakcs H 112 C2
Szakmár H 112 C3
Szalánta H 125 B4
Szałas PL 87 A4
Szalkszentmárton H 112 C3
Szalonna H 99 C4
Szamocin PL 76 A2
Szamotuły PL 75 B5
Szany H 111 B4
Szarvas H 113 C4
Szarvaskö H 113 B4
Szászvár H 125 A4
Százhalombatta H 112 B2
Szczawa PL 99 B4
Szczawnica PL 99 B4
Szczecin PL 74 A3
Szczecinek PL 68 B1
Szczekociny PL 87 B3
Szczerców PL 86 A3
Szczucin PL 87 B5
Szczuczarz PL 75 A5
Szczuki PL 77 B5
Szczurowa PL 87 B4
Szczyrk PL 99 B3
Szczytna PL 85 B4
Szczytno PL 77 A5
Szczyty PL 86 A2
Szécsény H 112 A3
Szederkény H 125 B4
Szedres H 112 C2
Szeged H 126 A2
Szeghalom H 113 B5
Szegvár H 113 C4
Székesfehérvár H 112 B2
Székkutas H 113 C4
Szekszárd H 125 A4
Szemplino Czarne PL 77 A5
Szemud PL 68 A3
Szendehely H 112 B3
Szendrö H 99 C4
Szentendre H 112 B3
Szentes H 113 C4
Szentgotthárd H 111 C3
Szentlászló H 125 A3
Szentlörinc H 125 A3
Szentmártonkáta H 113 B3
Szenyér H 111 C4
Szeremle H 125 A4
Szerencs H 113 A5
Szerep H 113 B5
Szigetszentmiklós H 112 B3
Szigetvár H 125 A3
Szikáncs H 126 A2
Szikszó H 113 A4
Szil H 111 B4
Szilvásvárad H 113 A4
Szklarska Poreba PL 84 B3
Szlichtyngowa PL 85 A4
Szob H 112 B2
Szolnok H 113 B4
Szombathely H 111 B3
Szorosad H 112 C2
Szpetal Graniczny PL 77 B4
Szprotawa PL 84 A3
Szreńsk PL 77 A5
Sztum PL 69 B4
Sztutowo PL 69 A4
Szubin PL 76 A2
Szücsi H 113 B3
Szulmierz PL 77 B5
Szulok H 124 A3
Szumanie PL 77 B4
Szwecja PL 75 A5
Szydłów
Łódzkie PL 86 A3
Świętokrzyskie PL 87 B5
Szydłowiec PL 87 A4
Szydlowo PL 77 A5
Szydłowo PL 75 A5
Szymanów PL 77 B5
Szynkielów PL 86 A2

T

Taastrup DK 61 D2
Tab H 112 C2
Tabanera la Luenga E 151 A3
Tabaqueros E 158 B2
Tábara E 149 A4
Tabenera de Cerrato E 142 B2
Taberg S 62 A2
Tabernas E 164 B2
Tabiano Bagni I 120 C3
Taboada E 140 B3
Taboadela E 140 B3
Tábor CZ 96 B2
Táborfalva H 112 B3
Taborište HR 124 B2
Tábua P 148 B1
Tabuaco P 148 A2
Tabuenca E 152 A2
Tabuyo del Monte E 141 B4
Täby S 57 A4
Tác H 112 B2
Tachov CZ 95 B4
Tadcaster GB 40 B2
Tadley GB 44 B2
Tafalla E 144 B2
Tafjord N 198 C4
Taganheira P 160 B1
Tågarp S 61 D2
Tággia I 133 B3
Tagliacozzo I 169 A3
Táglio di Po I 121 B5
Tagnon F 91 B4
Tahal E 164 B2
Tahitótfalu H 112 B3
Tahtaköprü TR 187 C4
Tailfingen D 107 A4
Taillis F 101 A4
Tain GB 32 D2
Tain-l'Hermitage F 117 B4
Taipadas P 154 C2
Taivalkoski FIN 197 D11
Takene S 55 A4
Takovo SRB 127 C2
Taksony H 112 B3
Tal E 140 B2
Talachyn BY 13 A8
Talamello I 135 B5
Talamone I 168 A1
Talant F 105 B3
Talarrubias E 156 A2
Talaván E 155 B4
Talavera de la Reina E 150 C3
Talavera la Real E 155 C4
Talayuela E 150 C2
Talayuelas E 159 B2
Talgarth GB 39 C3
Talgje N 52 A1
Talhadas P 148 B1
Táliga E 155 C3
Talizat F 116 B3
Tálknafjörður IS 190 B2
Talla I 135 B4
Talladale GB 31 B3
Tallaght IRL 30 A2
Tallard F 132 A2
Tällberg S 50 B1
Tallberg S 196 C5
Tallinn EST 8 C4
Talloires F 118 B3
Tallow IRL 29 B3
Tallsjö S 200 B4
Tallvik S 196 C5
Talmay F 105 B4
Talmont-St Hilaire F 114 B2
Talmont-sur-Gironde F 114 C3
Talne UA 13 D9
Talsano I 173 B3
Talsi LV 8 D3
Talvik N 192 B6
Talybont GB 39 B3
Tal-Y-Llyn GB 38 B3
Tamajón E 151 B4
Tamame E 149 A4
Tamames E 149 B3
Tamarit de Mar E 147 C2
Tamarite de Litera E 145 C4
Tamariu E 147 C4
Tamási H 112 C2
Tambach-Dietharz D 82 B2
Tameza E 141 A4
Tammisaari FIN 8 B3
Tampere FIN 8 B3
Tamsweg A 109 B4
Tamurejo E 156 B3
Tamworth GB 40 C2
Tana bru N 193 B12
Tañabueyes E 143 B3
Tanakajd H 111 B3
Tananger N 52 B1
Tanaunella I 178 B3
Tancarville F 89 A4
Tandsjöborg S 199 D11
Tånga S 61 C2
Tangelic H 112 C2
Tangen N 48 B3
Tangerhütte D 73 B4
Tangermünde D 73 B4
Tanhua FIN 197 B10
Taninges F 118 A3
Tankavaara FIN 197 A10
Tann D 82 B2
Tanna D 83 B3
Tannadice GB 35 B5
Tannåker S 60 C3
Tännäs S 199 C9
Tannay
Ardennes F 91 B4
Nièvre F 104 B2
Tannenbergsthal D 83 B4
Tännesberg D 95 B4
Tannheim A 108 B1
Tannila FIN 197 D8
Tanowo PL 74 A3
Tanum S 54 B2
Tanumshede S 54 B2
Tanus F 130 A1
Tanvald CZ 84 B3
Taormina I 177 B4
Tapa EST 8 C4
Tapfheim D 94 C2
Tapia de Casariego E 141 A4
Tapio F 146 A2
Tápióbicske H 112 B3
Tápiógyörgye H 113 B3
Tápióság H 112 B3
Tápiószecsö H 112 B3
Tápiószele H 113 B3
Tápiószentmárton H 113 B3
Tapolca H 111 C4
Tapolcafö H 111 B4
Tar HR 122 B2
Tarabo S 60 B2
Taradell E 147 C3
Taraklı TR 187 B5
Taramundi E 141 A3
Tarancón E 151 B4
Táranto I 173 B3
Tarare F 117 B4
Tarascon F 131 B3
Tarascon-sur-Ariège F 146 B2
Tarashcha UA 13 D9
Tarazona E 144 C2
Tarazona de la Mancha E 158 B2
Tarbena E 159 C3
Tarbert
GB 34 C2
IRL 29 B2
Tarbes F 145 A4
Tarbet GB 34 B3
Tarbolton GB 36 A2
Tarcento I 122 A2
Tarčin BIH 139 B4
Tarczyn PL 77 C5
Tardajos E 143 B3
Tardelcuende E 151 A5
Tardets-Sorholus F 144 A3
Tardienta E 145 C3
Tärendö S 196 B5
Targon F 128 B2
Târgovişte RO 17 C6
Târgu-Jiu RO 17 C5
Târgu Mureş RO 17 B6
Târgu Ocna RO 17 B7
Târgu Secuiesc RO 17 C7
Tarifa E 162 B2
Tariquejas E 161 B2
Tarján H 112 B2
Tárkany H 112 B2
Tarland GB 33 D4
Tarłów PL 87 A5
Tarm DK 59 C1
Tarmstedt D 72 A2
Tärnaby S 195 E6
Tarnalelesz H 113 A4
Tarnaörs H 113 B4
Târnăveni RO 17 B6
Tårnet N 193 C14
Tarnobrzeg PL 87 B5
Tarnos F 128 C1
Tarnów
Lubuskie PL 75 B3
Małopolskie PL 87 B4
Tarnowo Podgórne PL 75 B5
Tarnowskie Góry PL 86 B2
Tärnsjö S 51 B3
Tårnvik N 194 C6
Tarouca P 148 A2
Tarp D 64 B2
Tarquínia I 168 A1
Tarquínia Lido I 168 A1
Tarragona E 147 C2
Tårrajaur S 196 C2
Tàrrega E 147 C2
Tarrenz A 108 B1
Tårs
Nordjyllands DK 58 A3
Storstrøms DK 65 B4
Tarsia I 174 B2
Tarsus TR 23 C8
Tartas F 128 C2
Tartu EST 8 C5
Tarves GB 33 D4
Tarvísio I 109 C4
Taşağıl TR 189 C6
Täsch CH 119 A4
Taşköprü TR 23 A8
Tasov CZ 97 B4
Tasovčići BIH 139 B3
Taşucuo TR 23 C7
Tát H 112 B2
Tata H 112 B2
Tatabánya H 112 B2
Tataháza H 126 A1
Tatarbunary UA 17 C8
Tatárszentgyörgy H 112 B3
Tatranská-Lomnica SK 99 B4
Tau N 52 A1
Tauberbischofsheim D 94 B1
Taucha D 83 A4
Taufkirchen D 95 C4
Taufkirchen an der Pram A 96 C1
Taulé F 100 A2
Taulignan F 131 A3
Taulov DK 59 C2
Taunton GB 43 A3
Taunusstein D 81 B4
Tauragė LT 12 A5
Taurianova I 175 C2
Taurisano I 173 C4
Tauste E 144 C2
Tauves F 116 B2
Tavankut SRB 126 A1
Tavannes CH 106 B2
Tavarnelle val di Pesa I 135 B4
Tavas TR 188 B4
Tavaux F 105 B4
Tävelsås S 62 B2
Taverna I 175 B2
Taverne CH 120 A1
Tavernelle I 135 B5
Tavernes de la Valldigna E 159 B3
Tavérnola Bergamasca I 120 B3
Taverny F 90 B2
Tavescan E 146 B2
Taviano I 173 C4
Tavira P 160 B2
Tavistock GB 42 B2
Tavşanlı TR 187 C4
Tayinloan GB 34 C2
Taynuilt GB 34 B2
Tayport GB 35 B5
Tázlár H 112 C3
Tazones E 142 A1
Tczew PL 69 A3
Tczów PL 87 A5
Teangue GB 31 B3
Teano I 170 B2
Teba E 162 B3
Tebay GB 37 B4
Techendorf A 109 C4
Tecklenburg D 71 B4
Tecko-matorp S 61 D3
Tecuci RO 17 C7
Tefenni TR 189 B4
Tegelsmora S 51 B4
Tegernsee D 108 B2
Teggiano I 172 B1
Tegoleto I 135 B4
Teichel D 82 B3
Teignmouth GB 43 B3
Teillay F 101 B4
Teillet F 130 B1
Teisendorf D 109 B3
Teistungen D 82 A2
Teixeiro E 140 A2
Tejada de Tiétar E 150 B2
Tejado E 152 A1
Tejares E 150 B2
Tejn DK 67 A3
Teke TR 187 A4
Tekirdağ TR 186 B2
Tekovské-Lužany SK 112 A2
Telavåg N 46 B1
Telč CZ 97 B3
Telese Terme I 170 B2
Telford GB 38 B4
Telfs A 108 B2
Telgárt SK 99 C4
Telgte D 71 C4
Tellingstedt D 64 B2
Telšiai LT 8 E3
Telti I 178 B3
Teltow D 74 B2
Tembleque E 157 A4
Temelín CZ 96 B2
Temerin SRB 126 B1
Temiño E 143 B3
Témpio Pausánia I 178 B3
Templederry IRL 28 B3
Templemore IRL 28 B4
Temple Sowerby GB 37 B4
Templin D 74 A2
Temse B 79 A4
Tenay F 118 B2
Ten Boer NL 71 A3
Tenbury Wells GB 39 B4
Tenby GB 39 C2
Tence F 117 B4
Tende F 133 A3
Tenhult S 62 A2
Tenja HR 125 B4
Tenneville B 92 A1
Tennevoll N 194 B8
Tensta S 51 B4
Tenterden GB 45 B4

Teo E 140 B2
Teora I 172 B1
Tepasto FIN 196 B7
Tepelenë AL 182 C2
Teplá CZ 95 B4
Teplice CZ 84 B1
Teplička nad Váhom SK 98 B2
Tepsa FIN 197 B8
Tera E 143 C4
Téramo I 169 A3
Ter Apel NL 71 B4
Terborg NL 71 C3
Terchová SK 99 B3
Terebovlya UA 13 D6
Teremia Mare RO 126 B2
Terena P 155 C3
Teresa de Cofrentes E 159 B2
Terešov CZ 96 B1
Terezín CZ 84 B2
Terezino Polje HR 124 B3
Tergnier F 90 B3
Teriberka RUS 3 B14
Terlizzi I 171 B4
Termas de Monfortinho P 155 A4
Terme di Súio I 169 B3
Terme di Valdieri I 133 A3
Termens E 145 C4
Termes F 116 C3
Términi Imerese I 176 B2
Terminillo I 169 A2
Térmoli I 170 B3
Termonfeckin IRL 27 C4
Ternberg A 110 B1
Terndrup DK 58 B3
Terneuzen NL 79 A3
Terni I 168 A2
Ternitz A 111 B3
Ternopil UA 13 D6
Terpni GR 183 C5
Terracina I 169 B3
Terråk N 195 E3
Terralba I 179 C2
Terranova di Pollino I 174 B2
Terranova di Sibari I 174 B2
Terras do Bouro P 148 A1
Terrasini I 176 A2
Terrassa E 147 C3
Terrasson-la-Villedieu F 129 A4
Terrazos E 143 B3
Terriente E 152 B2
Terrugem P 155 C3
Tertenía I 179 C3
Teruel E 152 B2
Tervola FIN 196 C7
Tervuren B 79 B4
Terzaga E 152 B2
Tešanj BIH 125 C3
Tesáske-Mlyňany SK 98 C2
Teslić BIH 125 C3
Tessin D 66 B1
Tessy-sur-Vire F 88 B2
Tét H 111 B4
Tetbury GB 43 A4
Teterchen F 92 B2
Teterow D 65 C5
Teteven BG 17 D6
Tetiyev UA 13 D8
Tetovo MK 182 A2
Tettau D 82 B3
Tettnang D 107 B4
Teublitz D 95 B4
Teuchern D 83 A4
Teulada
E 159 C4
I 179 D2
Teupitz D 74 B2
Teurajärvi S 196 C5
Teutschenthal D 83 A3
Tevel H 112 C2
Teviothead GB 36 A4
Tewkesbury GB 39 C4
Thale D 82 A3
Thalfang D 92 B2
Thalgau A 109 B4
Thalkirch CH 107 C4
Thalmässing D 95 B3
Thalwil CH 107 B3
Thame GB 44 B3
Thann F 106 B2
Thannhausen D 94 C2
Thaon-les-Vosges F 105 A5
Tharandt D 83 B5
Tharsis E 161 B2
Thasos GR 183 C6
Thatcham GB 44 B2
Thaxted GB 45 B4
Thayngen CH 107 B3
Theale GB 44 B2
The Barony GB 33 B3
Thebes = Thiva GR 185 A4
Theding-hausen D 72 B2
Theessen D 73 B5
The Hague = 's-Gravenhage NL 70 B1
Themar D 82 B2
The Mumbles GB 39 C3
Thénezay F 102 C1
Thenon F 129 A4
Therouanne F 78 B2
Thessaloniki = Salonica GR 182 C4
Thetford GB 45 A4
Theux B 80 B1
Thézar-les-Corbières F 146 A3
Thèze F 145 A3
Thiberville F 89 A4
Thibie F 91 C4
Thiéblemont-Farémont F 91 C4
Thiendorf D 84 A1
Thiene I 121 B4
Thierrens CH 106 C1
Thiers F 117 B3
Thiesi I 178 B2
Thiessow D 66 B2
Thiezac F 116 B2
Þingeyri IS 190 B2
Þingvellir IS 190 C4
Thionville F 92 B2
Thira GR 185 C6
Thiron-Gardais F 89 B4
Thirsk GB 37 B5
Thisted DK 58 B1
Thiva = Thebes GR 185 A4
Thivars F 90 C1
Thiviers F 115 C4
Thizy F 117 A4
Tholen NL 79 A4
Tholey D 92 B3
Thomas Street IRL 28 A3
Thomastown IRL 30 B1
Thônes F 118 B3
Thonnance-les-Joinville F 91 C5
Thonon-les-Bains F 118 A3
Thorame-Basse F 132 A2
Thorame-Haute F 132 A2
Thorens-Glières F 118 A3
Thorigny-sur-Oreuse F 91 C3
Thörl A 110 B2
Þorlákshöfn IS 190 D4
Thornaby on Tees GB 37 B5
Thornbury GB 43 A4
Thorne GB 40 B3
Thornhill
Dumfries & Galloway GB 36 A3
Stirling GB 35 B3
Thornthwaite GB 36 B3
Thornton-le-Dale GB 40 A3
Þórshöfn IS 191 A10
Thouarcé F 102 B1
Thouars F 102 C1
Thrapston GB 44 A3
Threlkeld GB 36 B3
Thrumster GB 32 C3
Thueyts F 117 C4
Thuin B 79 B4
Thuir F 146 B3
Thumau D 95 A3
Thun CH 106 C2
Thuret F 116 B3
Thurey F 105 C4
Thüringen A 107 B4
Thurins F 117 B4
Thürkow D 65 C5
Thurles IRL 29 B4
Thurmaston GB 40 C2
Thurø By DK 65 A3
Thursby GB 36 B3
Thurso GB 32 C3
Thury-Harcourt F 89 B3
Thusis CH 107 C4
Thyborøn DK 58 B1
Þykkvibær IS 190 D5
Thyregod DK 59 C2
Tibi E 159 C3
Tibro S 55 B5
Tidaholm S 55 B4
Tidan S 55 B5
Tidersrum S 62 A3
Tiedra E 150 A2
Tiefenbach D 95 B4
Tiefencastel CH 107 C4
Tiefenort D 82 B2
Tiefensee D 74 B2
Tiel NL 79 A5
Tielmes E 151 B4
Tielt B 78 A3
Tienen B 79 B4
Tiengen D 106 B3
Tiercé F 102 B1
Tierga E 152 A2
Tiermas E 144 B2
Tierp S 51 B4
Tierrantona E 145 B4
Tighina MD 17 B8
Tighnabruaich GB 34 C2
Tignes F 119 B3
Tigy F 103 B4
Tihany H 112 C1
Tijnje NL 70 A2
Tijola E 164 B2
Tikhvin RUS 9 C8
Tilburg NL 79 A5
Til Châtel F 105 B4
Tilh F 128 C2
Tillac F 145 A4
Tillberga S 56 A2
Tille F 90 B2
Tillicoultry GB 35 B4
Tilloy Bellay F 91 B4
Tilly F 115 B5
Tilly-sur-Seulles F 88 A3
Tim DK 59 B1
Timau I 109 C4
Timbaki GR 185 D5
Timi CY 181 B1
Timişoara RO 126 B3
Timmele S 60 B3
Timmendorfer Strand D 65 C3
Timmernabben S 62 B4
Timmersdala S 55 B4
Timoleague IRL 29 C3
Timolin IRL 30 B2
Timrå S 200 D3
Timsfors S 61 C3
Timsgearraidh GB 31 A1
Tinajas E 152 B1
Tinalhas P 155 B3
Tinchebray F 88 B3
Tincques F 78 B2
Tineo E 141 A4
Tinglev DK 64 B2
Tingsryd S 63 B2
Tingstäde S 57 C4
Tingvoll N 198 C5
Tinlot B 79 B5
Tinnoset N 53 A5
Tinos GR 185 B6
Tintagel GB 42 B2
Tinténiac F 101 A4
Tintern GB 39 C4
Tintigny B 92 B1
Tione di Trento I 121 A3
Tipperary IRL 29 B3
Tiptree GB 45 B4
Tirana = Tiranë AL 182 B1
Tiranë= Tirana AL 182 B1
Tirano I 120 A3
Tiraspol MD 17 B8
Tire TR 188 A2
Tires I 108 C2
Tiriez E 158 C1
Tirig E 153 B4
Tiriolo I 175 C2
Tirnavos GR 182 D4
Tirrénia I 134 B3
Tirschenreuth D 95 B4
Tirstrup DK 59 B3
Tirteafuera E 157 B3
Tisno HR 137 B4
Tišnov CZ 97 B4
Tisovec SK 99 C3
Tisselskog S 54 B3
Tistedal N 54 A2
Tistrup DK 59 C1
Tisvildeleje DK 61 C2
Tiszaalpár H 113 C3
Tiszabö H 113 B4
Tiszacsége H 113 B5
Tiszadorogma H 113 B4
Tiszaföldvár H 113 C4
Tiszafüred H 113 B4
Tiszajenö H 113 B4
Tiszakécske H 113 C4
Tiszakeszi H 113 B4
Tiszakürt H 113 C4
Tiszalök H 113 A5
Tiszalúc H 113 A5
Tiszanána H 113 B4
Tiszaörs H 113 B4
Tiszaroff H 113 B4
Tiszasüly H 113 B4
Tiszasziget H 126 A2
Tiszaszőlős H 113 B4
Tiszaújváros H 113 B5
Tiszavasvári H 113 B5
Titaguas E 159 B2
Titel SRB 126 B2
Titisee-Neustadt D 106 B3
Tito I 172 B1
Titova Korenica HR 123 C4
Titran N 198 B5
Tittling D 96 C1
Tittmoning D 109 A3
Titz D 80 A2
Tiurajärvi FIN 196 B7
Tived S 55 B5
Tiverton GB 43 B3
Tivisa E 153 A4
Tívoli I 168 B2
Tizsadob H 113 A5
Tjällmo S 56 B1
Tjåmotis S 195 D9
Tjæreborg DK 59 C1
Tjautjas S 196 B3
Tjøme N 54 A1
Tjong N 195 D4
Tjonnefoss N 53 B4
Tjörn IS 190 B5
Tjörnarp S 61 D3
Tjøtta N 195 E3
Tkon HR 137 B4
Tleń PL 68 B3
Tlmače SK 98 C2
Tłuchowo PL 77 B4
Tlumačov CZ 98 B1
Tóalmas H 112 B3
Toano I 134 A3
Toba D 82 A2
Tobarra E 158 C2
Tobermore GB 27 B4
Tobermory GB 34 B1
Toberonochy GB 34 B2
Tobha Mor GB 31 B1
Tobo S 51 B4
Tocane-St Apre F 129 A3
Tocha P 148 B1
Tocina E 162 A2
Töcksfors S 54 A2
Tocón E 163 A4
Todal N 198 C5
Todi I 136 C1
Todmorden GB 40 B1
Todorici BIH 138 A3
Todtmoos D 106 B3
Todtnau D 106 B2
Toén E 140 B3
Tofta
Gotland S 57 C4
Skaraborg S 55 B4
Toftbyn S 50 B2
Tofte N 54 A1
Töftedal S 54 B2
Tofterup DK 59 C1
Toftlund DK 59 C2
Tófü H 125 A4
Tohmo FIN 197 C10
Tokaj H 113 A5
Tokarnia PL 87 B4
Tokary PL 76 C3
Tokod H 112 B2
Tököl H 112 B2
Tolastadh bho Thuath GB 31 A2
Toledo E 151 C3
Tolentino I 136 B2
Tolfa I 168 A1
Tolg S 62 A2
Tolga N 199 C8
Tolkmicko PL 69 A4
Tollarp S 61 D3
Tollered S 60 B2
Tølløse DK 61 D1
Tolmachevo RUS 9 C6
Tolmezzo I 122 A2
Tolmin SLO 122 A2
Tolna H 112 C2
Tolnanémedi H 112 C2
Tolob GB 33 B5
Tolosa
E 144 A1
P 155 B3
Tolox E 162 B3
Tolpuddle GB 43 B4
Tolva
E 145 B4
FIN 197 C11
Tolve I 172 B2
Tomar P 154 B2
Tomaševac SRB 126 B2
Tomašica BIH 124 C2
Tomášikovo SK 111 A4
Tomašouka BY 13 C5
Tomášovce SK 99 C3
Tomaszów Mazowiecki PL 87 A4
Tomatin GB 32 D3
Tombeboeuf F 129 B3
Tomdoun GB 32 D1
Tomelilla S 66 A2
Tomellosa E 151 B5
Tomelloso E 157 A4
Tomiño E 140 C2
Tomintoul GB 32 D3
Tomislavgrad BIH 138 B3
Tomisław PL 84 A3
Tomisławice PL 76 B3
Tomnavoulin GB 32 D3
Tompa H 126 A1
Tompaládony H 111 B3
Tomra N 198 C3
Tomter N 54 A1
Tona E 147 C3
Tonara I 179 B3
Tonbridge GB 45 B4
Tondela P 148 B1
Tønder DK 64 B1
Tongeren B 79 B5
Tongue GB 32 C2
Tönisvorst D 80 A2
Tønjum N 47 A4
Tonkopuro FIN 197 C11
Tonnay-Boutonne F 114 C3
Tonnay-Charente F 114 C3
Tonneins F 129 B3
Tonnerre F 104 B2
Tonnes N 195 D4
Tönning D 64 B1
Tonsåsen N 47 B6
Tønsberg N 54 A1
Tonstad N 52 B2
Toomyvara IRL 28 B3
Toormore IRL 29 C2
Topares E 164 B2
Topas E 150 A2
Topliţa RO 17 B6
Topola SRB 127 C2
Topolčani MK 182 B3
Topol'čany SK 98 C2
Topol'čianky SK 98 C2
Topolje HR 124 B2
Topólka PL 76 B3
Topol'niky SK 111 B4
Topolovăţu Mare RO 126 B3
Toponár H 125 A3
Toporów PL 75 B4
Topsham GB 43 B3
Topusko HR 124 B1
Toques E 140 B3
Torà E 147 C2
Toral de los Guzmanes E 142 B1
Toral de los Vados E 141 B4
Torbalı TR 188 A2
Torbjörntorp S 55 B4
Torbole I 121 B3
Torchiarolo I 173 B4
Torcross GB 43 B3
Torcy-le-Petit F 89 A5
Torda SRB 126 B2
Tørdal N 53 A4
Tordehumos E 142 C1
Tordera E 147 C3
Tordesillas E 150 A2
Tordesilos E 152 B2
Töre S 196 D5
Töreboda S 55 B5
Toreby DK 65 B4
Torekov S 61 C2
Torella dei Lombardi I 170 C3
Torellò E 147 B3
Toreno E 141 B4
Torfou F 114 A2
Torgau D 83 A5
Torgelow D 74 A3
Torgueda P 148 A2
Torhamn S 63 B3
Torhop N 193 B11
Torhout B 78 A3
Torigni-sur-Vire F 88 A3
Torija E 151 B4
Toril E 152 B2
Torino = Turin I 119 B4
Toritto I 171 C4
Torkovichi RUS 9 C7
Torla E 145 B3
Tormac RO 126 B3
Törmänen FIN 193 D11
Tormestorp S 61 C3
Tórmini I 121 B3
Tornada P 154 B1
Tornal'a SK 99 C4
Tornavacas E 150 B2
Tornby DK 58 A2
Tornesch D 72 A2
Torness GB 32 D2
Torniella I 135 B4
Tornimparte I 169 A3
Torning DK 59 B2
Tornio FIN 196 D7
Tornjoš SRB 126 B1
Tornos E 152 B2
Toro E 150 A2
Törökszentmiklós H 113 B4
Toropets RUS 9 D7
Torpa S 61 C3
Torpè I 178 B3
Torphins GB 33 D4
Torpo N 47 B5
Torpoint GB 42 B2
Torpsbruk S 62 A2
Torquay GB 43 B3
Torquemada E 142 B2
Torralba de Burgo E 151 A5
Torralba de Calatrava E 157 A4
Torrão P 154 C2
Torre Annunziata I 170 C2
Torreblacos E 143 C4
Torreblanca E 153 B4
Torreblascopedro E 157 B4
Torrecaballeros E 151 A3
Torrecampo E 156 B3
Torre Canne I 173 B3
Torre Cardela E 163 A4
Torrecilla E 152 B1
Torrecilla de la Jara E 156 A3
Torrecilla de la Orden E 150 A2
Torrecilla del Pinar E 151 A3
Torrecilla en Cameros E 143 B4
Torrecillas de la Tiesa E 156 A2
Torre das Vargens P 154 B3
Torre de Coelheiros P 154 C3
Torre de Dom Chama P 149 A2
Torre de Juan Abad E 157 B4
Torre de la Higuera E 161 B3
Torre del Bierzo E 141 B4
Torre del Burgo E 151 B4
Torre del Campo E 163 A4
Torre del Greco I 170 C2
Torre del Lago Puccini I 134 B3
Torre dell'Orso I 173 B4
Torre del Mar E 163 B3
Torredembarra E 147 C2
Torre de Miguel Sesmero E 155 C4
Torre de Moncorvo P 149 A2
Torre de Santa Maria E 156 A1
Torredonjimeno E 163 A4
Torre do Terranho P 148 B2
Torre Faro I 177 A4
Torregrosa E 147 C1
Torreira P 148 B1
Torrejoncillo E 155 B4
Torrejón de Ardoz E 151 B4
Torrejón de la Calzada E 151 B4
Torrejón del Rey E 151 B4
Torrejon el Rubio E 156 A1
Torrelaguna E 151 B4
Torrelapaja E 152 A2
Torre la Ribera E 145 B4
Torrelavega E 142 A2
Torrelobatón E 150 A2
Torrelodones E 151 B4
Torre los Negros E 152 B2
Torremaggiore I 171 B3
Torremanzanas E 159 C3
Torremayor E 155 C4
Torremezzo di Falconara I 174 B2
Torremocha E 156 A1
Torremolinos E 163 B3
Torrenieri I 135 B4
Torrenostra E 153 B4
Torrenova I 168 B2
Torrent E 159 B3
Torrente de Cinca E 153 A4
Torrenueva
Ciudad Real E 157 B4
Granada E 163 B4
Torreorgaz E 155 B4
Torre Orsáia I 172 B1
Torre-Pacheco E 165 B4
Torre Péllice I 119 C4
Torreperogil E 157 B4
Torres E 163 A4
Torresandino E 143 C3
Torre Santa Susanna I 173 B3
Torres-Cabrera E 163 A3
Torres de la Alameda E 151 B4
Torres Novas P 154 B2
Torres Vedras P 154 B1
Torrevieja E 165 B4
Torricella I 173 B3
Torri del Benaco I 121 B3
Torridon GB 31 B3
Torriglia I 134 A2
Torrijos E 151 C3
Tørring DK 59 C2
Torrita di Siena I 135 B4
Torroal P 154 C2
Torroella de Montgr ì E 147 B4
Torrox E 163 B4
Torrskog S 54 A3
Torsåker S 50 B3
Torsang S 50 B2
Torsås S 63 B4
Torsby S 49 B4
Torsetra N 48 B2
Torshälla S 56 A2
Tórshavn FO 4 A3
Torslanda S 60 B1
Torsminde DK 59 B1
Torsnes N 46 B3
Törtel H 113 B3
Tórtoles E 150 B2
Tórtoles de Esgueva E 142 C2
Tortol ì I 179 C3
Tortona I 120 C1
Tórtora I 174 B1
Tortoreto Lido I 136 C2
Tortorici I 177 A3
Tortosa E 153 B4
Tortosendo P 148 B2
Tortuera E 152 B2
Tortuero E 151 B4
Toruń PL 76 A3
Torup S 60 C3
Tor Vaiánica I 168 B2
Torver GB 36 B3
Tørvikbygde N 46 B3
Torviscón E 163 B4
Torzhok RUS 9 D9
Torzym PL 75 B4
Tosbotn N 195 E3
Toscelanor-Maderno I 121 B3
Tosno RUS 9 C7
Tossa de Mar E 147 C3
Tossåsen S 199 C10
Tosse F 128 C1
Tösse S 54 B3
Tossicía I 169 A3
Tostedt D 72 A2
Tosya TR 23 A8
Tószeg H 113 B4
Toszek PL 86 B2
Totana E 165 B3
Totebo S 62 A4
Tôtes F 89 A5
Tótkomlós H 113 C4
Totland N 198 D2
Tøtlandsvik N 52 A2
Totnes GB 43 B3
Tótszerdahely H 124 A2
Tøttdal N 199 A8
Totton GB 44 C2
Touça P 149 A2

Toucy F 104 B2
Toul F 92 C1
Toulon F 132 B1
Toulon-sur-Allier F 104 C2
Toulon-sur-Arroux
F 104 C3
Toulouse F 129 C4
Tourcoing F 78 B3
Tour de la Parata F 180 B1
Tourlaville F 88 A2
Tournai B 78 B3
Tournan-en-Brie F 90 C2
Tournay F 145 A4
Tournon-d'Agenais
F 129 B3
Tournon-St Martin
F 115 B4
Tournon-sur-Rhône
F 117 B4
Tournus F 105 C3
Touro
E 140 B2
P 148 B2
Tourouvre F 89 B4
Tourriers F 115 C4
Tours F 102 B2
Tourteron F 91 B4
Tourves F 132 B1
Toury F 103 A3
Touvedo P 148 A1
Touvois F 114 B2
Toužim CZ 83 B4
Tovačov CZ 98 B1
Tovariševo SRB 126 B1
Tovarnik HR 125 B5
Tovdal N 53 B4
Towcester GB 44 A3
Town Yetholm GB 35 C5
Tråastølen N 47 B4
Trabada E 141 A3
Trabadelo E 141 B4
Trabanca E 149 A3
Trabazos E 149 A3
Traben-Trarbach D 92 B3
Trabia I 176 B2
Tradate I 120 B1
Trädet S 60 B3
Trafaria P 154 C1
Tragacete E 152 B2
Tragwein A 96 C2
Traiguera E 153 B4
Trainel F 91 C3
Traisen A 110 A2
Traismauer A 97 C3
Traitsching D 95 B4
Trákhonas CY 181 A2
Tralee IRL 29 B2
Tramacastilla de Tena
E 145 B3
Tramagal P 154 B2
Tramariglio I 178 B2
Tramatza I 179 B2
Tramelan CH 106 B2
Tramonti di Sopra
I 122 A1
Tramore IRL 30 B1
Trampot F 92 C1
Trana I 119 B4
Tranås S 55 B5
Tranbjerg DK 59 B3
Tranby N 54 A1
Trancoso P 148 B2
Tranebjerg DK 59 C3
Tranekær DK 65 B3
Tranemo S 60 B3
Tranent GB 35 C5
Tranevåg N 52 B2
Trängslet S 49 A5
Tranhult S 60 B3
Trani I 171 B4
Trans-en-Provence
F 132 B2
Transtrand S 49 A5
Tranum DK 58 A2
Tranvik S 57 A4
Trápani I 176 A1
Trappes F 90 C2
Traryd S 61 C3
Trasacco I 169 B3
Trasierra E 156 B1
Träslövsläge S 60 B2
Trasmiras E 140 B3
Traspinedo E 150 A3
Trate SLO 110 C2
Trauchgau D 108 B1
Traun A 110 A1
Traunreut D 109 B3
Traunstein D 109 B3
Traunwalchen D 109 B3
Tråvad S 55 B4
Travemünde D 65 C3
Traversétolo I 120 C3
Travnik
BIH 139 A3
SLO 123 B3
Travo
F 180 B2
I 120 C2
Trawsfynydd GB 38 B3
Trbovlje SLO 123 A4
Trbušani SRB 127 D2
Treban F 116 A3
Třebařov CZ 97 B4
Trebatsch D 74 B3
Trebbin D 74 B2
Třebechovice pod
Orebem CZ 85 B3
Trebel D 73 B4
Třebenice CZ 84 B1
Trébeurden F 100 A2
Třebíč CZ 97 B3
Trebinje BIH 139 C4
Trebisacce I 174 B2
Trebitz D 83 A4
Trebnje SLO 123 B4
Třeboň CZ 96 B2
Třebovice CZ 97 B4
Trebsen D 83 A4
Trebujena E 161 C3
Trecastagni I 177 B4
Trecate I 120 B1
Trecenta I 121 B4
Tredegar GB 39 C3
Tredózio I 135 A4
Treffen A 109 C4
Treffort F 118 A2
Treffurt D 82 A2
Trefnant GB 38 A3
Tregaron GB 39 B3
Trégastel-Plage F 100 A2
Tregnago I 121 B4
Tregony GB 42 B2
Tréguier F 100 A2
Trégunc F 100 B2
Treharris GB 39 C3
Trehörningsjö S 200 C4
Tréia I 136 B2
Treignac F 116 B1
Treignat F 116 A2
Treignes B 91 A4
Treis-Karden D 80 B3
Trekanten S 63 B4
Trélazé F 102 B1
Trelech GB 39 C2
Trélissac F 129 A3
Trelleborg S 66 A2
Trélon F 91 A4
Trélou-sur-Marne F 91 B3
Tremblay-le-Vicomte
F 89 B5
Tremés P 154 B2
Tremezzo I 120 B2
Třemošná CZ 96 B1
Tremp E 145 B4
Trenčianska Stankovce
SK 98 C1
Trenčianska Turná
SK 98 C2
Trenčianske Teplá
SK 98 C2
Trenčianske Teplice
SK 98 C2
Trenčín SK 98 C2
Trendelburg D 81 A5
Trengereid N 46 B2
Trensacq F 128 B2
Trent D 66 B2
Trento I 121 A4
Treorchy GB 39 C3
Trept F 118 B2
Trepuzzi I 173 B4
Trescore Balneário
I 120 B2
Tresenda I 120 A3
Tresfjord N 198 C4
Tresigallo I 121 C4
Trešnjevica SRB 127 D3
Tresnurághes I 178 B2
Trespaderne E 143 B3
Třešť CZ 97 B3
Trestina I 135 B5
Tretower GB 39 C3
Trets F 132 B1
Tretten N 48 A2
Treuchtlingen D 94 C2
Treuen D 83 B4
Treuenbrietzen D 74 B1
Treungen N 53 A4
Trevelez E 163 B4
Trevi I 136 C1
Treviana E 143 B3
Treviglio I 120 B2
Trevignano Romano
I 168 A2
Trevi nel Lázio I 169 B3
Treviso I 122 B1
Trévoux F 117 B4
Treysa D 81 B5
Trézelles F 117 A3
Trezzo sull'Adda I 120 B2
Trhová Kamenice
CZ 97 B3
Trhové Sviny CZ 96 C2
Triacastela E 141 B3
Triaize F 114 B2
Trianda GR 188 C3
Triaucourt-en-Argonne
F 91 C5
Tribanj Kruščica
HR 137 A4
Triberg D 106 A3
Tribsees D 66 B1
Tribuče SLO 123 B4
Tricárico I 172 B2
Tricase I 173 C4
Tricésimo I 122 A2
Trieben A 110 B1
Triebes D 83 B4
Triepkendorf D 74 A2
Trier D 92 B2
Trieste I 122 B2
Trie-sur-Baïse F 145 A4
Triggiano I 173 A2
Triglitz D 73 A5
Trignac F 101 B3
Trigueros E 161 B3
Trigueros del Valle
E 142 C2
Trikala GR 182 D3
Trikeri GR 183 D5
Trikomo CY 181 A2
Trilj HR 138 B2
Trillo E 152 B1
Trilport F 90 C2
Trim IRL 30 A2
Trimdon GB 37 B5
Trindade
Beja P 160 B2
Bragança P 149 A2
Třinec CZ 98 B2
Tring GB 44 B3
Trinità d'Agultu I 178 B2
Trinitápoli I 171 B4
Trino I 119 B5
Trinta P 148 B2
Triora I 133 B3
Tripoli GR 184 B3
Triponzo I 136 C1
Triptis D 83 B3
Triste E 144 B3
Trittau D 72 A3
Trivento I 170 B2
Trivero I 119 B5
Trivigno I 172 B1
Trn BIH 124 C3
Trnava
HR 125 B4
SK 98 C1
Trnovec SK 112 A1
Trnovo BIH 139 B4
Trnovska vas SLO 110 C2
Troarn F 89 A3
Trochtelfingen D 94 C1
Trödje S 51 B4
Troense DK 65 A3
Trofa P 148 A1
Trofaiach A 110 B2
Trofors N 195 E4
Trogir HR 138 B2
Trøgstad N 54 A2
Tróia I 171 B3
Troia P 154 C2
Troina I 177 B3
Troisdorf D 80 B3
Trois-Ponts B 80 B1
Troisvierges L 92 A2
Trojane SLO 123 A3
Troldhede DK 59 C1
Trollhättan S 54 B3
Trolog BIH 138 B2
Tromello I 120 B1
Tromøy N 53 B4
Tromsø N 192 C3
Trondheim N 199 B7
Tronget F 116 A3
Trönninge S 61 C2
Trönningeby S 60 B2
Trönö S 51 A3
Tronzano-Vercellese
I 119 B5
Trôo F 102 B2
Troon GB 36 A2
Tropea I 175 C1
Tropy Sztumskie PL 69 B4
Trosa S 57 B3
Trösken S 50 B3
Trosly-Breuil F 90 B3
Trossingen D 107 A3
Trostberg D 109 A3
Trouville-sur-Mer F 89 A4
Trowbridge GB 43 A4
Troyes F 104 A3
Trpanj HR 138 B3
Trpinja HR 125 B4
Tršće HR 123 B3
Tršice CZ 98 B1
Trstená SK 99 B3
Trstenci BIH 125 B3
Trsteno HR 139 C3
Trstice SK 111 A4
Trstín SK 98 C1
Trubia E 141 A5
Trubjela MNE 139 C4
Truchas E 141 B4
Trujillanos E 155 C4
Trujillo E 156 A2
Trumieje PL 69 B4
Trun
CH 107 C3
F 89 B4
Truro GB 42 B1
Trusetal D 82 B2
Truskavets' UA 13 D5
Trustrup DK 59 B3
Trutnov CZ 85 B3
Tryserum S 56 B2
Trysil N 49 A4
Tryszczyn PL 76 A2
Trzcianka PL 75 A5
Trzciel PL 75 B4
Trzcińsko Zdrój PL 74 B3
Trzebiatów PL 67 B4
Trzebiel PL 84 A2
Trzebielino PL 68 A2
Trzebień PL 84 A3
Trzebiez PL 74 A3
Trzebinia PL 86 B3
Trzebnica PL 85 A5
Trzebnice PL 85 A4
Trzeciewiec PL 76 A3
Trzemeszno PL 76 B2
Trzemeszno-Lubuskie
PL 75 B4
Trzetrzewina PL 99 B4
Tržič SLO 123 A3
Tsamandas GR 182 D2
Tschagguns A 107 B4
Tschernitz D 84 A2
Tsebrykove UA 17 B9
Tsyelyakhany BY 13 B6
Tua P 148 A2
Tuam IRL 28 A3
Tubbercurry IRL 26 B2
Tubbergen NL 71 B3
Tubilla del Lago E 143 C3
Tübingen D 93 C5
Tubize B 79 B4
Tučapy CZ 96 B2
Tučepi HR 138 B3
Tuchan F 146 B3
Tüchen D 73 A5
Tuchola PL 76 A2
Tuchomie PL 68 A2
Tuchów PL 99 B5
Tuczno PL 75 A5
Tuddal N 53 A4
Tudela E 144 B2
Tudela de Duero E 150 A3
Tudweiliog GB 38 B2
Tuejar E 159 B2
Tuffé F 102 A2
Tufsingdalen N 199 C8
Tuhaň CZ 84 B2
Tui E 140 B2
Tukhkala RUS 197 D13
Tukums LV 8 D3
Tula I 178 B2
Tulcea RO 17 C8
Tul'chyn UA 13 D8
Tulette F 131 A3
Tuliszków PL 76 B3
Tulla IRL 28 B3
Tullamore IRL 30 A1
Tulle F 116 B1
Tullins F 118 B2
Tulln A 97 C4
Tullow IRL 30 B2
Tułowice PL 85 B5
Tulppio FIN 197 B12
Tulsk IRL 28 A3
Tumba S 57 A3
Tummel Bridge GB 35 B3
Tun S 55 B3
Tuna
Kalmar S 62 A4
Uppsala S 51 B5
Tuna Hästberg S 50 B2
Tunçbilek TR 187 C4
Tunes P 160 B1
Tungelsta S 57 A4
Tunnerstad S 55 B5
Tunnhovd N 47 B5
Tunstall GB 45 A5
Tuohikotti FIN 8 B5
Tuoro sul Trasimeno
I 135 B5
Tupadły PL 76 B3
Tupanari BIH 139 A4
Tupik RUS 9 E8
Tuplice PL 84 A2
Tura H 112 B3
Turanj HR 137 B4
Turany SK 99 B3
Turbe BIH 139 A3
Turbenthal CH 107 B3
Turcia E 141 B5
Turčianske Teplice
SK 98 C2
Turcifal P 154 B1
Turckheim F 106 A2
Turda RO 17 B5
Turégano E 151 A4
Turek PL 76 B3
Tŭrgovishte BG 17 D7
Turgutlu TR 188 A2
Turi I 173 B3
Turin = Torino I 119 B4
Turis E 159 B3
Türje H 111 C4
Turka UA 12 D5
Túrkeve H 113 B4
Türkheim D 108 A1
Türkmenli TR 186 C1
Turku FIN 8 B3
Turleque E 157 A4
Turňa nad Bodvou
SK 99 C4
Turnberry GB 36 A2
Turnhout B 79 A4
Türnitz A 110 B2
Turnov CZ 84 B3
Turnu RO 126 A3
Turnu Măgurele RO 17 D6
Turón E 164 C1
Turoszów PL 84 B2
Turowo PL 77 A5
Turquel P 154 B1
Turri I 179 C2
Turries F 132 A2
Turriff GB 33 D4
Tursi I 174 A2
Turtmann CH 119 A4
Turtola FIN 196 C6
Turze PL 86 A1
Turzovka SK 98 B2
Tusa I 177 B3
Tuscánia I 168 A1
Tuse DK 61 D1
Tušilovic HR 123 B4
Tuszyn PL 86 A3
Tutow D 66 C2
Tutrakan BG 17 C7
Tuttlingen D 107 B3
Tutzing D 108 B2
Tuzla
BIH 125 C4
TR 23 C8
Tuzlukçu TR 189 A6
Tvååker S 60 B2
Tvärålund S 200 B5
Tvärskog S 63 B4
Tvedestrand N 53 B4
Tveit
Hordaland N 47 B4
Rogaland N 52 A2
Tver RUS 9 D9
Tverrelvmo N 192 D3
Tversted DK 58 A3
Tving S 63 B3
Tvrdošin SK 99 B3
Tvrdošovce SK 112 A2
Twardogóra PL 85 A5
Twatt GB 33 B3
Twello NL 70 B3
Twimberg A 110 C1
Twist D 71 B4
Twistringen D 72 B1
Tworóg PL 86 B2
Twyford
Hampshire GB 44 B2
Wokingham GB 44 B3
Tyachiv UA 17 A5
Tychówka PL 67 C5
Tychowo PL 67 C5
Tychy PL 86 B2
Tydal N 199 B8
Týec nad Labem CZ 97 A3
Tyfors S 49 B6
Tygelsjö S 61 D2
Tylldal N 199 C7
Tylstrup DK 58 A2
Tymbark PL 99 B4
Tymowa PL 99 B4
Tyndrum GB 34 B3
Týnec nad Sázavou
CZ 96 B2
Tynemouth GB 37 A5
Tyngsjö S 49 B5
Týniště nad Orlicí
CZ 85 B4
Týn nad Vltavou CZ 96 B2
Tynset N 199 C7
Tyresö S 57 A4
Tyringe S 61 C3
Tyrislöt S 56 B2
Tyristrand N 48 B2
Tyrrellspass IRL 30 A1
Tysnes N 46 B2
Tysse N 46 B2
Tyssebotn N 46 B2
Tyssedal N 46 B3
Tystberga S 56 B3
Tysvær N 52 A1
Tywyn GB 39 B2
Tzermiado GR 185 D6
Tzummarum NL 70 A2

U

Ub SRB 127 C2
Ubby DK 61 D1
Úbeda E 157 B4
Überlingen D 107 B4
Ubidea E 143 A4
Ubli HR 138 C2
Ubrique E 162 B2
Ucero E 143 C3
Uchaud F 131 B3
Uchte D 72 B1
Uckerath D 80 B3
Uckfield GB 45 C4
Ucklum S 54 B2
Uclés E 151 C5
Ucria I 177 A3
Udbina HR 137 A4
Uddebo S 60 B3
Uddeholm S 49 B5
Uddevalla S 54 B2
Uddheden S 49 C4
Uden NL 80 A1
Uder D 82 A2
Udiča SK 98 B2
Údine I 122 A2
Udvar H 125 B4
Ueckermünde D 74 A3
Uelsen D 71 B3
Uelzen D 73 B3
Uetendorf CH 106 C2
Uetersen D 72 A2
Uetze D 72 B3
Uffculme GB 43 B3
Uffenheim D 94 B2
Ugarana E 143 A4
Ugento I 173 C4
Ugerldse DK 61 D1
Uggerby DK 58 A3
Uggerslev DK 59 C3
Uggiano la Chiesa
I 173 B4
Ugíjar E 164 C1
Ugine F 118 B3
Uglejevik BIH 125 C5
Uglenes N 46 B2
Uglich RUS 9 D11
Ugljane HR 138 B2
Ugod H 111 B4
Uherské Hradiště
CZ 98 B1
Uherský Brod CZ 98 B1
Uherský Ostroh CZ 98 C1
Uhingen D 94 C1
Uhlířské-Janovice
CZ 96 B3
Uhřiněves CZ 96 A2
Uhyst D 84 A2
Uig GB 31 B2
Uitgeest NL 70 B1
Uithoorn NL 70 B1
Uithuizen NL 71 A3
Uithuizermeeden NL 71 A3
Uivar RO 126 B2
Ujazd
Łódzkie PL 87 A3
Opolskie PL 86 B2
Ujezd u Brna CZ 97 B4
Ujhartyán H 112 B3
Újkígyós H 113 C5
Ujpetre H 125 B4
Ujście PL 75 A5
Ujsolt H 112 C3
Újszász H 113 B4
Újszentmargita H 113 B5
Ujué E 144 B2
Ukanc SLO 122 A2
Ukmergė LT 13 A6
Ukna S 56 B2
Ula TR 188 B3
Ul'anka SK 99 C3
Ulaş TR 186 A2
Ulássai I 179 C3
Ulbjerg DK 58 B2
Ulbster GB 32 C3
Ulceby GB 40 B3
Ulcinj MNE 16 E3
Uldum DK 59 C2
Ulefoss N 53 A5
Uleila del Campo E 164 B2
Ulëz AL 182 B1
Ulfborg DK 59 B1
Uljma SRB 127 B3
Ullånger S 200 C4
Ullapool GB 32 D1
Ullared S 60 B2
Ullatti S 196 B4
Ullatun N 52 A2
Ulldecona E 153 B4
Ulldemolins E 147 C1
Ullerslev DK 59 C3
Ullervad S 55 B4
Üllés H 126 A1
Üllő H 112 B3
Ulm D 94 C1
Ulme P 154 B2
Ulmen D 80 B2
Ulnes N 47 B6
Ulog BIH 139 B4
Ulricehamn S 60 B3
Ulrichstein D 81 B5
Ulrika S 56 B1
Ulriksfors S 200 C1
Ulrum NL 71 A3
Ulsberg N 198 C6
Ulsta GB 33 A5
Ulsted DK 58 A3
Ulsteinvik N 198 C2
Ulstrup
Vestsjællands Amt.
DK 59 C3
Viborg Amt. DK 59 B2
Ulsvåg N 194 B6
Ulubey TR 188 A4
Uluborlu TR 189 A5
Ulukışla TR 23 C8
Ulverston GB 36 B3
Ulvik N 46 B3
Umag HR 122 B2
Uman UA 13 D9
Umba RUS 3 C14
Umbértide I 135 B5
Umbriático I 174 B2
Umčari SRB 127 C2
Umeå S 200 C6
Umgransele S 200 B4
Umhausen A 108 B1
Umka SRB 127 C2
Umljanovic HR 138 B2
Umnäs S 195 E7
Umurbey TR 186 B1
Unaðsdalur IS 190 A3
Unapool GB 32 C1
Unari FIN 197 B8
Unbyn S 196 D4
Uncastillo E 144 B2
Undenäs S 55 B5
Undersaker S 199 B10
Undredal N 46 B4
Unešić HR 138 B2
Úněšov CZ 96 B1
Ungheni MD 17 B7
Unhais da Serra P 148 B2
Unhošť CZ 84 B2
Unichowo PL 68 A2
Uničov CZ 98 B1
Uniejów PL 76 C3
Unisław PL 76 A3
Unkel D 80 B3
Unken A 109 B3
Unna D 81 A3
Unnaryd S 60 C3
Unquera E 142 A2
Unterach A 109 B4
Unterägeri CH 107 B3
Unterammergau D 108 B2
Unterhaching D 108 A2

Unteriberg CH 107 B3
Unterkochen D 94 C2
Unter Langkampfen A 108 B3
Unterlaussa A 110 B1
Unterlüss D 72 B3
Untermünkheim D 94 B1
Unterschächen CH 107 C3
Unterschleissheim D 95 C3
Unterschwaningen D 94 B2
Untersiemau D 82 B2
Unter-steinbach D 94 B2
Unterweissenbach A 96 C2
Unterzell D 95 B4
Upavon GB 44 B2
Úpice CZ 85 B4
Upiłka PL 68 B2
Upphärad S 54 B3
Uppingham GB 40 C3
Upplands-Väsby S 57 A3
Uppsala S 51 C4
Uppsjøhytta N 48 A1
Upton-upon-Severn GB 39 B4
Ur F 146 B2
Uras I 179 C2
Uraz PL 85 A4
Urbánia I 136 B1
Urbino I 136 B1
Urçay F 103 C4
Urda E 157 A4
Urdax E 144 A2
Urdilde E 140 B2
Urdos F 145 B3
Urk NL 70 B2
Úrkút H 111 B4
Urla TR 188 A1
Urlingford IRL 30 B1
Urnäsch CH 107 B4
Urnes N 47 A4
Uroševac KOS 16 D4
Urracal E 164 B2
Urries E 144 B2
Urroz E 144 B2
Ursensollen D 95 B3
Urshult S 63 B2
Uršna Sela SLO 123 B4
Urszulewo PL 77 B4
Ury F 90 C2
Urziceni RO 17 C7
Urzulei I 178 B3
Usagre E 156 B1
Uşak TR 187 D4
Usedom D 66 C2
Useldange L 92 B1
Uséllus I 179 C2
Ushakovo RUS 69 A5
Usingen D 81 B4
Usini I 178 B2
Usk GB 39 C4
Uskedal N 46 C2
Üsküdar TR 186 A4
Uslar D 82 A1
Úsov CZ 97 B5
Usquert NL 71 A3
Ussássai I 179 C3
Ussé F 102 B2
Usséglio I 119 B4
Ussel
Cantal F 116 B2
Corrèze F 116 B2
Usson-du-Poitou F 115 B4
Usson-en-Forez F 117 B3
Usson-les-Bains F 146 B3
Ustaoset N 47 B5
Ustaritz F 144 A2
Uštěk CZ 84 B2
Uster CH 107 B3
Ústi CZ 98 B1
Ustikolina BIH 139 B4
Ústínad Labem CZ 84 B2
Ústínad Orlicí CZ 97 B4
Ustipračà BIH 139 B5
Ustka PL 68 A1
Ust Luga RUS 8 C6
Ustroń PL 98 B2
Ustronie Morskie PL 67 B4
Ustyuzhna RUS 9 C10
Uszód H 112 C2
Utåker N 52 A1
Utansjö S 200 D3
Utebo E 152 A3
Utena LT 13 A6
Utery CZ 95 B5
Uthaug N 198 B6
Utiel E 159 B2
Utne N 46 B3
Utö S 57 B4
Utrecht NL 70 B2
Utrera E 162 A2
Utrillas E 153 B3
Utsjoki FIN 193 C11
Utstein kloster N 52 A1
Uttendorf A 109 B3
Uttenweiler D 107 A4
Utterslev DK 65 B4
Uttoxeter GB 40 C2
Utvälinge S 61 C2
Utvorda N 199 A7
Uusikaarlepyy FIN 3 E8
Uusikaupunki FIN 8 B2
Uvaly CZ 96 A2
Uvdal N 47 B5
Uza F 128 B1
Uzdin SRB 126 B2
Uzdowo PL 77 A5
Uzein F 145 A3
Uzel F 100 A3
Uzerche F 116 B1
Uzès F 131 A3
Uzhhorod UA 12 D5
Uzhok UA 12 D5
Užice SRB 127 D1
Uznach CH 107 B3
Üzümlü
Konya TR 189 B6
Muğla TR 188 C4
Uzunköprü TR 186 A1

V

Vaalajärvi FIN 197 B9
Vaas F 102 B2
Vaasa FIN 8 A2
Vaasen NL 70 B2
Vabre F 130 B1
Vác H 112 B3
Vacha D 82 B2
Váchartyán H 112 B3
Väckelsång S 63 B2
Vacqueyras F 131 A3
Vad S 50 B2
Vada I 134 B3
Väddö S 51 C5
Väderstad S 55 B5
Vadheim N 46 A2
Vadillo de la Sierra E 150 B2
Vadillos E 152 B1
Vadla N 52 A2
Vado I 135 A4
Vado Lígure I 133 A4
Vadsø N 193 B13
Vadstena S 55 B5
Vadum DK 58 A2
Vaduz FL 107 B4
Vafos N 53 B5
Vág H 111 B4
Vågåmo N 198 D6
Væggerløse DK 65 B4
Vaggeryd S 62 A2
Vaghia GR 184 A4
Vaglia I 135 B4
Váglio Basilicata I 172 B1
Vagney F 106 A1
Vagnhärad S 57 B3
Vagnsunda S 57 A4
Vagos P 148 B1
Vai GR 185 D7
Vaiano I 135 B4
Vaiges F 102 A1
Vaihingen D 93 C4
Vaillant F 105 B4
Vailly-sur-Aisne F 91 B3
Vailly-sur Sauldre F 103 B4
Vairano Scalo I 170 B2
Vaison-la-Romaine F 131 A4
Vaite F 105 B4
Väjern S 54 B2
Vajszló H 125 B3
Vaksdal N 46 B2
Vál H 112 B2
Valaam RUS 9 B7
Valada P 154 B2
Vålådalen S 199 B10
Valadares P 148 A1
Valado P 154 B1
Valandovo MK 182 B4
Valaská SK 99 C3
Valaská Belá SK 98 C2
Valaská Dubová SK 99 B3
Valašská Polanka CZ 98 B1
Valašské Klobouky CZ 98 B2
Valašské Meziříčí CZ 98 B1
Valberg F 132 A2
Vålberg S 55 A4
Valbo S 51 B4
Valbom P 148 A1
Valbondione I 120 A3
Valbonnais F 118 C2
Valbuena de Duero E 142 C2
Vălcani RO 126 B2
Valdagno I 121 B4
Valdahon F 105 B5
Valdaracete E 151 B4
Valday RUS 9 D8
Valdealgorfa E 153 B3
Valdecaballeros E 156 A2
Valdecabras E 152 B1
Valdecarros E 150 B2
Valdeconcha E 151 B5
Valdeflores E 161 B3
Valdefresno E 142 B1
Valdeganga E 158 B2
Valdelacasa E 150 B2
Valdelacasa de Tajo E 156 A2
Valdelarco E 161 B3
Valdelosa E 149 A4
Valdeltormo E 153 B4
Valdelugeros E 142 B1
Valdemanco de Esteras E 156 B3
Valdemarsvik S 56 B2
Valdemorillo E 151 B3
Valdemoro E 151 B4
Valdemoro Sierra E 152 B2
Valdenoceda E 143 B3
Valdeobispo E 149 B3
Valdeolivas E 152 B1
Valdepeñas E 157 B4
Valdepeñas de Jaén E 163 A4
Valdepiélago E 142 B1
Valdepolo E 142 B1
Valderas E 142 B1
Valdérice I 176 A1
Valderrobres E 153 B4
Valderrueda E 142 B2
Val de San Lorenzo E 141 B4
Val de Santo Domingo E 150 B3
Val d'Esquières F 132 B2
Valdestillas E 150 A3
Valdetorres E 156 B1
Valdetorres de Jarama E 151 B4
Valdeverdeja E 150 C2
Valdevimbre E 142 B1
Valdieri I 133 A3
Valdilecha E 151 B4
Val-d'Isère F 119 B3
Valdobbiádene I 121 B4
Valdocondes E 143 C3
Valdoviño E 140 A2
Valea lui Mihai RO 16 B5
Vale de Açor
Beja P 160 B2
Portalegre P 154 B3
Vale de Agua P 160 B1
Vale de Cambra P 148 B1
Vale de Lobo P 160 B1
Vale de Prazeres P 148 B2
Vale de Reis P 154 C2
Vale de Rosa P 160 B2
Vale de Santarém P 154 B2
Vale de Vargo P 160 B2
Vale do Peso P 155 B3
Valega P 148 B1
Valéggio sul Mincio I 121 B3
Valeiro P 154 C2
Valença P 140 B2
Valençay F 103 B3
Valence
Charente F 115 C4
Drôme F 117 C4
Valence d'Agen F 129 B3
Valence d'Albigeois F 130 A1
Valence-sur-Baise F 129 C3
Valencia E 159 B3
Valencia de Alcántara E 155 B3
Valencia de Don Juan E 142 B1
Valencia de las Torres E 156 B1
Valencia del Ventoso E 161 A3
Valencia de Mombuey E 161 A2
Valenciennes F 79 B3
Valensole F 132 B1
Valentano I 168 A1
Valentigney F 106 B1
Valentine F 145 A4
Valenza I 120 B1
Valenzuela E 163 A3
Valenzuela de Calatrava E 157 B4
Våler
Hedmark N 48 B3
Østfold N 54 A1
Valera de Abajo E 158 B1
Valeria E 158 B1
Valestrand N 52 A1
Valestrandsfossen N 46 B2
Valevåg N 52 A1
Valfabbrica I 136 B1
Valflaunes F 131 B2
Valga EST 8 D5
Valgorge F 131 A3
Valgrisenche I 119 B4
Valguarnera Caropepe I 177 B3
Valhelhas P 148 B2
Valjevo SRB 127 C1
Valka LV 8 D4
Valkeakoski FIN 8 B4
Valkenburg NL 80 B1
Valkenswaard NL 79 A5
Valkó H 112 B3
Valla S 56 A2
Vallada E 159 C3
Vallado E 141 A4
Valladolid E 150 A3
Vallåkra S 61 D2
Vallata I 172 A1
Vallberga S 61 C3
Vall d'Alba E 153 B3
Valldemossa E 166 B2
Valle N 52 A3
Valle Castellana I 136 C2
Valle de Abdalajís E 163 B3
Valle de Cabuérniga E 142 A2
Valle de la Serena E 156 B2
Valle de Matamoros E 155 C4
Valle de Santa Ana E 155 C4
Valledolmo I 176 B2
Valledoria I 178 B2
Vallelado E 150 A3
Vallelunga Pratameno I 176 B2
Valle Mosso I 119 B5
Vallendar D 81 B3
Vallentuna S 57 A4
Vallerås S 49 B5
Valleraugue F 130 A2
Vallermosa I 179 C2
Vallet F 101 B4
Valletta M 175 C3
Valley GB 38 A2
Vallfogona de Riucorb E 147 C2
Valli del Pasúbio I 121 B4
Vallo della Lucánia I 172 B1
Valloire F 118 B3
Vallombrosa I 135 B4
Vallon-Pont-d'Arc F 131 A3
Vallorbe CH 105 C5
Vallouise F 118 C3
Valls E 147 C2
Vallset N 48 B3
Vallsta S 50 A3
Vallstena S 57 C4
Valmadrid E 153 A3
Valmiera LV 8 D4
Valmojado E 151 B3
Valmont F 89 A4
Valmontone I 169 B2
Valö S 51 B5
Valognes F 88 A2
Valonga P 148 B1
Valongo P 148 A1
Válor E 164 C1
Valoria la Buena E 142 C2
Valøy N 199 A7
Valozhyn BY 13 A7
Valpaços P 148 A2
Valpelline I 119 B4
Valpiana I 135 B3
Valpovo HR 125 B4
Valras-Plage F 130 B2
Valréas F 131 A3
Vals CH 107 C4
Valsavarenche I 119 B4
Vålse DK 65 B4
Valsequillo E 156 B2
Valsjöbyn S 199 A11
Vals-les-Bains F 117 C4
Valsonne F 117 B4
Valstagna I 121 B4
Val-Suzon F 105 B3
Valtablado del Rio E 152 B1
Valþjofsstaður IS 191 B11
Val Thorens F 118 B3
Valtice CZ 97 C4
Valtiendas E 151 A4
Valtierra E 144 B2
Valtopina I 136 B1
Valtorta I 120 B2
Valtournenche I 119 B4
Valverde E 144 C2
Valverde de Burguillos E 155 C4
Valverde de Júcar E 158 B1
Valverde de la Vera E 150 B2
Valverde de la Virgen E 142 B1
Valverde del Camino E 161 B3
Valverde del Fresno E 149 B3
Valverde de Llerena E 156 B2
Valverde de Mérida E 156 B1
Valvträsk S 196 C4
Vamberk CZ 85 B4
Vamdrup DK 59 C2
Våmhus S 50 A1
Vamlingbo S 57 D4
Vammala FIN 8 B3
Vamos GR 185 D5
Vámosmikola H 112 B2
Vámosszabadi H 111 B4
Vanault-les-Dames F 91 C4
Vandel DK 59 C2
Vandenesse F 104 C2
Vandenesse-en-Auxois F 104 B3
Vandóies I 108 C2
Väne-Åsaka S 54 B3
Vänersborg S 54 B3
Vänersnäs S 54 B3
Vang N 47 A5
Vänge S 51 C4
Vangsnes N 46 A3
Vänjaurbäck S 200 B4
Vännacka S 54 A3
Vannareid N 192 B3
Vännäs S 200 C5
Vannes F 101 B3
Vannsätter S 51 A3
Vannvåg N 192 B3
Vansbro S 49 B6
Vanse N 52 B2
Vantaa FIN 8 B4
Vanttauskoski FIN 197 C9
Vanviken N 199 B7
Vanyarc H 112 B3
Vaour F 129 B4
Vapnyarka UA 13 D8
Vaprio d'Adda I 120 B2
Vaqueiros P 160 B2
Vara S 55 B3
Varacieux F 118 B2
Varades F 101 B4
Varages F 132 B1
Varaldsøy N 46 B2
Varallo I 119 B5
Varangerbotn N 193 B12
Varano de'Melegari I 120 C3
Varaždin HR 124 A2
Varaždinske Toplice HR 124 A2
Varazze I 133 A4
Varberg S 60 B2
Vardal N 48 B2
Varde DK 59 C1
Vårdö FIN 51 B7
Vardø N 193 B15
Vardomb H 125 A4
Varejoki FIN 196 C7
Varel D 71 A5
Varėna LT 13 A6
Vårenes N 52 A1
Varengeville-sur-Mer F 89 A4
Varenna I 120 A2
Varennes-en-Argonne F 91 B5
Varennes-le-Grand F 105 C3
Varennes-St Sauveur F 105 C4
Varennes-sur-Allier F 117 A3
Varennes-sur-Amance F 105 B4
Vareš BIH 139 A4
Varese I 120 B1
Varese Ligure I 134 A2
Vârfurile RO 16 B5
Vårgårda S 60 A2
Vargas
E 143 A3
P 154 B2
Vargön S 54 B3
Varhaug N 52 B1
Variaş RO 126 A2
Variaşu Mic RO 126 A3
Varilhes F 146 A2
Varin SK 98 B2
Väring S 55 B4
Váriz P 149 A3
Varkaus FIN 8 A5
Varmahlíð IS 190 B6
Varmaland IS 190 C4
Värmlands Bro S 55 A4
Värmskog S 55 A3
Varna
BG 17 D7
SRB 127 C1
Värnamo S 60 B4
Varnhem S 55 B4
Varnsdorf CZ 84 B2
Värö S 60 B2
Varoška Rijeka BIH 124 B2
Városlöd H 111 B4
Várpalota H 112 B2
Varreddes F 90 C2
Vars F 118 C3
Varsi I 120 C2
Varsseveld NL 71 C3
Vårsta S 57 A3
Vartdal N 198 C3
Vartofta S 55 B4
Vårvik S 54 A3
Várvölgy H 111 C4
Varzi I 120 C2
Varzjelas P 148 B1
Varzo I 119 A5
Varzy F 104 B2
Vasad H 112 B3
Väse S 55 A4
Vašica SRB 125 B5
Vasilevichi BY 13 B8
Väskinde S 57 C4
Vaskút H 125 A4
Vaslui RO 17 B7
Vassbotn N 53 B4
Vassenden N 47 A6
Vassieux-en-Vercors F 118 C2
Vassmolösa S 63 B4
Vassy F 88 B3
Västansjö S 195 E6
Västanvik S 50 B1
Västerås S 56 A2
Västerby S 50 B2
Västerfärnebo S 50 C3
Västergarn S 57 C4
Västerhaninge S 57 A4
Västervik S 62 A4
Vasto I 170 A2
Västra Ämtervik S 55 A4
Västra-Bodarne S 60 B2
Västra Karup S 61 C2
Vasvár H 111 B3
Vasylkiv UA 13 C9
Vát H 111 B3
Vatan F 103 B3
Väte S 57 C4
Vathia GR 184 C3
Vatican City = Cittádel Vaticano I 168 B2
Vatili CY 181 A2
Vatin SRB 126 B3
Vatland N 52 B3
Vatnar N 53 A5
Vatnås N 48 C1
Vatne N 53 B3
Vatnestrøm N 53 B4
Vätö S 51 C5
Vatra-Dornei RO 17 B6
Vatry F 91 C4
Vattholma S 51 B4
Vättis CH 107 C4
Vauchamps F 91 C3
Vauchassis F 104 A2
Vaucouleurs F 92 C1
Vaudoy-en-Brie F 90 C3
Vaulen N 52 B1
Vaulruz CH 106 C1
Vaulx Vraucourt F 90 A2
Vaumas F 104 C2
Vausseroux F 115 B3
Vauvenargues F 132 B1
Vauvert F 131 B3
Vauvillers F 105 B5
Vaux-sur-Sure B 92 B1
Vawkavysk BY 13 B6
Vaxholm S 57 A4
Växjö S 62 B2
Våxtorp S 61 C3
Vayrac F 129 B4
Važec SK 99 B3
Veberöd S 61 D3
Vechelde D 72 B3
Vechta D 71 B5
Vecinos E 149 B4
Vecsés H 112 B3
Vedavågen N 52 A1
Veddige S 60 B2
Vedersø DK 59 B1
Vedeseta I 120 B2
Vedevåg S 56 A1
Vedra E 140 B2
Vedum S 55 B3
Veendam NL 71 A3
Veenendaal NL 70 B2
Vega
Asturias E 142 A1
Asturias E 142 A1
Vega de Espinareda E 141 B4
Vega de Infanzones E 142 B1
Vegadeo E 141 A3
Vega de Pas E 143 A3
Vega de Valcarce E 141 B4
Vega de Valdetronco E 150 A2
Vegårshei N 53 B4
Vegas de Coria E 149 B3
Vegas del Condado E 142 B1
Vegby S 60 B3
Vegger DK 58 B2
Veggli N 47 B6
Veghel NL 80 A1
Veglast D 66 B1
Véglie I 173 B3
Veguillas E 151 B4
Vegusdal N 53 B4
Veidholmen N 198 B4
Veidnes N 193 B10
Veikåker N 48 B1
Veinge S 61 C3
Vejbystrand S 61 C2
Vejen DK 59 C2
Vejer de la Frontera E 162 B2
Vejle DK 59 C2
Vejprty CZ 83 B5
Velada E 150 B3
Vela Luka HR 138 C2
Velayos E 150 B3
Velbert D 80 A3
Velburg D 95 B3
Velde N 199 A8
Velden
Bayern D 95 B3
Bayern D 95 C4
Velden am Worther See A 109 C5
Velefique E 164 B2
Velen D 80 A2
Velenje SLO 123 A4
Veles MK 182 B3
Velesevec HR 124 B2
Velešin CZ 96 C2
Velestino GR 182 D4
Velez Blanco E 164 B2
Vélez de Benaudalla E 163 B4
Vélez-Málaga E 163 B3
Vélez Rubio E 164 B2
Veliiki Radinci SRB 127 B1
Velika HR 125 B3
Velika Gorica HR 124 B2

Velika Grdevac HR 124 B3
Velika Greda SRB 126 B3
Velika Ilova BIH 125 C3
Velika Kladuša BIH 124 B1
Velika Kopanica HR 125 B4
Velika Krsna SRB 127 C2
Velika Obarska BIH 125 C5
Velika Pisanica HR 124 B3
Velika Plana SRB 127 C3
Velika Zdenci HR 124 B3
Velike Lašče SLO 123 B3
Velike Središte SRB 126 B3
Veliki Gaj SRB 126 B3
Veliki Popović SRB 127 C3
Velikiye Luki RUS 9 D7
Veliko Gradište SRB 127 C3
Veliko Orašje SRB 127 C3
Veliko Selo SRB 127 C3
Veliko Tŭrnovo BG 17 D6
Velilla del Río Carrió E 142 B2
Velilla de San Antonio E 151 B4
Veli Lošinj HR 137 A3
Velingrad BG 183 A5
Velizh RUS 9 E7
Veljun HR 123 B4
Velká Bíteš CZ 97 B4
Velka Hled'scbe CZ 95 B4
Velká Lomnica SK 99 B4
Velkánad Veličkou CZ 98 C1
Velké Bystřice CZ 98 B1
Velké Heraltice CZ 98 B1
Velké Karlovice CZ 98 B2
Vel'ke'Kostol'any SK 98 C1
Vel'ké Leváre SK 97 C5
Velké Losiny CZ 98 A1
Velké Meziříčí CZ 97 B4
Velké Pavlovice CZ 97 C4
Vel'ké Rovné SK 98 B2
Vel'ké Uherce SK 98 C2
Vel'ké Zálužie SK 98 C1
Vel'ký Blahovo SK 99 C4
Velky Bor CZ 96 B1
Vel'ký Cetin SK 112 A2
Vel'ký Krtíš SK 112 A3
Vel'ký Meder SK 111 B4
Velky Ujezd CZ 98 B1
Vellahn D 73 A3
Vellberg D 94 B1
Velles F 103 C3
Velletri I 168 B2
Vellinge S 66 A2
Vellisca E 151 B5
Velliza E 150 A3
Vellmar D 81 A5
Velp NL 70 B2
Velten D 74 B2
Velvary CZ 84 B2
Velvendos GR 182 C4
Vemb DK 59 B1
Vemdalen S 199 C10
Veme N 48 B2
Véménd H 125 A4
Vemmedrup DK 61 D2
Vena S 62 A3
Venaco F 180 A2
Venafro I 169 B4
Venarey-les-Laumes F 104 B3
Venaría I 119 B4
Venasca I 133 A3
Venčane SRB 127 C2
Vence F 132 B3
Venda Nova
Coimbra P 154 A2
Leiria P 154 B2
Vendas Novas P 154 C2
Vendays-Montalivet F 114 C2
Vendel S 51 B4
Vendelso S 57 A4
Vendouil F 91 B3
Vendeuvre-sur-Barse F 104 A3
Vendoeuvres F 115 B5
Vendôme F 103 B3
Venelles F 131 B4
Veness GB 33 B4
Venézia = Venice I 122 B1
Venialbo E 150 A2
Venice = Venézia I 122 B1
Vénissieux F 117 B4
Venjan S 49 B5
Venlo NL 80 A2
Vennesla N 53 B3
Vennesund N 195 E3
Vennezey F 92 C2
Venn Green GB 42 B2
Venosa I 172 B1
Venray NL 80 A1
Vent A 108 C1
Venta de Baños E 142 C2
Venta del Moro E 158 B2
Venta de los Santos E 157 B4
Venta las Ranas E 142 A1
Ventanueva E 141 A4
Ventas de Huelma E 163 A4
Ventas de Zafarraya E 163 B3
Ventavon F 132 A1
Ventimíglia I 133 B3
Ventnor GB 44 C2
Ventosa de la Sierra E 143 C4
Ventosilla E 143 C4
Ventspils LV 8 D2
Venturina I 134 B3
Venzolasca F 180 A2
Venzone I 122 A2
Vép H 111 B3
Vera
E 164 B3
N 199 B9
Vera Cruz P 160 A2
Vera de Bidasoa E 144 A2
Vera de Moncayo E 144 C2
Verbánia I 119 B5
Verberie F 90 B2
Verbicaro I 174 B1
Verbier CH 119 A4
Vercelli I 119 B5
Vercel-Villedieu-le-Camp F 105 B5
Verchen D 66 C1
Vercheny F 118 C2
Verclause F 131 A4
Verdalsøra N 199 B8
Verden D 72 B2
Verdens Ende N 54 A1
Verdikoussa GR 182 D3
Verdille F 115 C3
Verdú E 147 C2
Verdun F 92 B1
Verdun-sur-Garonne F 129 C4
Verdun-sur-le-Doubs F 105 C4
Veresegyház H 112 B3
Verfeil F 129 C4
Vergato I 135 A4
Vergel E 159 C4
Vergeletto CH 120 A1
Verges E 147 B4
Vergiate I 120 B1
Vergt F 129 A3
Veria GR 182 C4
Verín E 141 C3
Veringenstadt D 107 A4
Verl D 81 A4
Verma N 198 C5
Vermand F 90 B3
Vermelha P 154 B1
Vermenton F 104 B2
Vernago I 108 C1
Vernante I 133 A3
Vernantes F 102 B2
Vernár SK 99 C4
Vernasca I 120 C2
Vernayaz CH 119 A4
Vernazza I 134 A2
Vern-d'Anjou F 102 B1
Verneřice CZ 84 B2
Vernet F 146 A2
Vernet-les-Bains F 146 B3
Verneuil F 91 B3
Verneuil-sur-Avre F 89 B4
Vernier CH 118 A3
Vérnio I 135 A4
Vérnole I 173 B4
Vernon F 90 B1
Vernoux-en-Vivarais F 117 C4
Veróce H 112 B3
Verolanuova I 120 B3
Véroli I 169 B3
Verona I 121 B4
Verpelét H 113 B4
Verrabotn N 199 B7
Verrès I 119 B4
Verrey-sous-Salmaise F 104 B3
Verrières F 115 B4
Versailles F 90 C2
Versam CH 107 C4
Verseg H 112 B3
Versmold D 71 B5
Versoix CH 118 A3
Verteillac F 115 C4
Vértesacsa H 112 B2
Vertou F 101 B4
Vertus F 91 C3
Verviers B 80 B1
Vervins F 91 B3
Verwood GB 43 B5
Veryan GB 42 B2
Veržej SLO 111 C3
Verzuolo I 133 A3
Verzy F 91 B4
Vescovato F 180 A2
Vése H 124 A3
Veselínad Lužnicí CZ 96 B2
Veselínad Moravou CZ 98 C1
Veseliy BG 17 D7
Vésime I 119 C5
Veskoniemi FIN 193 D11
Vesoul F 105 B5
Vespolate I 120 B1
Vessigebro S 60 C2
Vestbygd N 52 B2
Vestenanova I 121 B4
Vester Husby S 56 B2
Vester Nebel DK 59 C2
Vesterøhavn DK 58 A3
Vester Torup DK 58 A2
Vester Vedsted DK 59 C1
Vestervig DK 58 B1
Vestfossen N 53 A5
Vestmannaeyjar IS 190 D5
Vestmarka N 48 C3
Vestnes N 198 C4
Vestone I 120 B3
Vestre Gausdal N 48 A2
Vestre Jakobselv N 193 B13
Vestre Slidre N 47 A5
Vesyegonsk RUS 9 C10
Veszprém H 112 B1
Veszprémvarsány H 112 B1
Vésztő H 113 C5
Vetlanda S 62 A3
Vetovo HR 125 B3
Vetralla I 168 A2
Větrný Jeníkov CZ 97 B3
Vétroz CH 119 A4
Vetschau D 84 A2
Vettasjärvi S 196 B4
Vetto I 134 A3
Vetulónia I 135 C3
Veules-les-Roses F 89 A4
Veulettes-sur-Mer F 89 A4
Veum N 53 A4
Veurne B 78 A2
Veverská Bitýška CZ 97 B4
Vevey CH 106 C1
Vevi GR 182 C3
Vevring N 46 A2
Vex CH 119 A4
Veynes F 132 A1
Veyre-Monton F 116 B3
Veyrier F 118 B3
Vézelay F 104 B2
Vézelise F 92 C2
Vézenobres F 131 A3
Vezins F 102 B1
Vézins-de-Lévézou F 130 A1
Vezirhan TR 187 B5
Vezirköprü TR 23 A8
Vezza di Óglio I 120 A3
Vezzani F 180 A2
Vezzano I 121 A4
Vezzano sul Cróstolo I 121 C3
Vi S 200 D3
Viadana I 121 C3
Via Gloria P 160 B2
Viana E 143 B4
Viana do Alentejo P 154 C2
Viana do Bolo E 141 B3
Viana do Castelo P 148 A1
Vianden L 92 B2
Viannos GR 185 D6
Viaréggio I 134 B3
Viator E 164 C2
Vibble S 57 C4
Viborg DK 58 B2
Vibo Valéntia I 175 C2
Vibraye F 102 A2
Vic E 147 C3
Vícar E 164 C2
Vicarello I 134 B3
Vicari I 176 B2
Vicchio I 135 B4
Vicdesses F 146 B2
Vic-en-Bigorre F 145 A4
Vicenza I 121 B4
Vic-Fézensac F 129 C3
Vichy F 117 A3
Vickan S 60 B2
Vickerstown GB 36 B3
Vic-le-Comte F 116 B3
Vico F 180 A1
Vico del Gargano I 171 B3
Vico Equense I 170 C2
Vicopisano I 134 B3
Vicosoprano CH 120 A2
Vicovaro I 169 A2
Vic-sur-Aisne F 90 B3
Vic-sur-Cère F 116 C2
Victoria = Rabat M 175 C3
Vidago P 148 A2
Vidauban F 132 B2
Vide P 148 B2
Videbæk DK 59 B1
Videm SLO 123 B3
Videseter N 198 D4
Vidigueira P 160 A2
Vidin BG 16 D5
Vidlin GB 33 A5
Vidsel S 196 D3
Vidzy BY 13 A7
Viechtach D 95 B4
Vieille-Brioude F 117 B3
Vieira P 154 B2
Vieira do Minho P 148 A1
Vieiros P 155 C3
Vielha E 145 B4
Vielle-Aure F 145 B4
Viellespesse F 116 B3
Viellevigne F 114 B2
Vielmur-sur-Agout F 130 B1
Vielsalm B 80 B1
Viels Maison F 91 C3
Vienenburg D 73 C3
Vienna = Wien A 111 A3
Vienne F 117 B4
Vieritz D 73 B5
Viernheim D 93 B4
Vierraden D 74 A3
Viersen D 80 A2
Vierville-sur-Mer F 88 A3
Vierzon F 103 B4
Vieselbach D 82 B3
Vieste I 171 B4
Vietas S 194 C9
Vieteren B 78 B2
Vietri di Potenza I 172 B1
Vietri sul Mare I 170 C2
Vieux-Boucau-les-Bains F 128 C1
Vif F 118 B2
Vig DK 61 D1
Vigásio I 121 B3
Vigaun A 109 B4
Vigeland N 52 B3
Vigeois F 116 B1
Vigévano I 120 B1
Viggianello I 174 B2
Viggiano I 174 A1
Vigliano I 169 A3
Vigmostad N 52 B3
Vignale I 119 B5
Vignanello I 168 A2
Vigneulles-lès-Hattonchâtel F 92 C1
Vignevieille F 146 B3
Vignola I 135 A4
Vignory F 105 A4
Vignoux-sur Barangeon F 103 B4
Vigo E 140 B2
Vigo di Fassa I 121 A4
Vigone I 119 C4
Vigrestad N 52 B1
Vihiers F 102 B1
Viitasaari FIN 8 A4
Vik IS 190 D6
Vik
Nordland N 195 E3
Rogaland N 52 B1
Sogn og Fjordane N 46 A3
S 63 C2
Vika S 50 B2
Vikajärvi FIN 197 C9
Vikane N 54 A1
Vikarbyn S 50 B2
Vike N 46 B2
Vikedal N 52 A1
Vikeland N 53 B3
Viken
Jämtland S 199 A10
Skåne S 61 C2
Viker N 48 B2
Vikersund N 48 C1
Vikeså N 52 B2
Vikevåg N 52 A1
Vikingstad S 56 B1
Vikmanshyttan S 50 B2
Vikna N 199 A7
Vikøy N 46 B3
Vikran
Troms N 192 C2
Troms N 194 B7
Viksjö S 200 D3
Viksøyri N 46 A3
Viksta S 51 B4
Vila Boim P 155 C3
Vila Chãde Ourique P 154 B2
Viladamat E 147 B4
Vila de Cruces E 140 B2
Vila de Rei P 154 B2
Vila do Bispo P 160 B1
Vila do Conde P 148 A1
Viladrau E 147 C3
Vila Flor P 149 A2
Vila Franca das Navas P 149 B2
Vilafranca del Maestrat E 153 B3
Vilafranca del Penedès E 147 C2
Vila Franca de Xira P 154 C1
Vila Fresca P 154 C1
Vilagarcía de Arousa E 140 B2
Vilajuiga E 147 B4
Vilamarin E 140 B3
Vilamartín de Valdeorras F 141 B3
Vila Nogueira P 154 C1
Vila Nova da Baronia P 154 C2
Vilanova de Castelló E 159 B3
Vila Nova de Cerveira P 140 C2
Vila Nova de Famalicão P 148 A1
Vila Nova de Foz Côa P 149 A2
Vila Nova de Gaia P 148 A1
Vila Nova de Milfontes P 160 B1
Vila Nova de Paiva P 148 B2
Vila Nova de São Bento P 161 B2
Vilanova de Sau E 147 C3
Vilanova i la Geltrú E 147 C2
Vilapedre E 140 A3
Vila Pouca de Aguiar P 148 A2
Vila Praja de Ancora P 148 A1
Vilarandelo P 148 A2
Vilar de Santos E 140 B3
Vilardevós E 141 C3
Vila Real P 148 A2
Vila-real de los Infantes E 159 B3
Vila Real de Santo António P 160 B2
Vilar Formosa P 149 B3
Vila-Rodona E 147 C2
Vila Ruiva P 160 A2
Vilasantar E 140 A2
Vilaseca E 147 C2
Vila Seca P 148 B1
Vilassar de Mar E 147 C3
Vilasund S 195 D5
Vila Velha de Ródão P 155 B3
Vila Verde
Braga P 148 A1
Lisboa P 154 B1
Vila Verde de Filcalho P 161 B2
Vila Viçosa P 155 C3
Vilches E 157 B4
Vildbjerg DK 59 B1
Vilémov CZ 97 B3
Vileyka BY 13 A7
Vilhelmina S 200 B2
Vilia GR 184 A4
Viljandi EST 8 C4
Villabáñez E 150 A3
Villablanca E 161 B2
Villablino E 141 B4
Villabona E 144 A1
Villabragima E 142 C1
Villabuena del Puente E 150 A2
Villacadima E 151 A4
Villacañas E 157 A4
Villacarriedo E 143 A3
Villacarrillo E 164 A1
Villa Castelli I 173 B3
Villacastín E 150 B3
Villach A 109 C4
Villacidro I 179 C2
Villaconejos E 151 B4
Villaconejos de Trabaque E 152 B1
Villa Cova de Lixa P 148 A1
Villada E 142 B2
Villadangos del Páramo E 141 B5
Villadecanes E 141 B4
Villa del Prado E 150 B3
Villa del Río E 157 C3
Villadepera E 149 A3
Villa de Peralonso E 149 A3
Villa di Chiavenna I 120 A2
Villadiego E 142 B2
Villadompardo E 163 A3
Villadóssola I 119 A5
Villaeles de Valdavia E 142 B2
Villaescusa de Haro E 158 B1
Villafáfila E 142 C1
Villafeliche E 152 A2
Villaflores E 150 A2
Villafrades de Campos E 142 B2
Villafranca
Avila E 150 B2
Navarra E 144 B2
Villafranca de Córdoba E 157 C3
Villafranca del Bierzo E 141 B4
Villafranca de los Barros E 155 C4
Villafranca de los Caballeros E 157 A4
Villafranca di Verona I 121 B3
Villafranca in Lunigiana I 134 A2
Villafranca-Montes de Oca E 143 B3
Villafranca Tirrena I 177 A4
Villafranco del Campo E 152 B2
Villafranco del Guadalquivir E 161 B3
Villafrati I 176 B2
Villafrechós E 142 C1
Villafruela E 143 C3
Villagarcia de las Torres E 156 B1
Villaggio Mancuso I 175 B2
Villagonzalo E 156 B1
Villagotón E 141 B4
Villagrains F 128 B2
Villaharta E 156 B3
Villahermosa E 158 C1
Villaherreros E 142 B2
Villahoz E 143 B3
Villaines-la-Juhel F 89 B3
Villajoyosa E 159 C3
Villalago I 169 B3
Villalba
E 140 A3
I 176 B2
Villalba de Calatrava E 157 B4
Villalba de Guardo E 142 B2
Villalba del Alcor E 161 B3
Villalba de la Sierra E 152 B1
Villalba de los Alcores E 142 C2
Villalba de los Barros E 155 C4
Villalba del Rey E 151 B5
Villalcampo E 149 A3
Villalcázar de Sirga E 142 B2
Villalengua E 152 A2
Villalgordo del Júcar E 158 B1
Villalgordo del Marquesado E 158 B1
Villalmóndar E 143 B3
Villalón de Campos E 142 B1
Villalonga E 159 C3
Villalonso E 150 A2
Villalpando E 142 C1
Villaluenga E 151 B4
Villalumbroso E 142 B2
Villálvaro E 143 C3
Villamalea E 158 B2
Villamanán E 142 B1
Villamanín E 142 B1
Villamanrique E 157 B5
Villamanrique de la Condesa E 161 B3
Villamanta E 151 B3
Villamantilla E 151 B3
Villamar I 179 C2
Villamartín E 162 B2
Villamartín de Campos E 142 B2
Villamartín de Don Sancho E 142 B1
Villamassárgia I 179 C2
Villamayor E 142 A1
Villamayor de Calatrava E 157 B3
Villamayor de Campos E 142 C1
Villamayor de Santiago E 157 A5
Villamblard F 129 A3
Villamejil E 141 B4
Villamesias E 156 A2
Villaminaya E 157 A4
Villa Minozzo I 134 A3
Villamor de los Escuderos E 150 A2
Villamoronta E 142 B2
Villamuelas E 151 C4
Villamuriel de Cerrato E 142 C2
Villandraut F 128 B2
Villanova I 173 B3
Villanova d'Asti I 119 C4
Villanova del Battista I 171 B3
Villanova Mondov ì I 133 A3
Villanova Monteleone I 178 B2
Villante E 143 B3
Villantério I 120 B2
Villanubla E 142 C2
Villanueva de Alcardete E 157 A4
Villanueva de Alcorón E 152 B1
Villanueva de Algaidas E 163 A3
Villanueva de Argaña E 143 B3
Villanueva de Bogas E 157 A4
Villanueva de Córdoba E 156 B3
Villanueva de Gállego E 144 C3
Villanueva del Aceral E 150 A3
Villanueva de la Concepcion E 163 B3
Villanueva de la Fuente E 158 C1
Villanueva de la Jara E 158 B2
Villanueva de la Reina E 157 B4
Villanueva del Arzobispo E 164 A2
Villanueva de la Serena E 156 B2
Villanueva de la Sierra E 149 B3
Villanueva de las Manzanas E 142 B1
Villanueva de las Peras E 141 C5
Villanueva de las Torres E 164 B1

Villanueva de la Vera E 150 B2
Villanueva del Campo E 142 C1
Villanueva del Duque E 156 B3
Villanueva del Fresno E 155 C3
Villanueva del Huerva E 152 A2
Villanueva de los Castillejos E 161 B2
Villanueva de los Infantes E 157 B5
Villanueva del Rey E 156 B2
Villanueva del Rio E 162 A2
Villanueva del Río y Minas E 162 A2
Villanueva del Rosario E 163 B3
Villanueva del Trabuco E 163 A3
Villanueva de Mesia E 163 A4
Villanueva de Nía E 142 B2
Villanueva de Oscos E 141 A4
Villanueva de San Carlos E 157 B4
Villanueva de San Juan E 162 A2
Villanueva de Tapia E 163 A3
Villanueva de Valdegovia E 143 B3
Villány H 125 B4
Villaputzu I 179 C3
Villaquejida E 142 B1
Villaquilambre E 142 B1
Villaquiran de los Infantes E 142 B2
Villaralto E 156 B3
Villarcayo E 143 B3
Villard-de-Lans F 118 B2
Villar de Barrio E 140 B3
Villar de Cañas E 158 B1
Villar de Chinchilla E 158 C2
Villar de Ciervo E 149 B3
Villardeciervos E 141 C4
Villar de Domingo Garcia E 152 B1
Villardefrades E 142 C1
Villar del Arzobispo E 159 B3
Villar del Buey E 149 A3
Villar del Cobo E 152 B2
Villar del Humo E 158 B2
Villar de los Navarros E 152 A2
Villar del Pedroso E 156 A2
Villar del Rey E 155 B4
Villar del Rio E 143 B4
Villar del Saz de Navalón E 152 B1
Villar de Rena E 156 A2
Villarejo E 151 A4
Villarejo de Fuentes E 158 B1
Villarejo de Orbigo E 141 B5
Villarejo de Salvanes E 151 B4
Villarejo-Periesteban E 158 B1
Villares del Saz E 158 B1
Villaretto I 119 B4
Villargordo del Cabriel E 158 B2
Villarino E 149 A3
Villarino de Conso E 141 B3
Villarluengo E 153 B3
Villarobe E 143 B3
Villarosa I 177 B3
Villar Perosa I 119 C4
Villarramiel E 142 B2
Villarrasa E 161 B3
Villarreal de San Carlos E 150 C1
Villarrin de Campos E 142 C1
Villarrobledo E 158 B1
Villarroya de la Sierra E 152 A2
Villarroya de los Pinares E 153 B3
Villarrubia de los Ojos E 157 A4
Villarrubia de Santiago E 151 C4
Villarrubio E 151 C5
Villars-les-Dombes F 117 A5
Villarta E 158 B2
Villarta de los Montes E 156 A3
Villarta de San Juan E 157 A4
Villasana de Mena E 143 A3
Villasandino E 142 B2
Villa San Giovanni I 175 C1
Villa Santa Maria I 169 B4
Villasante E 143 A3
Villa Santina I 122 A1
Villasarracino E 142 B2
Villasayas E 151 A5
Villasdardo E 149 A3
Villaseca de Henares E 151 B5
Villaseca de Laciana E 141 B4
Villaseca de la Sagra E 151 C4
Villaseco de los Gamitos E 149 A3
Villaseco de los Reyes E 149 A3
Villasequilla de Yepes E 151 C4
Villasimius I 179 C3
Villasmundo I 177 B4
Villasor I 179 C2
Villastar E 152 B2
Villastellone I 119 C4
Villatobas E 151 C4
Villatorp E 150 B2
Villatoya E 158 B2
Villavaliente E 158 B2
Villavelayo E 143 B4
Villavella E 141 B3
Villaver de de Guadalimar E 158 C1
Villaverde del Rio E 162 A2
Villaviciosa E 142 A1
Villaviciosa de Córdoba E 156 B3
Villaviciosa de Odón E 151 B4
Villavieja de Yeltes E 149 B3
Villayón E 141 A4
Villé F 93 C3
Villebois-Lavalette F 115 C4
Villecerf F 90 C2
Villecomtal F 130 A1
Villedieu-les-Poêles F 88 B2
Villedieu-sur-Indre F 103 C3
Ville-di-Pietrabugno F 180 A2
Villedômain F 103 B3
Villefagnan F 115 B4
Villefontaine F 118 B2
Villefort F 131 A2
Villefranche-d'Albigeois F 130 B1
Villefranche-d'Allier F 116 A2
Villefranche-de-Lauragais F 146 A2
Villefranche-de-Lonchat F 128 B3
Villefranche-de-Panat F 130 A1
Villefranche-de-Rouergue F 130 A1
Villefranche-du-Périgord F 129 B4
Villefranche-sur-Cher F 103 B3
Villefranche-sur-Mer F 133 B3
Villefranche-sur-Saône F 117 A4
Villegenon F 103 B4
Villel E 152 B2
Villemaur-sur-Vanne F 104 A2
Villemontais F 117 B3
Villemur-sur-Tarn F 129 C4
Villena E 159 C3
Villenauxe-la-Grande F 91 C3
Villenave-d'Ornon F 128 B2
Villeneuve
CH 119 A3
F 129 B5
Villeneuve-d'Ascq F 78 B3
Villeneuve-de-Berg F 131 A3
Villeneuve-de-Marsan F 128 C2
Villeneuve-de-Rivière F 145 A4
Villeneuve-la-Guyard F 90 C3
Villeneuve-l'Archevêque F 104 A2
Villeneuve-le-Comte F 90 C2
Villeneuve-lès-Avignon F 131 B3
Villeneuve-les-Corbières F 146 B3
Villeneuve-St Georges F 90 C2
Villeneuve-sur-Allier F 104 C2
Villeneuve-sur-Lot F 129 B3
Villeneuve-sur-Yonne F 104 A2
Villeréal F 129 B3
Villerias E 142 C2
Villeromain F 103 B3
Villers-Bocage
Calvados F 88 A3
Somme F 90 B2
Villers-Bretonneux F 90 B2
Villers-Carbonnel F 90 B2
Villers-Cotterêts F 90 B3
Villersexel F 105 B5
Villers-Farlay F 105 C4
Villers-le-Gambon B 79 B4
Villers-le-Lac F 106 B1
Villers-sur-Mer F 89 A3
Villerupt F 92 B1
Villerville F 89 A4
Villeseneux F 91 C4
Ville-sous-la-Ferté F 105 A3
Ville-sur-Illon F 105 A5
Ville-sur-Tourbe F 91 B4
Villetrun F 103 B3
Villetta Barrea I 169 B3
Villeurbanne F 117 B4
Villeveyrac F 130 B2
Villevocance F 117 B4
Villiers-St Benoit F 104 B2
Villiers-St Georges F 91 C3
Villingen D 106 A3
Villmar D 81 B4
Villoldo E 142 B2
Villon F 104 B3
Villoria E 150 B2
Vilnes N 46 A1
Vilnius LT 13 A6
Vils
A 108 B1
DK 58 B1
Vilsbiburg D 95 C4
Vilseck D 95 B3
Vilshofen D 96 C1
Vilshult S 63 B2
Vilusi MNE 139 C4
Vilvestre E 149 A3
Vilvoorde B 79 B4
Vimeiro P 154 B1
Vimercate I 120 B2
Vimianzo E 140 A1
Vimieiro P 154 C3
Vimioso P 149 A3
Vimmerby S 62 A3
Vimoutiers F 89 B4
Vimperk CZ 96 B1
Vimy F 78 B2
Vinadi CH 108 C1
Vinadio I 133 A3
Vinaixa E 147 C1
Vinarós E 153 B4
Vinäs S 50 B1
Vinay F 118 B2
Vinberg S 60 C2
Vinca F 146 B3
Vinča SRB 127 C2
Vinchiaturo I 170 B2
Vinci I 135 B3
Vindeby DK 65 A3
Vindelgransele S 195 E9
Vindeln S 200 B5
Vinderup DK 58 B1
Vindsvik N 52 A2
Vinets F 91 C4
Vineuil F 103 B3
Vinga RO 126 A3
Vingåker S 56 A1
Vingnes N 48 A2
Vingrau F 146 B3
Vingrom N 48 A2
Vinhais P 149 A3
Vinica
HR 124 A2
MK 182 B4
SK 112 A3
SLO 123 B4
Viniegra de Arriba E 143 B4
Vinje
Hordaland N 46 B3
Sør-Trøndelag N 198 B6
Telemark N 53 A3
Vinkovci HR 125 B4
Vinliden S 200 B3
Vinninga S 55 B4
Vinnytsya UA 13 D8
Vinon F 103 B4
Vinon-sur-Verdon F 132 B1
Vinslöv S 61 C3
Vinstra N 48 A1
Vintjärn S 50 B3
Vintrosa S 55 A5
Viñuela E 163 B3
Viñuela de Sayago E 149 A4
Viñuelas E 151 B4
Vinuesa E 143 C4
Vinzelberg D 73 B4
Viöl D 64 B2
Viola I 133 A3
Violay F 117 B4
Vipava SLO 122 B2
Vipiteno I 108 C2
Vipperow D 74 A1
Vir
BIH 138 B3
Vir *continued*
HR 137 A4
Vira CH 120 A1
Vire F 88 B3
Vireda S 62 A2
Vireux F 91 A4
Virgen A 109 B3
Virgen de la Cabeza E 157 B3
Virginia IRL 27 C3
Virieu F 118 B2
Virieu-le-Grand F 118 B2
Virje HR 124 A2
Virkkunen FIN 197 D10
Virklund DK 59 B2
Virovitica HR 124 B3
Virsbo S 50 C3
Virserum S 62 A3
Virtaniemi FIN 193 D12
Virton B 92 B1
Virtsu EST 8 C3
Viry F 118 A3
Vis HR 138 B2
Visbek D 71 B5
Visby
DK 64 A1
S 57 C4
Visé B 80 B1
Višegrad BIH 139 B5
Viserba I 136 A1
Viseu P 148 B2
Visiedo E 152 B2
Viskafors S 60 B2
Visland N 52 B2
Vislanda S 62 B2
Visnes N 52 A1
Višnja Gora SLO 123 B3
Višnjan HR 122 B2
Višnové CZ 97 C4
Visnums-Kil S 55 A5
Viso del Marqués E 157 B4
Visoko
BIH 139 B4
SLO 123 A3
Visone I 119 C5
Visp CH 119 A4
Vissefjärda S 63 B3
Visselhövede D 72 B2
Vissenbjerg DK 59 C3
Visso I 136 C2
Vistabella del Maestrat E 153 B3
Vistheden S 196 D3
Vita I 176 B1
Vitanje SLO 123 A4
Vitebsk = Vitsyebsk BY 13 A9
Viterbo I 168 A2
Vitez BIH 139 A3
Vithkuq AL 182 C2
Vitigudino E 149 A3
Vitina
BIH 138 B3
GR 184 B3
Vitis A 97 C3
Vítkov CZ 98 B1
Vitoria-Gasteiz E 143 B4
Vitré F 101 A4
Vitrey-sur-Mance F 105 B4
Vitry-en-Artois F 78 B2
Vitry-le-François F 91 C4
Vitry-sur-Seine F 90 C2
Vitsand S 49 B4
Vitsyebsk = Vitebsk BY 13 A9
Vittangi S 196 B4
Vittaryd S 60 C3
Vitteaux F 104 B3
Vittel F 105 A4
Vittinge S 51 C4
Vittória I 177 C3
Vittório Véneto I 122 B1
Vittsjö S 61 C3
Viù I 119 B4
Viul N 48 B2
Vivario F 180 A2
Viveiro E 140 A3
Vivel del Rio Martin E 152 B3
Viver E 159 B3
Viverols F 117 B3
Viveros E 158 C1
Viviers F 131 A3
Vivonne F 115 B4
Vivy F 102 B1
Vize TR 186 A2
Vizille F 118 B2
Viziňada HR 122 B2
Viziru RO 17 C7
Vizovice CZ 98 B1
Vizvár H 124 A3
Vizzavona F 180 A2
Vizzini I 177 B3
Vlachiotis GR 184 C3
Vlachovice CZ 98 B1
Vlachovo SK 99 C4
Vláchovo Březi CZ 96 B1
Vladimirci SRB 127 C1
Vladimirovac SRB 127 B2
Vladislav CZ 97 B3
Vlagtwedde NL 71 A4
Vlajkovac SRB 127 B3
Vlasenica BIH 139 A4
Vlašim CZ 96 B2
Vlatkovići BIH 138 A3
Vledder NL 70 B3
Vlissingen NL 79 A3
Vlkolínec SK 99 B3
Vlorë AL 182 C1
Vlotho D 72 B1
Vnanje Gorice SLO 123 B3
Vobarno I 121 B3
Voćin HR 124 B3
Vöcklabruck A 109 A4
Vöcklamarkt A 109 B4
Vodanj SRB 127 C2
Voderady SK 98 C1
Vodice
Istarska HR 123 B3
Šibenska HR 137 B4
SLO 123 A3
Vodňany CZ 96 B2
Vodnjan HR 122 C2
Vodskov DK 58 A3
Voe GB 33 A5
Voerså DK 58 A3
Voghera I 120 C2
Vogogna I 119 A5
Vogošća BIH 139 B4
Vogüé F 131 A3
Vohburg D 95 C3
Vohenstrauss D 95 B4
Vöhl D 81 A4
Vöhrenbach D 106 A3
Vöhringen D 94 C2
Void-Vacon F 92 C1
Voiron F 118 B2
Voise F 90 C1
Voisey F 105 B4
Voiteg RO 126 B3
Voiteur F 105 C4
Voitsberg A 110 B2
Vojakkala FIN 196 D7
Vojens DK 59 C2
Vojka SRB 127 C2
Vojlovica SRB 127 C2
Vojnić HR 123 B4
Vojnice SK 112 B2
Vojnik SLO 123 A4
Vojvoda Stepa SRB 126 B2
Volada GR 188 D2
Volargne I 121 B3
Volary CZ 96 C1
Volče SLO 122 A2
Volda N 198 C3
Volendam NL 70 B2
Volga RUS 9 C11
Volimes GR 184 B1
Volissos GR 185 A6
Volkach D 94 B2
Völkermarkt A 110 C1
Volkhov RUS 9 C8
Völklingen D 92 B2
Volkmarsen D 81 A5
Voll N 198 C4
Vollenhove NL 70 B2
Vollore-Montagne F 117 B3
Vollsjö S 61 D3
Volodymyr-Volyns'kyy UA 13 C6
Volokolamsk RUS 9 D9
Volos GR 182 D4
Volosovo RUS 9 C6
Volovets UA 13 D5
Voltággio I 120 C1
Volta Mantovana I 121 B3
Volterra I 135 B3
Voltri I 133 A4
Volturara Áppula I 170 B3
Volturara Irpina I 170 C2
Volvic F 116 B3
Volx F 132 B1
Volyně CZ 96 B1
Vonitsa GR 182 E2
Vönöck H 111 B4
Vonsild DK 59 C2
Voorschoten NL 70 B1
Vopnafjörður IS 191 B11
Vorau A 110 B2
Vorbasse DK 59 C2
Vorchdorf A 109 B4
Vorden
D 71 B5
NL 71 B3
Vordernberg A 110 B1
Vordingborg DK 65 A4
Vorë AL 182 B1
Voreppe F 118 B2
Vorey F 117 B3
Vorgod DK 59 B1
Vormsund N 48 B3
Võru EST 8 D5
Voskopojë AL 182 C2
Voss N 46 B3
Votice CZ 96 B2
Voué F 91 C4
Vouillé F 115 B4
Voulx F 90 C2
Voussac F 116 A3
Vouvray F 102 B2
Vouvry CH 119 A3
Vouzela P 148 B1
Vouziers F 91 B4
Voves F 103 A3
Voxna S 50 A2
Voy GB 33 B3
Voynitsa RUS 3 D12
Voznesenye RUS 9 B9
Vrå
DK 58 A2
S 60 C3
Vráble SK 98 C2
Vračenovići MNE 139 C4
Vračev Gaj SRB 127 C3
Vraćevsnica SRB 127 C2
Vrådal N 53 A4
Vrakneika GR 184 A2
Vrana HR 123 C3
Vranduk BIH 139 A3
Vrångö S 60 B1
Vrani RO 127 B3
Vranić SRB 127 C2
Vraniči BIH 139 B4
Vranja HR 123 B3
Vranjak BIH 125 C4
Vranje SRB 16 D4
Vranovice CZ 97 C4
Vranov nad Dyje CZ 97 C3
Vransko SLO 123 A3
Vrapčići BIH 139 B3
Vratimov CZ 98 B2
Vratsa BG 17 D5
Vrbanja HR 125 C4
Vrbanjci BIH 124 C3
Vrbas SRB 126 B1
Vrbaška BIH 124 B3
Vrbnik
Primorsko-Goranska HR 123 B3
Zadarsko-Kninska HR 138 A2
Vrbno pod Pradědem CZ 85 B5
Vrboska HR 138 B2
Vrbov SK 99 B4
Vrbovce SK 98 C1
Vrbové SK 98 C1
Vrbovec HR 124 B2
Vrbovski SRB 127 C2
Vrbovsko HR 123 B4
Vrchlabí CZ 84 B3
Vrčin SRB 127 C2
Vrdy CZ 97 B3
Vrebac HR 137 A4
Vreden D 71 B3
Vreoci SRB 127 C2
Vretstorp S 55 A5
Vrginmost HR 124 B1
Vrgorac HR 138 B3
Vrhnika SLO 123 B3
Vrhovine HR 123 C4
Vrhpolie SRB 127 C1
Vriezenveen NL 71 B3
Vrigne-aux-Bois F 91 B4
Vrigstad S 62 A2
Vrlika HR 138 B2
Vrnograč BIH 124 B1
Vron F 78 B1
Vroomshoop NL 71 B3
Vroutek CZ 83 B5
Vrpolje HR 125 B4
Vršac SRB 126 B3
Vrsar HR 122 B2
Vrsi HR 137 A4
Vrtoče BIH 124 C2
Vrútky SK 98 B2
Všeruby CZ 95 B4
Všestary CZ 85 B3
Vsetín CZ 98 B1
Vučkovica SRB 127 D2
Vught NL 79 A5
Vuillafans F 105 B5
Vukovar HR 125 B5
Vuku N 199 B8
Vulcan RO 17 C5
Vulcăneşti MD 17 C8
Vuoggatjålme S 195 D7
Vuojärvi FIN 197 B9
Vuolijoki FIN 3 D10
Vuollerim S 196 C3
Vuotso FIN 197 A10
Vuzenica SLO 110 C2
Vyartsilya RUS 9 A7
Vyborg RUS 9 B6
Výčapy CZ 97 B3
Výčapy-Opatovce SK 98 C2
Východna SK 99 B3
Vydrany SK 111 A4
Vyerkhnyadzvinsk BY 13 A7
Vyhne SK 98 C2
Vy-lès Lure F 105 B5
Vylkove UA 17 C8
Vynohradiv UA 17 A5
Vyshniy Volochek RUS 9 D9
Vyškov CZ 97 B5
Vysokánad Kysucou SK 98 B2
Vysoké Mýto CZ 97 B4
Vysokovsk RUS 9 D10
Vyšší Brod CZ 96 C2
Vytegra RUS 9 B10

W

Waabs D 64 B2
Waalwijk NL 79 A5
Waarschoot B 79 A3
Wabern D 81 A5
Wąbrzeźno PL 69 B3
Wąchock PL 87 A5
Wachow D 74 B1
Wachów PL 86 B2
Wächtersbach D 81 B5
Wackersdorf D 95 B4
Waddington GB 40 B3
Wadebridge GB 42 B2
Wadelsdorf D 84 A2

Wädenswil CH 107 B3
Wadern D 92 B2
Wadersloh D 81 A4
Wadlew PL 86 A3
Wadowice PL 99 B3
Wagenfeld D 72 B1
Wageningen NL 70 C2
Waghäusel D 93 B4
Waging D 109 B3
Wagrain A 109 B4
Wagrowiec PL 76 B2
Wahlsdorf D 74 C2
Wahlstedt D 64 C3
Wahrenholz D 73 B3
Waiblingen D 94 C1
Waidhaus D 95 B4
Waidhofen an der Thaya A 97 C3
Waidhofen an der Ybbs A 110 B1
Waimes B 80 B2
Wainfleet All Saints GB 41 B4
Waizenkirchen A 96 C1
Wakefield GB 40 B2
Wałbrzych PL 85 B4
Walchensee D 108 B2
Walchsee A 109 B3
Wałcz PL 75 A5
Wald CH 107 B3
Waldaschaff D 94 B1
Waldbach A 110 B2
Waldböckelheim D 93 B3
Waldbröl D 81 B3
Waldeck D 81 A5
Waldenburg D 83 B4
Waldfischbach-Burgalben D 93 B3
Waldheim D 83 A5
Waldkappel D 82 A1
Waldkirch D 106 A2
Waldkirchen D 96 C1
Waldkirchen am Wesen A 96 C1
Waldkraiburg D 109 A3
Wald-Michelbach D 93 B4
Waldmohr D 93 B3
Waldmünchen D 95 B4
Waldring A 109 B3
Waldsassen D 95 A4
Waldshut D 106 B3
Waldstatt CH 107 B4
Waldwisse F 92 B2
Walenstadt CH 107 B4
Walentynów PL 87 A5
Walichnowy PL 86 A2
Walincourt F 90 A3
Walkenried D 82 A2
Walkeringham GB 40 B3
Wallasey GB 38 A3
Walldürn D 94 B1
Wallenfells D 82 B3
Wallenhorst D 71 B5
Wallers F 78 B3
Wallersdorf D 95 C4
Wallerstein D 94 C2
Wallingford GB 44 B2
Wallitz D 74 A1
Walls GB 33 A5
Wallsbüll D 64 B2
Walmer GB 45 B5
Walsall GB 40 C2
Walshoutem B 79 B5
Walsrode D 72 B2
Waltenhofen D 107 B5
Waltershausen D 82 B2
Waltham Abbey GB 45 B4
Waltham on the Wolds GB 40 C3
Walton-on-Thames GB 44 B3
Walton-on-the-Naze GB 45 B5
Wamba E 142 C2
Wanderup D 64 B2
Wandlitz D 74 B2
Wanfried D 82 A2
Wangen im Allgäu D 107 B4
Wangerooge D 71 A4
Wangersen D 72 A2
Wängi CH 107 B3
Wanna D 64 C1
Wansford GB 40 C3
Wantage GB 44 B2
Wanzleben D 73 B4
Waplewo PL 77 A5
Wapnica PL 75 A4
Wapno PL 76 B2
Warburg D 81 A5
Wardenburg D 71 A5
Ware GB 44 B3
Waregem B 79 B3
Wareham GB 43 B4
Waremme B 79 B5
Waren D 74 A1
Warendorf D 71 C4
Warga NL 70 A2
Warin D 65 C4
Wark GB 37 A4
Warka PL 87 A5
Warkworth GB 37 A5
Warlubie PL 69 B3
Warminster GB 43 A4
Warnemünde D 65 B5
Warnow D 65 C4
Warnsveld NL 70 B3
Warrenpoint GB 27 B4
Warrington GB 38 A4
Warsaw = Warszawa PL 77 B6
Warsingsfehn D 71 A4
Warsow D 73 A4
Warstein D 81 A4
Warszawa = Warsaw PL 77 B6
Warta PL 86 A2
Wartberg A 110 B1
Warth A 107 B5
Warwick GB 44 A2
Warza D 82 B2
Wasbister GB 33 B3
Washington GB 37 B5
Wąsosz PL 85 A4
Wasselonne F 93 C3
Wassen CH 107 C3
Wassenaar NL 70 B1
Wasserauen CH 107 B4
Wasserburg D 108 A3
Wassertrüdingen D 94 B2
Wassy F 91 C4
Wasungen D 82 B2
Watchet GB 43 A3
Waterford IRL 30 B1
Watergrasshill IRL 29 B3
Waterloo B 79 B4
Waterville IRL 29 C1
Watford GB 44 B3
Wathlingen D 72 B3
Watten
F 78 B2
GB 32 C3
Wattens A 108 B2
Watton GB 41 C4
Wattwil CH 107 B4
Waunfawr GB 38 A2
Wavignies F 90 B2
Wavre B 79 B4
Wearhead GB 37 B4
Węchadlow PL 87 B4
Wedel D 72 A2
Wedemark D 72 B2
Weedon Bec GB 44 A2
Weener D 71 A4
Weert NL 80 A1
Weesp NL 70 B2
Weeze D 80 A2
Weferlingen D 73 B4
Wegeleben D 82 A3
Weggis CH 106 B3
Węgierska-Górka PL 99 B3
Wegliniec PL 84 A3
Węgorzyno PL 75 A4
Węgrzynice PL 75 B4
Wegscheid D 96 C1
Wehdel D 72 A1
Wehr D 106 B2
Weibersbrunn D 94 B1
Weichering D 95 C3
Weida D 83 B4
Weiden D 95 B4
Weidenberg D 95 B3
Weidenhain D 83 A4
Weidenstetten D 94 C1
Weierbach D 93 B3
Weikersheim D 94 B1
Weil D 108 A1
Weil am Rhein D 106 B2
Weilburg D 81 B4
Weil der Stadt D 93 C4
Weilerswist D 80 B2
Weilheim
Baden-Württemberg D 94 C1
Bayern D 108 B2
Weilmünster D 81 B4
Weiltensfeld A 110 C1
Weimar D 82 B3
Weinberg D 94 B2
Weinfelden CH 107 B4
Weingarten
Baden-Württemberg D 93 B4
Baden-Württemberg D 107 B4
Weinheim D 93 B4
Weinstadt D 94 C1
Weismain D 82 B3
Weissbriach A 109 C4
Weissenbach A 108 B1
Weissenberg D 84 A2
Weissenbrunn D 82 B3
Weissenburg D 94 B2
Weissenfels D 83 A3
Weissenhorn D 94 C2
Weissenkirchen A 97 C3
Weissensee D 82 A3
Weissenstadt D 83 B3
Weisskirchen im Steiermark A 110 B1
Weisstannen CH 107 C4
Weisswasser D 84 A2
Weitendorf D 65 C5
Weitersfeld A 97 C3
Weitersfelden A 96 C2
Weitnau D 107 B5
Wéitra A 96 C2
Weiz A 110 B2
Wejherowo PL 68 A3
Welkenraedt B 80 B1
Wellaune D 83 A4
Wellin B 91 A5
Wellingborough GB 44 A3
Wellington
Somerset GB 43 B3
Wellington *continued*
Telford & Wrekin GB 38 B4
Wellingtonbridge IRL 30 B2
Wells GB 43 A4
Wells-next-the-Sea GB 41 C4
Wels A 109 A5
Welschenrohr CH 106 B2
Welshpool GB 38 B3
Welver D 81 A3
Welwyn Garden City GB 44 B3
Welzheim D 94 C1
Welzow D 84 A2
Wem GB 38 B4
Wembury GB 42 B2
Wemding D 94 C2
Wenden D 81 B3
Wendisch Rietz D 74 B3
Wendlingen D 94 C1
Weng A 109 A4
Weng bei Admont A 110 B1
Wengen CH 106 C2
Wenigzell A 110 B2
Wennigsen D 72 B2
Wenns A 108 B1
Wenzenbach D 95 B4
Weppersdorf A 111 B3
Werben D 73 B4
Werbig D 74 C2
Werdau D 83 B4
Werder D 74 B1
Werdohl D 81 A3
Werfen A 109 B4
Werkendam NL 79 A4
Werl D 81 A3
Werlte D 71 B4
Wermelskirchen D 80 A3
Wermsdorf D 83 A4
Wernberg Köblitz D 95 B4
Werne D 81 A3
Werneck D 94 B2
Werneuchen D 74 B2
Wernigerode D 82 A2
Wertach D 108 B1
Wertheim D 94 B1
Wertingen D 94 C2
Weseke D 80 A2
Wesel D 80 A2
Wesenberg D 74 A1
Wesendorf D 73 B3
Wesołowo PL 77 A5
Wesselburen D 64 B1
Wesseling D 80 B2
West Bridgford GB 40 C2
West Bromwich GB 40 C2
Westbury
Shropshire GB 38 B4
Wiltshire GB 43 A4
Westbury-on-Severn GB 39 C4
Westendorf A 108 B3
Westensee D 64 B2
Westerbork NL 71 B3
Westerburg D 81 B3
Westerhaar NL 71 B3
Westerholt D 71 A4
Westerkappeln D 71 B4
Westerland D 64 B1
Westerlo B 79 A4
Westerstede D 71 A4
West Haddon GB 44 A2
Westheim D 94 B2
Westhill GB 33 D4
Westkapelle
B 78 A3
NL 79 A3
West Kilbride GB 34 C3
West Linton GB 35 C4
West Lulworth GB 43 B4
West Mersea GB 45 B4
Westminster GB 44 B3
Weston GB 40 C1
Weston-super-Mare GB 43 A4
Westport IRL 28 A2
Westruther GB 35 C5
West-Terschelling NL 70 A2
Westward Ho! GB 42 A2
West Woodburn GB 37 A4
Wetheral GB 37 B4
Wetherby GB 40 B2
Wetter
Hessen D 81 B4
Nordrhein-Westfalen D 80 A3
Wetteren B 79 A3
Wettin D 83 A3
Wettringen D 71 B4
Wetzikon CH 107 B3
Wetzlar D 81 B4
Wewelsfleth D 64 C2
Wexford IRL 30 B2
Weybridge GB 44 B3
Weyerbusch D 81 B3
Weyer Markt A 110 B1
Weyersheim F 93 C3
Weyhe D 72 B1
Weyhill GB 44 B2
Weymouth GB 43 B4
Weyregg A 109 B4
Węzyska PL 75 B3
Whalton GB 37 A5
Whauphill GB 36 B2
Wheatley GB 44 B2
Whickham GB 37 B5
Whipsnade GB 44 B3
Whitburn GB 35 C4
Whitby GB 37 B6
Whitchurch
Hampshire GB 44 B2
Herefordshire GB 39 C4
Shropshire GB 38 B4
White Bridge GB 32 D2
Whitegate IRL 29 C3
Whitehaven GB 36 B3
Whitehead GB 27 B5
Whithorn GB 36 B2
Whitley Bay GB 37 A5
Whitstable GB 45 B5
Whittington GB 38 B4
Whittlesey GB 41 C3
Wiązów PL 85 B5
Wick GB 32 C3
Wickede D 81 A3
Wickford GB 45 B4
Wickham GB 44 C2
Wickham Market GB 45 A5
Wicklow IRL 30 B2
Wicko PL 68 A2
Widawa PL 86 A2
Widdrington GB 37 A5
Widecombe in the Moor GB 42 B3
Widemouth GB 42 B2
Widnes GB 38 A4
Widuchowo PL 74 A3
Więcbork PL 76 A2
Wiefelstede D 71 A5
Wiehe D 82 A3
Wiehl D 81 B3
Wiek D 66 B2
Większyce PL 86 B1
Wielbark PL 77 A5
Wiele PL 68 B2
Wieleń PL 75 B5
Wielgie
Kujawsko-Pomorskie PL 77 B4
Łódzkie PL 86 A2
Mazowieckie PL 87 A5
Wielgomłyny PL 87 A3
Wielichowo PL 75 B5
Wieliczka PL 99 B4
Wielka Łąka PL 76 A3
Wielowies PL 86 B2
Wieluń PL 86 A2
Wien = Vienna A 111 A3
Wiener Neustadt A 111 B3
Wiepke D 73 B4
Wierden NL 71 B3
Wieren D 73 B3
Wieruszów PL 86 A2
Wierzbica
Mazowieckie PL 77 B6
Mazowieckie PL 87 A5
Wierzbie PL 86 A2
Wierzbięcin PL 75 A4
Wierzchowo PL 75 A5
Wierzchucino PL 68 A3
Wierzchy PL 86 A2
Wies A 110 C2
Wiesau D 95 B4
Wiesbaden D 93 A4
Wieselburg A 110 A2
Wiesen CH 107 C4
Wiesenburg D 73 B5
Wiesenfelden D 95 B4
Wiesensteig D 94 C1
Wiesentheid D 94 B2
Wiesloch D 93 B4
Wiesmath A 111 B3
Wiesmoor D 71 A4
Wietmarschen D 71 B4
Wietze D 72 B2
Wigan GB 38 A4
Wiggen CH 106 C2
Wigston GB 40 C2
Wigton GB 36 B3
Wigtown GB 36 B2
Wijchen NL 80 A1
Wijhe NL 70 B3
Wijk bij Duurstede NL 70 C2
Wil CH 107 B4
Wilamowice PL 99 B3
Wilczęta PL 69 A4
Wilczkowice PL 77 B4
Wilczna PL 76 B3
Wilczyn PL 76 B3
Wildalpen A 110 B1
Wildbad D 93 C4
Wildberg
Baden-Württemberg D 93 C4
Brandenburg D 74 B1
Wildegg CH 106 B3
Wildendürnbach A 97 C4
Wildeshausen D 72 B1
Wildon A 110 C2
Wilfersdorf A 97 C4
Wilhelmsburg
A 110 A2
D 74 A2
Wilhelmsdorf D 107 B4
Wilhelmshaven D 71 A5
Wilków PL 77 B5
Willebadessen D 81 A5
Willebroek B 79 A4
Willgottheim F 93 C3
Willhermsdorf D 94 B2
Willich D 80 A2
Willingen D 81 A4
Willington GB 37 B5
Willisau CH 106 B3
Wilmslow GB 40 B1
Wilsdruff D 83 A5
Wilster D 64 C2
Wilsum D 71 B3
Wilton GB 44 B2
Wiltz L 92 B1
Wimborne Minster GB 43 B5
Wimereux F 78 B1
Wimmenau F 93 C3
Wimmis CH 106 C2
Wincanton GB 43 A4
Winchcombe GB 44 B2
Winchelsea GB 45 C4
Winchester GB 44 B2
Windermere GB 36 B4
Windischeschenbach D 95 B4
Windischgarsten A 110 B1
Windorf D 96 C1
Windsbach D 94 B2
Windsor GB 44 B3
Wingene B 78 A3
Wingham GB 45 B5
Winkleigh GB 42 B3
Winklern A 109 C3
Winnenden D 94 C1
Winnica PL 77 B5
Winnigstedt D 73 B3
Winnweiler D 93 B3
Winschoten NL 71 A4
Winsen
Niedersachsen D 72 A3
Niedersachsen D 72 B2
Winsford GB 38 A4
Wińsko PL 85 A4
Winslow GB 44 B3
Winsum
Friesland NL 70 A2
Groningen NL 71 A3
Winterberg D 81 A4
Winterfeld D 73 B4
Winterswijk NL 71 C3
Winterthur CH 107 B3
Wintzenheim F 106 A2
Winzer D 95 C5
Wipperdorf D 82 A2
Wipperfürth D 80 A3
Wirksworth GB 40 B2
Wisbech GB 41 C4
Wischhafen D 64 C2
Wishaw GB 35 C4
Wisła PL 98 B2
Wisła Wielka PL 98 B2
Wislica PL 87 B4
Wismar D 65 C4
Wisniewo PL 77 A5
Wiśniowa PL 99 B4
Wissant F 78 B1
Wissembourg F 93 B3
Wissen D 81 B3
Witanowice PL 99 B3
Witham GB 45 B4
Withern GB 41 B4
Withernsea GB 41 B4
Witkowo PL 76 B2
Witmarsum NL 70 A2
Witney GB 44 B2
Witnica PL 75 B3
Witonia PL 77 B4
Witry-les-Reims F 91 B4
Wittdün D 64 B1
Wittelsheim F 106 B2
Witten D 80 A3
Wittenberge D 73 A4
Wittenburg D 73 A4
Wittenheim F 106 B2
Wittichenau D 84 A2
Wittighausen D 94 B1
Wittingen D 73 B3
Wittislingen D 94 C2
Wittlich D 92 B2
Wittmannsdorf A 110 C2
Wittmund D 71 A4
Wittorf D 72 A2
Wittstock D 73 A5
Witzenhausen D 82 A1
Wiveliscombe GB 43 A3
Wivenhoe GB 45 B4
Władysławowo PL 69 A3
Wleń PL 84 A3
Włocławek PL 77 B4
Włodawa PL 13 C5
Włodzimierzów PL 87 A3
Włosień PL 84 A3
Włostow PL 87 B5
Włoszakowice PL 75 C5
Włoszczowa PL 87 B3
Wöbbelin D 73 A4
Woburn GB 44 B3
Wodzisław PL 87 B4
Wodzisław Śląski PL 98 B2
Woerden NL 70 B1
Woerth F 93 C3
Wohlen CH 106 B3
Woippy F 92 B2
Wojcieszow PL 85 B3
Wojkowice Kościelne PL 86 B3
Wojnicz PL 99 B4
Woking GB 44 B3
Wokingham GB 44 B3
Wola Jachowa PL 87 B4
Wola Niechcicka PL 86 A3
Wolbórz PL 87 A3
Wolbrom PL 87 B3
Wołczyn PL 86 A2
Woldegk D 74 A2
Wolfach D 93 C4
Wolfegg D 107 B4
Wolfen D 83 A4
Wolfenbüttel D 73 B3
Wolfersheim D 81 B4
Wolfhagen D 81 A5
Wolfratshausen D 108 B2
Wolfsberg A 110 C1
Wolfsburg D 73 B3
Wolf's Castle GB 39 C2
Wolfshagen D 74 A2
Wolfstein D 93 B3
Wolfurt A 107 B4
Wolgast D 66 B2
Wolhusen CH 106 B3
Wolin PL 67 C3
Wolka PL 87 A4
Wolkenstein D 83 B5
Wolkersdorf A 97 C4
Wöllersdorf A 111 B3
Wollin D 73 B5
Wöllstadt D 81 B4
Wolmirstedt D 73 B4
Wolnzach D 95 C3
Wołów PL 85 A4
Wolsztyn PL 75 B5
Wolvega NL 70 B2
Wolverhampton GB 40 C1
Wolverton GB 44 A3
Wombwell GB 40 B2
Woodbridge GB 45 A5
Woodhall Spa GB 41 B3
Woodstock GB 44 B2
Wookey Hole GB 43 A4
Wool GB 43 B4
Woolacombe GB 42 A2
Wooler GB 37 A4
Woolwich GB 45 B4
Wooperton GB 37 A5
Worb CH 106 C2
Worbis D 82 A2
Worcester GB 39 B4
Wördern A 97 C4
Wörgl A 108 B3
Workington GB 36 B3
Worksop GB 40 B2
Workum NL 70 B2
Wörlitz D 83 A4
Wormer NL 70 B1
Wormhout F 78 B2
Wormit GB 35 B5
Worms D 93 B4
Worpswede D 72 A1
Wörrstadt D 93 B4
Wörschach A 110 B1
Worsley GB 38 A4
Wörth
Bayern D 93 B5
Bayern D 95 B4
Bayern D 95 C4
Rheinland-Pfalz D 93 B4
Worthing GB 44 C3
Woudsend NL 70 B2
Woumen B 78 A2
Woźniki PL 86 B3
Wragby GB 41 B3
Wrangle GB 41 B4
Wręczyca Wlk. PL 86 B2
Wredenhagen D 73 A5
Wremen D 72 A1
Wrentham GB 45 A5
Wrexham GB 38 A3
Wriedel D 72 A3
Wriezen D 74 B3
Wrist D 64 C2
Wróblewo
Mazowieckie PL 77 B5
Wielkopolskie PL 75 B5
Wrocki PL 69 B4
Wrocław PL 85 A5
Wronki PL 75 B5
Wroxham GB 41 C5
Września PL 76 B2
Wrzosowo PL 67 B4
Wschowa PL 85 A4
Wulfen D 80 A3
Wülfen D 83 A3
Wulkau D 73 B5
Wünnenberg D 81 A4
Wünsdorf D 74 B2
Wunsiedel D 95 A4
Wunstorf D 72 B2
Wuppertal D 80 A3
Wurmannsquick D 95 C4
Würselen D 80 B2
Wurzbach D 82 B3
Würzburg D 94 B1
Wurzen D 83 A4
Wust D 74 B1
Wusterhausen D 73 B5
Wusterwitz D 73 B5
Wustrau-Altfriesack D 74 B1
Wustrow D 66 B1
Wuustwezel B 79 A4
Wye GB 45 B4
Wyględów PL 87 A5
Wyk D 64 B1
Wykroty PL 84 A3
Wylye GB 43 A5
Wymiarki PL 84 A3

Wymondham GB **41** C5
Wyrzysk PL **76** A2
Wyśmierzyce PL **87** A4
Wysoka
Dolnośląskie PL **85** A3
Wielkopolskie PL **76** A2
Wyszanów PL **86** A2
Wyszogród PL **77** B5

X

Xanten D **80** A2
Xanthi GR **183** B6
Xarrë AL **182** D2
Xátiva E **159** C3
Xeraco E **159** B3
Xert E **153** B4
Xerta E **153** B4
Xertigny F **105** A5
Xilagani GR **183** C7
Xilokastro GR **184** A3
Xinzo de Limia E **140** B3
Xixón = Gijón E **142** A1
Xove E **140** A3
Xubia E **140** A2
Xunqueira de Ambia
E **140** B3
Xunqueira de Espadañedo E **140** B3
Xylophagou CY **181** B2

Y

Yablanitsa BG **17** D6
Yağcılar TR **186** C3
Yahyalı TR **23** B8
Yakoruda BG **183** A5
Yalova TR **187** B4
Yalvaç TR **189** A6
Yambol BG **17** D7
Yampil UA **13** D8
Yaniskoski RUS **193** D12
Yantarnyy RUS **69** A4
Yarbasan TR **186** D3
Yarcombe GB **43** B3
Yaremcha UA **13** D6
Yarm GB **37** B5
Yarmouth GB **44** C2
Yarrow GB **35** C4
Yasinya UA **17** A6
Yatağan TR **188** B3
Yate GB **43** A4
Yatton GB **43** A4
Yavoriv UA **13** D5
Yaxley GB **41** C3
Yazıca TR **187** B6
Yazıköy TR **188** C2
Ybbs A **110** A2
Ybbsitz A **110** B1
Ydby DK **58** B1
Yddal N **46** B2
Ydes F **116** B2
Yealmpton GB **42** B3
Yebra de Basa E **145** B3
Yecla E **159** C2
Yecla de Yeltes E **149** B3
Yelsk BY **13** C8
Yelverton GB **42** B2
Yena RUS **197** B14
Yenice
Ankara TR **23** B7
Aydın TR **188** B3
Çanakkale TR **186** C2
Edirne TR **183** C8
Yenifoça TR **186** D1
Yenihisar TR **188** B2
Yeniköy TR **186** D4
Yeniköy Plaji TR **186** B3
Yenipazar TR **188** B3
Yenişarbademli TR **189** B6
Yenişehir TR **187** B4
Yenne F **118** B2
Yeovil GB **43** B4
Yepes E **151** C4
Yerköy TR **23** B8
Yerólakkos CY **181** A2
Yeroskipos CY **181** B1
Yerseke NL **79** A4
Yerville F **89** A4
Yeşildağ TR **189** B6
Yeşilhisar TR **23** B8
Yeşilköy TR **186** B3
Yeşilova TR **189** B4
Yeşilyurt TR **188** A3
Yeste E **164** A2
Yezerishche BY **9** E6
Y Felinheli GB **38** A2
Ygos-St Saturnin F **128** C2
Ygrande F **104** C1
Yialousa CY **181** A3
Yığılca TR **187** B6
Yli-Ii FIN **197** D8
Yli-Kärppä FIN **197** D8
Yli-Muonia FIN **196** A6
Ylitornio FIN **196** C6
Ylivieska FIN **3** D9
Ylläsjärvi FIN **196** B7
Ymonville F **103** A3
Yngsjö S **63** C2
York GB **40** B2
Youghal IRL **29** C4
Yoğuntaş TR **186** A2
Yozgat TR **23** B8
Yport F **89** A4
Ypres = Ieper B **78** B2
Yssingeaux F **117** B4
Ystad S **66** A2
Ystalyfera GB **39** C3
Ystebrød N **52** B1
Ystradgynlais GB **39** C3
Ytre Arna N **46** B2
Ytre Enebakk N **54** A2
Ytre Rendal N **199** D8
Ytteran S **199** B11
Ytterhogdal S **199** C11
Yttermalung S **49** B5
Yunak TR **187** D6
Yuncos E **151** B4
Yunquera E **162** B3
Yunquera de Henares
E **151** B4
Yushkozero RUS **3** D13
Yverdon-les-Bains
CH **106** C1
Yvetot F **89** A4
Yvignac F **101** A3
Yvoir B **79** B4
Yvonand CH **106** C1
Yxnerum S **56** B2
Yzeure F **104** C2

Z

Zaamslag NL **79** A3
Zaanstad NL **70** B1
Žabalj SRB **126** B2
Zabar H **113** A4
Žabari SRB **127** C3
Zabiče SLO **123** B3
Zabierzów PL **87** B3
Ząbki PL **77** B6
Ząbkowice Śląskie
PL **85** B4
Zablaće HR **138** B1
Žabljak MNE **139** B5
Žabno PL **87** B4
Zabok HR **124** A1
Žabokreky SK **98** C2
Zabor PL **75** C4
Żabowo PL **75** A4
Zabrdje BIH **125** C4
Zábřeh CZ **97** B4
Zabrežje SRB **127** C2
Ząbrowo PL **67** C4
Zabrze PL **86** B2
Zabrzeż PL **99** B4
Zacharo GR **184** B2
Zadar HR **137** A4
Zadzim PL **86** A2
Zafarraya E **163** B3
Zafferana Etnea I **177** B4
Zafra E **155** C4
Žaga SLO **122** A2
Zagajica SRB **127** C3
Żagań PL **84** A3
Zaglav HR **137** B4
Zaglavak SRB **127** D1
Zagnańsk PL **87** B4
Zagora GR **183** D5
Zagorc SLO **110** C2
Zagorićani BIH **138** B3
Zagorje SLO **123** A4
Zagórów PL **76** B2
Zagradje SRB **127** C2
Zagreb HR **124** B1
Zagrilla E **163** A3
Zagvozd HR **138** B3
Zagwiździe PL **86** B1
Zagyvarekas H **113** B4
Zagyvaróna H **113** A3
Zahara E **162** B2
Zahara de los Atunes
E **162** B2
Zahinos E **155** C4
Zahna D **83** A4
Záhoři CZ **96** B2
Zahrádka CZ **97** B3
Zahrensdorf D **73** A3
Zaidin E **153** A4
Zaječar SRB **16** D5
Zákamenné SK **99** B3
Zákány H **124** A2
Zákányszék H **126** A1
Zakliczyn PL **99** B4
Zakopane PL **99** B3
Zakroczym PL **77** B5
Zakrzew PL **87** A5
Zakrzewo PL **76** B3
Zakupy CZ **84** B2
Zakynthos GR **184** B1
Zalaapáti H **111** C4
Zalabaksa H **111** C3
Zalaegerszeg H **111** C3
Zalakomár H **111** C4
Zalakoppány H **111** C4
Zalalövö H **111** C3
Zalamea de la Serena
E **156** B2
Zalamea la Real E **161** B3
Zalaszentgrót H **111** C4
Zalaszentiván H **111** C3
Zalău RO **17** B5
Zalavár H **111** C4
Zalcsie PL **86** A3
Zaldibar E **143** A4
Žalec SLO **123** A4
Zalesie PL **77** A5
Zalewo PL **69** B4
Zalishchyky UA **13** D6
Zalla E **143** A3
Zaltbommel NL **79** A5
Zamárdi H **112** C1
Zamarte PL **68** B2
Zamberk CZ **85** B4
Zambra E **163** A3
Zambugueira do Mar
P **160** B1
Zámoly H **112** B2
Zamora E **149** A4
Zamość PL **13** C5
Zamoście PL **86** A3
Zams A **108** B1
Zandhoven B **79** A4
Žandov CZ **84** B2
Zandvoort NL **70** B1
Zangliveri GR **183** C5
Zánka H **111** C4
Zaorejas E **152** B1
Zaovine SRB **127** D1
Zapadnaya Dvina
RUS **9** D8
Zapfend D **94** A2
Zapole PL **86** A2
Zapolyarnyy RUS **193** C14
Zapponeta I **171** B3
Zaprešić HR **124** B1
Zaragoza E **153** A3
Zarasai LT **13** A7
Zarautz E **144** A1
Zarcilla de Ramos
E **164** B3
Zaręby PL **77** A6
Žarki PL **86** B3
Zarko GR **182** D4
Žarnovica SK **98** C2
Zarnow PL **87** A4
Zarnowiec PL **68** A3
Zarošice CZ **97** B4
Żarów PL **85** B4
Zarren B **78** A2
Zarrentin D **73** A3
Żary PL **84** A3
Zarza Capilla E **156** B2
Zarza de Alange E **156** B1
Zarza de Granadilla
E **149** B3
Zarza de Tajo E **151** B4
Zarzadilla de Totana
E **164** B3
Zarza la Mayor E **155** B4
Zarzuela del Monte
E **150** B3
Zarzuela del Pinar
E **151** A3
Zas E **140** A2
Zasavica SRB **127** C1
Zasieki PL **84** A2
Zásmuky CZ **96** B3
Žatec CZ **83** B5
Zaton HR **139** C4
Zatonie PL **84** A3
Zator PL **99** A3
Zauchwitz D **74** B2
Zavala BIH **139** C3
Zavalje BIH **124** C1
Zavattarello I **120** C2
Zavidovići BIH **139** A4
Zavlaka SRB **127** C1
Zawady PL **77** C5
Zawadzkie PL **86** B2
Zawdy PL **86** A2
Zawidów PL **84** A3
Zawidz PL **77** B4
Zawiercie PL **86** B3
Zawoja PL **99** B3
Zawonia PL **85** A5
Žažina HR **124** B2
Zázrivá SK **99** B3
Zbarazh UA **13** D6
Zbąszyń PL **75** B4
Zbąszynek PL **75** B4
Zbehy SK **98** C2
Zbiersk PL **76** C3
Zbiroh CZ **96** B1
Zblewo PL **69** B3
Zbójno PL **77** A4
Zbrachlin PL **76** A3
Zbraslav CZ **96** B2
Zbraslavice CZ **97** B3
Ždala HR **124** A3
Ždánice CZ **98** B1
Žďár nad Sázavov
CZ **97** B3
Zdbice PL **75** A5
Zdenci HR **125** B3
Ždiar SK **99** B4
Zdice CZ **96** B1
Zdirec nad Doubravou
CZ **97** B3
Zdolbuniv UA **13** C7
Zdounky CZ **98** B1
Ždrelo SRB **127** C3
Zduńska Wola PL **86** A2
Zduny
Łódzkie PL **77** B4
Wielkopolskie PL **85** A5
Żdżary PL **87** A4
Zdziechowice
Opolskie PL **86** A2
Wielkopolskie PL **76** B2
Zdziszowice PL **86** B2
Zeberio E **143** A4
Žebrák CZ **96** B1
Zebreira P **155** B3
Zebrzydowa PL **84** A3
Zechlin D **74** A1
Zechlinerhütte D **74** A1
Zederhaus A **109** B4
Žednik SRB **126** B1
Zeebrugge B **78** A3
Zegrze PL **77** B6
Zehdenick D **74** B2
Zehren D **83** A5
Zeil D **94** A2
Zeilarn D **95** C4
Zeist NL **70** B2
Zeithain D **83** A5
Zeitz D **83** A4
Želatava CZ **97** B3
Żelazno PL **68** A2
Zele B **79** A4
Zelenoborskiy RUS **3** C13
Zelenogorsk RUS **9** B6
Zelenograd RUS **9** D10
Zelenogradsk RUS **12** A4
Železná Ruda CZ **96** B1
Železnice CZ **84** B3
Železnik SRB **127** C2
Zelezniki SLO **123** A3
Železny Brod CZ **84** B3
Zelhem NL **71** B3
Želiezovce SK **112** A2
Żelkowo PL **68** A2
Zell
CH **106** B2
Baden-Württemberg D **93** C4
Baden-Württemberg D **106** B2
Rheinland-Pfalz D **92** A3
Zella-Mehlis D **82** B2
Zell am See A **109** B3
Zell am Ziller A **108** B2
Zell an der Pram A **96** C1
Zell bei Zellhof A **96** C2
Zellerndorf A **97** C3
Zellingen D **94** B1
Želovce SK **112** A3
Zelów PL **86** A3
Zeltweg A **110** B1
Zelzate B **79** A3
Zemberovce SK **98** C2
Zembrzyce PL **99** B3
Zemianske-Kostol'any
SK **98** C2
Zemitz D **66** C2
Zemné SK **112** B1
Zemst B **79** B4
Zemun SRB **127** C2
Zemunik Donji HR **137** A4
Zenica BIH **139** A3
Zennor GB **42** B1
Žepa BIH **139** B5
Žepče BIH **139** A4
Zepponami I **168** A2
Zerbst D **73** C5
Zerf D **92** B2
Zerind RO **113** C5
Żerków PL **76** B2
Zermatt CH **119** A4
Zernez CH **107** C5
Zerpen-schleuse D **74** B2
Zestoa E **144** A1
Zetel D **71** A4
Zeulenroda D **83** B3
Zeven D **72** A2
Zevenaar NL **70** C3
Zevenbergen NL **79** A4
Zévio I **121** B4
Zeytinbaği TR **186** B3
Zeytindağ TR **186** D2
Zgierz PL **86** A3
Zgorzelec PL **84** A3
Zgošča BIH **139** A4
Zhabinka BY **13** B6
Zharkovskiy RUS **9** E8
Zhashkiv UA **13** D9
Zhlobin BY **13** B9
Zhmerynka UA **13** D8
Zhodzina BY **13** A8
Zhytomyr UA **13** C8
Žiar nad Hronom
SK **98** C2
Zicavo F **180** B2
Zickhusen D **65** C4
Zidani Most SLO **123** A4
Ziddorf D **73** A5
Židlochovice CZ **97** B4
Ziębice PL **85** B5
Ziegendorf D **73** A4
Ziegenrück D **83** B3
Zieleniec
Dolnośląskie PL **85** B4
Warmińsko-Mazurskie PL **77** A6
Zachodnio-Pomorskie PL **75** A4
Zielona PL **77** A4
Zielona Góra PL **75** C4
Zieluń-Osada PL **77** A4
Ziemetshausen D **94** C2
Zierenberg D **81** A5
Zierikzee NL **79** A3
Ziersdorf A **97** C3
Zierzow D **73** A4
Ziesar D **73** B5
Ziesendorf D **65** C5
Ziethen D **74** B2
Žihle CZ **96** A1
Žilina SK **98** B2
Ziltendorf D **74** B3
Zimandu Nou RO **126** A3
Zimna Woda PL **77** A5
Zimnicea RO **17** D6
Zinal CH **119** A4
Zinasco I **120** B2
Zingst D **66** B1
Zinkgruvan S **55** B6
Žinkovy CZ **96** B1
Zinnowitz D **66** B2
Zirc H **112** B1
Žiri SLO **123** A3
Zirl A **108** B2
Zirndorf D **94** B2
Žirovnica SRB **127** C3
Žirovnice CZ **97** B3
Zisterdorf A **97** C4
Žitište SRB **126** B2
Zitsa GR **182** D2
Zittau D **84** B2
Živaja HR **124** B2
Živinice BIH **139** A4
Zlatar HR **124** A2
Zlatar Bistrica HR **124** A2
Zlate Hory CZ **85** B5
Zlaté Klasy SK **111** A4
Zlaté Moravce SK **98** C2
Zlatnána Ostrove
SK **112** B1
Zlatniky SK **98** C2
Zlatograd BG **183** B7
Žlebič SLO **123** B3
Zlín CZ **98** B1
Złocieniec PL **75** A5
Złoczew PL **86** A2
Zlonice CZ **84** B2
Złotniki Kujawskie
PL **76** B3
Złotoryja PL **85** A3
Złotów PL **68** B2
Złoty Stok PL **85** B4
Zlutice CZ **83** B5
Zmajevac BIH **124** C2
Zmajevo SRB **126** B1
Żmigród PL **85** A4
Zmijavci HR **138** B3
Žminj HR **122** B2
Żnin PL **76** B2
Znojmo CZ **97** C4
Zöblitz D **83** B5
Zocca I **135** A3
Zoetermeer NL **70** B1
Zofingen CH **106** B2
Zogno I **120** B2
Zohor SK **111** A3
Zolling D **95** C3
Zolochiv UA **13** D6
Zomba H **112** C2
Zomergem B **79** A3
Zoñán E **141** A3
Zonguldak TR **187** A6
Zonhoven B **79** B5
Zonza F **180** B2
Zörbig D **83** A4
Zorita E **156** A2
Żory PL **98** A2
Zossen D **74** B2
Zottegem B **79** B3
Zoutkamp NL **71** A3
Zovi Do BIH **139** B4
Zreče SLO **123** A4
Zrenjanin SRB **126** B2
Žrnovica HR **138** B2
Zručnad Sazavou
CZ **97** B3
Zsadány H **113** C5
Zsámbék H **112** B2
Zsámbok H **112** B3
Zsana H **126** A1
Zschopau D **83** B5
Zuberec SK **99** B3
Zubieta E **144** A2
Zubiri E **144** B2
Zubtsov RUS **9** D9
Zucaina E **153** B3
Zudar D **66** B2
Zuera E **144** C3
Zufre E **161** B3
Zug CH **107** B3
Zuheros E **163** A3
Zuidhorn NL **71** A3
Zuidlaren NL **71** A3
Zuidwolde NL **71** B3
Zújar E **164** B2
Żukowo PL **69** A3
Žuljana HR **138** C3
Žulová CZ **85** B5
Zülpich D **80** B2
Zumaia E **144** A1
Zumárraga E **143** A4
Zundert NL **79** A4
Županja HR **125** B4
Zurgena E **164** B2
Zürich CH **107** B3
Żuromin PL **77** A4
Zurzach CH **106** B3
Zusmarshausen D **94** C2
Zusow D **65** C4
Züssow D **66** C2
Žuta Lovka HR **123** C4
Zutphen NL **70** B3
Žužemberk SLO **123** B3
Zvenyhorodka UA **13** D9
Zvikovské Podhradi
CZ **96** B2
Zvolen SK **99** C3
Zvolenská Slatina
SK **99** C3
Zvornik BIH **139** A5
Zwartsluis NL **70** B3
Zweibrücken D **93** B3
Zweisimmen CH **106** C2
Zwettl A **97** C3
Zwettl an der Rodl
A **96** C2
Zwickau D **83** B4
Zwiefalten D **107** A4
Zwieryn PL **75** B4
Zwierzno PL **69** A4
Zwiesel D **96** B1
Zwieselstein A **108** C2
Zwoleń PL **87** A5
Zwolle NL **70** B3
Zwönitz D **83** B4
Żychlin PL **77** B4
Zydowo
Wielkopolskie PL **76** B2
Zachodnio-Pomorskie PL **68** A1
Żyrardów PL **77** B5
Żytno PL **86** B3
Żywiec PL **99** B3
Zyyi CY **181** B2